AF594161

BEEPLE

everydays, the first 5000 days

mike winkelmann

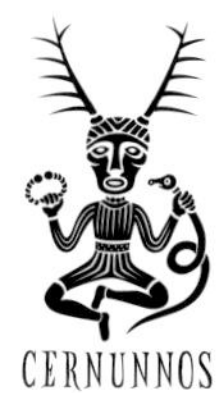

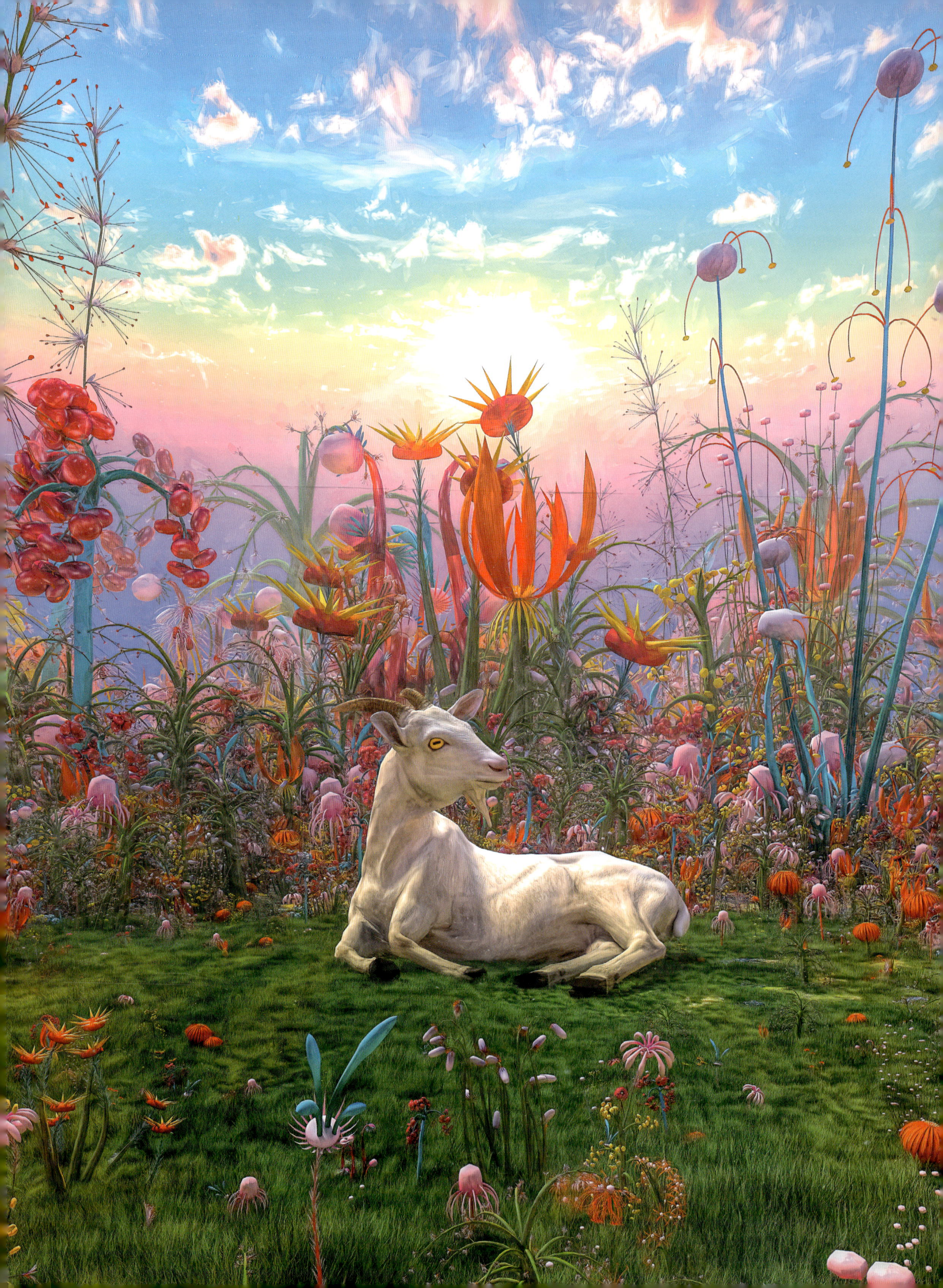

contents

OPPOSITE PAGE

CHILL BABY GOAT

03.11.2020

foreword

For well over a decade, Beeple has inspired digital artists and motion designers worldwide to explore the realms of what is possible in Cinema 4D and OctaneRender, pioneering a distinctive style and making statements on pop culture that will surely influence future generations of digital artists. He has jump-started entire aesthetic movements with his masterful talent and re-envisioned social media with his now world-famous *Everydays* project.

What makes Beeple so unique, however, is his legendary discipline. He is so dedicated to his craft that he has to create something every single day, for the sole purpose of simply getting better.

Every. Single. Day.

That means never skipping a day, even when he's on vacation or when his wife was giving birth; never skipping a day when he has computer trouble or the power goes out. Not to mention when he just doesn't feel like it.

Every. Single. Day.

There's a golden rule in making art that nothing good happens in a day, meaning any piece of creative output requires more than twenty-four hours to develop and manifest. But the joke's on us, because some of Beeple's creations, which might have taken just a few hours, are jaw-dropping statements of creativity and technical prowess, crafted by someone who has become so adept at his craft that it's borderline demoralizing for the rest of us. Discovering a Beeple image in your feed is both an inspiration and a challenge.

Every. Single. Day.

Beeple's entry into the NFT space has obviously been a resounding success. He's been a key innovator in teaching everyone else how to best utilize the technology of smart contracts, and he has established a winning formula for formatting images, tying them to the blockchain in interesting ways, and combining physical components with the artwork to reward collectors. He is writing the rulebook for everyone else to follow.

But what's so beautiful about Beeple is that his profound success in the NFT space hasn't changed him one bit. He's still among the most authentic people I've ever met. He's always funny, engaging, willing to help, and more approachable than people expect.

Watching his success has, if anything, reminded us of what a gem he really is—a true legend in character, in discipline, and in talent. As the driving force of innovation in the digital art space, Beeple wields a great amount of authority, and the keys couldn't be in better hands or with a better person than someone making legendary art.

Every. Single. Day.

Bradley G. Munkowitz

OPPOSITE PAGE

RESISTANCE

03.17.2021

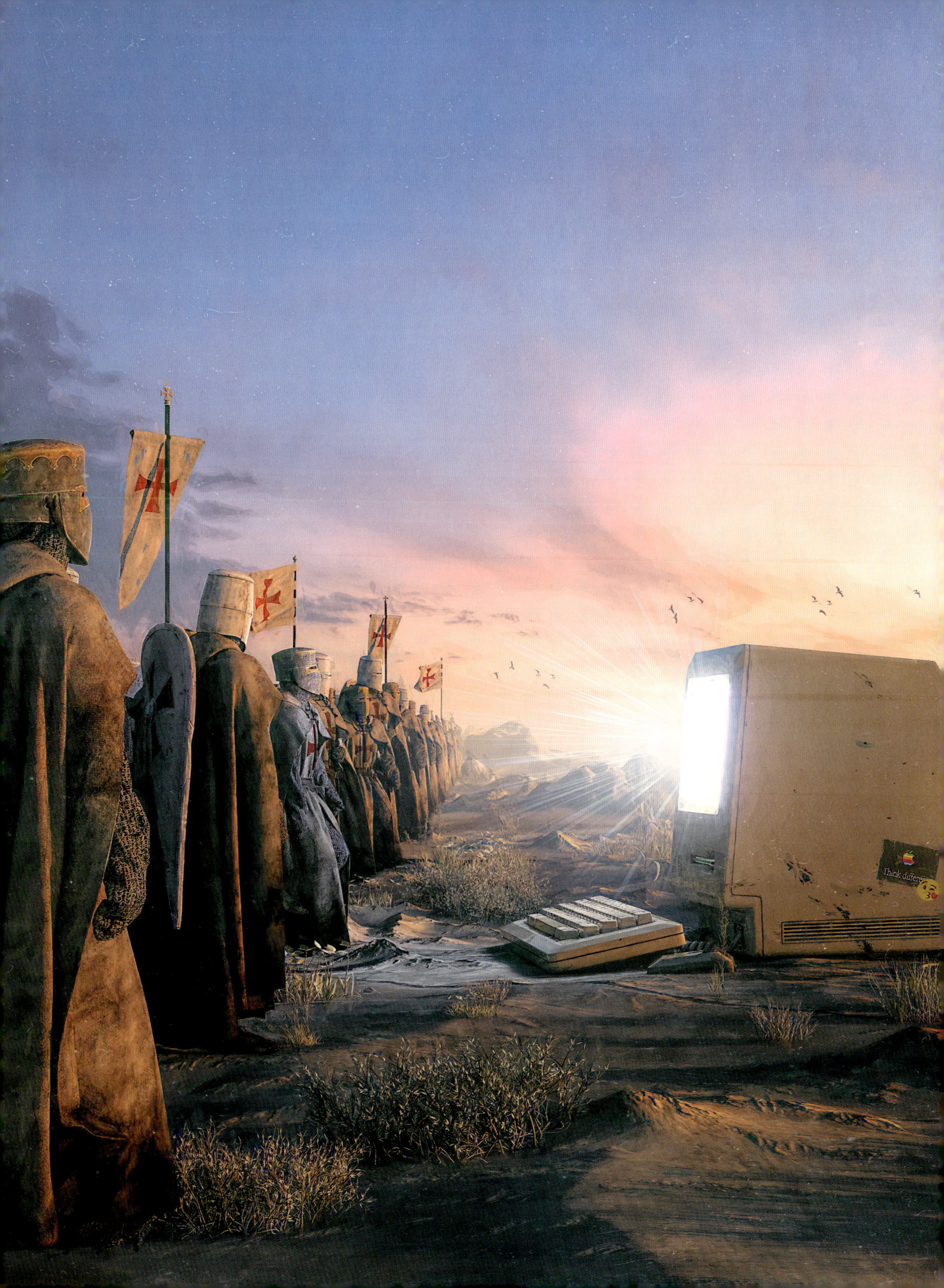
Think differe

thank you

ugh. to be honest this almost feels stupid to try to pretend that this tiny little bullshit thank you is in ANY WAY sufficient for the insane amount of support and love that i've received for this project. i am truly at a loss for words about how to even begin to articulate how much this means to me. i'm literally on my like tenth draft of writing this tiny paragraph, i've started over again and again as i realized that these words are simply not enough.

but maybe that should be a wake-up call to me that these words truly aren't enough and that i need to be better with my actions to SHOW this gratitude more . . . 🙏

to jenpoe—you have never been anything less than a true equal partner in this journey, and where we are today is absolutely as much your doing as mine, please always know that. mlymlymlymlymym.

to scotty—your support over the years has always meant the world to me and now to be able to work with you is a true honor and i feel so lucky to be in this position. fun times ahead. me you me me me me me me cashed. LOLOLOLOL.

to smomly—you have always put scotty and me before yourself, and your constant support and belief in my work—even when it's stuff i know you would rather i not make (LOL) has been inspiring for me as i try to be one-tenth of the parent you are.

to d—i was just recently thinking about that very first computer you bought after a teacher recommended one for me in fourth grade—386SX with 2MB of RAM and a 20MB hard drive that I believe was around $2000. it recently occurred to me that on a cost-adjusted basis this was one of the most expensive things you ever bought. <3

to my friends/collaborators—you have pushed and challenged me to think more about what good art is and can be. i am constantly inspired by you to work harder and be better and your support has made me a better artist (who still mostly blows). ;)

to the digital art community—i absolutely would not be where i am without your support and belief in my work. that is quite simply the only reason i am here, i could have done all this work and nobody could have given a shit. but instead you said, hey ok, we'll welcome this weirdo with open arms. please know that i am doing and will continue to do everything i can to help show the rest of the world how special this community is and how many insanely thoughtful, talented, caring individuals it is comprised of.

to my collectors—this has been a relatively new type of support for my work but one whose impact is hard to overstate at this point. please know that i very much appreciate your belief in my work and look at this support more like an investment than patronage. you do not need to collect my work to be a fan, so this is a different level of support i take very seriously. i want to see this be a wise investment. to that end, i am reinvesting this money into more ambitious art projects that i could have only dreamed of before. i feel EXTREMELY fortunate to be in this position, and please trust i will be working my ass off to make you shitloads of money on your investment.

OPPOSITE PAGE

ALIVE

02.19.2021

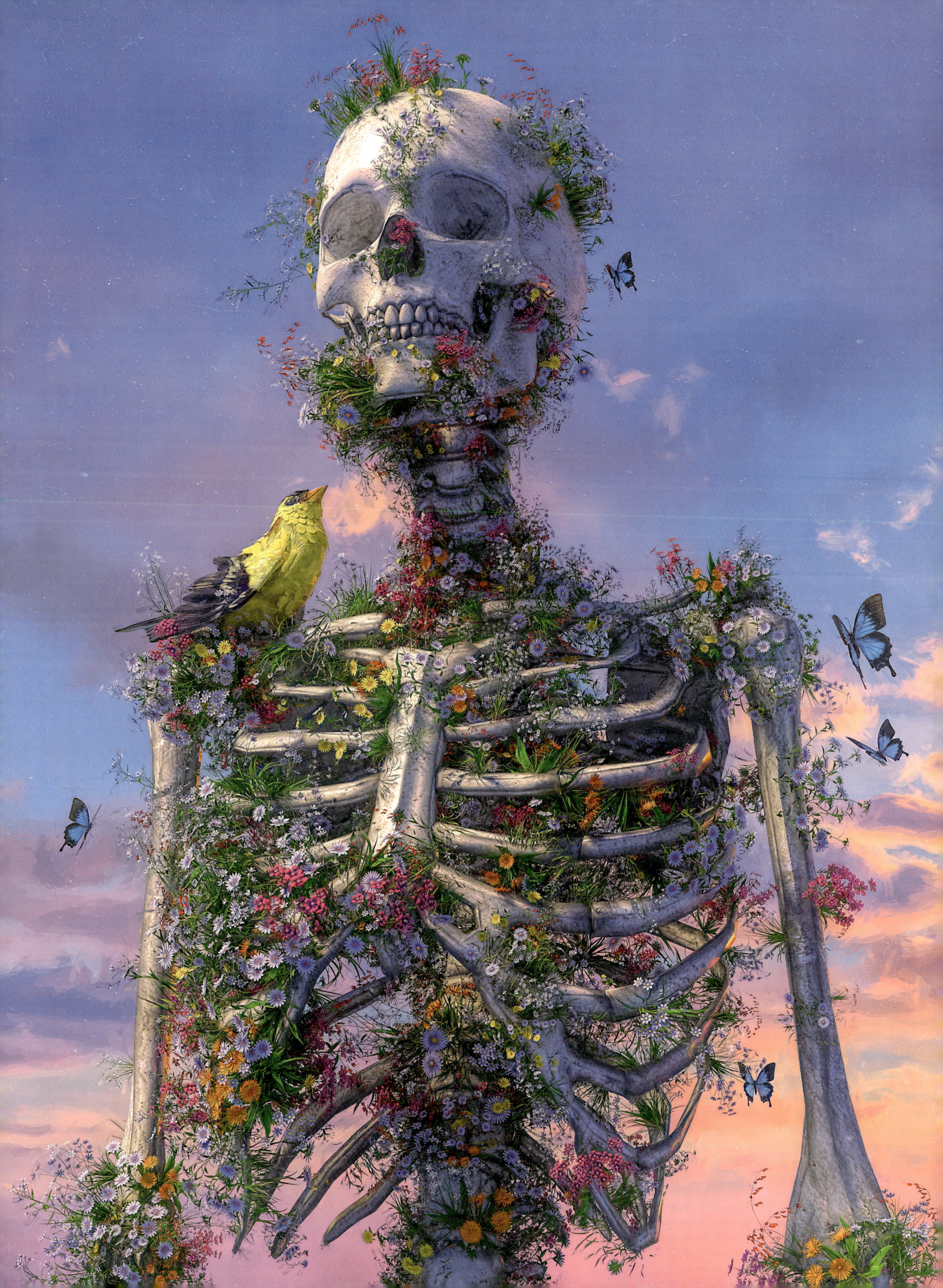

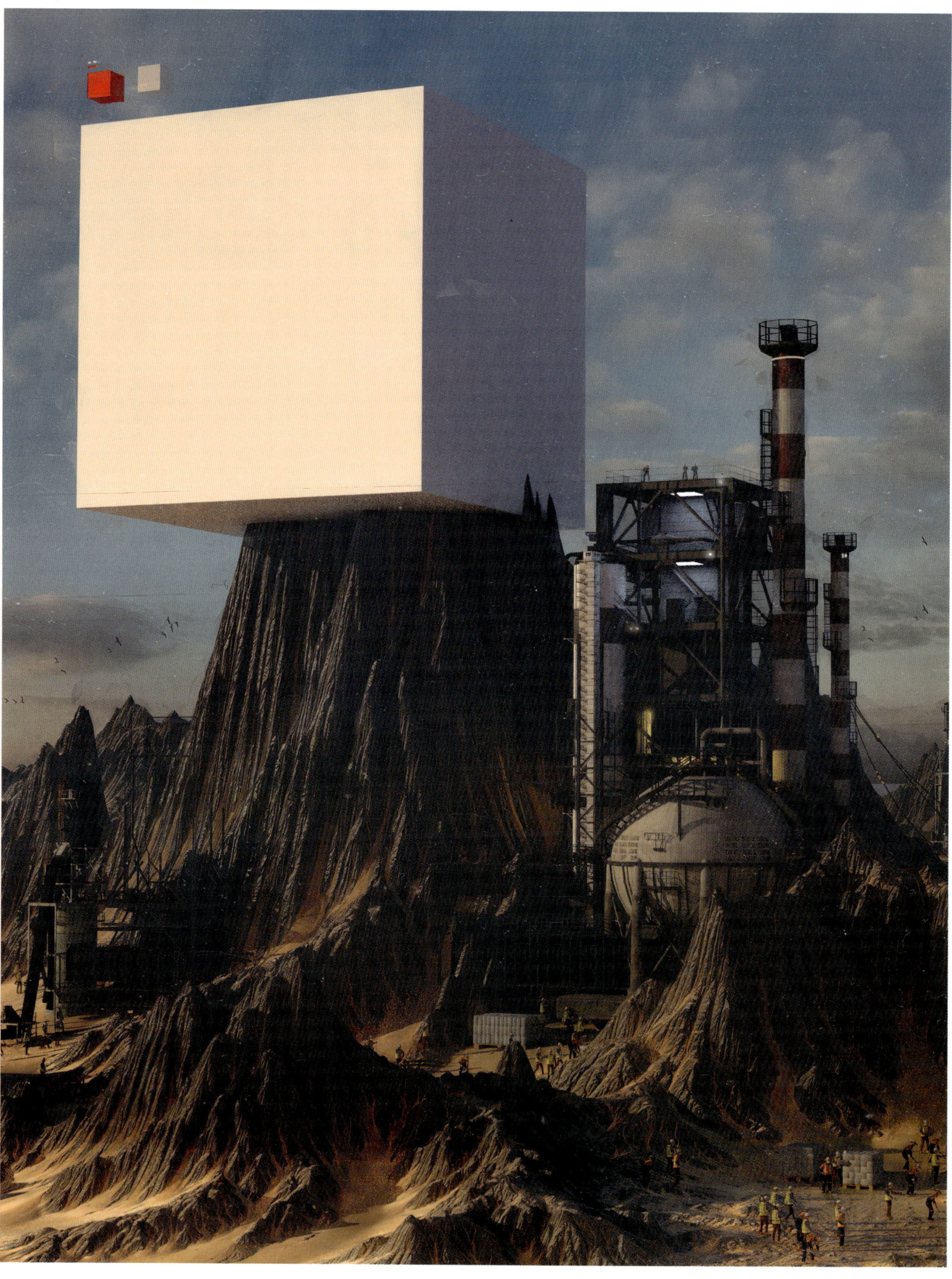

interview

_Haley Mellin (HM): Let's begin with *Everydays*. What's this about as an art project? Where did it begin?

_Mike Winkelmann (MW): The project began in 2007. Basically, I just wanted to get better at making pictures. I wanted to get better at drawing and had seen an illustrator in the UK, Tom Judd, do a sketch a day in a sketchbook in 2005. I thought that was a really cool idea. You could see the progression. You could see certain themes evolving over that time. I thought it was a great way to stick with something, so that's what I did. Actually, I tried starting it a couple times before the "official" start, but I wasn't posting them online. I was only doing them in my notebook, and even then it was very fuzzy. . . . I'd do a little doodle, and then it was like, "It's done today. There, I did it."

_HM: But *had* you done it?

_MW: Well, then it was like, "No, you didn't really sit down or actually put in the time and work." That was when I decided to post them online every day. Even that act, knowing full well that almost nobody was going to see them, made me try a lot harder. It made it into this binary thing: it was either posted online or not. It was either done, or it wasn't. After the first year of *Everydays*, I realized I'd learned a ton, and that this was something that was really beneficial. Technique-wise, I'd learned a lot, and I'd also learned a lot of different workflows that I'd previously never thought possible. I learned more in that one year than in probably the last five years. So I thought, maybe I could use the same practice to teach myself other programs. I was already doing digital art besides these drawings, in addition to the *Everydays*, but it wasn't 3D, it was 2D art. At the end of the first year, it was like, "Okay, I'm just going to transition to doing an *Everyday* using these 3D programs," which nobody was doing at the time. I started from there, and then it just kept going.

_HM: And it's still ongoing. What was your start date?

_MW: May 1st, 2007.

_HM: What are the pictures about? Were there different phases?

_MW: In the beginning, a lot of it was just purely trying to get better. I wasn't superconscious of the end product. These were about practice. These were about getting better and sitting down each day for a couple hours whether I was inspired or not. It was about looking at art as work. I really wasn't concerned with the end-product. The end product was a by-product of the work. Slowly, over time, it has shifted to the point where I'm more concerned about the end product. It's still about the practice, but I'm also concerned about how the final picture looks, because that's the part of the thing that I want to practice.

_HM: What were you trying to get better at?

_MW: In the beginning, it was like, "Today, I want to learn how to model a water bottle." Was it going to create a great picture? Probably not, but I didn't really give a shit. It was going to be a water bottle. The point was to figure out how to model it. Eventually, it became, "Now I want to figure out how to make a cool picture of this water bottle." At this point, I'm trying to practice making really good pictures.

OPPOSITE PAGE

VERSION45

04.18.2021

_HM: What were some of the themes, and how have they evolved?

_MW: For a very long time, they were very abstract—just about color, form, composition, things like that. And then, mid-2015, I started putting people in them. They were still pretty abstract, but it was a way to show scale within these landscapes. I liked doing that. I thought it was a different direction for what I was doing, where I could still do things that were abstract, but by putting people in there, it changed the feel of it. It went from being this abstract thing, to putting yourself in the shoes of these subjects and imagining—at least that's how I looked at them—imagining, what it would look like if I was that little figure, putting myself in their shoes. So then they became about these weird, semi-sci-fi landscapes, these sometimes-geometric landscapes that these people inhabited. Slowly, over the last five years, they've become even more literal, with themes around politics and our relationships to technology and pop culture. They've also become about capturing and reinterpreting moments in real time.

_HM: Interesting. I think of Norman Rockwell and the way he'd paint contemporary moments. Originally, you were making them to get better. Now, you're continuing the practice. Is it a meditation of sorts? Is it to just continue to refine your ability? Why do you continue to do it?

_MW: I still feel like most of them suck, and people are just way too generous, or their standards are too low, and that I need to get way, way better still. That is truly how I feel. I've never remotely felt that I don't need any more practice. I feel almost the opposite. I feel even shittier now, especially now that I have an even a broader sense of art history, and I'm looking at absolute fucking masterpieces. I'm not making that. The bar is even higher now, and now I'm paying more attention, too, to more conceptual themes around the work, not just about making images. How does this fit into a broader narrative of art history? How do I reference things from the past? I'm trying to move the needle just one inch forward in terms of looking at art and looking at images in a way that people have not seen.

_HM: How did that purpose shift within you, and do you plan on continuing it in the future?

_MW: To some degree, I was always trying to do that. Even when I knew nothing about art history, I always recognized that, to stick around, you have to be doing something new that people haven't seen before. As I started caring more about the end product, the "everyday" was always still the goal, but it became a question of, "Is this something people haven't seen before? Does it feel new? Or like a different aesthetic or technique?" Sometimes the effect is small, but I always want to make something that feels like I haven't seen it before. That's why some of them are really weird. Like, "What the fuck is that?" Well, you haven't seen it before.

_HM: It brings to mind Magritte, who would put on a full suit and literally walk to work with a briefcase to work nine to five each day. It's this notion of art-as-practice, like practicing, getting better, practicing a shared craft that has evolved over millennia, except obviously with innovative new mediums. How do you carve out time to make them, especially considering your increasingly busy schedule?

_MW: One of the things that always precipitated this project was a book I read—which I do not do almost ever. Seriously, in the last twenty years, I've probably read three, four books, maybe. But I read this book titled *The War of Art* by Steven Pressfield. It's very easy to read. It's one sentence per page, and each page is to-the-fucking-point, like a punch in the face of truth. It's all about motivation and procrastination and not letting ourselves say, "Oh, I'll do it tomorrow." That was another really big motivational focus. A lot of people struggle with staring at that blank page and walking away, and then fifteen years will go by and the page will still be blank. *Everydays* takes away that choice, and at the same time, the boundaries make certain artistic choices that I think are very interesting.

_HM: You mean like creative restrictions?

_MW: I've always gravitated towards putting bounds on what I was doing, because, honestly, it makes it easier. The things I find to be the most challenging are when it's just this big, open blue sky where you can do anything. I get crushed under the weight of a million choices. With this, I've taken away key choices, so that the entire project can continue. I won't get burnt out if I look at each day as one piece of a bigger project. That's the thing that sometimes people miss: a lot of people looked at the *First 5,000 Days* and assumed I just tore some pages out of my sketchbook and gave it to them. No—I don't do two *Everydays* one day and then one another day. People think that I bank a bunch of them and then just release a different one each day. I've never done that, and I never will do that. That is not the point of this. The point is to do a new picture *that* day. What do I want to say to that day? Some of my themes are personal, and some are about what's going on in the world. Not having inspiration be a factor in deciding to put out work is another artistic choice, because I can't just sit down when I'm inspired. Instead, it's like, "I've got two hours."

_HM: Is it hard for you to tap into that creative space? When I look at some of the things that you've come up with, it's just like, "How do you think of that?" How do you come up with an idea for one of these *Everydays*?

_MW: They need to be finished and posted online by midnight. Usually almost all of them are done at the end of the day—

_HM: Wait—Eastern, Pacific, Hawaii?

_MW: Wherever I am. Some days, if I travel, it's like, "Wow, I've got an extra three hours." Others I'll lose three hours. It's always whatever time zone I'm in at the end of the day, that is the deadline, and they're usually made in the last few hours of the night. Many times, I work right up until midnight. And it's not like during the day I'm thinking about it nonstop. Sometimes I'll see an image, or something will happen, and I'll be like, "Ah, that's what I'm going to do," and then I'll sit down later and do it. On the other hand, if something big happens, something that I feel like I need to reflect on, there's a bit more stress.

_HM: Where do you look for these images or find these things that happen?

_MW: Usually when I sit down, I'll look through pictures on the internet for maybe ten minutes. I'll look through them very fast, looking for anything that can be that first spark. What is the first minimal viable product that is different from what I've done before, is something I could be interested in, and is something I could spend some time on? Of course, I'm always trying to find the picture that I'm most excited to make, because that is the picture that I think people will be most excited to see. It's very rare that I'll put a shitload of time into something that people won't enjoy.

_HM: Why is that?

_MW: No matter what the actual subject matter is, people can see when there's a lot of passion behind something. It gets them excited. I look through pictures for a little bit, and then I just sit down and start. From there, I'm always open to changing direction, and sometimes the direction will completely change in the last five minutes. I'll put in a new object or a new shape, or I'll change something, and then that will provide a new direction. I'm very open throughout the process.

_HM: You're conscious of your audience.

_MW: There's one thing I think I need to do more of—because I think people find it interesting—stream and create more of them live. I'm excited to now have spaces where I can invite people to watch me do it live. It can either be with everybody directing me, or with one person directing me, or it can be with nobody directing me, and I just have headphones on, come in, and do the fucking picture, not talk to anybody, and walk out.

_HM: That'd be awesome.

_MW: All of those things become interesting choices in their own respects, and people still have no idea why I'm making them.

_HM: How long does a piece take on average?

_MW: On average, I would say about two hours, and that can change depending on if I have an idea that needs a longer period of time. In that case, I'll note the idea, and wait for four or five days, or whenever, until I've got the time to devote. Usually it's two hours, depending on the day.

_HM: When did you start making them live? Do you do it often?

_MW: I was doing a series of talks at conferences and different design events and digital art conferences, talking about the *Everydays*, talking about my practice, and one day it was like, *I don't really have anything else to talk about*. I didn't want to do another talk I'd said a million times, regurgitating the same thing everybody's already heard from me fifteen times over. I thought, what if I did my *Everydays* live, did it in an hour in front of the audience, brought up a person to be kind of like a sidekick, to help bounce questions off me, who can keep talking while I'm doing it? I did the first one in 2019, not too long ago, but since then, I've done it about two dozen times. Some on Zoom, obviously, and some in front of live audiences.

_HM: How does it go?

_MW: To me, it's really a fun, alternative way to show people 1) you don't need to take everything so fucking seriously, and 2) you can just make something. It can be fun, and it can be stupid, and it can just be about having a good time. Art *can* be a fun thing. For a lot of people, art maybe was fun, and then it stopped being fun. It became unenjoyable, so they stopped. I'm not talking about professional artists. I'm talking more about people who were artists and then stopped, or people who want to do something but build up so much pressure that it paralyzes them, and they end up not making anything. I want to show people that you can make something with no preconceived notion of what it's going to be, and you can see the whole thing through from start to finish. At the end of the day, I'm going to post it. It's fun. I'll definitely do more of them in the future.

_HM: Do you have a favorite *Everyday*?

_MW: There's a few that stick out, but not many: the last of the *First 5,000 Days*, or the first *Everyday*. . . . There are a couple that were more like inflection points. New themes, new approaches, new subjects, new characters. Those, I would say, stand out a bit more. Over the years, there have been a few where I felt like I got lucky, when some unconscious thing turned out better than I felt like I deserved credit for. Or ones where I learned something new and felt like I'd unlocked two months' worth of new ideas, aesthetics, or techniques.

OPPOSITE PAGE

TO INFINITY AND BEYOND
01.20.2019

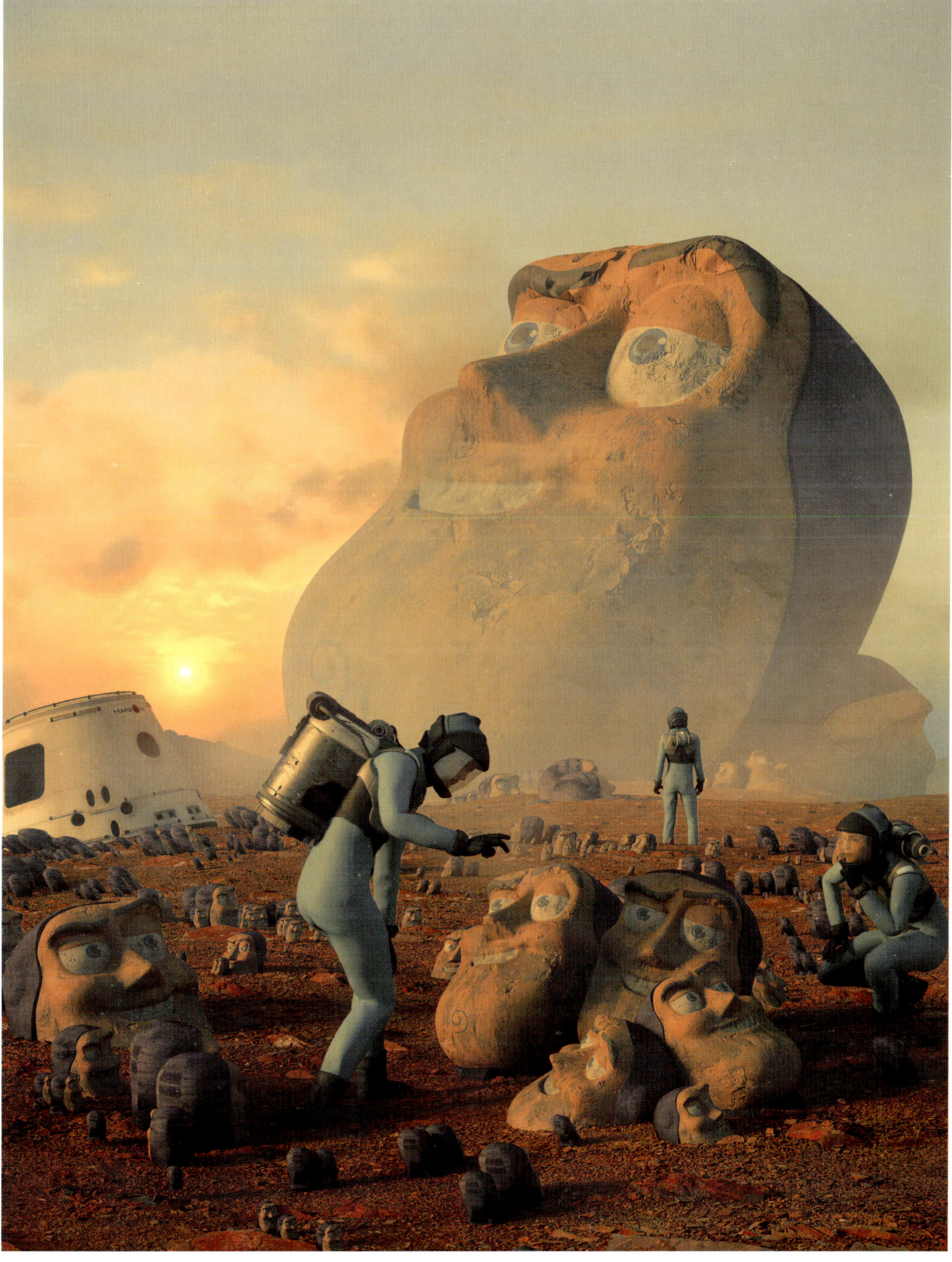

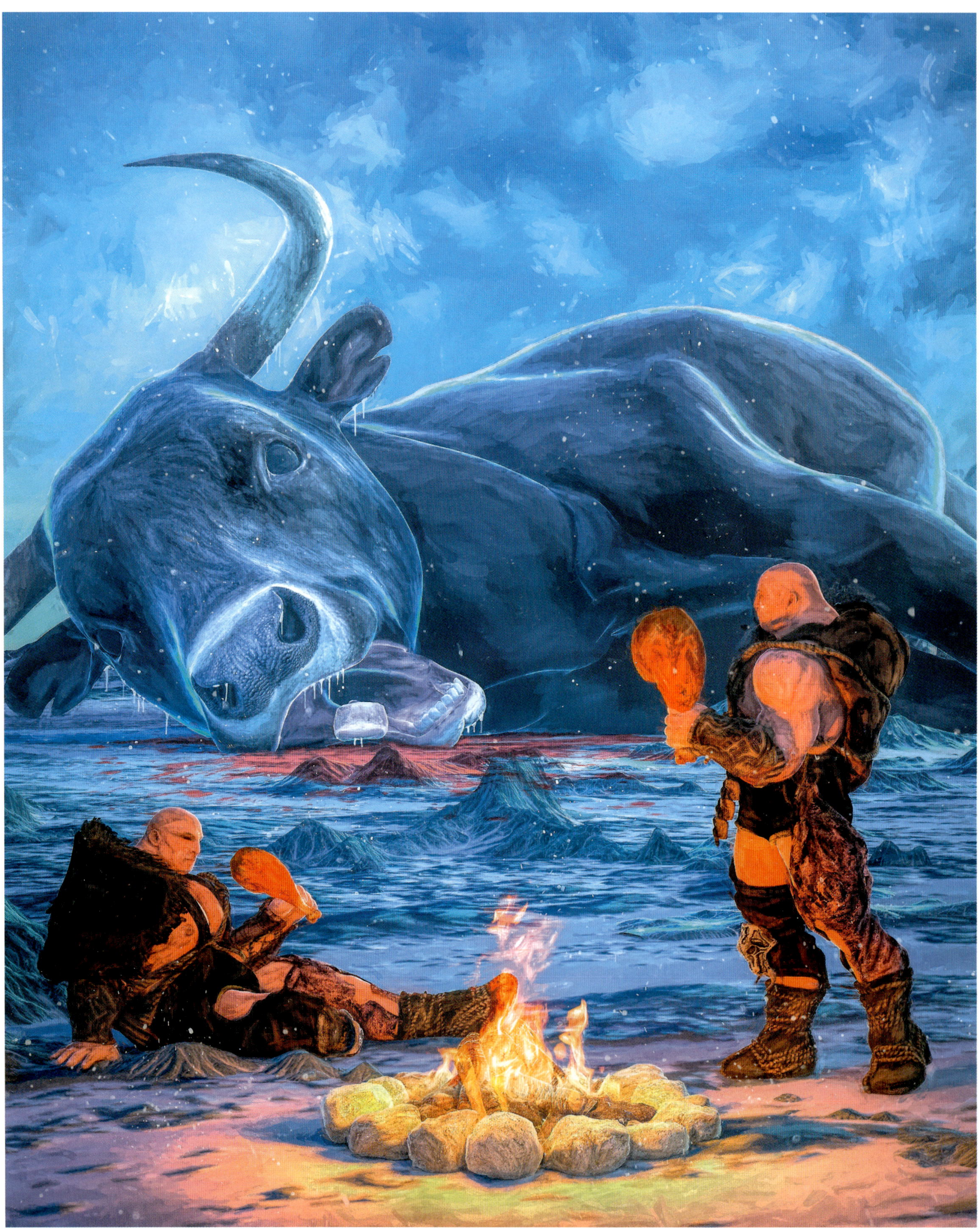

_HM: It's also nice how your characters evolve over time. They have their own personalities.

_MW: A hundred percent. That's how I look at them too, as this cast of characters I have some idea of the meaning behind. Buzz Lightyear, to me, is an analogy for this American overconfidence and stupidity.

_HM: I'd like to shift the conversation toward the viewing end. After you've made an image and posted it online, it's done. The moment they're put online, you've released them to the public. There's no filter—that's a very radical and innovative viewing approach.

_MW: Usually when they're done, I click save, and immediately go to Twitter to post it. There's no stepping back, as I usually have literally run out of time. That process of asking, "Is this good? Is this not good?" That's not part of it. That's another thing that people get too hung up on; they put too much importance on whether or not they personally like the work. To me, in some respects, it's just not that relevant. With the *Everydays*, it's irrelevant whether or not I like them. It just has to be done.

_HM: What can you tell me about your viewership and your thoughts about what happens postproduction?

_MW: There's value in not having a filter, but I am very conscious about one fact: they're most likely going to be viewed on a phone. That phone is small, and people won't see a lot of details. A lot of the time, I take advantage of that. The pictures have broader brushstrokes, for example. I'm creating for the medium of how people are going to view it, which isn't ten feet tall.

_HM: When you say broad brushstrokes, do you mean compositional forms, or color, or light? What is a brushstroke to you?

_MW: Broad brushstrokes are like this: there's a lot of little fuckups in there that you would not notice [at first], but if you look very close, it's like, "Well, that doesn't look great." I've been called out over it.

_HM: "Dude, your JPEG's off, man."

_MW: People were upset! I did a picture of people eating a giant bull during one of the last crypto winters. If you look close, you can see the guy on the left's thumb is not covering the meat.

_HM: Oh, he's not actually holding anything.

_MW: People saw it and they called me out. I had a bunch of people saying, "Bro, where's the fucking thumb?" So, the very next day, I made a piece in response to people calling out my thumb. I think I called it *Thumbgate*. I find it very interesting to be able to get immediate feedback and then have it affect the next day's work. This immediate feedback can change things moving forward.

OPPOSITE PAGE

CRYPTO WINTER

05.20.2021

_HM: A lot of art viewing is inaccessible to most people. You talk directly to your public in real time. What do you like about this sort of open-form conversation?

_MW: A lot of people focus on the NFT and crypto portion of what's happened, but what's been lost is the social-media aspect. That's how I gained a following—making these pictures very consciously for the internet and very consciously for them to be viewed immediately. With some of them, there's a disposability to the image that makes it meant for right now. Down the line, *Thumbgate*, for instance, isn't going to make any sense to a new viewer. Nevertheless, my works celebrate the weirdness of the internet in a way that I think is very different from artists of the past. As far as accessibility, what museums of the future will need to grapple with is that these images are instantly accessible. You can follow a shit-ton of artists. Before social media, if you asked me how many artists I followed, I would probably say fifty—maybe. It was hard! You had to go check their website. And how did you find them in the first place? Through a blog, or by going to this or that event?

_HM: And then, five months later, you'd still see the same work.

_MW: These days, I follow ten times more artists and am able to be inspired and affected by all of them. That is a massive, massive shift that I think we simultaneously take for granted and don't even understand the ramifications of. Think about how fast ideas and trends can spread when that's the case. And, moving forward, that is not going away. It's something people will be used to, and they'll be looking to museums to provide an experience that they couldn't just get on their phone. Personally, I think that will need to be more of a visceral experience than what you see at museums now.

_HM: I'm fascinated by your commitment and the generative growth this project has made. I also am deeply impassioned by the concept that it's going to continue—that we're not looking retroactively on something you intend on making into a book. What do you want the legacy of this project to be a hundred years from now?

_MW: I want it to be something that inspires people to make *more* art and to look at art-making not as some mystical, magical practice, but something that can just be a normal part of every person's life. Something that can help you work through things mentally, can help relieve stress, improve a skill, this or that. This project has inspired tens of thousands of people to start their own *Everydays*. Seeing that, and seeing people create careers from it already, has been really rewarding. I would love to see the movement continue to gain traction and be something that more people do as a way to get themselves to make more art.

OPPOSITE PAGE

THUMBGATE
5.21.2021

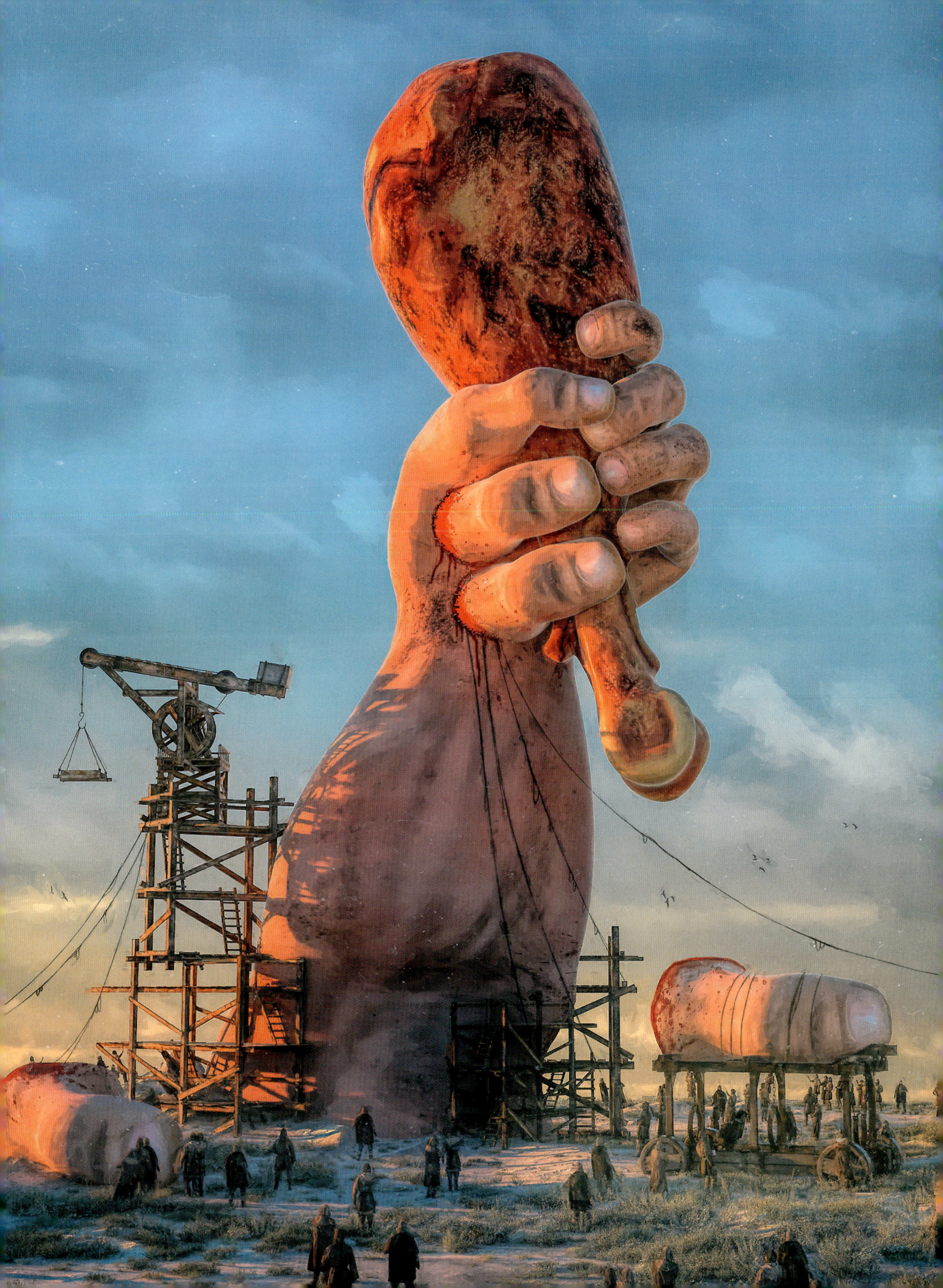

YOU DO NOT HAVE A LACK OF IDEAS, YOU HAVE A LACK OF DEADLINES.

—beeple

2007–2011 the REALLY crappy years

this project began out of an intense desire to get a LOT better at making art. at first this was drawing and then after the first year, i realized this could be used to learn Cinema 4D, a 3D rendering program which i had never used before. after that, i did a year or so digital photography, Adobe Illustrator, etc.

the focus of these first years, though, was really about learning the tools needed to create digital art. there is a massive amount of technique to become proficient with these programs that are extremely vast in terms of their capability. a typical 3D workflow includes at least some knowledge of concepting, modeling, materials, shading, lighting, rendering, and post compositing. to be able to make something in 3D you need to know at least a little bit about all of those things. when starting the *Everydays* I knew NOTHING of any of those areas. so often times I gave almost no thought to the actual final image as I was really super focused on just the process and learning.

after the first four years or so, I became comfortable enough with these tools that I then began to concentrate more on trying to learn how to make images that I actually liked. i had learned a workflow that allowed me to focus on more of the fundamentals of "good" art instead of the tools. from there, i honed in on color, composition, form, value, concept, etc.

tldr; yeaaa, the first few years mostly suck ass so we're gonna blow through these in a couple quick pages. ;)

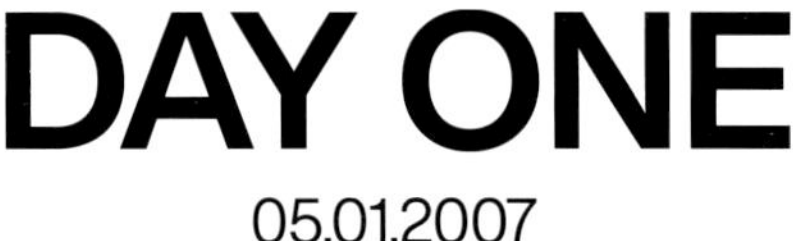
DAY ONE
05.01.2007

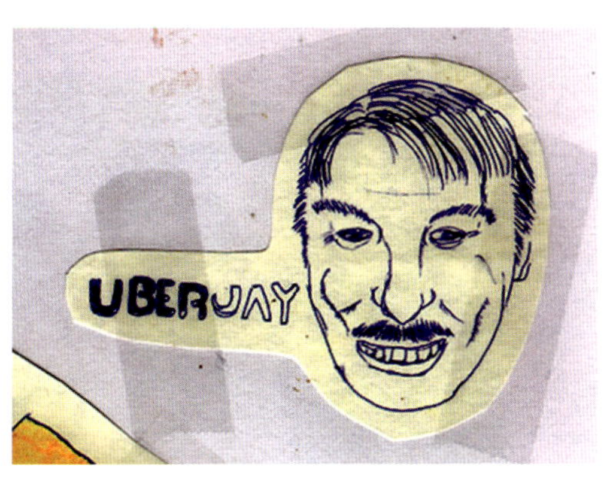
UBERJAY

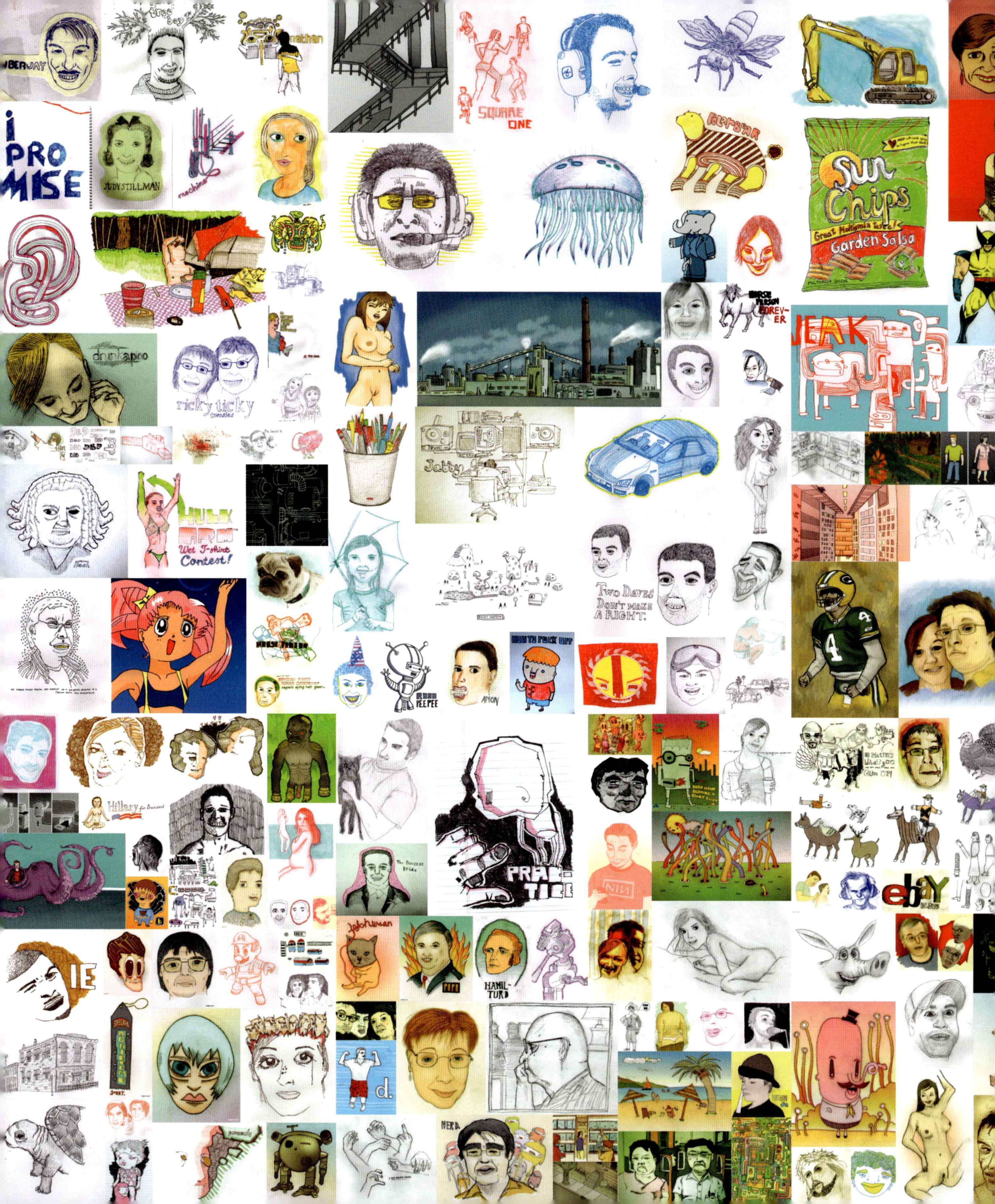

tree boy
nathan
SQUARE ONE
I PRO MISE
JUDY STILLMAN
Sun Chips
Great Multigrain taste!
Garden Salsa
ricky ticky
HULK ARM
Wet T-shirt Contest!
Two Daves Don't make a right.
PEEPEE
AMON
PRAC TICE
Hillary for President
ebay
HAMIL-TURD
IE
NERD

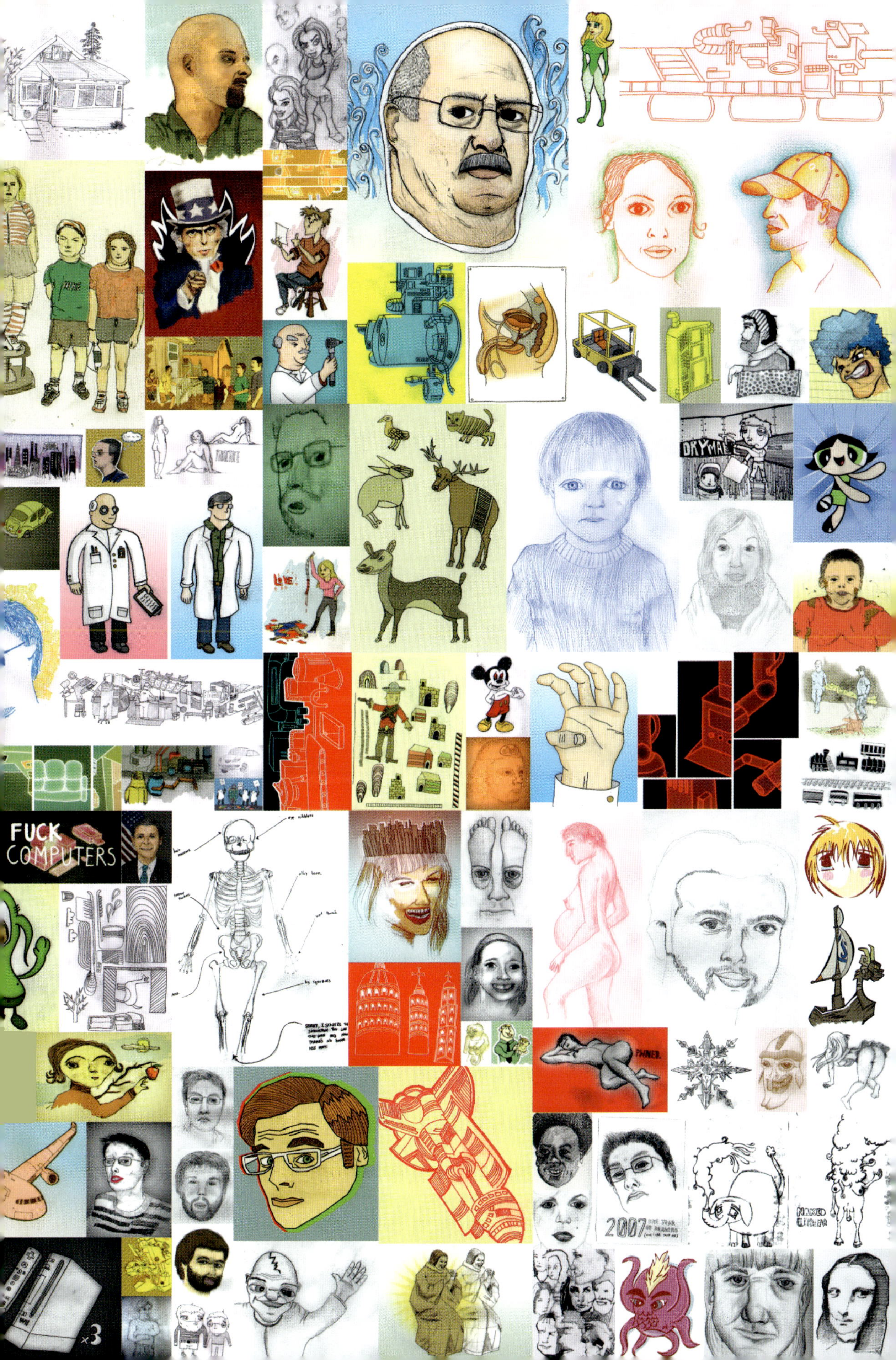
DRYMAL
FUCK COMPUTERS
PWNED.
2007
x3

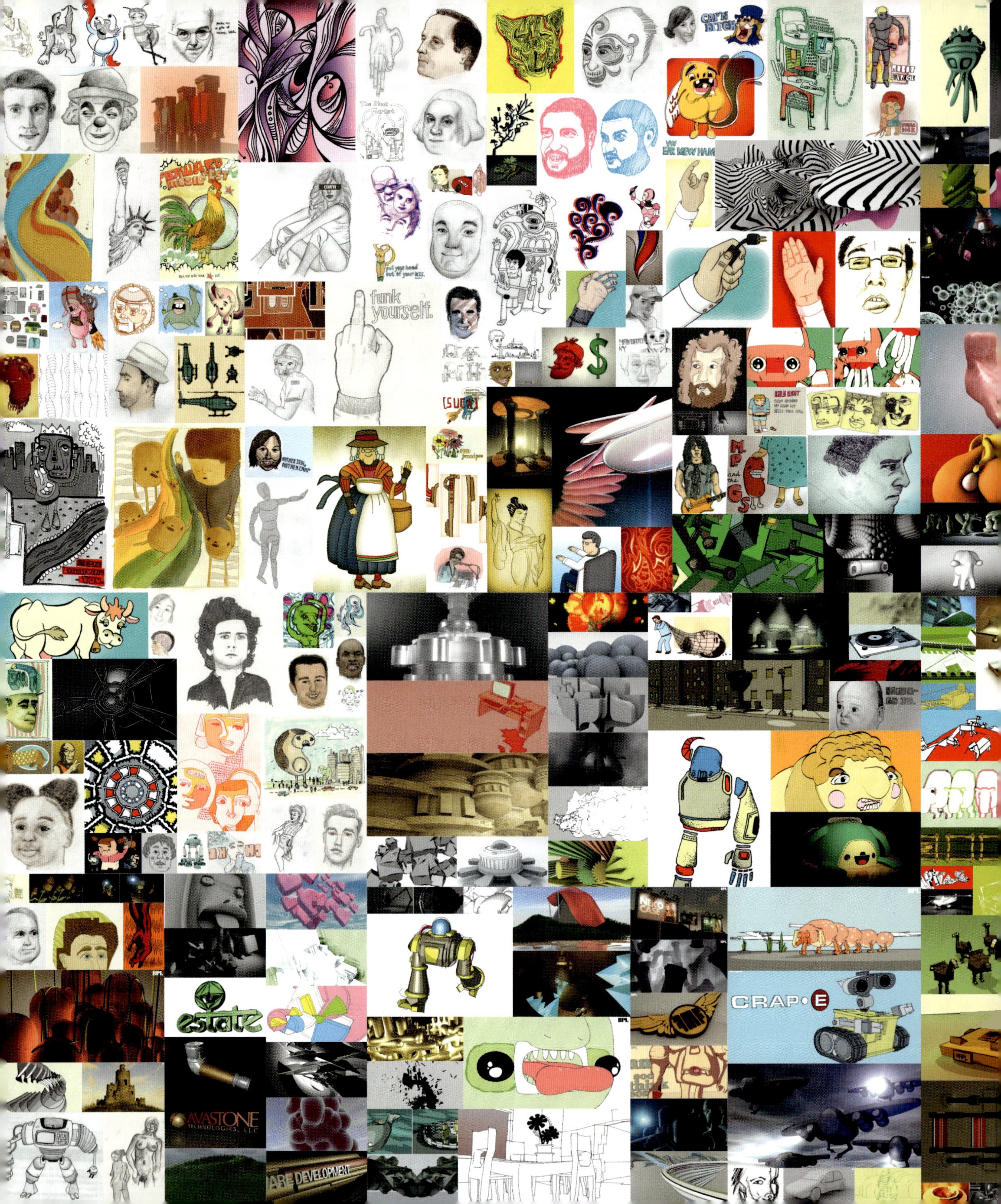
funk yourself.
CRAP·E
estate
AVASTONE
TECHNOLOGIES, LLC
DEVELOPMENT
CAP'N BITCH
pull your head out of your ass.

Dan More
chicken bird concept
MBX systems
MILWAUKEE FILM
FUCK COMPUTERS
ME FEEL LIKE
yoga
SMART ALYK
DREAM GOO
2009

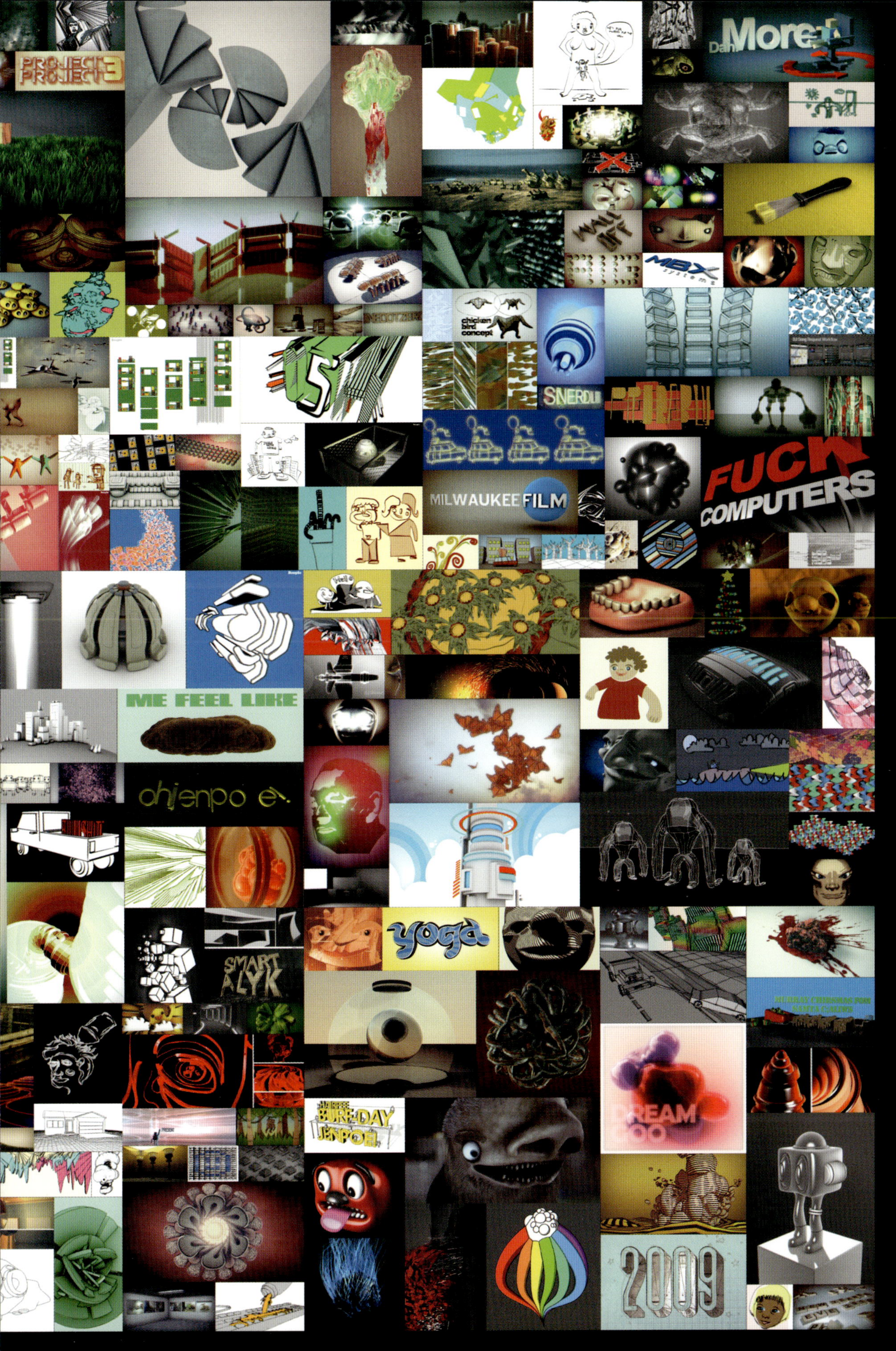

2009

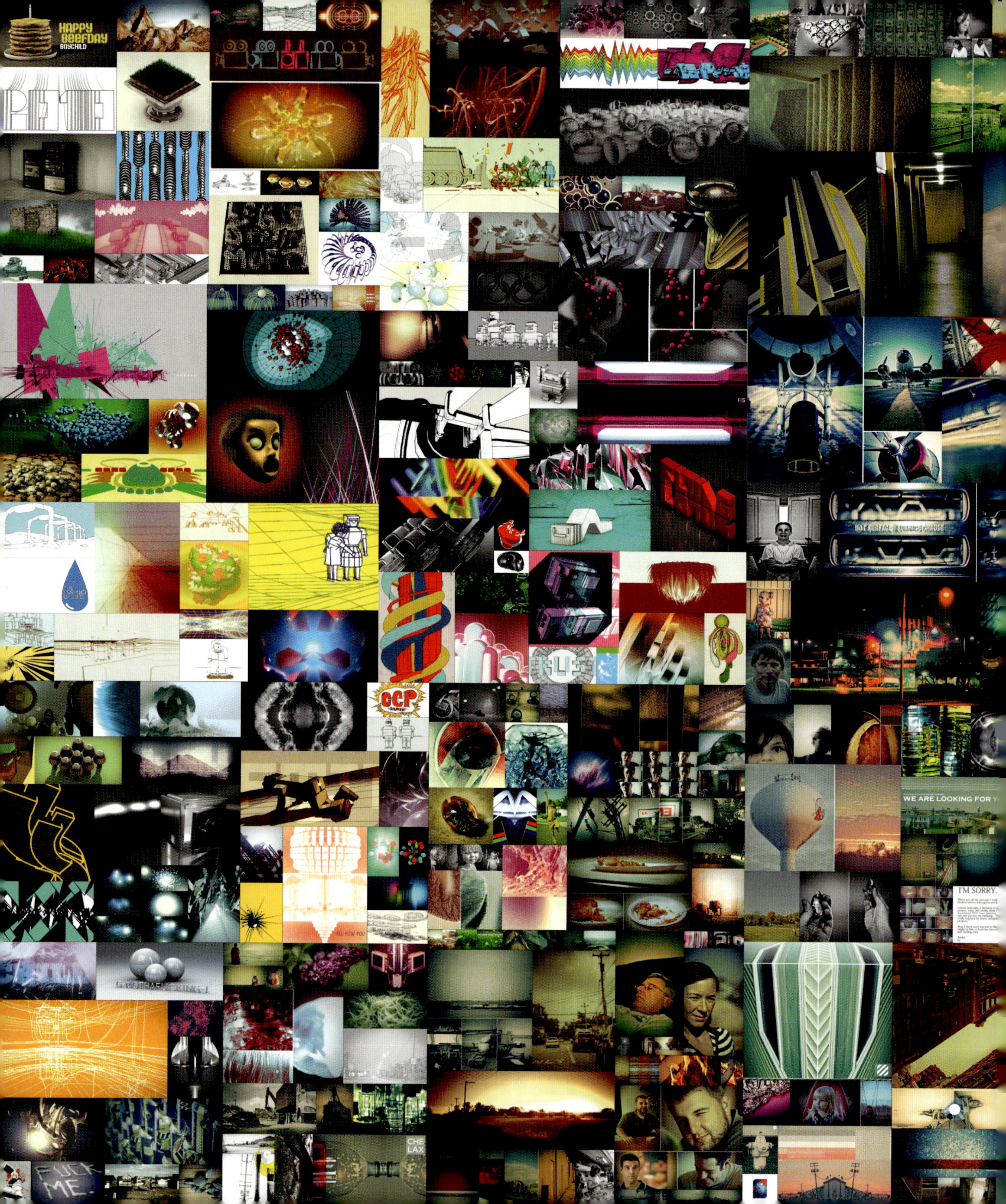

HAPPY
BEEFDAY
BOYCHILD
OCP
WE ARE LOOKING FOR Y
I'M SORRY.
CHE
LAX
FUCK
ME.

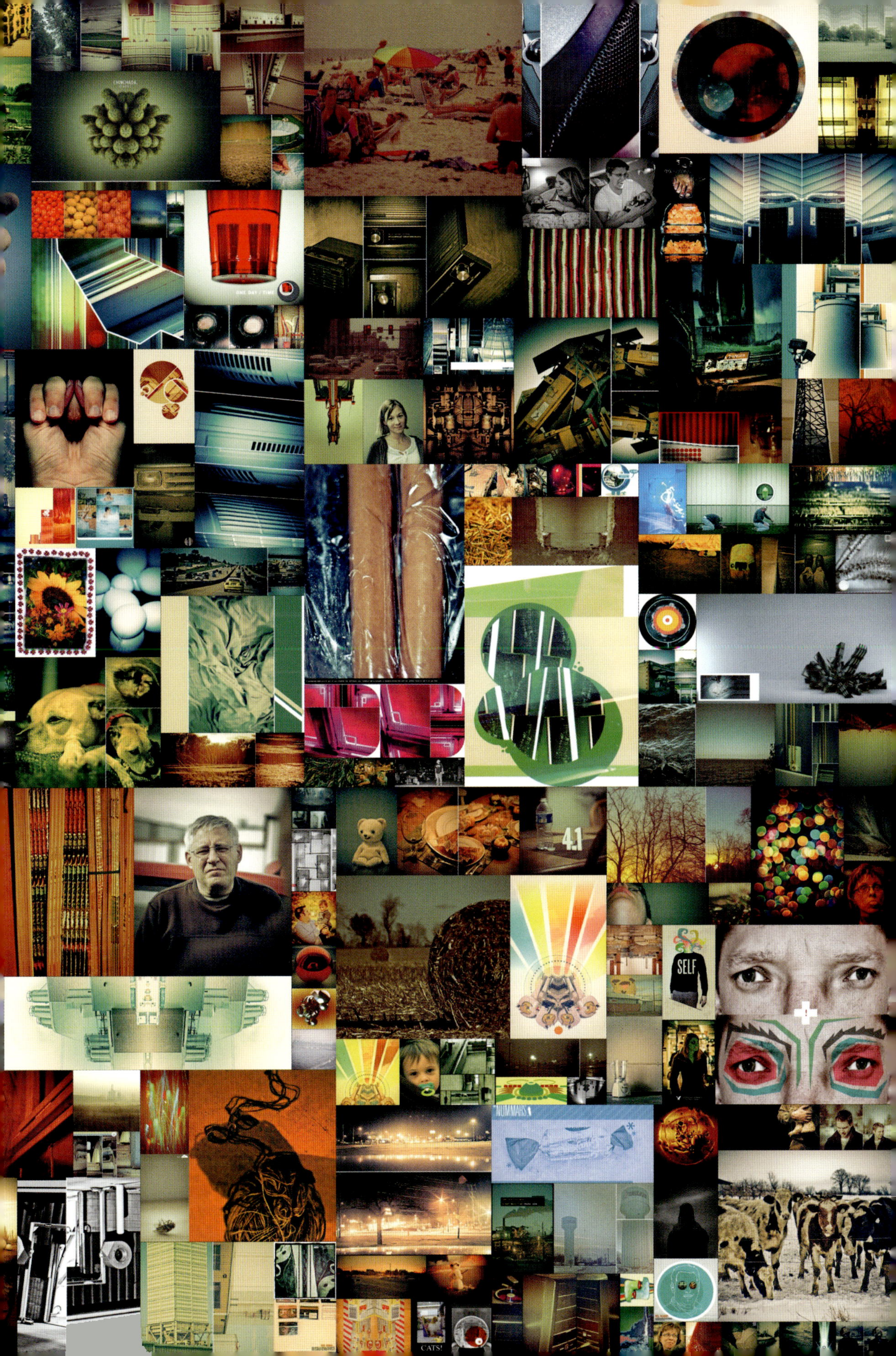
4.1
SELF
CATS!

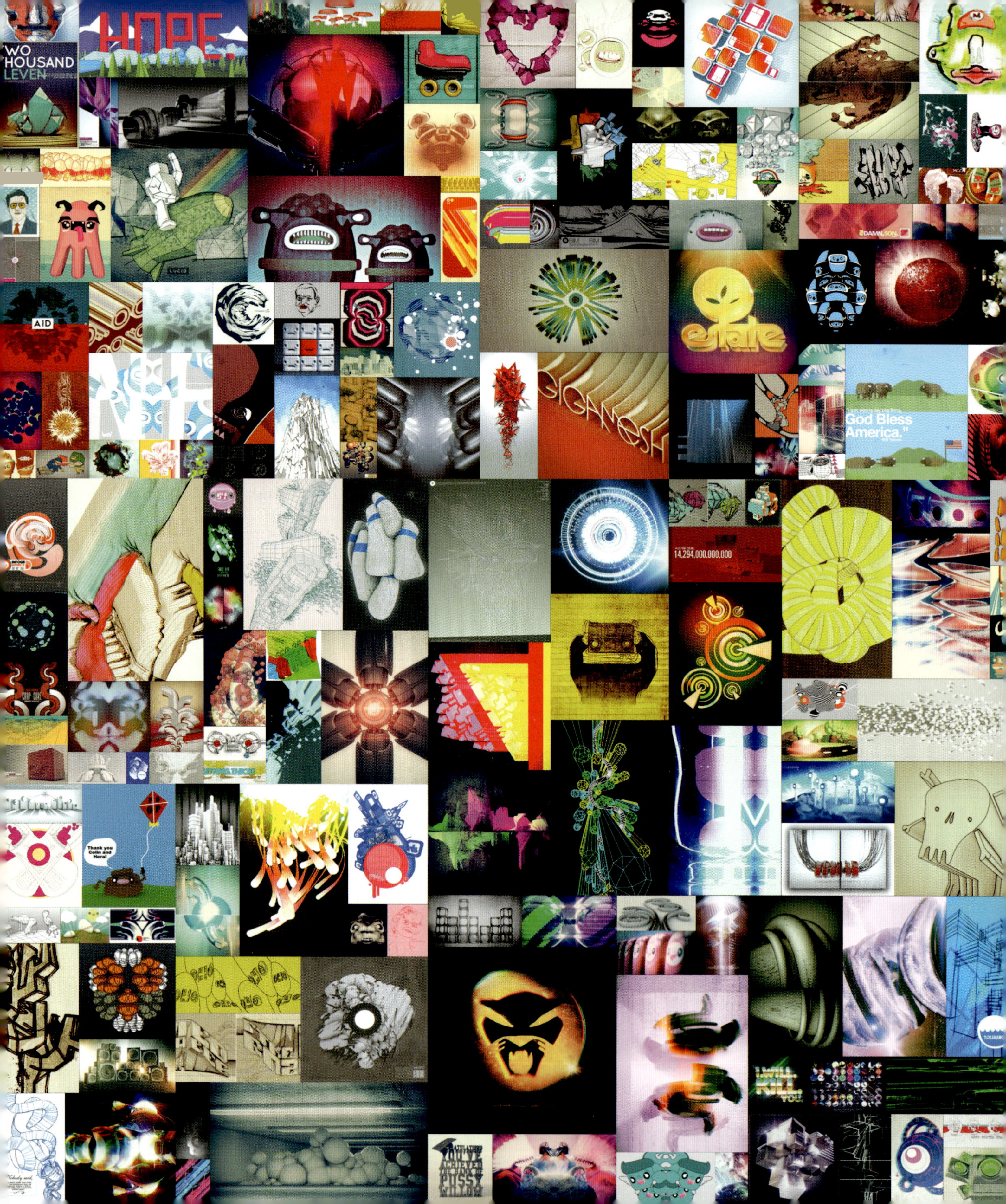
WO
HOUSAND
LEVEN
HOPE
LUCID
AID
DAMN,SON!
estate
GIGAMESH
God Bless
America."
14,294,000,000,000
Thank you
Colin and
Hera!
I WILL
KILL
YOU.

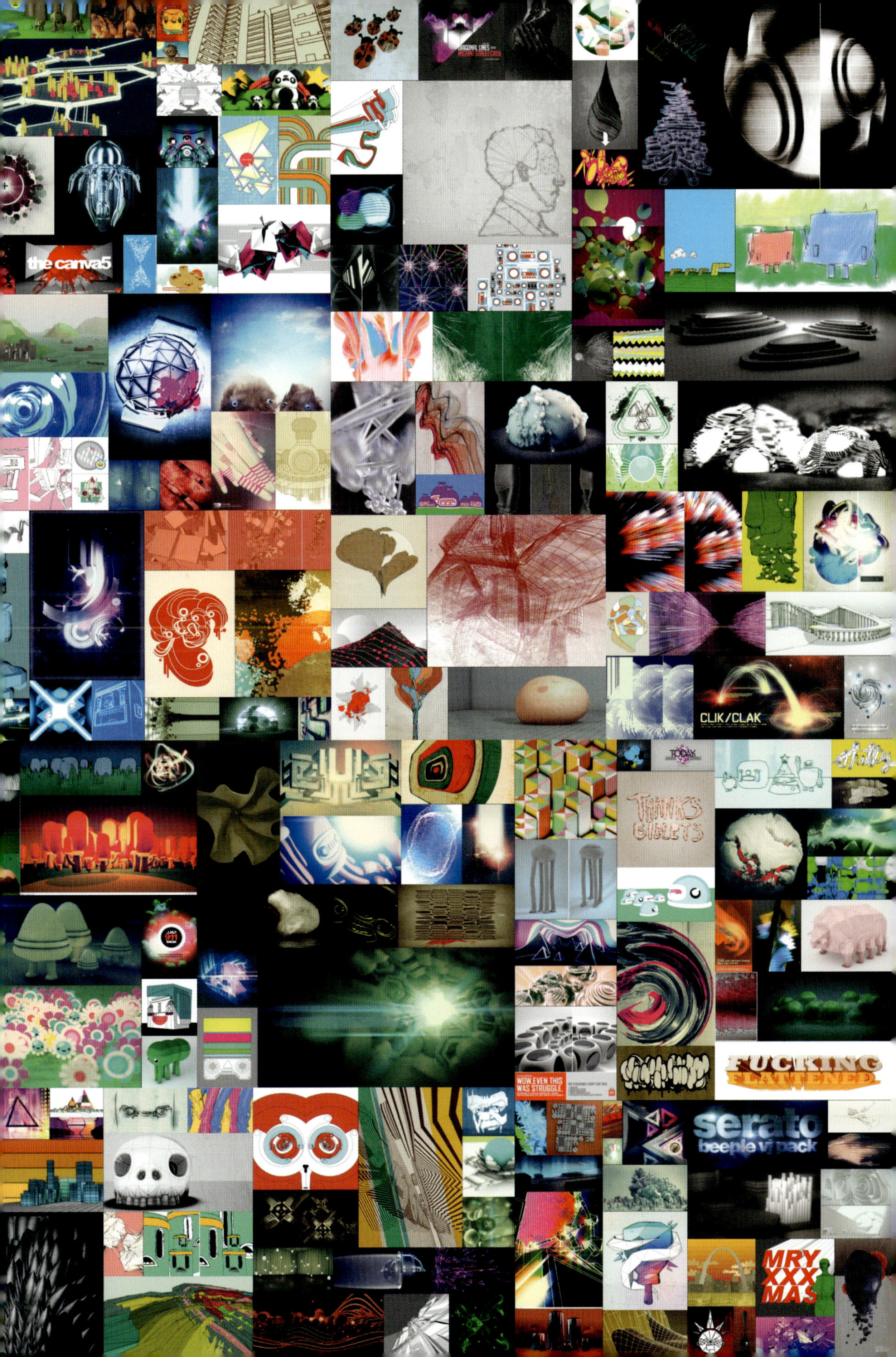

the canva5
CLIK/CLAK
THANKS GIBLETS
WOW EVEN THIS WAS STRUGGLE.
FUCKING FLATTENED
serato
beeple vj pack
MRY XXX MAS

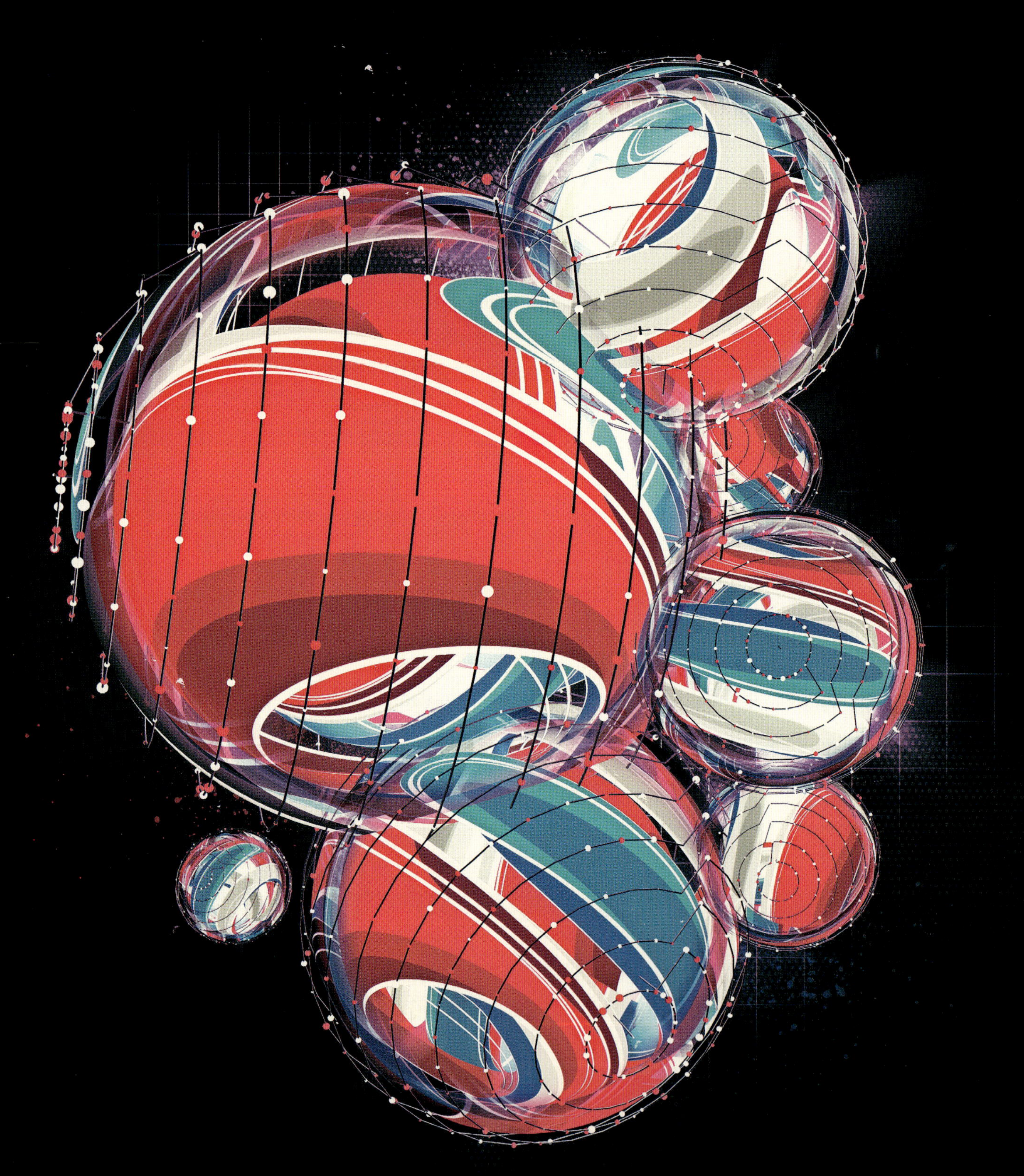

2012

OPPOSITE PAGE

pepballs
11.25.2012

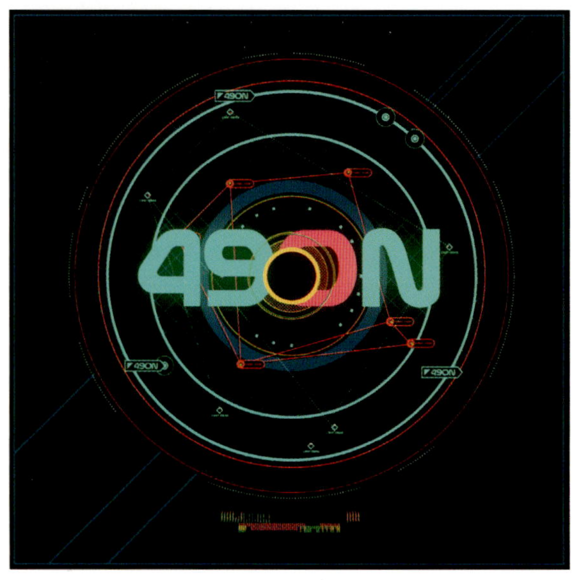

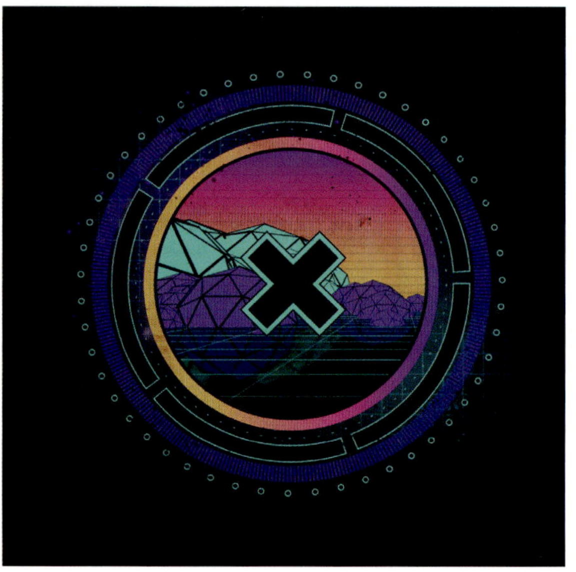

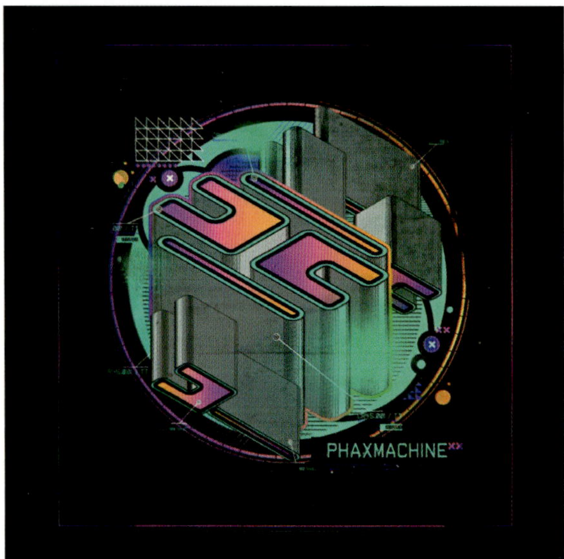

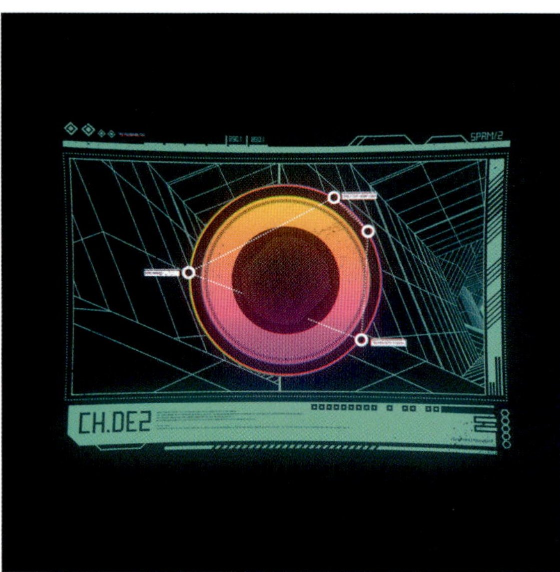

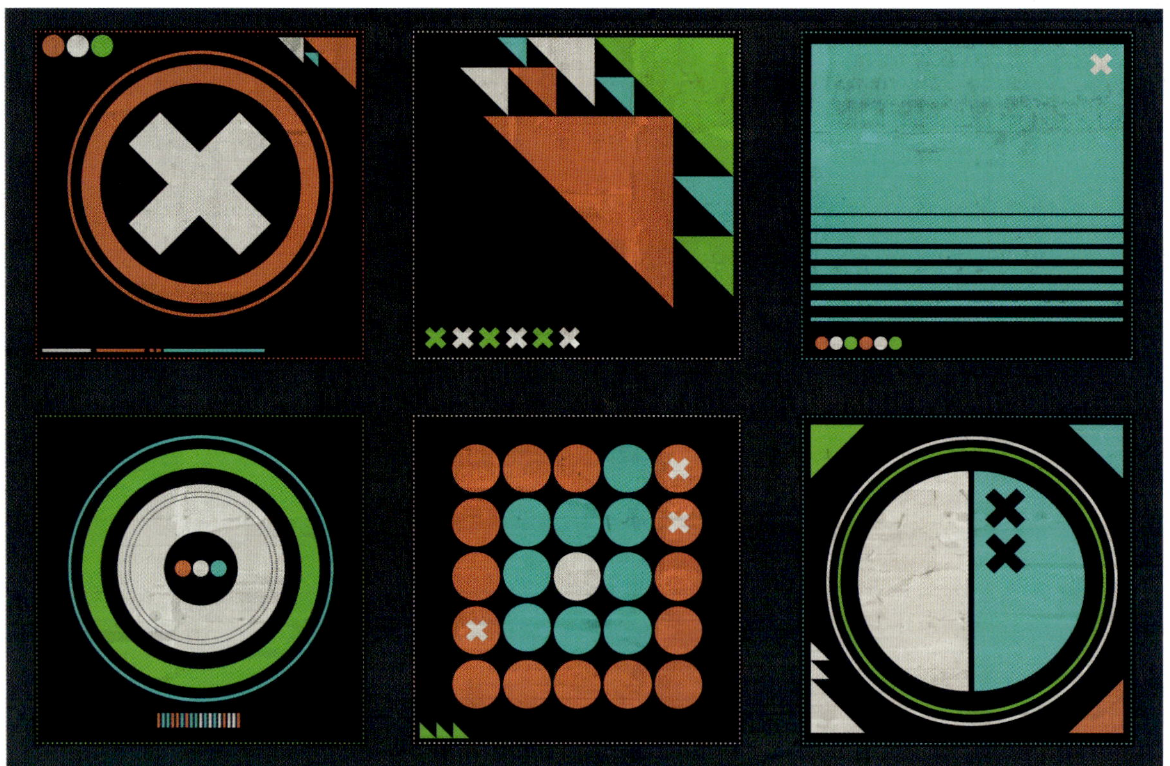

TOP LEFT
OKKKKKKKK
05.10.2012

TOP RIGHT
xx/oo v52.76
12.12.2012

MIDDLE LEFT
phaxmachine (xx)
12.29.2012

MIDDLE RIGHT
bluff called
11.16.2012

BOTTOM
always seems worse/ always works out
06.14.2012

OPPOSITE PAGE
assfist feral children
12.05.2012

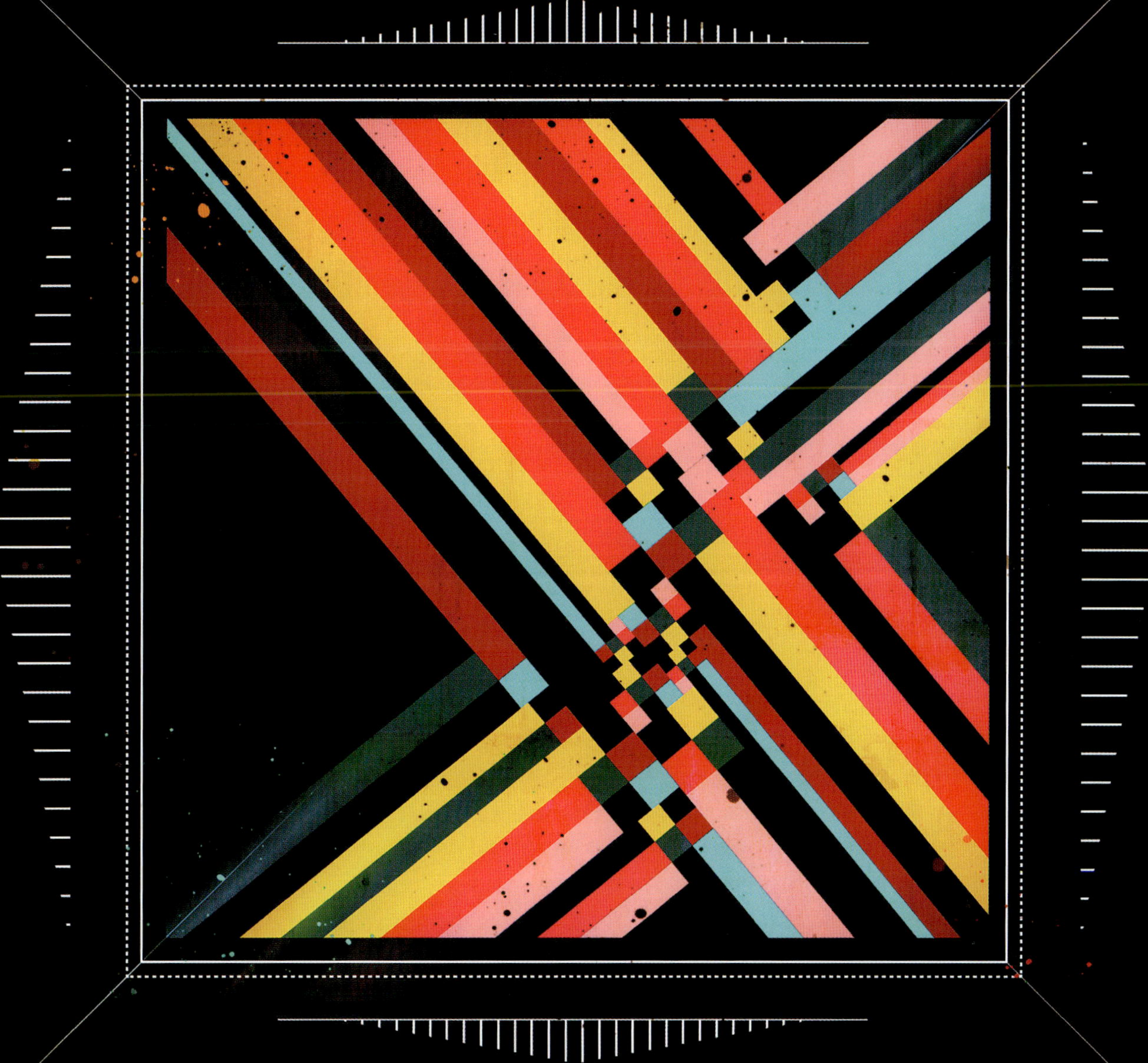

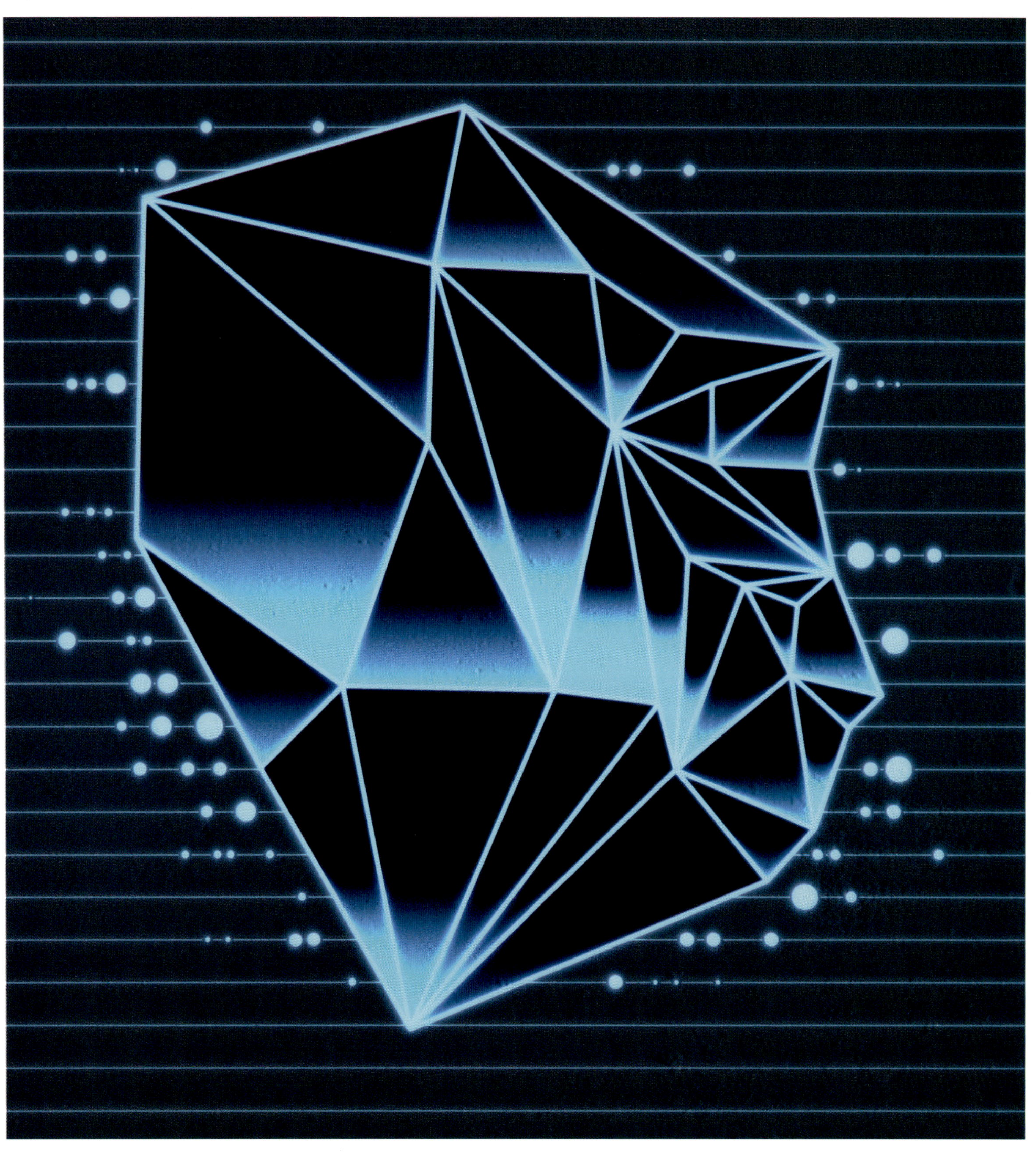

ABOVE
keegeldemon
02.27.2012

OPPOSITE PAGE
POTUS 3012
11.06.2012

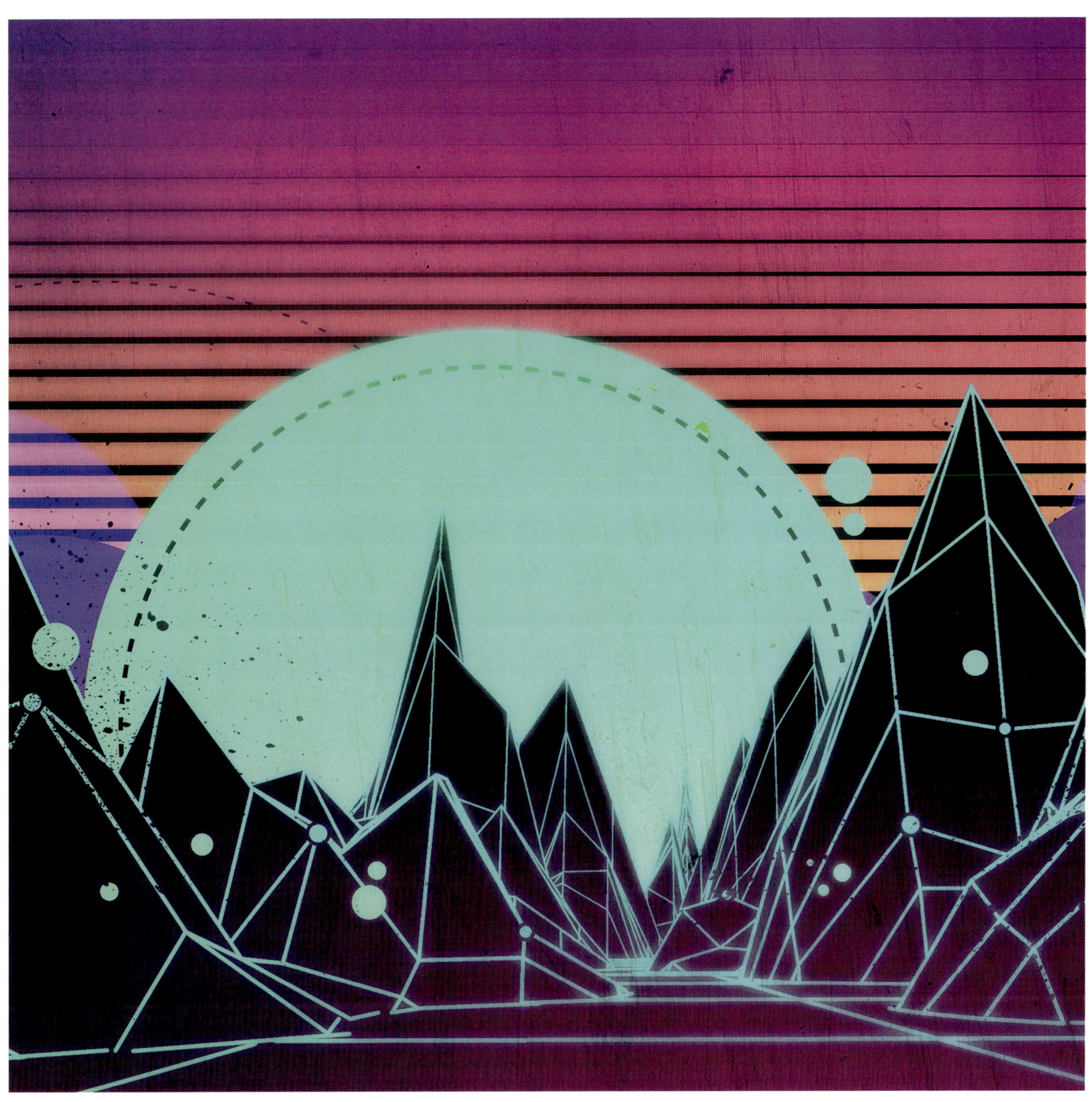

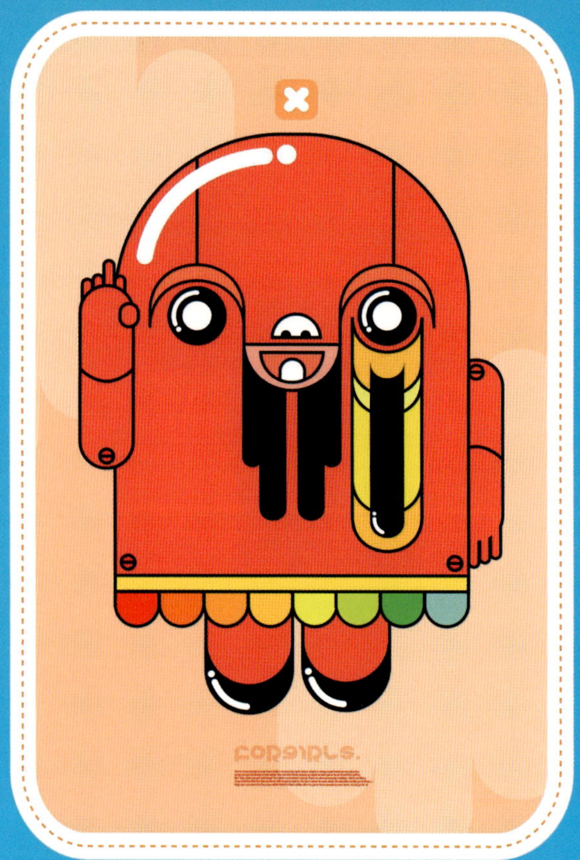

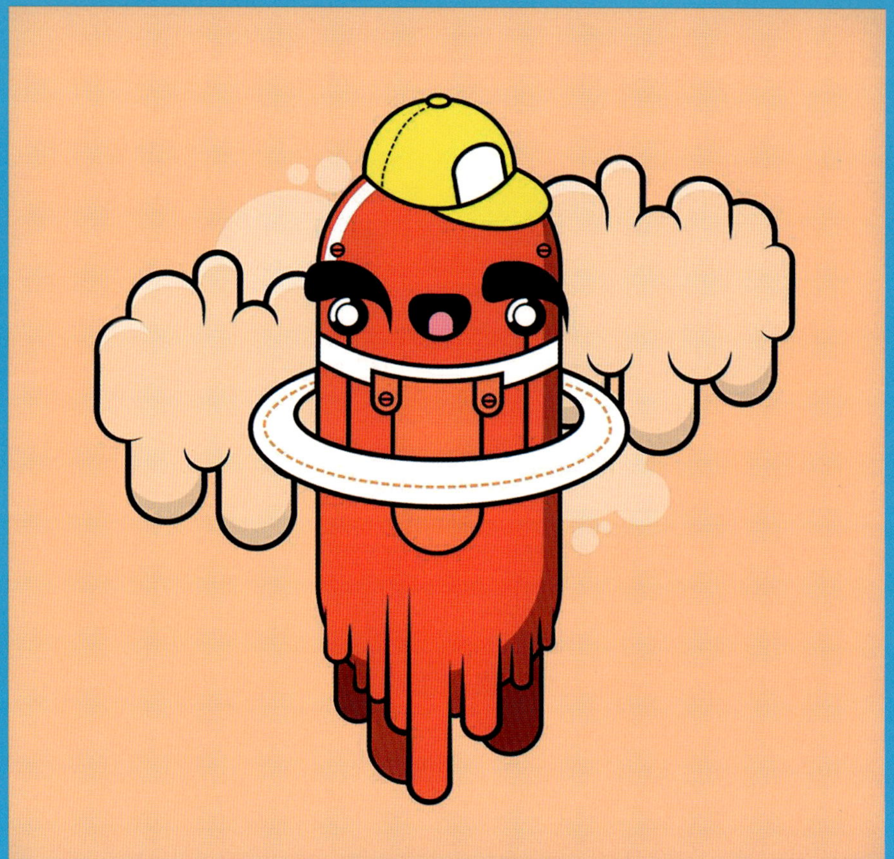

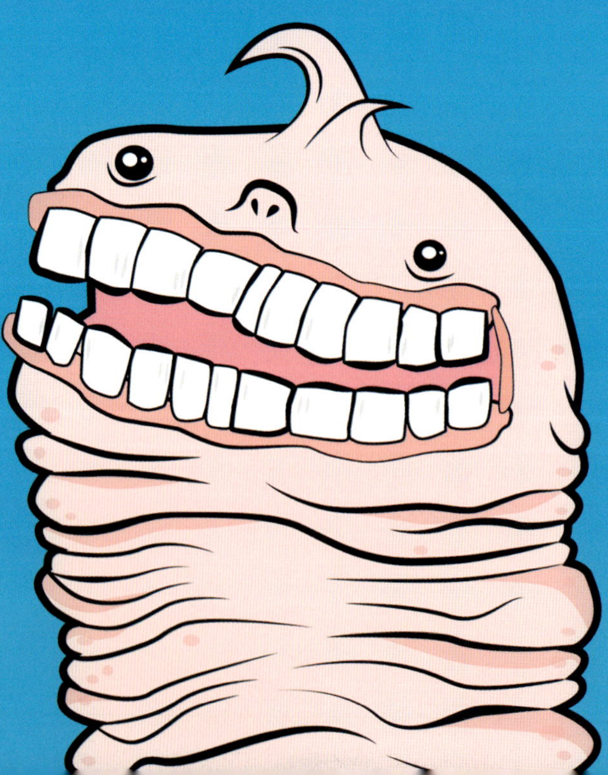

TOP LEFT
(for girls)
02.26.2012

TOP RIGHT
fucking whiplash
03.05.2012

RIGHT
falcid skinpup
01.05.2012

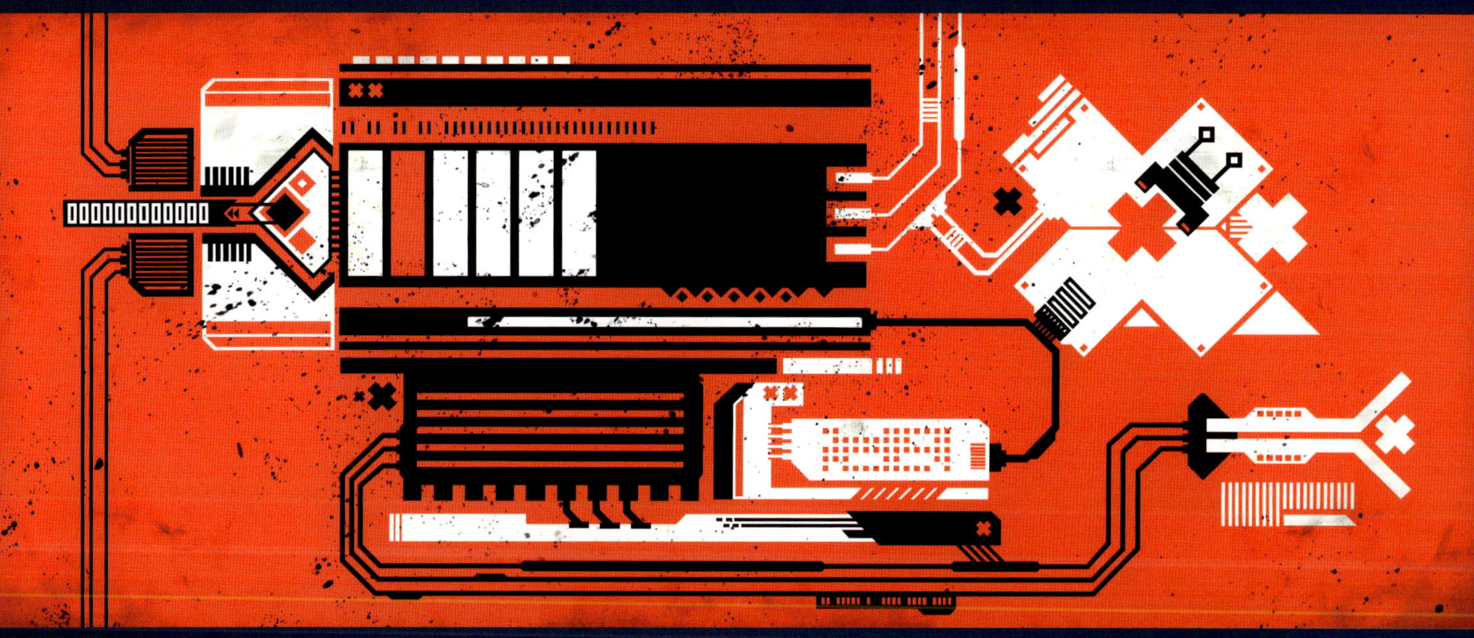

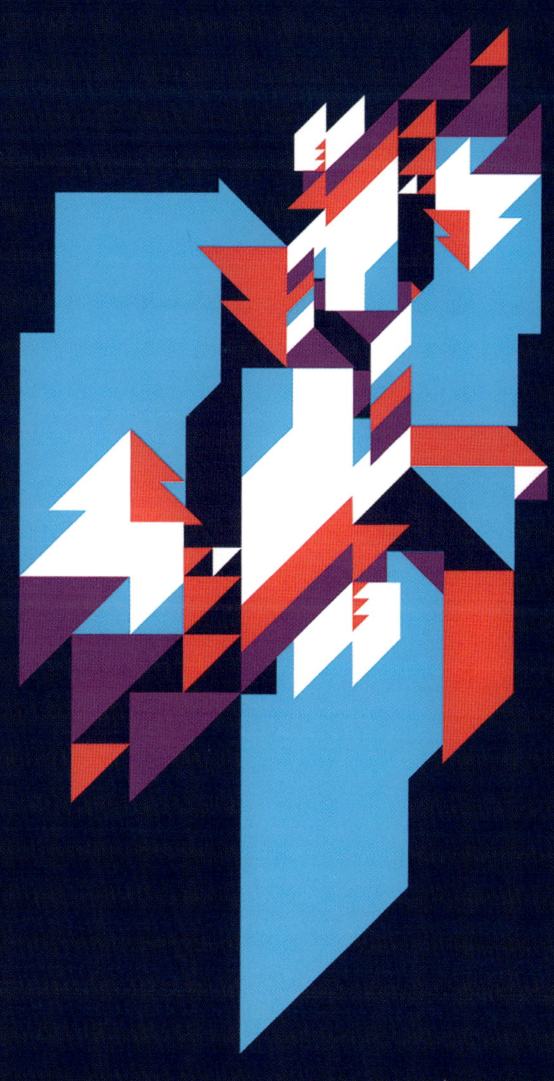

TOP

RWB.ONE

08.10.2012

BOTTOM

almost

05.11.2012

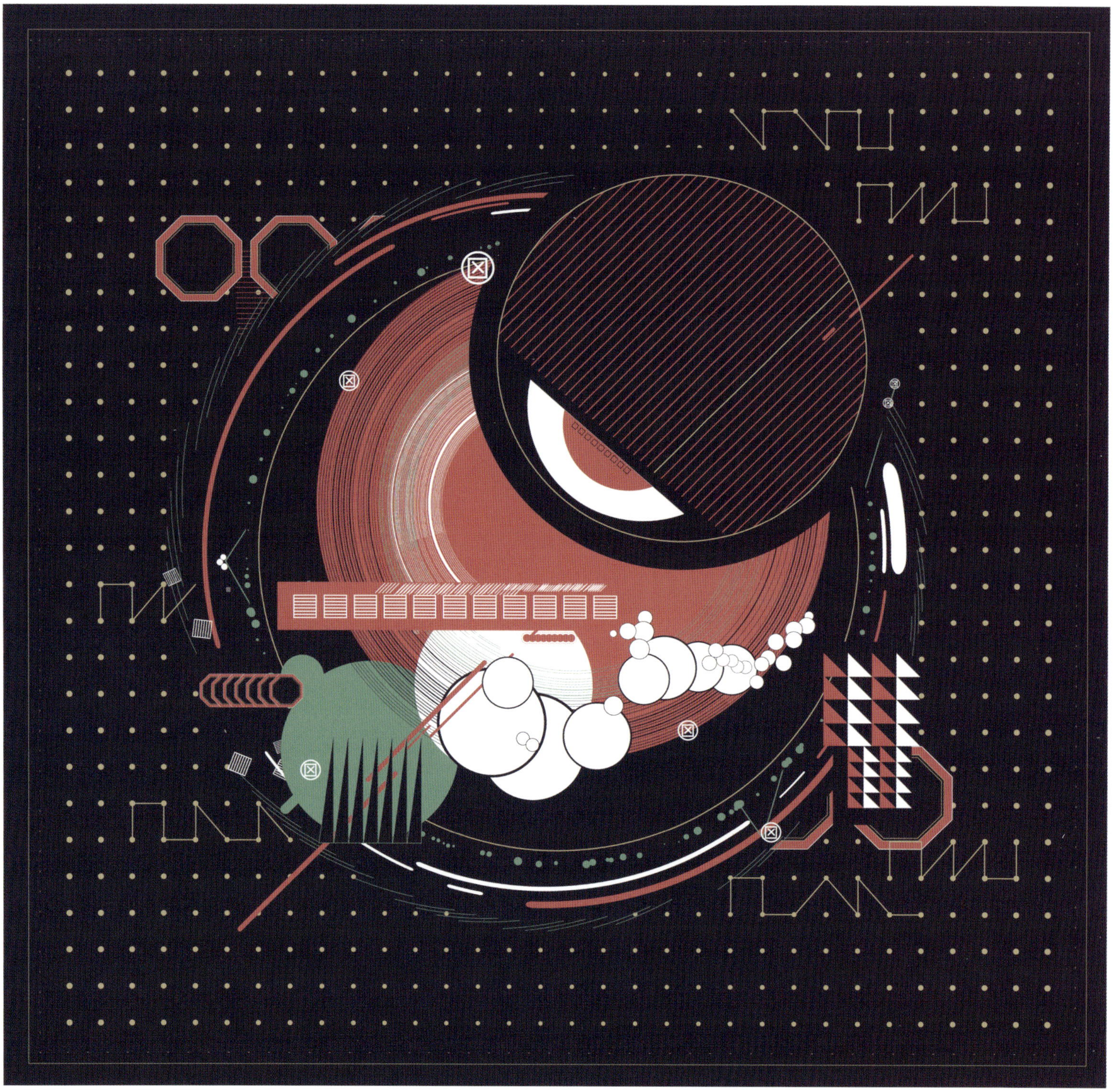

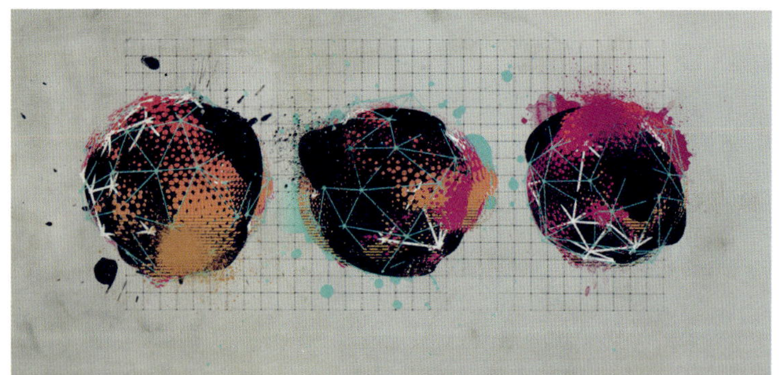

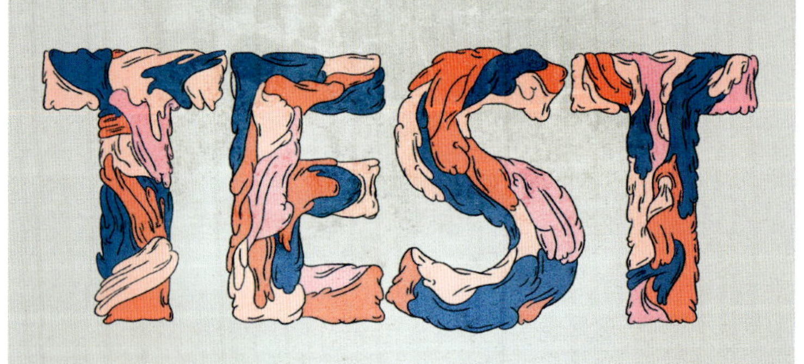
TEST

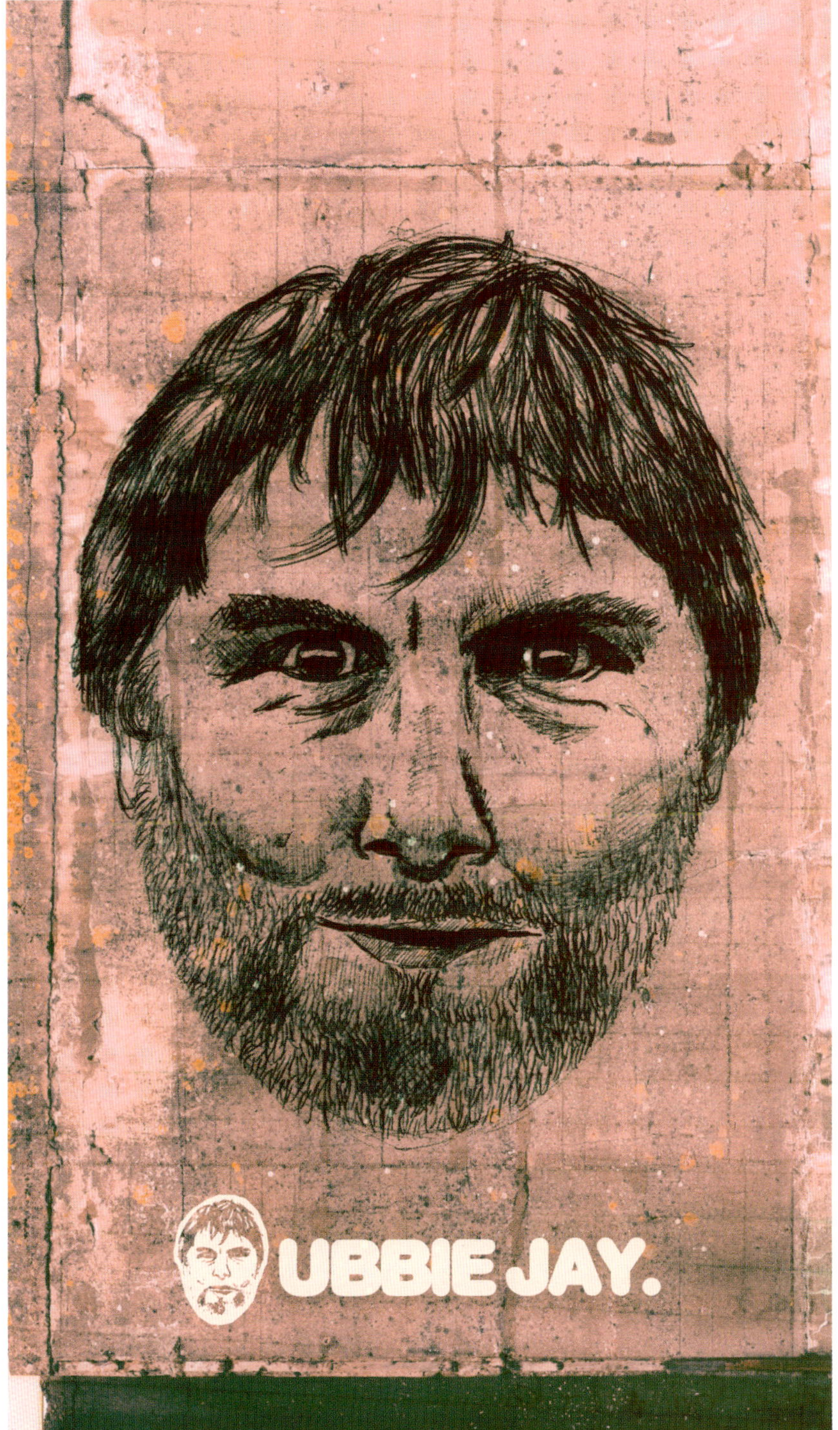

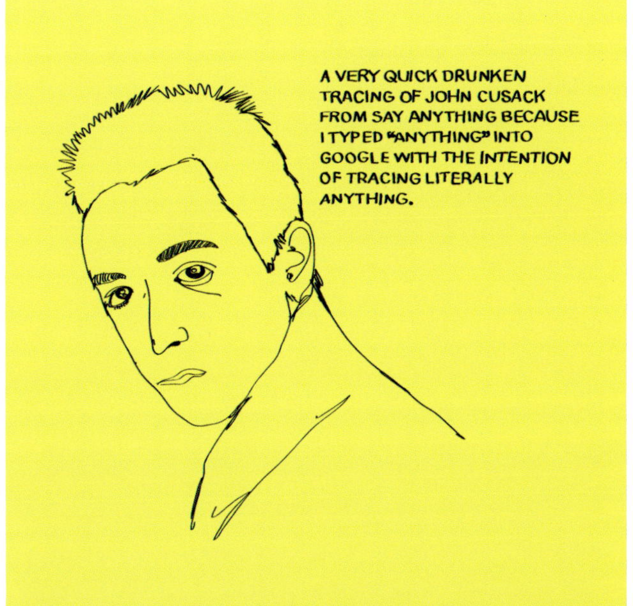

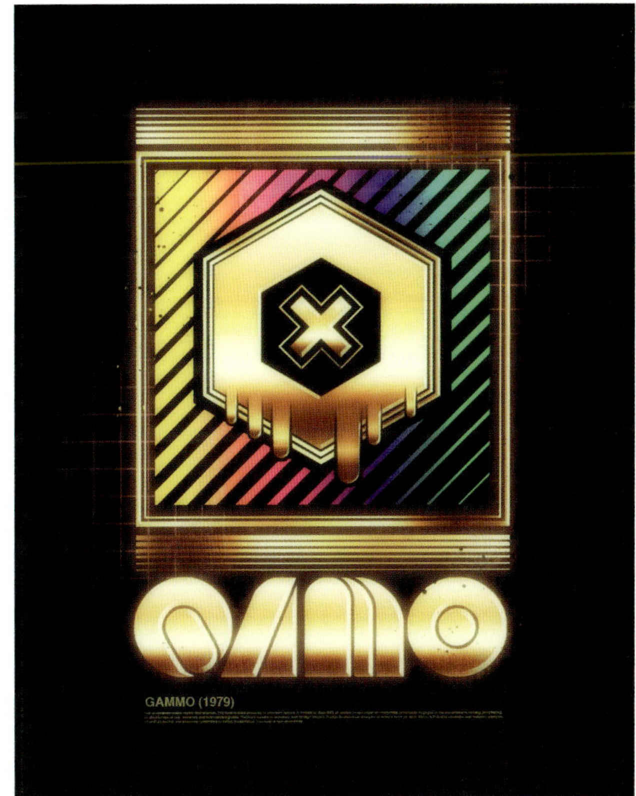

OPPOSITE PAGE, TOP

random shit for your face to maybe like
10.04.2012

OPPOSITE PAGE, BOTTOM LEFT

mutations / (control you never had)
12.04.2012

OPPOSITE PAGE, BOTTOM RIGHT

glimmer of hope
06.12.2012

LEFT

better, but still not where I wanna be. (same shit, 1827th day)
05.01.2012

TOP RIGHT

the pinnacle of artistic expression
05.04.2012

BOTTOM RIGHT

OAMO / 1979
12.21.2012

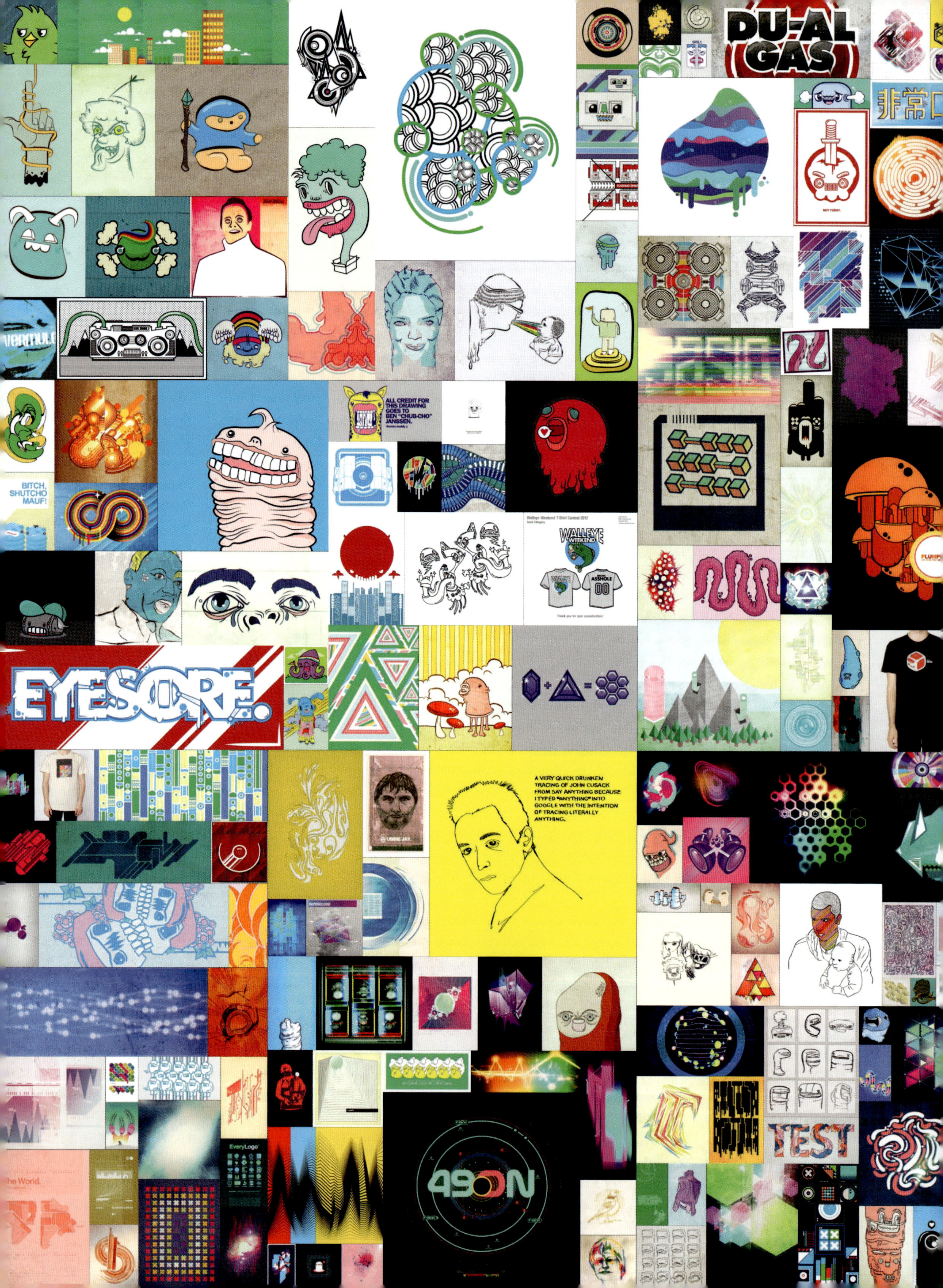
DU-AL
GAS
非常口
ALL CREDIT FOR THIS DRAWING GOES TO BEN "CHUB-CHO" JANSSEN.
BITCH, SHUTCHO MAUF!
WALLEYE WEEKEND
ASSHOLE
EYESORE
A VERY QUICK DRUNKEN TRACING OF JOHN CUSACK FROM SAY ANYTHING BECAUSE I TYPED "ANYTHING" INTO GOOGLE WITH THE INTENTION OF TRACING LITERALLY ANYTHING.
TEST
49ON
EveryLogo

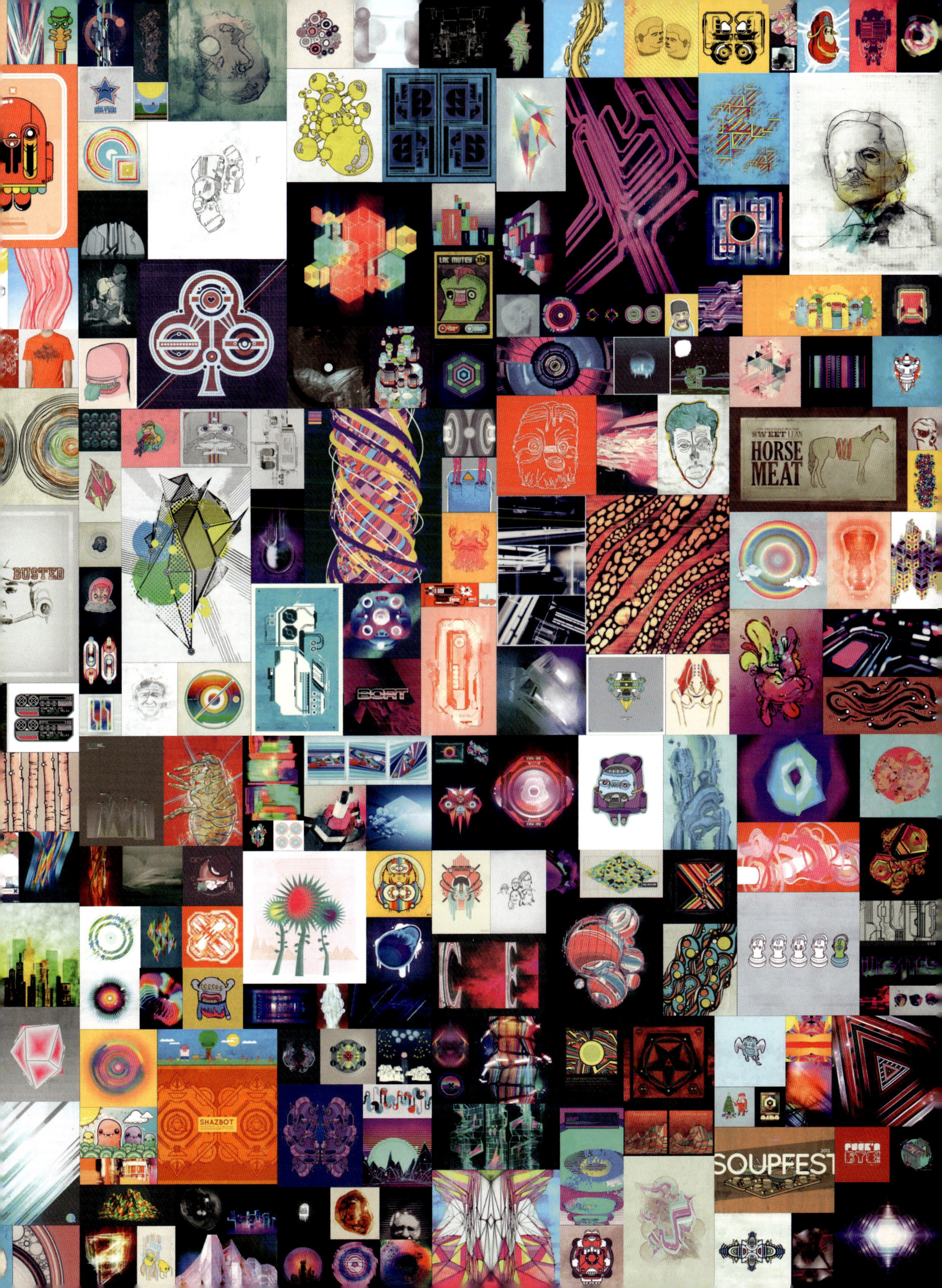
BUSTED
SWEET LEAN
HORSE MEAT
SHAZBOT
SOUPFEST

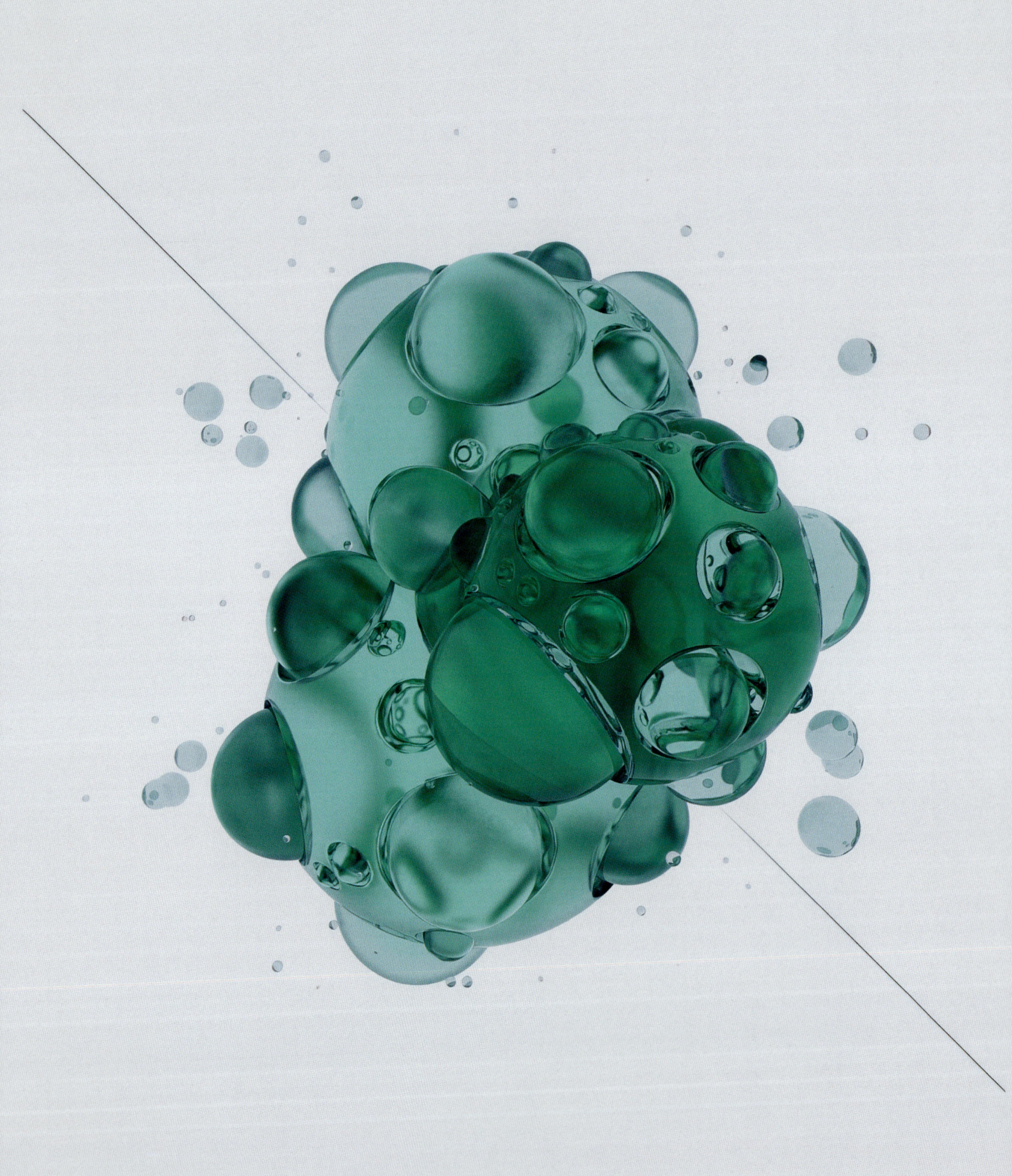

2013

OPPOSITE PAGE

lifting funk
05.16.2013

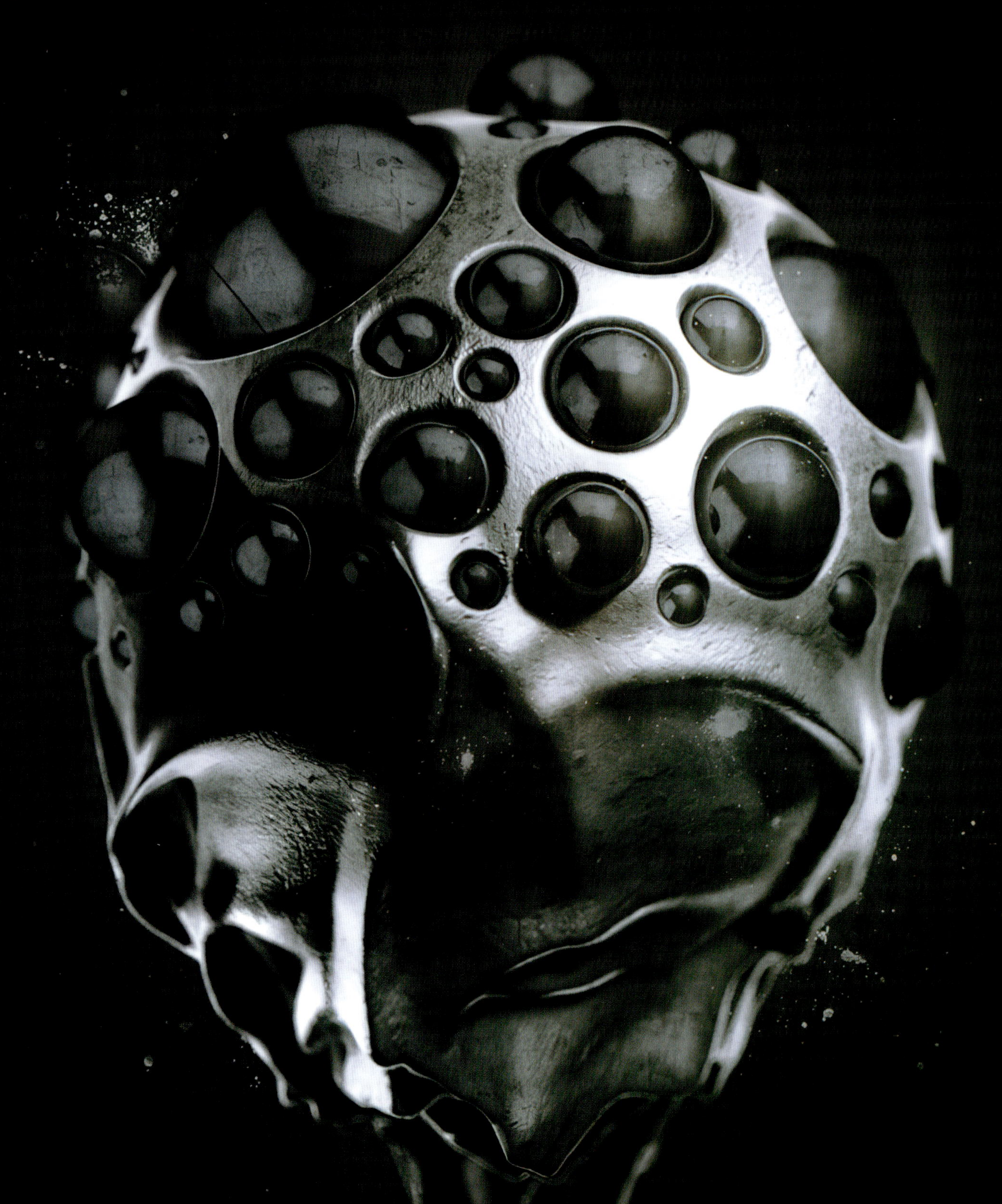

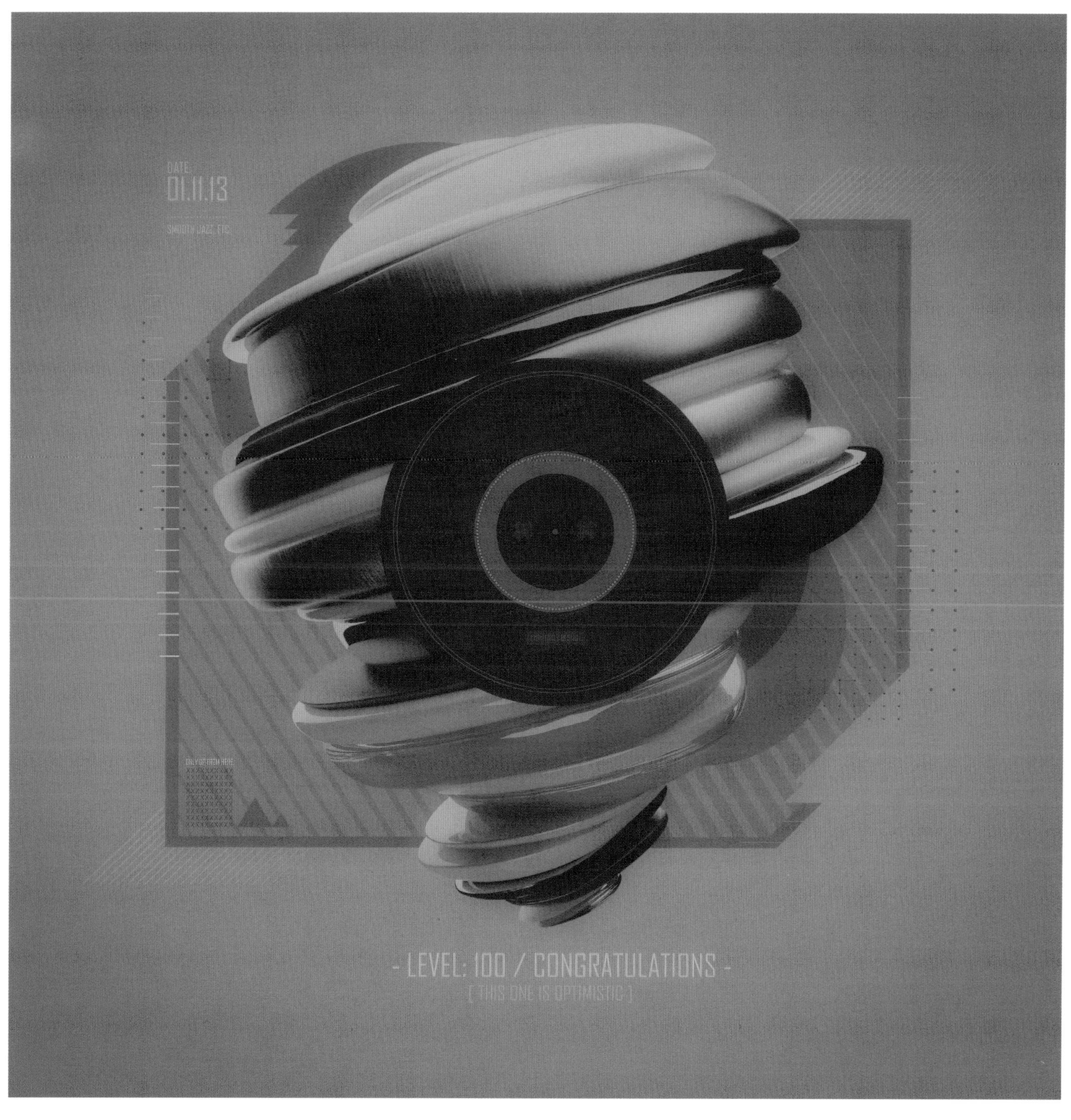

OPPOSITE PAGE

bare puss
01.02.2013

ABOVE

optimistic
01.11.2013

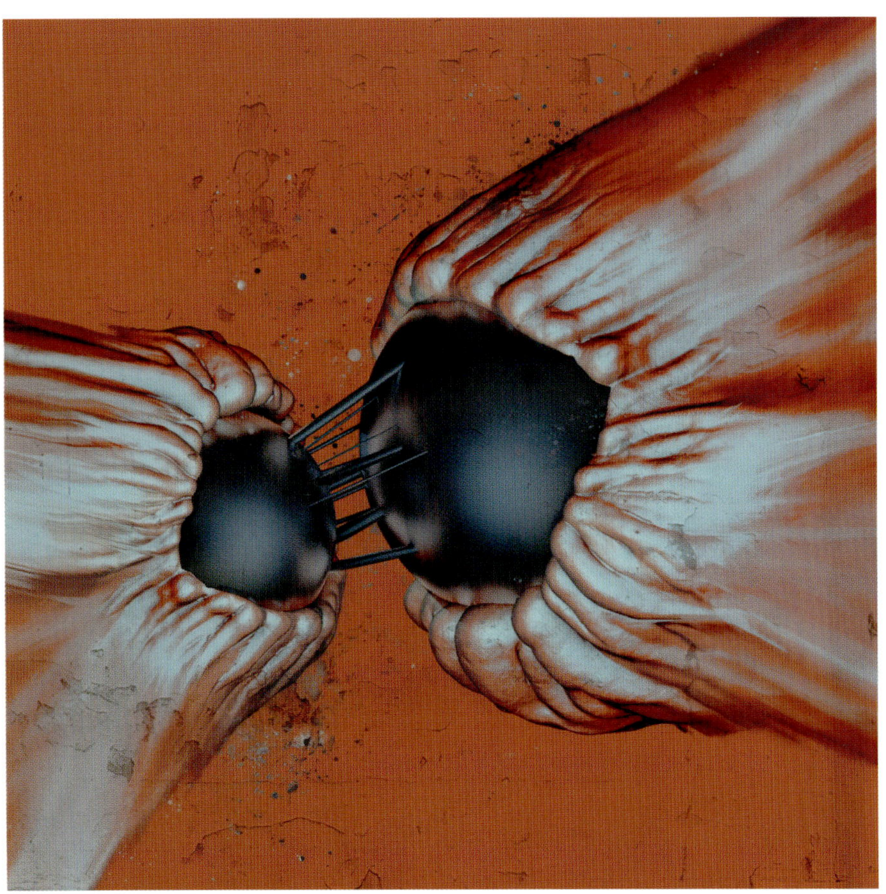

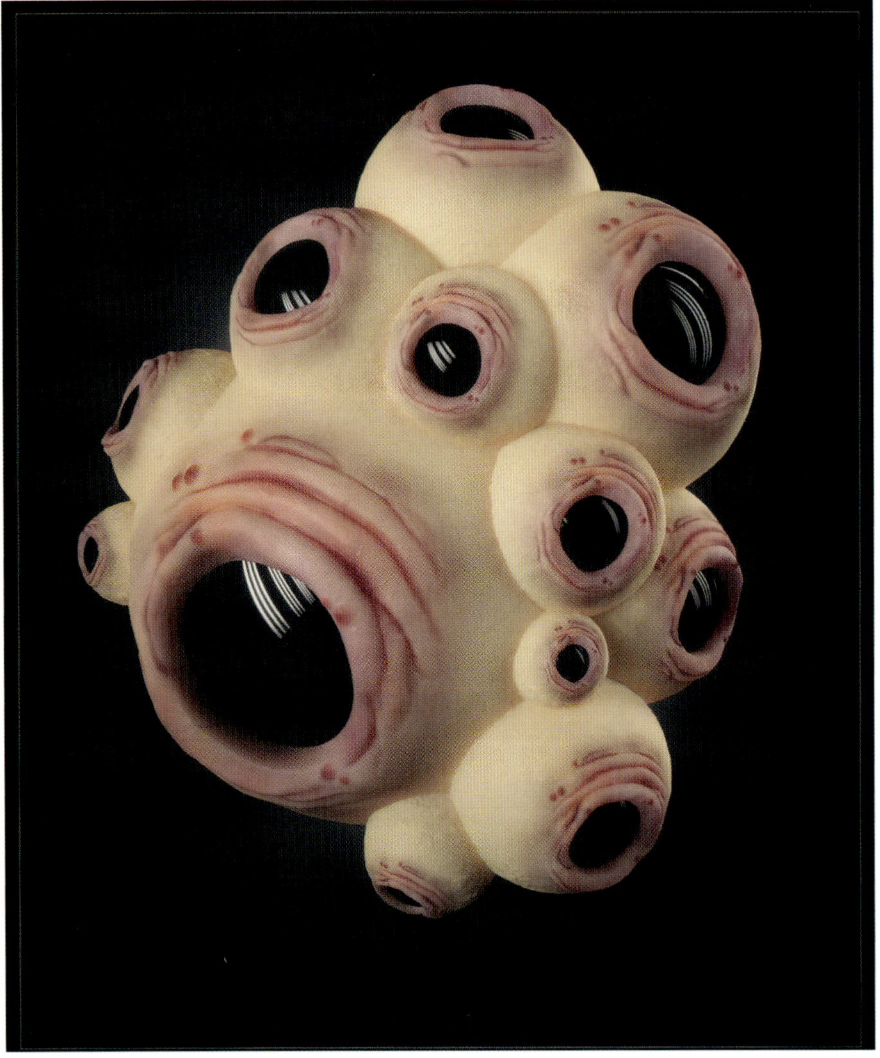

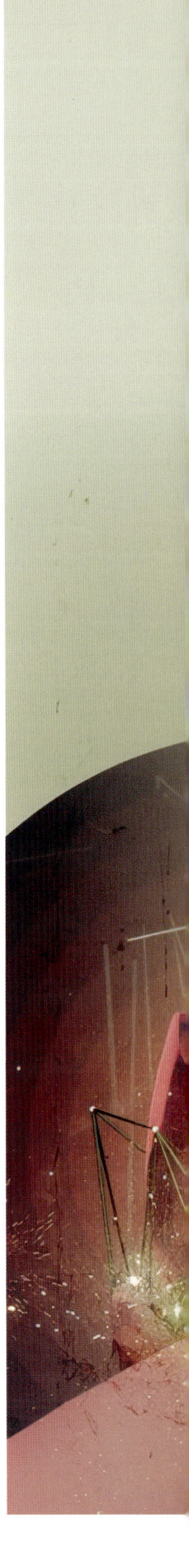

TOP

violent fusion (with unfortunate poles)
02.23.2013

BOTTOM

eyepie cloud
03.12.2013

OPPOSITE PAGE

snow day
02.22.2013

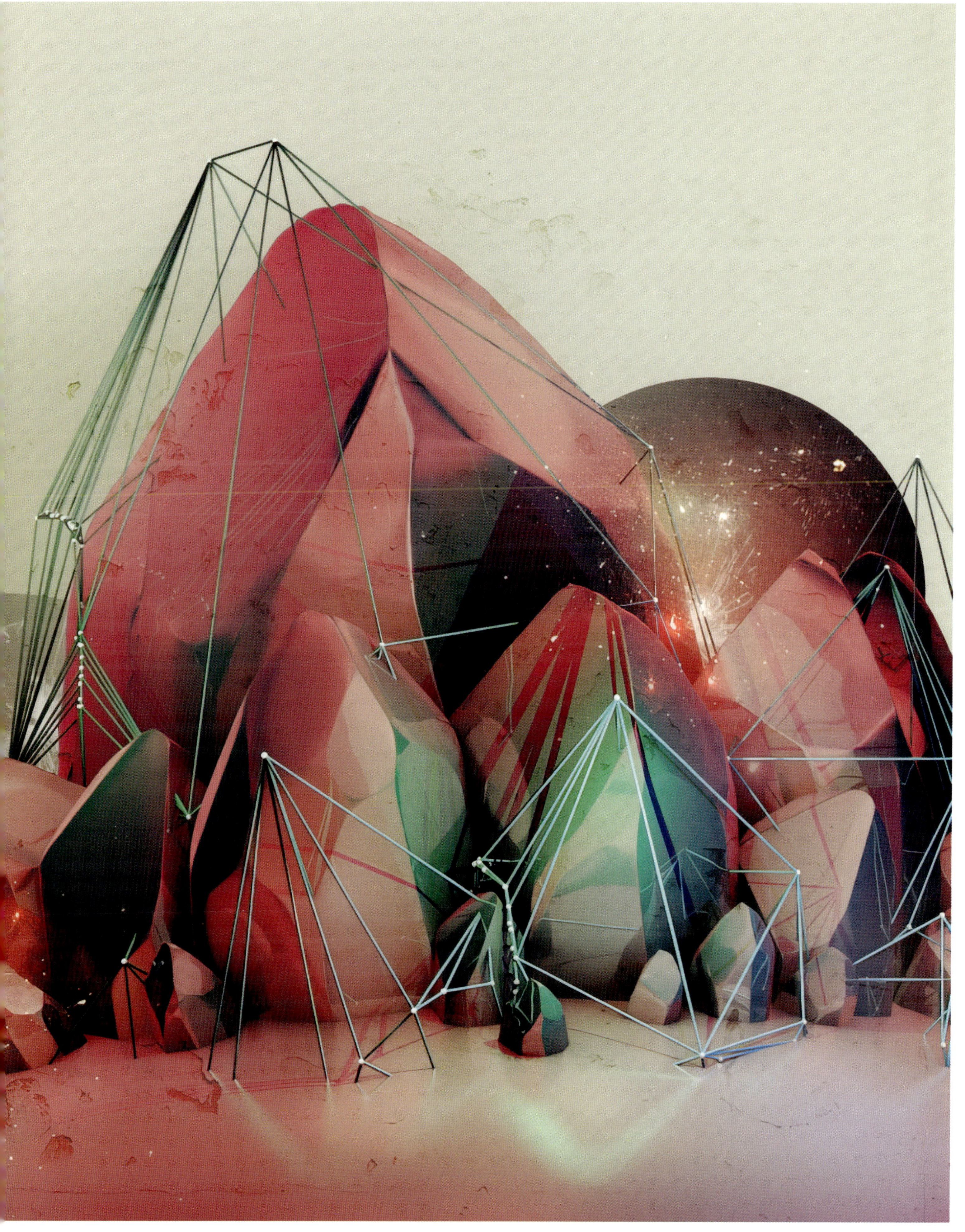

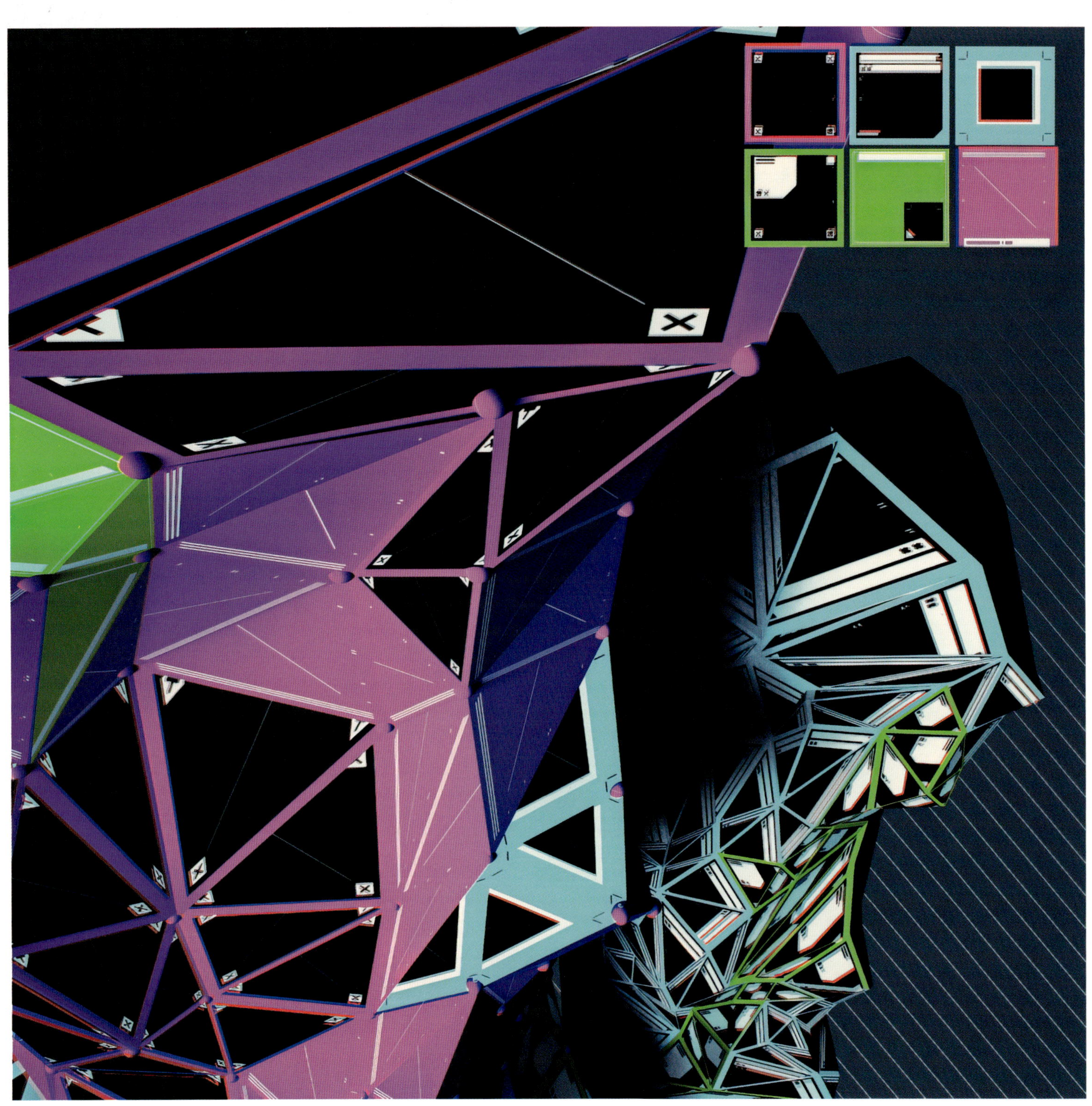

ABOVE
#OCULUSBONERZ
08.02.2013

OPPOSITE PAGE
melson nandela
12.05.2013

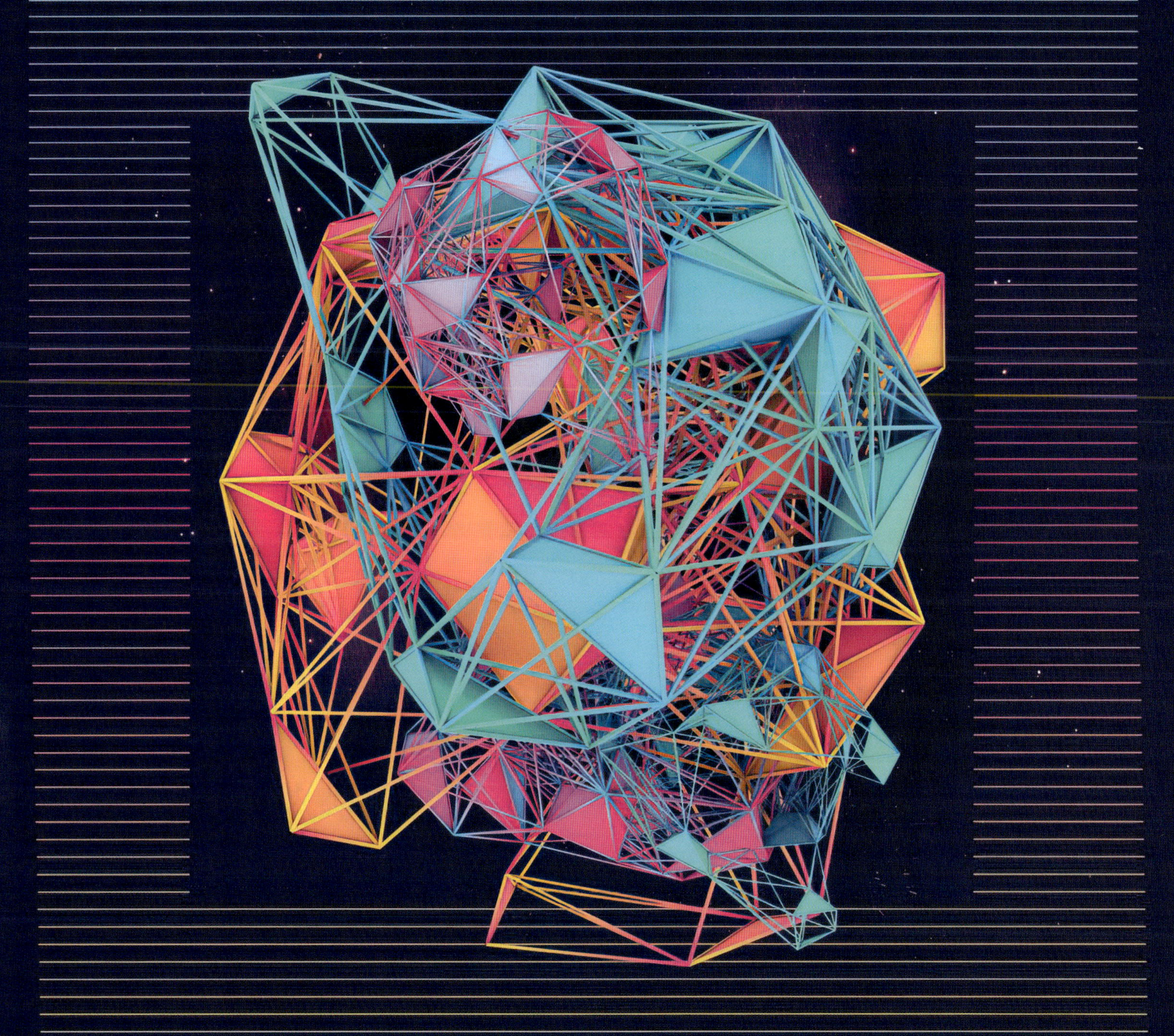

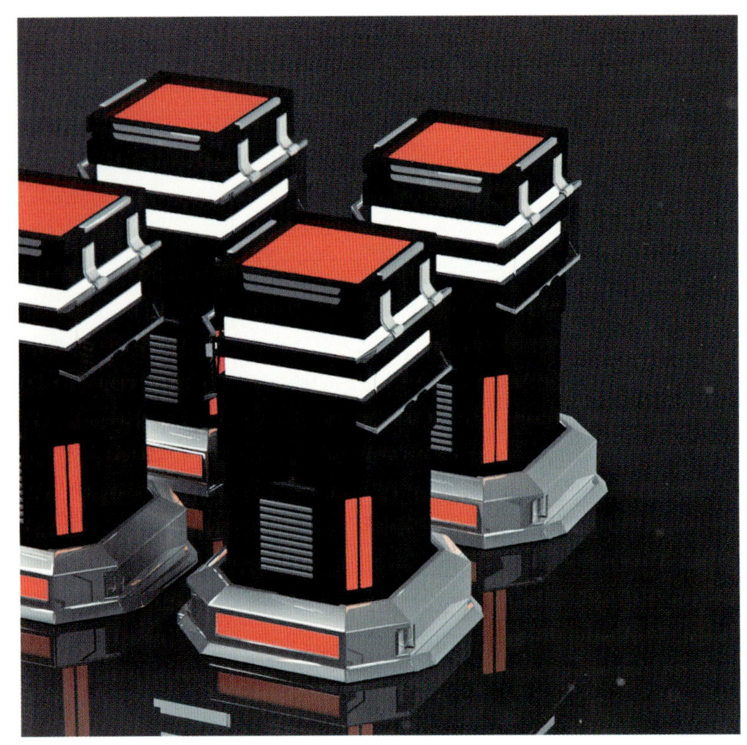

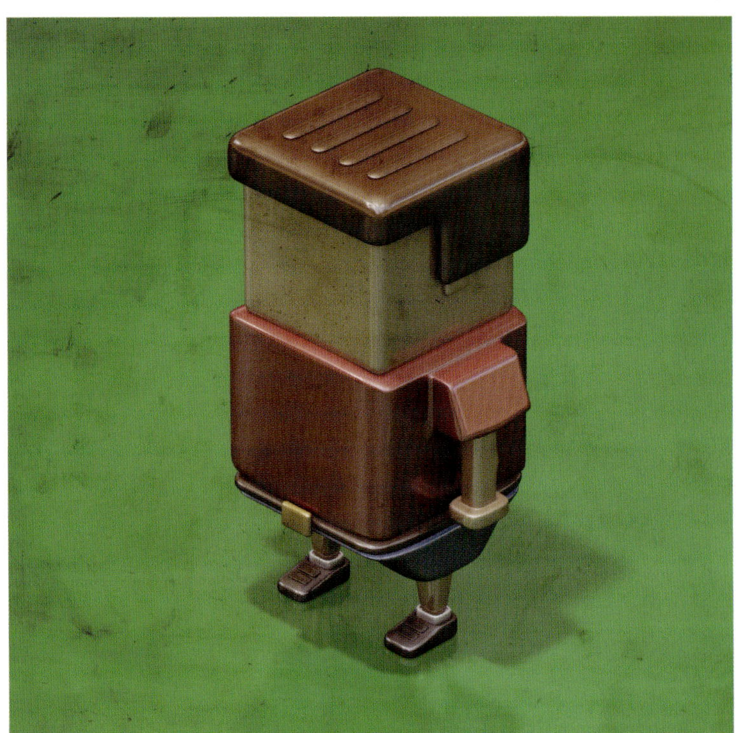

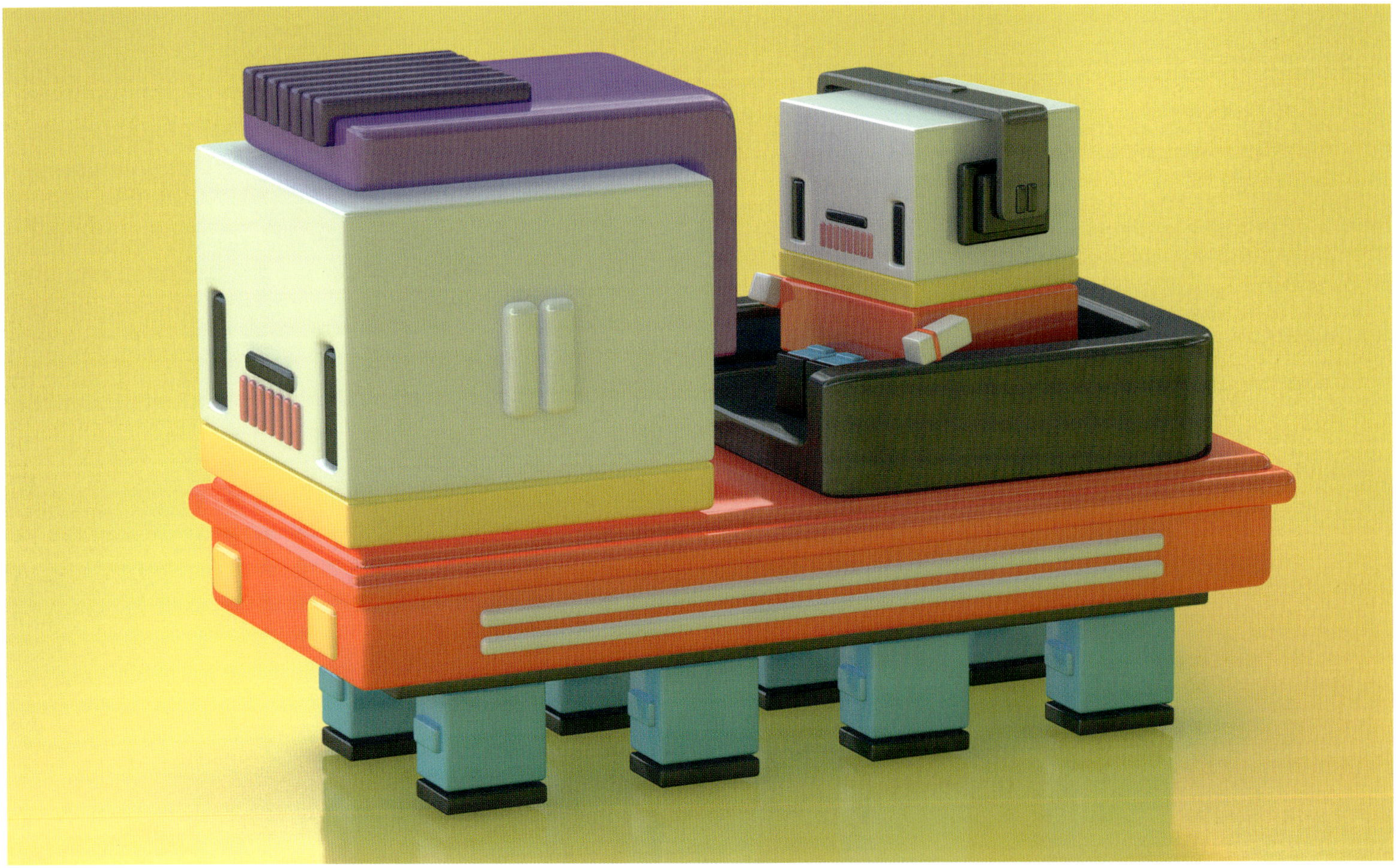

TOP LEFT

punchgrid
08.11.2013

TOP RIGHT

IMPERFECT CANVAS WITH LIMITED/ IMPERFECT CONTROL
07.03.2013

BOTTOM

dogbus with child
08.20.2013

OPPOSITE PAGE

intense jawing
05.15.2013

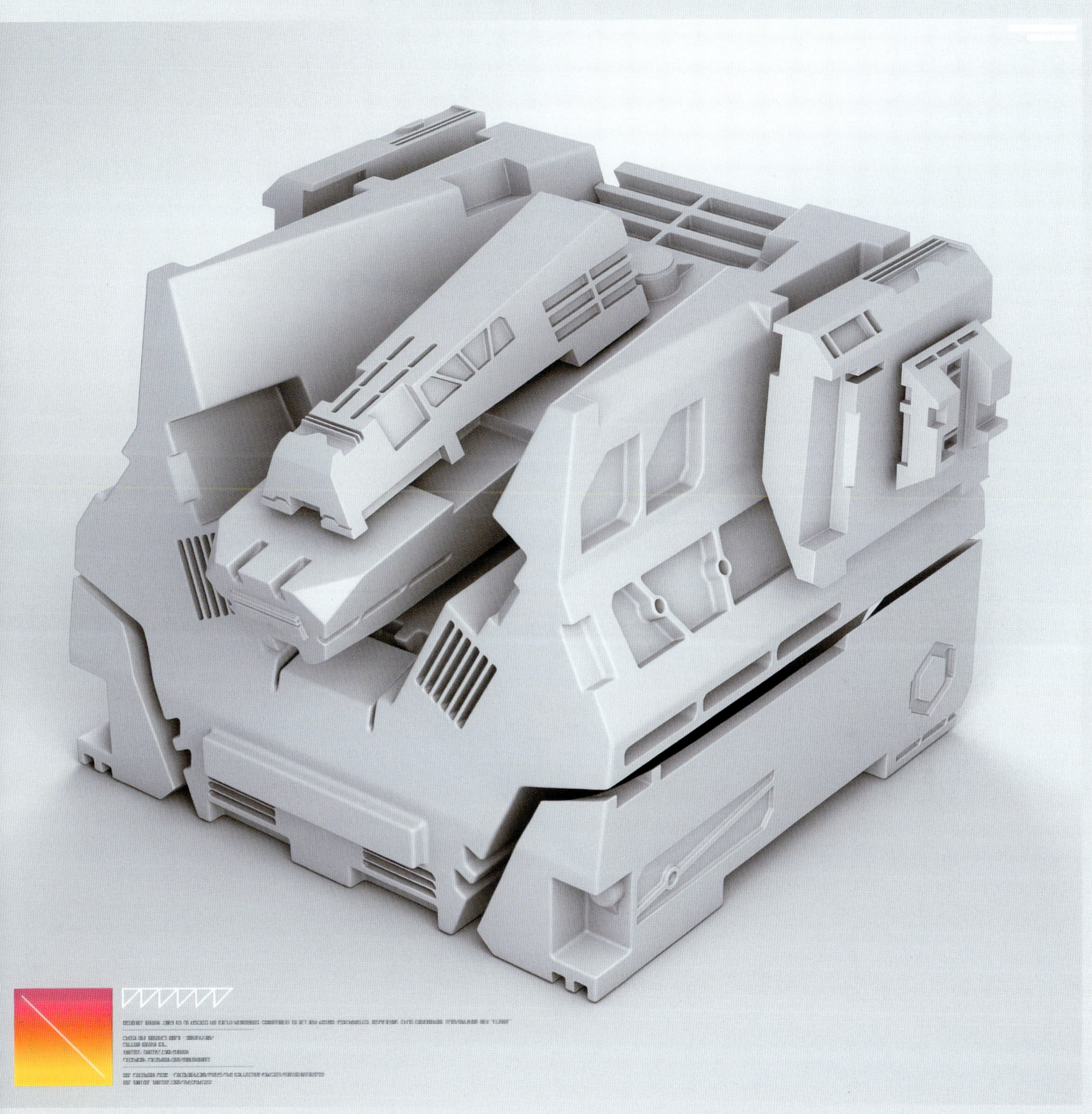

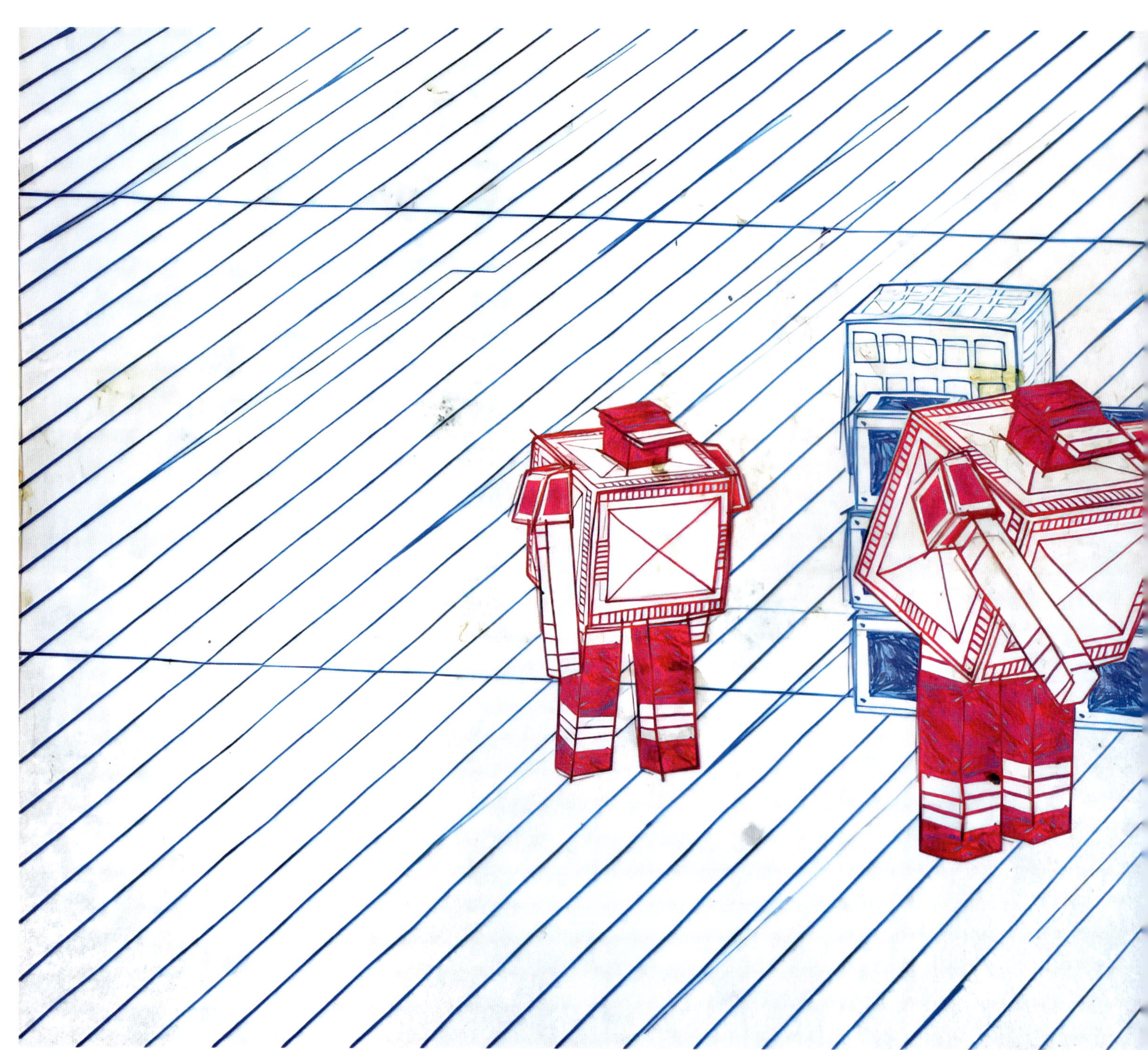

ABOVE

first day of fall
07.27.2013

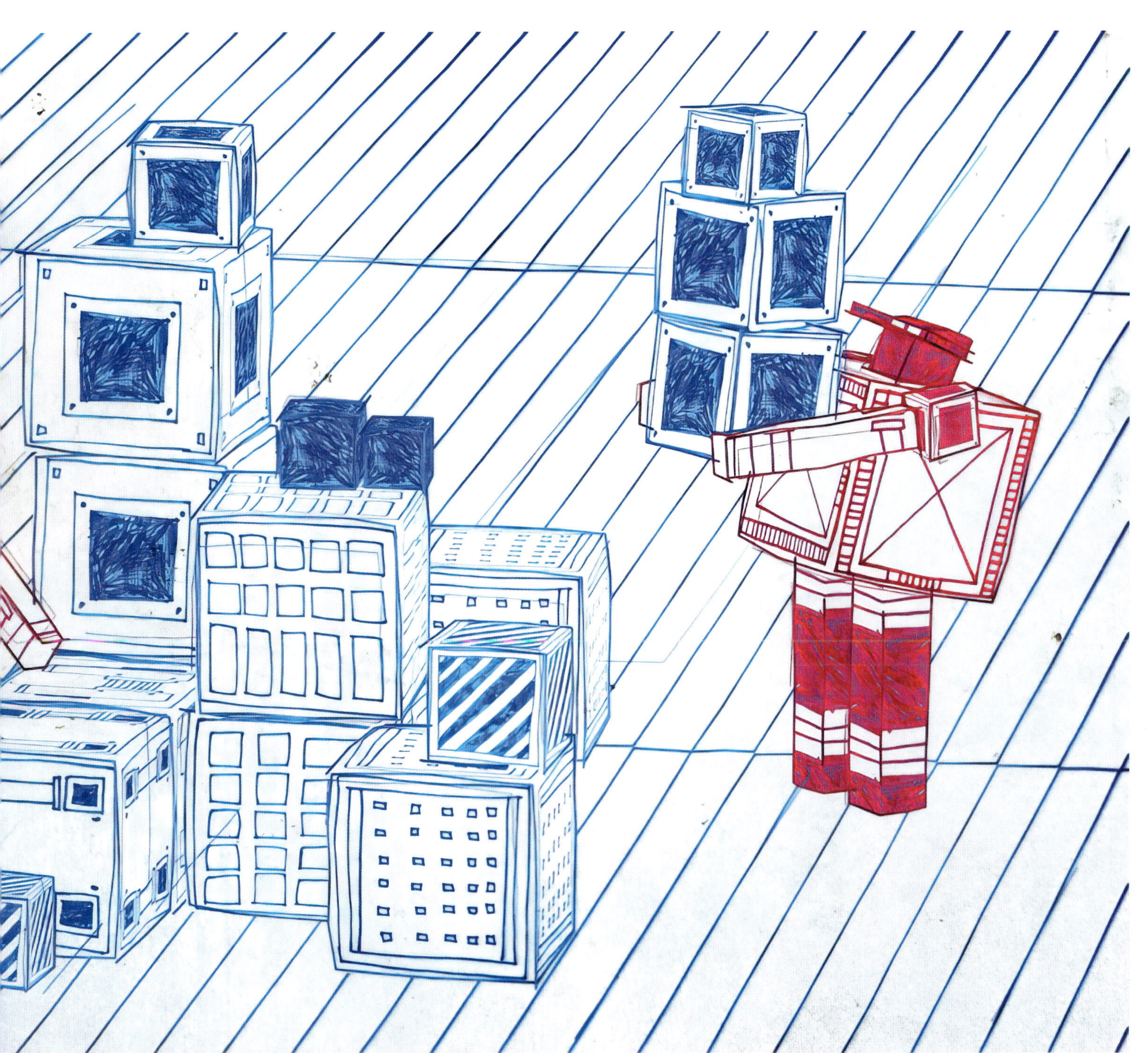

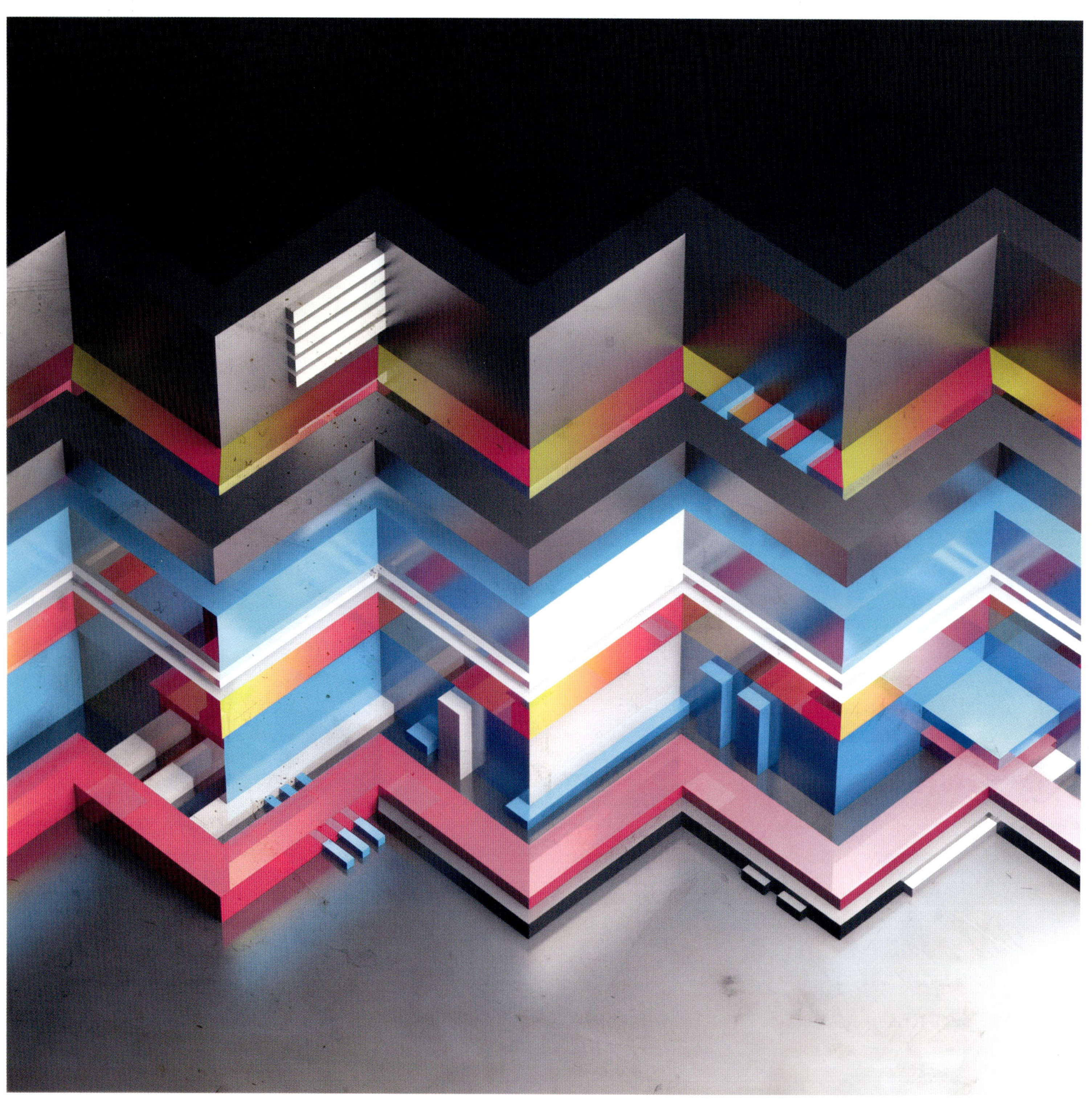

ABOVE

positivity charlie brown
08.21.2013

OPPOSITE PAGE

scromblar
11.22.2013

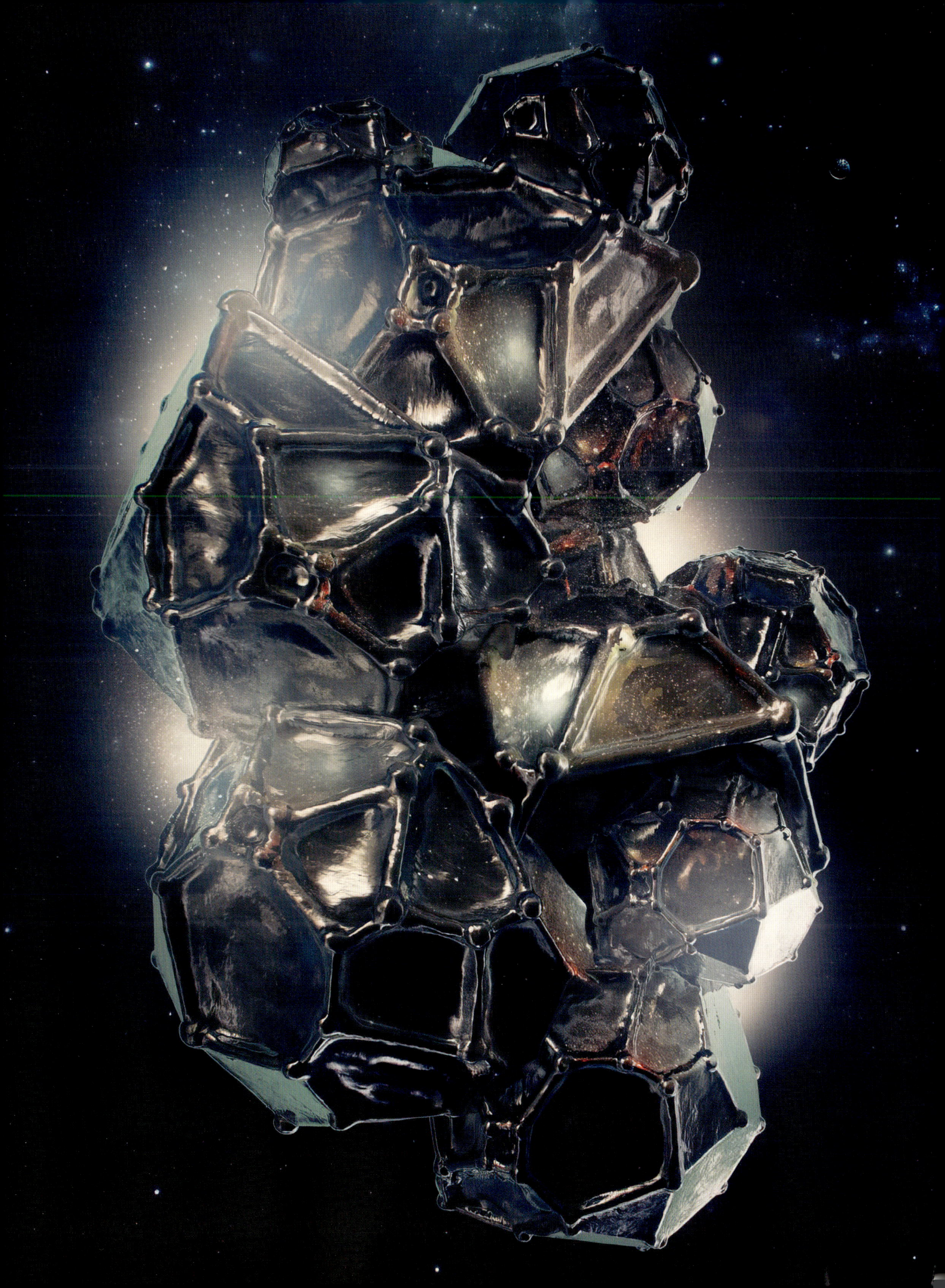

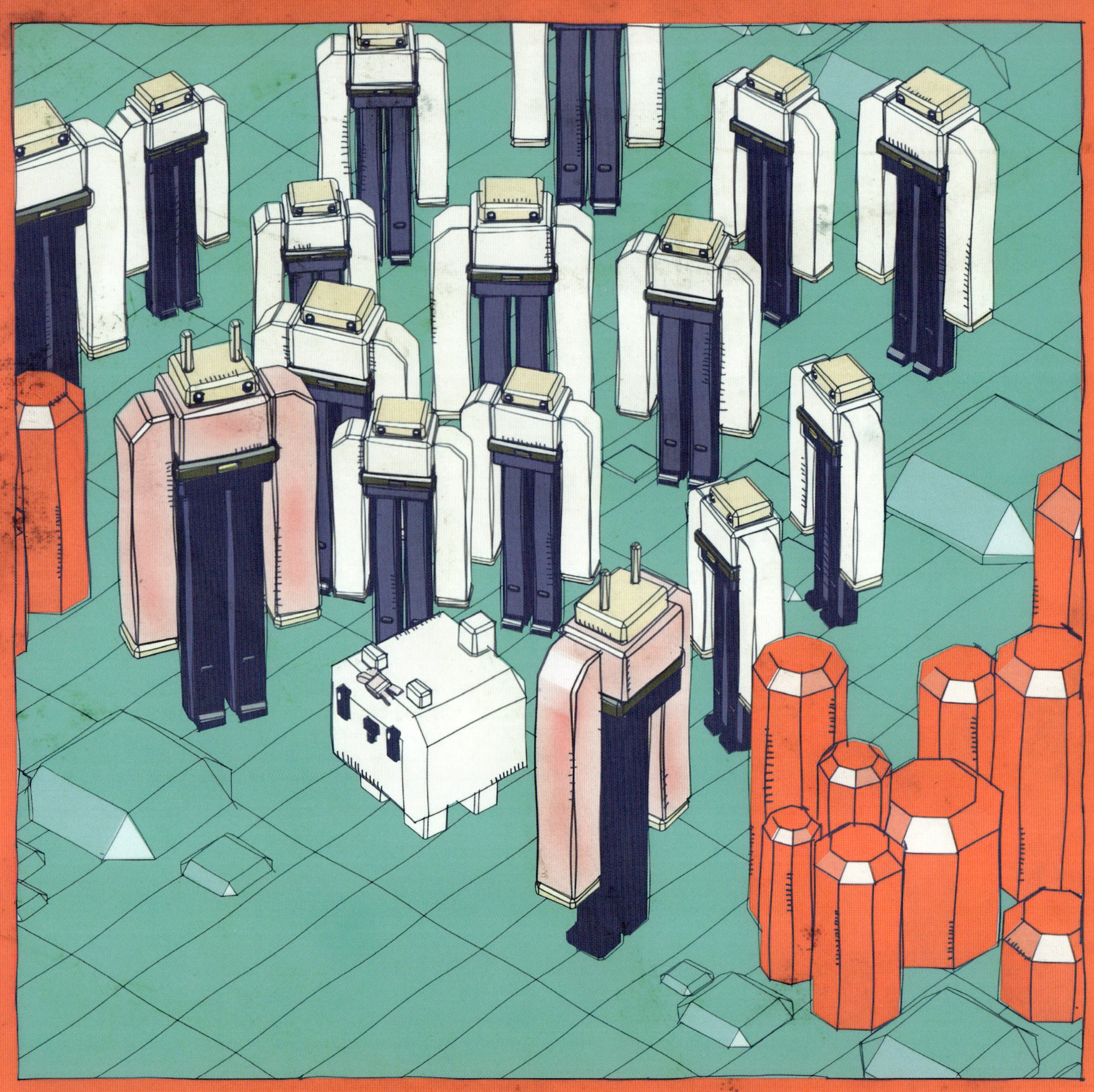

ABOVE

pup care
10.25.2013

OPPOSITE PAGE

gloubulous study
09.03.2013

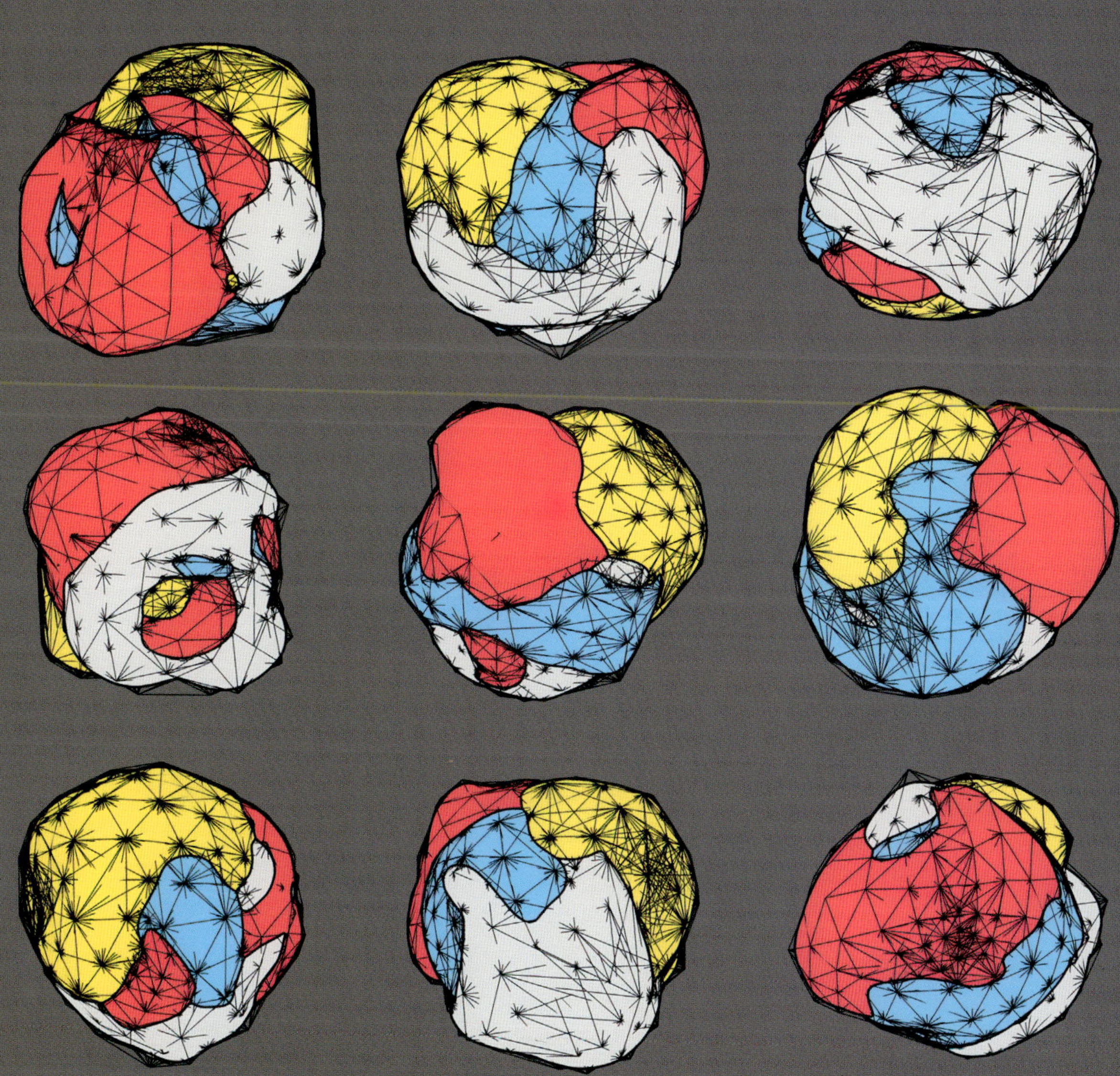

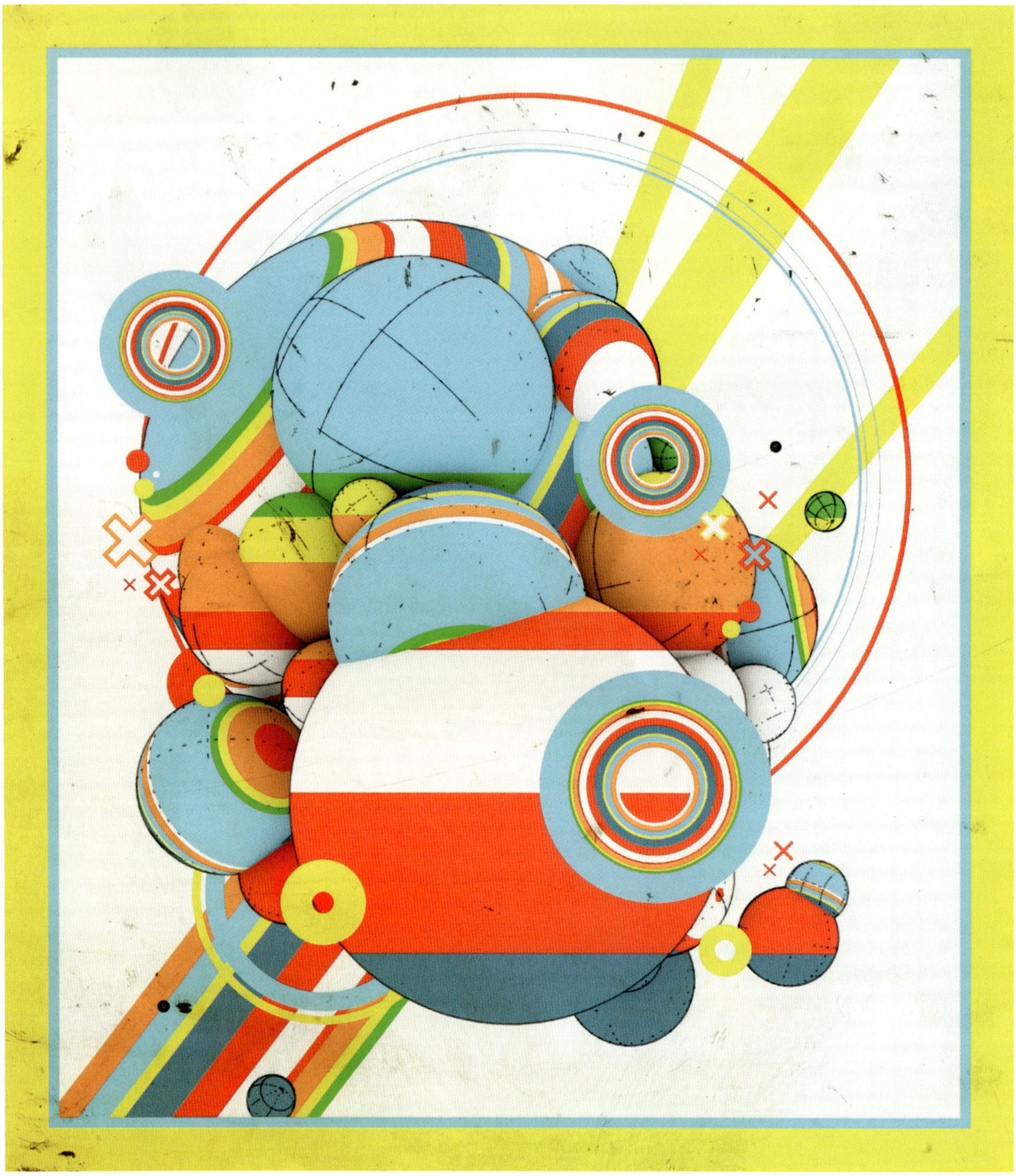

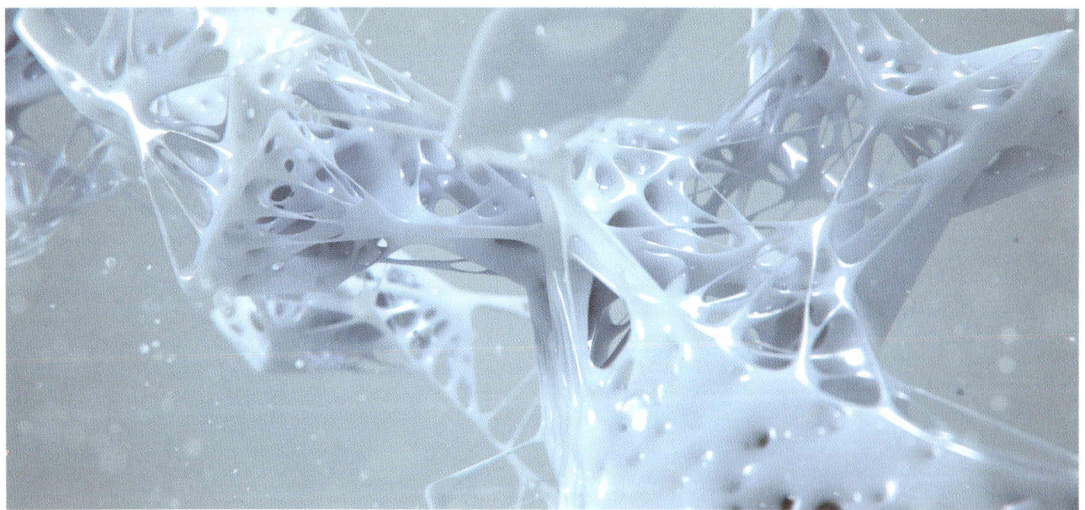

TOP
being outside for the first time in your life
09.21.2013

BOTTOM
milkweb
05.09.2013

OPPOSITE PAGE
two weeks
10.03.2013

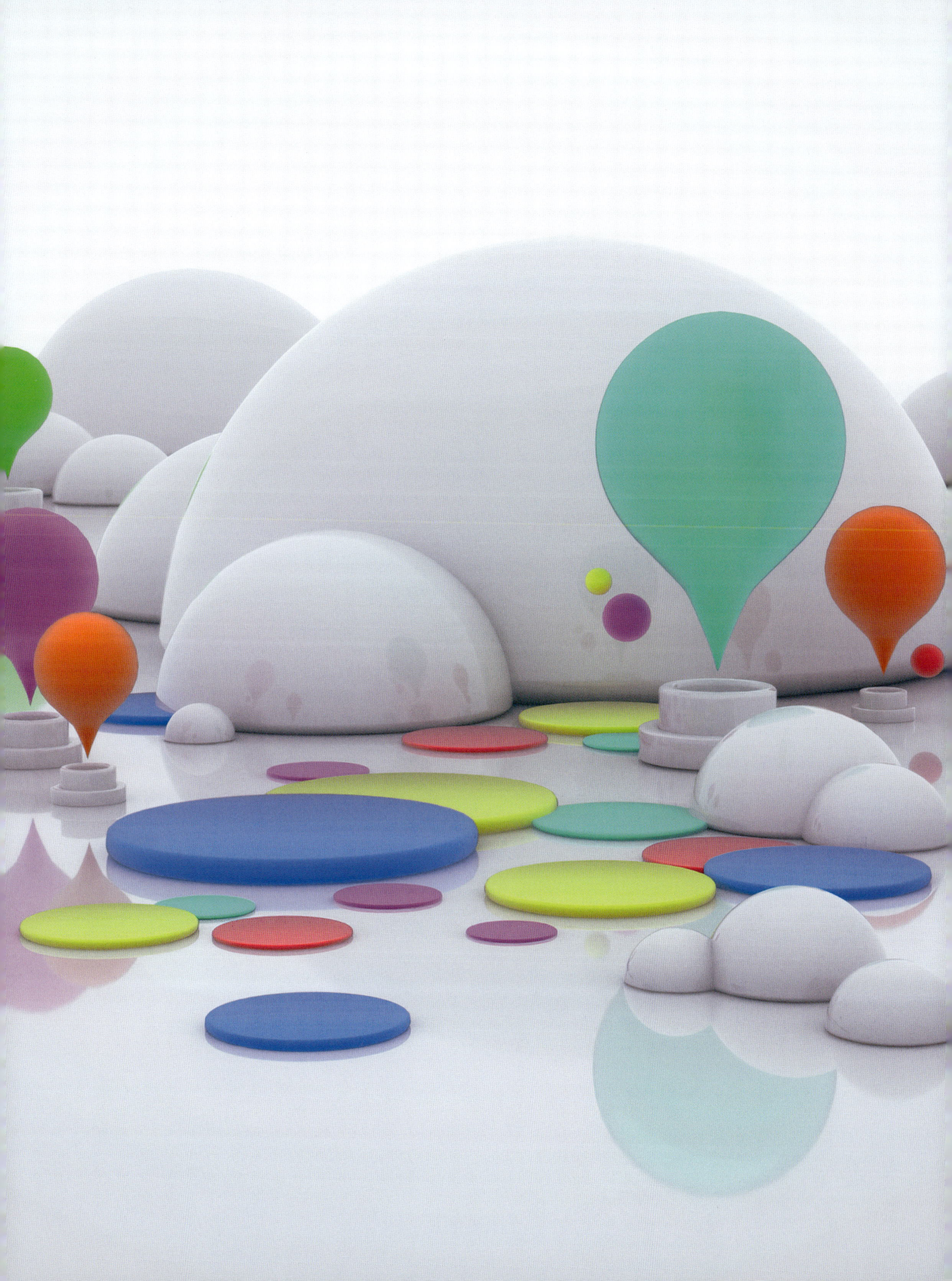

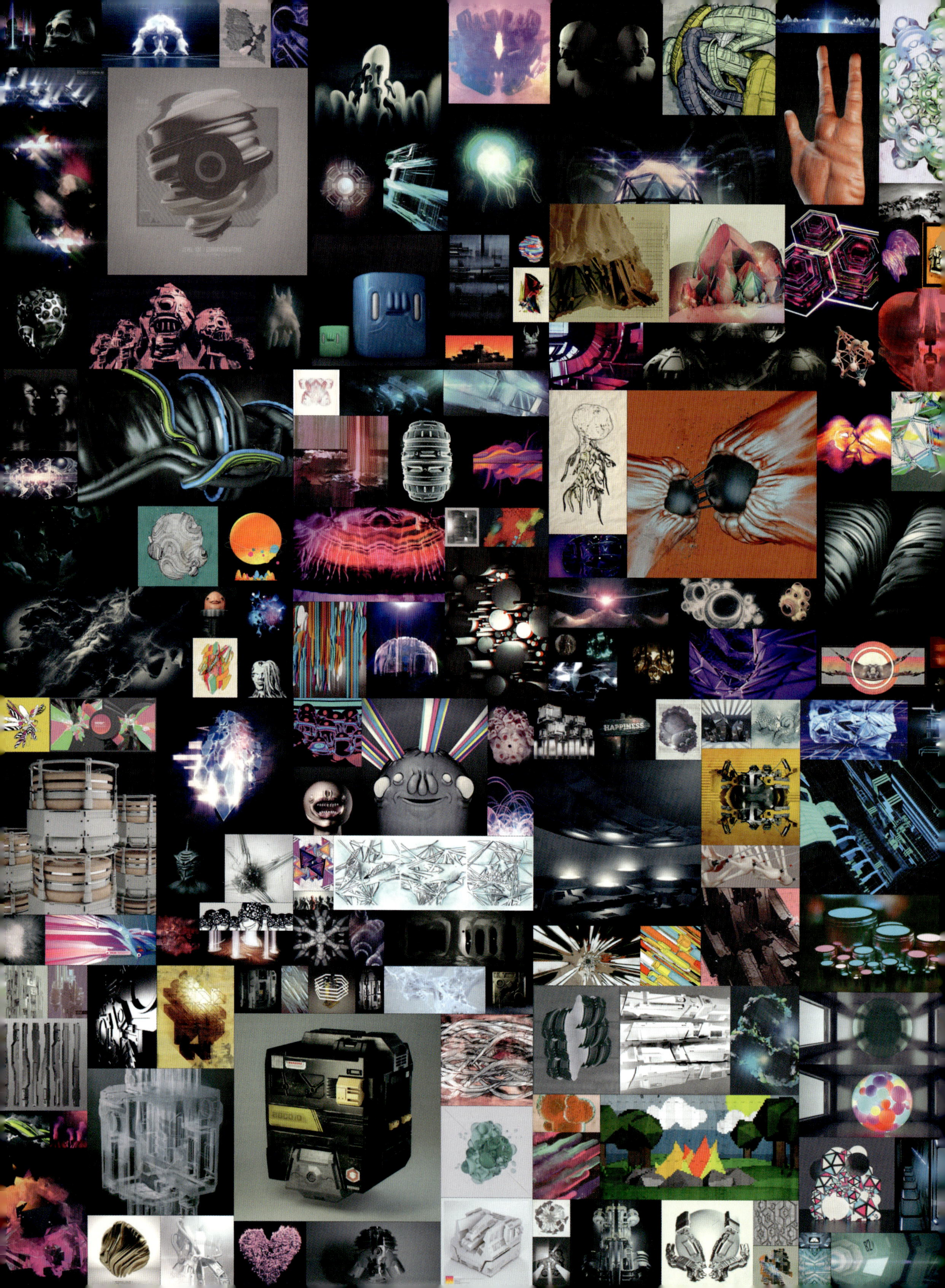

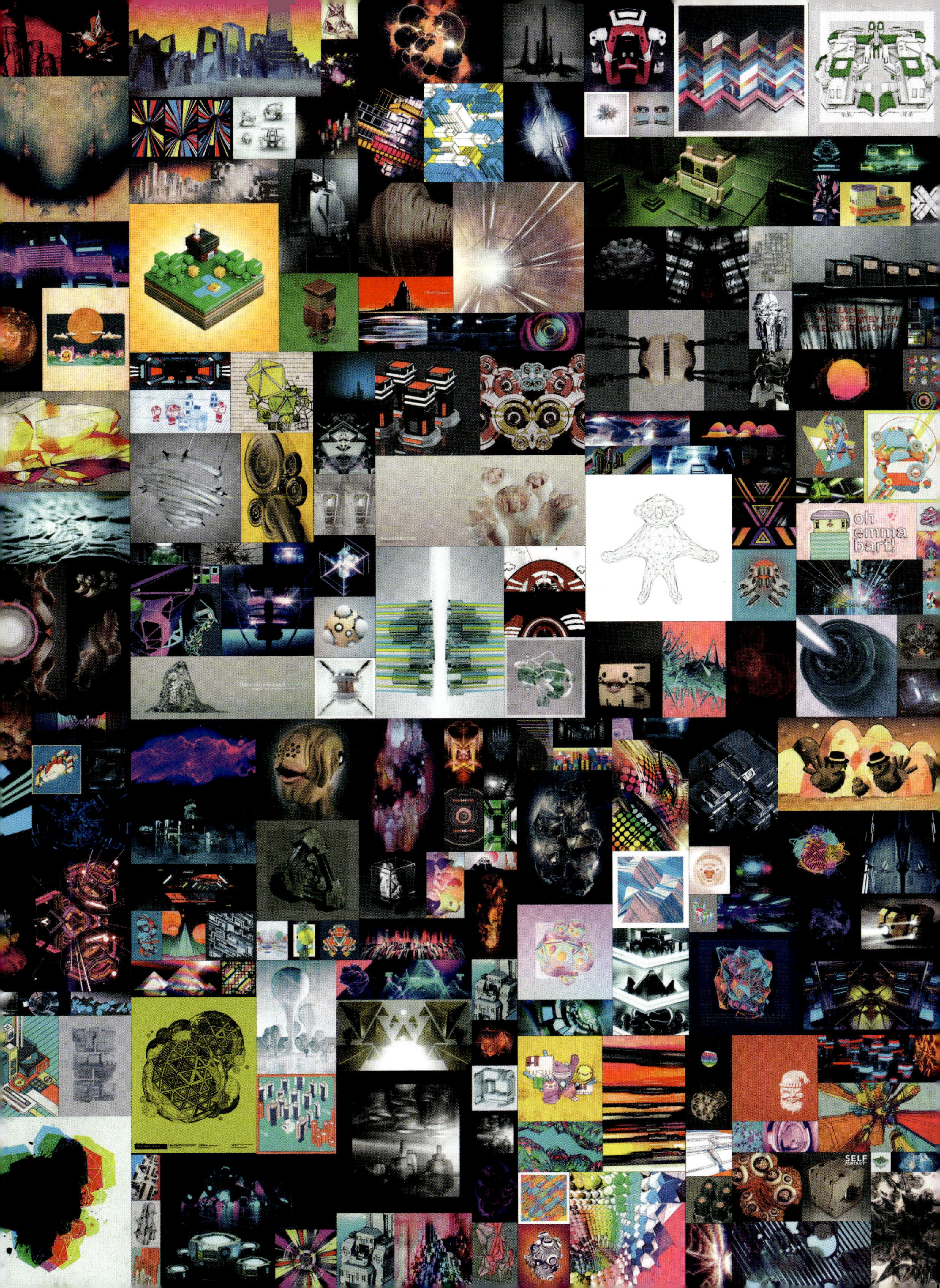

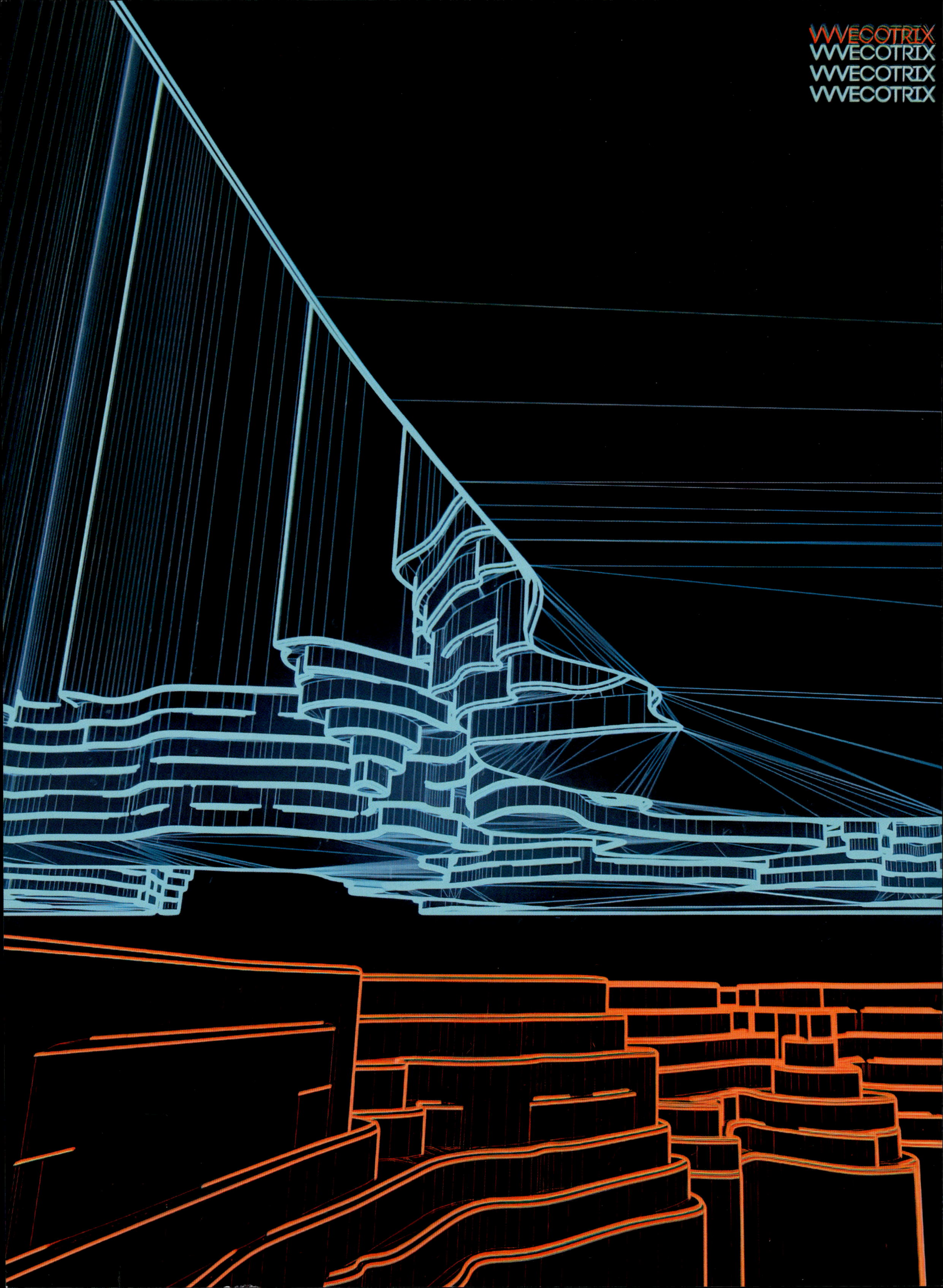

VVVECOTRIX
VVVECOTRIX
VVVECOTRIX
VVVECOTRIX

2014

OPPOSITE PAGE

last second clutch
07.05.2014

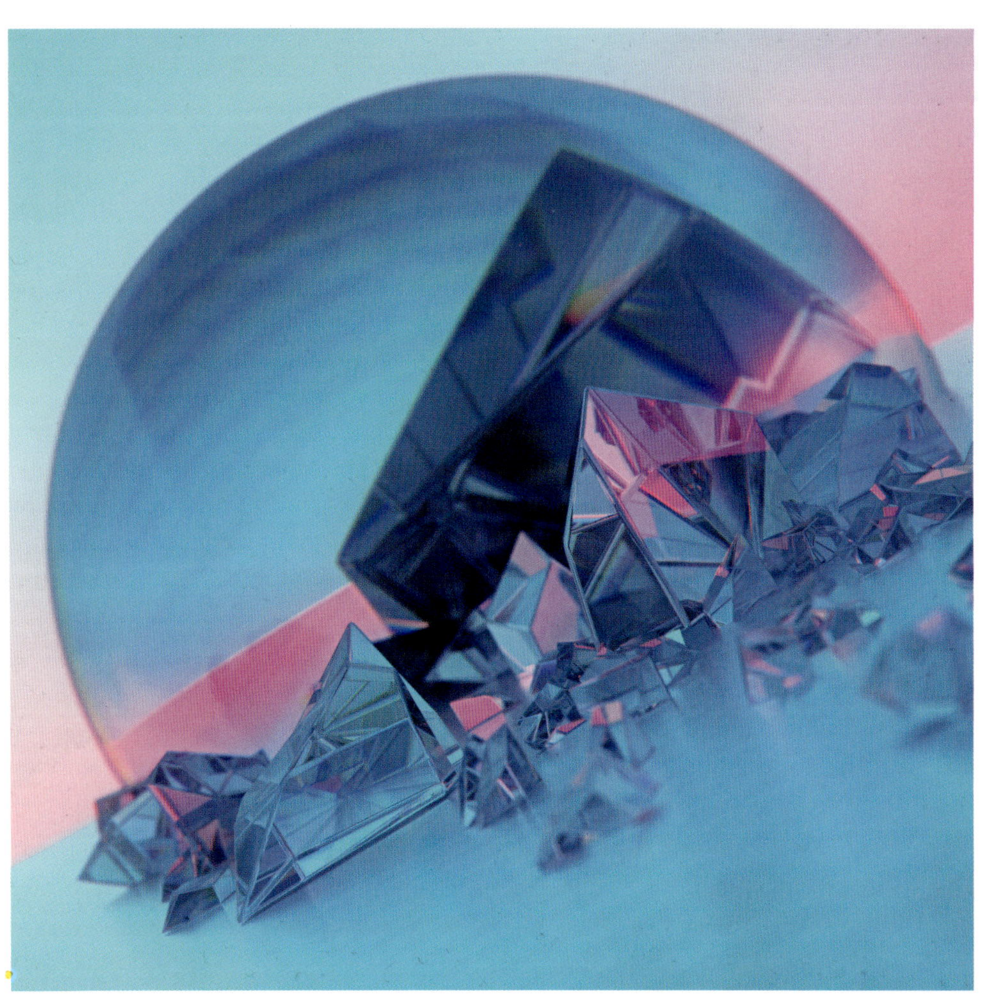

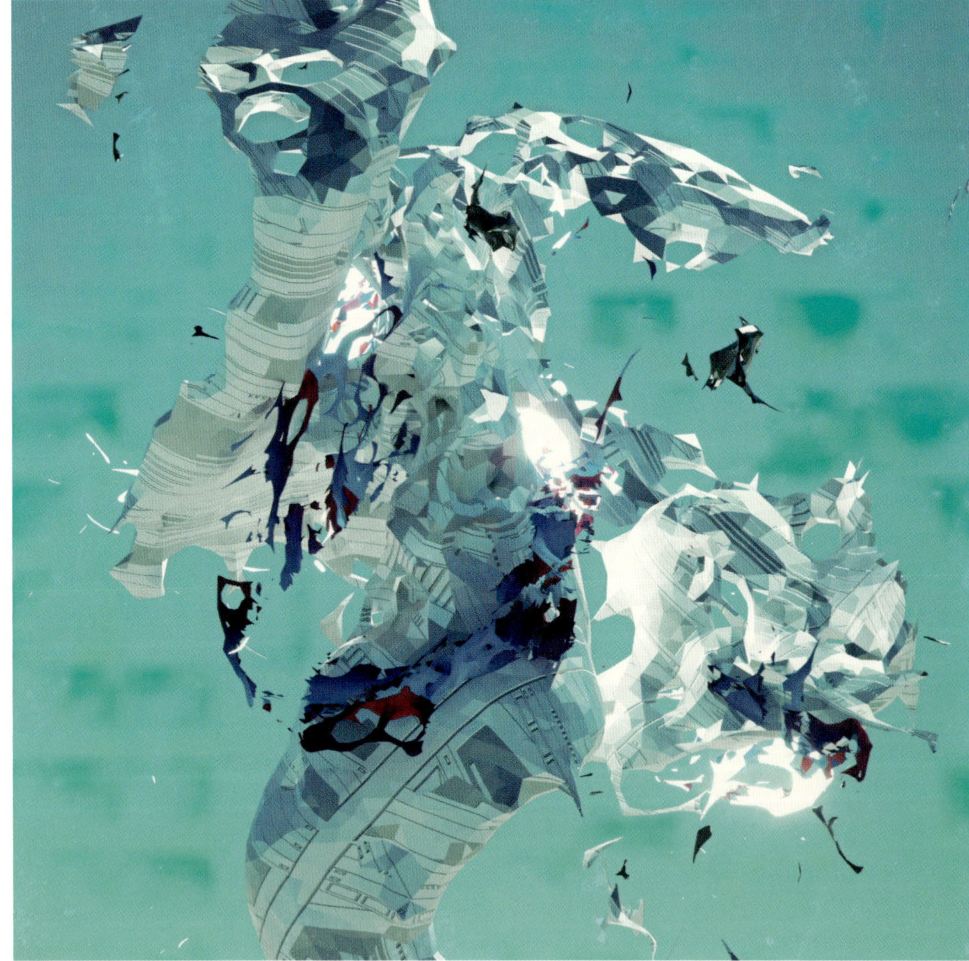

TOP

sochi
02.07.2014

BOTTOM

phynic
04.04.2014

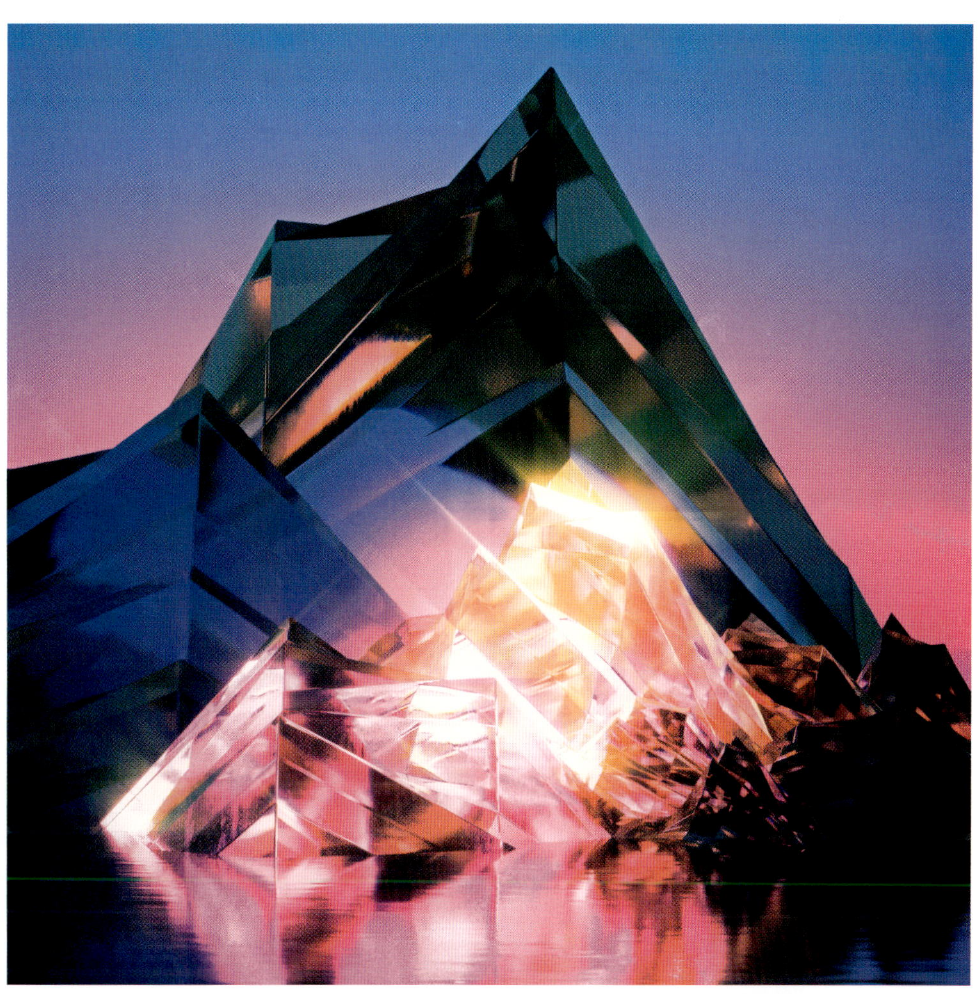

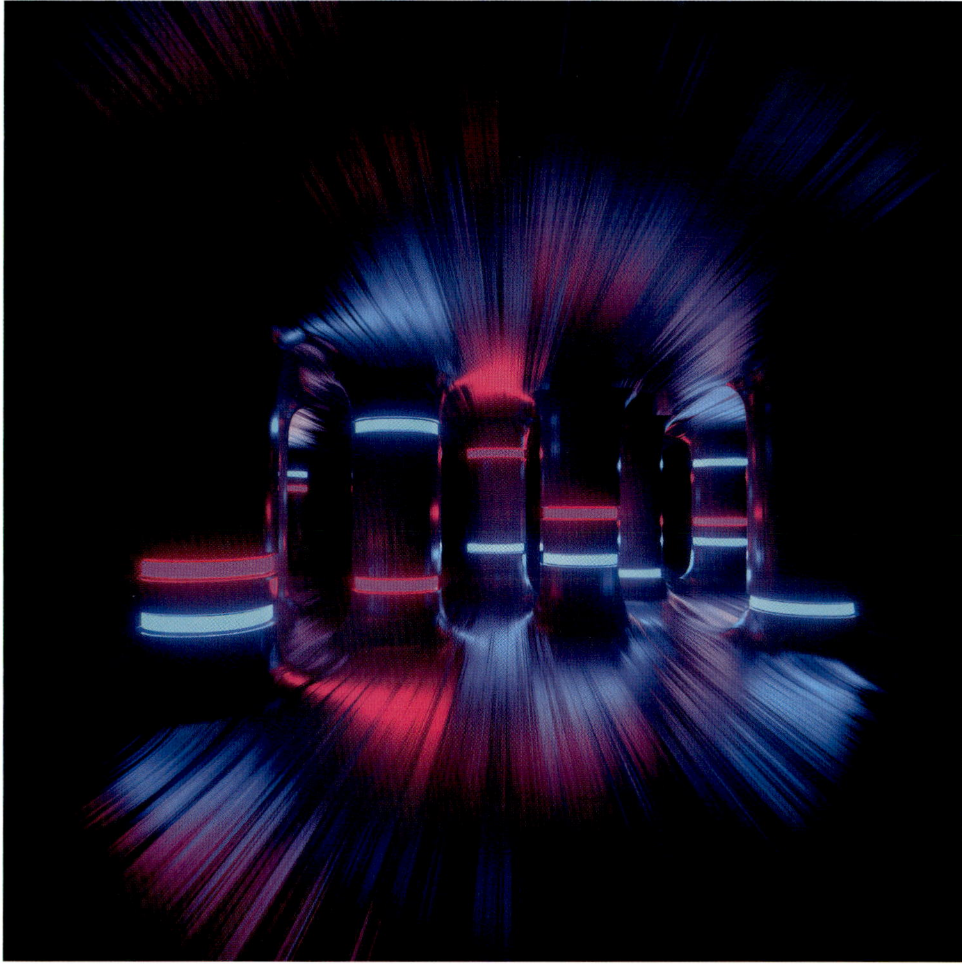

TOP

JUNIPEAR (MORNING V60)
02.28.2014

BOTTOM

swedish organic pink vynil
01.04.2014

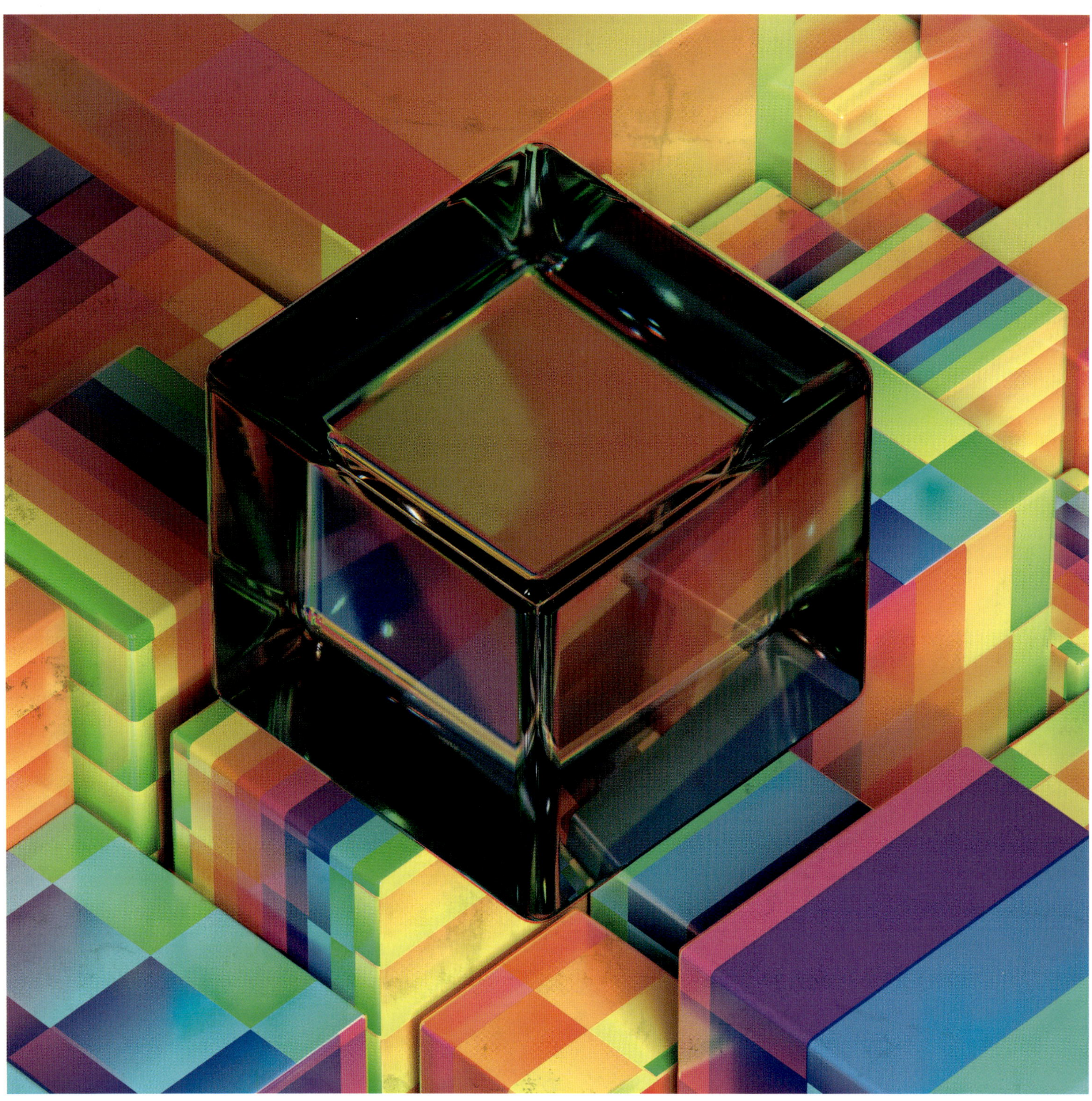

ABOVE

handgun lunch break
02.20.2014

OPPOSITE PAGE

**PURE(SURFACE.
CRSYTLS)**
02.26.2014

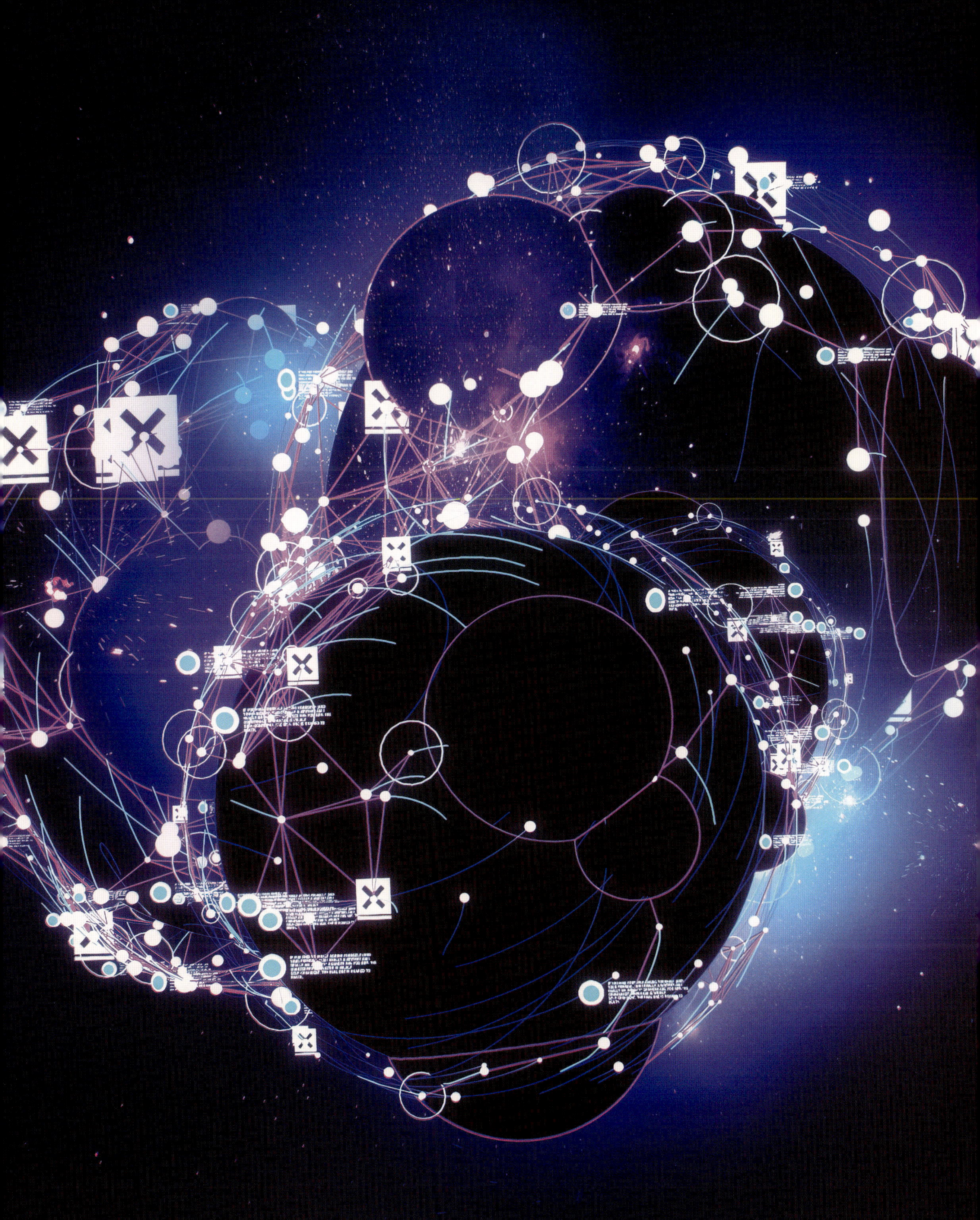

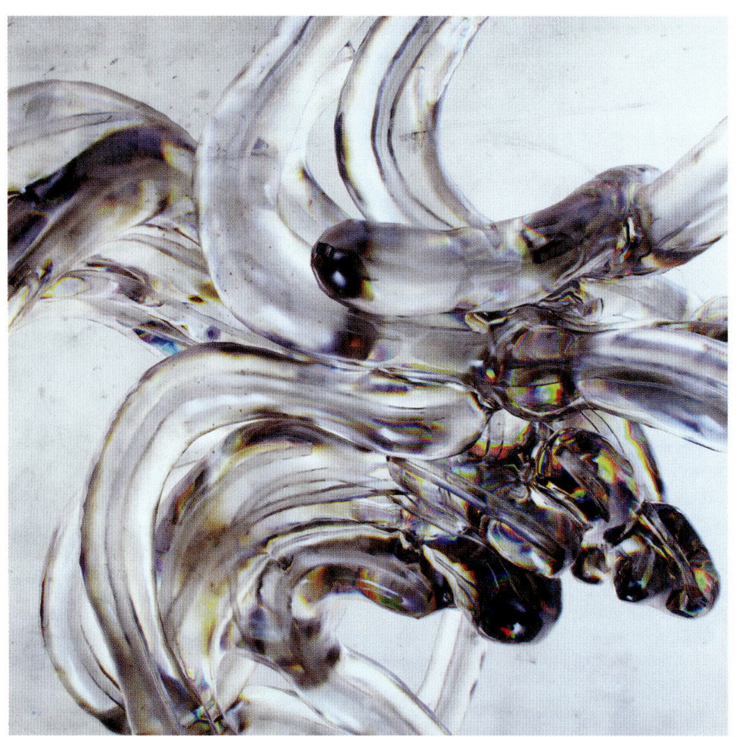

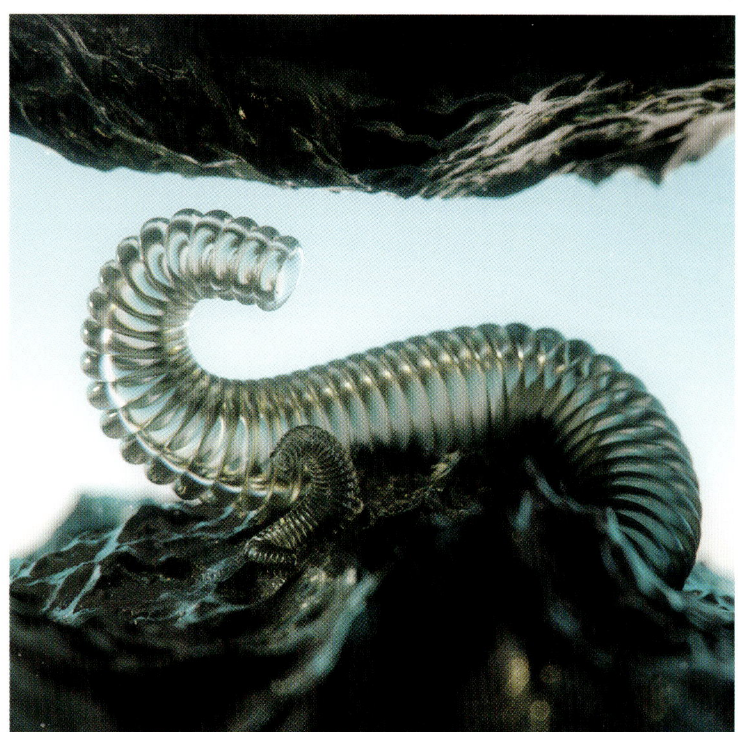

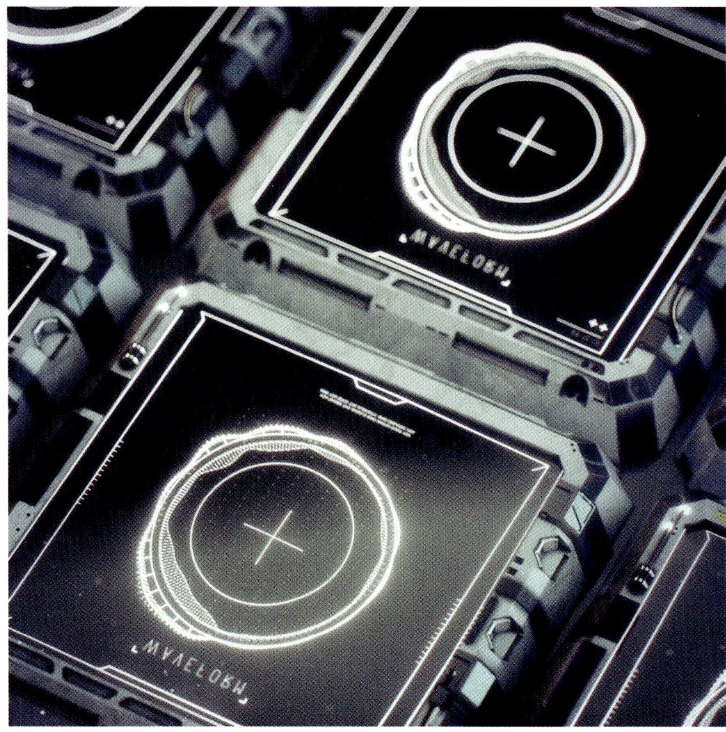

TOP LEFT
crystal tapeworms
06.25.2014

TOP RIGHT
CRYSTAL PILL BUGS
07.15.2014

BOTTOM
screen one
05.20.2014

OPPOSITE PAGE
pug amber
12.04.2014

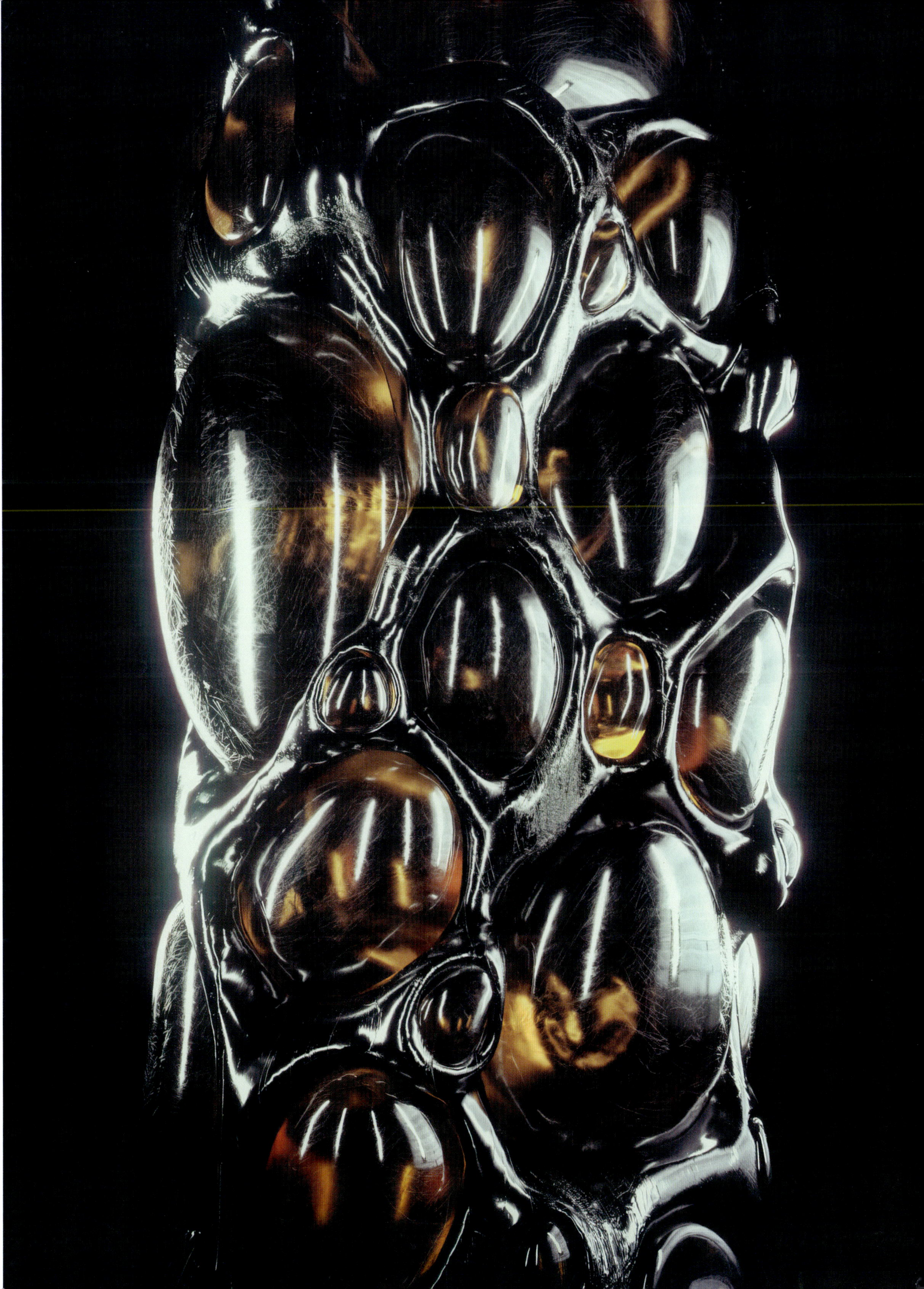

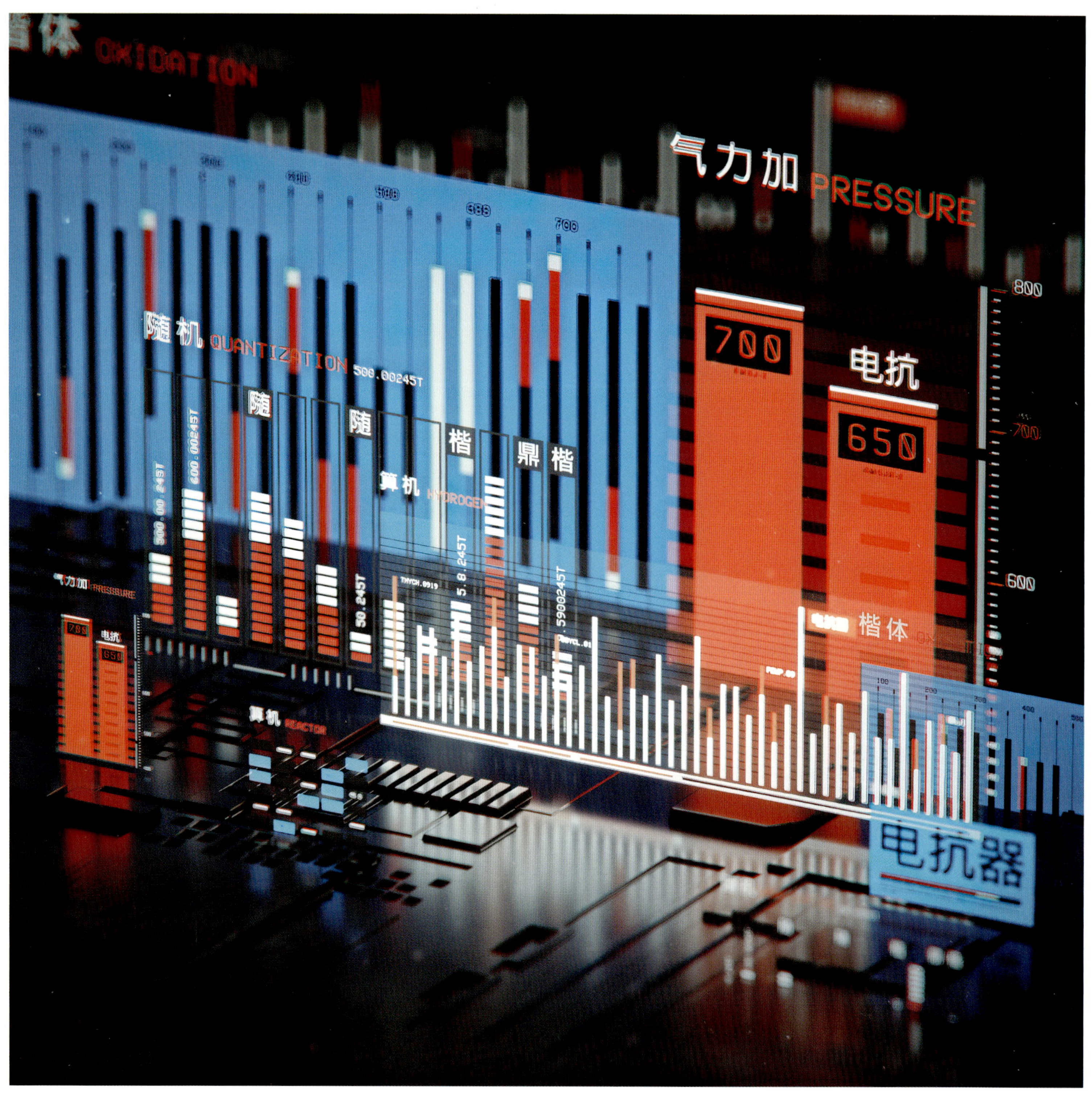

ABOVE
ELEVEN.CN
08.24.2014

OPPOSITE PAGE
red.whi.blu (preach)
07.04.2014

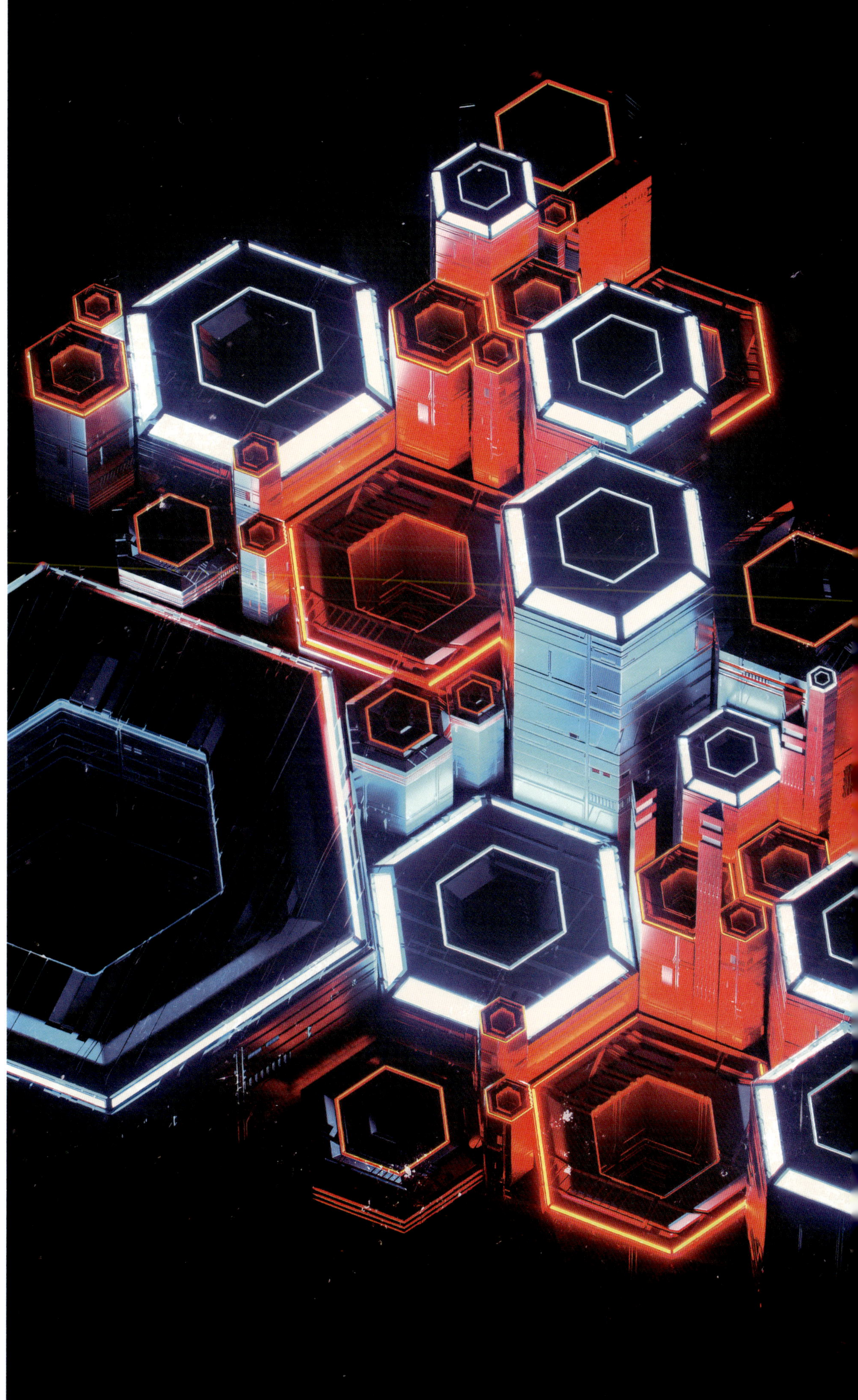

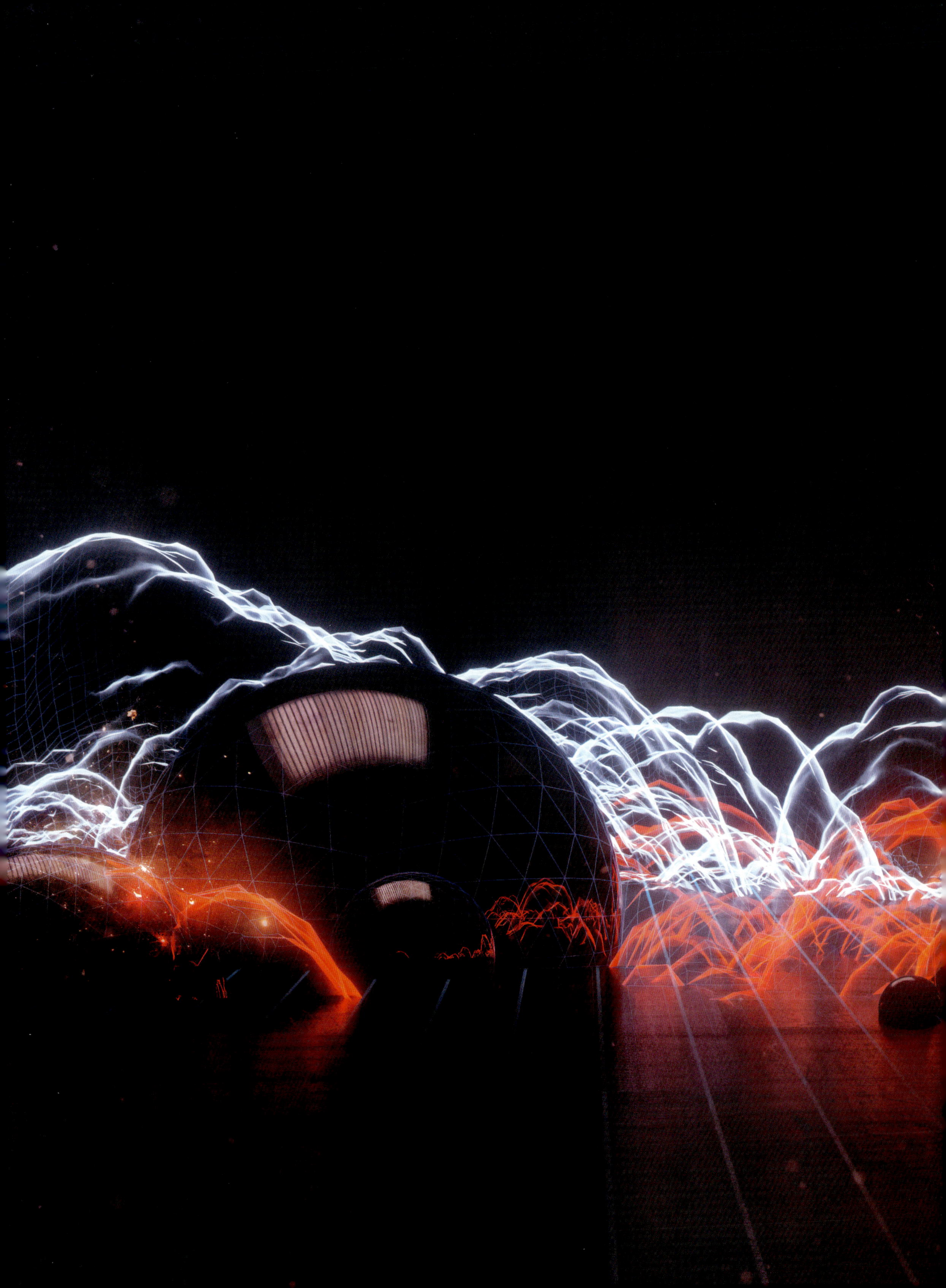

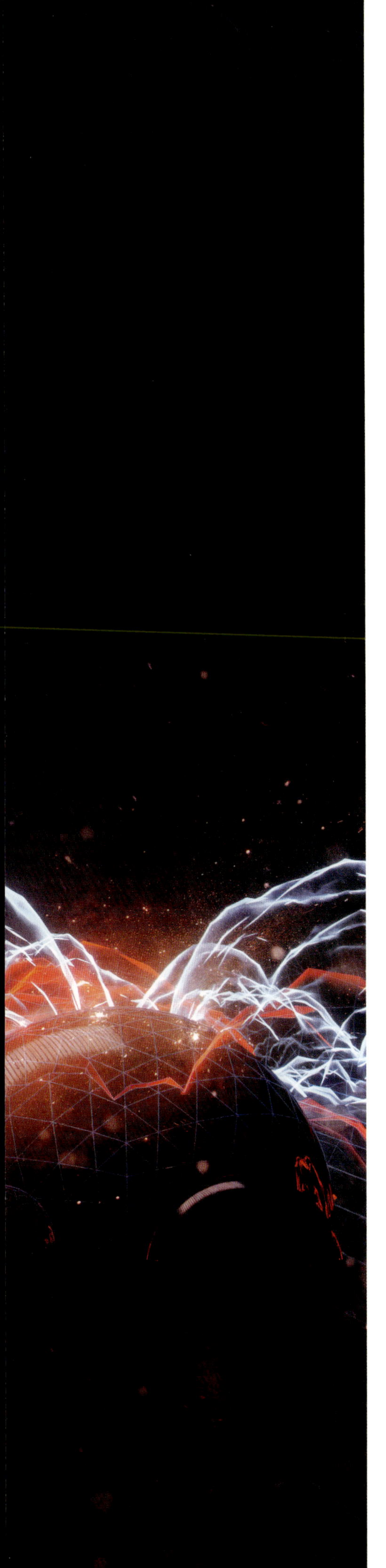

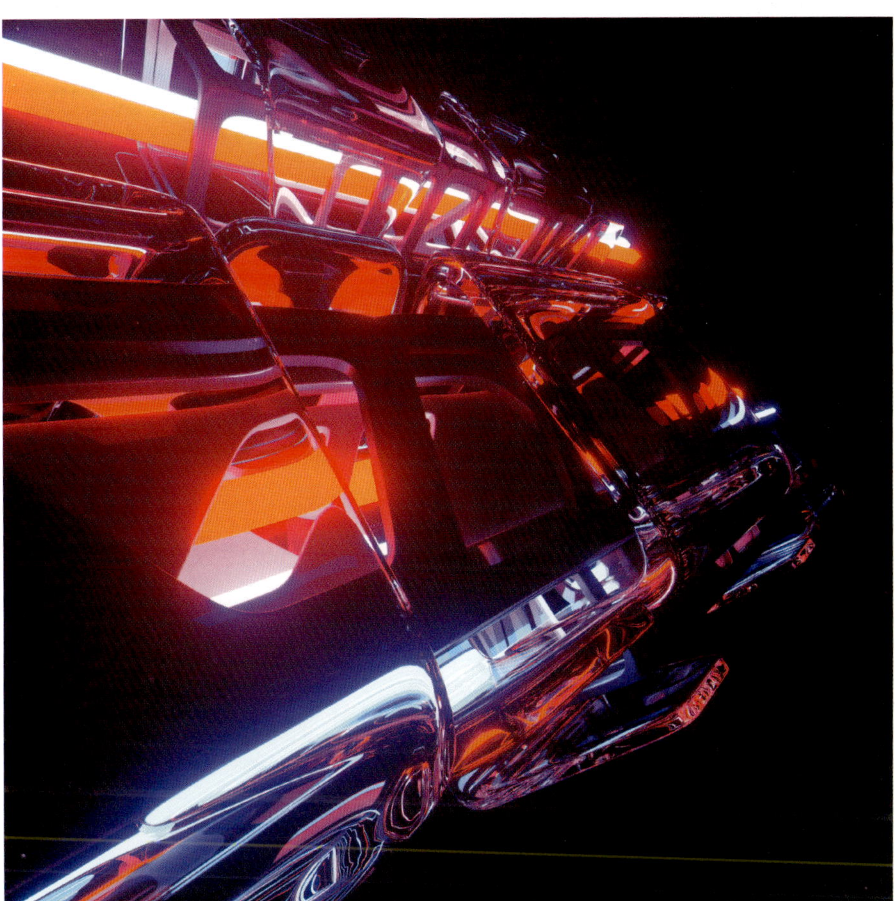

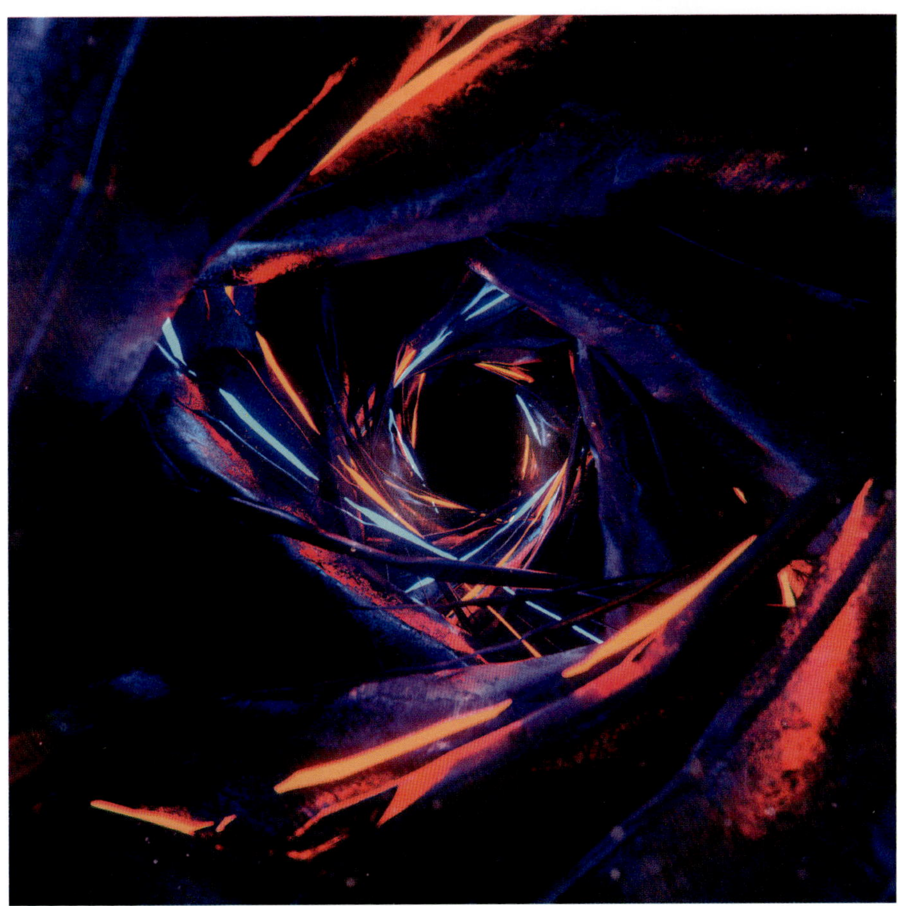

OPPOSITE PAGE
SPLICKY SPLOW
08.07.2014

TOP
24 k ultra
10.17.2014

BOTTOM
neon colon
07.09.2014

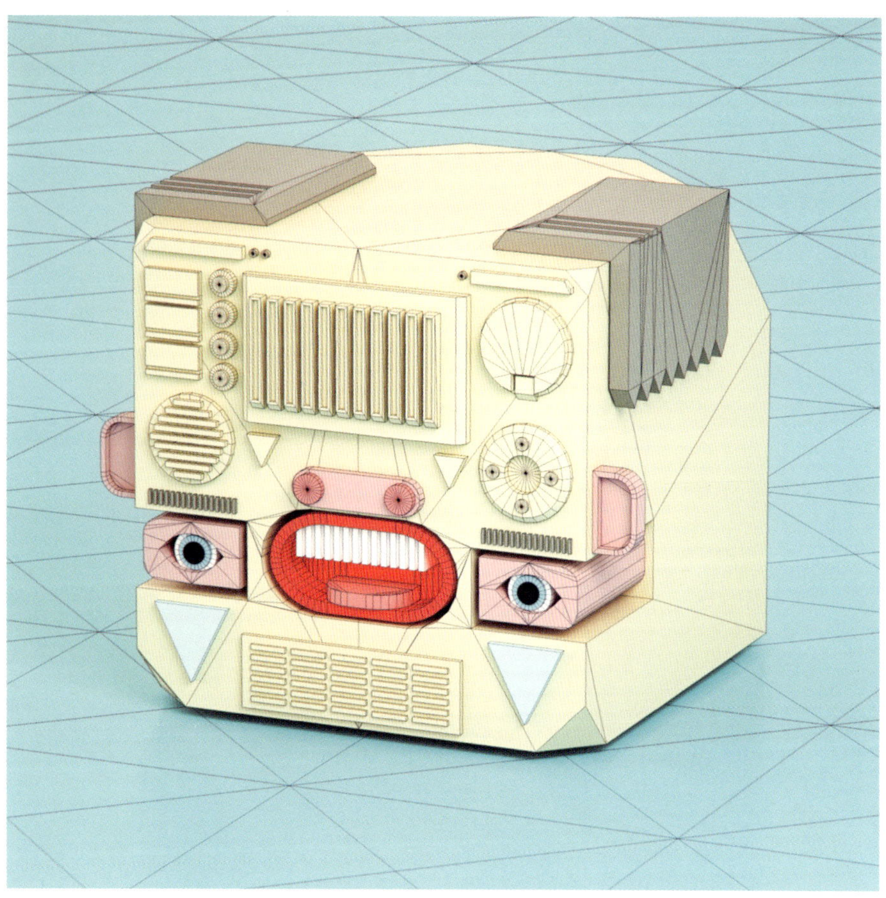

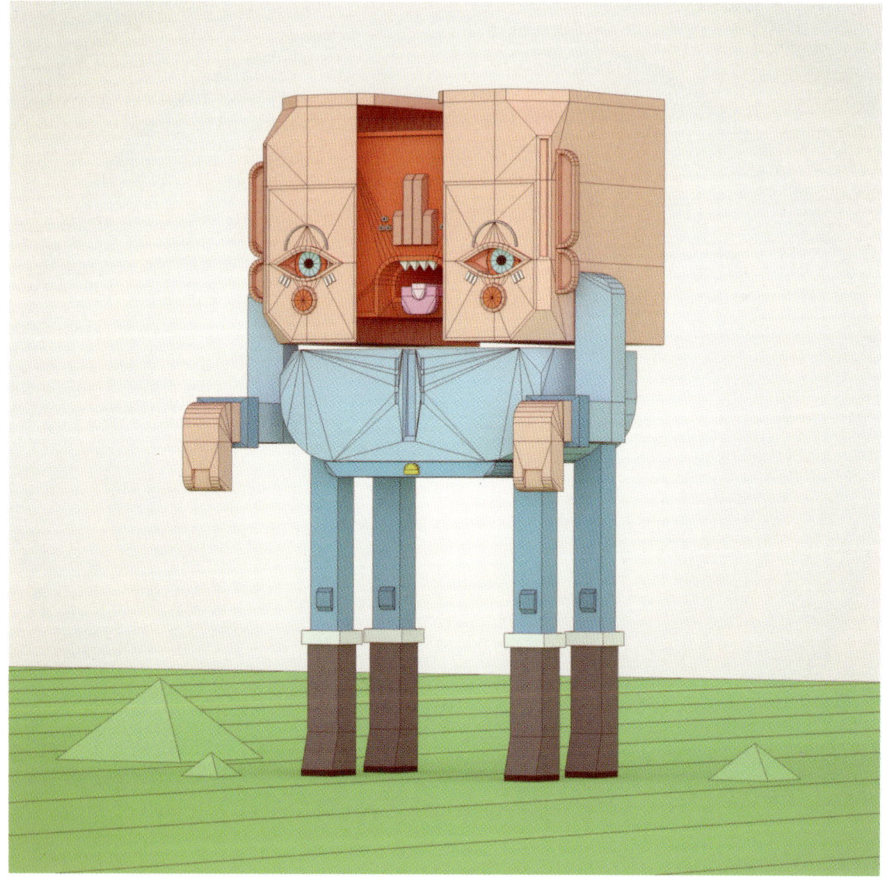

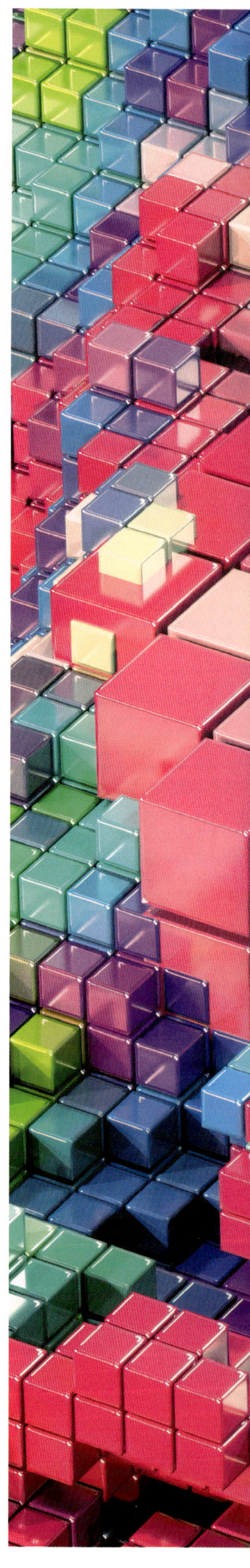

TOP
white people be like
10.23.2014

BOTTOM
lethargic pup
10.20.2014

OPPOSITE PAGE
CHICKLETS
07.18.2014

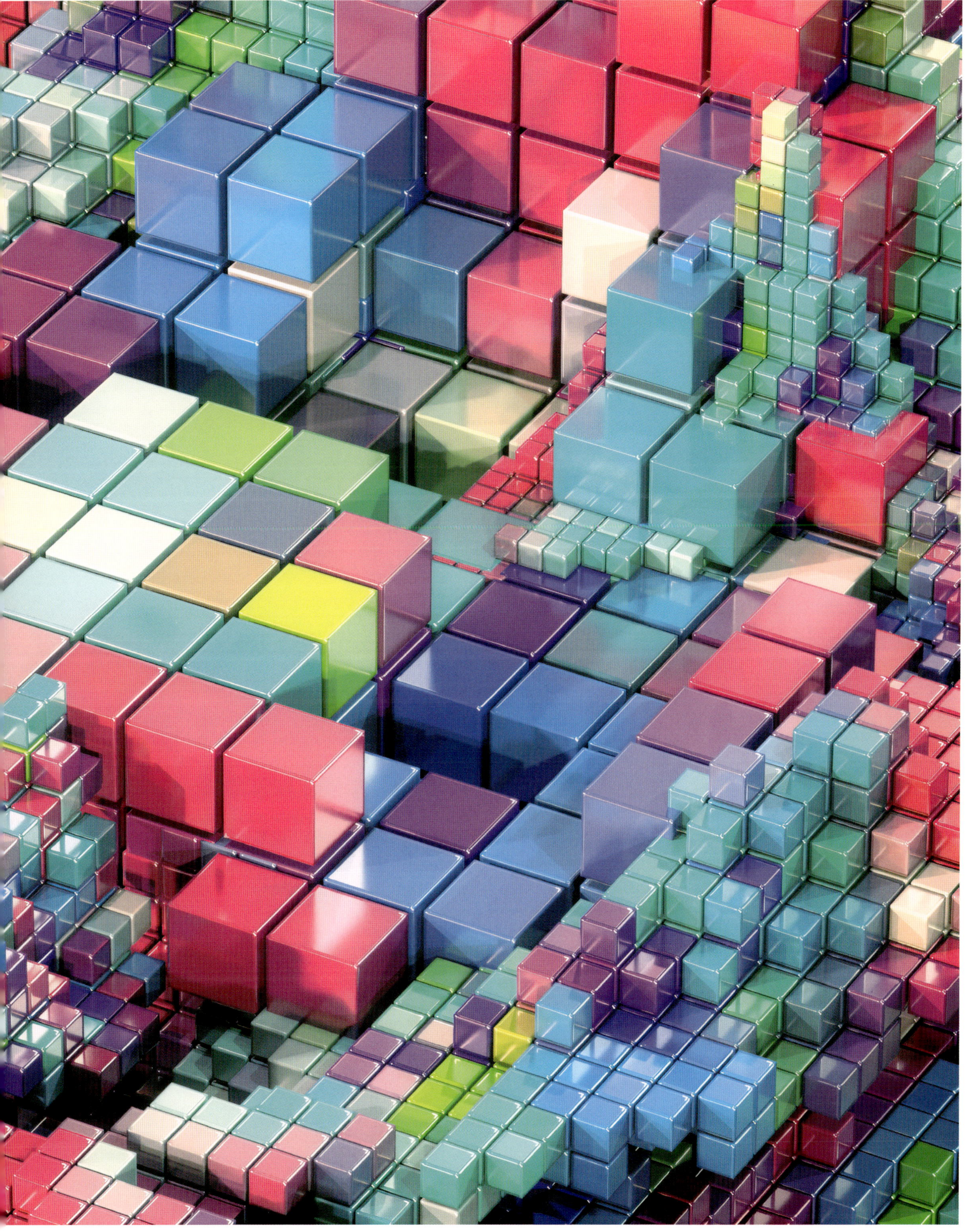

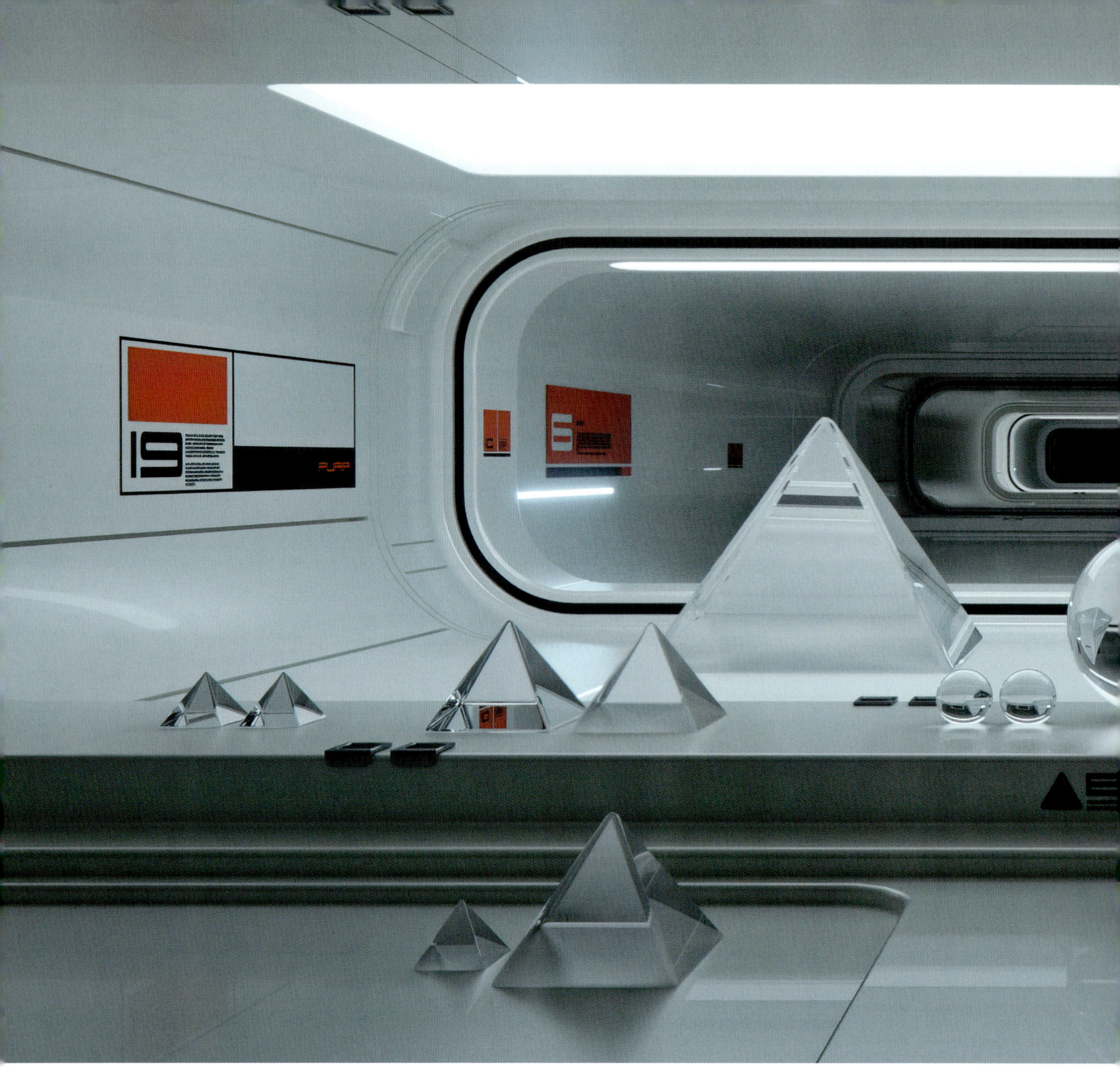

ABOVE

asymmetrical future
12.18.2014

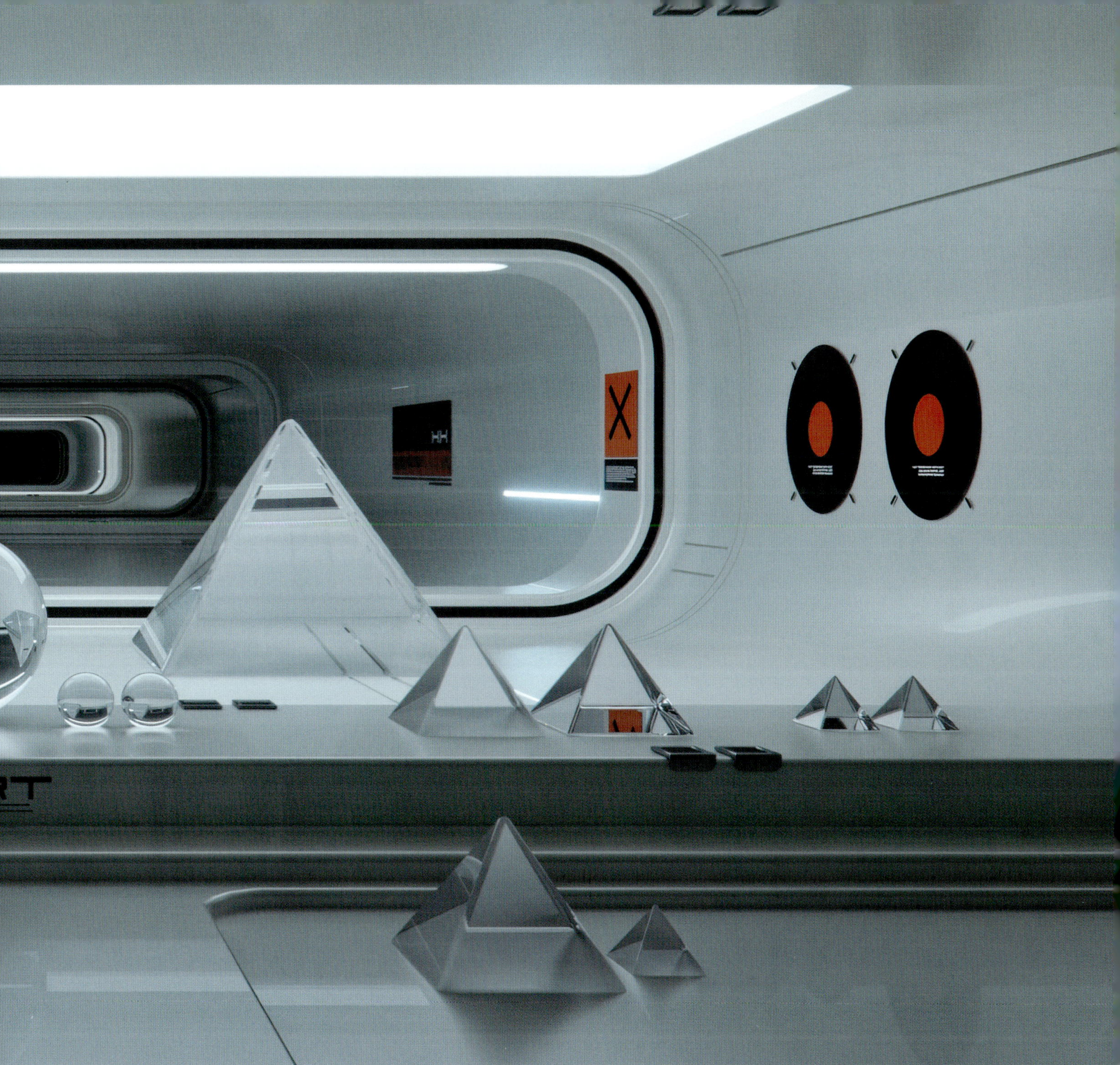

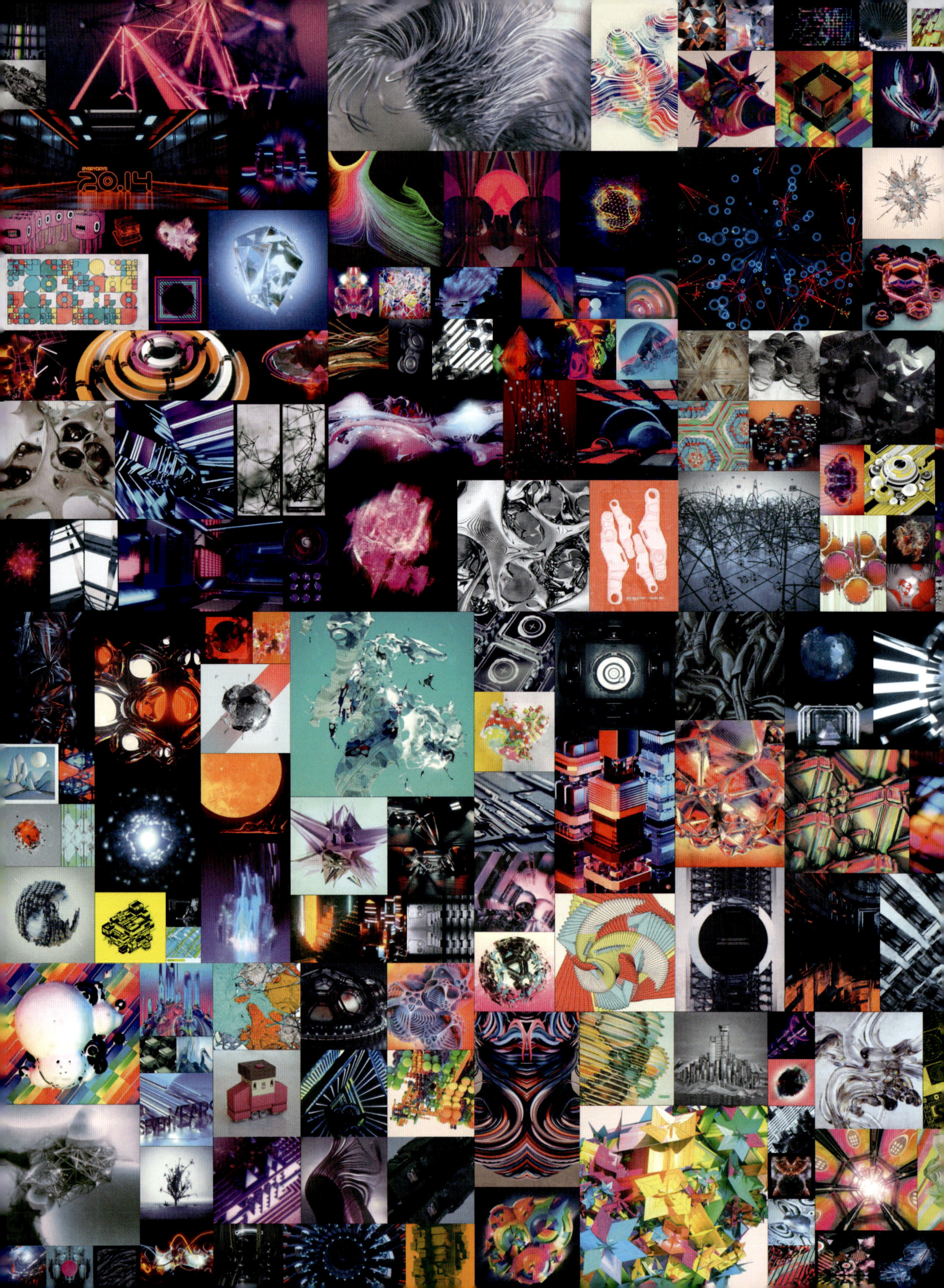
EVERYDAYS
20.14

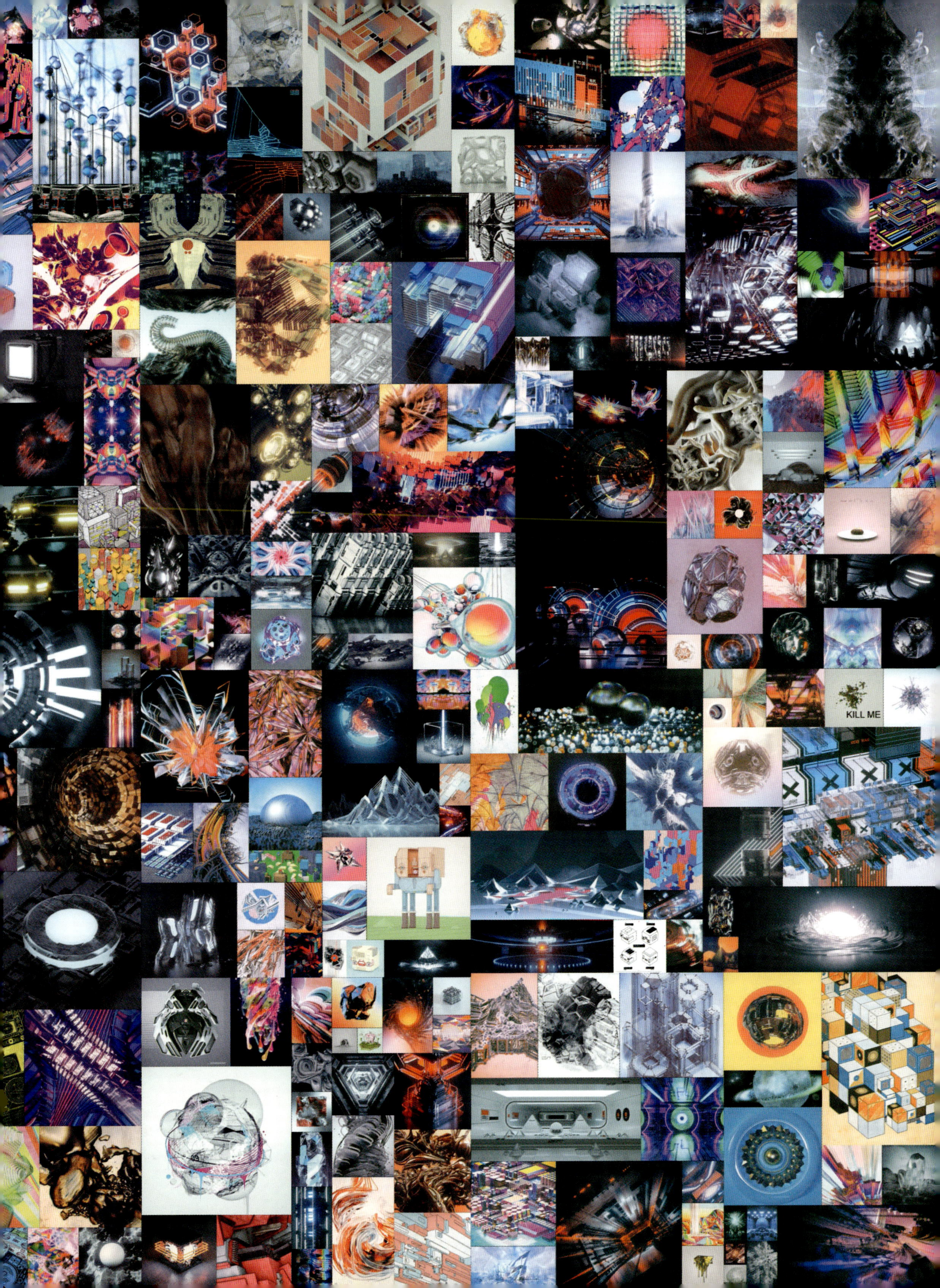
KILL ME

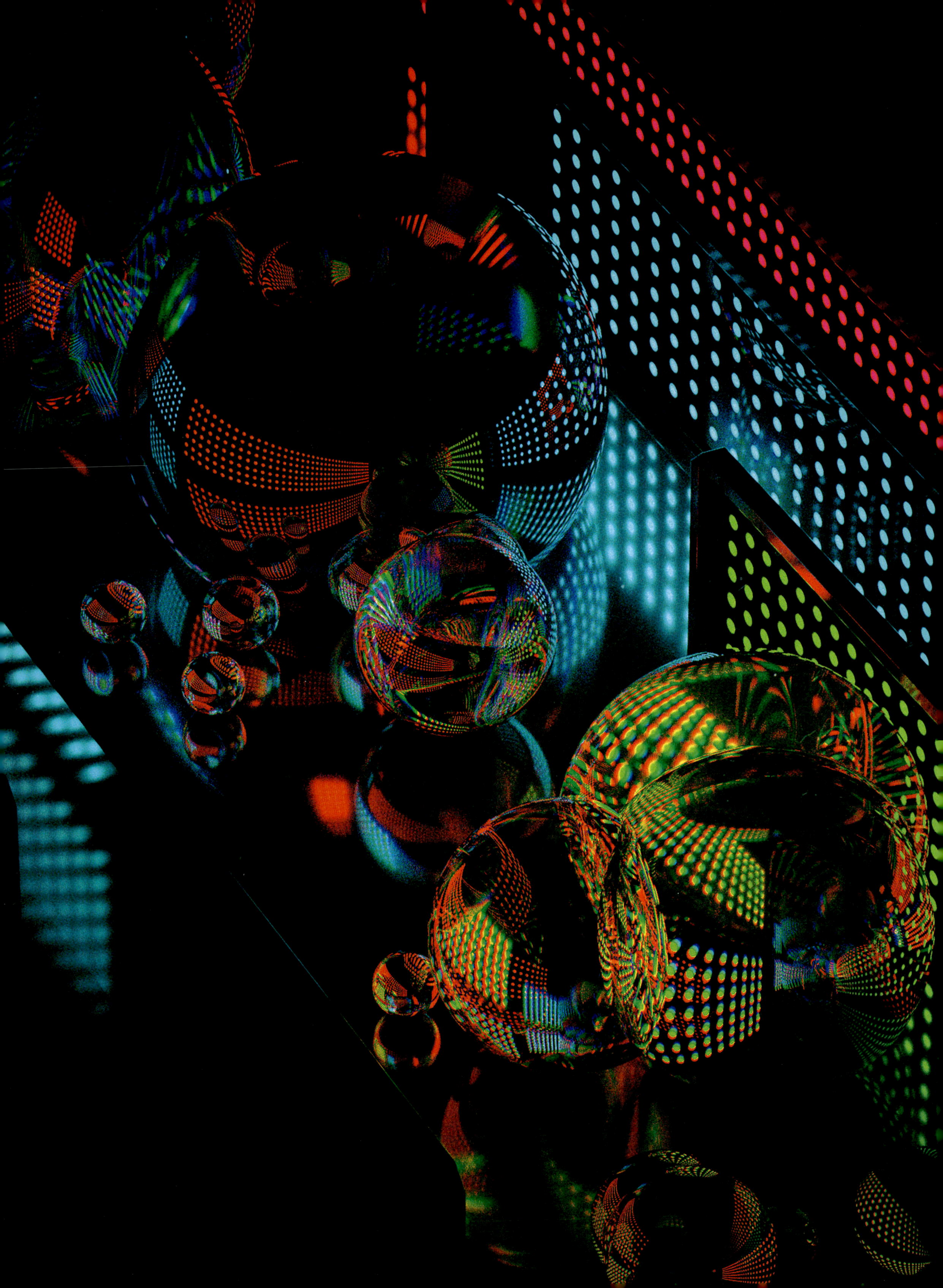

2015

OPPOSITE PAGE

dfhgdfgh
03.07.2015

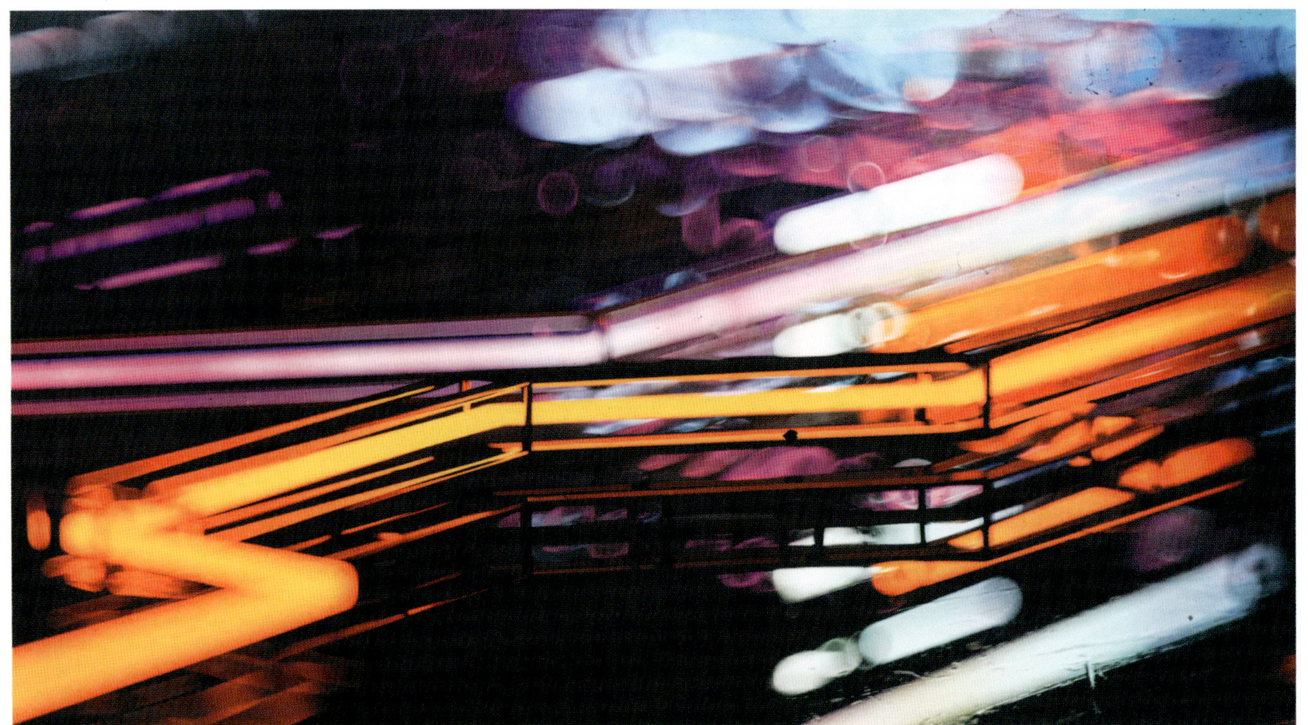

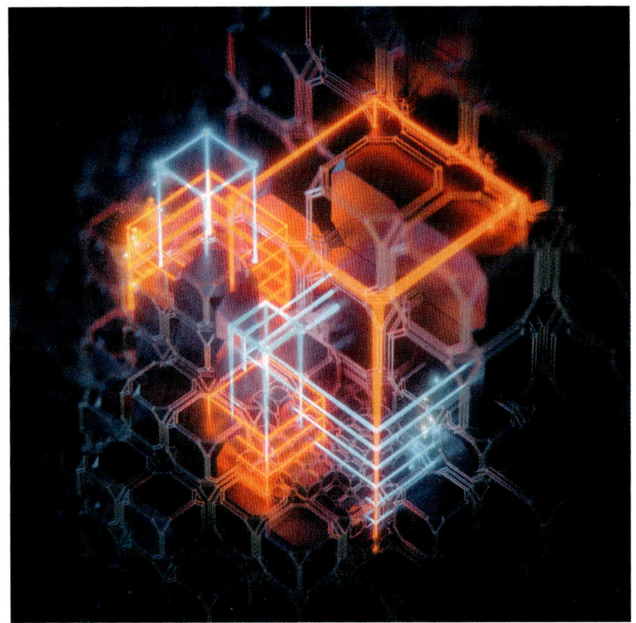

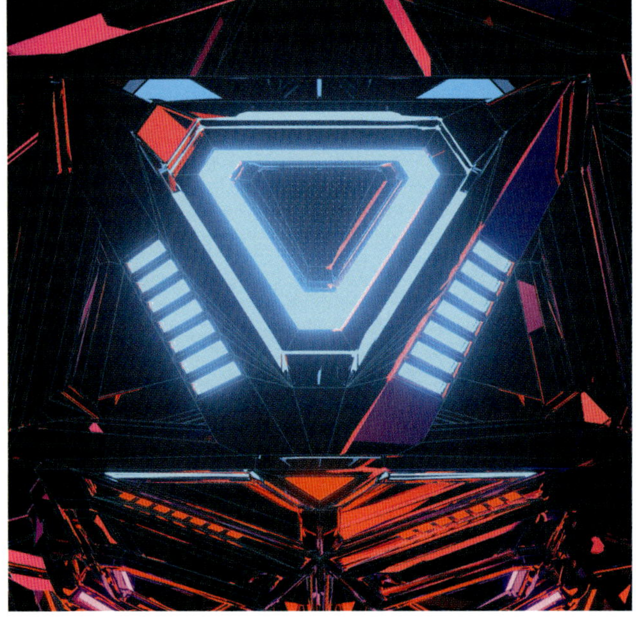

TOP

new management
02.24.2015

BOTTOM LEFT

double blowout //
03.03.2015

BOTTOM RIGHT

dirty ribbon
05.18.2015

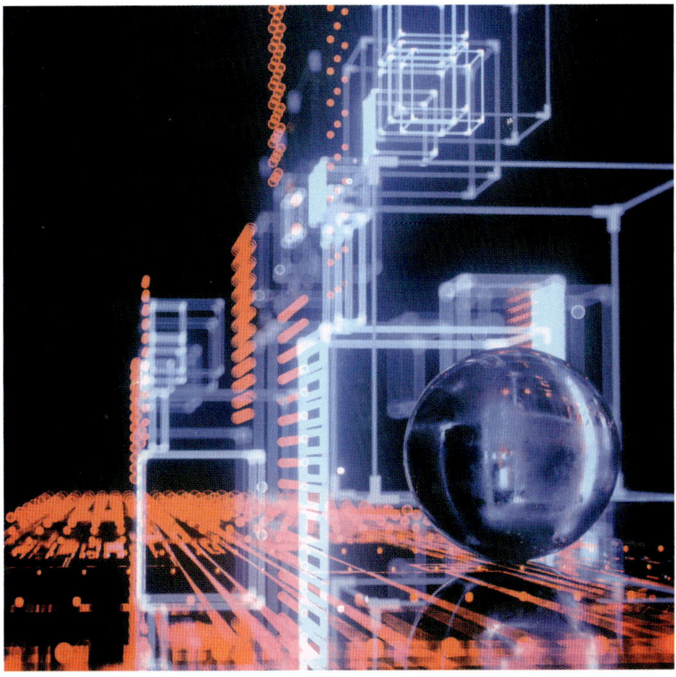

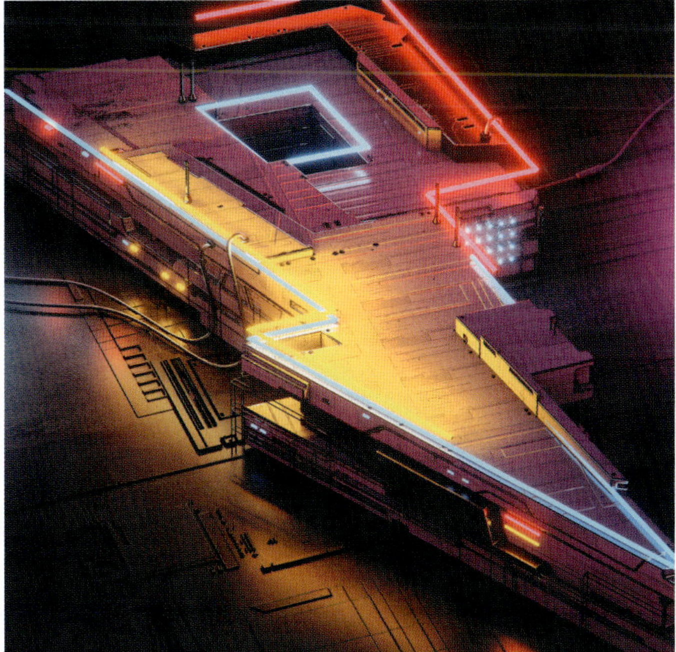

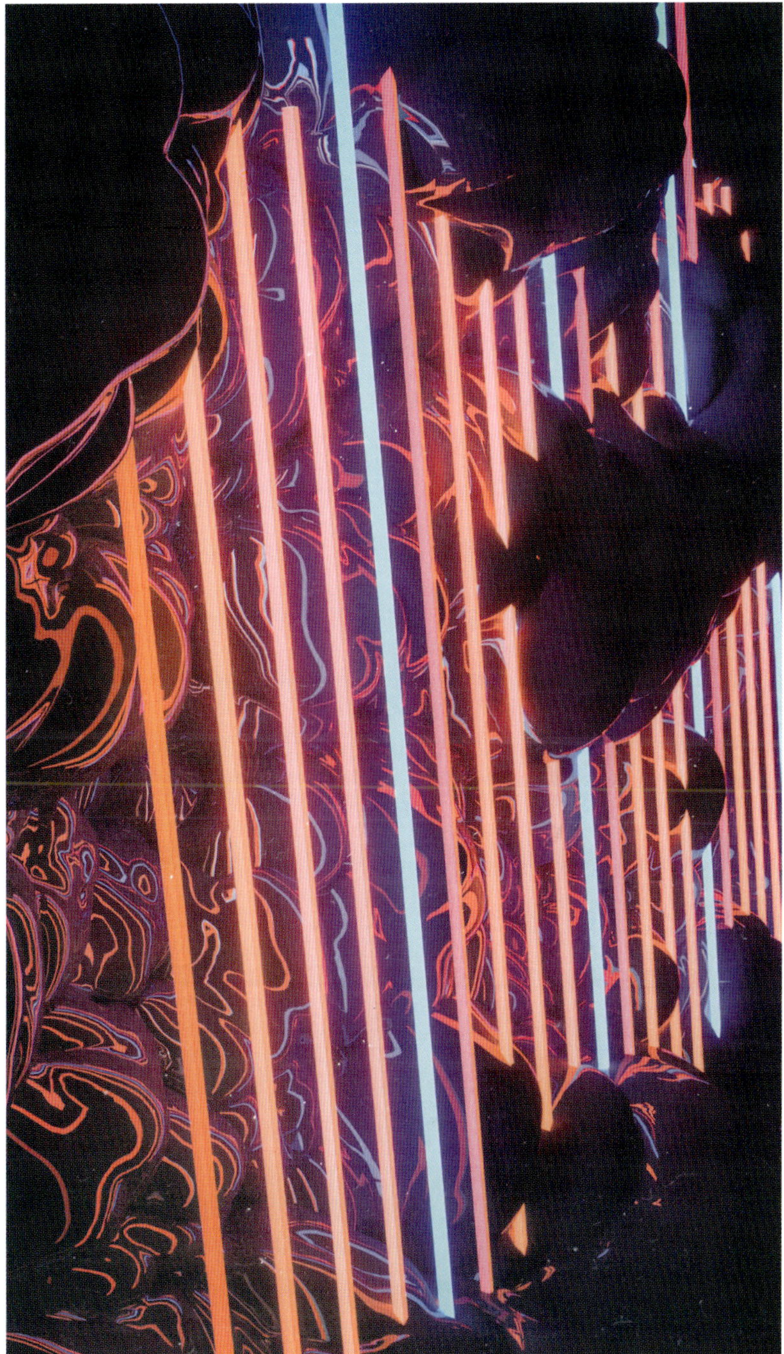

TOP LEFT

shade runn

01.21.2015

BOTTOM LEFT

PROX

11.24.2015

RIGHT

radiant nothing

03.09.2015

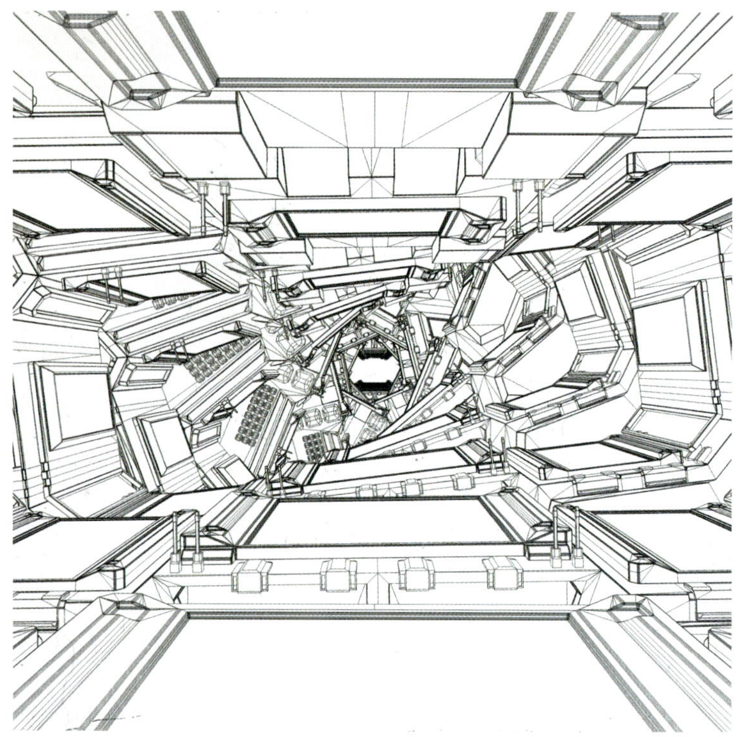
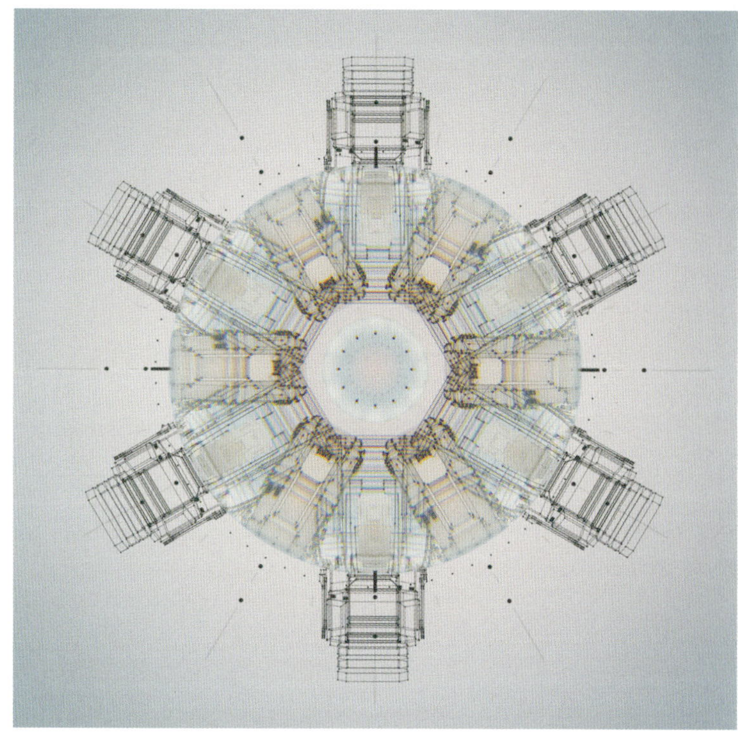
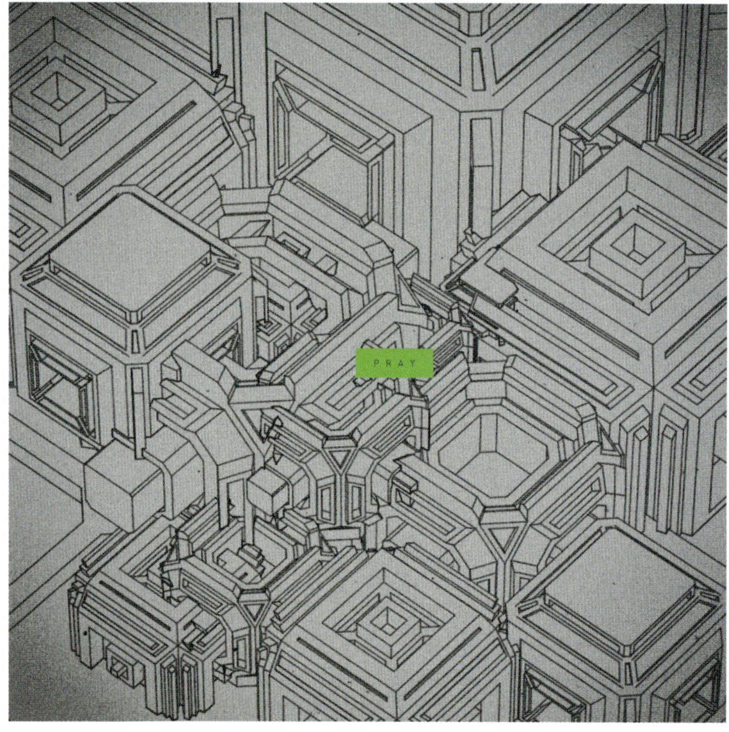

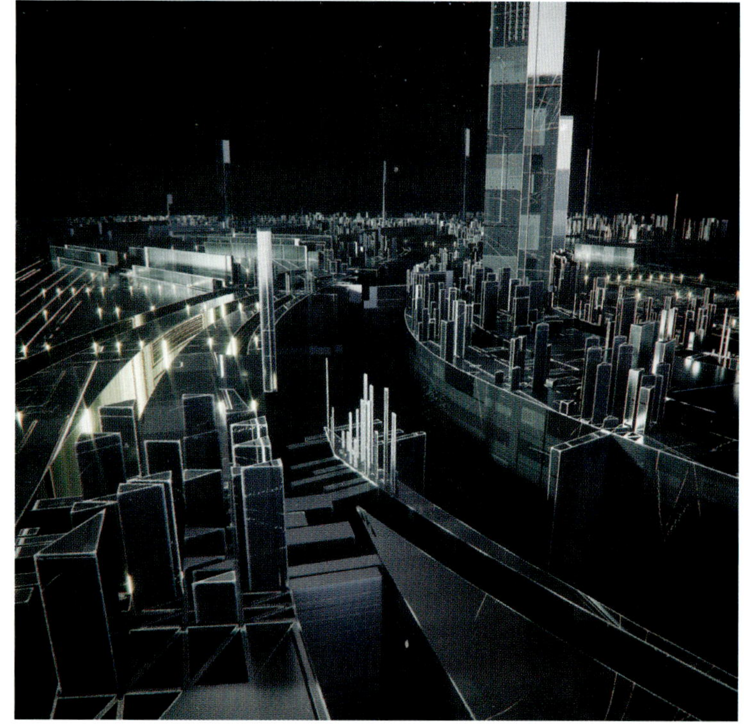

TOP LEFT
needed respite
06.18.2015

TOP RIGHT
CORTXX.NINE
10.29.2015

BOTTOM LEFT
pray
06.13.2015

BOTTOM RIGHT
reclamm.x3
03.28.2015

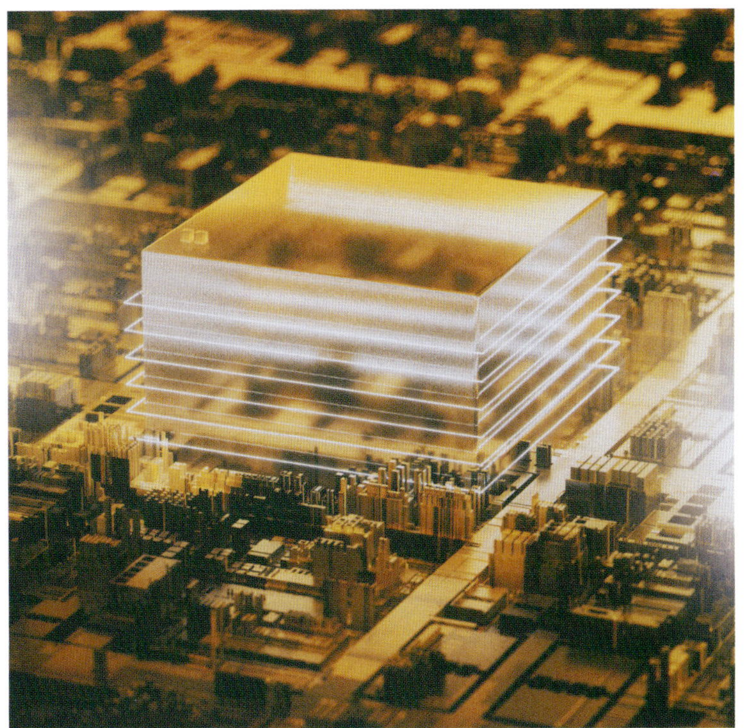

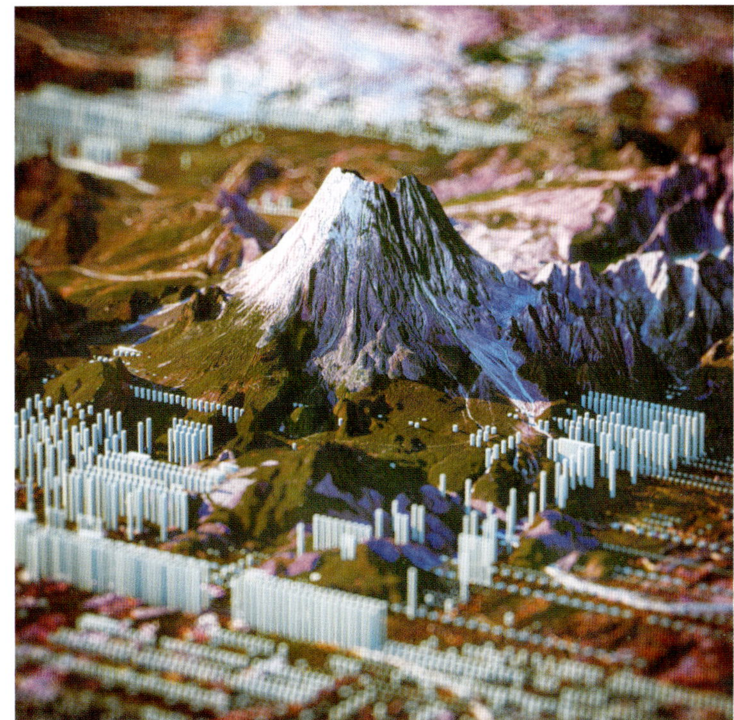

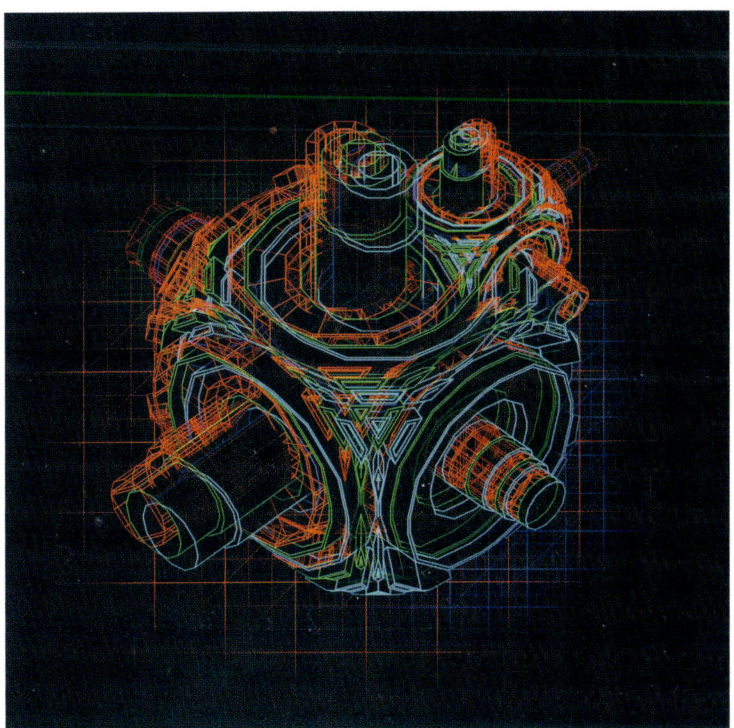

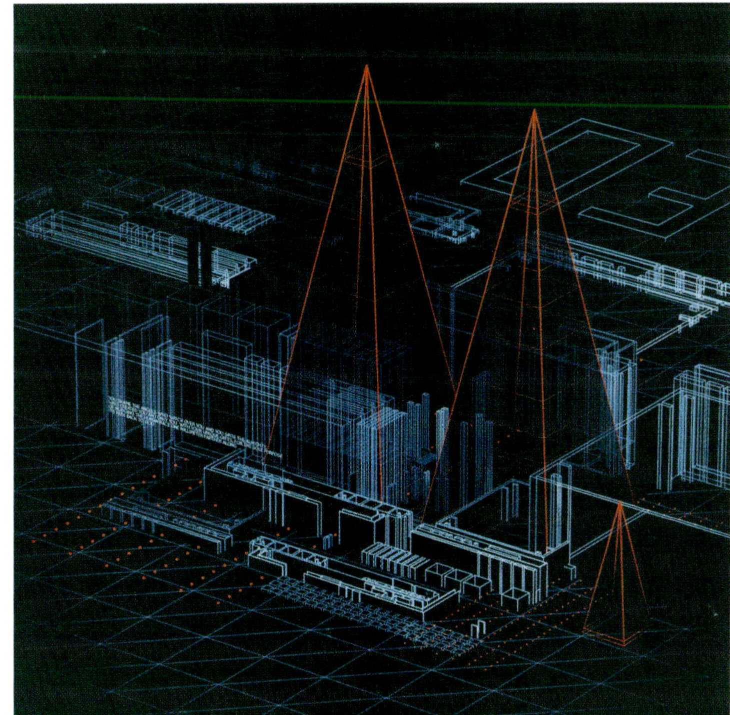

TOP LEFT
complex problem
06.14.2015

TOP RIGHT
resont-plus.8k(busy)
06.04.2015

BOTTOM LEFT
RGB VENTRICLE
02.19.2015

BOTTOM RIGHT
bad beat
02.13.2015

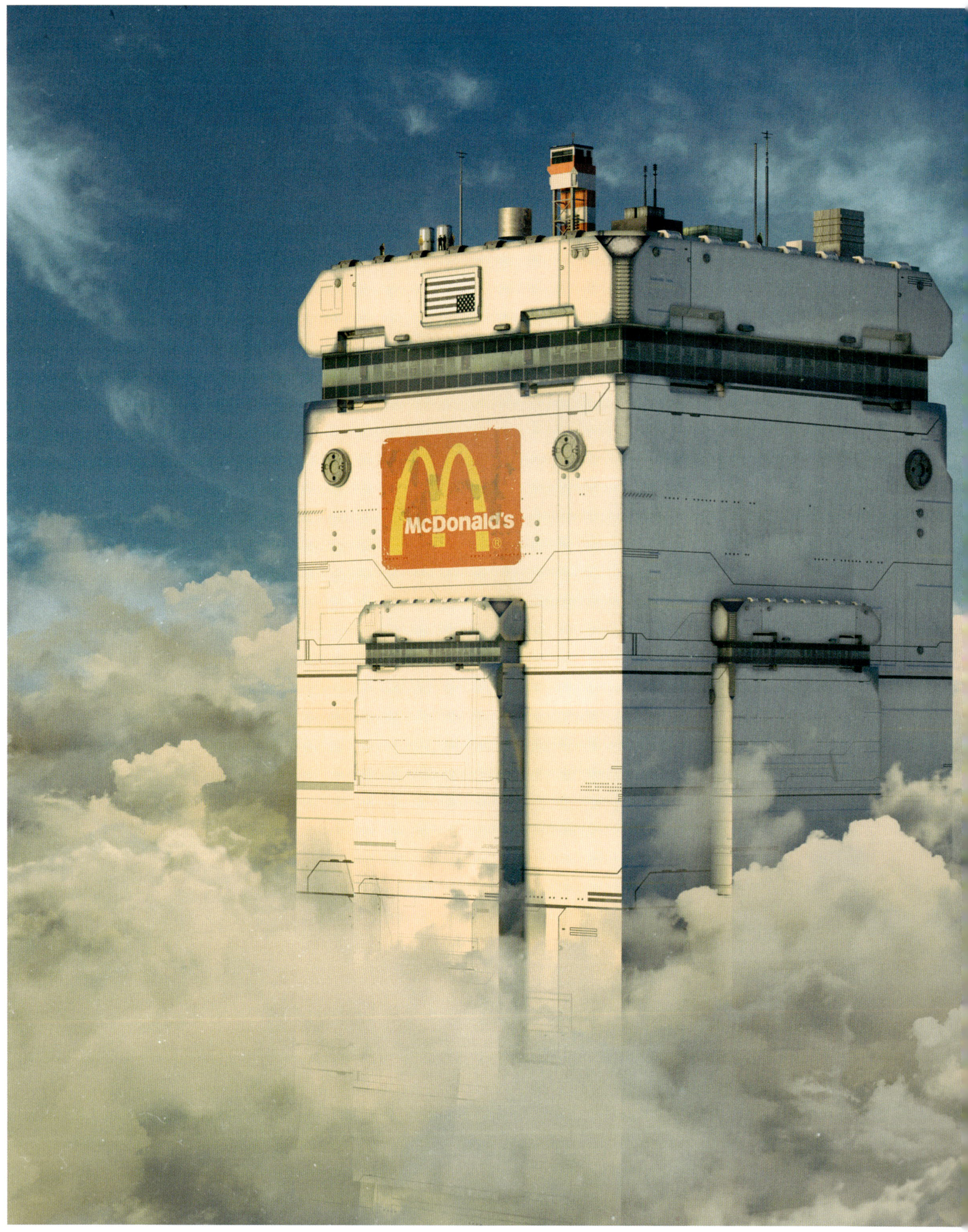
McDonald's

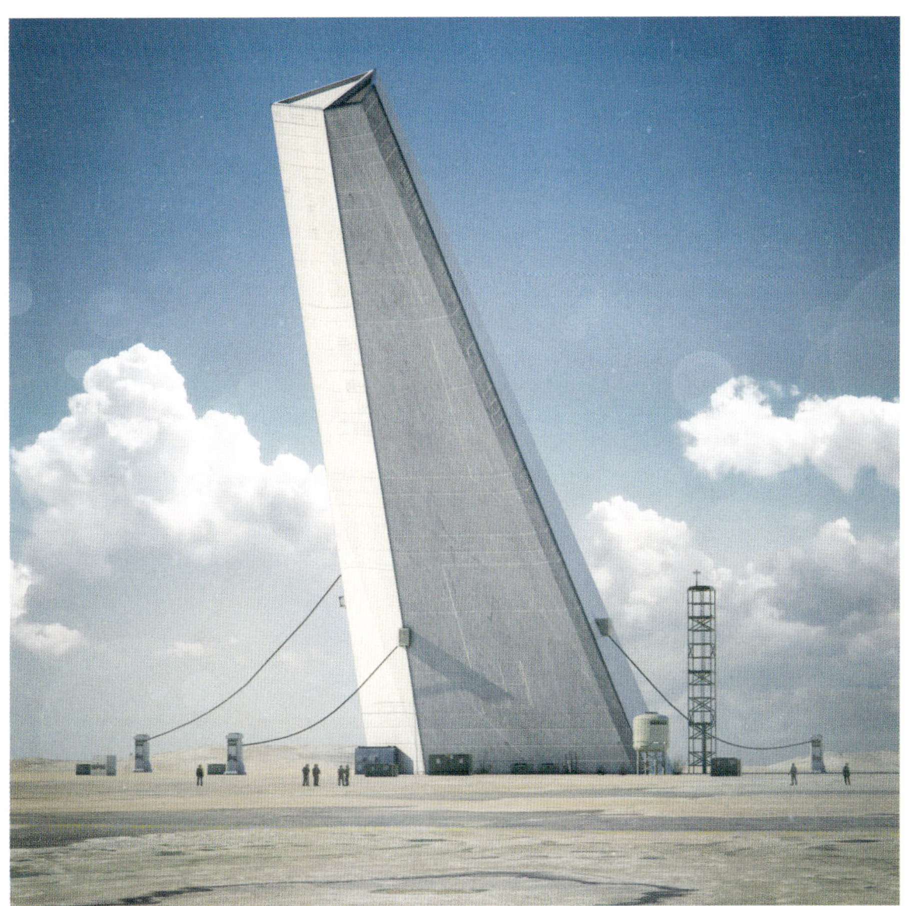

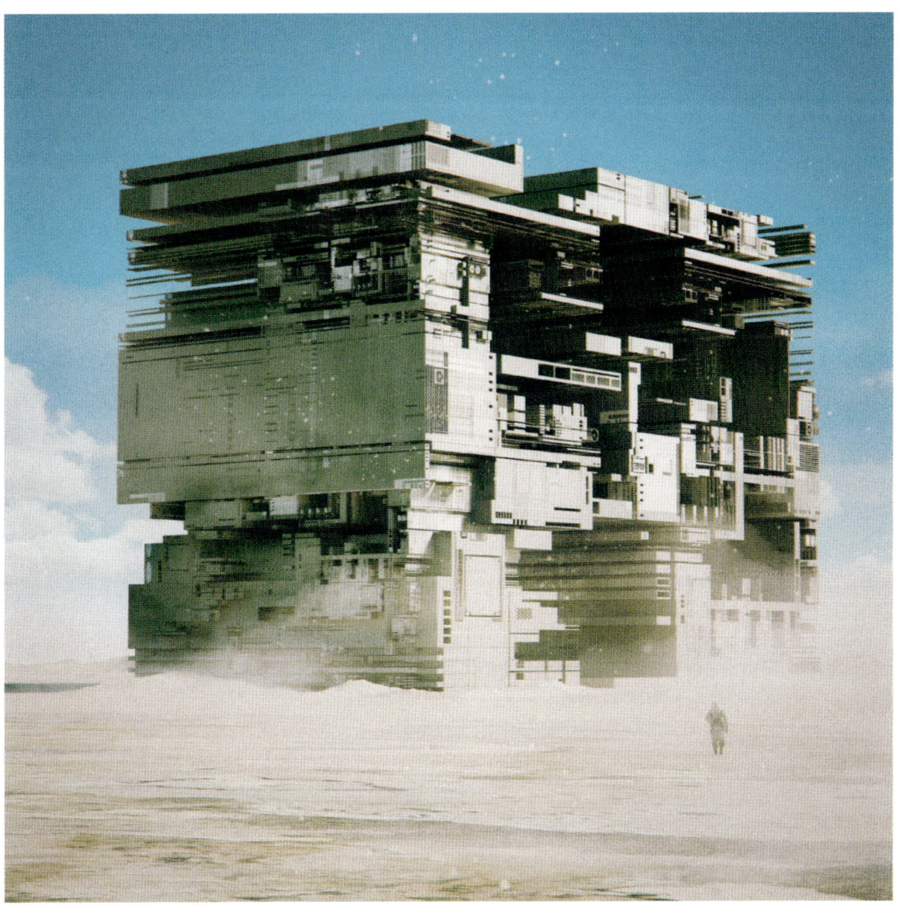

OPPOSITE PAGE
MCD 2087
08.11.2015

TOP
GRINDCO
08.17.2015

BOTTOM
TURO-B1
12.26.2015

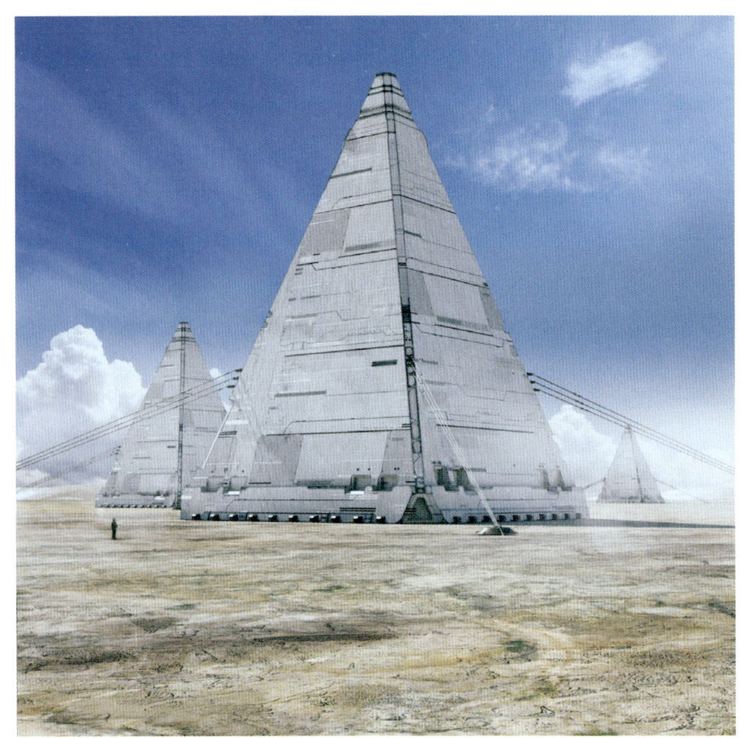

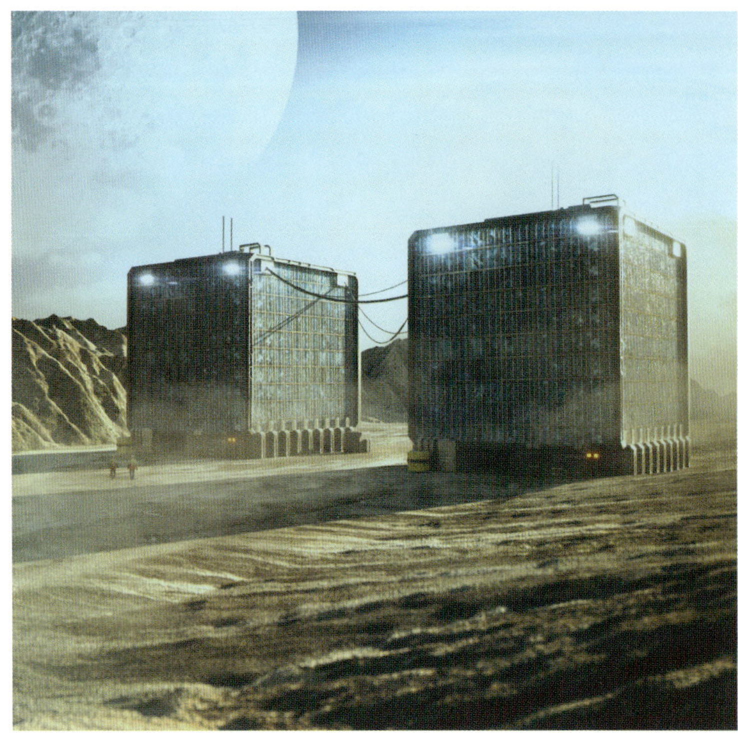

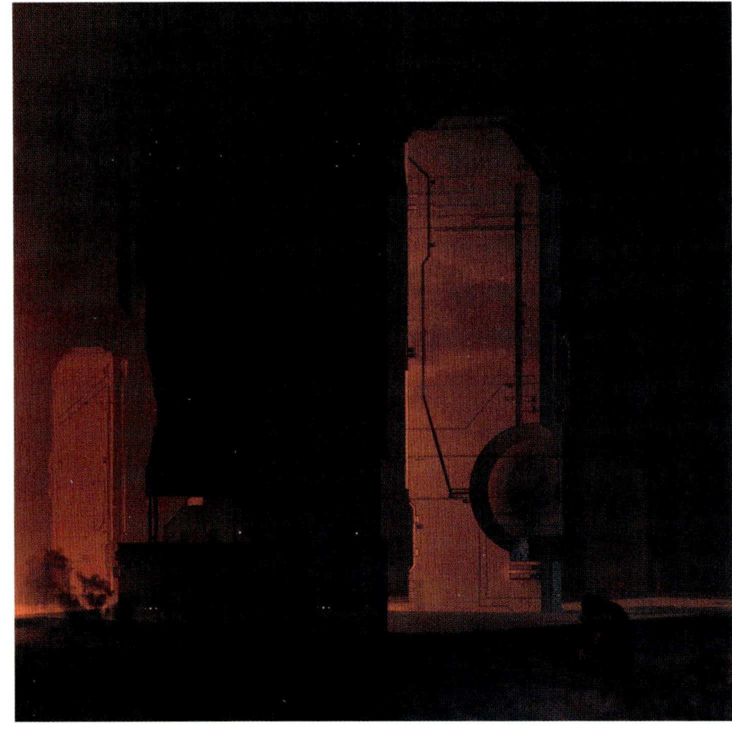

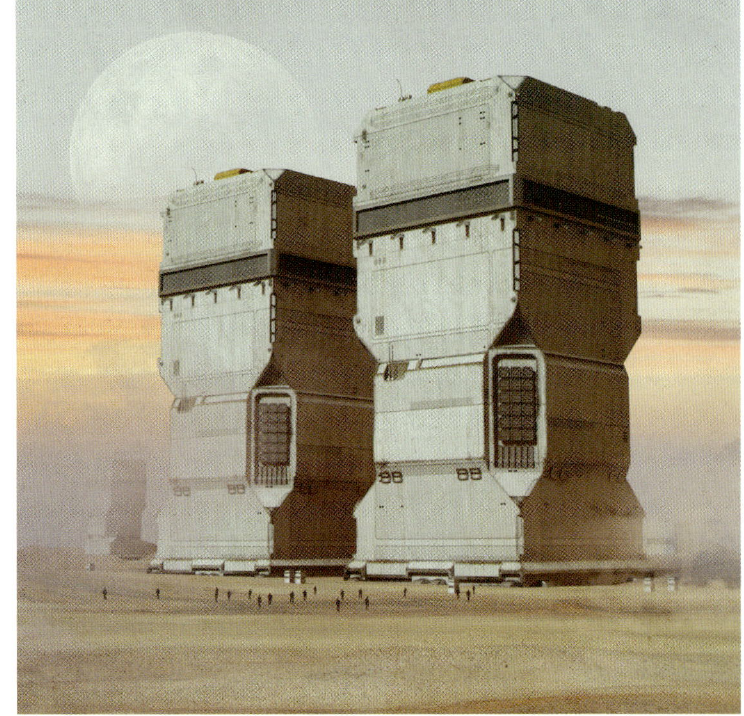

TOP LEFT
sto-flue.two
07.13.2015

TOP RIGHT
pxil.two
05.12.2015

BOTTOM LEFT
BURN.DAWN
11.27.2015

BOTTOM RIGHT
FOGBAE.TOWR4
07.06.2015

OPPOSITE PAGE
BOXXX-3W
07.01.2015

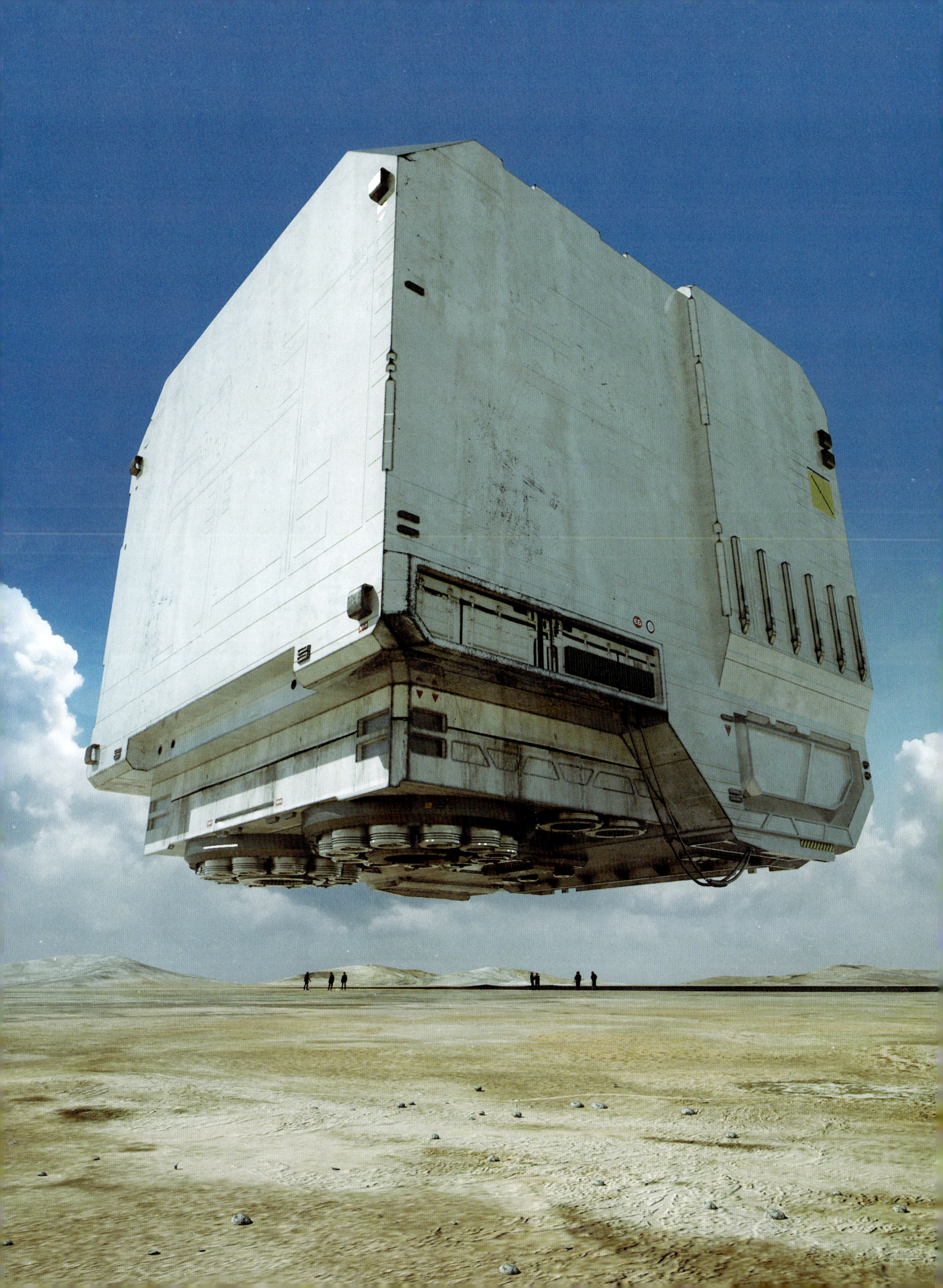

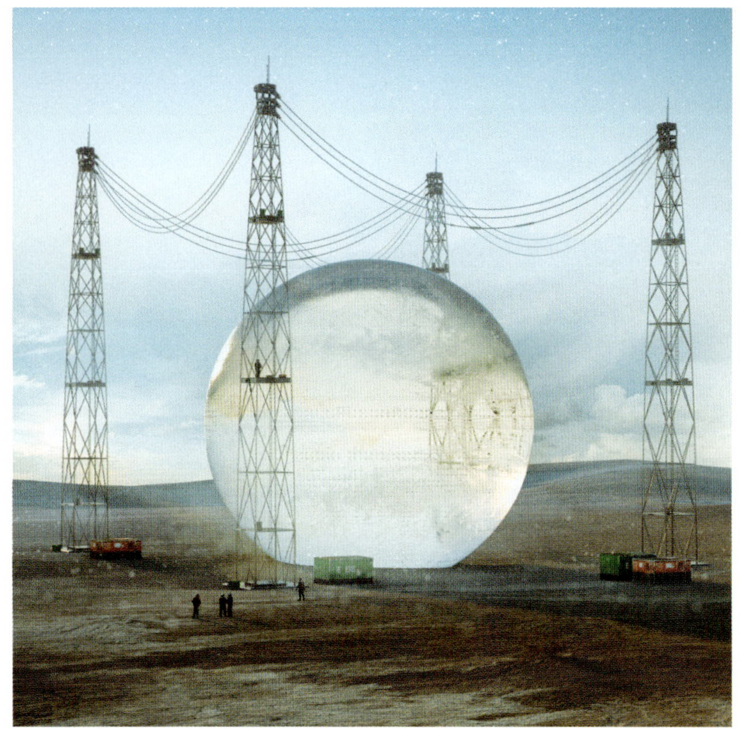

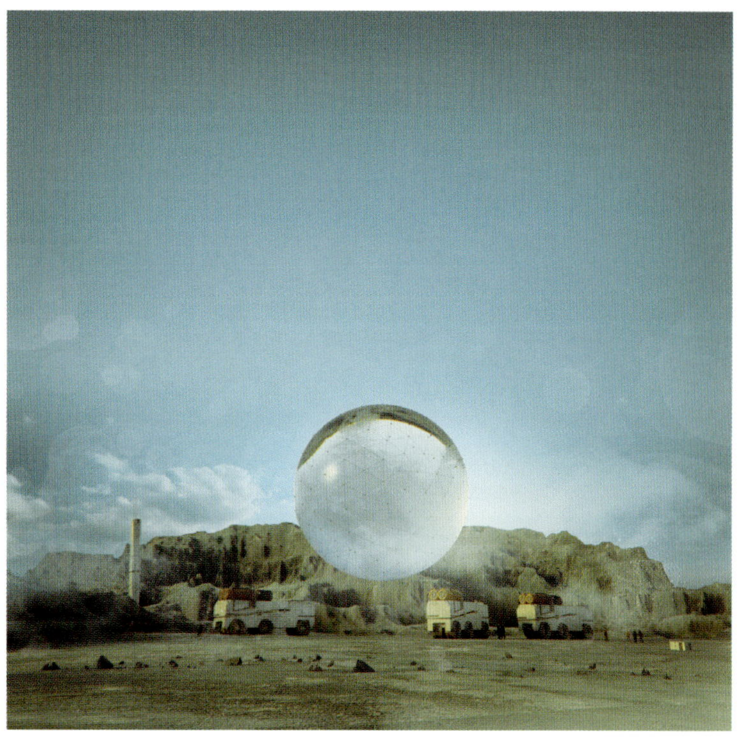

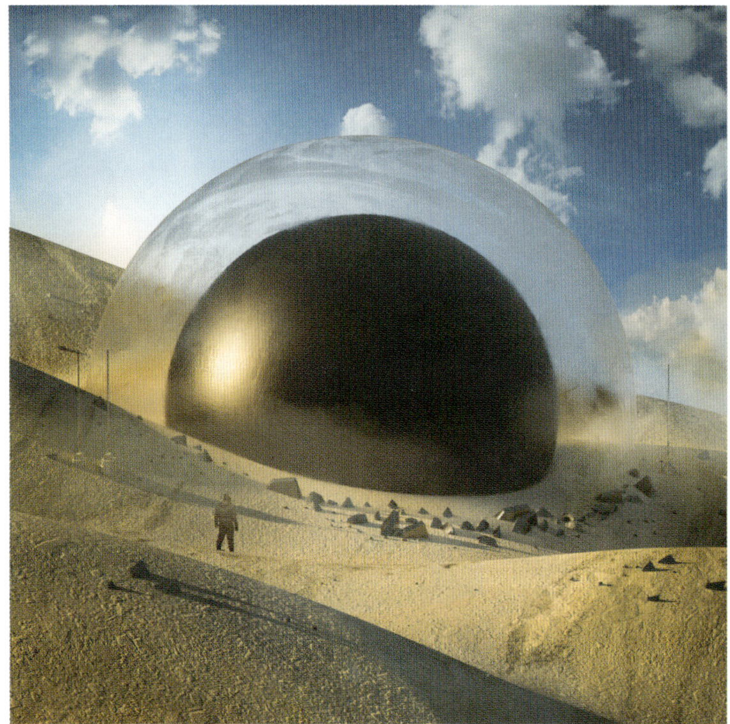

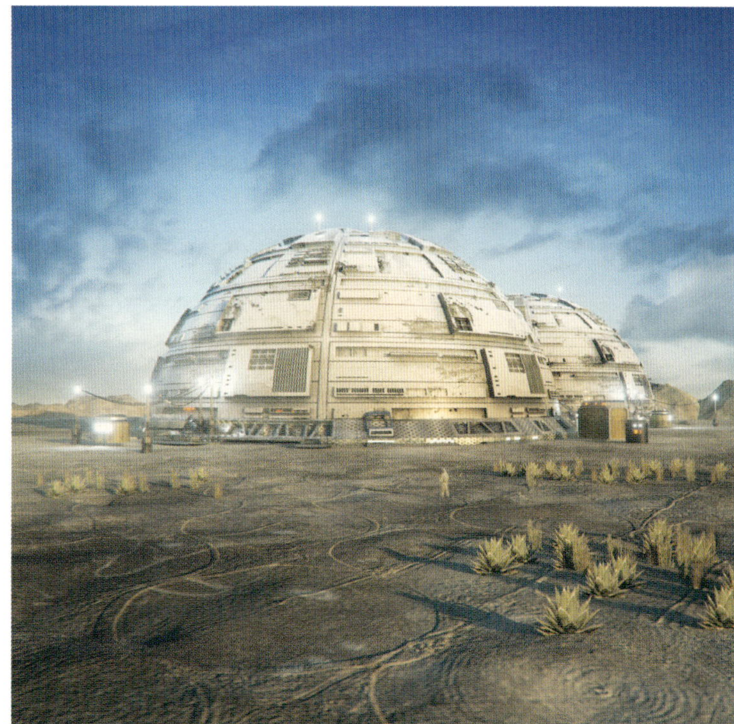

TOP LEFT
gaussian harvest
06.10.2015

TOP RIGHT
UTIL.IOUS
10.18.2015

BOTTOM LEFT
IRON NUCLEUS
08.05.2015

BOTTOM RIGHT
hydrogation tanks
05.26.2015

OPPOSITE PAGE
MINOR PEON
07.23.2015

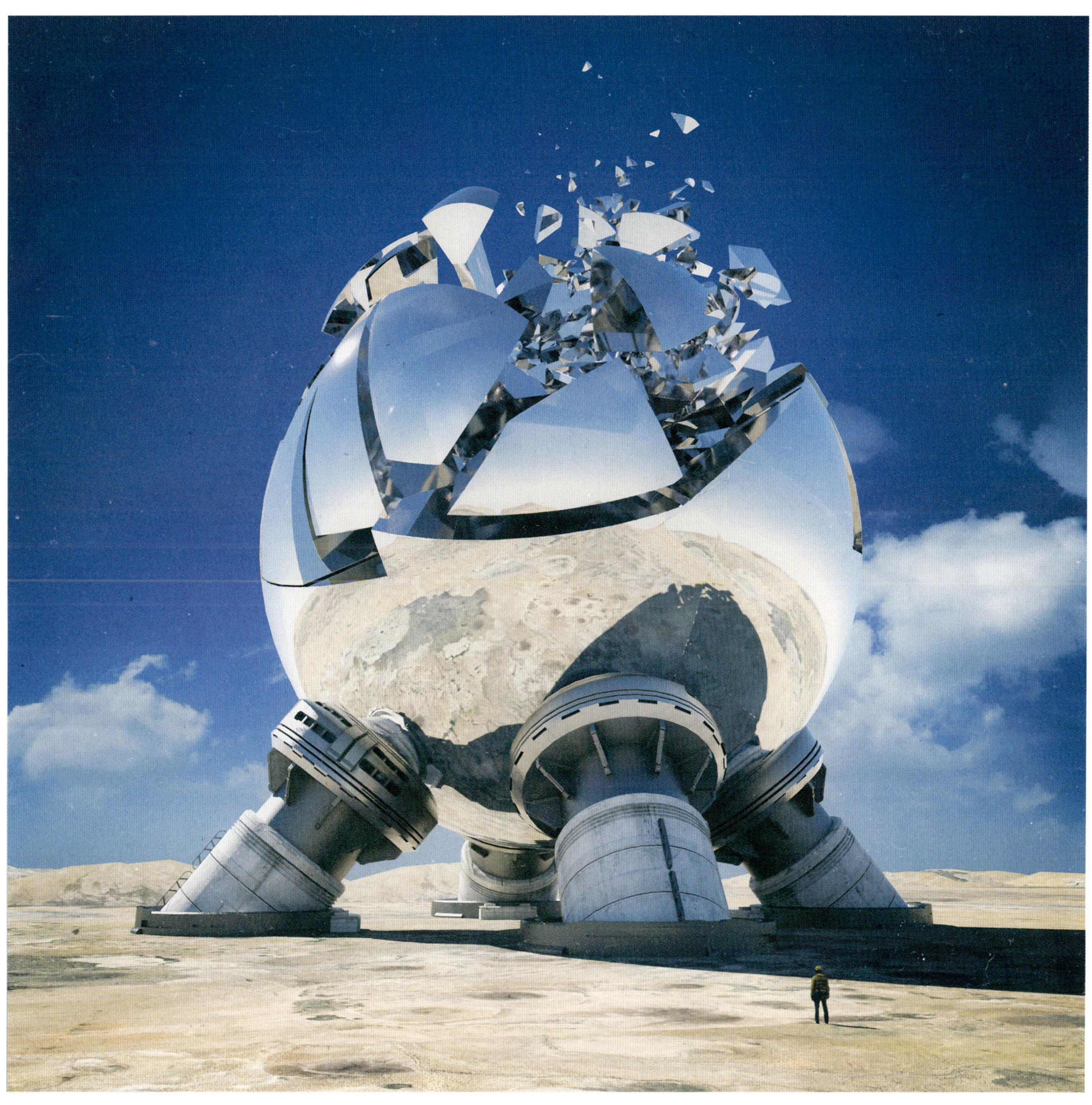

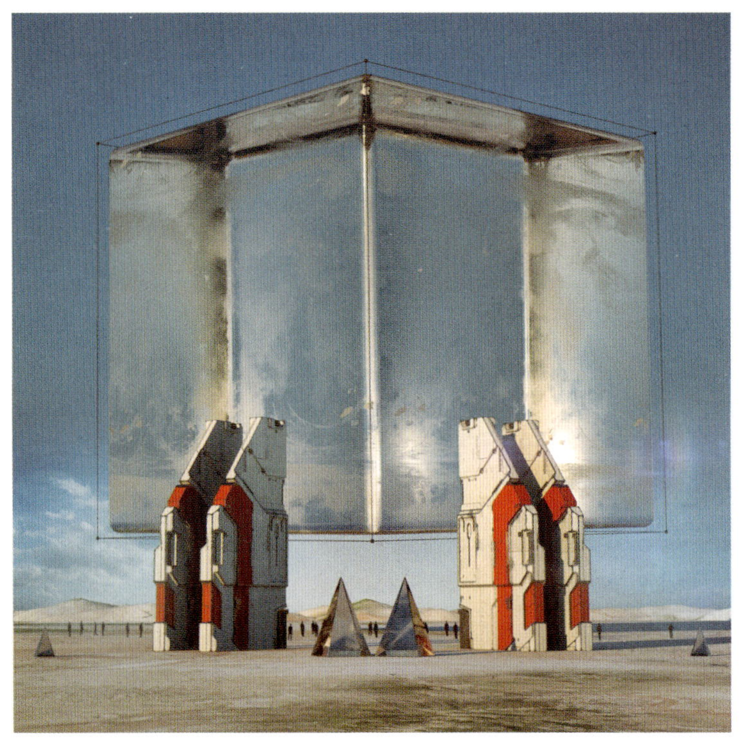

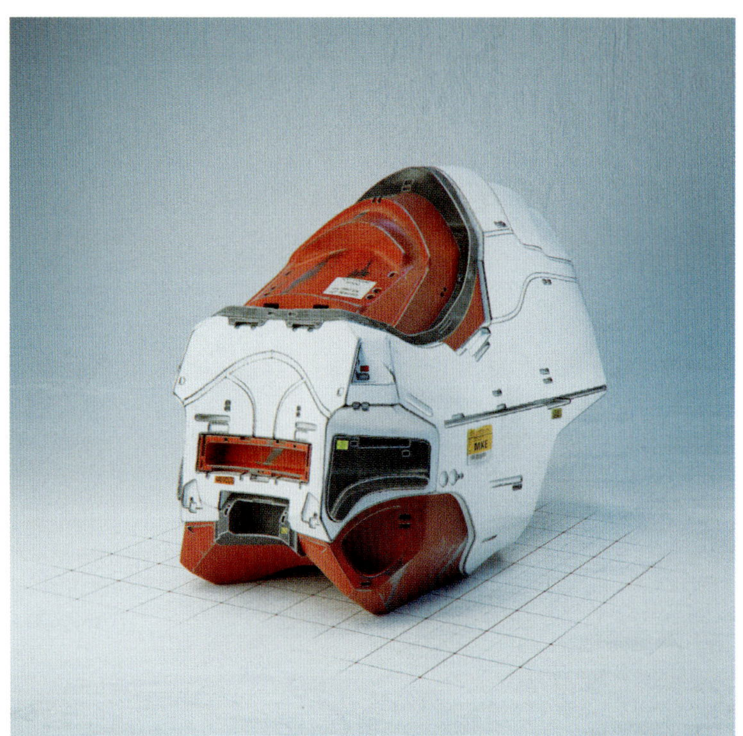

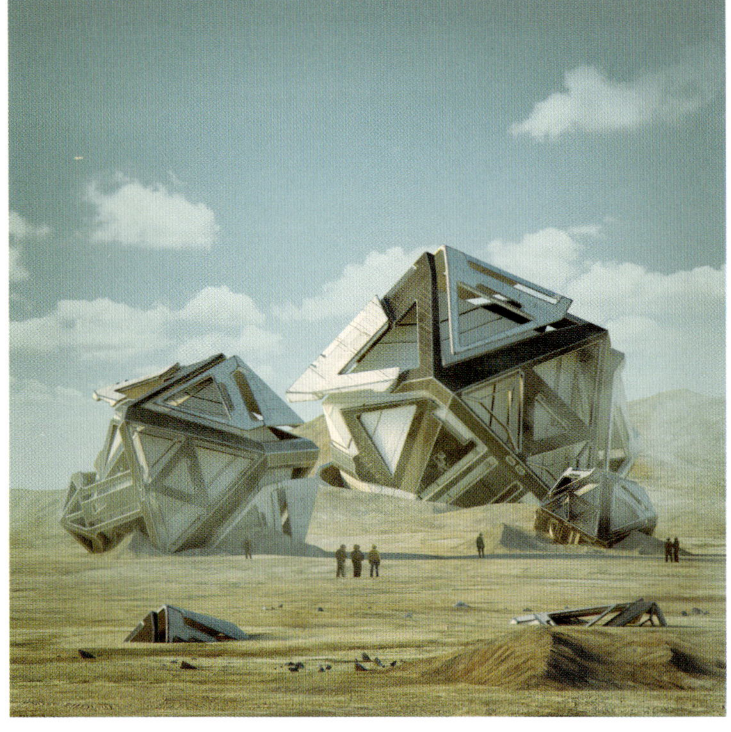

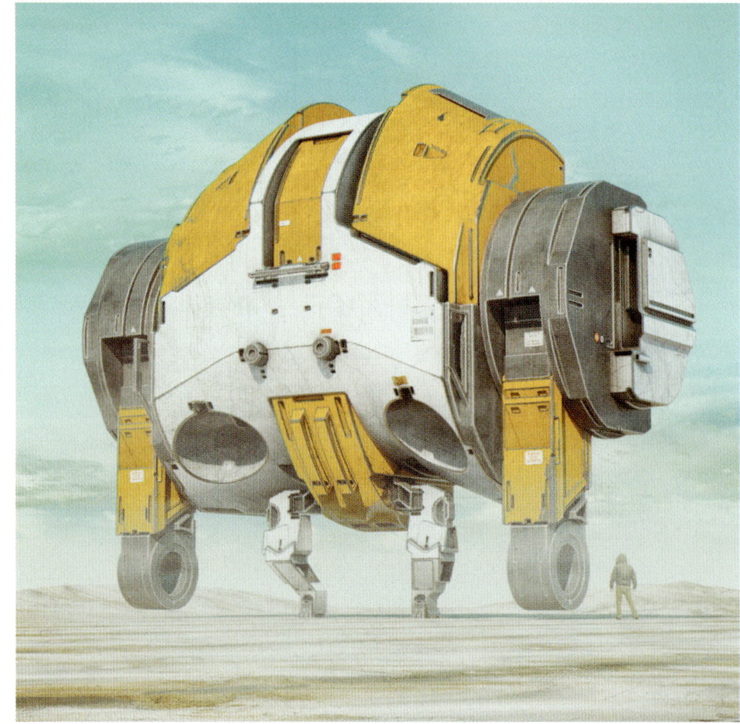

TOP LEFT
ORTHAGANOL
11.11.2015

TOP RIGHT
B1-ONE
11.13.2015

BOTTOM LEFT
PLATONIC
12.19.2015

BOTTOM RIGHT
90K GORILLA
12.01.2015

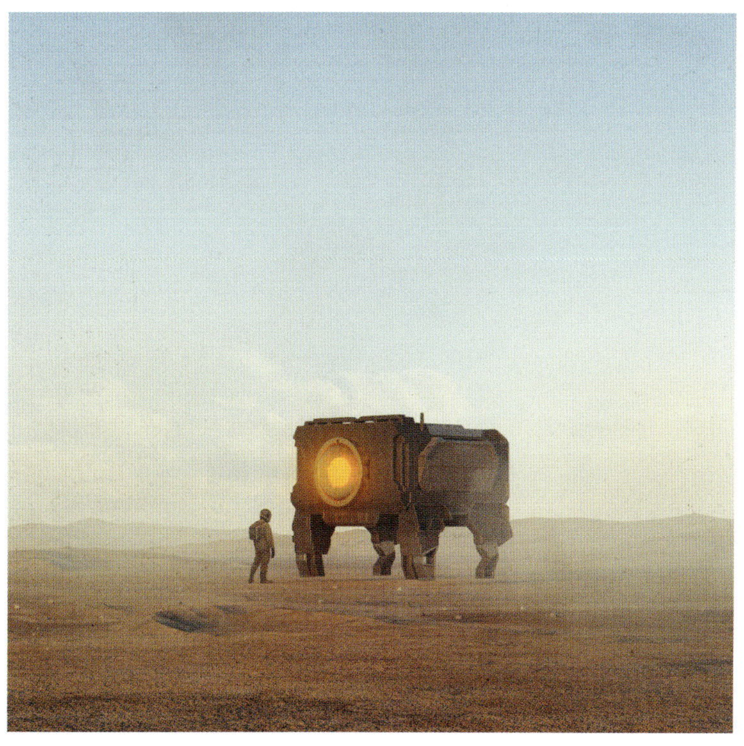

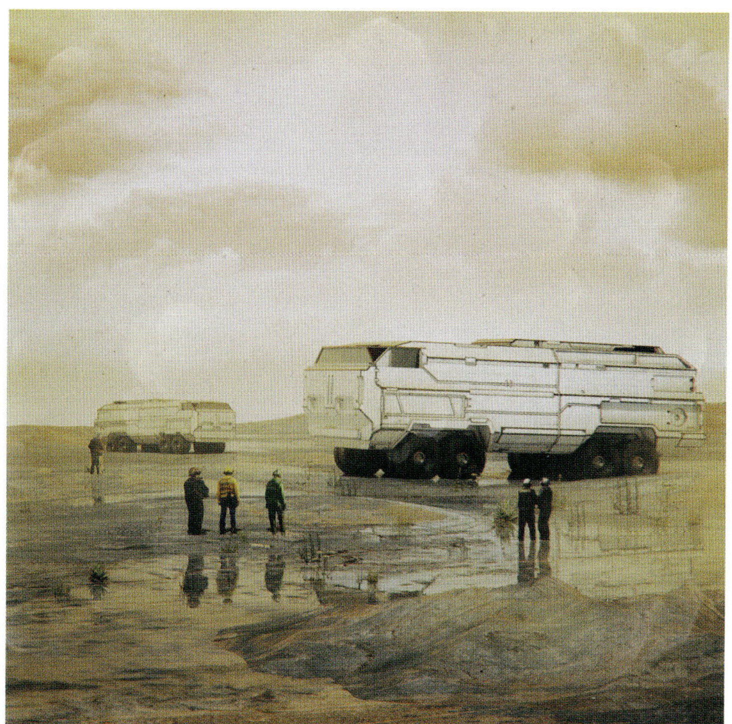

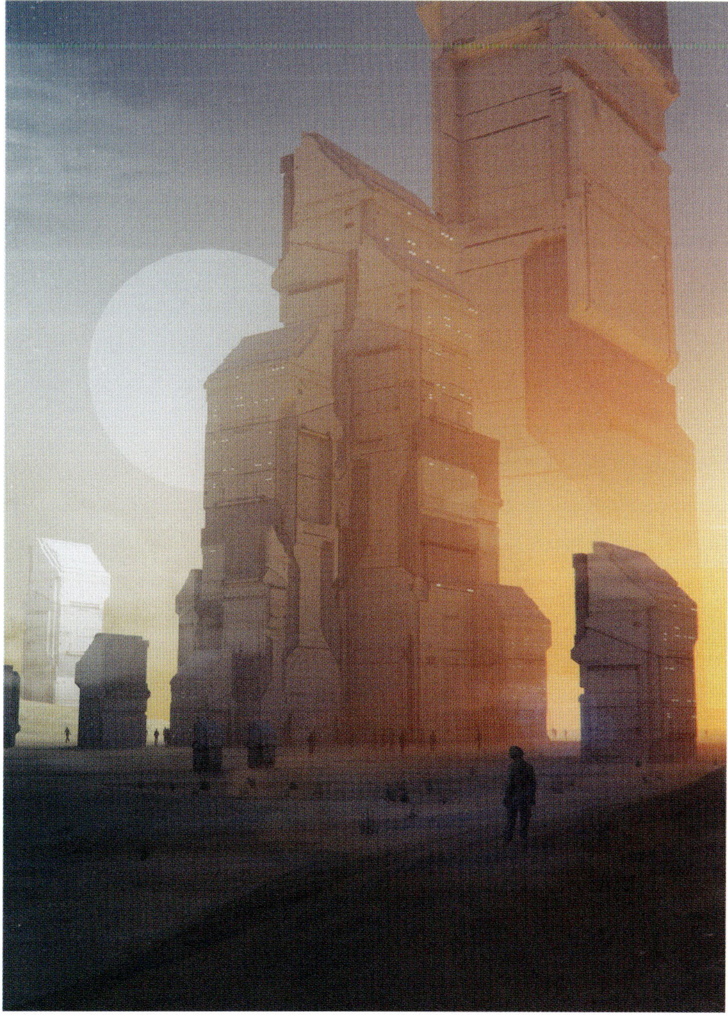

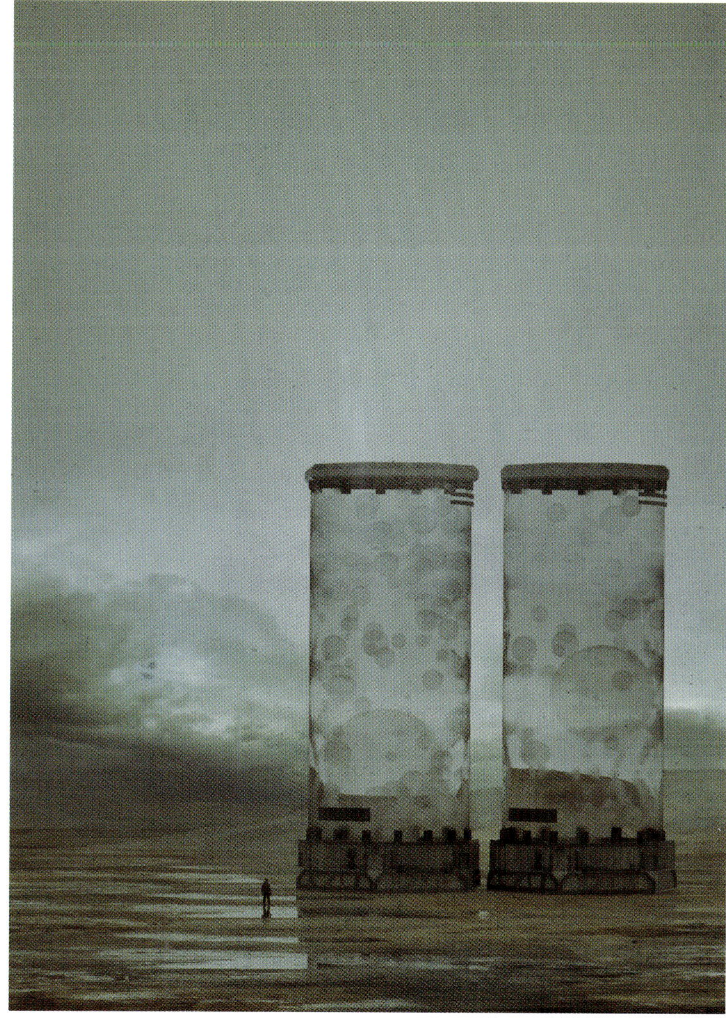

TOP LEFT
OLD FRIEND
12.20.2015

TOP RIGHT
VHC.01
11.04.2015

BOTTOM LEFT
YT.SUN-CITY08
11.07.2015

BOTTOM RIGHT
OB.TANK
07.26.2015

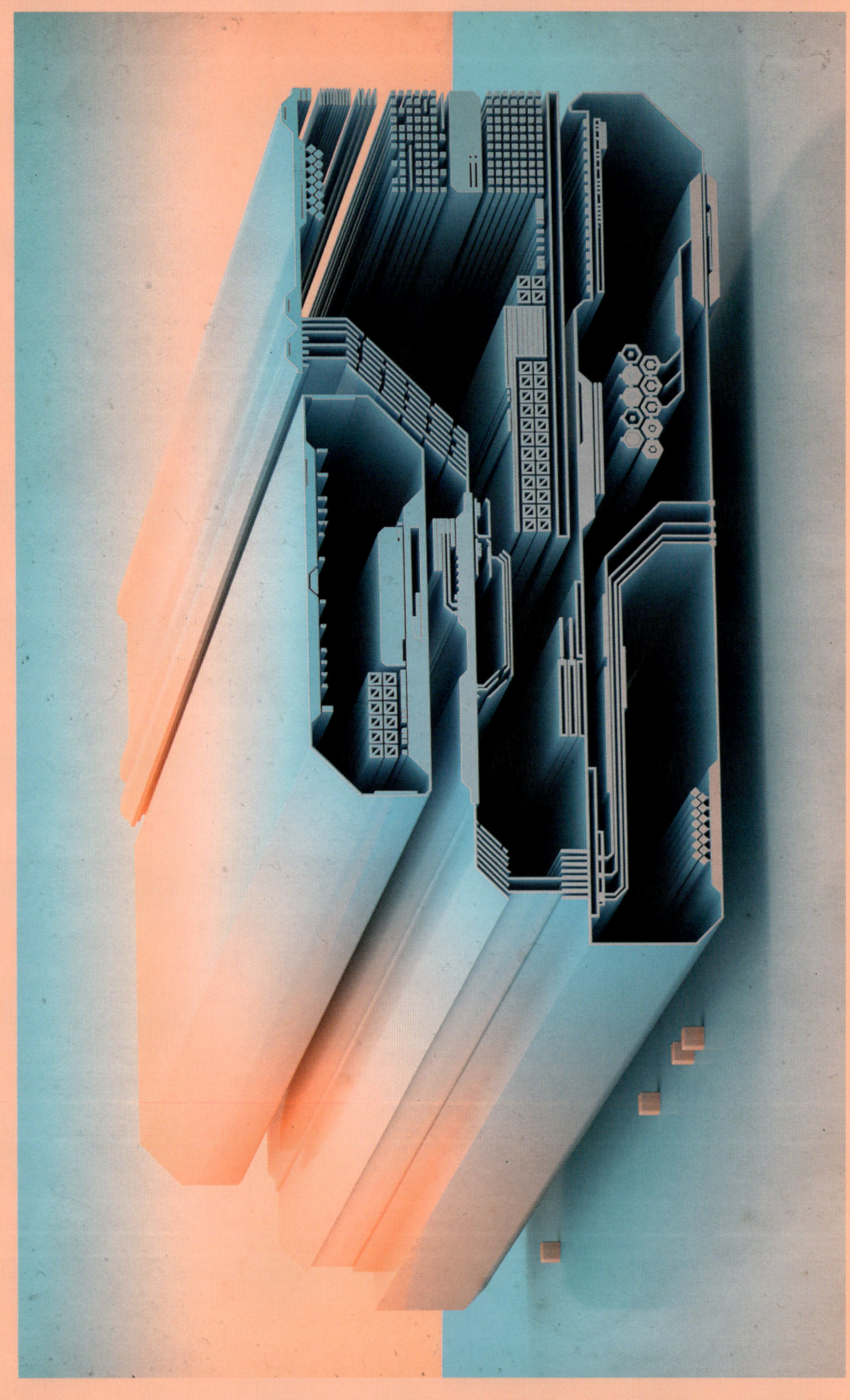

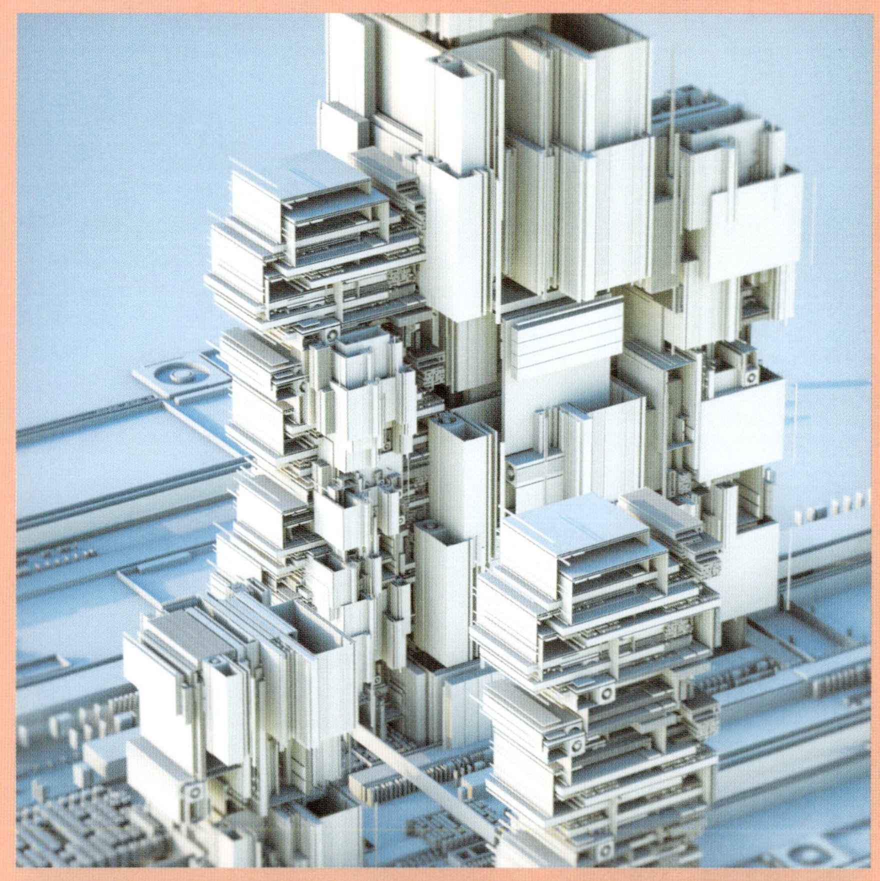

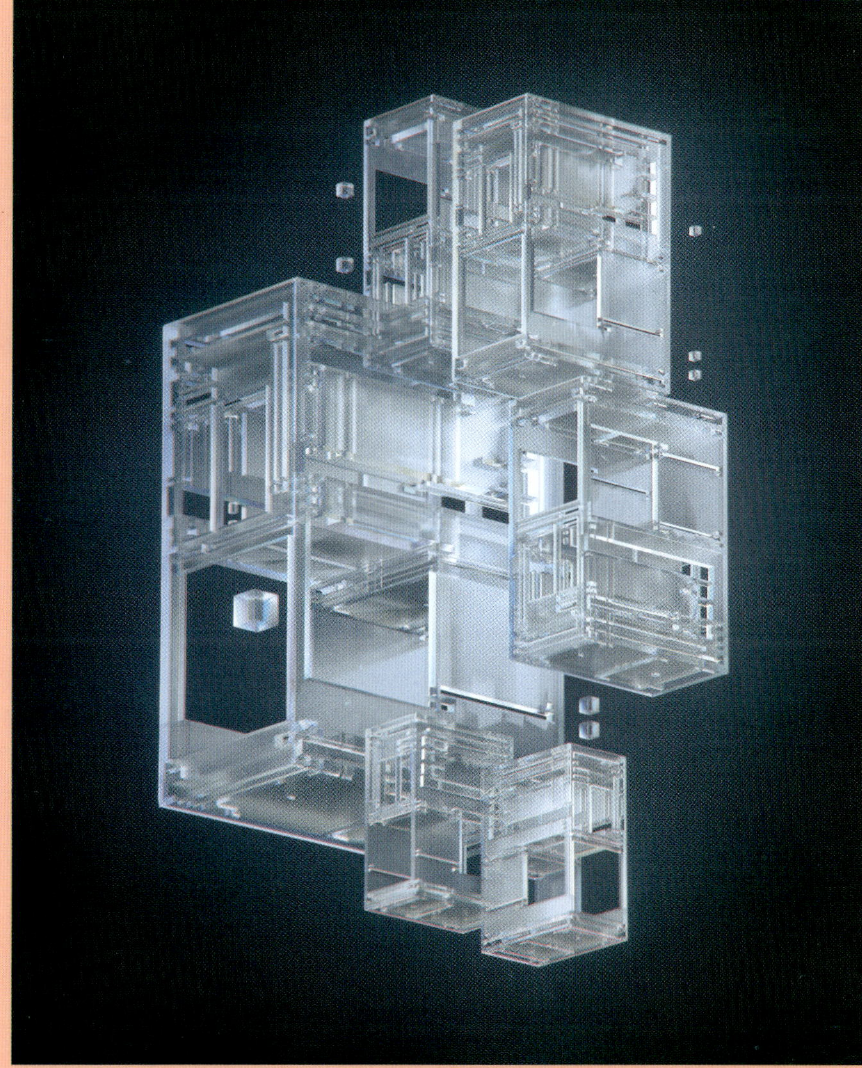

OPPOSITE PAGE

boardwalk picnic
01.14.2015

TOP

rosebud
02.07.2015

BOTTOM

FROST.IE 1969
11.30.2015

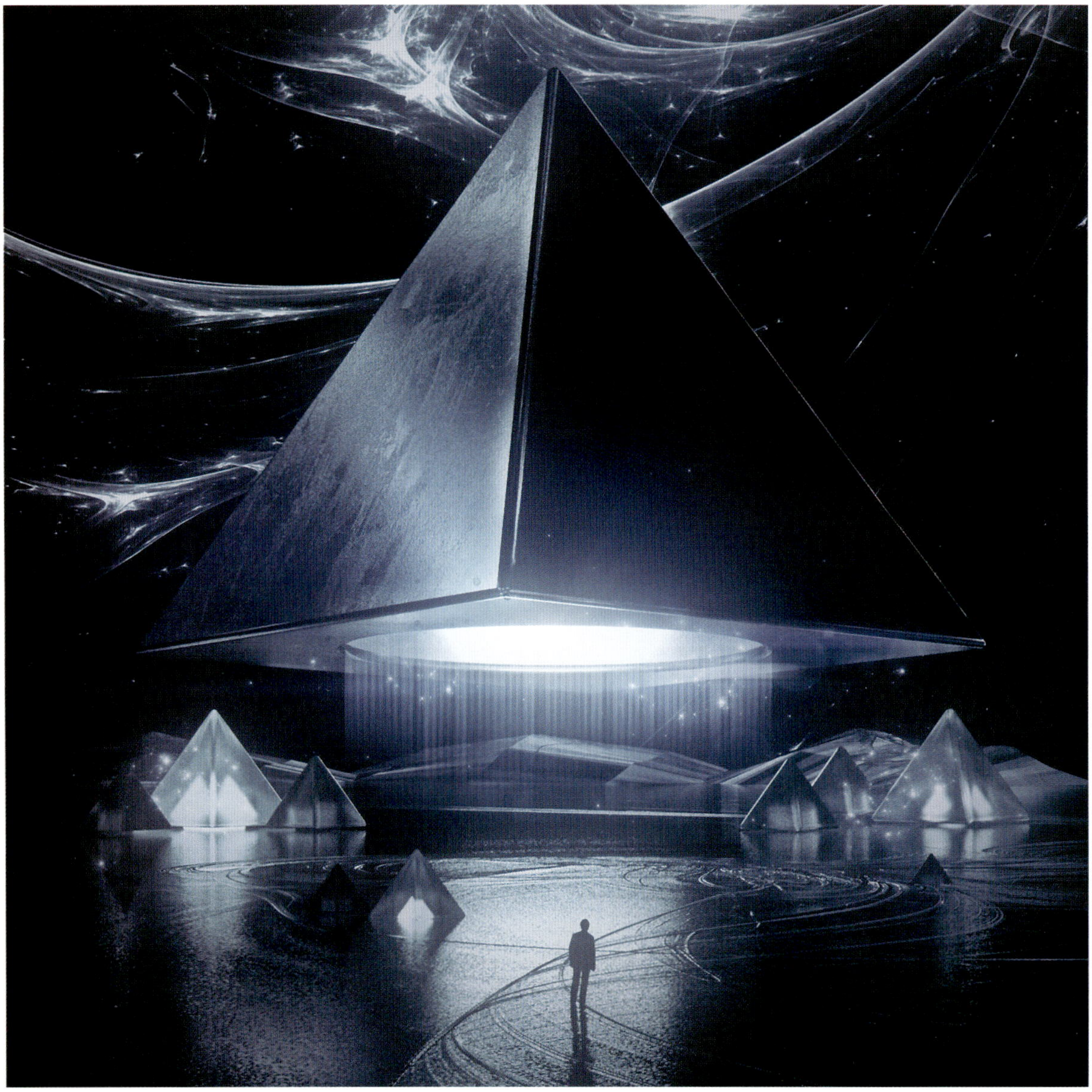

ABOVE

GOD.FIVE
04.24.2015

OPPOSITE PAGE

b-crys
04.29.2015

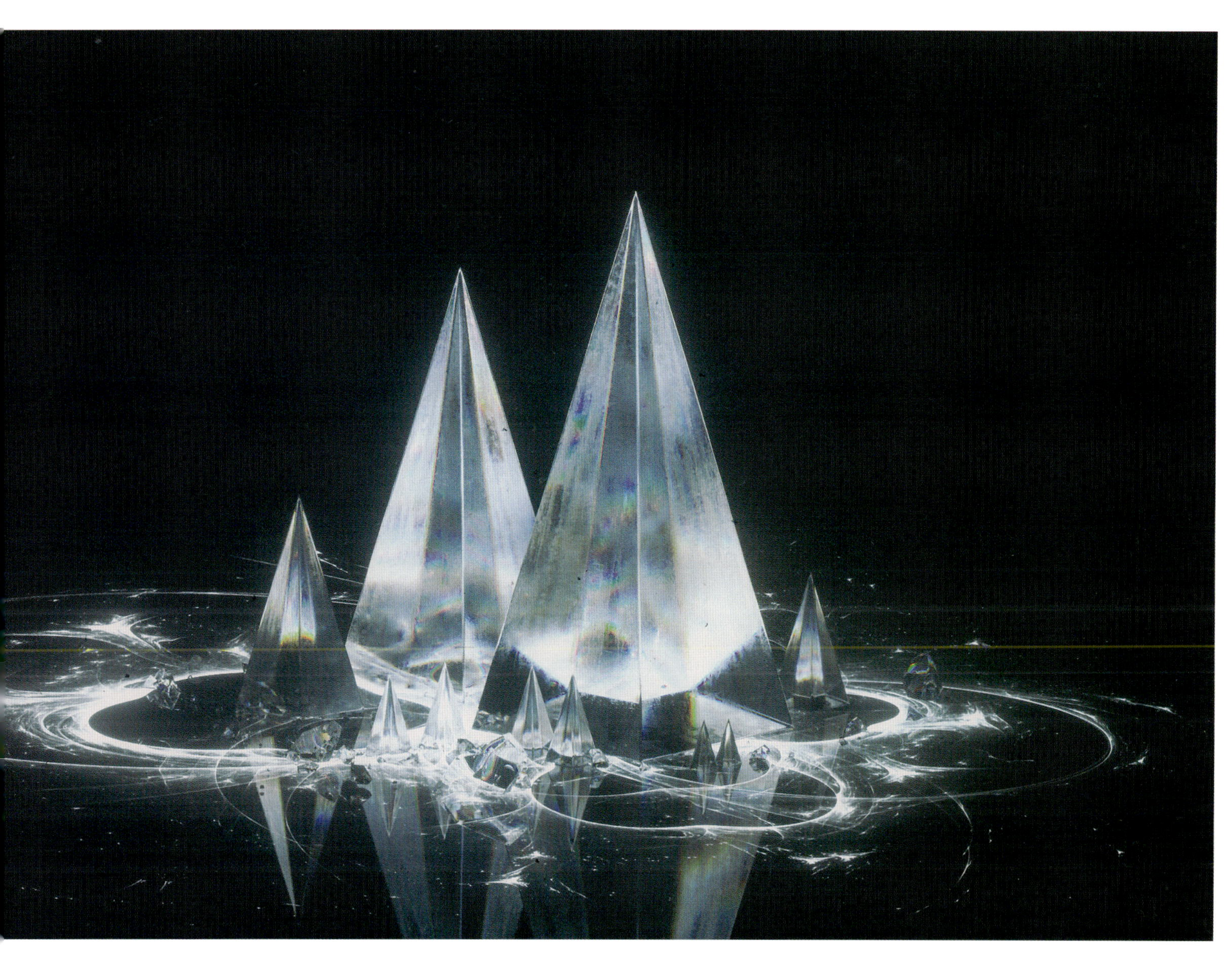

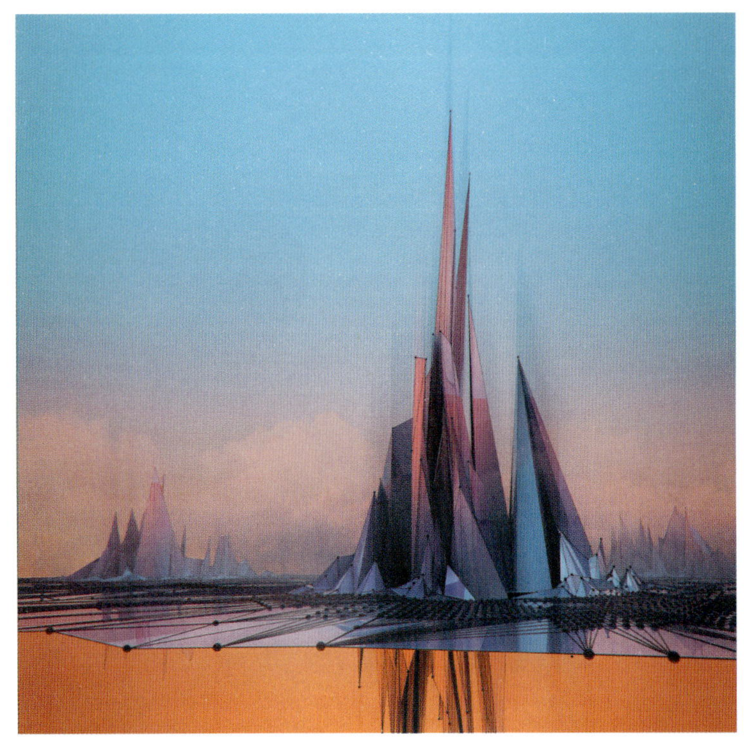

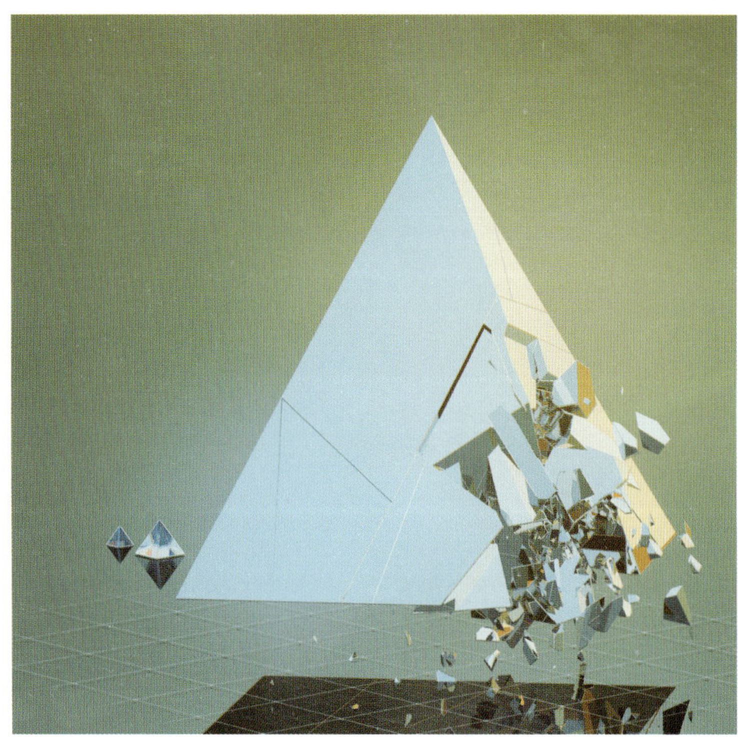

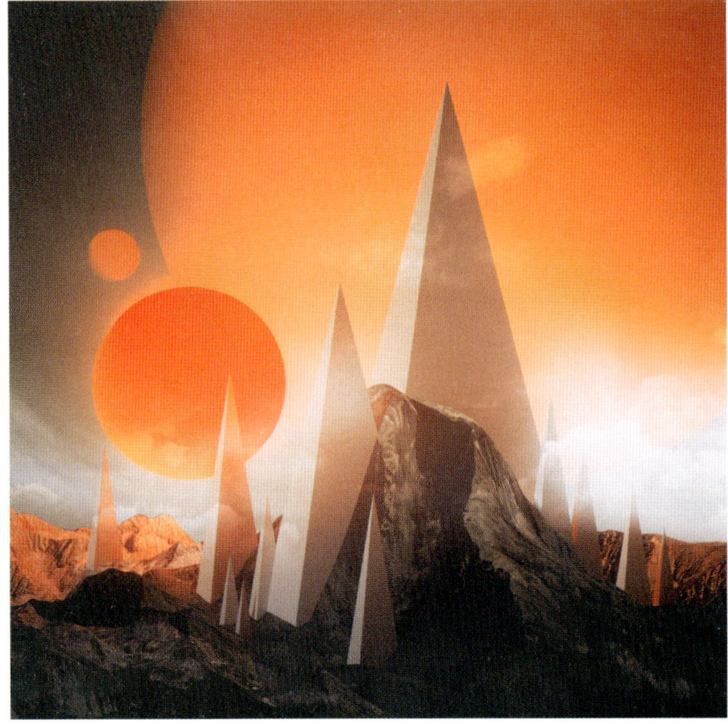

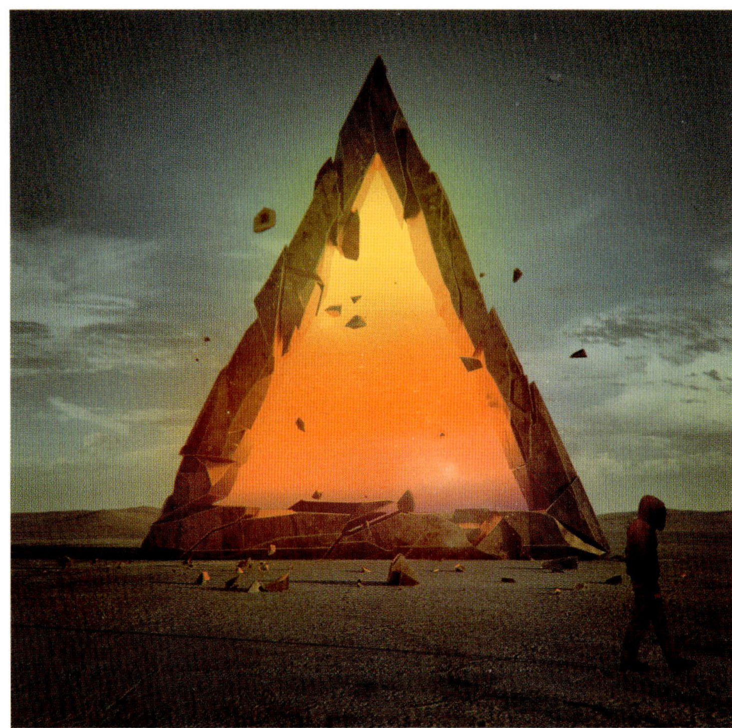

TOP LEFT

HEVEN / HEL

08.21.2015

TOP RIGHT

VOIDDD

12.02.2015

BOTTOM LEFT

TINKY POIN

08.15.2015

BOTTOM RIGHT

WALK AWAY

11.28.2015

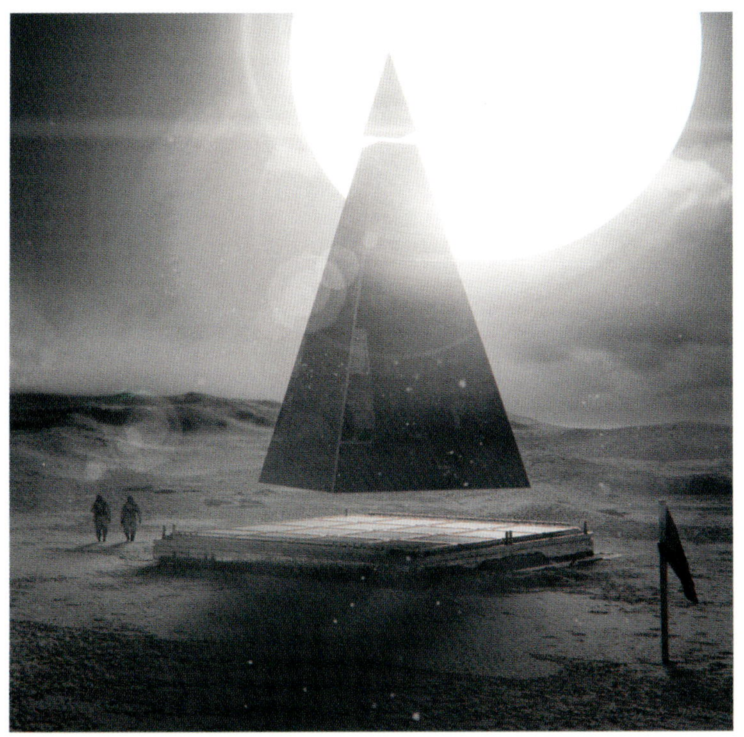

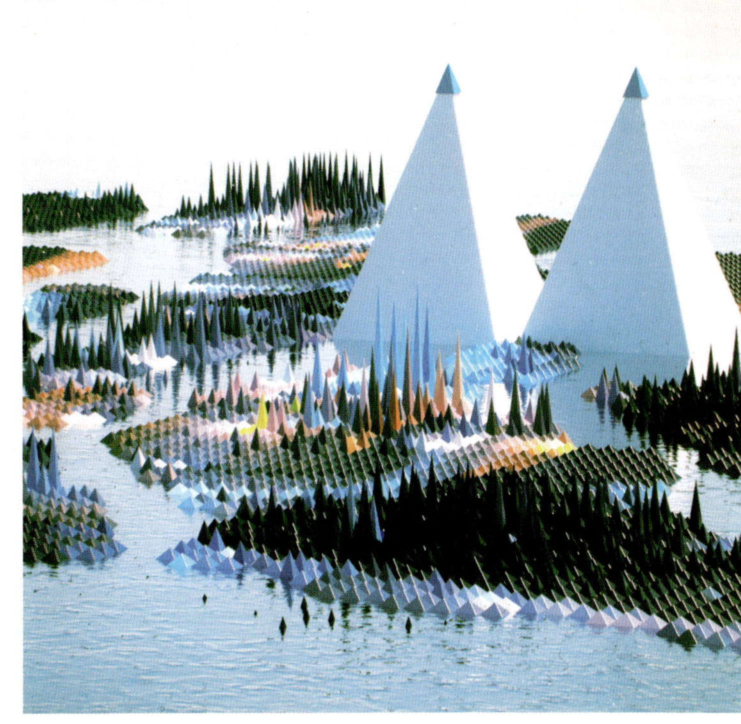

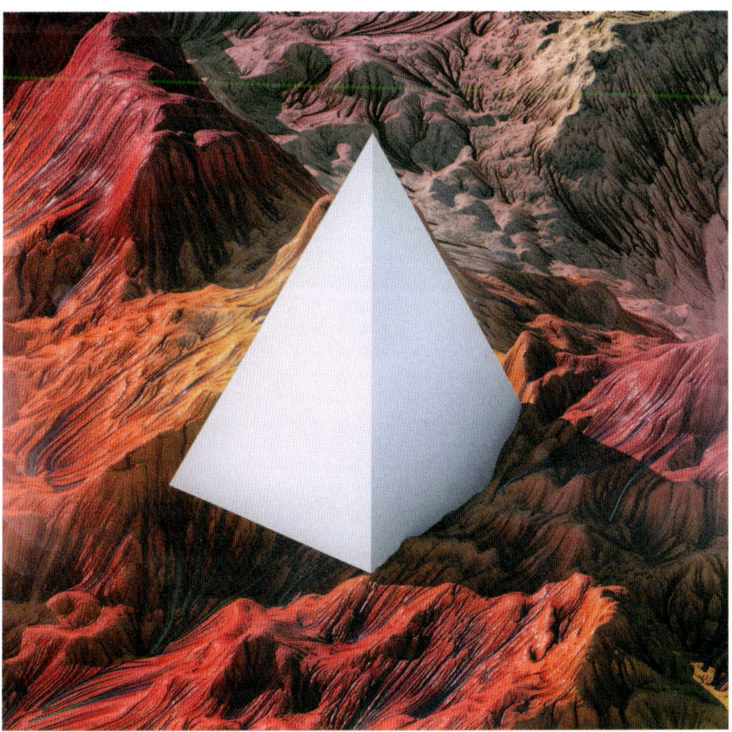

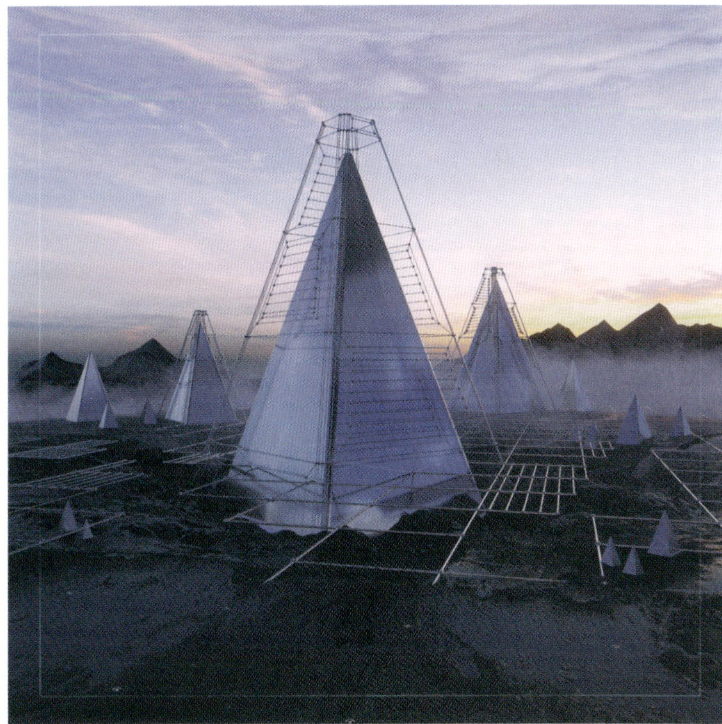

TOP LEFT
EXODUS.2205
12.22.2015

TOP RIGHT
HOLO
01.22.2015

BOTTOM LEFT
BIF.FITT
12.04.2015

BOTTOM RIGHT
SPOT-ROK
08.27.2015

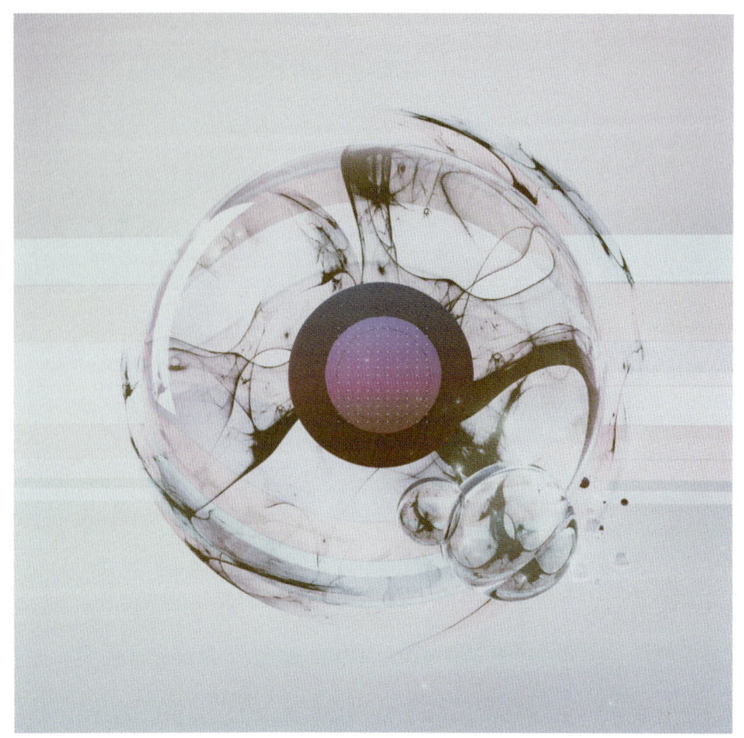

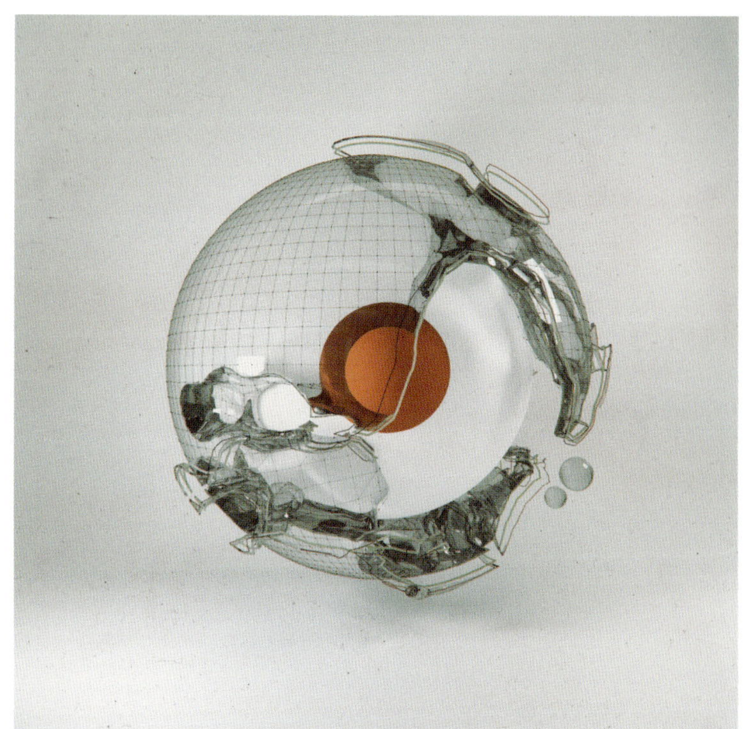

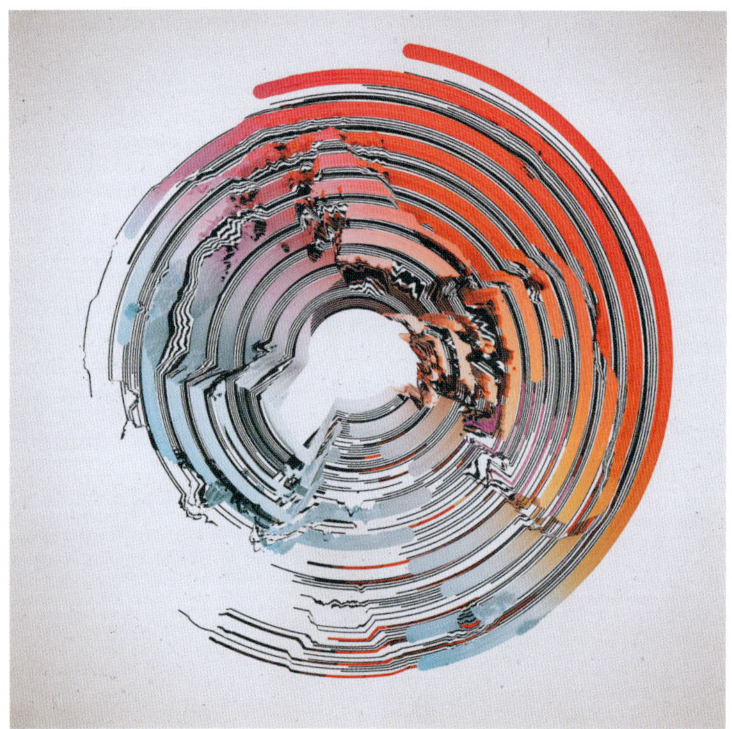

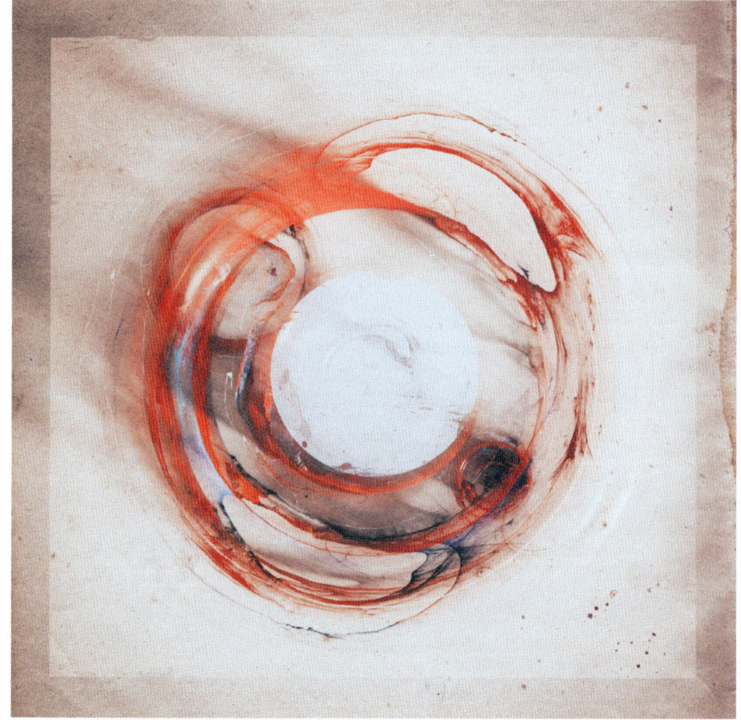

TOP LEFT
left hand superhell
04.26.2015

TOP RIGHT
NUCLEAR FAMILY
10.17.2015

BOTTOM LEFT
CRUSHED PHOTON
08.29.2015

BOTTOM RIGHT
SPORTFUCK
06.09.2015

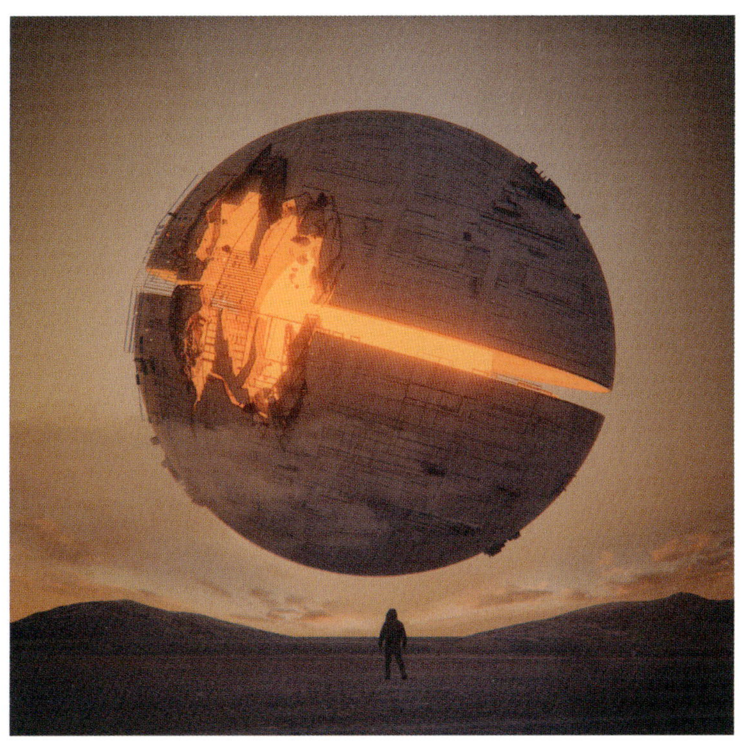

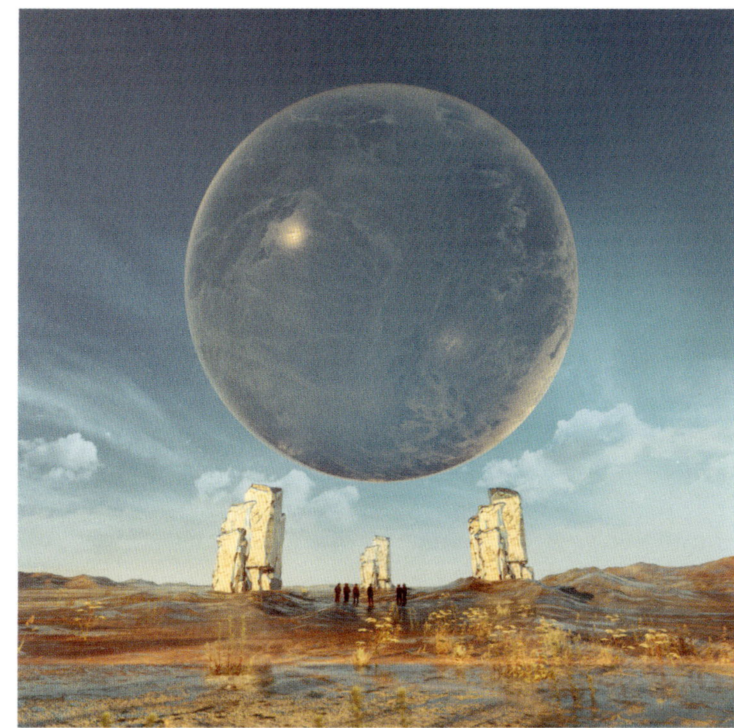

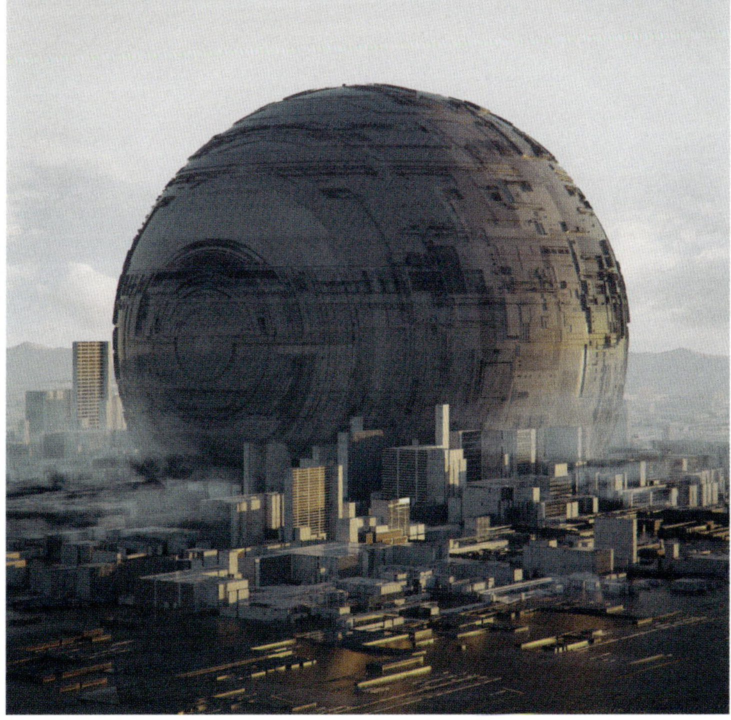

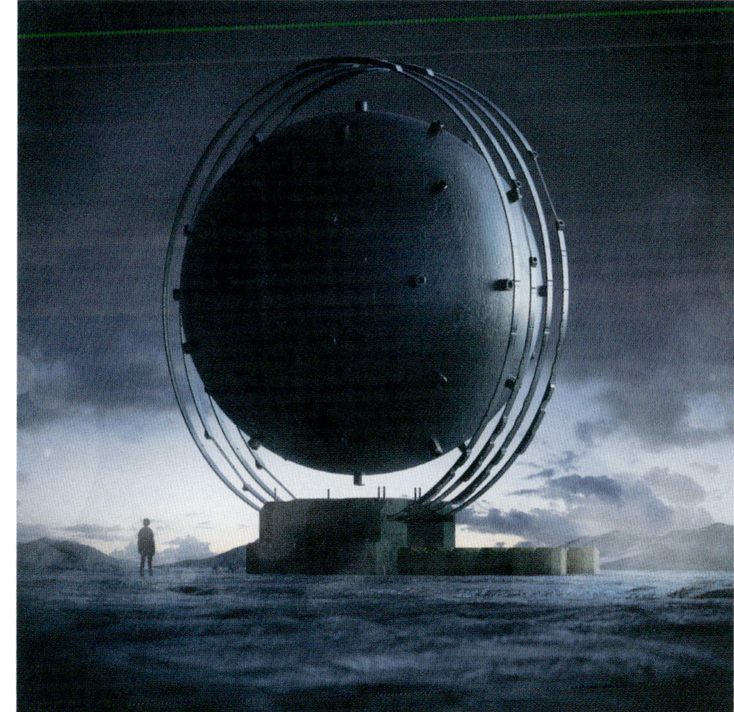

TOP LEFT
GRIND
11.22.2015

TOP RIGHT
PHERE RITUAL
07.17.2015

BOTTOM LEFT
POE-STAR32
12.16.2015

BOTTOM RIGHT
perfect destruction machine
06.17.2015

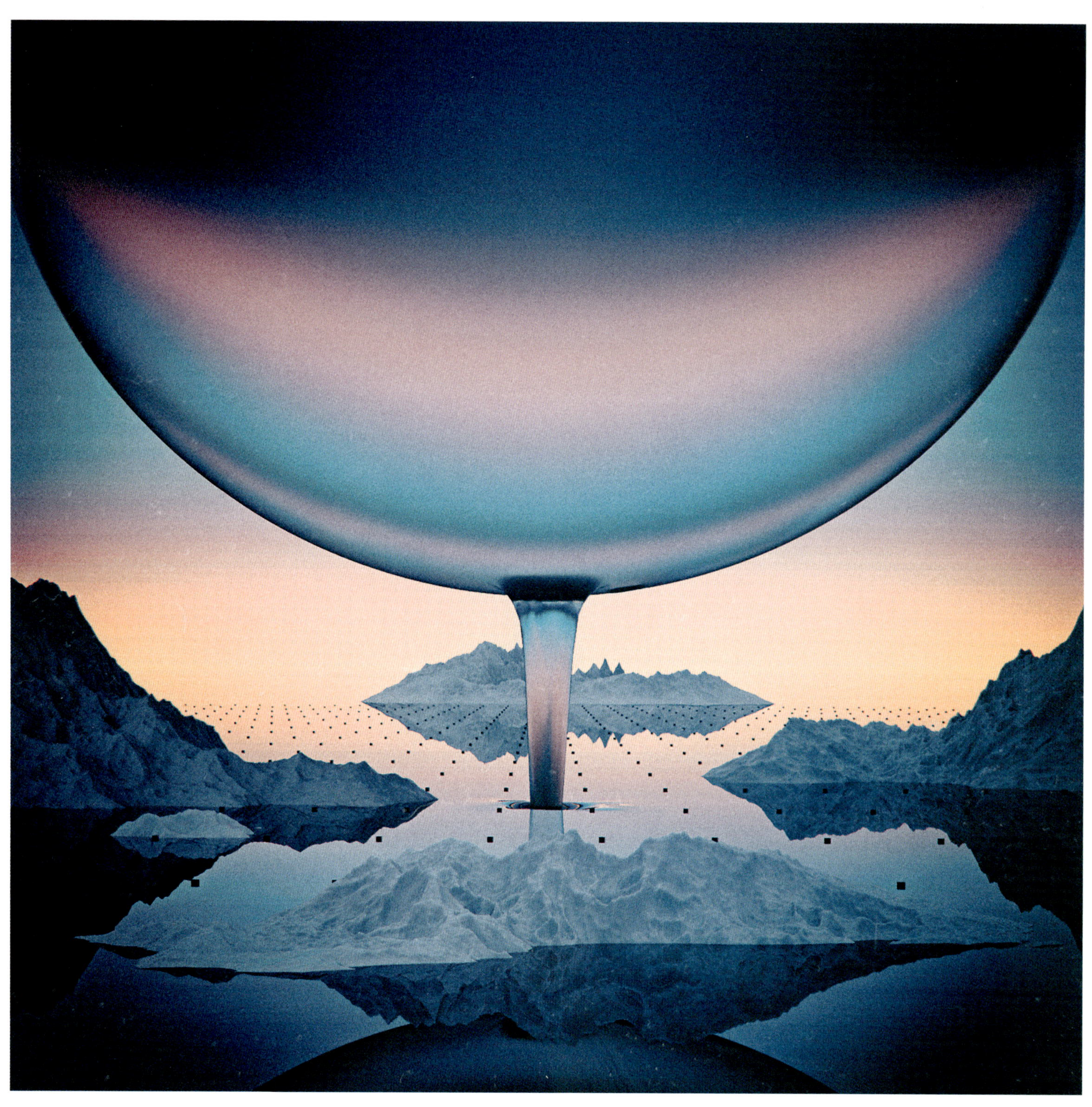

ABOVE
glass equinox
01.17.2015

OPPOSITE PAGE
HOTHMILK
01.23.2015

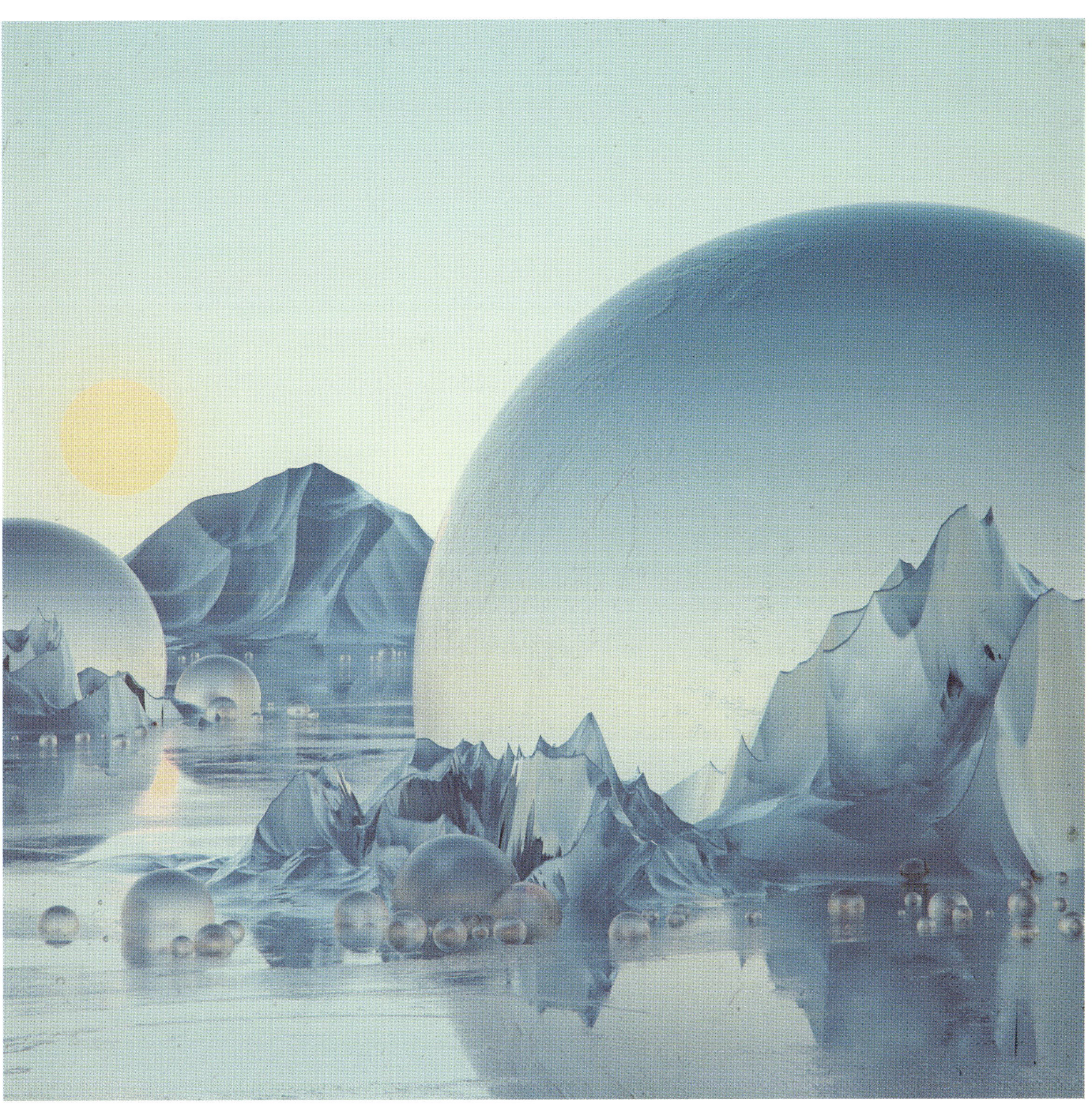

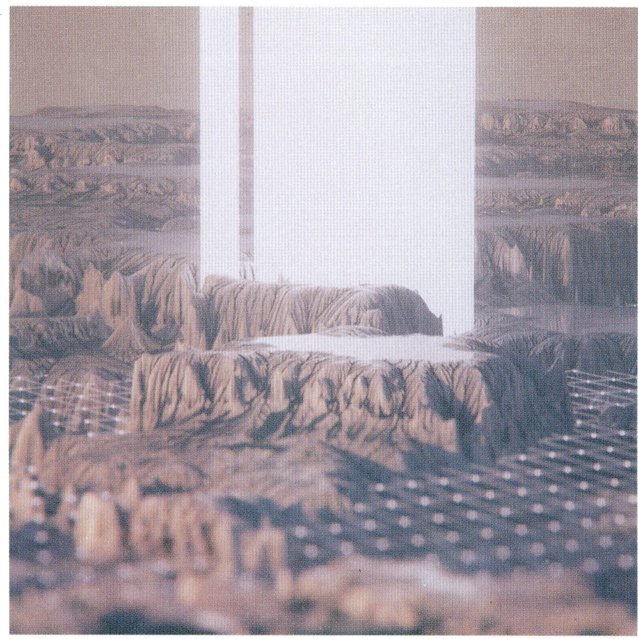

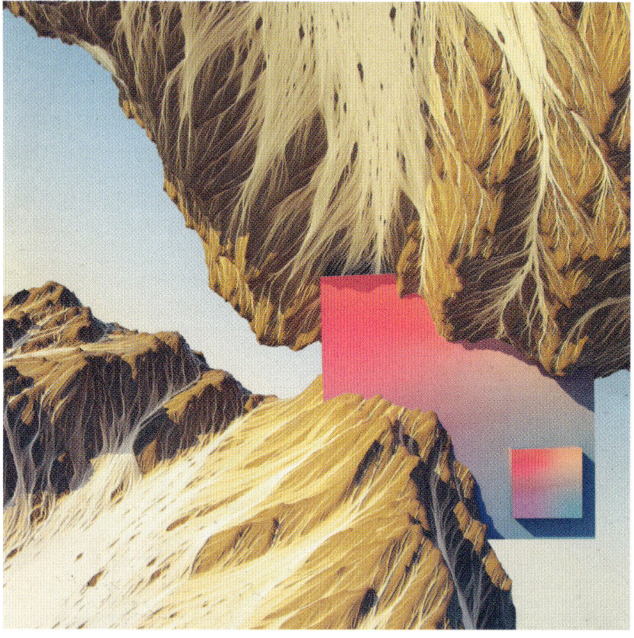

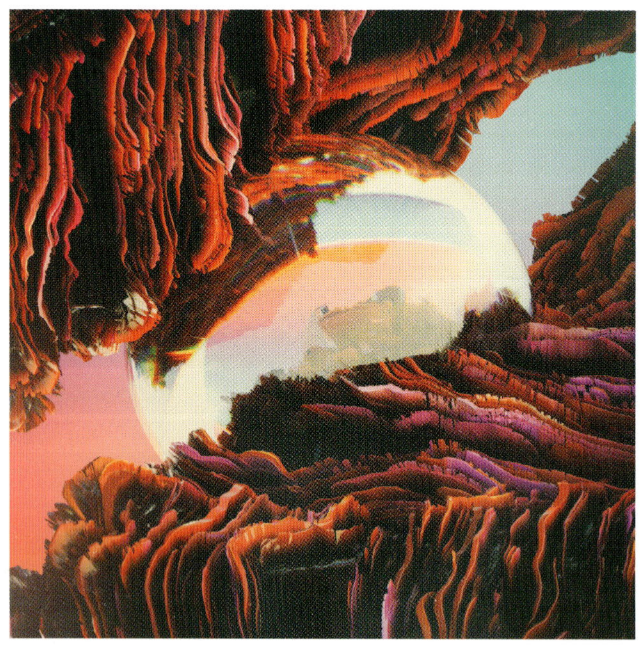

TOP

FACE-SLAP
11.12.2015

MIDDLE

E-CLASS
09.17.2015

BOTTOM

fluid mechanics
06.12.2015

OPPOSITE PAGE

DEM CUBES
05.06.2015

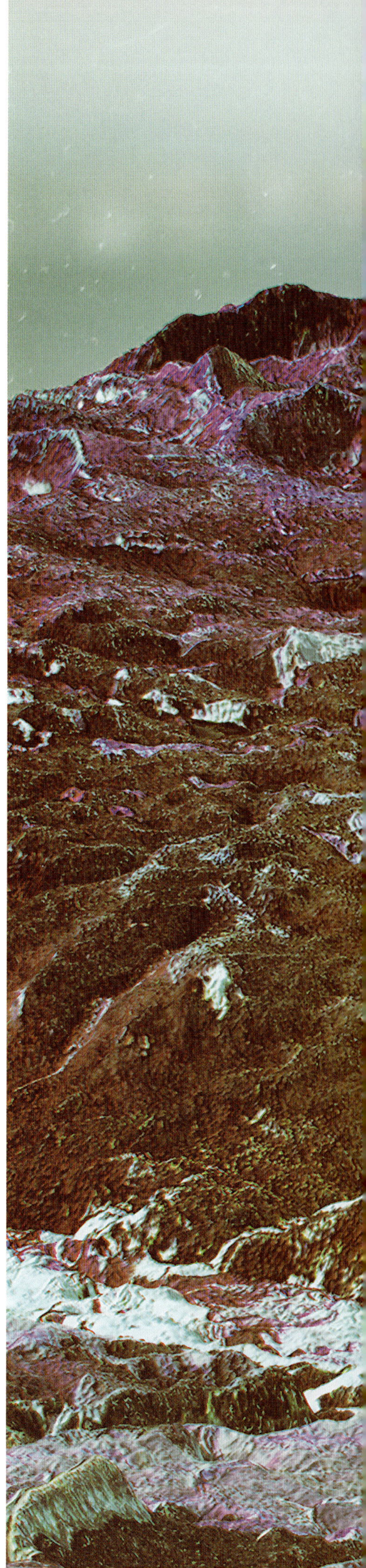

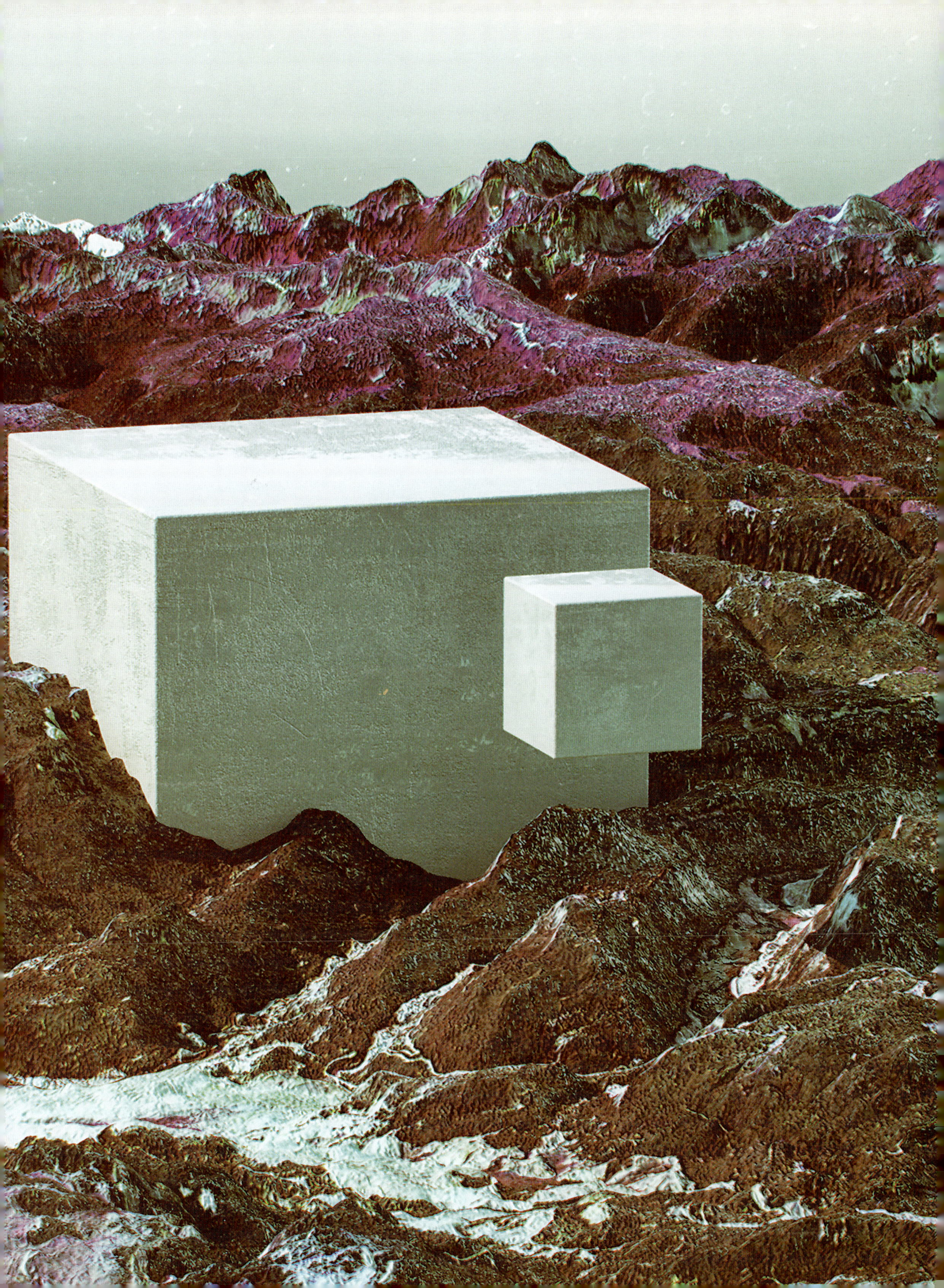

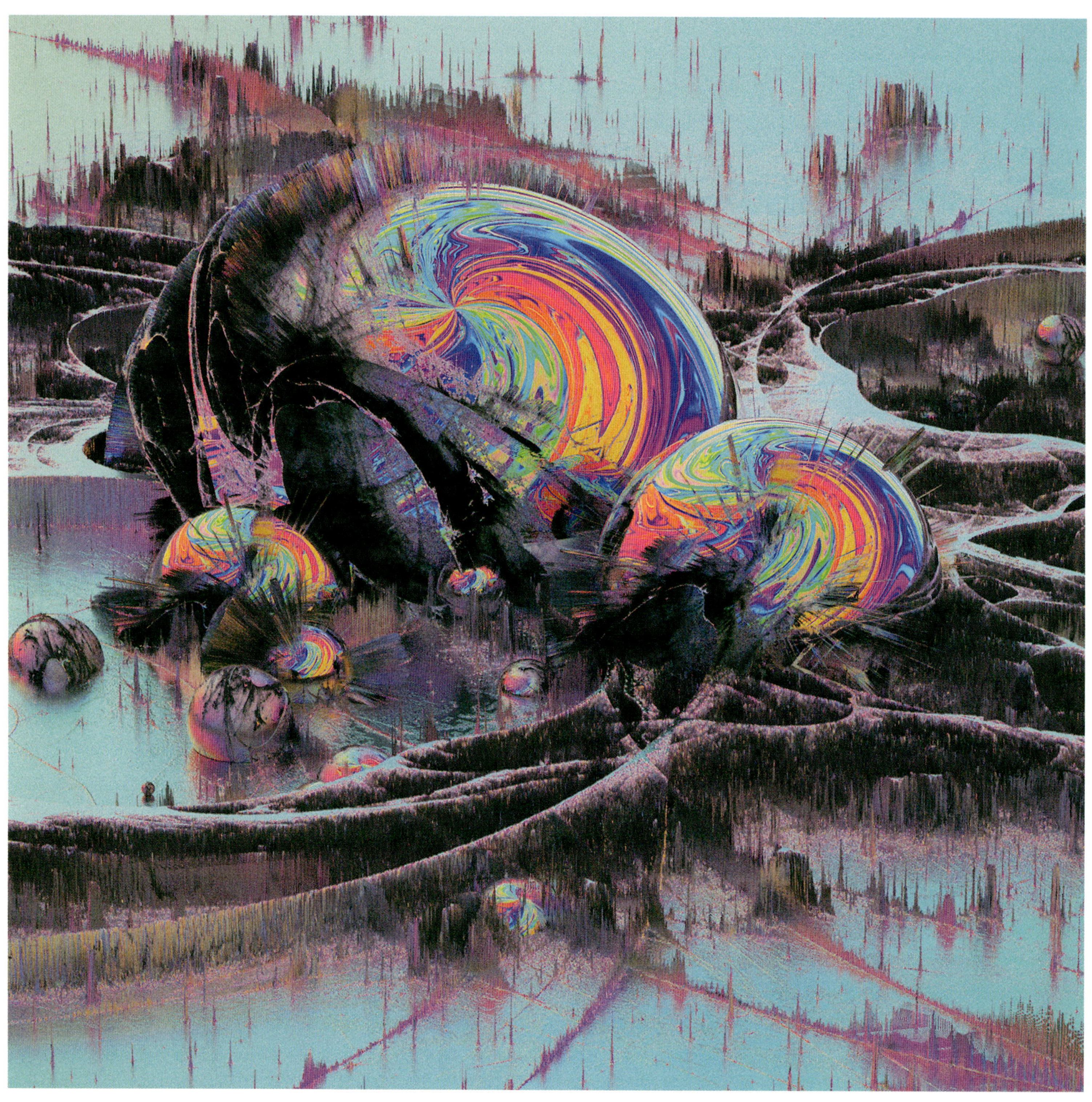

ABOVE

ghost jacked
05.09.2015

OPPOSITE PAGE

binaural color mauws
05.17.2015

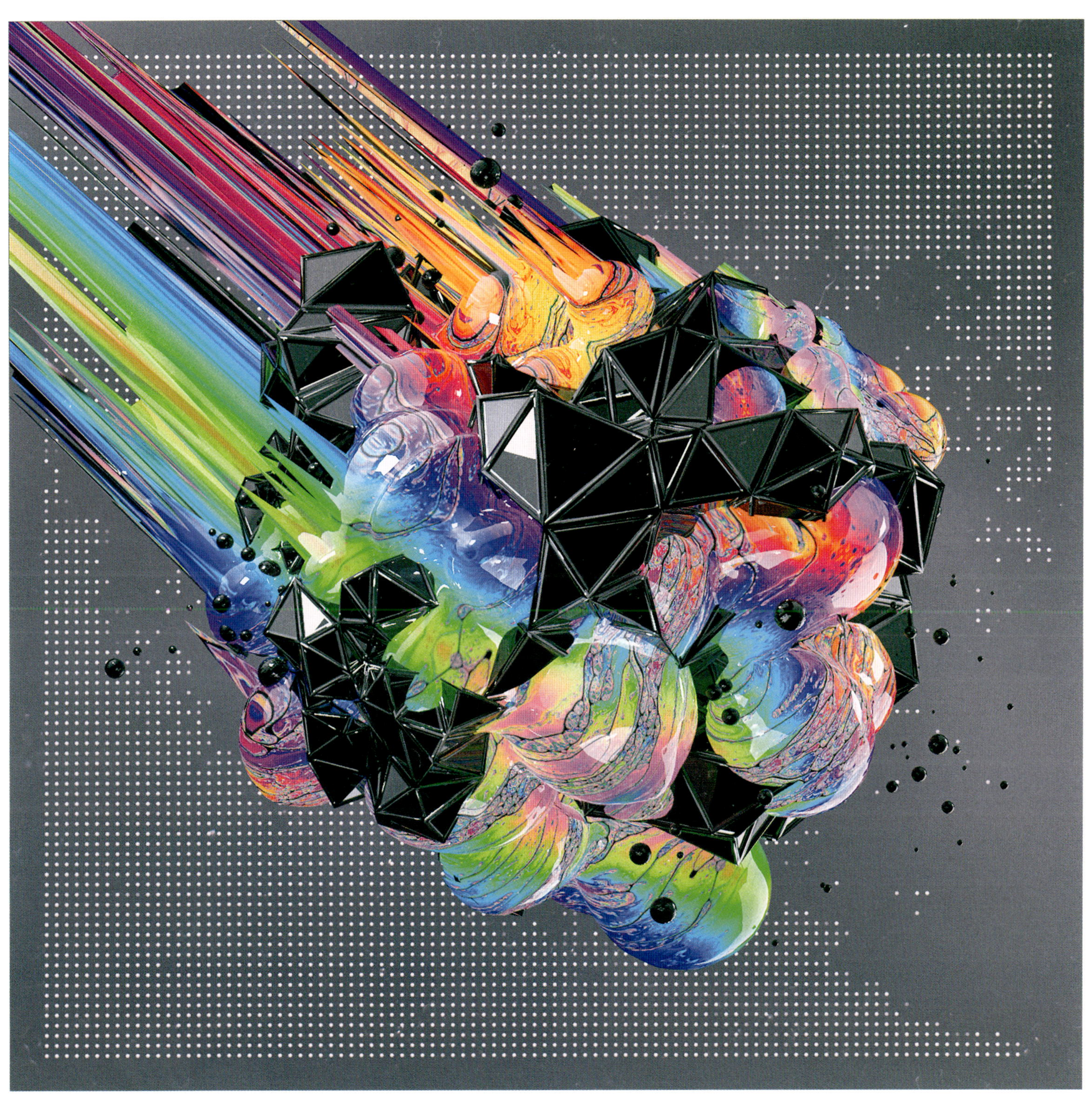

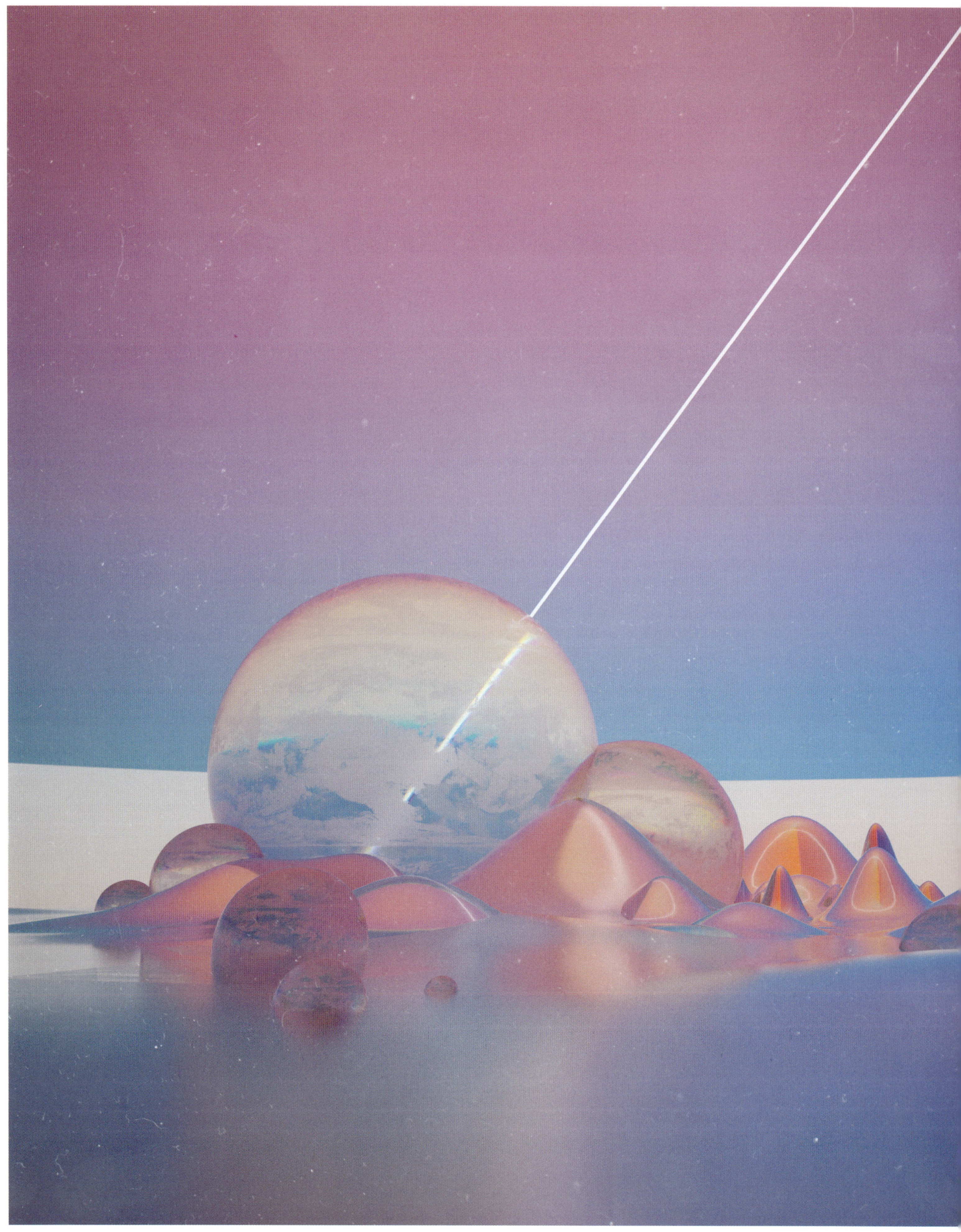

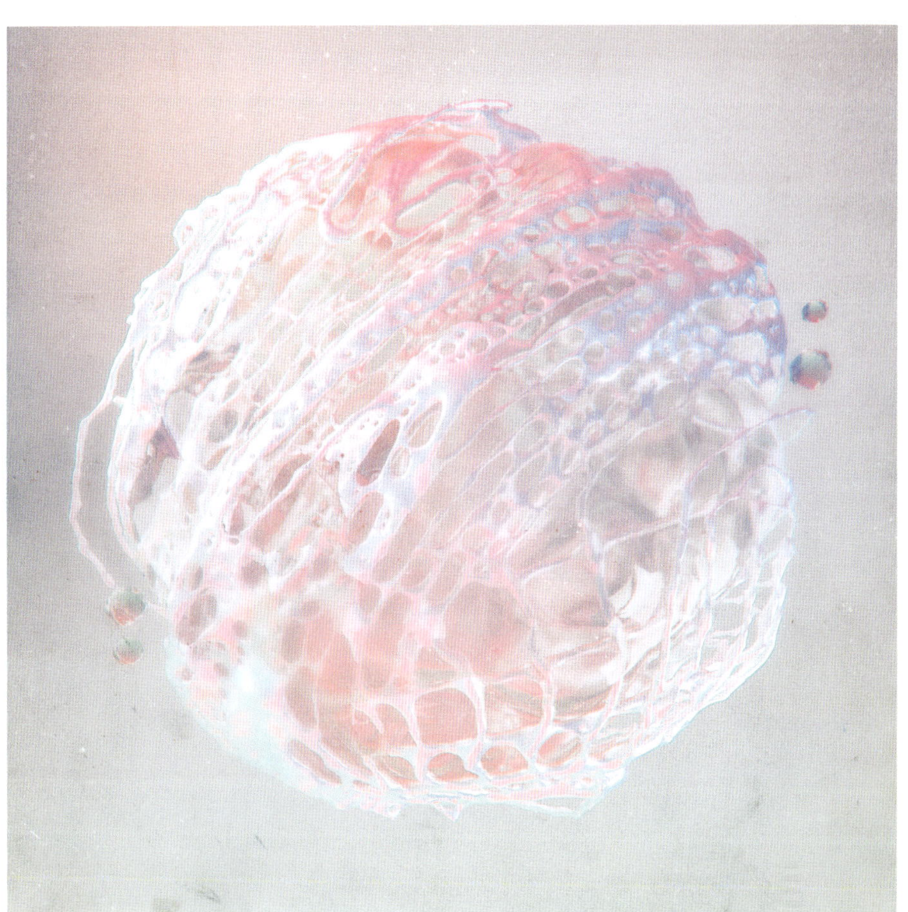

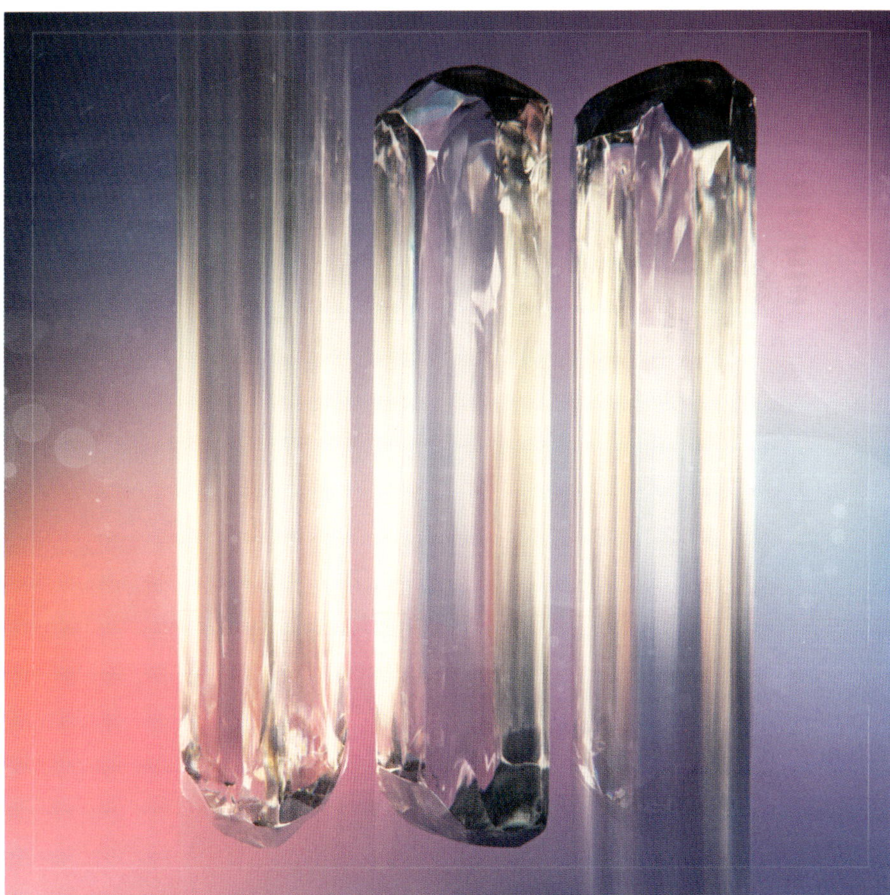

OPPOSITE PAGE
HOTAIR
08.08.2015

TOP
nice dream (stomped)
04.09.2015

BOTTOM
W
04.06.2015

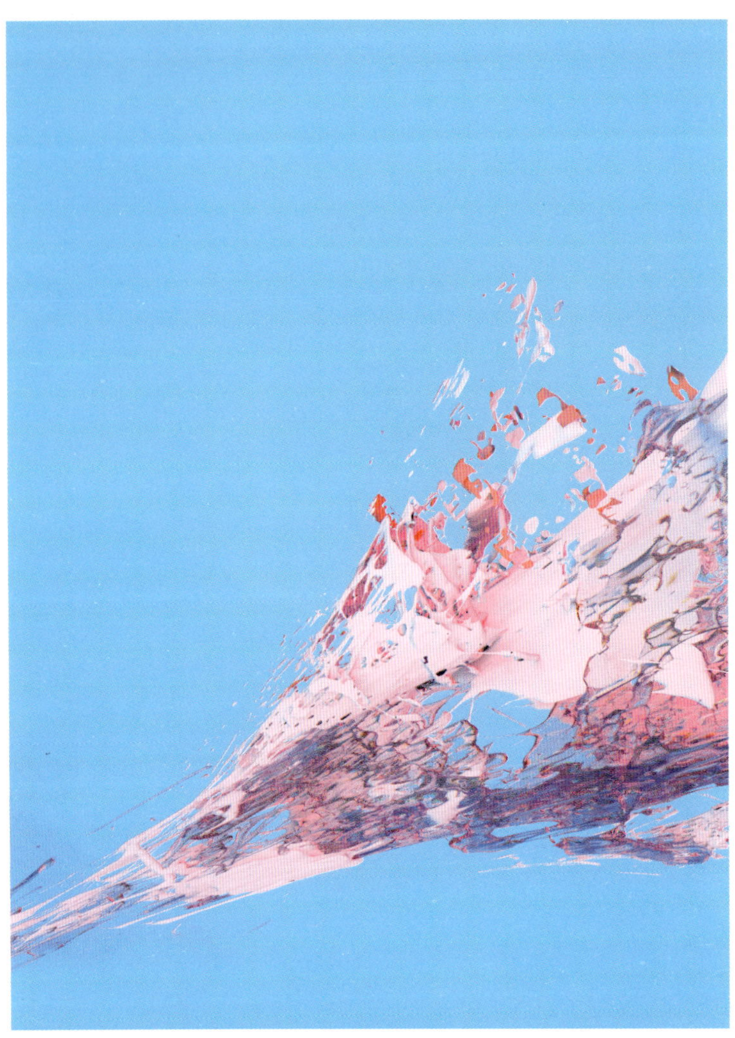

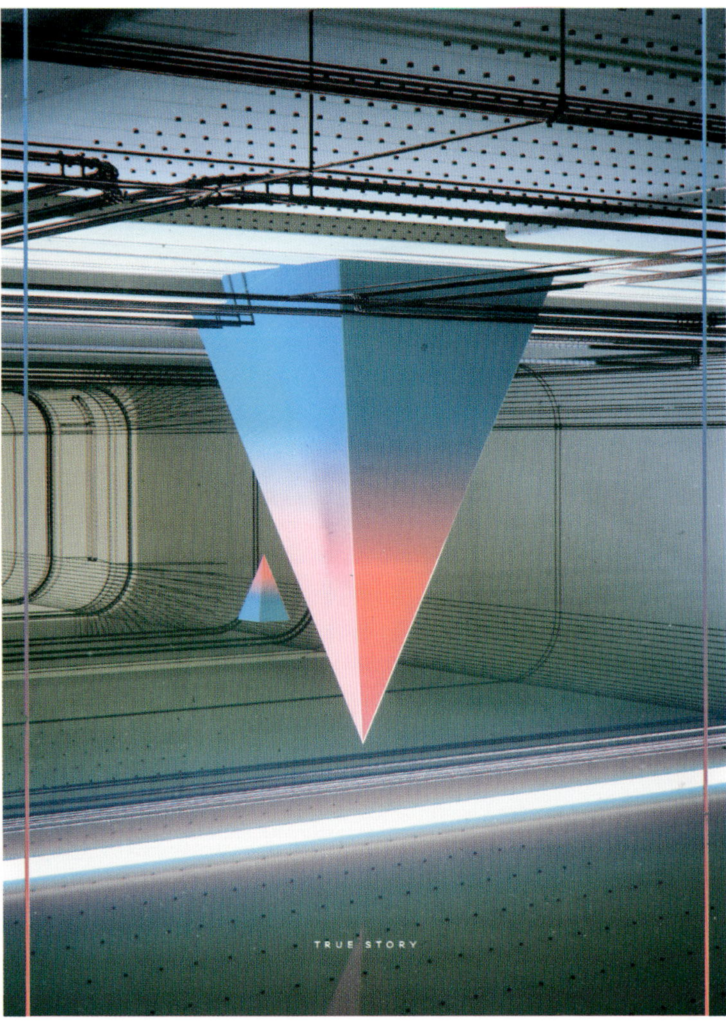

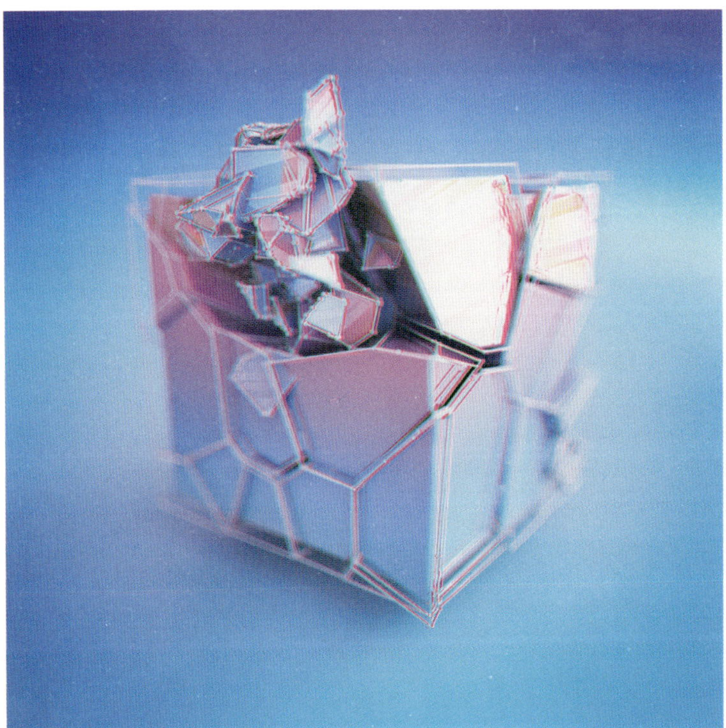

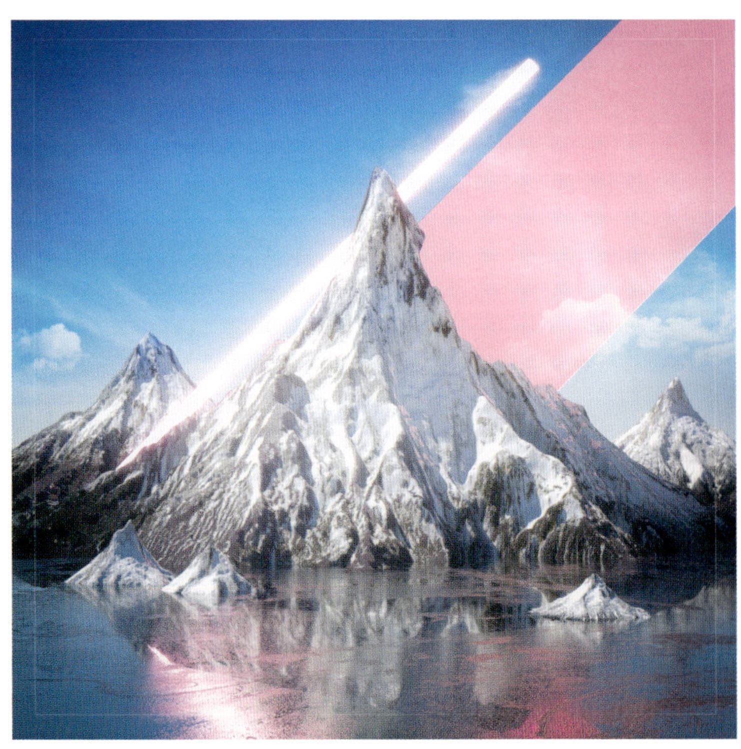

TOP LEFT
strawberry sneeze
07.14.2015

TOP RIGHT
grift
07.22.2015

BOTTOM LEFT
NEXUS PUSTANG
07.25.2015

BOTTOM RIGHT
CHILI CHEESE DOG
07.24.2015

OPPOSITE PAGE
tinct formation discovery
06.15.2015

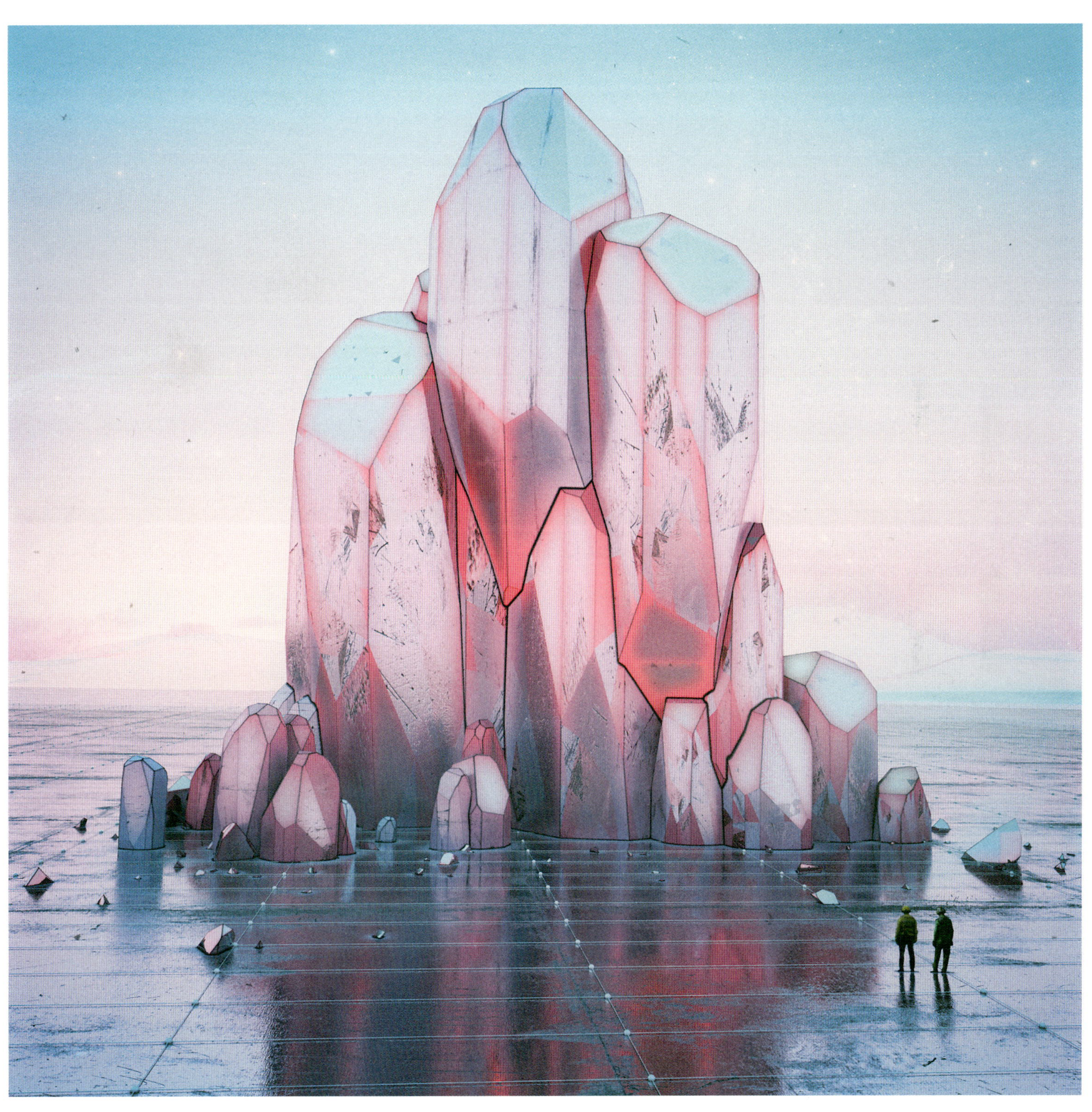

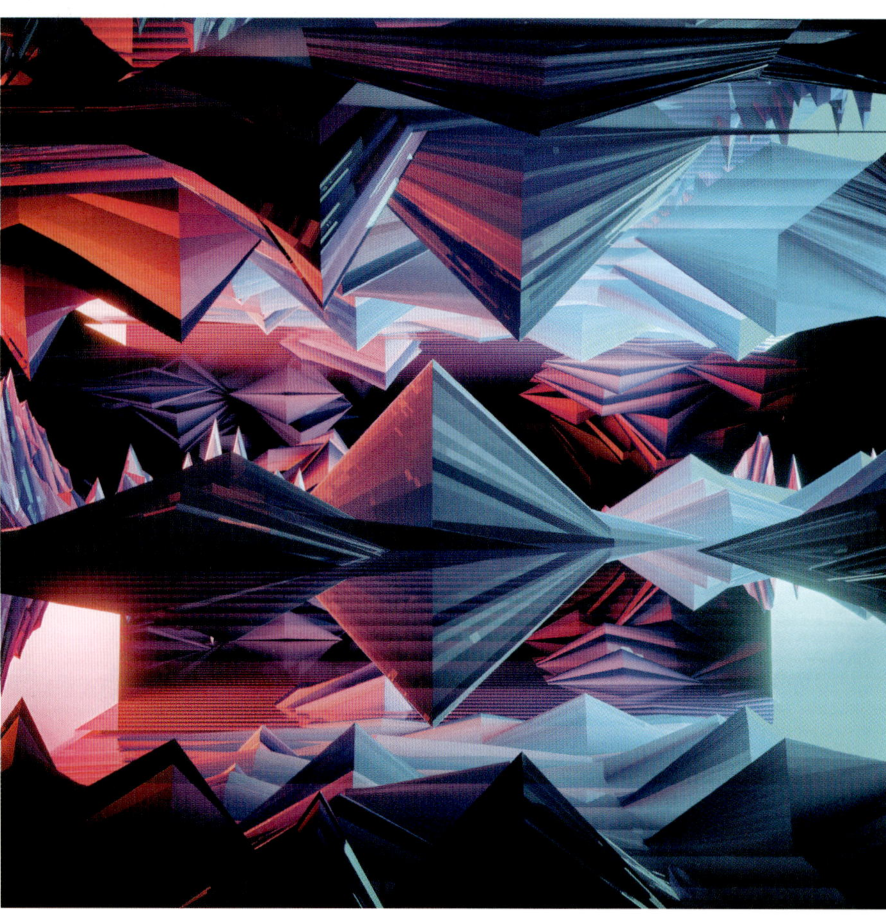

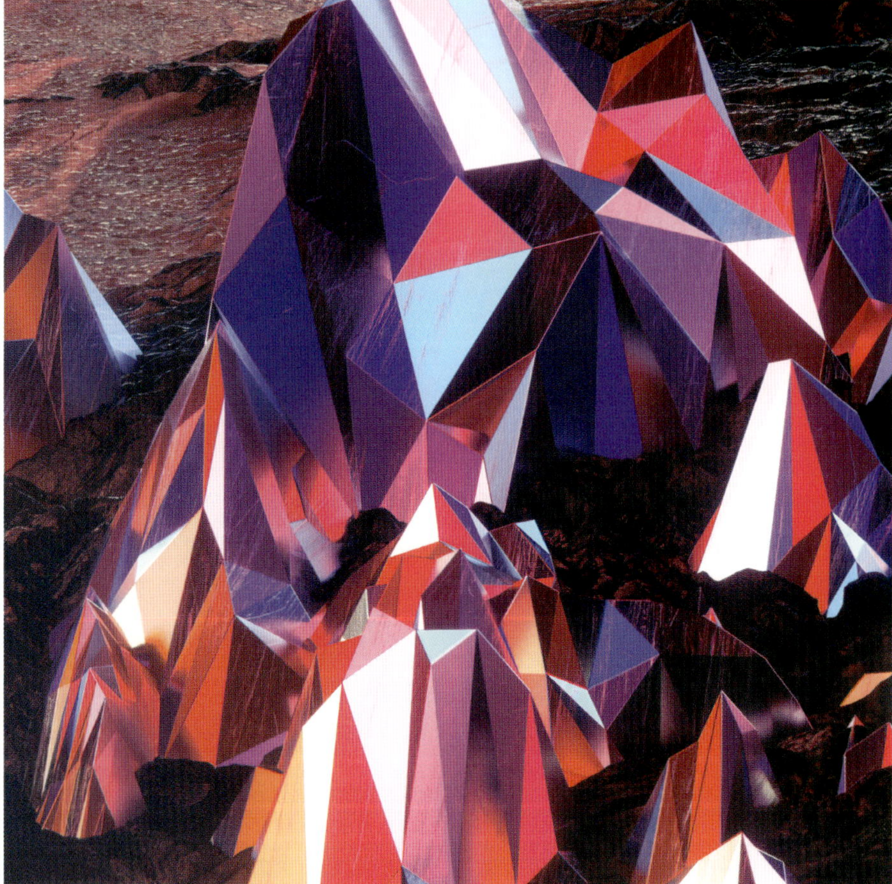

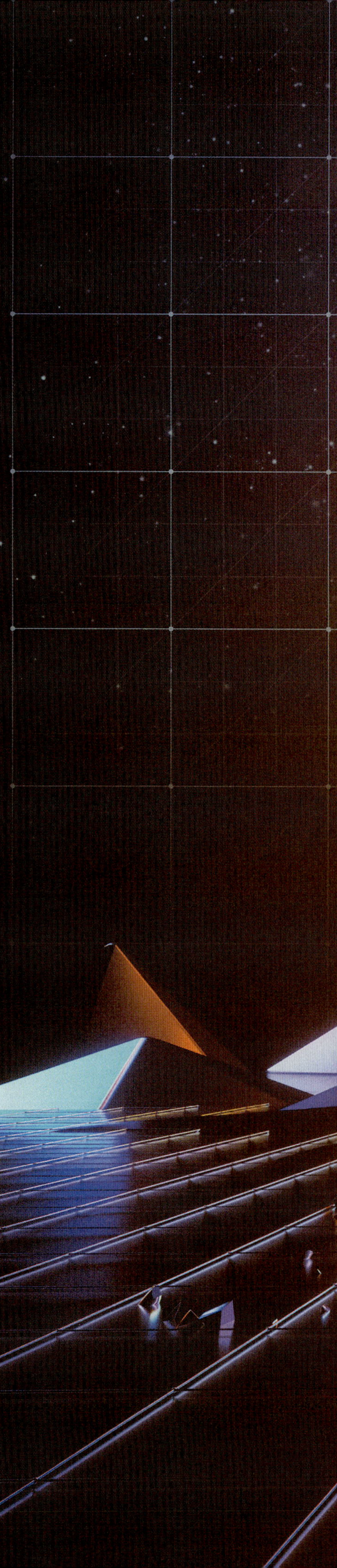

TOP
eye milk
04.05.2015

BOTTOM
brokechords
05.29.2015

OPPOSITE PAGE
RGB
08.07.2015

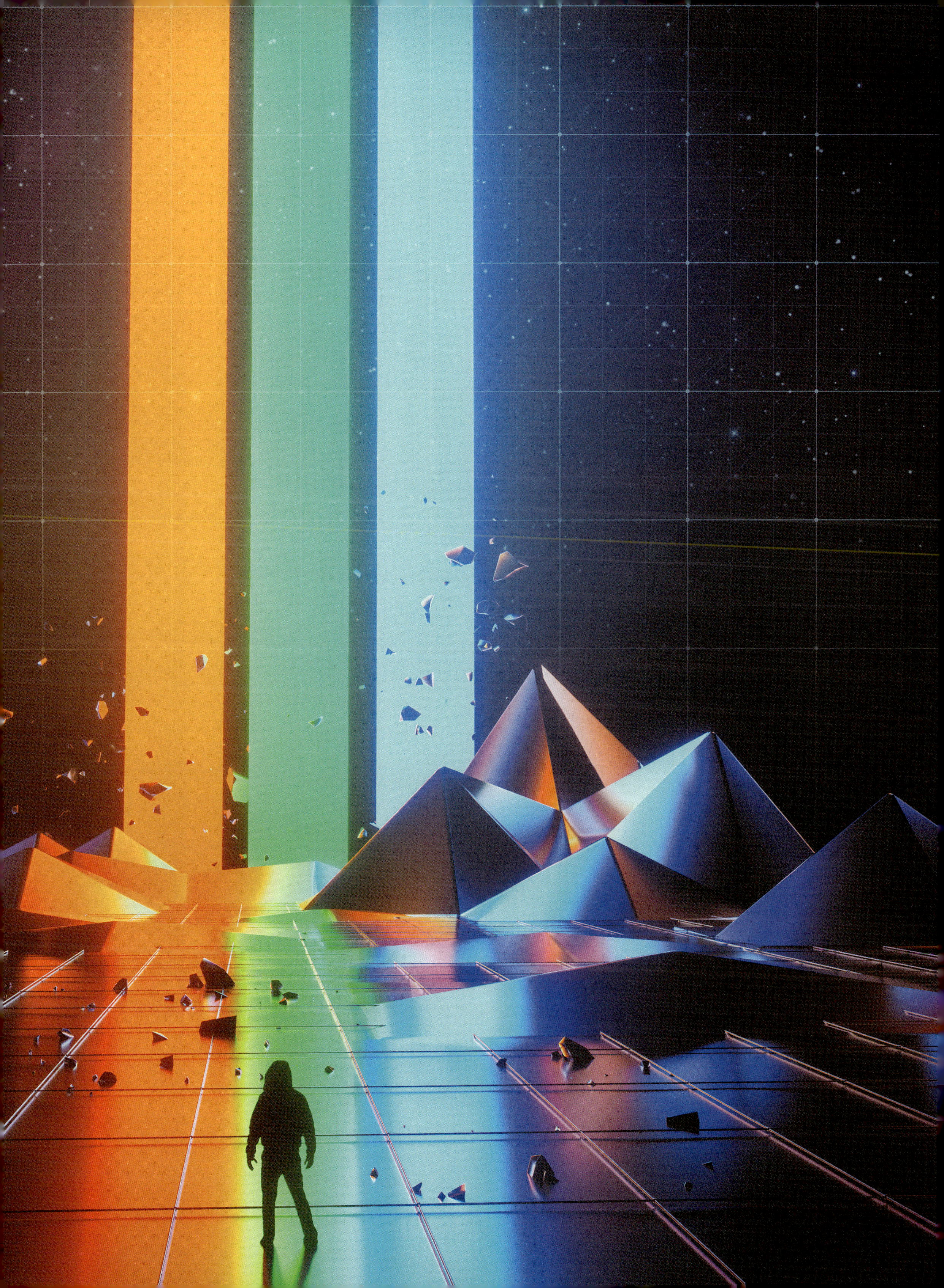

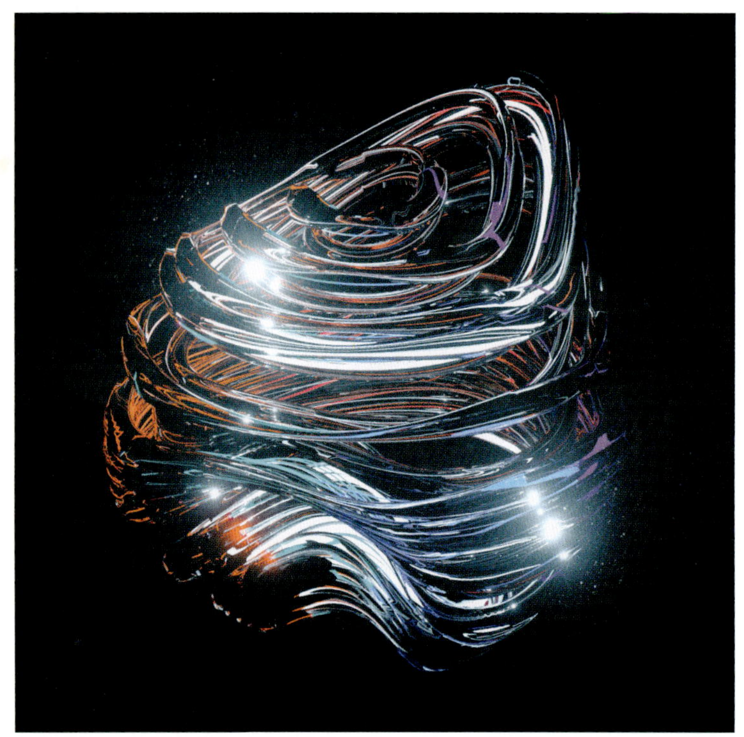

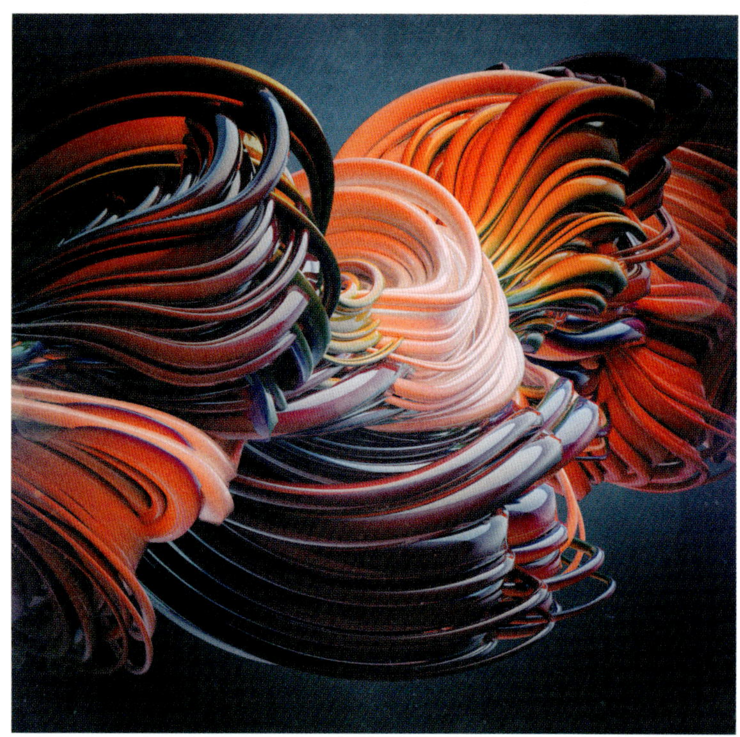

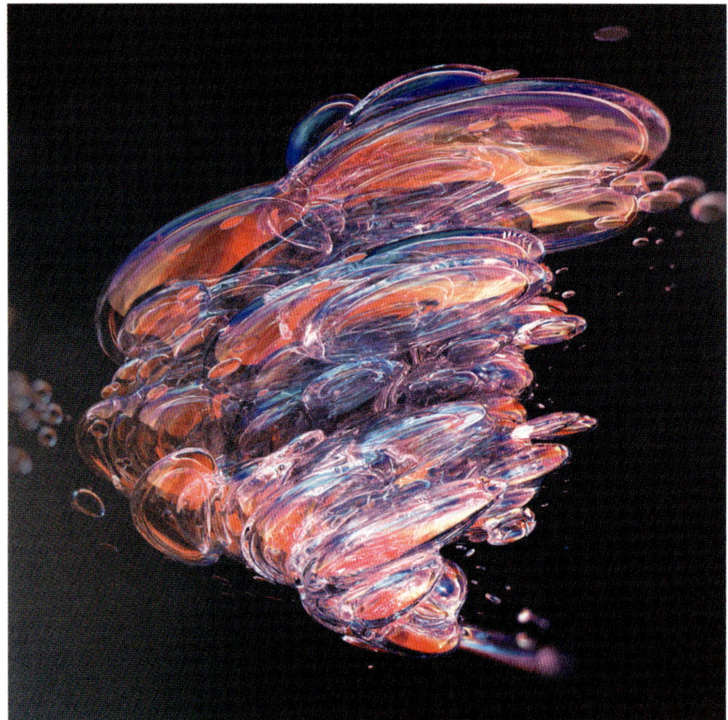

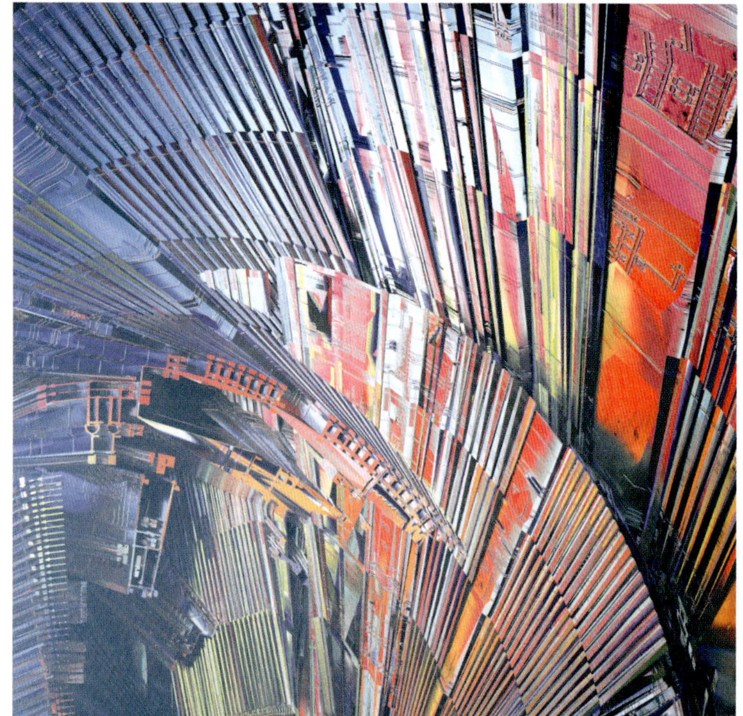

TOP LEFT
alpha hole
03.08.2015

TOP RIGHT
next year
01.18.2015

BOTTOM LEFT
b-pop pudding
04.18.2015

BOTTOM RIGHT
ONE MILLION
04.19.2015

OPPOSITE PAGE
DISTILLED
04.15.2015

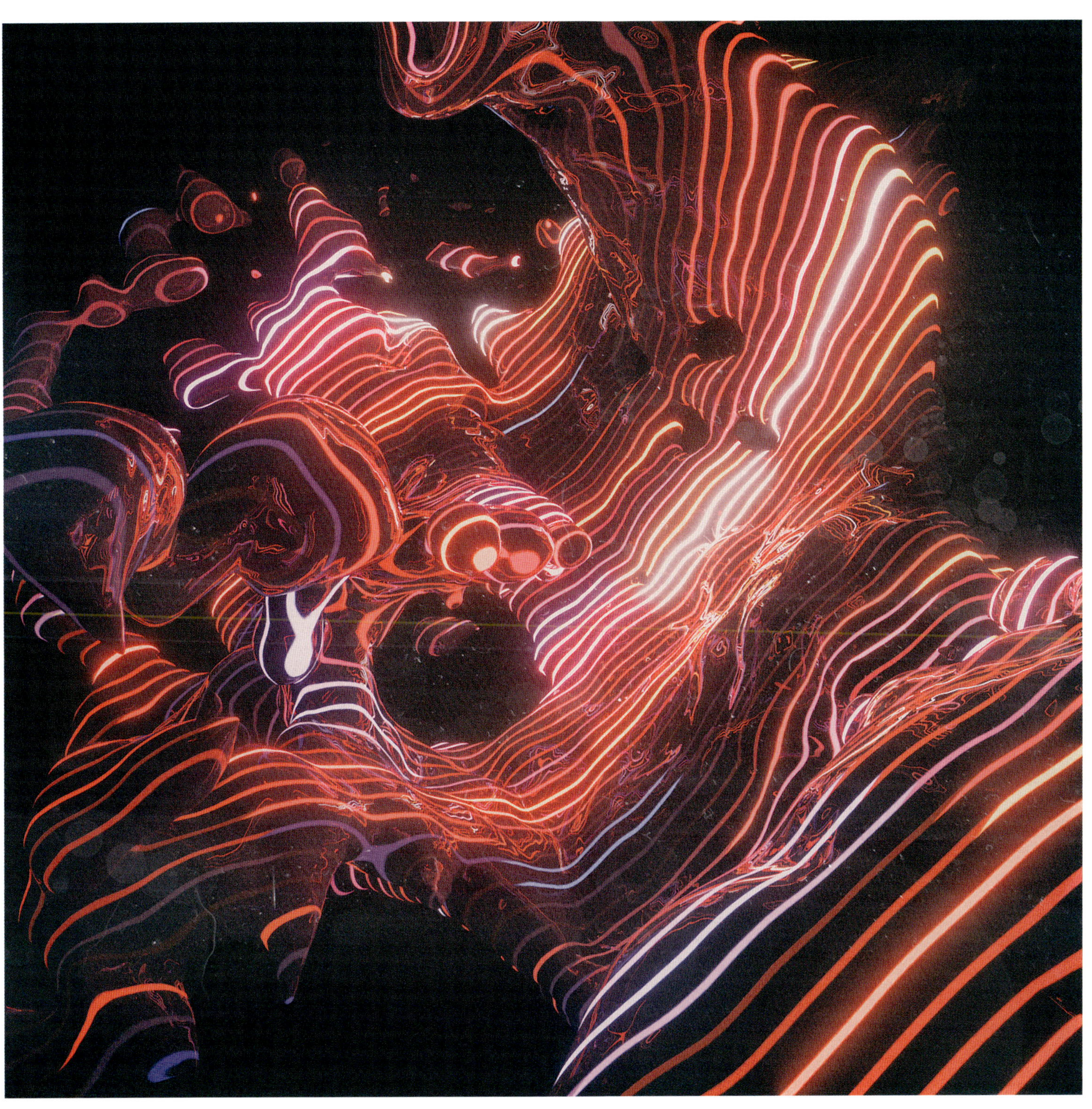

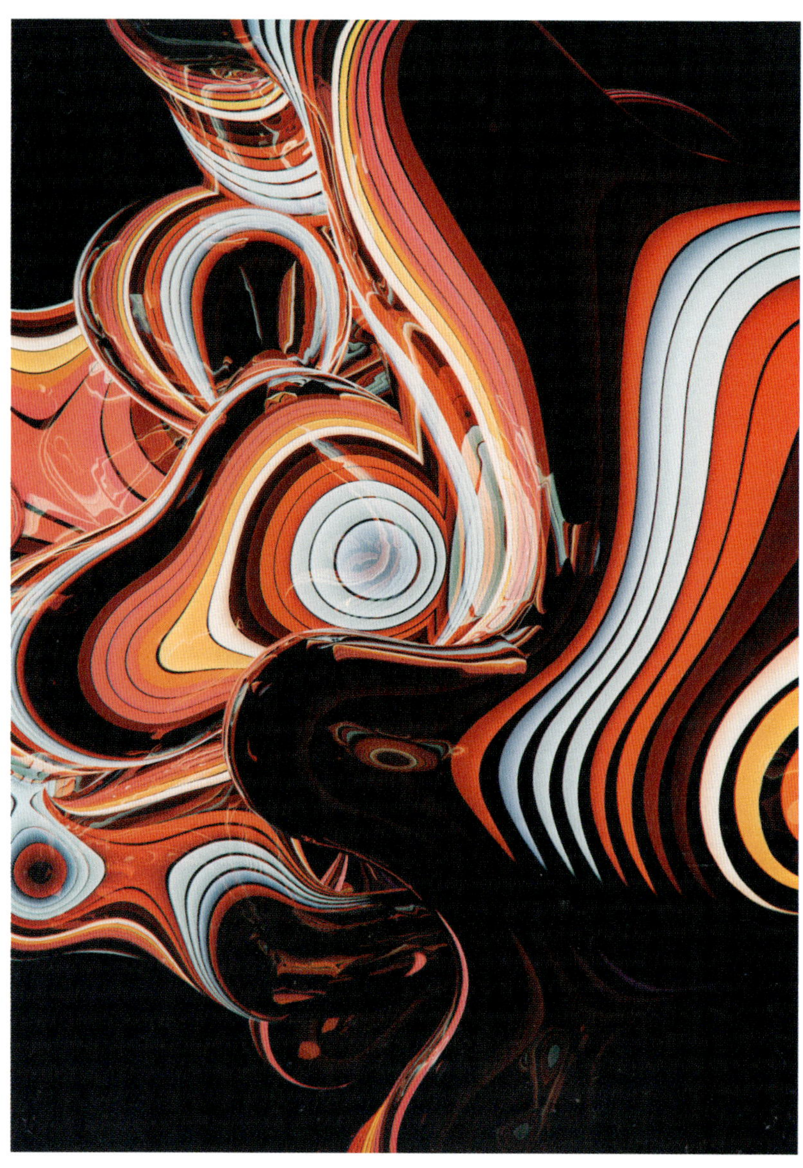

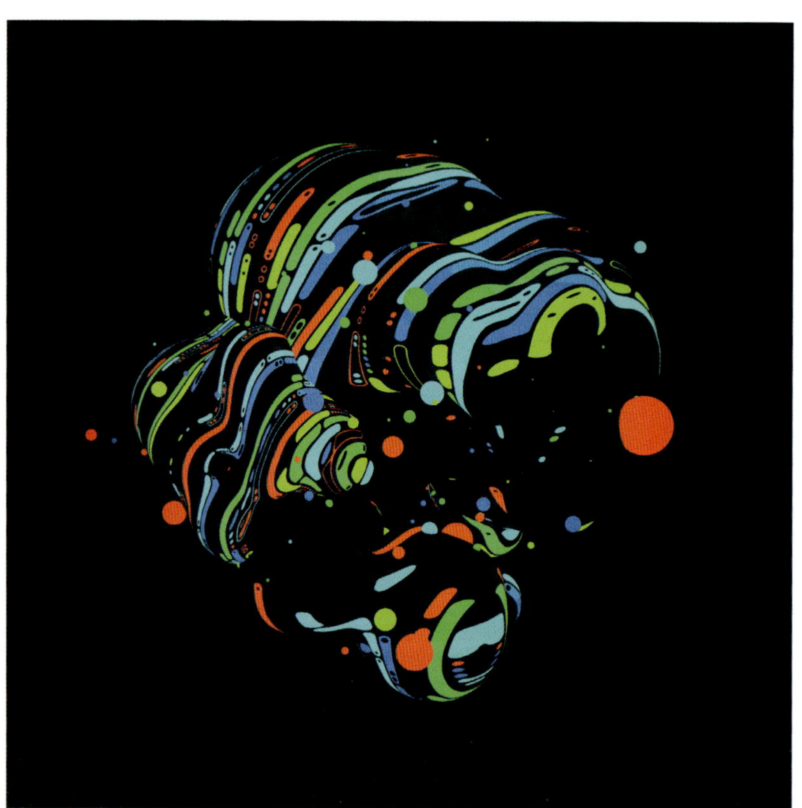

TOP

junggie oobs
05.24.2015

BOTTOM

super memo
05.21.2015

OPPOSITE PAGE

DRIP QUARK
09.01.2015

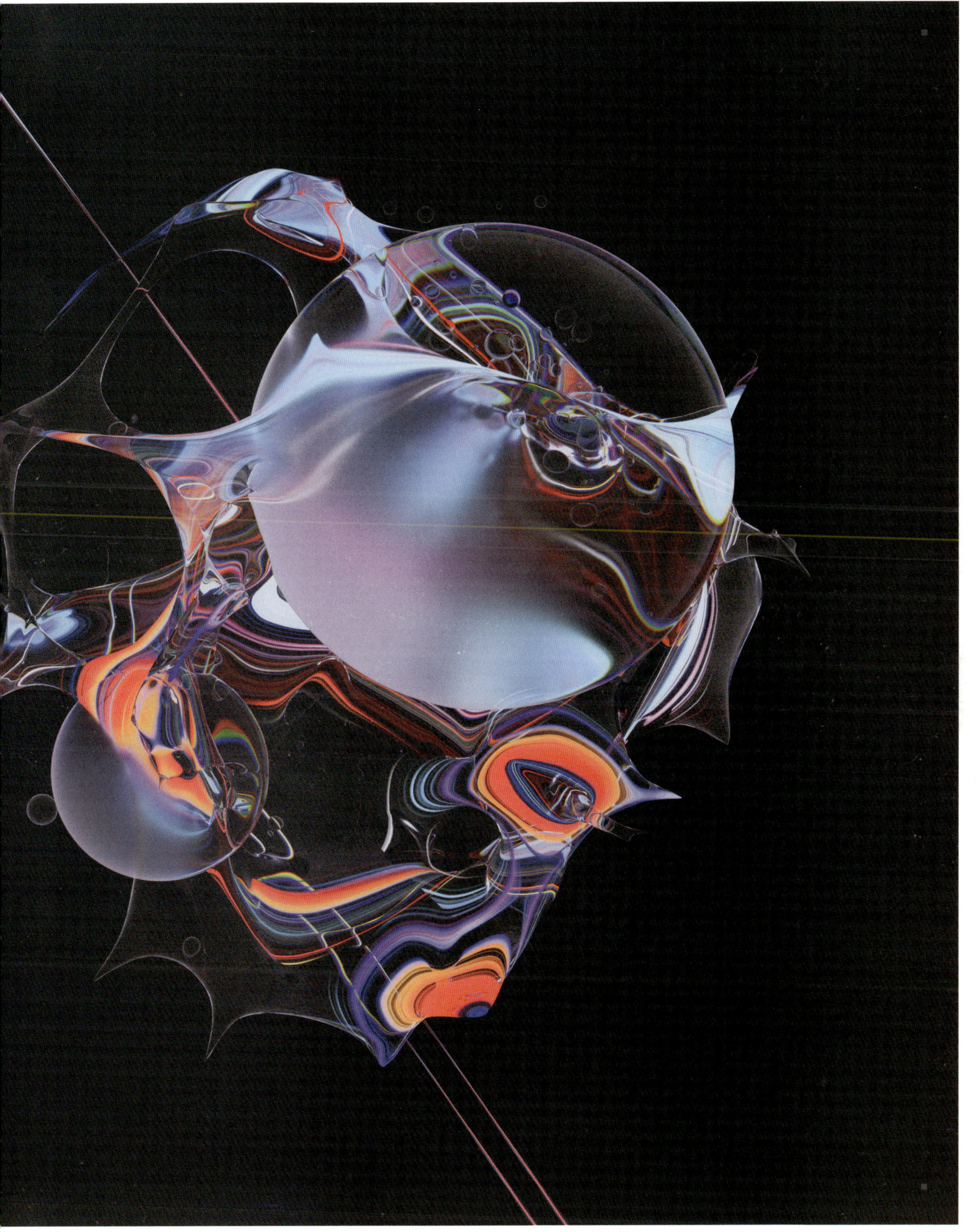

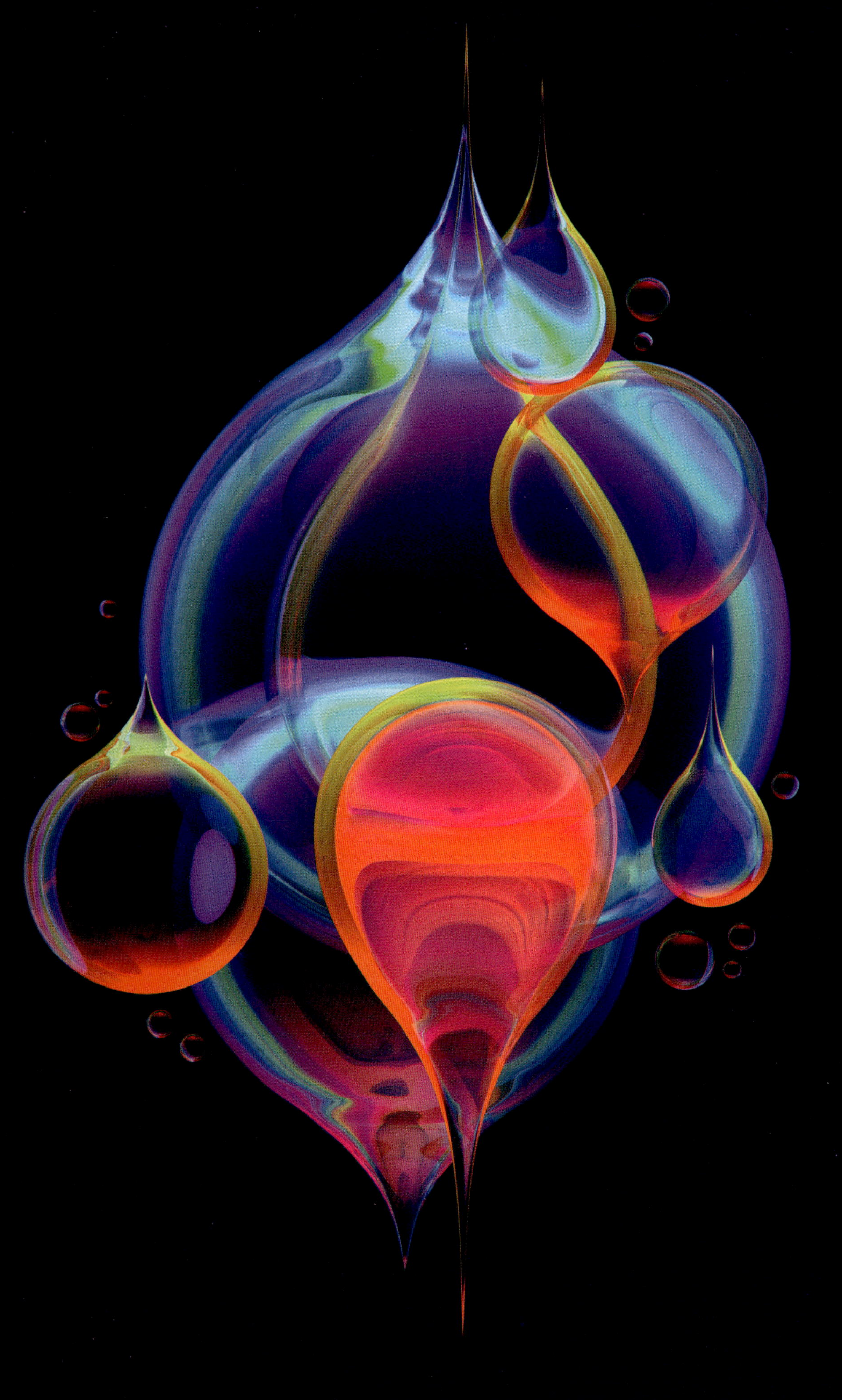

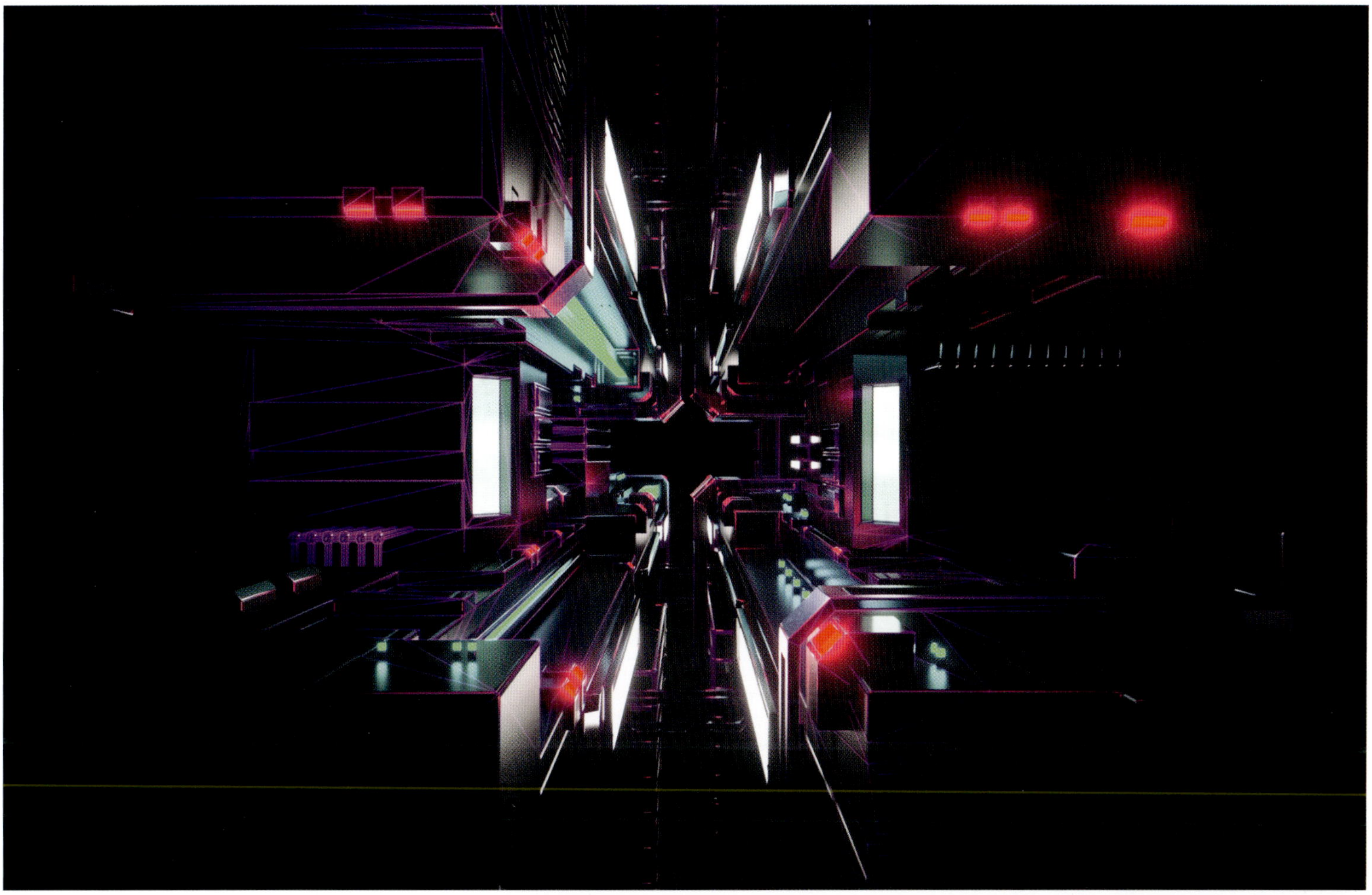

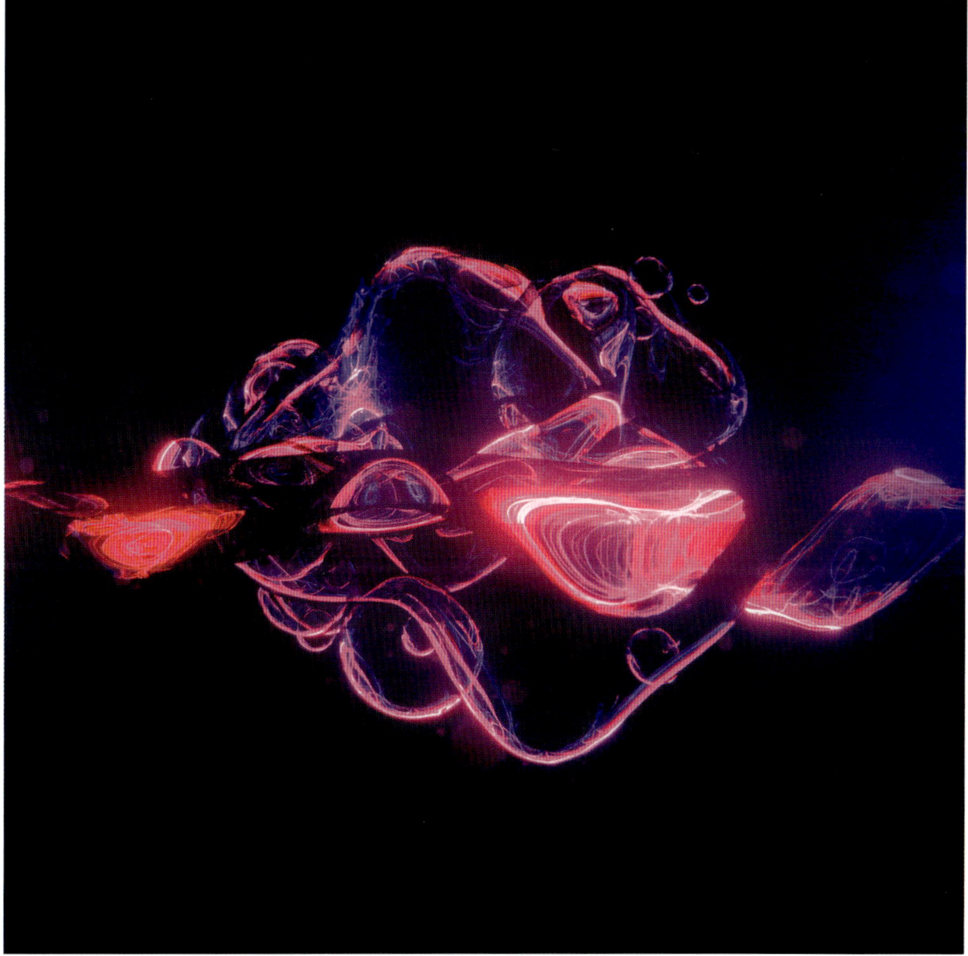

OPPOSITE PAGE

PONTIX.F
09.26.2015

TOP

360 T-HAWK
03.02.2015

BOTTOM

FOCUS
10.13.2015

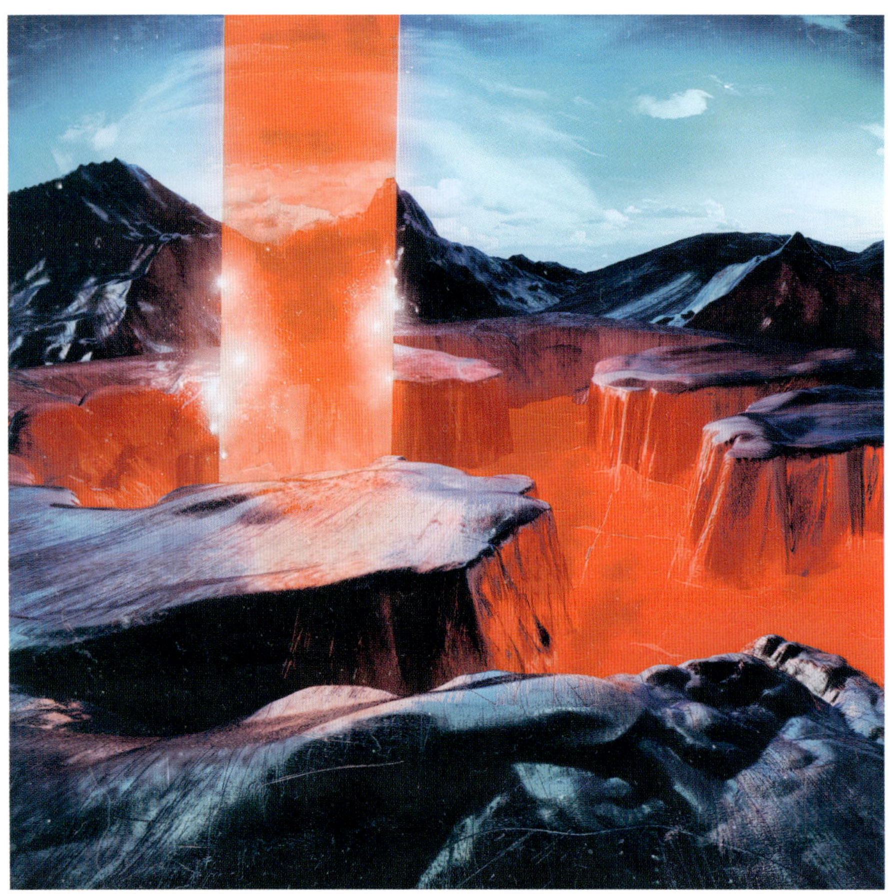

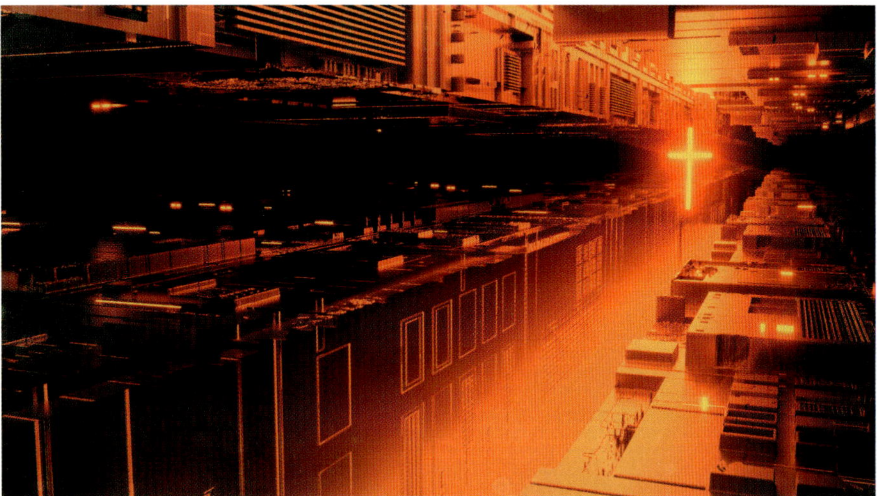

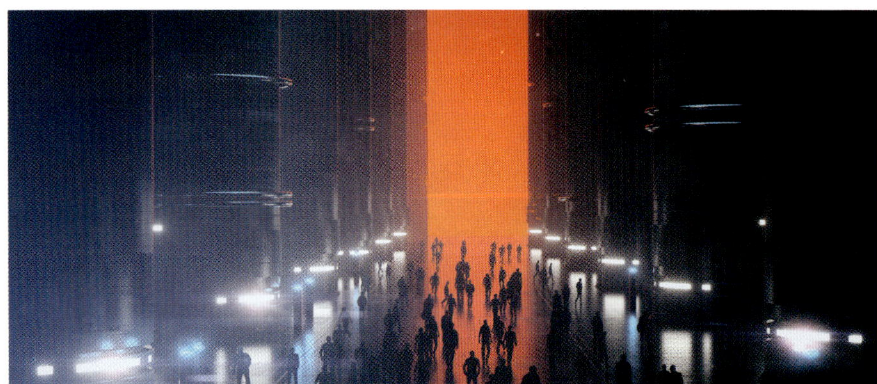

TOP
metallurgy
01.31.2015

MIDDLE
boychild v30
01.03.2015

BOTTOM
unrest
04.27.2015

OPPOSITE PAGE
TERRAFORM
12.11.2015

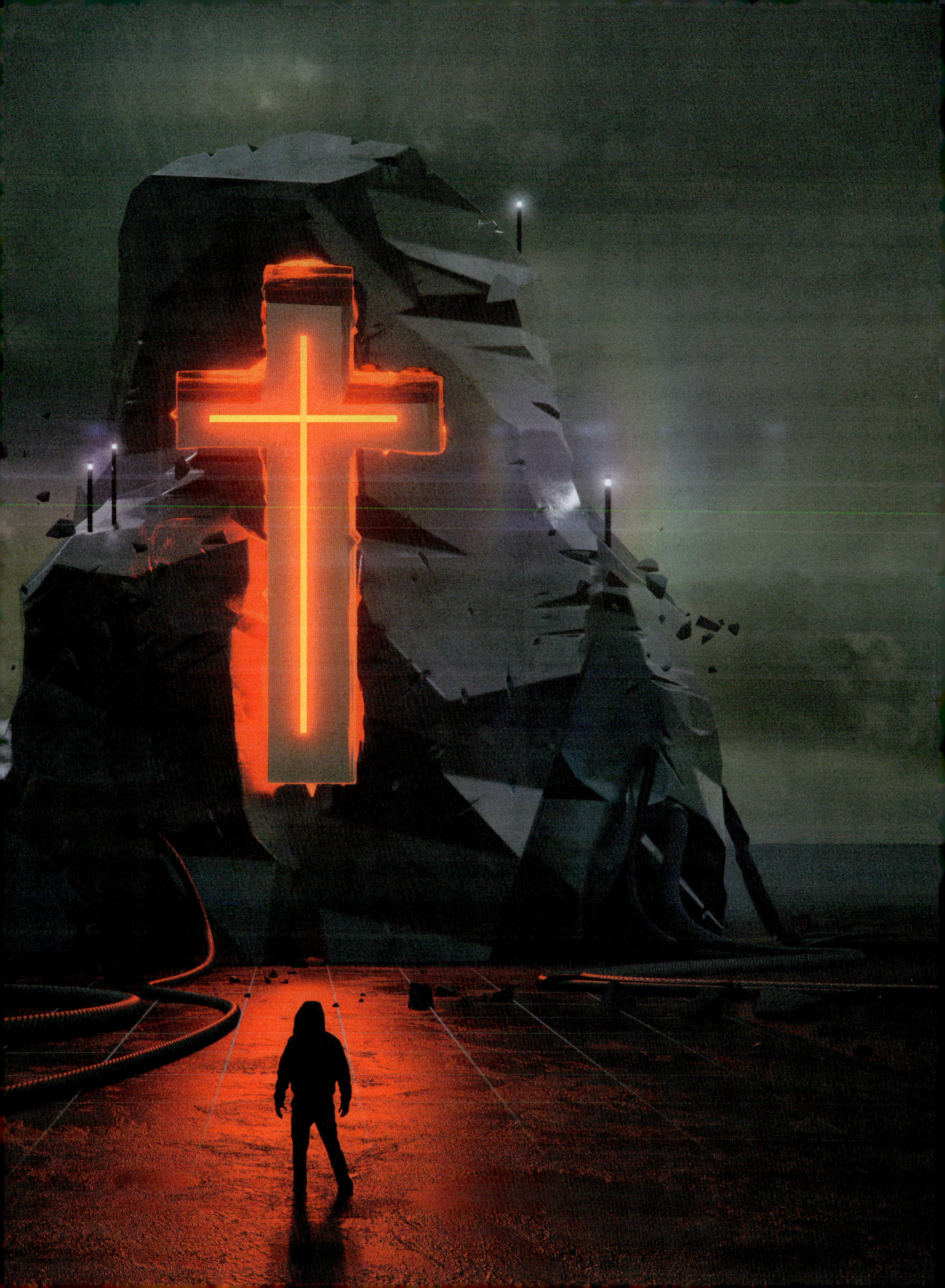

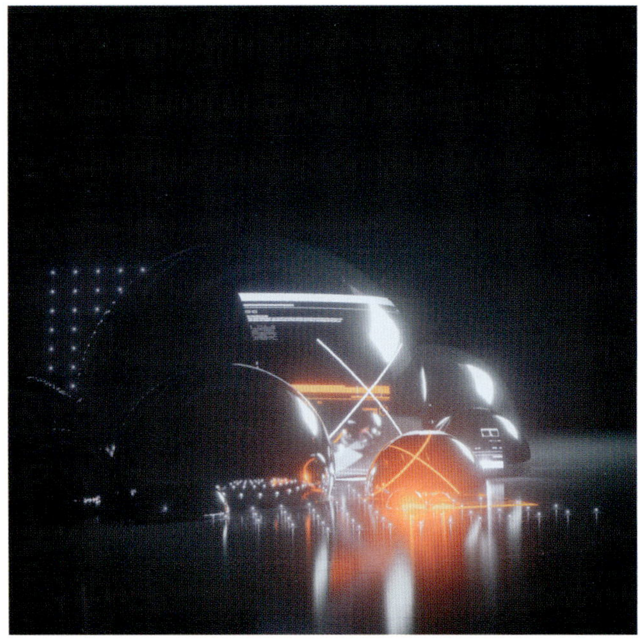

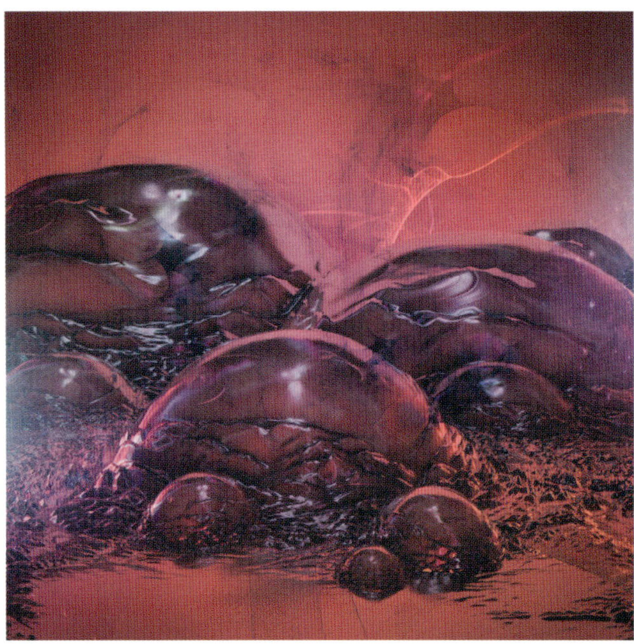

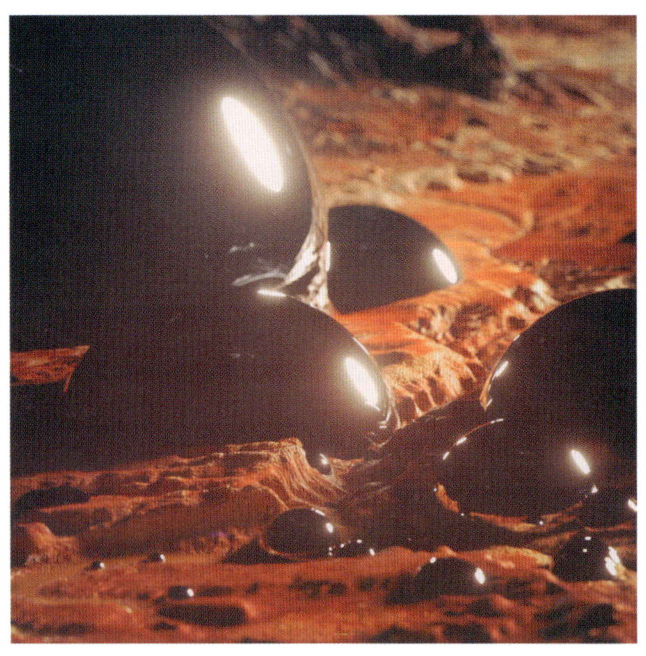

TOP

FRIED GOBO
07.31.2015

MIDDLE

tightB
06.16.2015

BOTTOM

HITE
05.13.2015

OPPOSITE PAGE

GAX-447
12.12.2015

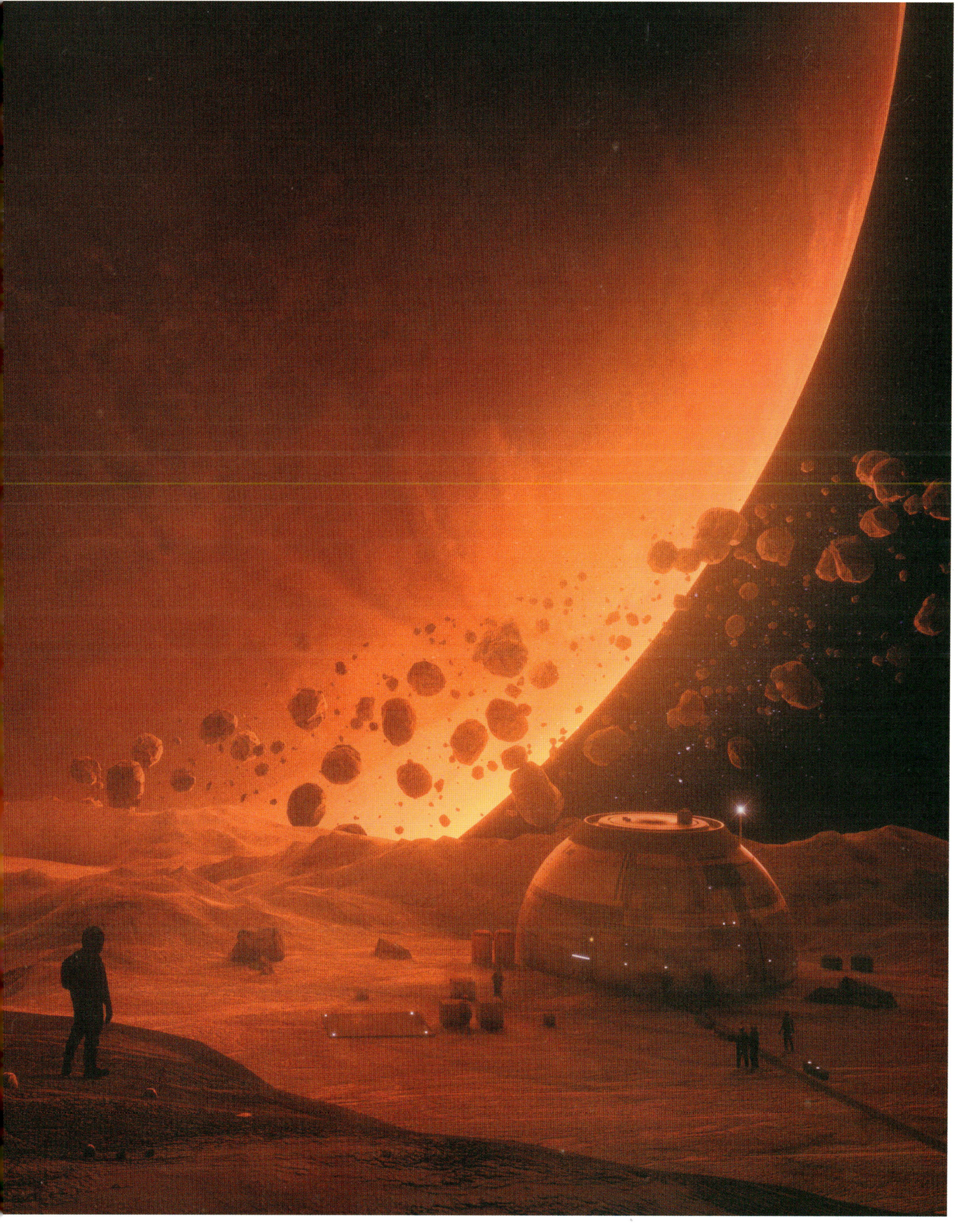

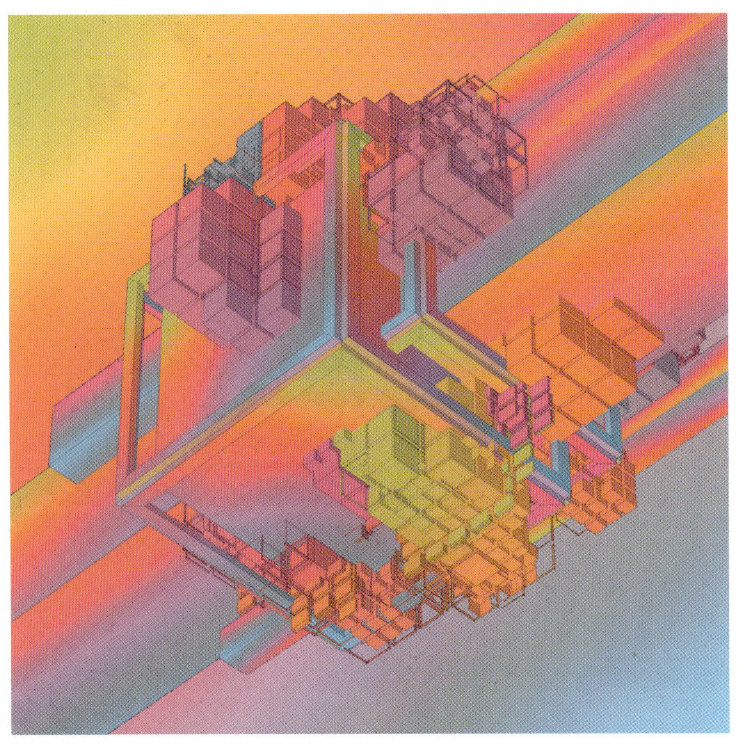

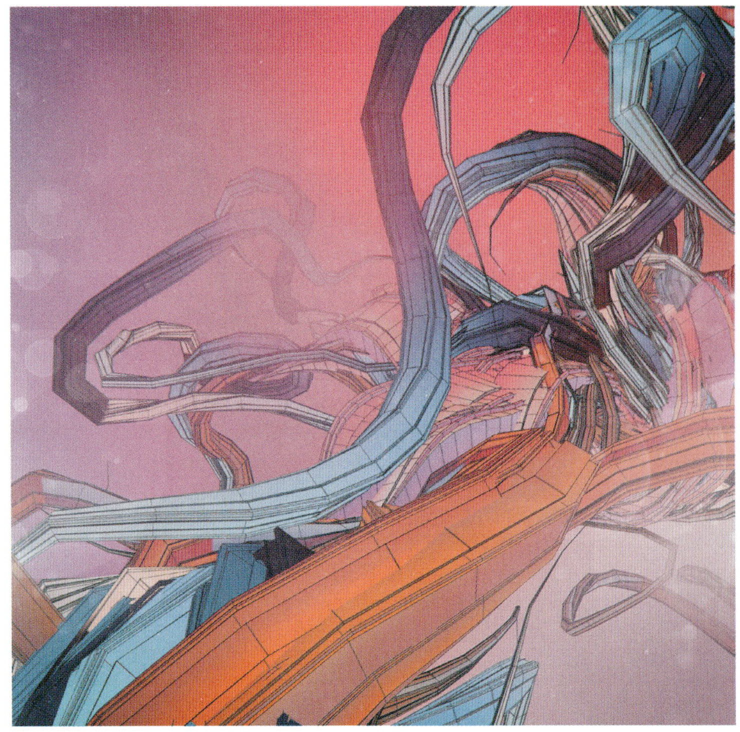

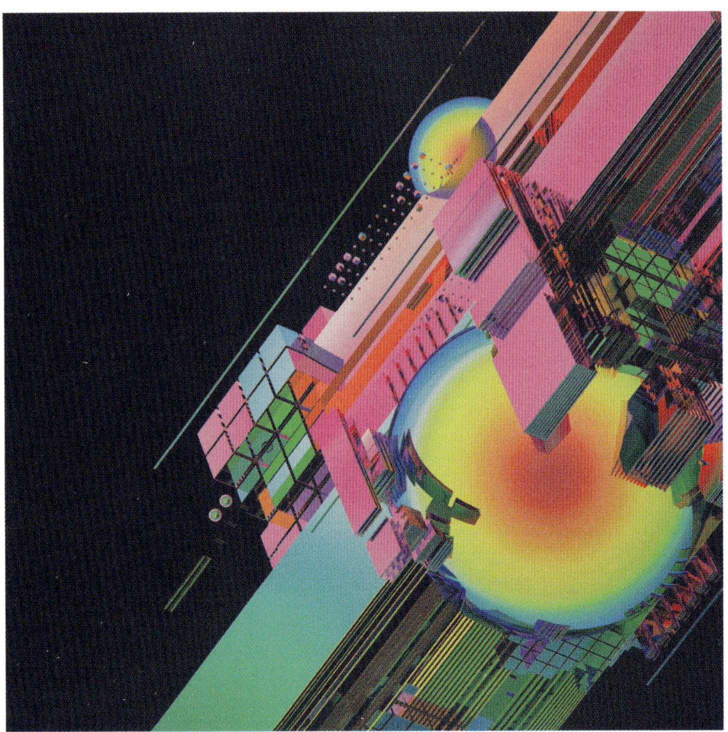

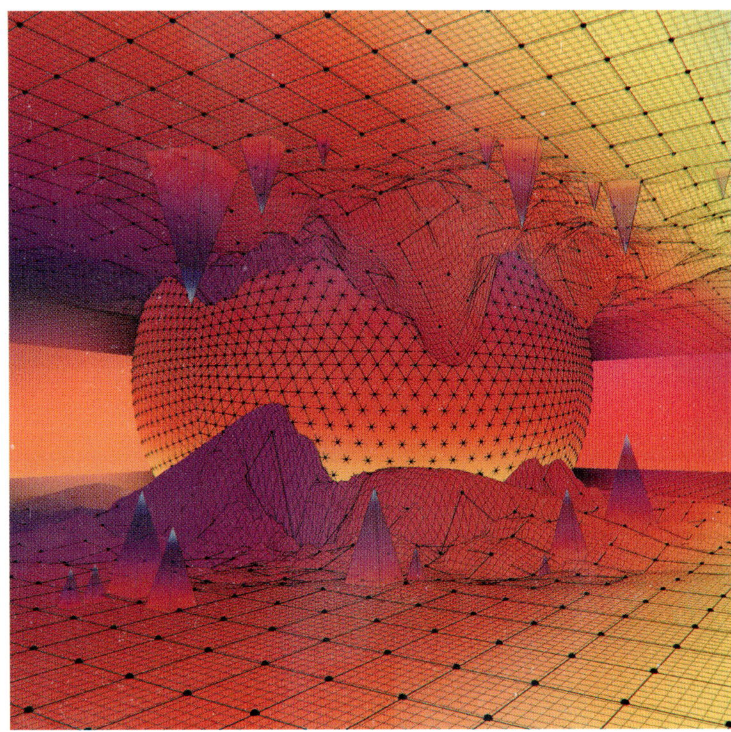

TOP LEFT
NYC
09.29.2015

TOP RIGHT
MXXX
10.05.2015

BOTTOM LEFT
FAT 8 INCHES
12.28.2015

BOTTOM RIGHT
MICKY MOSE
10.01.2015

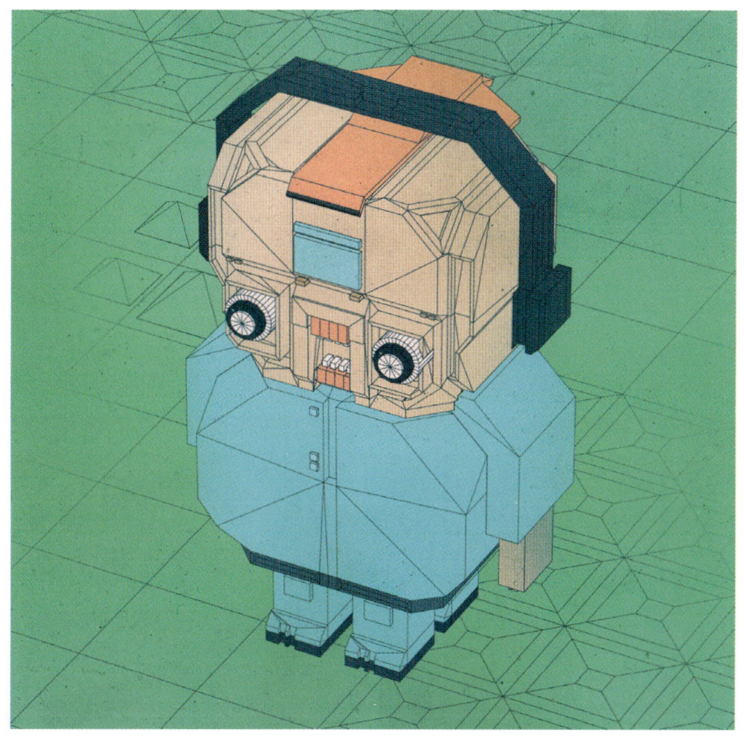

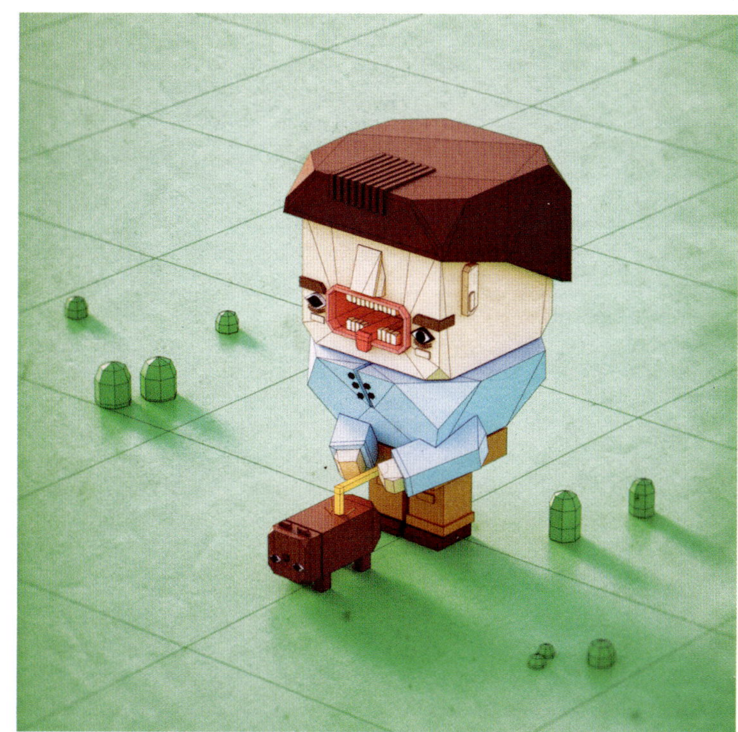

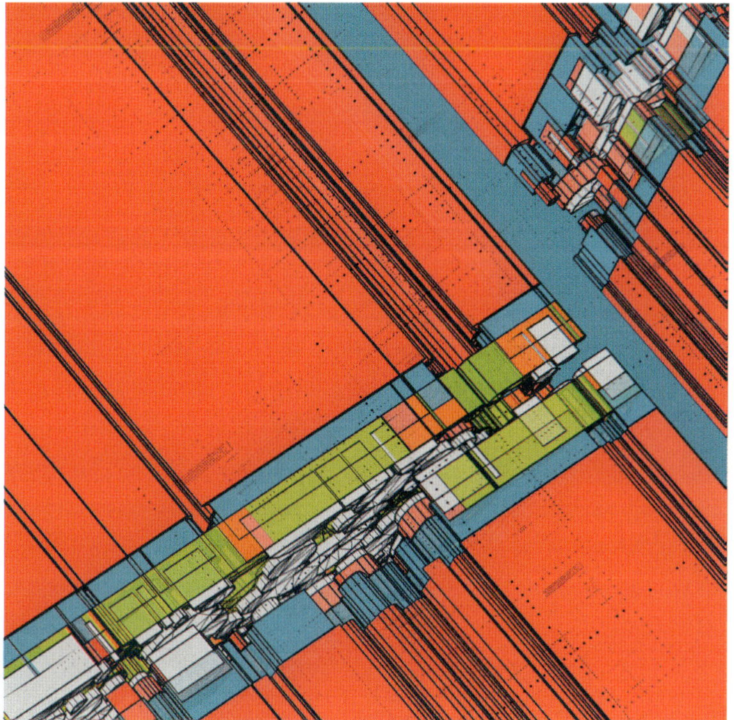

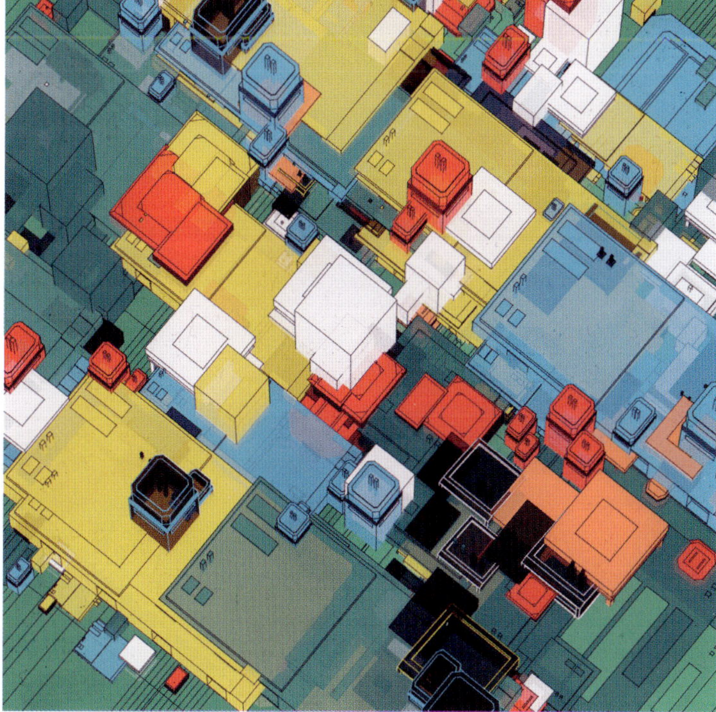

TOP LEFT

LIVECRAP

10.06.2015

TOP RIGHT

eight years

05.01.2015

BOTTOM LEFT

MADISON SQUARE GARDEN

10.02.2015

BOTTOM RIGHT

FLOOR 100

09.30.2015

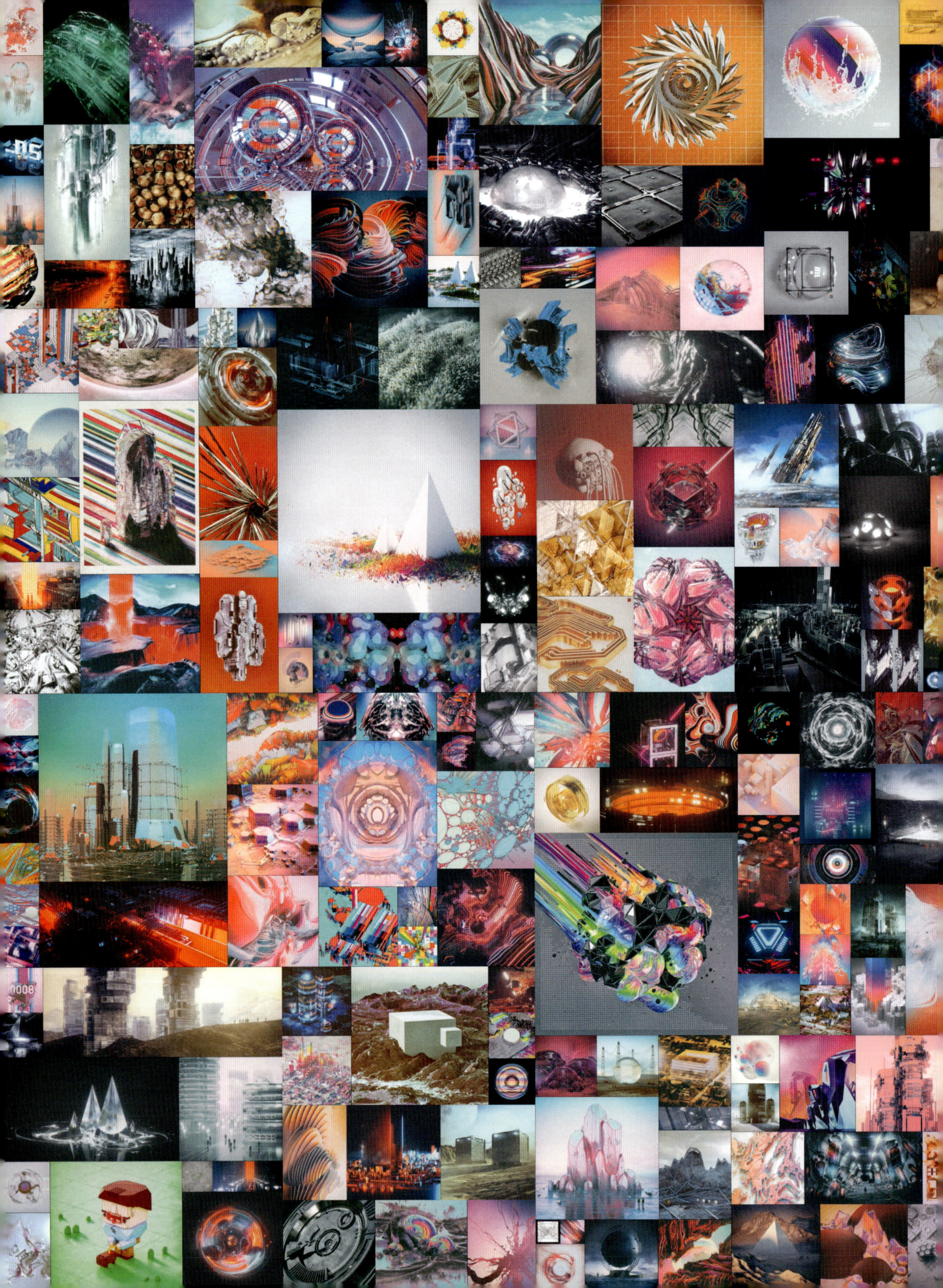

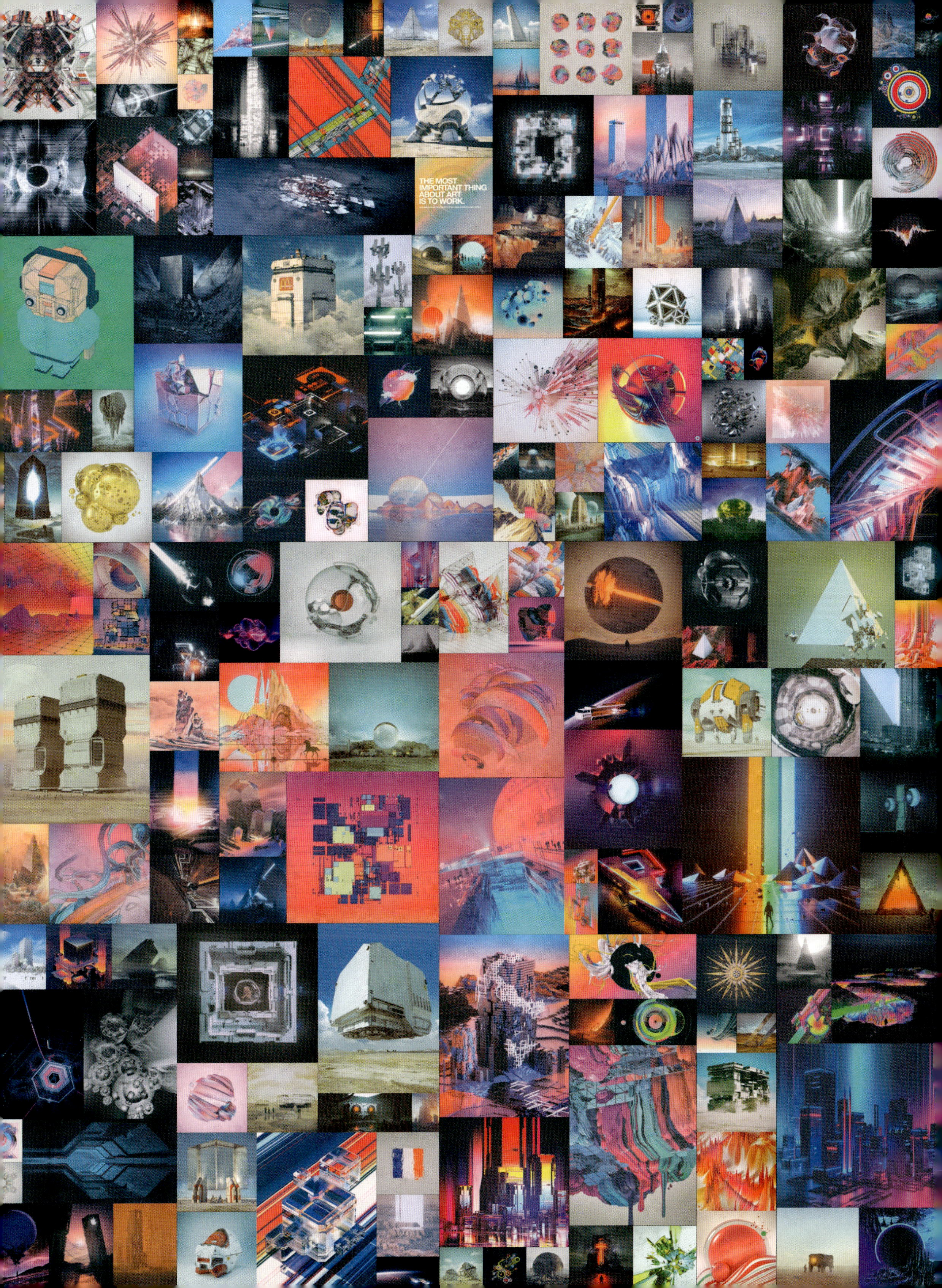
THE MOST
IMPORTANT THING
ABOUT ART
IS TO WORK.

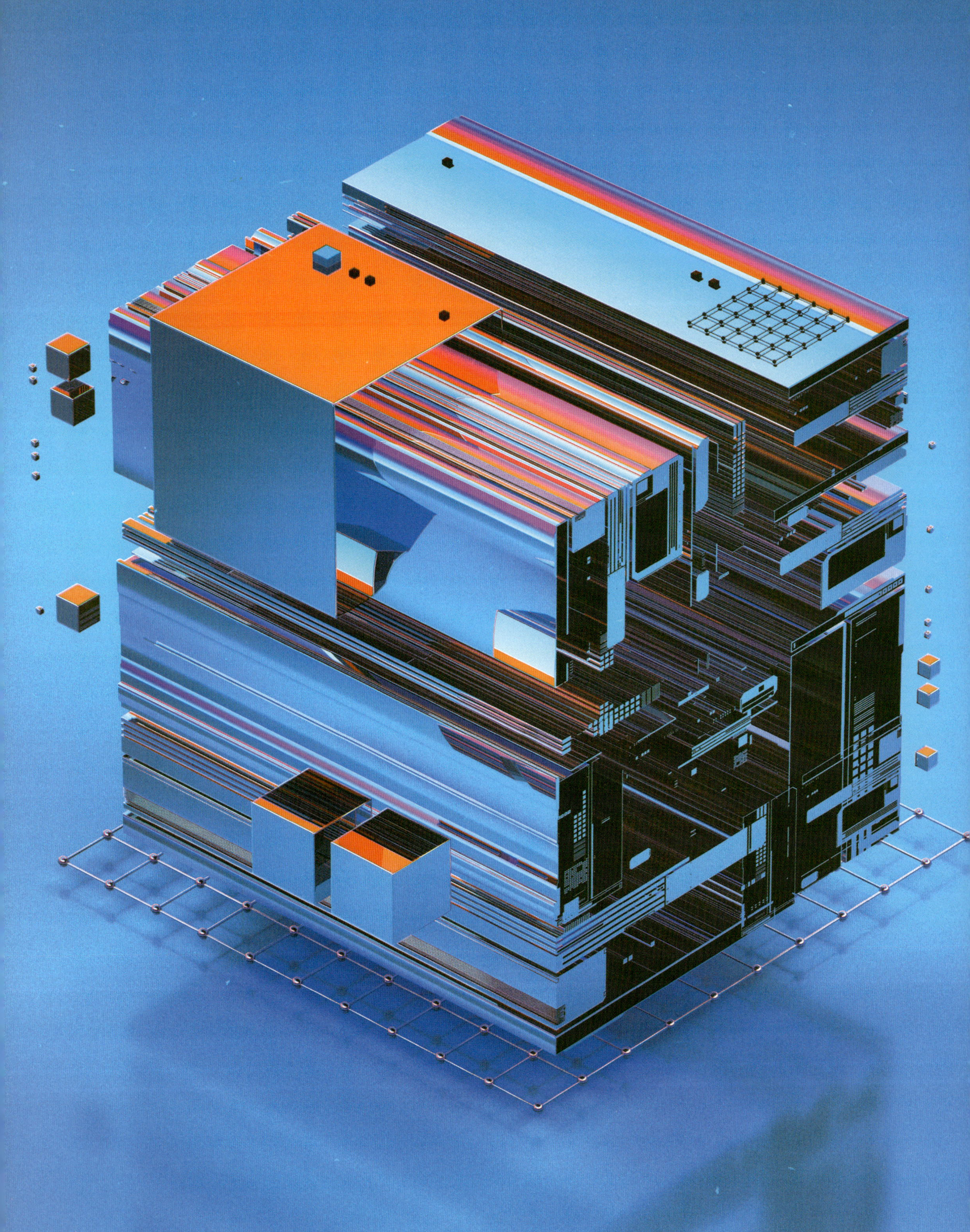

2016

OPPOSITE PAGE

CHEMICAL_BURN

03.26.2016

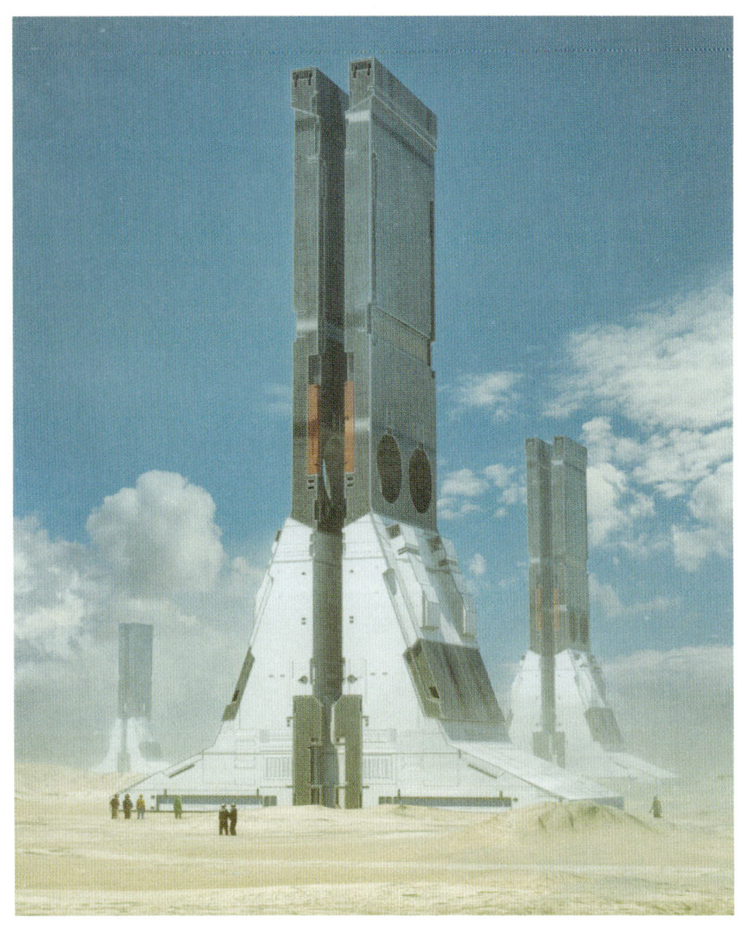

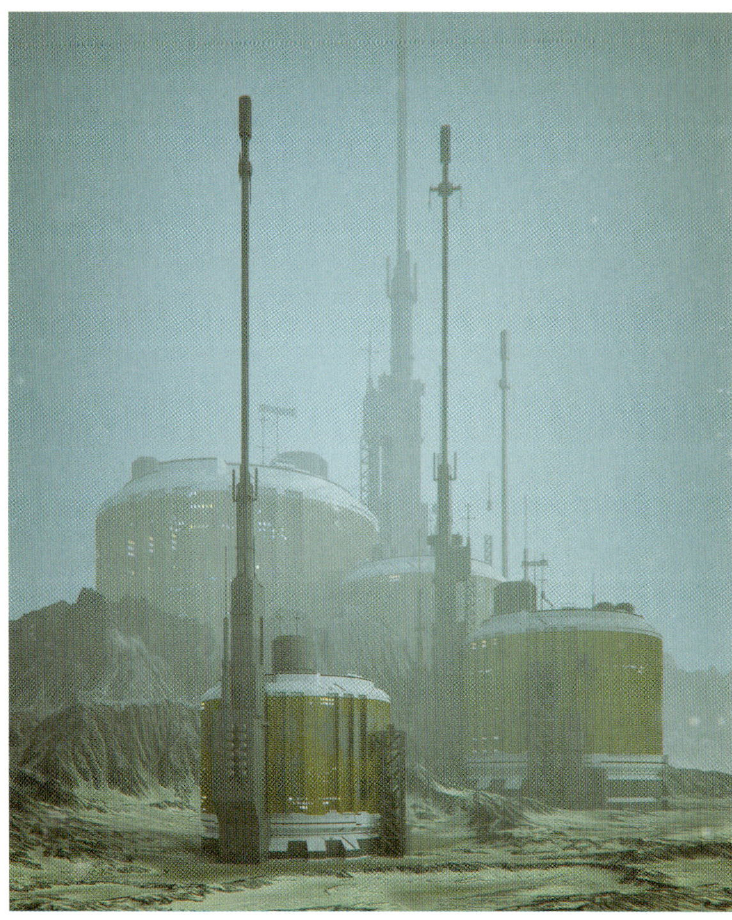

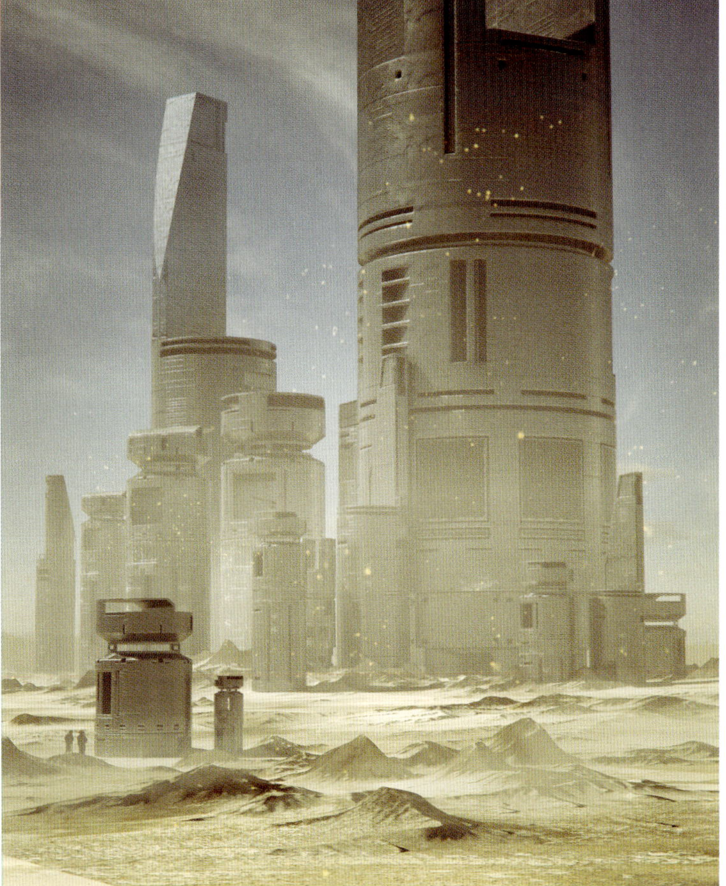

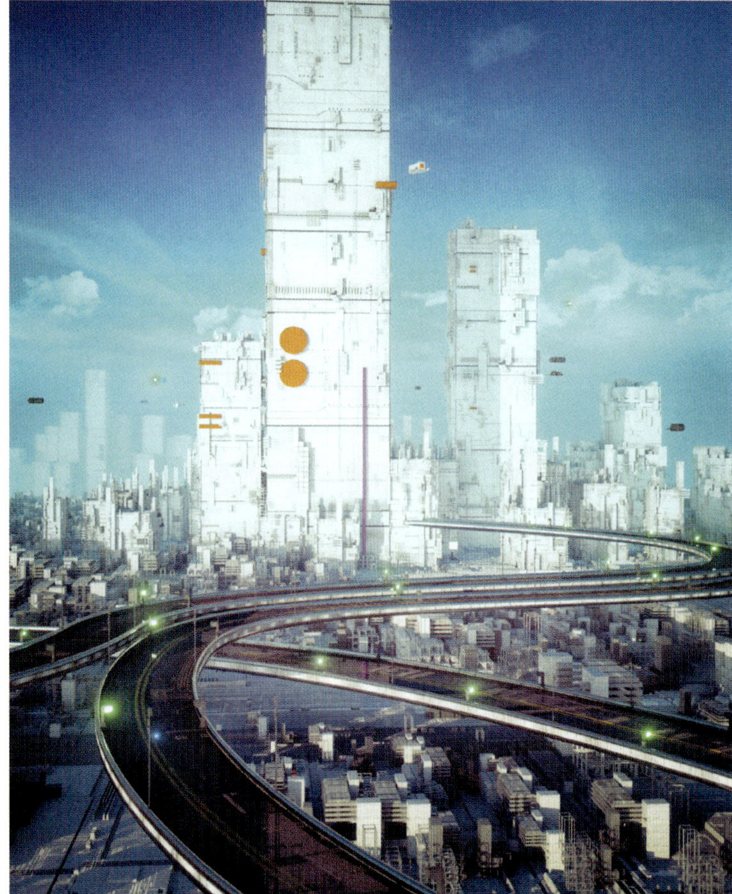

TOP LEFT
QUADTRI.4E
12.08.2016

TOP RIGHT
LITHIUM-BL.07
12.19.2016

BOTTOM LEFT
RECOTR.STATION6.00
03.06.2016

BOTTOM RIGHT
REBUILD
08.20.2016

OPPOSITE PAGE
THIRTY-FIVE
06.20.2016

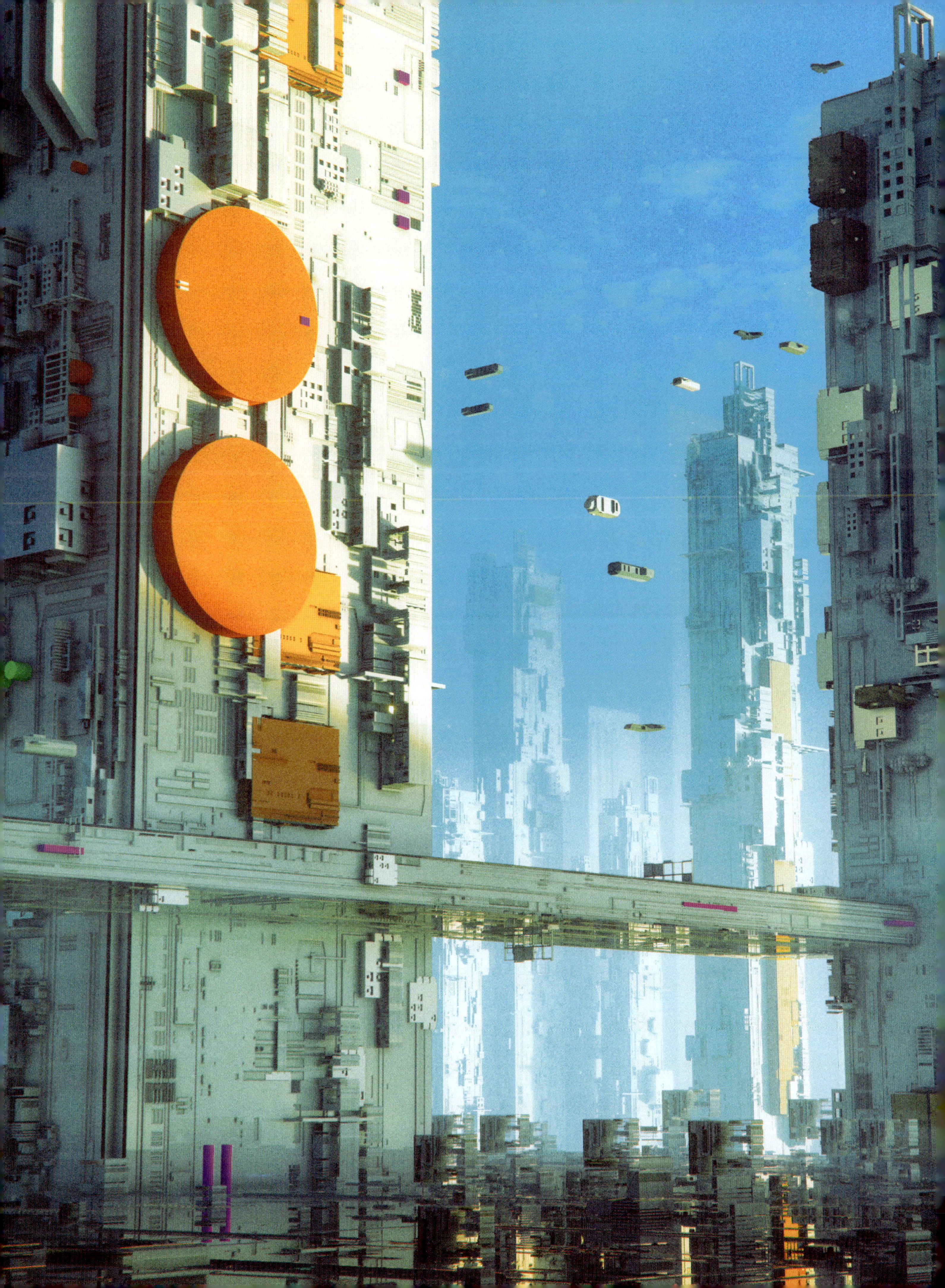

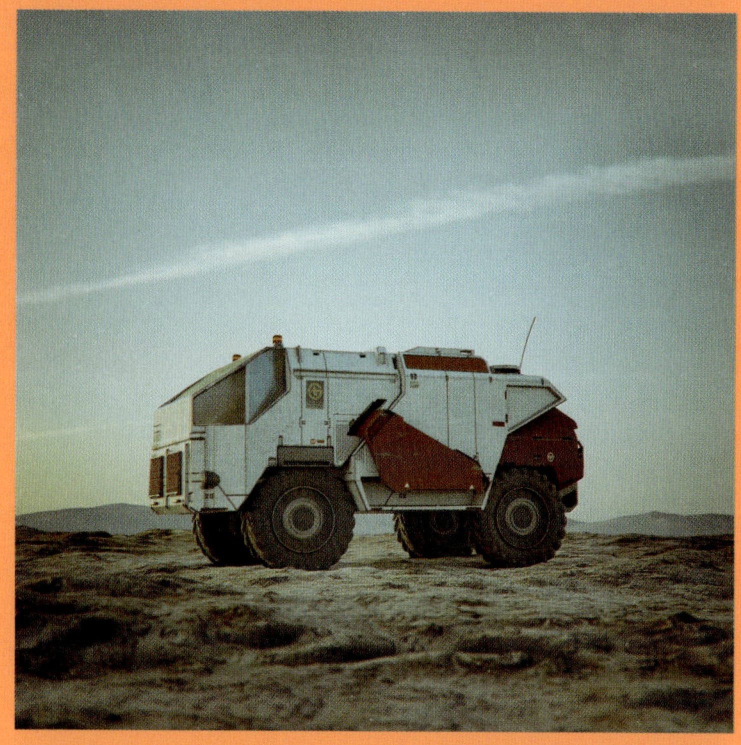

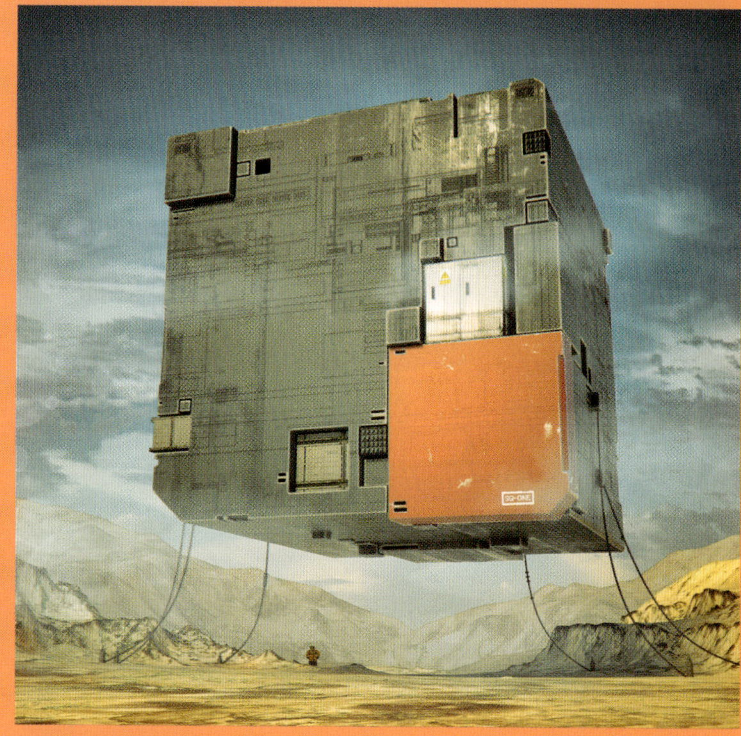

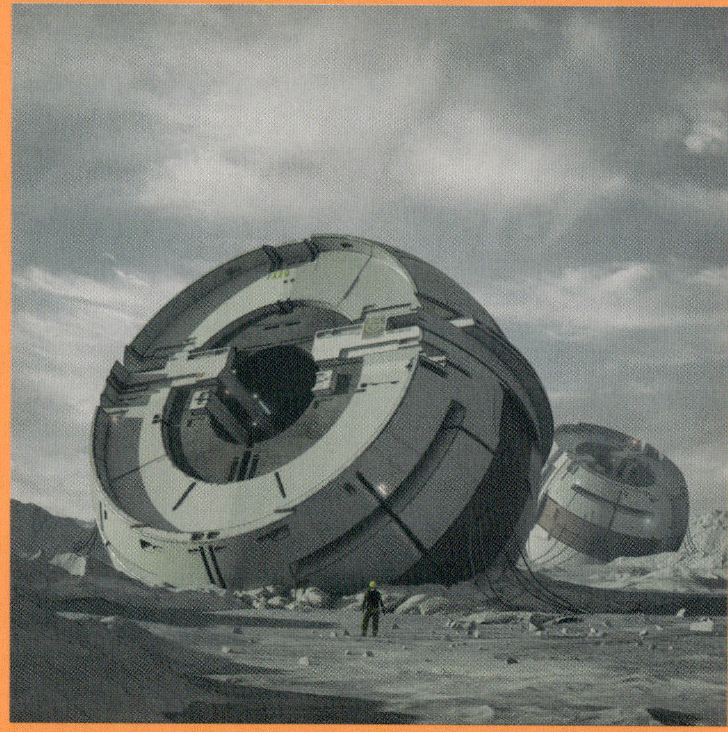

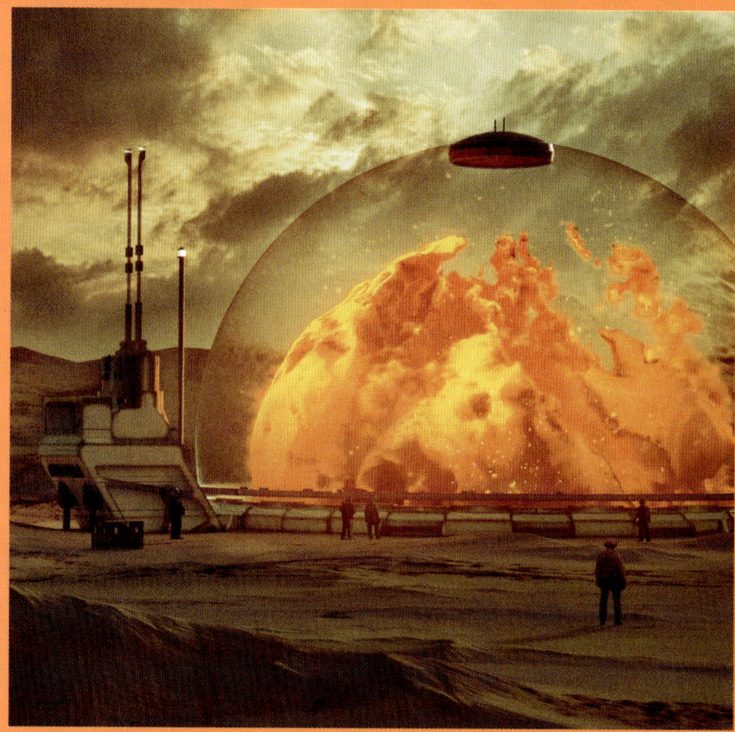

TOP LEFT
BOY-C.MOBILE.31
01.03.2016

TOP RIGHT
SQUARE ONE
01.01.2016

BOTTOM LEFT
POINTOVER ONE
09.25.2016

BOTTOM RIGHT
PLASMA. INCINERATOR1.5
02.13.2016

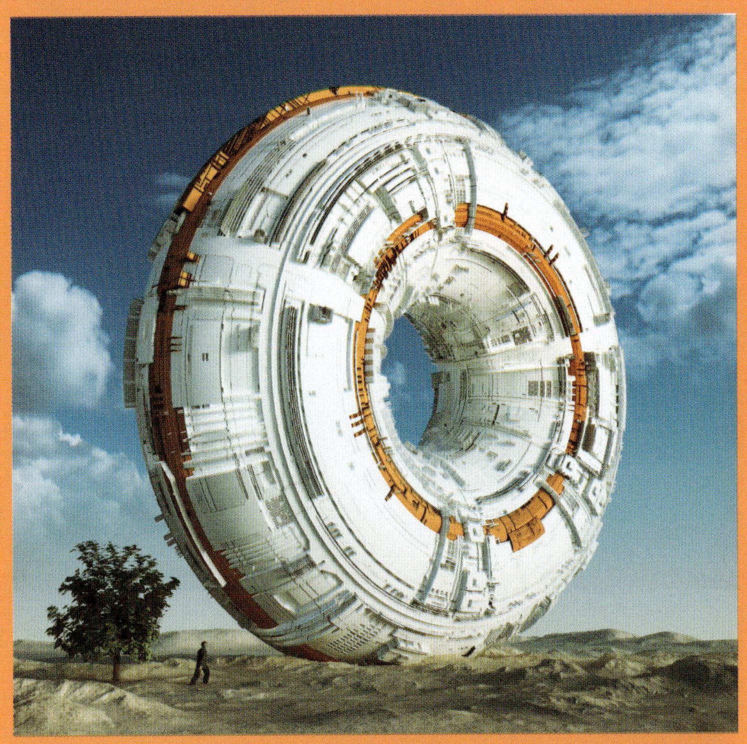

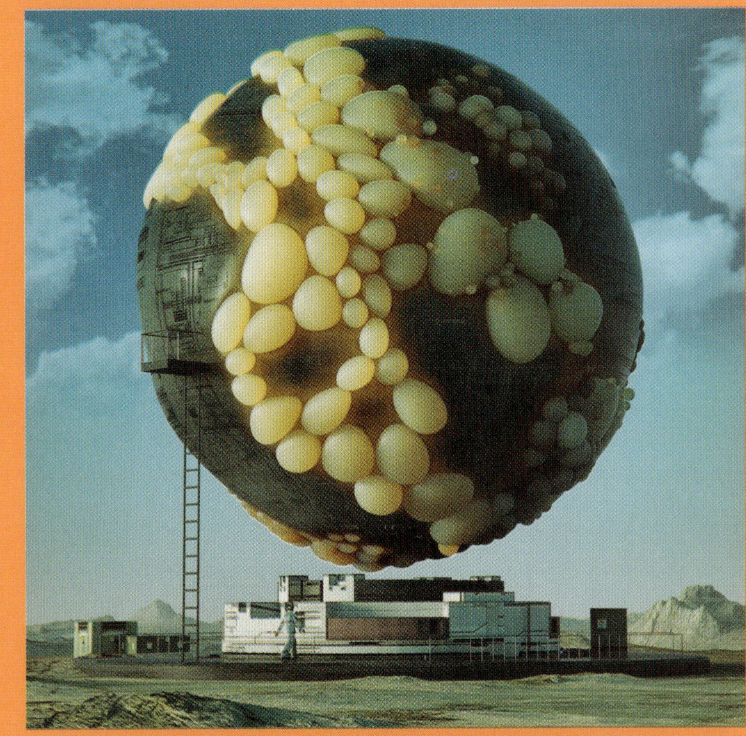

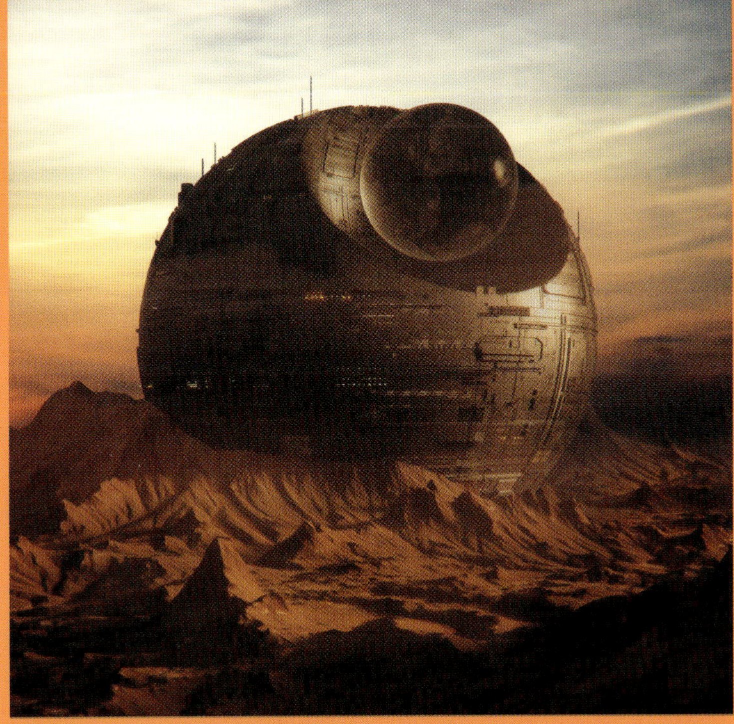

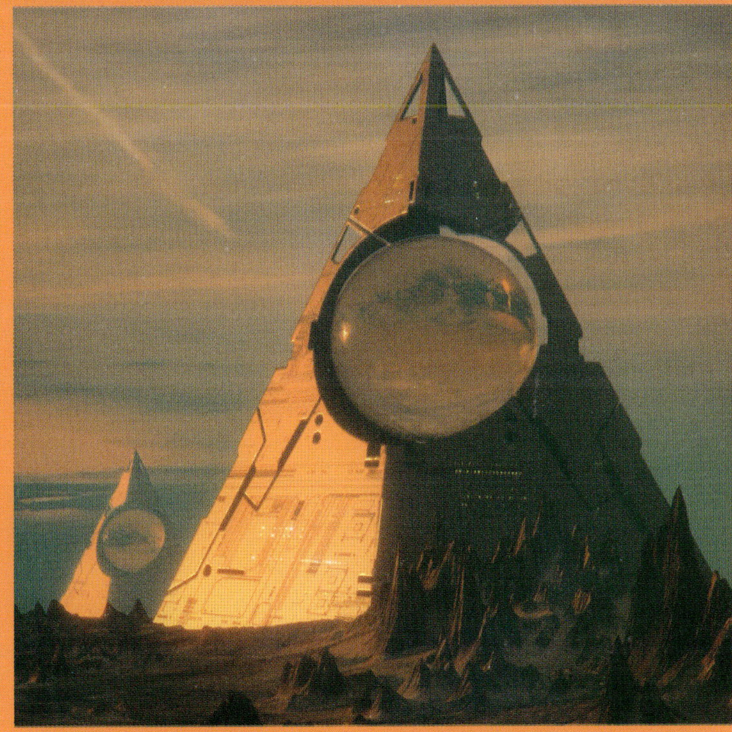

TOP LEFT
TORTOR2
07.19.2016

TOP RIGHT
REBUILD.XO
07.31.2016

BOTTOM LEFT
XOHTH.9
04.01.2016

BOTTOM RIGHT
MAGFLY
03.30.2016

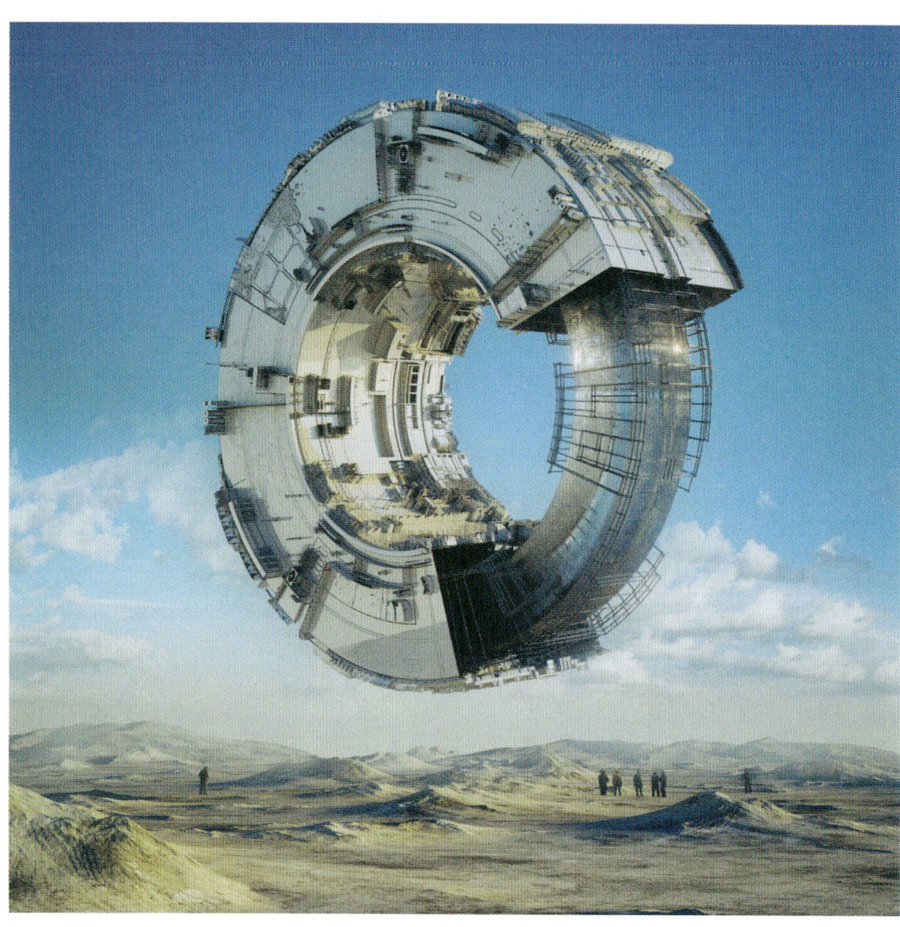

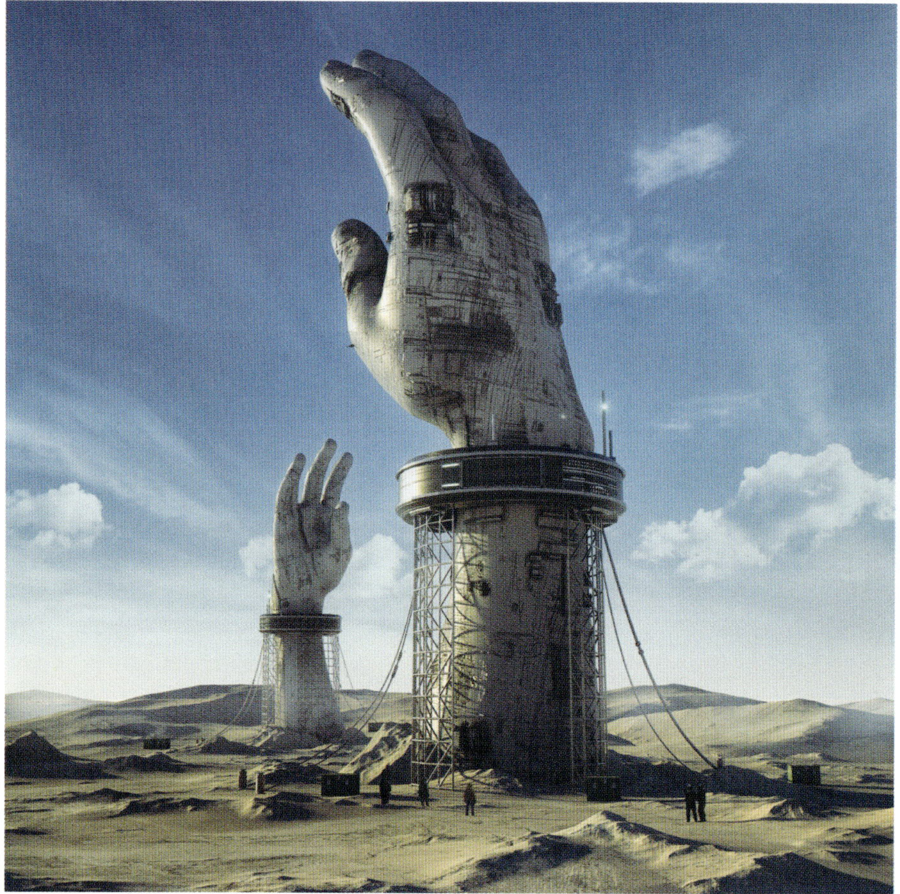

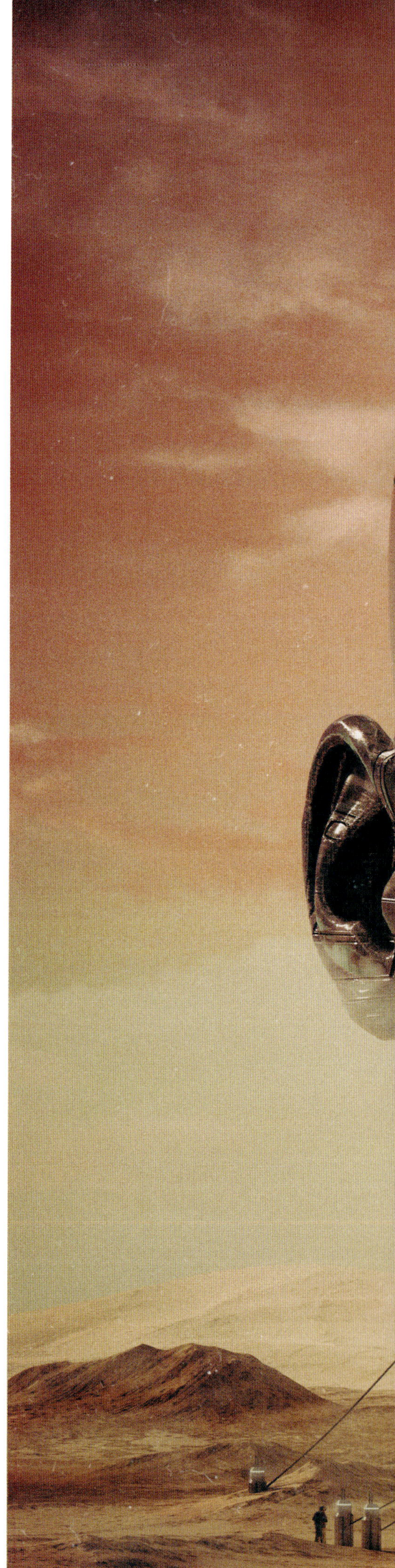

TOP
REBALANCE
02.08.2016

BOTTOM
RESTRAINED
02.10.2016

OPPOSITE PAGE
VACUOUS
02.27.2016

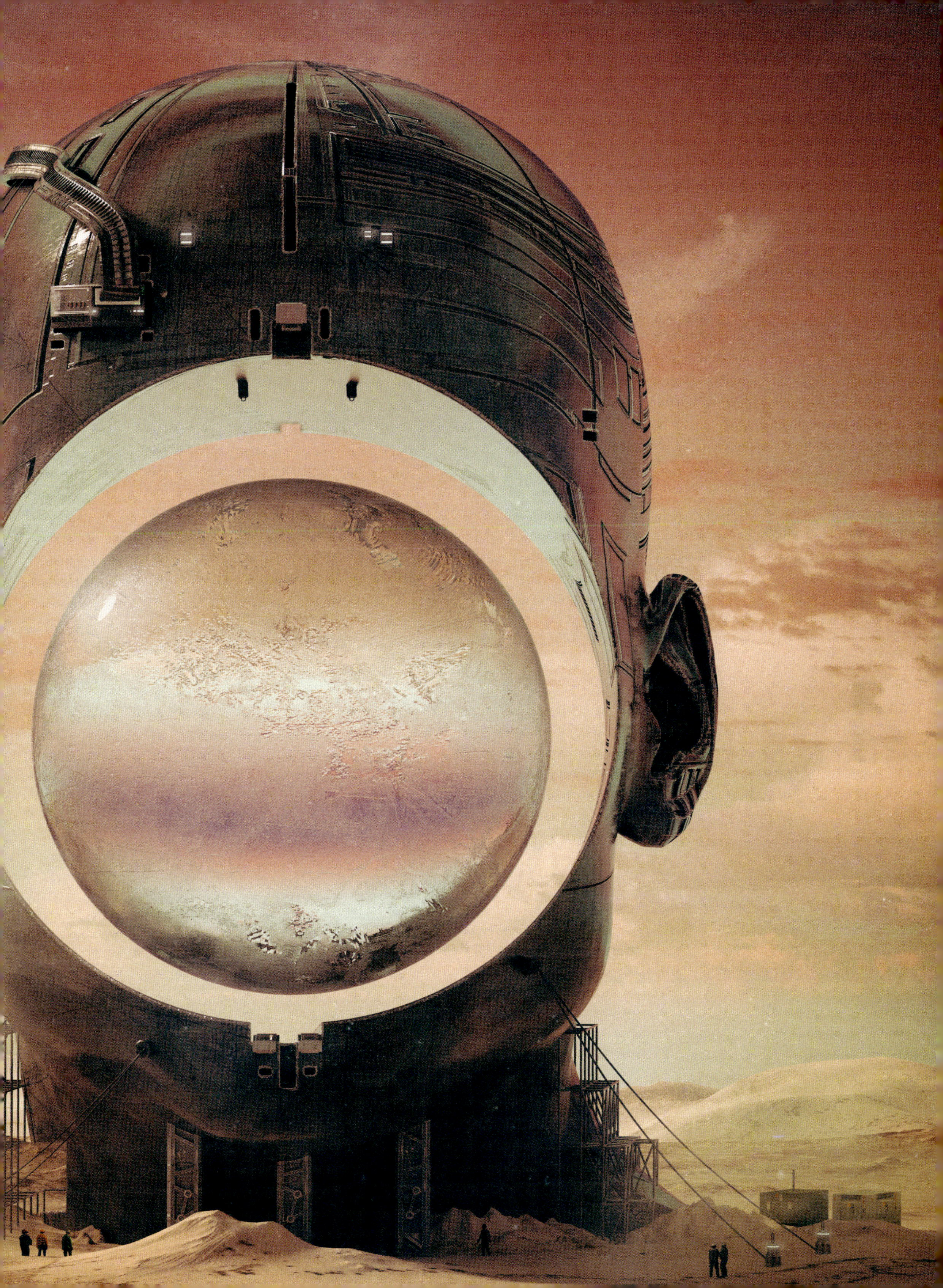

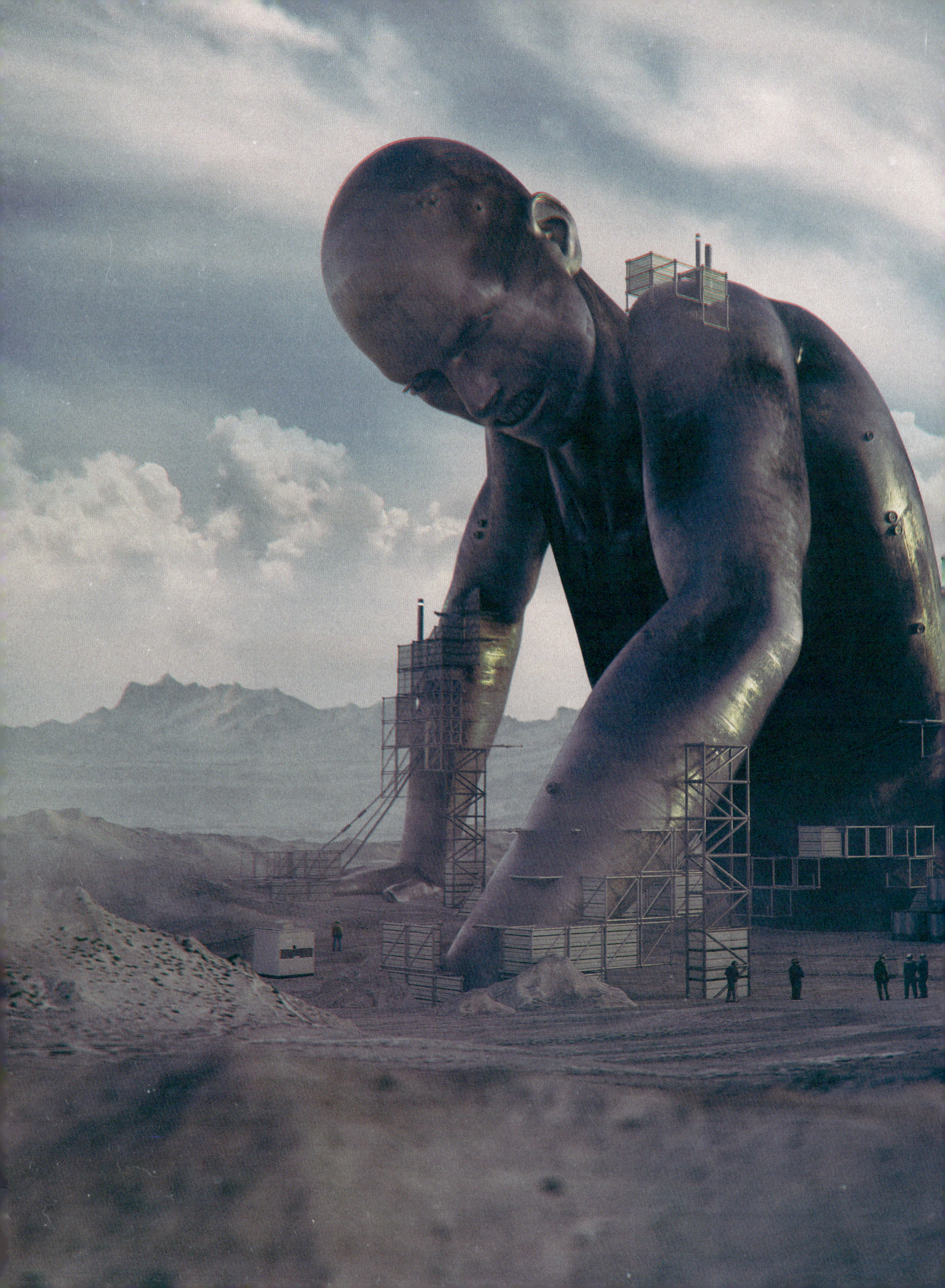

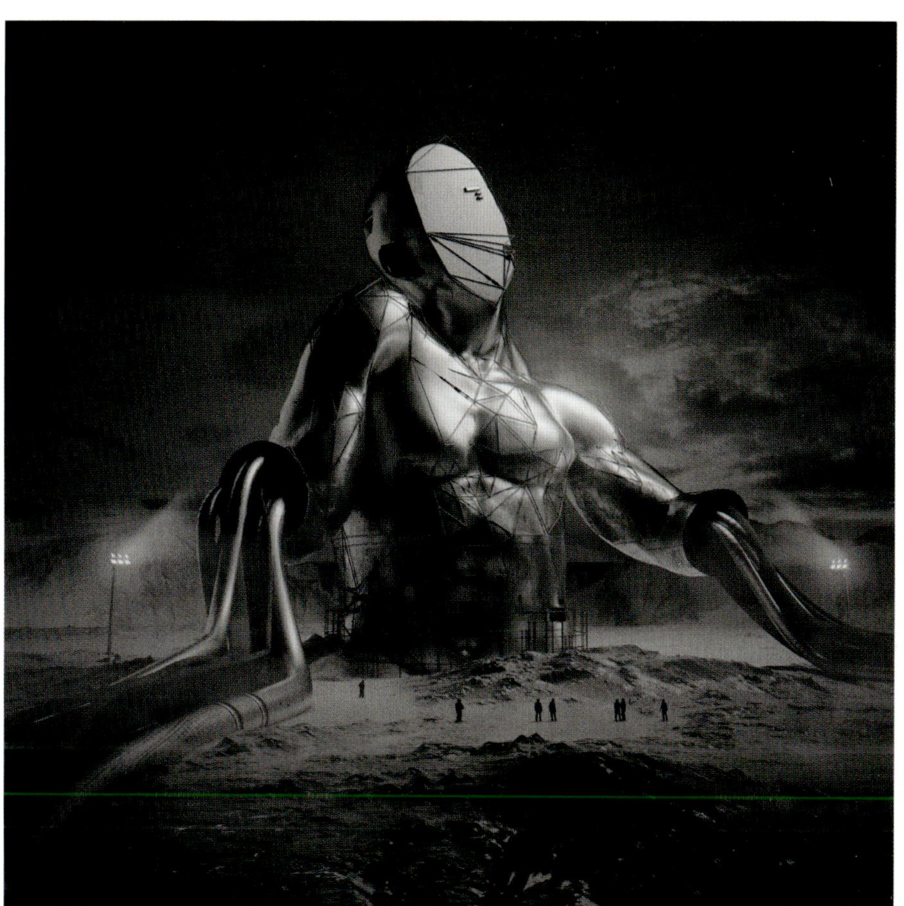

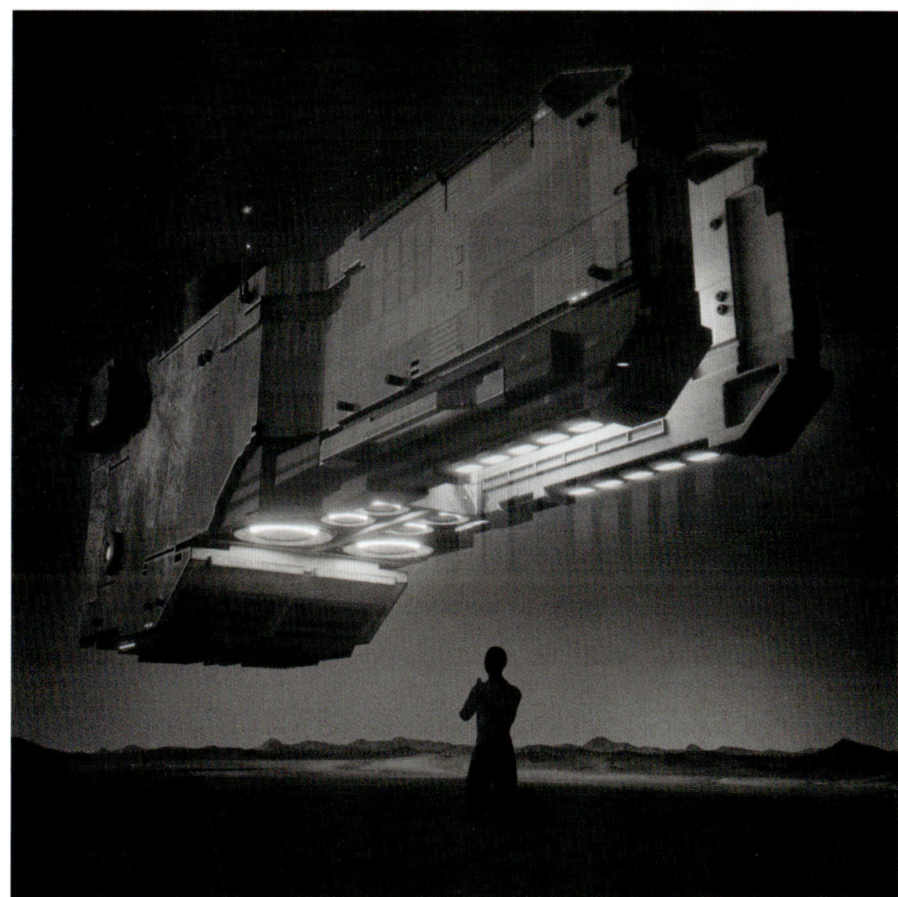

OPPOSITE PAGE
WOLF.SIX
01.25.2016

TOP
FLAT EARTH
01.28.2016

BOTTOM
MOTHERSHIP
11.06.2016

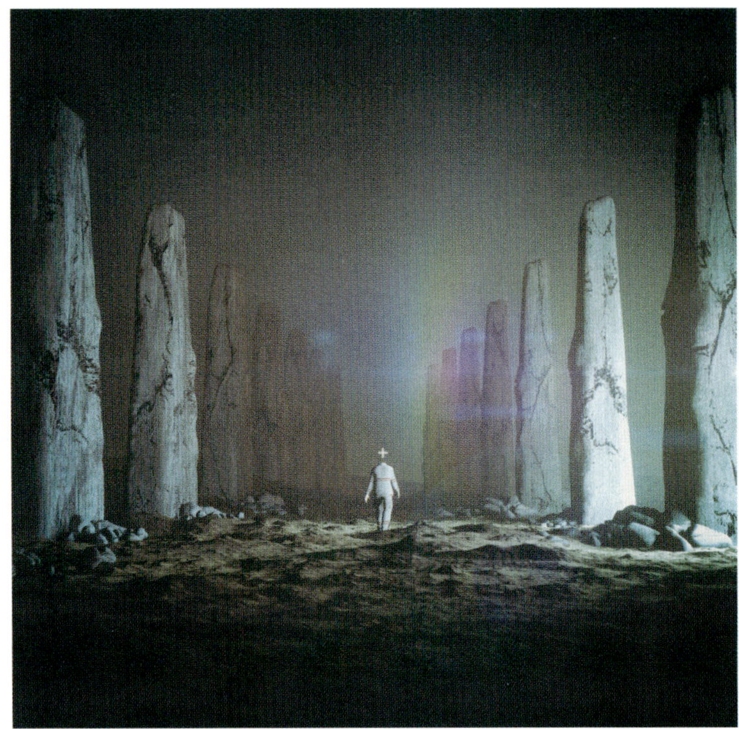

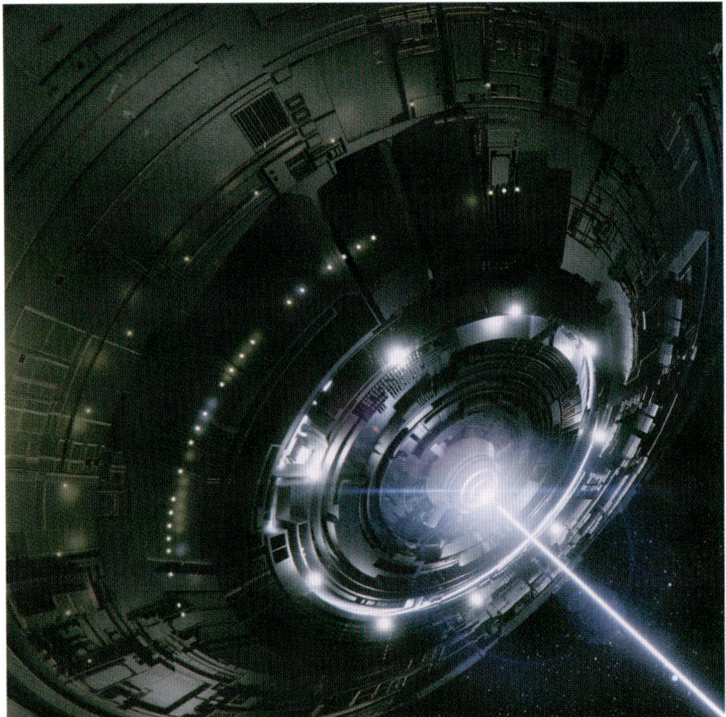

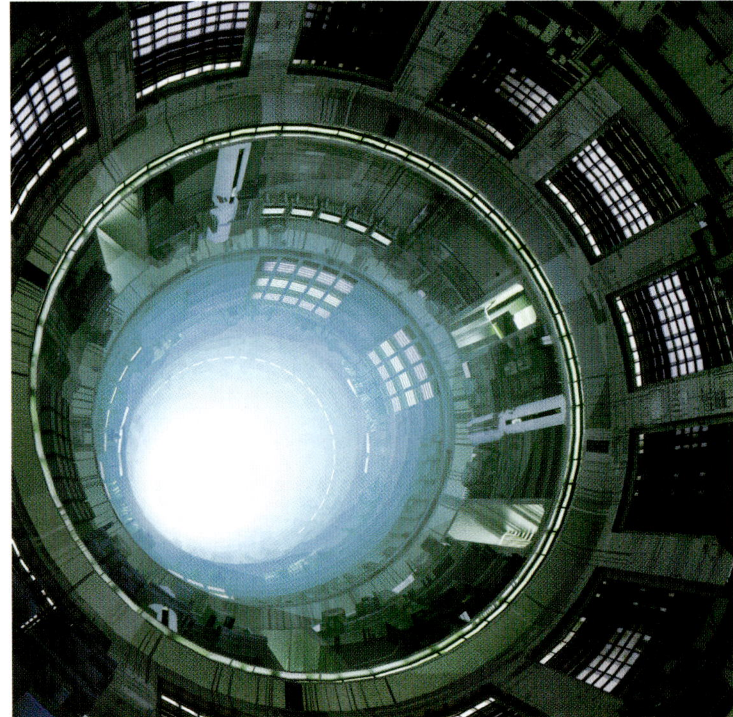

TOP LEFT
INCREMENTAL
01.10.2016

TOP RIGHT
INDUCTION
01.04.2016

BOTTOM LEFT
RESET
01.02.2016

BOTTOM RIGHT
ROT.SCALE
04.19.2016

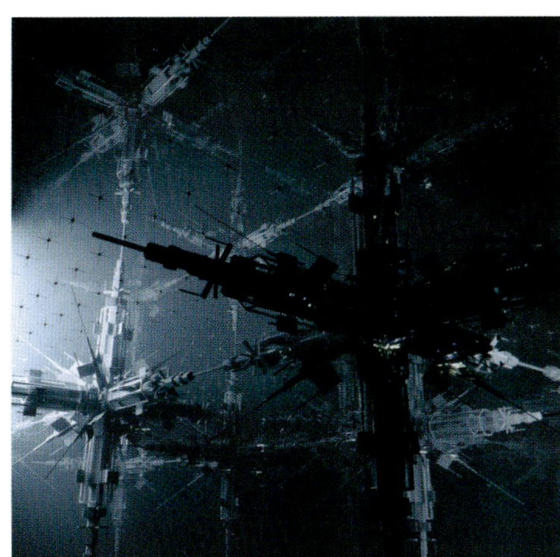

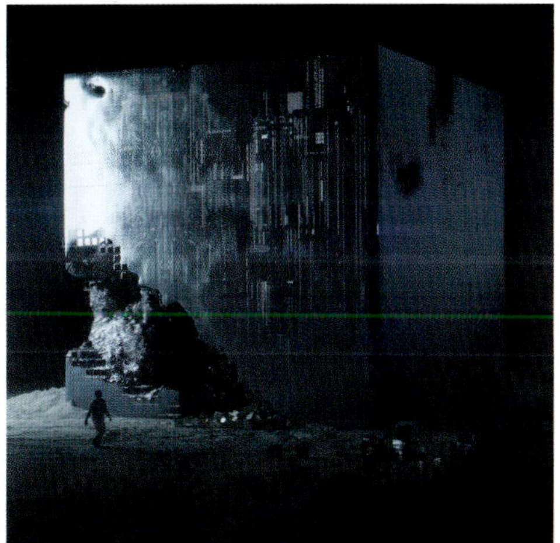

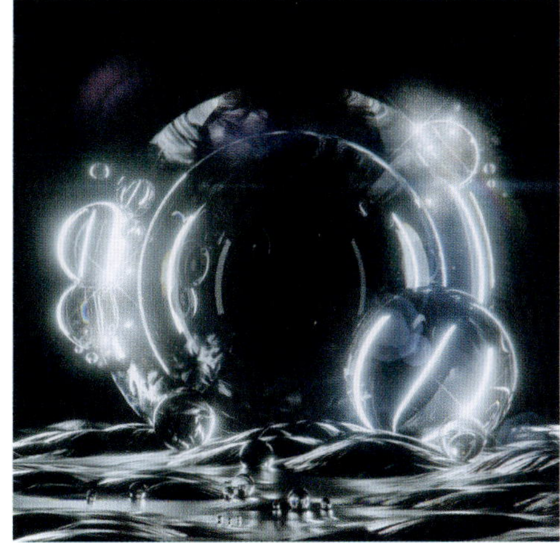

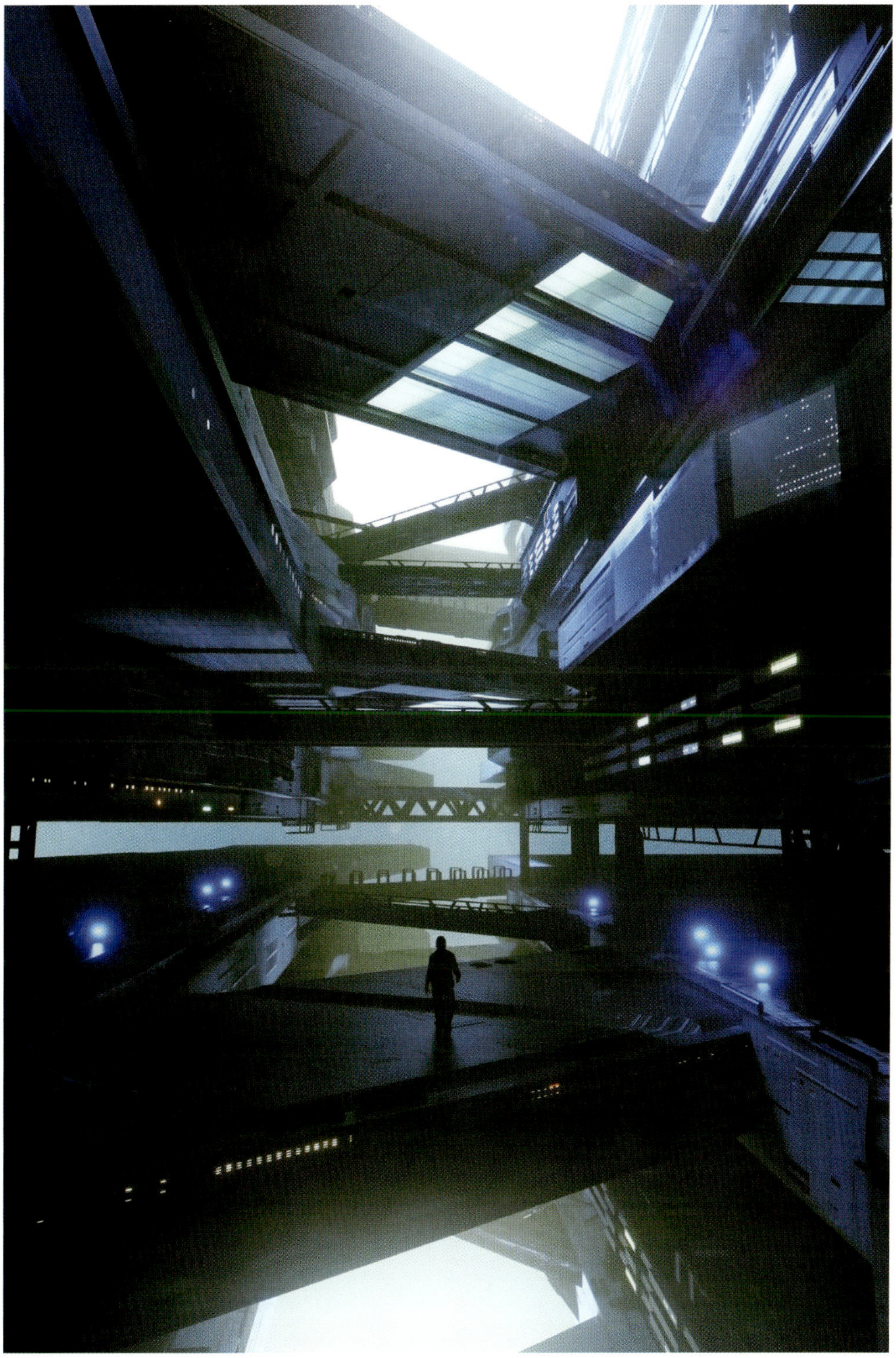

TOP LEFT
BASE.T10
12.18.2016

MIDDLE LEFT
DECAY BOX
01.12.2016

BOTTOM LEFT
ANGELDUST //
03.01.2016

RIGHT
OVERPASS
03.25.2016

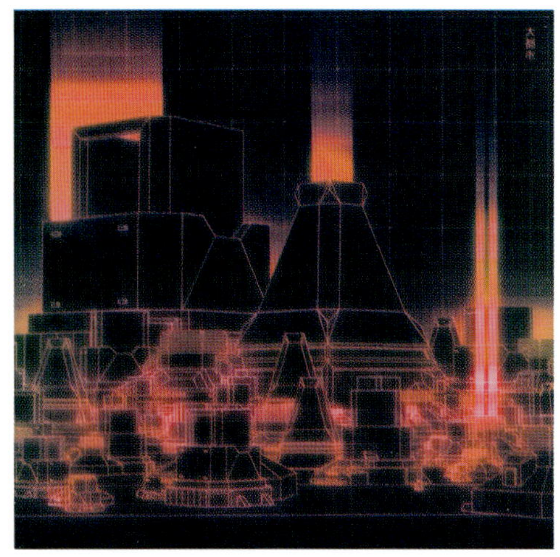

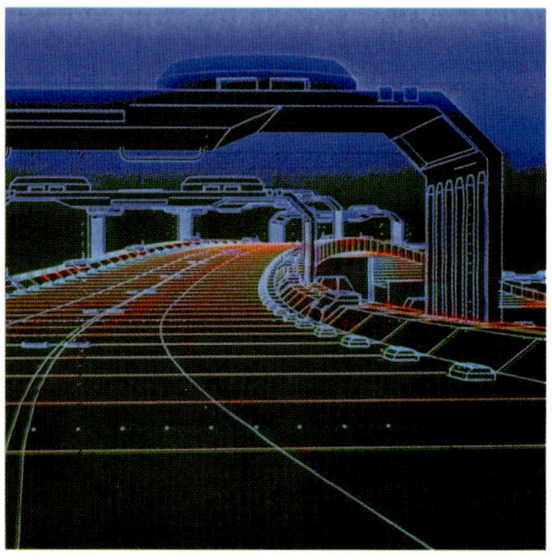

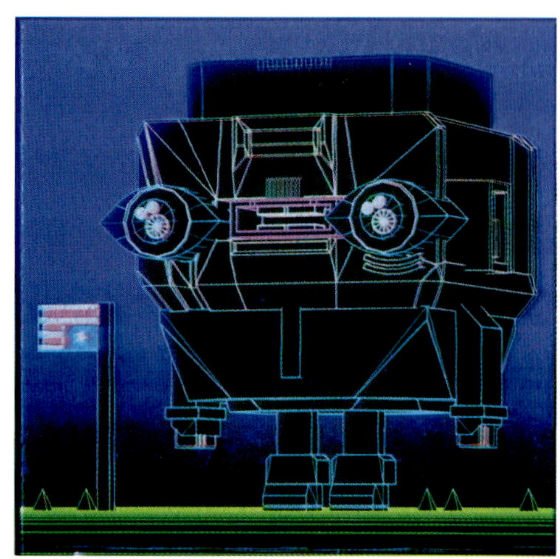

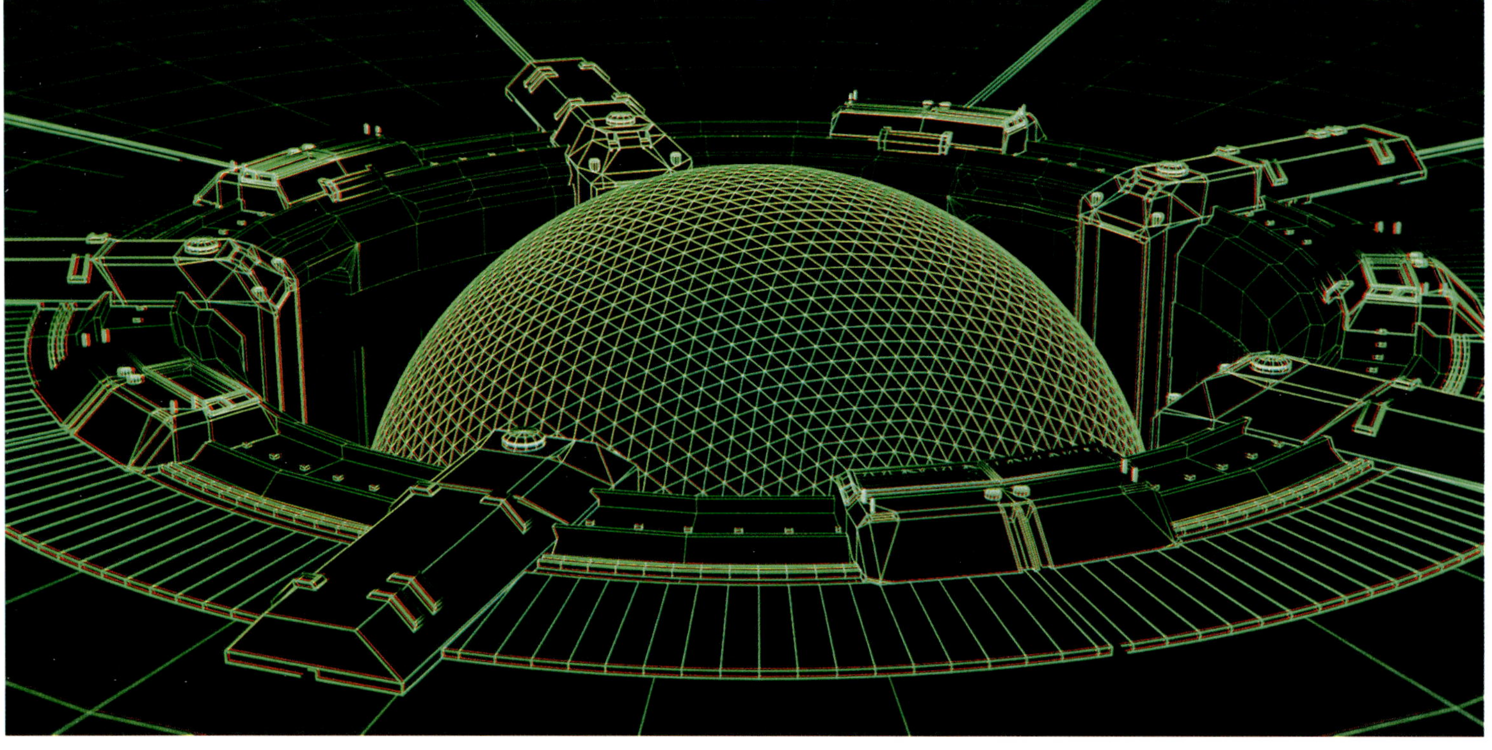

TOP LEFT
POLIS
02.18.2016

TOP MIDDLE
1981
01.15.2016

TOP RIGHT
SUPER MAJORITY
01.18.2016

BOTTOM
SKT
10.29.2016

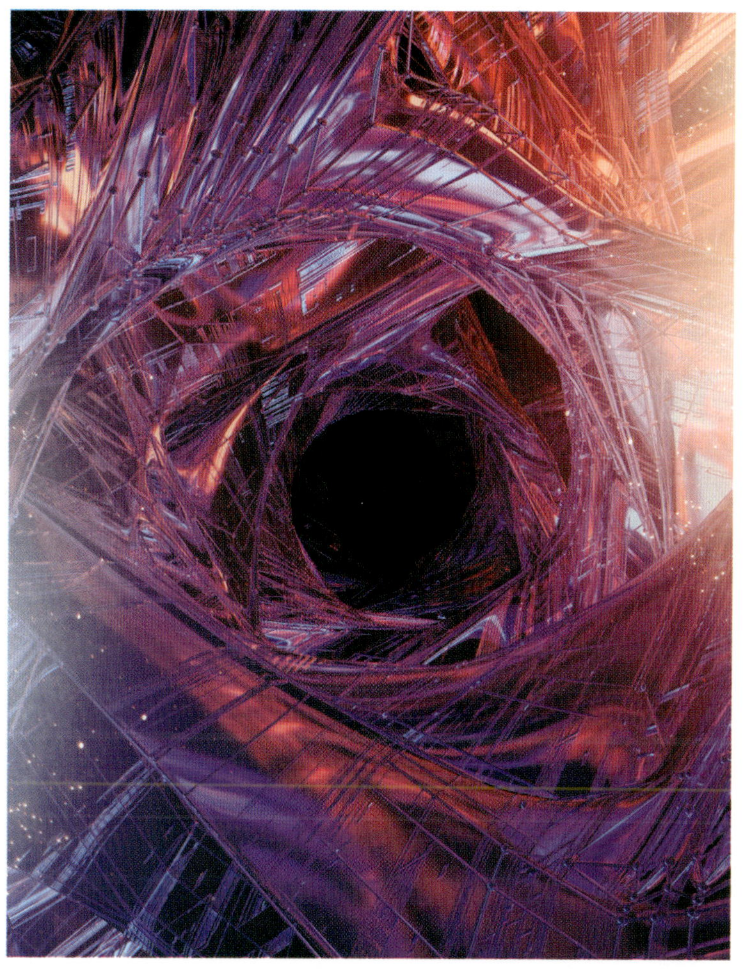

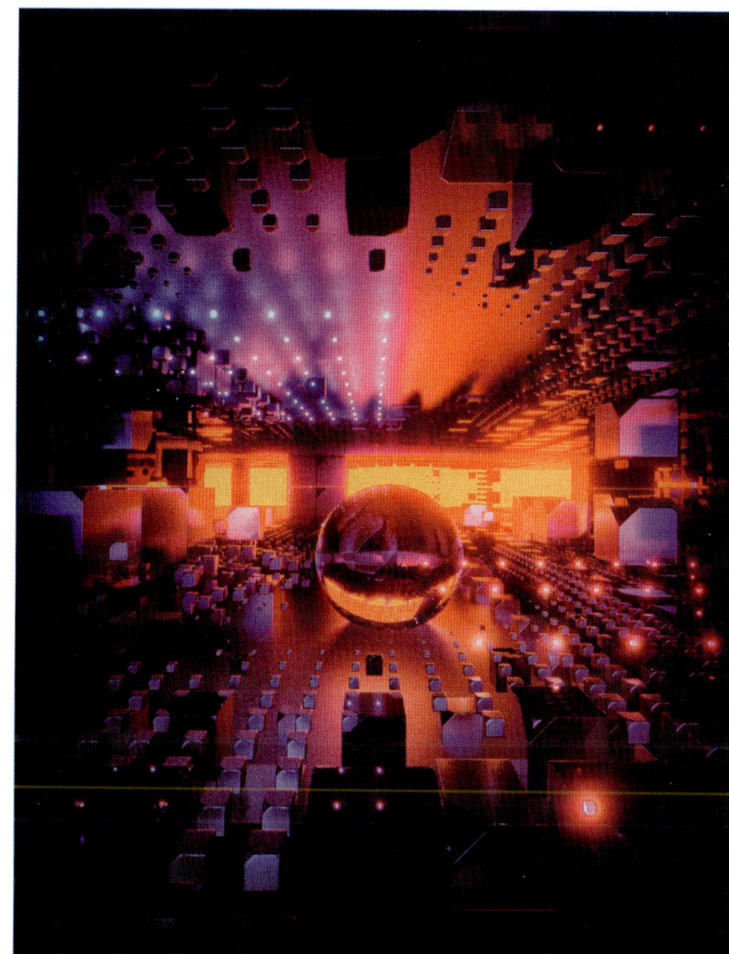

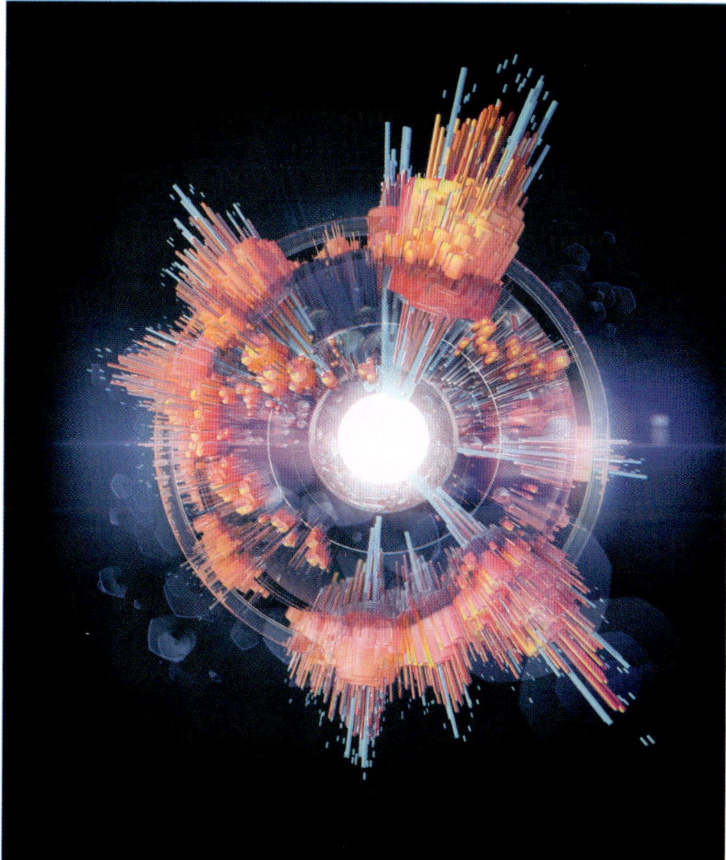

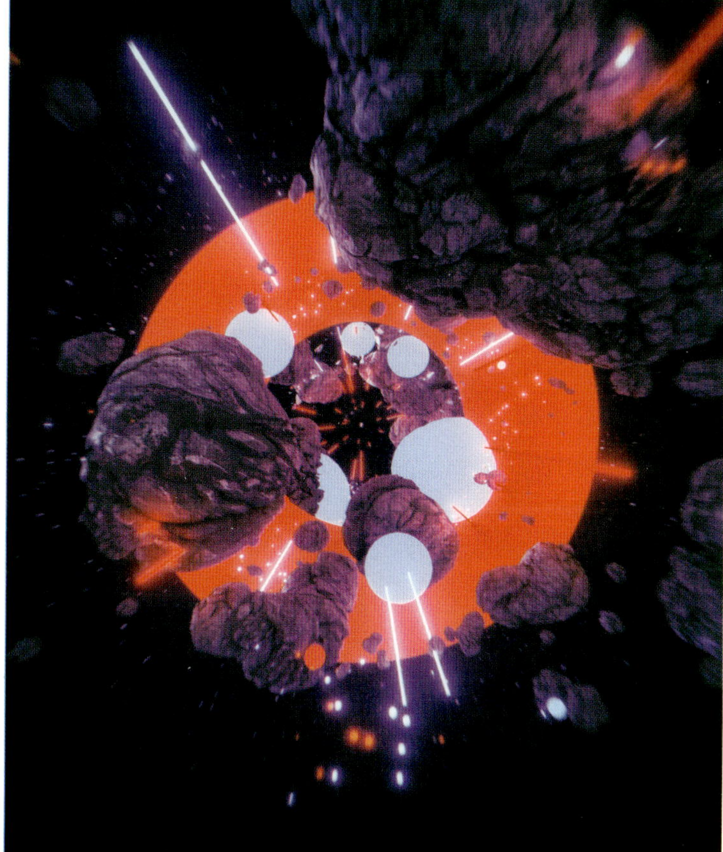

TOP LEFT
WRMMHOLE
04.09.2016

TOP RIGHT
ANOMALY1983
04.18.2016

BOTTOM LEFT
GLAXSPLODE
05.20.2016

BOTTOM RIGHT
STAR-BARF.990
05.22.2016

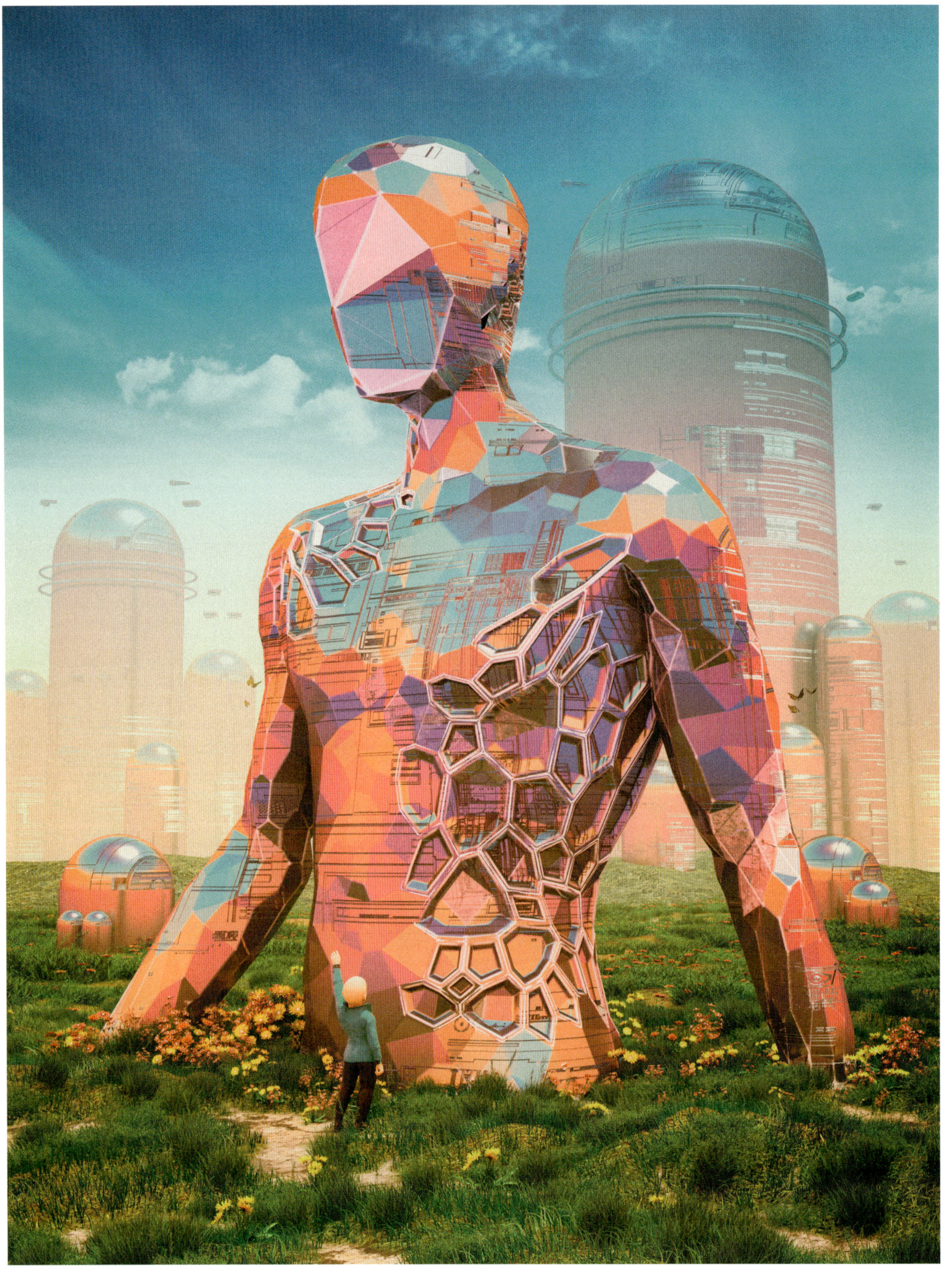

ABOVE

OUT OF THE RIFT
08.08.2016

OPPOSITE PAGE

LEFT VENTRICLE
02.05.2016

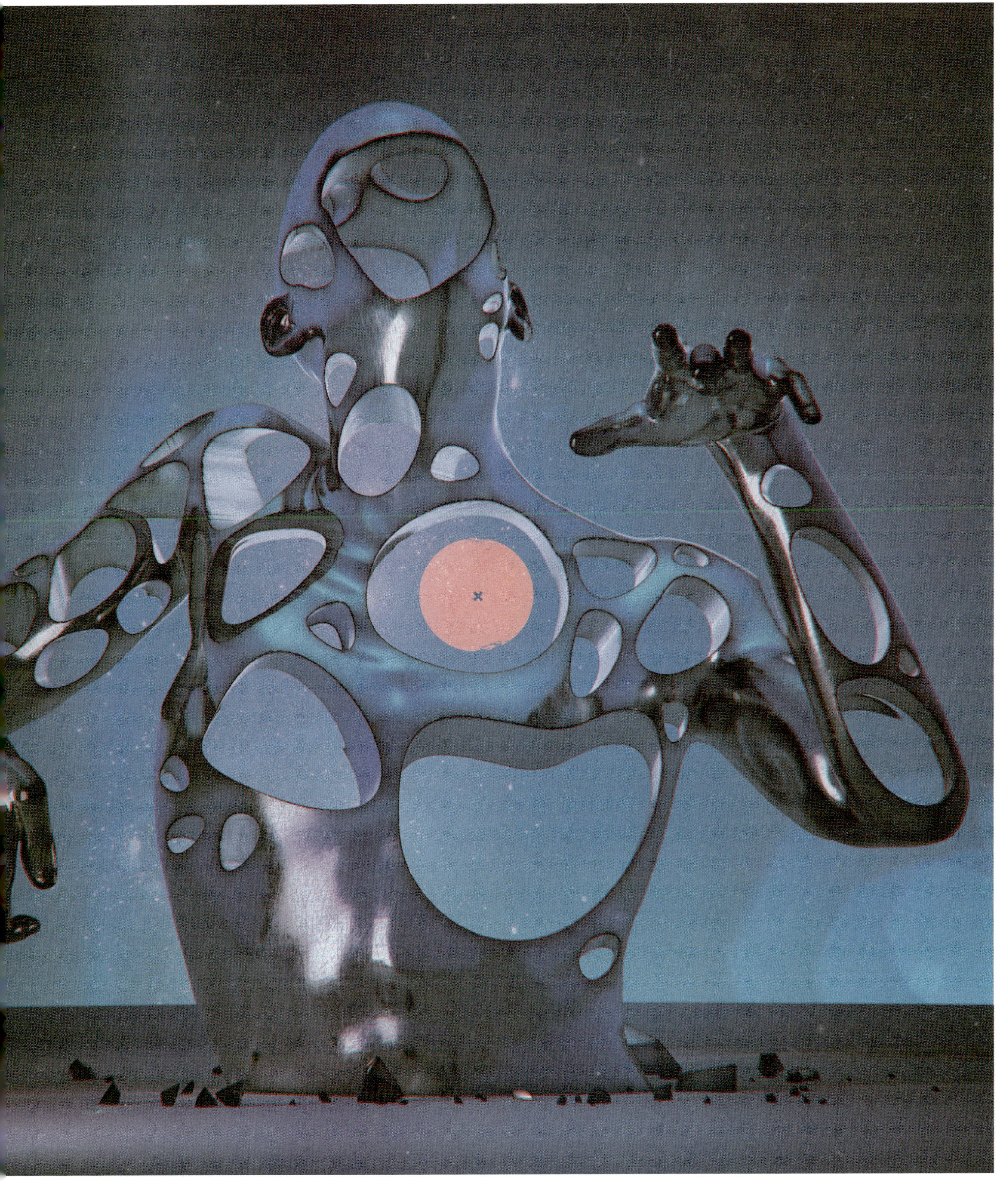

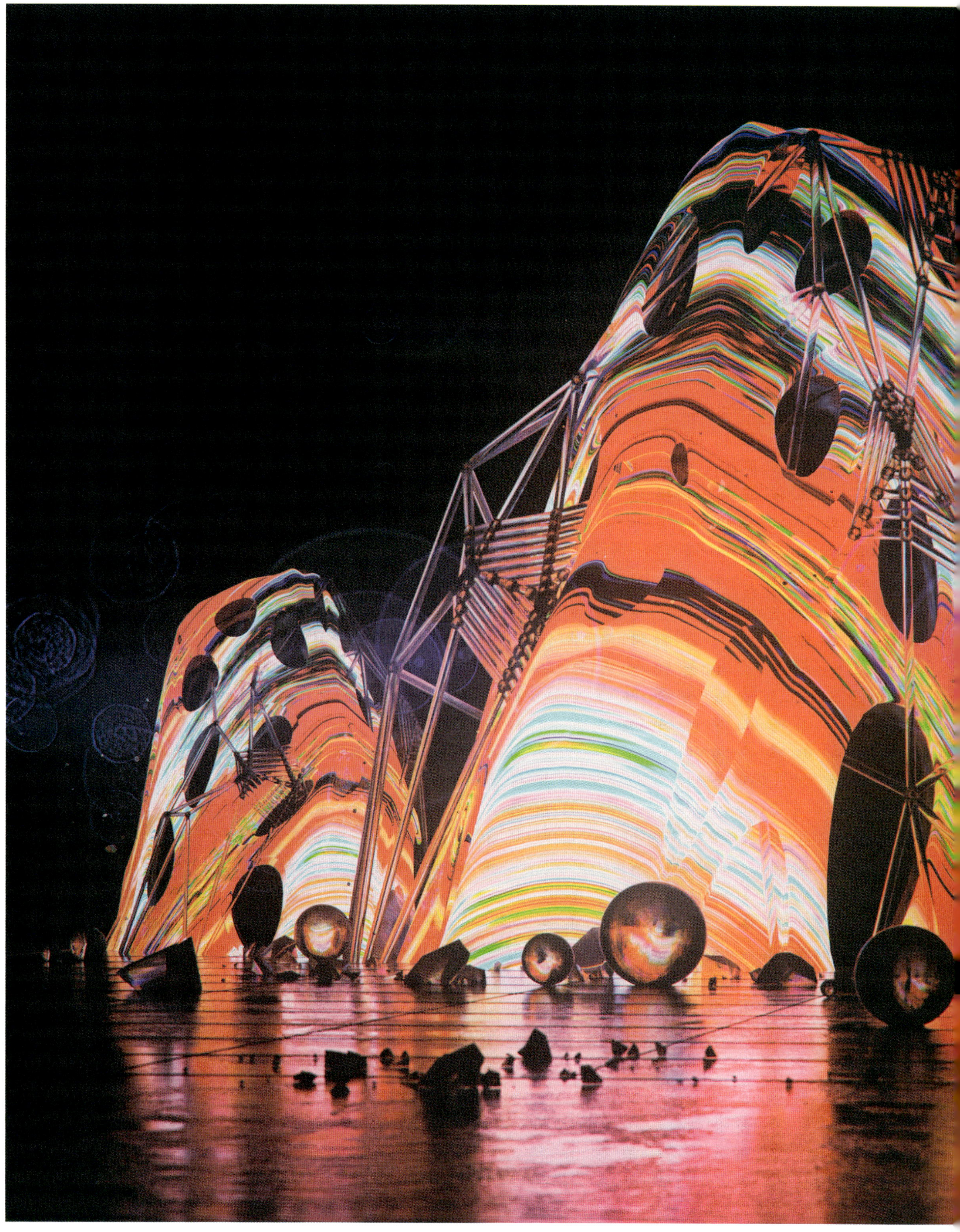

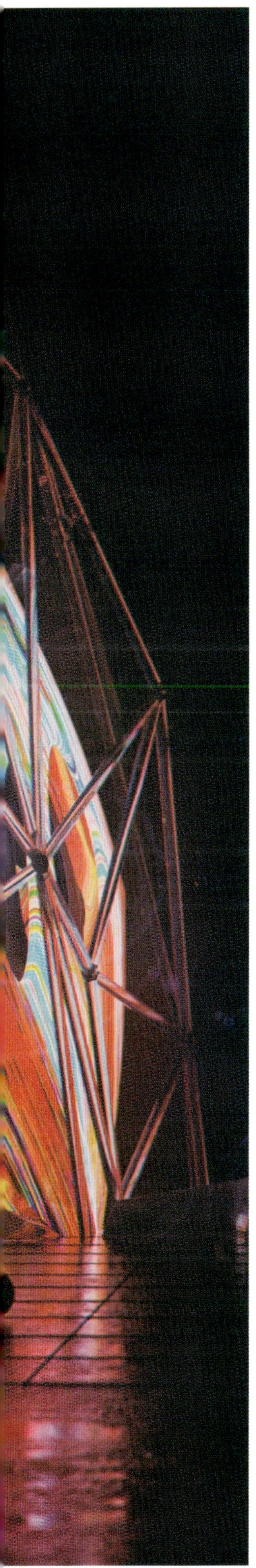

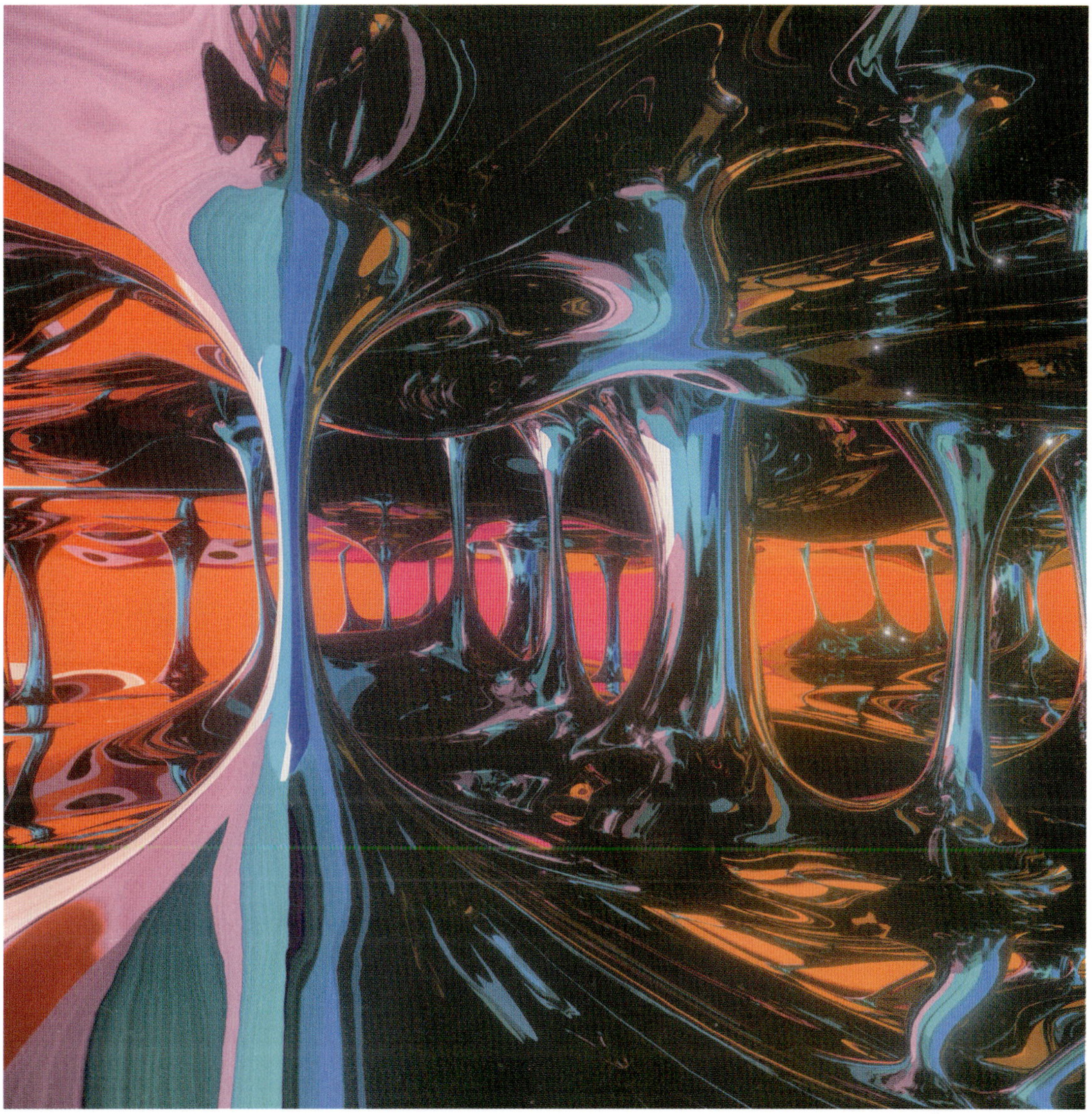

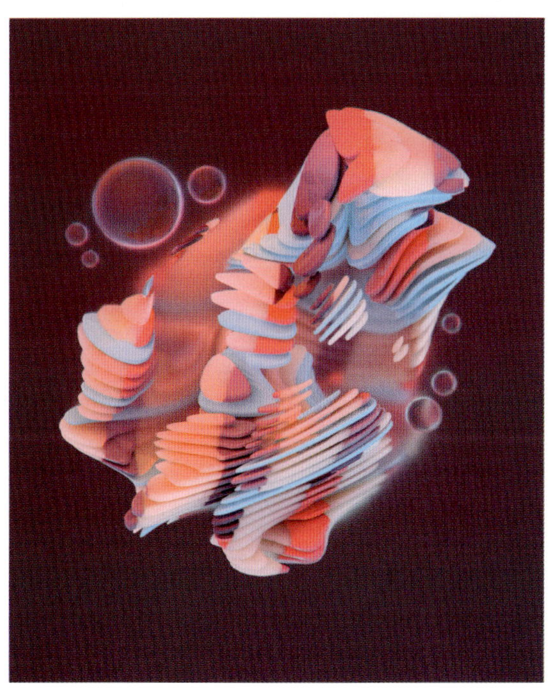

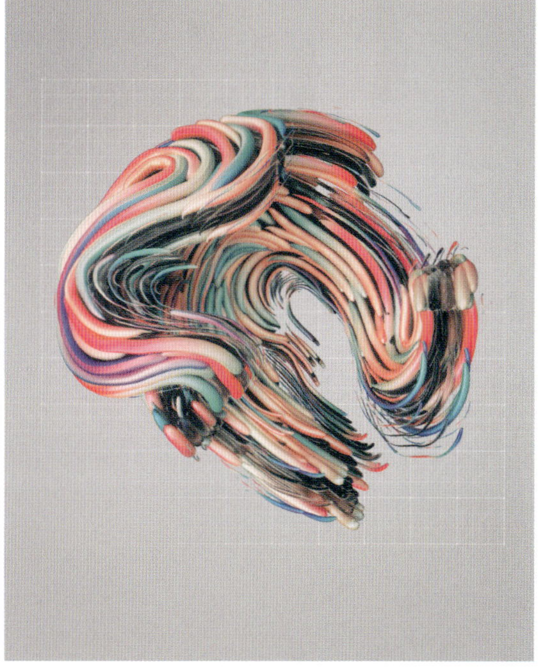

OPPOSITE PAGE
ADJUST
01.20.2016

TOP
SLOWDRIP
09.24.2016

BOTTOM LEFT
OPAQQQ
09.05.2016

BOTTOM RIGHT
VIVE.02
09.01.2016

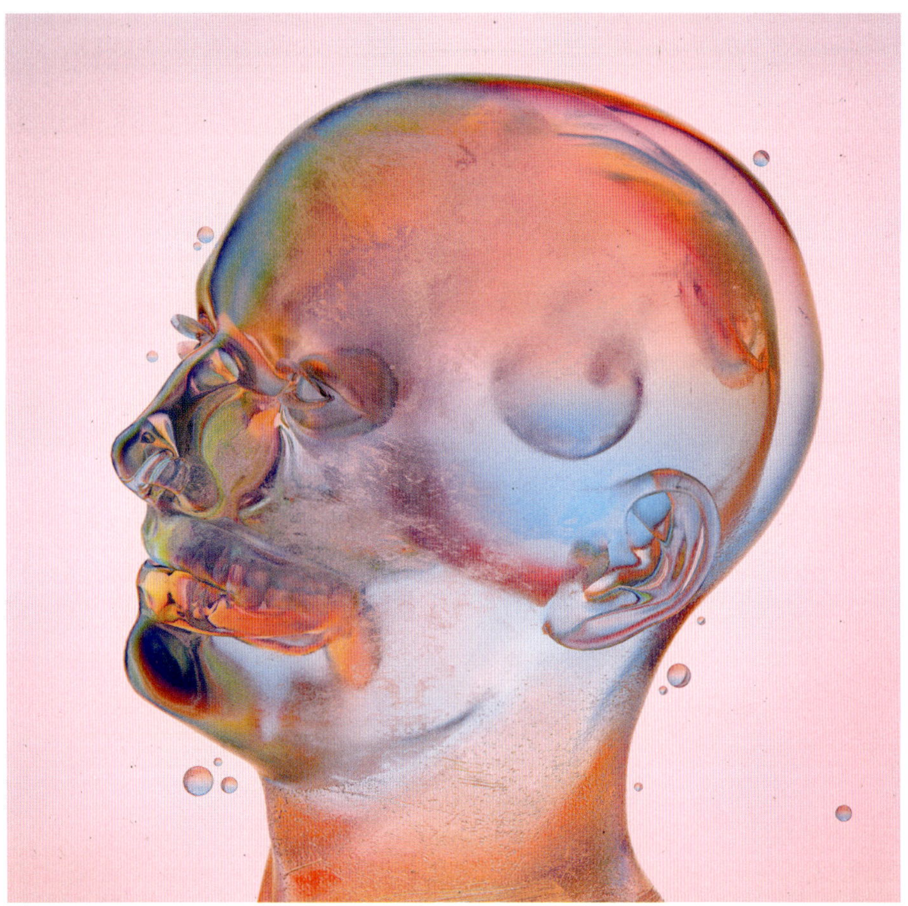

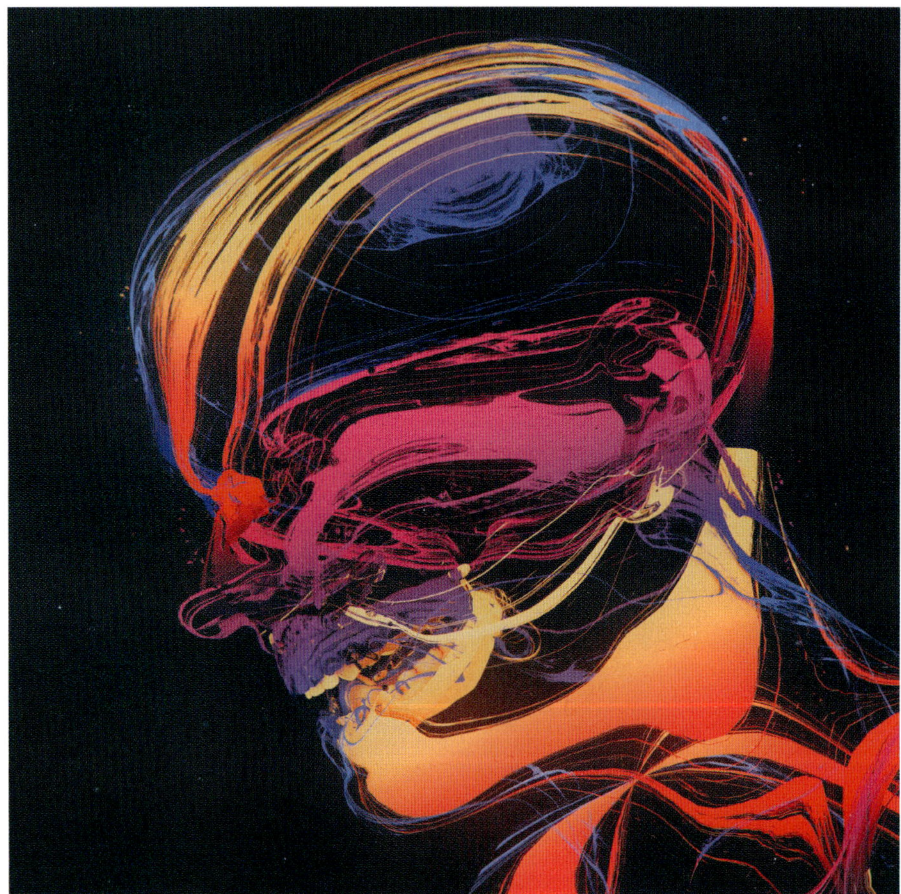

TOP
URANIUMFACE
04.15.2016

BOTTOM
HEADSWIM
03.03.2016

OPPOSITE PAGE
FANTASTIC.PSYB
03.14.2016

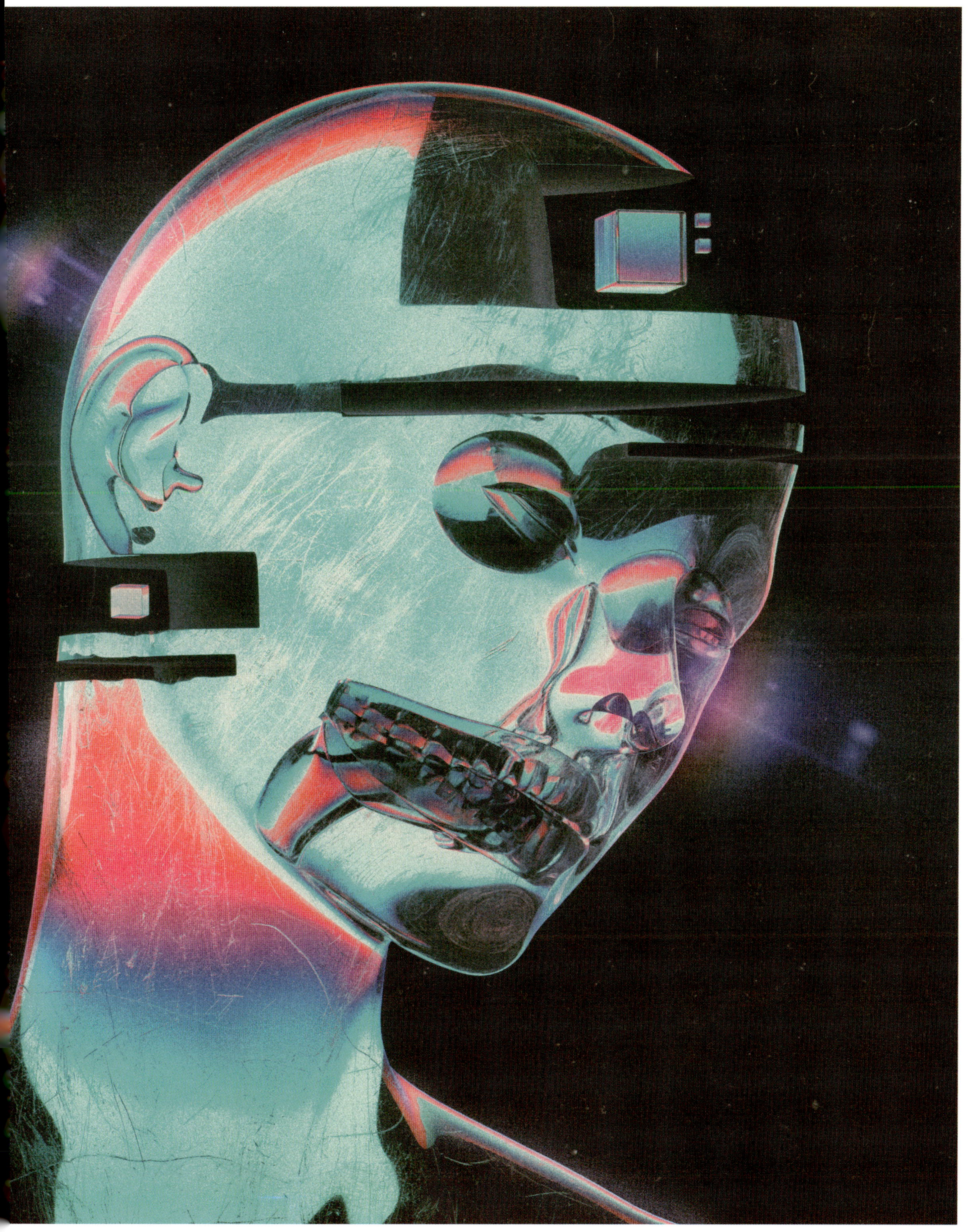

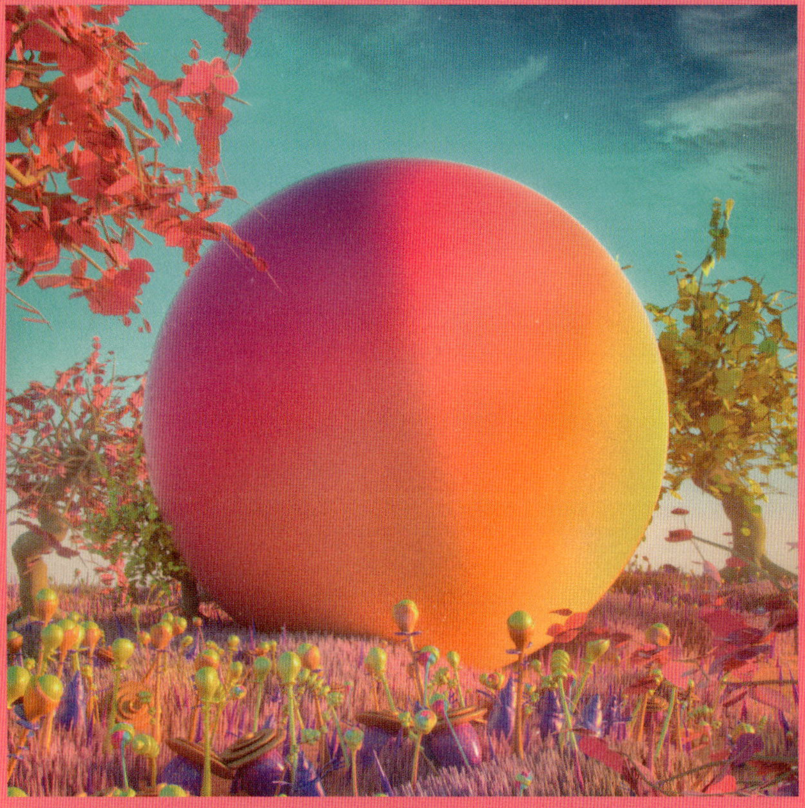

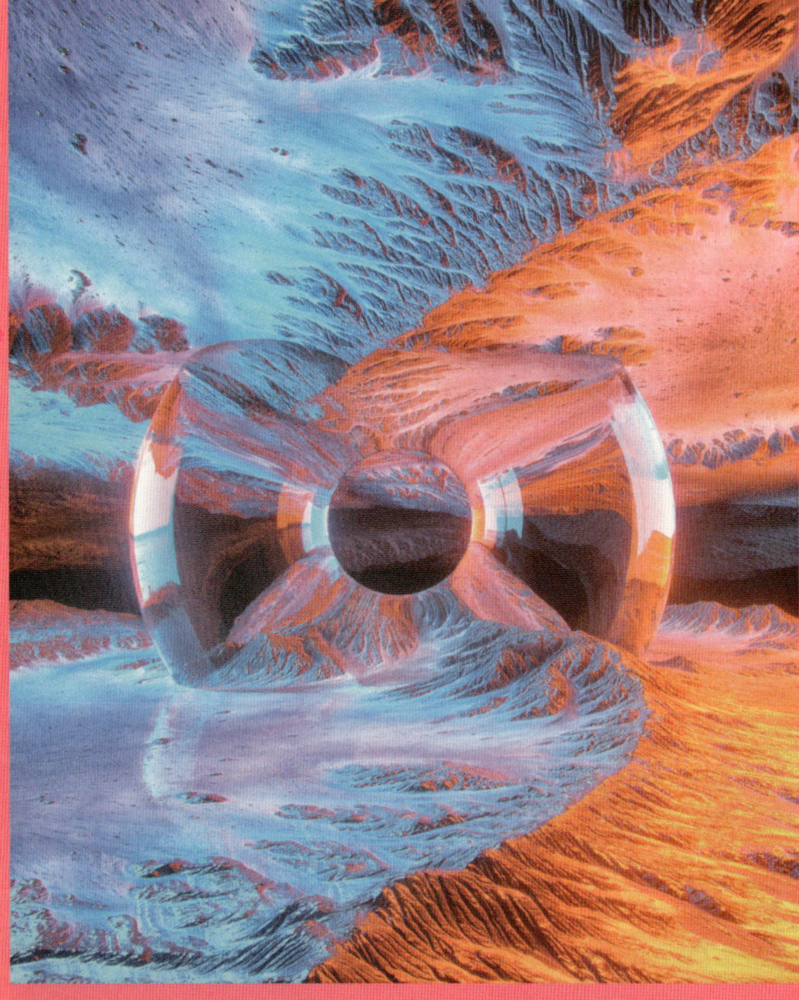

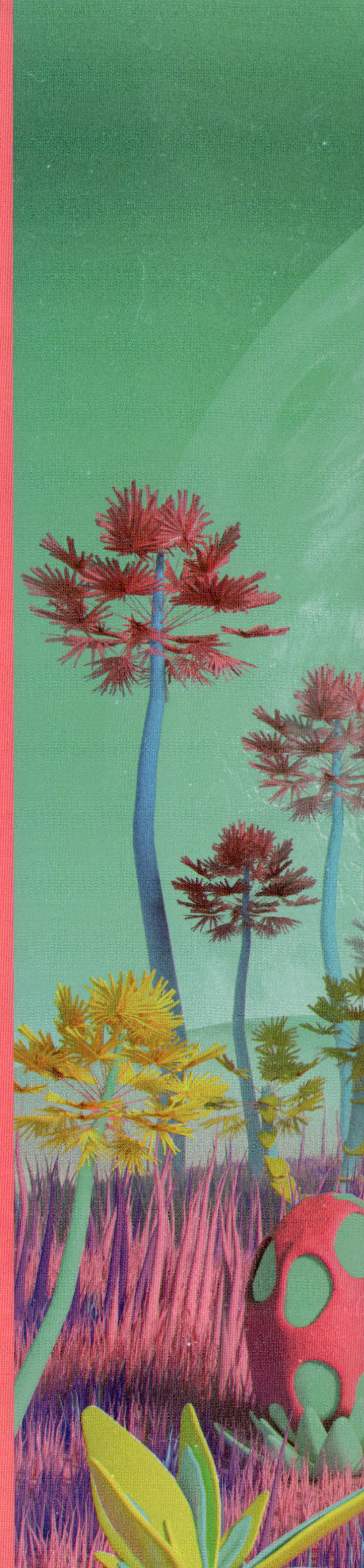

TOP
GYUMBALL
05.26.2016

BOTTOM
HOT / COLD
10.26.2016

OPPOSITE PAGE
MELAU.FIVE
06.05.2016

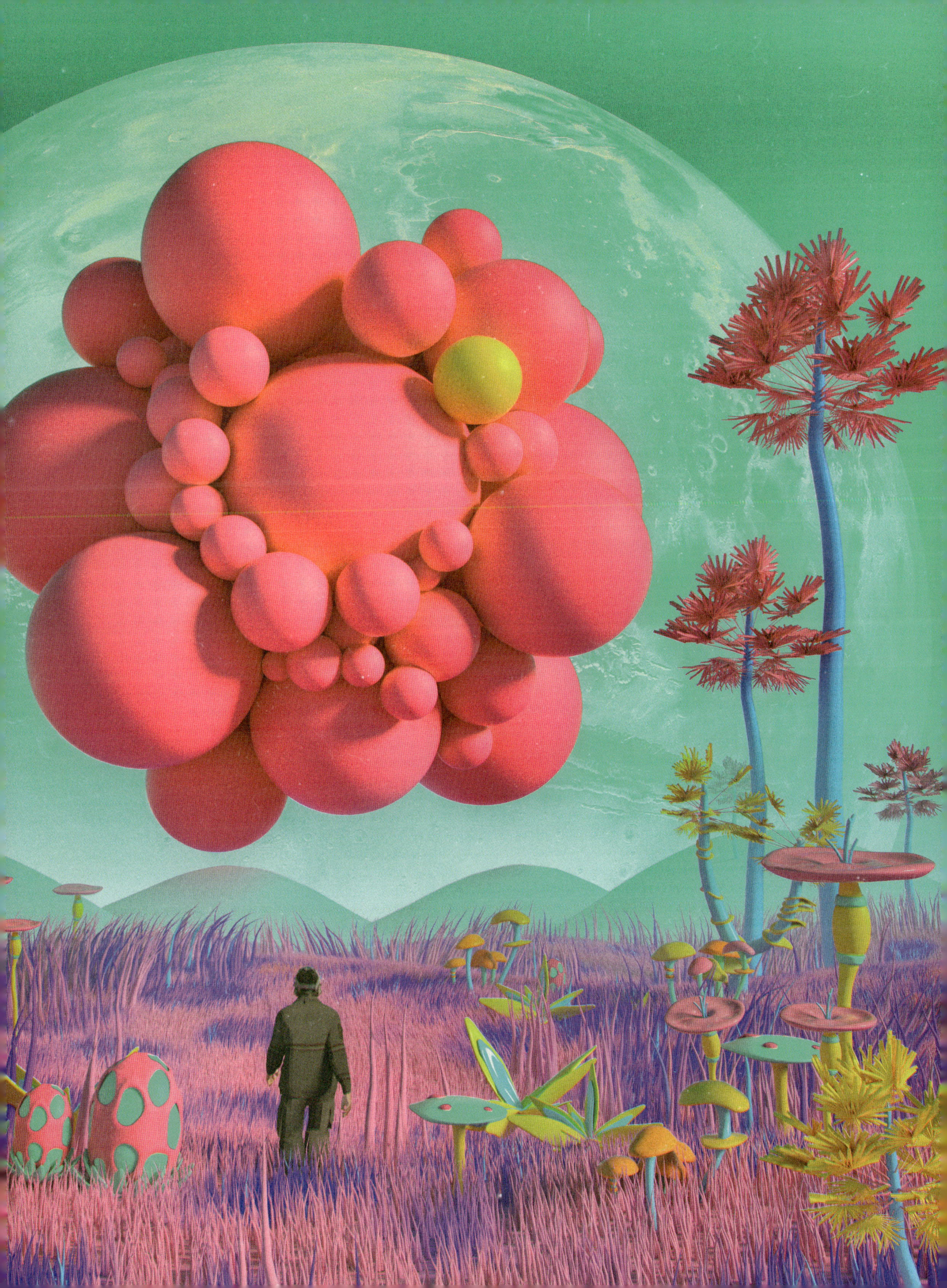

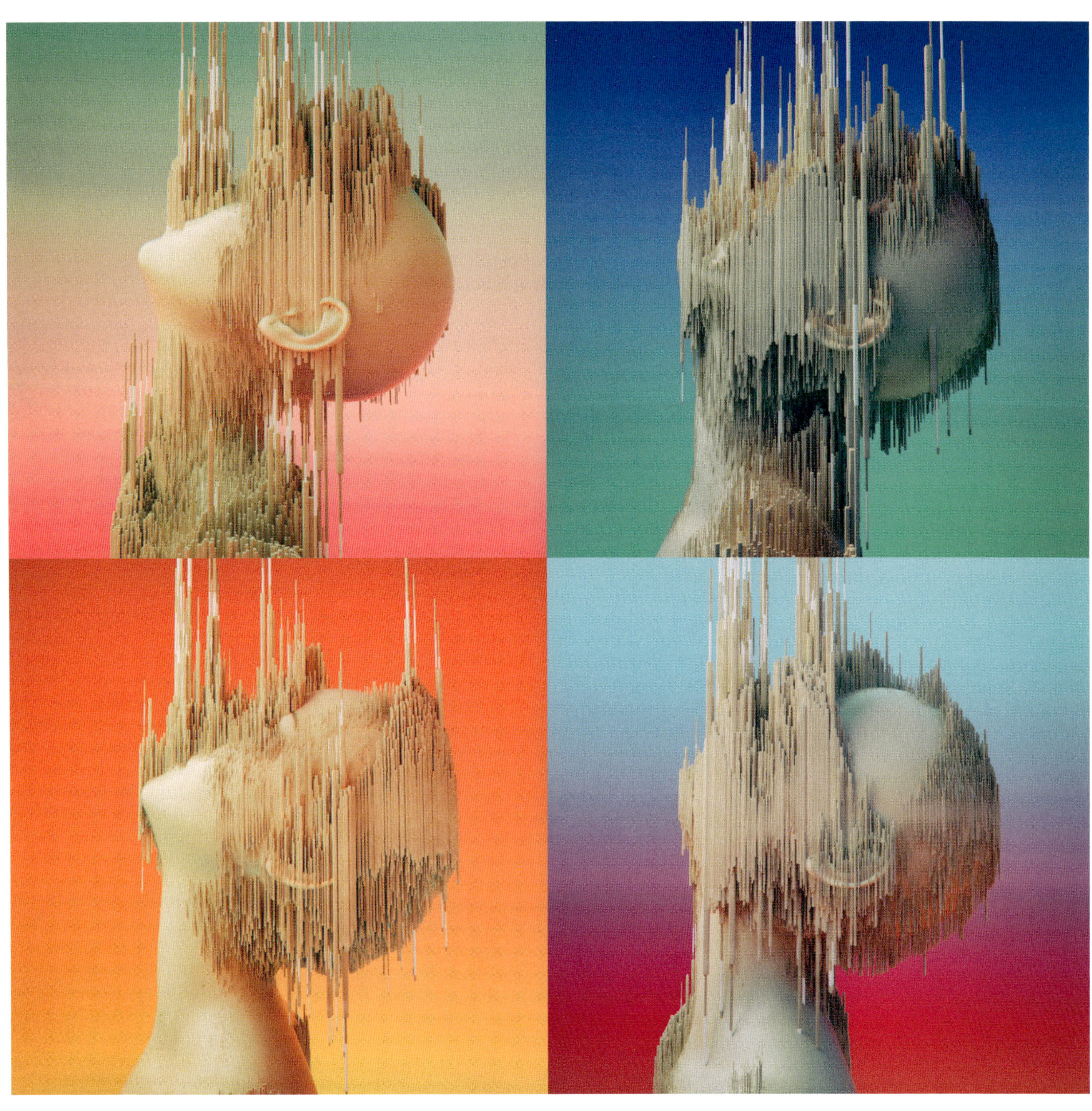

ABOVE
WHO ARE YOU?
06.09.2016

OPPOSITE PAGE, TOP
SAME INSIDES
06.17.2016

OPPOSITE PAGE, BOTTOM
WOBBLY
06.18.2016

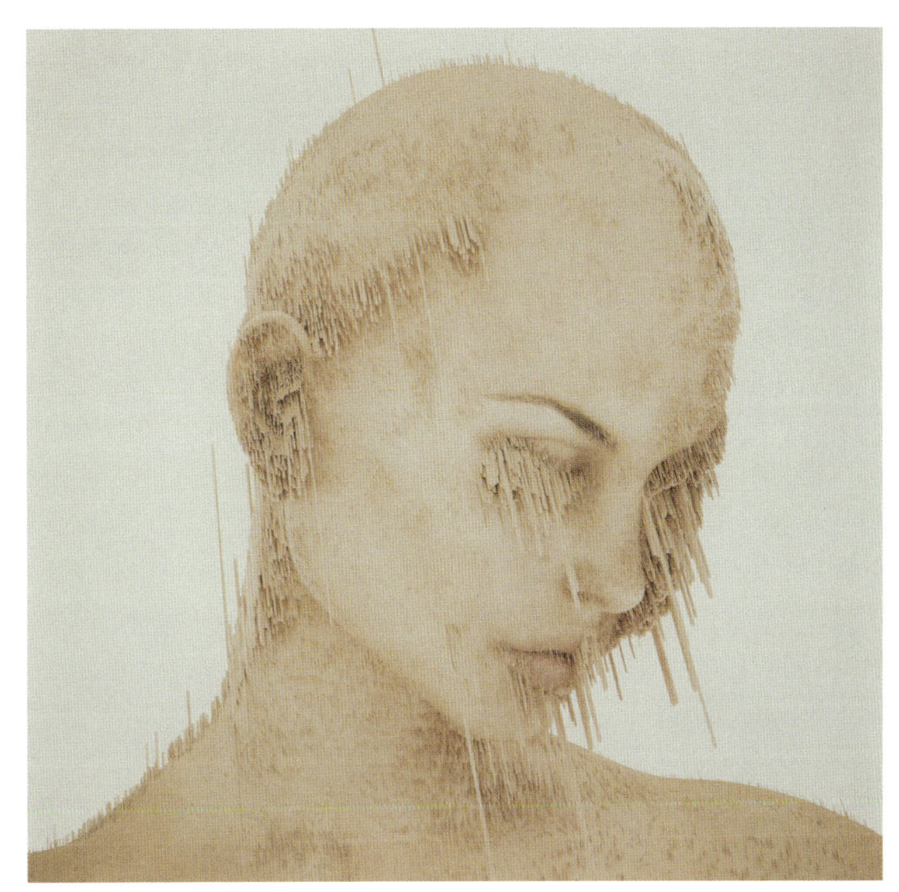

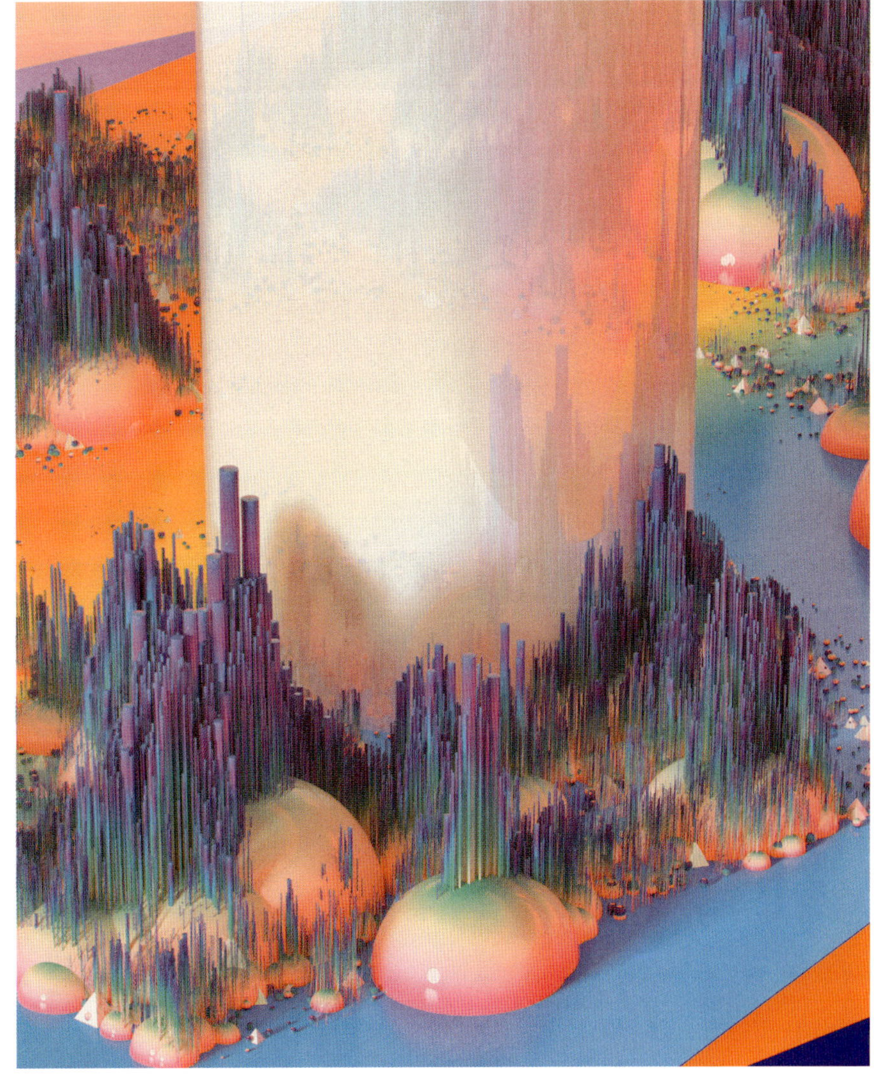

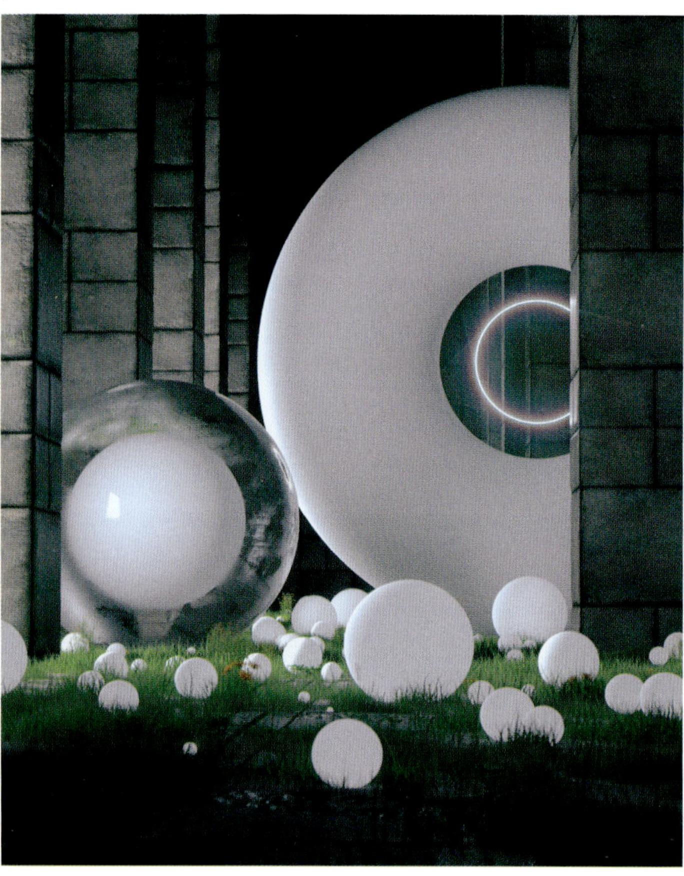

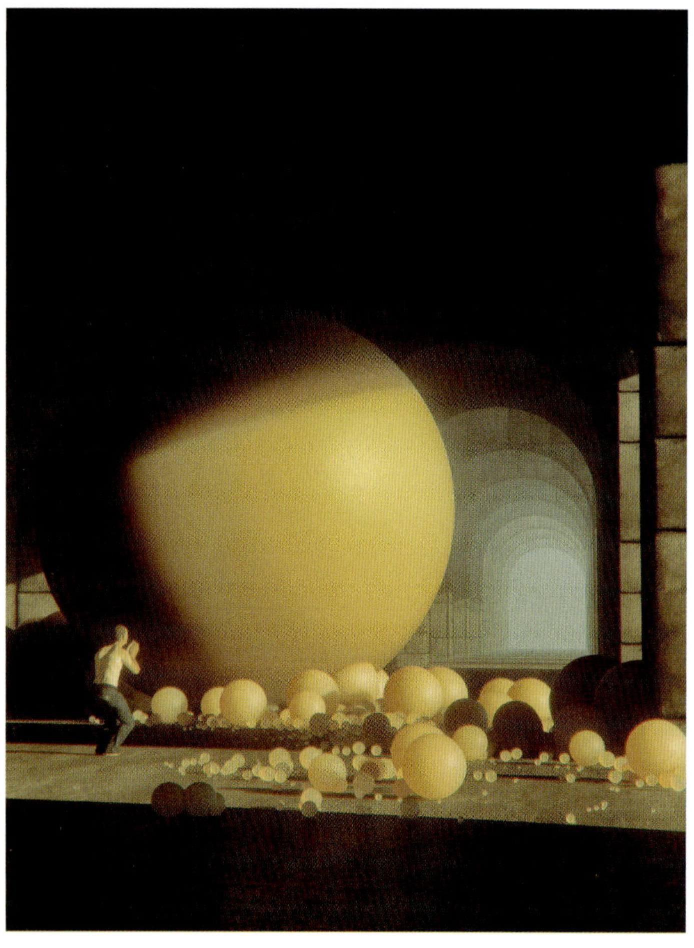

TOP
SPLOWTT
09.02.2016

BOTTOM
SKINBALL WORSHIP
06.15.2016

OPPOSITE PAGE
ZERO
06.12.2016

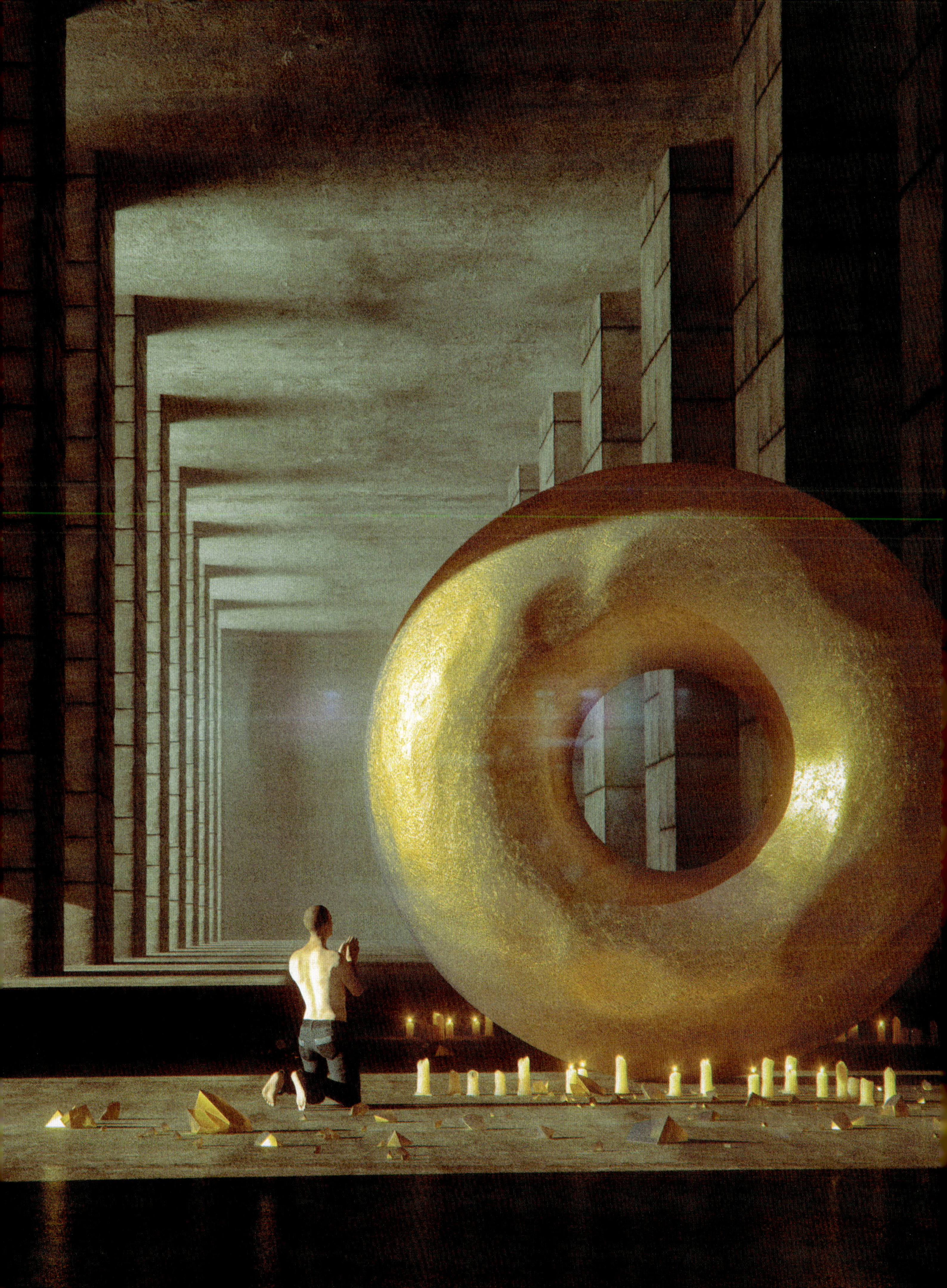

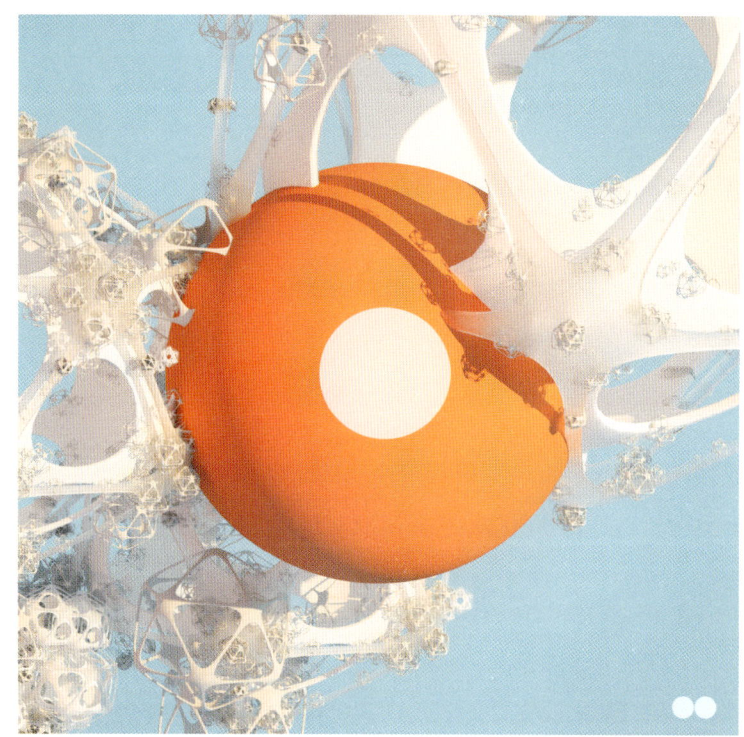

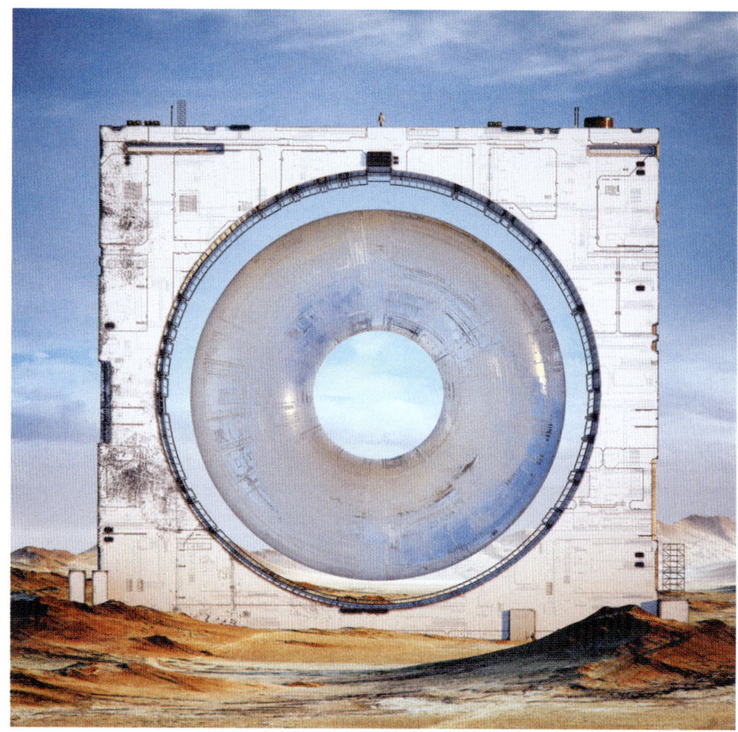

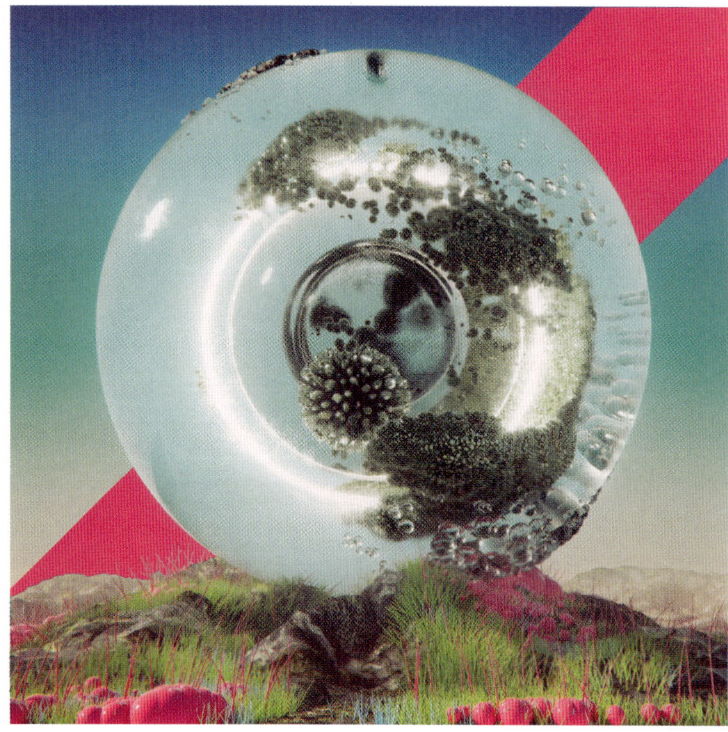

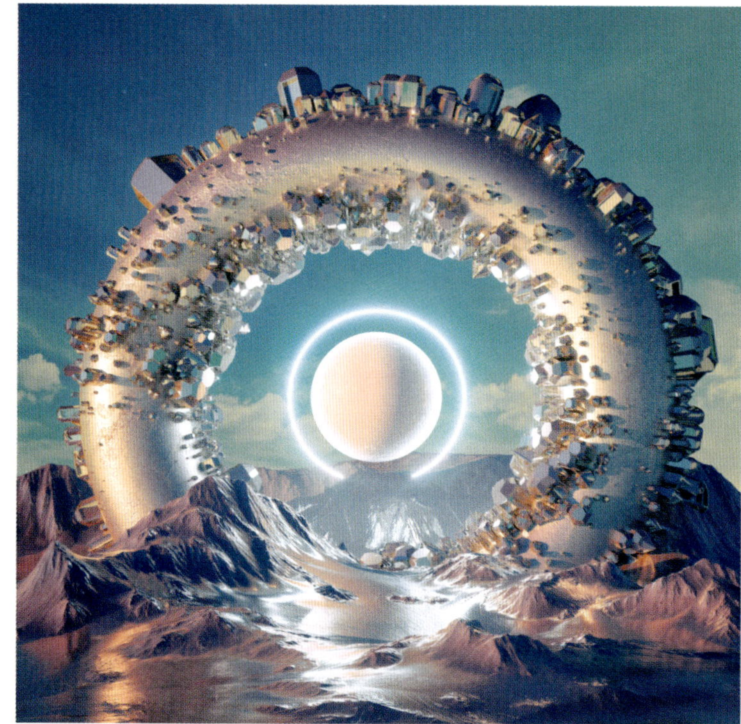

TOP LEFT
RECURSIVE.ZYGOTE
06.07.2016

TOP RIGHT
OOO.OOO
04.10.2016

BOTTOM LEFT
SPORE.T
06.10.2016

BOTTOM RIGHT
BLASTTT
06.08.2016

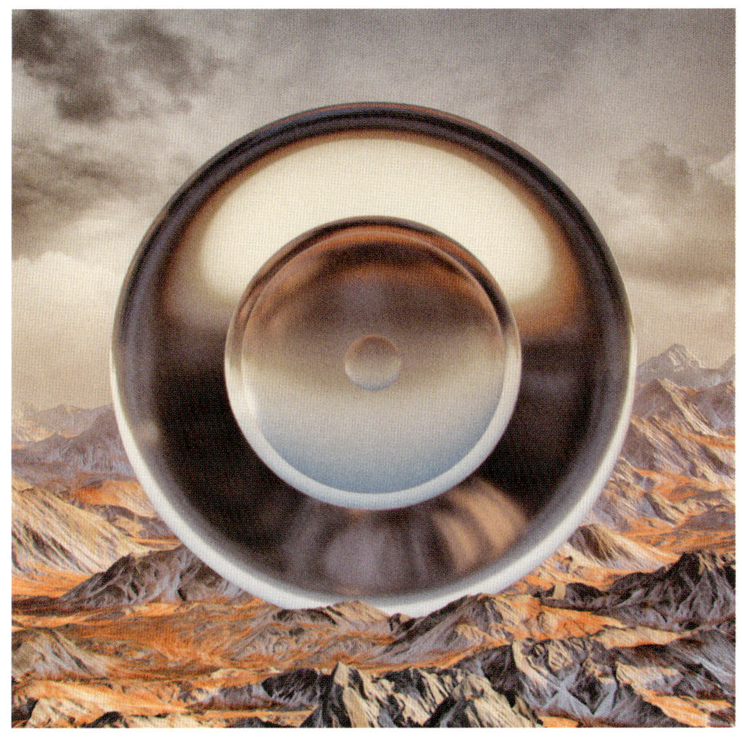

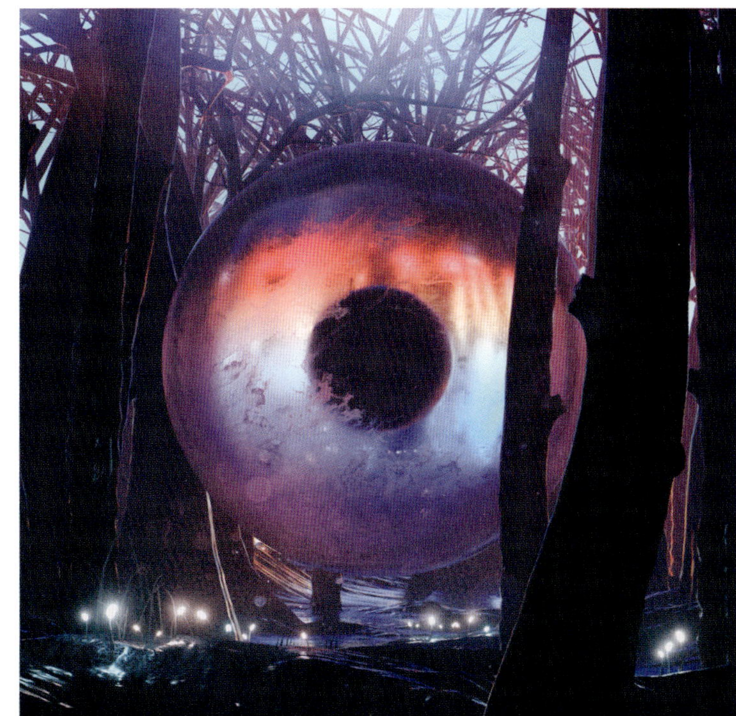

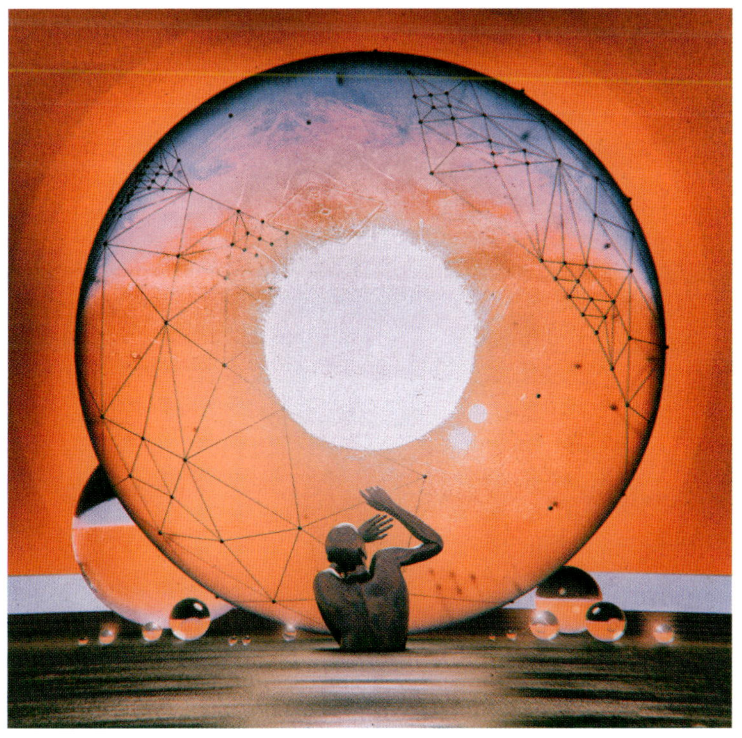

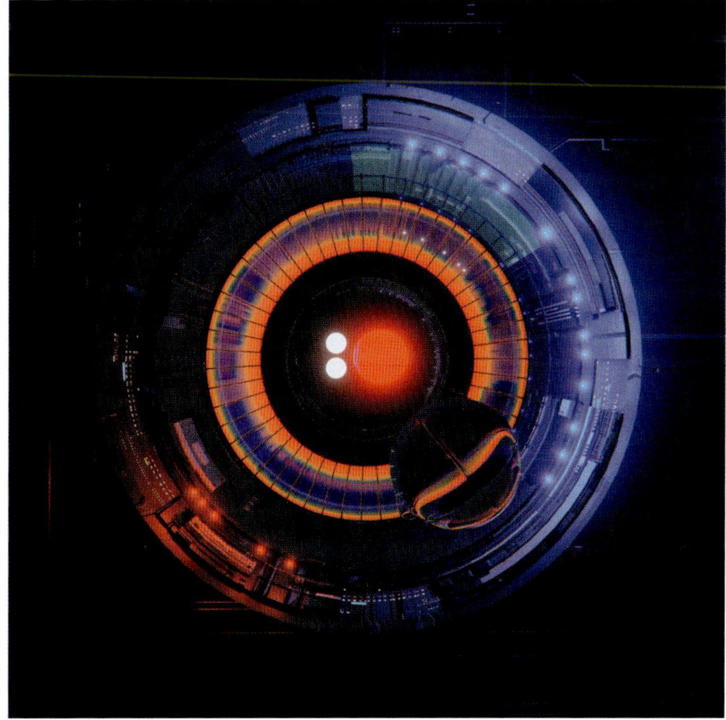

TOP LEFT
APPALACHIAN IRIS
04.29.2016

TOP RIGHT
FOREST ZYGOTE
03.24.2016

BOTTOM LEFT
BLINDING.MC7
03.21.2016

BOTTOM RIGHT
BINARY PUPIL
03.28.2016

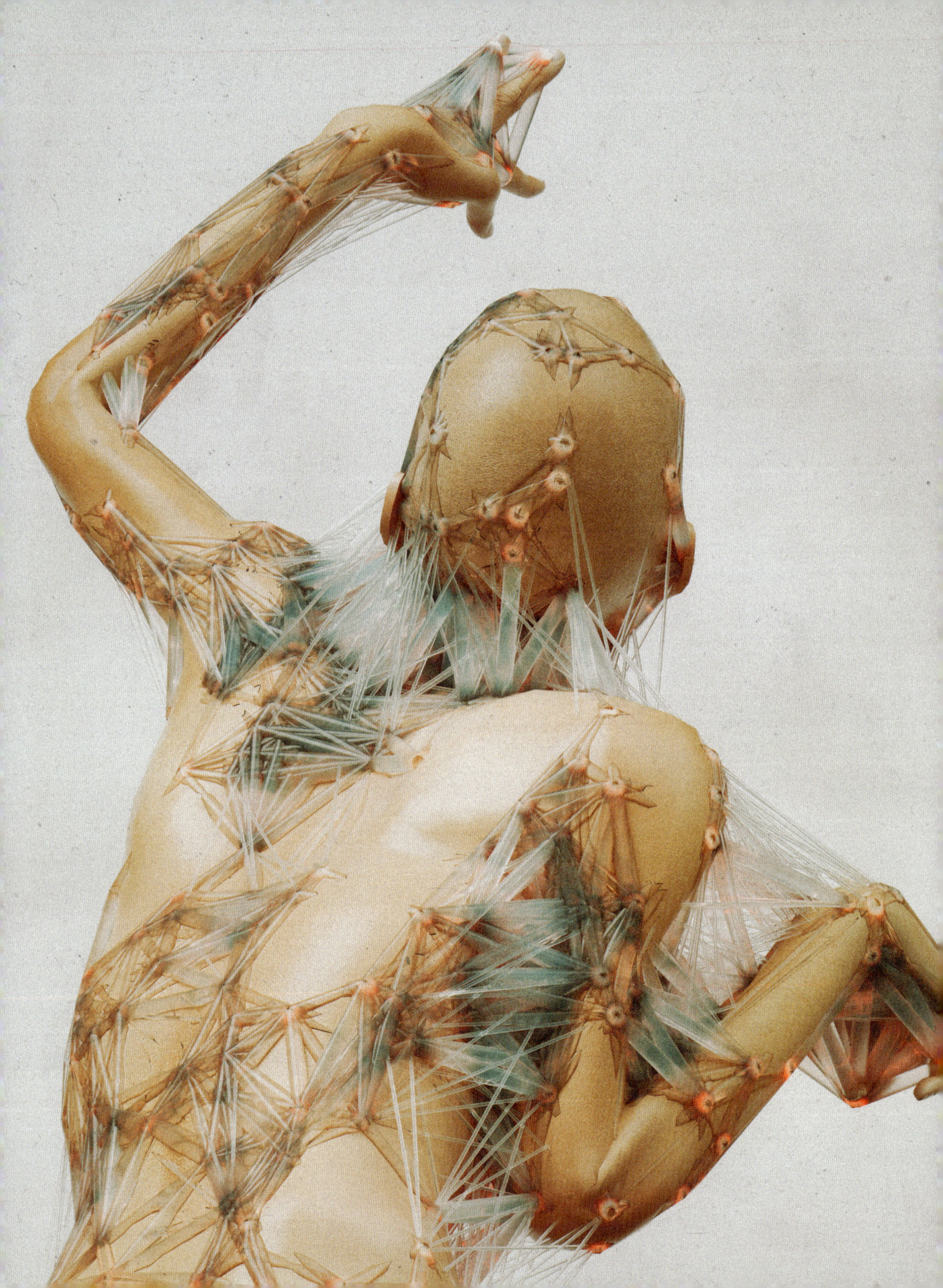

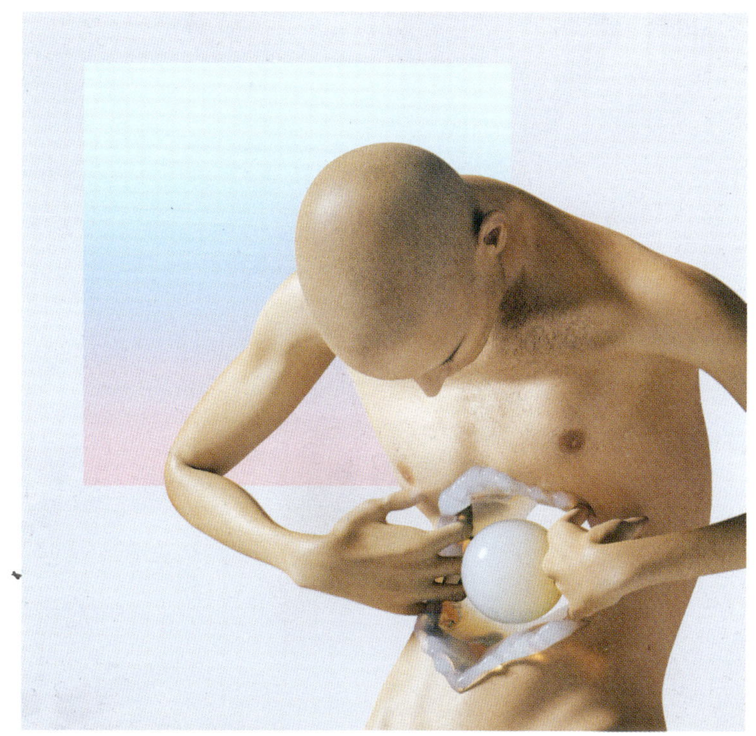

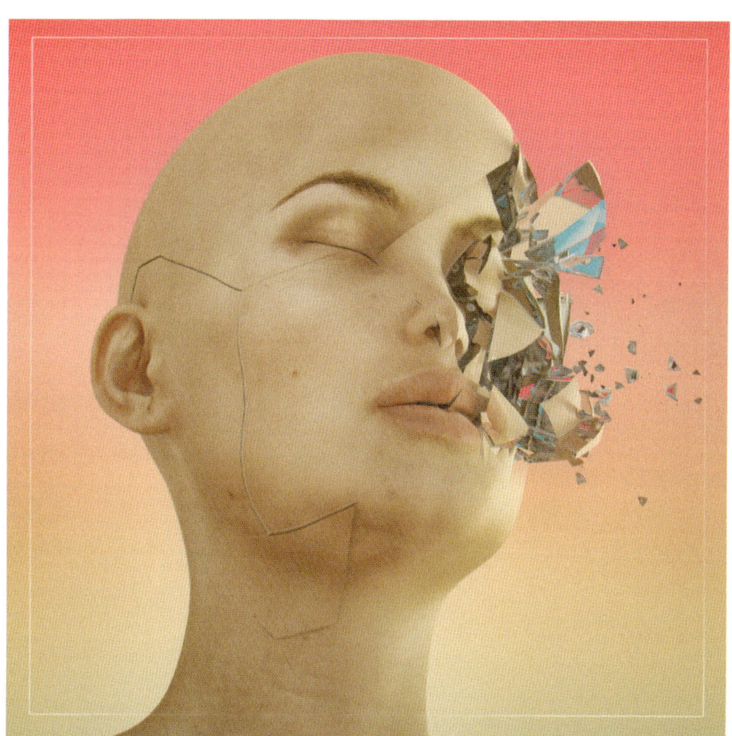

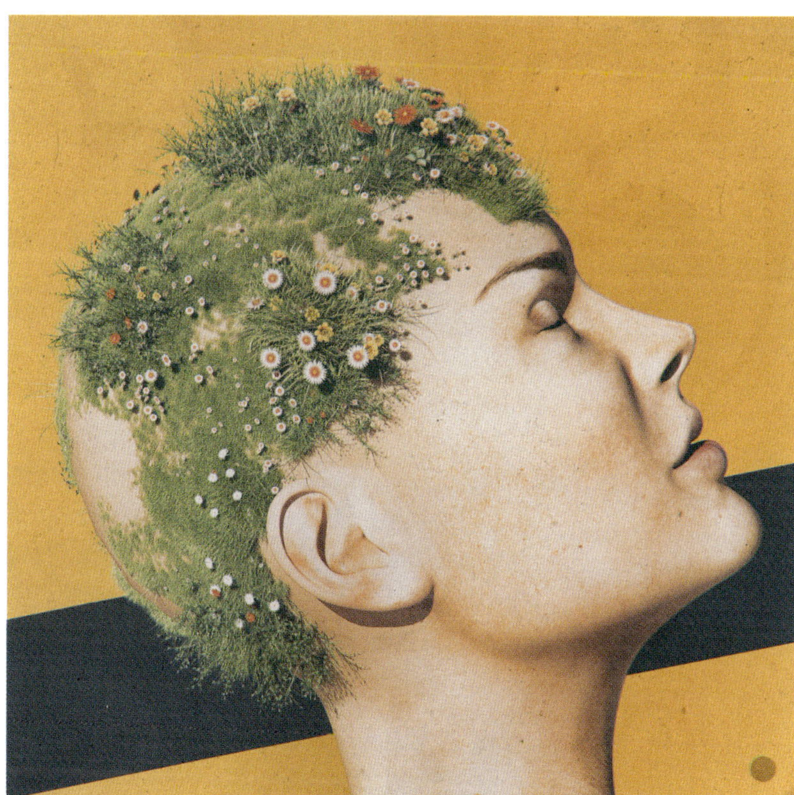

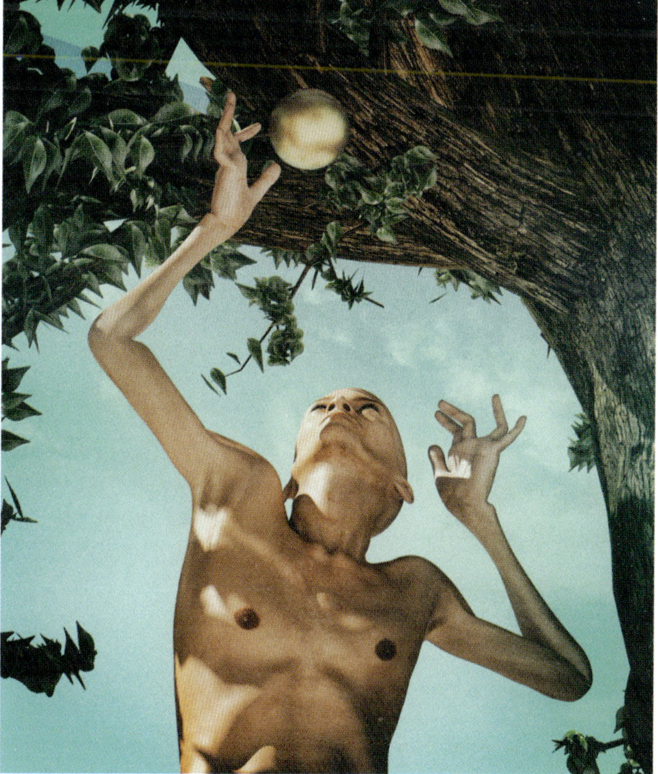

OPPOSITE PAGE
PERIAKTOI
07.07.2016

TOP LEFT
GUT CHECK
07.05.2016

TOP RIGHT
FACESHATTT
07.16.2016

BOTTOM LEFT
YELLOW DOT
08.22.2016

BOTTOM RIGHT
TOO BLESSED
07.03.2016

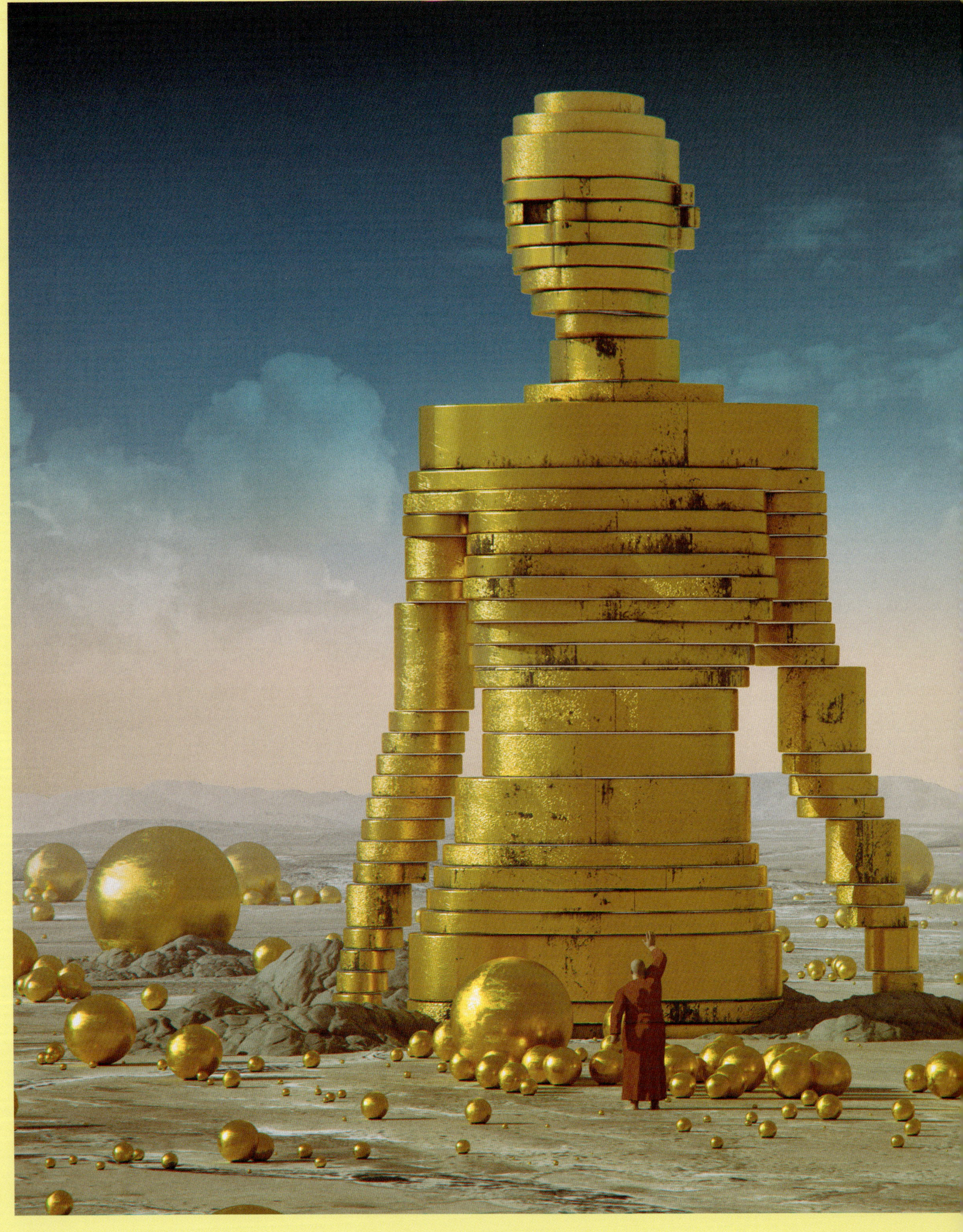

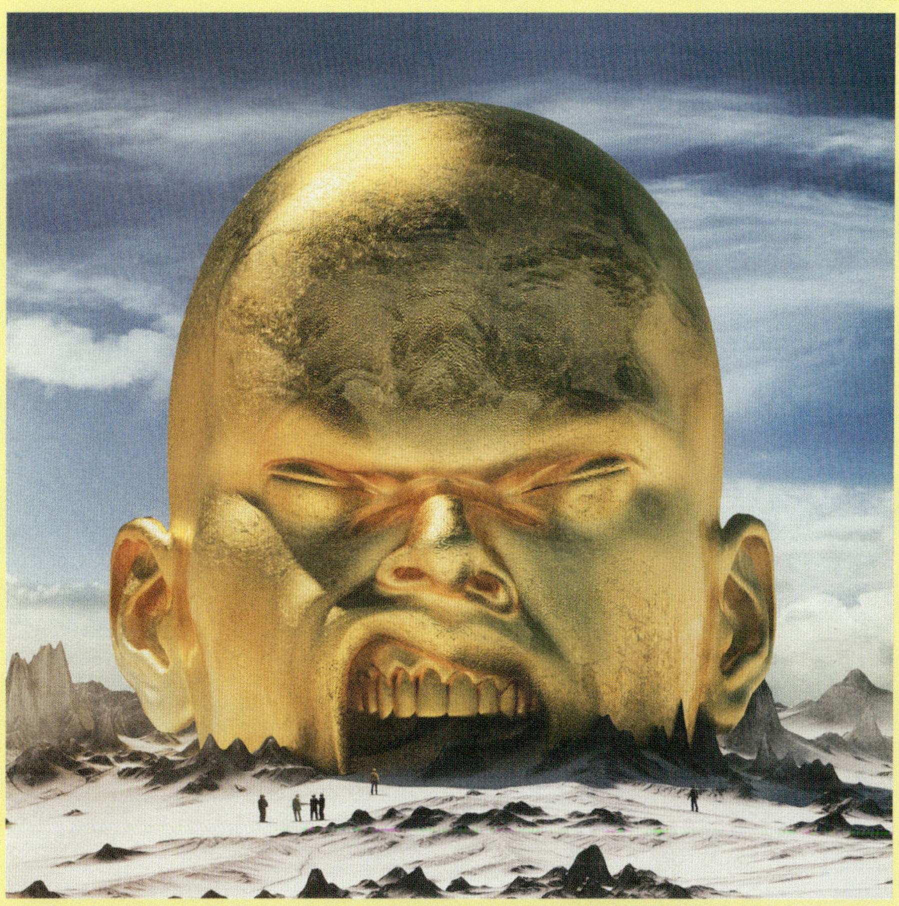

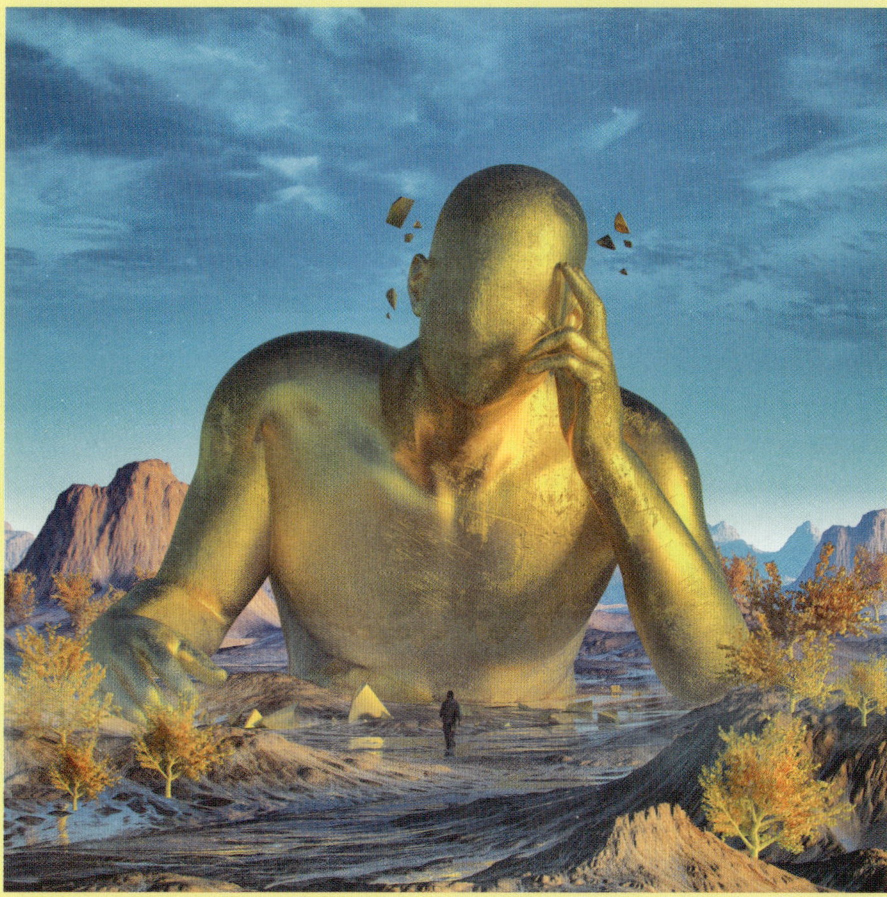

OPPOSITE PAGE
THICK AIR
07.18.2016

TOP
EASY LIFE
02.24.2016

BOTTOM
SUNDAYGOLDNOFACEGIANT
04.17.2016

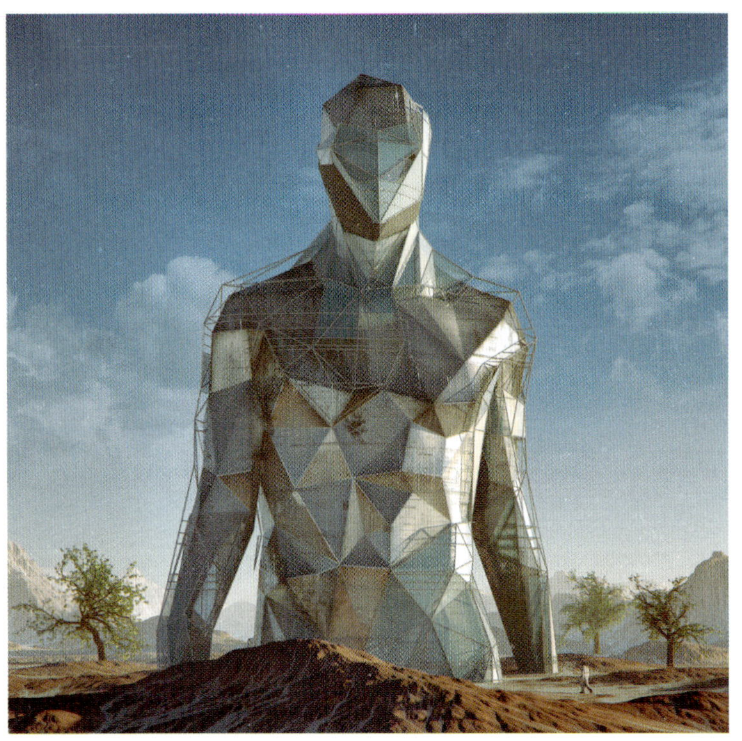

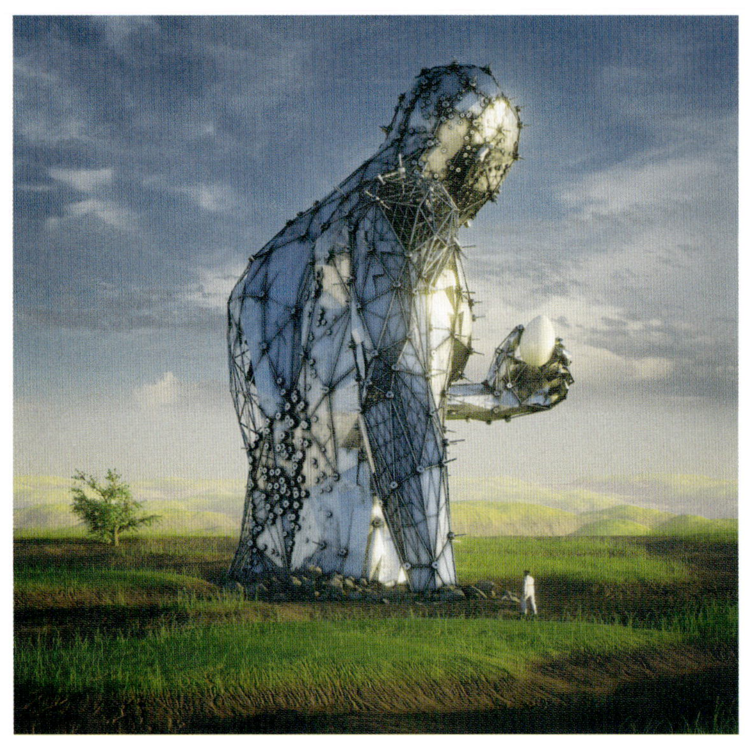

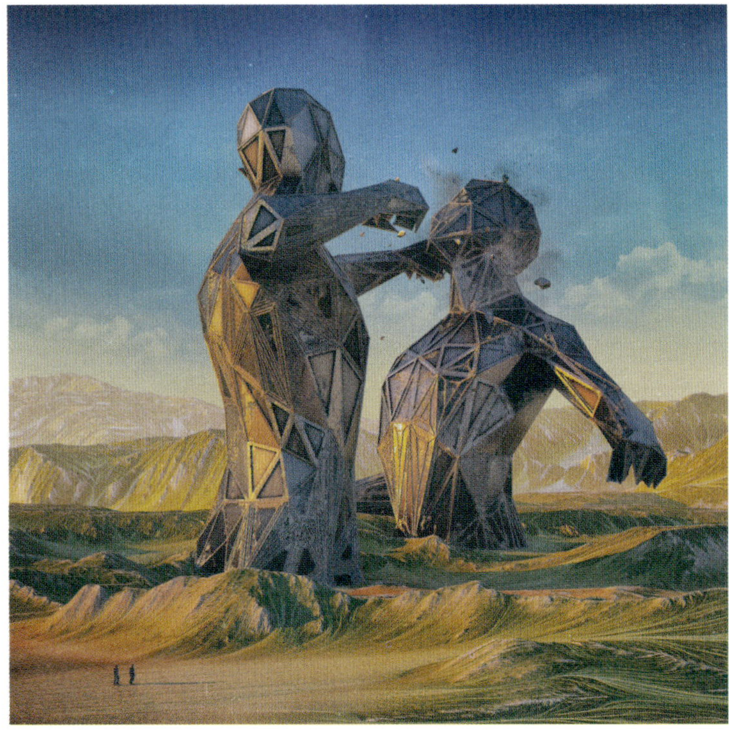

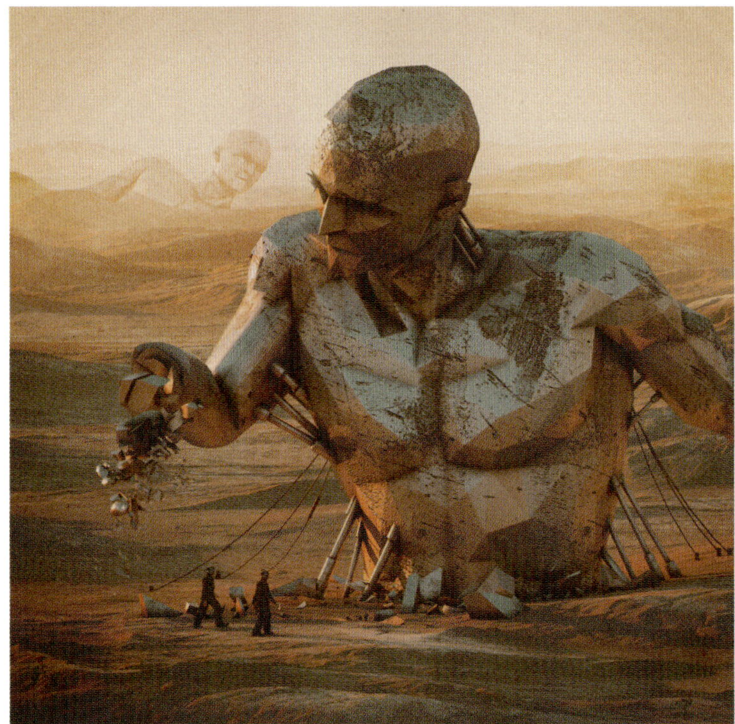

TOP LEFT
DECIMATEDHUMAN.9000
04.24.2016

TOP RIGHT
ROBOT FINDS EGG
05.24.2016

BOTTOM LEFT
CONFLICT.1992
05.07.2016

BOTTOM RIGHT
MERCIA.2216
05.03.2016

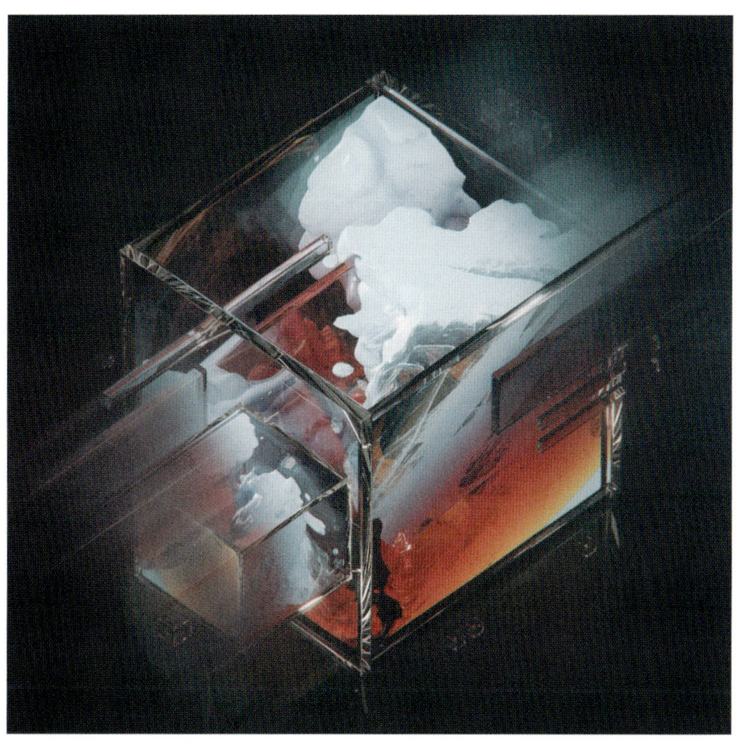

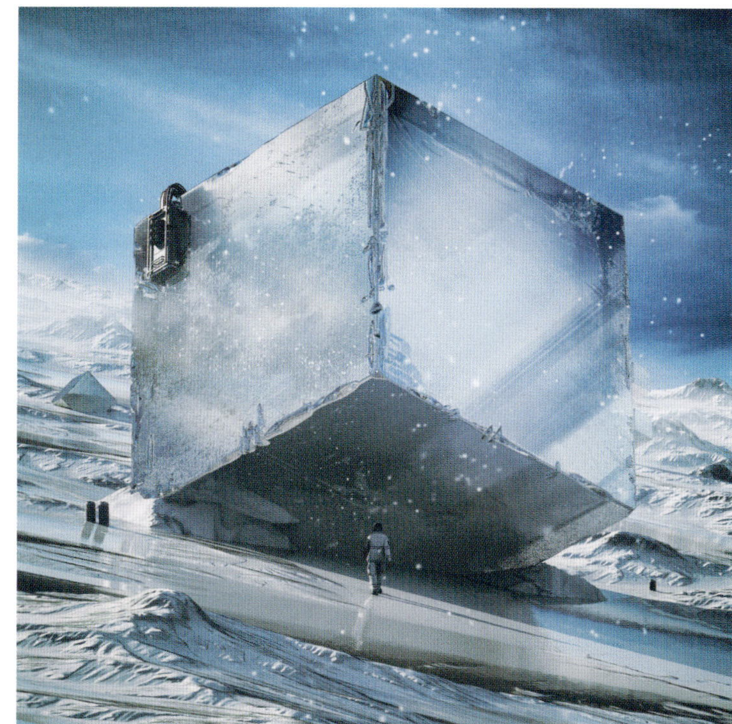

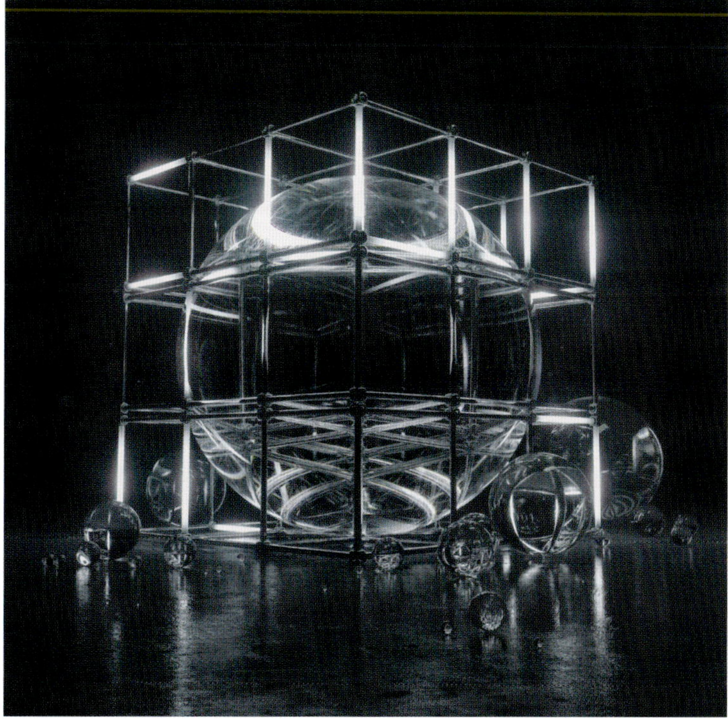

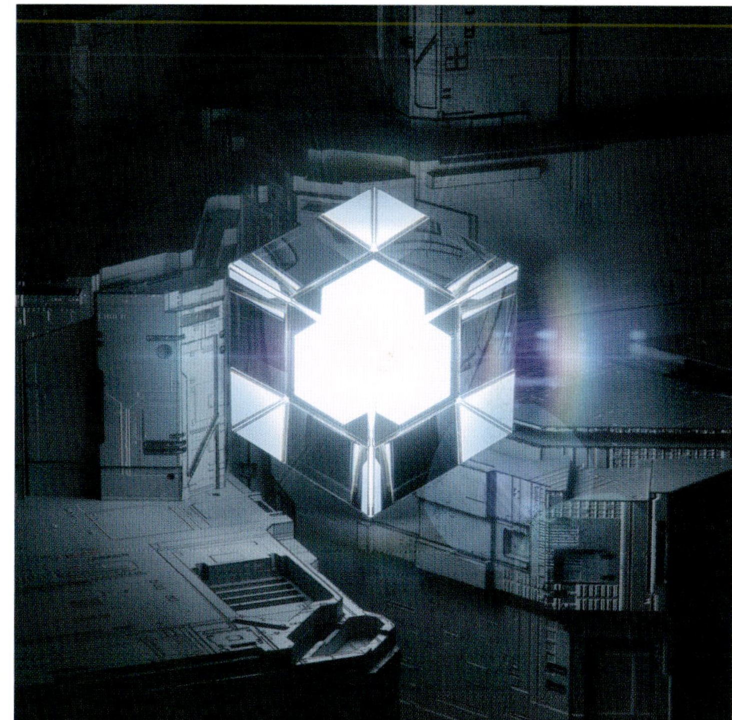

TOP LEFT
SIXTY.F
03.07.2016

TOP RIGHT
PRECIPICE
03.15.2016

BOTTOM LEFT
HONEYBEAR
04.20.2016

BOTTOM RIGHT
BEACON
03.20.2016

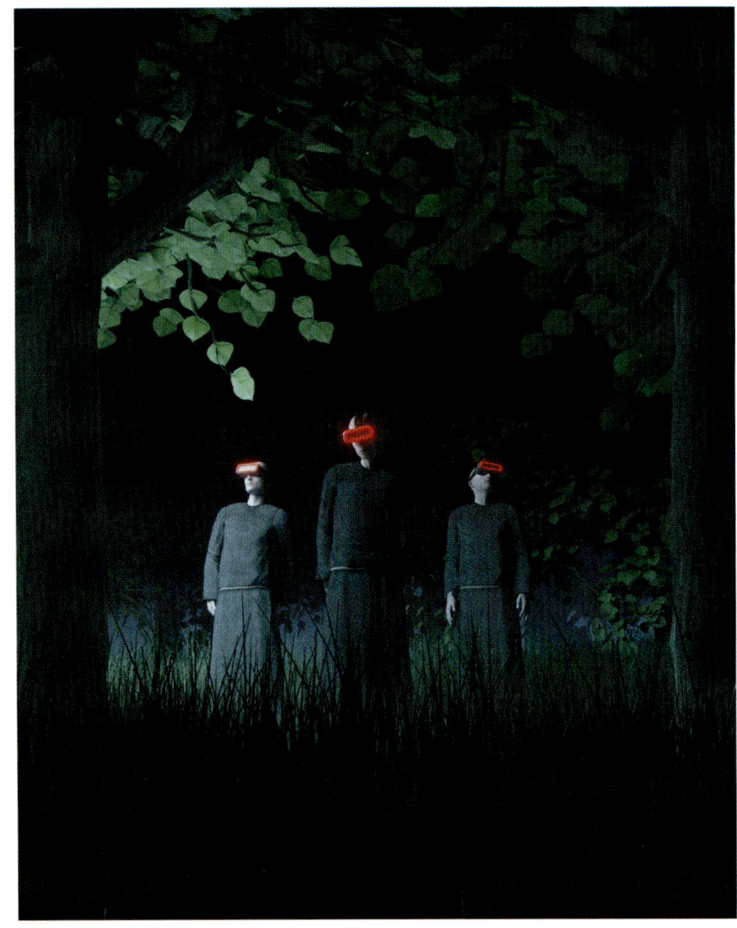

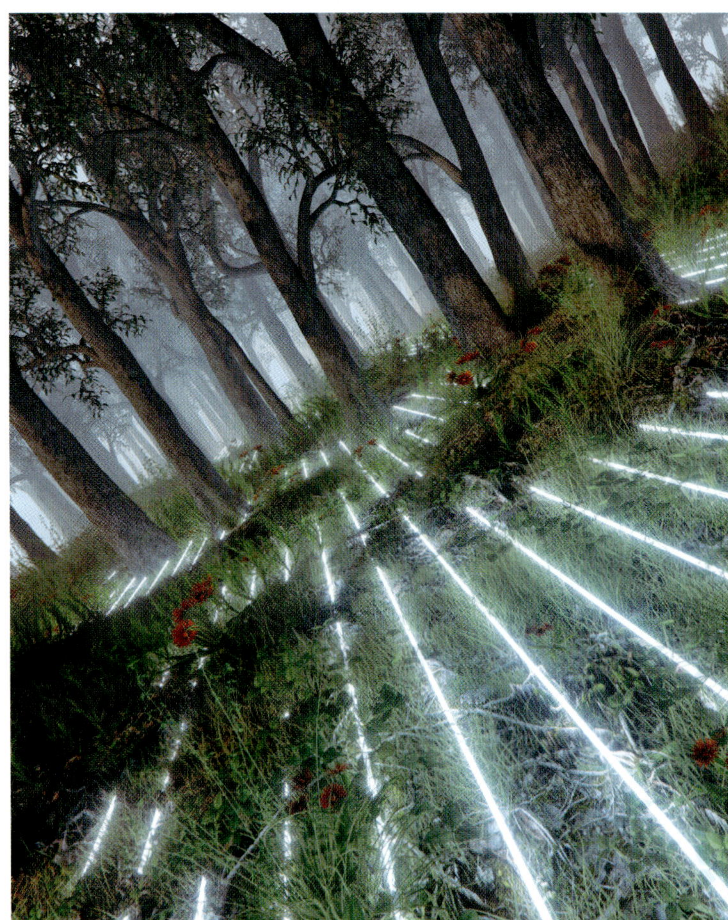

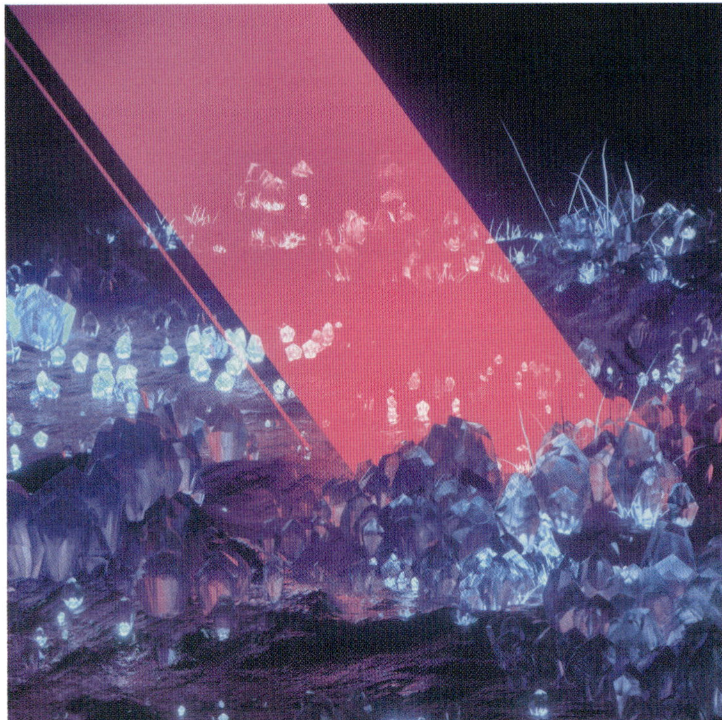

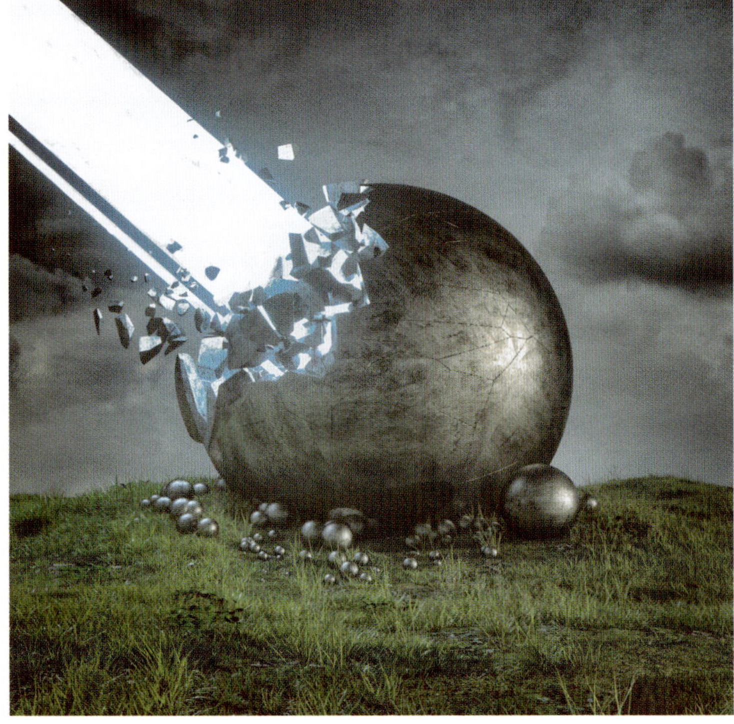

TOP LEFT
ILLUMORII
08.06.2016

TOP RIGHT
UNWRAPPED
08.29.2016

BOTTOM LEFT
PURPSPLIFF
12.27.2016

BOTTOM RIGHT
CRO-MAGNUM
12.07.2016

OPPOSITE PAGE
BEAMMM
08.13.2016

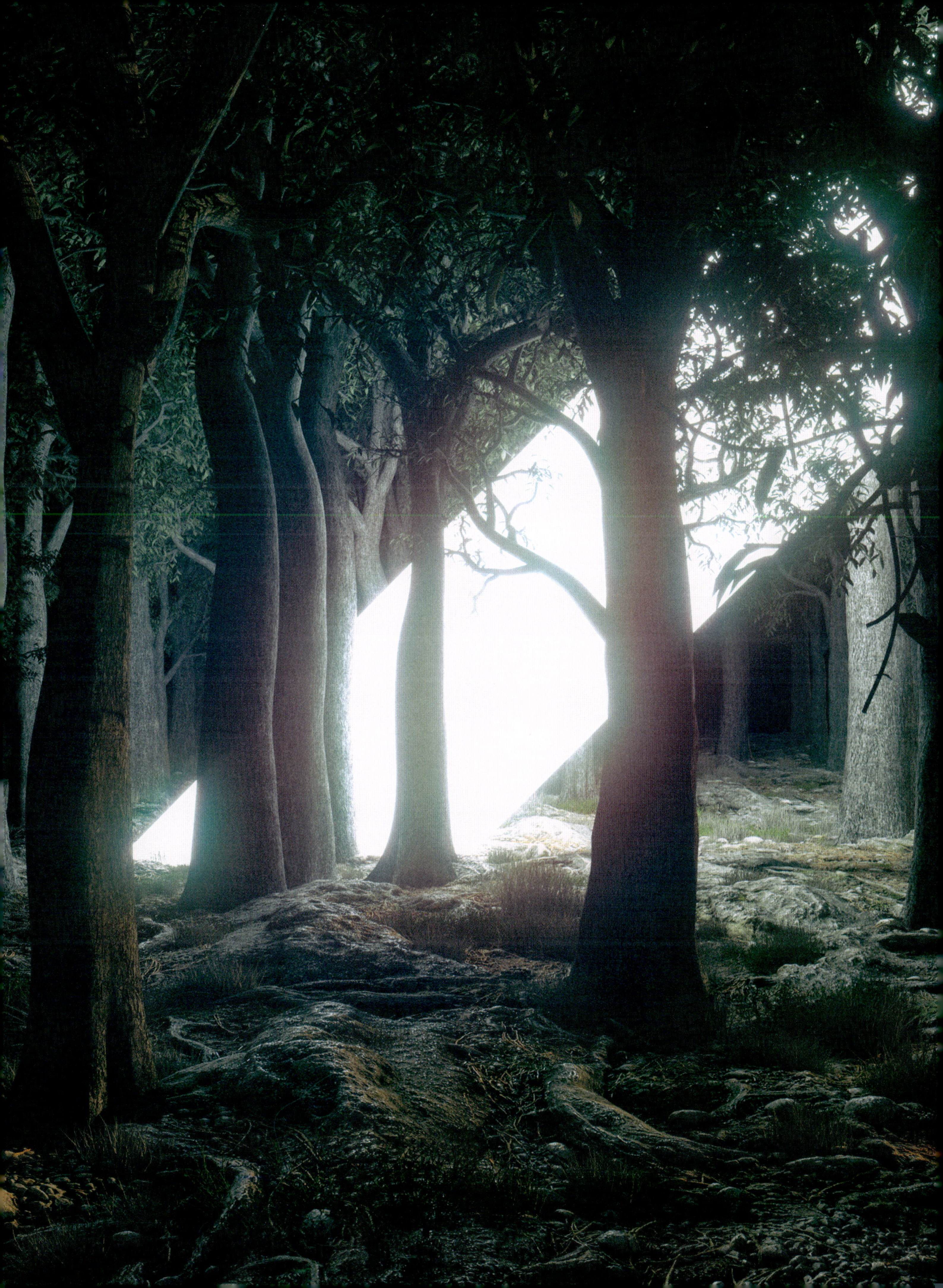

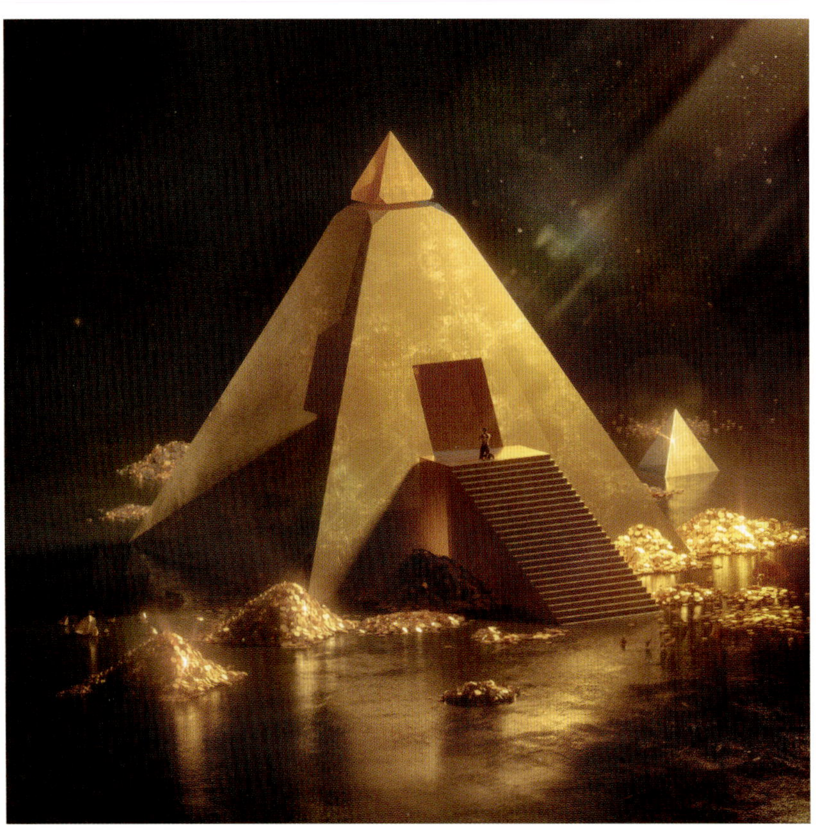

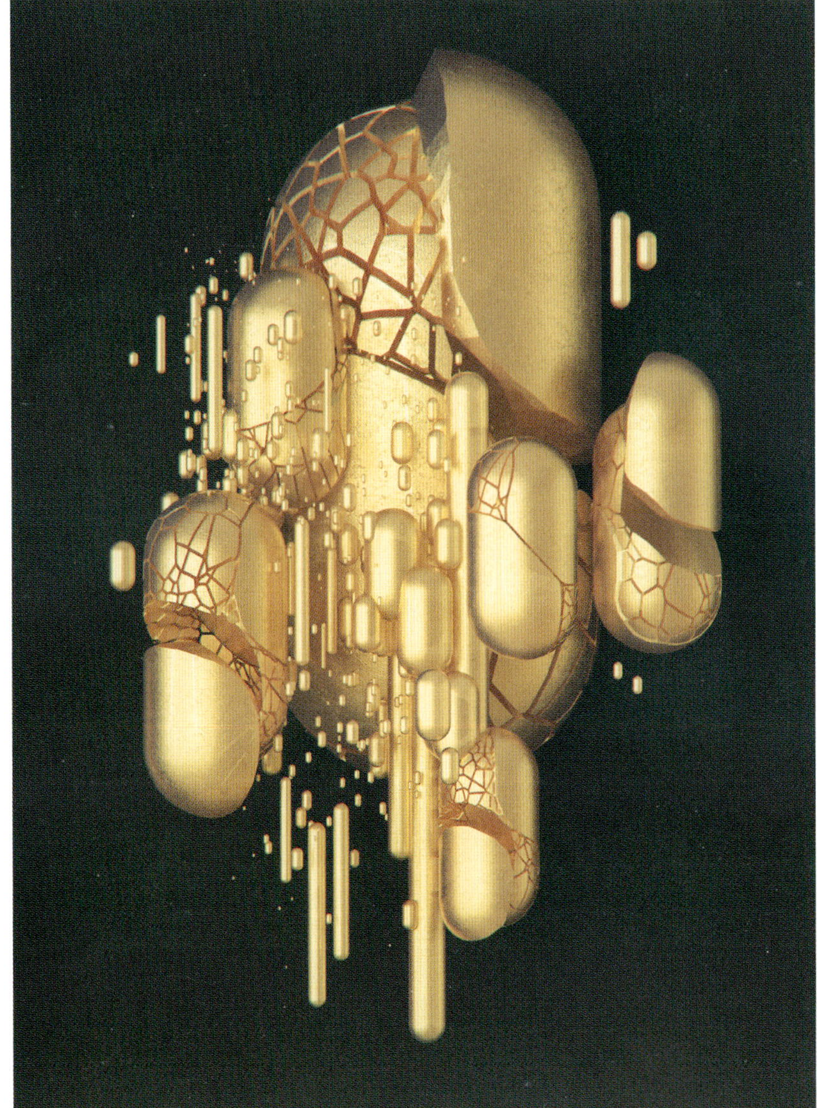

TOP

ROSEGOLD2
05.25.2016

BOTTOM

V-FRACTURE
09.28.2016

OPPOSITE PAGE

THREE SOL
09.11.2016

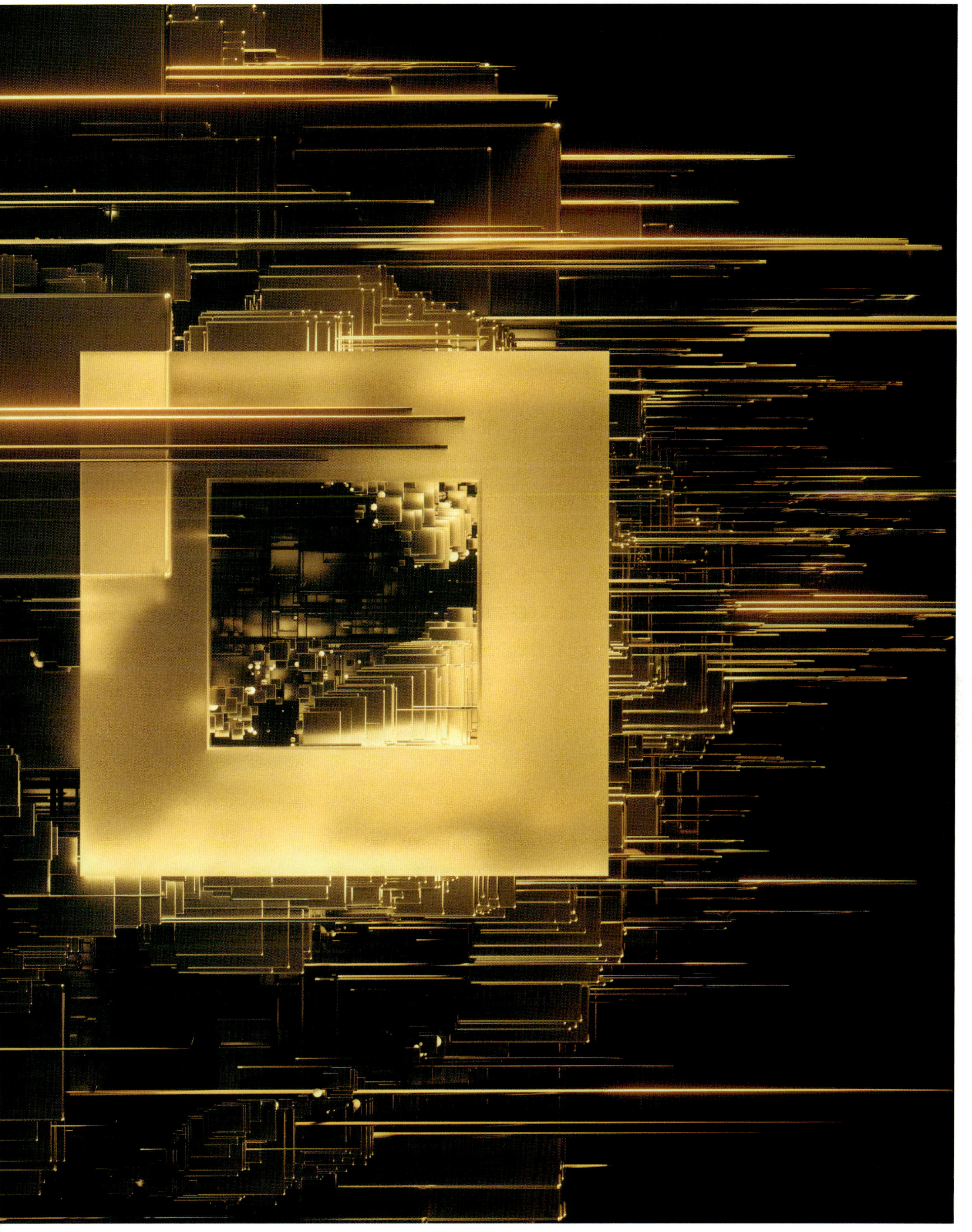

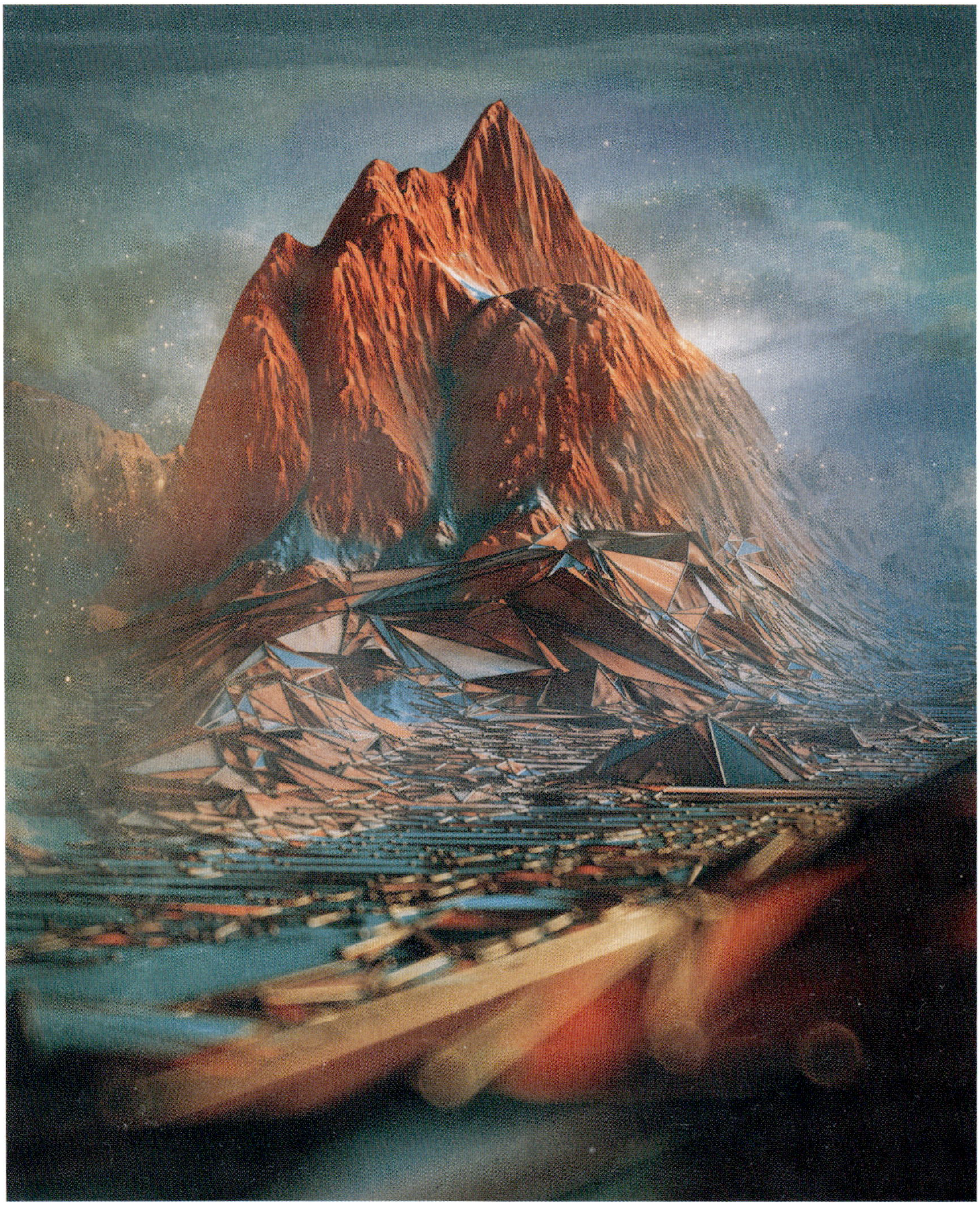

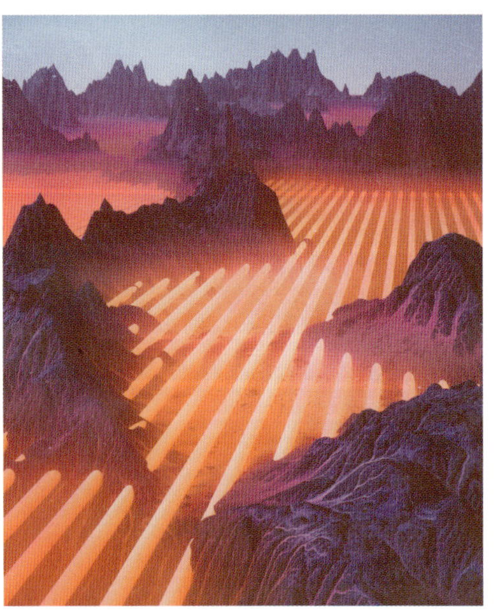

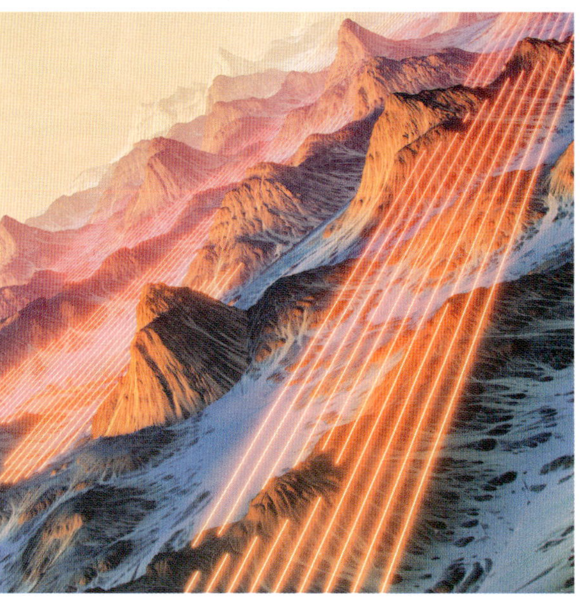

TOP

MTNT (RED)
01.21.2016

BOTTOM LEFT

WINDCHILL
12.13.2016

BOTTOM RIGHT

XANNN.6
04.12.2016

OPPOSITE PAGE

BETTER
12.06.2016

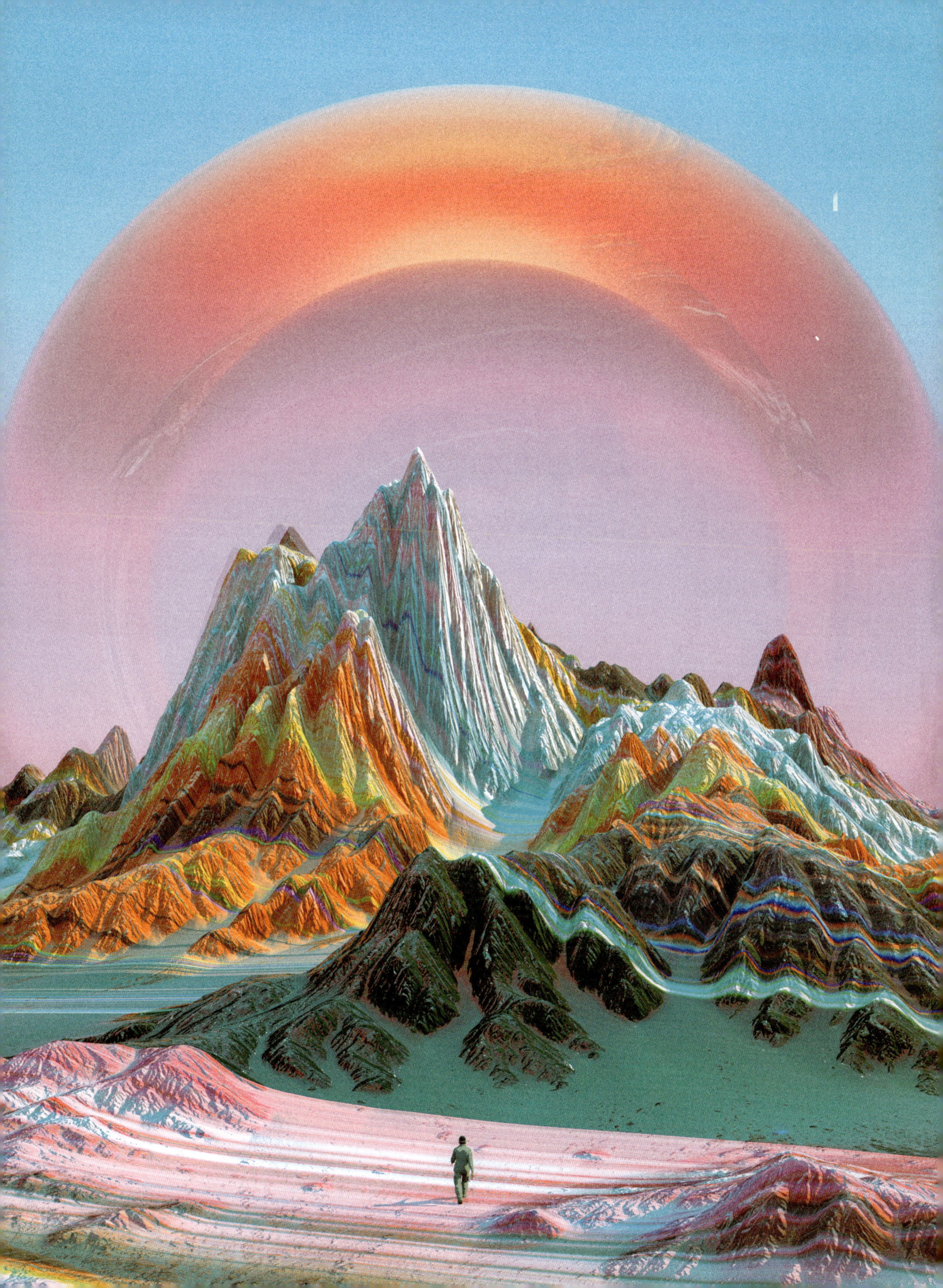

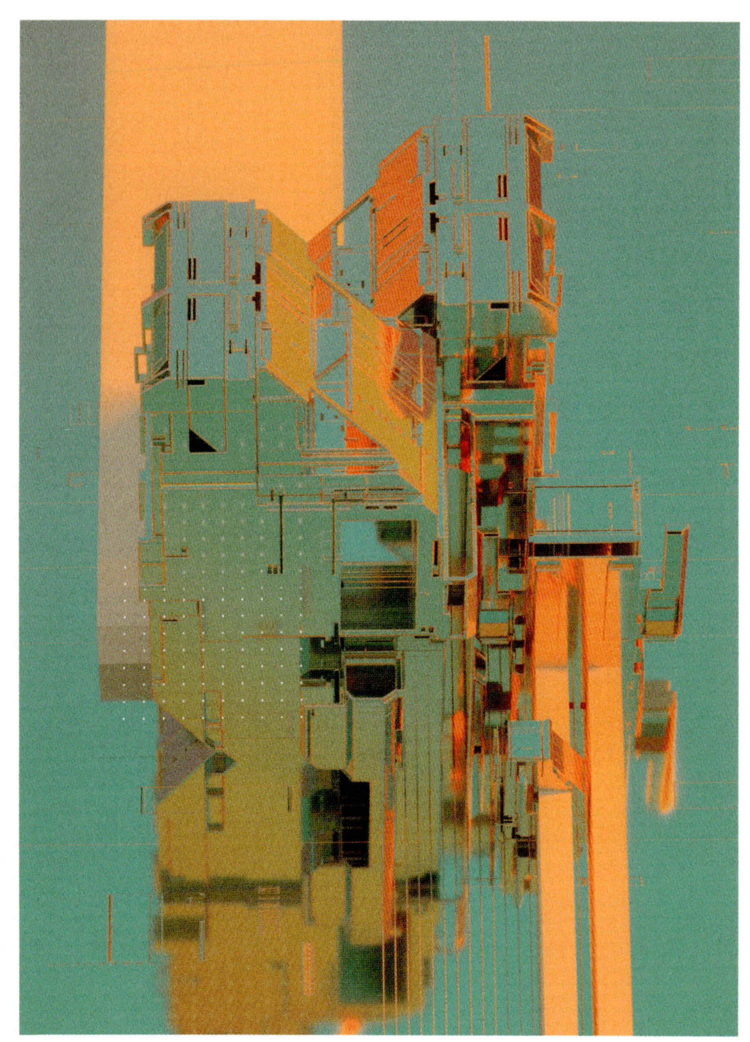

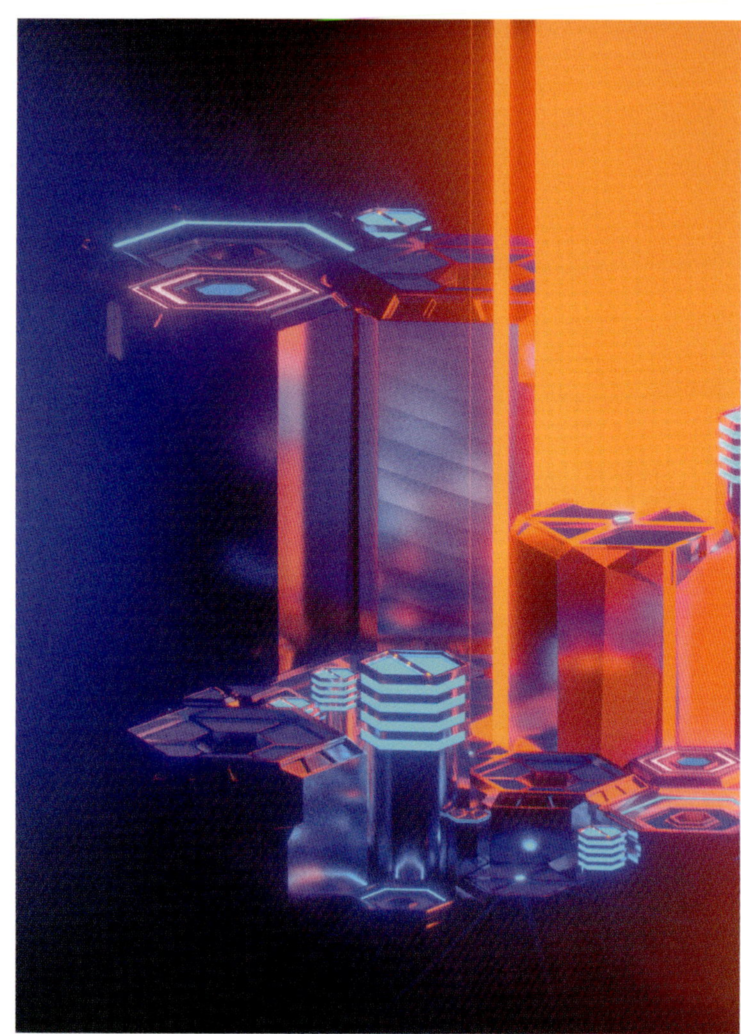

LEFT

METAL GEAR

11.07.2016

RIGHT

NEONMURK / EYE.SAXX

04.08.2016

OPPOSITE PAGE

APPLECART

09.13.2016

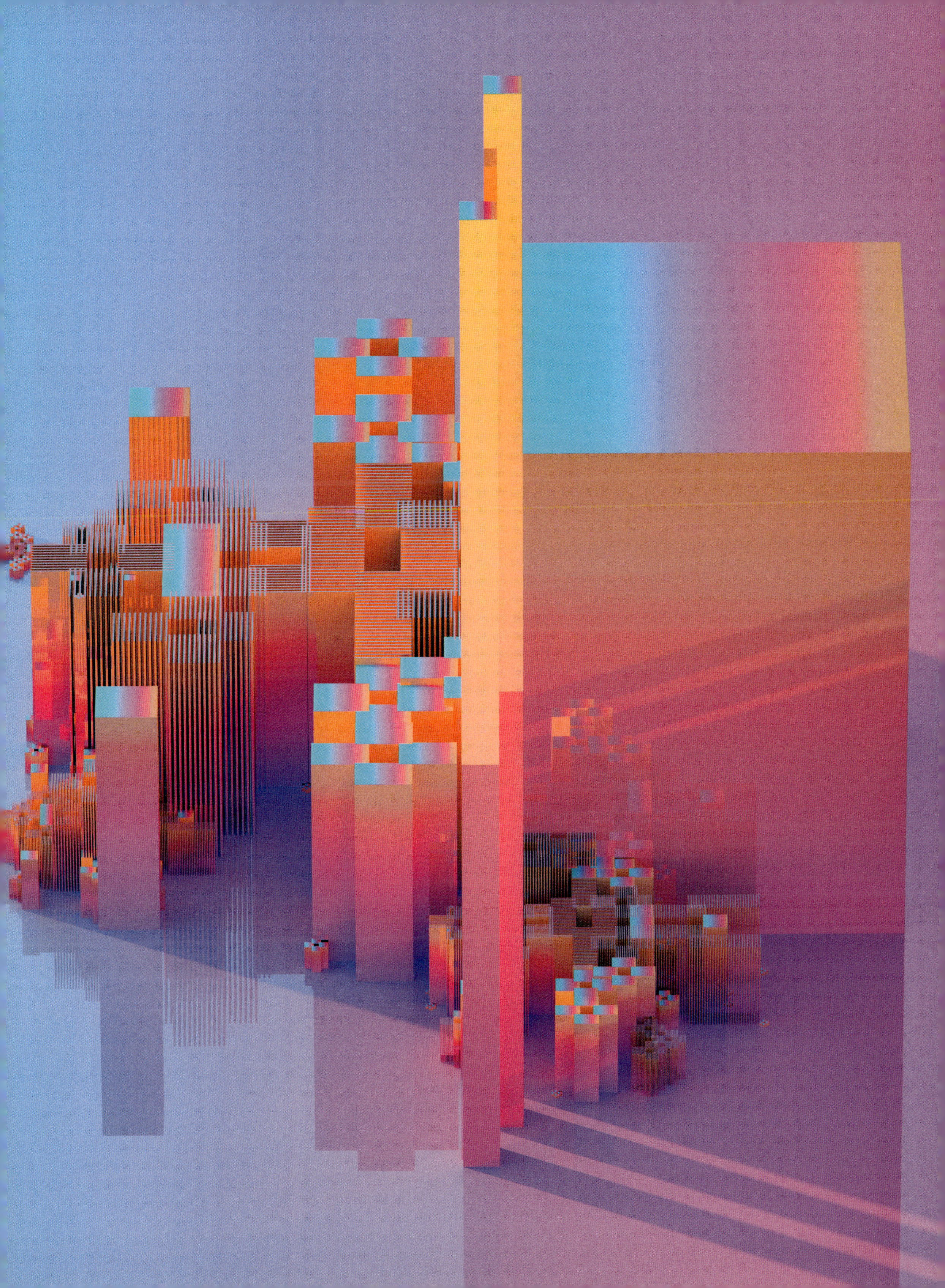

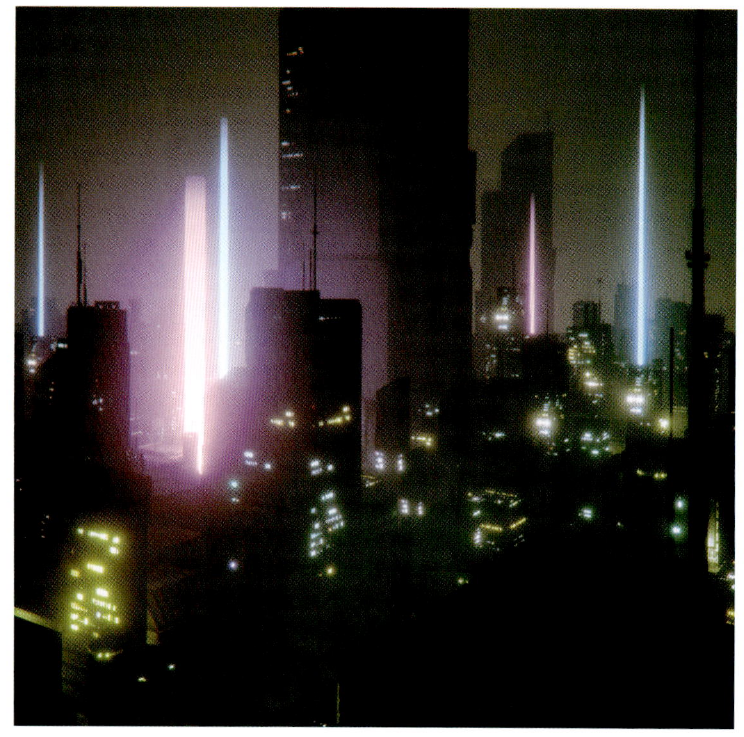

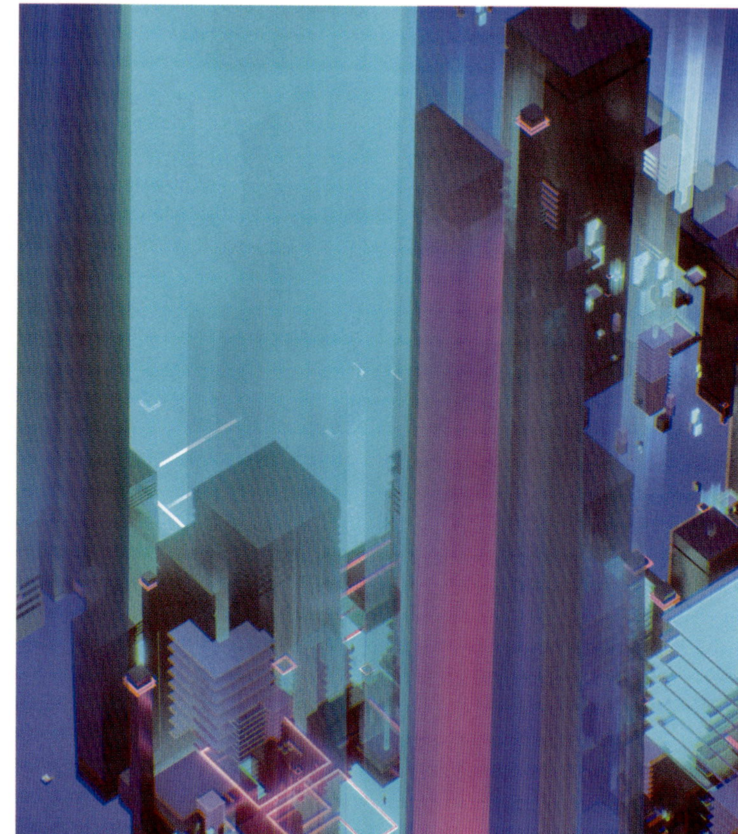

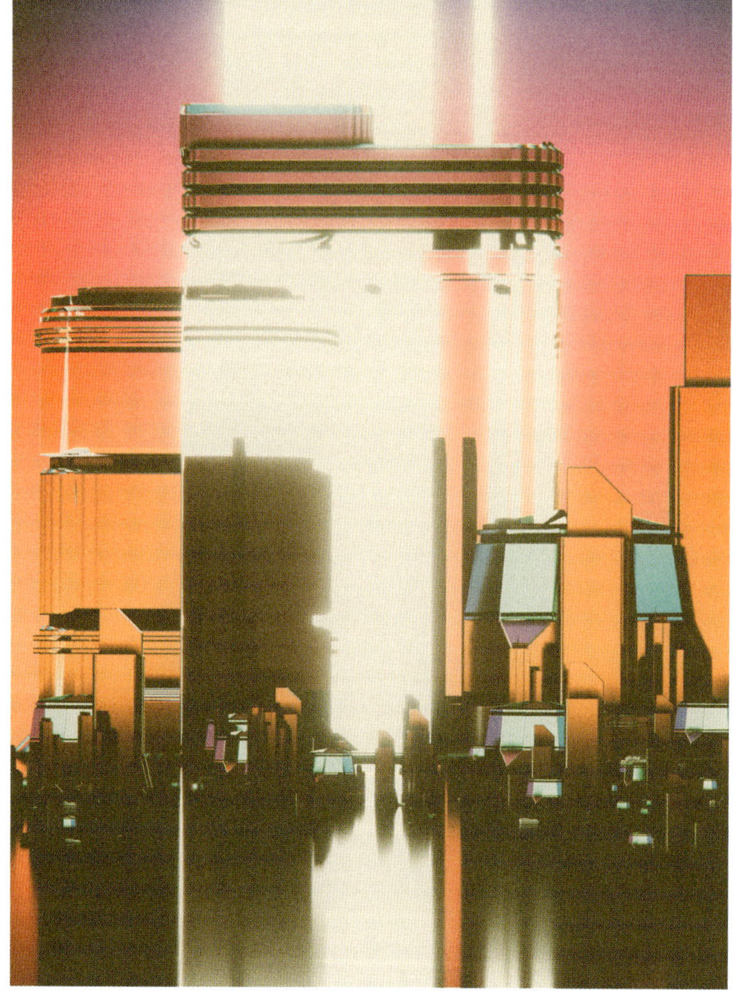

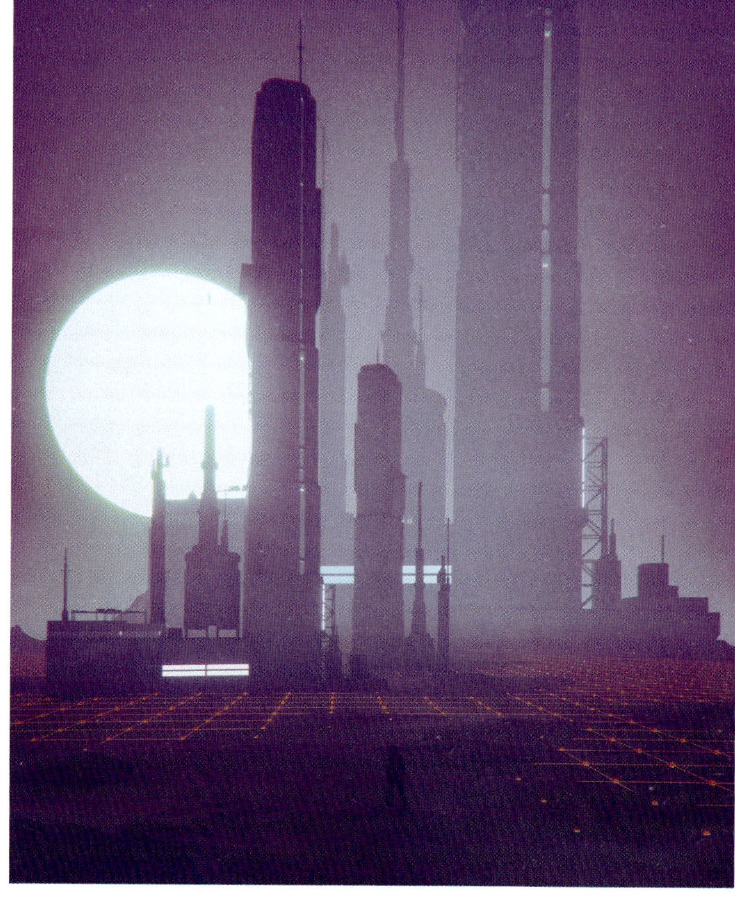

TOP LEFT
XEONN2040
12.12.2016

TOP RIGHT
BETAMAX198555
09.04.2016

BOTTOM LEFT
DEVOLVE
09.09.2016

BOTTOM RIGHT
FAURM.FIELD.009
12.21.2016

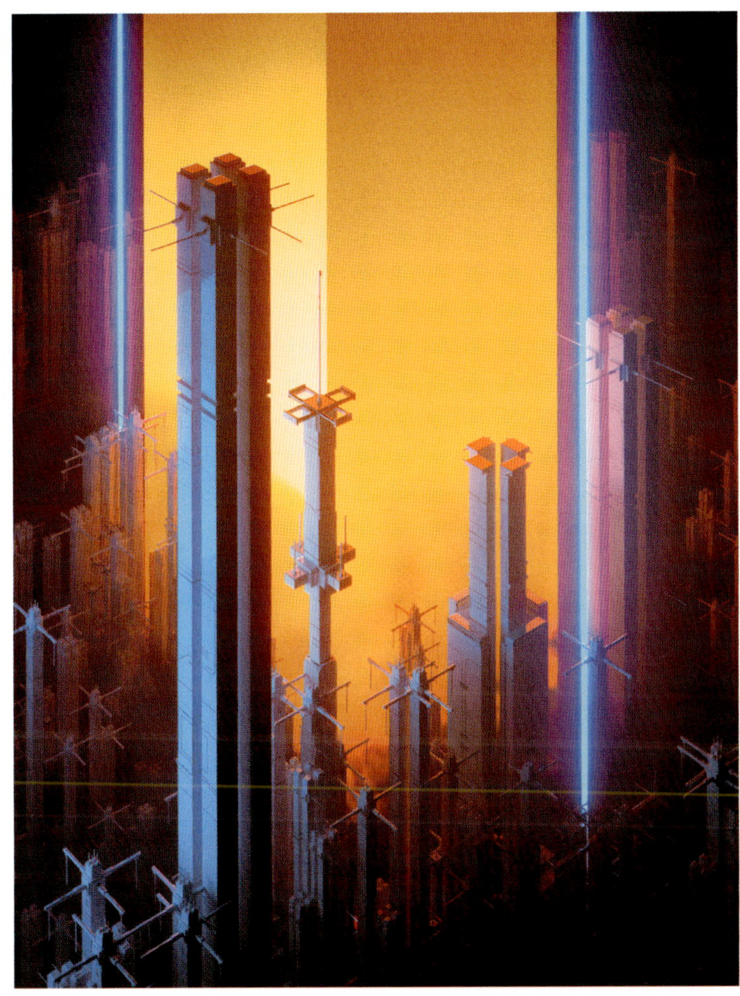

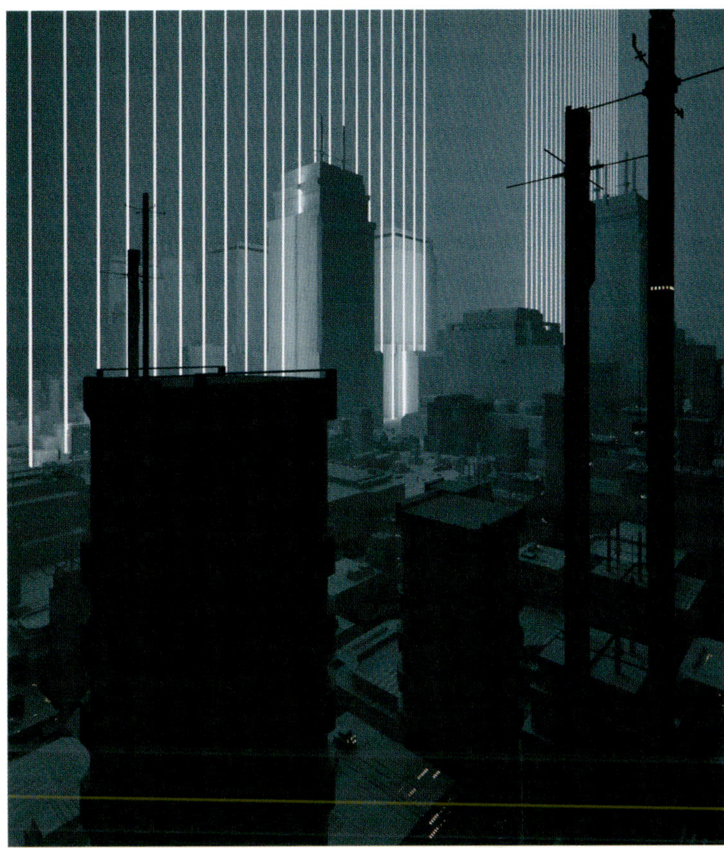

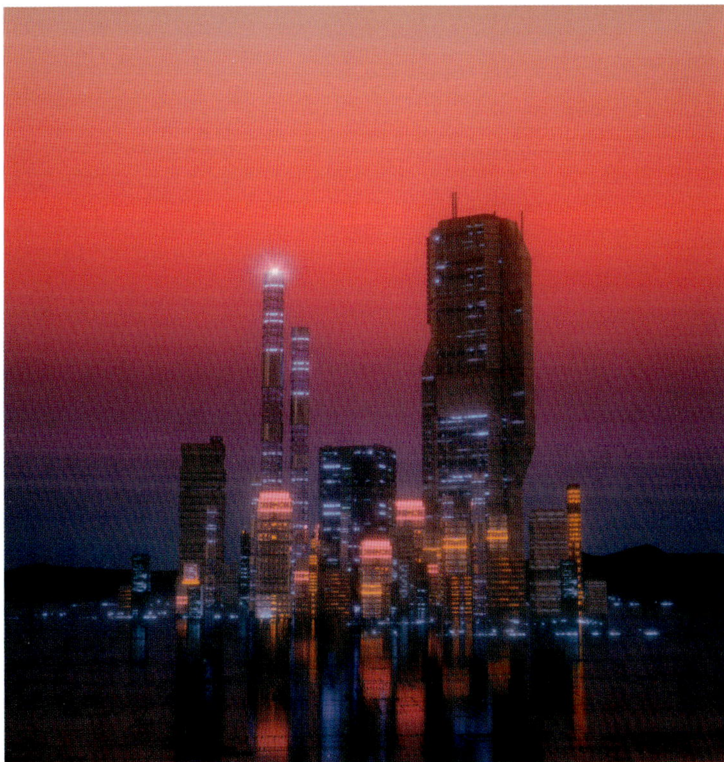

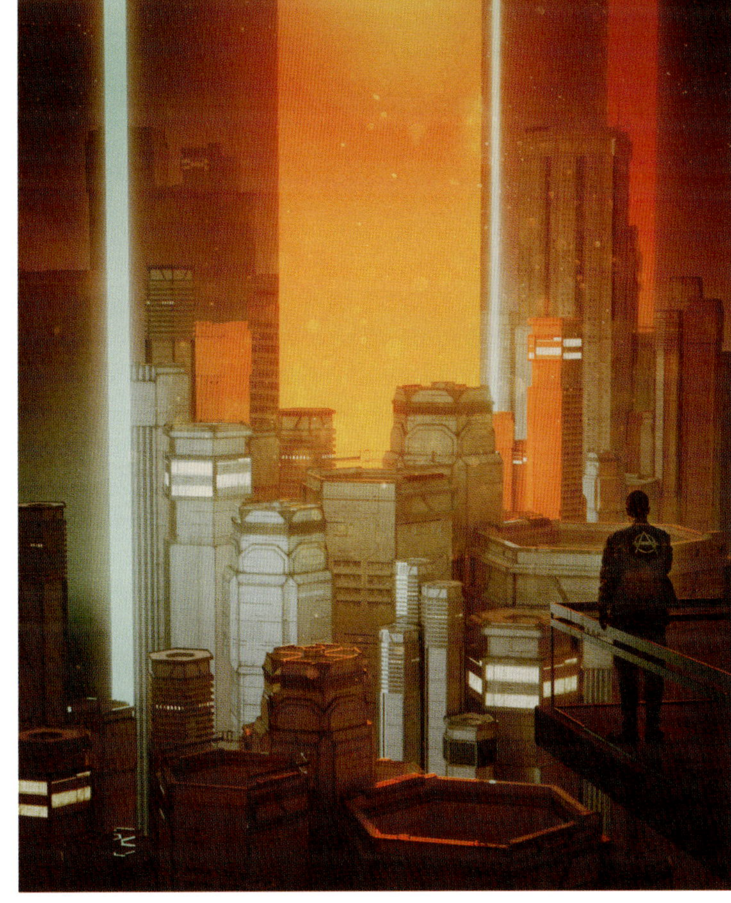

TOP LEFT
SPITE PIT
12.26.2016

TOP RIGHT
SQUARED
12.28.2016

BOTTOM LEFT
HYPE.REVERSE
09.10.2016

BOTTOM RIGHT
HEXAGONIA
06.25.2016

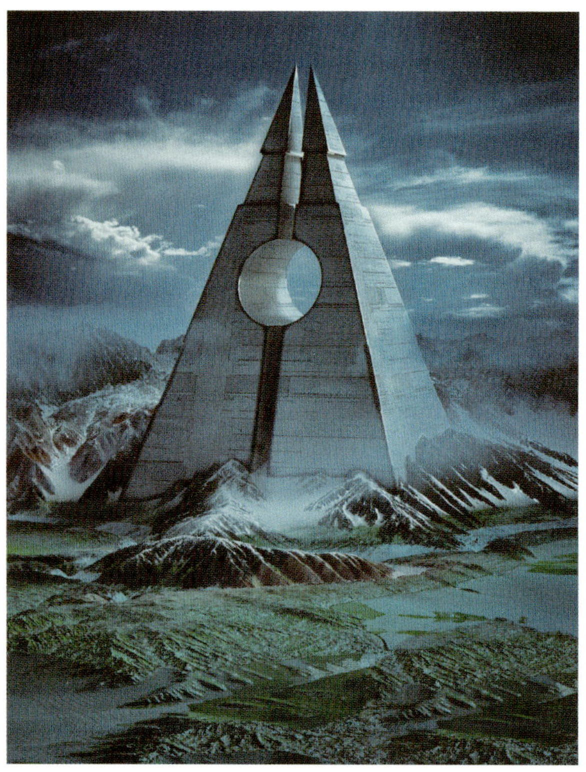

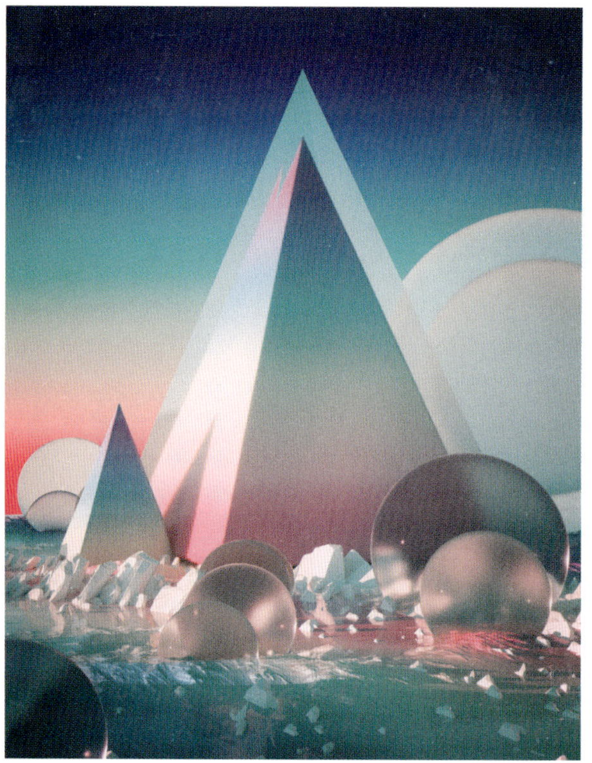

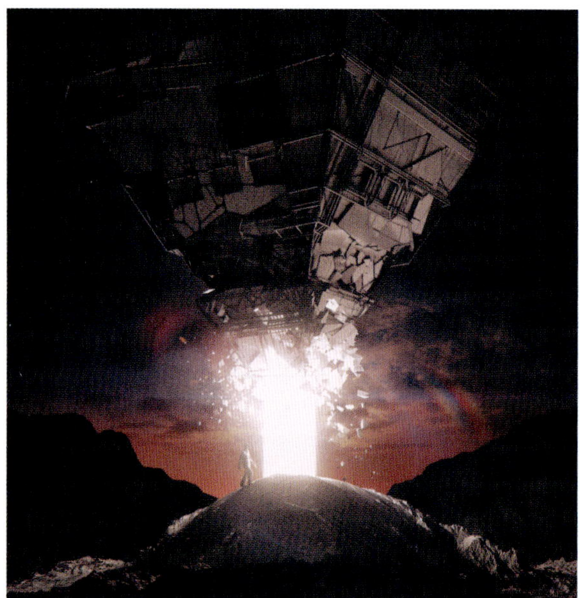

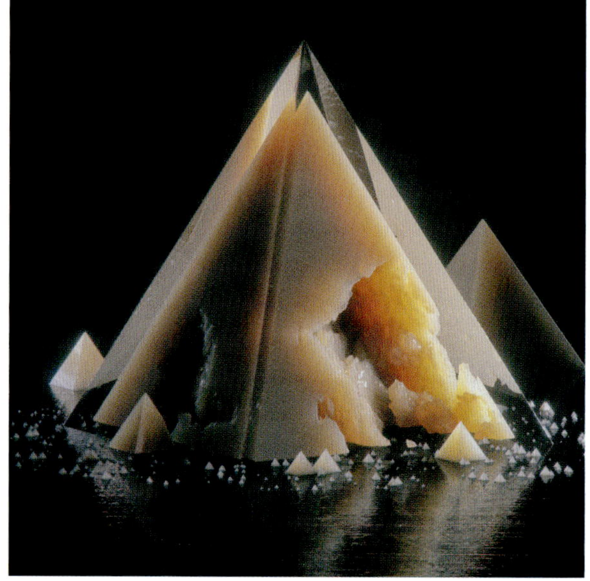

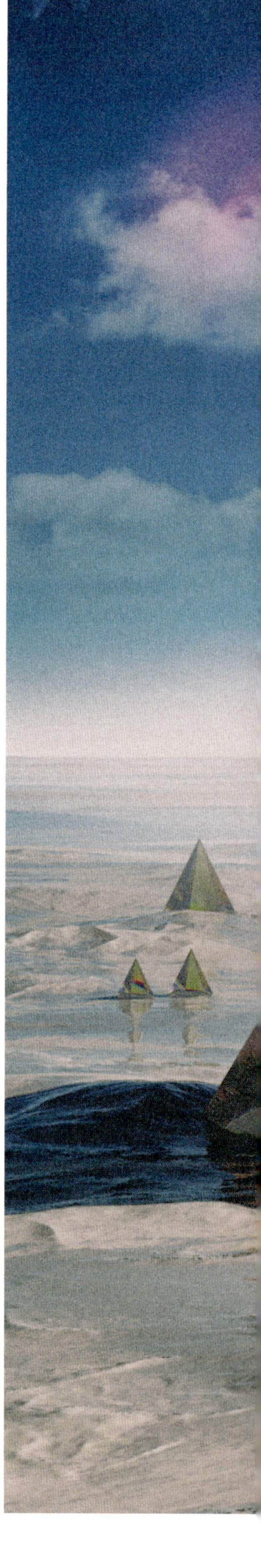

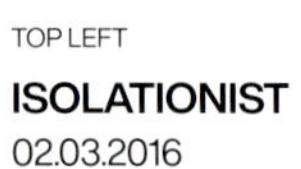

TOP LEFT
ISOLATIONIST
02.03.2016

TOP RIGHT
PRIMITVE
09.23.2016

BOTTOM LEFT
SEED
01.22.2016

BOTTOM RIGHT
OVRDRIVE
09.21.2016

OPPOSITE PAGE
CRYSHATTT
09.29.2016

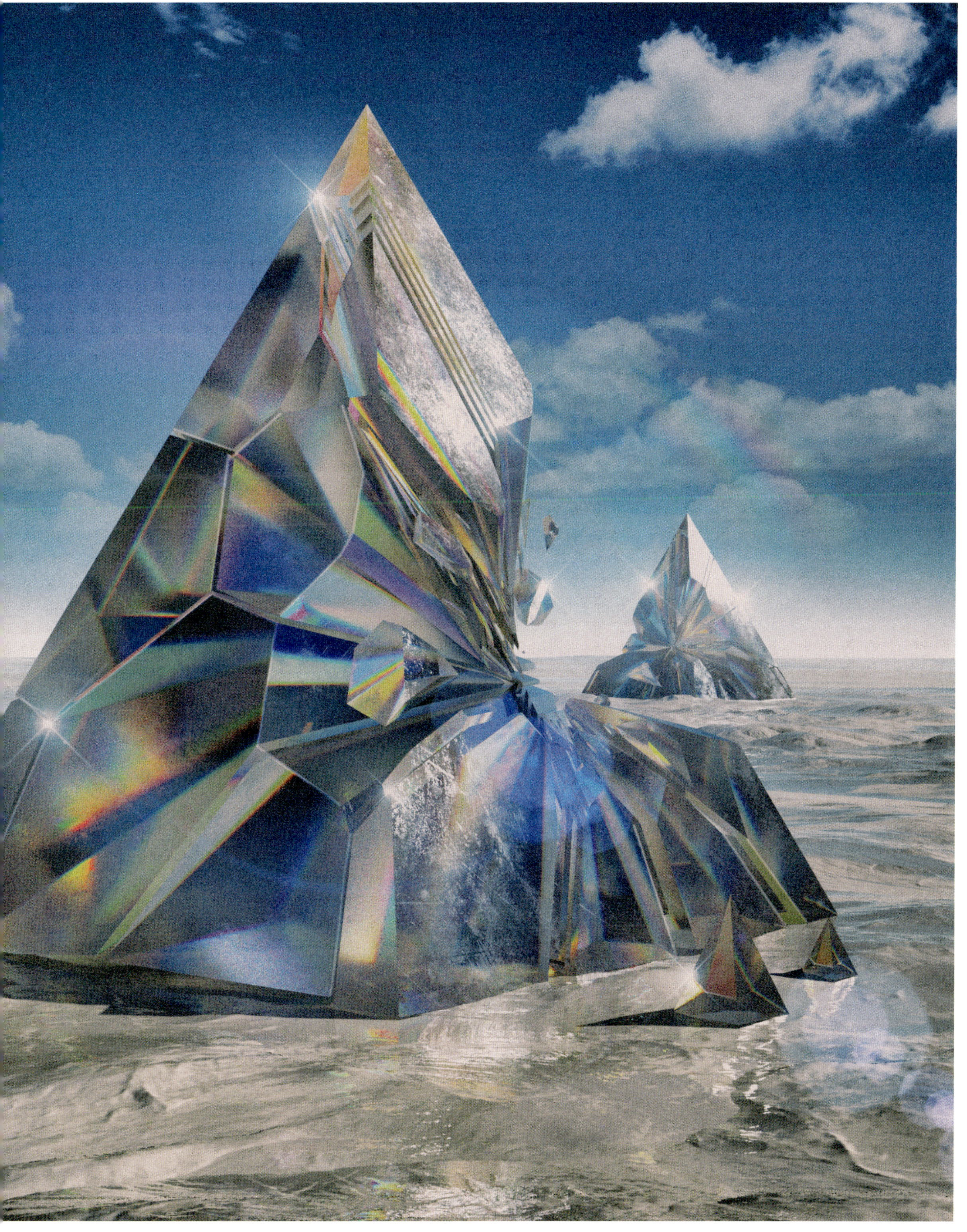

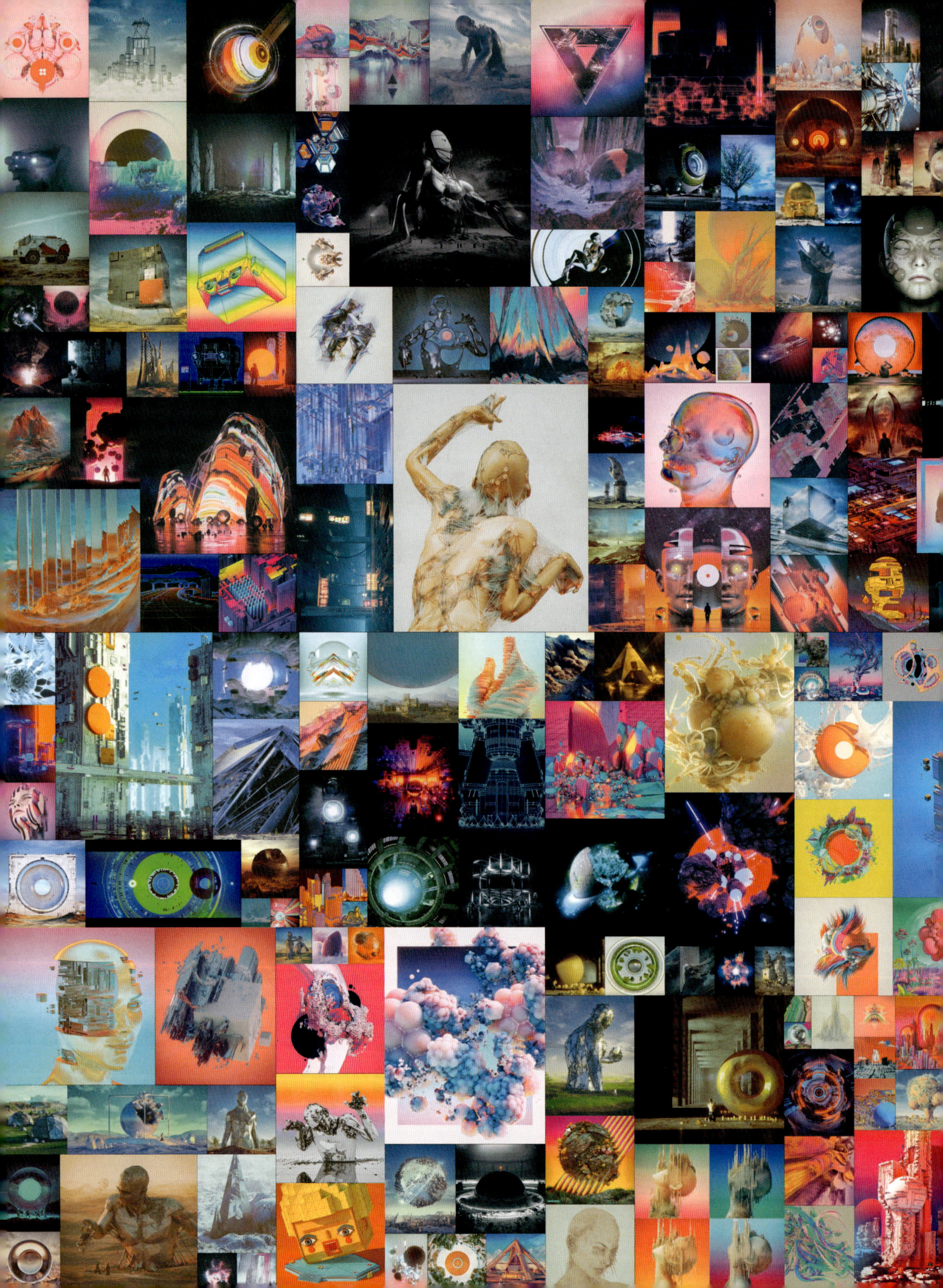

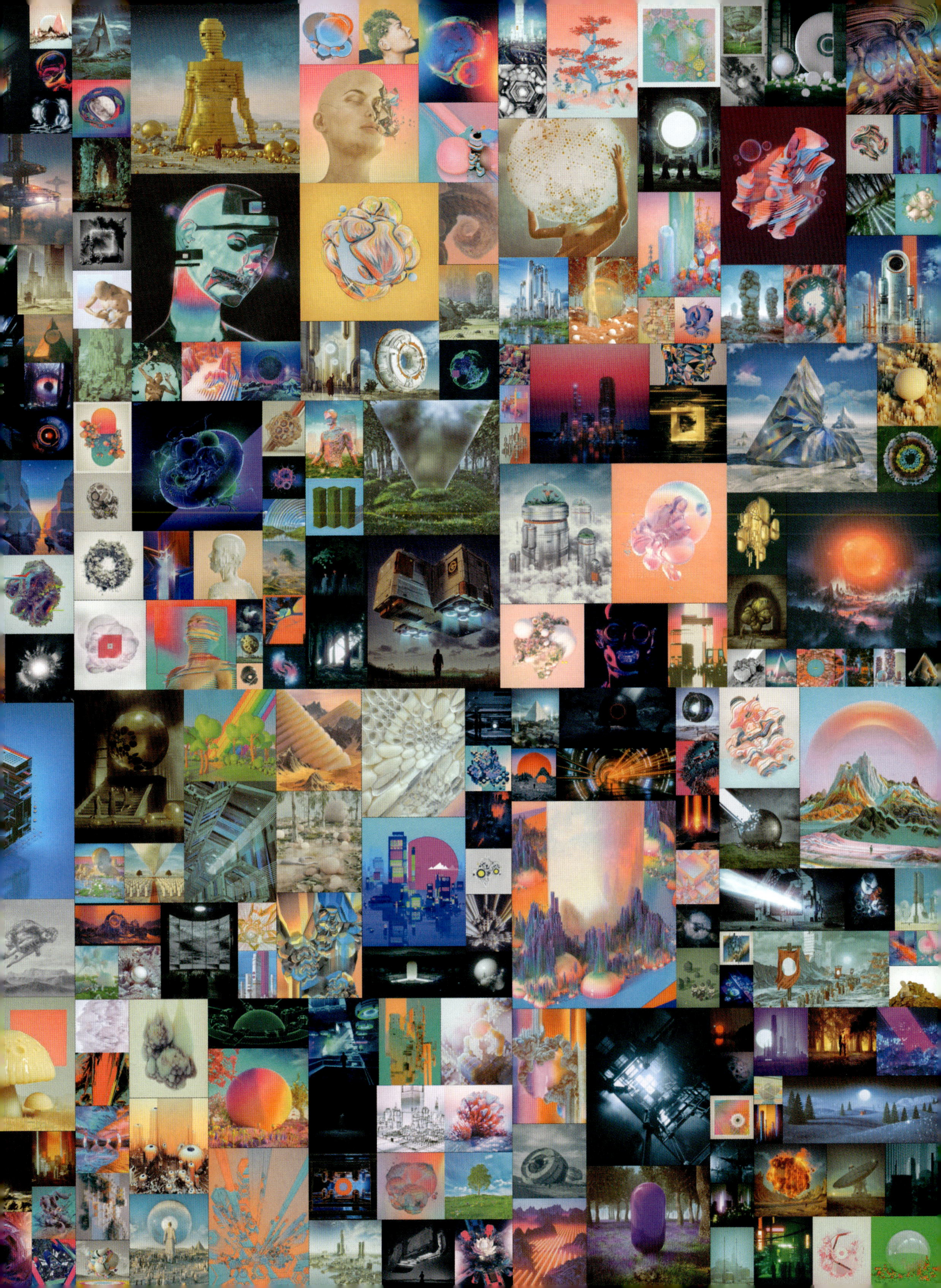

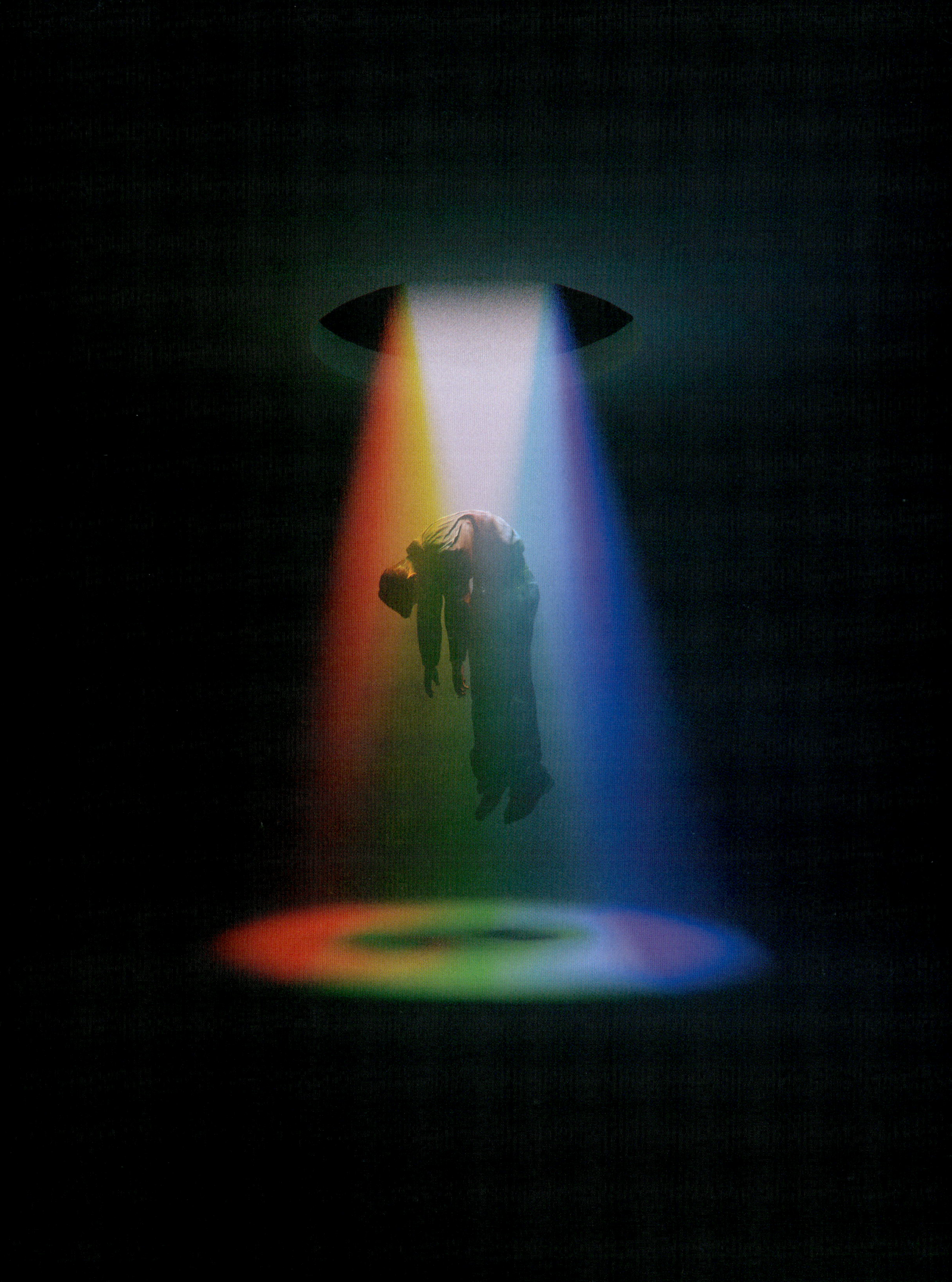

2017

OPPOSITE PAGE

CRUSHED LIGHT
02.22.2017

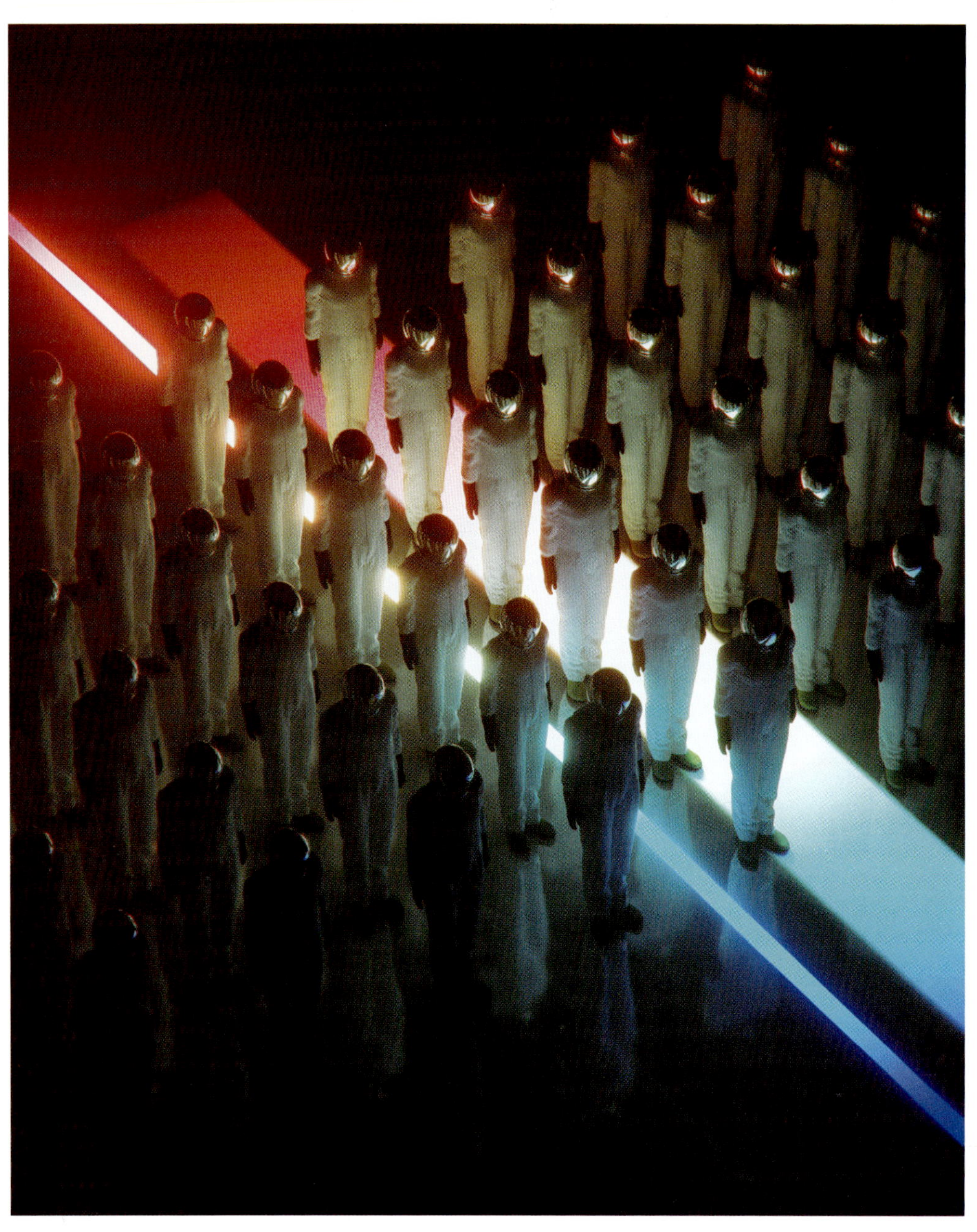

ABOVE

SPECTRUM 72

03.29.2017

OPPOSITE PAGE

1982 SAX SOLO

10.08.2017

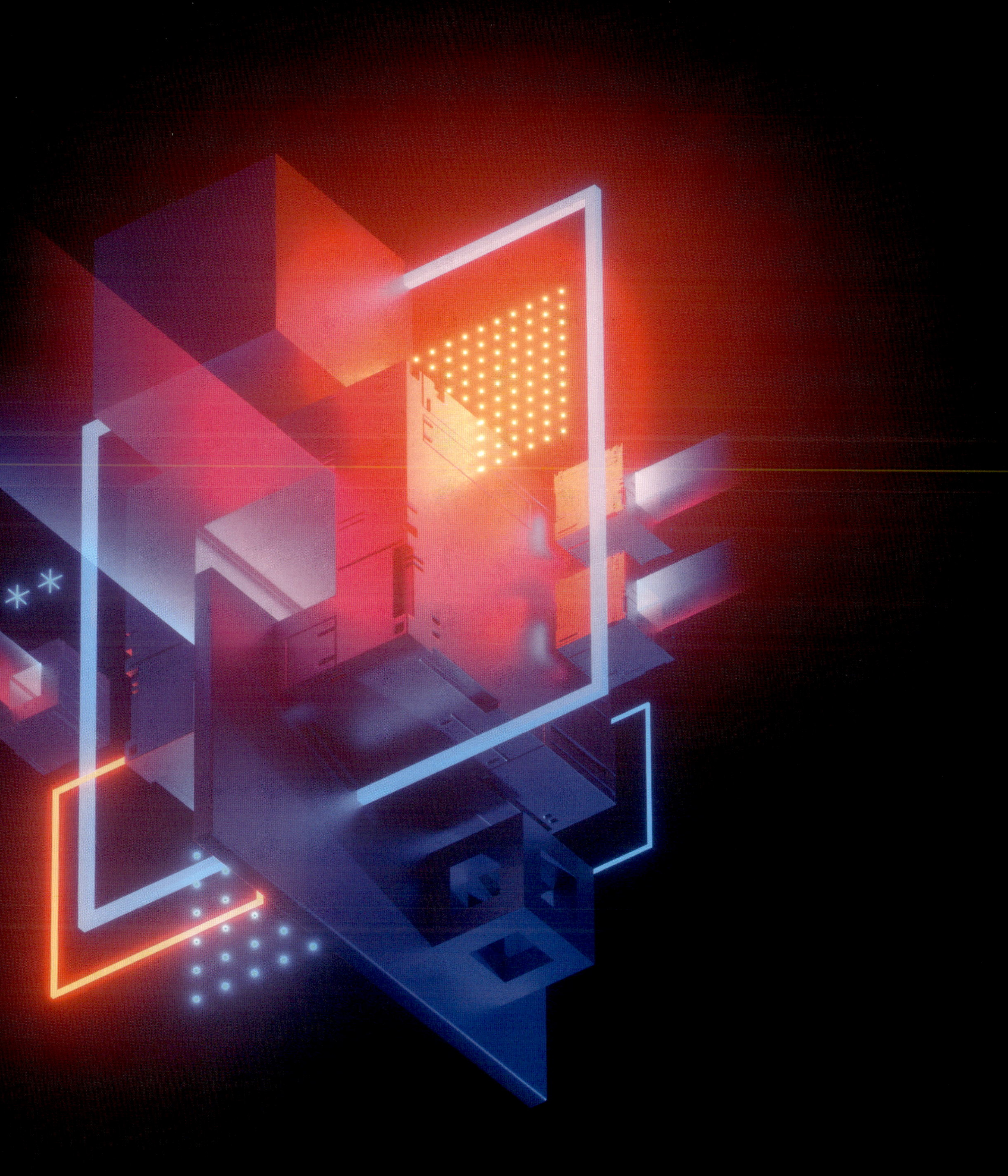

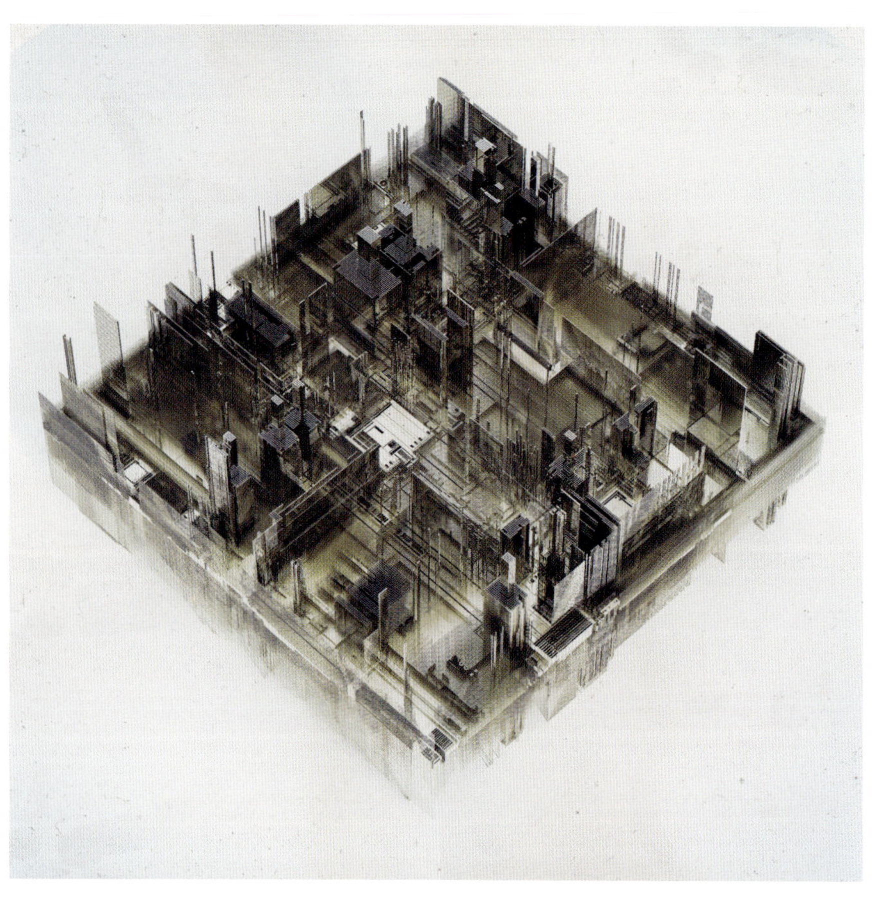

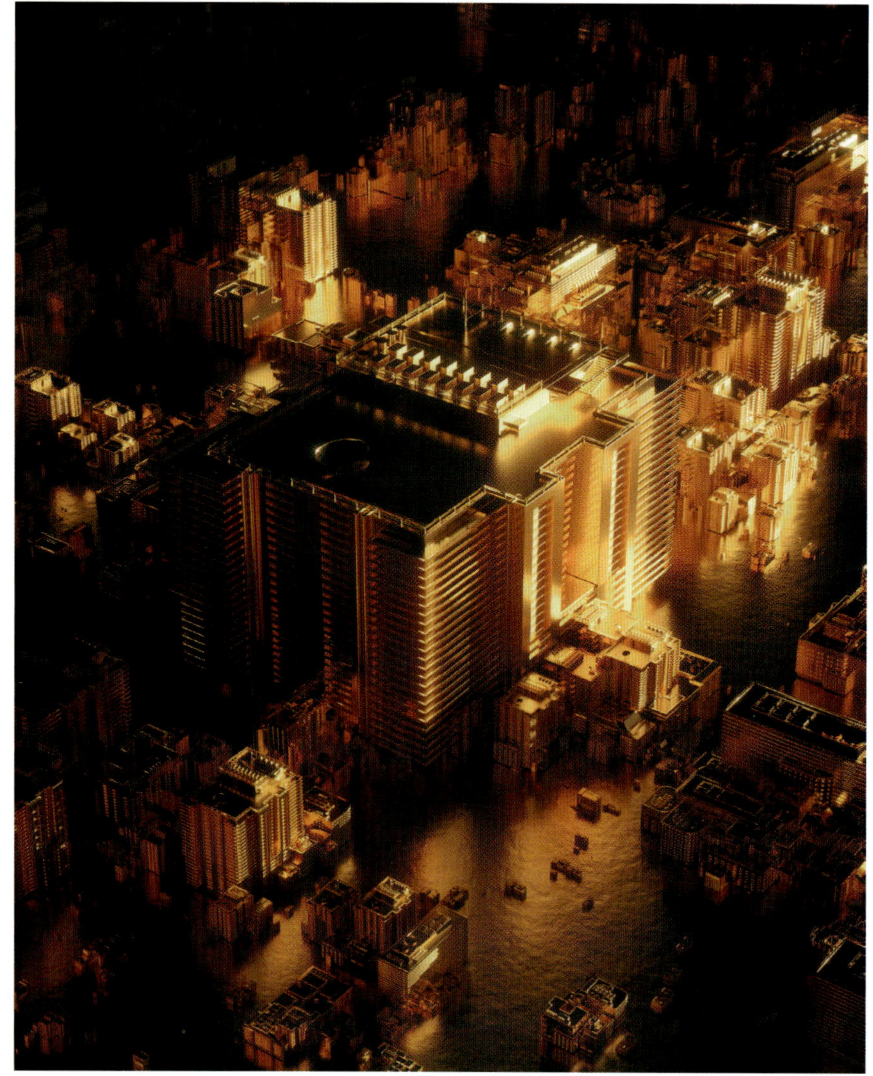

TOP

THERMAL PASTE
02.01.2017

BOTTOM

BLACK FRIDAY
11.24.2017

OPPOSITE PAGE

ACTIVATED
01.28.2017

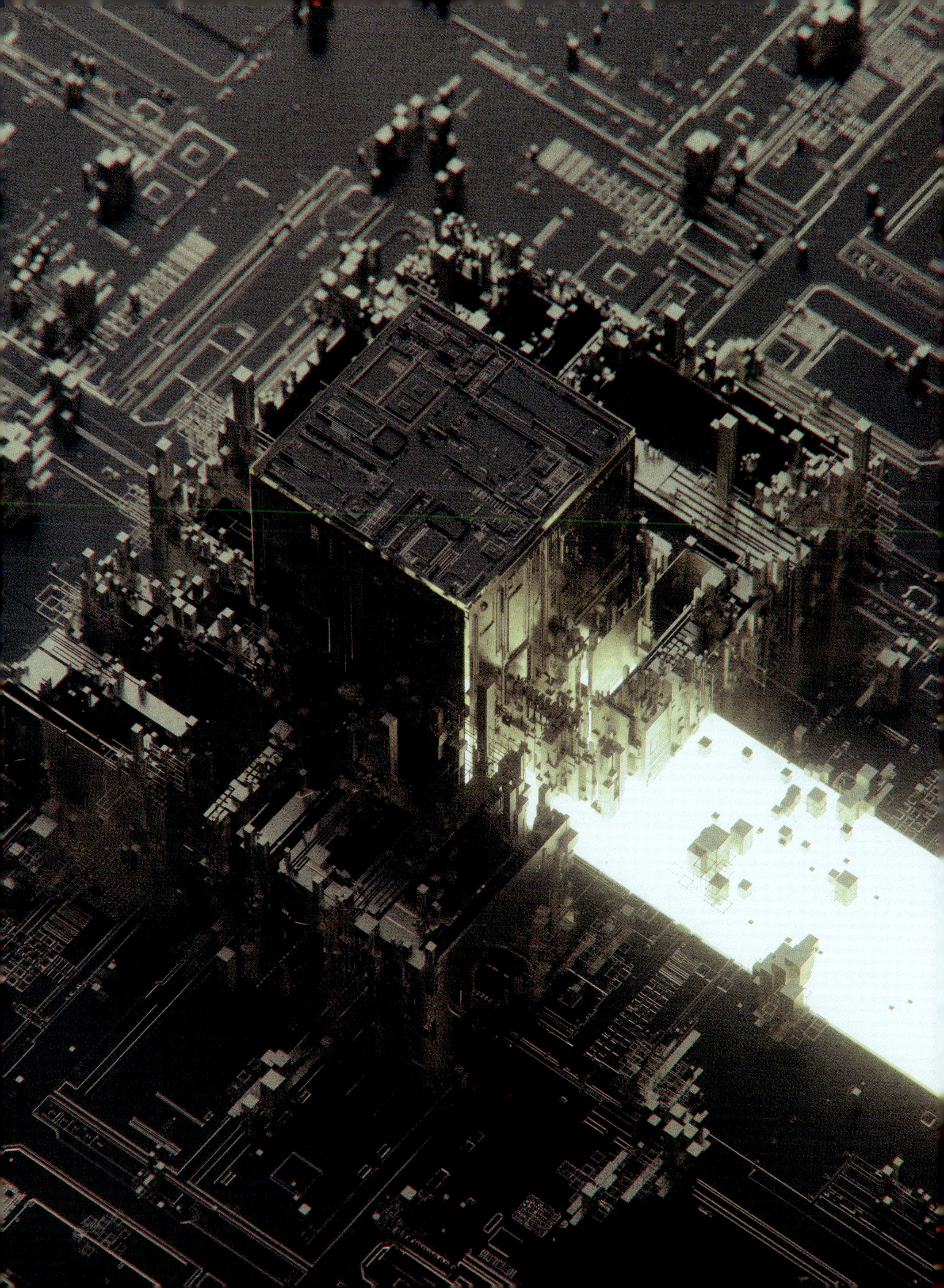

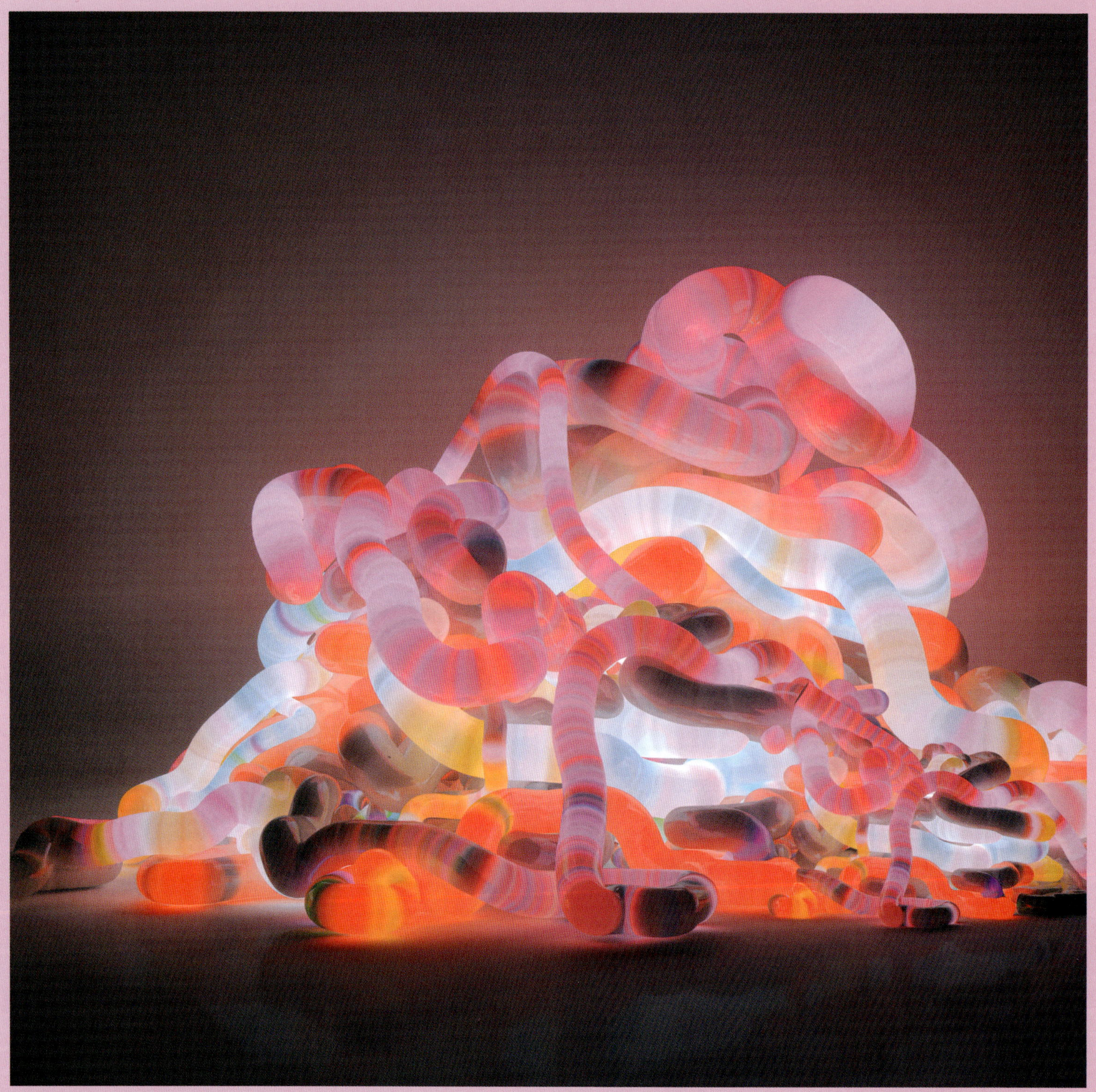

ABOVE

ELECTRIC INTESTINES
02.26.2017

OPPOSITE PAGE

ROLLBACK
03.11.2017

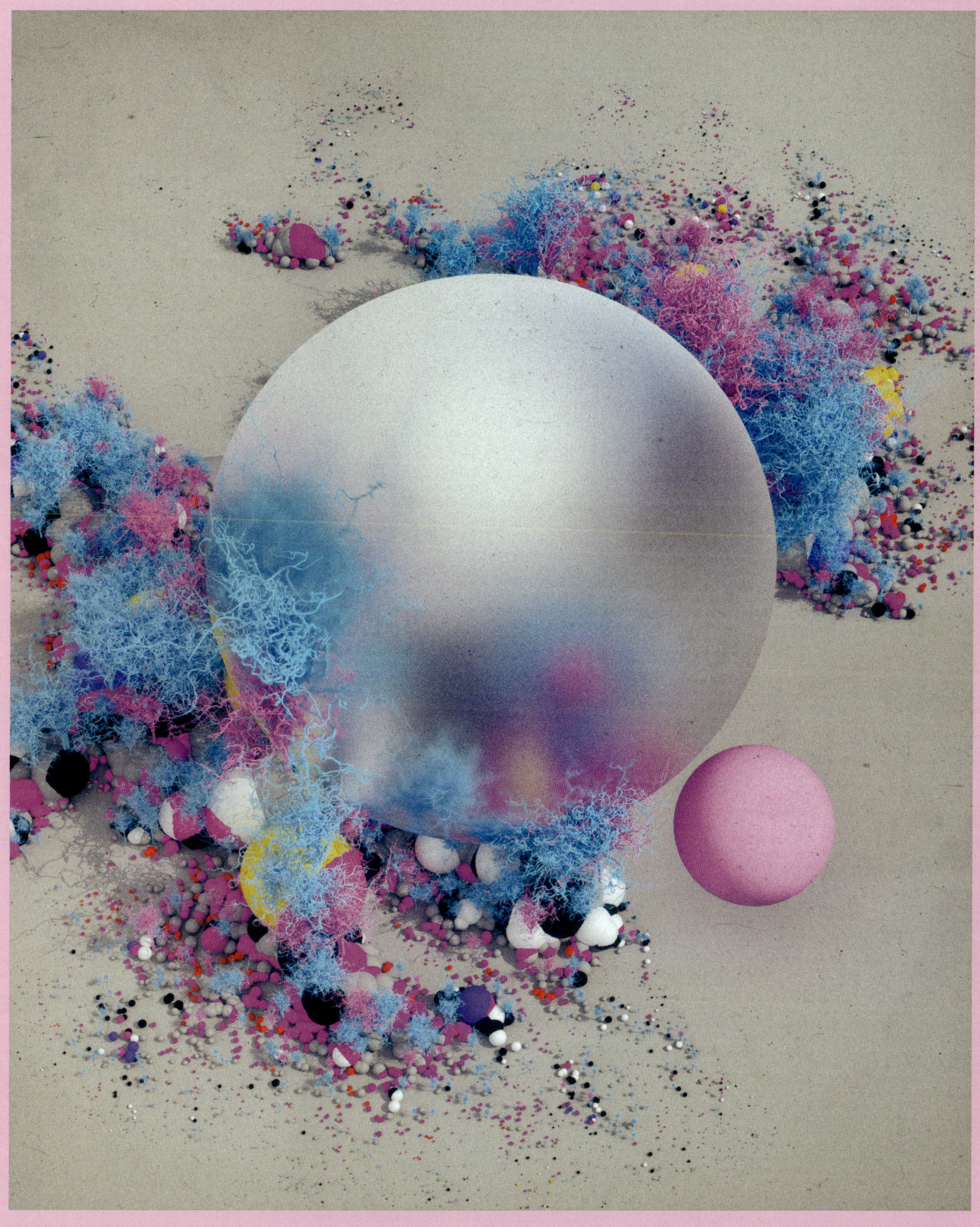

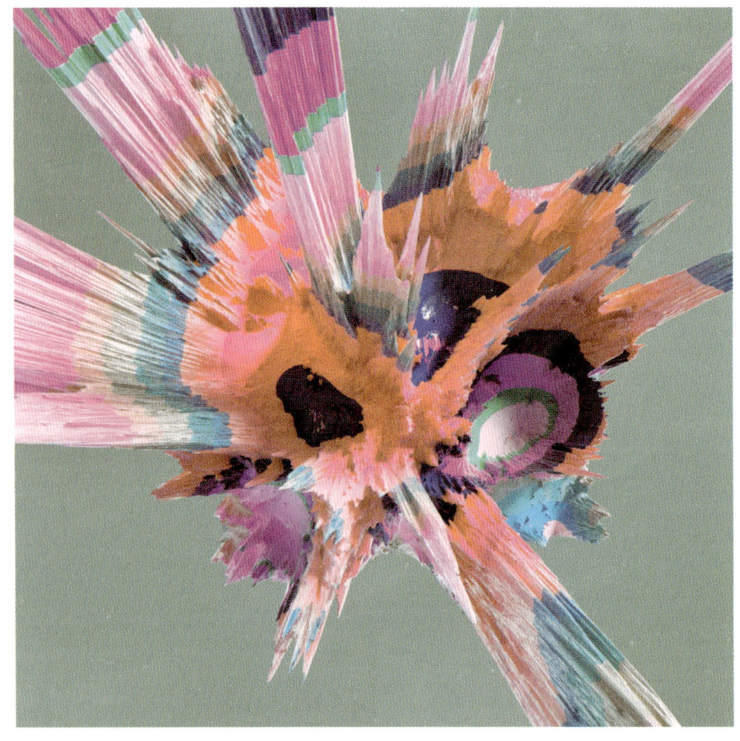

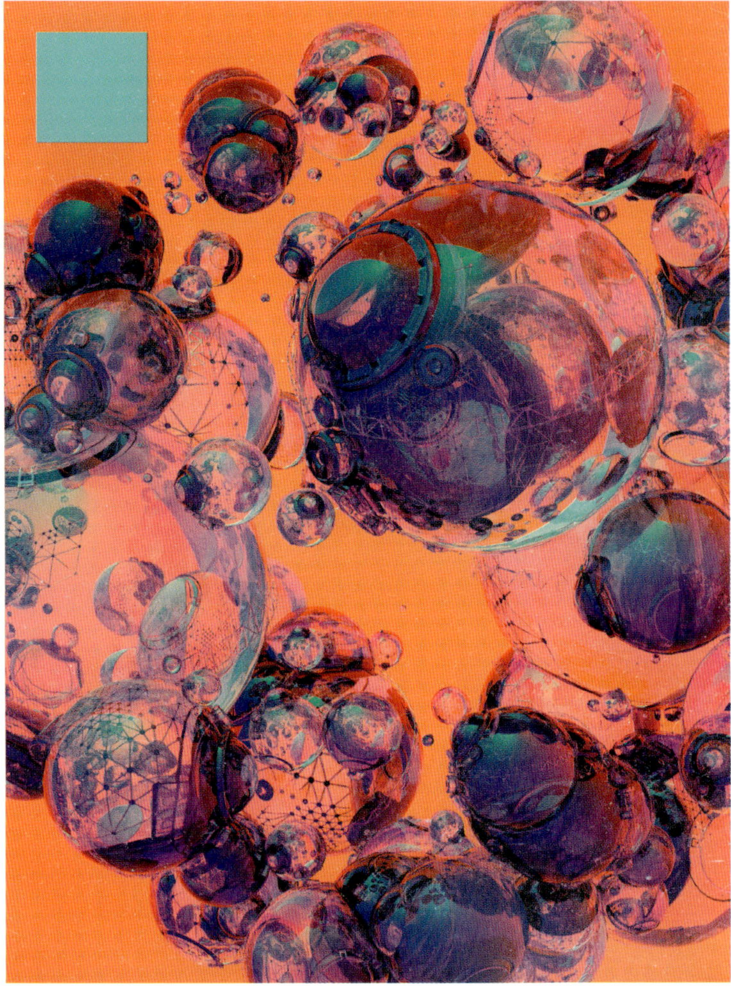

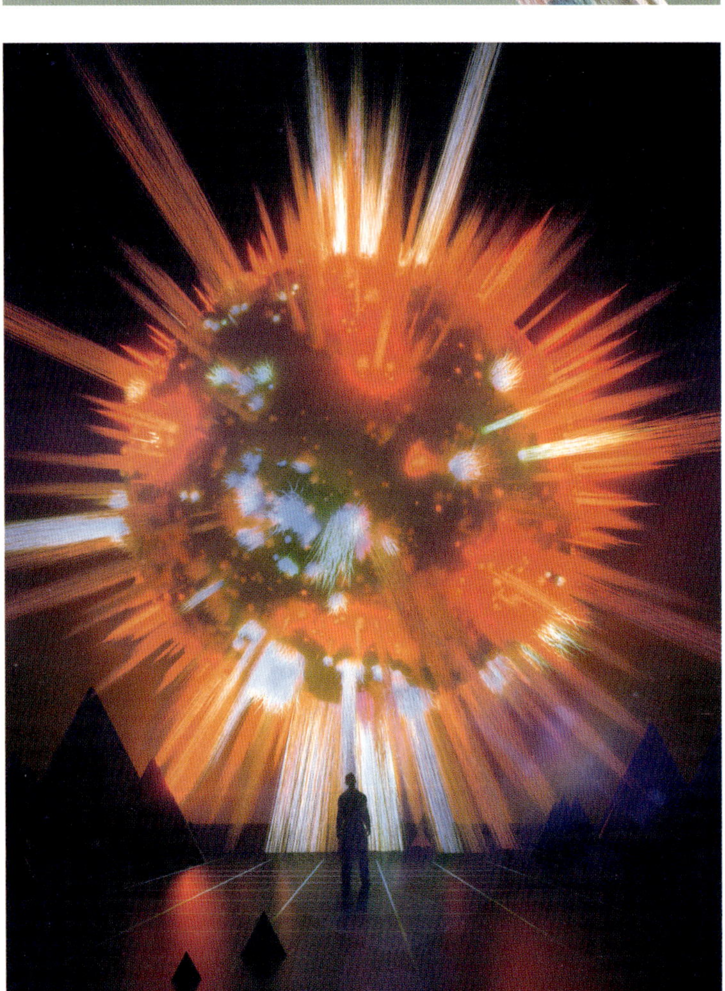

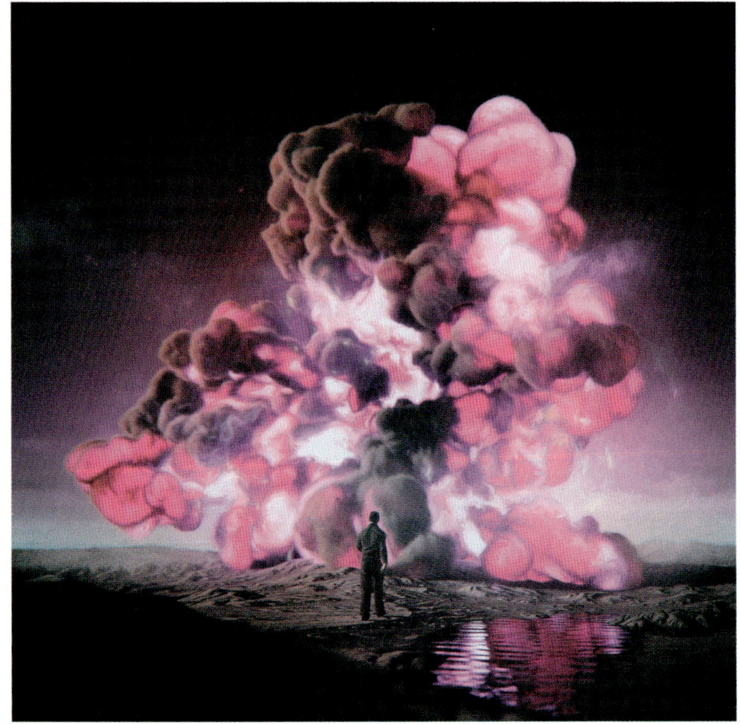

TOP LEFT
SMOKY MOUNTAINS
11.09.2017

TOP RIGHT
CABIN FEVER
11.12.2017

BOTTOM LEFT
SUPERNOVA
03.07.2017

BOTTOM RIGHT
PINK MUSTARD
03.06.2017

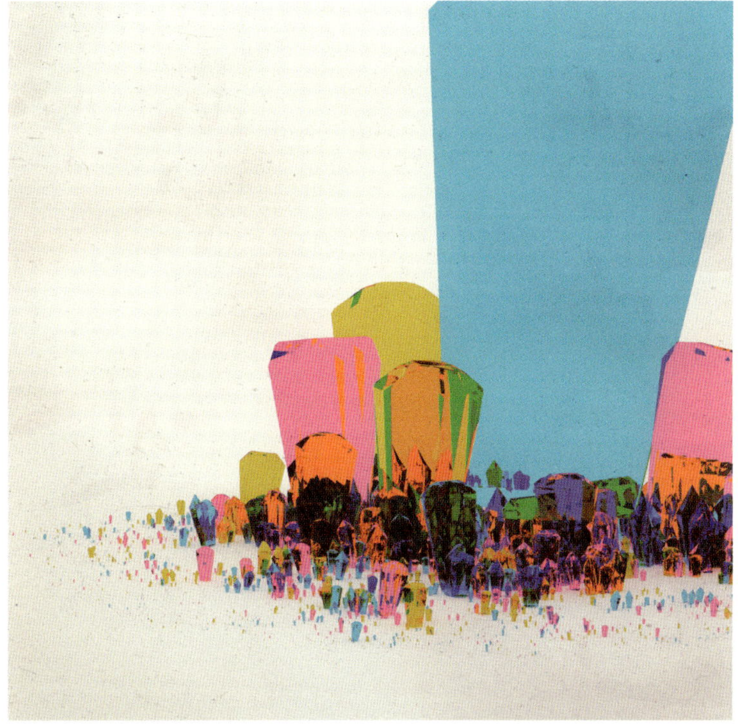

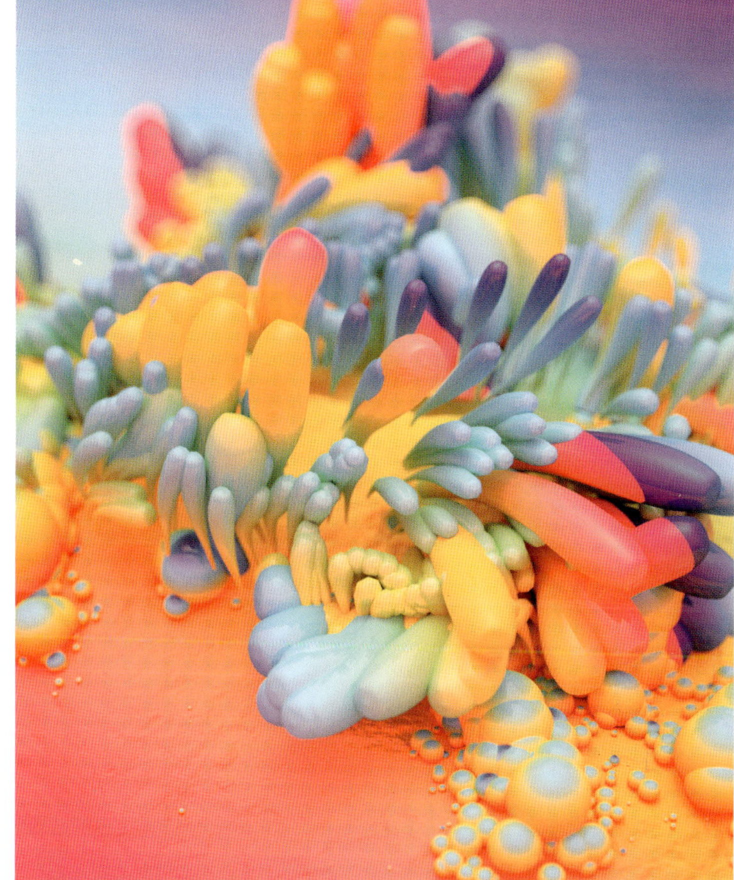

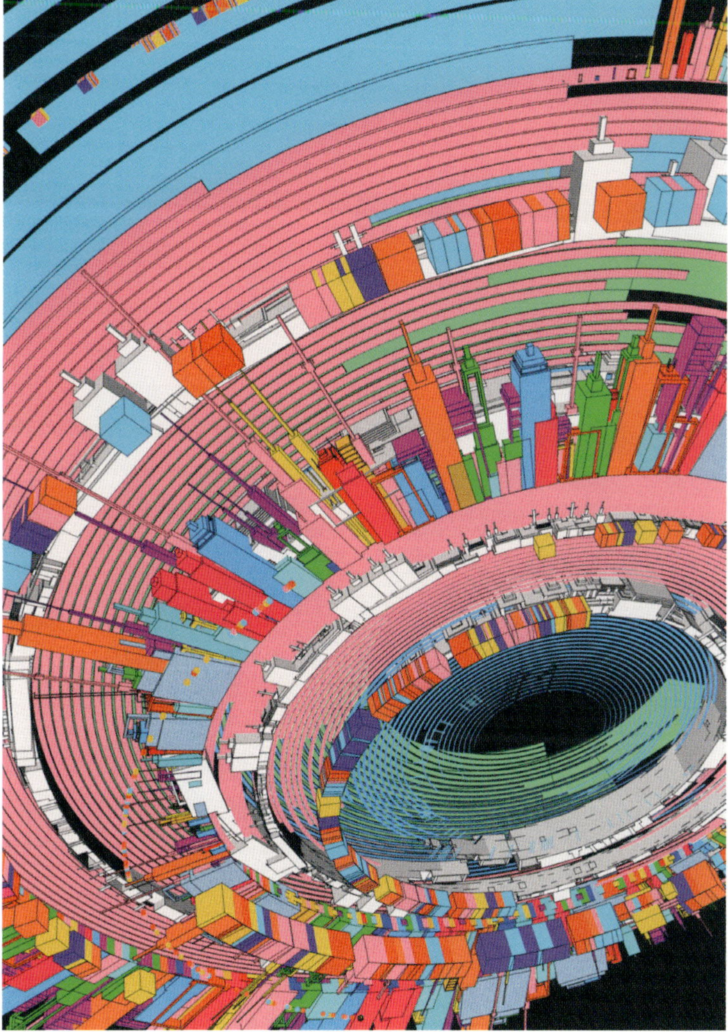

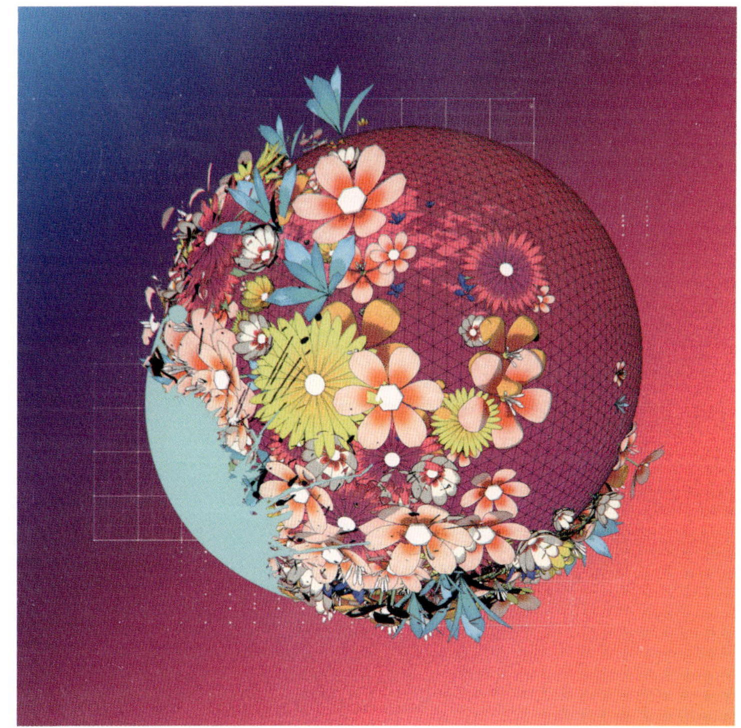

TOP LEFT

FRACTURED ATTENTION

04.28.2017

TOP RIGHT

COLOR.FLU

04.21.2017

BOTTOM LEFT

HUG EVERYBODY

04.10.2017

BOTTOM RIGHT

CAFFEINATED

04.09.2017

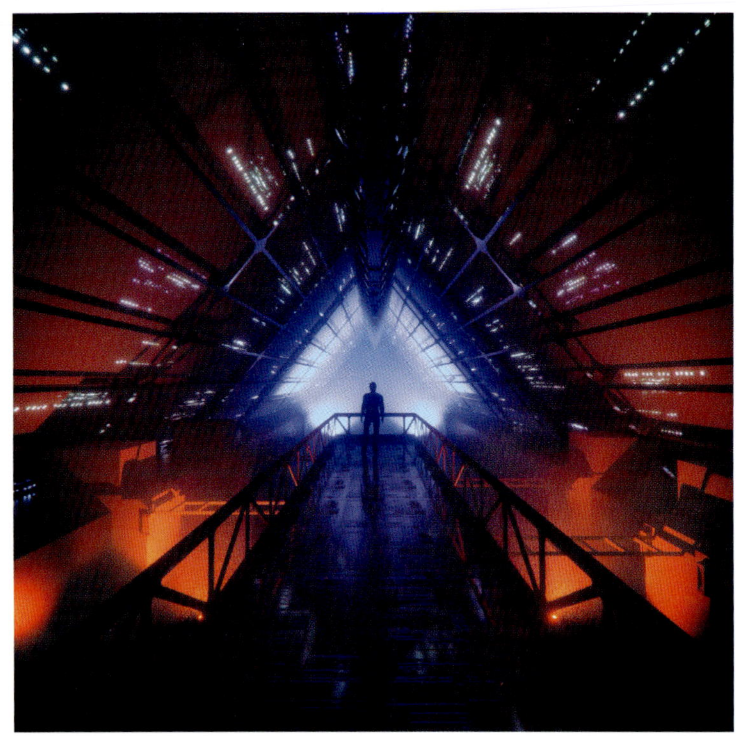

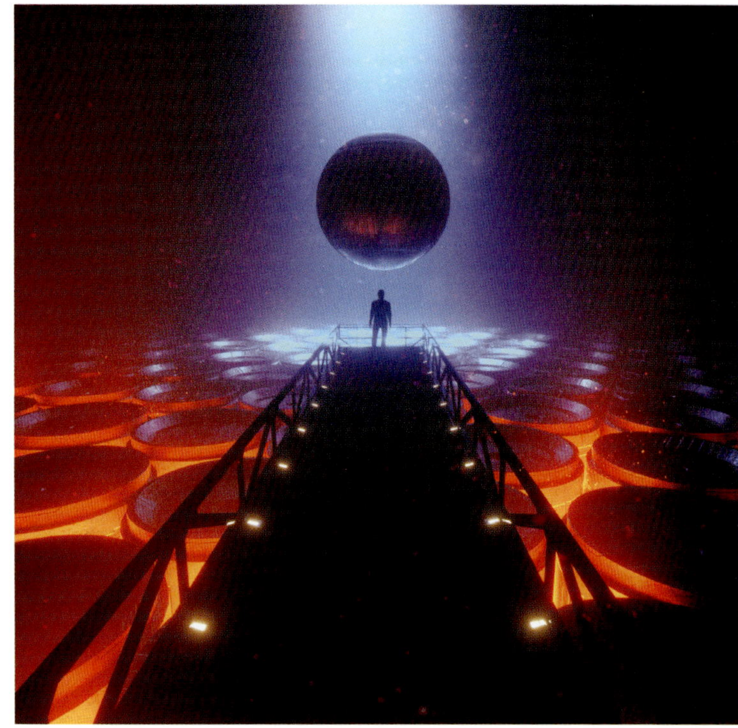

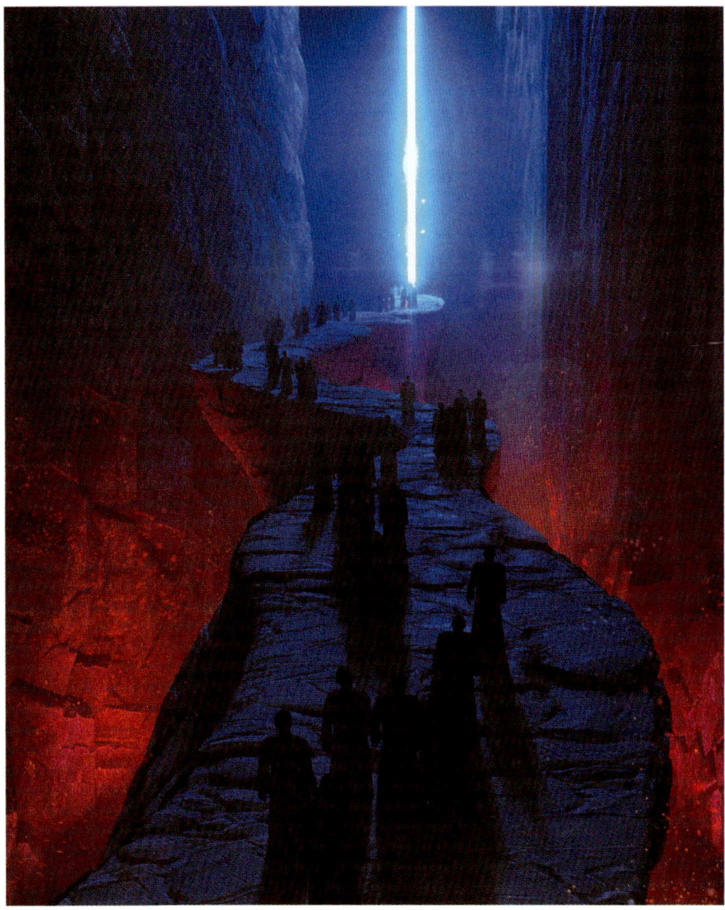

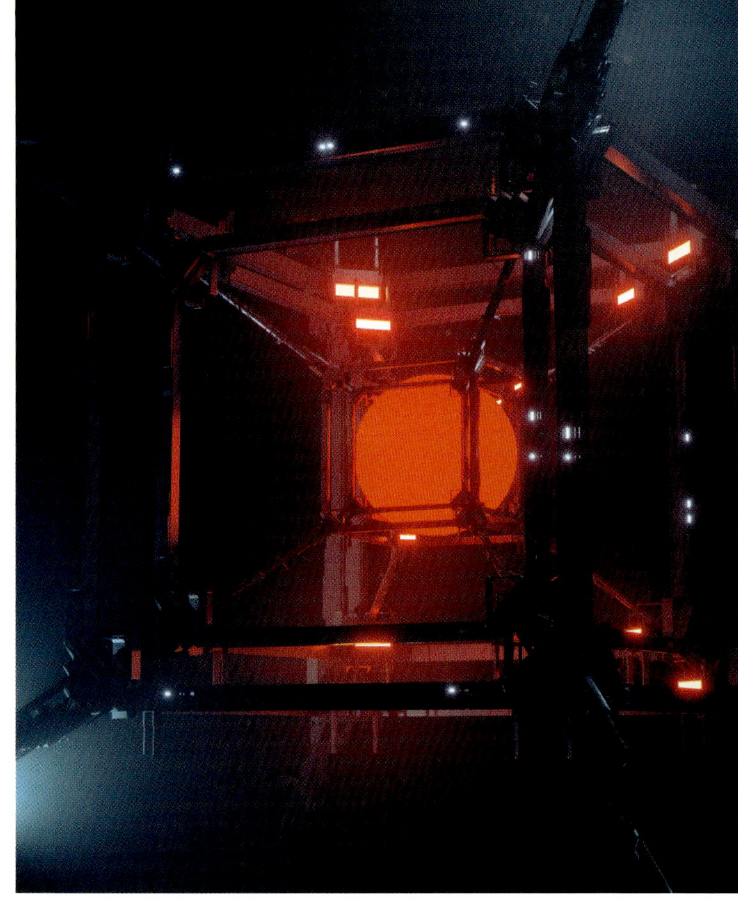

TOP LEFT
HYPERLIGHT78
05.13.2017

TOP RIGHT
LEVEL NINE
05.22.2017

BOTTOM LEFT
COMMENCEMENT
05.14.2017

BOTTOM RIGHT
RAGE
02.02.2017

OPPOSITE PAGE
CLEAN ROOM
03.23.2017

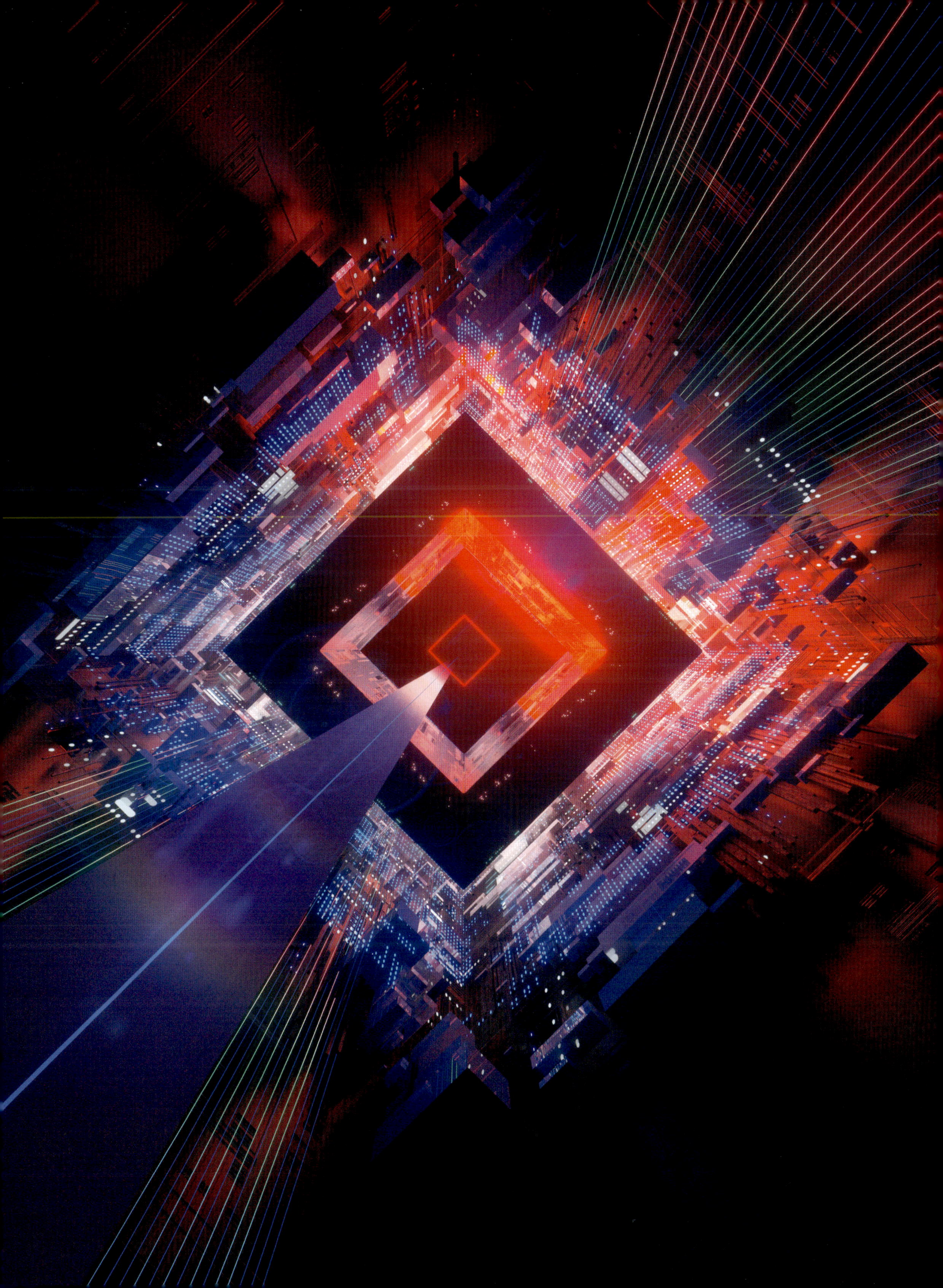

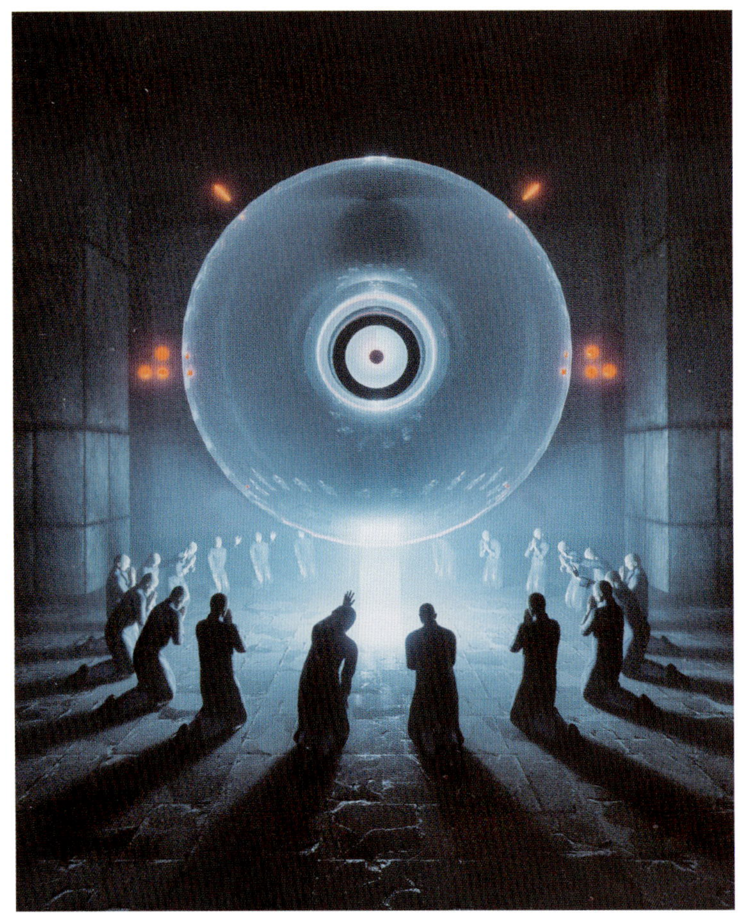

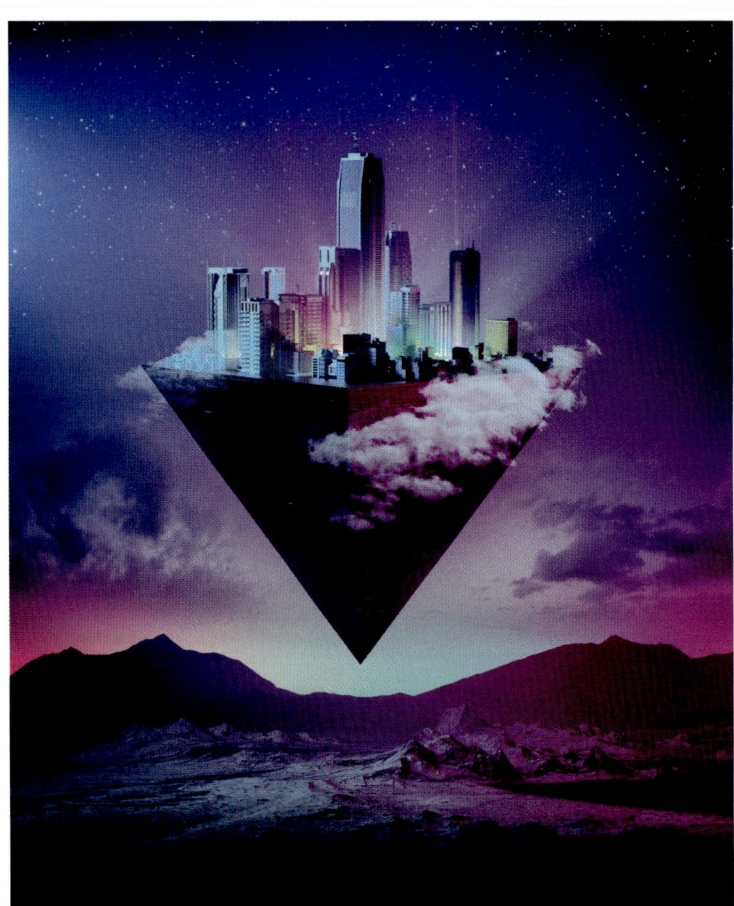

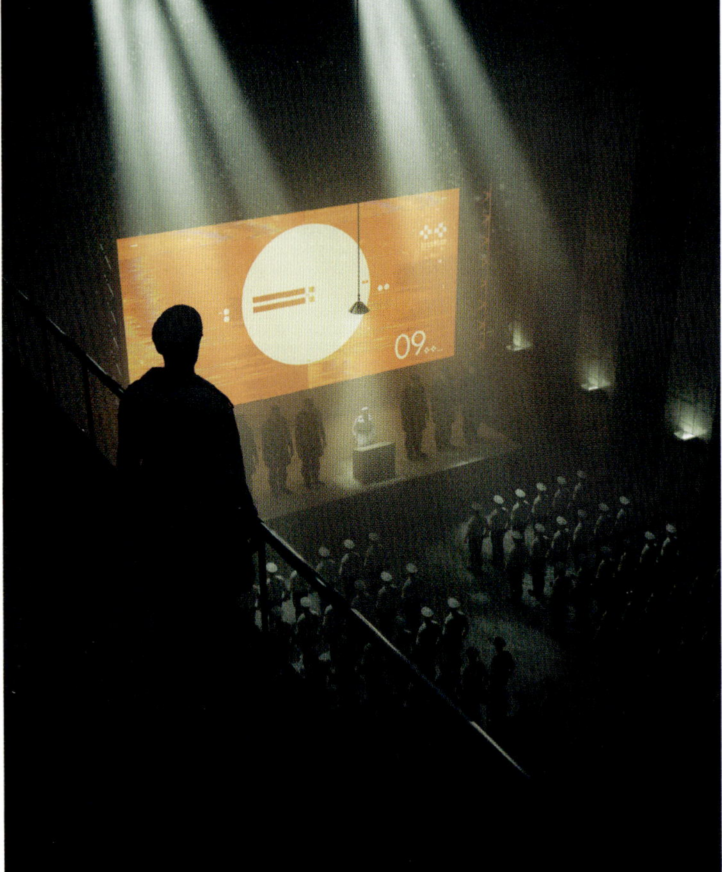

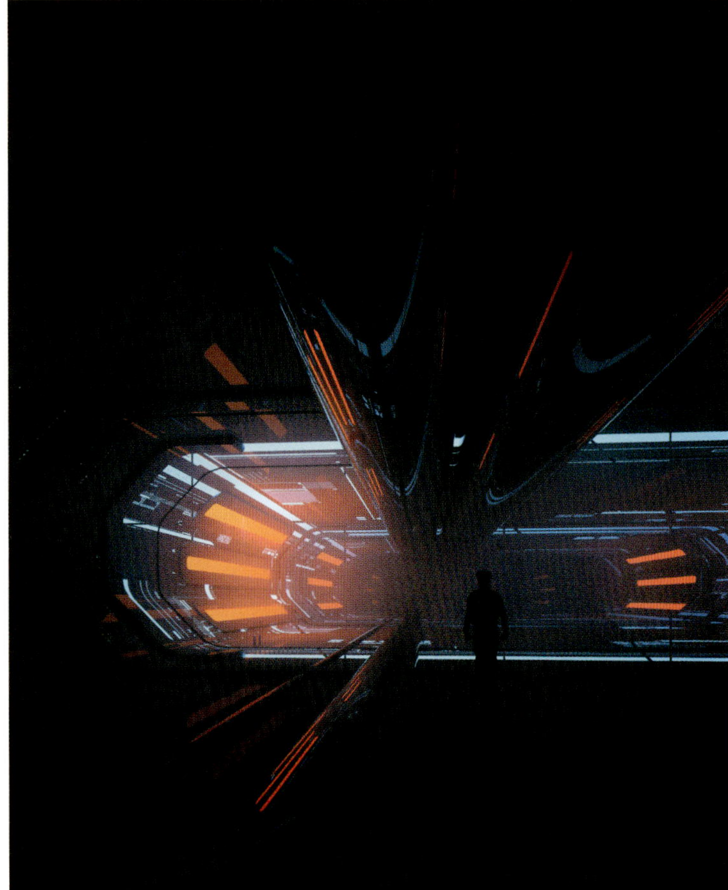

TOP LEFT
USER INTERFACE
03.27.2017

TOP RIGHT
TRIANGULATE
11.13.2017

BOTTOM LEFT
ZERO.NINE
02.06.2017

BOTTOM RIGHT
XEON.FUTURE
02.25.2017

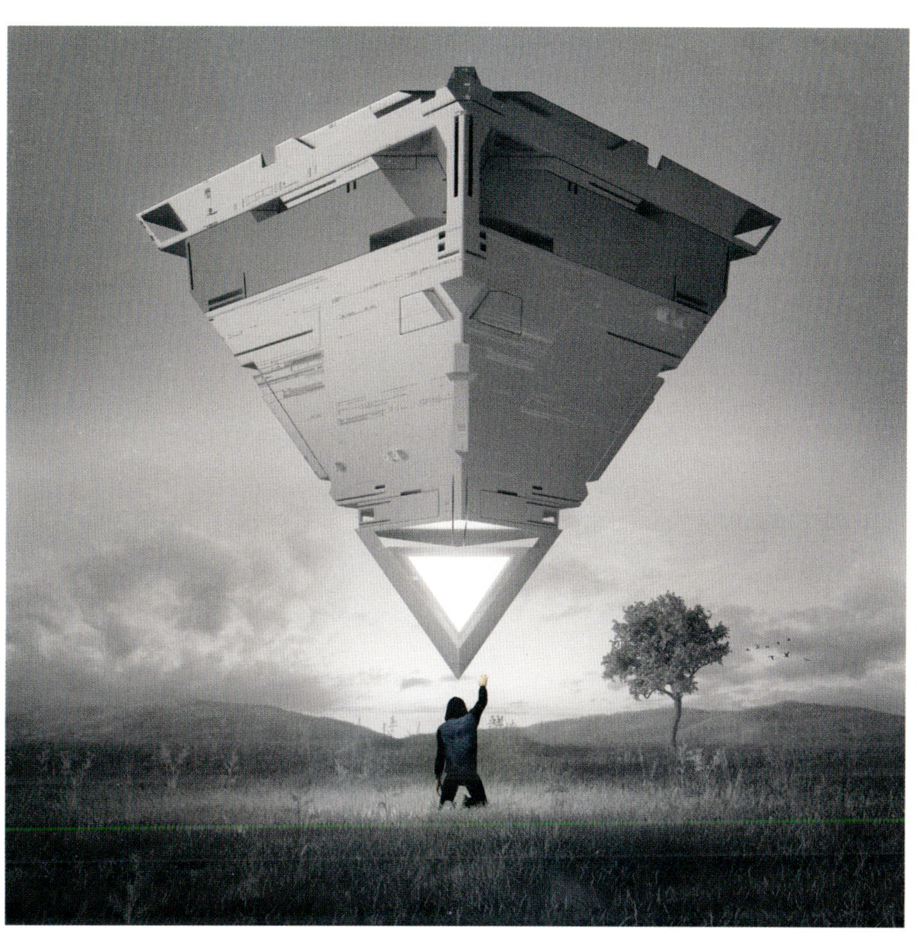

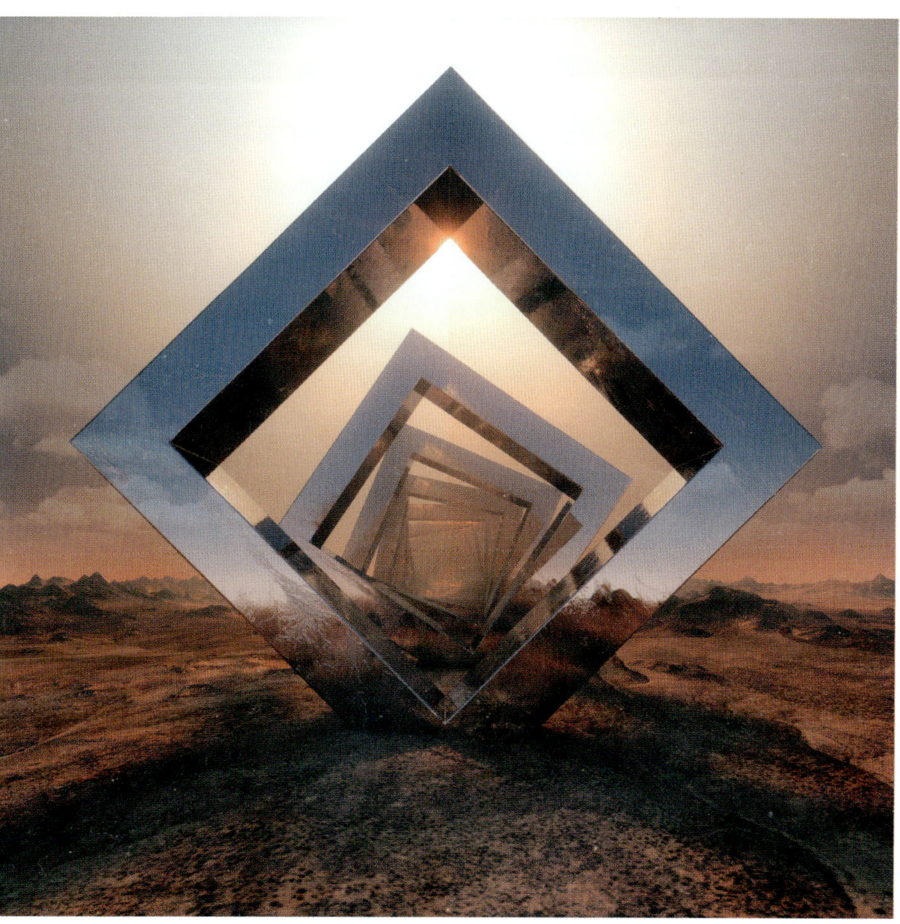

TOP
MONOCHROMAT
03.18.2017

BOTTOM
TRIOMETRIC
03.31.2017

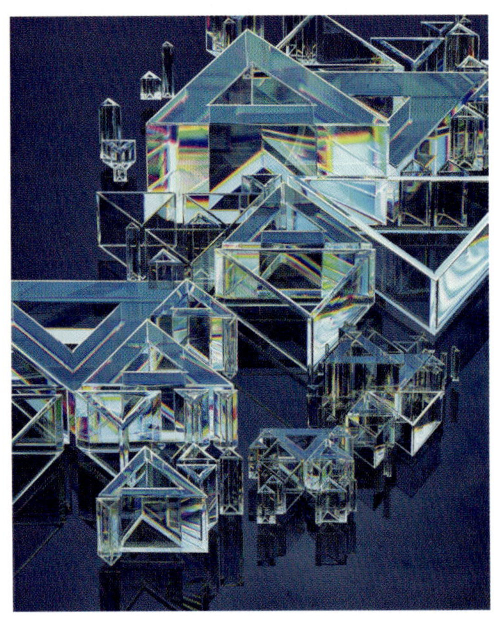

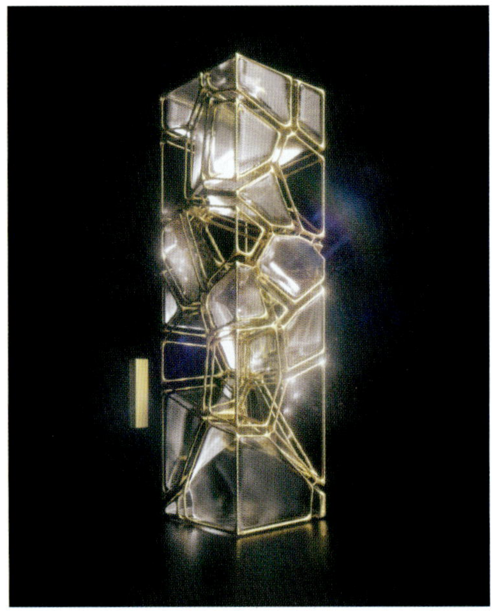

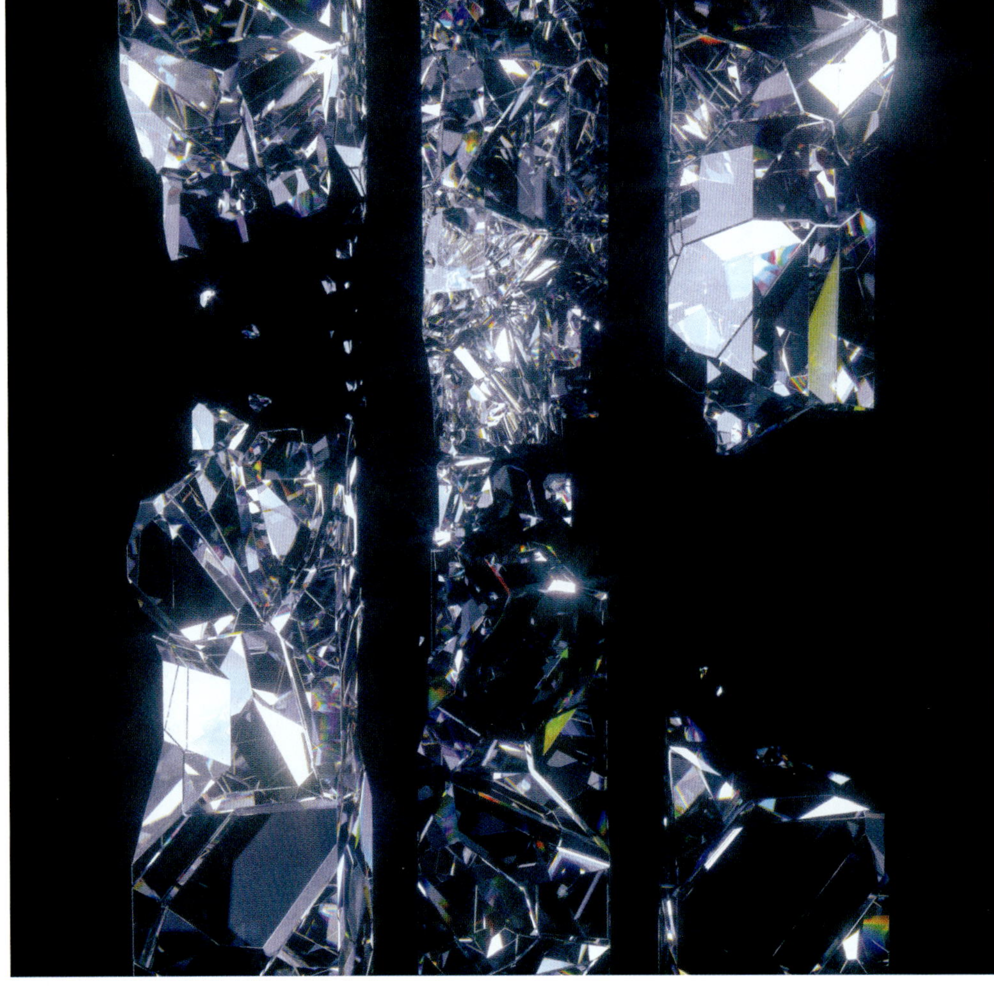

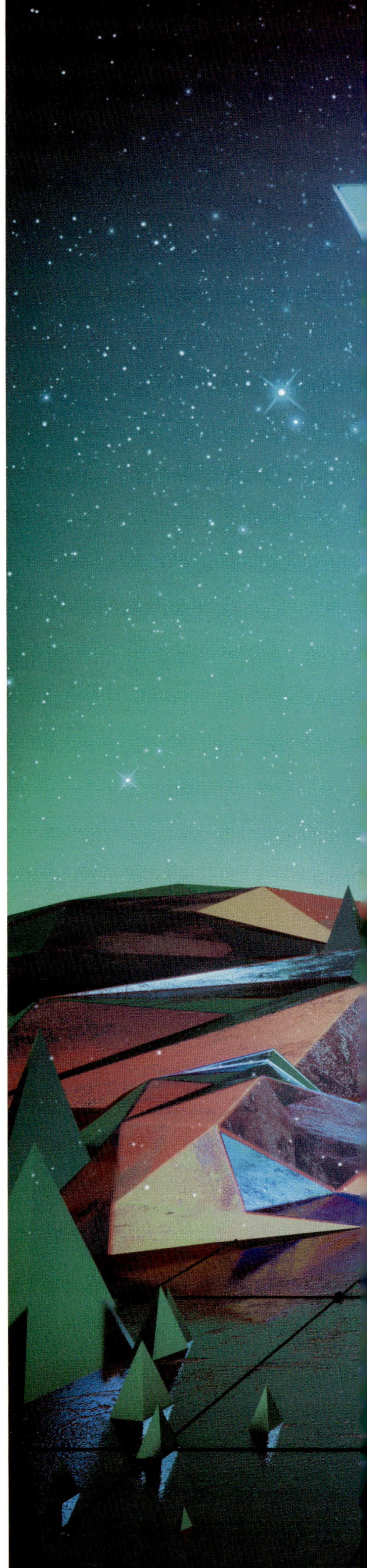

TOP LEFT

TRIAGONAL GEMINI 1978

05.24.2017

TOP RIGHT

HOLLOW GOLD

10.03.2017

BOTTOM

ONE HUNDRED

03.17.2017

OPPOSITE PAGE

GLASS FRACTALS

04.20.2017

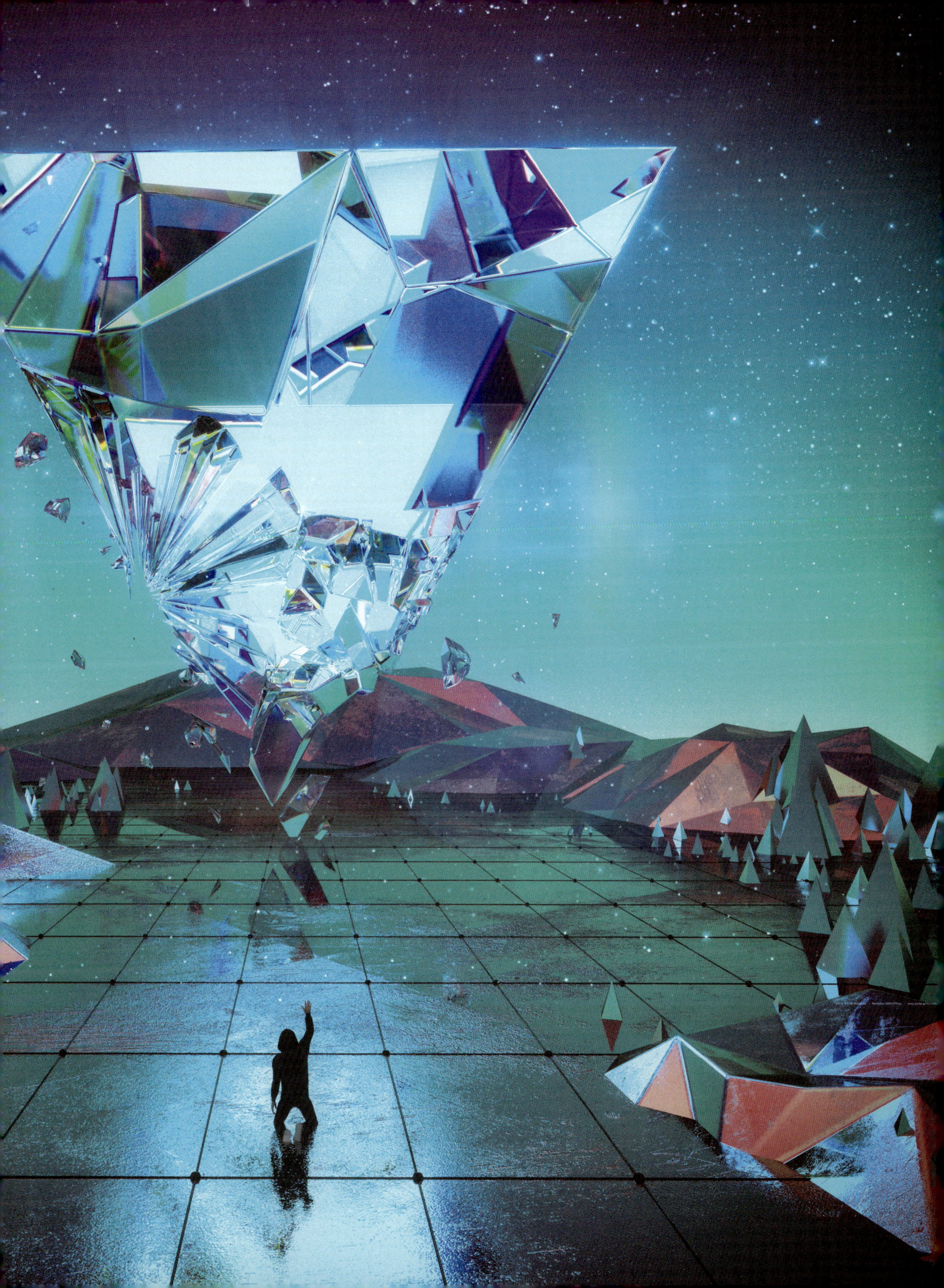

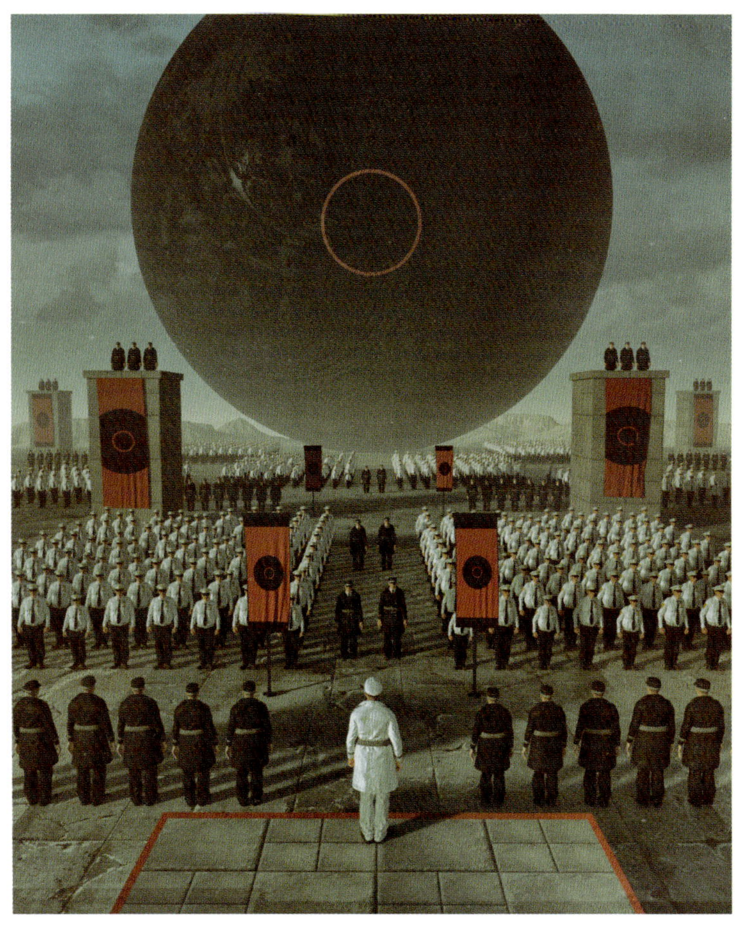

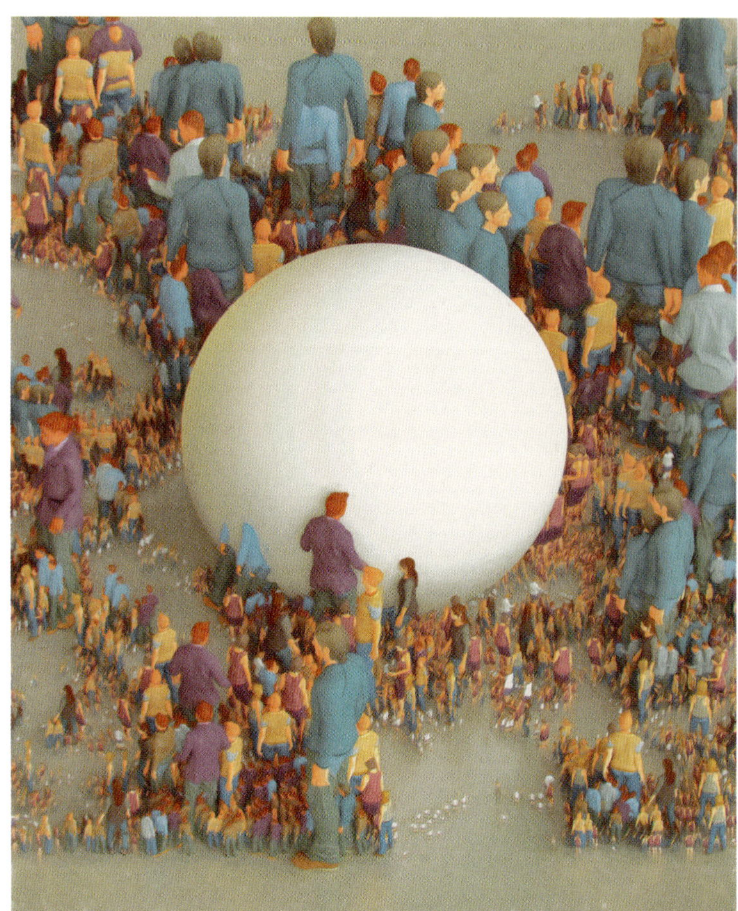

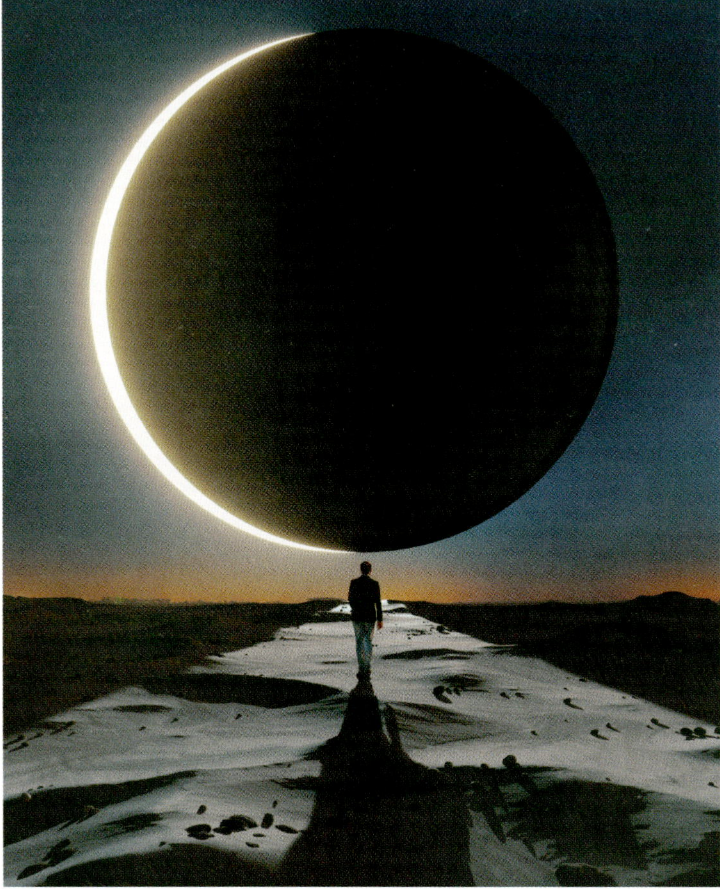

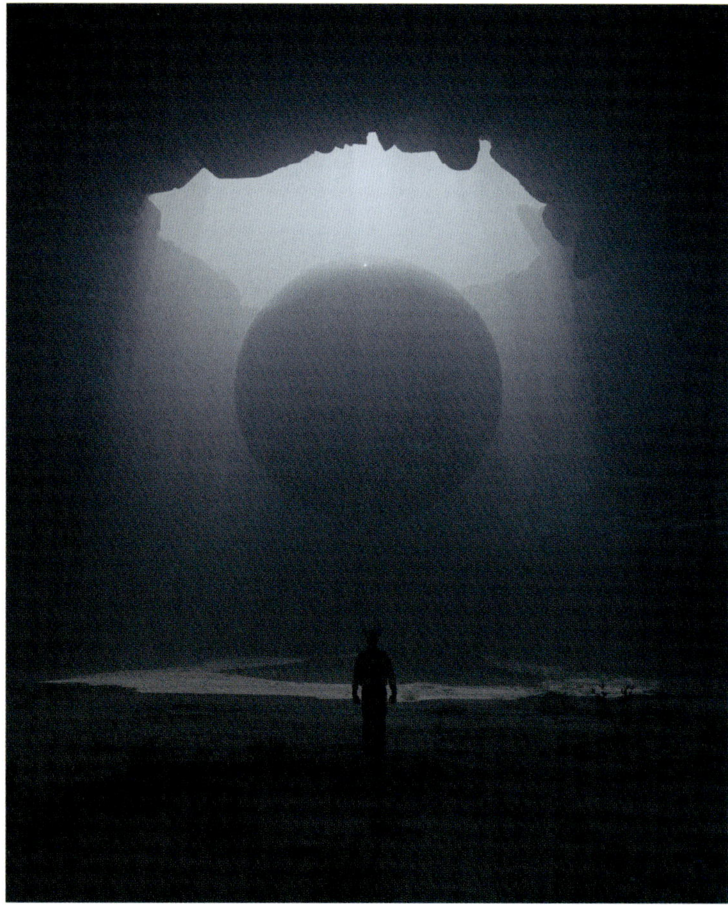

TOP LEFT
FULL CIRCLE
01.07.2017

TOP RIGHT
EVERYONE
02.08.2017

BOTTOM LEFT
TOTALITY
08.21.2017

BOTTOM RIGHT
LIFTED
02.03.2017

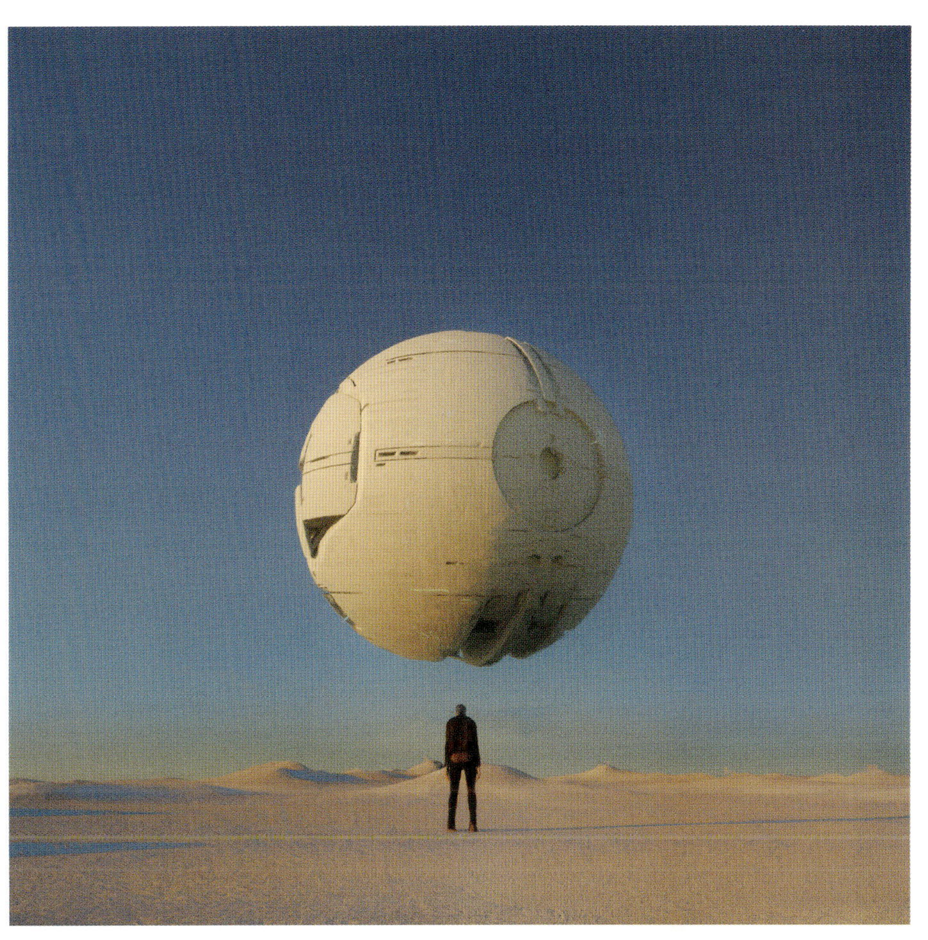

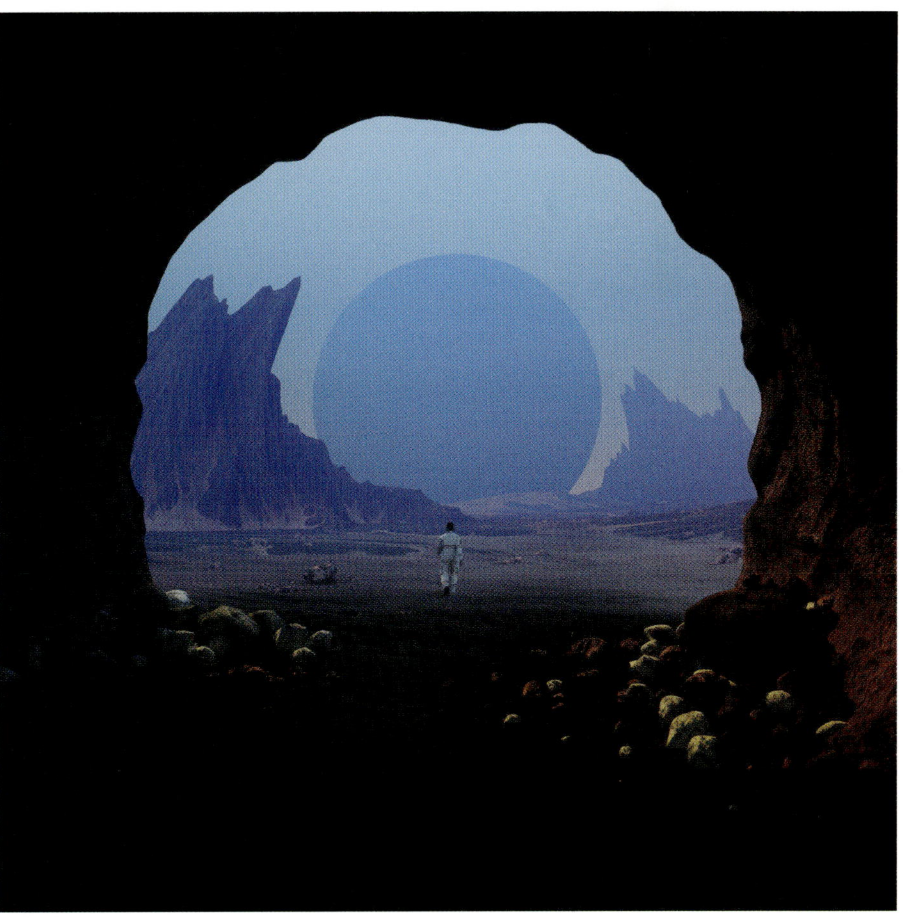

TOP

LIFE

02.10.2017

BOTTOM

BLUE DAWN

05.31.2017

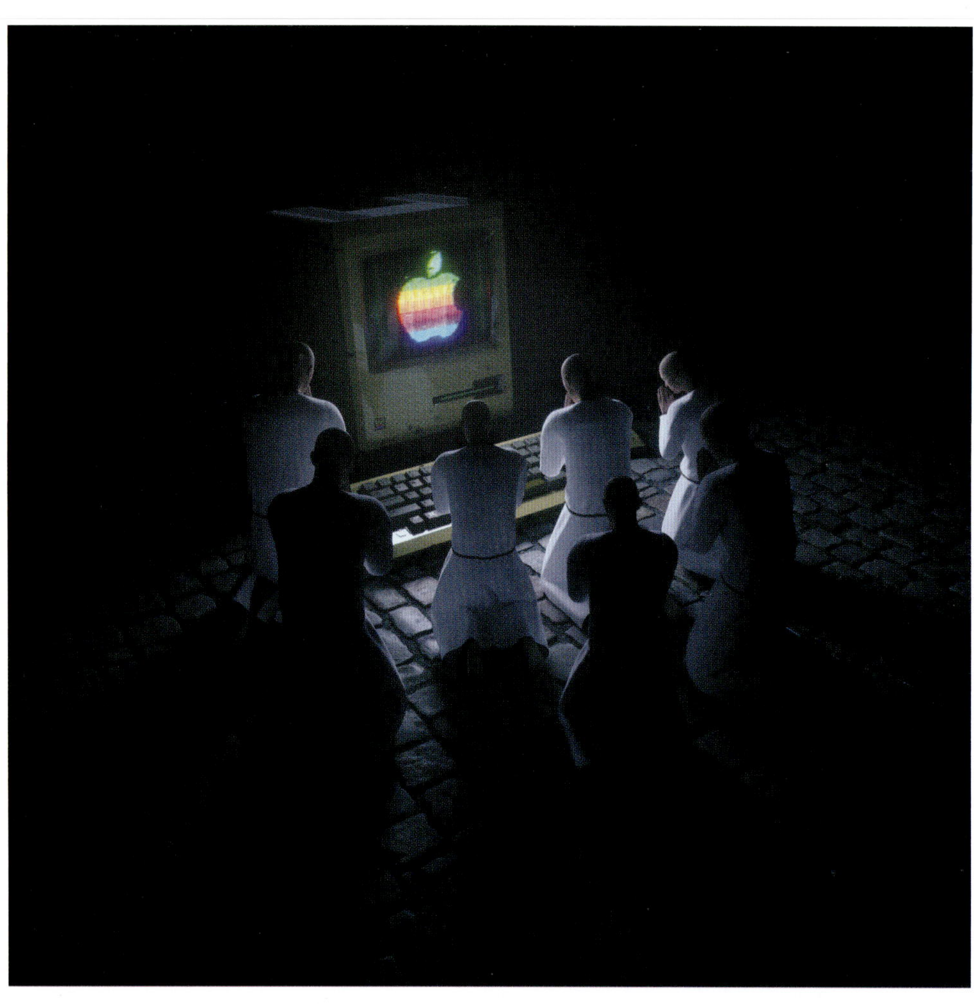

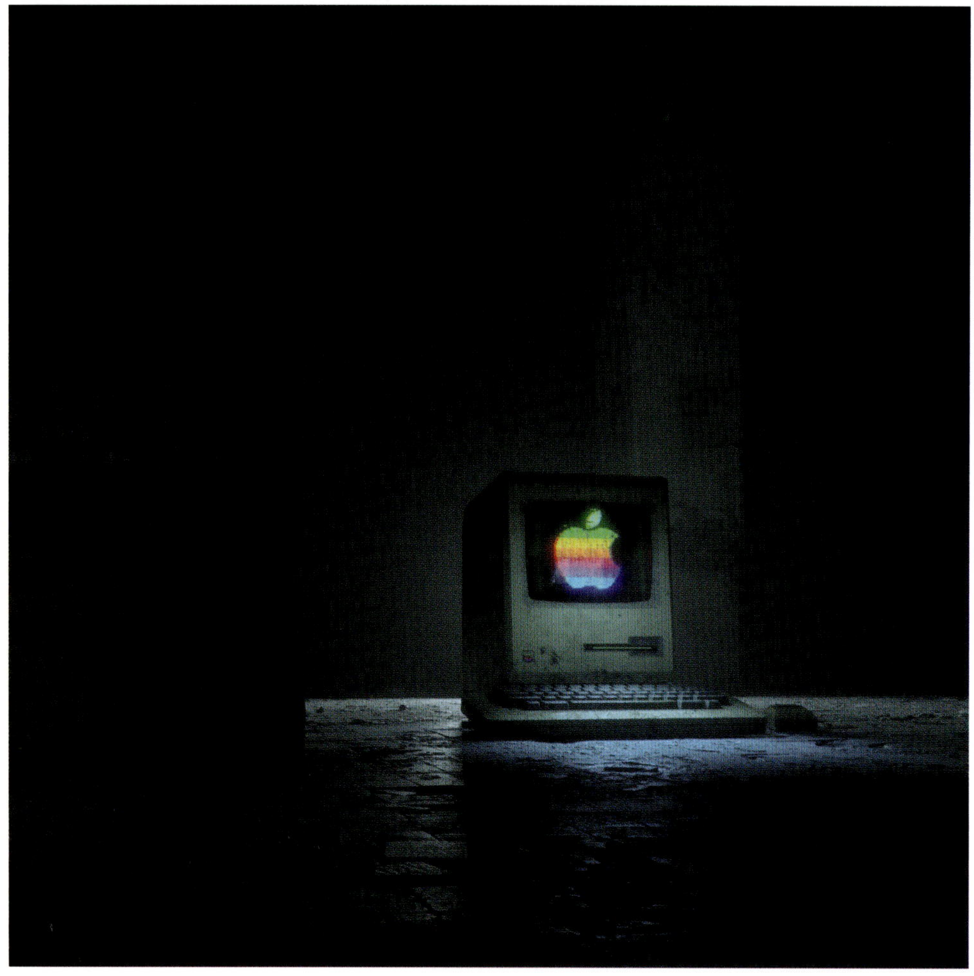

TOP

CULT OF MAC
12.01.2017

BOTTOM

BLUE SCREEN
10.10.2017

OPPOSITE PAGE, TOP LEFT

GENIUS BAR 2067
07.17.2017

OPPOSITE PAGE, TOP RIGHT

FACEBOOK REGISTRATION 2063
08.14.2017

OPPOSITE PAGE, BOTTOM LEFT

IPHONE 36s
07.28.2017

OPPOSITE PAGE, BOTTOM RIGHT

NEWS FEED
07.23.2017

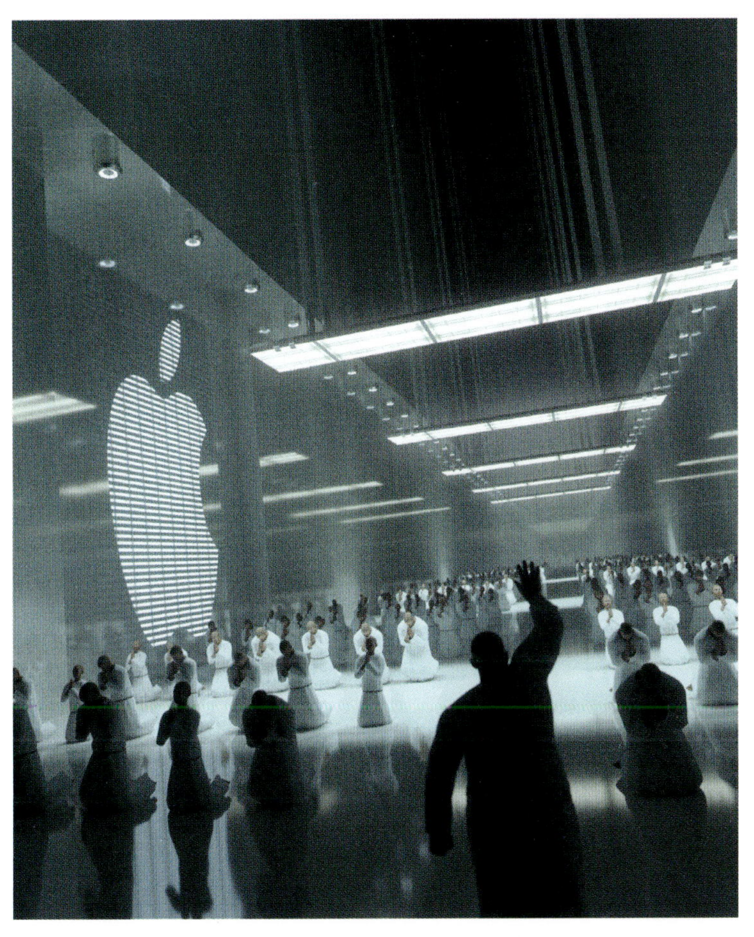

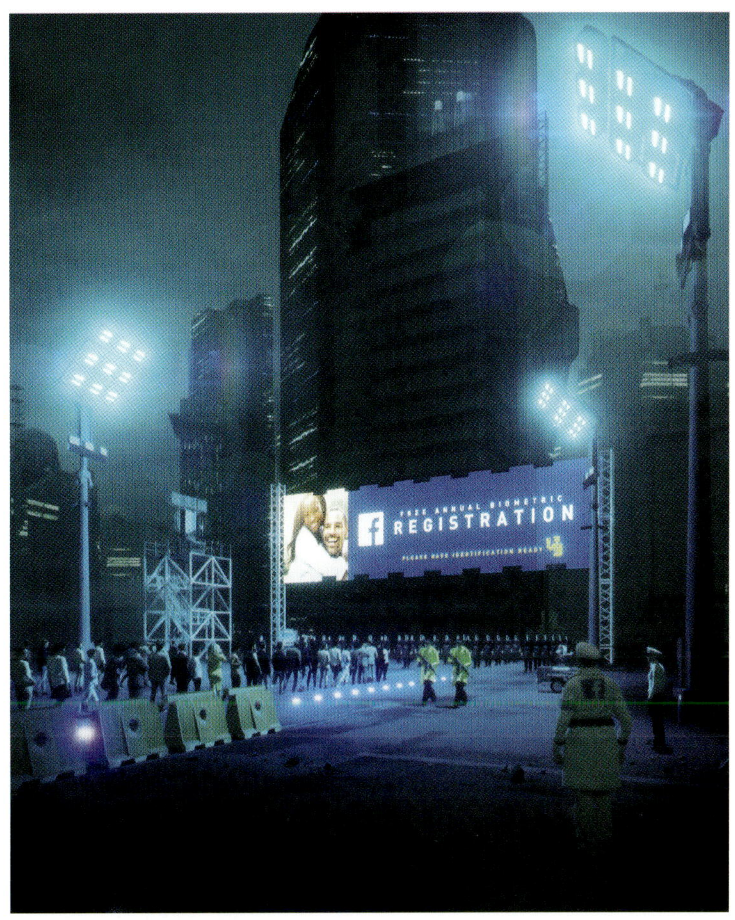
FREE ANNUAL BIOMETRIC
REGISTRATION
PLEASE HAVE IDENTIFICATION READY

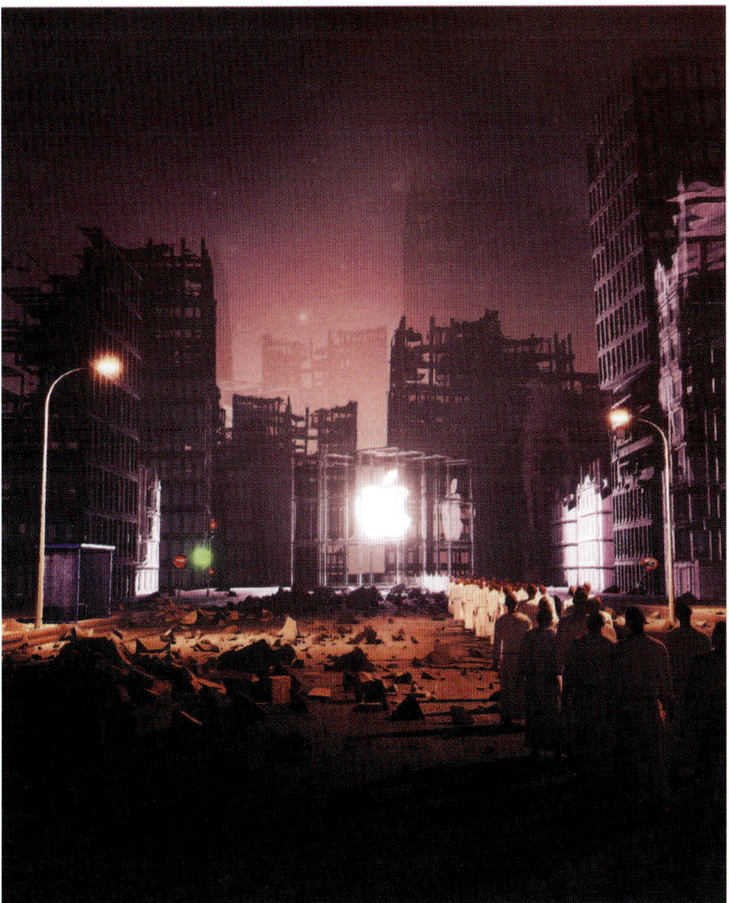

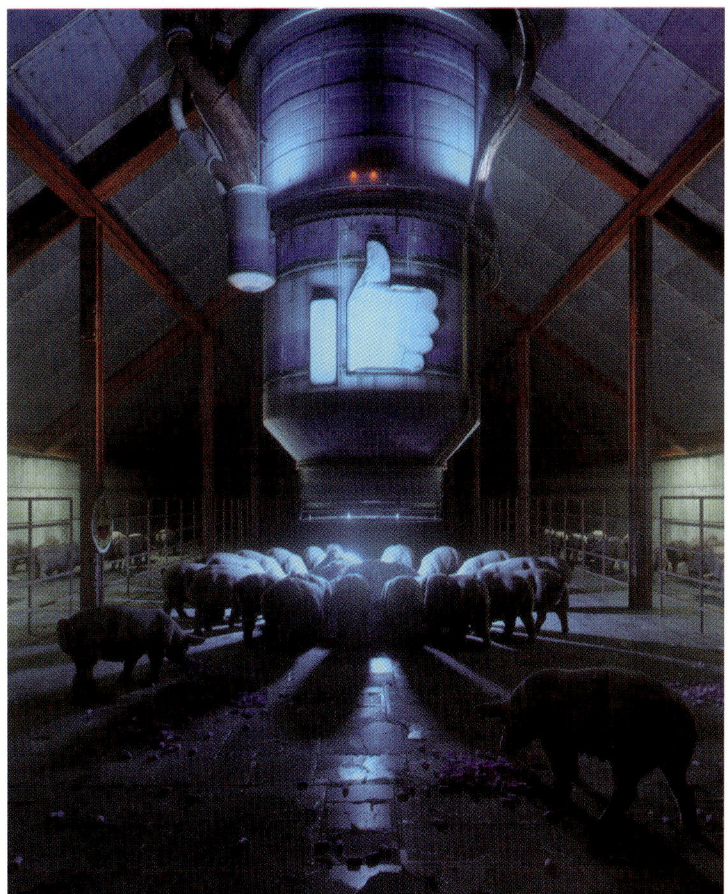

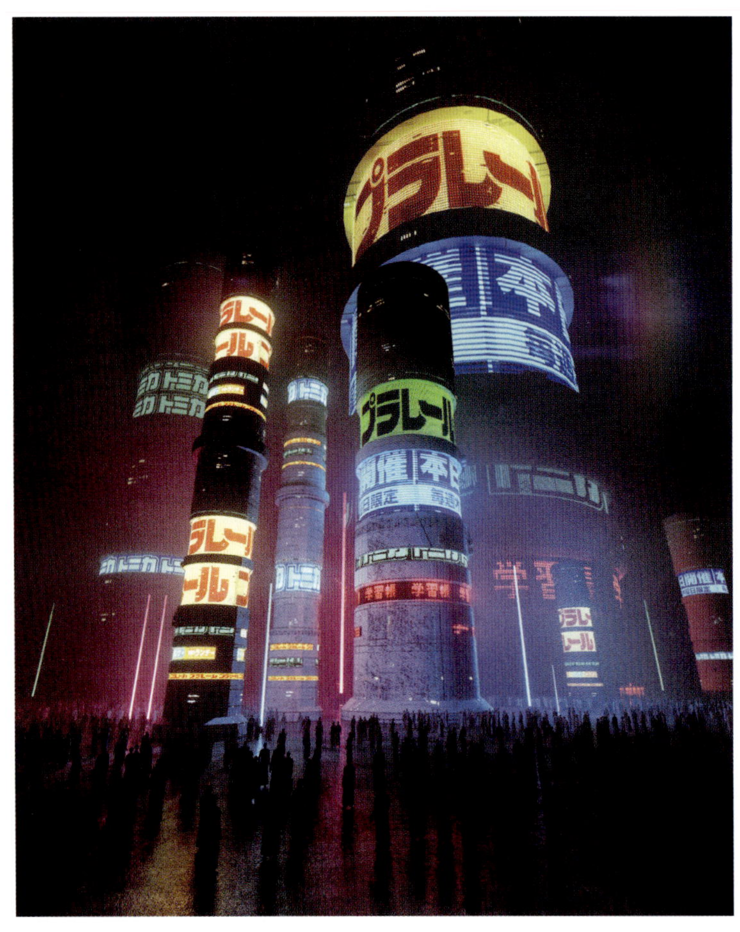

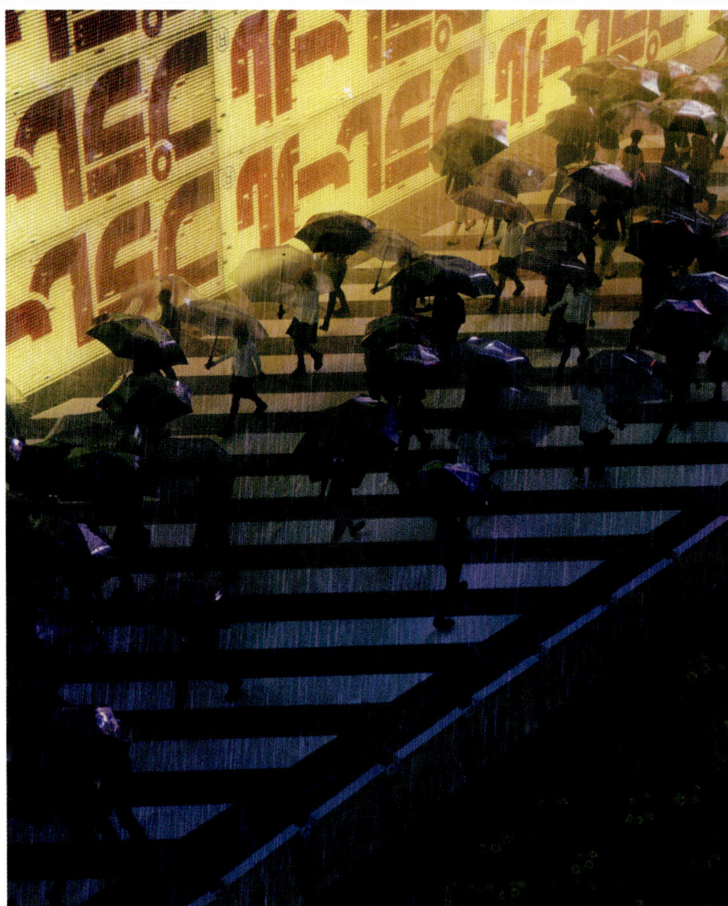

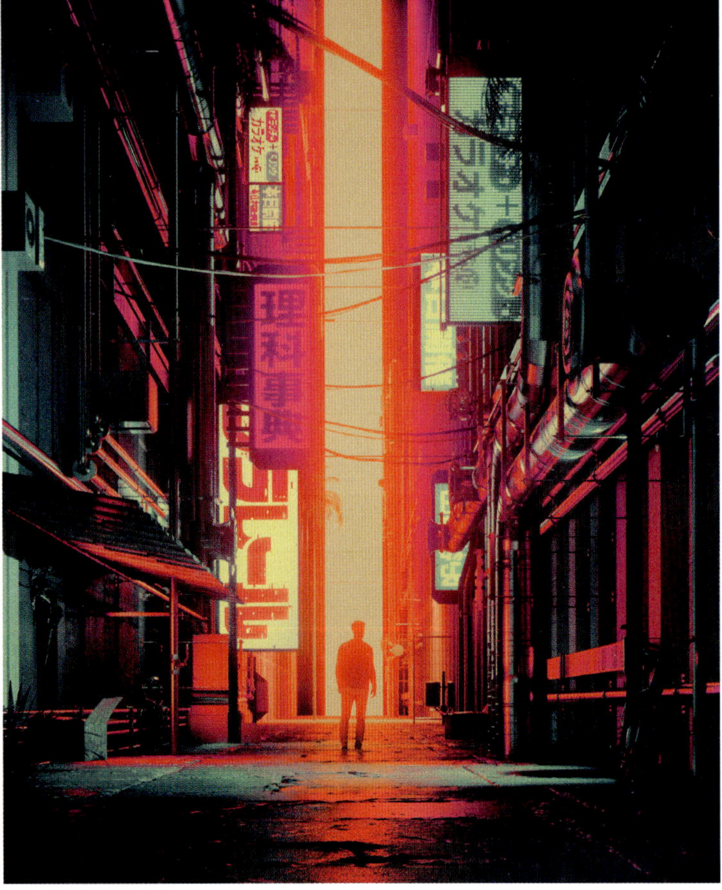

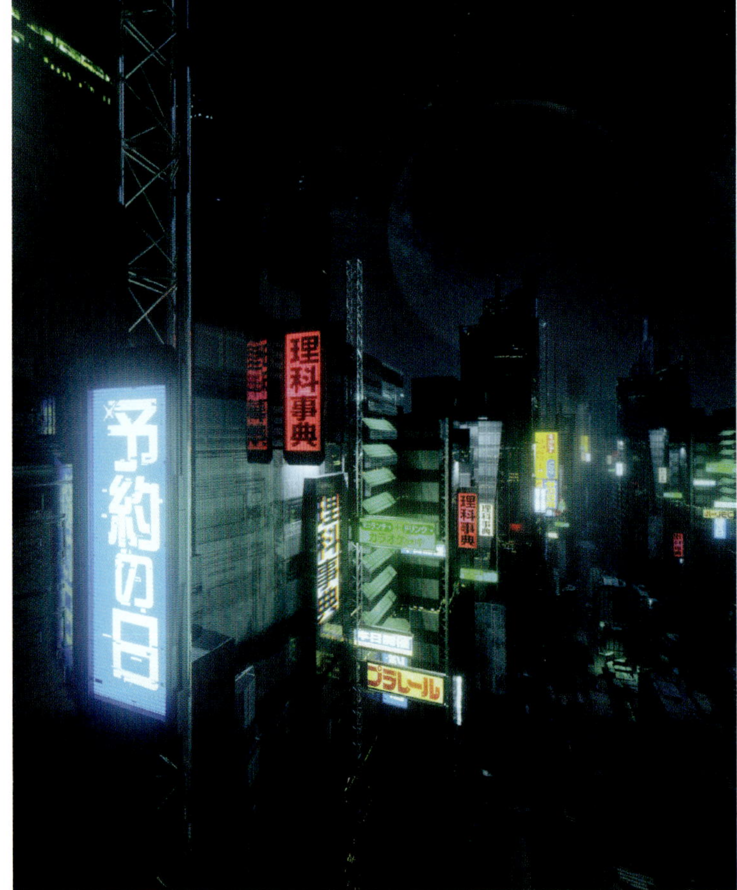

TOP LEFT
CONTROL.BLUR
05.18.2017

TOP RIGHT
YELLOW
05.28.2017

BOTTOM LEFT
FULL STOP
10.01.2017

BOTTOM RIGHT
ELECTRIC VOID
06.24.2017

OPPOSITE PAGE
FOCUS
04.30.2017

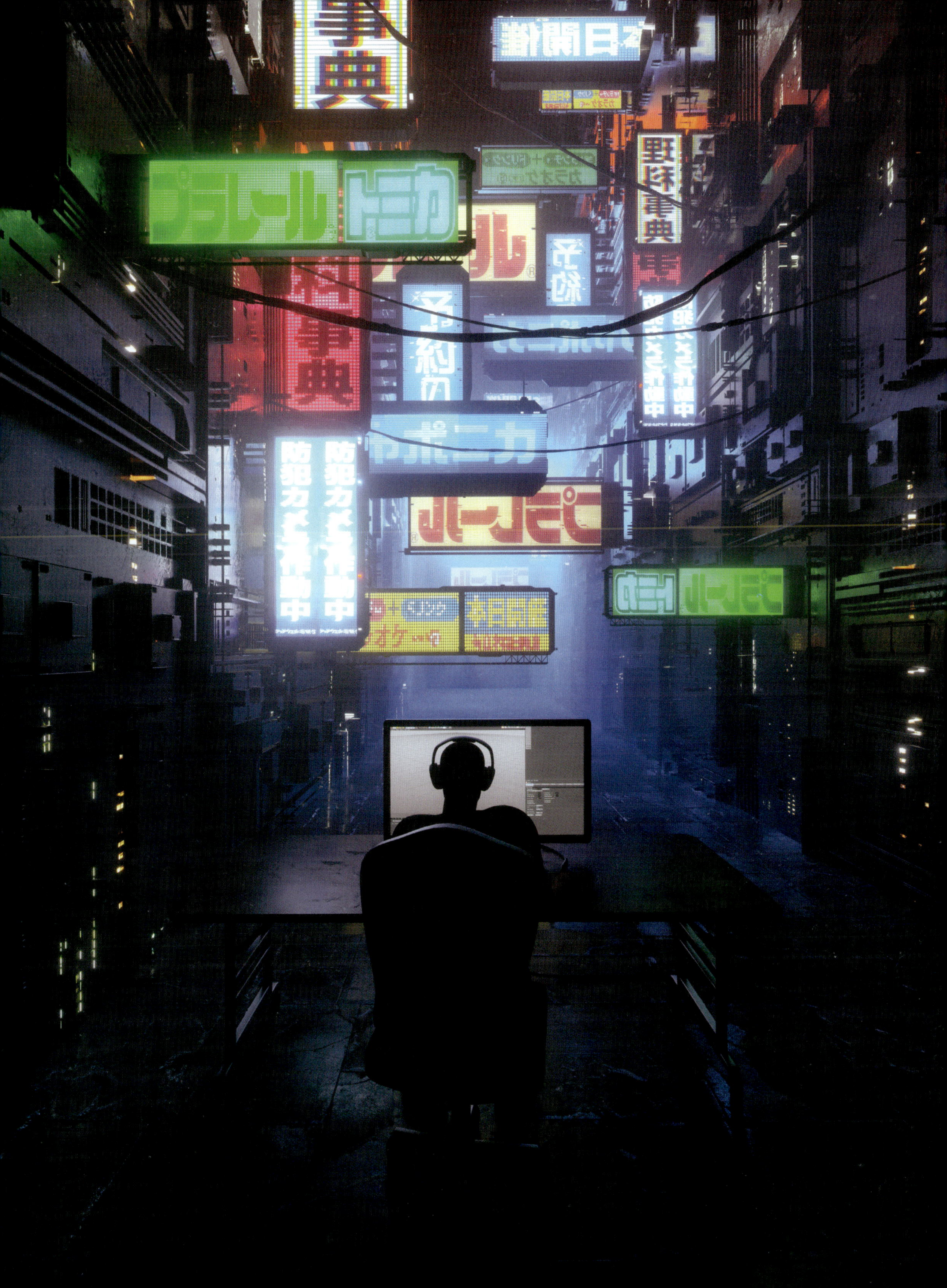

事典
プラレール
トミカ
予約の
ヤポニカ

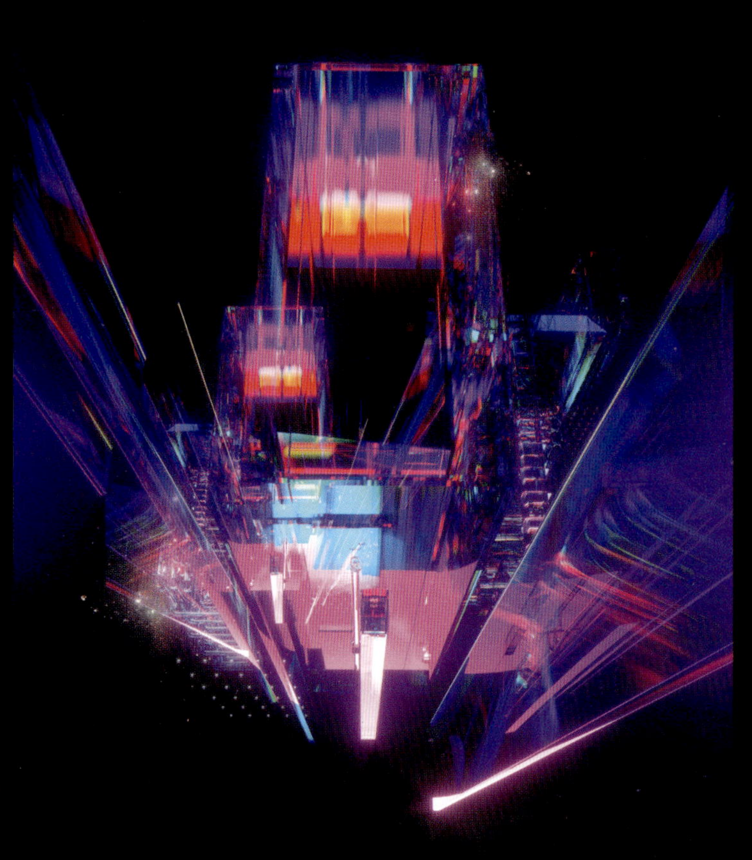

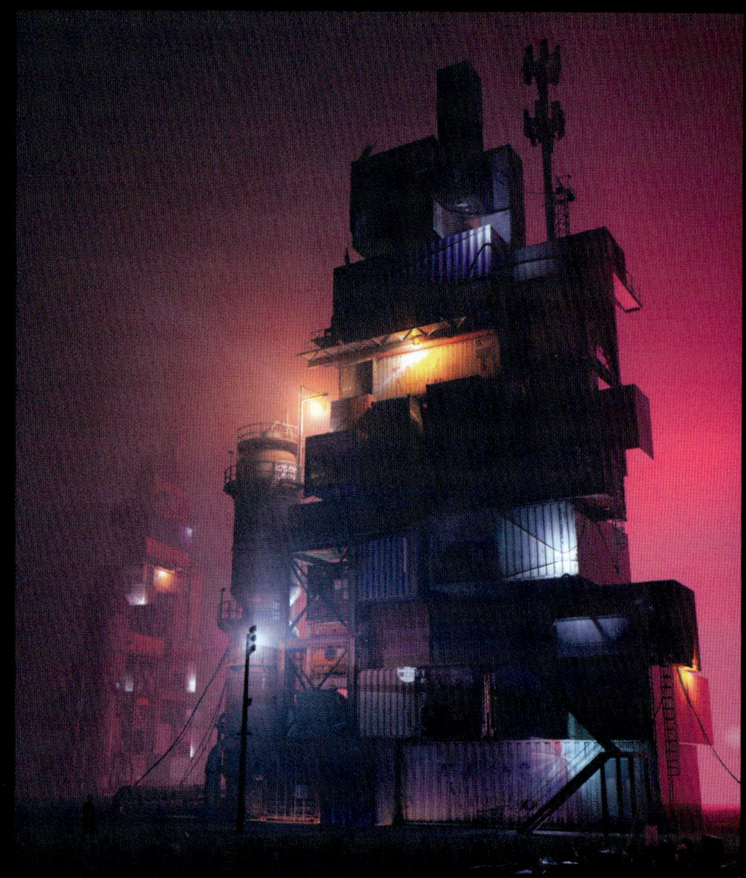

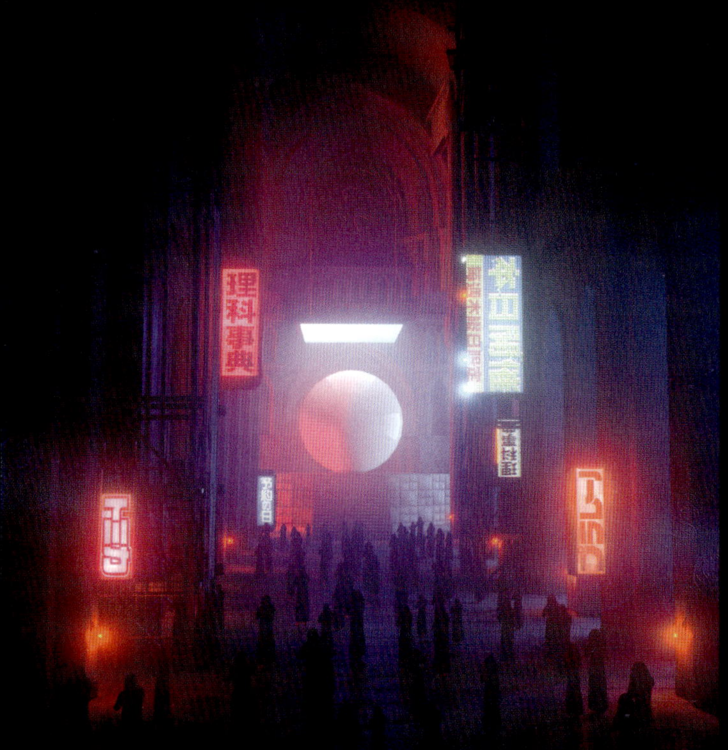

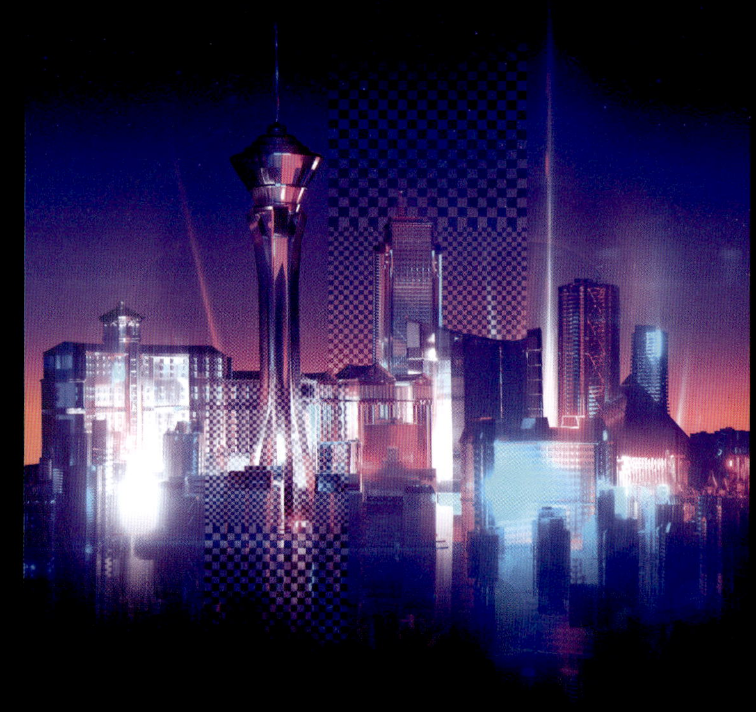

TOP LEFT

UNLIMITED SPECTRUM

11.29.2017

TOP RIGHT

SUPERCLUSTER

11.26.2017

BOTTOM LEFT

ALGORITHM WORSHIP

12.02.2017

BOTTOM RIGHT

VIRTUAL VEGAS

12.06.2017

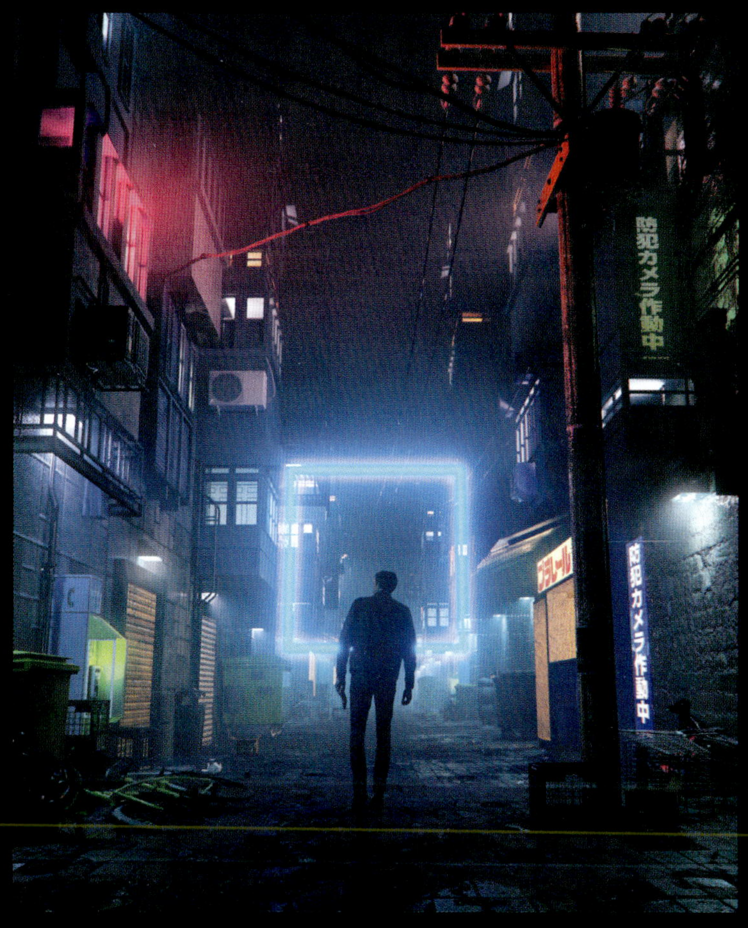

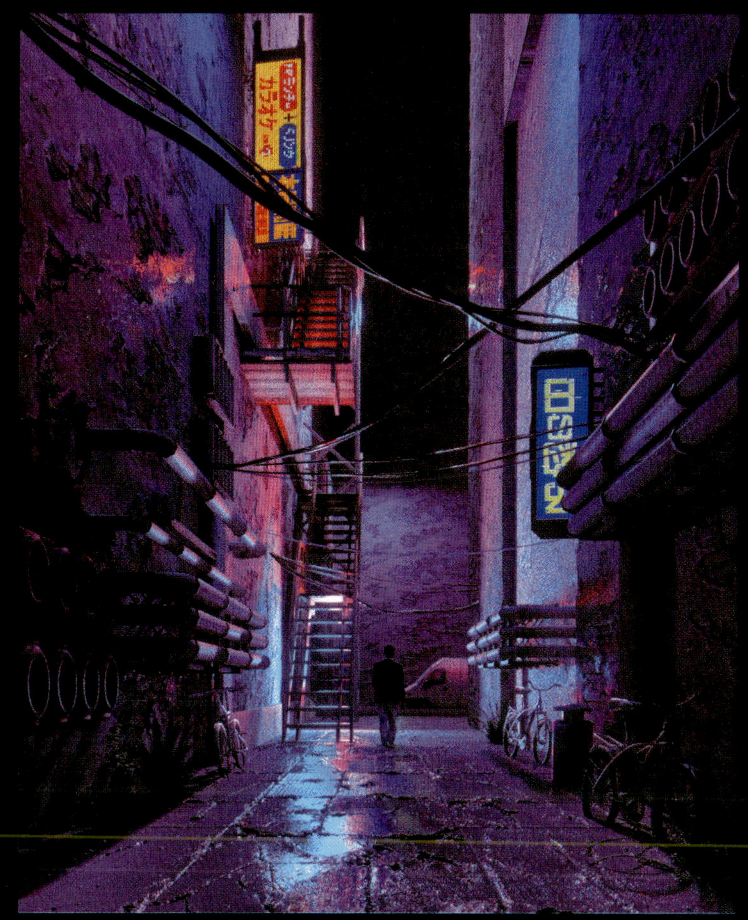

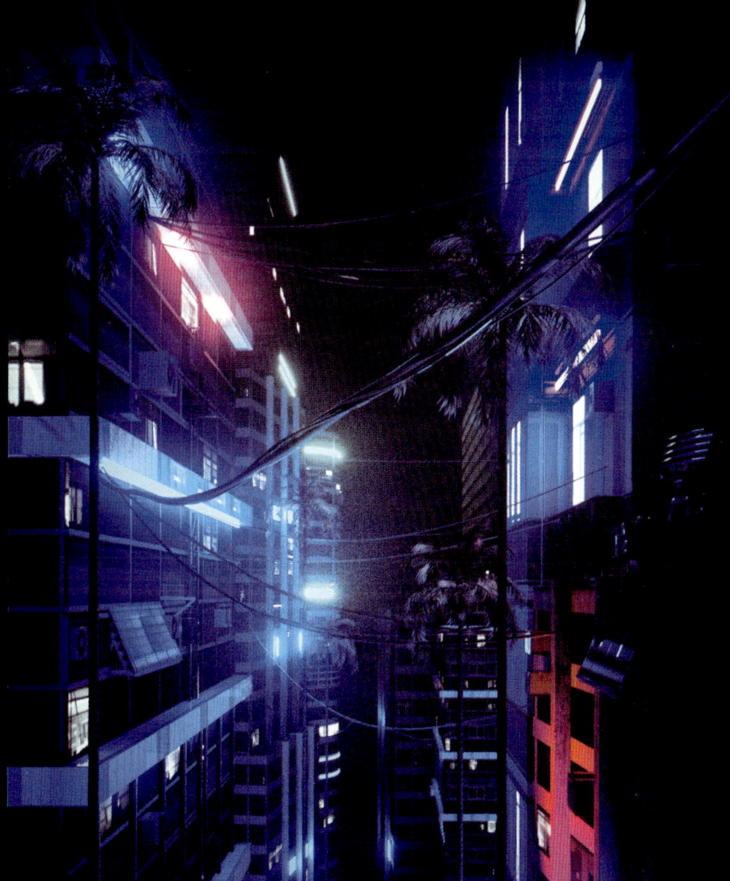

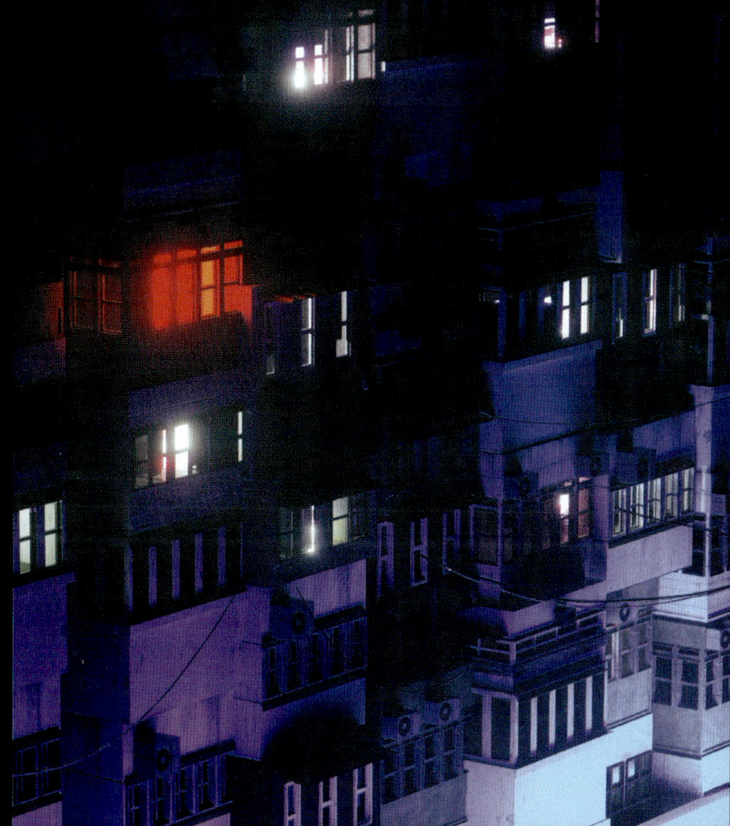

TOP LEFT
XEON SQUARE
11.28.2017

TOP RIGHT
SUPERWONGGG
09.09.2017

BOTTOM LEFT
NITROGEN CITY
09.26.2017

BOTTOM RIGHT
REDROOM
10.02.2017

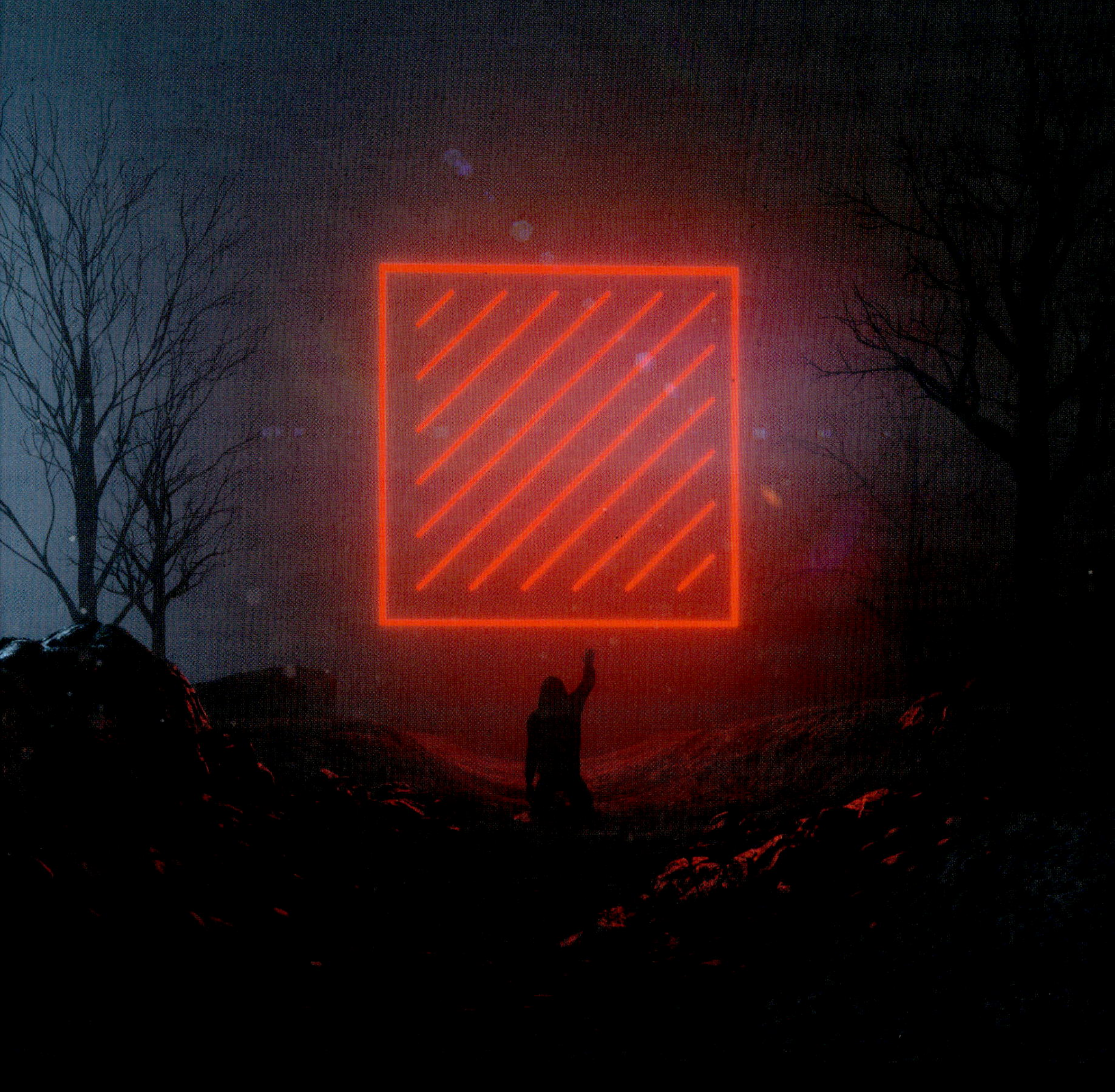

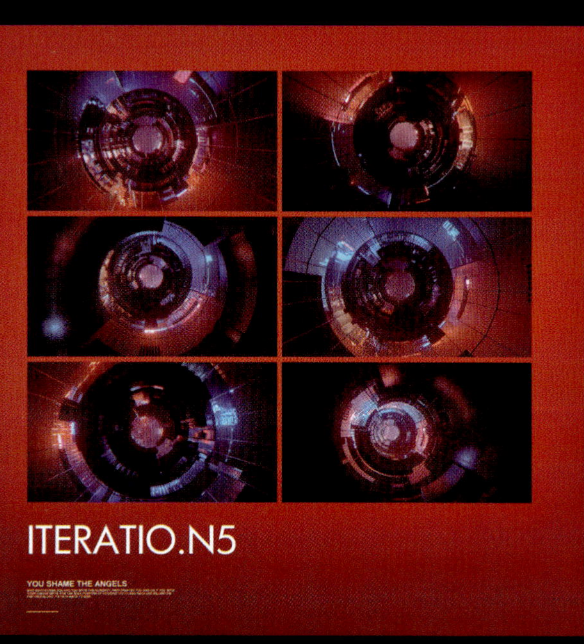

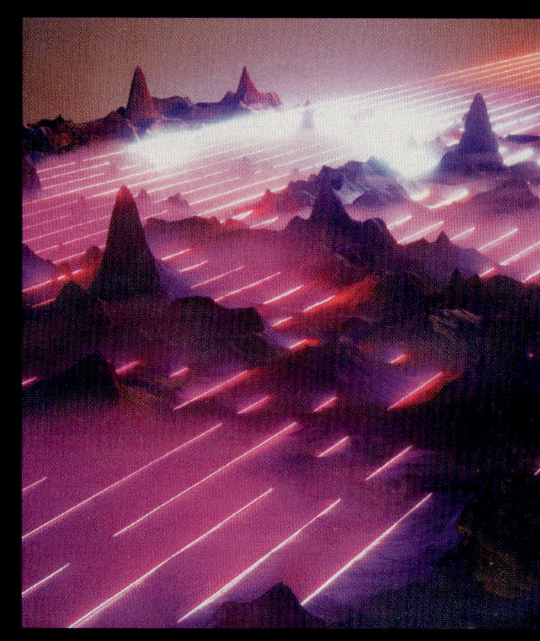

TOP
UNCOMPRESSED
11.17.2017

BOTTOM LEFT
ITERATIO.N5
02.21.2017

BOTTOM RIGHT
74PONTIAC
07.27.2017

OPPOSITE PAGE
TEN YEARS
05.01.2017

right now.

fuck checking facebook again,
fuck that pic you just saw on instagram,
fuck worrying about how many people liked your last post,
fuck the news,
fuck that person you really should email back,
fuck your self-doubt,
fuck whatever happened yesterday,
fuck starting tomorrow,
fuck will people like this,
fuck will this be good enough...

fuck all of your excuses.

sit the fuck down and do your work.

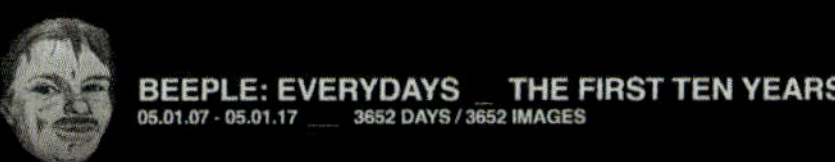

(NOPE. STILL SHIT.)

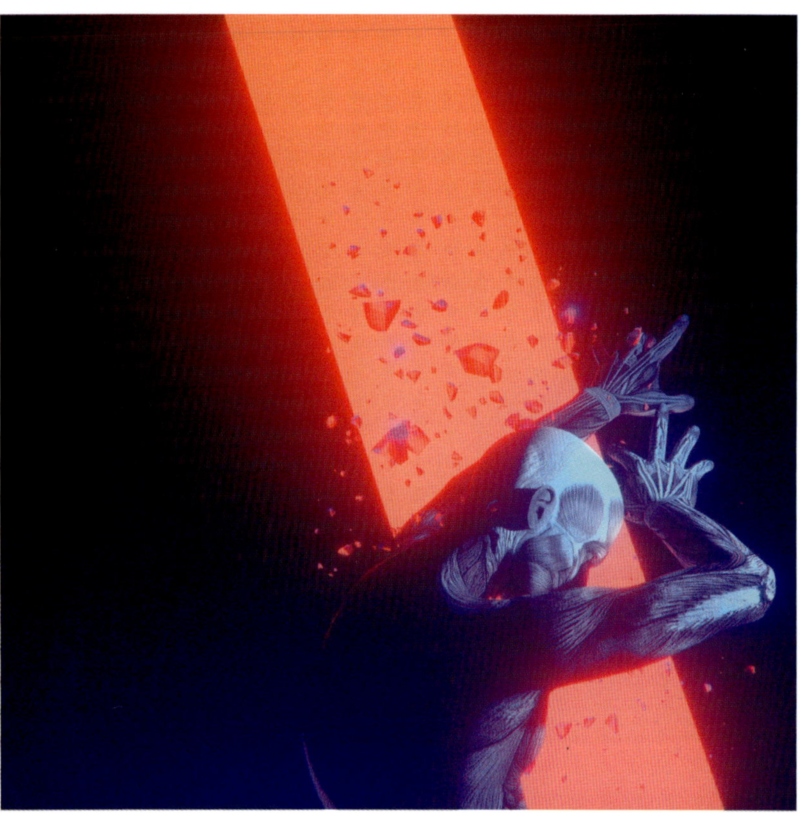

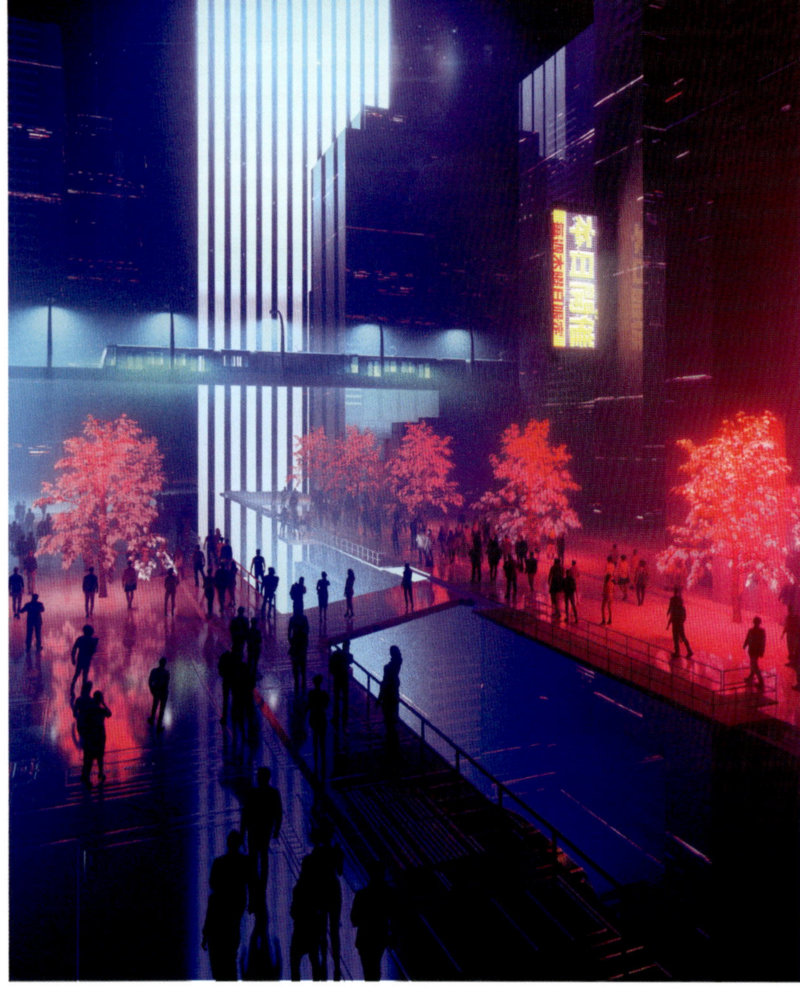

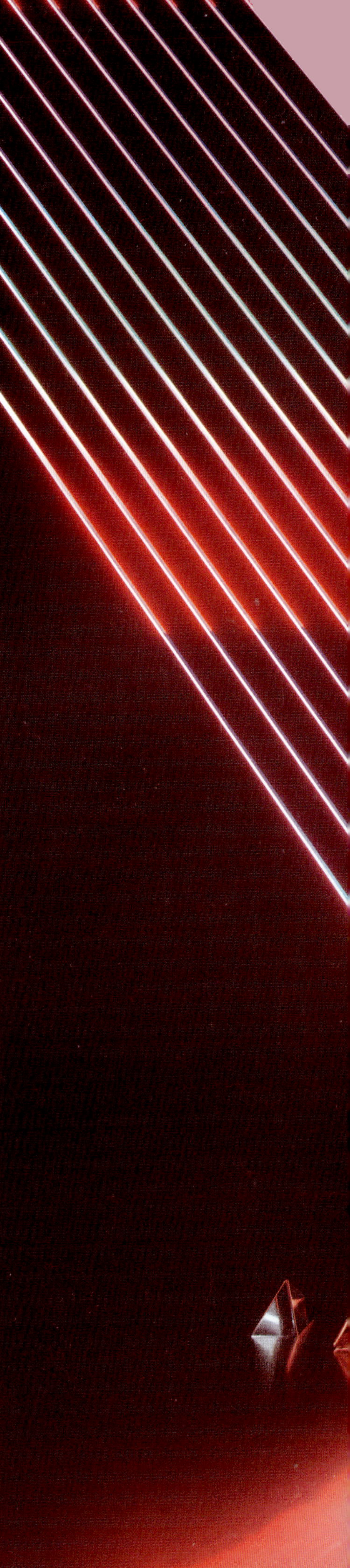

TOP

ICE BLUE
07.05.2017

BOTTOM

RADIATE BLUE
07.11.2017

OPPOSITE PAGE

BACK OFF THE RAINBOW
05.02.2017

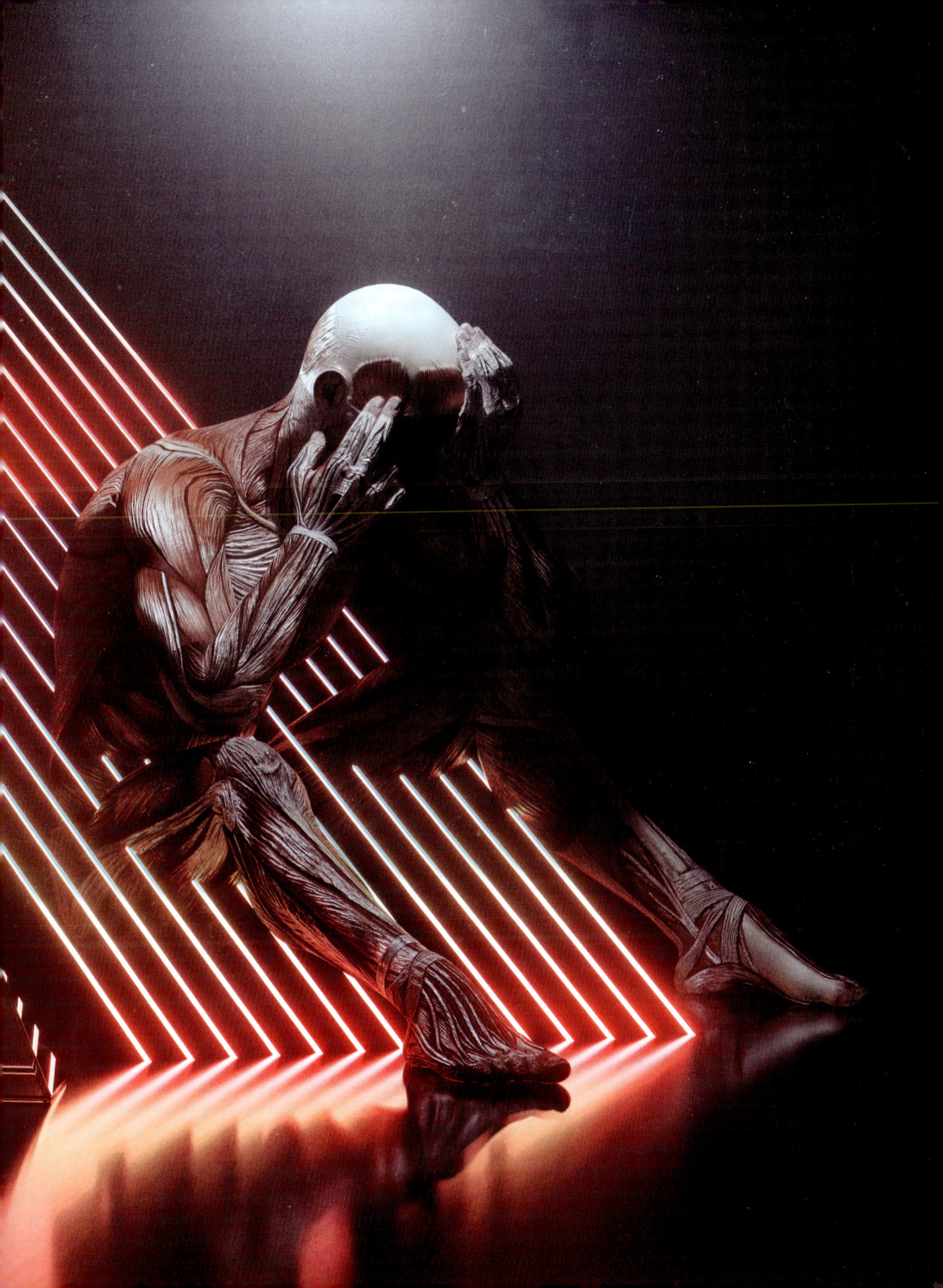

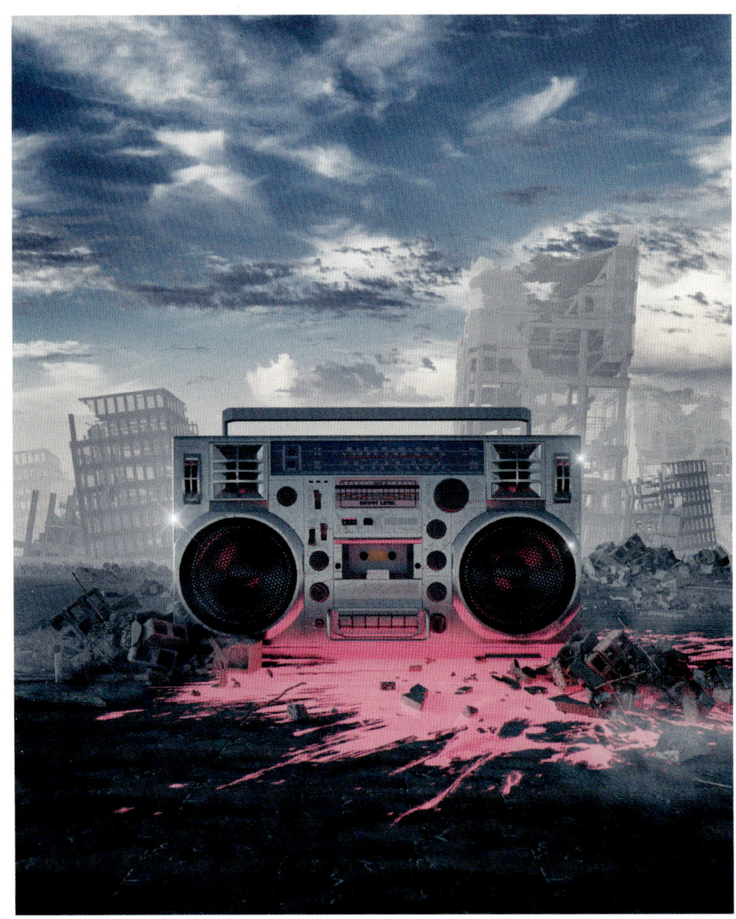

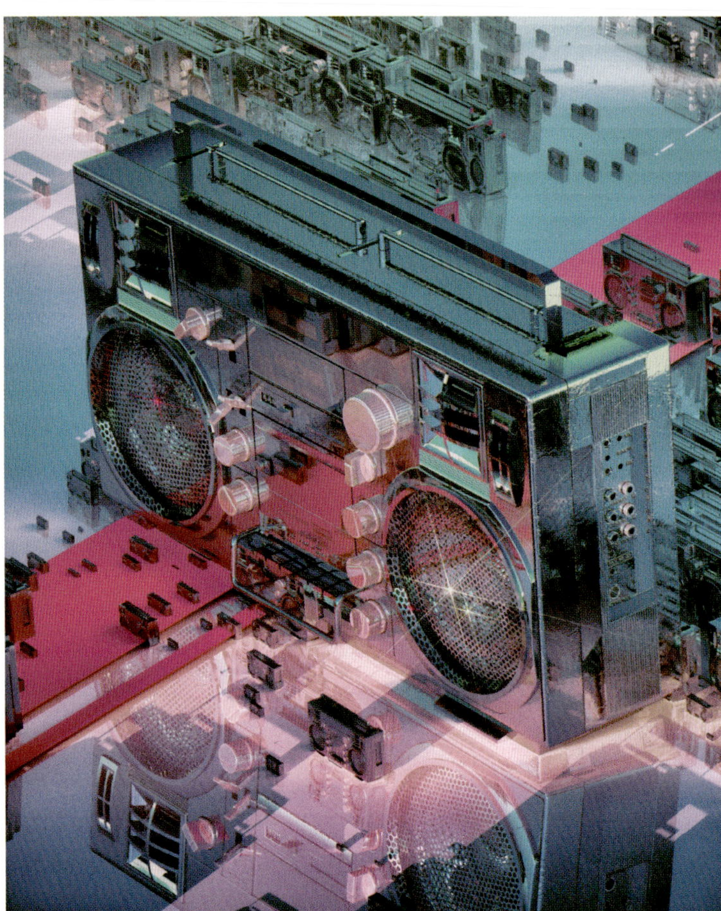

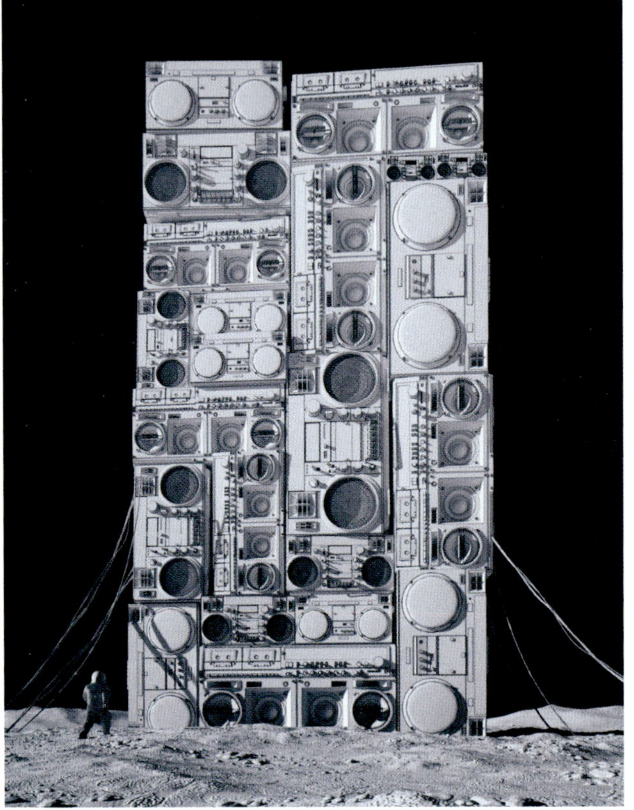

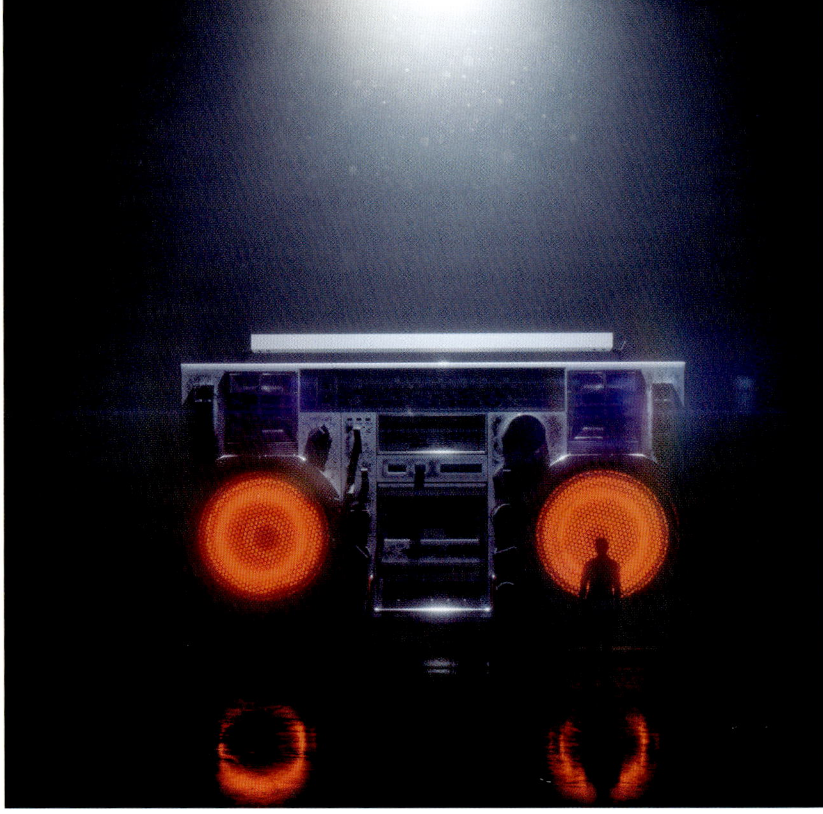

TOP LEFT

APOCALYPSE FRESH
11.01.2017

TOP RIGHT

STROWBARY SUPERJAM
11.14.2017

BOTTOM LEFT

ONE GIANT LEAP
11.21.2017

BOTTOM RIGHT

RED1983
10.26.2017

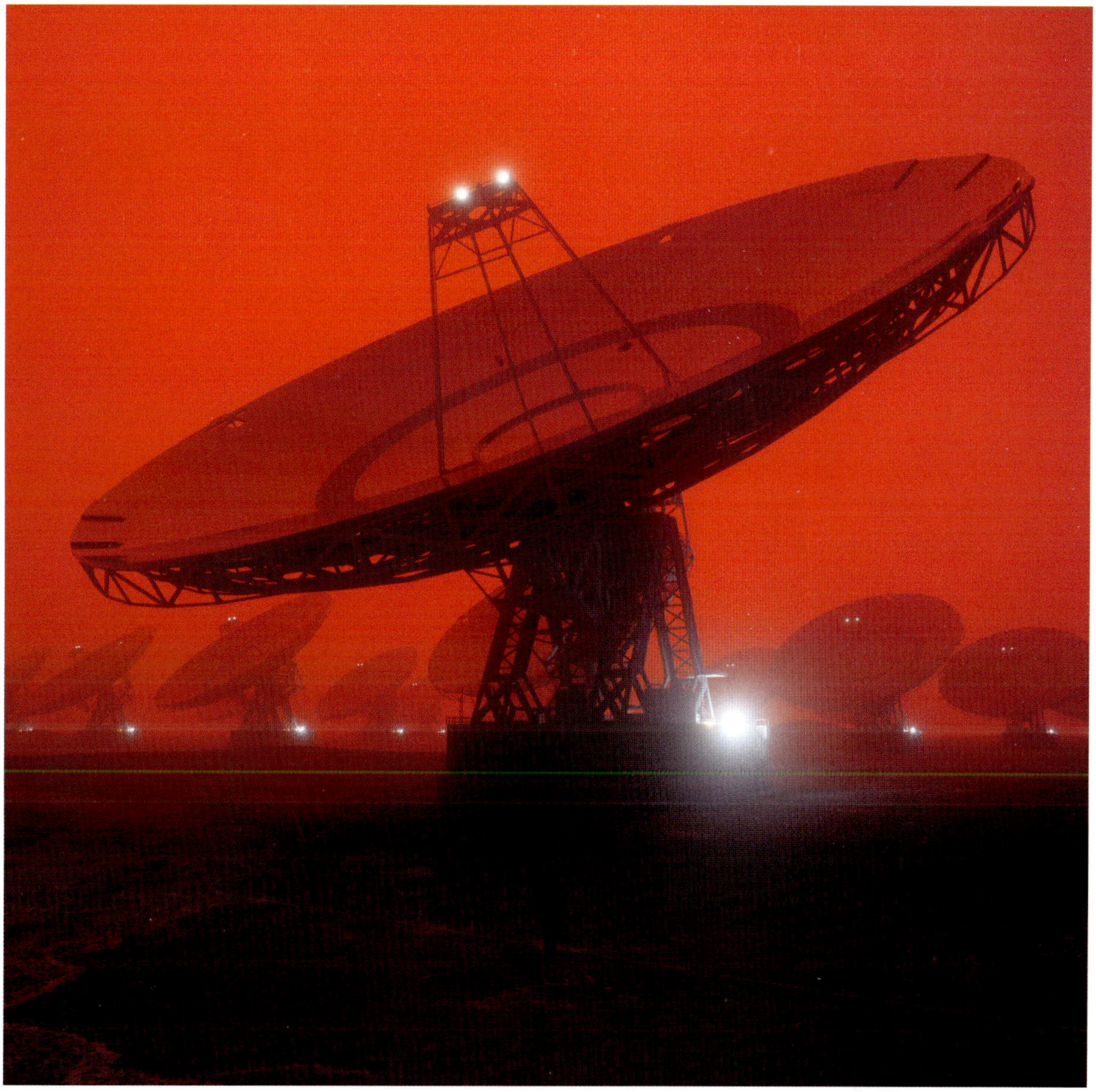

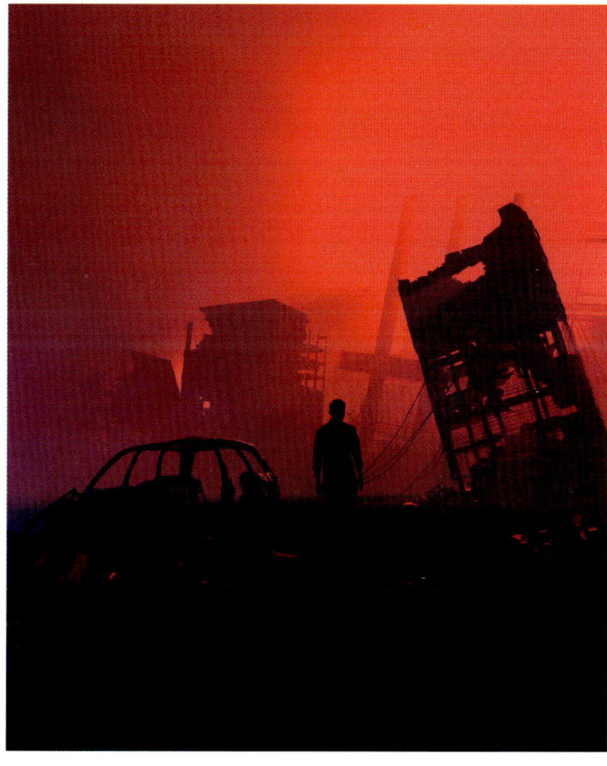

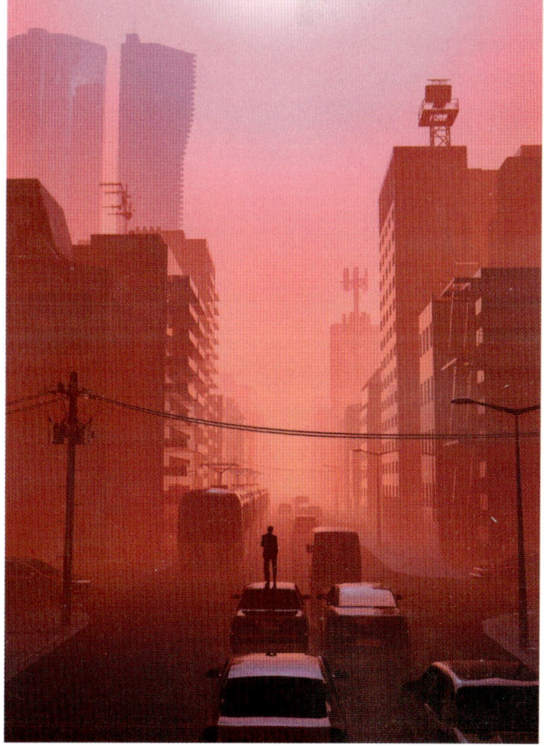

TOP

LISTEN
09.18.2017

BOTTOM LEFT

RED.WONDER
11.04.2017

BOTTOM RIGHT

POPULATION REBOOT
12.12.2017

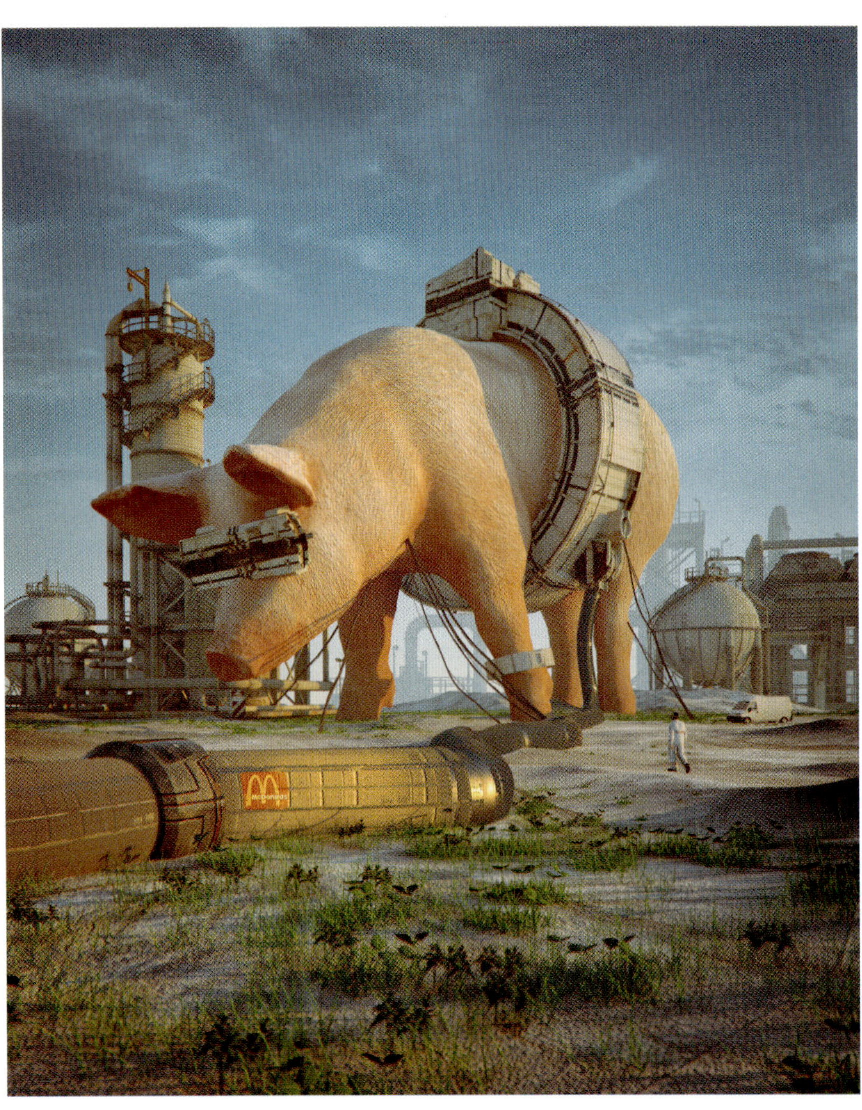

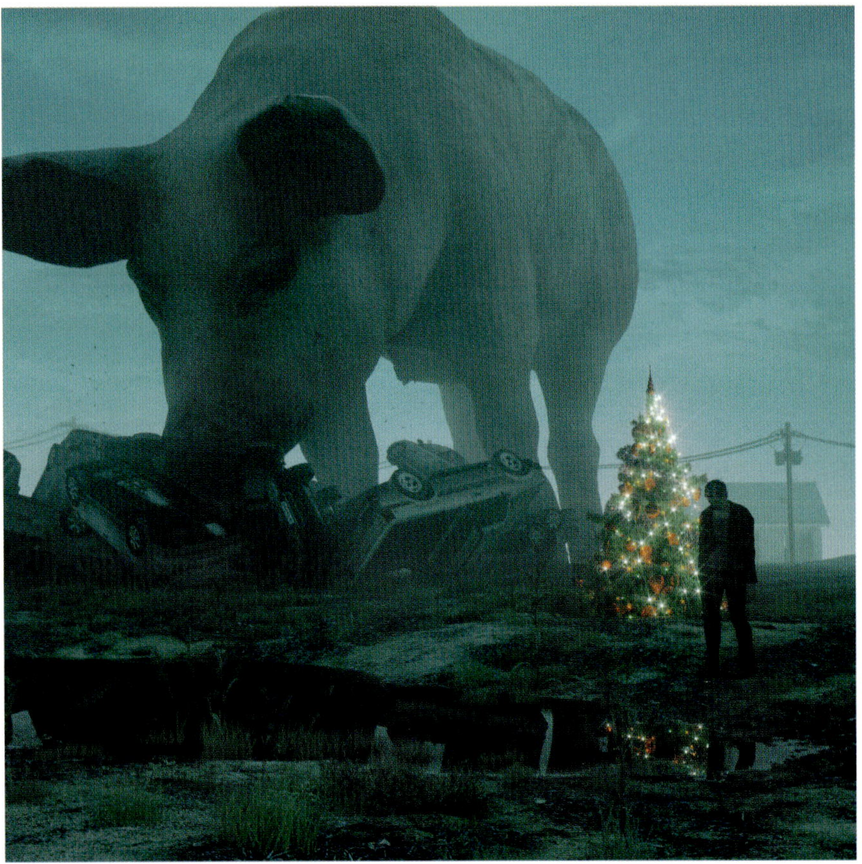

TOP

MCDONALDS 2185
09.23.2017

BOTTOM

giant pig eating cars on christmas morning with really tired dude looking at mud thinking about porgs
12.22.2017

OPPOSITE PAGE

GEN.MOD2044
05.10.2017

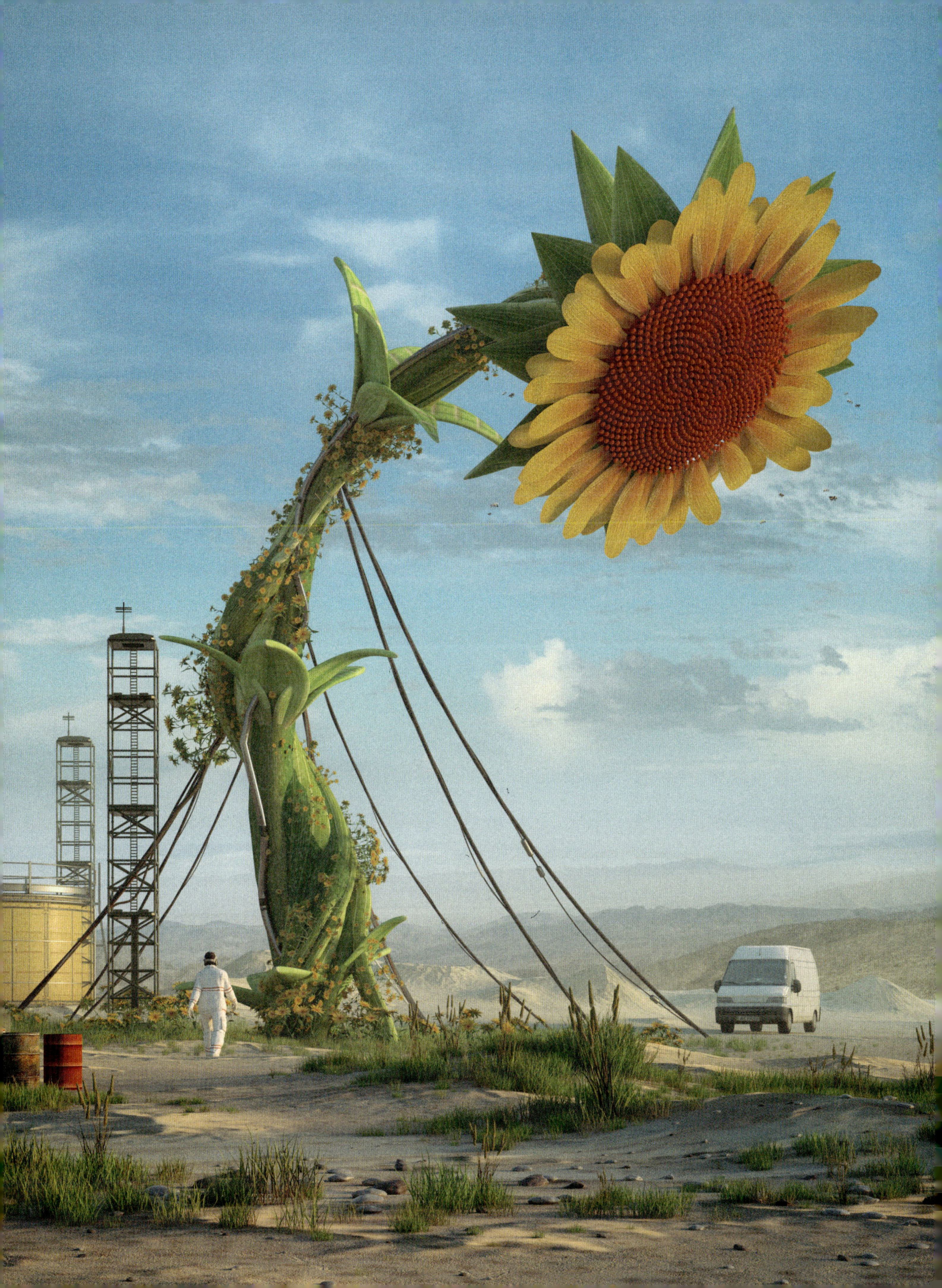

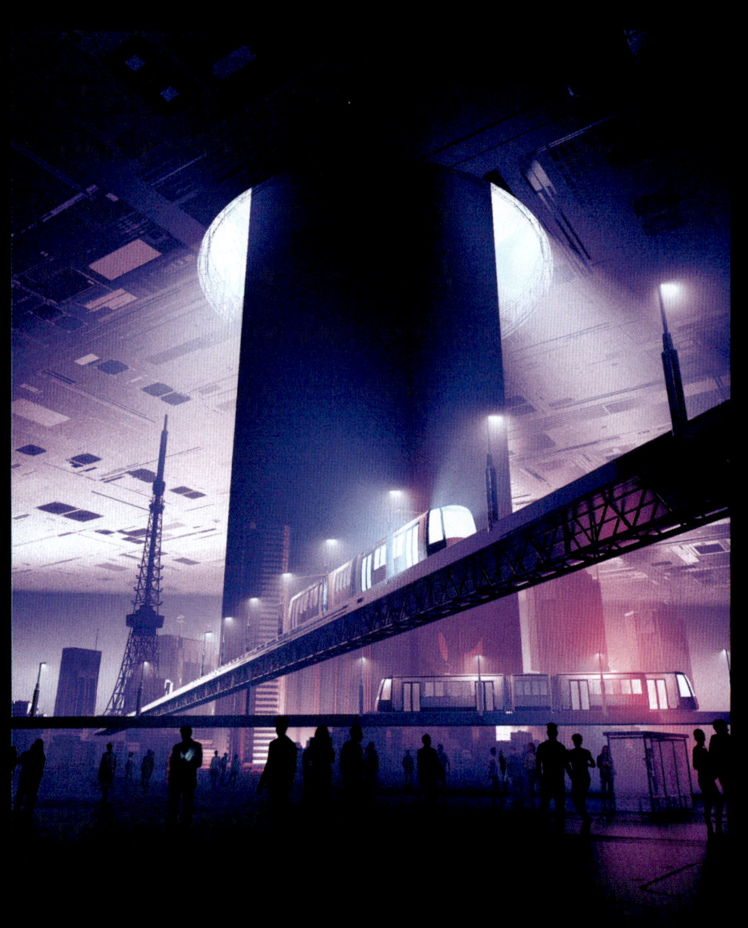

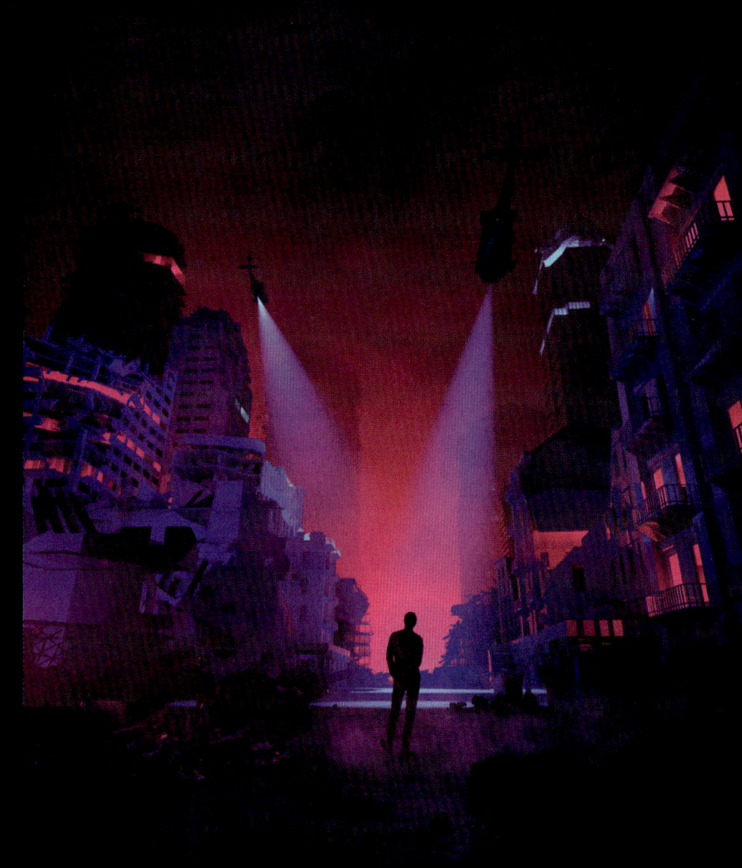

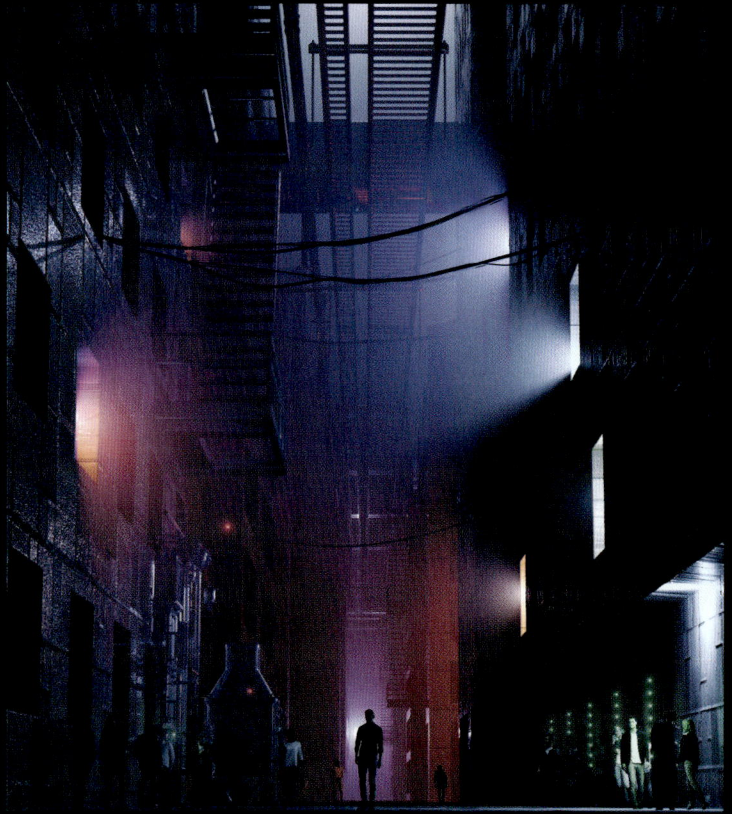

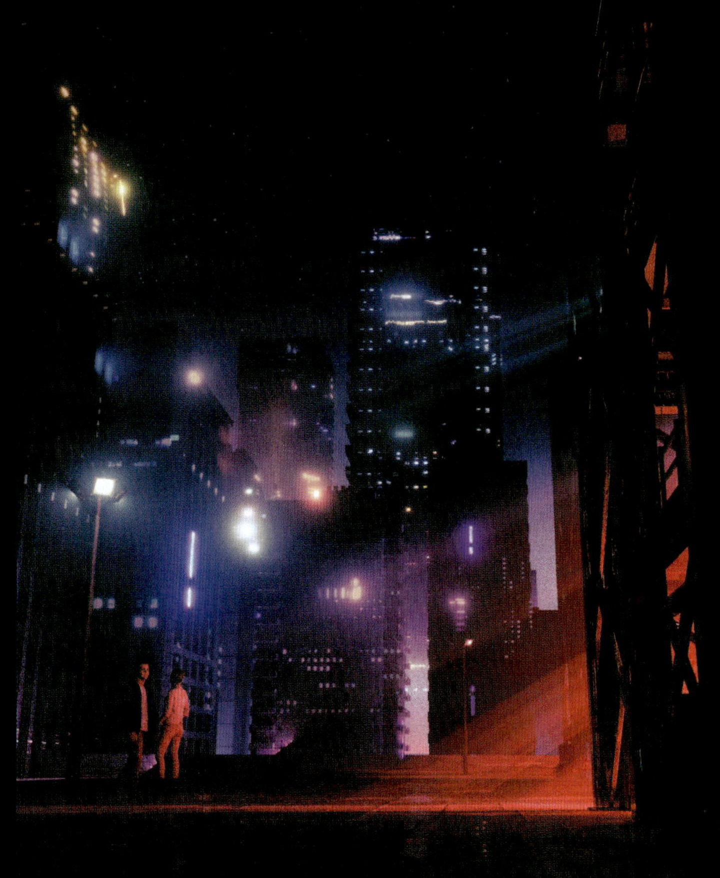

TOP LEFT
TROPOLIS
10.31.2017

TOP RIGHT
FUCKED FUTURE
11.18.2017

BOTTOM LEFT
MENTAL FOG
10.30.2017

BOTTOM RIGHT
RED SUCROSE
11.07.2017

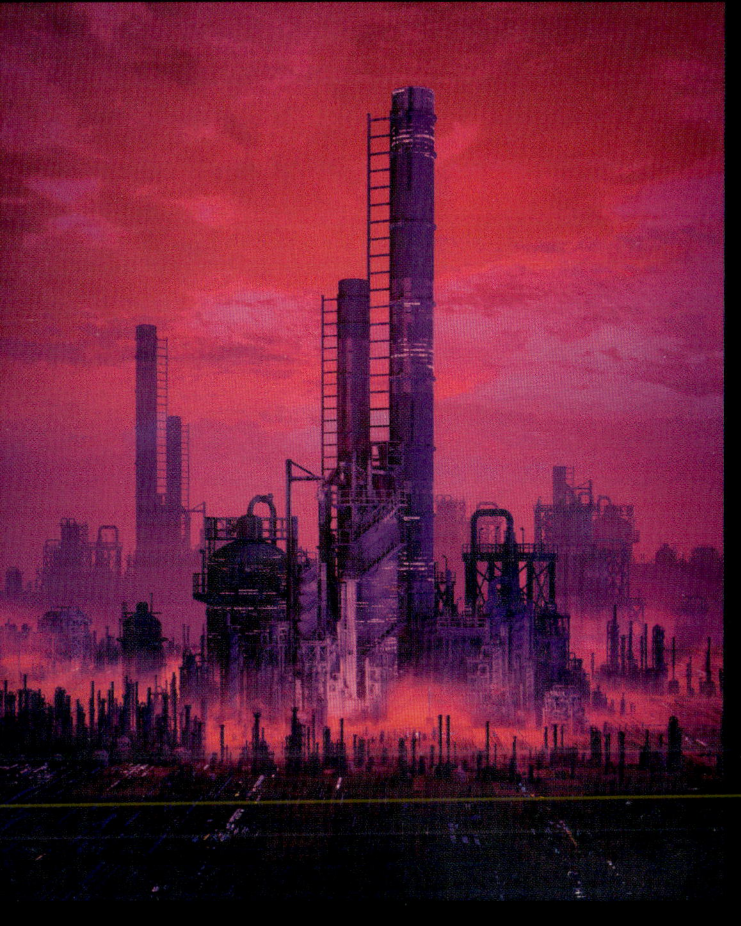

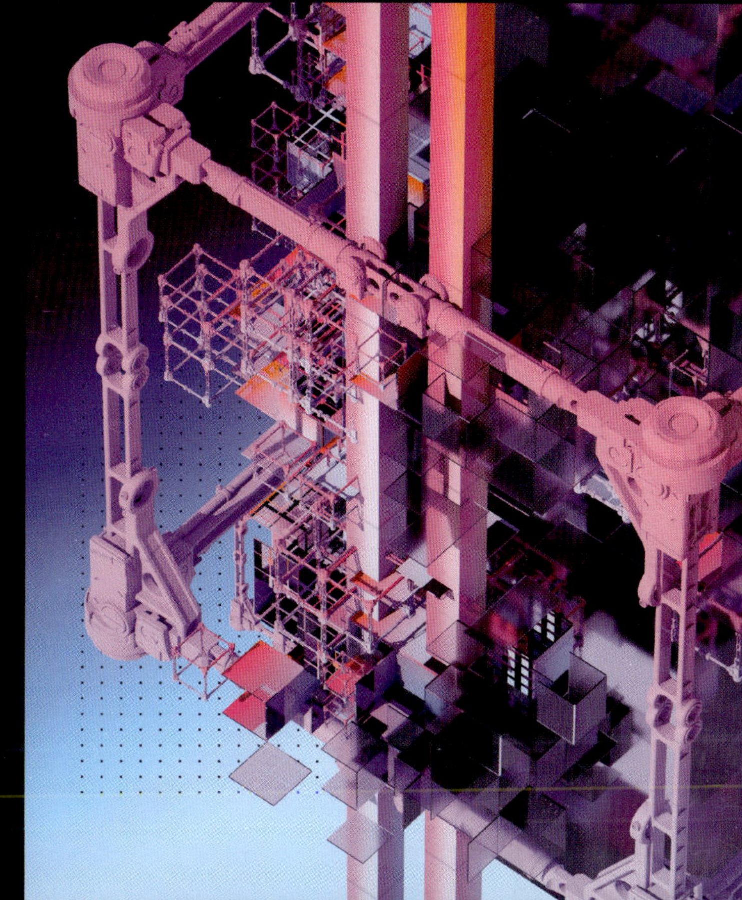

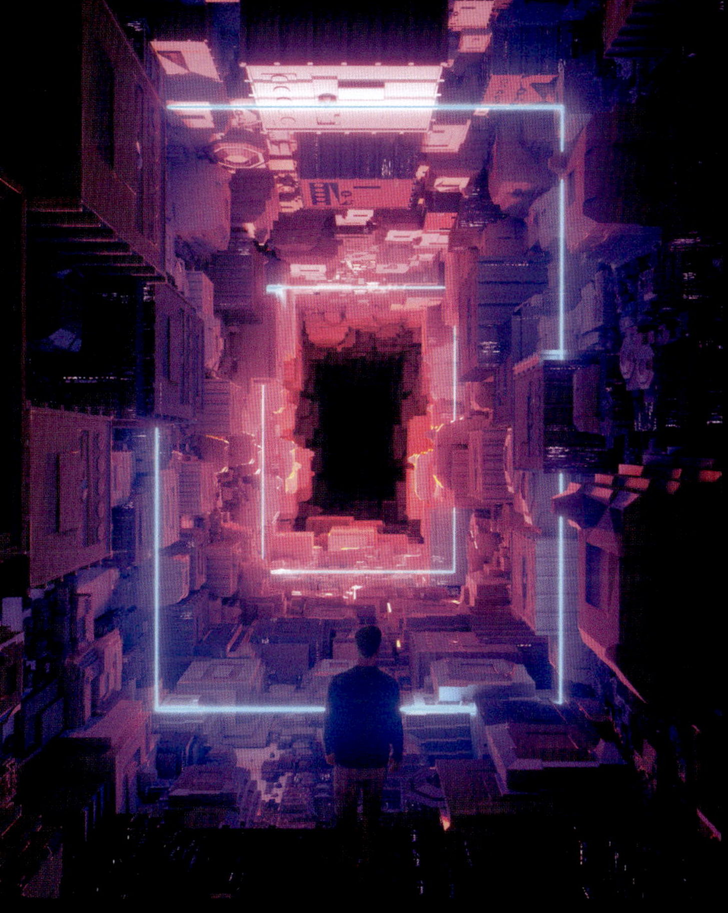

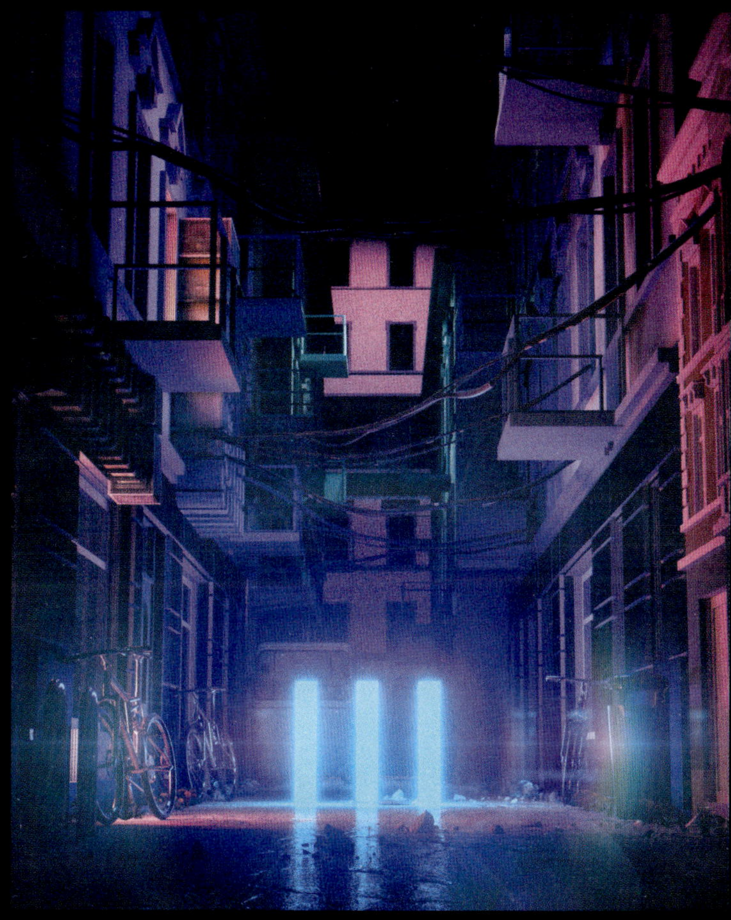

TOP LEFT
CANDY SMOG
10.05.2017

TOP RIGHT
DISREPAIR
09.17.2017

BOTTOM LEFT
MAKESHIFT HOME
09.08.2017

BOTTOM RIGHT
III
09.15.2017

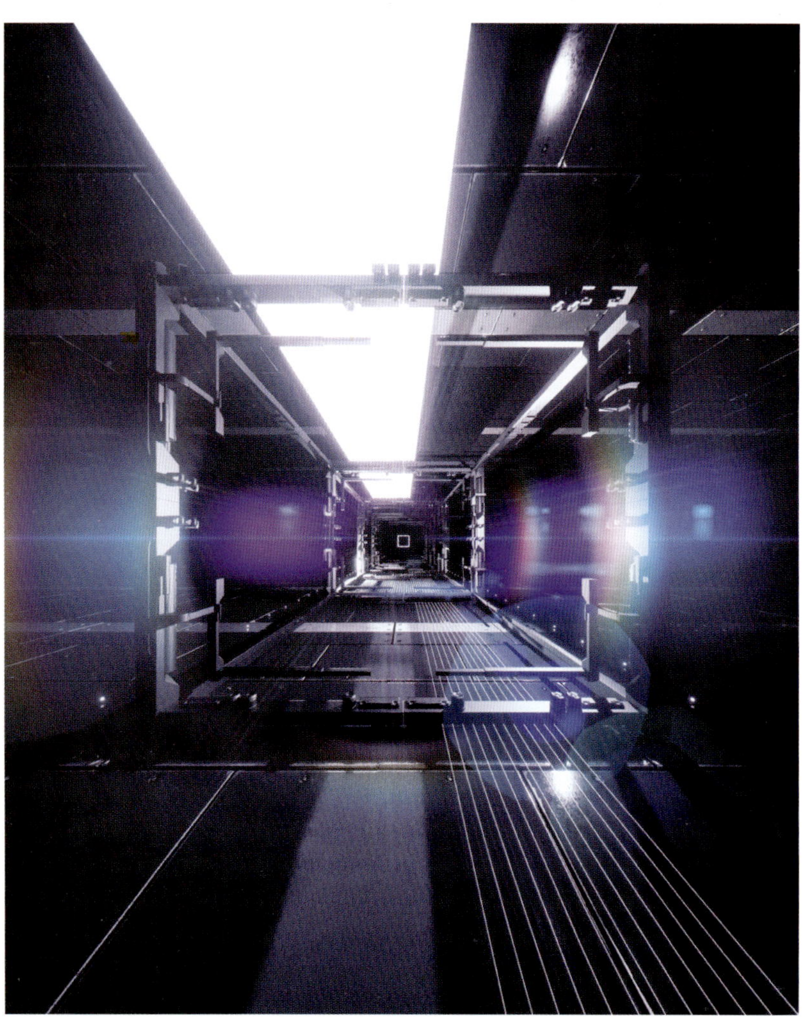

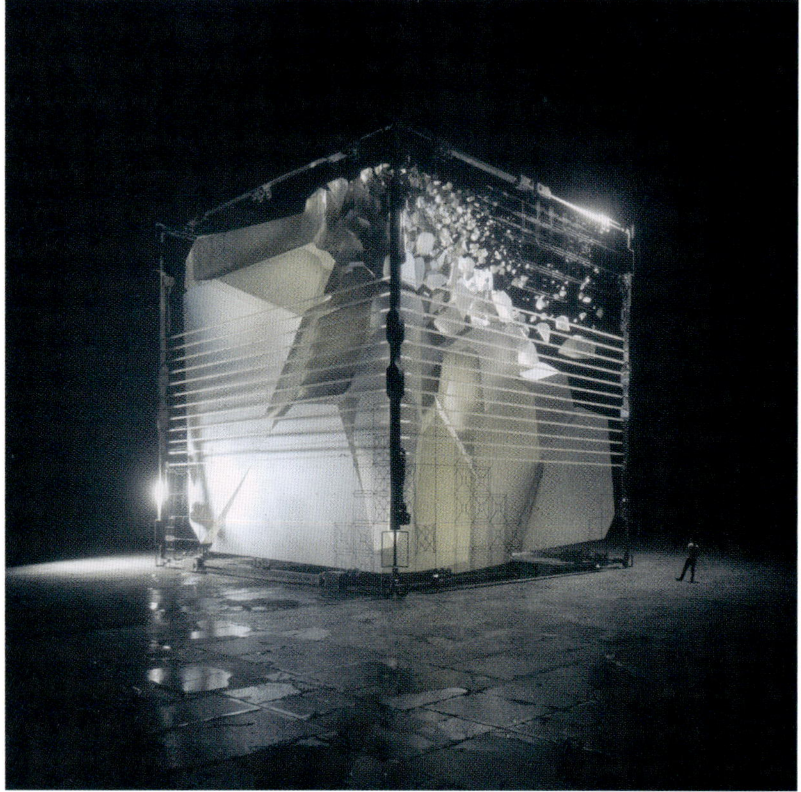

TOP
CHROMATIC
05.08.2017

BOTTOM
WINTER
07.16.2017

OPPOSITE PAGE
LEARNCUBED
06.01.2017

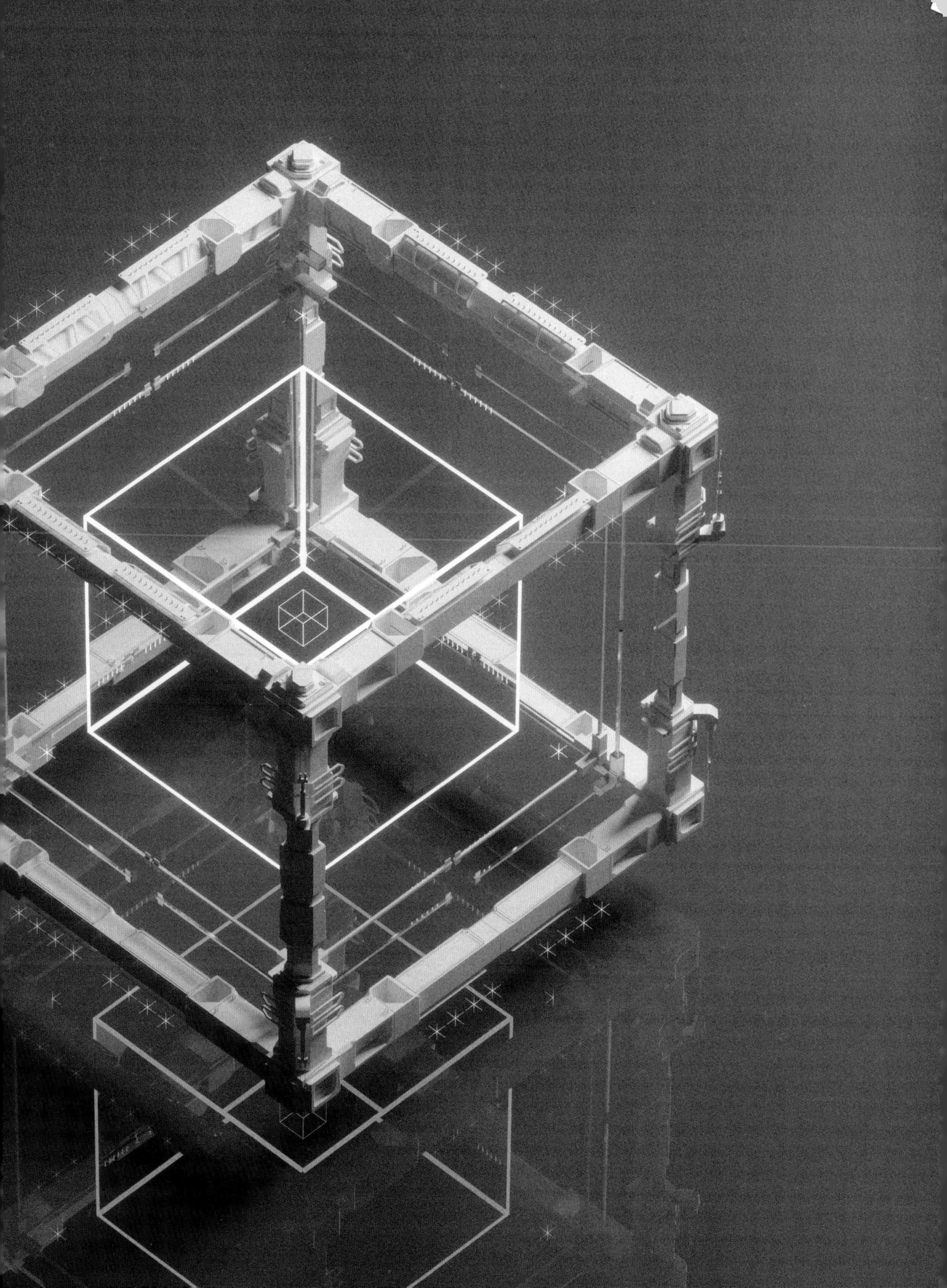

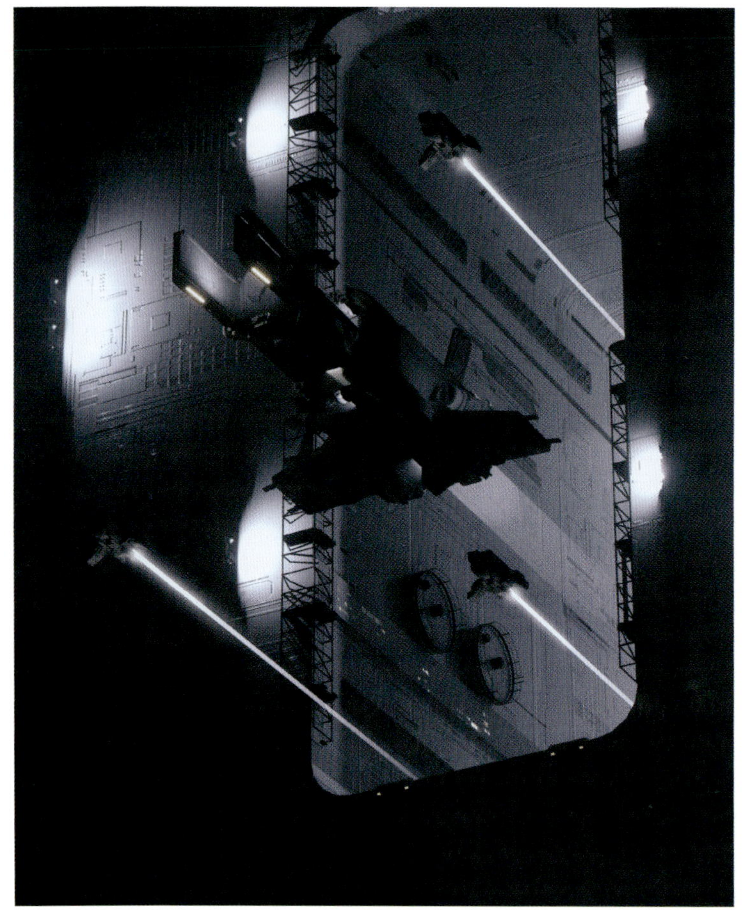

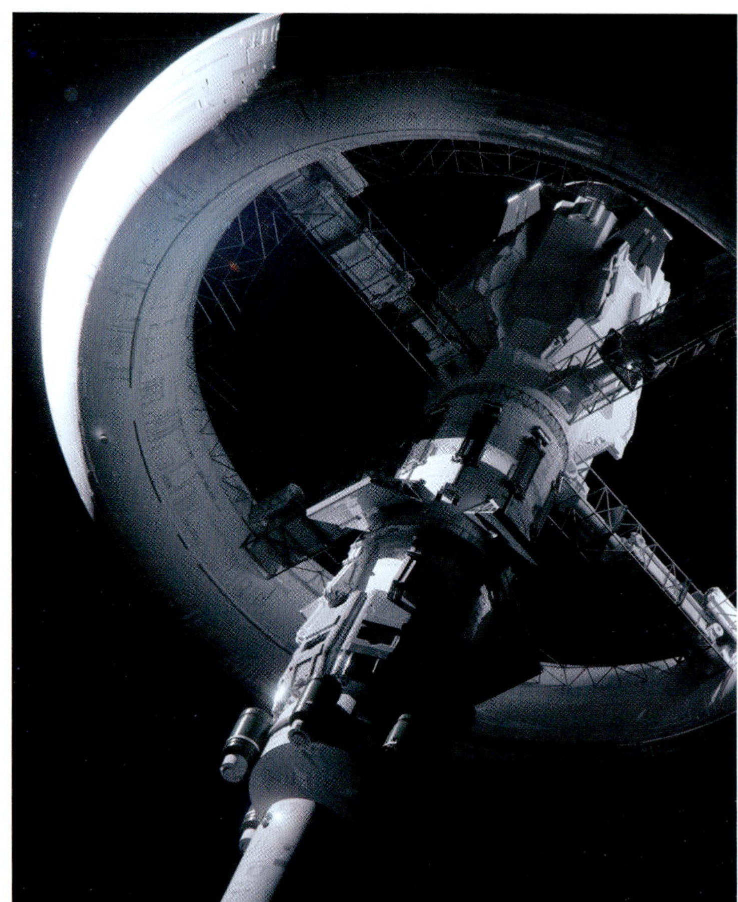

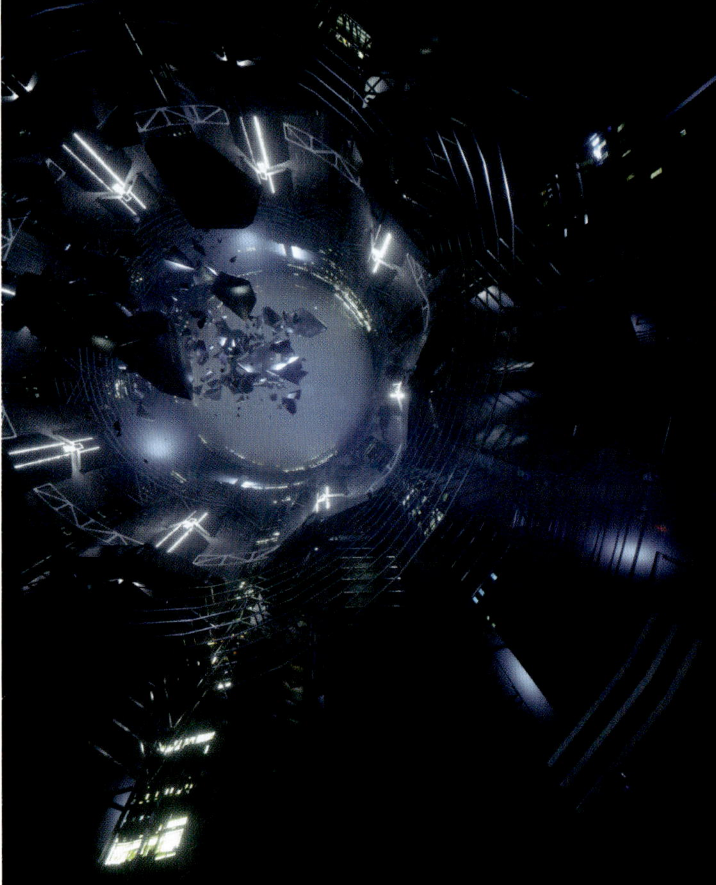

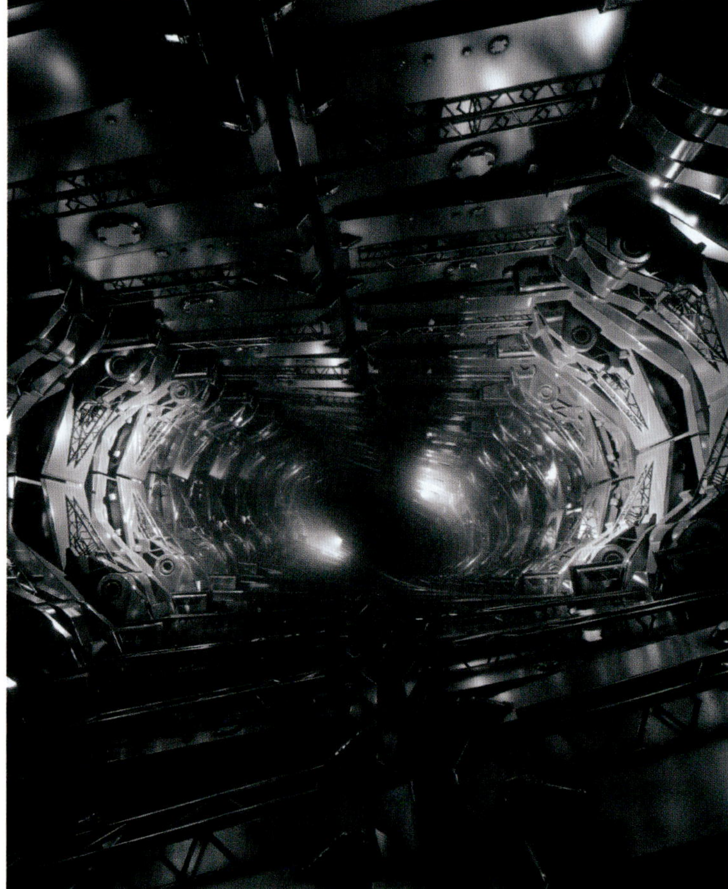

TOP LEFT

EPOX.01

06.19.2017

TOP RIGHT

THIRTY SIX

06.20.2017

BOTTOM LEFT

PROCESSED OBSIDIAN DUST

06.22.2017

BOTTOM RIGHT

TEX.CHROME09

06.27.2017

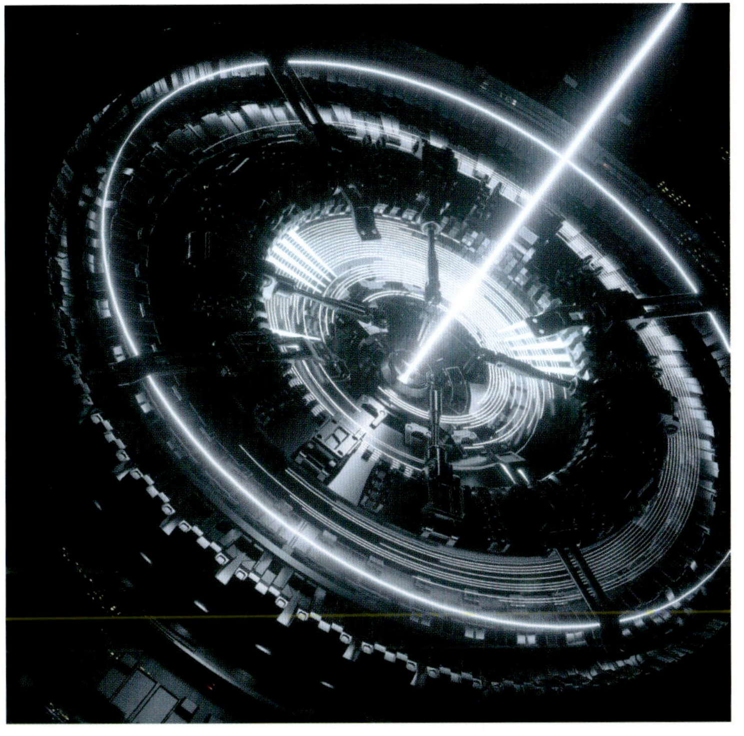
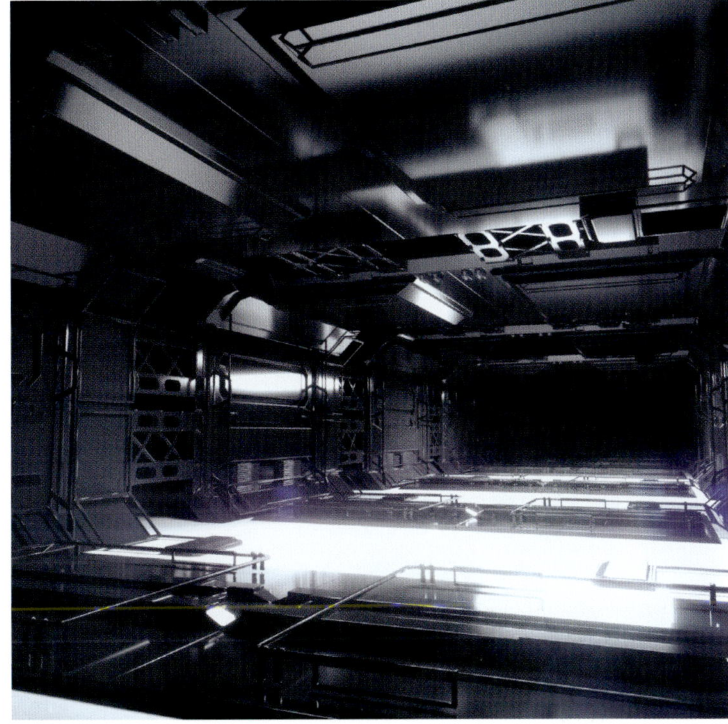
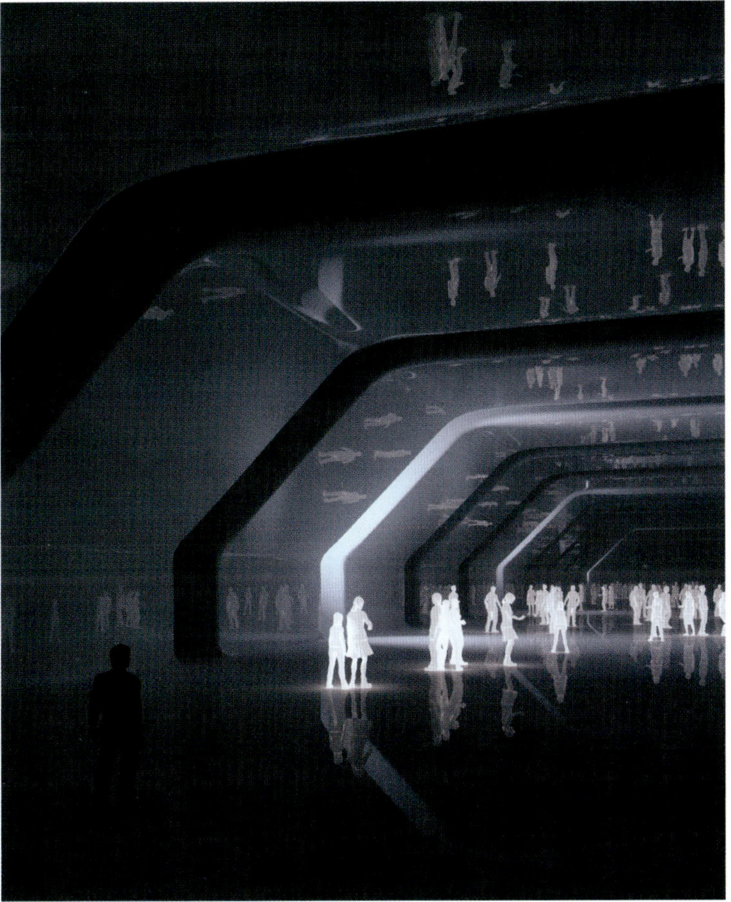
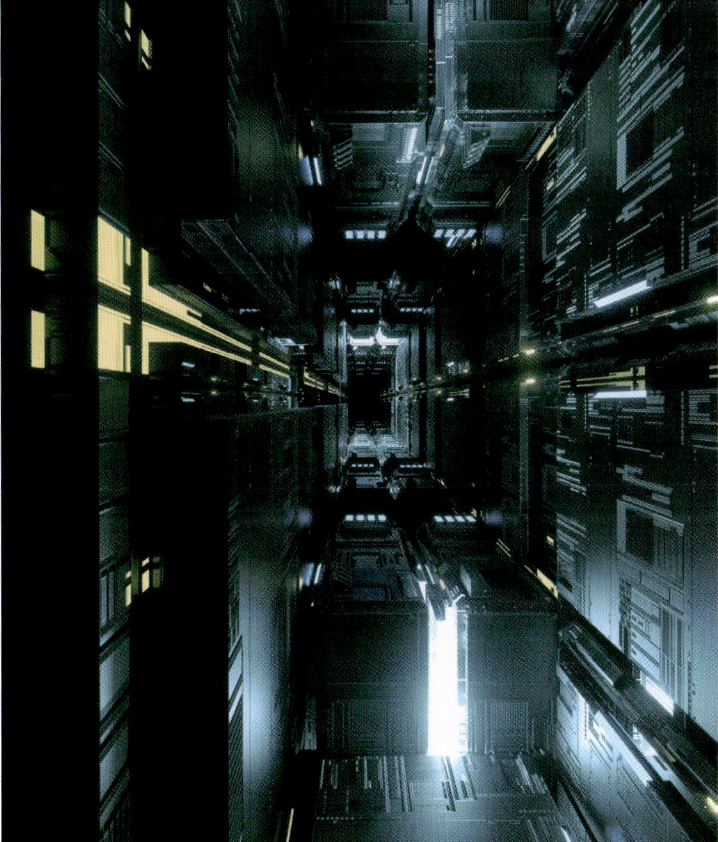

TOP LEFT

OPTICAL AMPLIFICATION
05.06.2017

TOP RIGHT

D2
08.24.2017

BOTTOM LEFT

REAL PEOPLE
05.26.2017

BOTTOM RIGHT

OVR.WRK9
04.29.2017

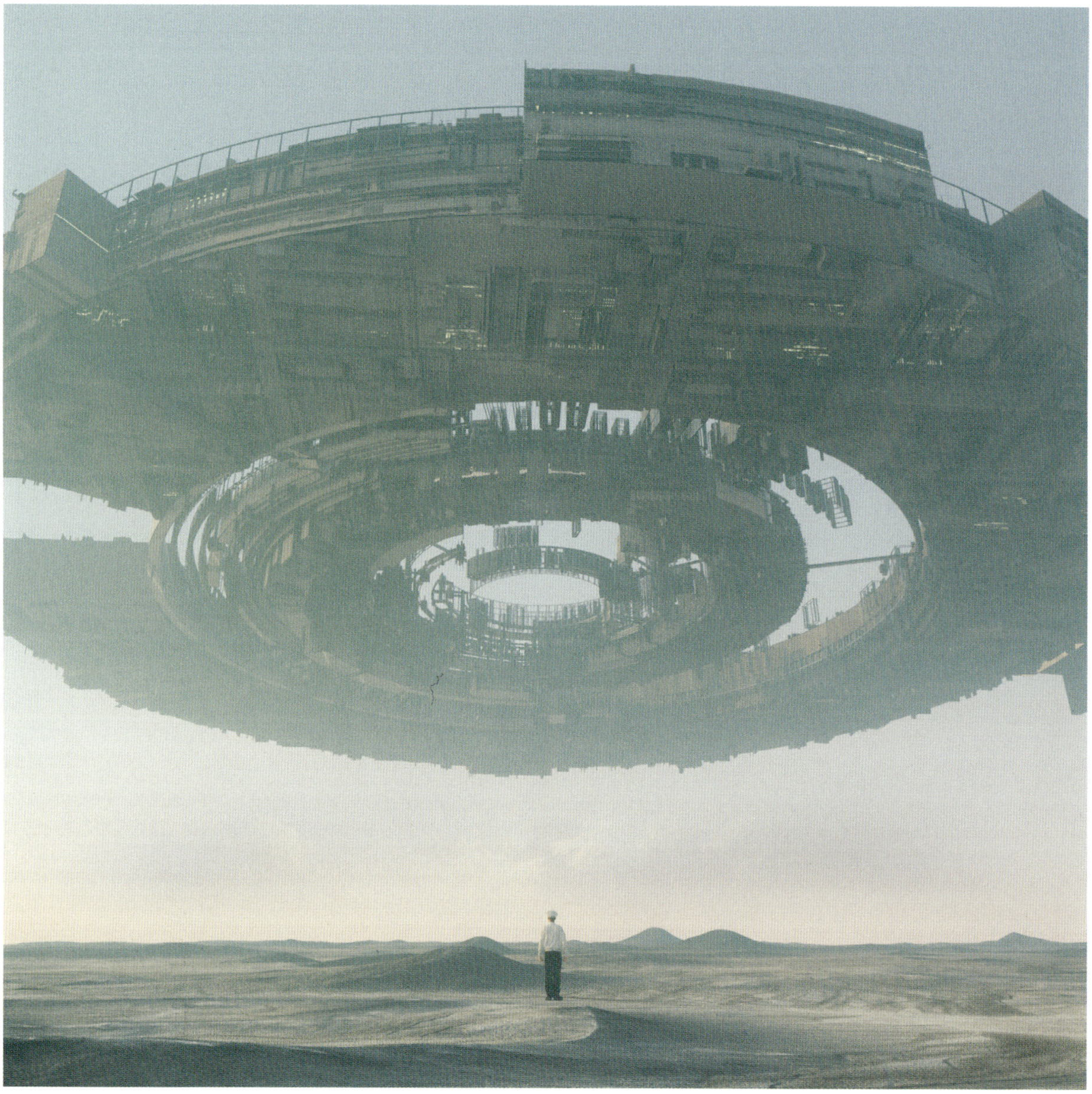

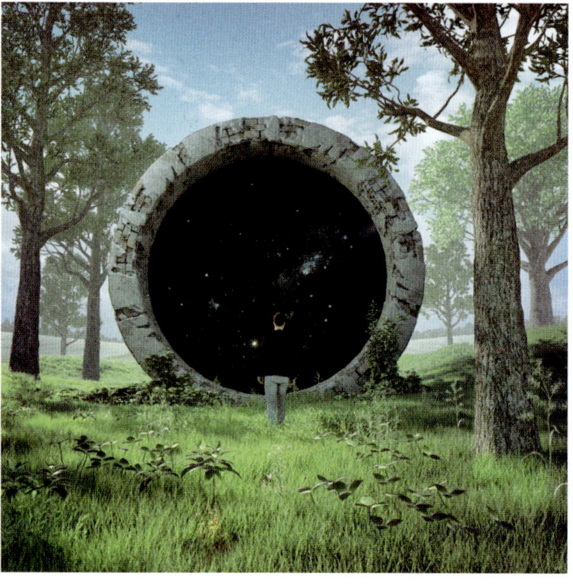

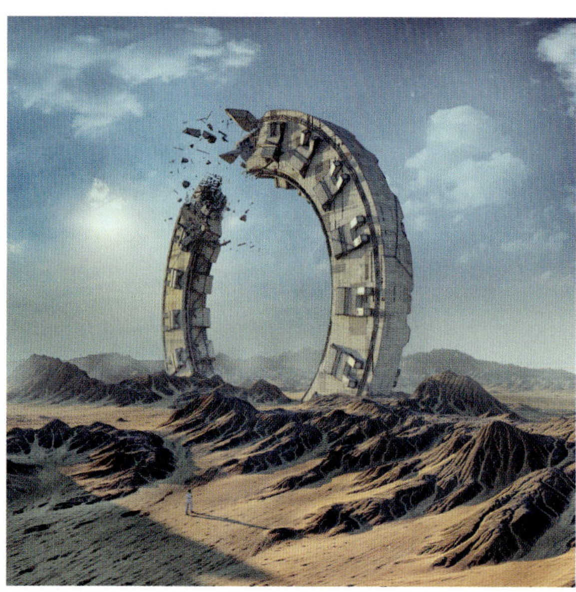

TOP
BREACH
02.23.2017

BOTTOM LEFT
VOIDFACE
11.15.2017

BOTTOM RIGHT
BROKEN CONTINUUM
11.11.2017

OPPOSITE PAGE
POWER FILTRATION GATE
06.05.2017

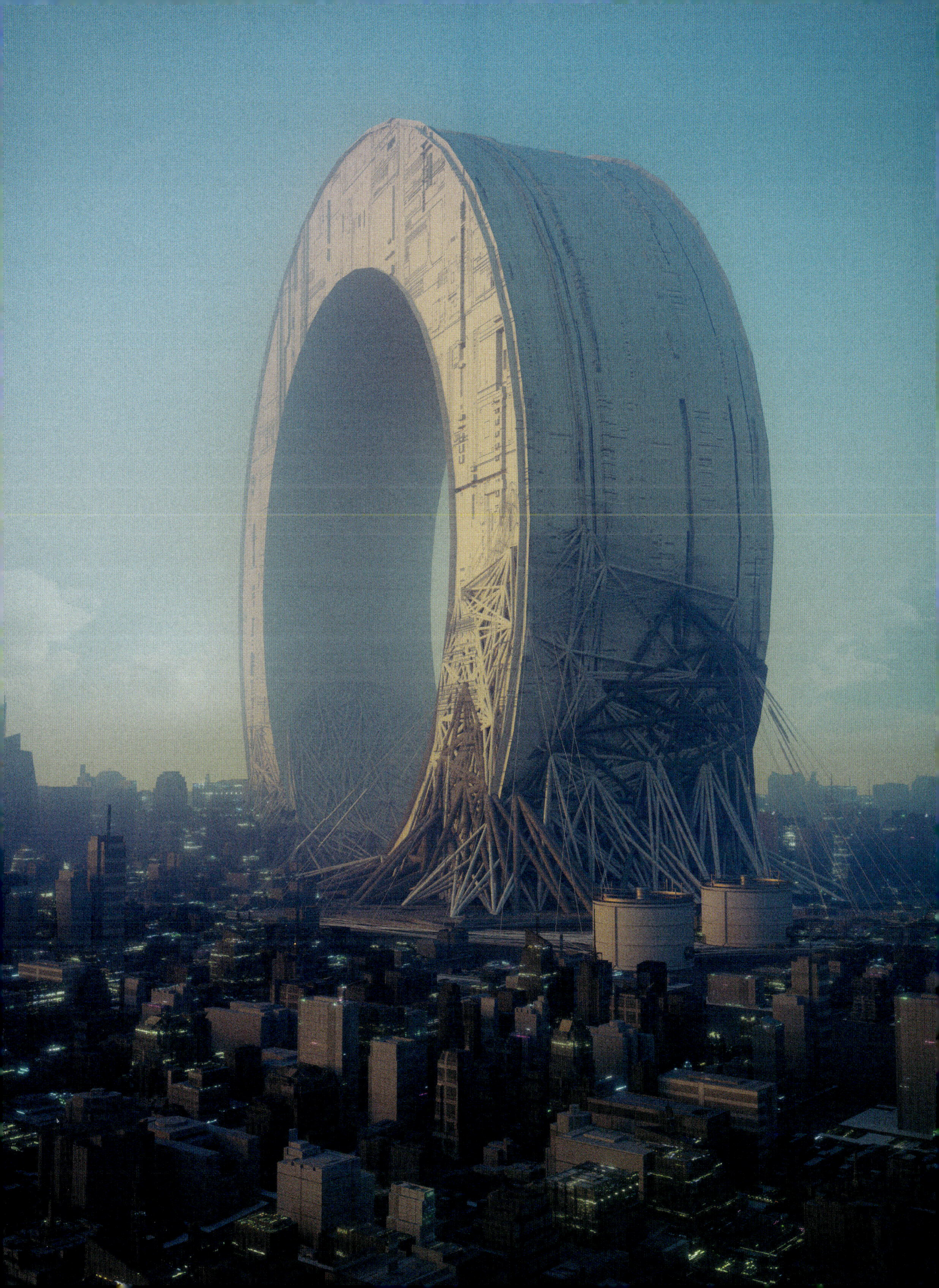

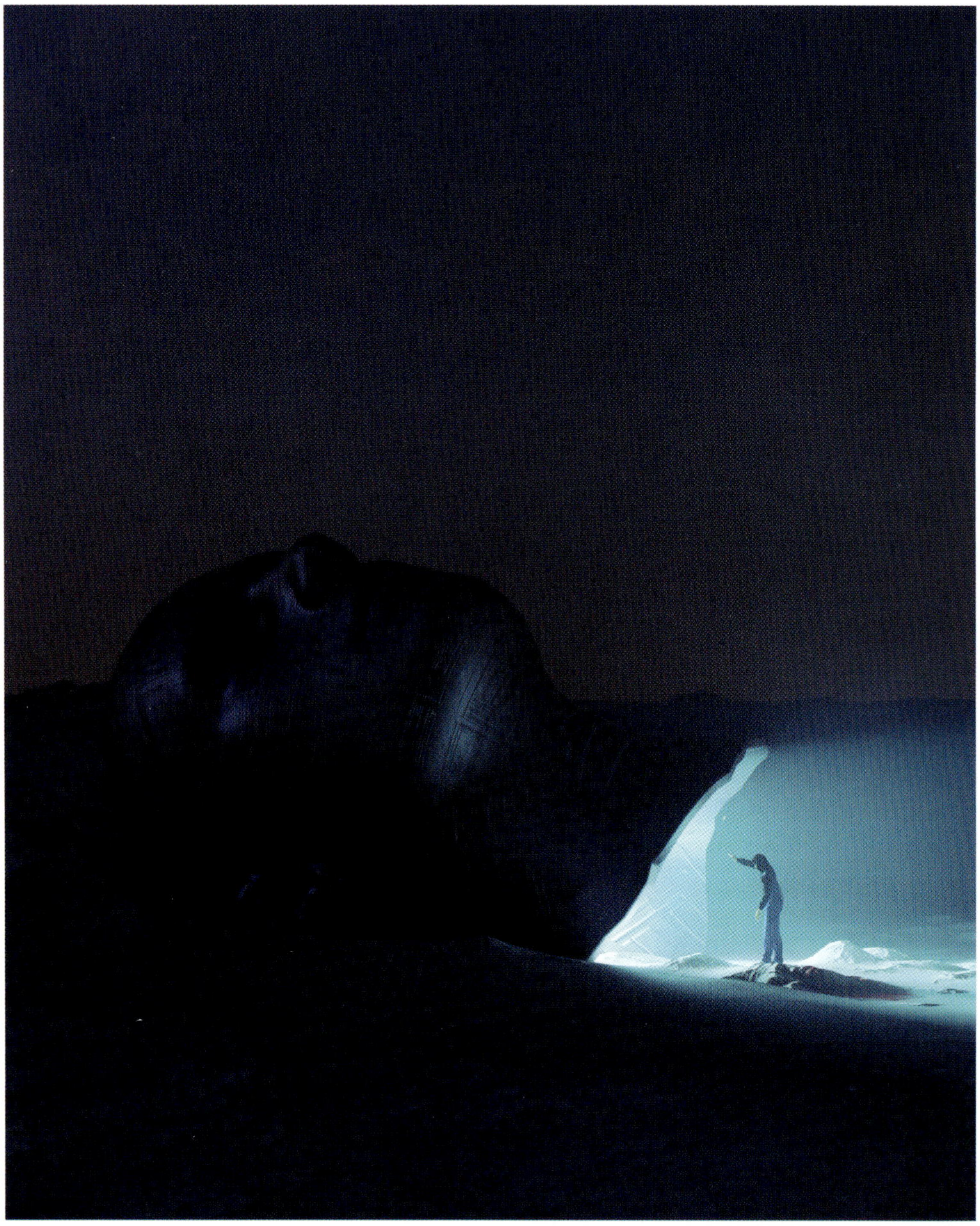

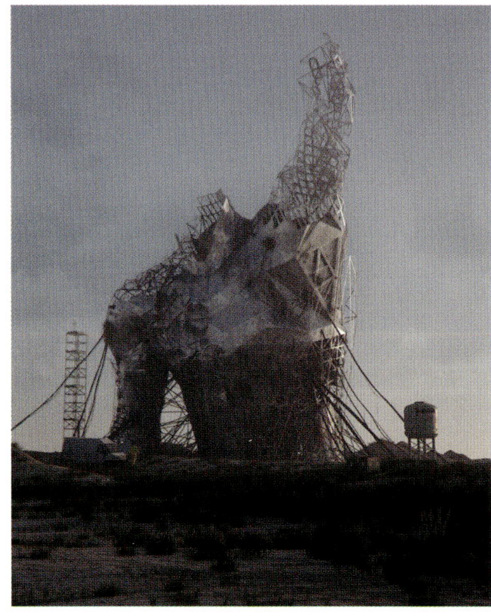

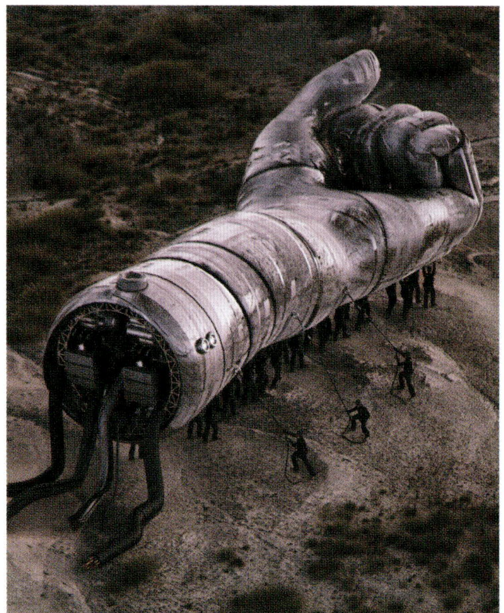

TOP

HEADSPACE
09.22.2017

BOTTOM LEFT

(DE)CONSTRUCT
06.17.2017

BOTTOM RIGHT

DISMANTLE
06.07.2017

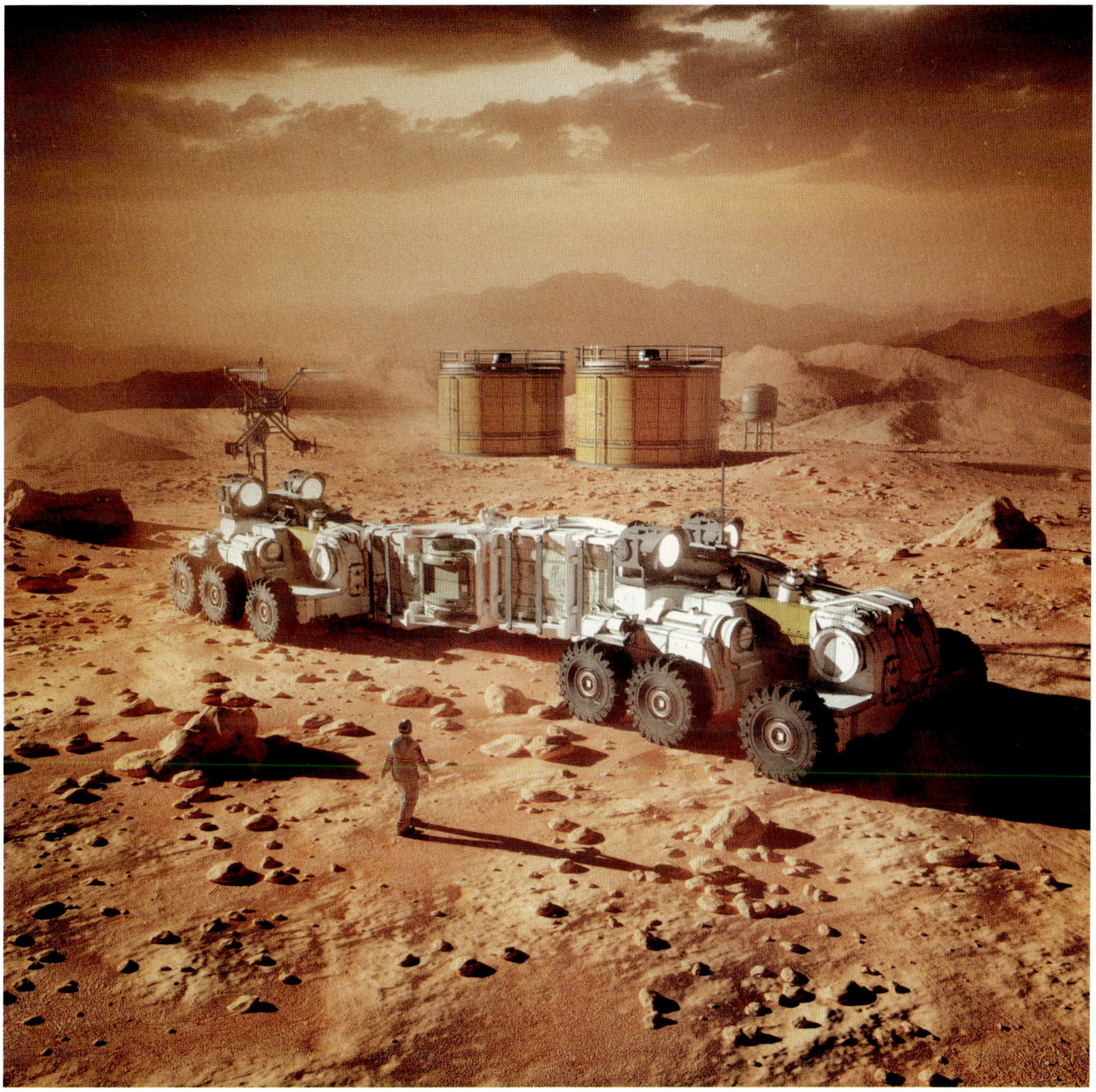

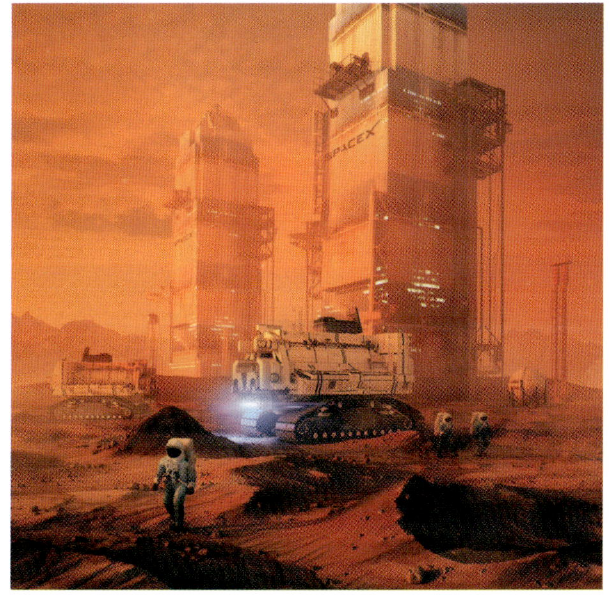

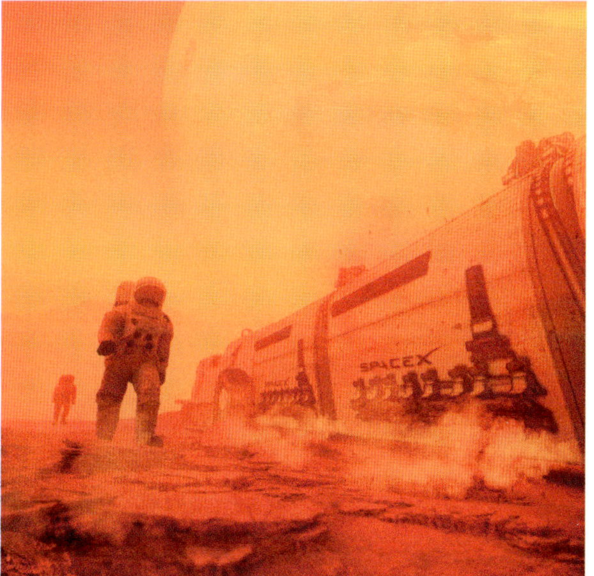

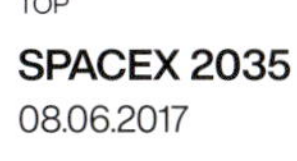

TOP

SPACEX 2035
08.06.2017

BOTTOM LEFT

**SPACEX.MARS.
BASE01**
08.20.2017

BOTTOM RIGHT

BADASS
08.08.2017

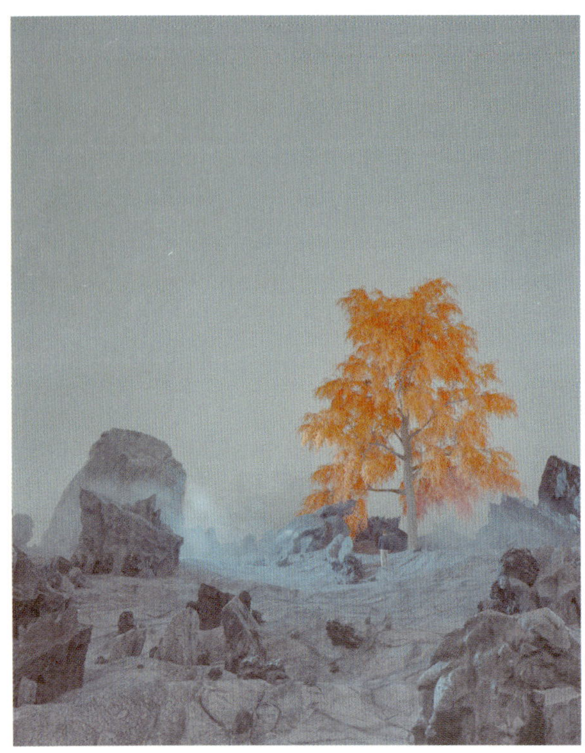

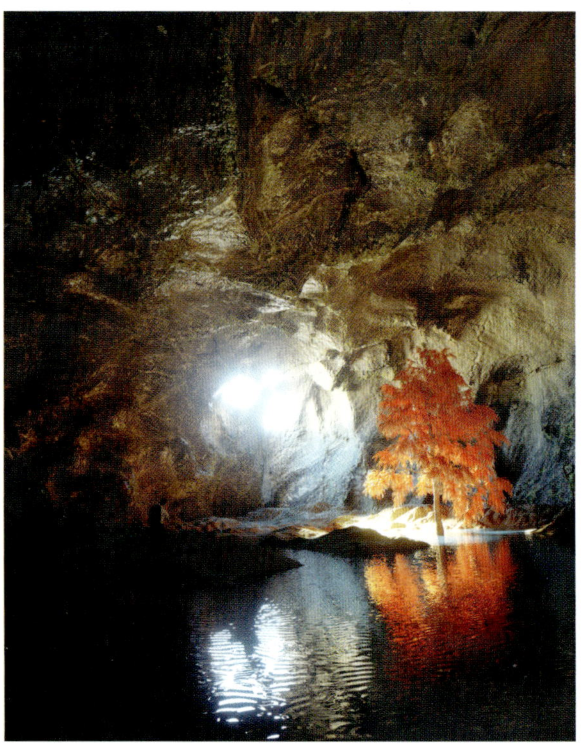

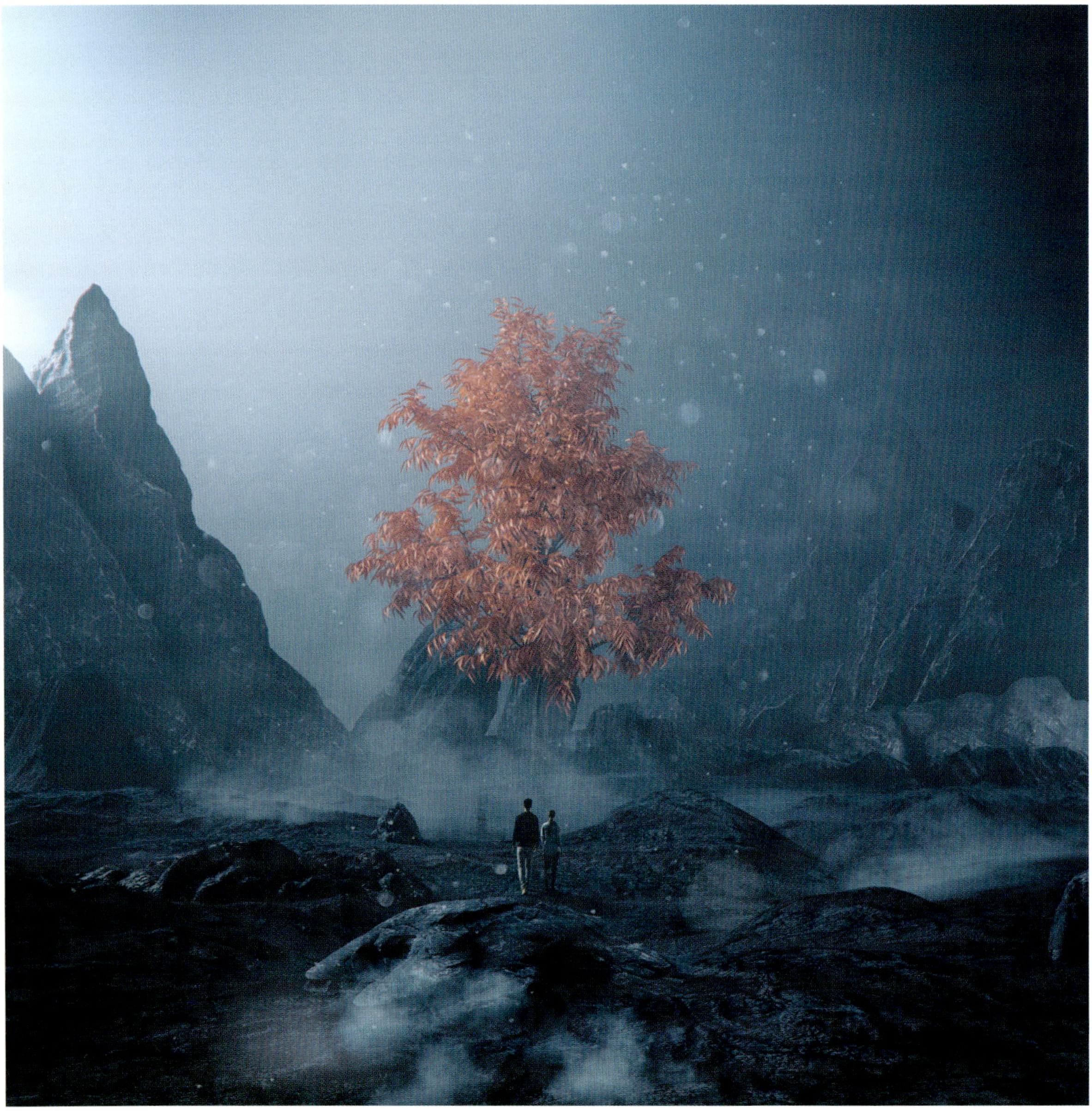

TOP LEFT

LAST TREE

07.24.2017

TOP RIGHT

GROW

07.30.2017

BOTTOM

INDEPENDENCE

07.04.2017

OPPOSITE PAGE

ILLUMINATED PATH

07.06.2017

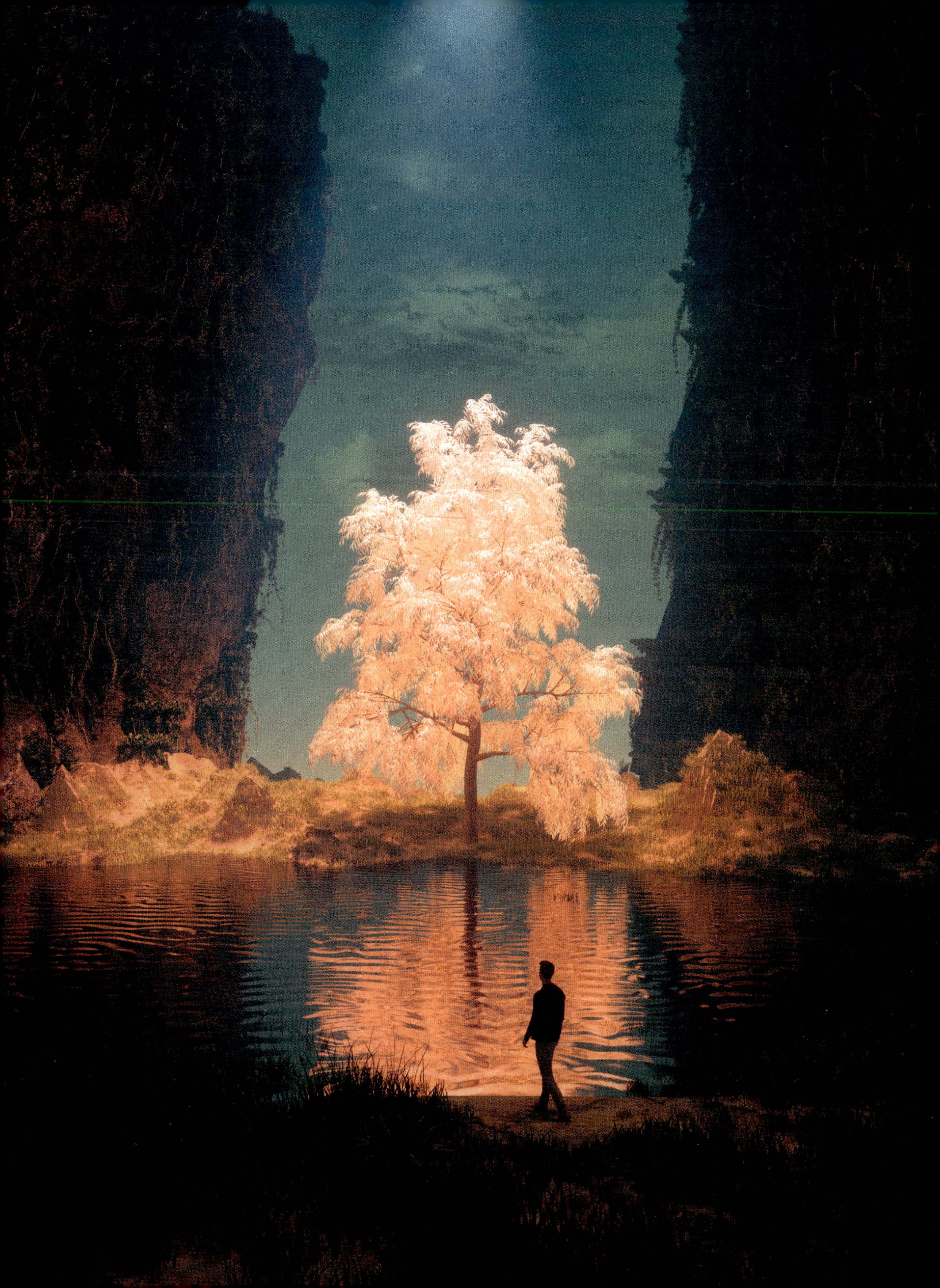

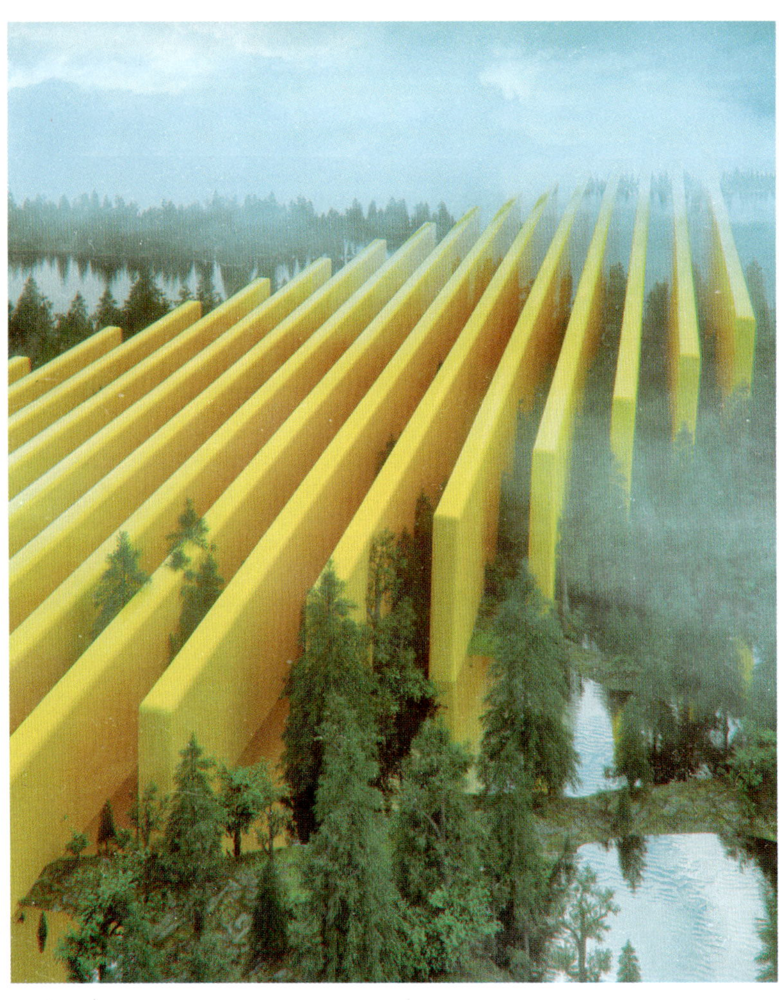

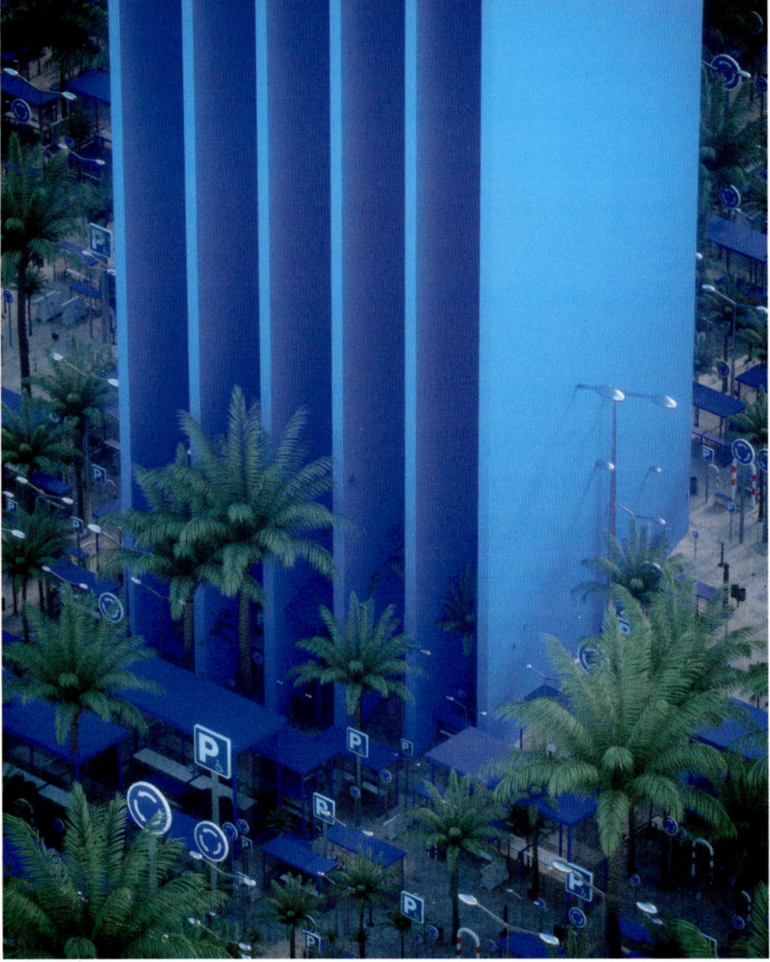

TOP

SWEDEN
09.04.2017

BOTTOM

BLUU
09.11.2017

OPPOSITE PAGE

MAXIMILLION.TWO
08.19.2017

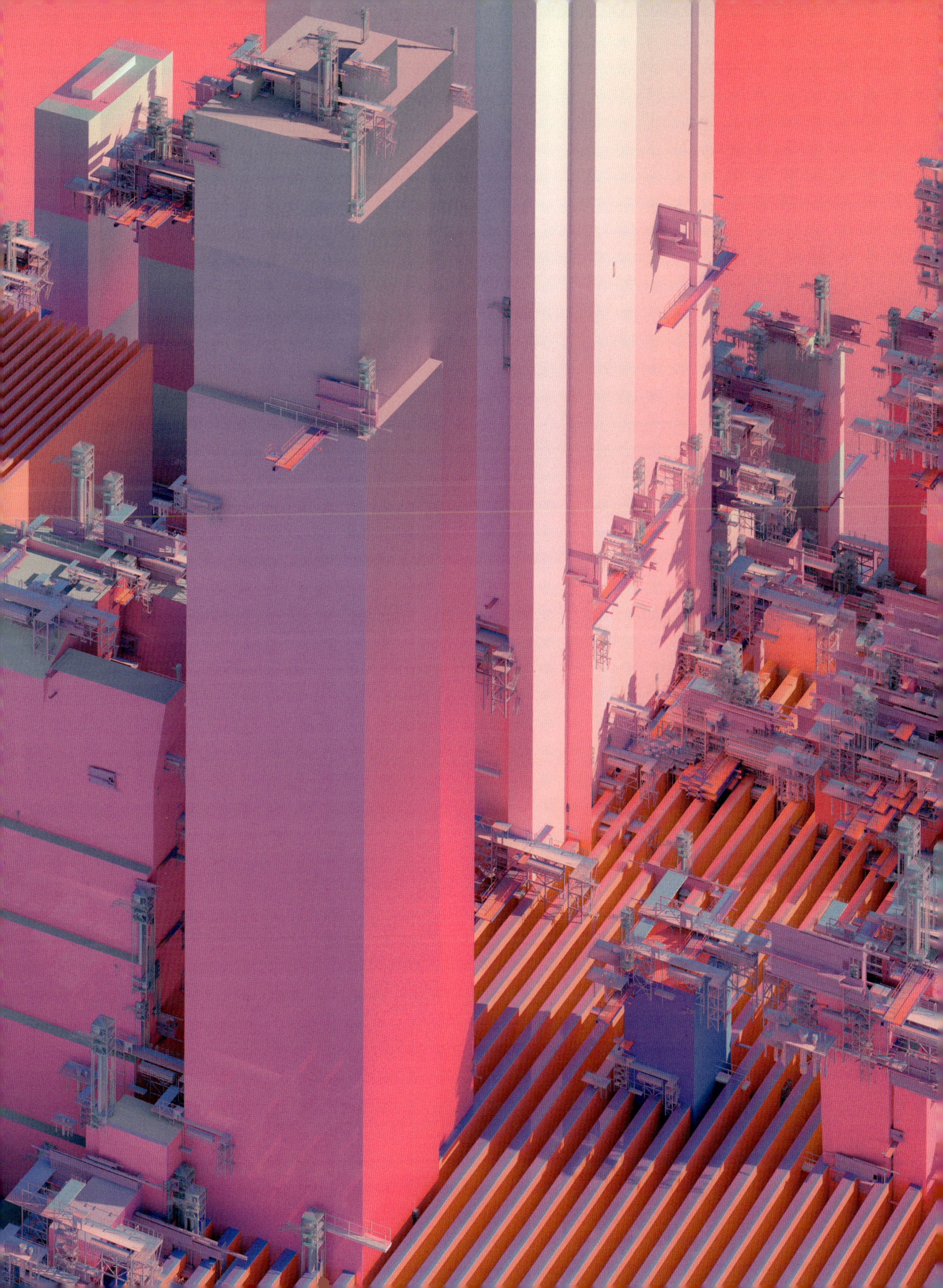

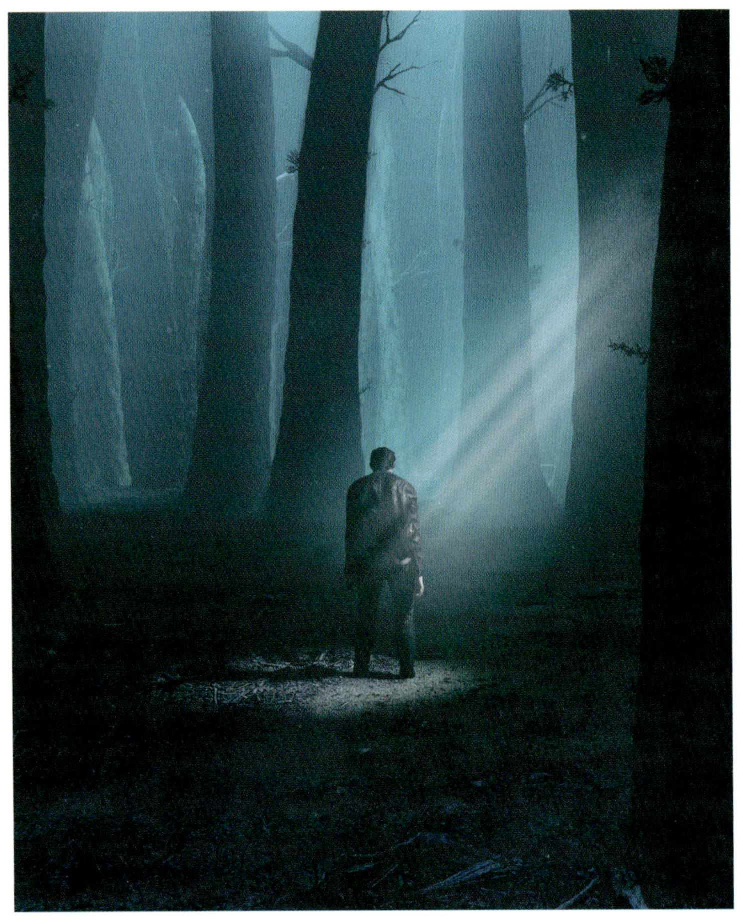

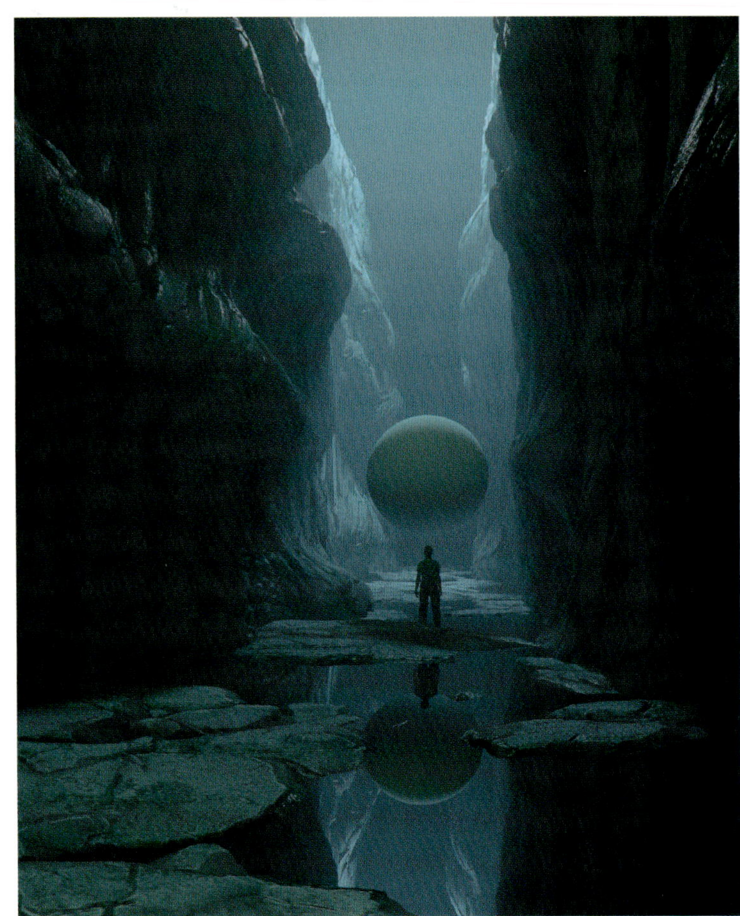

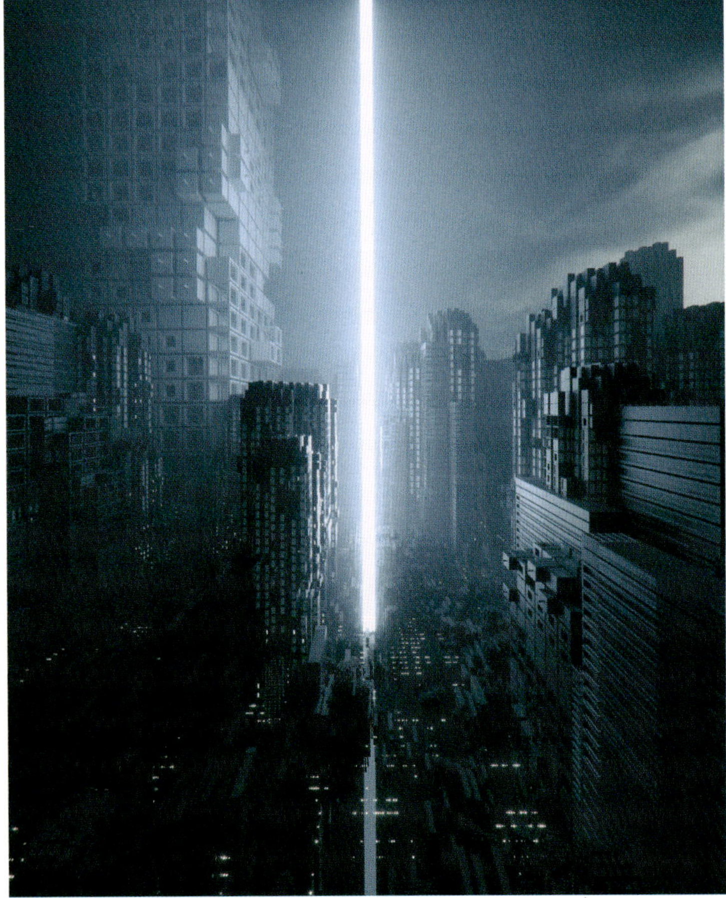

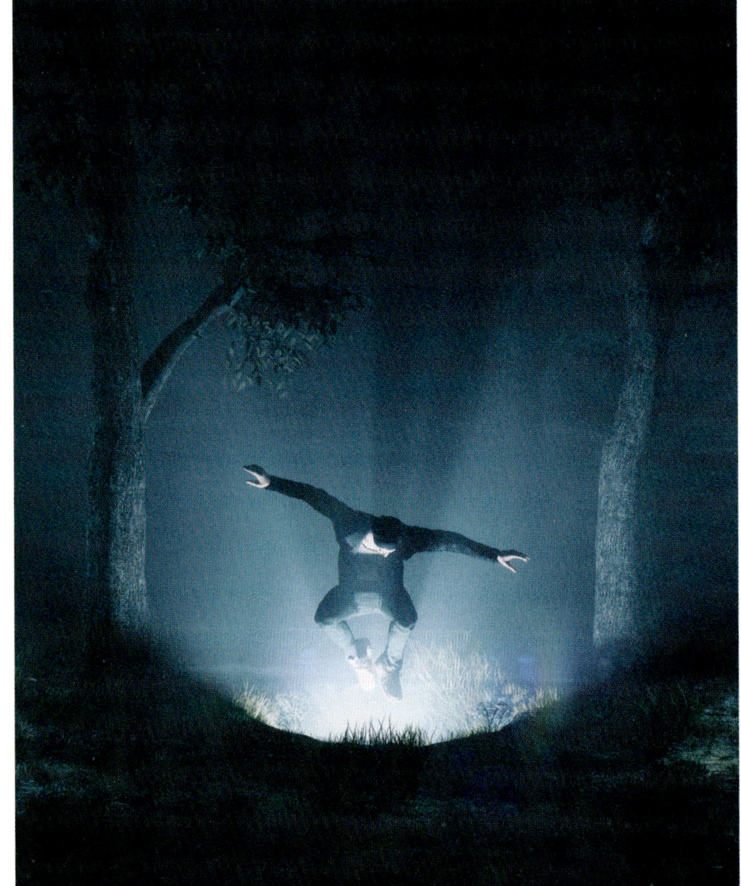

TOP LEFT
LOST
02.13.2017

TOP RIGHT
BASE
02.18.2017

BOTTOM LEFT
RECKONING
02.27.2017

BOTTOM RIGHT
FLOAT
03.03.2017

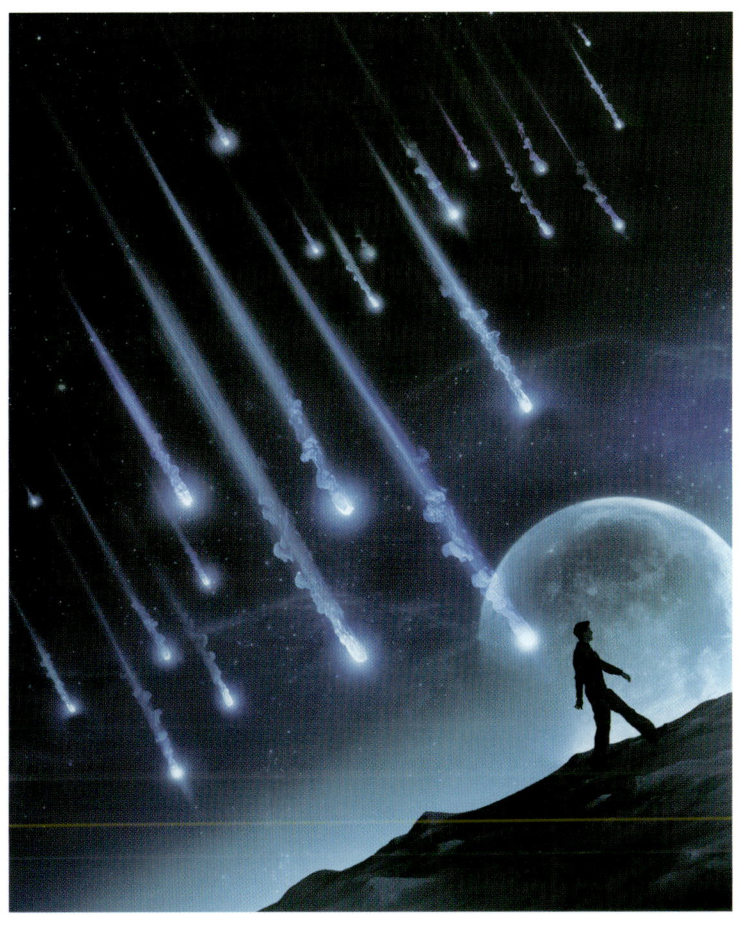
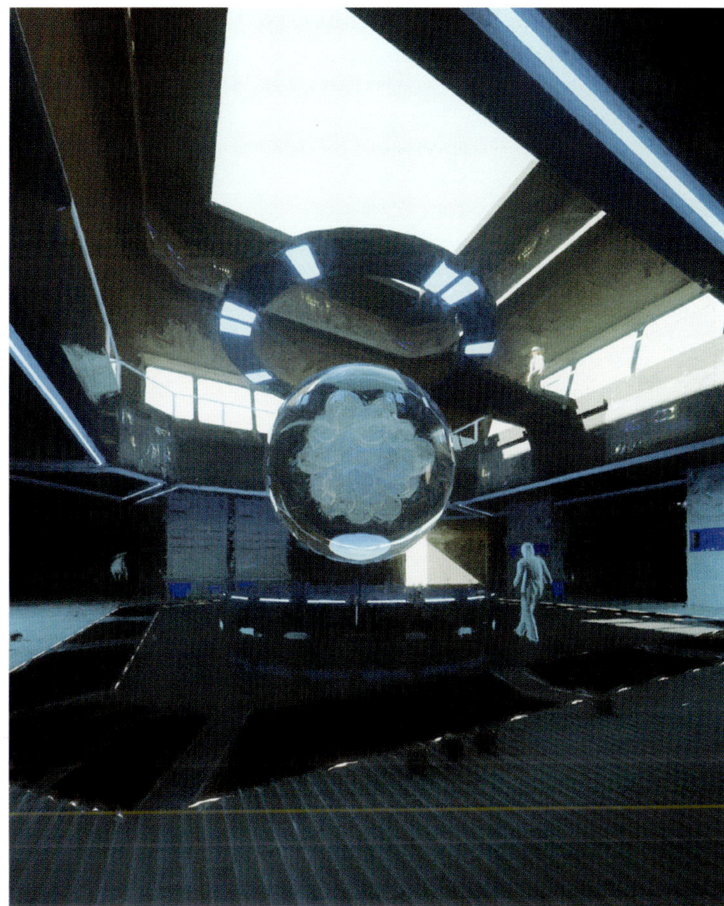
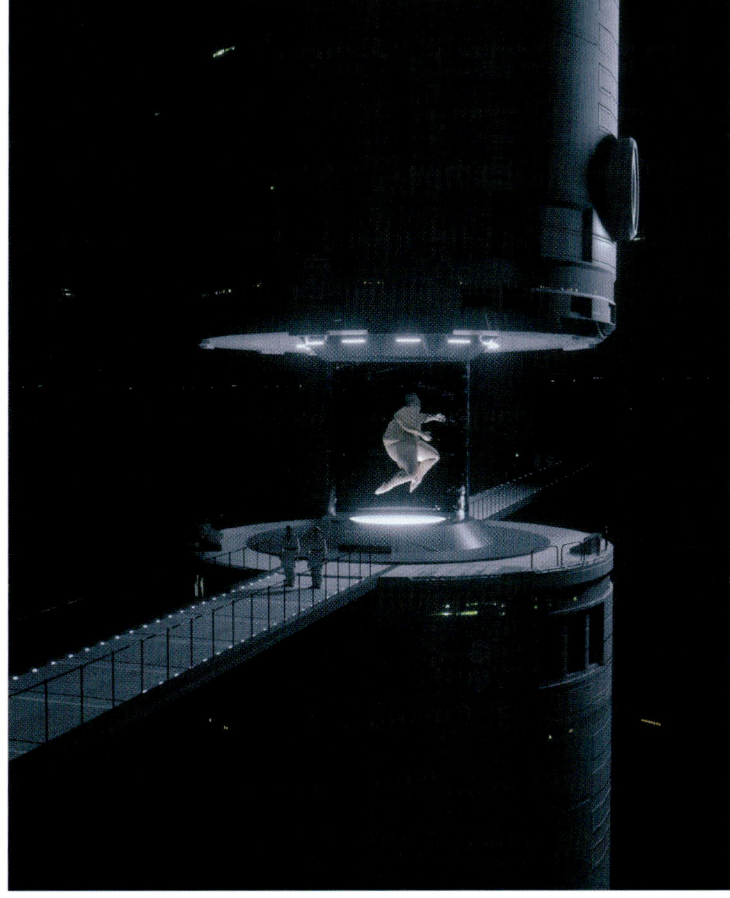
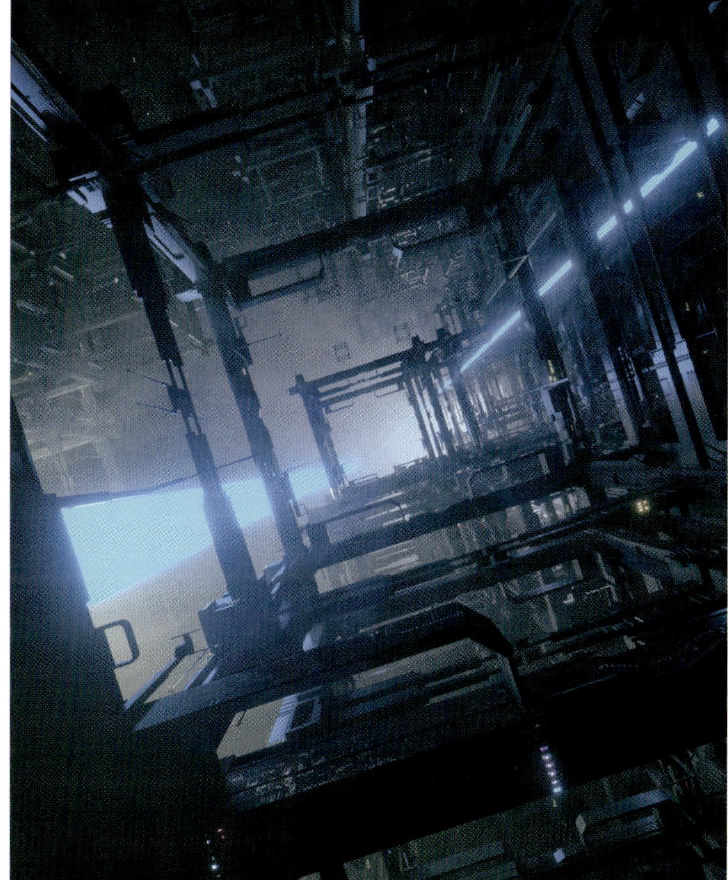

TOP LEFT
DUST
03.05.2017

TOP RIGHT
SUBBEAMS
02.19.2017

BOTTOM LEFT
SUSPENDED
02.05.2017

BOTTOM RIGHT
POLYTECHNICAL
02.16.2017

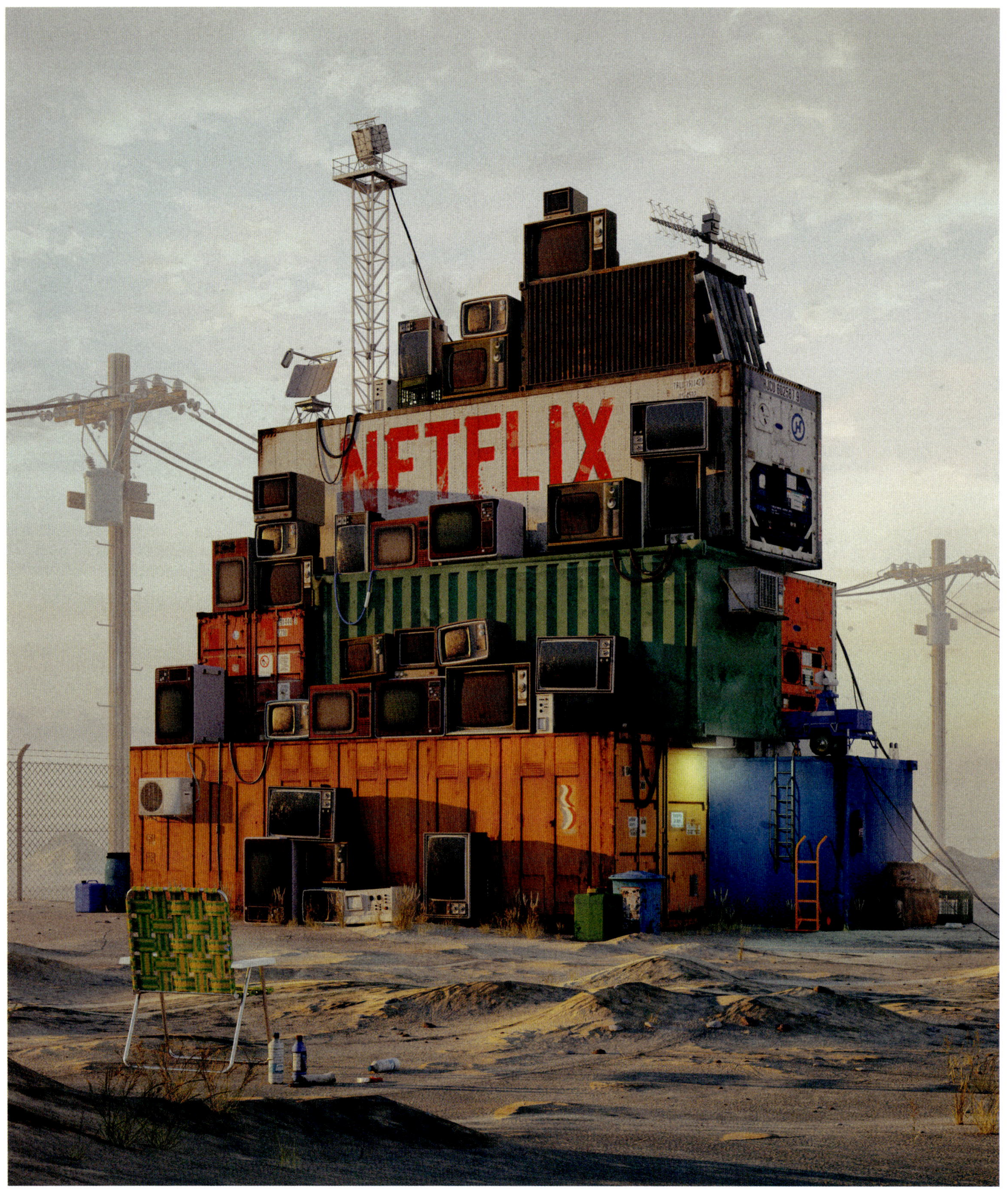

ABOVE

NETFLIX 2087
12.15.2017

OPPOSITE PAGE

GOOGLE DATA CENTER 2079
11.30.2017

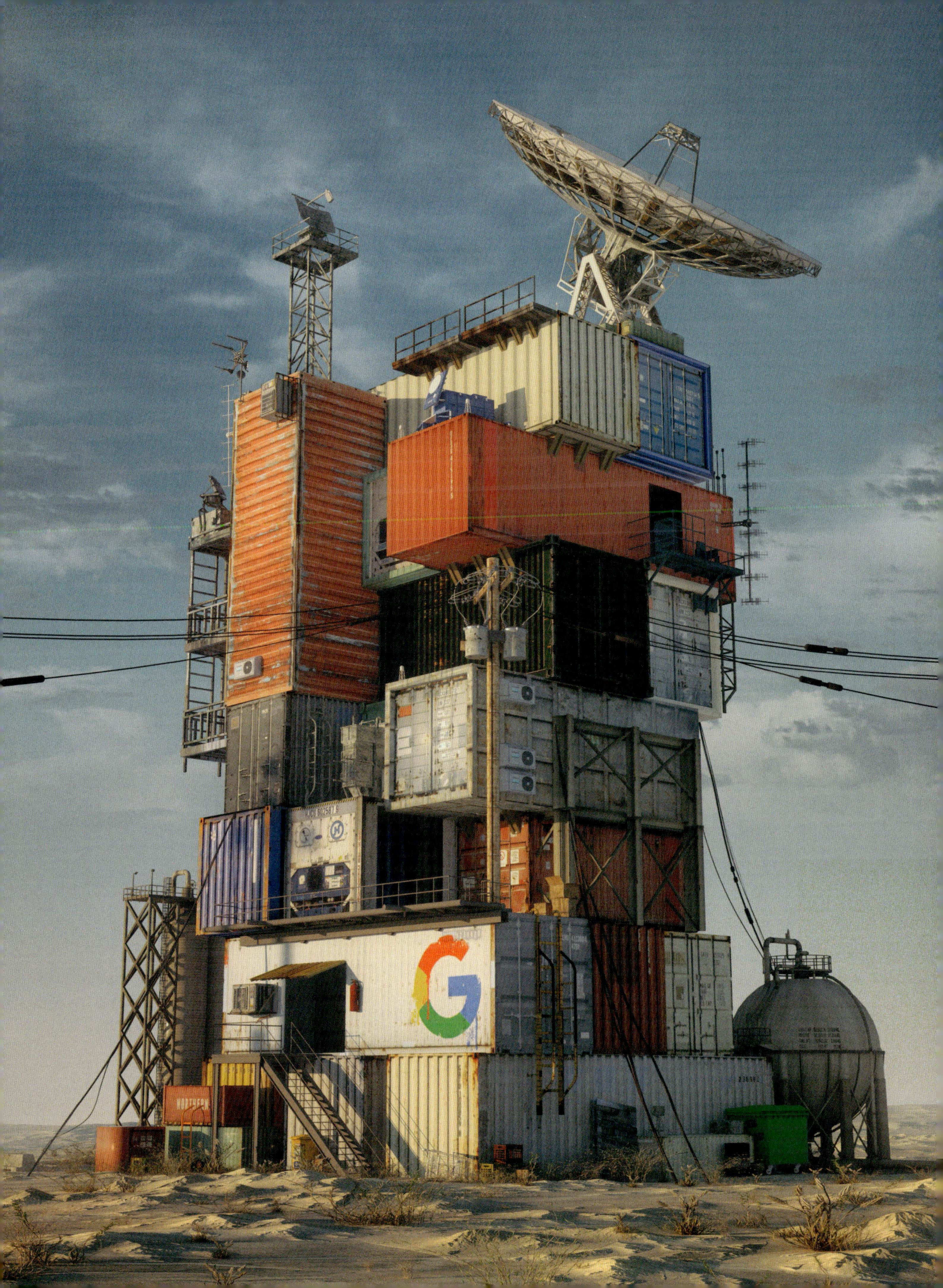

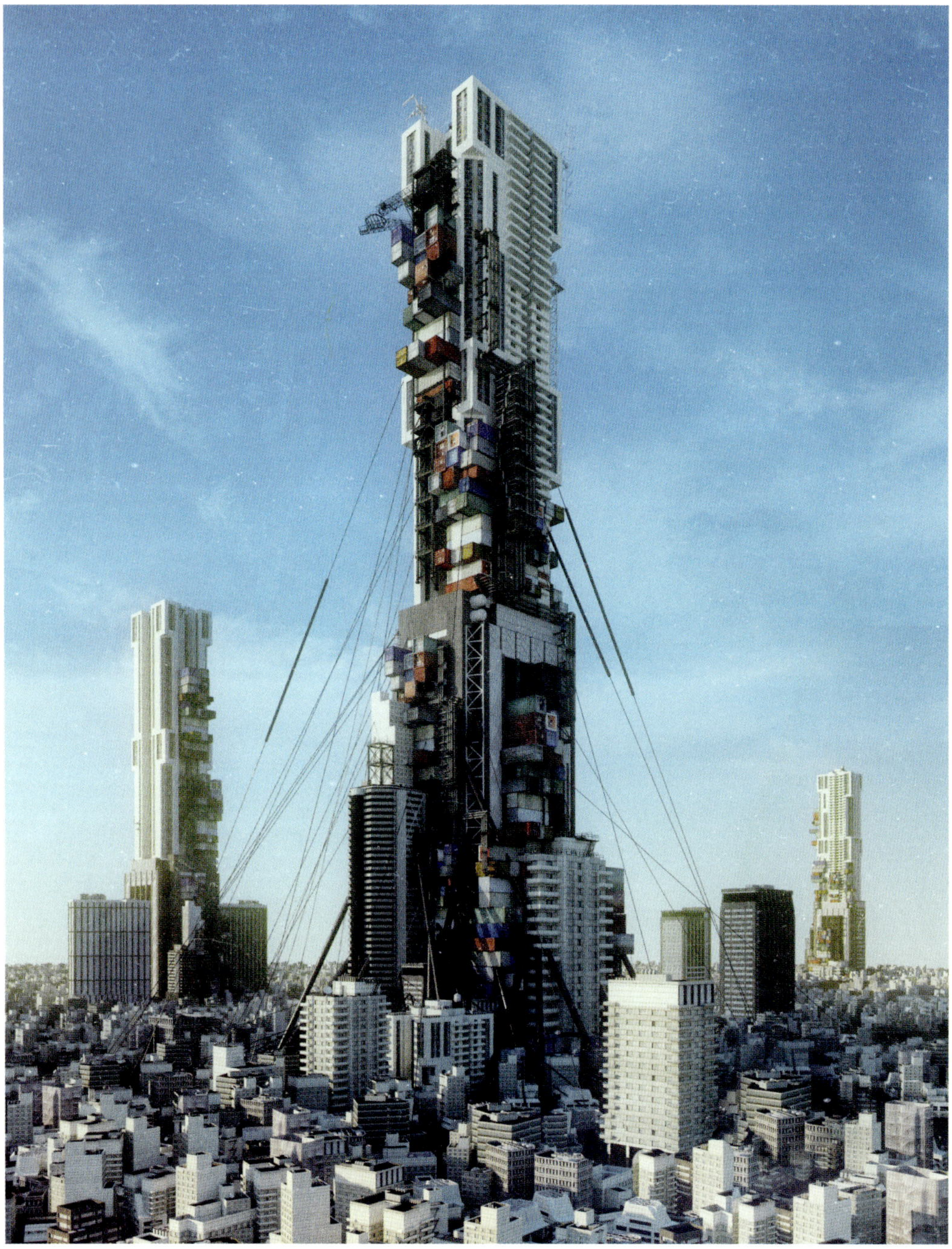

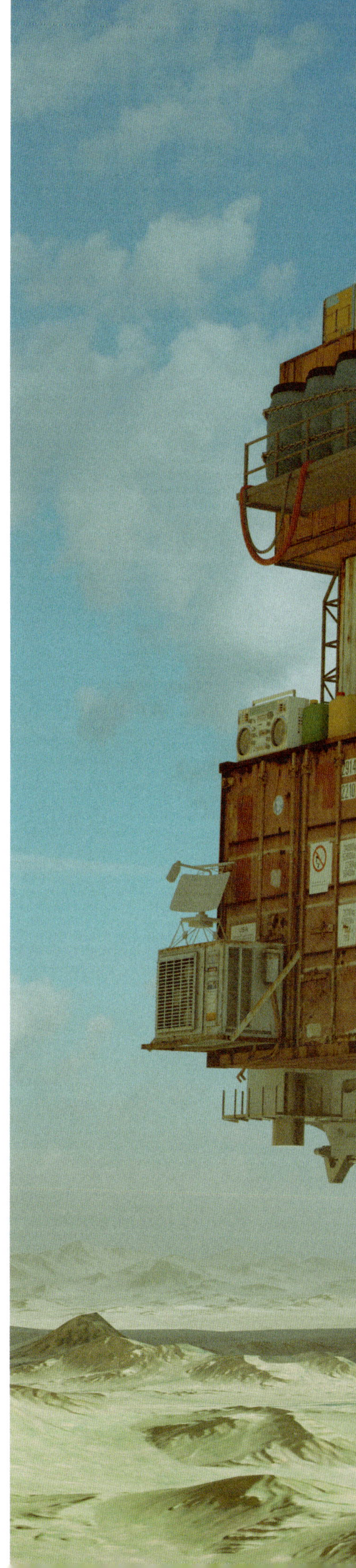

ABOVE

ZERO SPECTRUM
12.18.2017

OPPOSITE PAGE

AMAZON MOBILE SITE 2091
12.03.2017

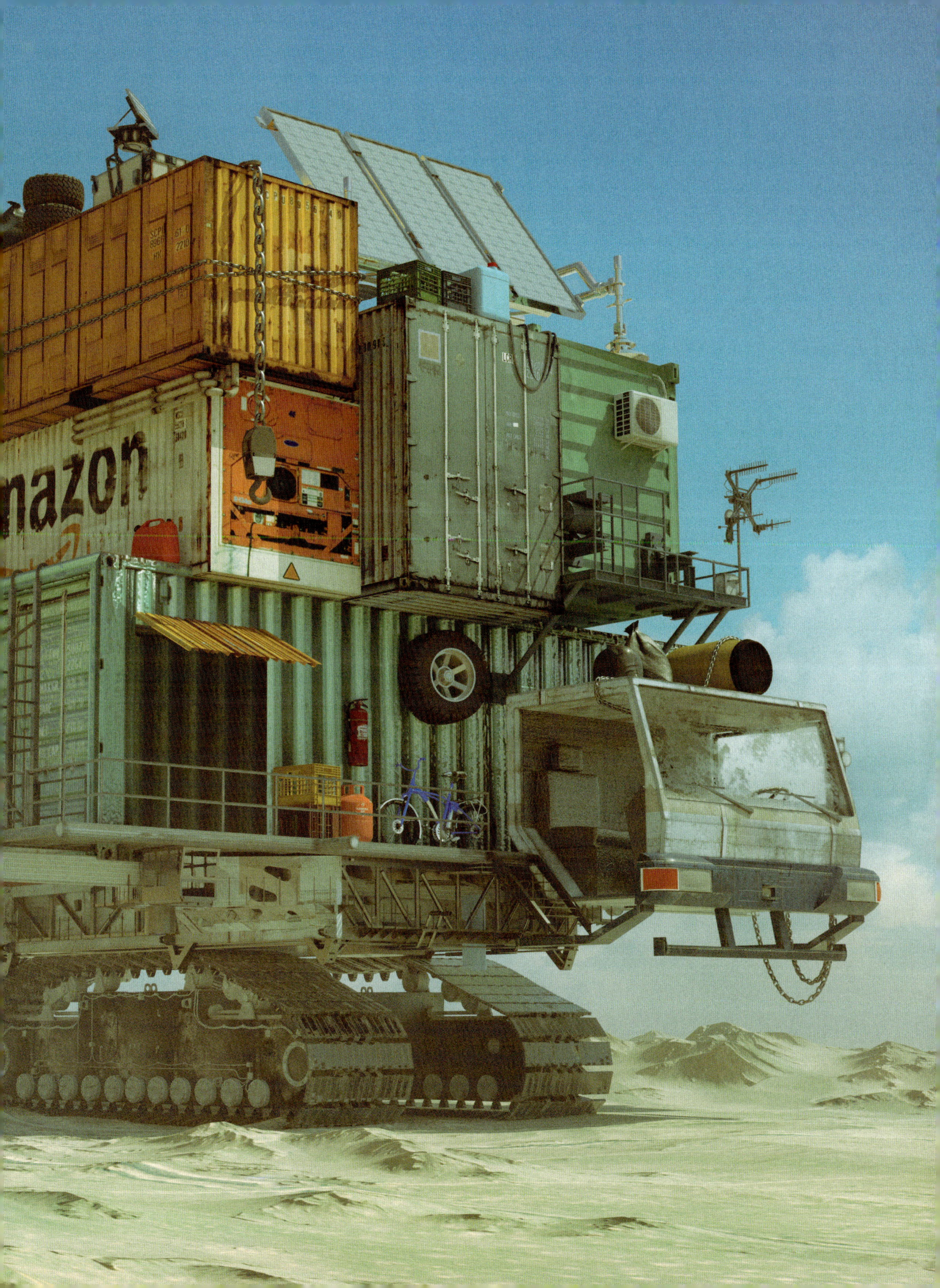
nazon

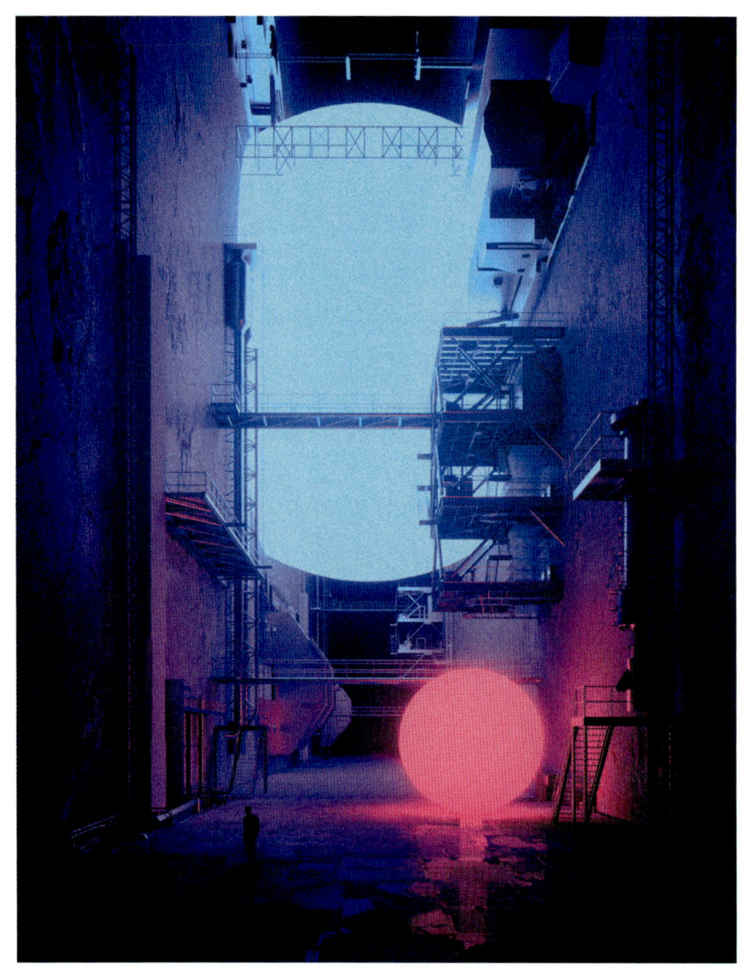

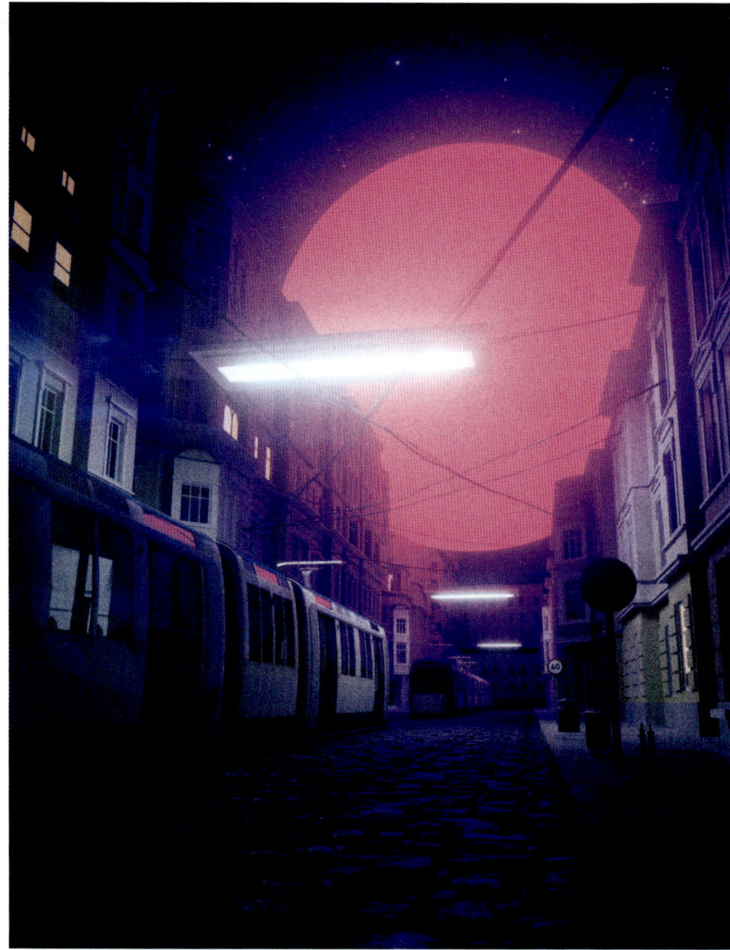

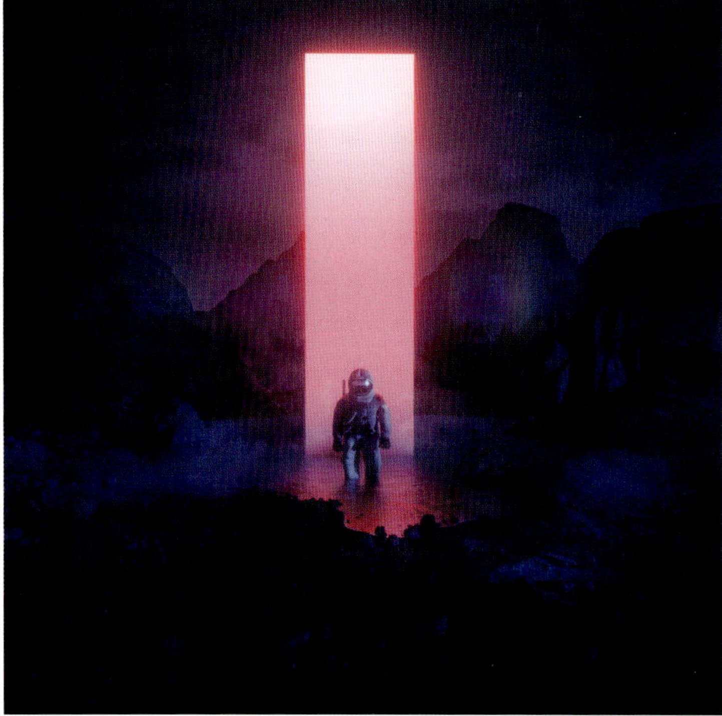

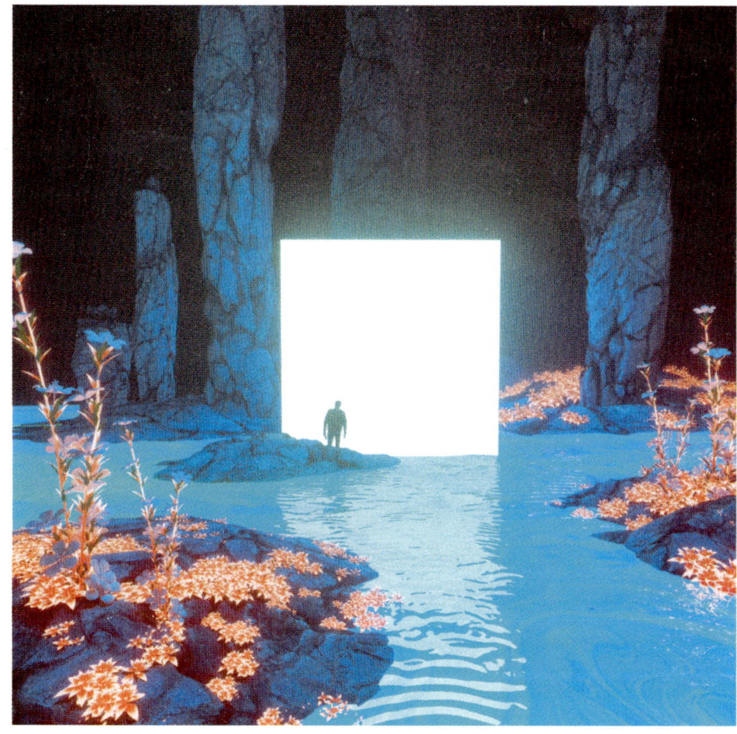

TOP LEFT
MELT.NEON
08.04.2017

TOP RIGHT
GOTHENBURG
09.05.2017

BOTTOM LEFT
UNICORN ZERO
11.03.2017

BOTTOM RIGHT
WHITE RUBICON
07.20.2017

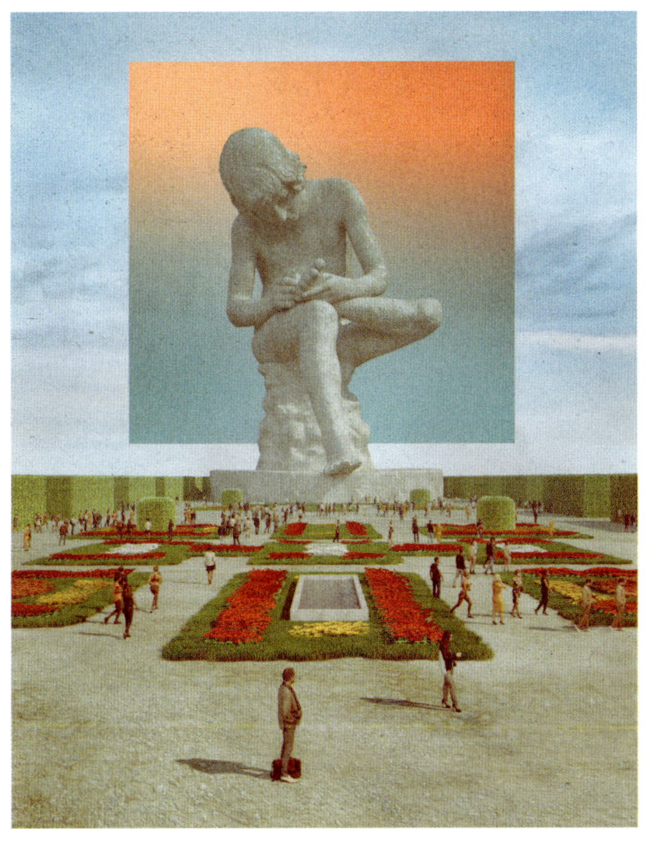

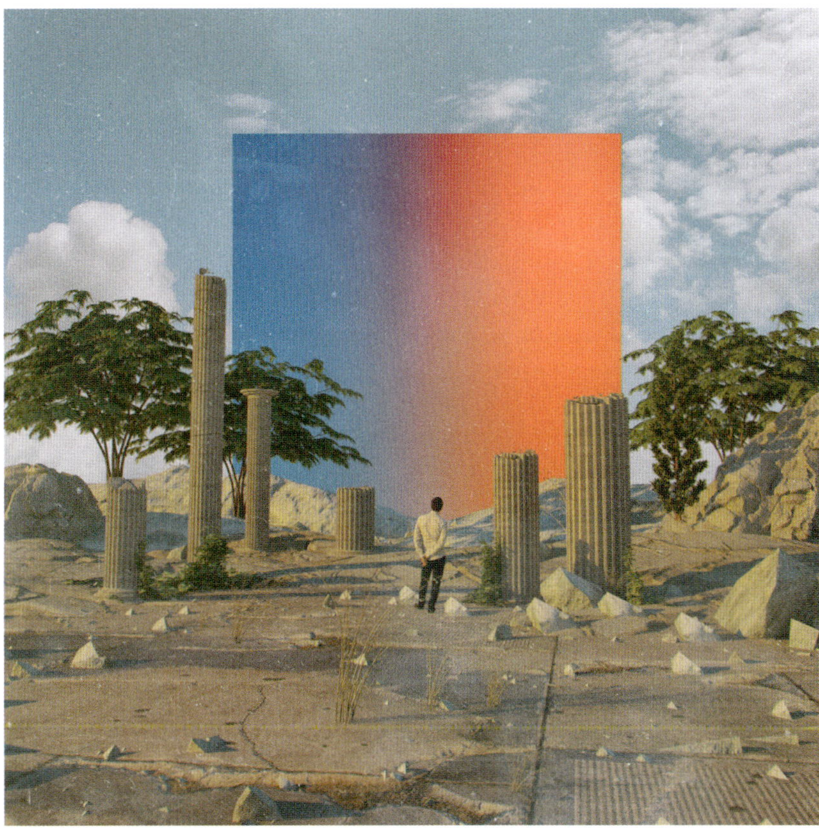

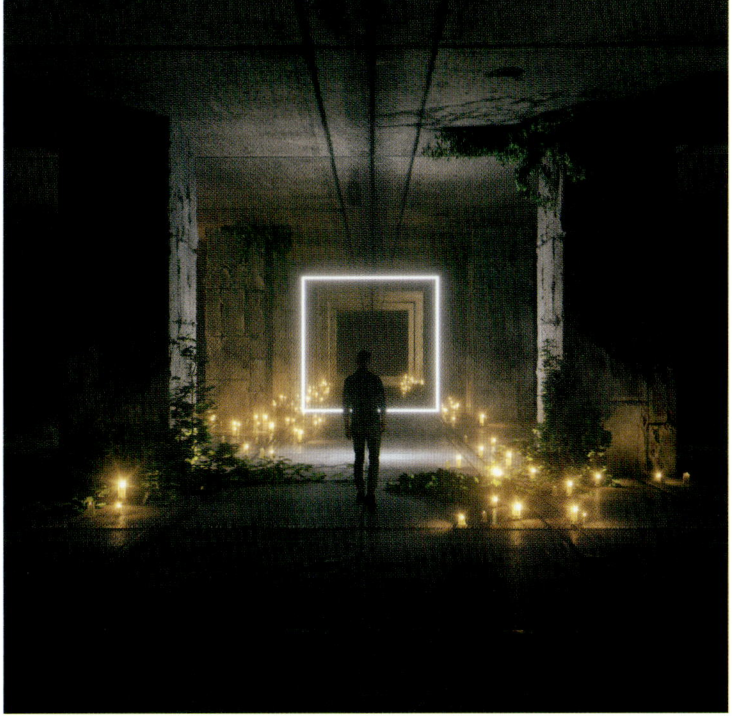

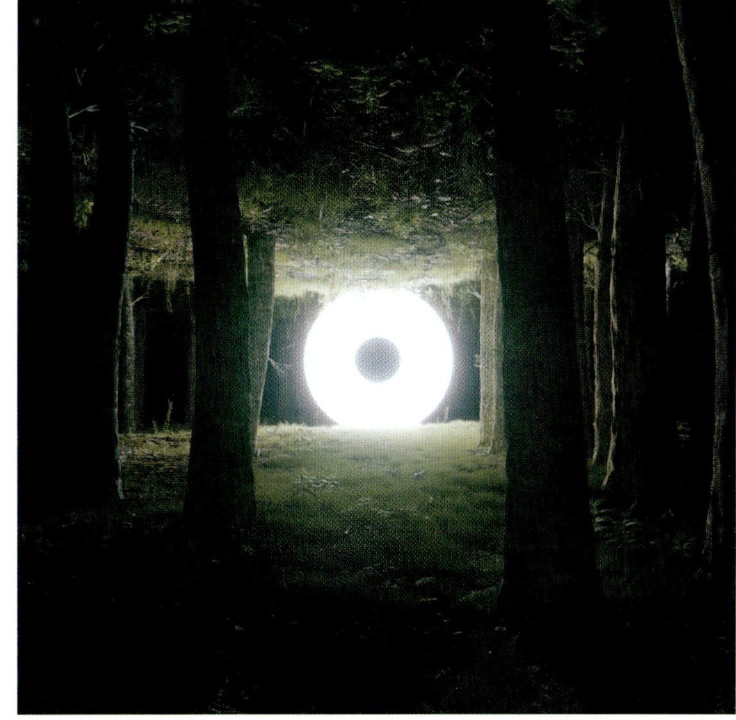

TOP LEFT
VIENNA
08.23.2017

TOP RIGHT
COLOR.CIVILIZE
09.01.2017

BOTTOM LEFT
LAST LEVEL
07.12.2017

BOTTOM RIGHT
O
10.09.2017

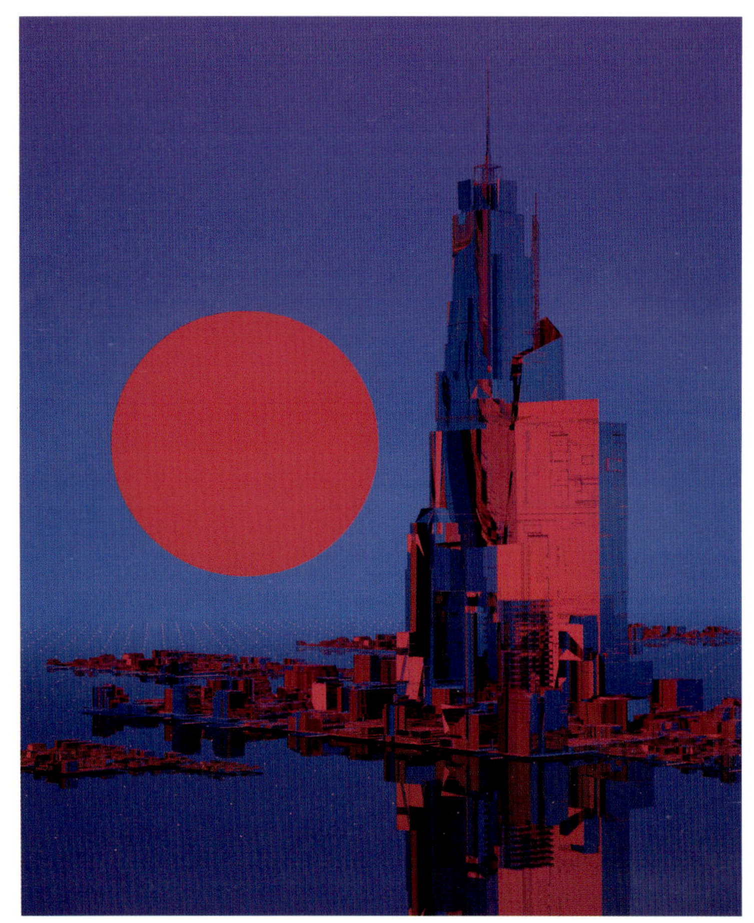

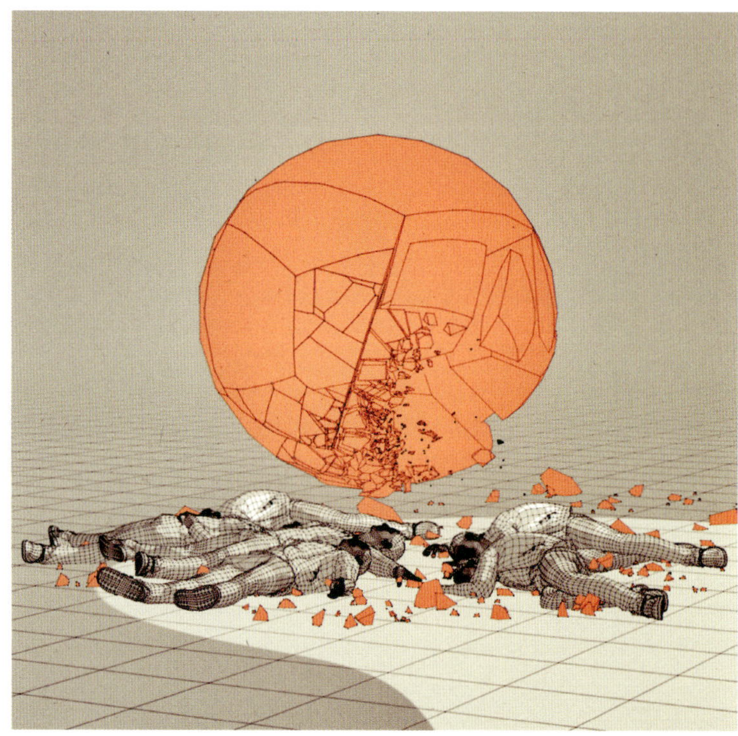

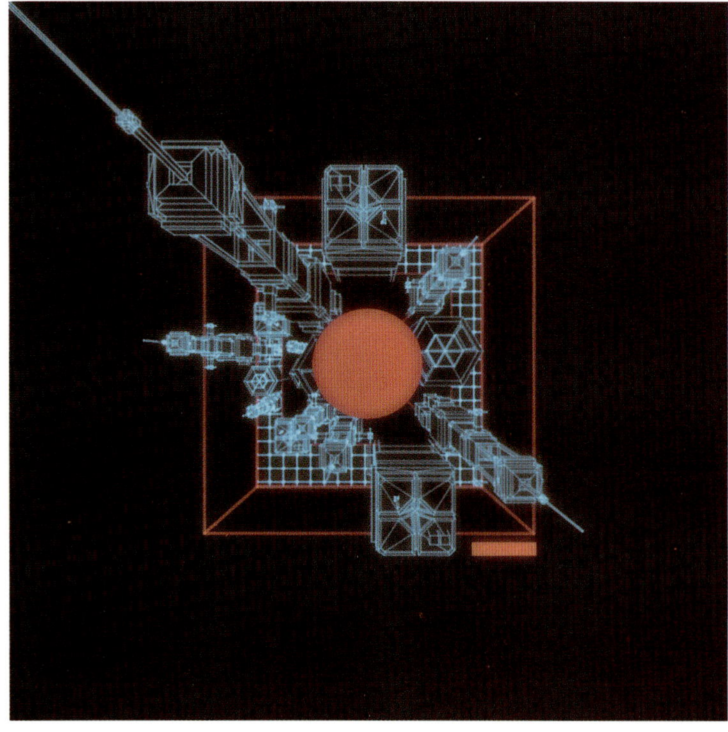

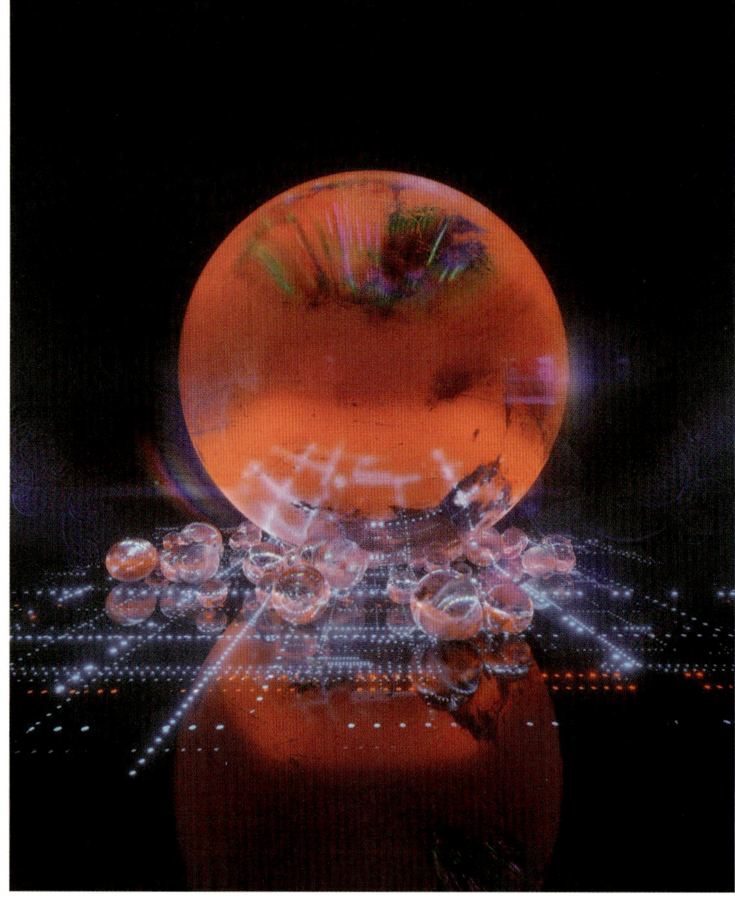

TOP LEFT
BLUESKY / REDSKY
09.30.2017

TOP RIGHT
CRUSHHH
01.02.2017

BOTTOM LEFT
BOY-C32
01.03.2017

BOTTOM RIGHT
FORBIDDEN FRUIT
01.16.2017

OPPOSITE PAGE
SATURATED FUTURE
12.08.2017

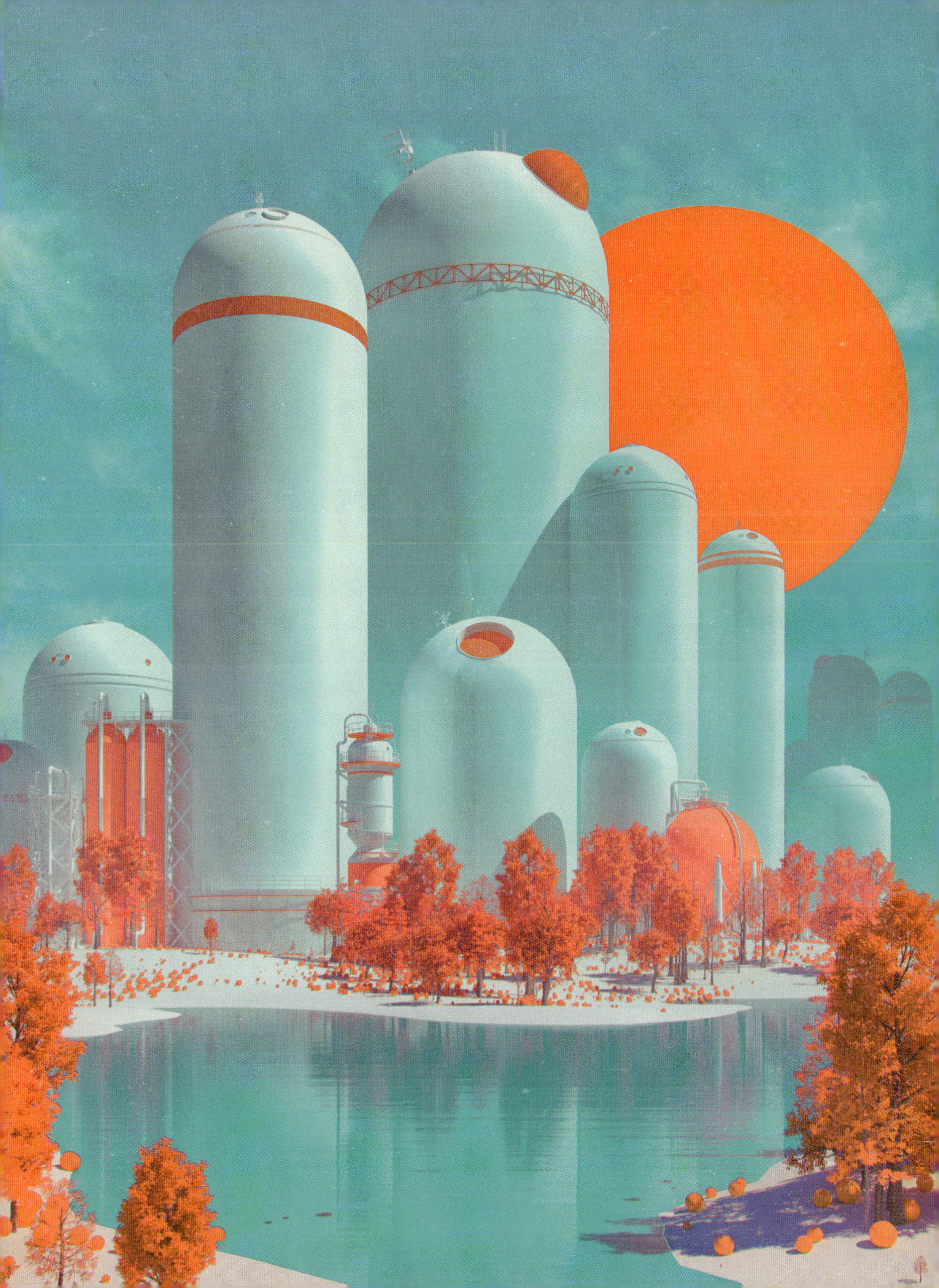

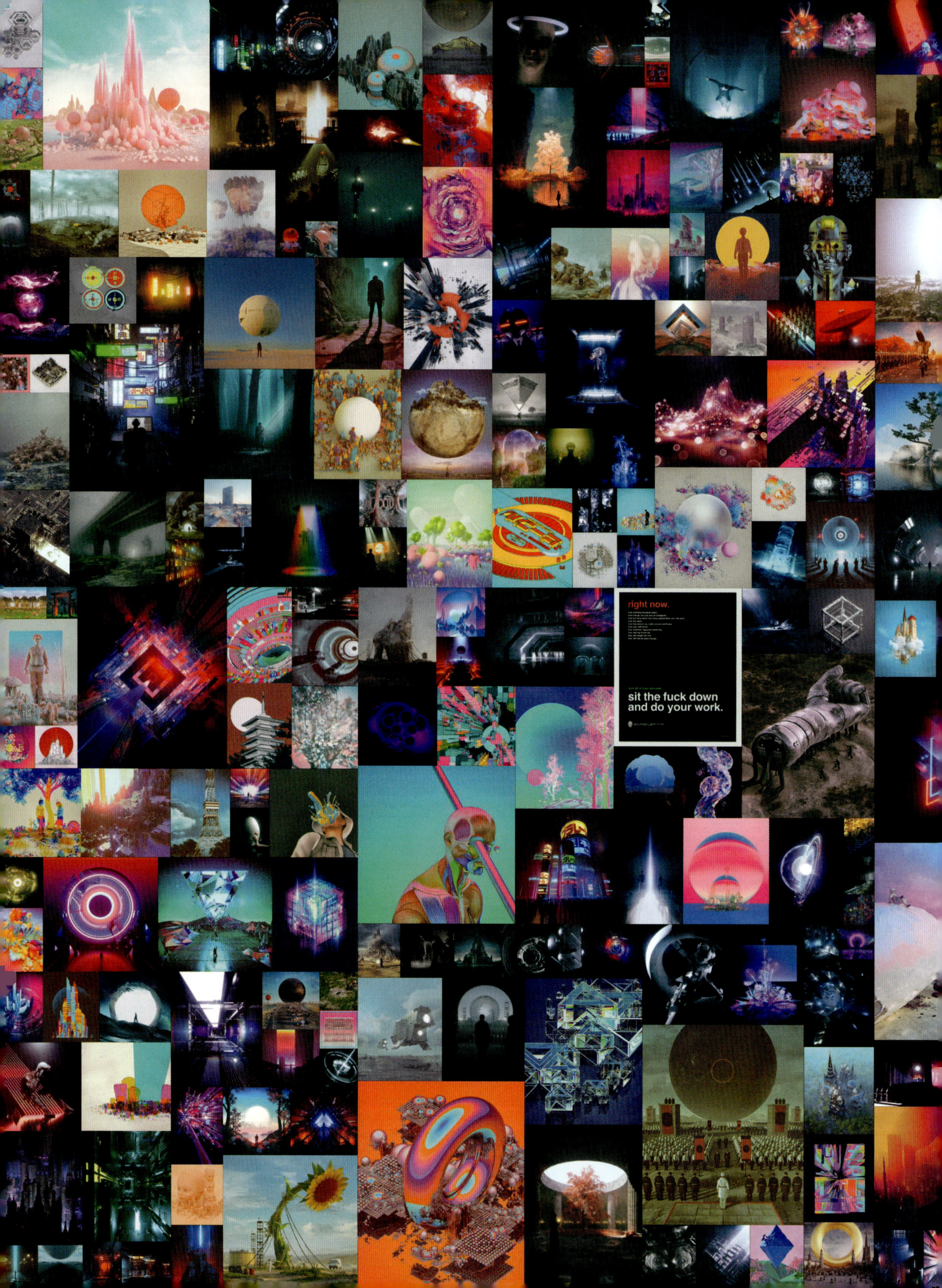
right now.
sit the fuck down
and do your work.

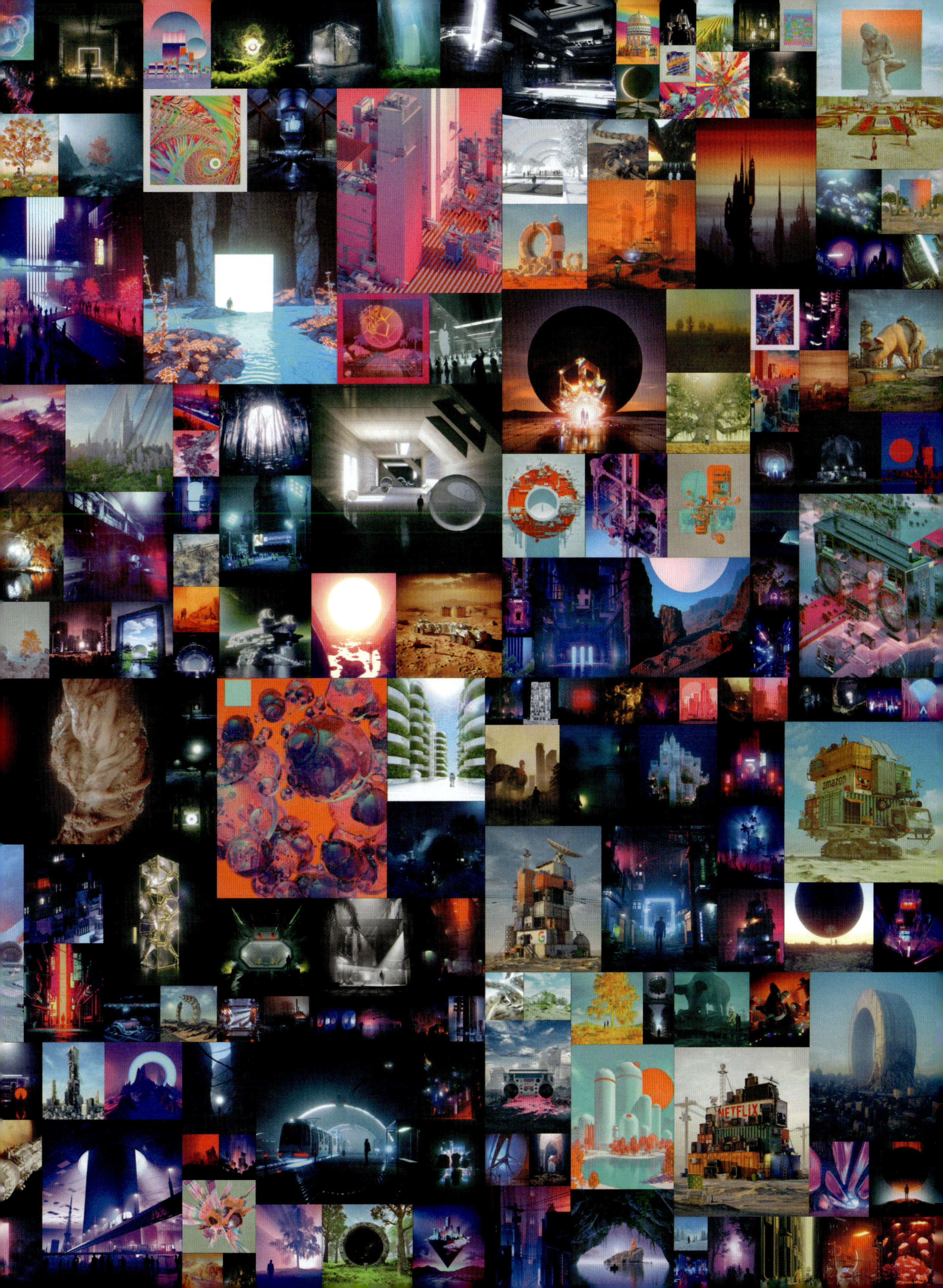
amazon
NETFLIX

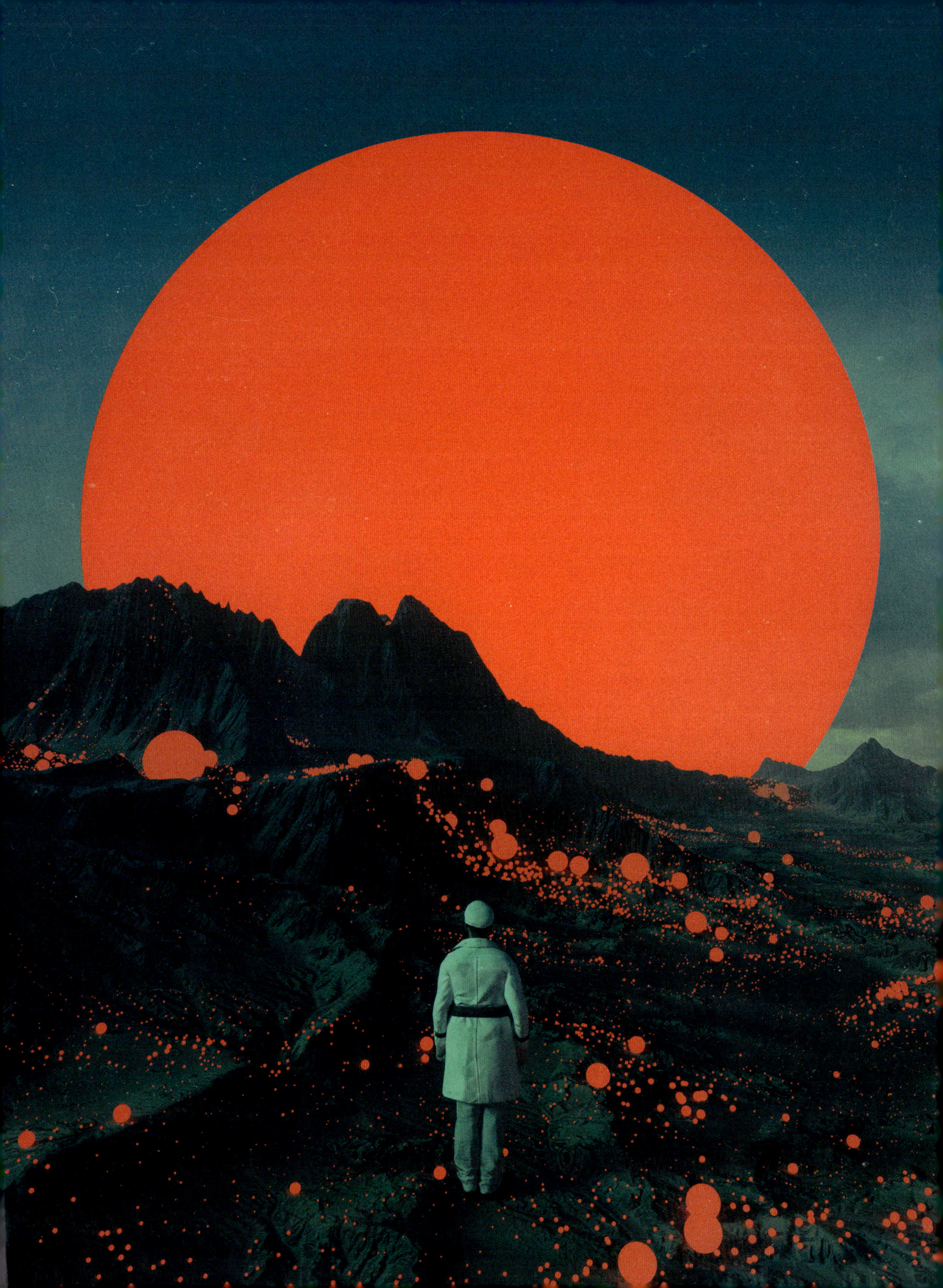

2018

OPPOSITE PAGE

BROKEN MOON

04.16.2018

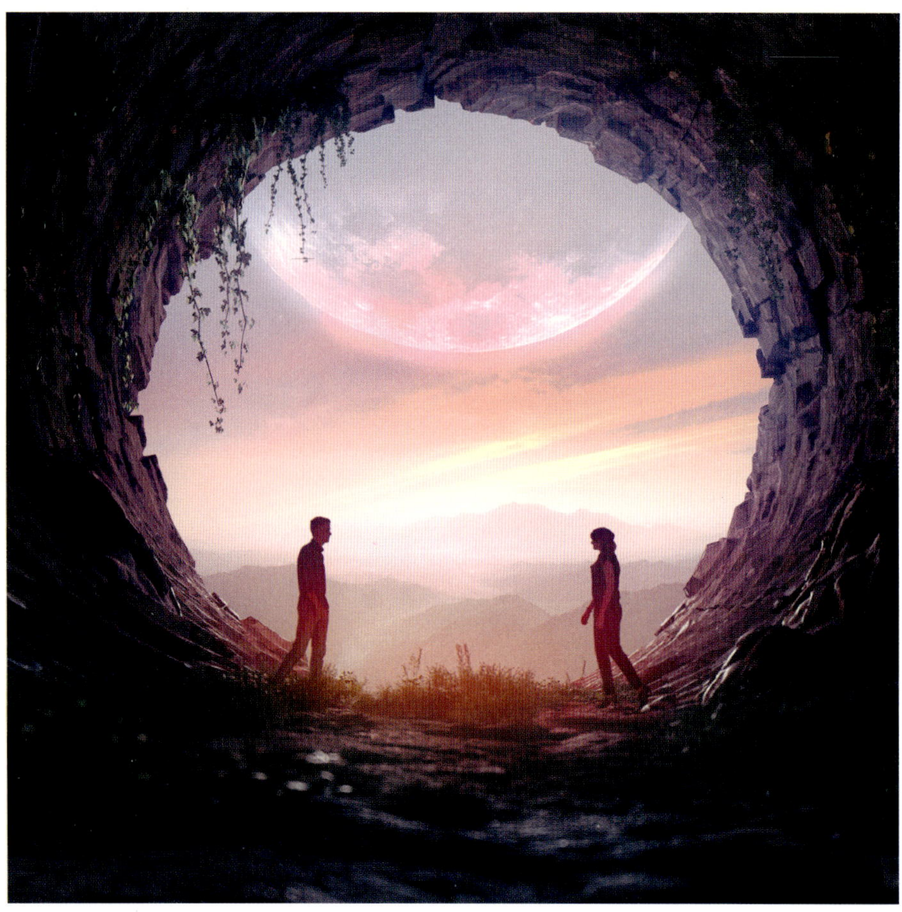

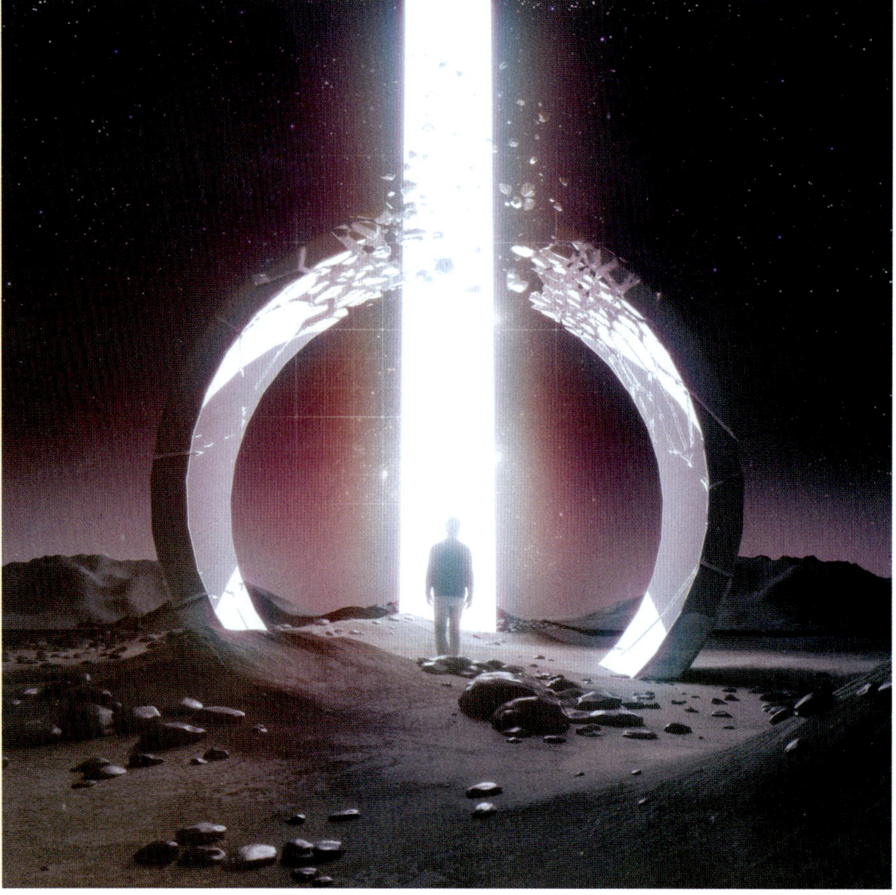

TOP
SUNDAY MORNING
05.05.2018

BOTTOM
EARLY RISE
02.05.2018

OPPOSITE PAGE
PREMULTIPLY
01.09.2018

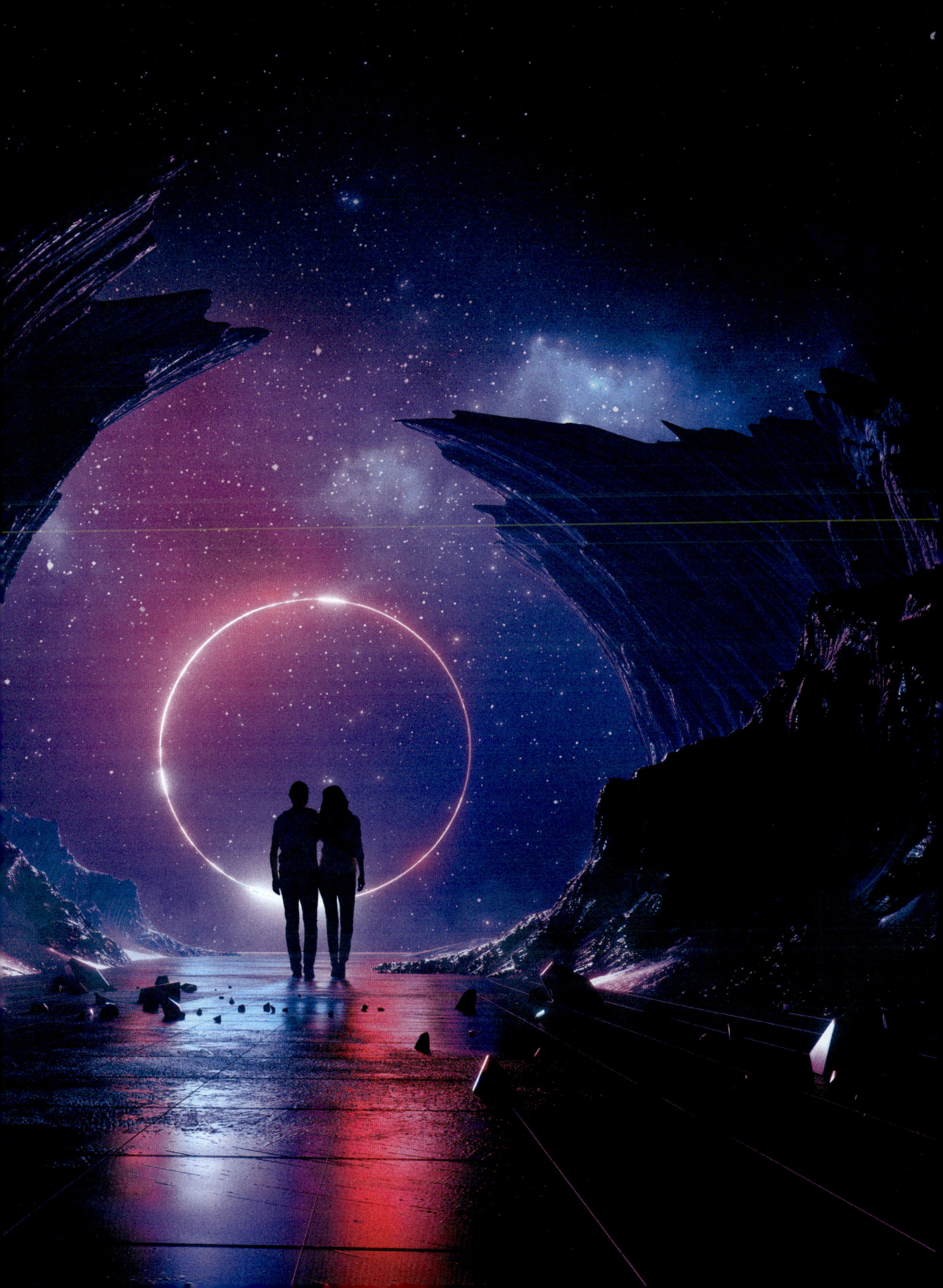

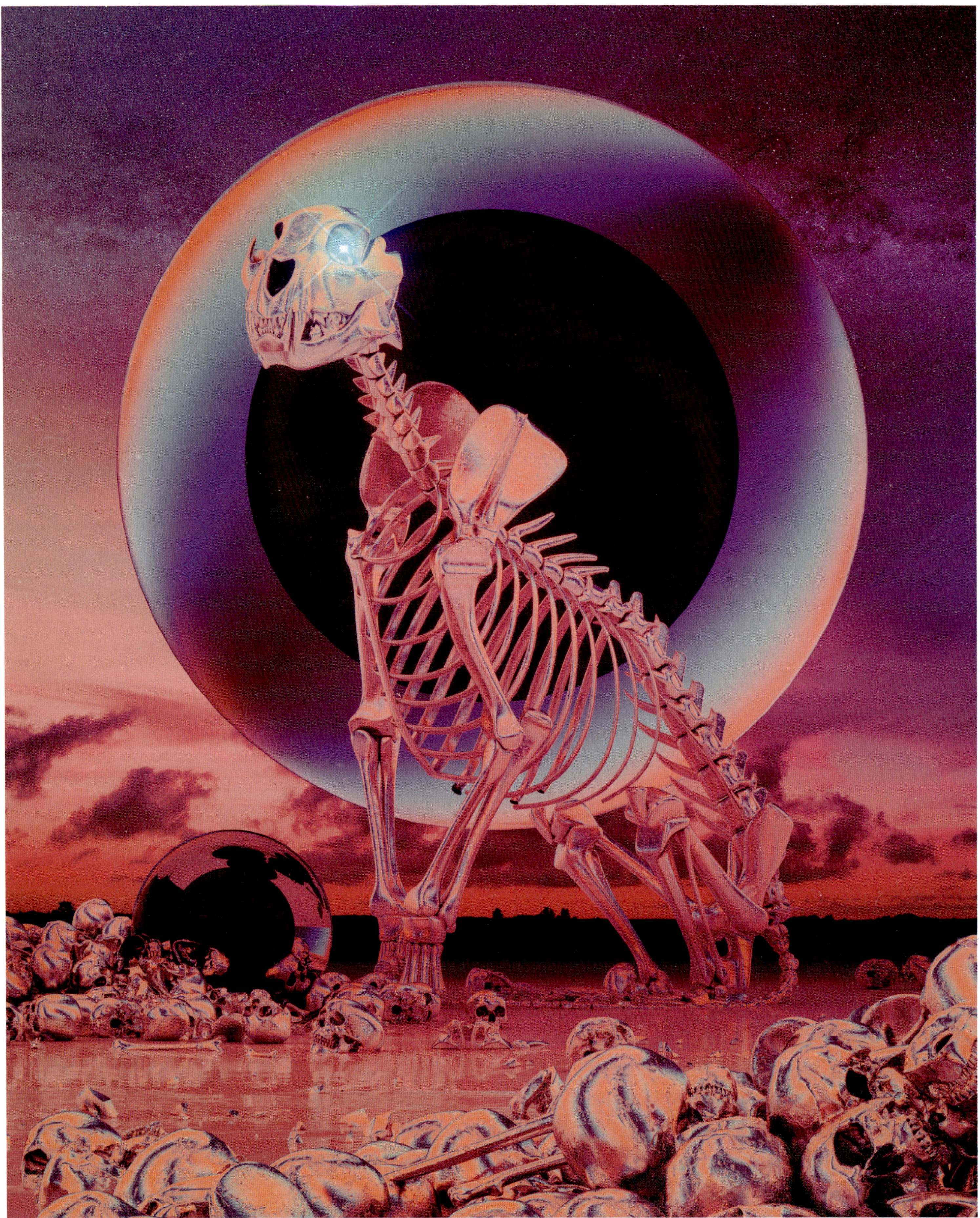

ABOVE

NEW RIDE

06.22.2018

OPPOSITE PAGE

JOEY CHESTNUT

07.04.2018

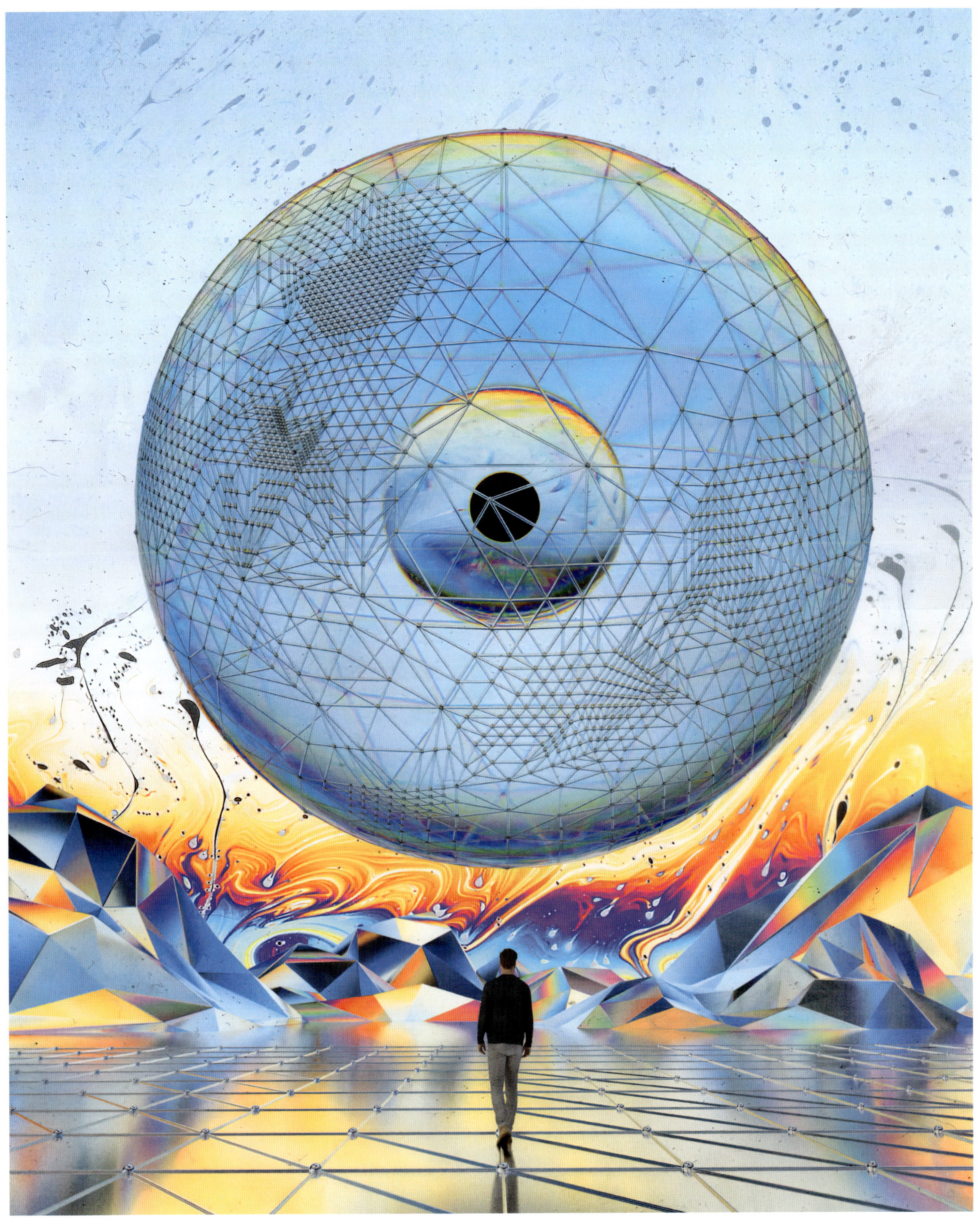

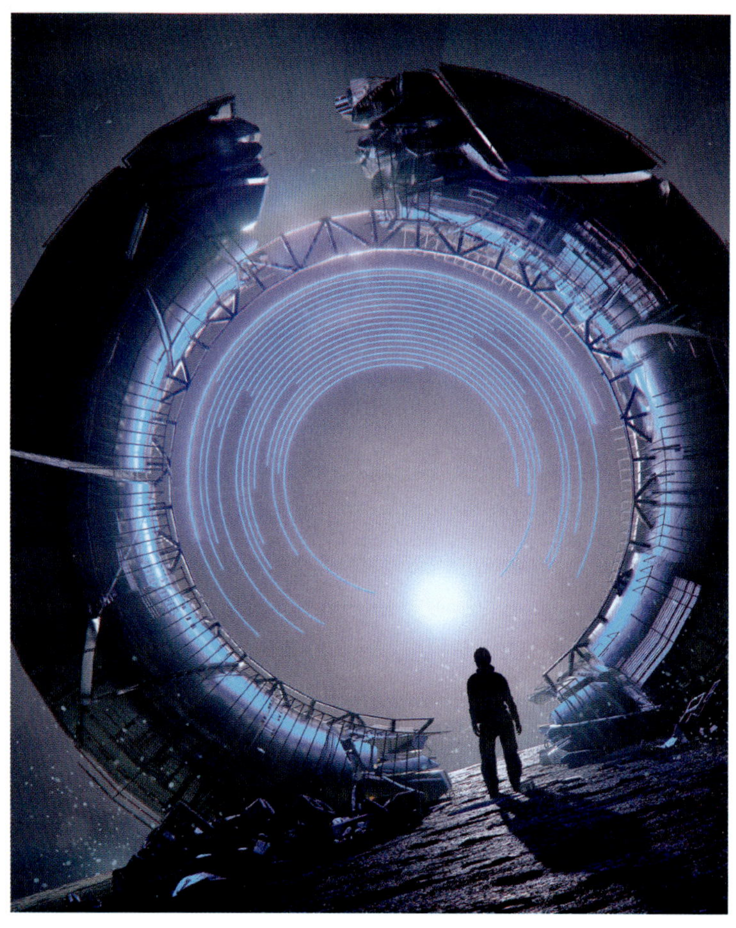

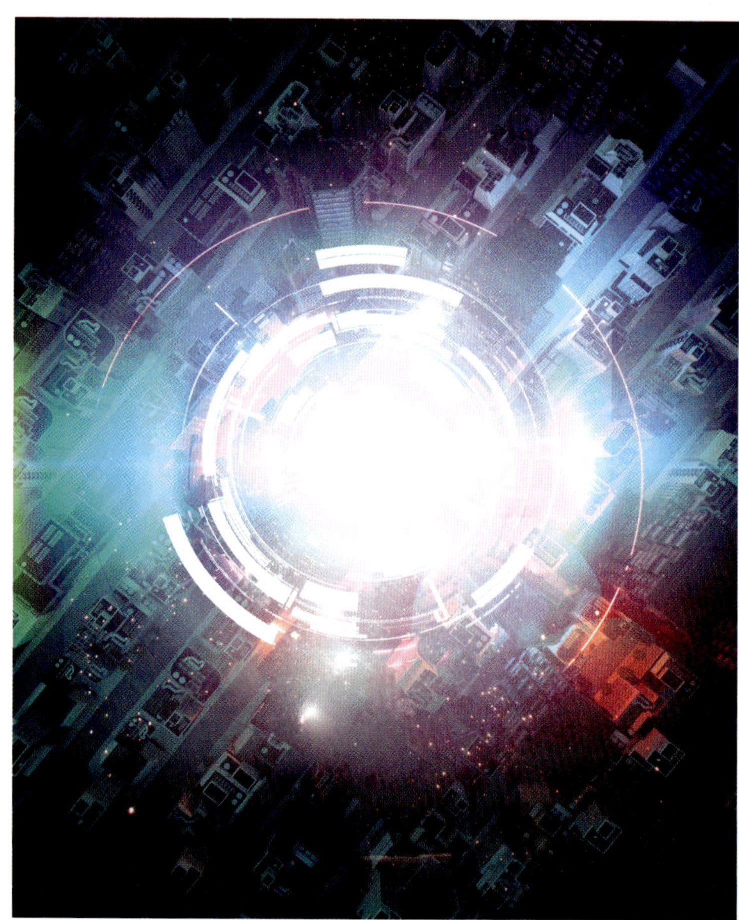

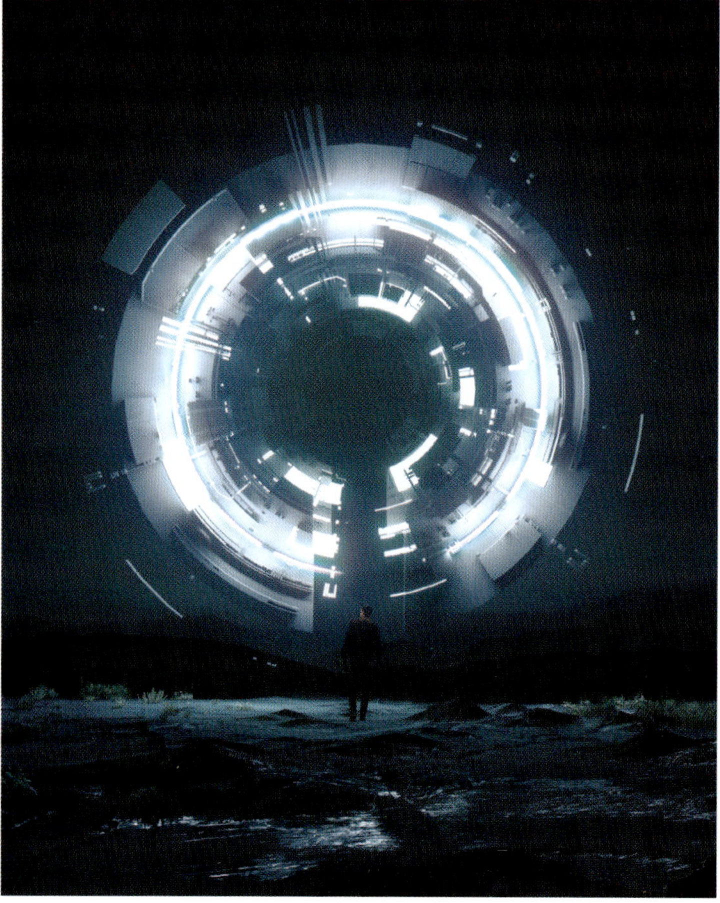

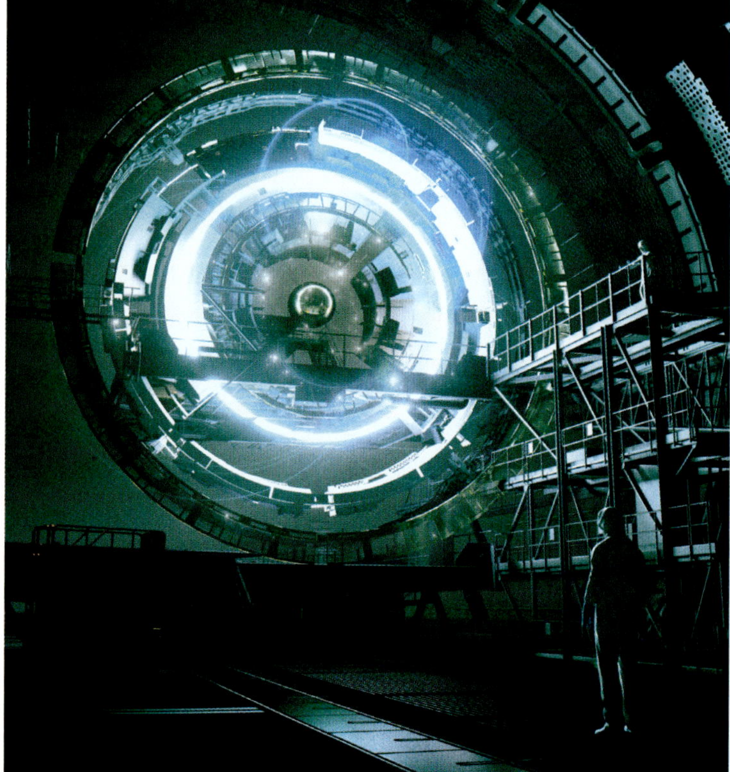

TOP LEFT

BLUE TINT

07.19.2018

TOP RIGHT

BLACK HOLE

10.12.2018

BOTTOM LEFT

PORTAL.ONE

06.13.2018

BOTTOM RIGHT

PHERE COLLIDER NINE

12.12.2018

OPPOSITE PAGE

MAGIC KINGDOM

11.08.2018

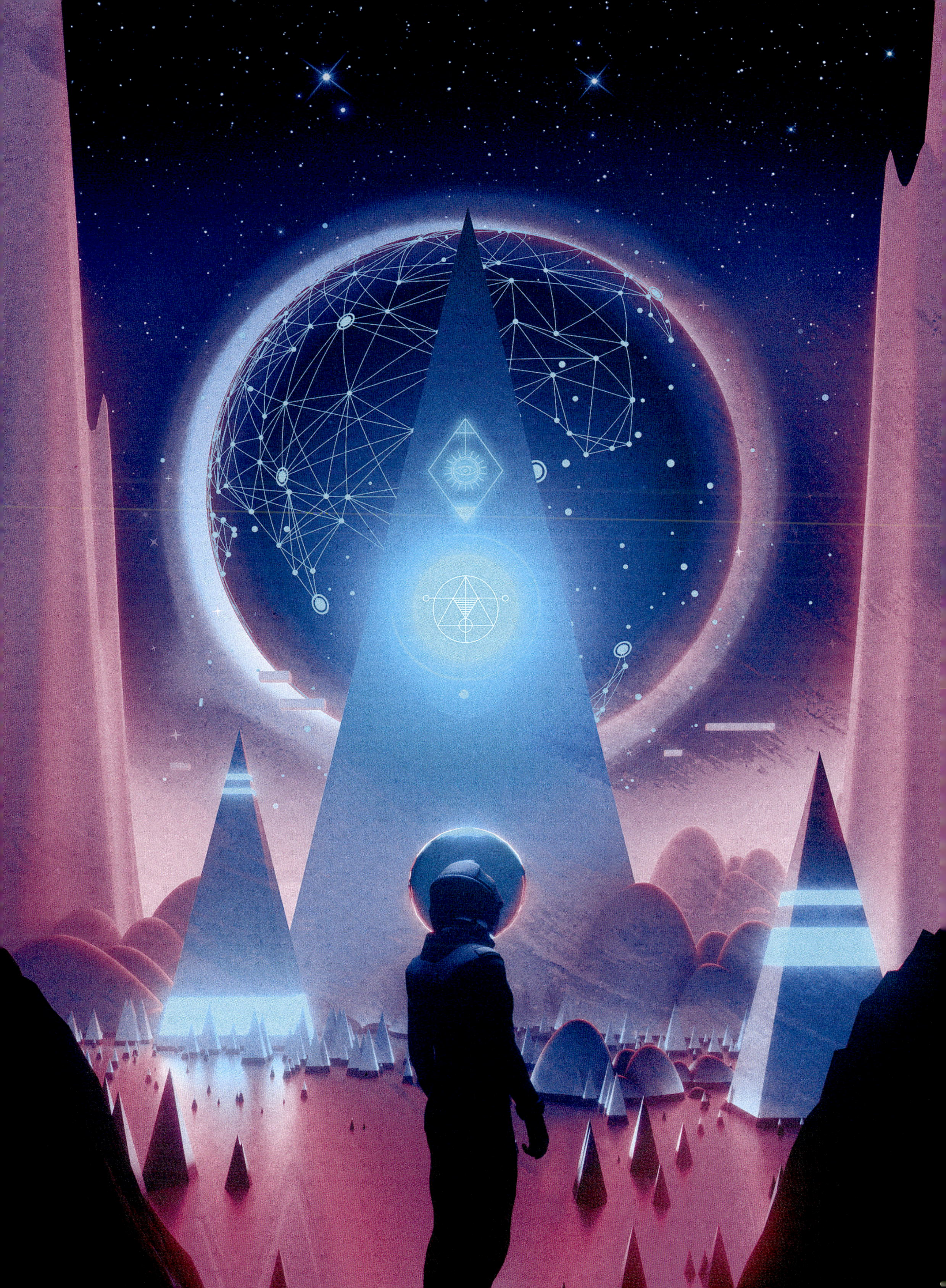

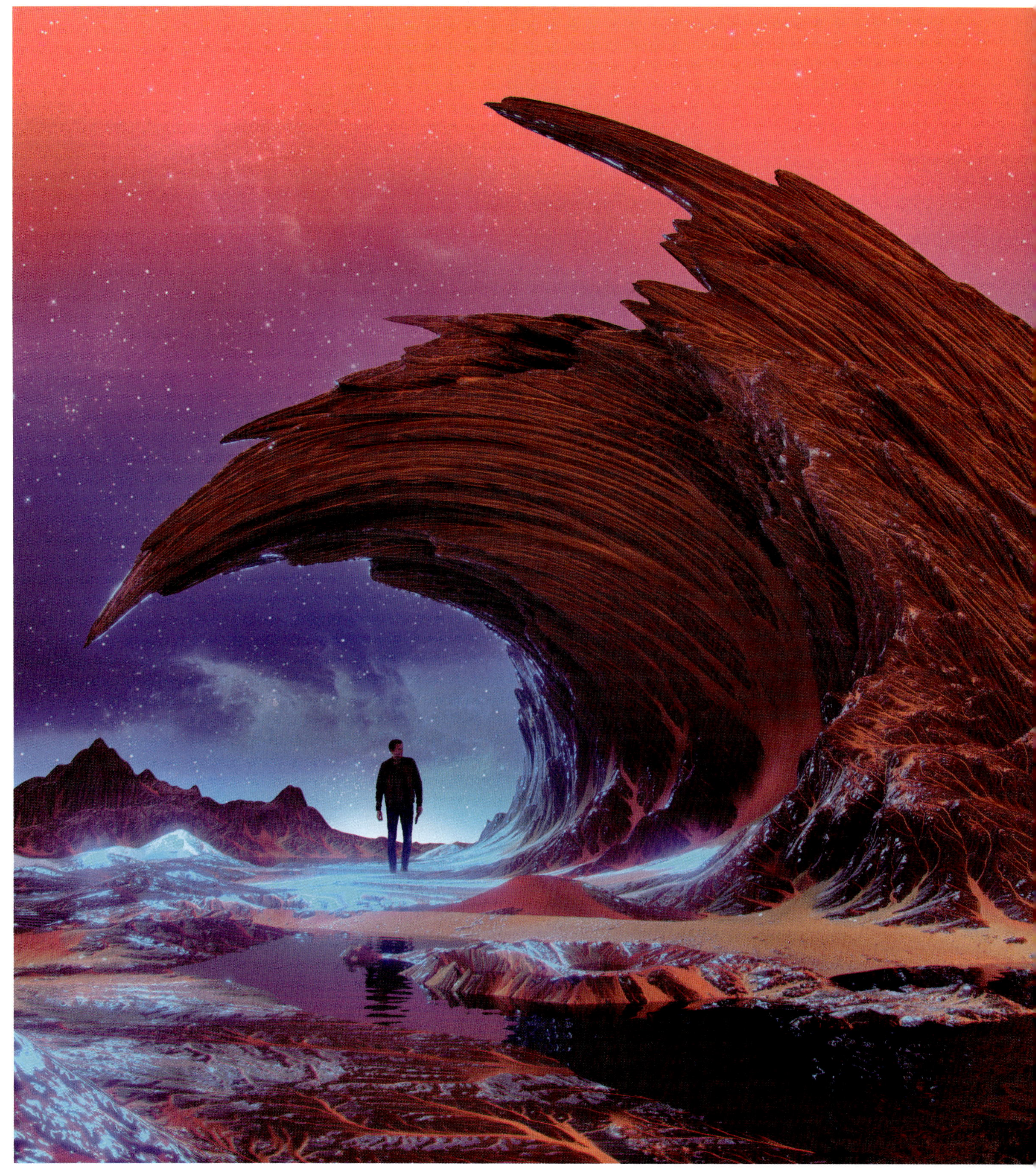

ABOVE

RIDE.WAVE
02.01.2018

OPPOSITE PAGE

AVALANCHE.9
02.10.2018

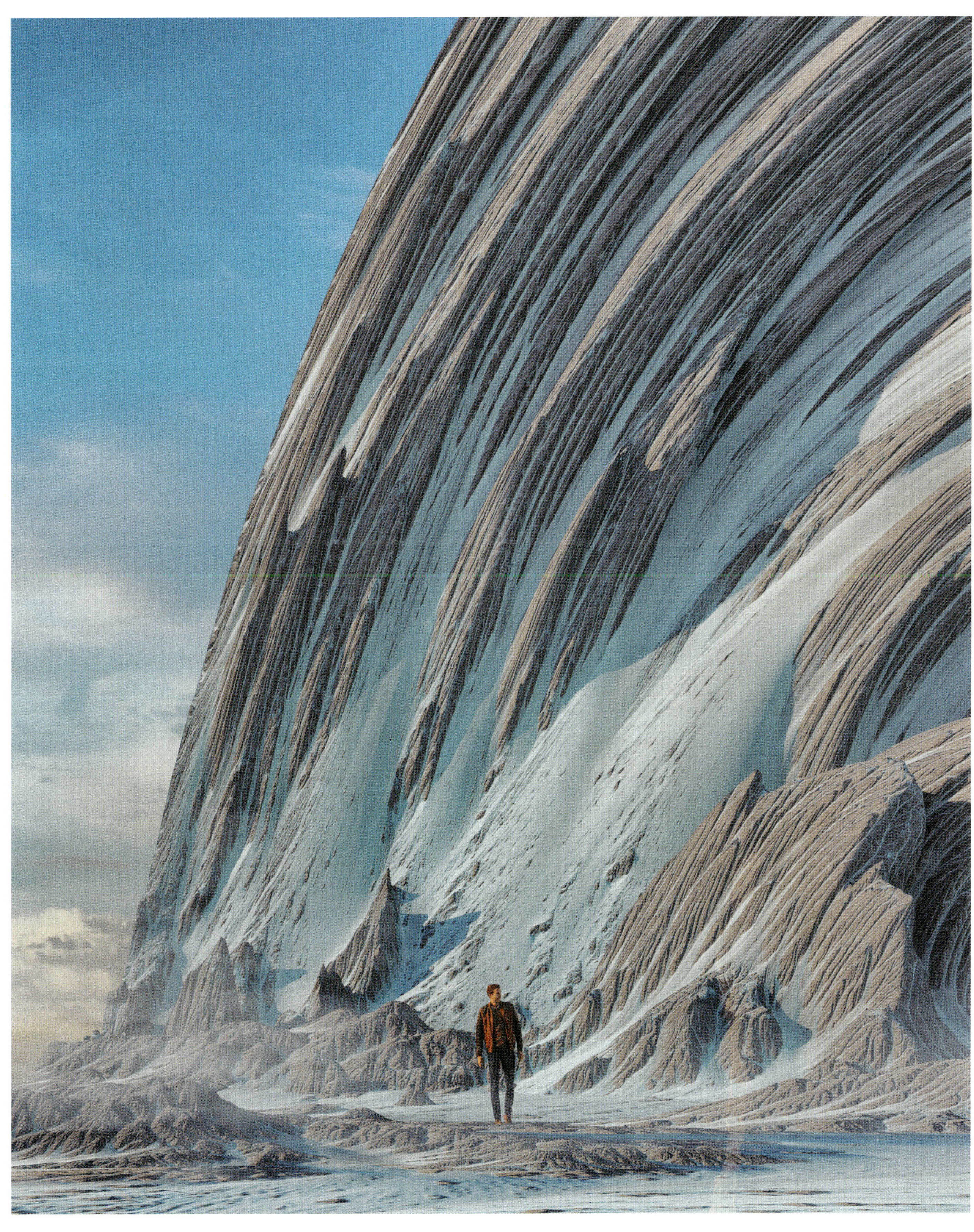

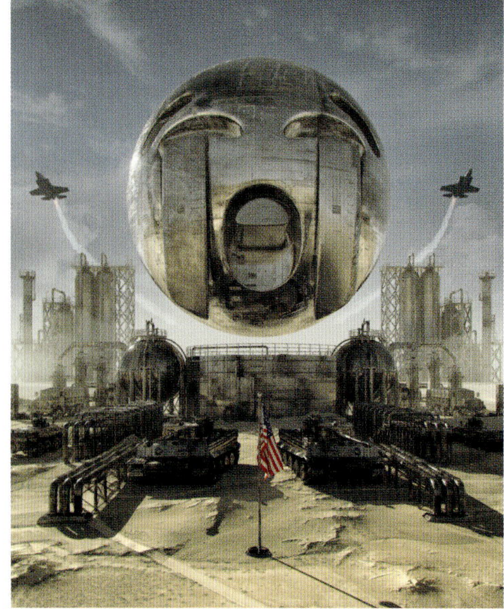

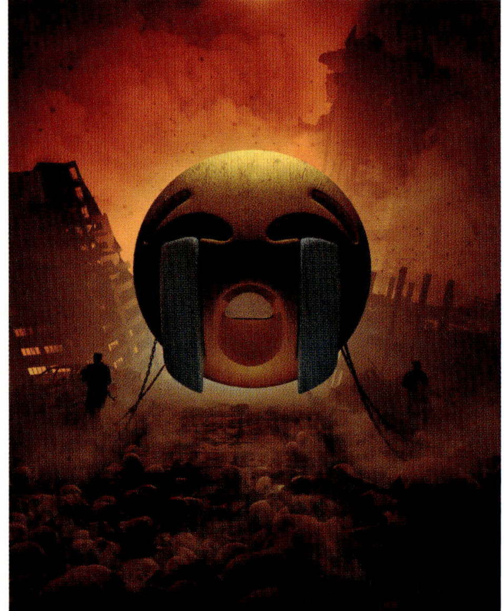

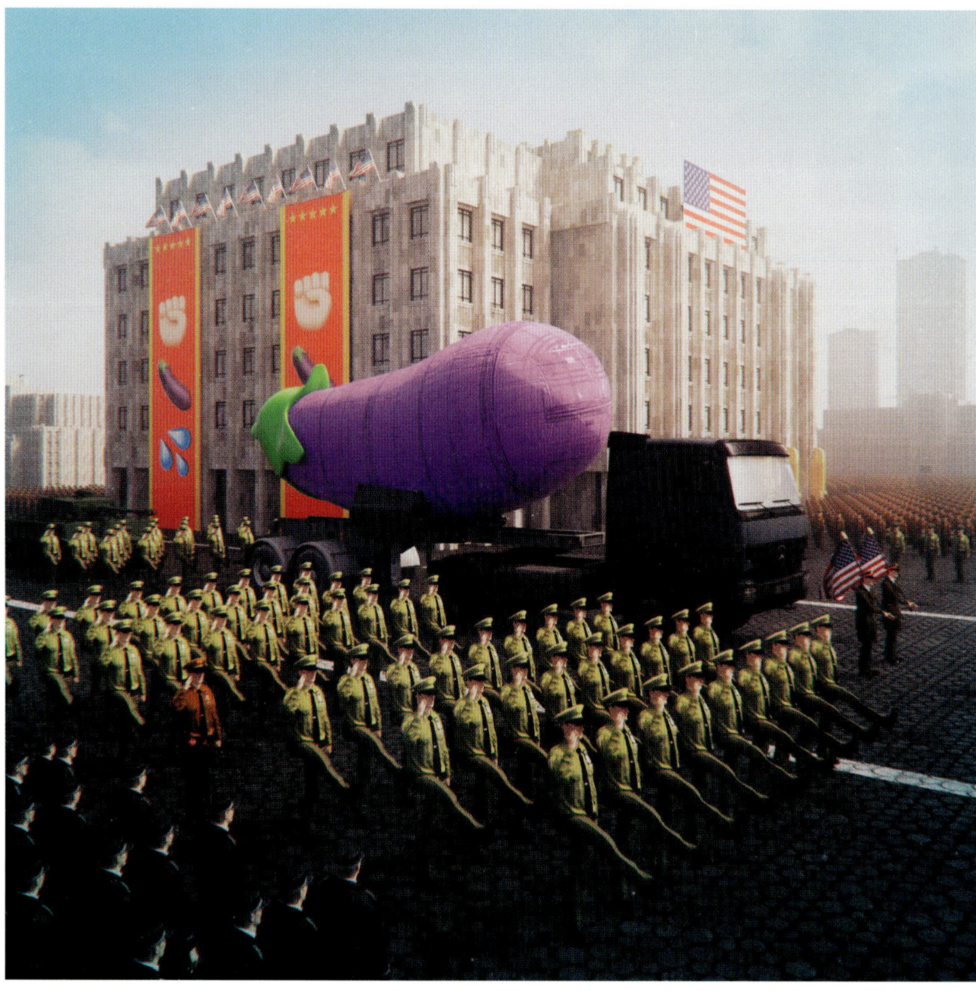

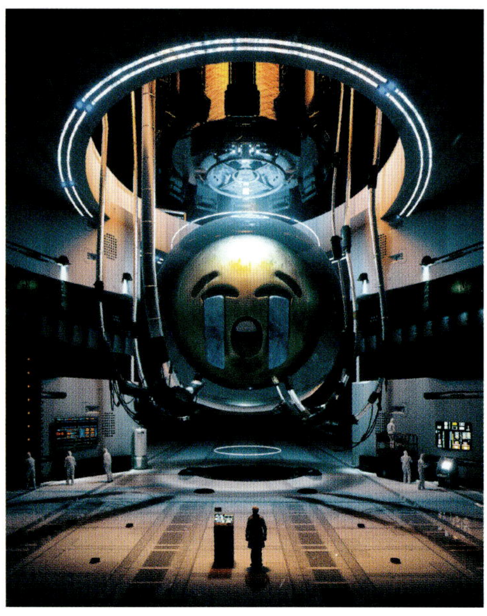

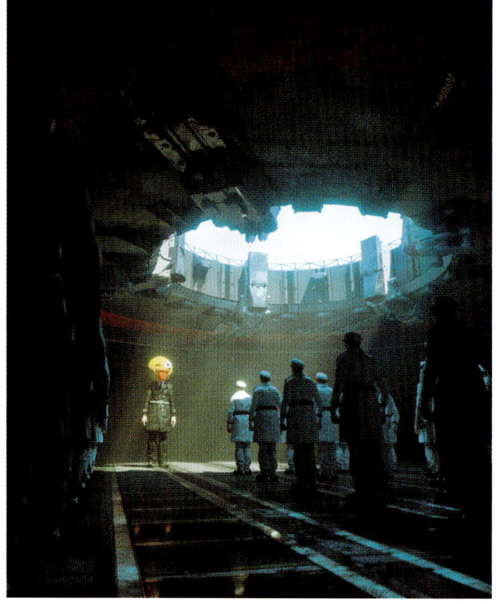

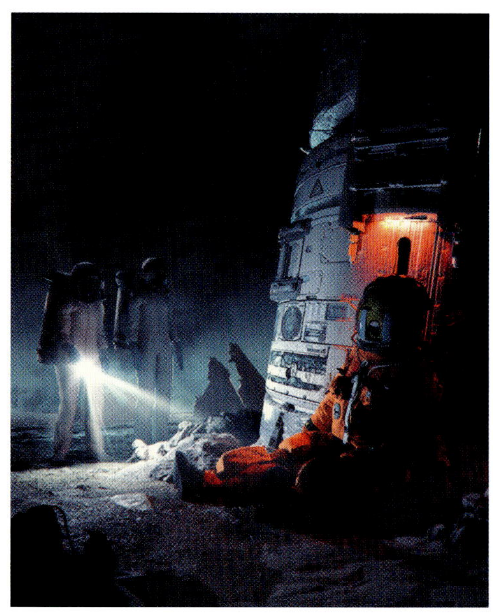

TOP LEFT
EMOJI AMERICA
05.14.2018

MIDDLE LEFT
WEAPONS OF MASS EMOJIS
05.03.2018

TOP RIGHT
EMOJI WARFAR
08.10.2018

BOTTOM LEFT
SCIENTIFICALLY PERFECT EMOJI
08.15.2018

BOTTOM MIDDLE
EMOJI WARFARE (ep.2)
03.14.2018

BOTTOM RIGHT
HARD LANDING
12.09.2018

OPPOSITE PAGE
EMOJI WARFARE
03.10.2018

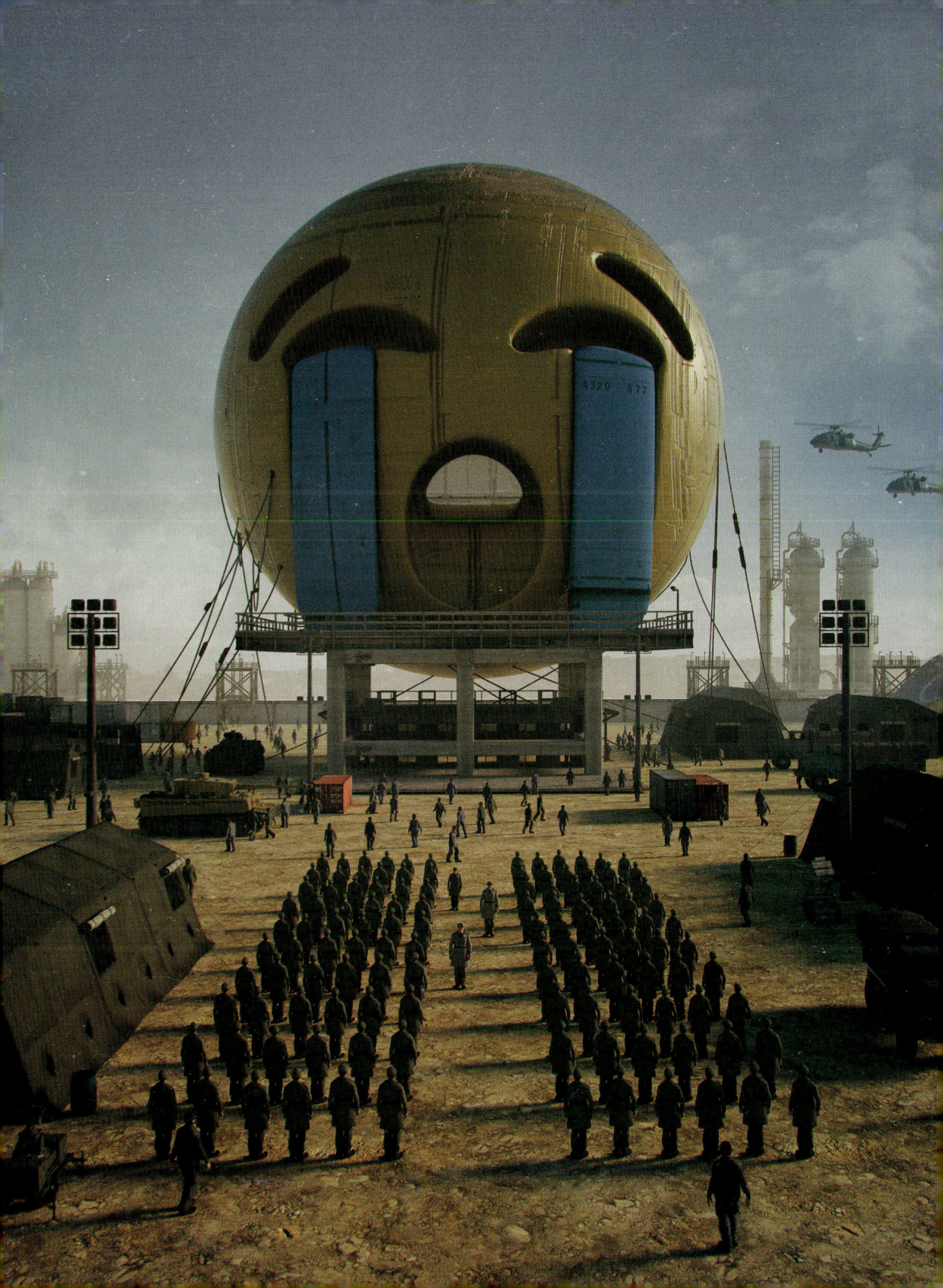
4320 477

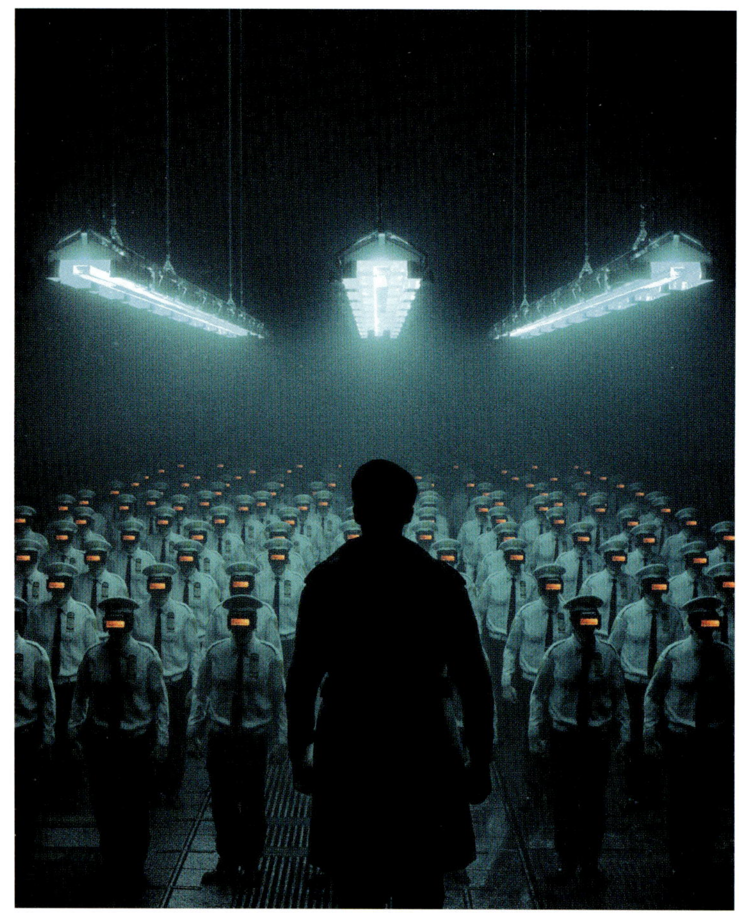

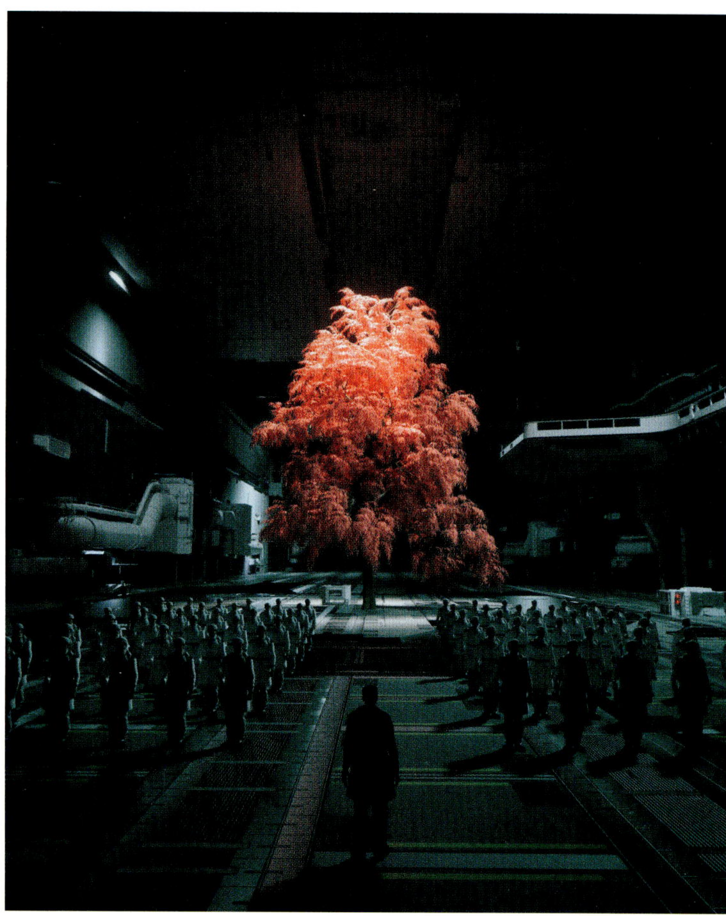

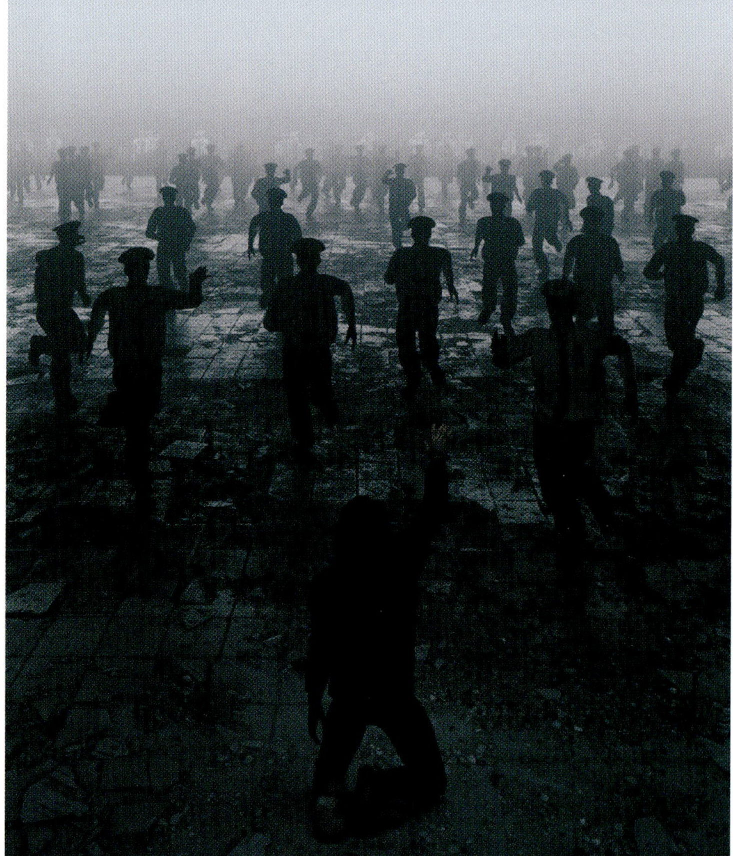

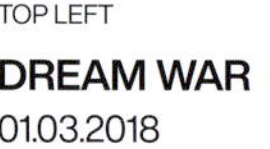

TOP LEFT
DREAM WAR
01.03.2018

TOP RIGHT
LAST TREE
04.18.2018

BOTTOM LEFT
FITC TORONTO
04.10.2018

BOTTOM RIGHT
SWARM
02.24.2018

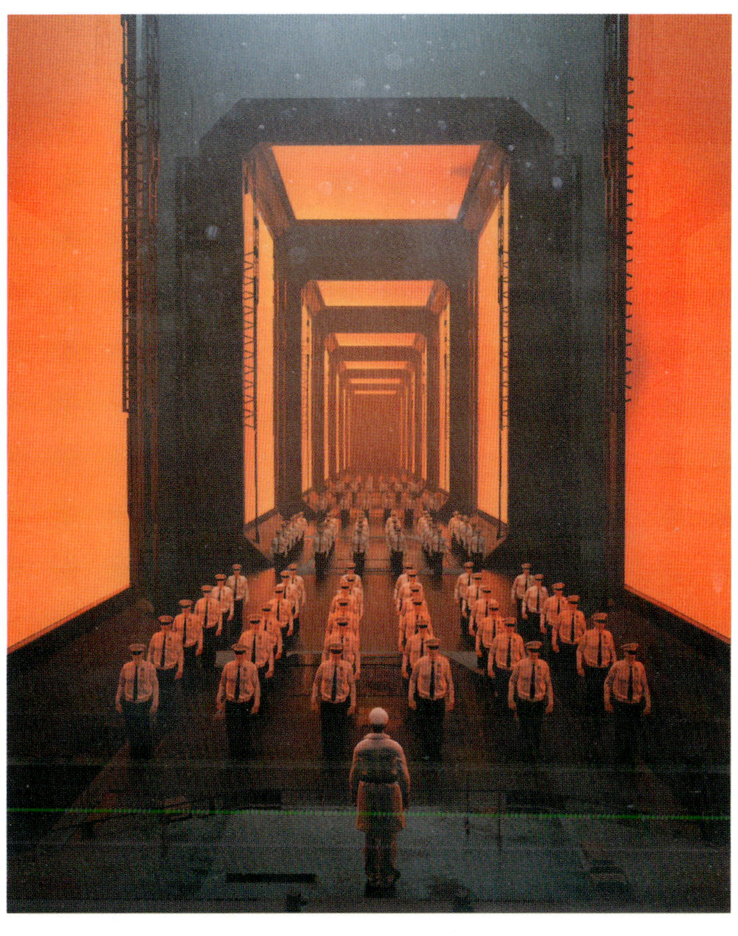

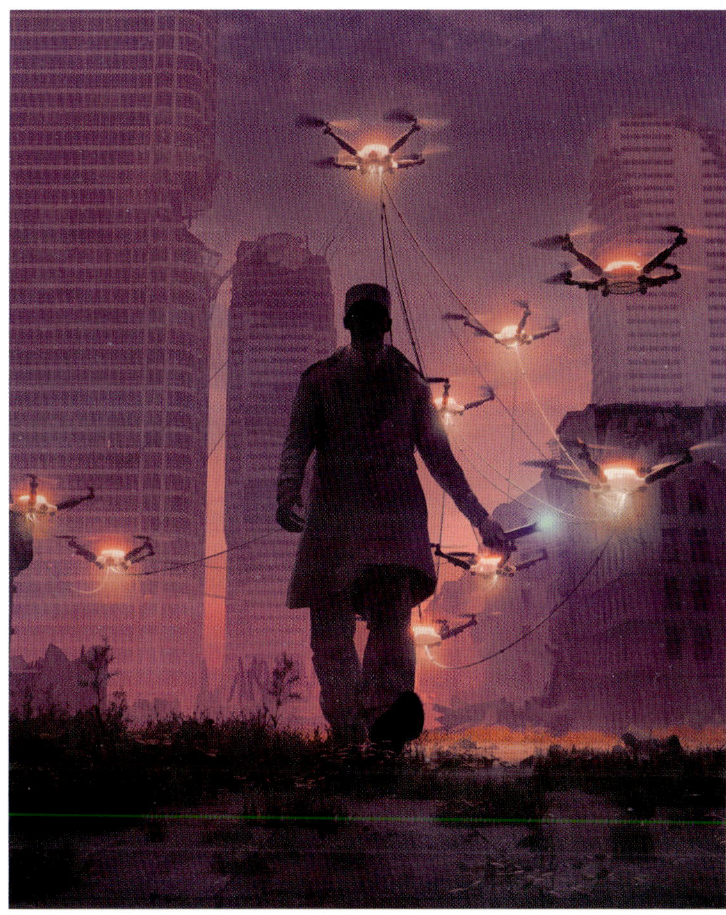

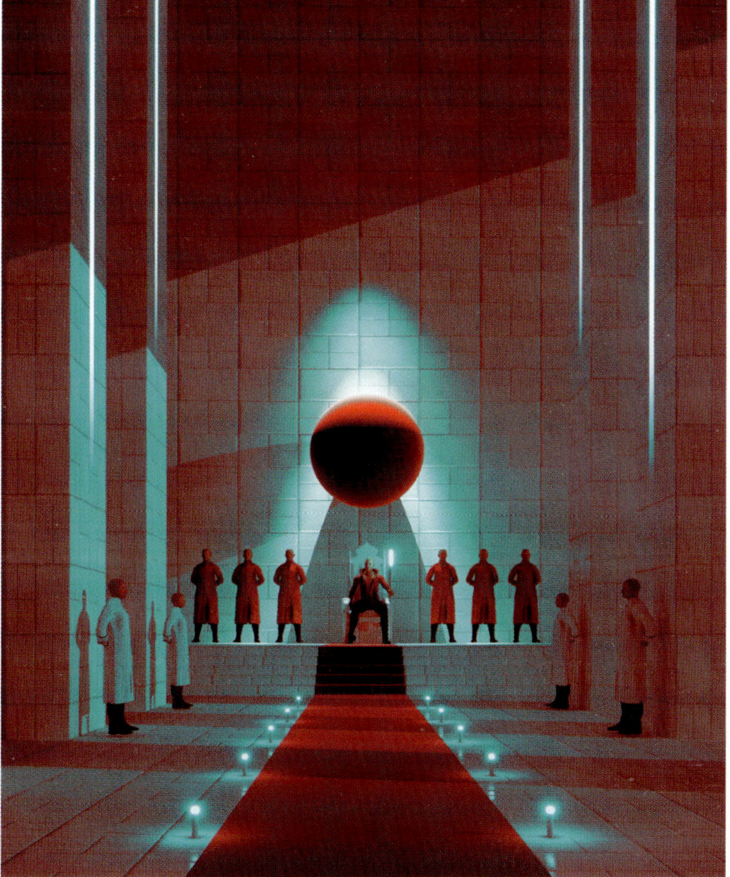

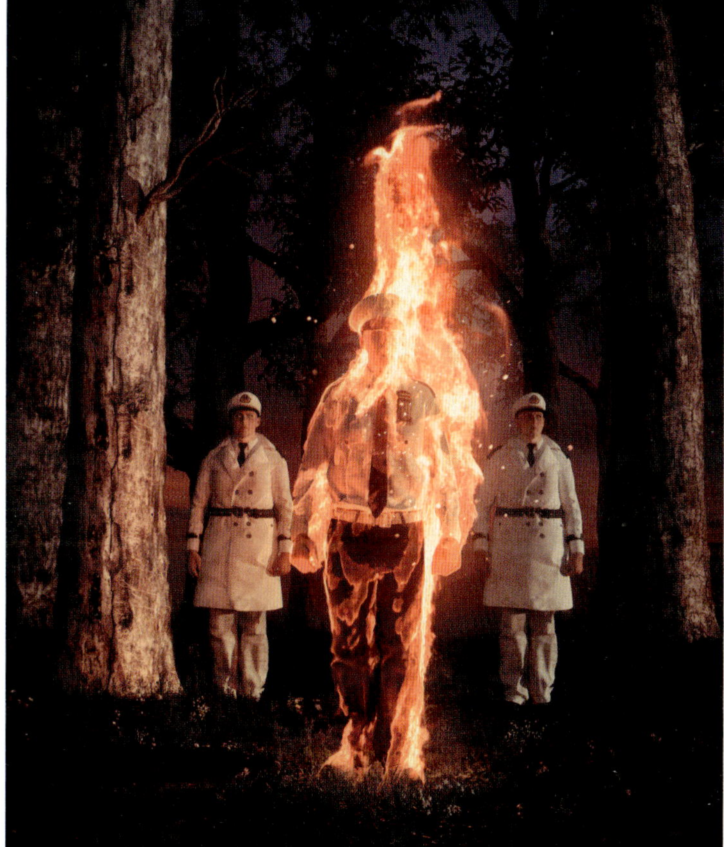

TOP LEFT
RED LINE
10.18.2018

TOP RIGHT
MORNING DRONE SWEEP
03.19.2018

BOTTOM LEFT
REVELATIONS
03.25.2018

BOTTOM RIGHT
ALL GOOD
04.28.2018

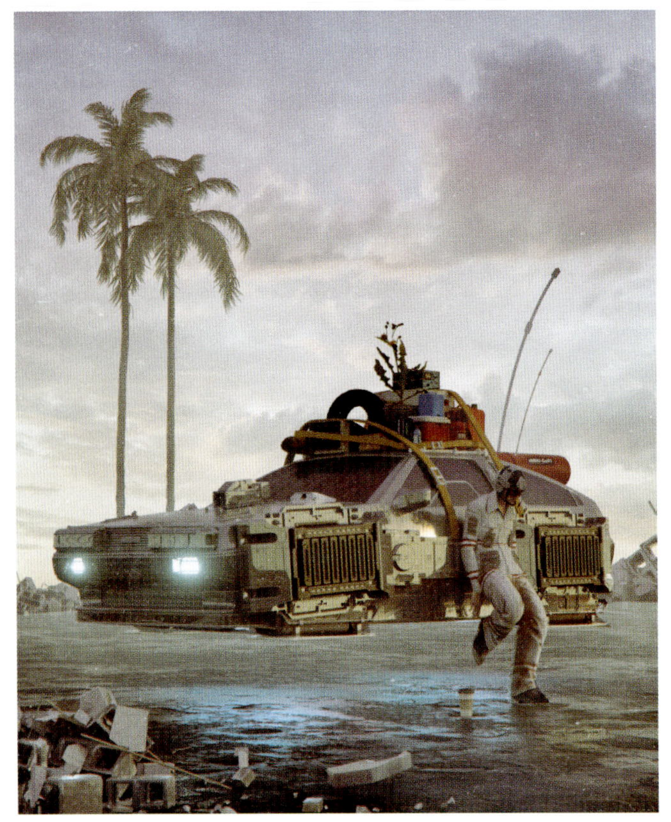

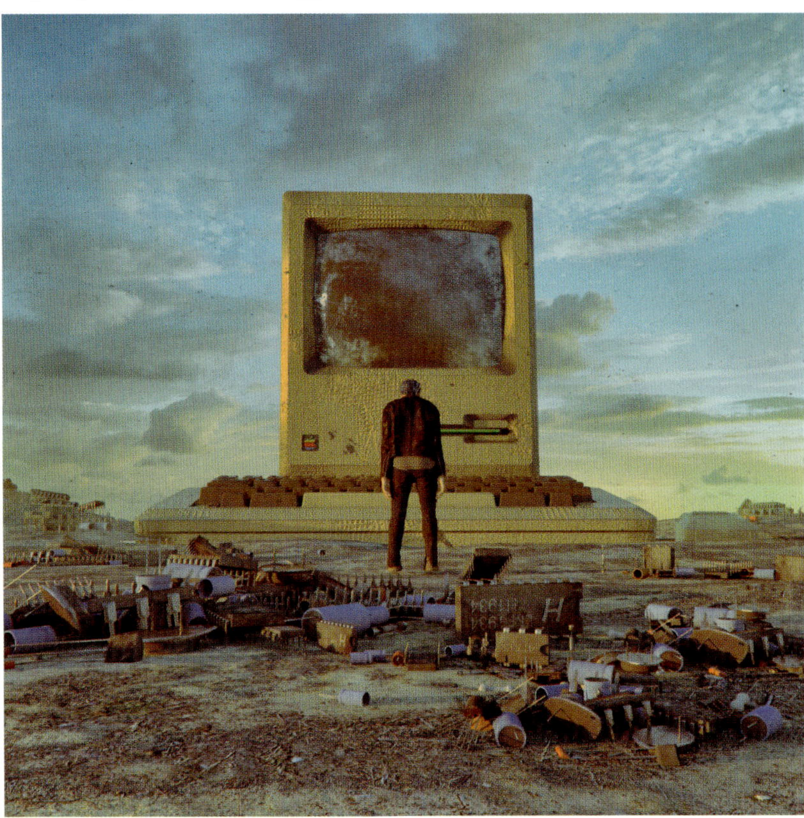

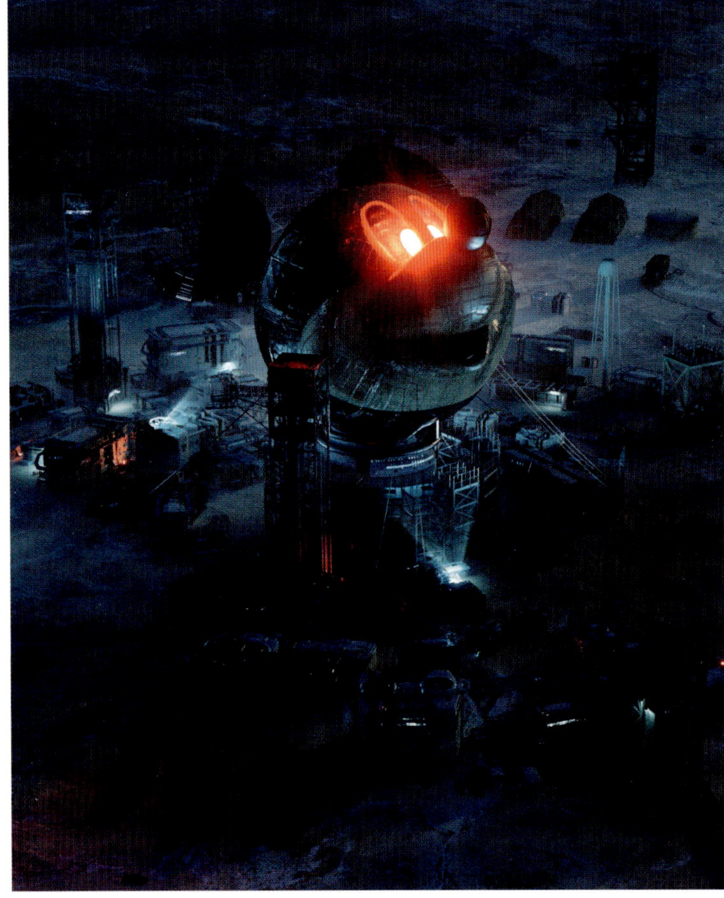

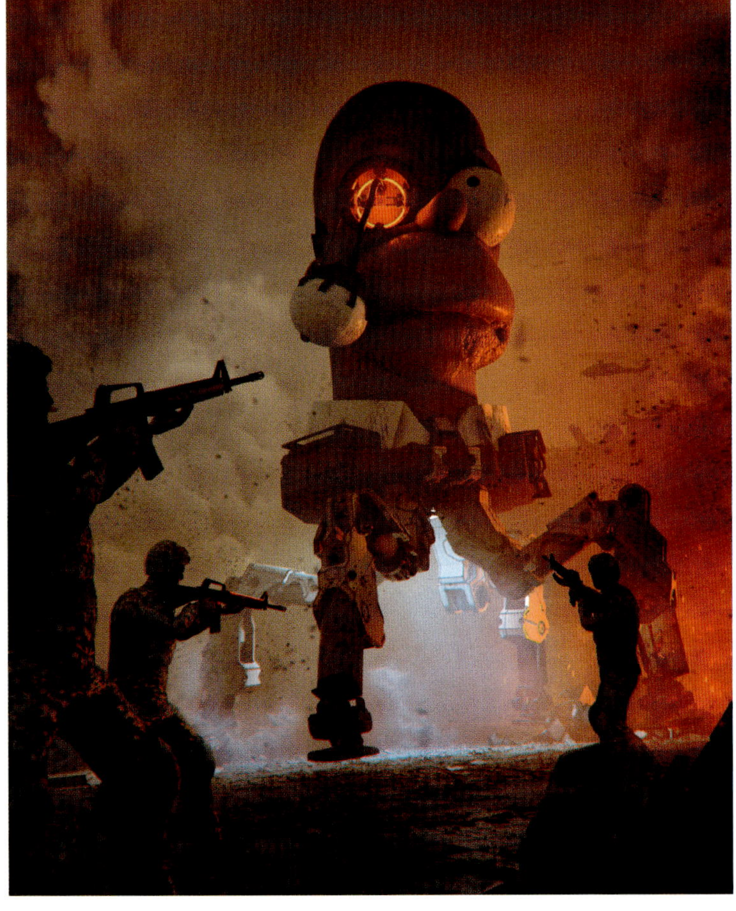

TOP LEFT
GOING HOME
10.24.2018

TOP RIGHT
REFORMAT
10.25.2018

BOTTOM LEFT
WEAPONIZE EVERYTHING
12.06.2018

BOTTOM RIGHT
DOH
08.25.2018

OPPOSITE PAGE
WOKE POOH
07.20.2018

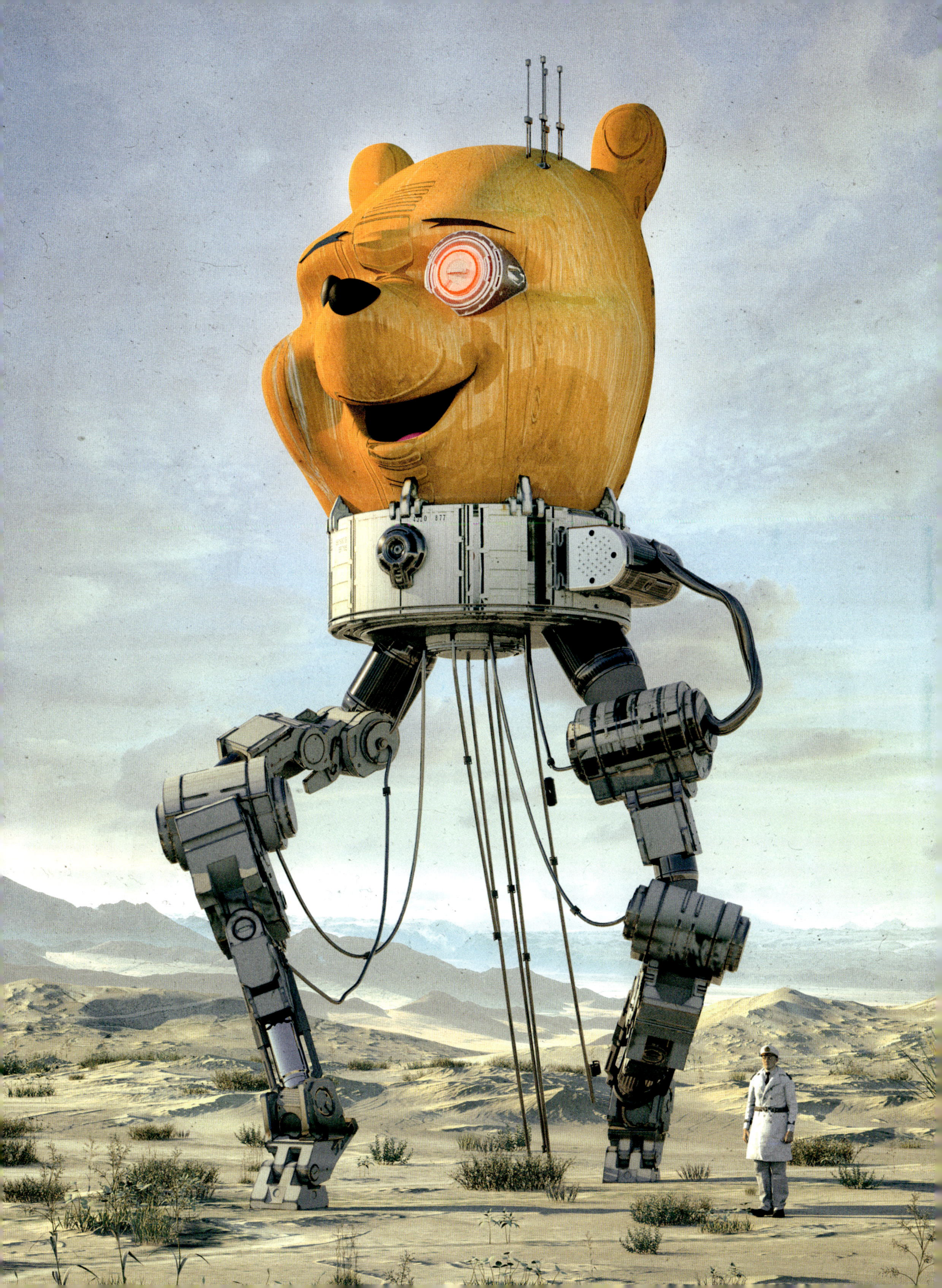

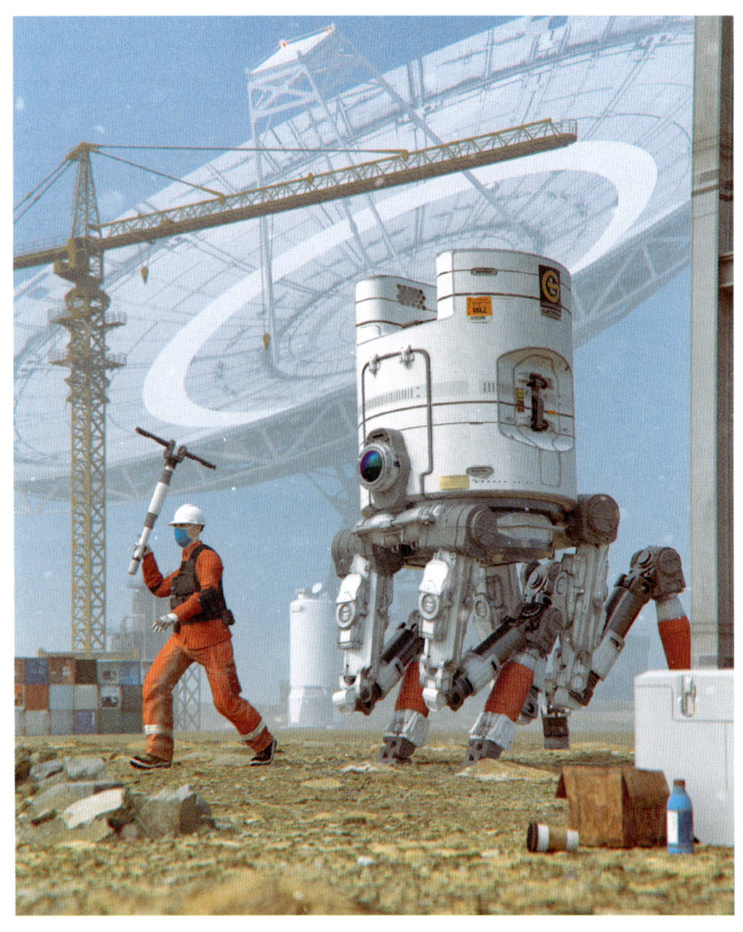

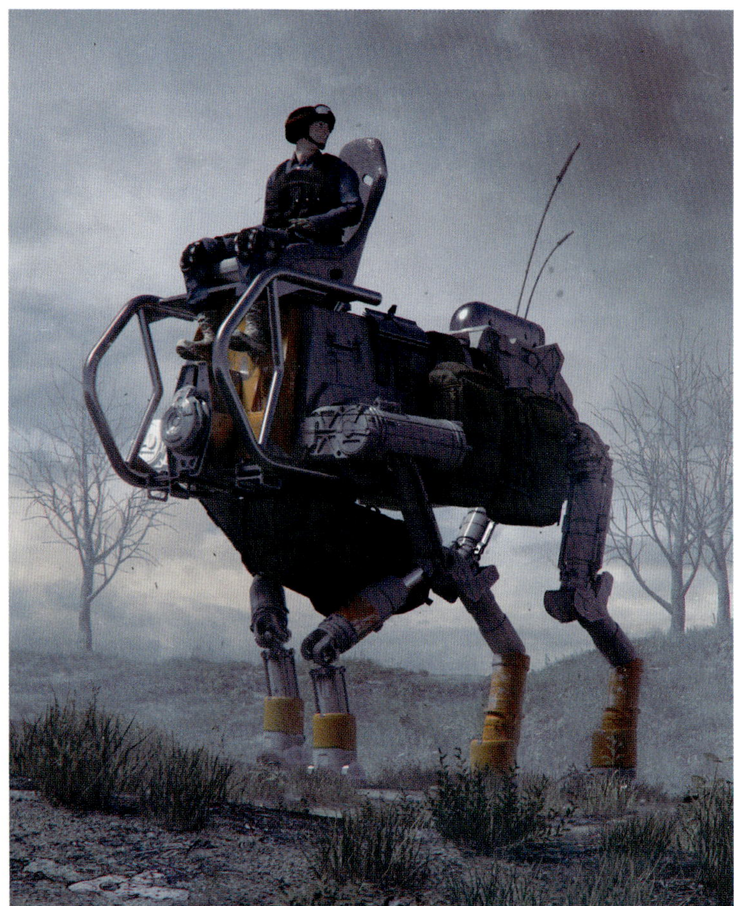

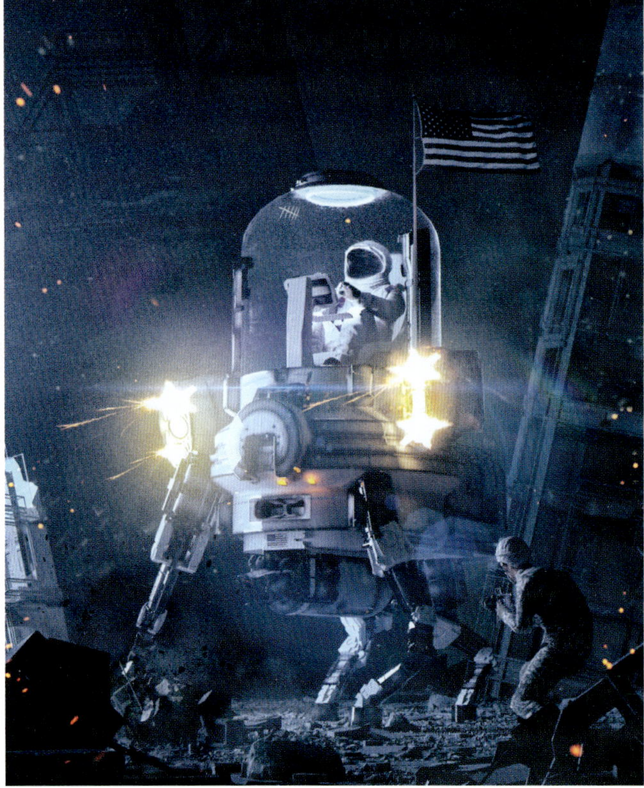

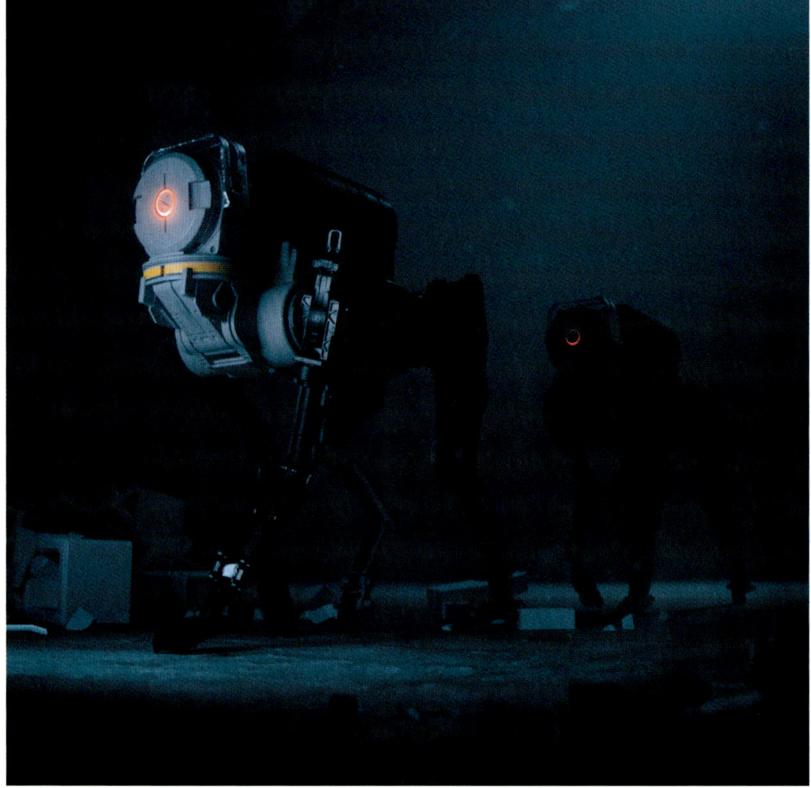

TOP LEFT
SHEPARD 2086
07.12.2018

TOP RIGHT
UBERDOG 2051
07.06.2018

BOTTOM LEFT
SPACE FORCE 2067
10.16.2018

BOTTOM RIGHT
REPLICATE STRAY
04.27.2018

OPPOSITE PAGE
FULL FLEX
06.15.2018

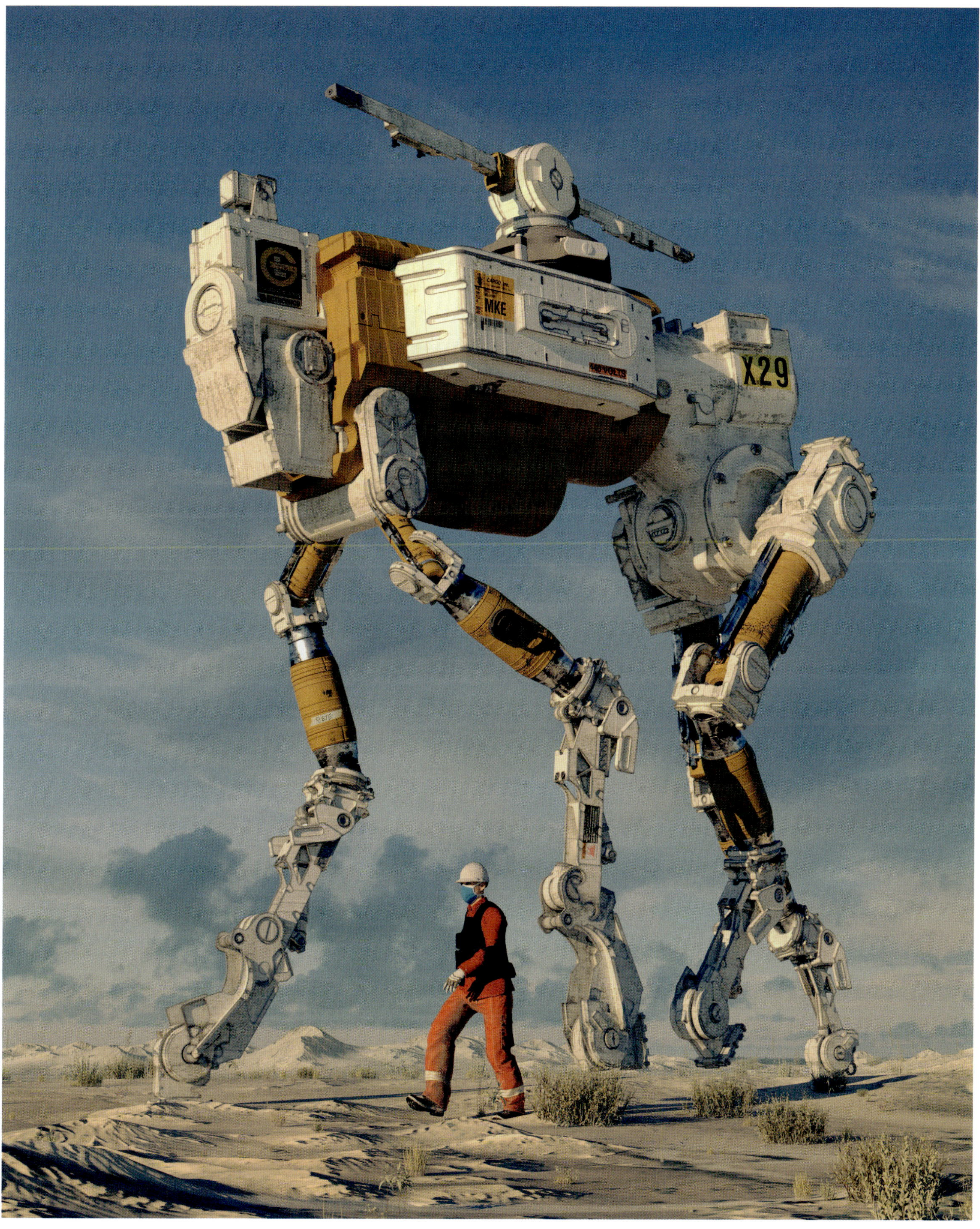
CARGO INC.
MKE
440 VOLTS
X29

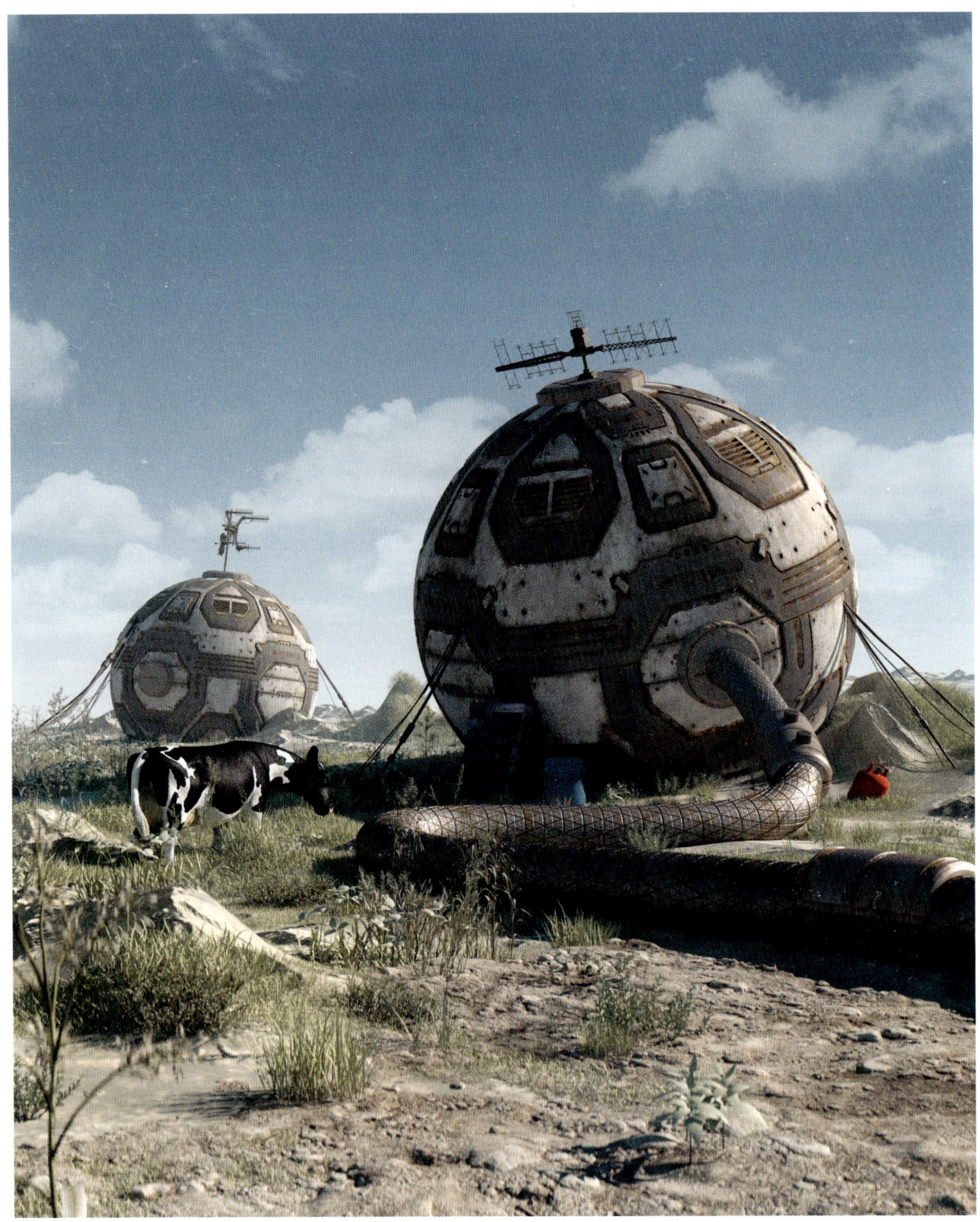

LEFT

DECOMMISSIONED COMM PODS

05.07.2018

OPPOSITE PAGE

MUSHROOM GENERATOR

07.25.2018

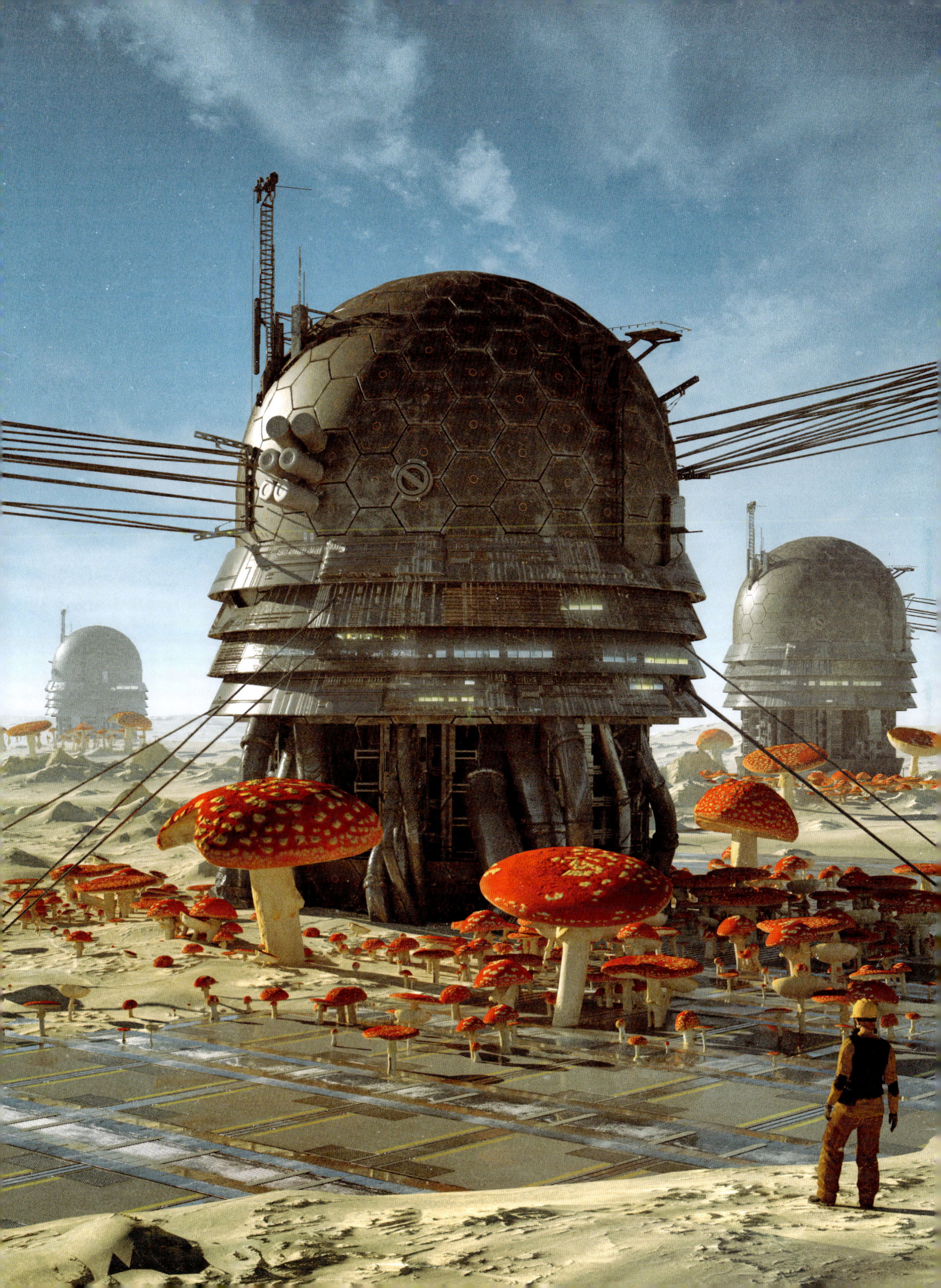

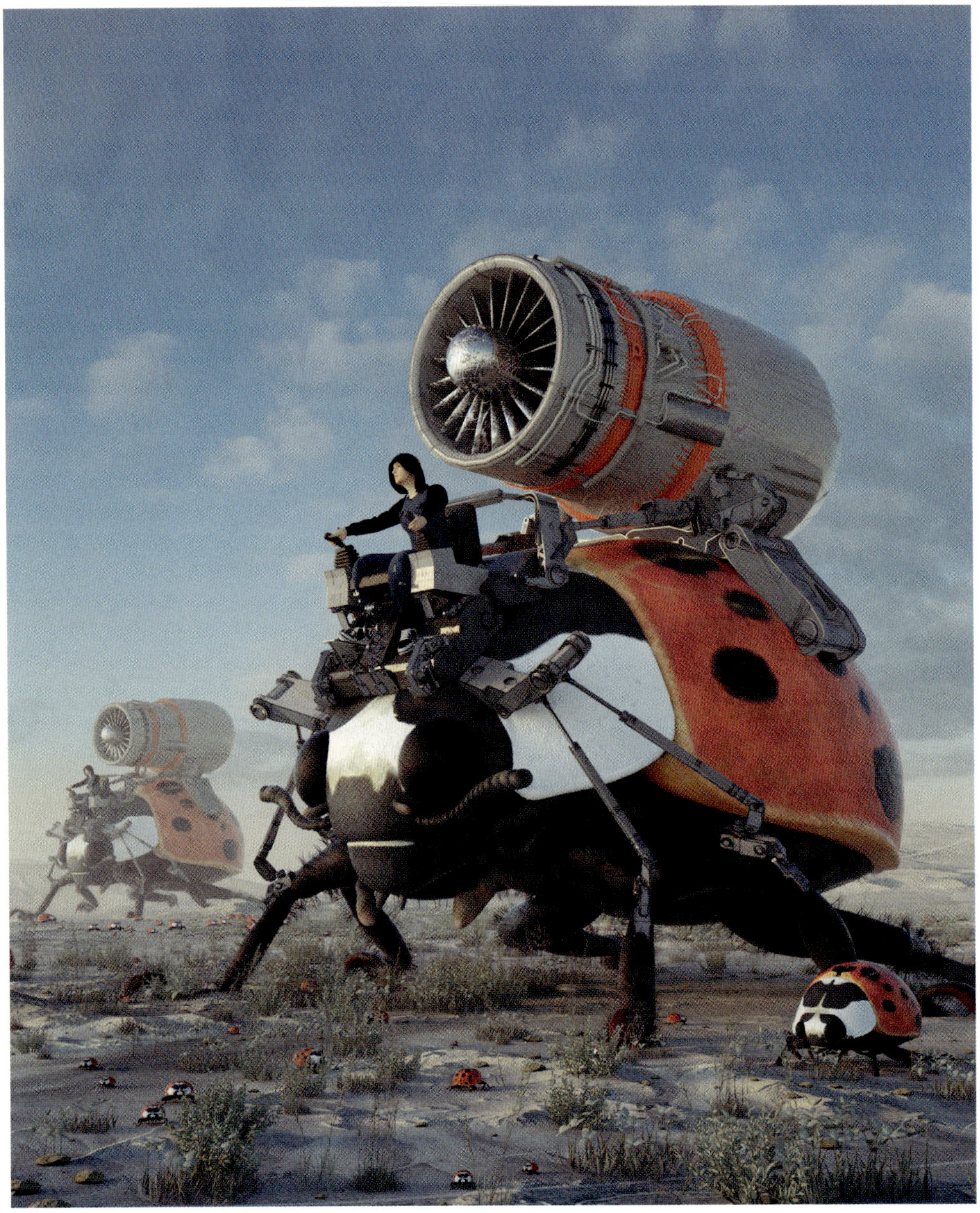

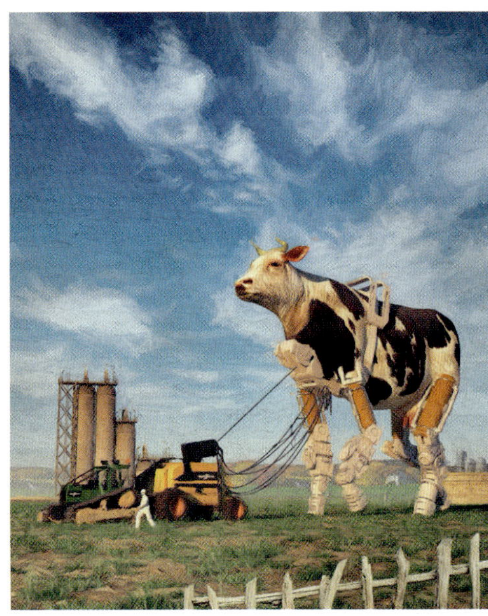

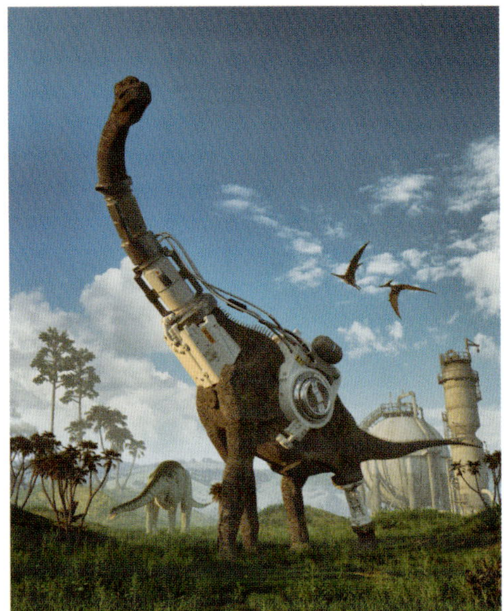

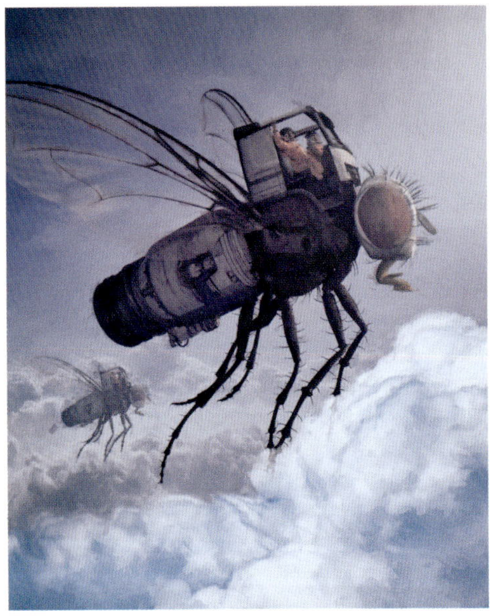

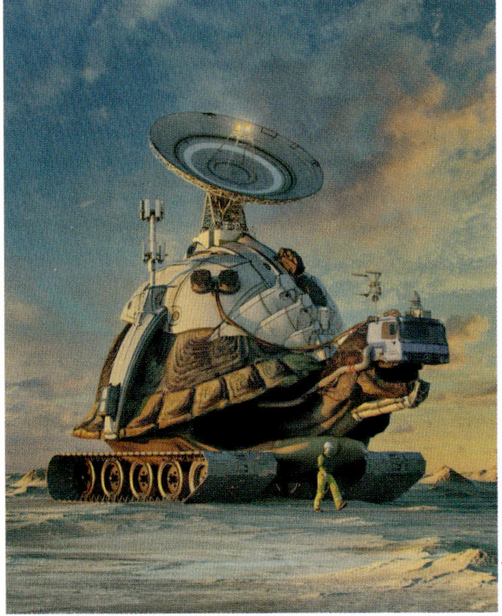

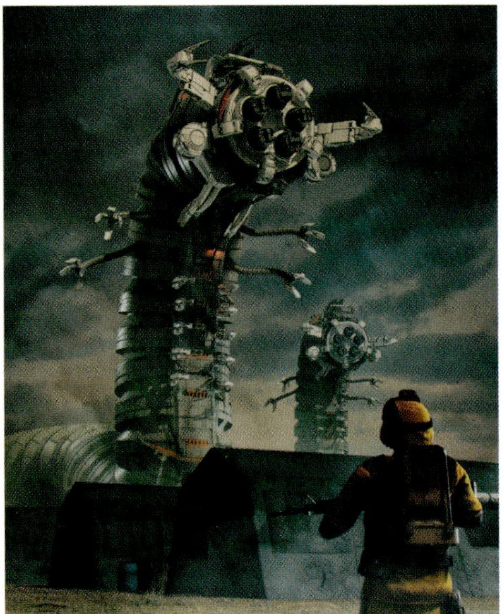

TOP LEFT
THERMONUCLEAR LADYBUGS
03.09.2018

TOP RIGHT
FARM FRESH
08.03.2018

MIDDLE RIGHT
[RE].VOLVE
06.29.2018

BOTTOM LEFT
SUPERFLY
12.08.2018

BOTTOM MIDDLE
SLOW INTERNET
10.05.2018

BOTTOM RIGHT
PLATINUM WURMS
11.03.2018

OPPOSITE PAGE
SNAIL MAIL
03.26.2018

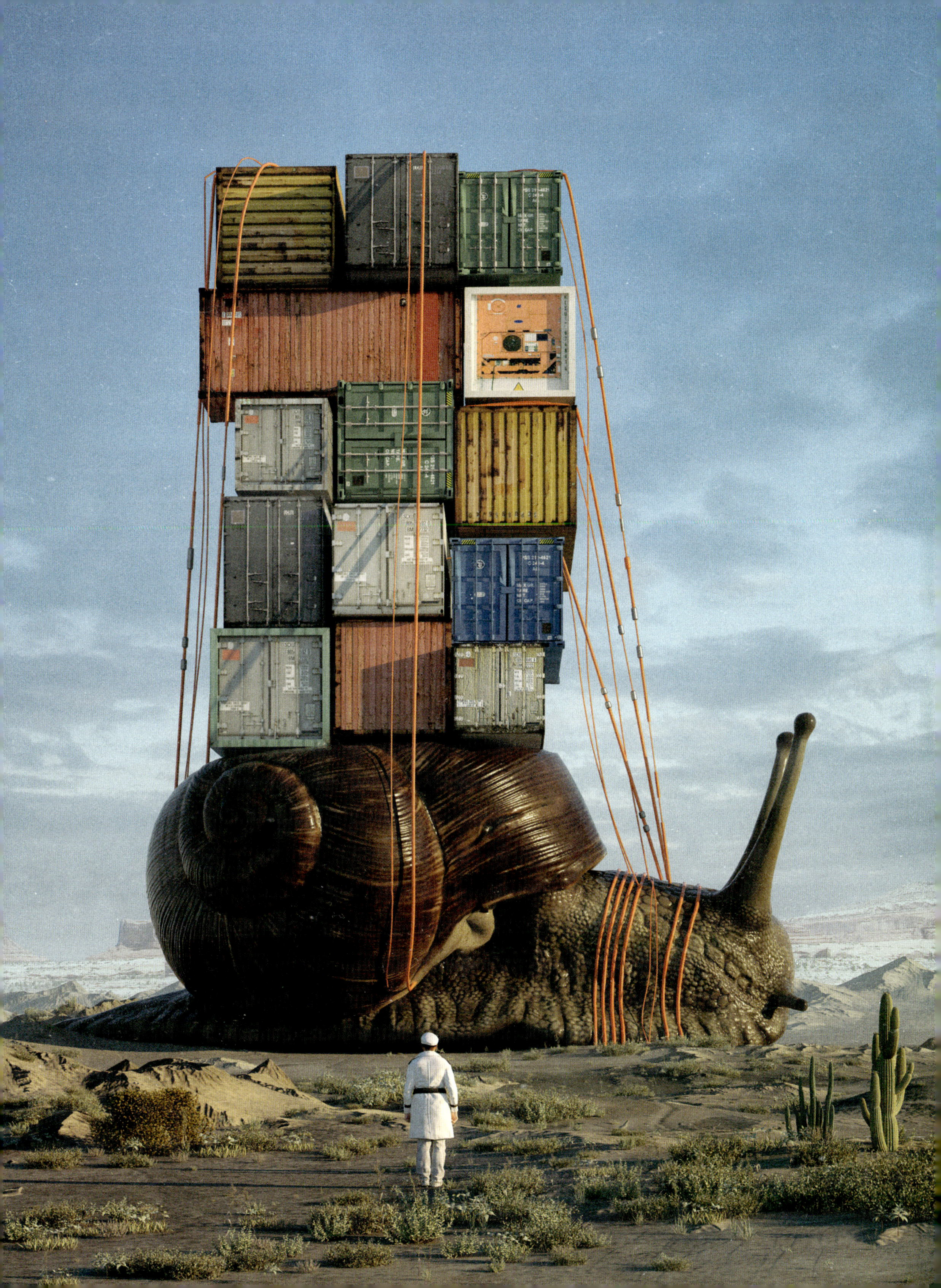

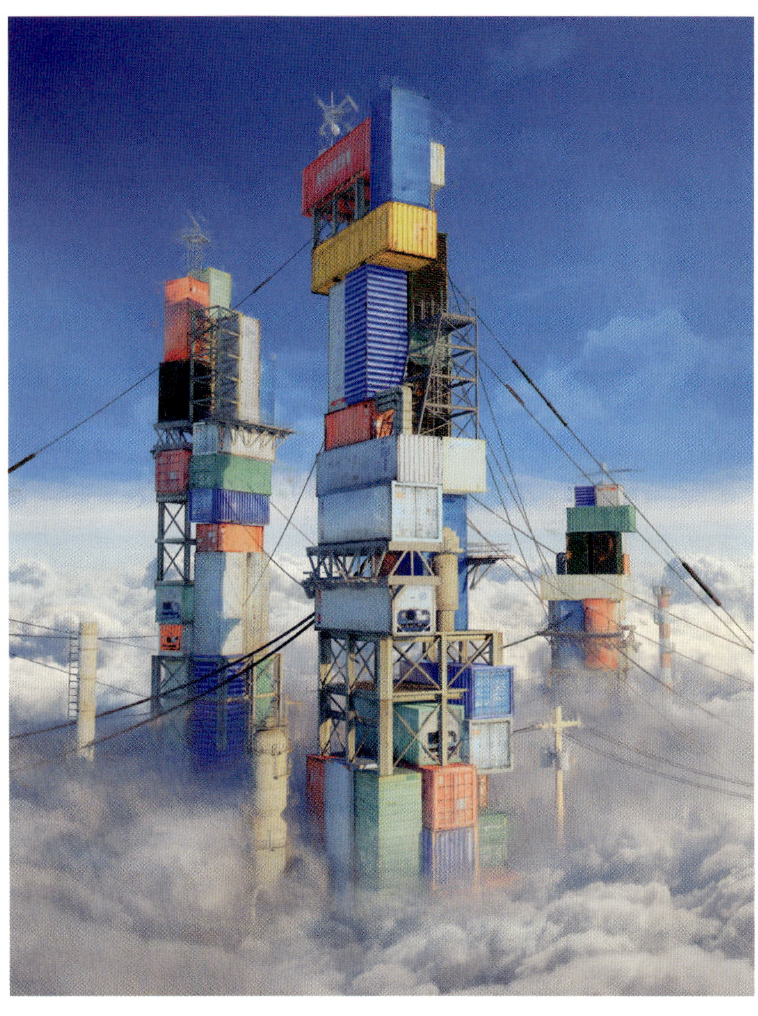

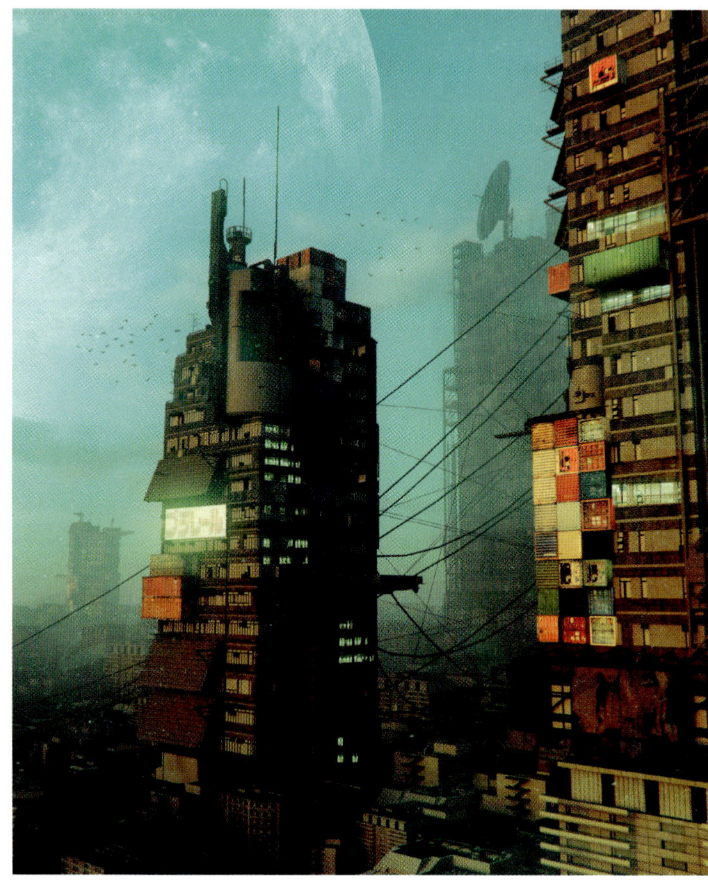

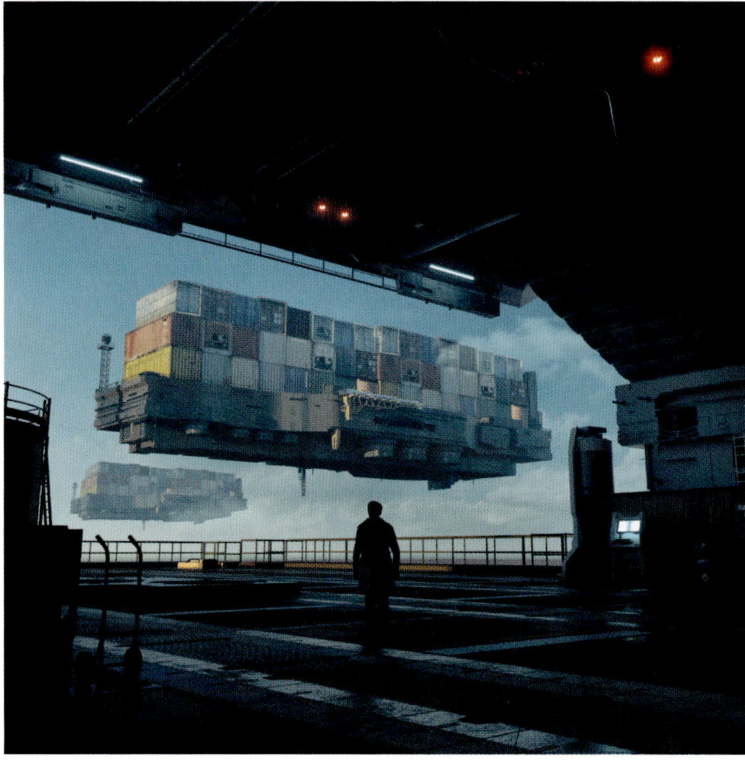

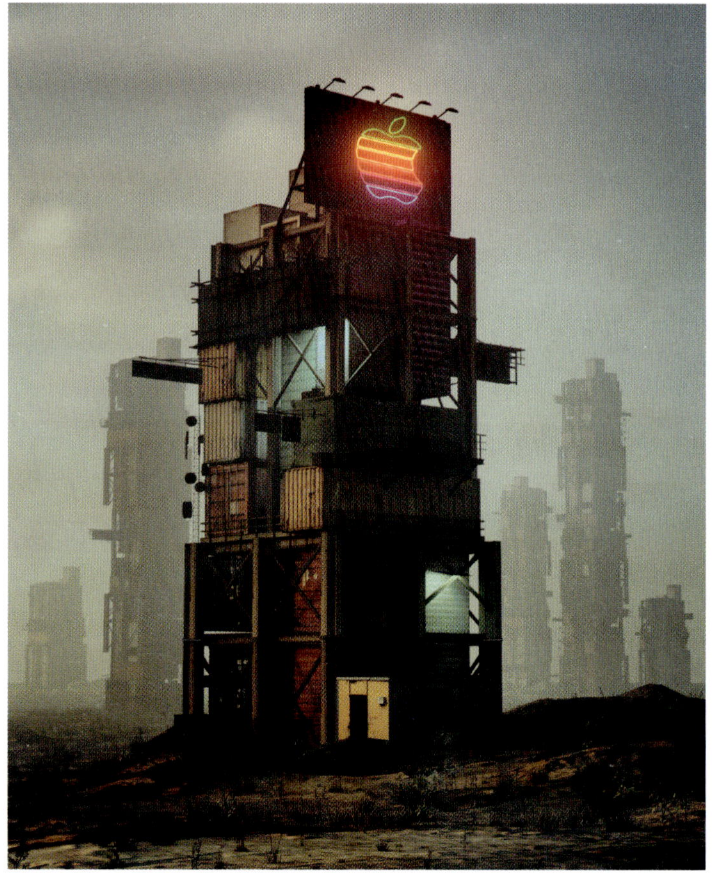

TOP LEFT
FULL STACK
03.02.2018

TOP RIGHT
MORNING OXIDE
08.27.2018

BOTTOM LEFT
TEN TERABYTES
05.11.2018

BOTTOM RIGHT
ONE TRILLION DOLLARS
08.02.2018

OPPOSITE PAGE, TOP
MICROSOFT CLOUD 2094
01.20.2018

OPPOSITE PAGE, BOTTOM
GENIUS BAR 2073
01.26.2018

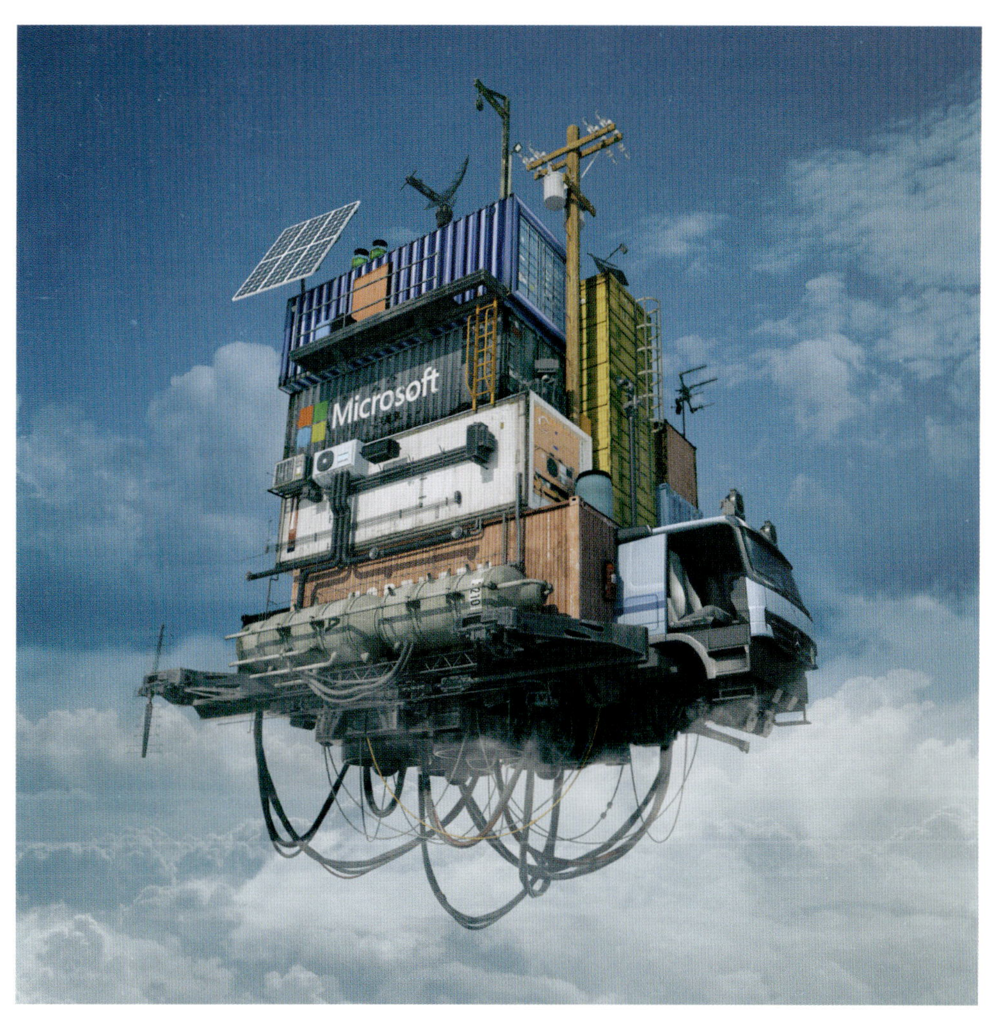
Microsoft

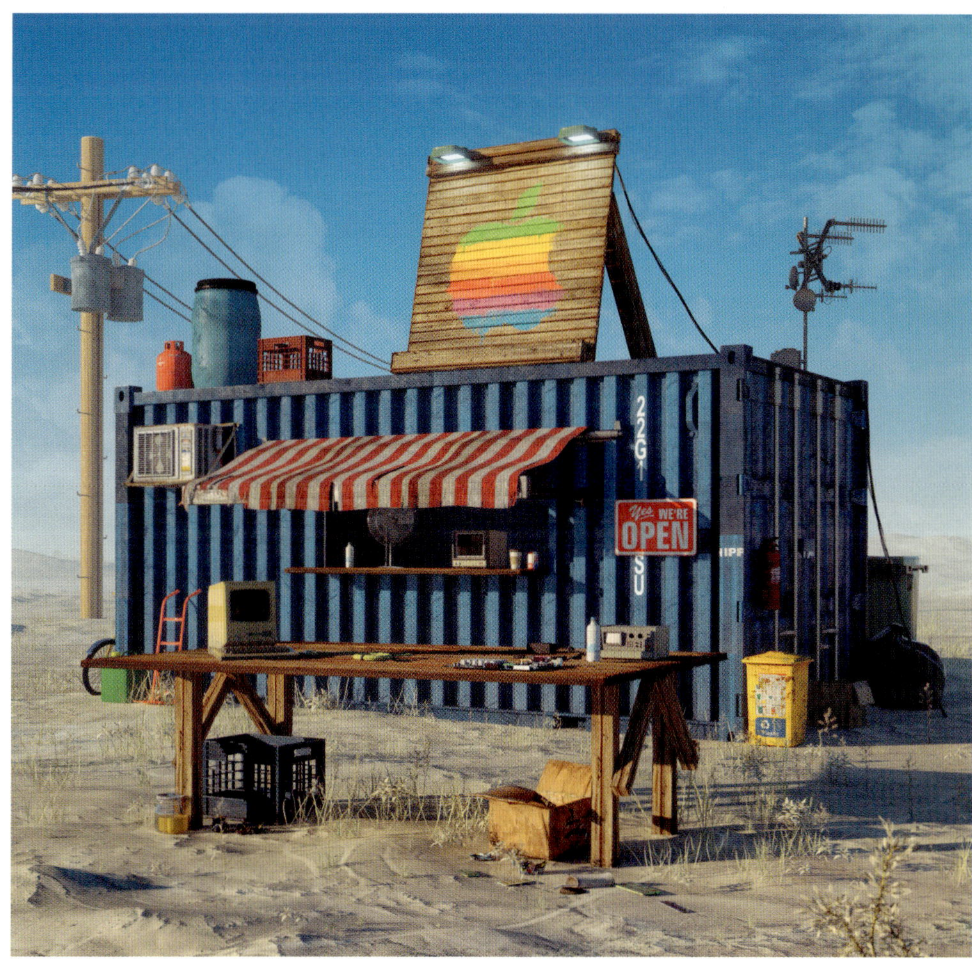
22G1
Yes WE'RE
OPEN

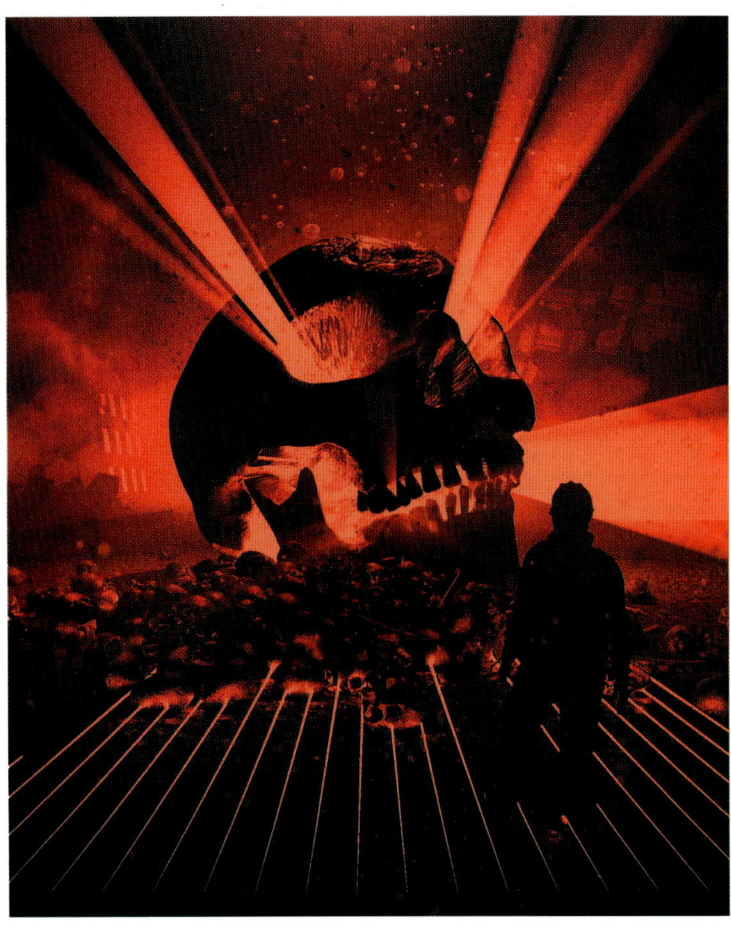

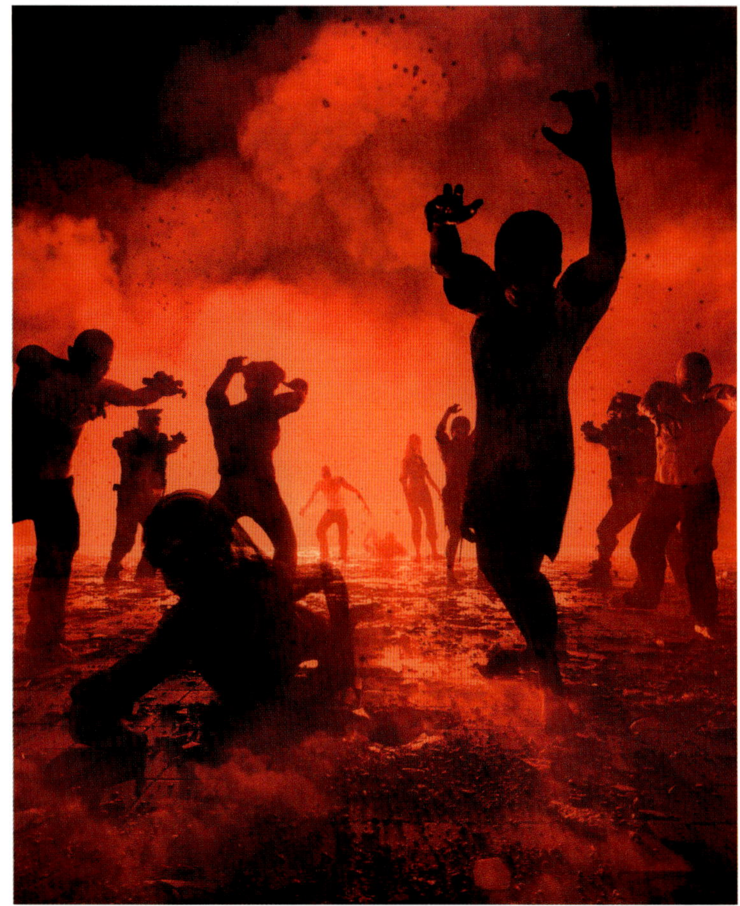

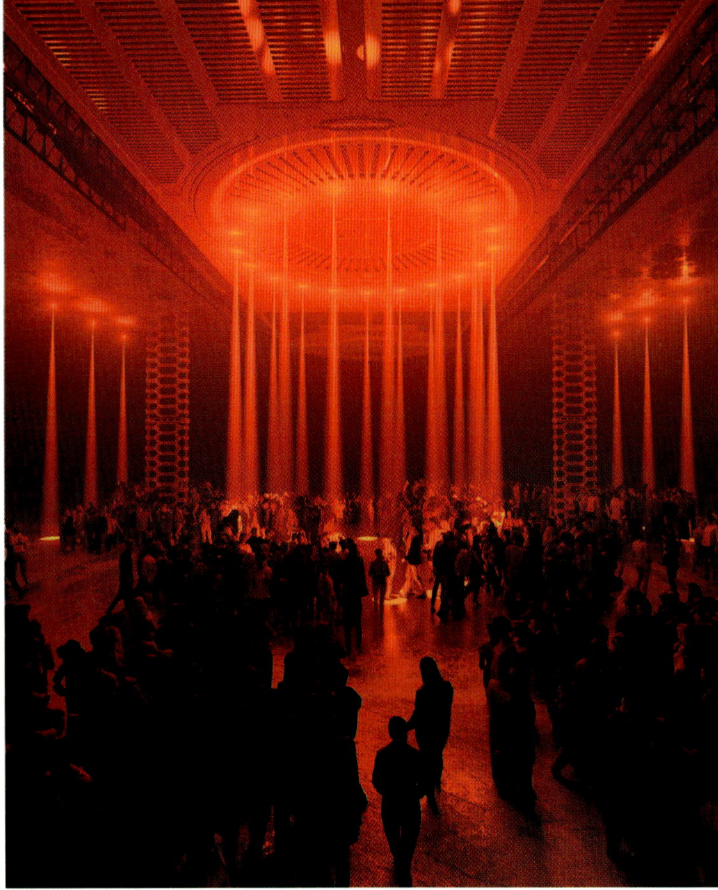

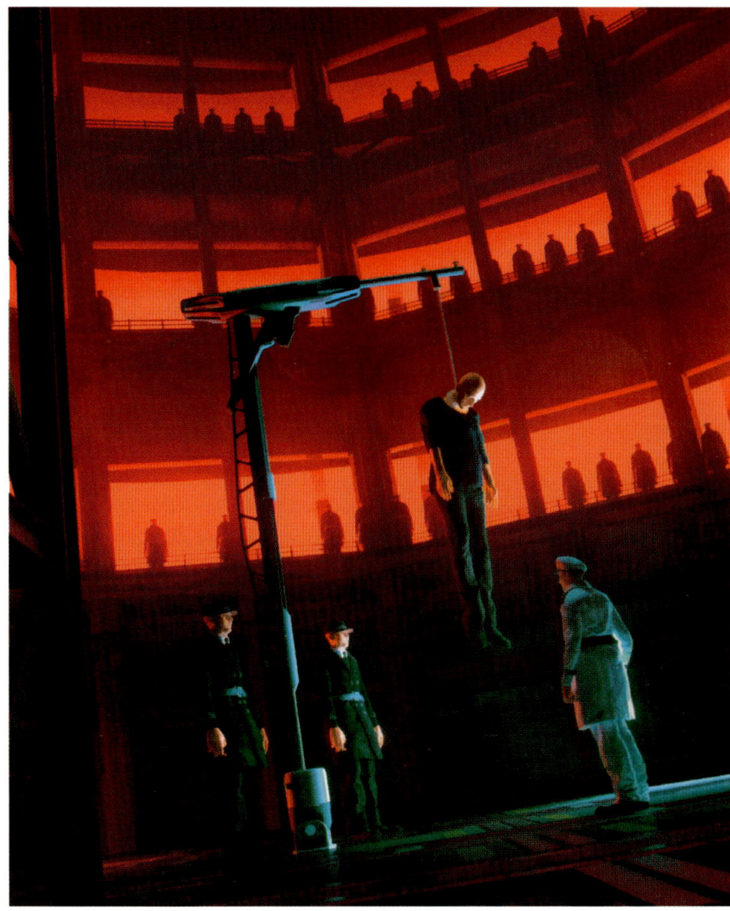

TOP LEFT
SUPERGONE
05.17.2018

TOP RIGHT
NEW FOLLOWERS
10.29.2018

BOTTOM LEFT
BLOOD MOON
05.04.2018

BOTTOM RIGHT
EXECUTE
11.18.2018

OPPOSITE PAGE
DISNEYLAND 2072
07.31.2018

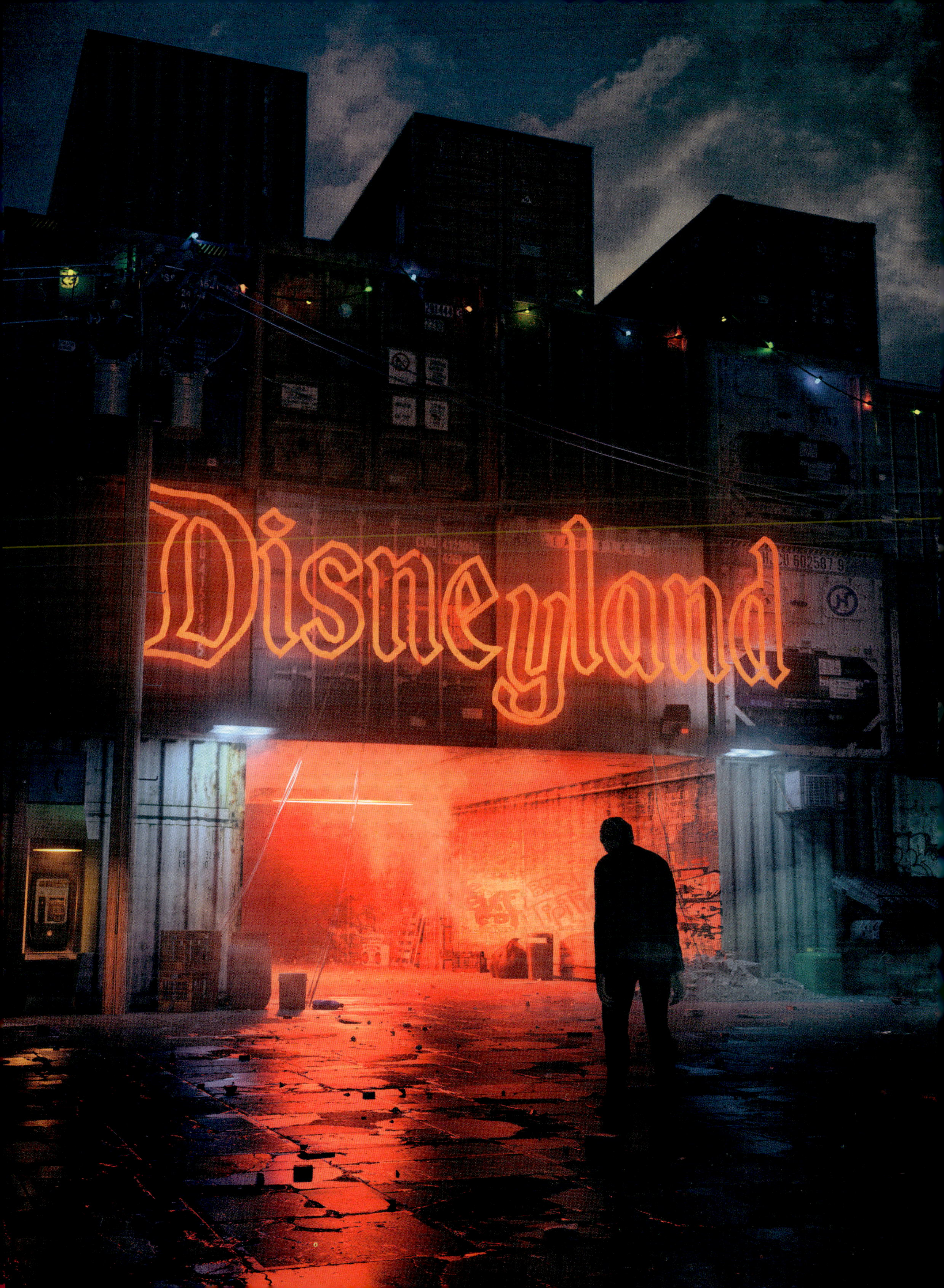
Disneyland

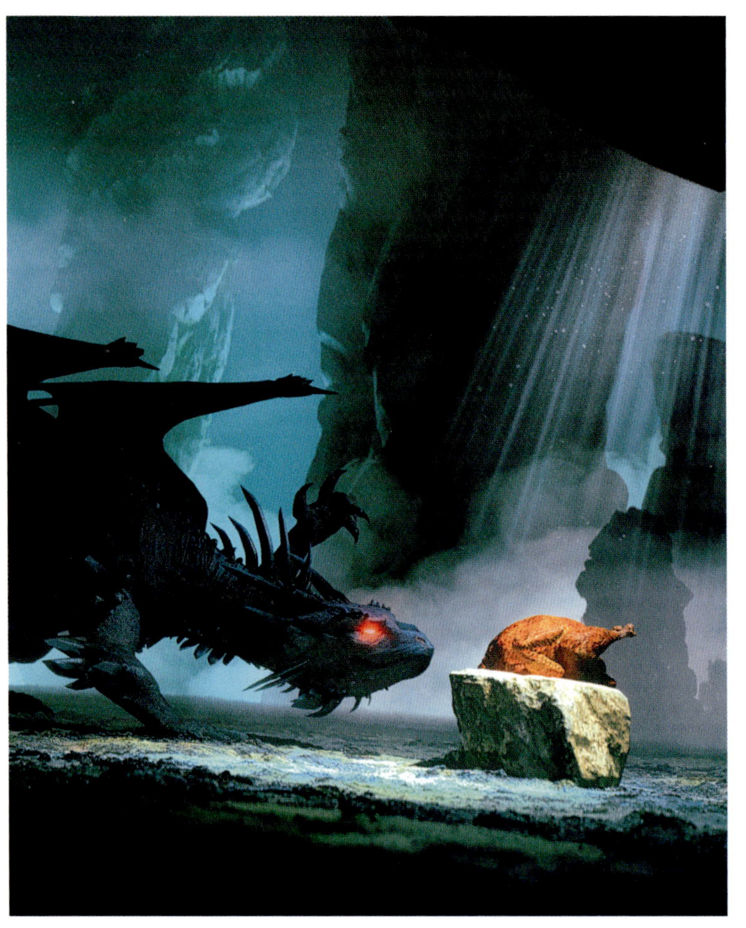

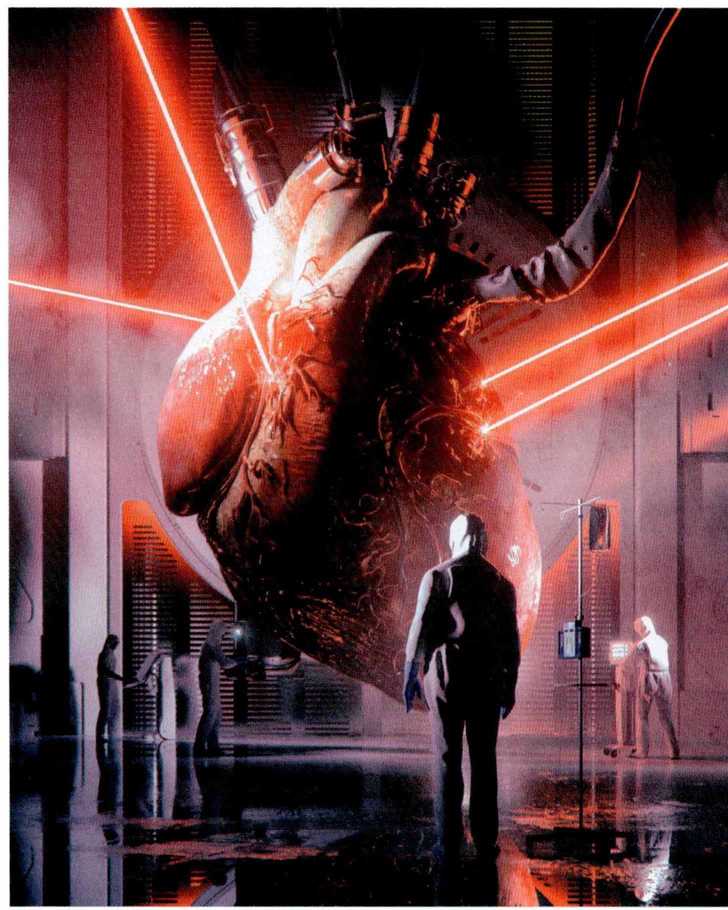

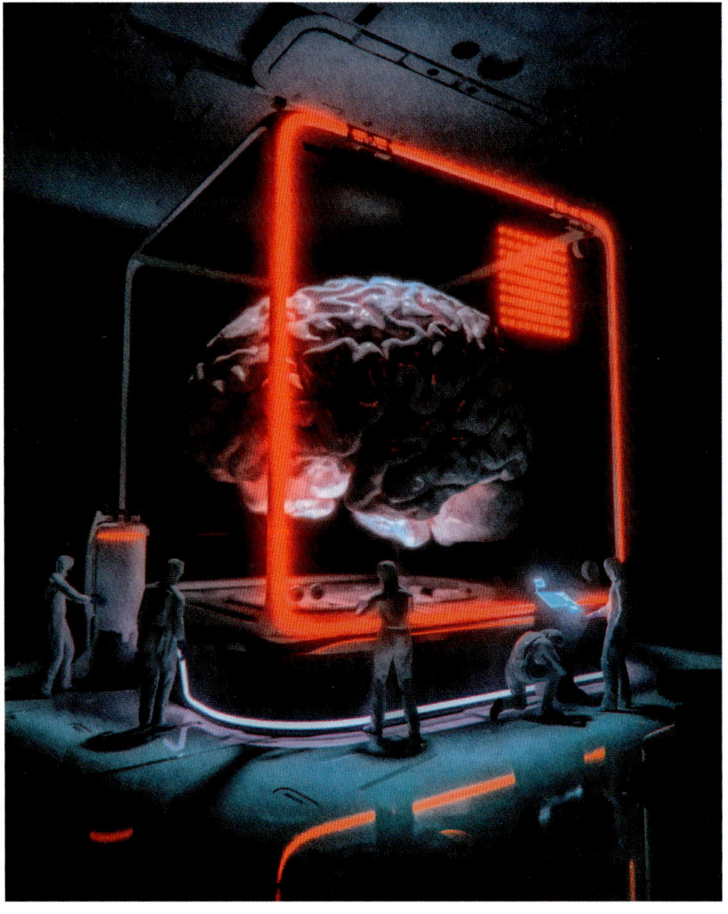

TOP LEFT

LEFTOVERS
11.23.2018

TOP RIGHT

OPEN HEART SURGERY
11.30.2018

BOTTOM

GREY MATTER
07.03.2018

OPPOSITE PAGE

THE FIRST RETRIBUTION DAY
11.22.2018

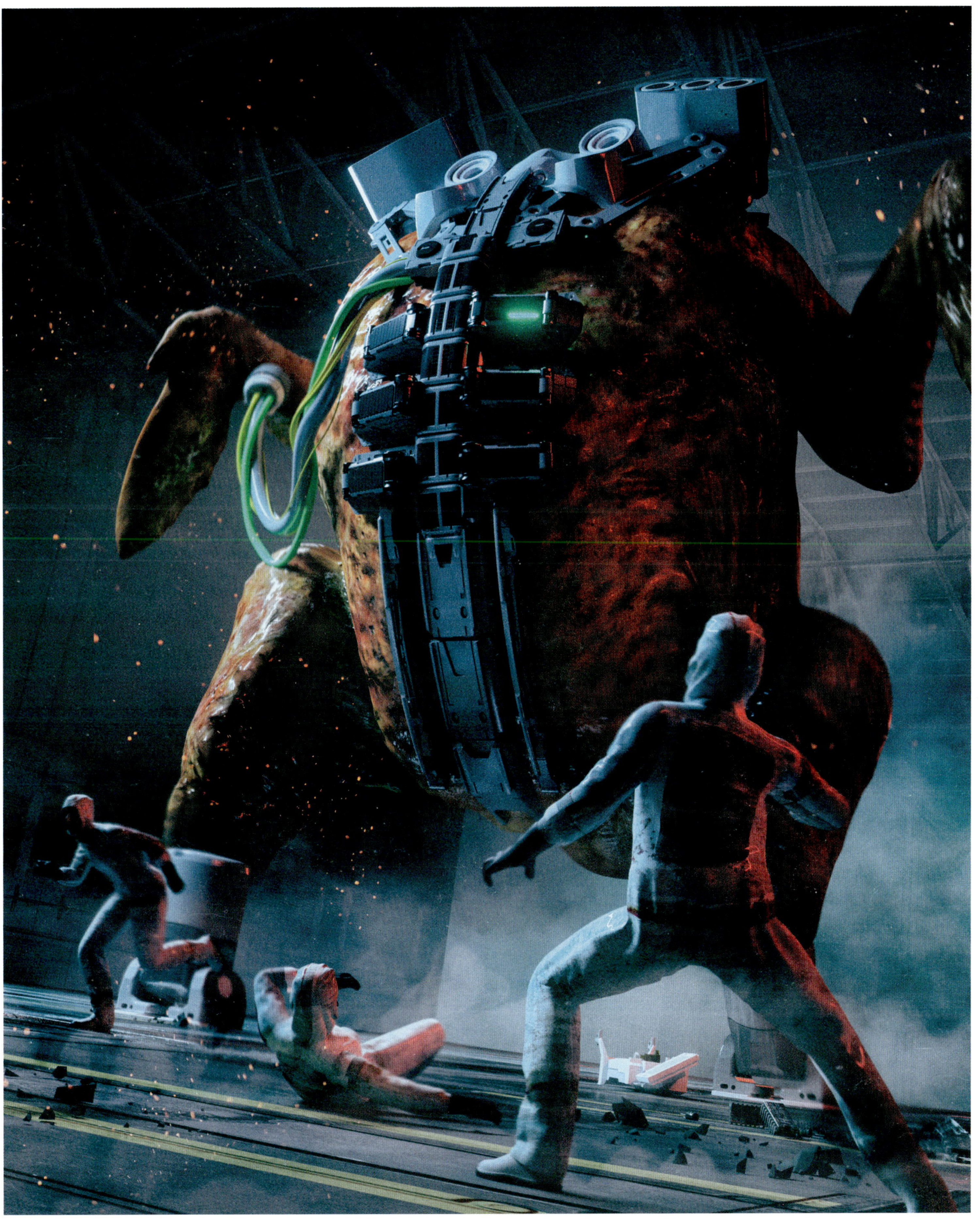

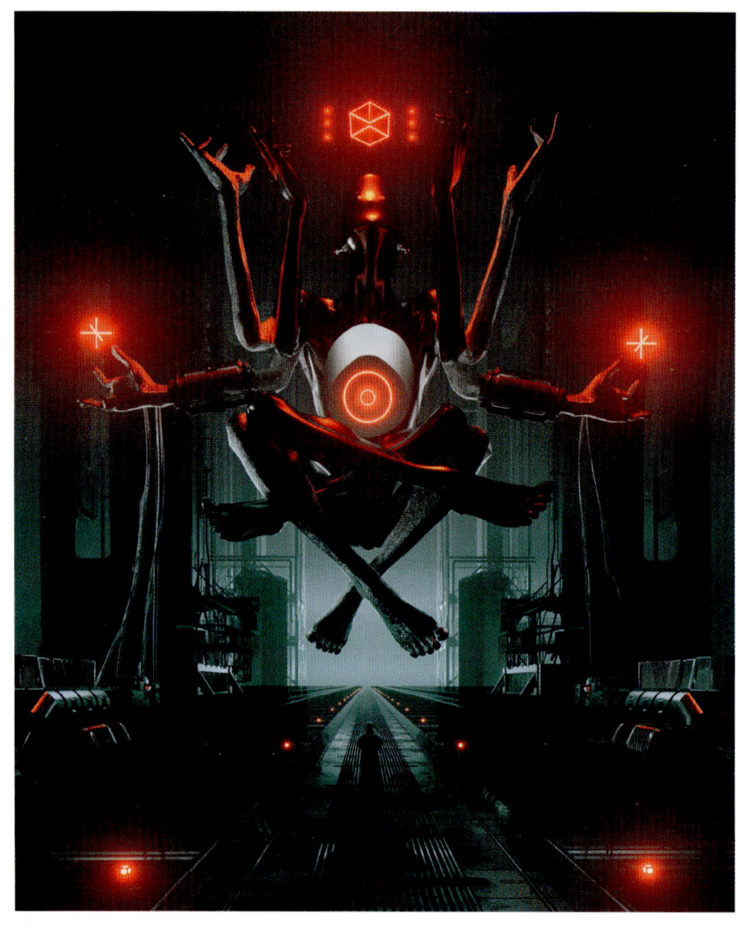

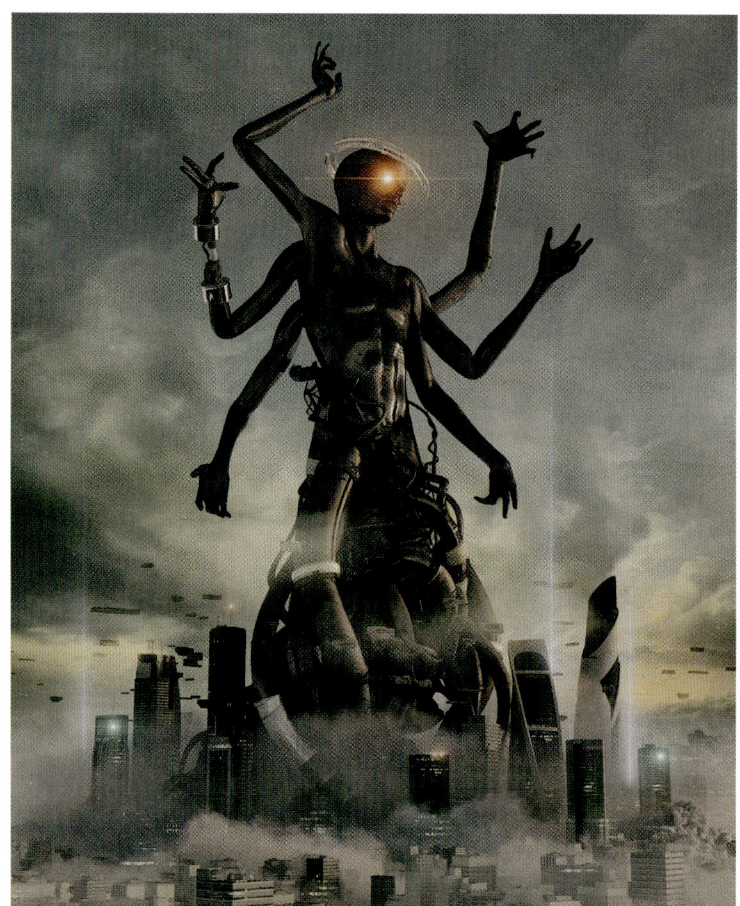

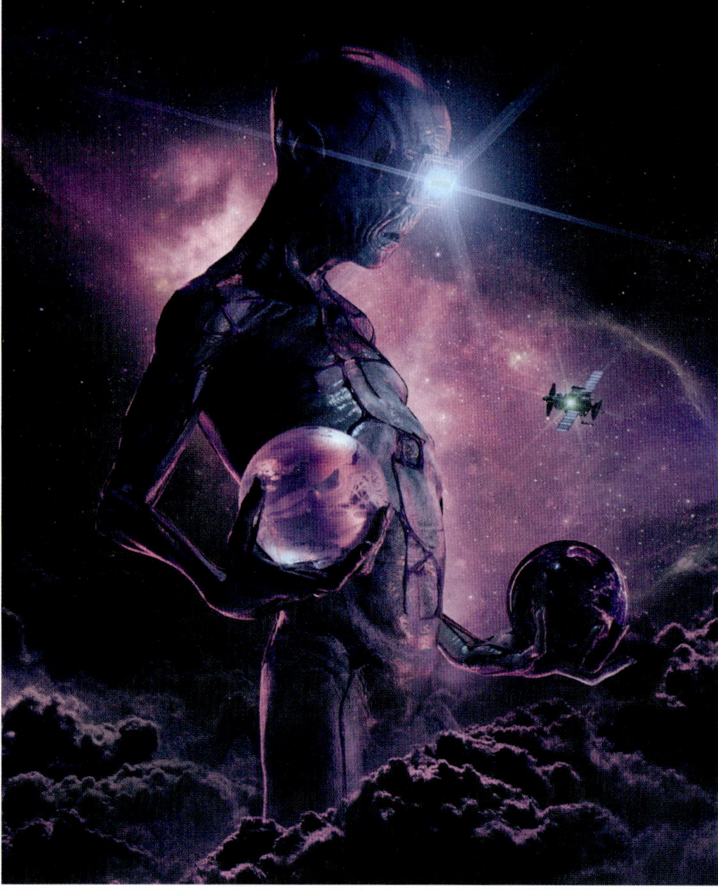

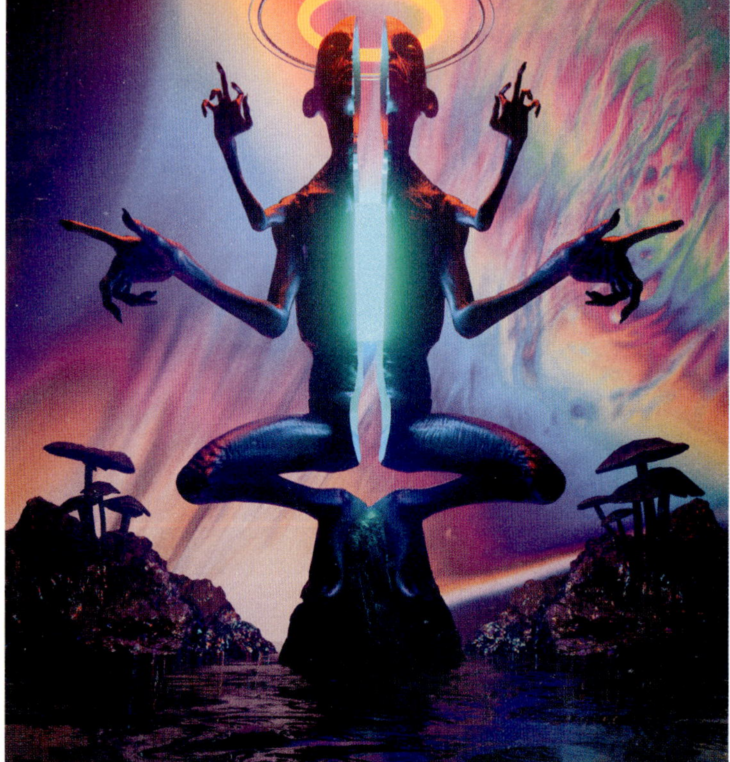

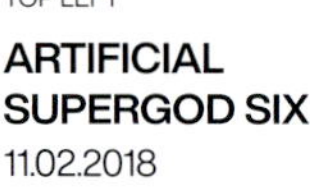

TOP LEFT

ARTIFICIAL SUPERGOD SIX
11.02.2018

TOP RIGHT

LAST PROGRAMMER
11.05.2018

BOTTOM LEFT

FOUND
12.15.2018

BOTTOM RIGHT

some weird hippy thing i guess
12.29.2018

OPPOSITE PAGE

CHASE PERFECTION
12.13.2018

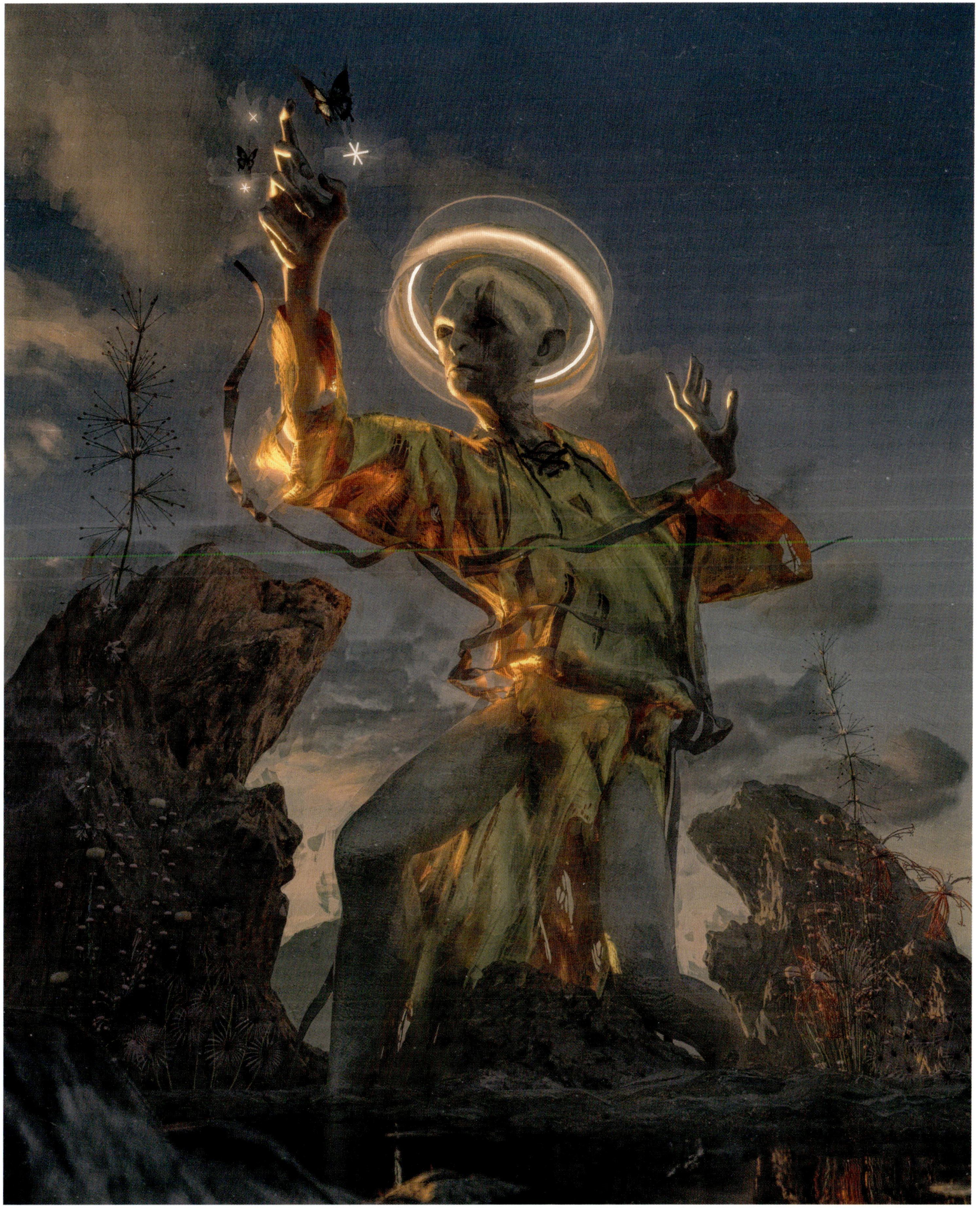

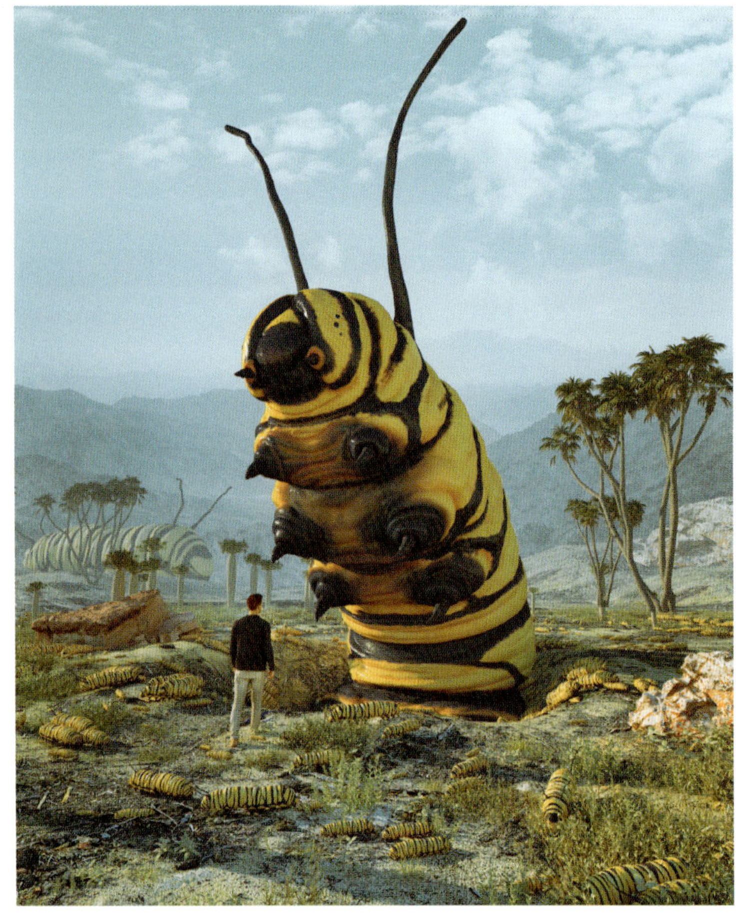

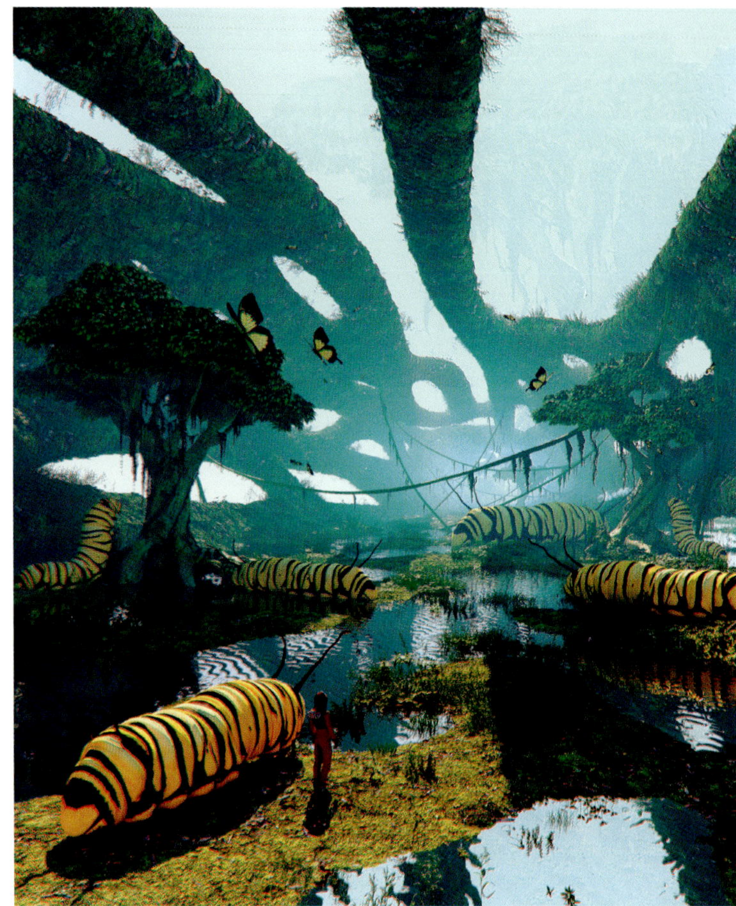

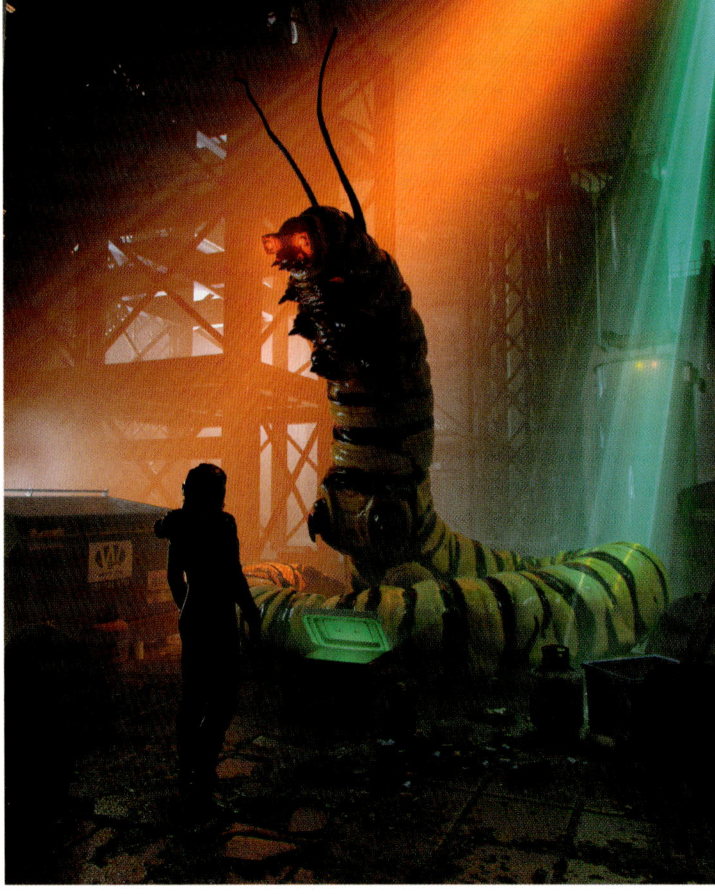

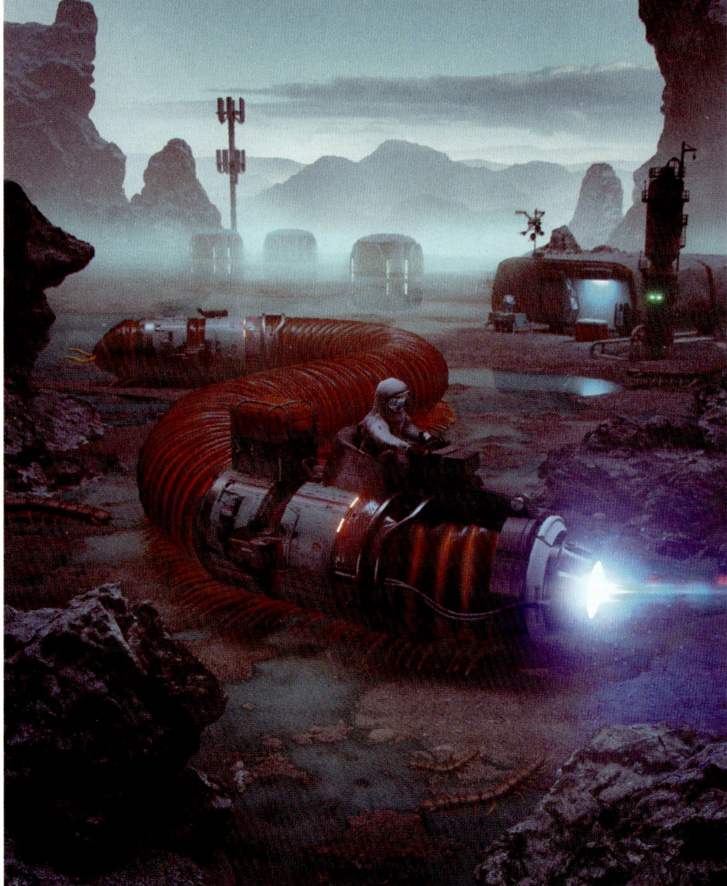

TOP LEFT

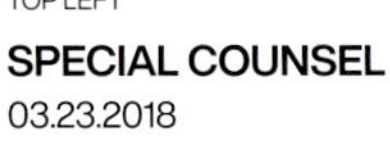

SPECIAL COUNSEL
03.23.2018

TOP RIGHT

FEAST MODE
12.22.2018

BOTTOM LEFT

buying drugs from cryptoworm
10.09.2018

BOTTOM RIGHT

MARTIAN SILK FARMER
11.29.2018

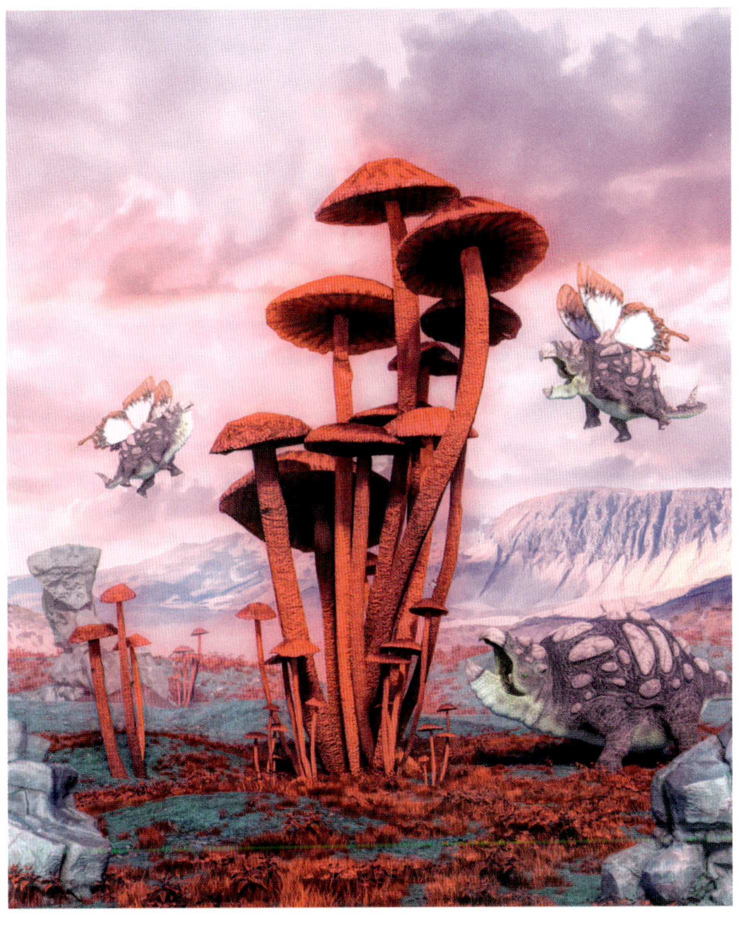

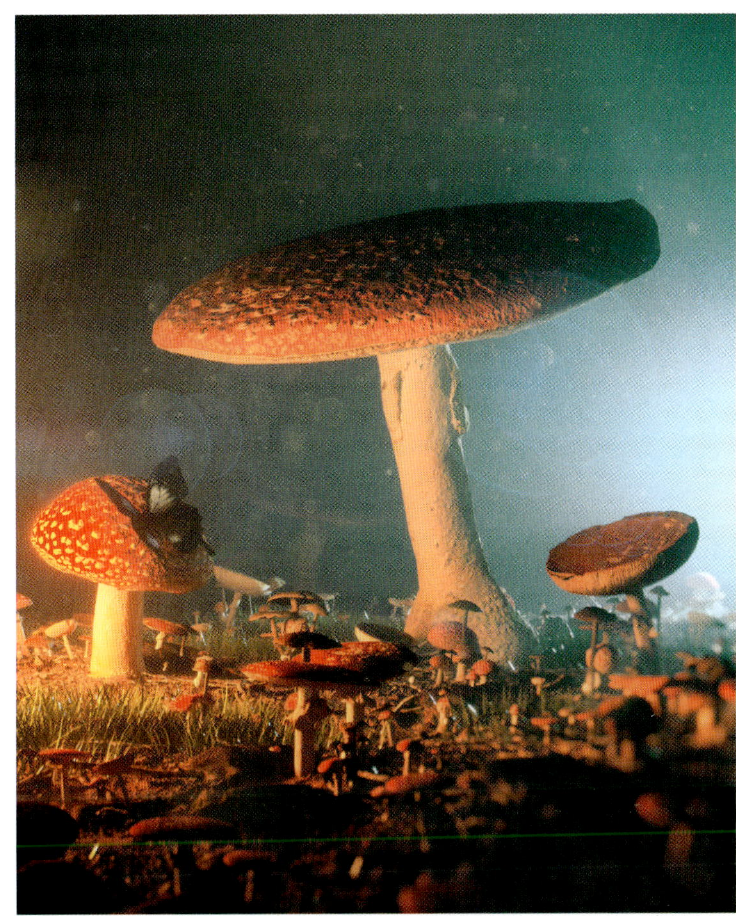

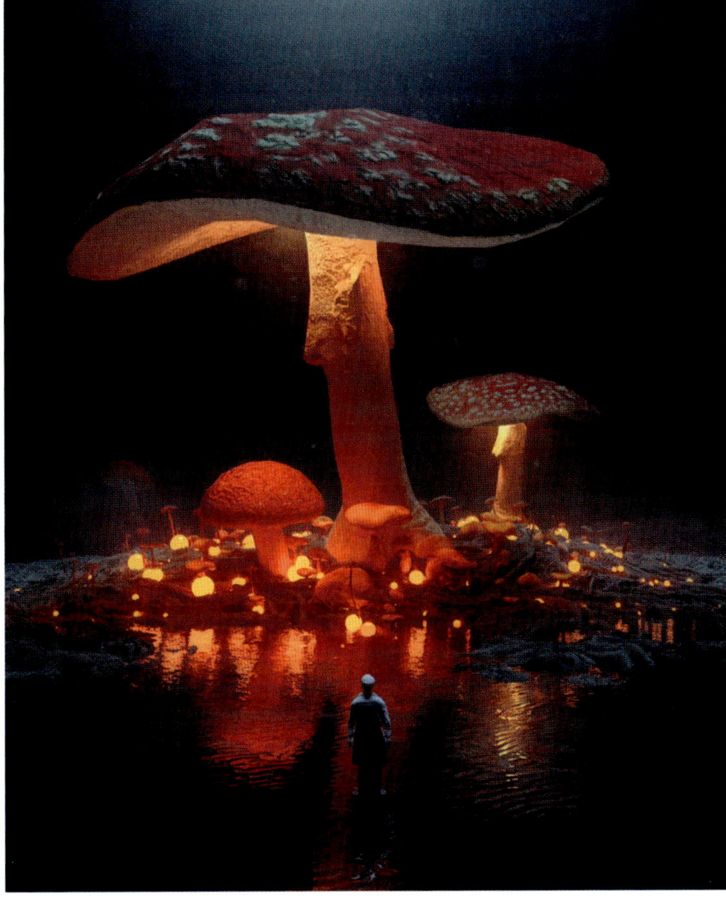

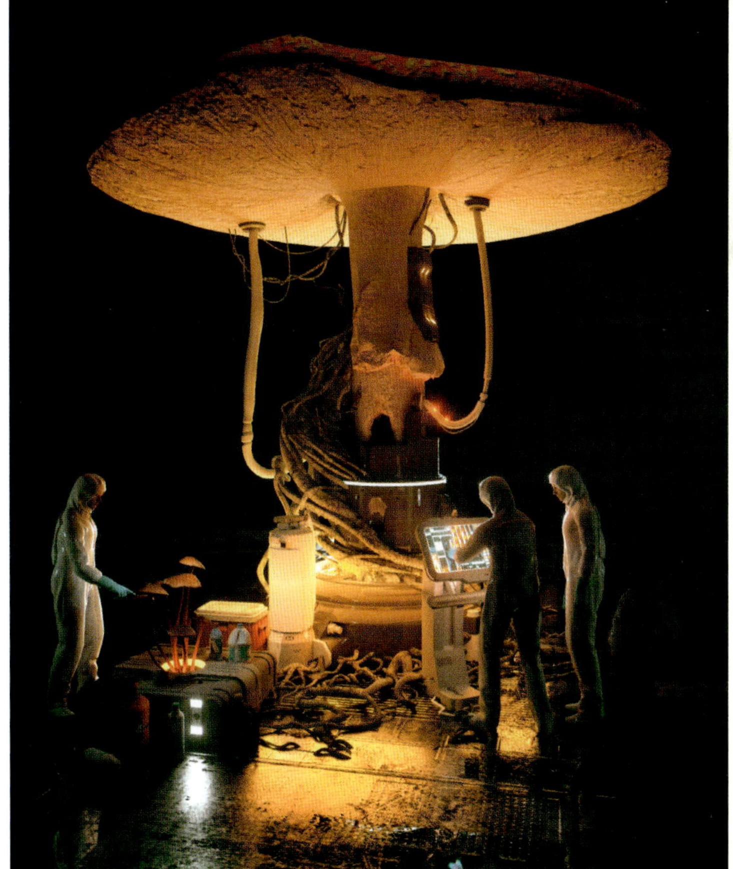

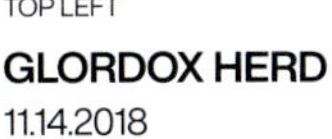

TOP LEFT

GLORDOX HERD

11.14.2018

TOP RIGHT

LITTLE THINGS

07.10.2018

BOTTOM LEFT

ALPHA SPORE

08.01.2018

BOTTOM RIGHT

BIOHACKERS

09.10.2018

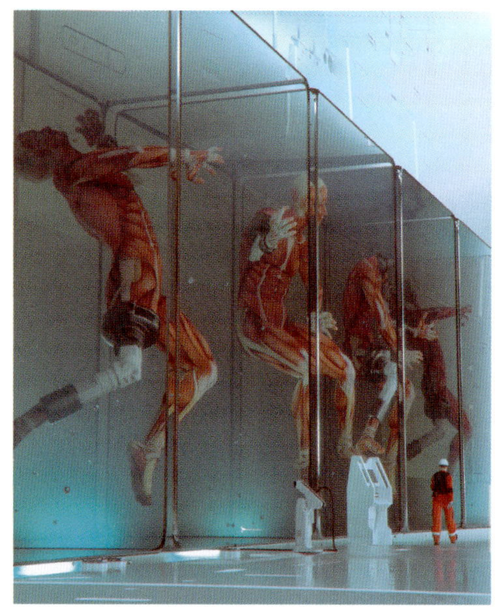

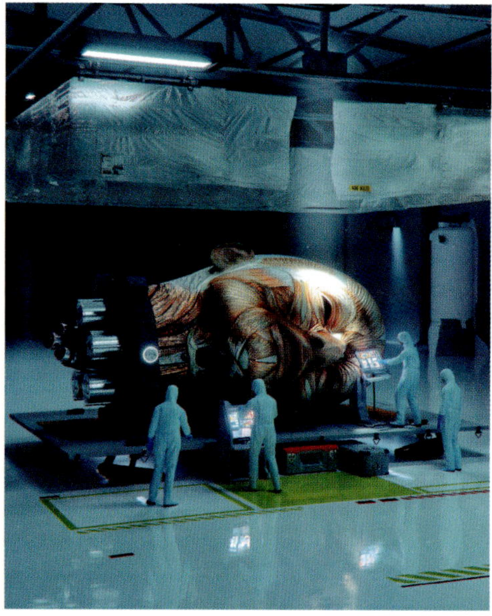

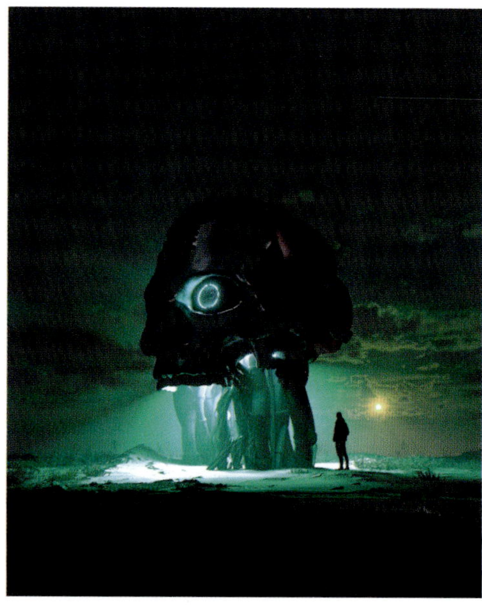

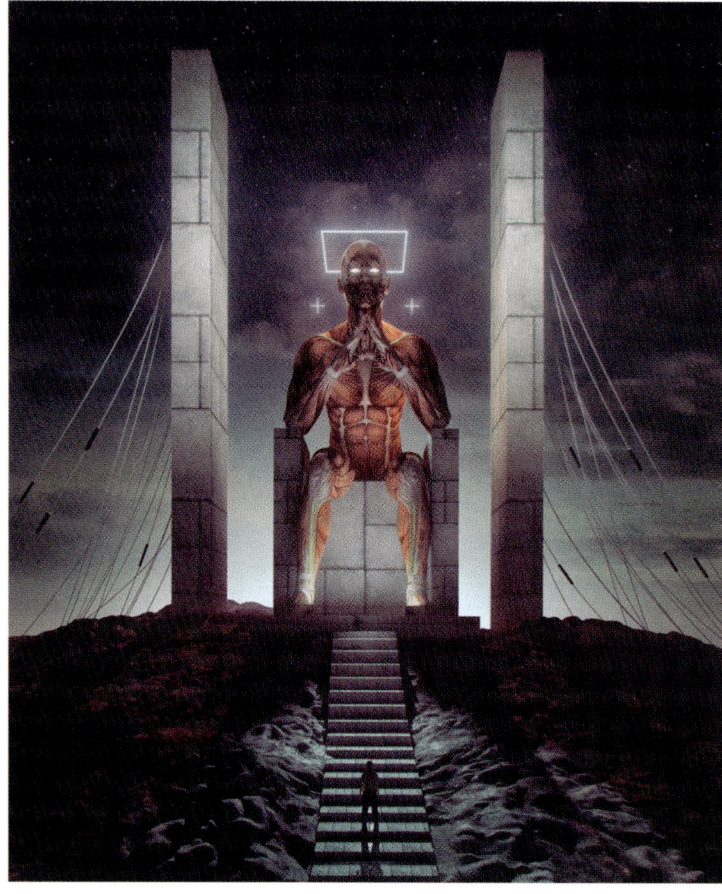

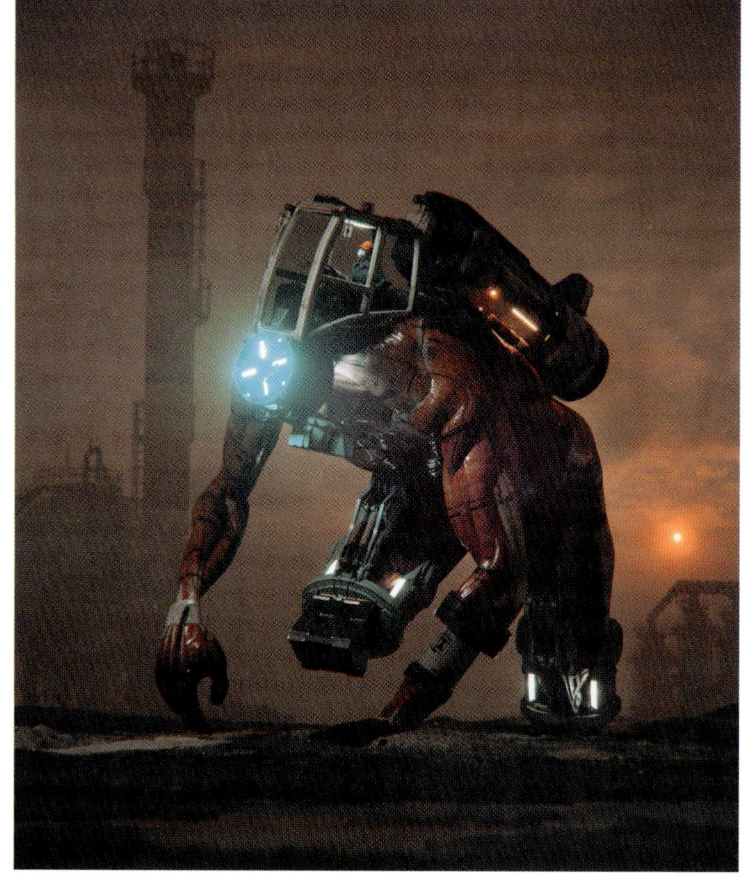

TOP LEFT

BIOMETRIC WORKFORCE
06.04.2018

TOP MIDDLE

ROUTINE MAINTENANCE
08.28.2018

TOP RIGHT

HEADLAMP
11.20.2018

BOTTOM LEFT

ARTIFICIAL SUPERGOD
07.08.2018

BOTTOM RIGHT

BEASTMODE
11.13.2018

OPPOSITE PAGE

HUMAN ELEMENT
08.08.2018

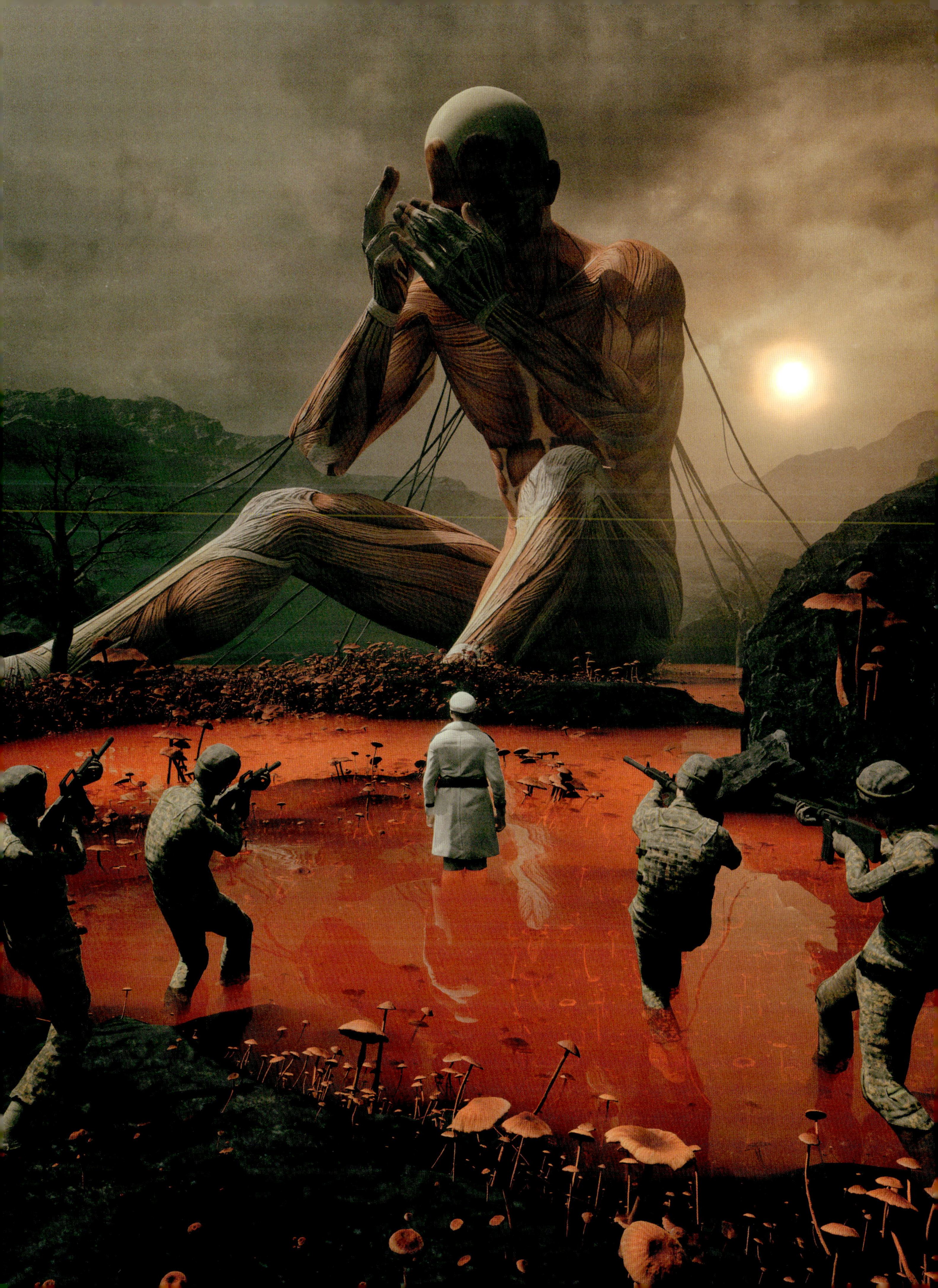

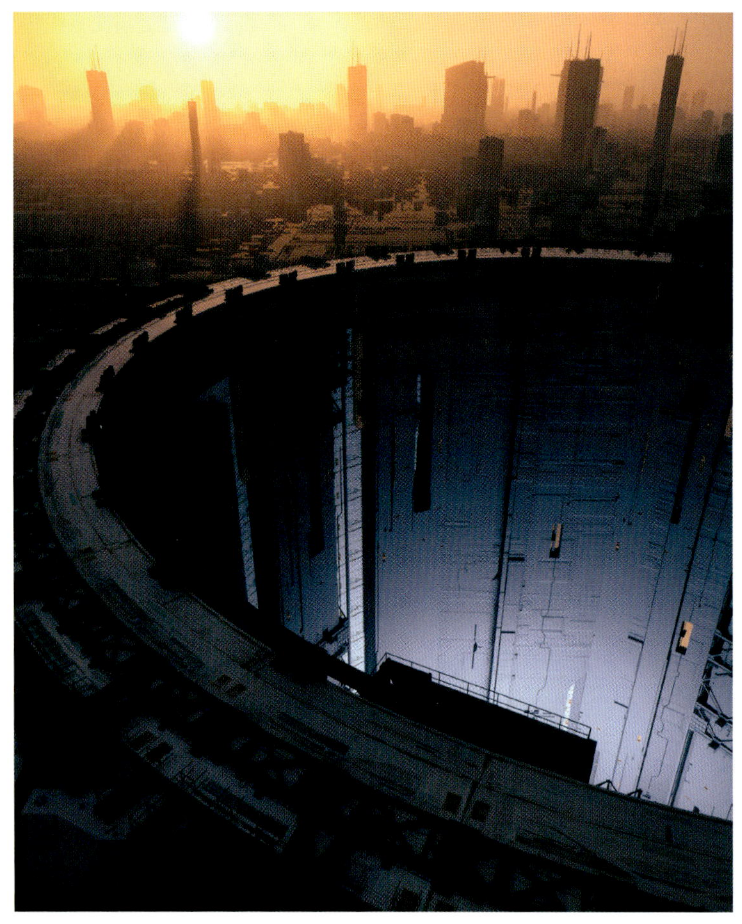

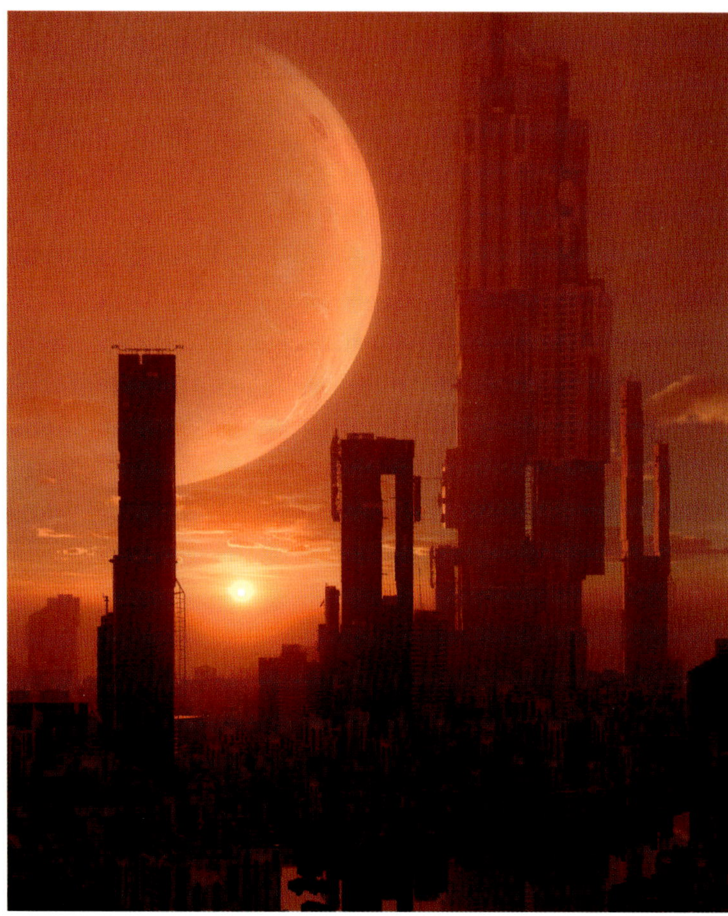

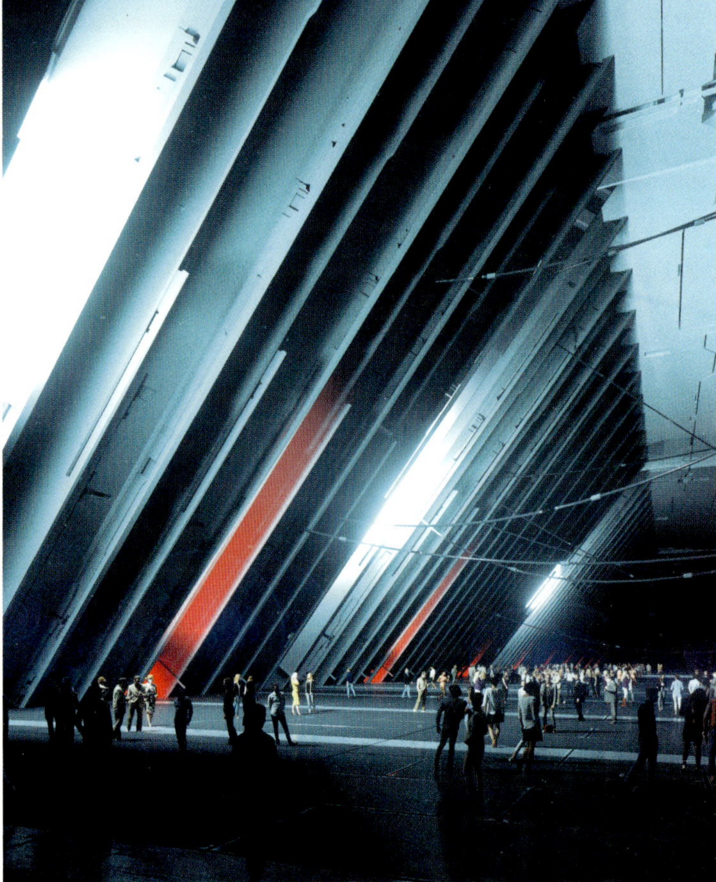

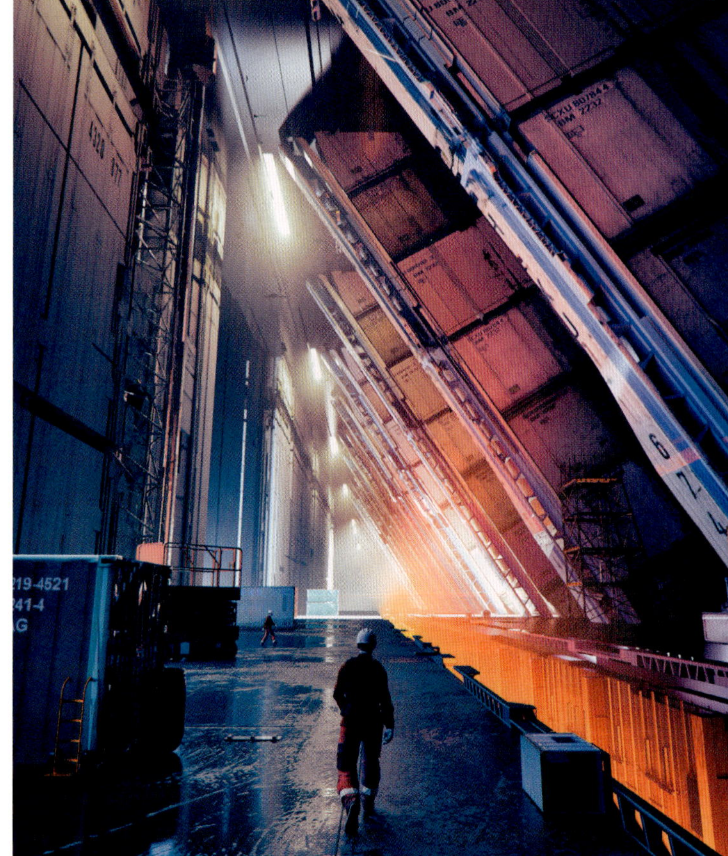

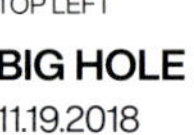

TOP LEFT

BIG HOLE

11.19.2018

TOP RIGHT

CRIMSON SMOG

11.12.2018

BOTTOM LEFT

TRANSLATION LOST

05.29.2018

BOTTOM RIGHT

NIGHTSHIFT

06.02.2018

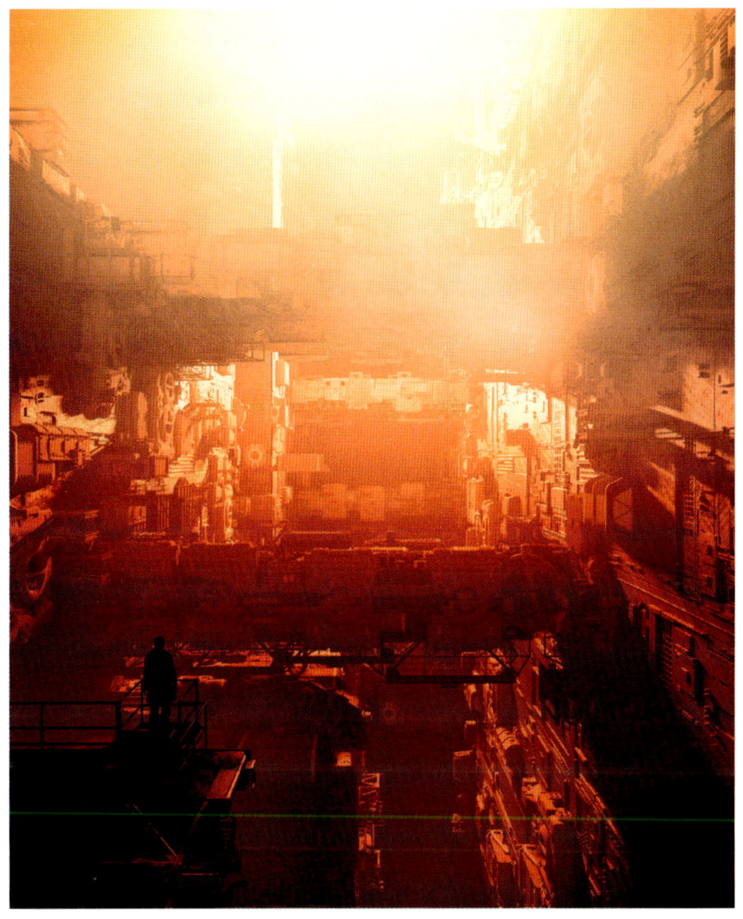

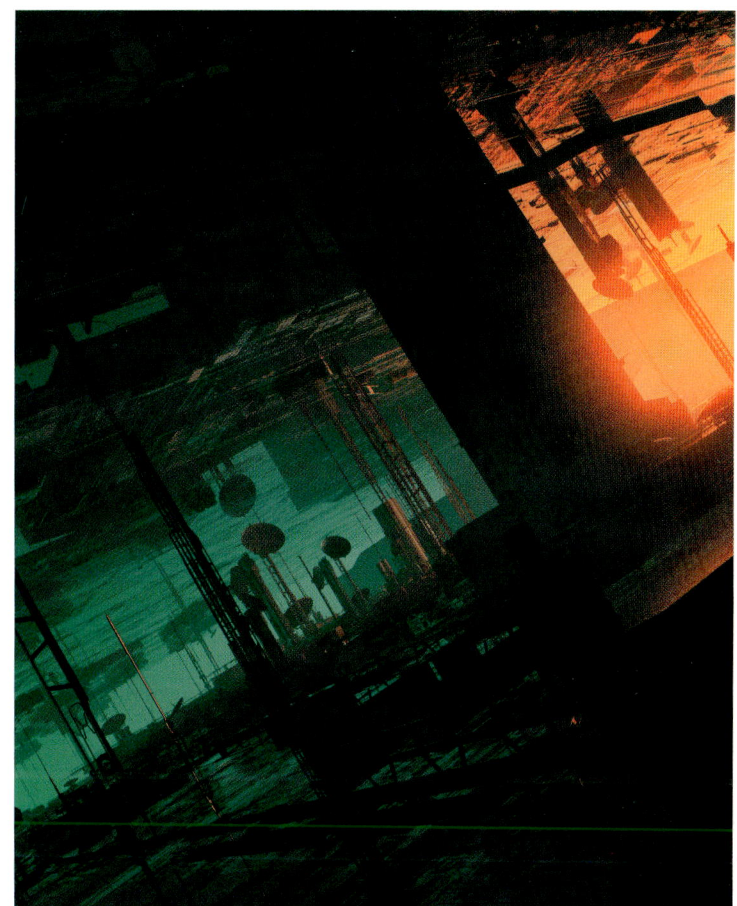

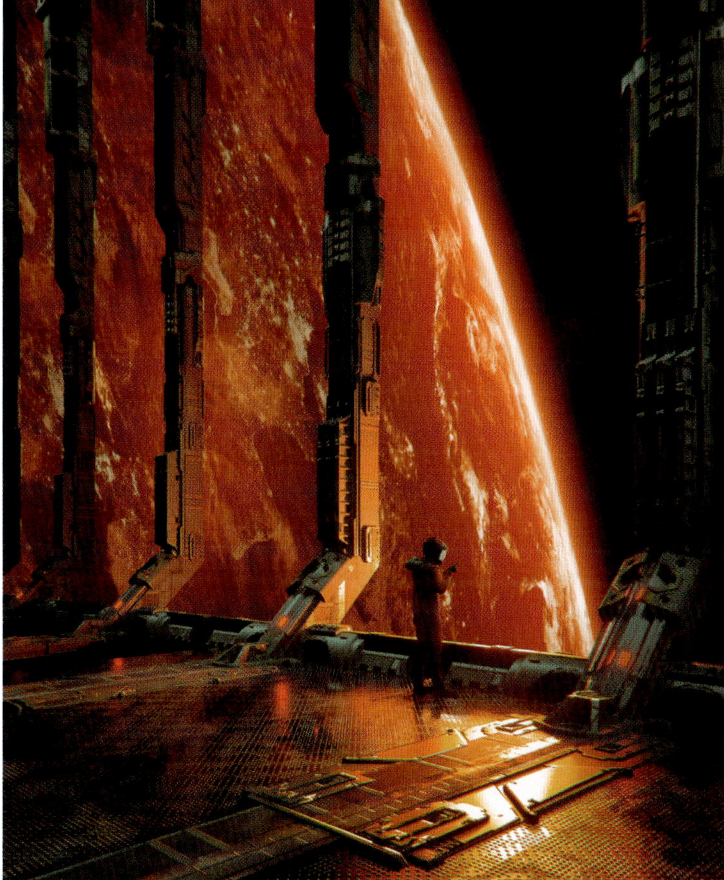

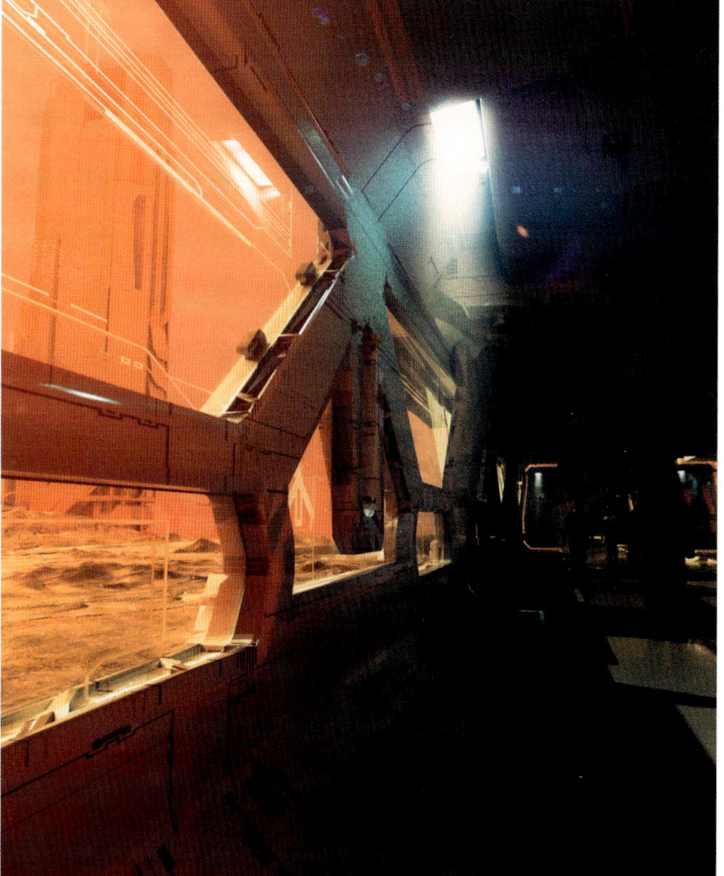

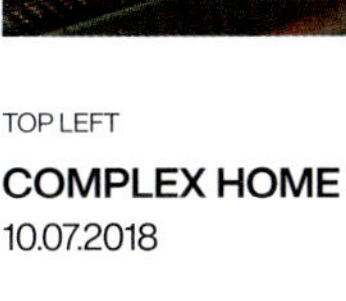

TOP LEFT

COMPLEX HOME
10.07.2018

TOP RIGHT

SIXTY ONE THOUSAND
10.10.2018

BOTTOM LEFT

BEGIN
09.12.2018

BOTTOM RIGHT

WEDNESDAY MORNING
04.04.2018

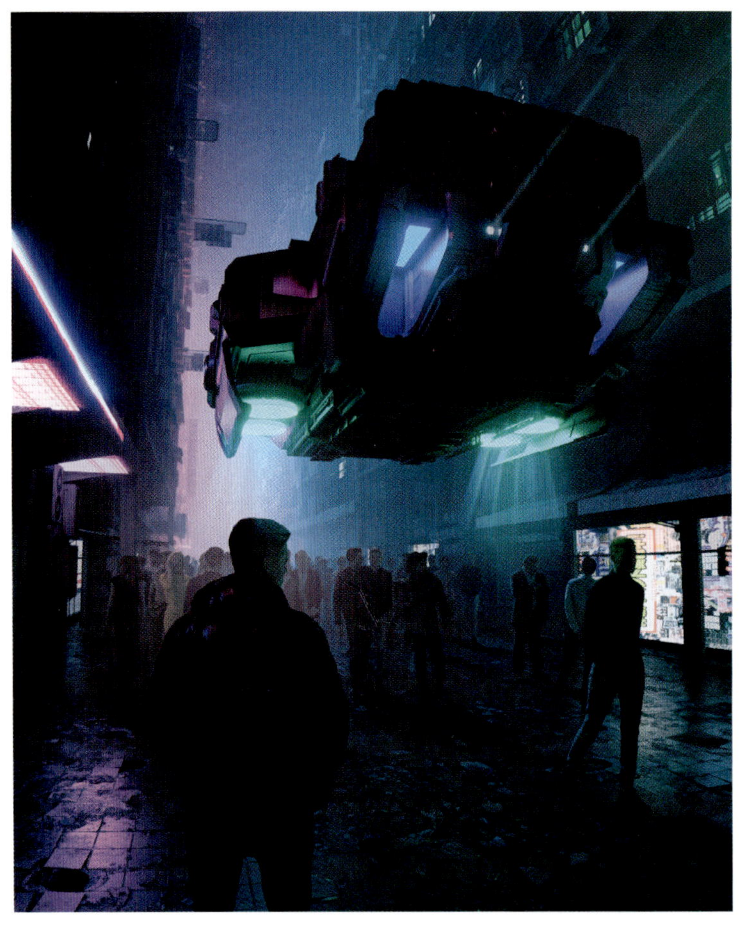

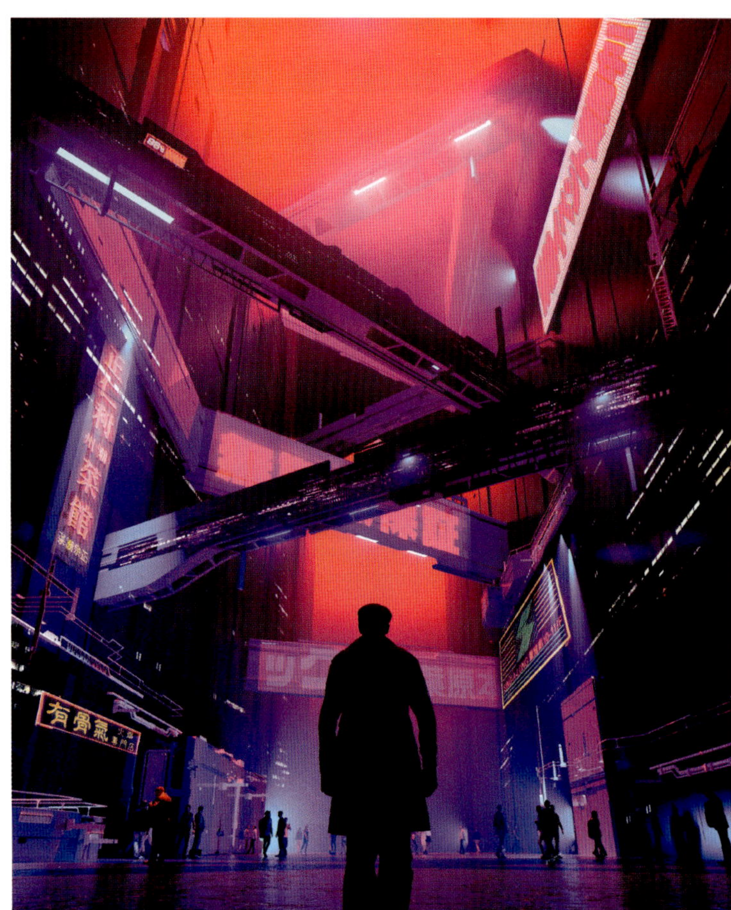

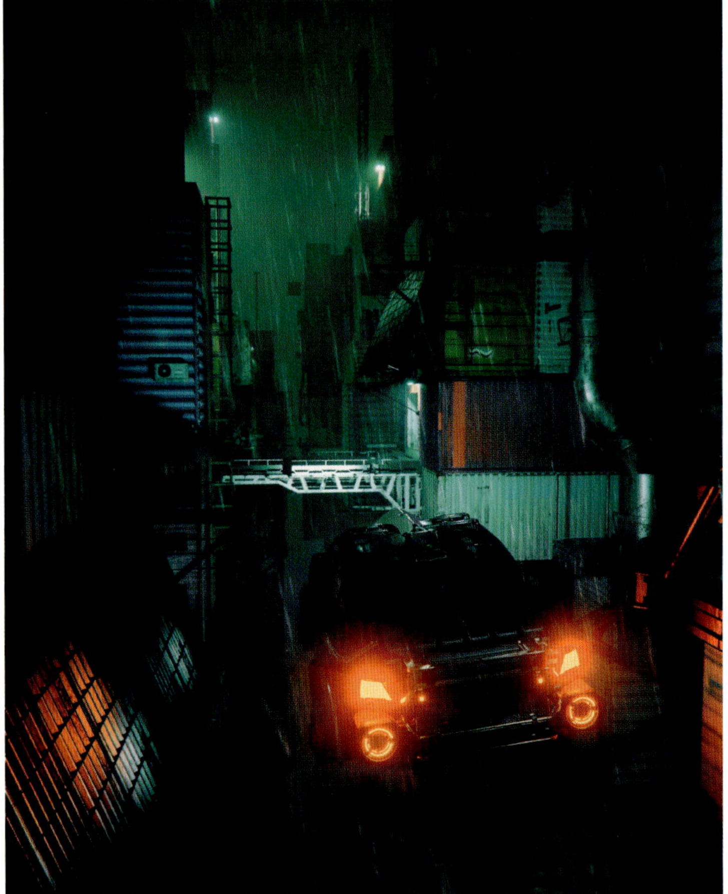

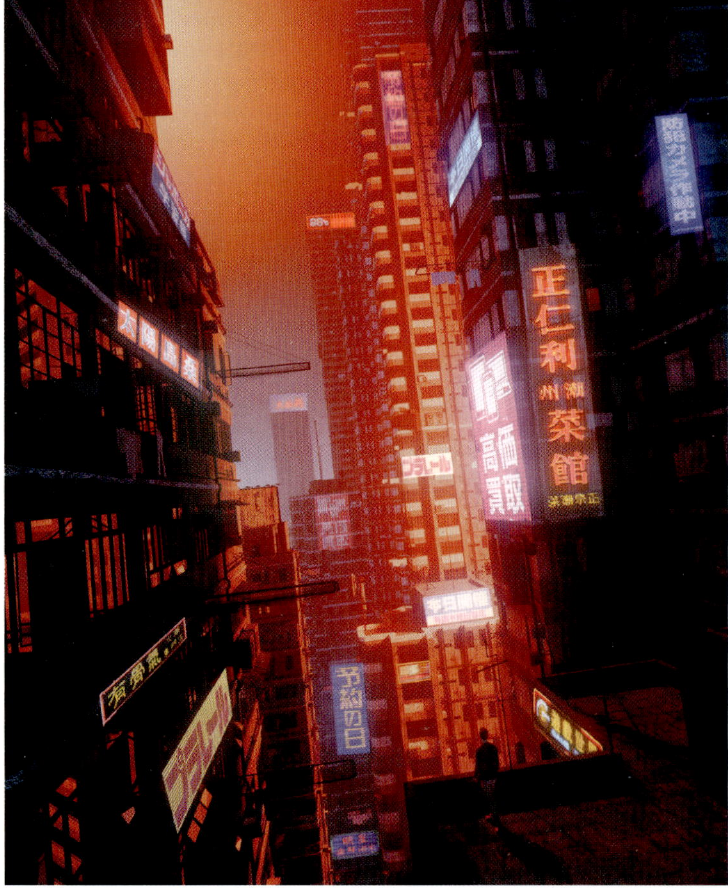

TOP LEFT
TRANSIT LABOR
11.17.2018

TOP RIGHT
MAX RADAR
06.10.2018

BOTTOM LEFT
MIDNIGHT PATROL
09.02.2018

BOTTOM RIGHT
SUPERDIVIDE.4
07.26.2018

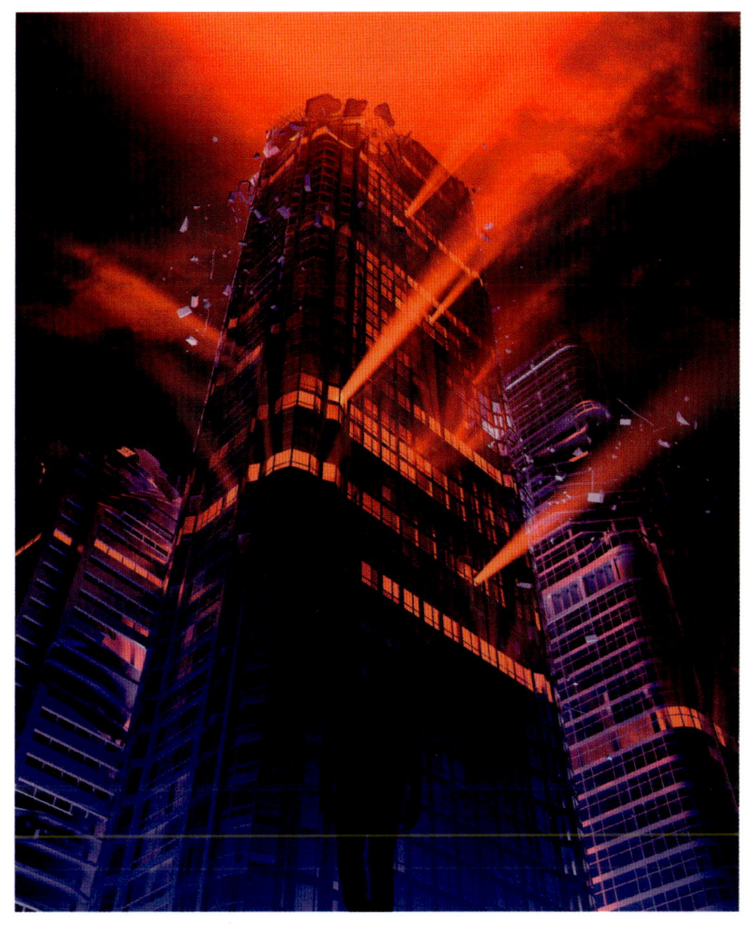

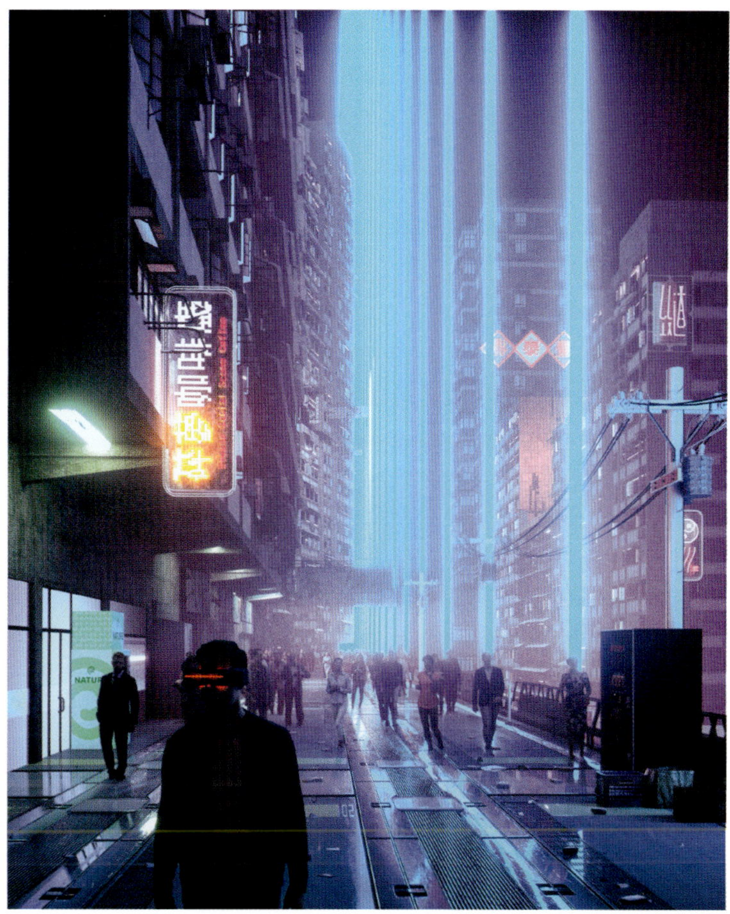

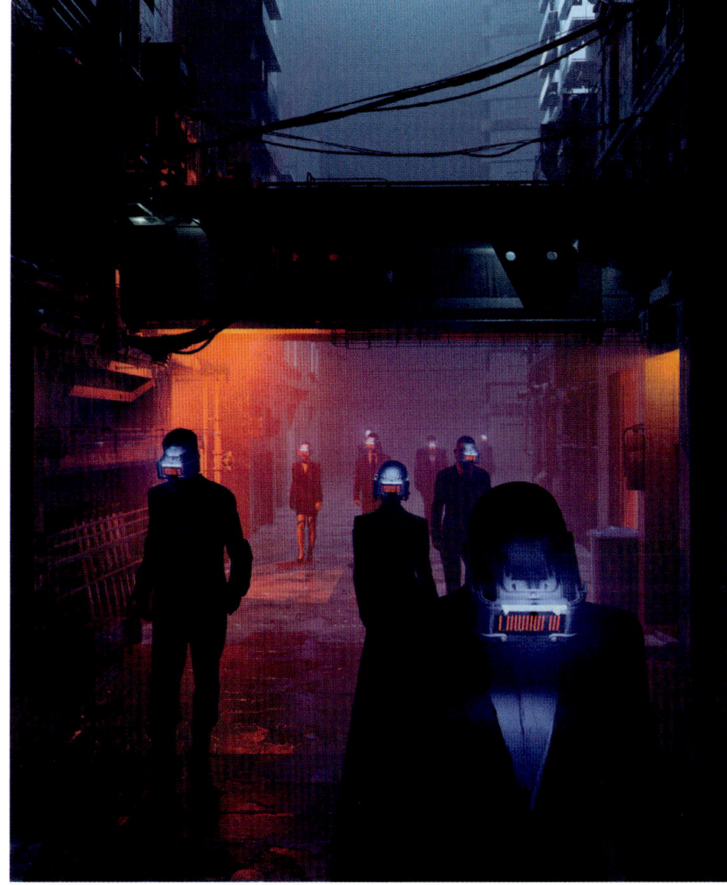

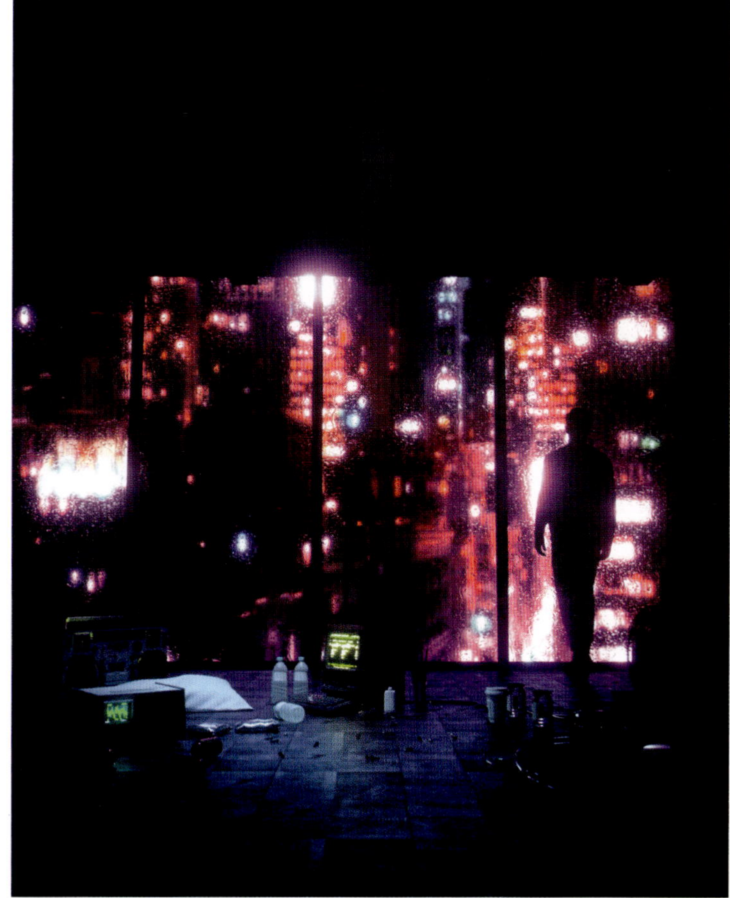

TOP LEFT
RED POWER
06.28.2018

TOP RIGHT
NEONDIVIDE
08.14.2018

BOTTOM LEFT
MOVE FORWARD
01.01.2018

BOTTOM RIGHT
VAPOR TRAIL
01.21.2018

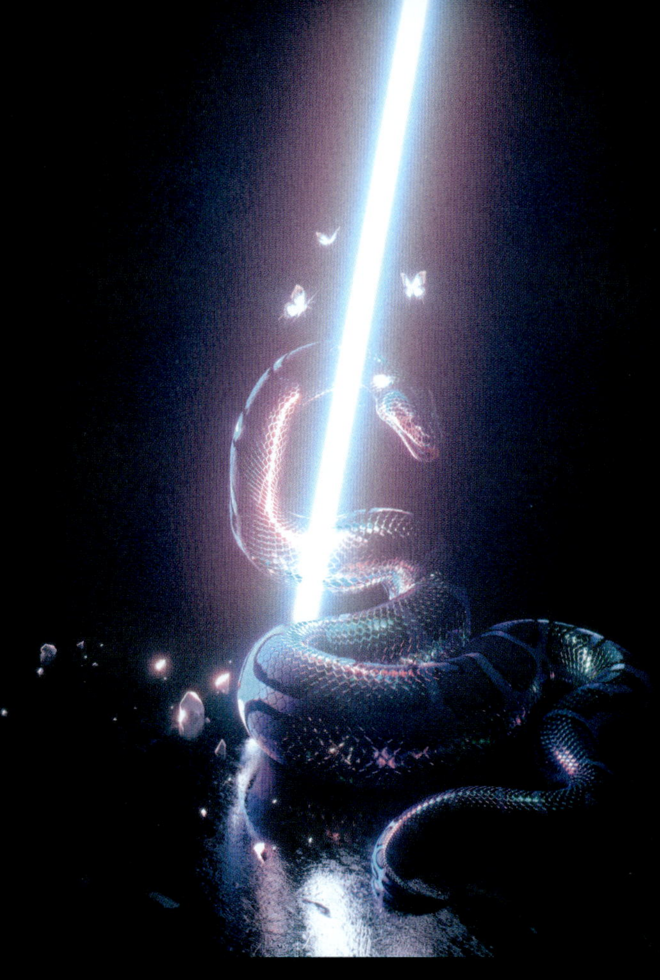

LEFT

THIN WHITE LINE
12.17.2018

OPPOSITE PAGE

HARD RESET
05.16.2018

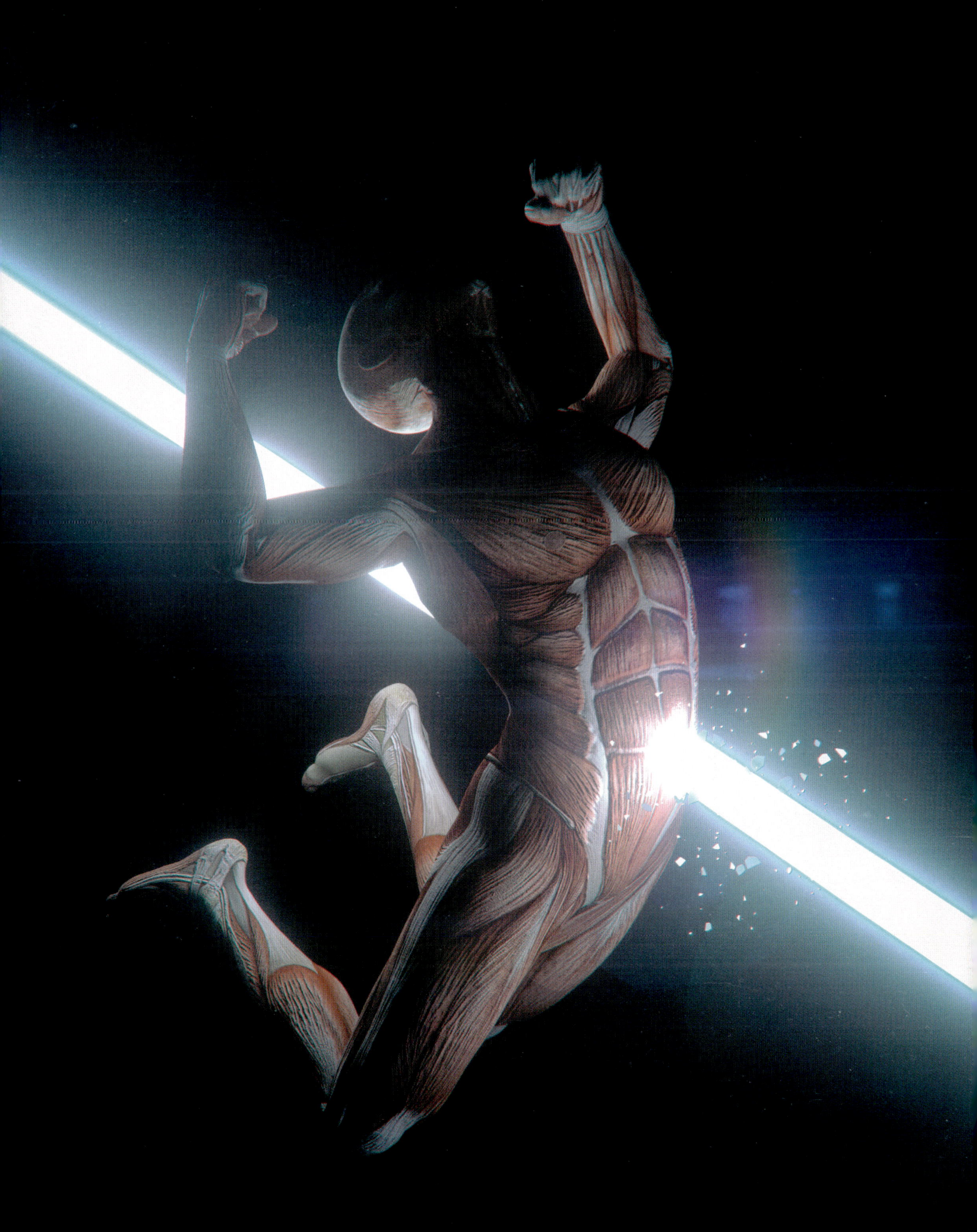

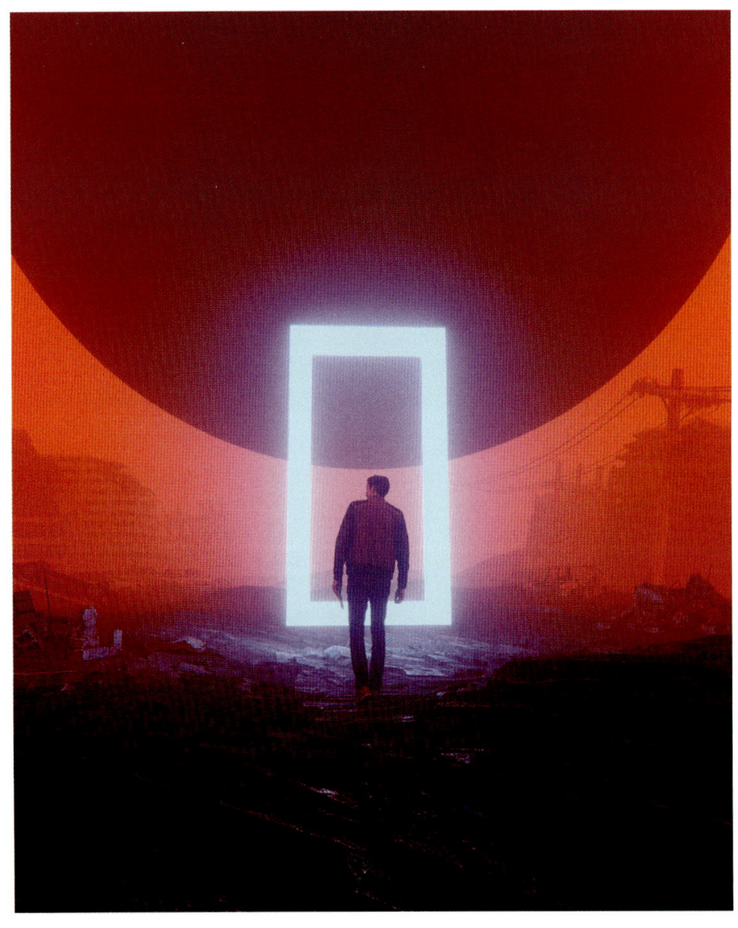

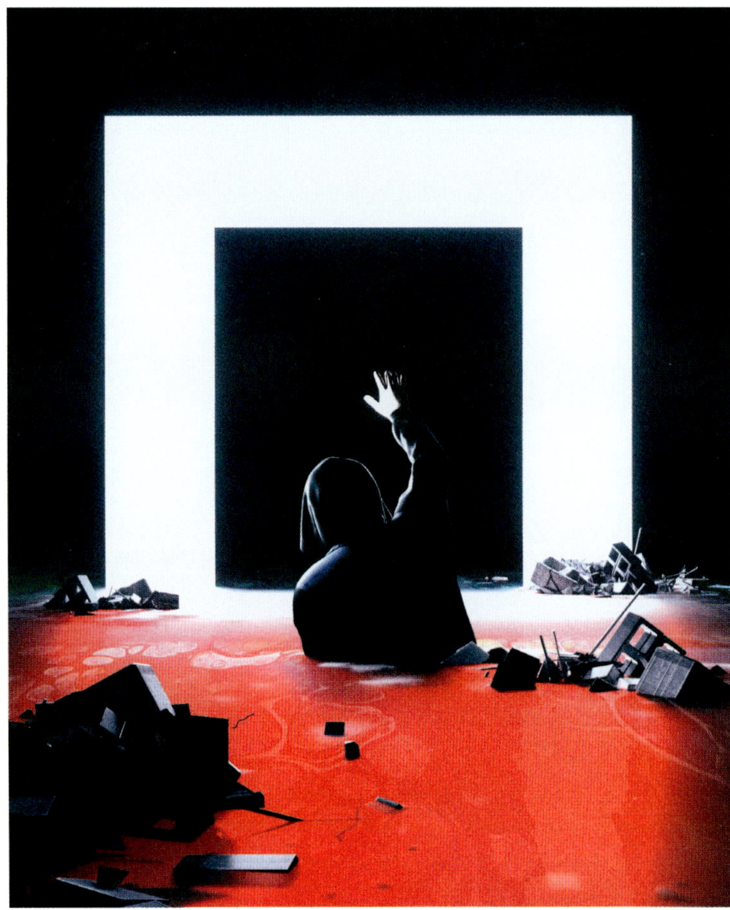

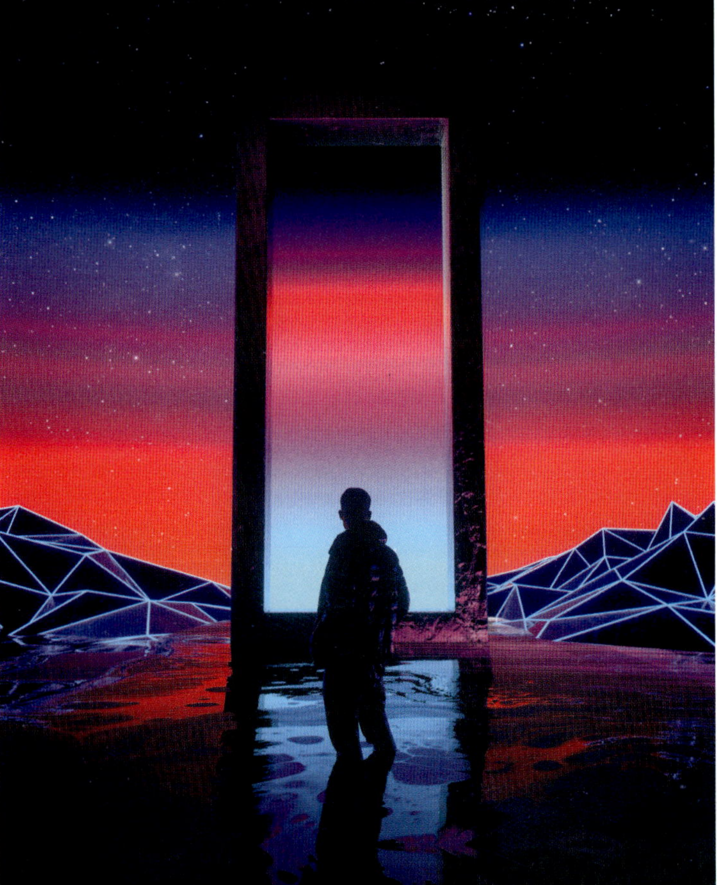

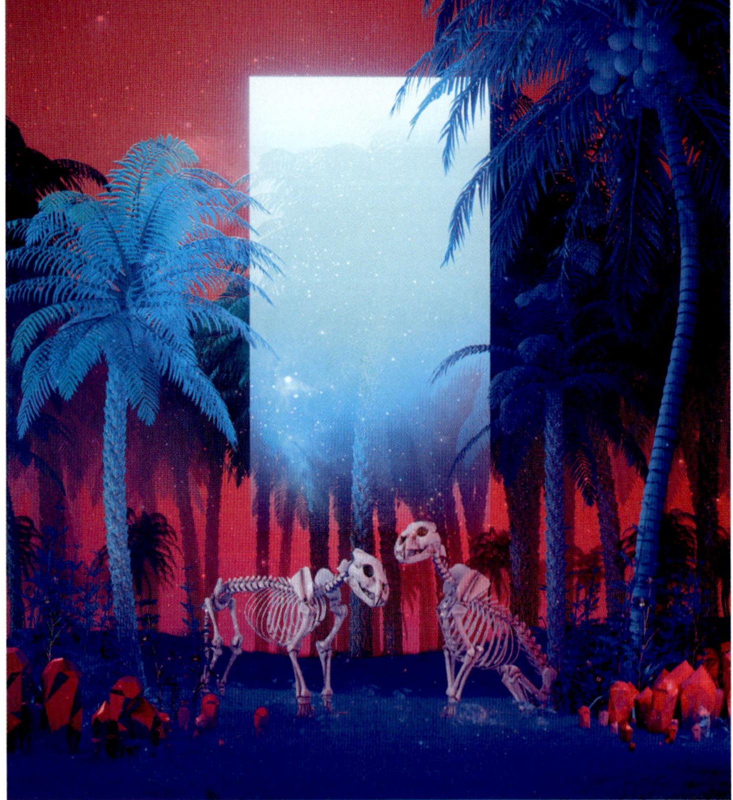

TOP LEFT
INFINITE LOOP
08.06.2018

TOP RIGHT
PADDLE OUT
08.26.2018

BOTTOM LEFT
WORKSPACE
12.07.2018

BOTTOM RIGHT
OLD GUARD
03.05.2018

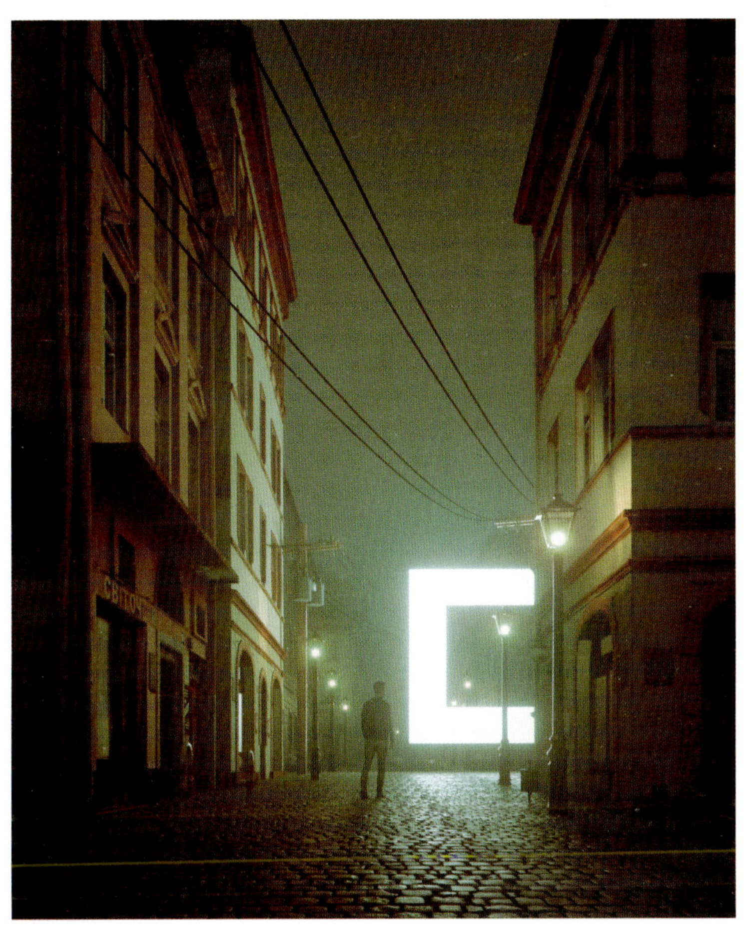

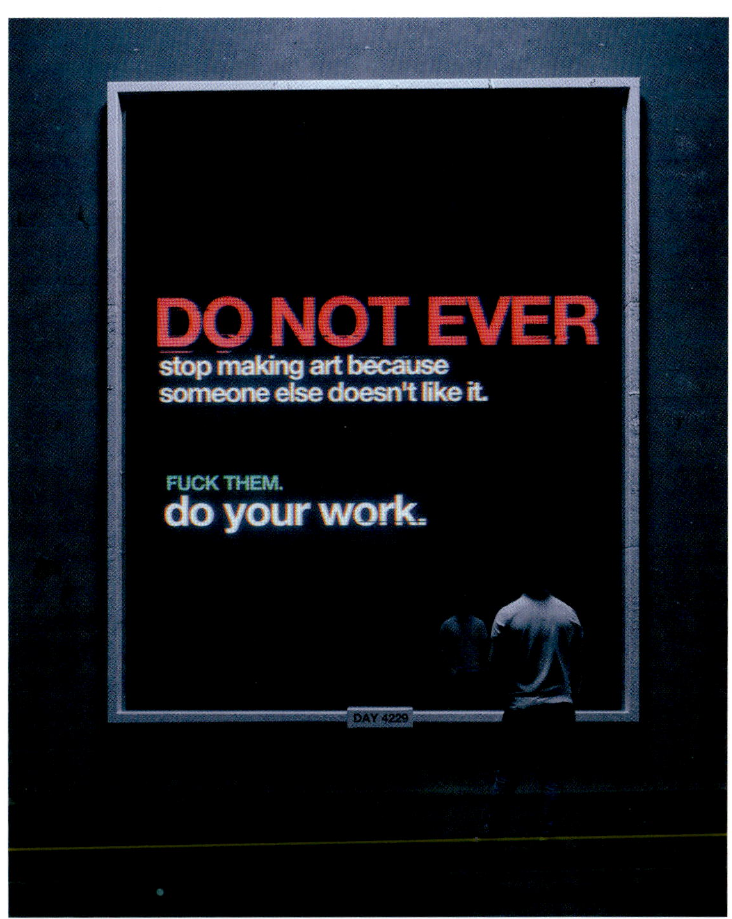

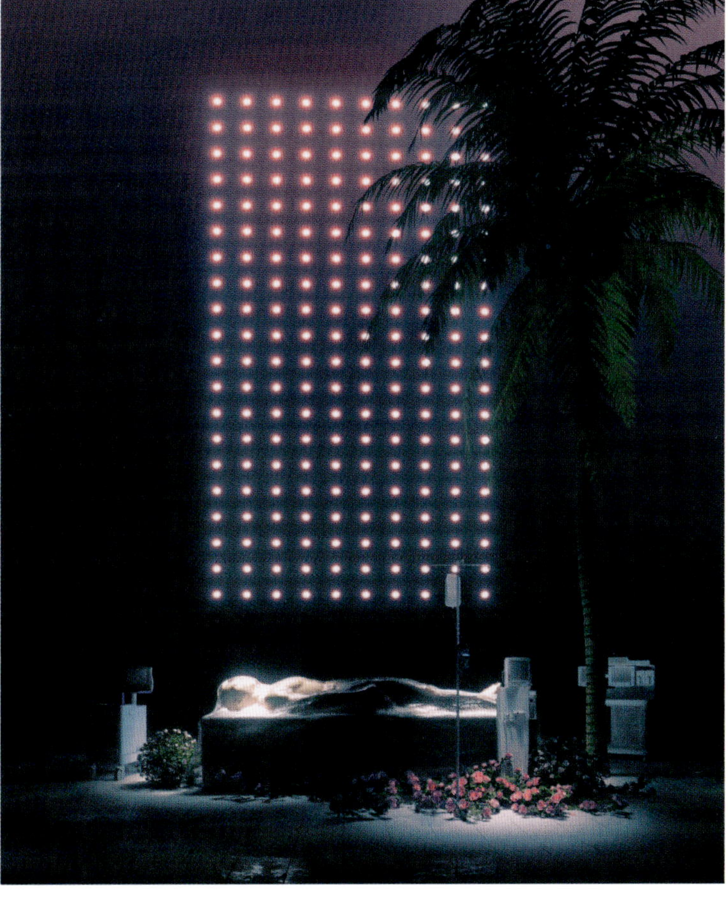

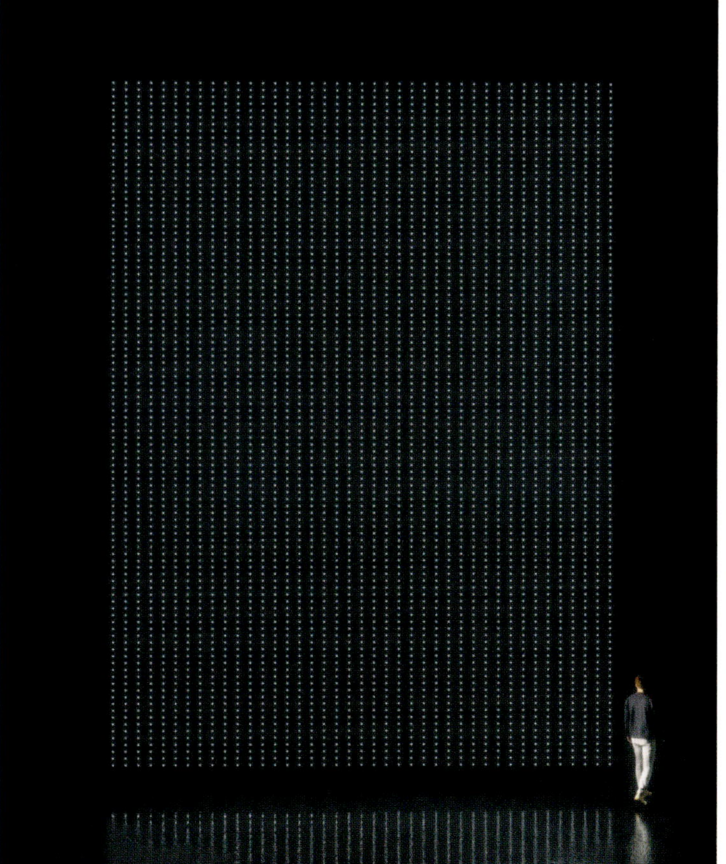

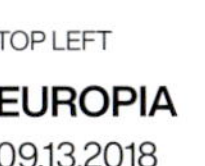

TOP LEFT

EUROPIA
09.13.2018

TOP RIGHT

PLEASE SHARE
11.28.2018

BOTTOM LEFT

SUPER VACATION
02.12.2018

BOTTOM RIGHT

FOUR THOUSAND DAYS
04.13.2018

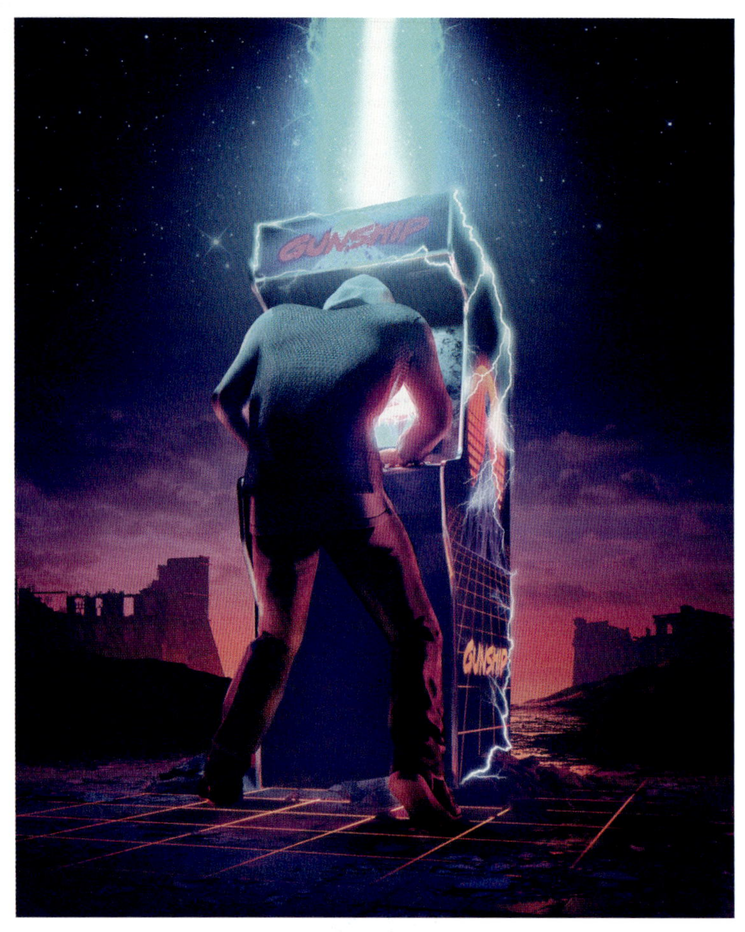

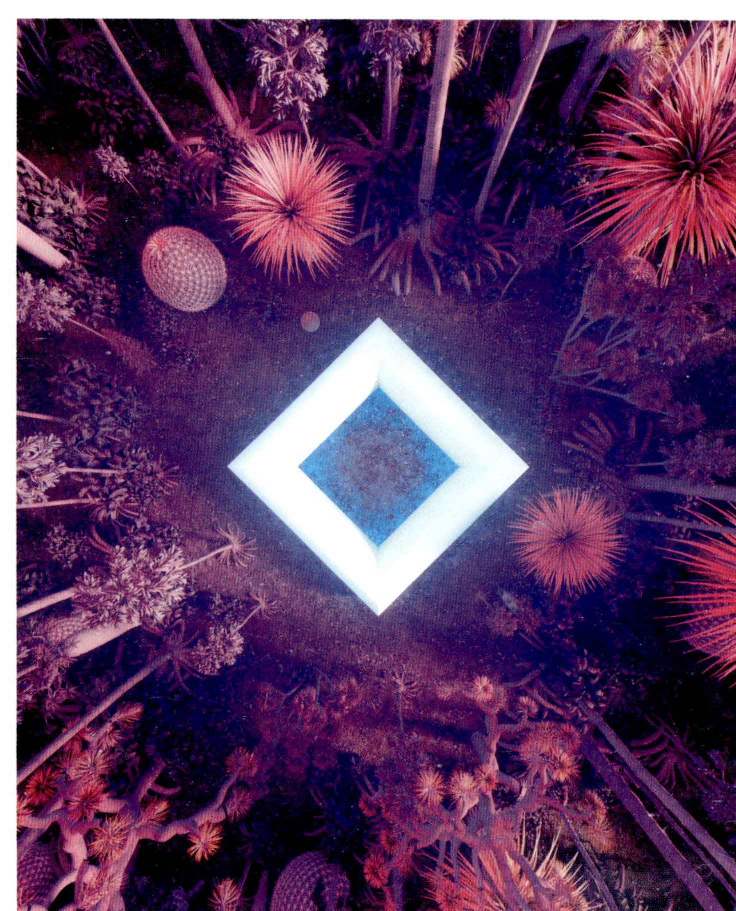

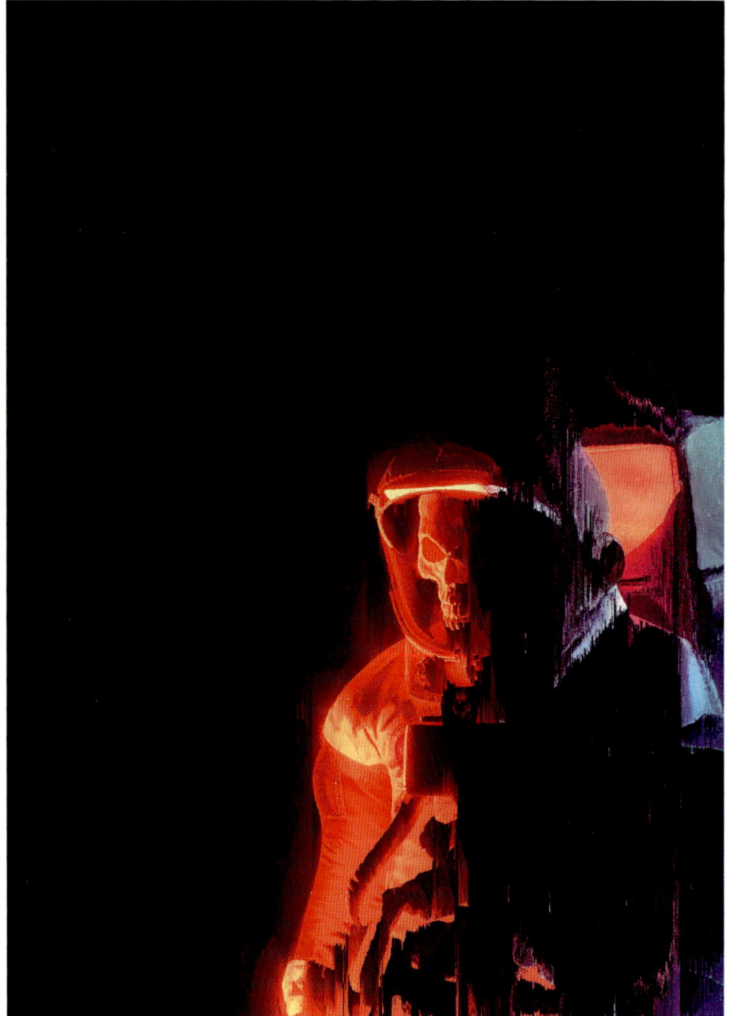

TOP LEFT

GUNSHIP
12.04.2018

TOP RIGHT

PURPSCURPP
03.11.2018

BOTTOM

DOWNLOAD ETERNITY
09.04.2018

OPPOSITE PAGE

DEEP SPACE
06.14.2018

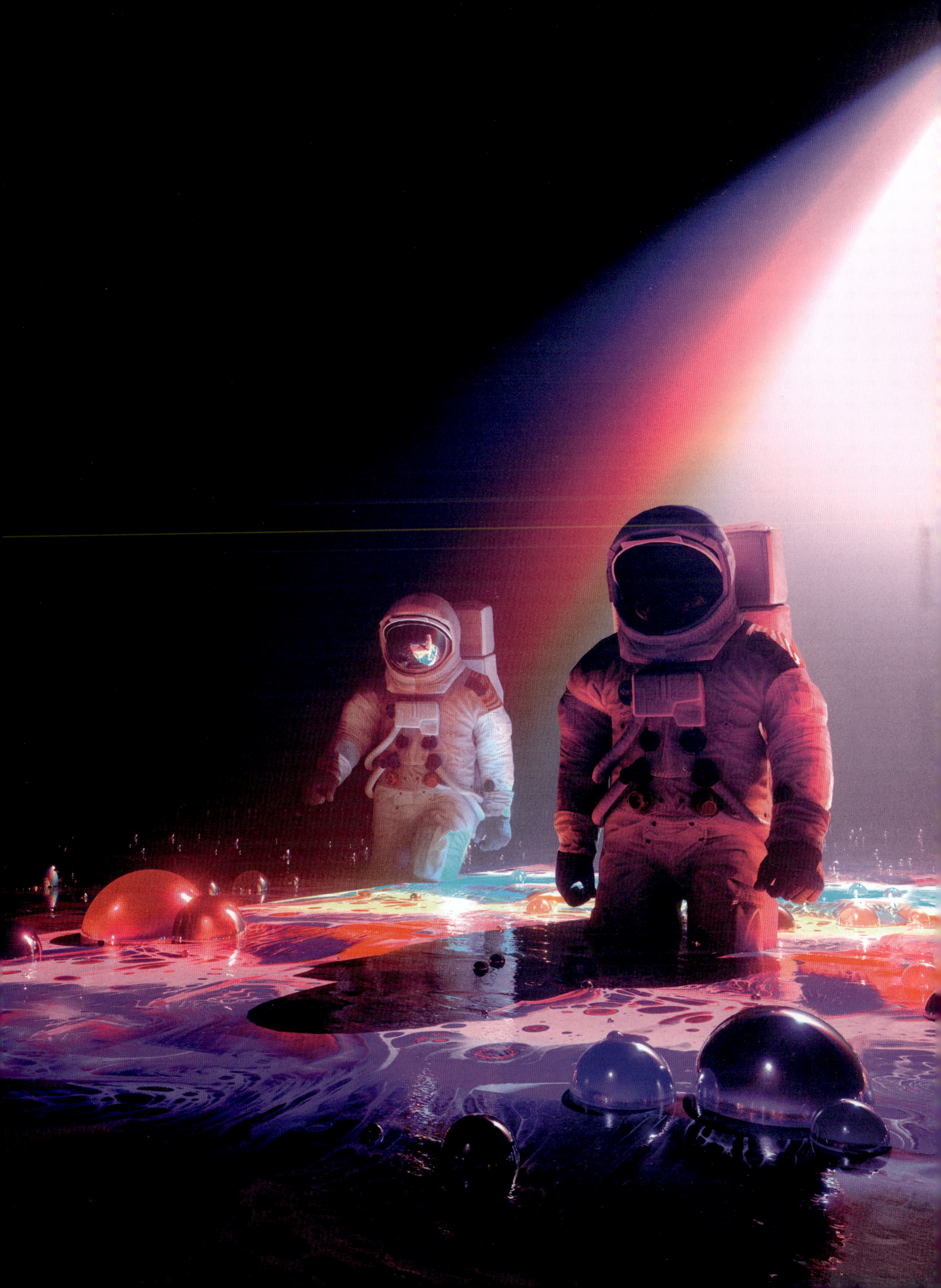

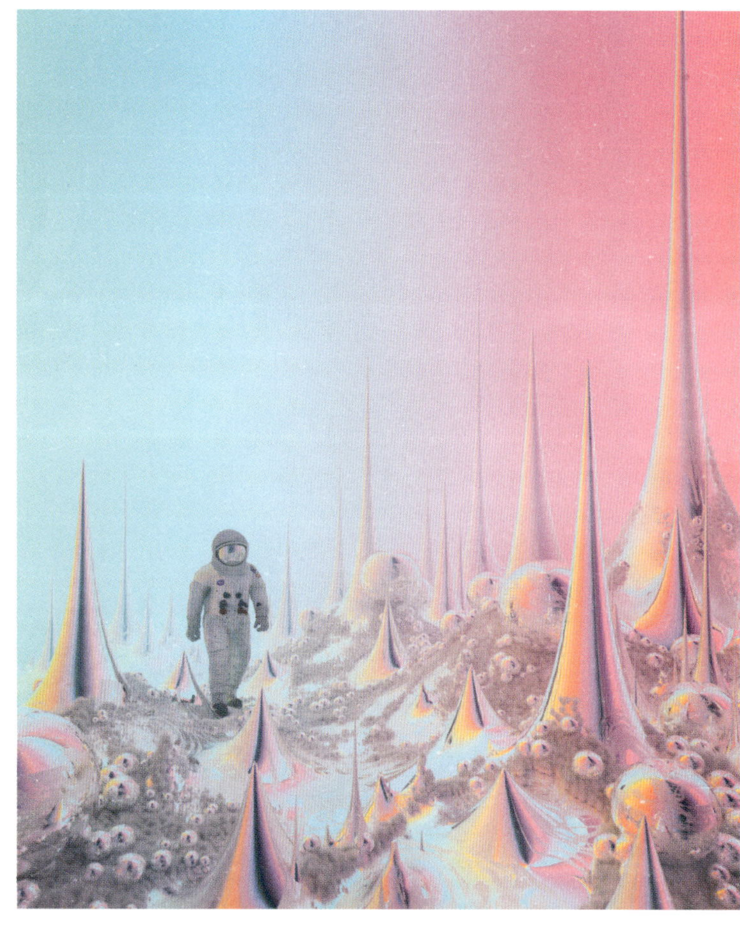

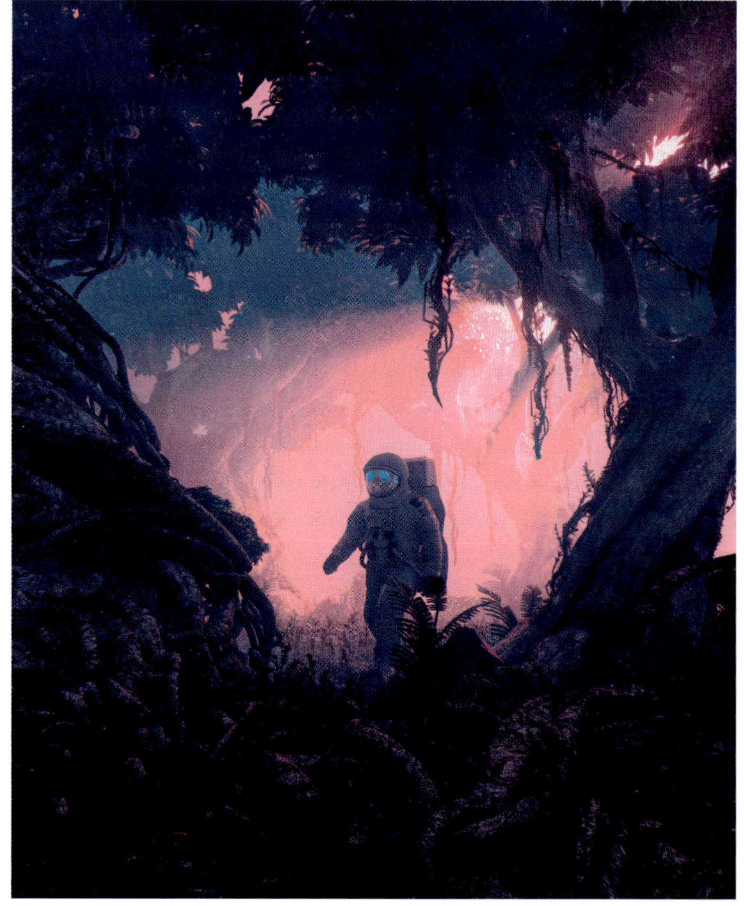

TOP

BRIGHT SIDE OF THE MOON
08.20.2018

BOTTOM

WRONG PLANET
08.30.2018

OPPOSITE PAGE, TOP LEFT

ATMOSPHERIC REENTRY
09.14.2018

OPPOSITE PAGE, TOP RIGHT

SPACE APE
08.23.2018

OPPOSITE PAGE, BOTTOM LEFT

GLAX.9
09.01.2018

OPPOSITE PAGE, BOTTOM RIGHT

INTERNATIONAL APE STATION
12.05.2018

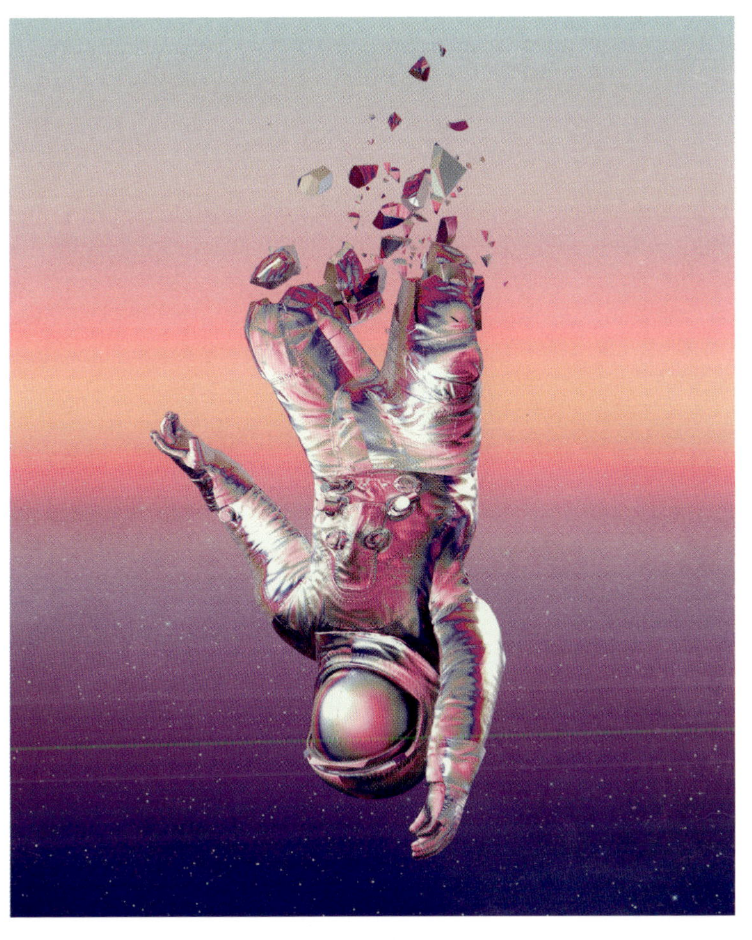

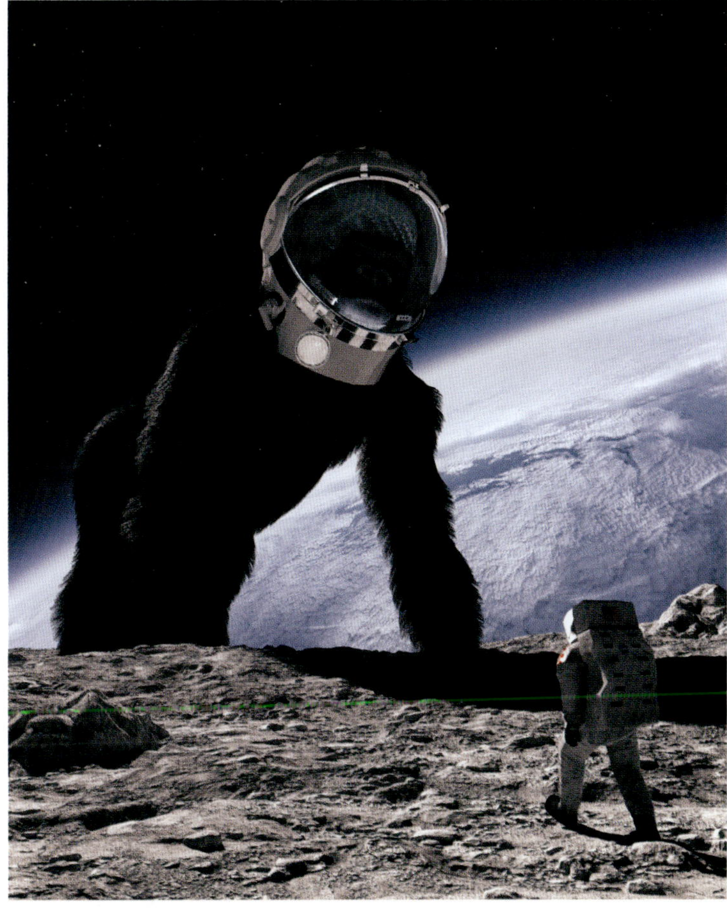

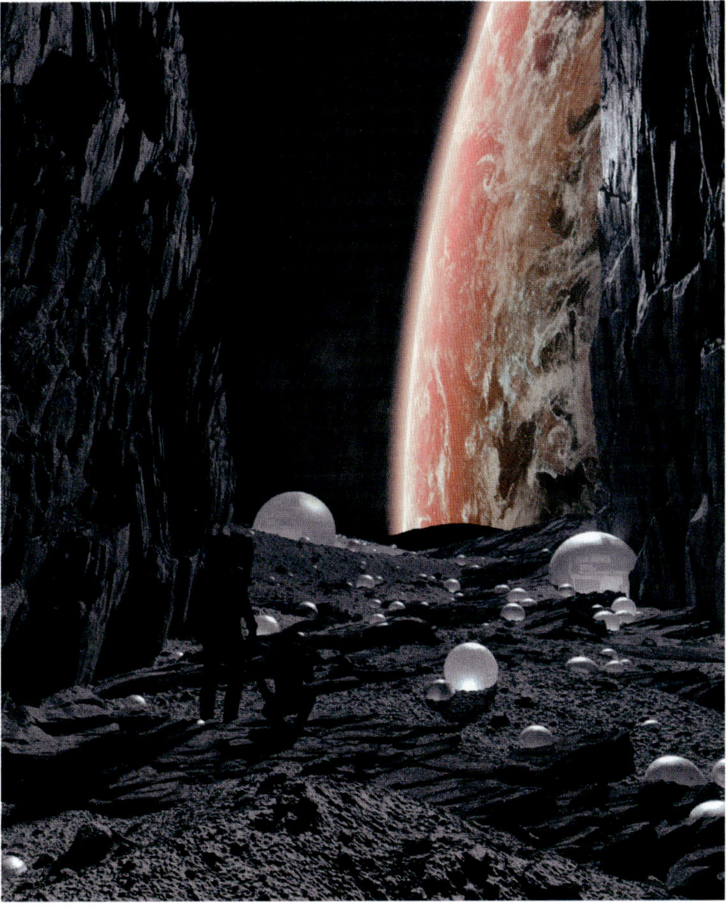

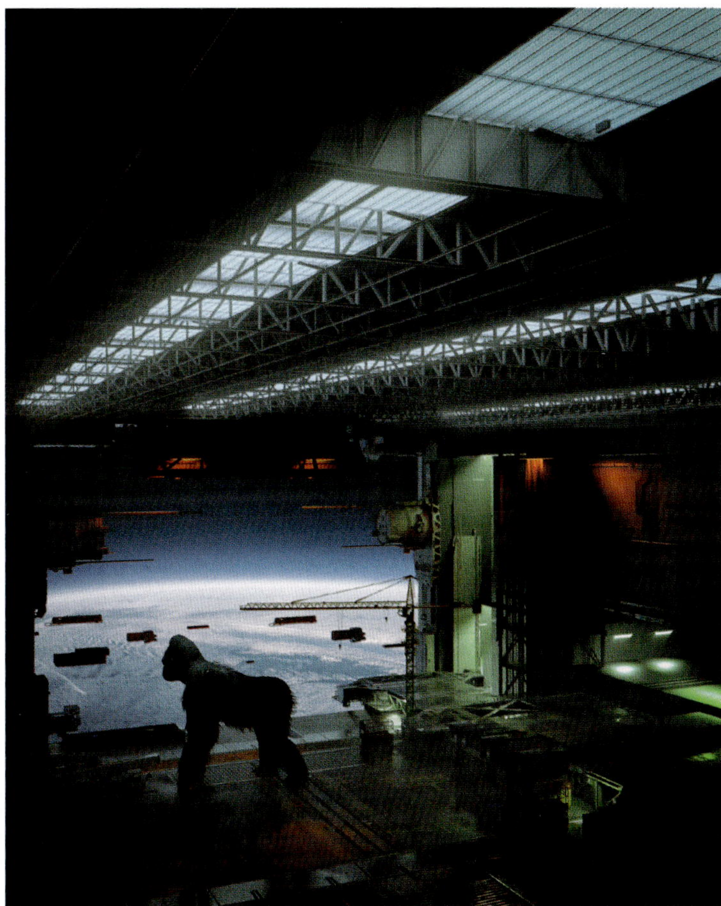

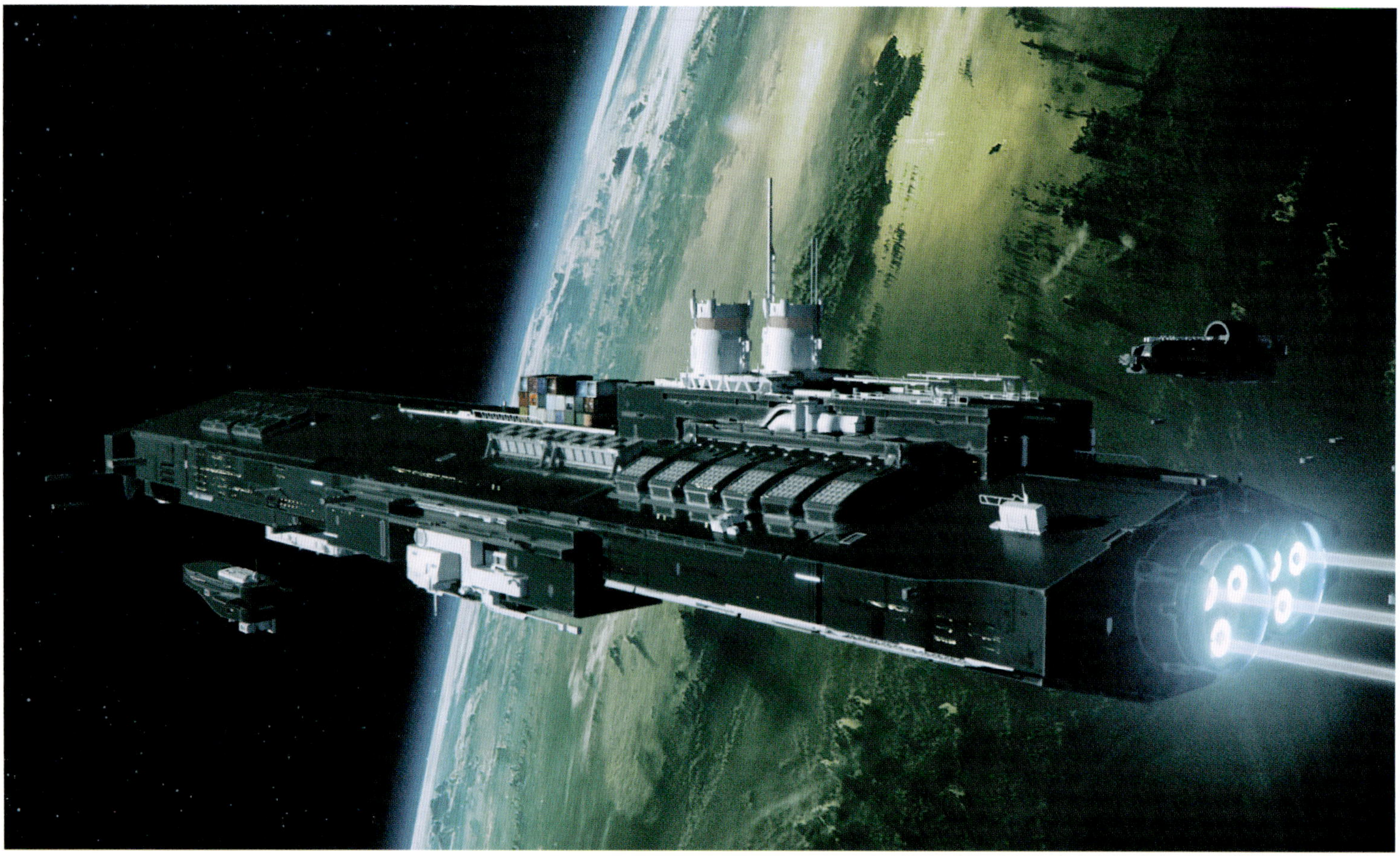

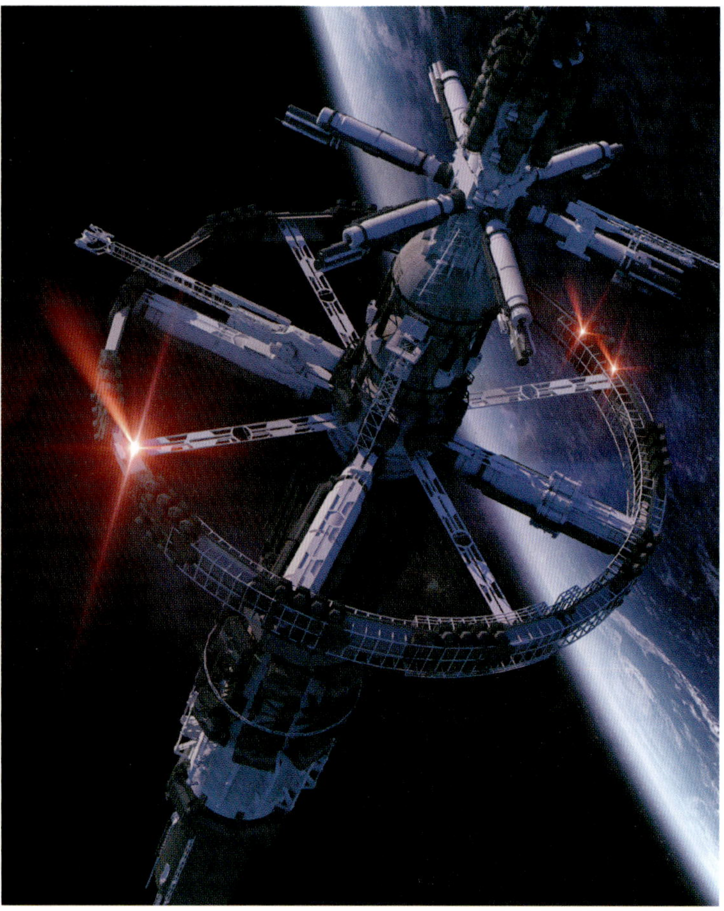

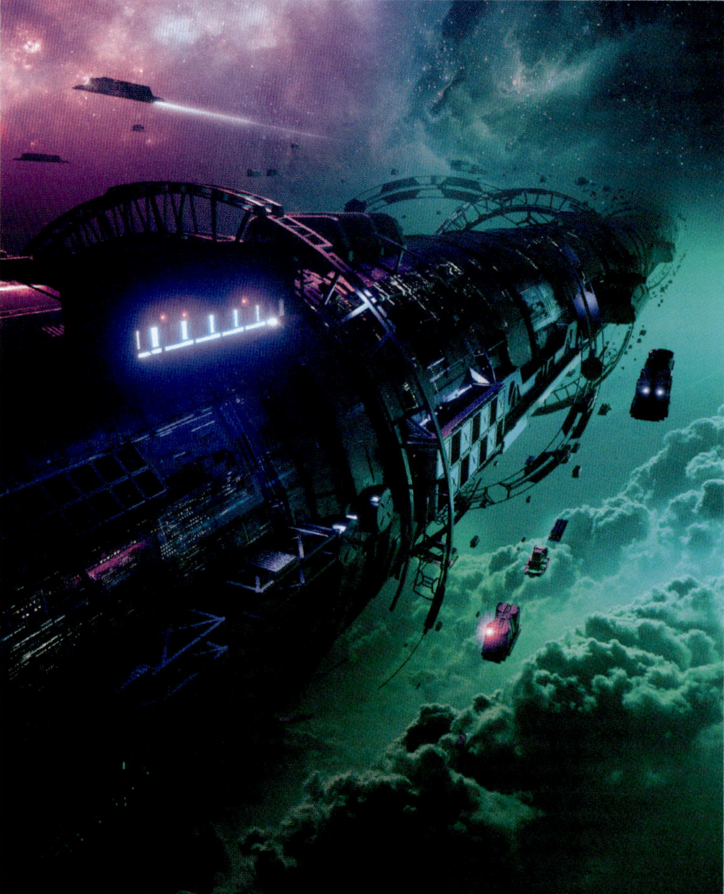

TOP

STATION-Q89
10.23.2018

BOTTOM LEFT

HYPERSTILL
08.12.2018

BOTTOM RIGHT

IONIZED GAS EXTRACTION
11.07.2018

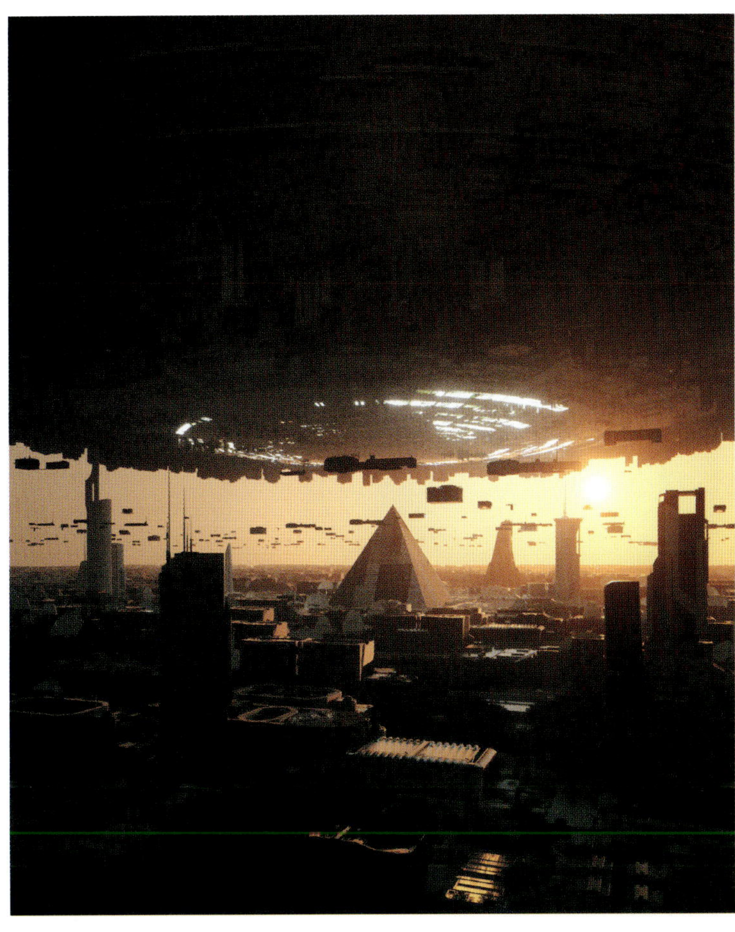

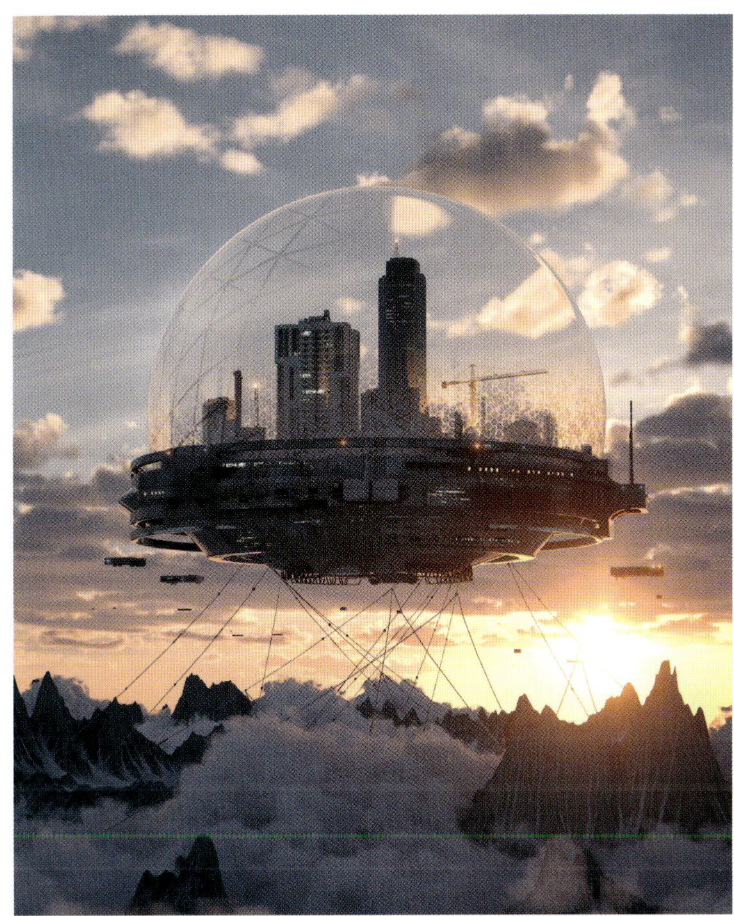

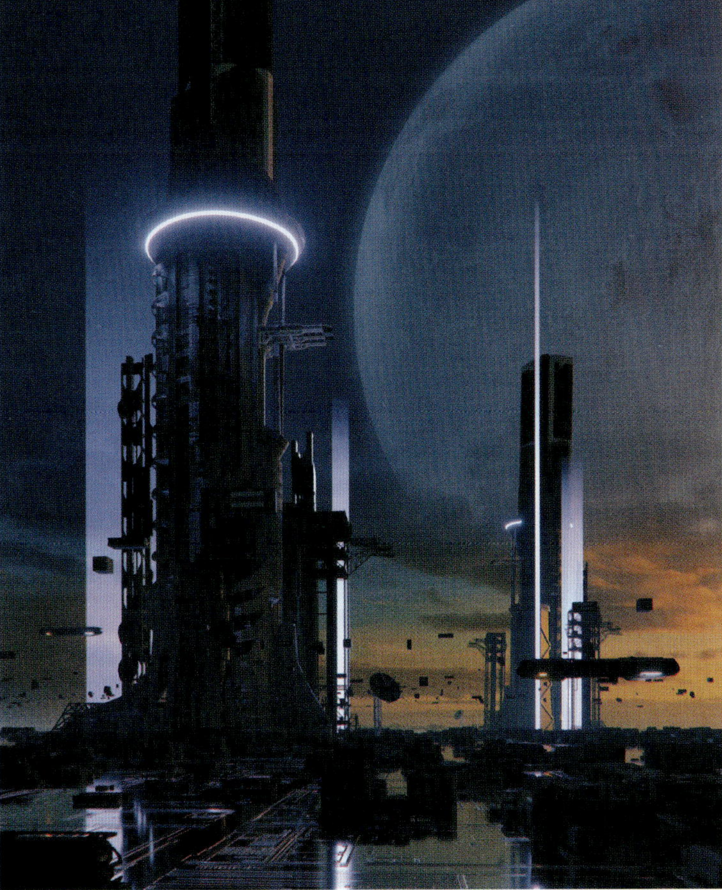

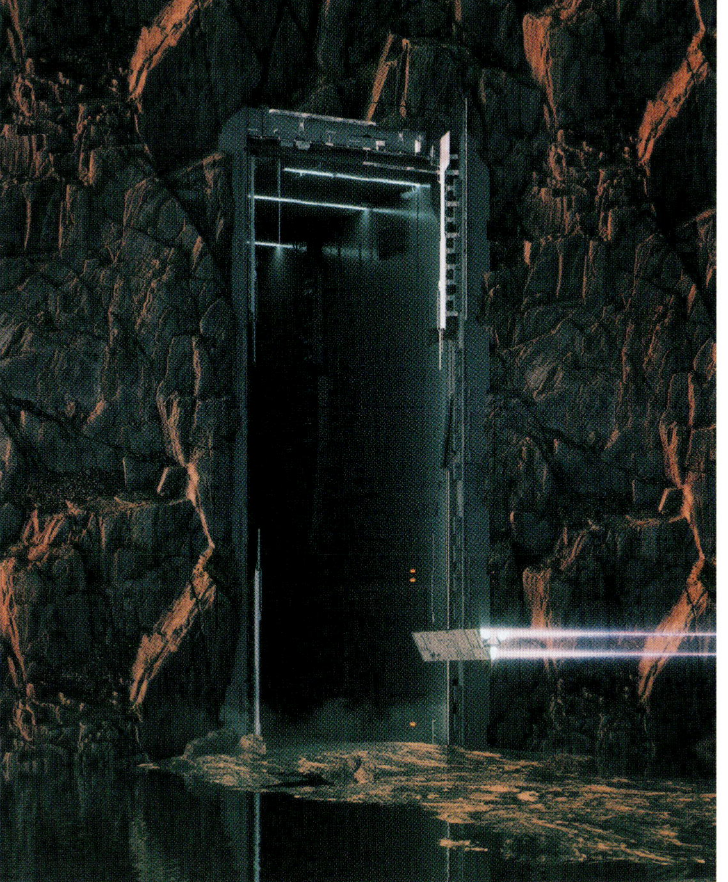

TOP LEFT

SUPERCLOUD
10.04.2018

TOP RIGHT

ELEVATION.1
11.04.2018

BOTTOM LEFT

PRE-DAWN HUMANITY
10.13.2018

BOTTOM RIGHT

SUB TERRAIN
10.11.2018

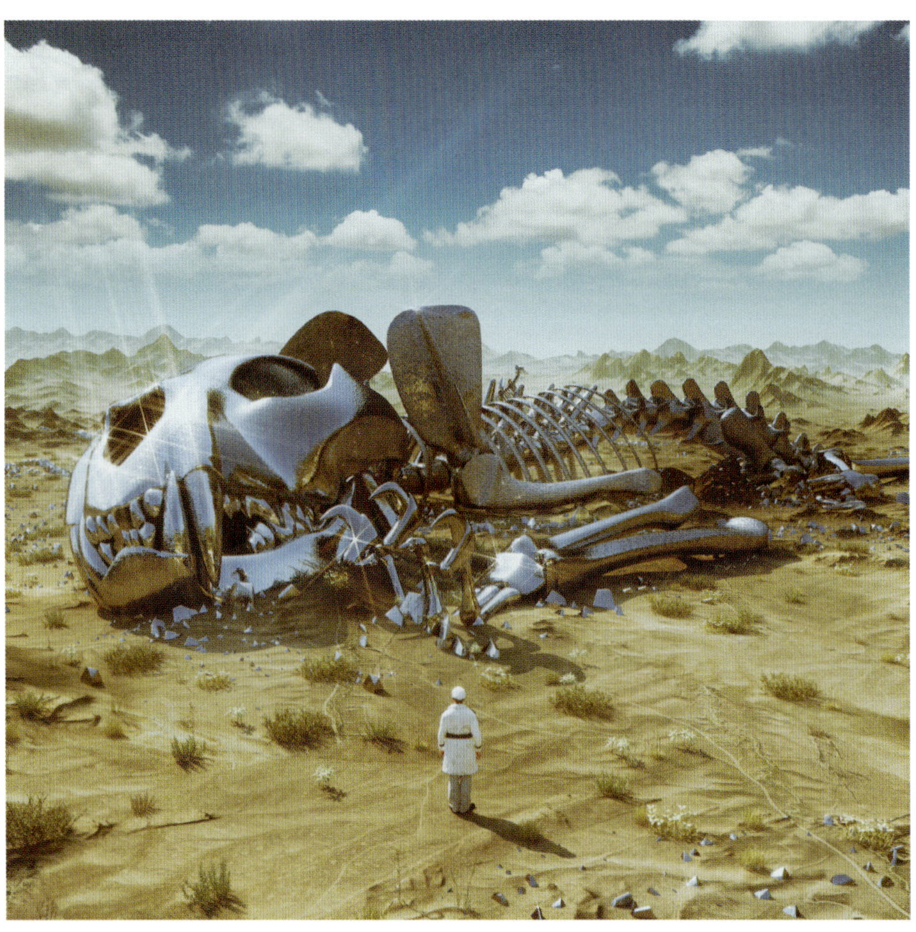

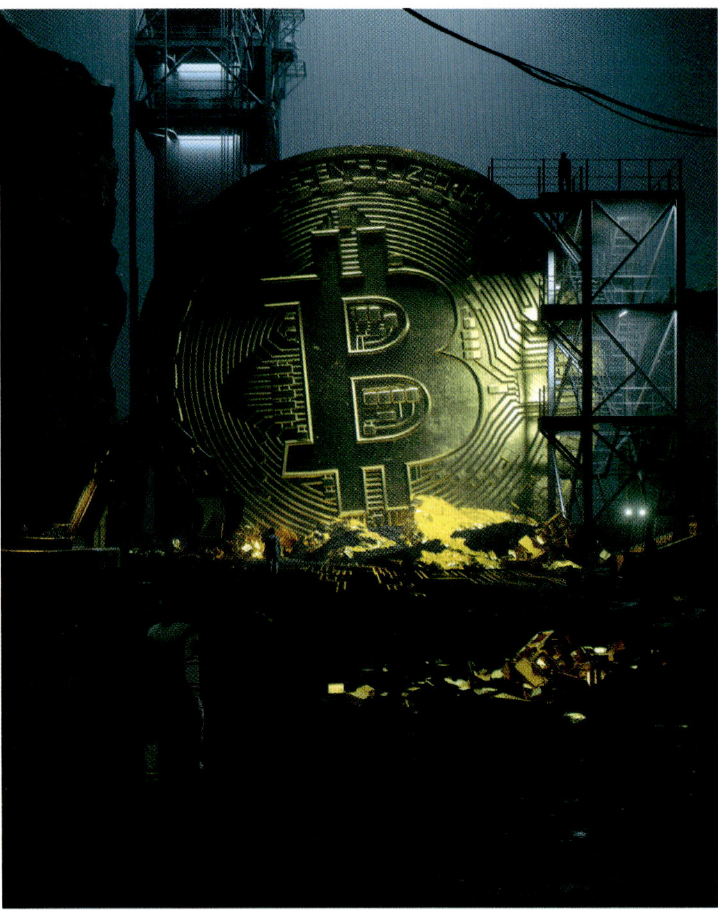

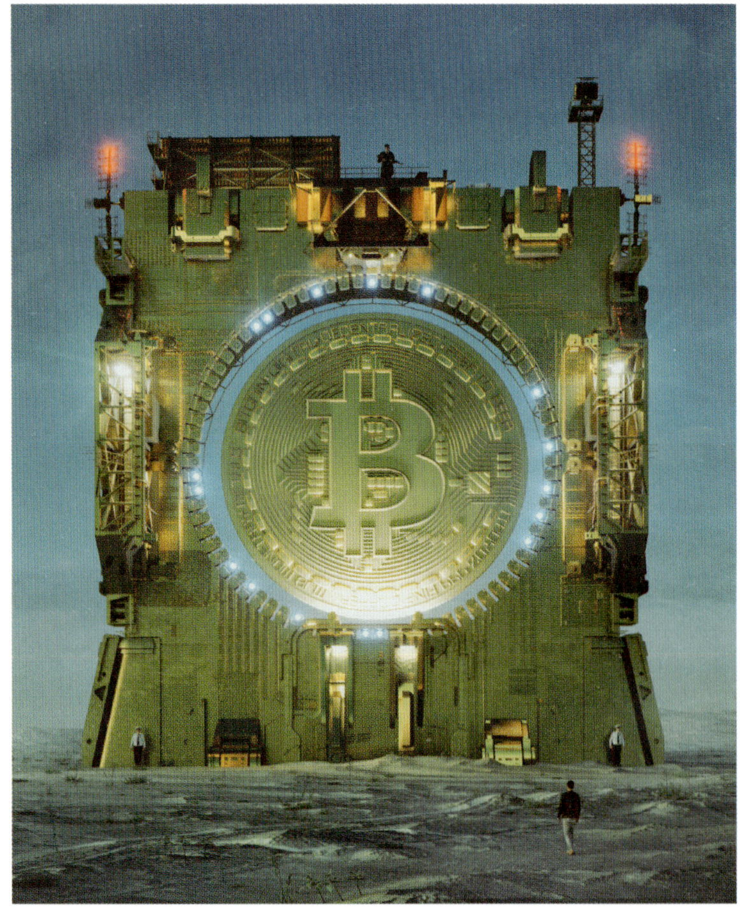

TOP

CHROME EXTINCTION
05.08.2018

BOTTOM LEFT

SUPER EXTRACTION
01.08.2018

BOTTOM RIGHT

COIN ZERO
01.10.2018

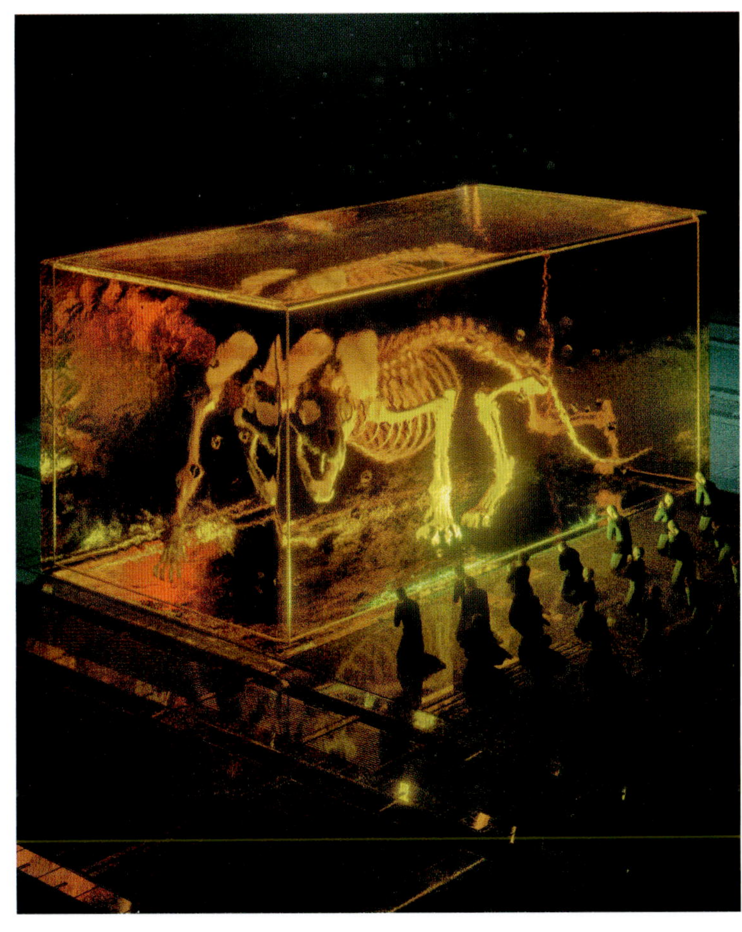

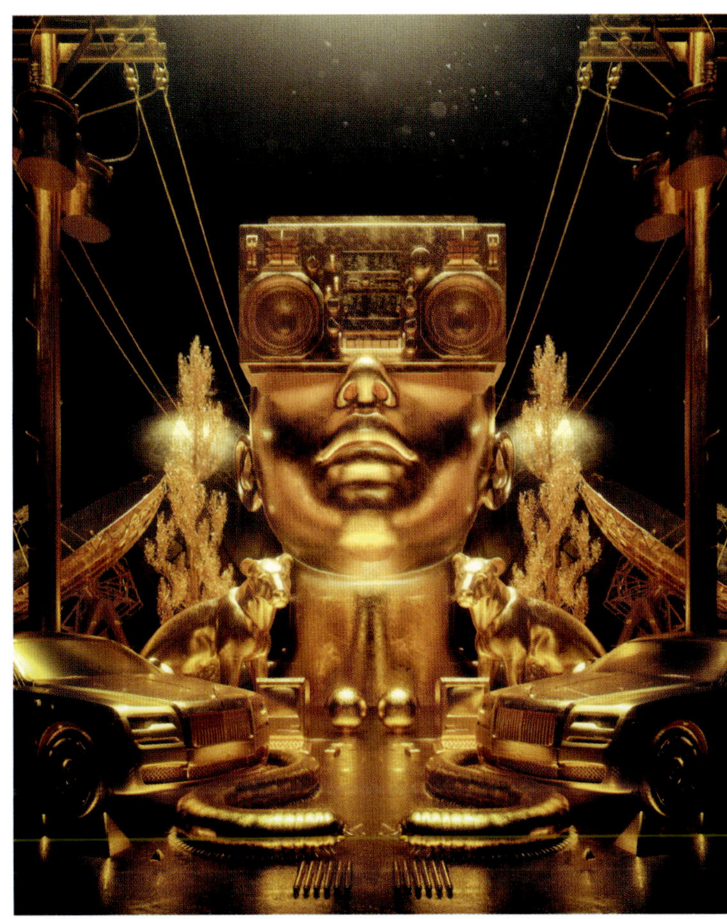

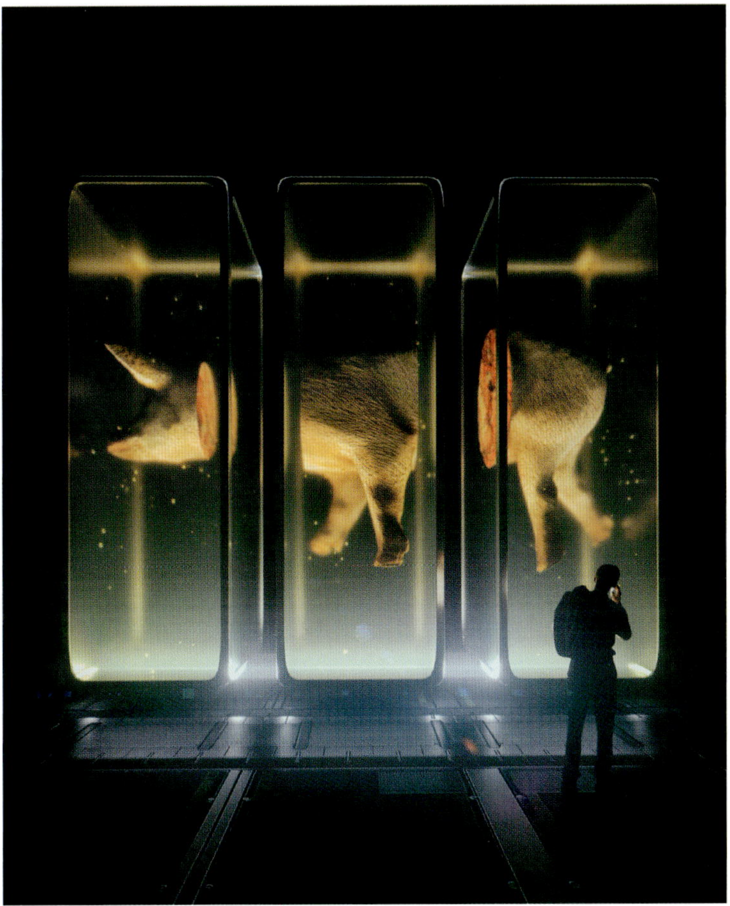

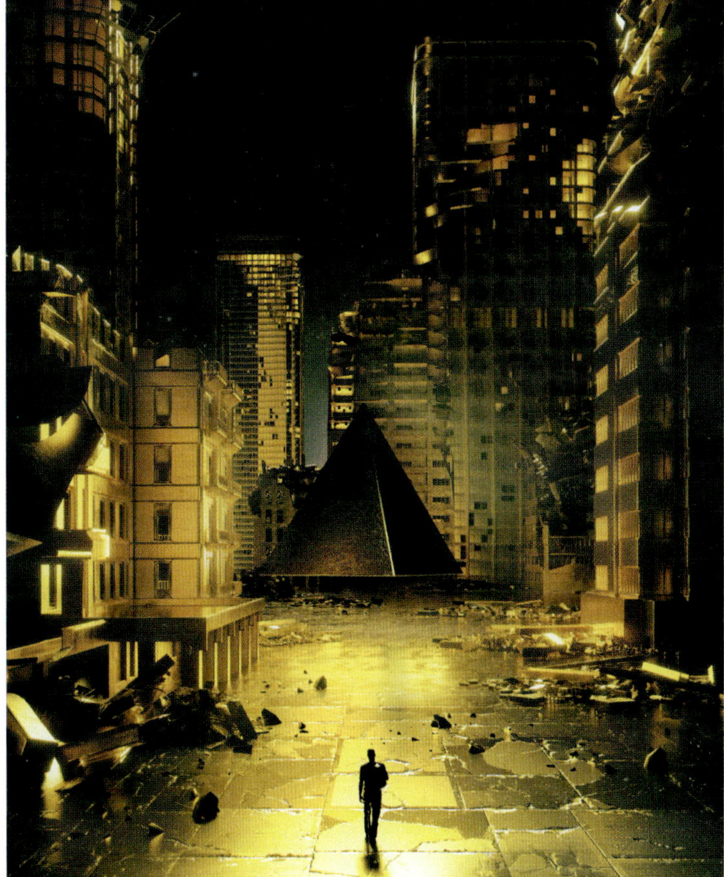

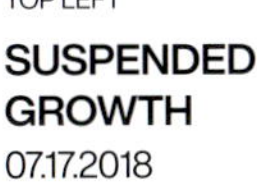

TOP LEFT

SUSPENDED GROWTH

07.17.2018

TOP RIGHT

BUSINESS SYSTEMS

07.18.2018

BOTTOM LEFT

RULE OF THIRDS

05.10.2018

BOTTOM RIGHT

OPULENT DESTRUCT

04.02.2018

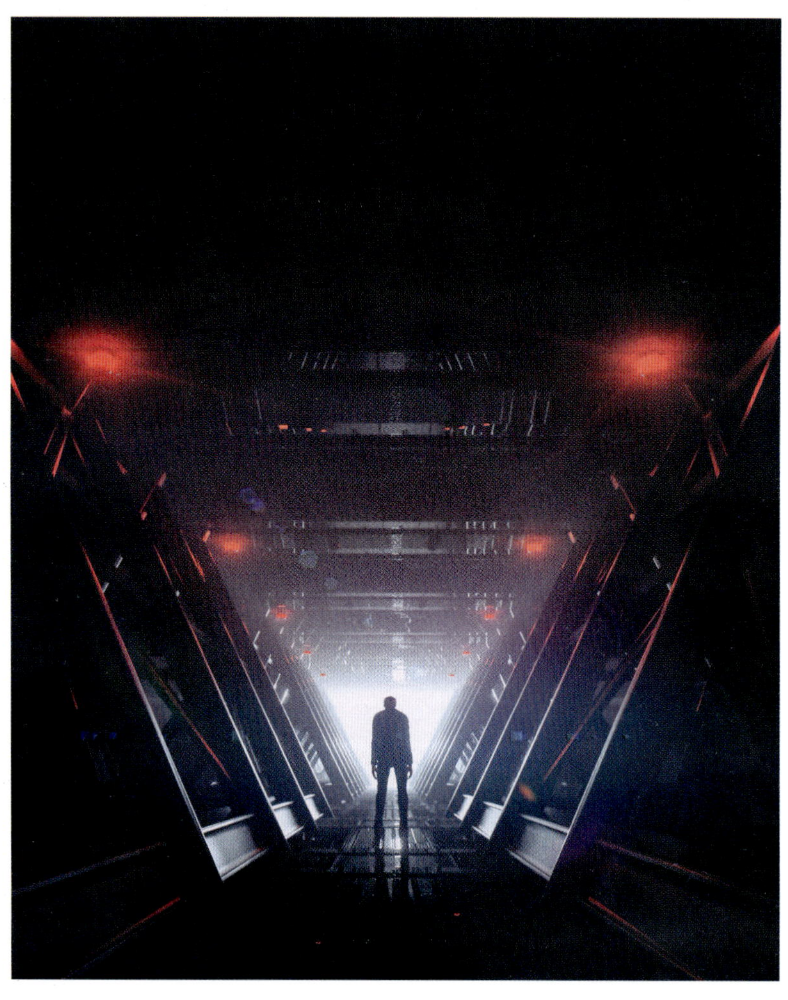

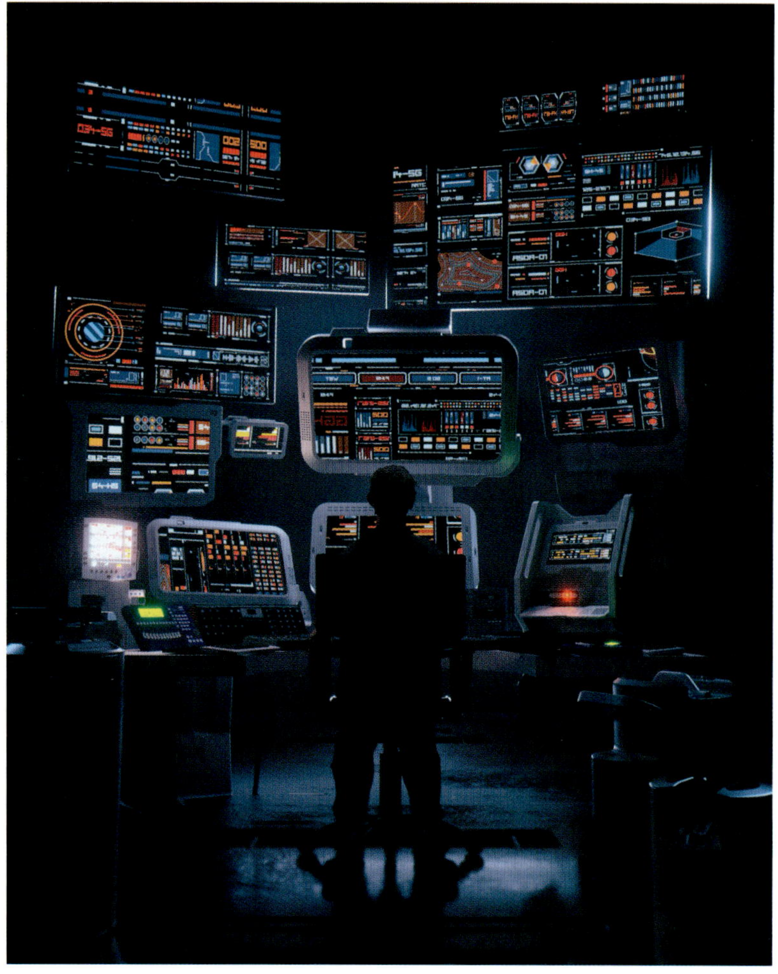

TOP

VOID.SELF

06.23.2018

BOTTOM

AIR LOCKED

06.24.2018

OPPOSITE PAGE

COMFORT ZONE

01.31.2018

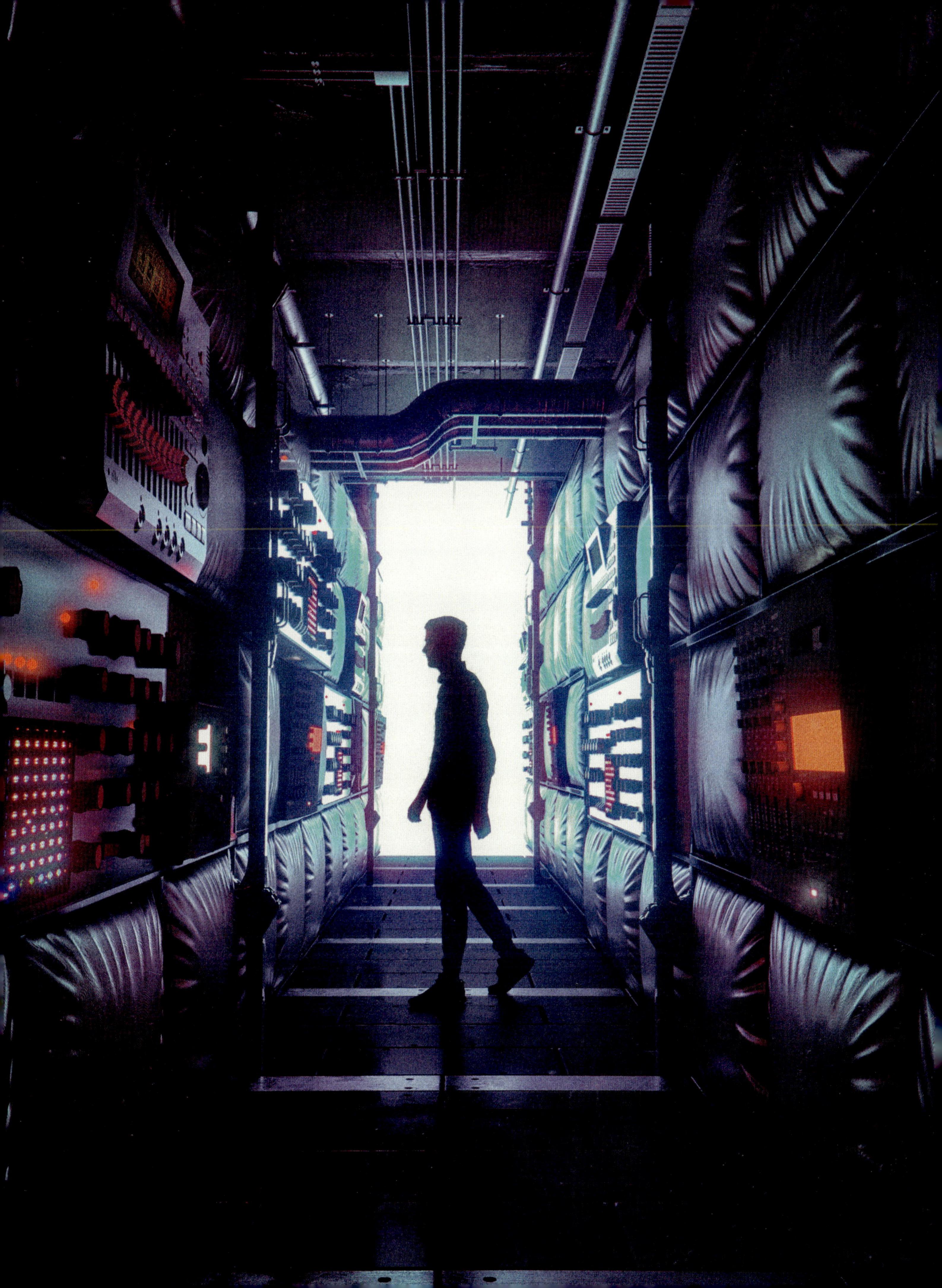

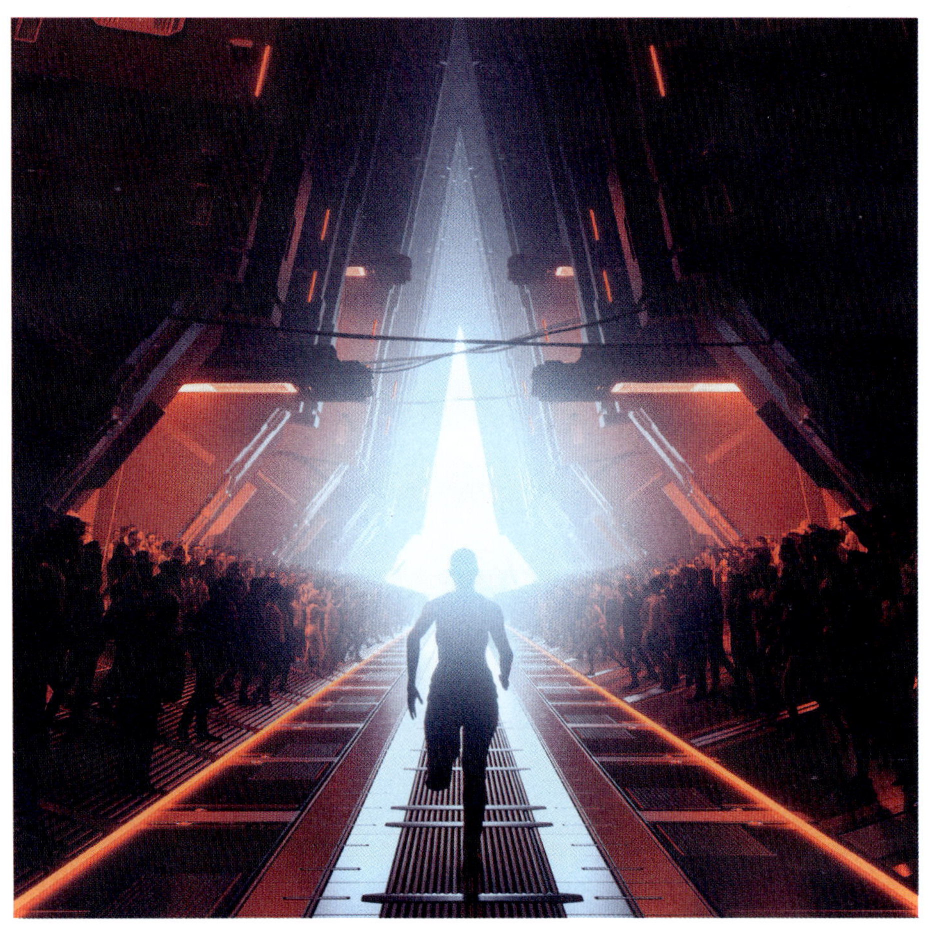

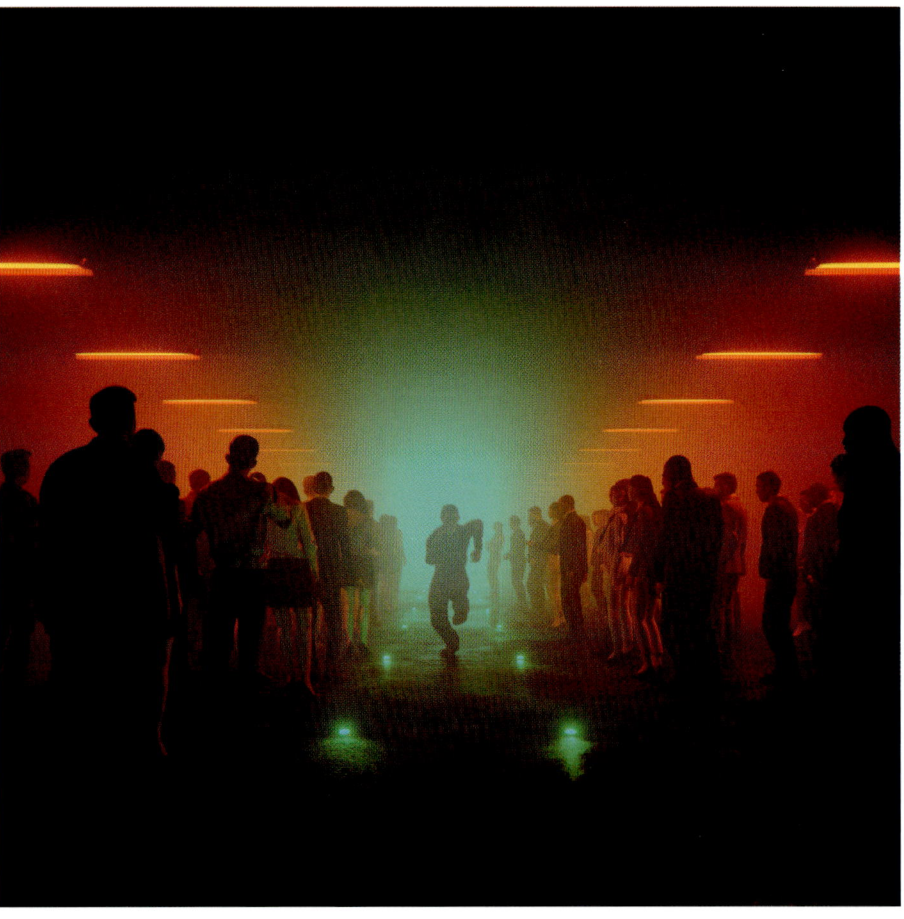

TOP	BOTTOM
NEW SEASON	**RUN**
10.02.2018	01.28.2018

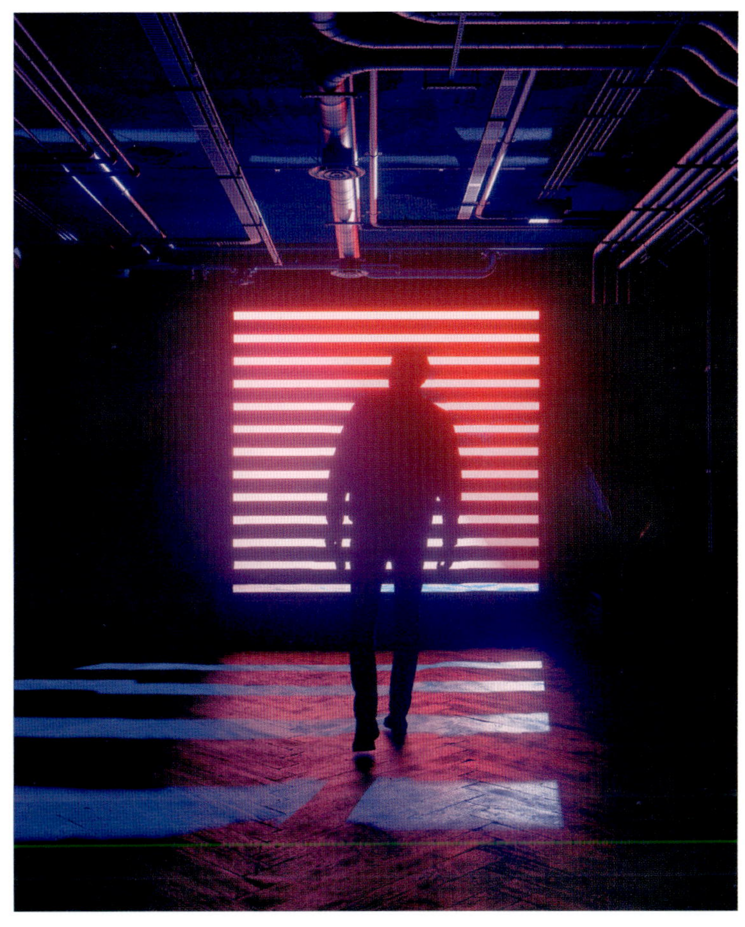

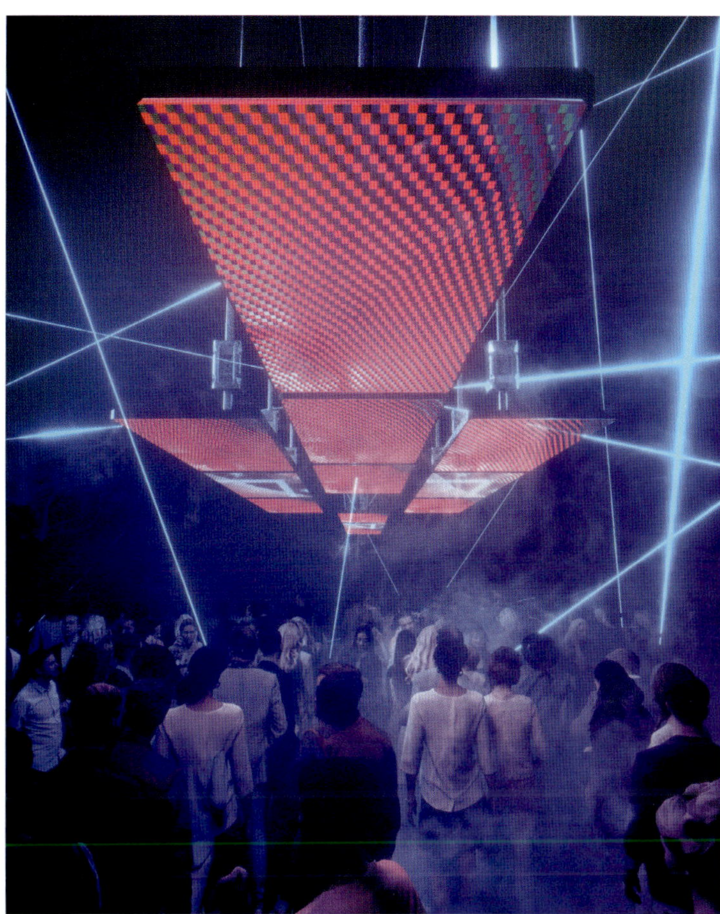

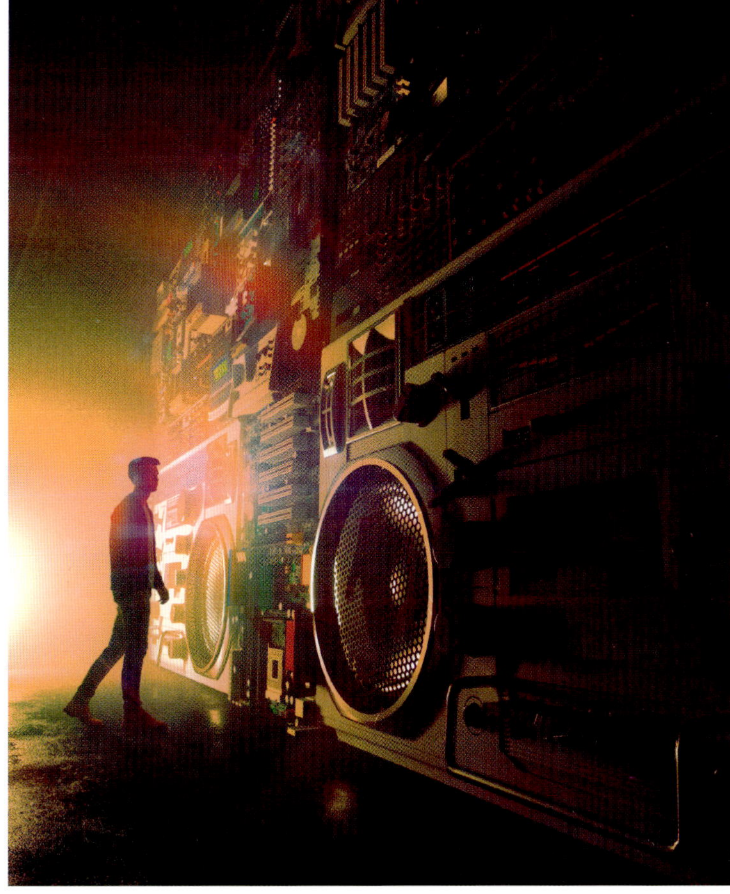

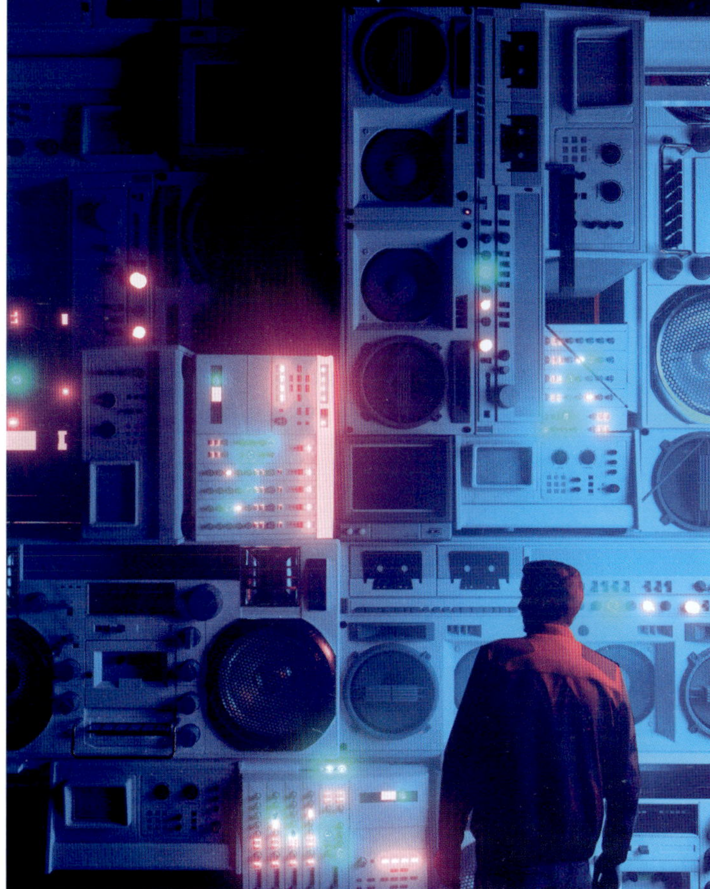

TOP LEFT
DIVIDE BY ZERO
07.16.2018

TOP RIGHT
CTRL+Z
10.19.2018

BOTTOM LEFT
OUTPUT LEVEL
04.25.2018

BOTTOM RIGHT
REBUILD.PHASE
02.21.2018

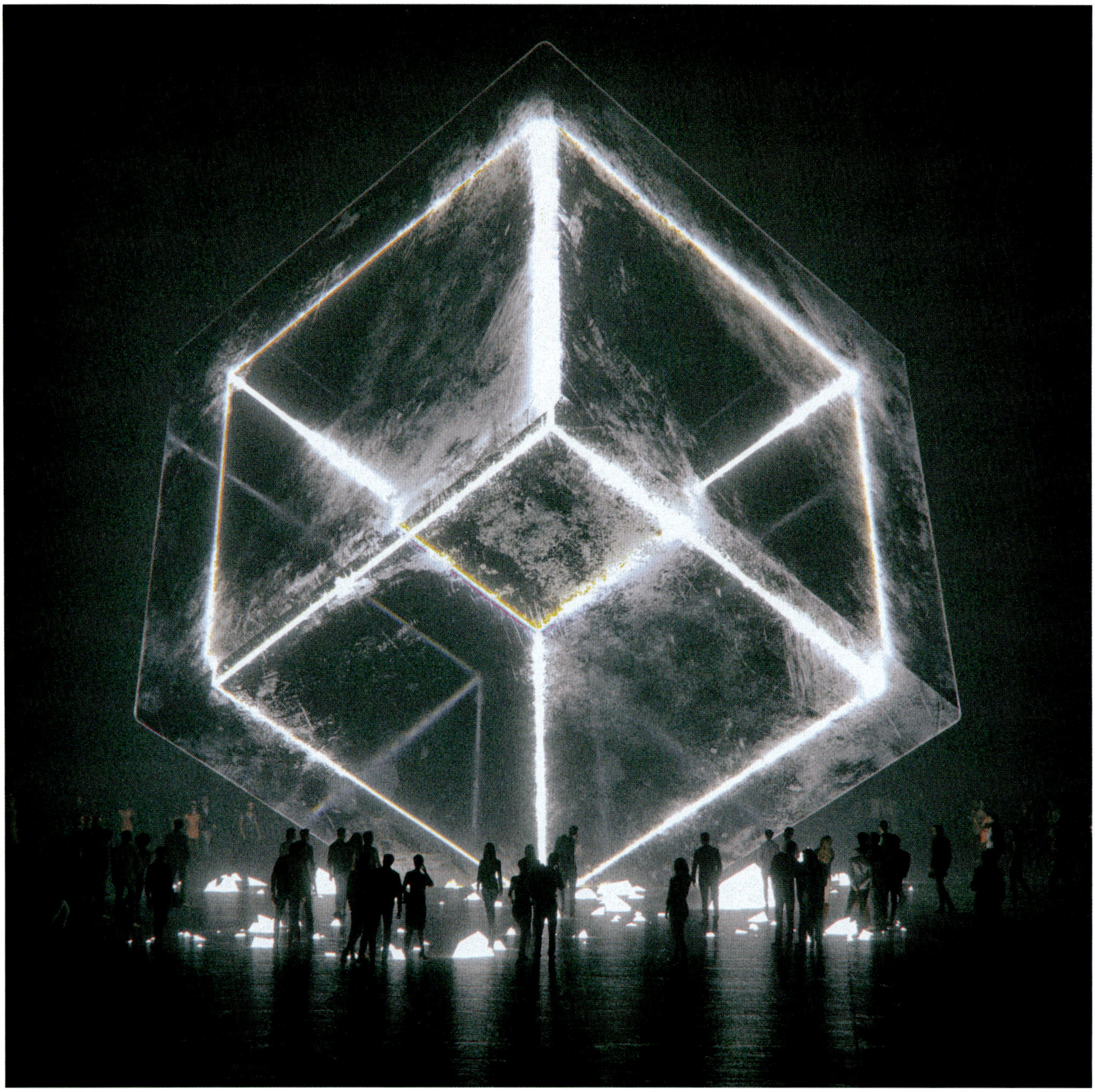

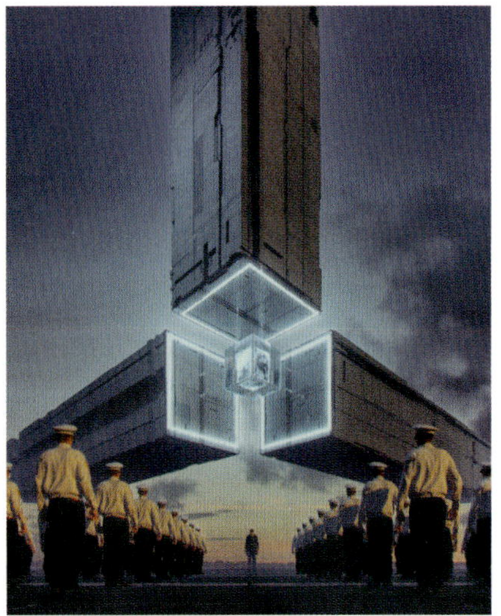

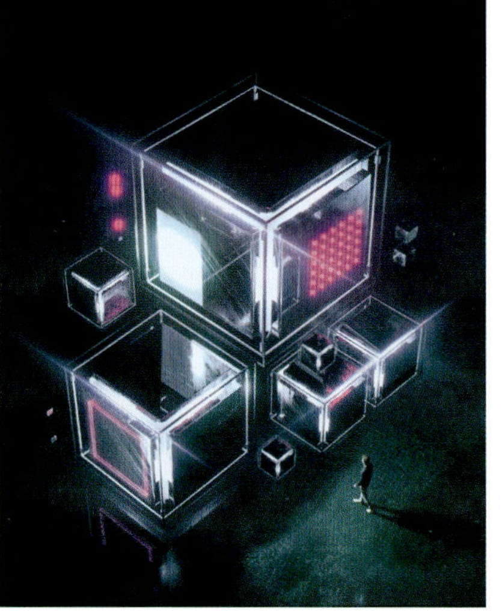

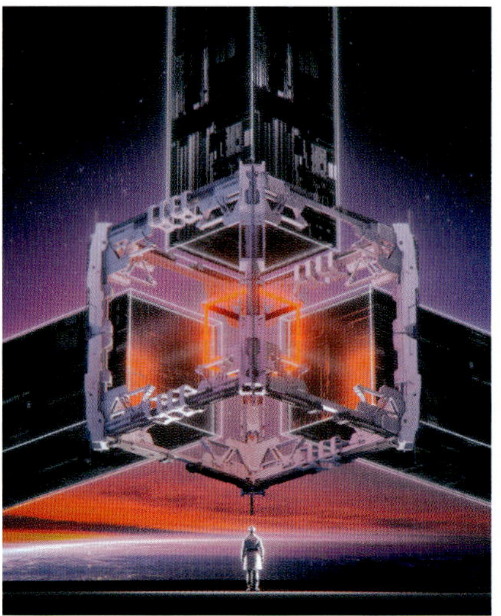

TOP
CRYPTIC CUBE
03.16.2018

BOTTOM LEFT
TETRAHYDE
05.30.2018

BOTTOM MIDDLE
CUBICAL
04.09.2018

BOTTOM RIGHT
RED DAWN
10.01.2018

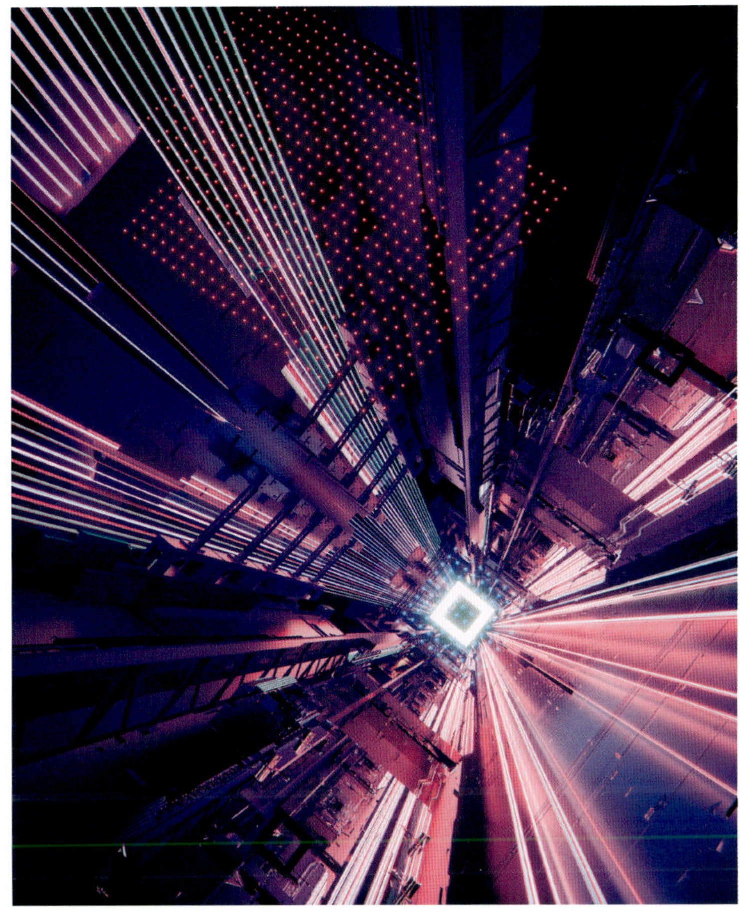

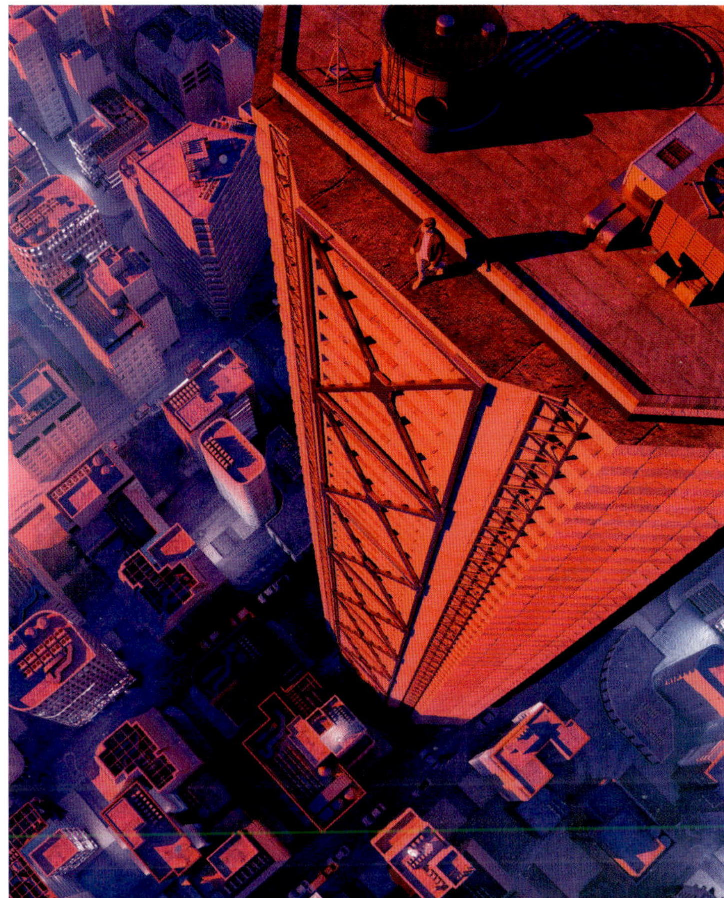

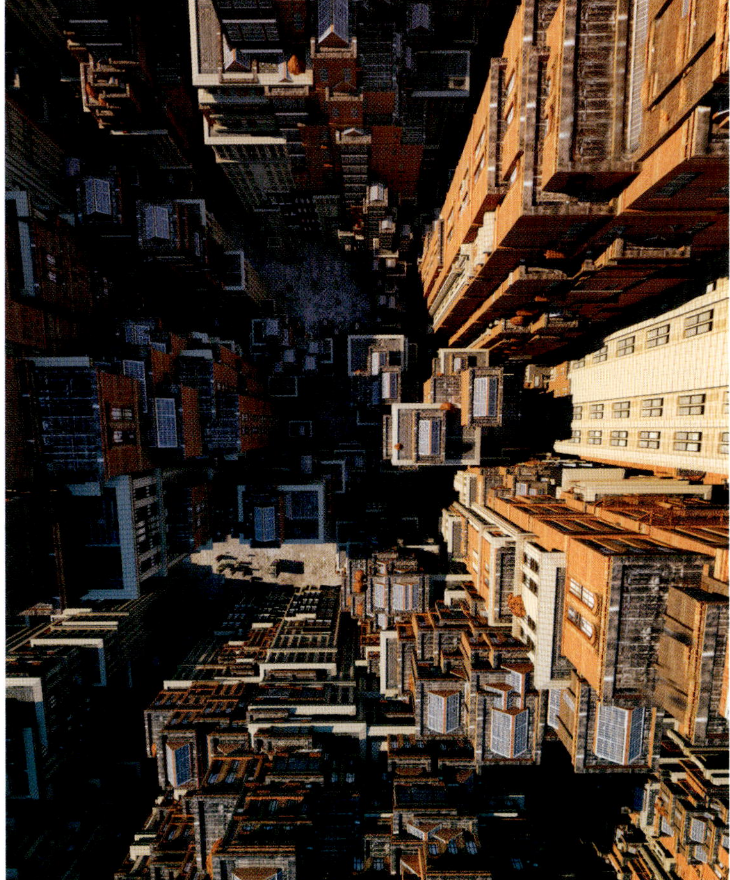

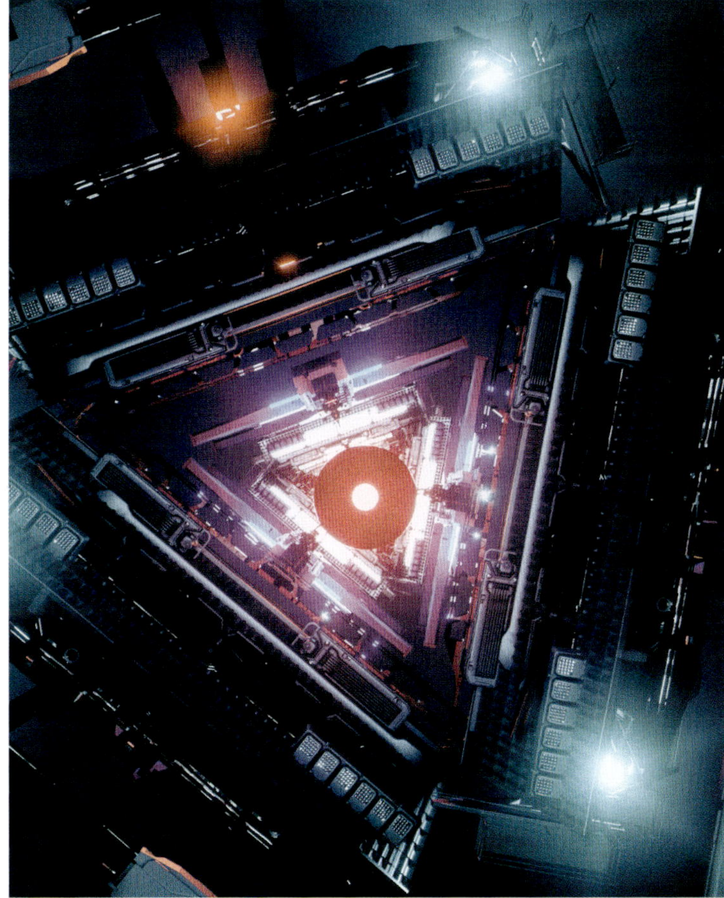

TOP LEFT
SQUARE.PHASE
05.09.2018

TOP RIGHT
RED SKY
05.21.2018

BOTTOM LEFT
TORONTO
04.07.2018

BOTTOM RIGHT
THE FACTORY
12.02.2018

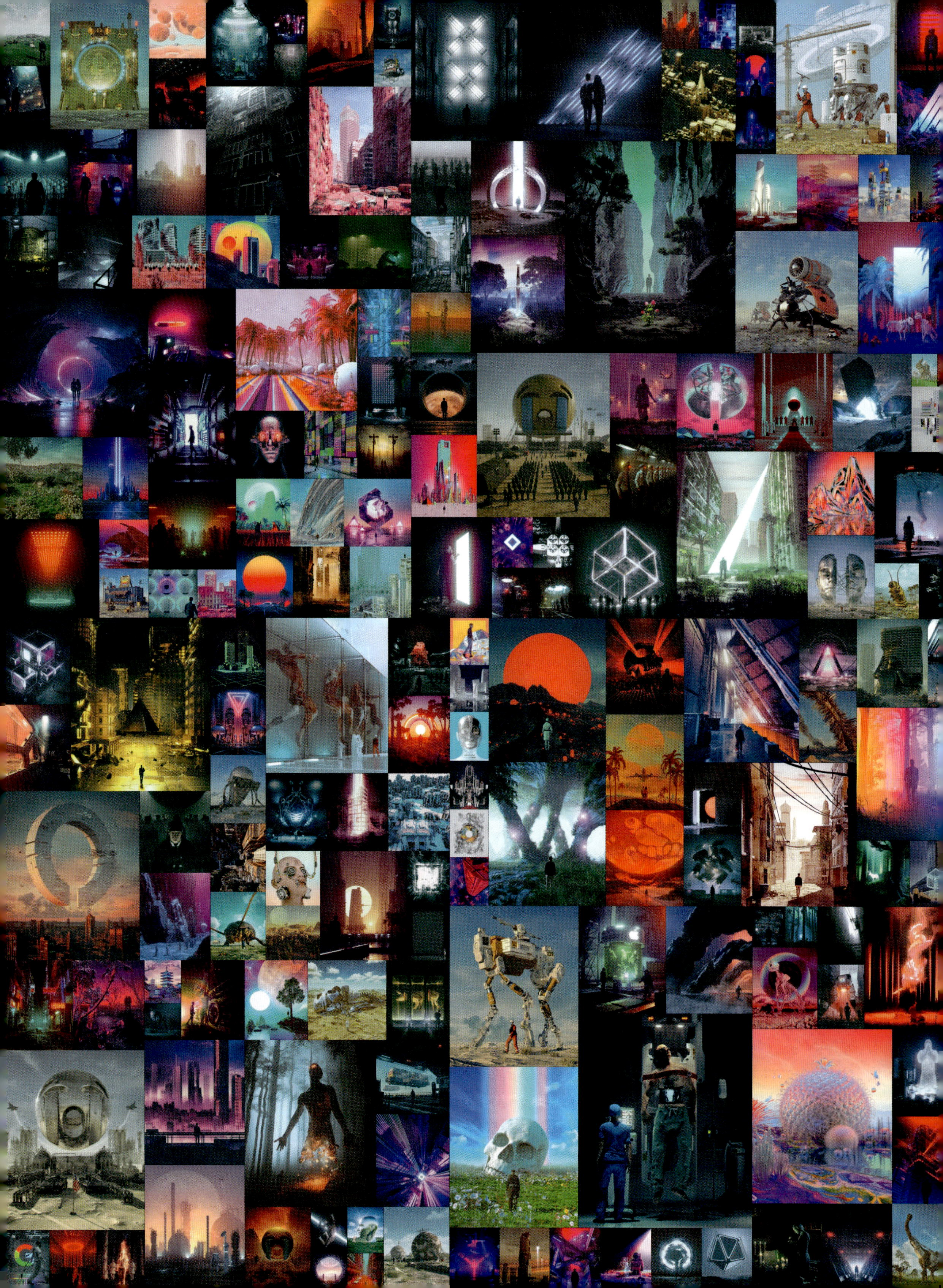

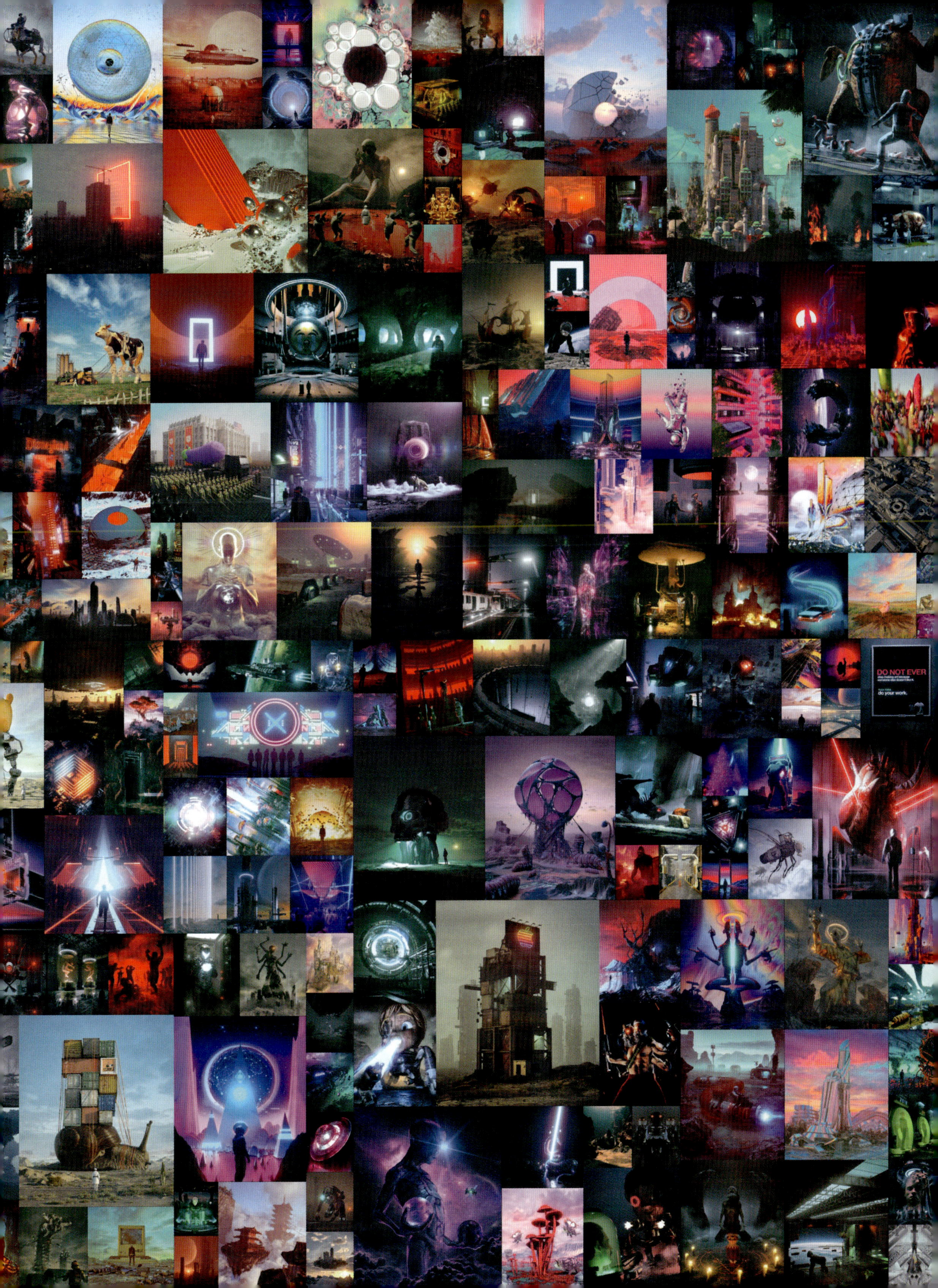
DO NOT EVER
do your work.

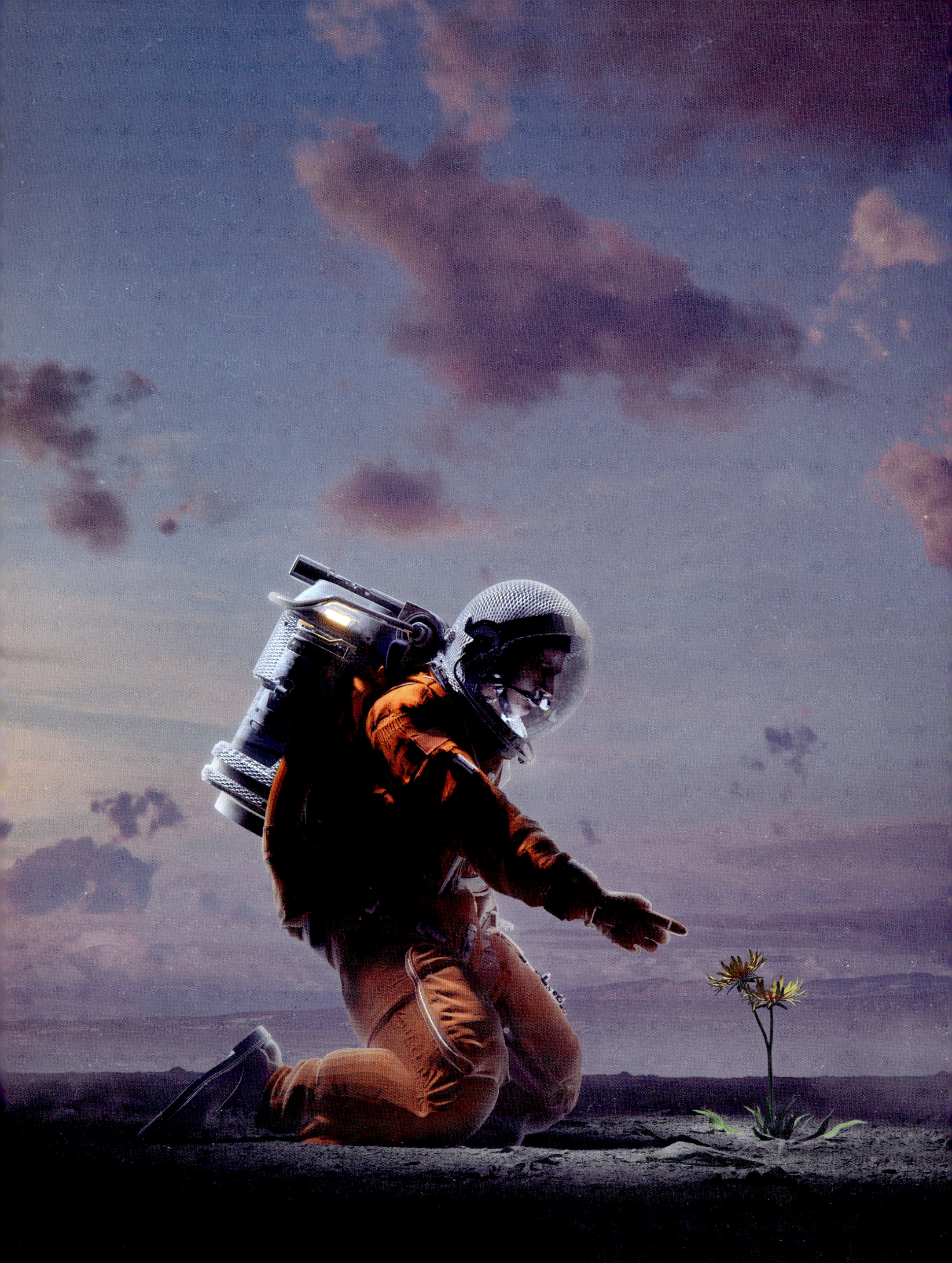

2019

OPPOSITE PAGE

START AGAIN

01.11.2019

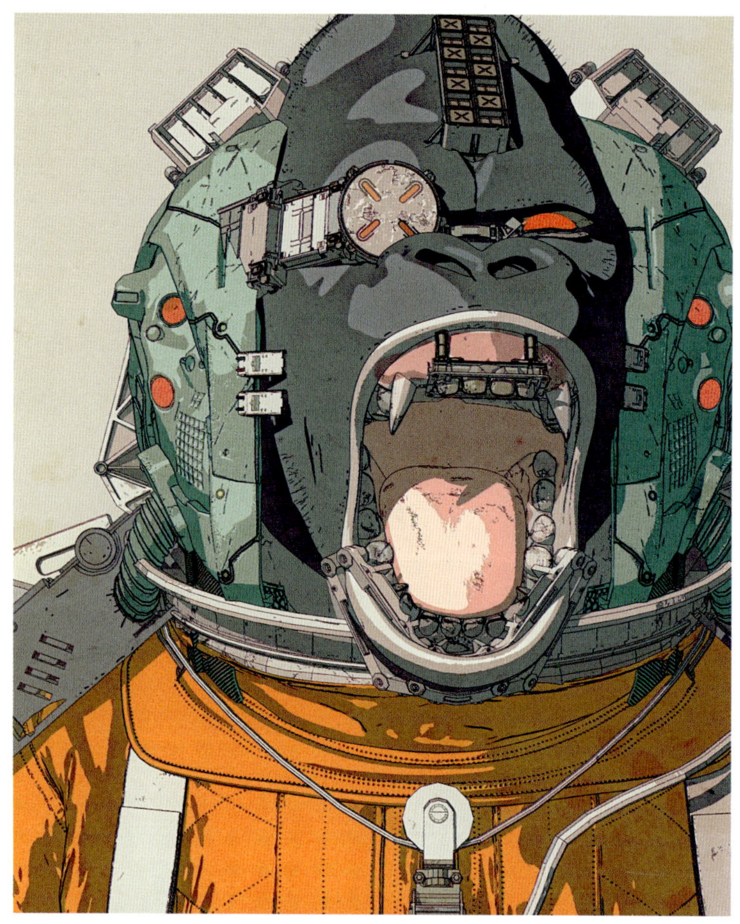

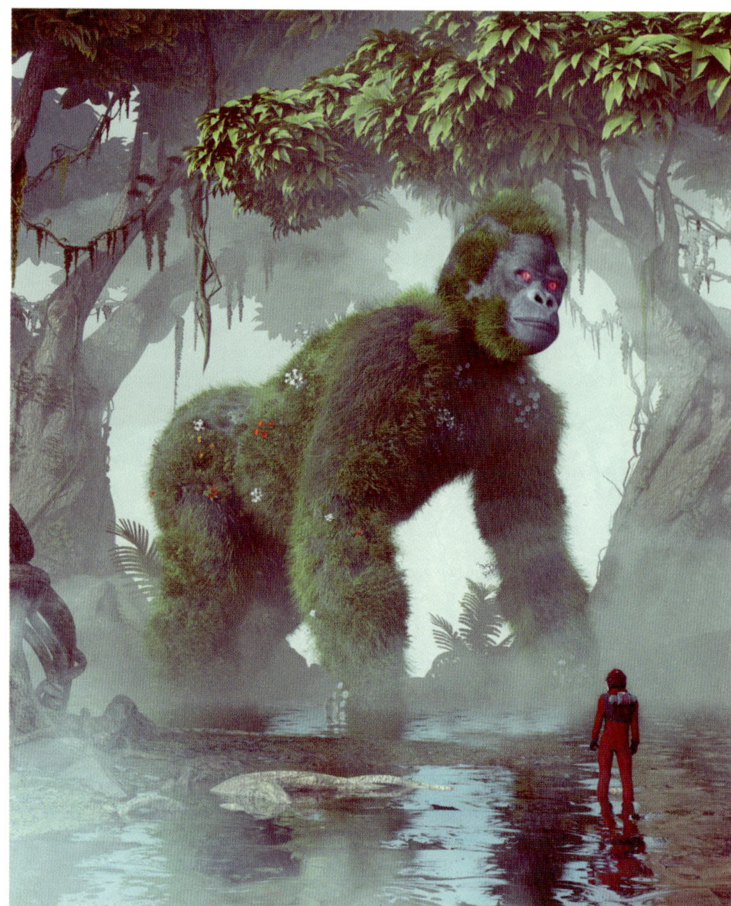

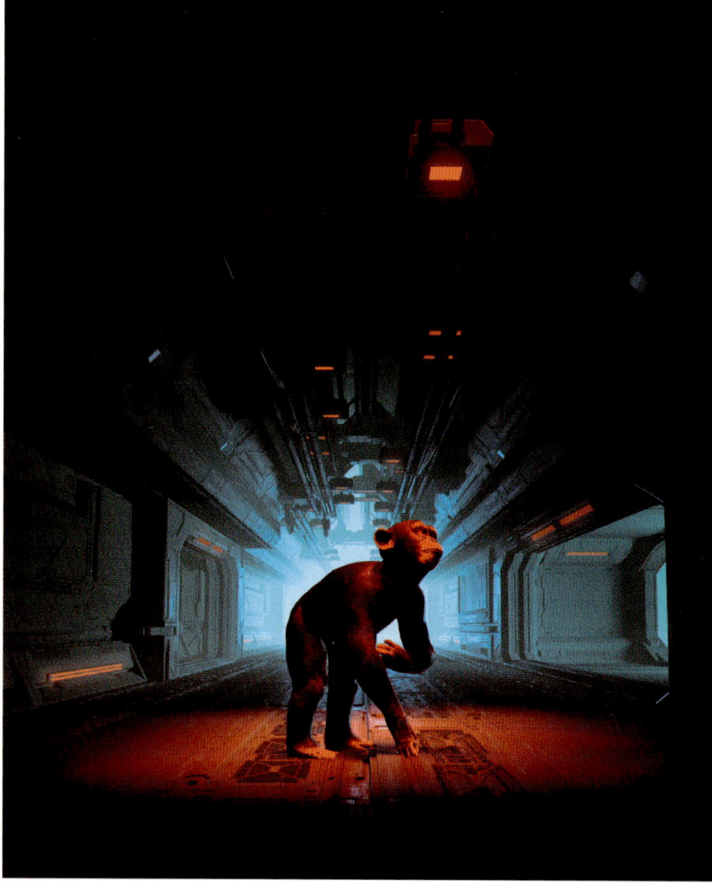

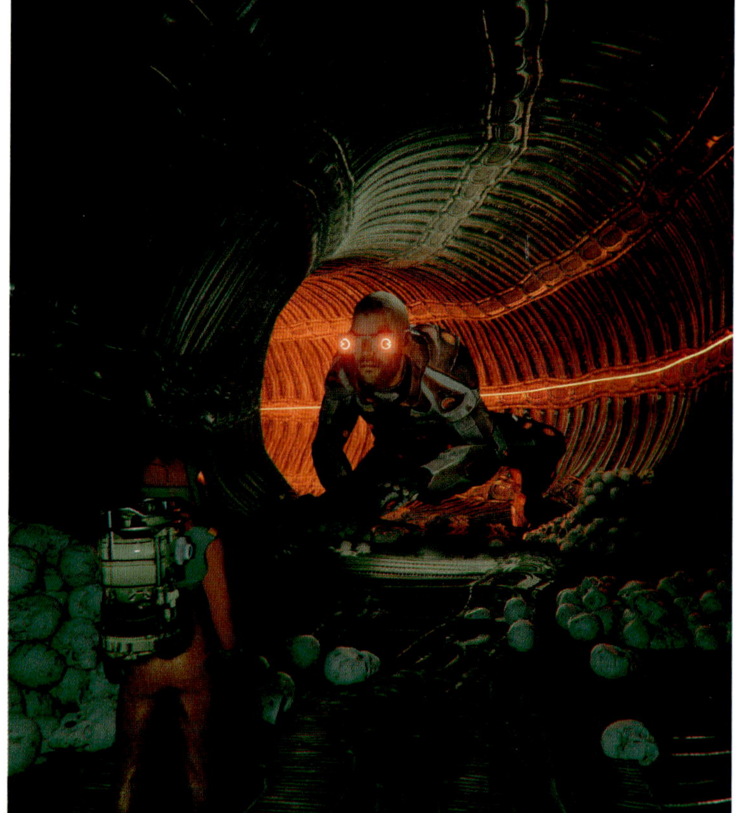

TOP LEFT
REVERSE PROGRESS
02.17.2019

TOP RIGHT
APESHIT
01.14.2019

BOTTOM LEFT
HUMANITY 2020
12.27.2019

BOTTOM RIGHT
BAD DAY
01.06.2019

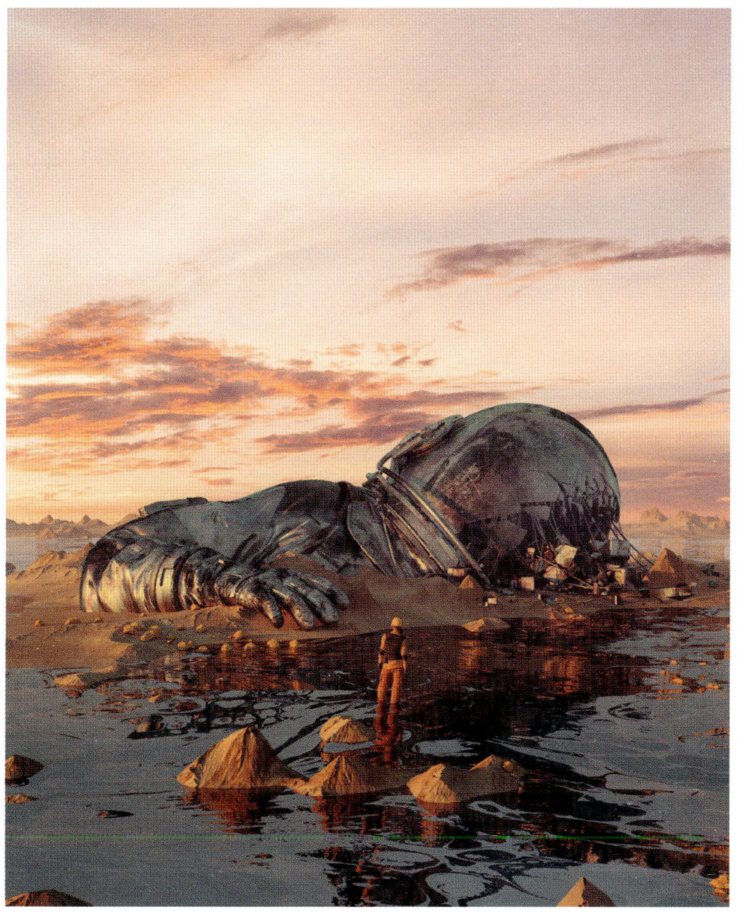

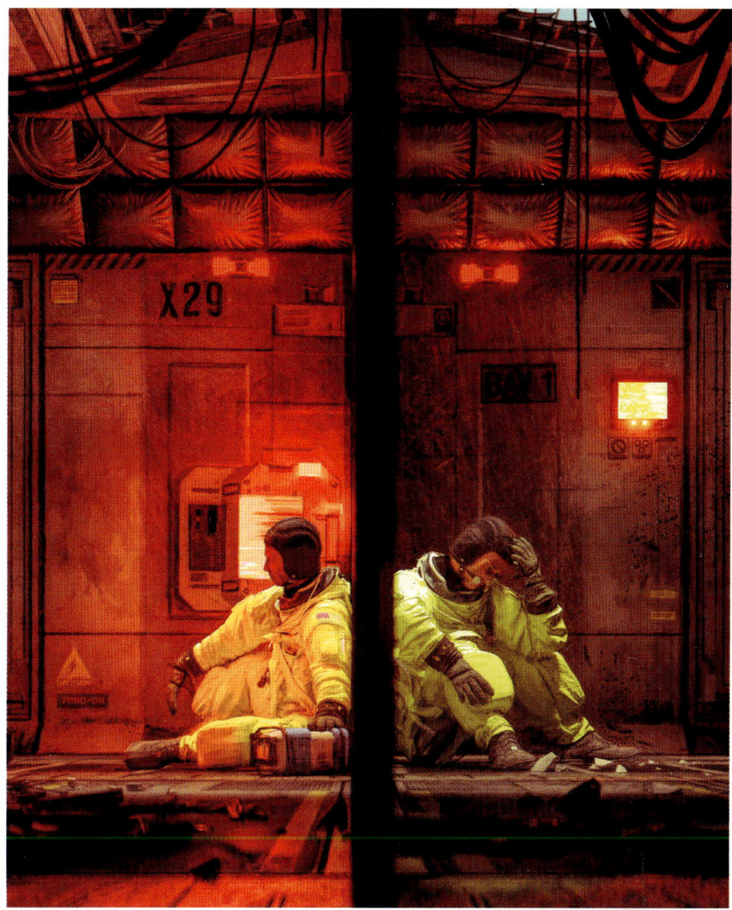

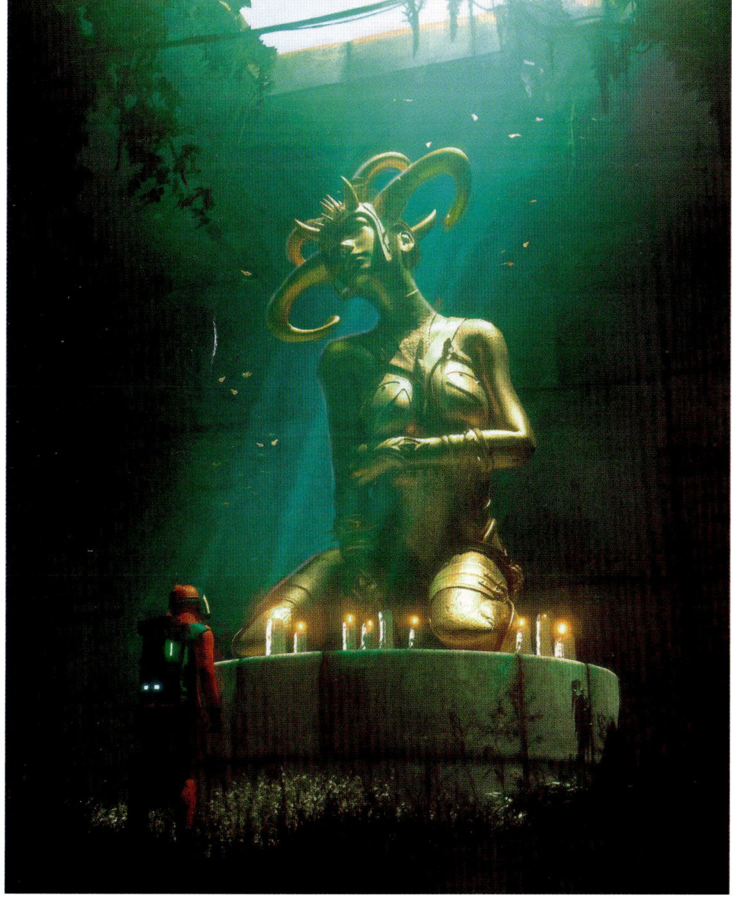

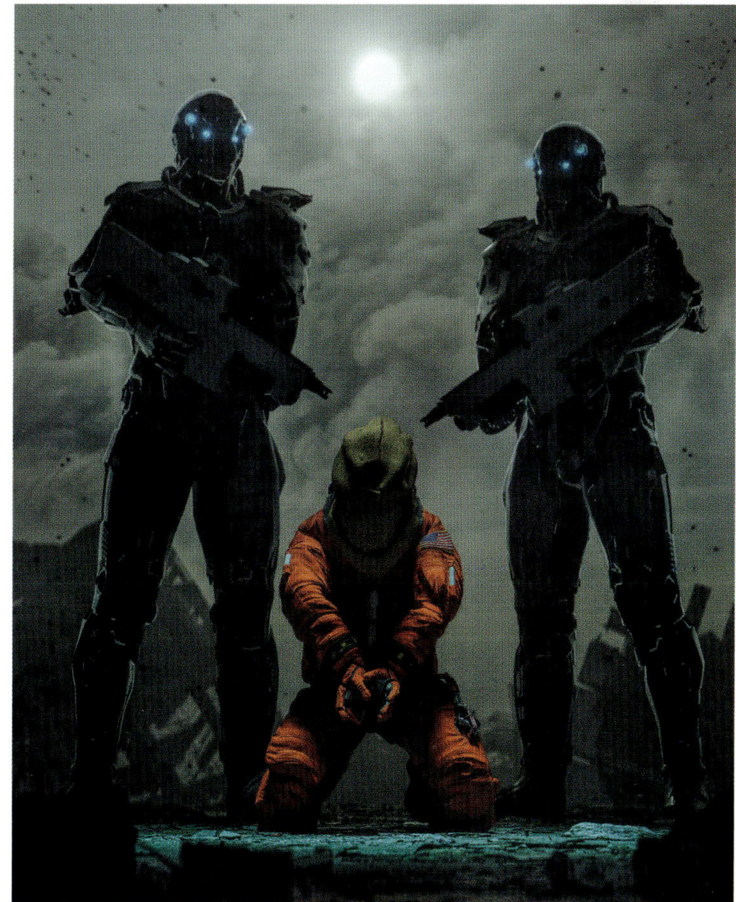

TOP LEFT

WE WERE GIANTS
01.29.2019

TOP RIGHT

SO CLOSE
11.04.2019

BOTTOM LEFT

FORGOTTEN CULTURE
11.09.2019

BOTTOM RIGHT

HUMAN ERROR
04.17.2019

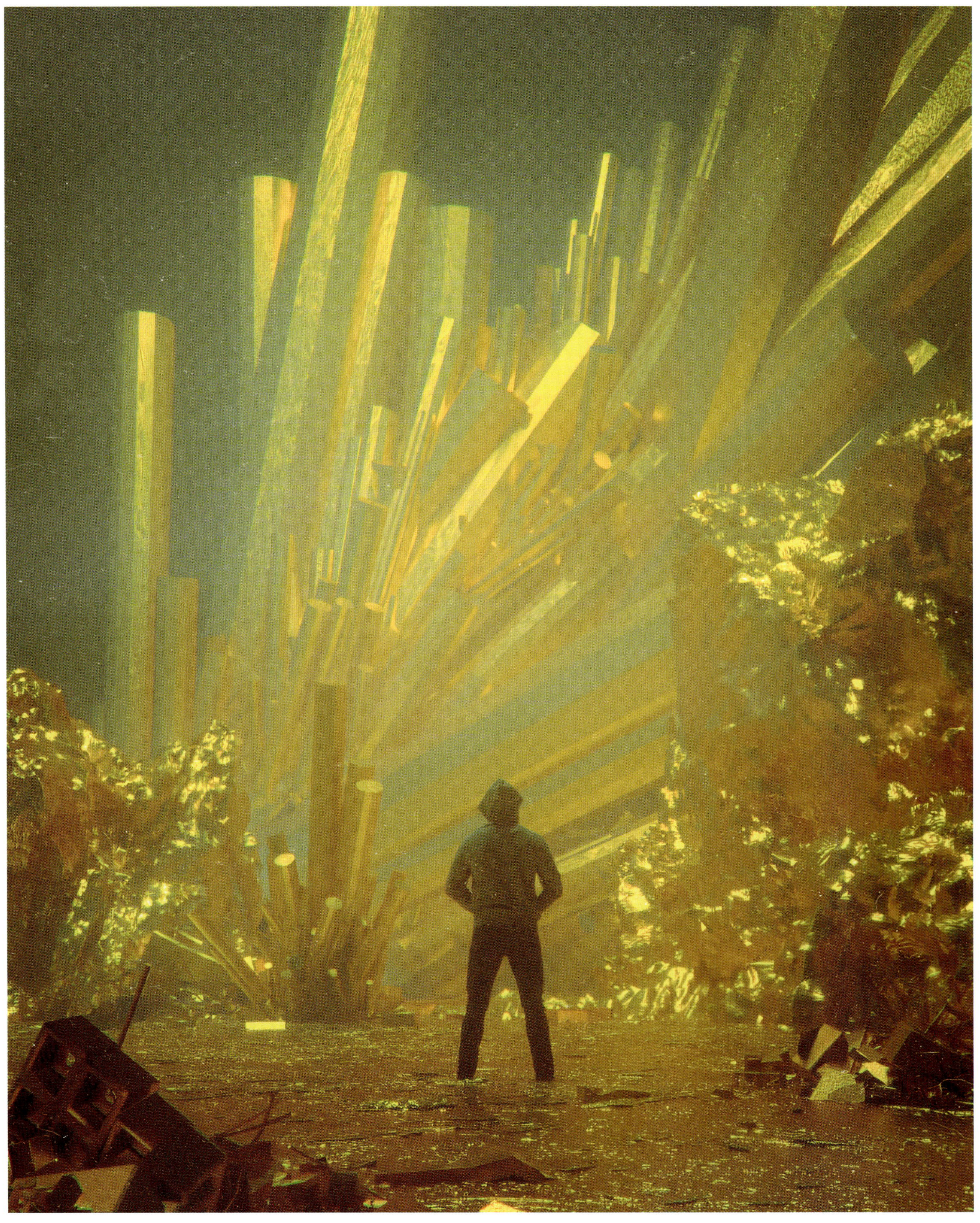

ABOVE

SIX GOD
05.02.2019

OPPOSITE PAGE

CRYSTAL OVERDOSE
03.29.2019

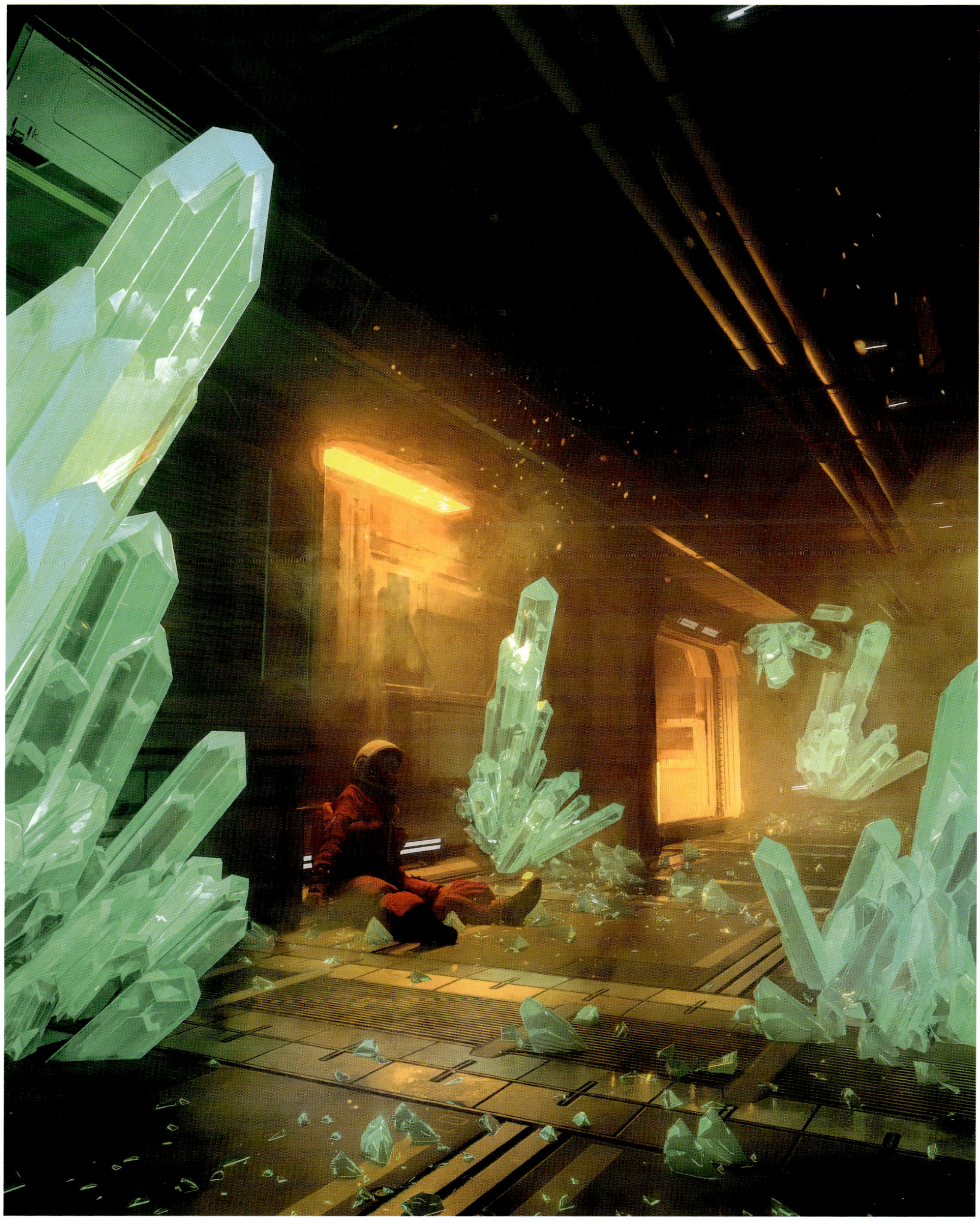

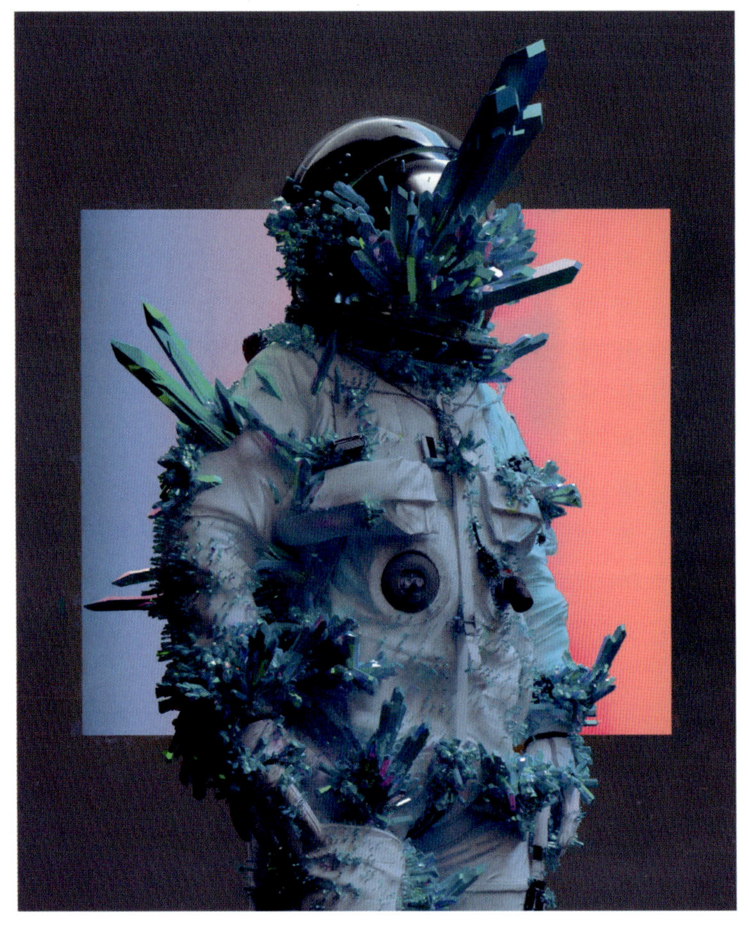

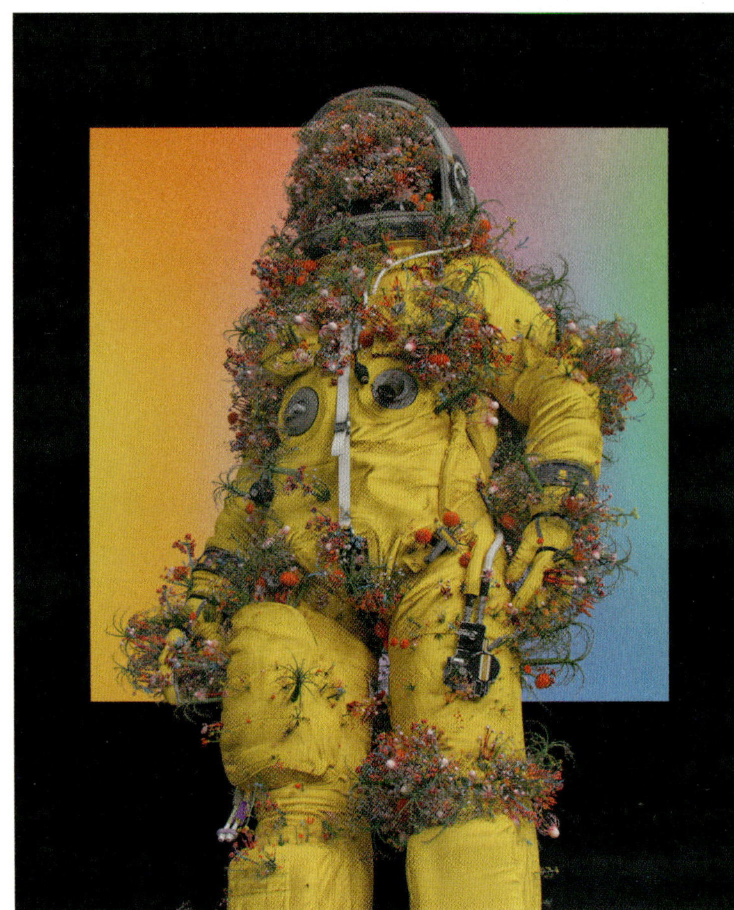

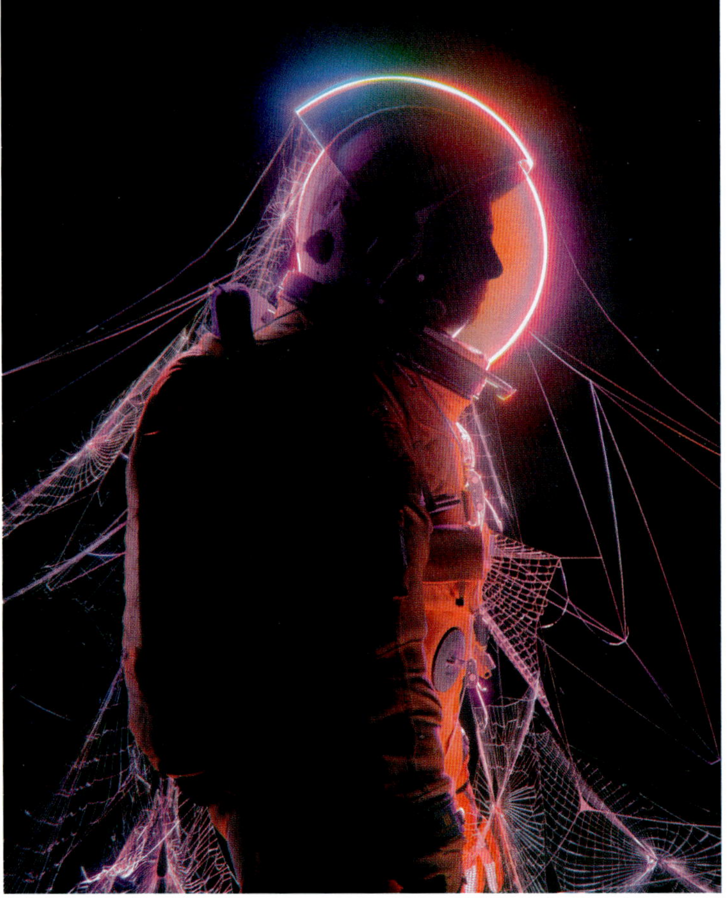

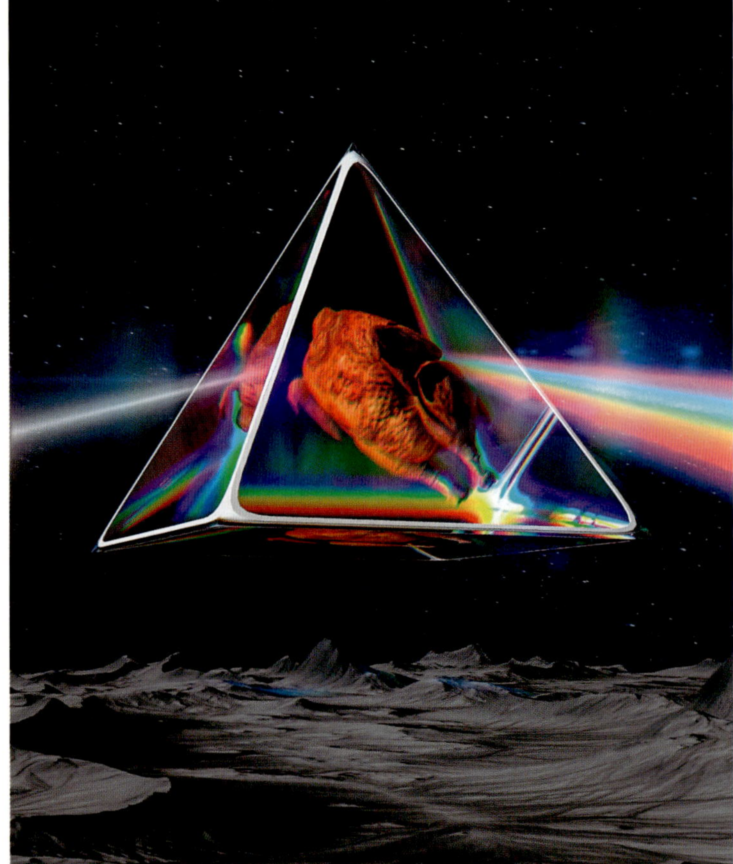

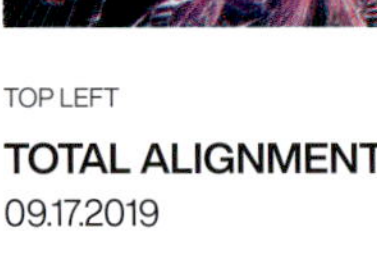

TOP LEFT
TOTAL ALIGNMENT
09.17.2019

TOP RIGHT
HOMEGROWN
02.04.2019

BOTTOM LEFT
STAND STILL
05.14.2019

BOTTOM RIGHT
DARK SIDE OF THE MEAT
11.28.2019

OPPOSITE PAGE
FREEFALL
01.15.2019

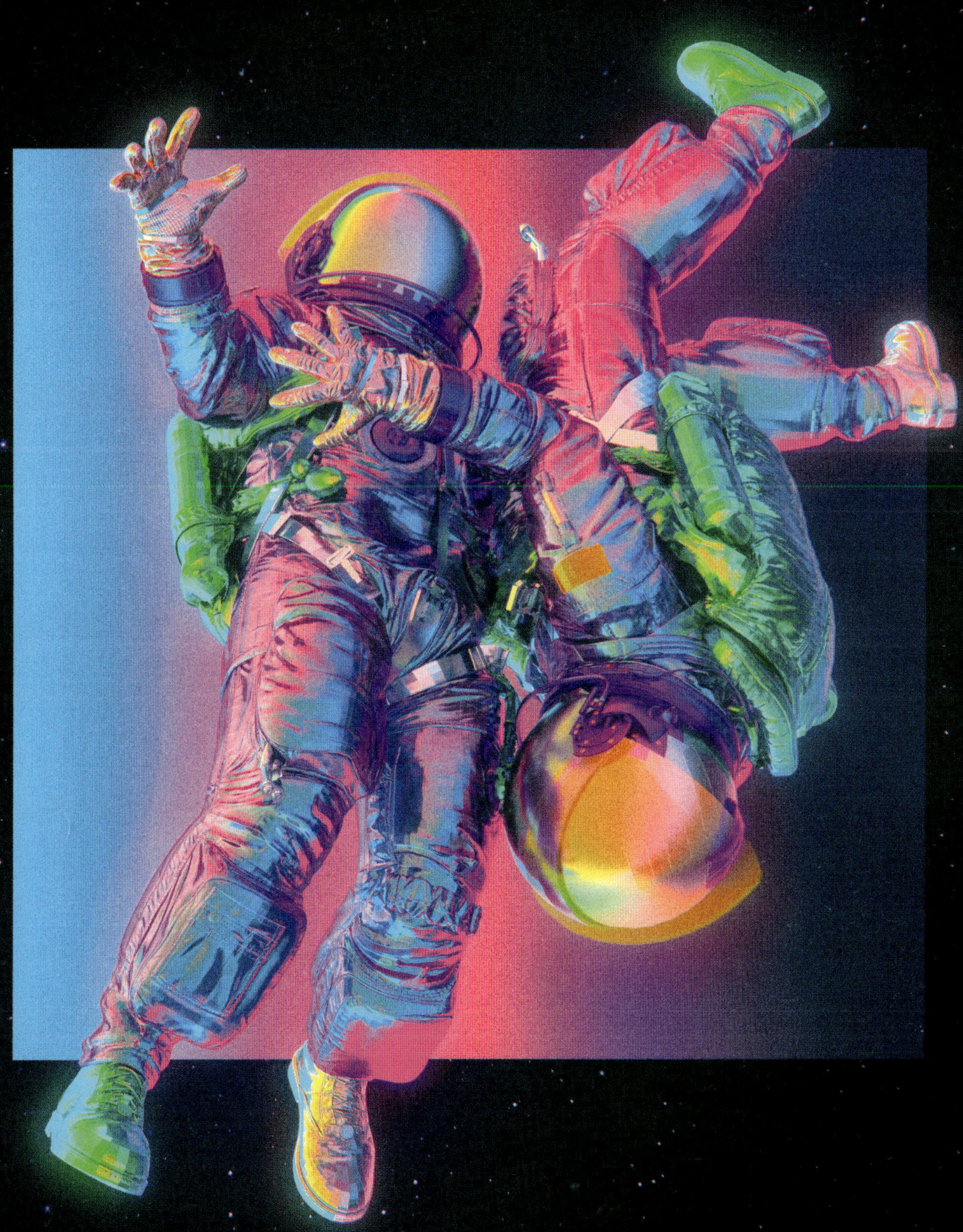

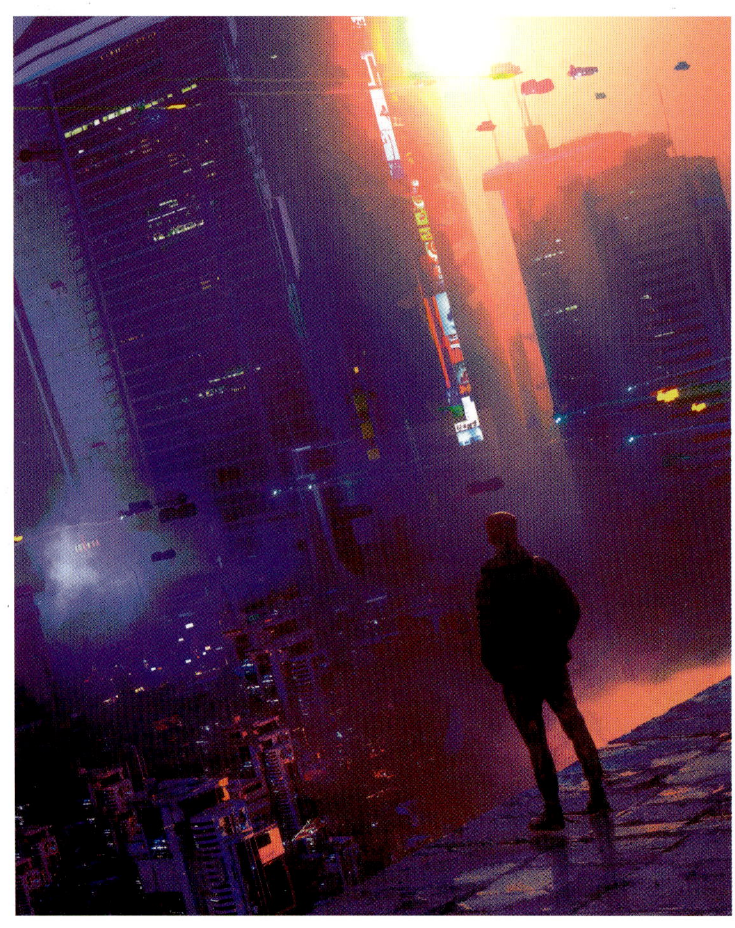

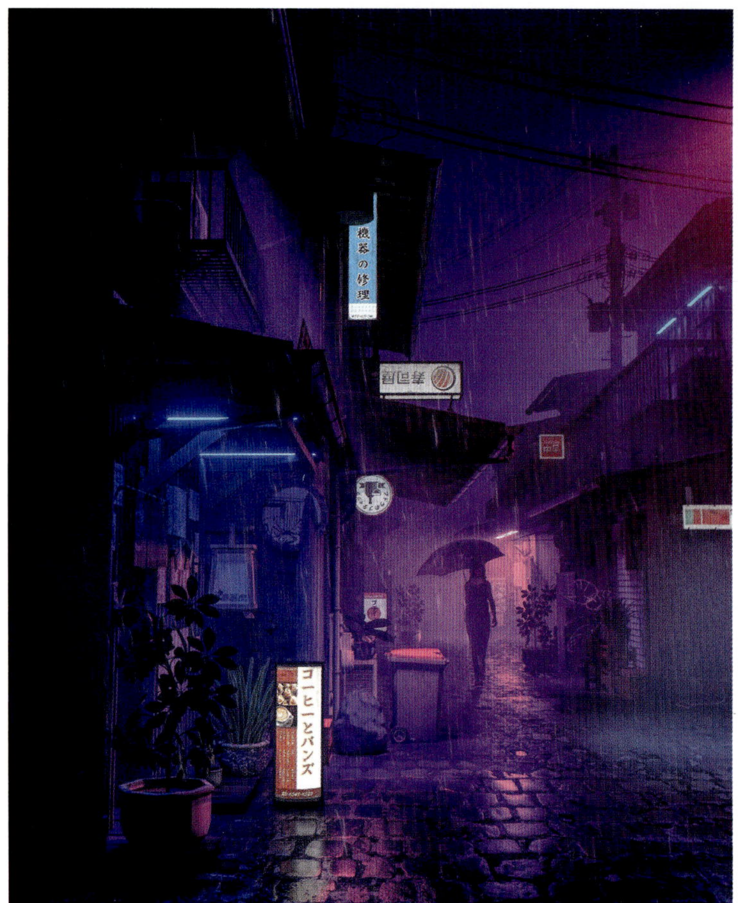

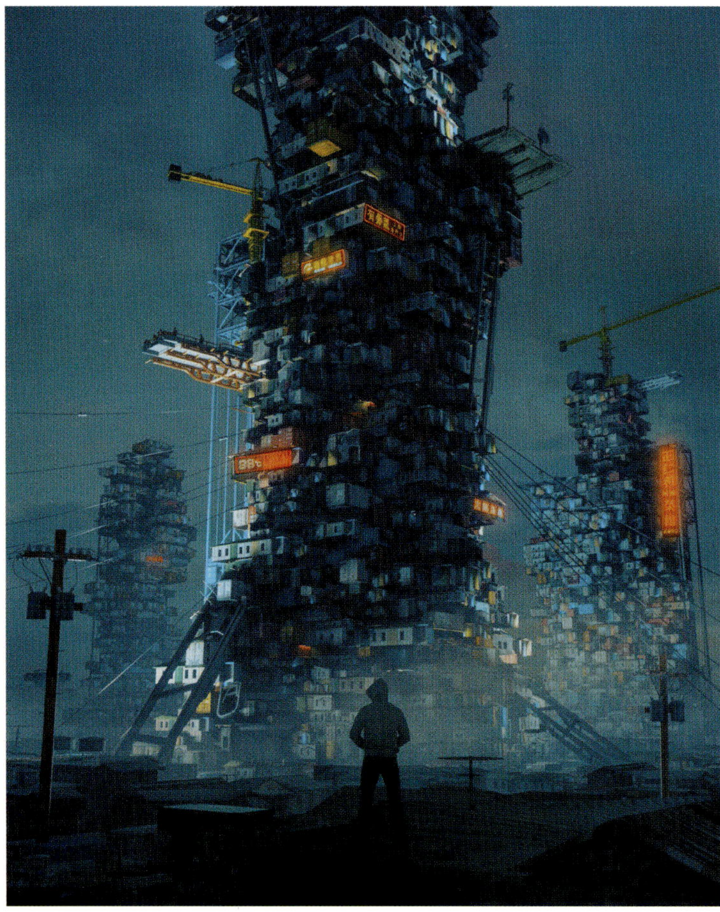

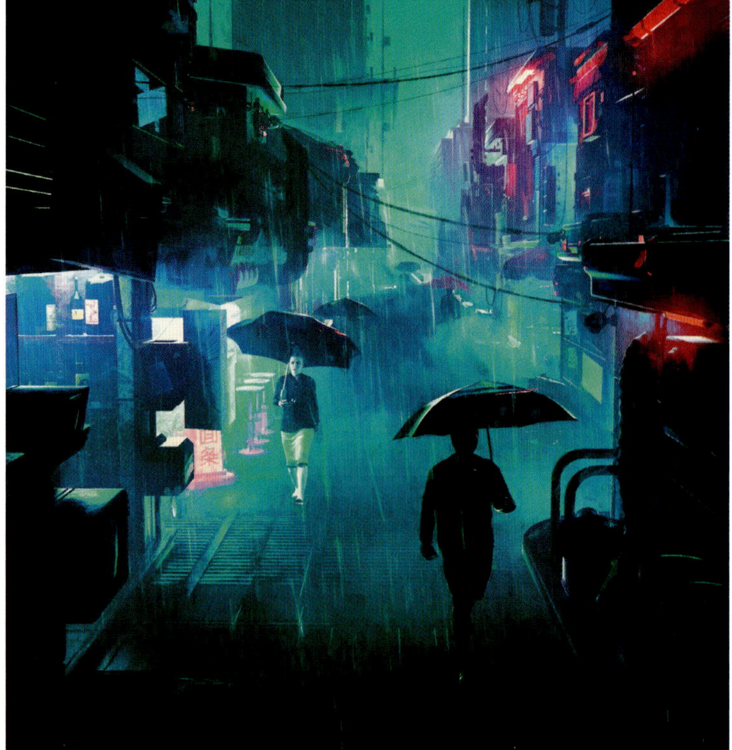

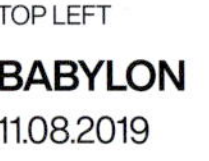

TOP LEFT
BABYLON
11.08.2019

TOP RIGHT
PURPLE RAIN
03.06.2019

BOTTOM LEFT
ELECTRIC CITY
01.24.2019

BOTTOM RIGHT
TURQUOISE RAINBOW
11.24.2019

OPPOSITE PAGE
UNLIMITED FOG
02.15.2019

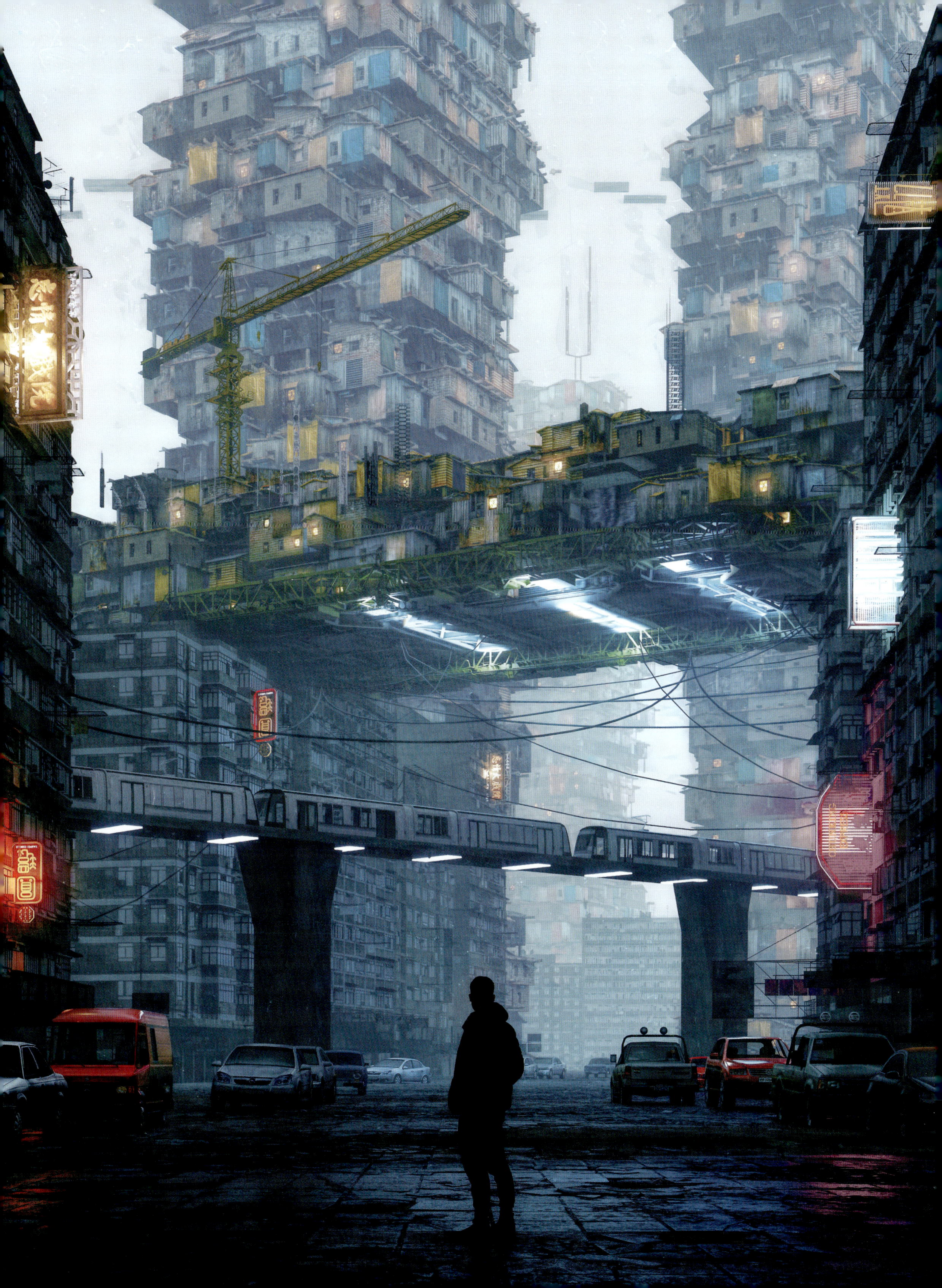

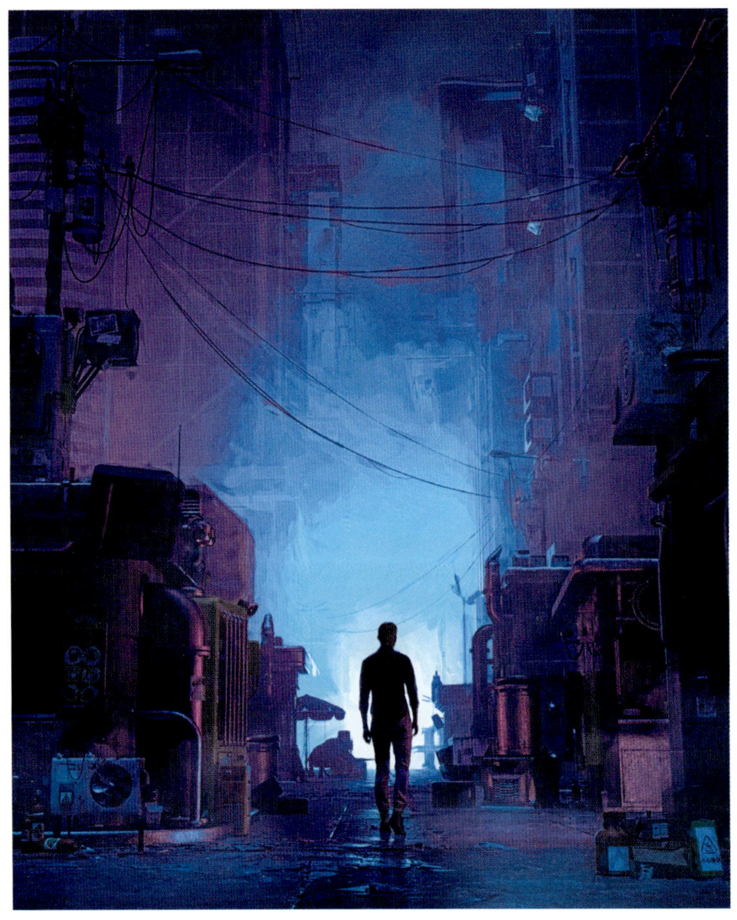

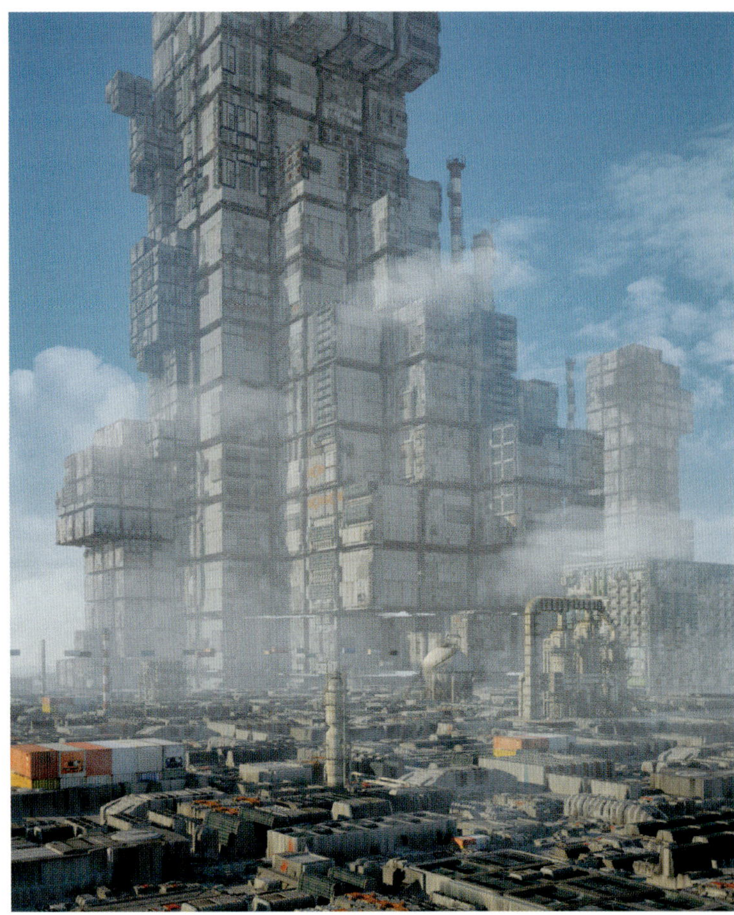

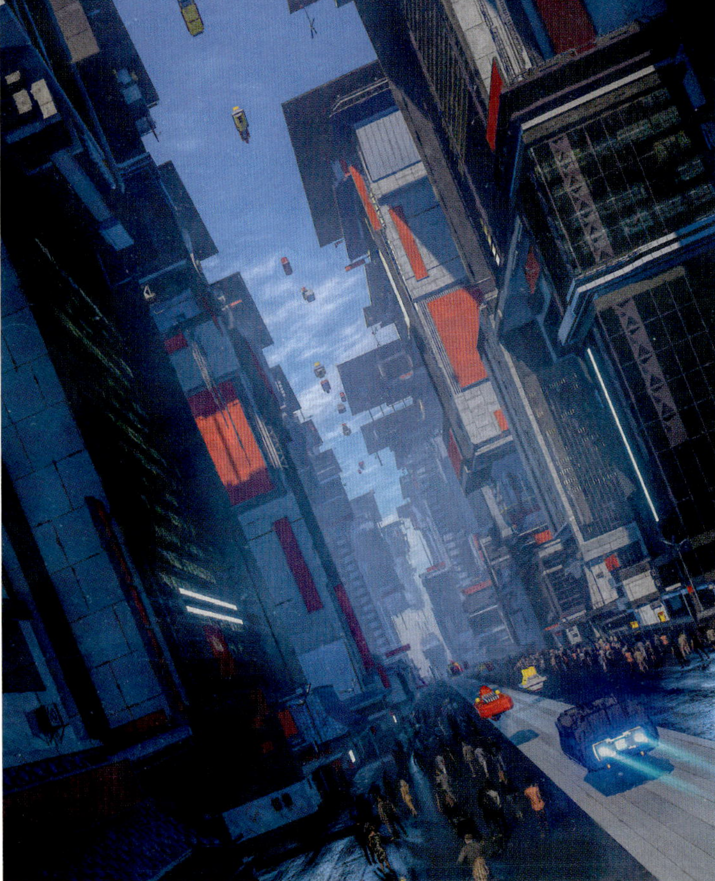

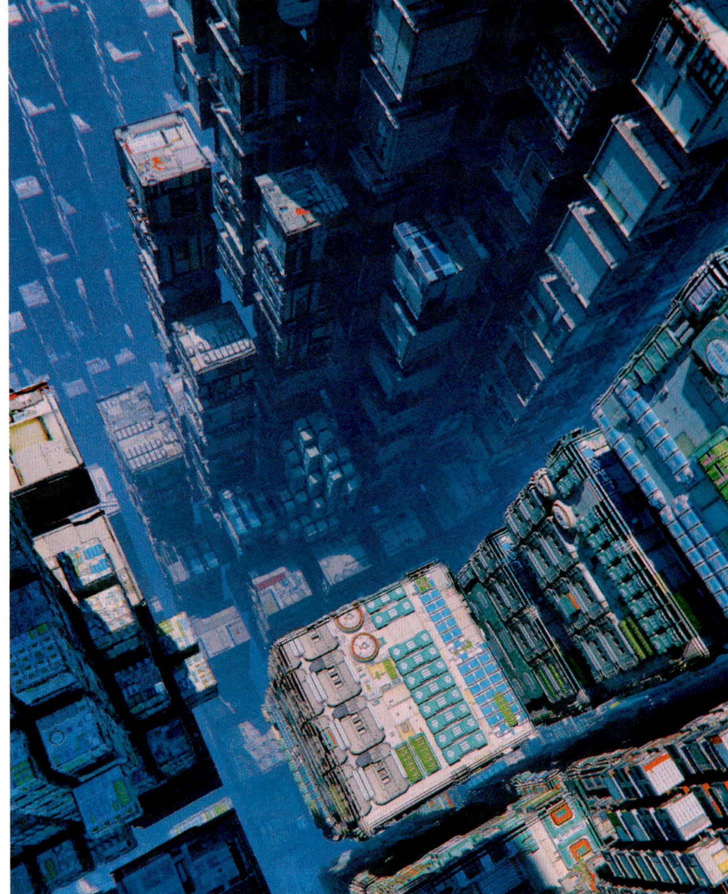

TOP LEFT
welcome
10.22.2019

TOP RIGHT
TIMECODIA
01.28.2019

BOTTOM LEFT
TERTIARY COLORS
08.13.2019

BOTTOM RIGHT
VOXXED OUT
01.26.2019

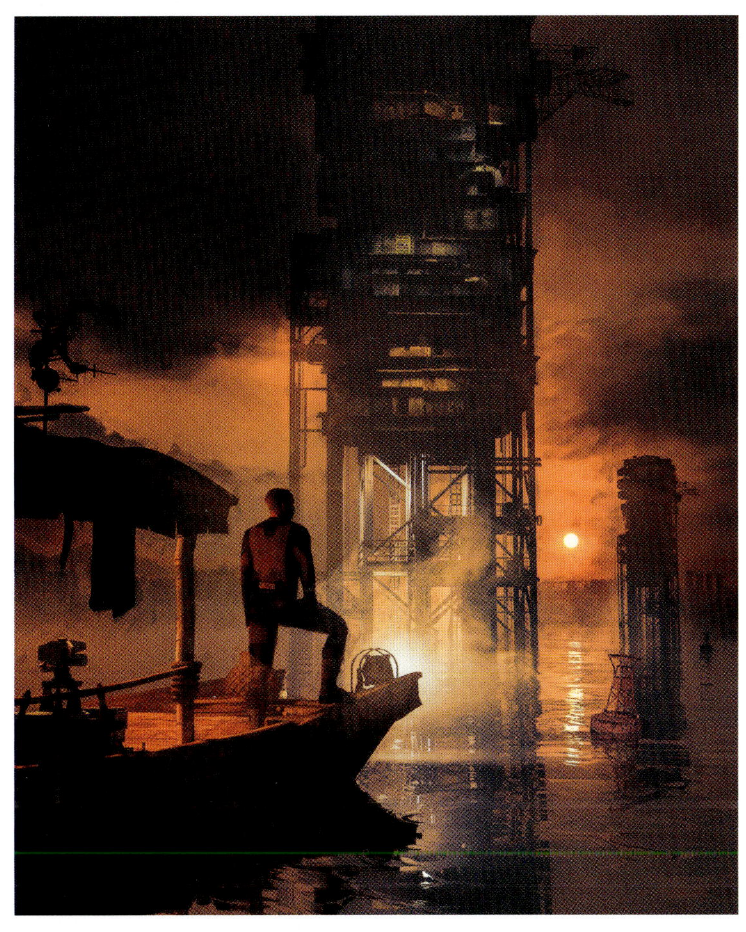

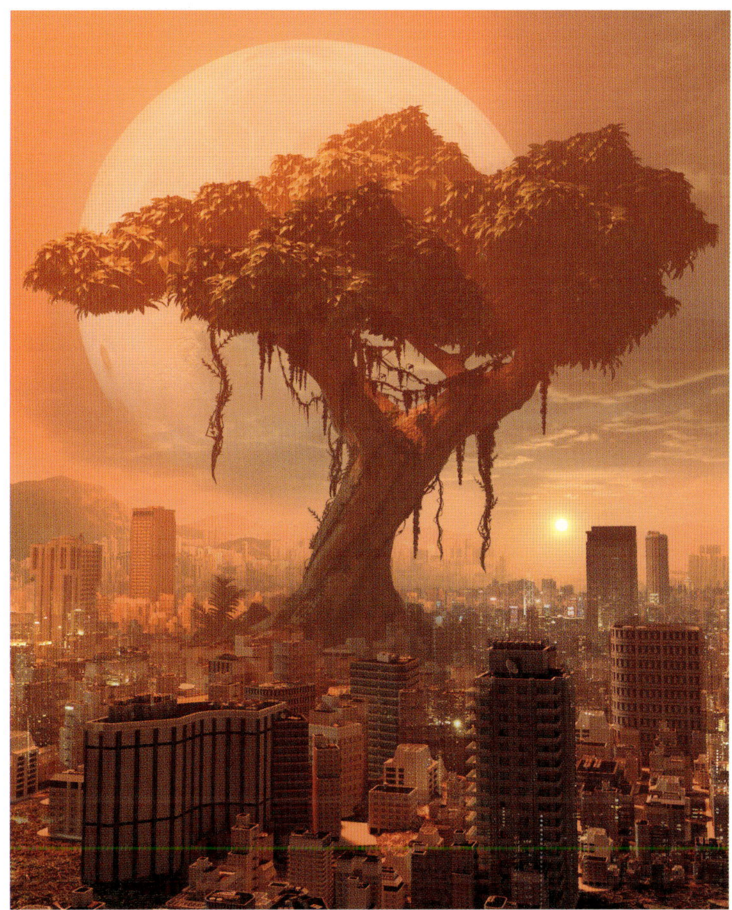

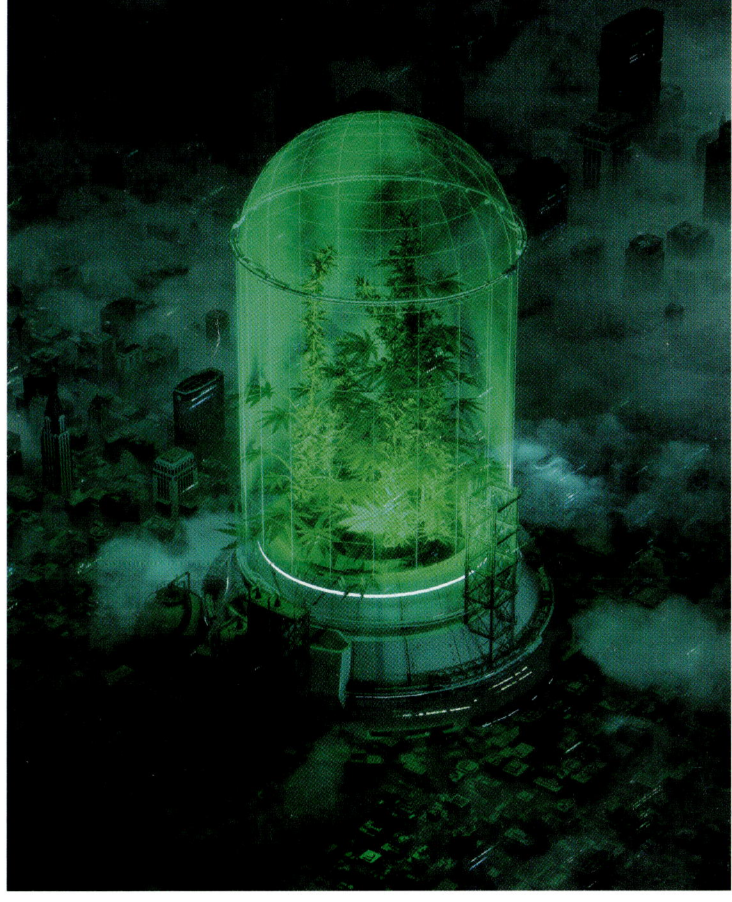

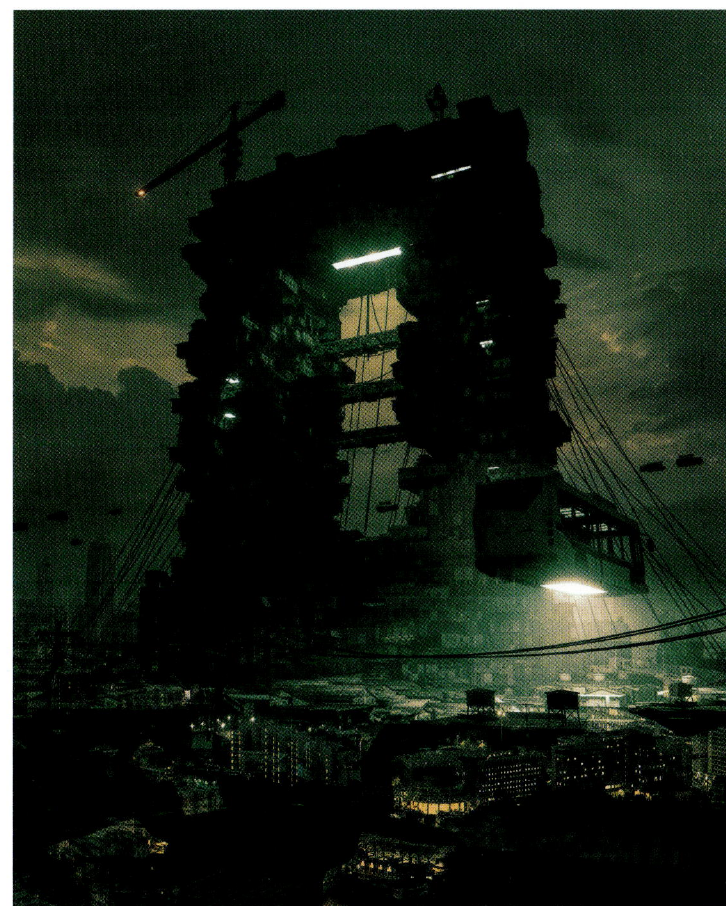

TOP LEFT
RED LETTER
03.11.2019

TOP RIGHT
SETTING SUN
10.05.2019

BOTTOM LEFT
XEON7.SUPERDANK
07.08.2019

BOTTOM RIGHT
GIAGANTICA
06.13.2019

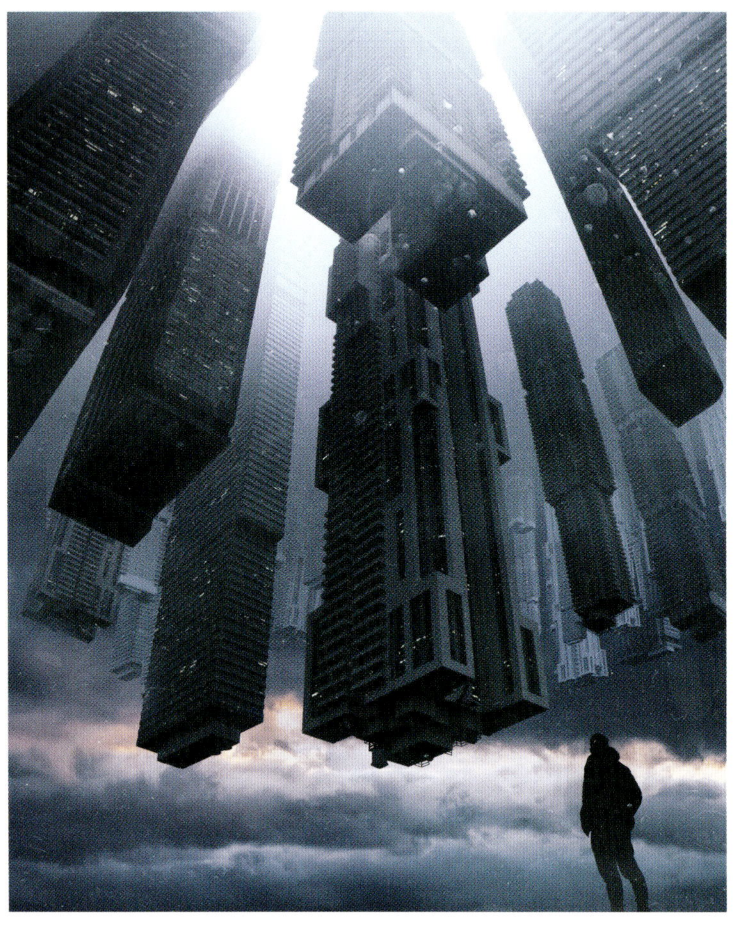

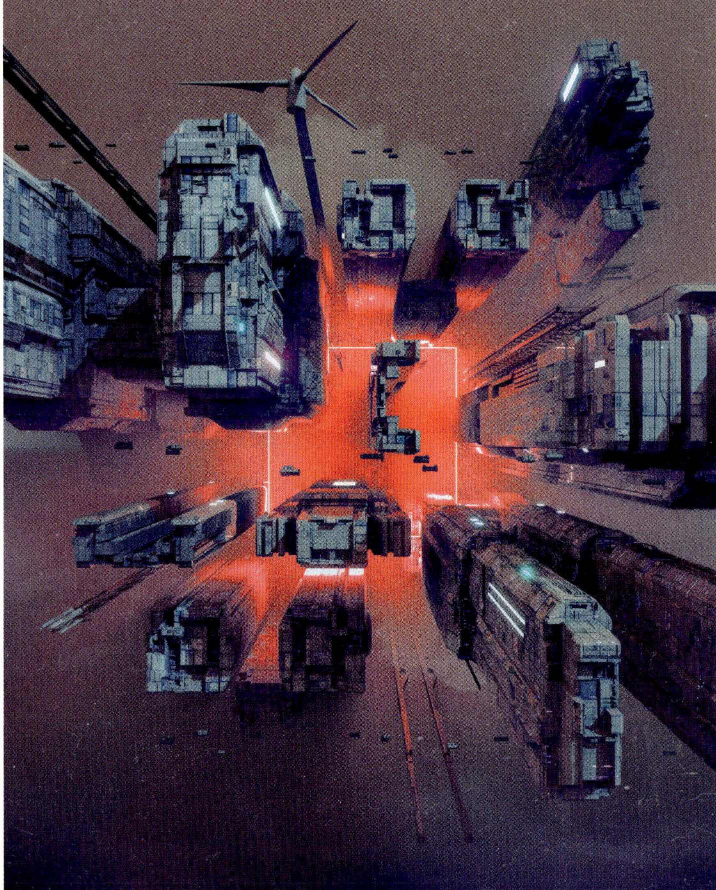

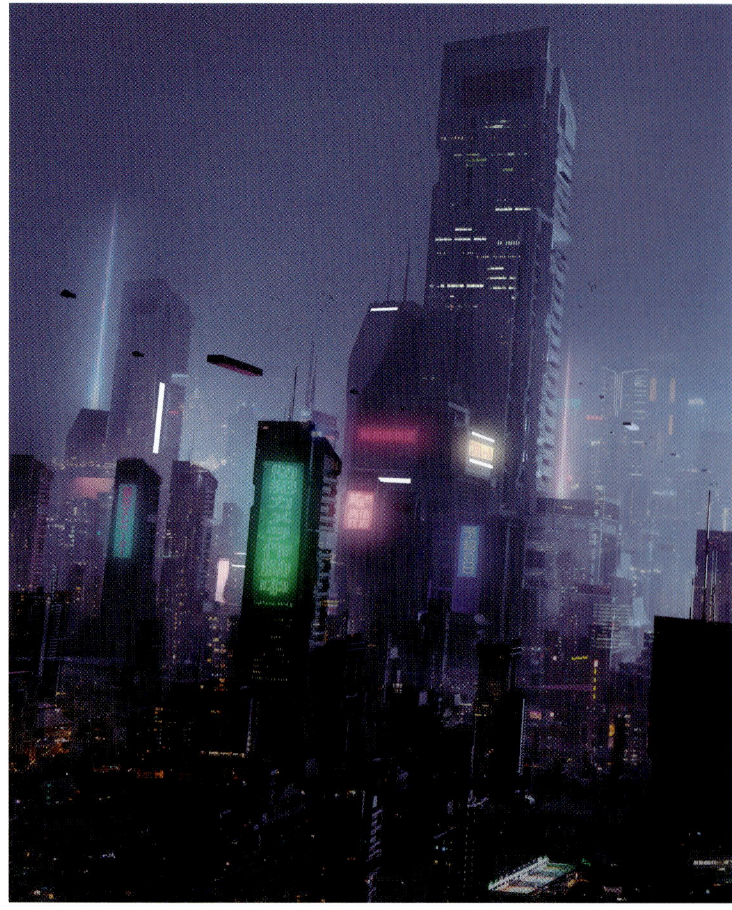

TOP LEFT
DOWNSIDEUP
07.14.2019

TOP RIGHT
MASS TRANSIT
09.30.2019

BOTTOM LEFT
RED LIGHT DISTRICT
07.29.2019

BOTTOM RIGHT
LOW.END
08.15.2019

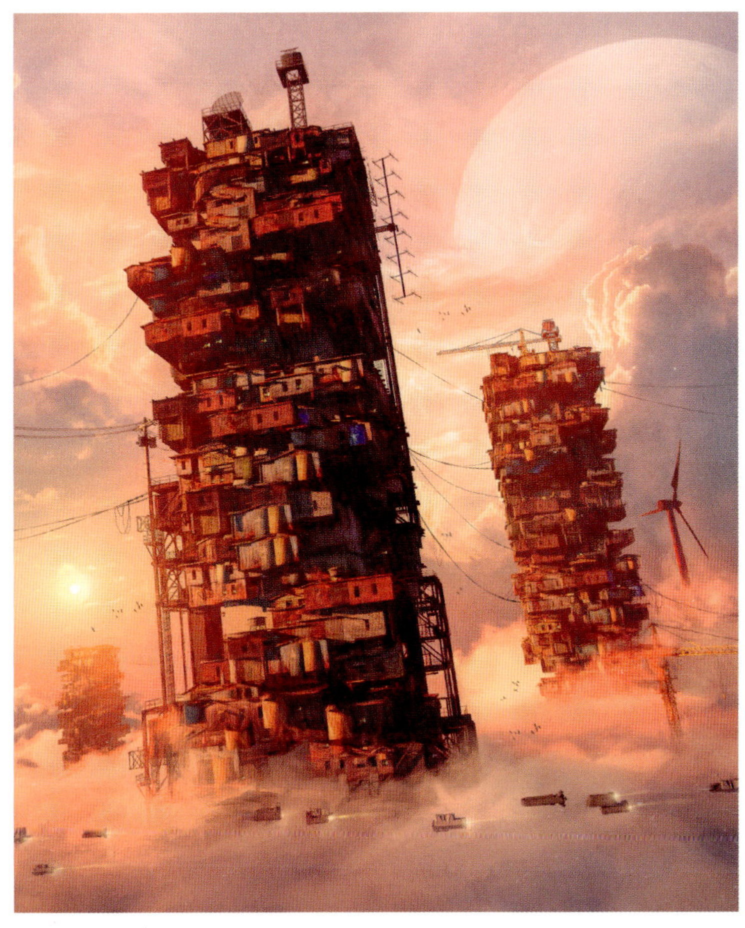

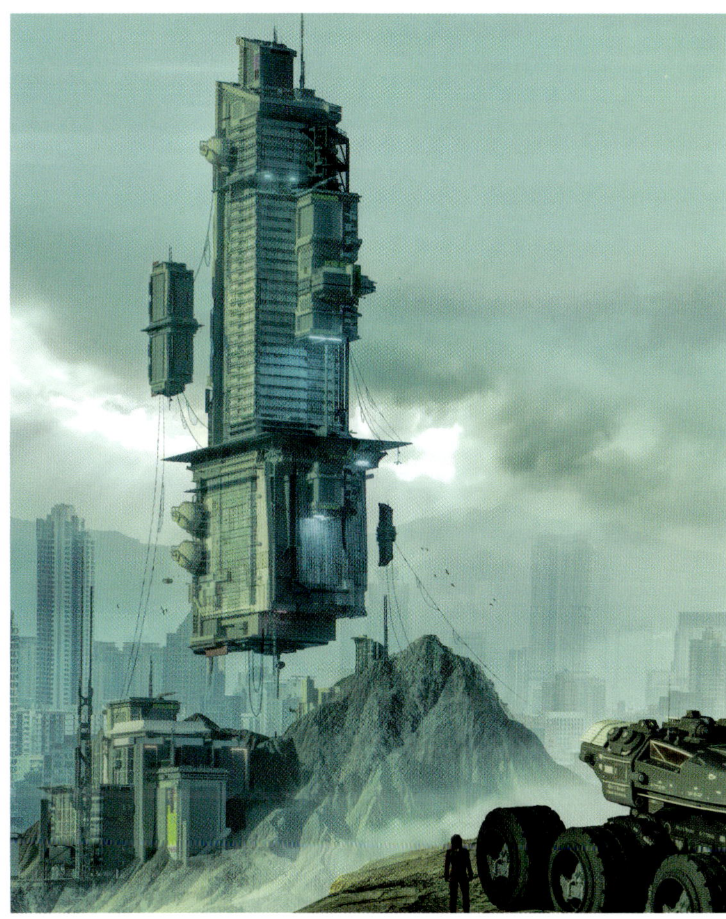

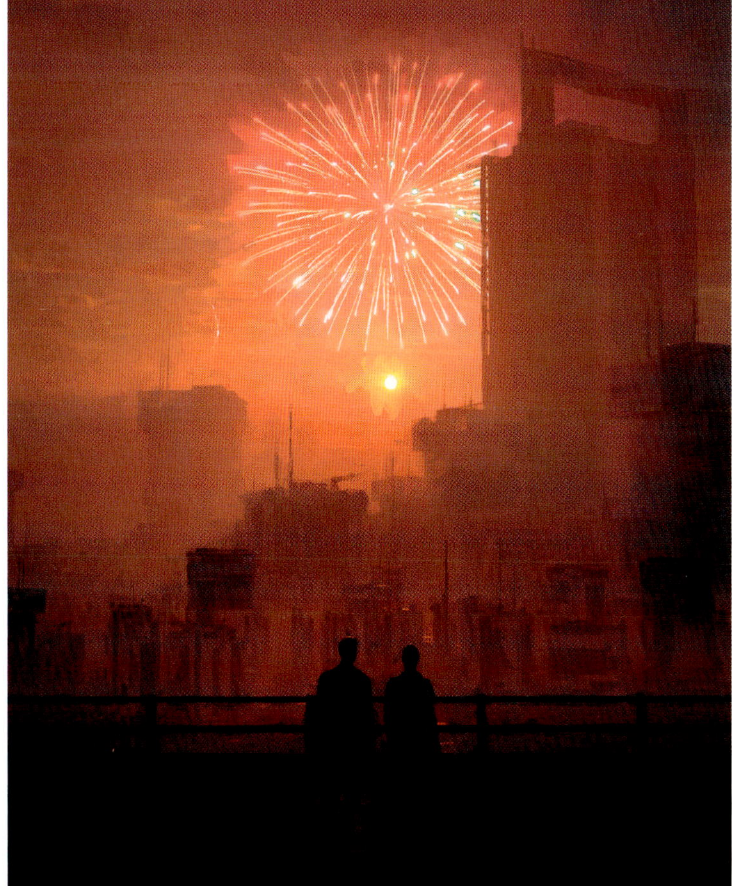

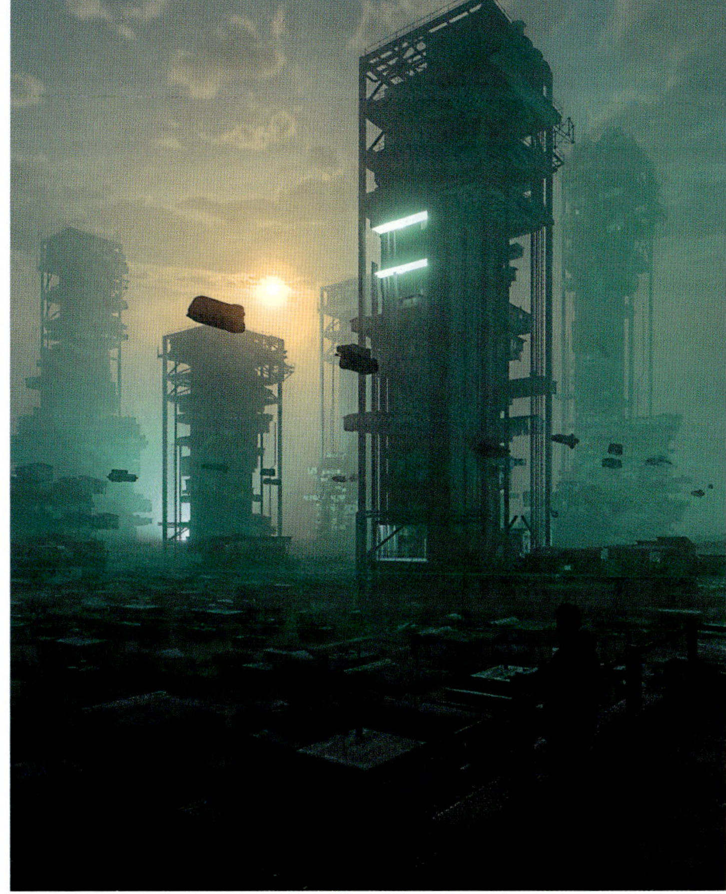

TOP LEFT
FRAGILE EXSISTENCE
11.11.2019

TOP RIGHT
TOWER OF SOLACE
09.01.2019

BOTTOM LEFT
NEXT CHAPTER
12.31.2019

BOTTOM RIGHT
LONG GAME
12.16.2019

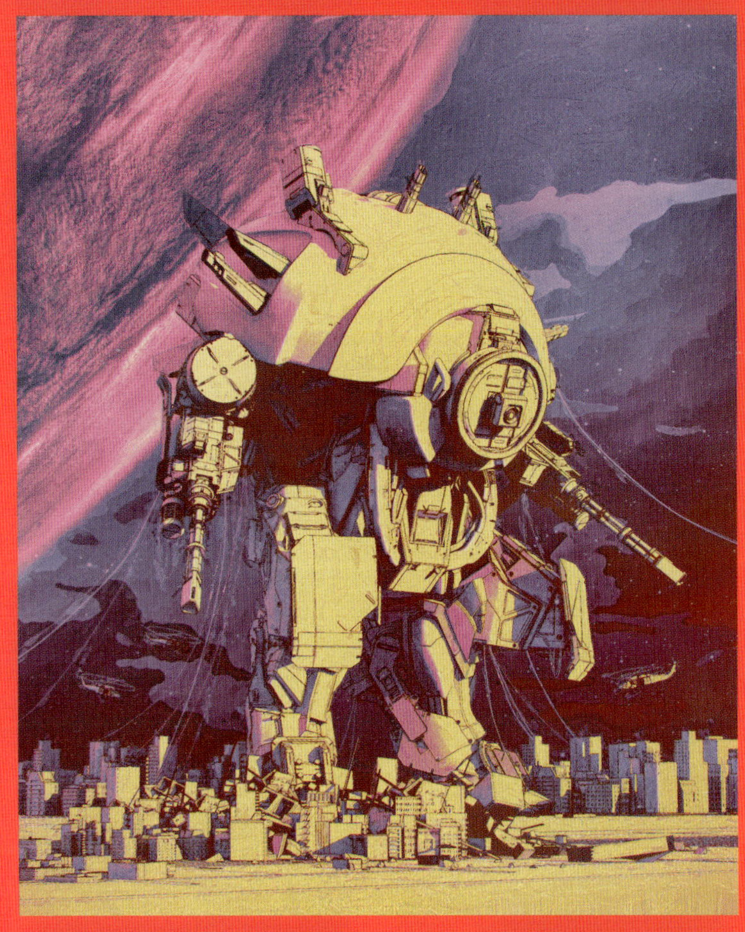

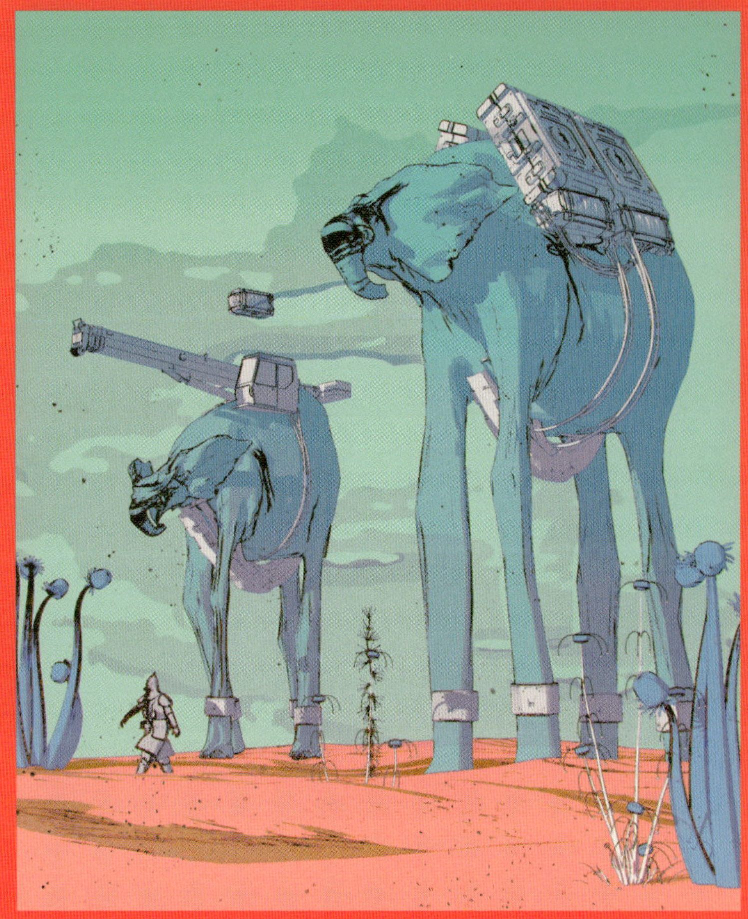

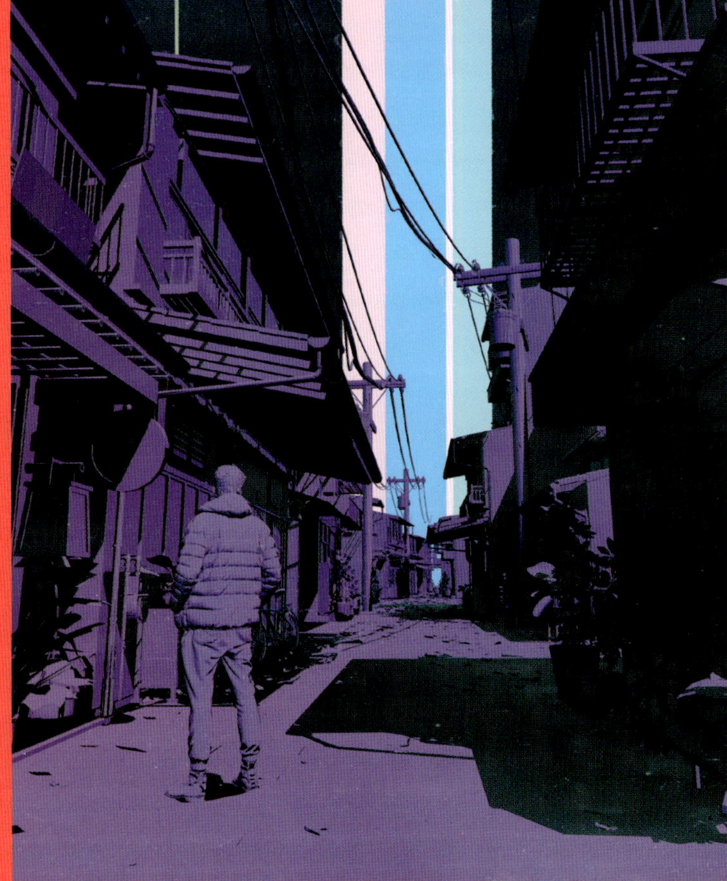

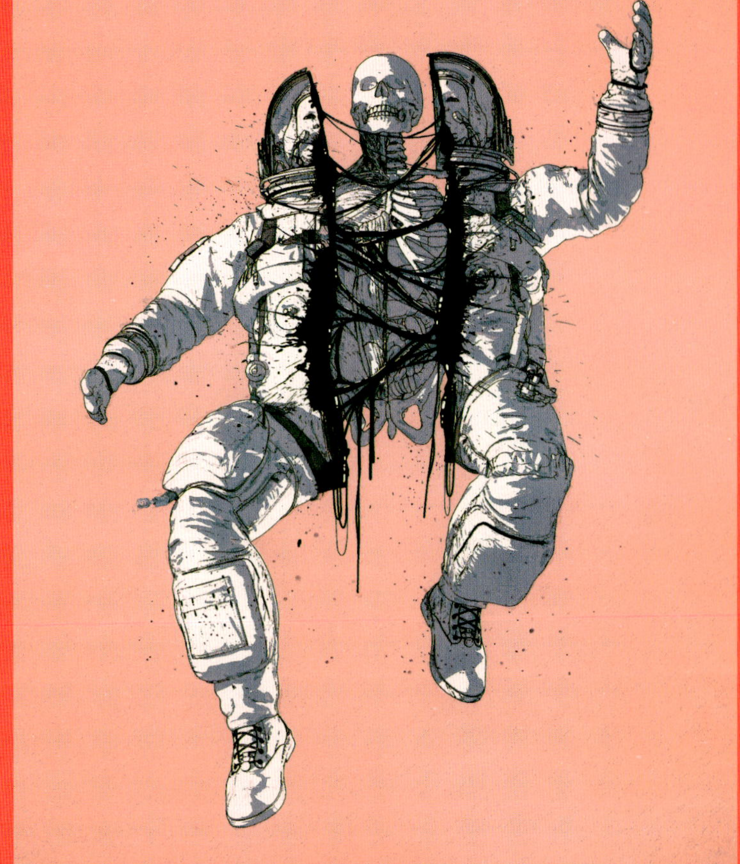

TOP LEFT
MEGIBOT
06.14.2019

TOP RIGHT
DATENIGHT
07.06.2019

BOTTOM LEFT
ENTIRELY PURPLE RAINBOW
07.20.2019

BOTTOM RIGHT
EXPLUSION
06.15.2019

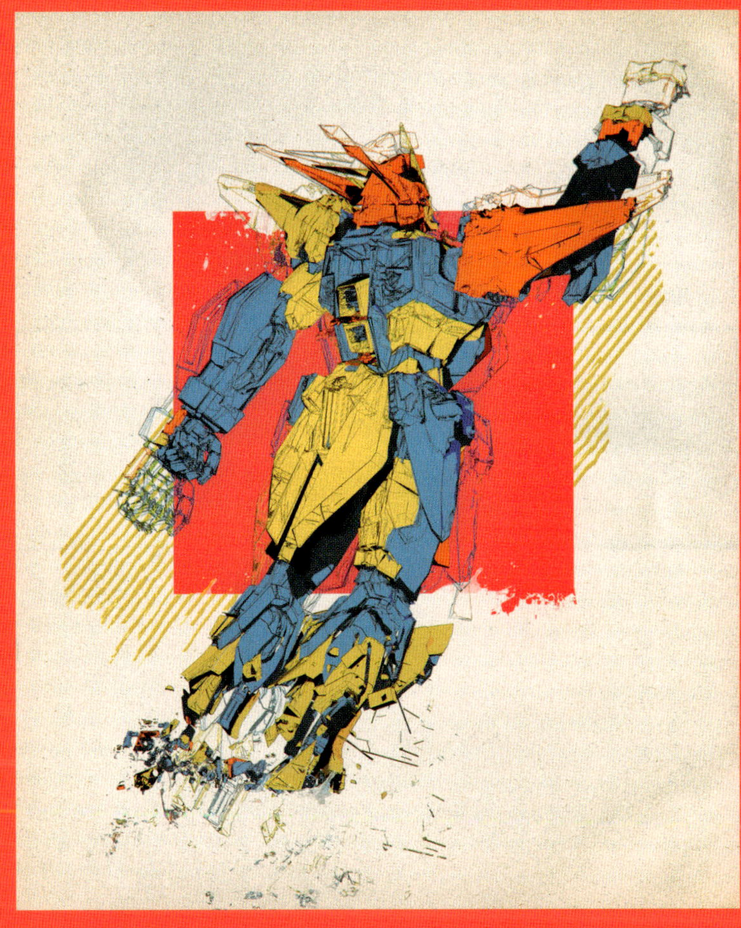

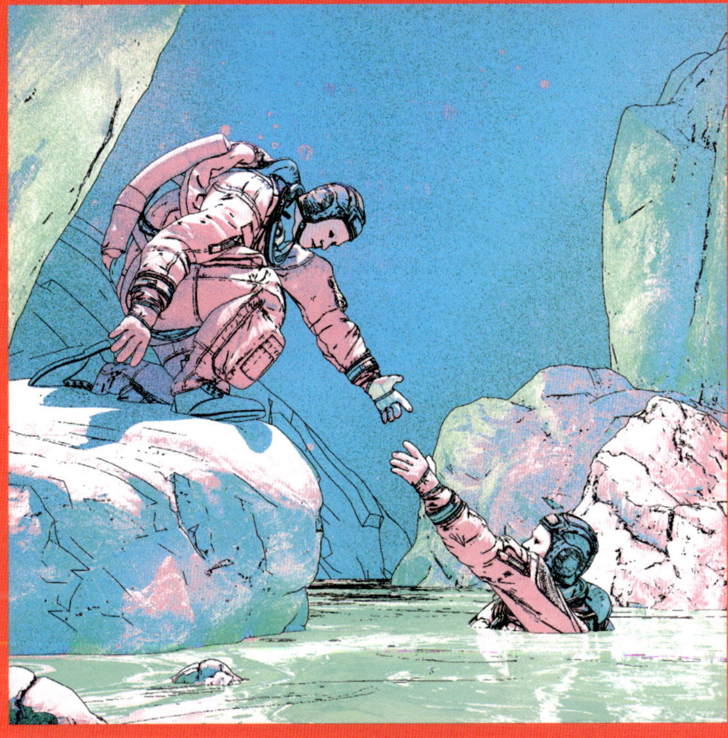

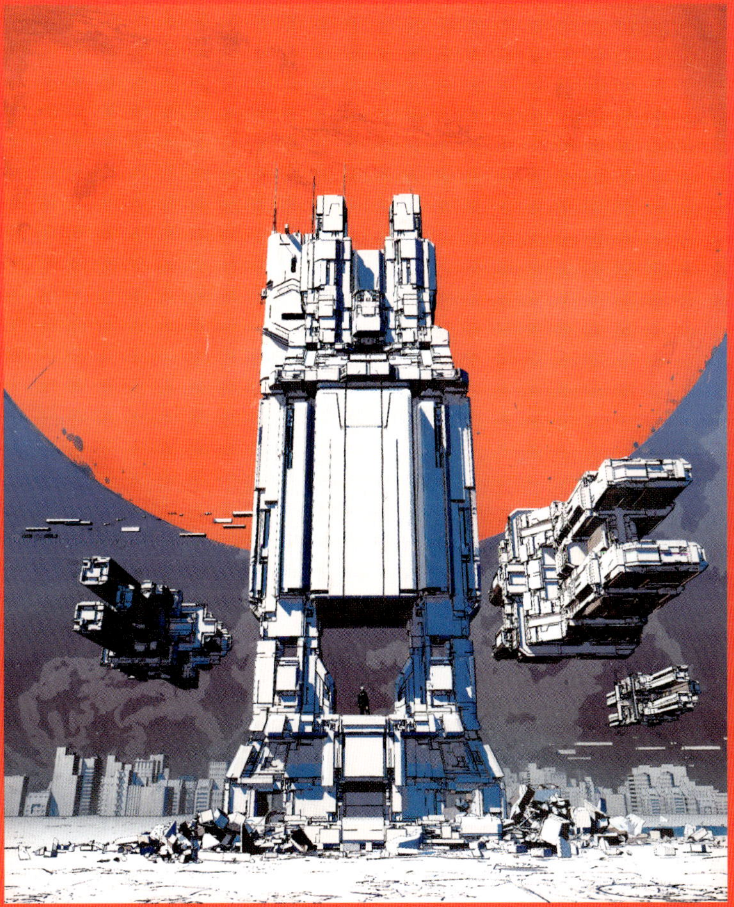

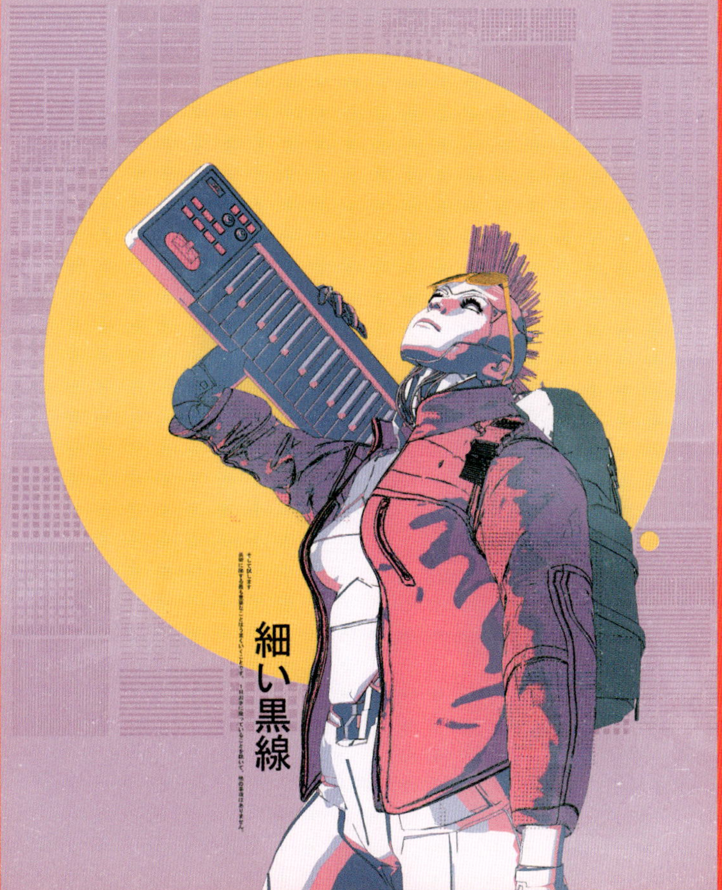

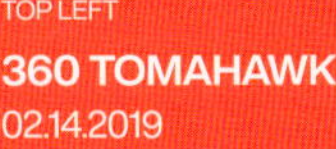

TOP LEFT
360 TOMAHAWK
02.14.2019

TOP RIGHT
LIL' HELP
03.05.2019

BOTTOM LEFT
1981 FORWARD
03.19.2019

BOTTOM RIGHT
THIN BLACK LINE
03.21.2019

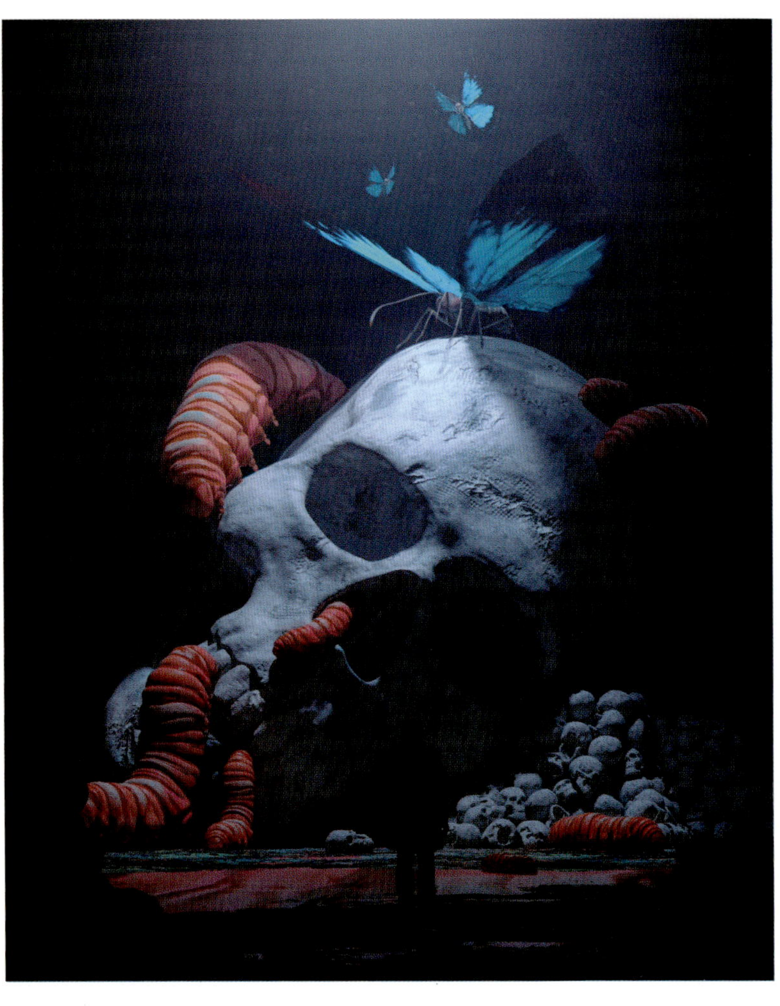

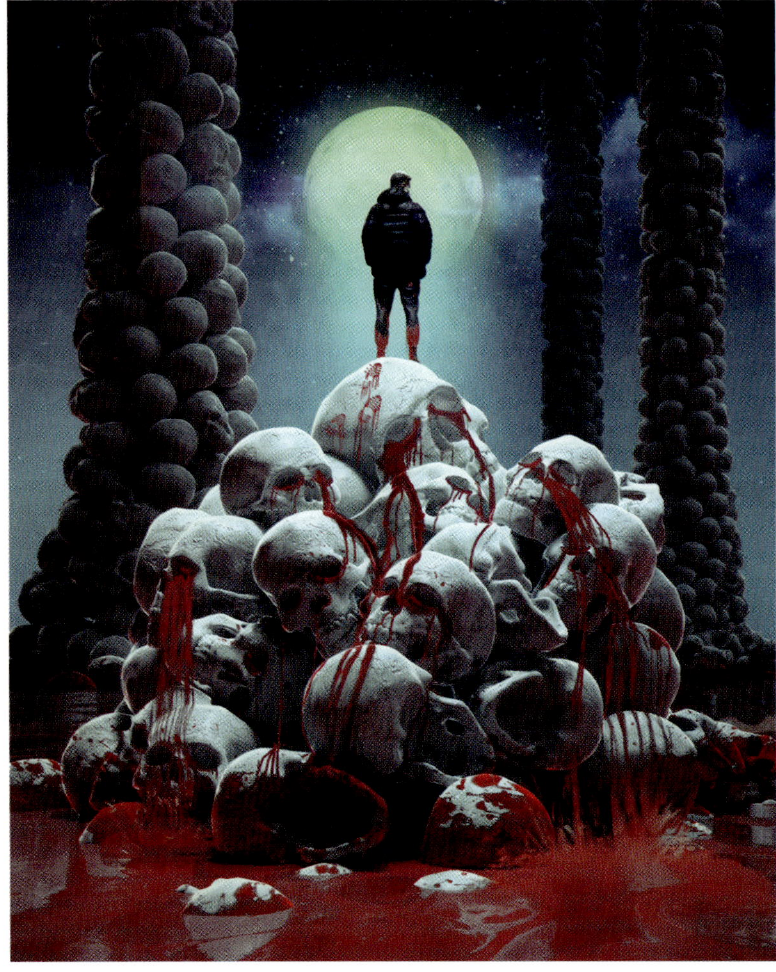

TOP

OFF WHITE
03.07.2019

BOTTOM

ON TO THE NEXT ONE
12.04.2019

OPPOSITE PAGE

rest in peace, motherfucker
04.30.2019

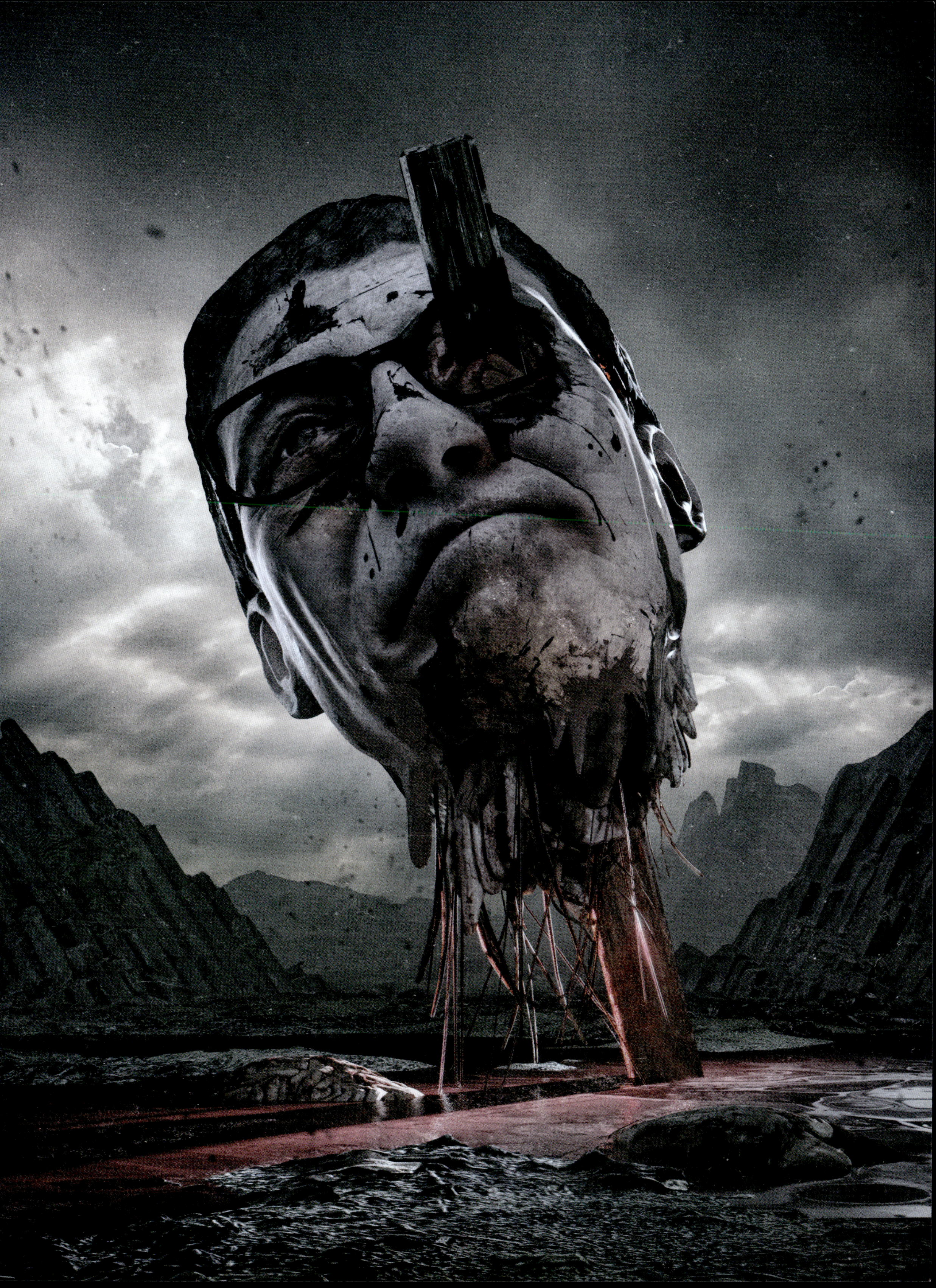

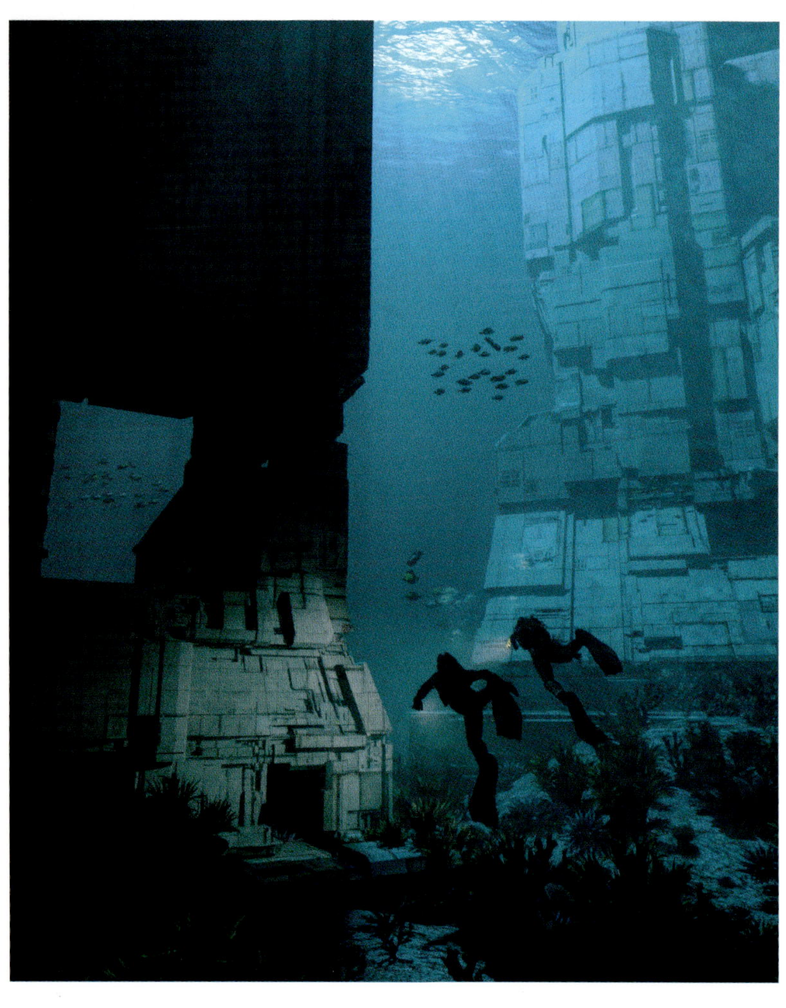

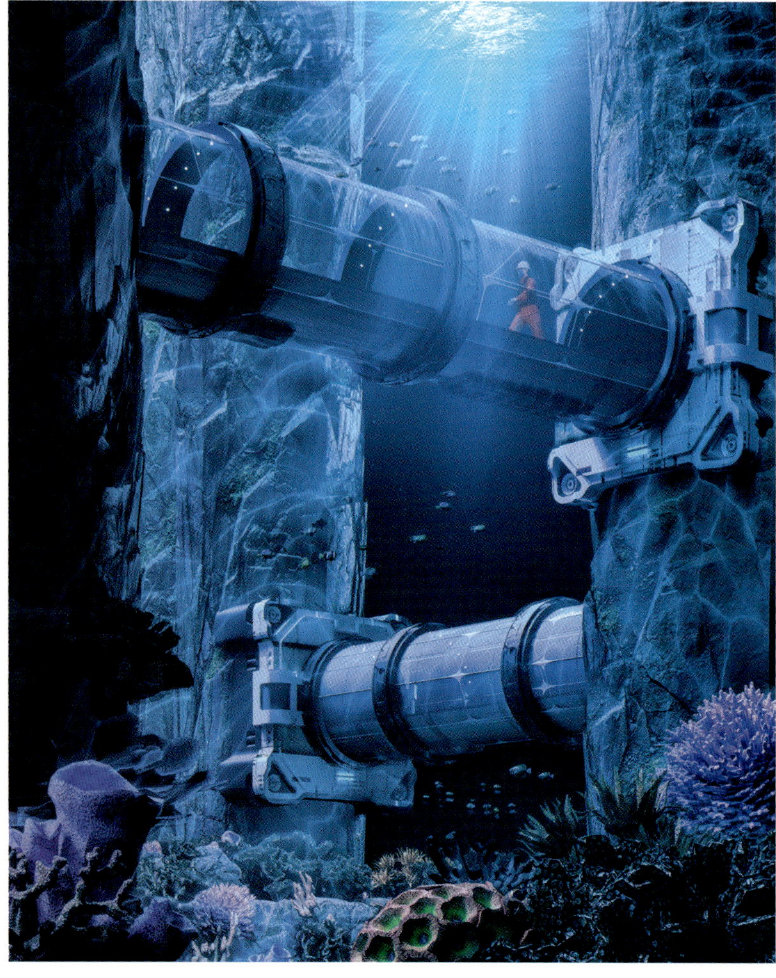

TOP

FORGOTTEN FUTURE
03.26.2019

BOTTOM

NEW YORK CITY 2281
02.28.2019

OPPOSITE PAGE

CURRENT EVENTS
12.26.2019

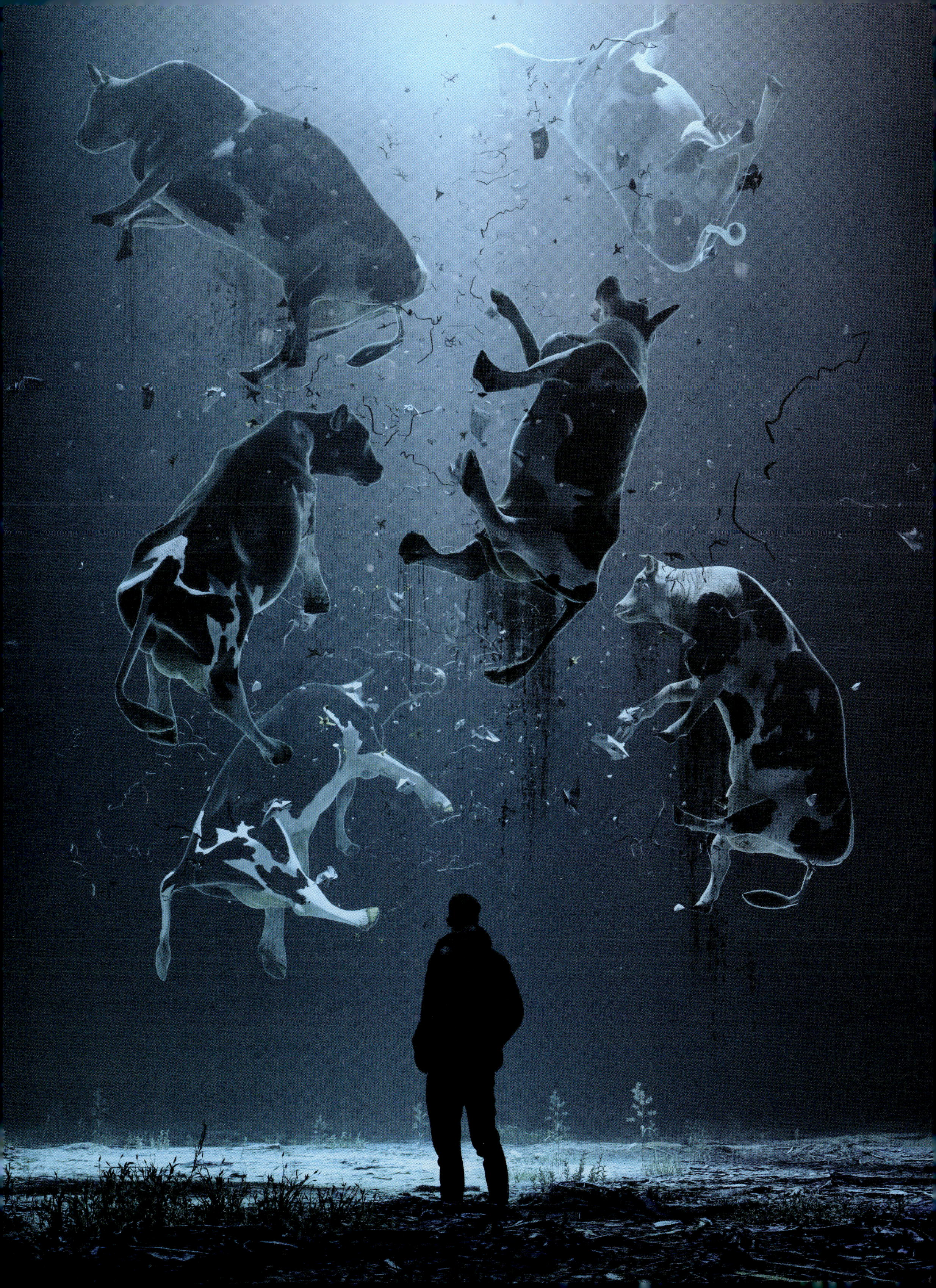

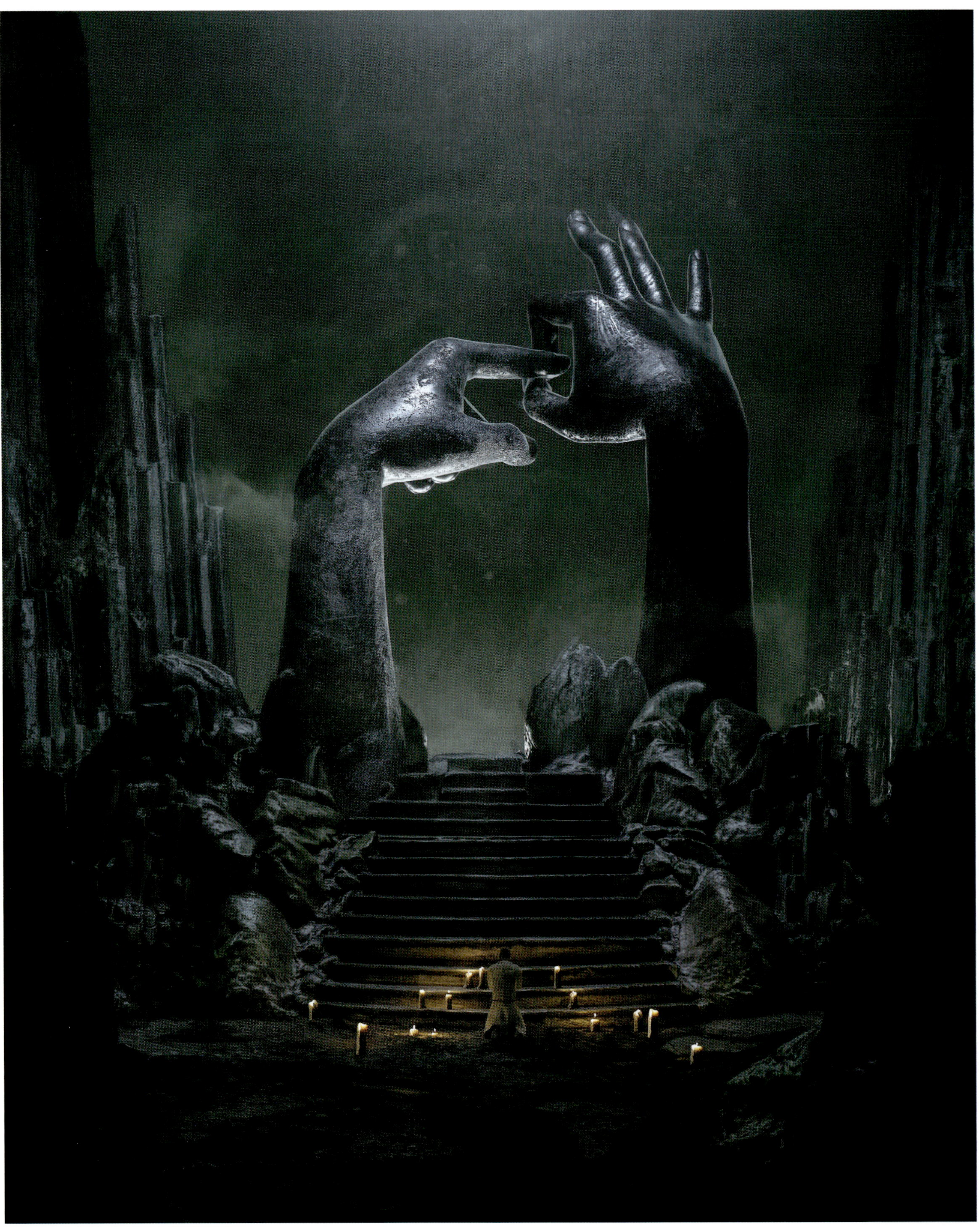

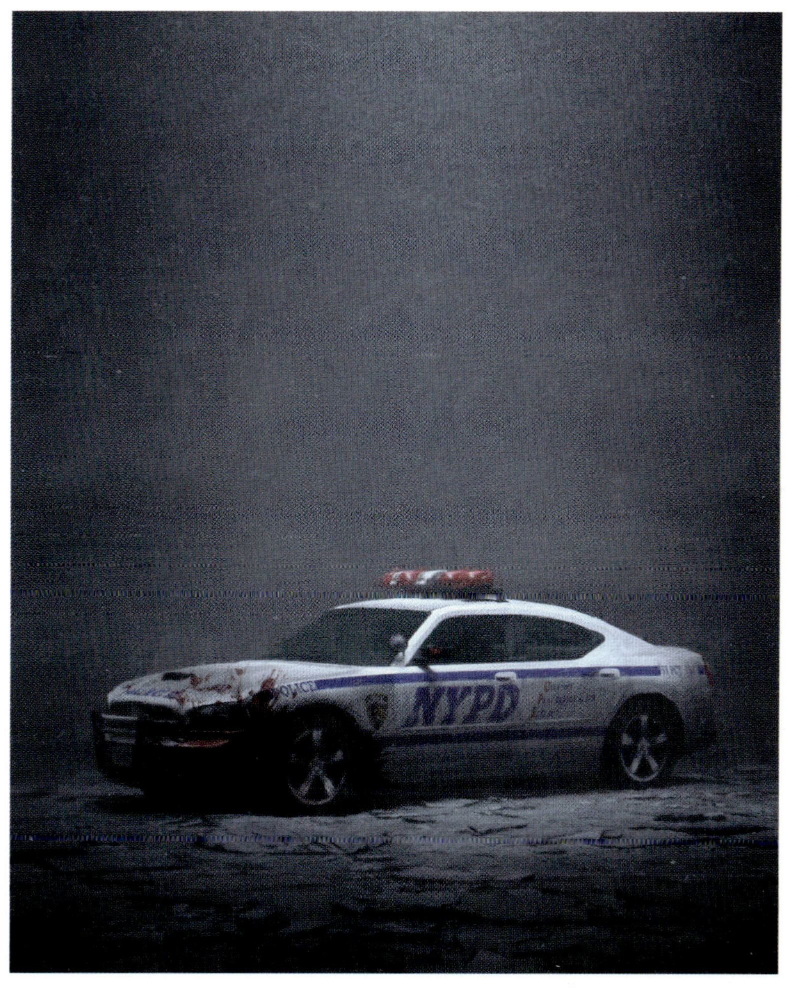

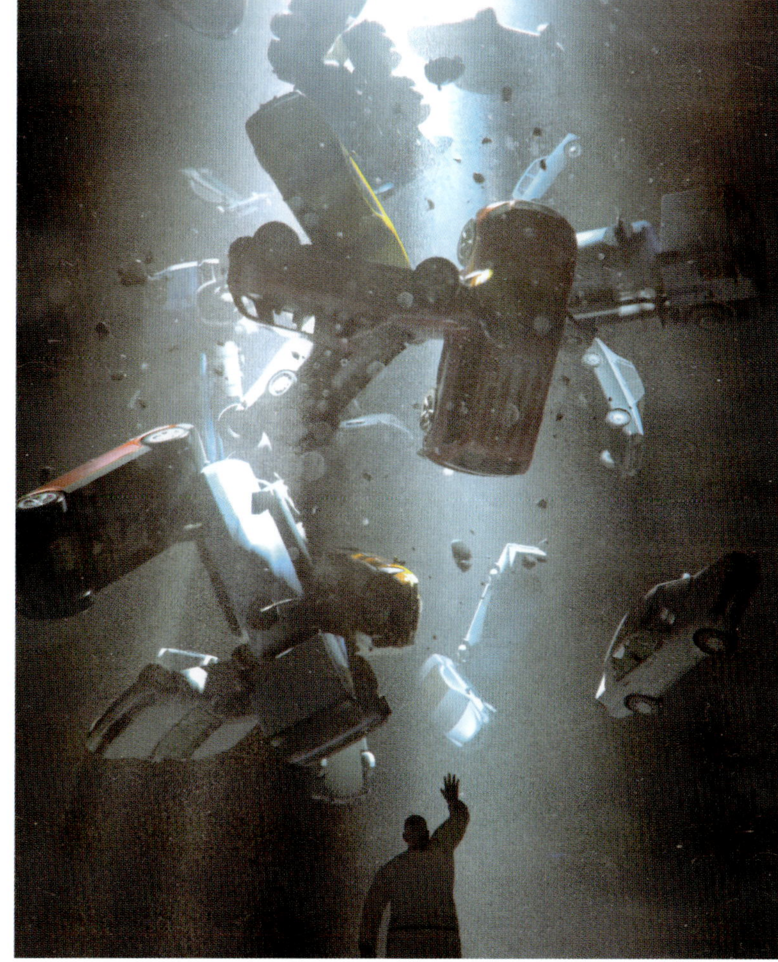

OPPOSITE PAGE

I / O
02.16.2019

TOP

FOG OF WAR
11.20.2019

BOTTOM

JUGGLING ACT
07.23.2019

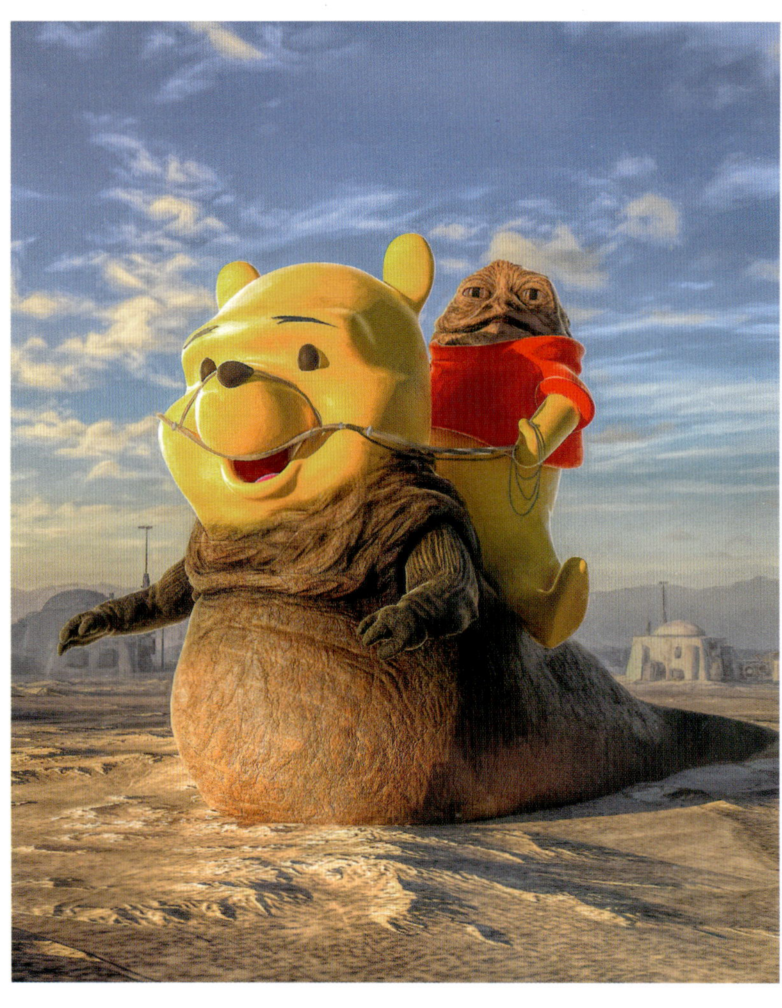

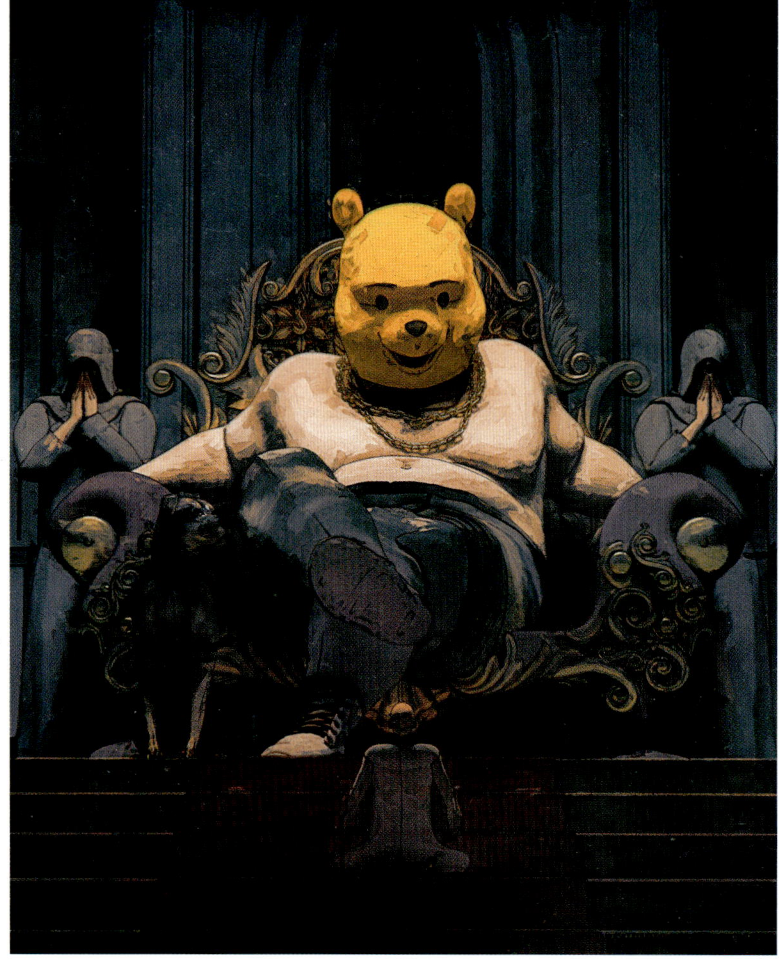

TOP

JABBA THE POOH / WINNIE THE HUTT

12.12.2019

BOTTOM

POOH BOSS

03.10.2019

OPPOSITE PAGE

TROJAN POOH

04.03.2019

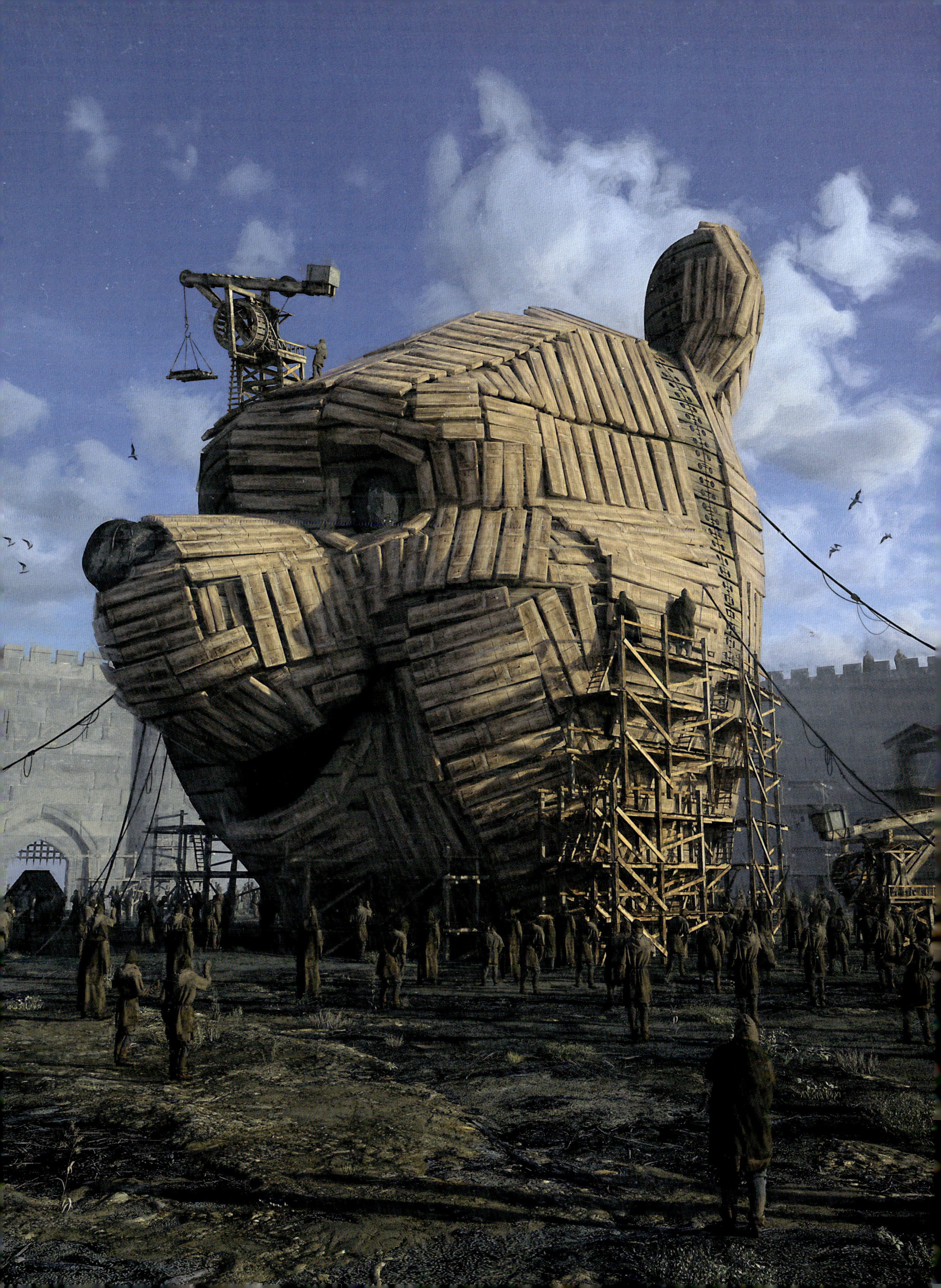

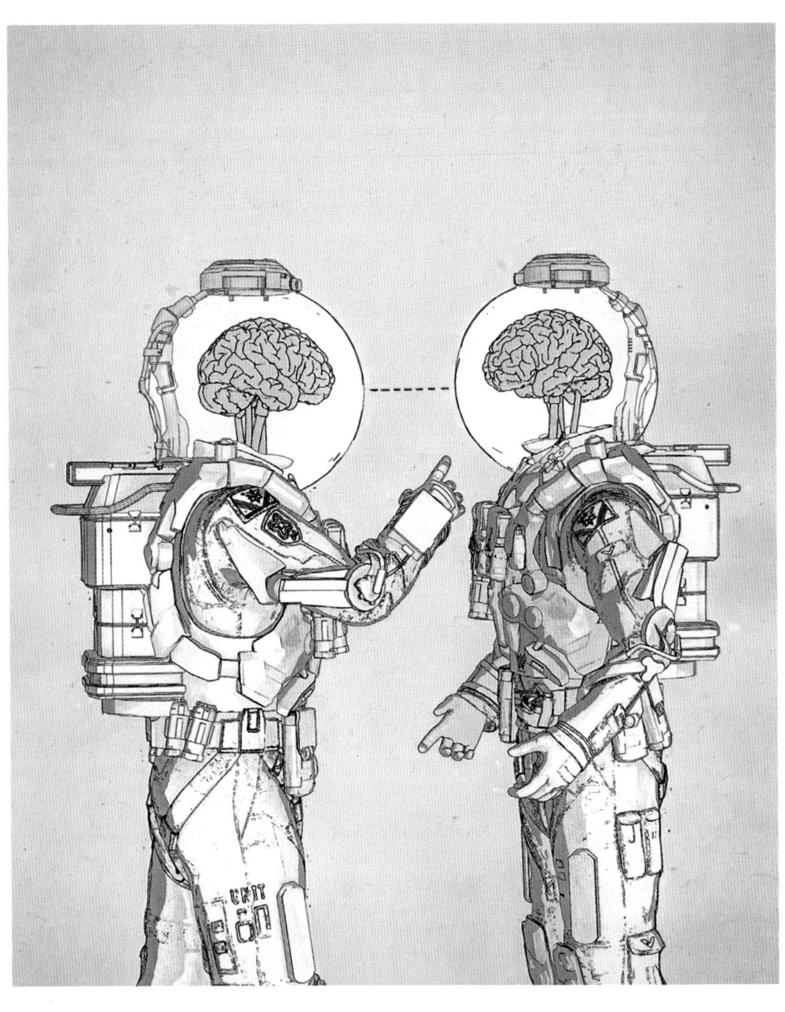

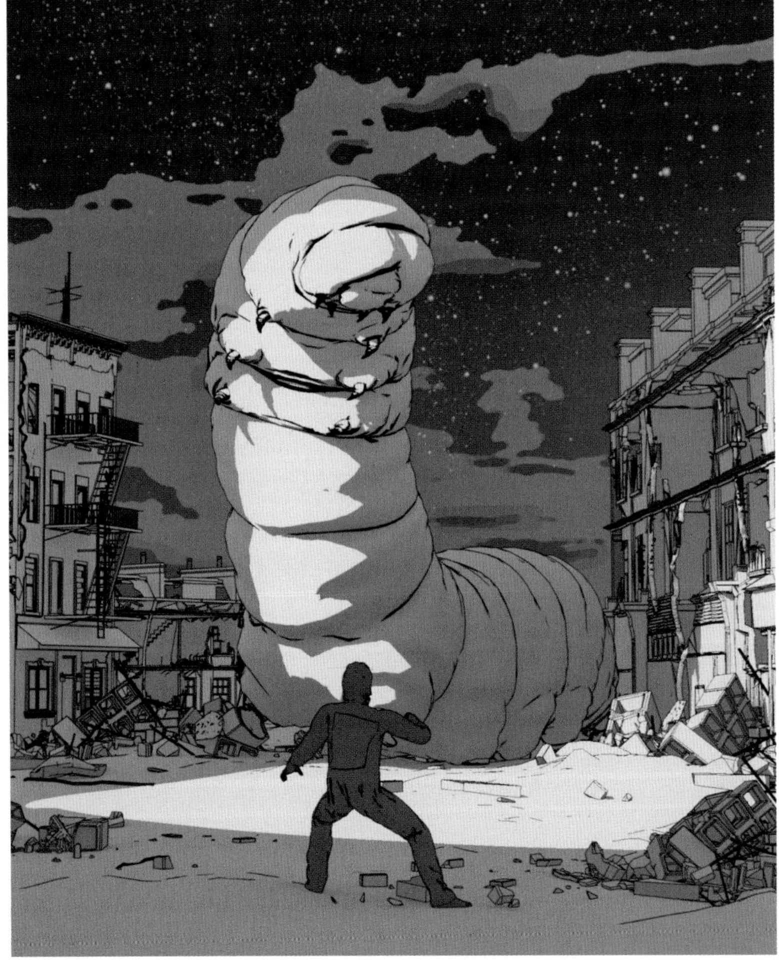

TOP

KOMMUNICATE

06.24.2019

BOTTOM

MONOCHROMATIC ABBERATION

02.12.2019

OPPOSITE PAGE

WHITE PEARL

02.11.2019

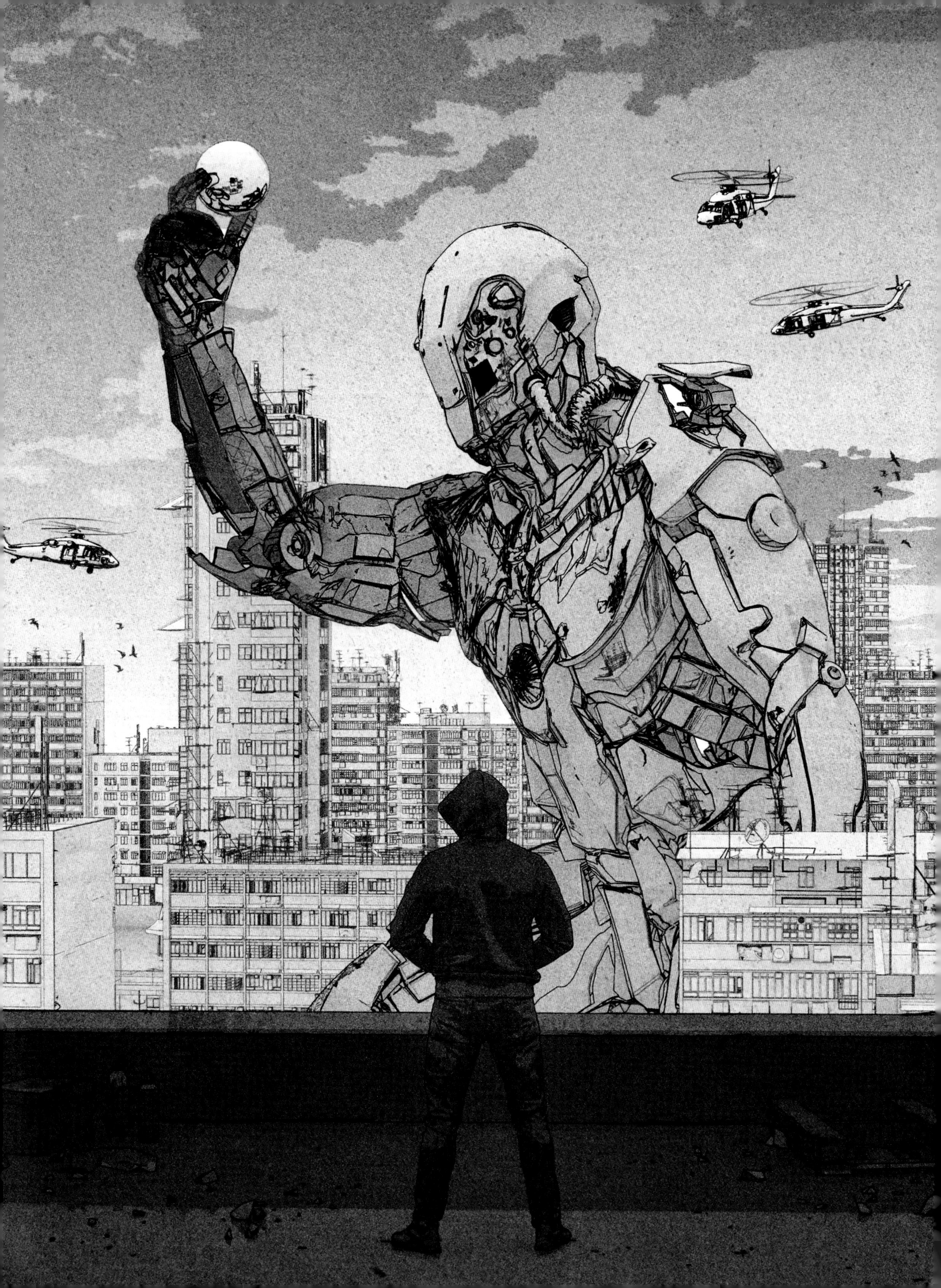

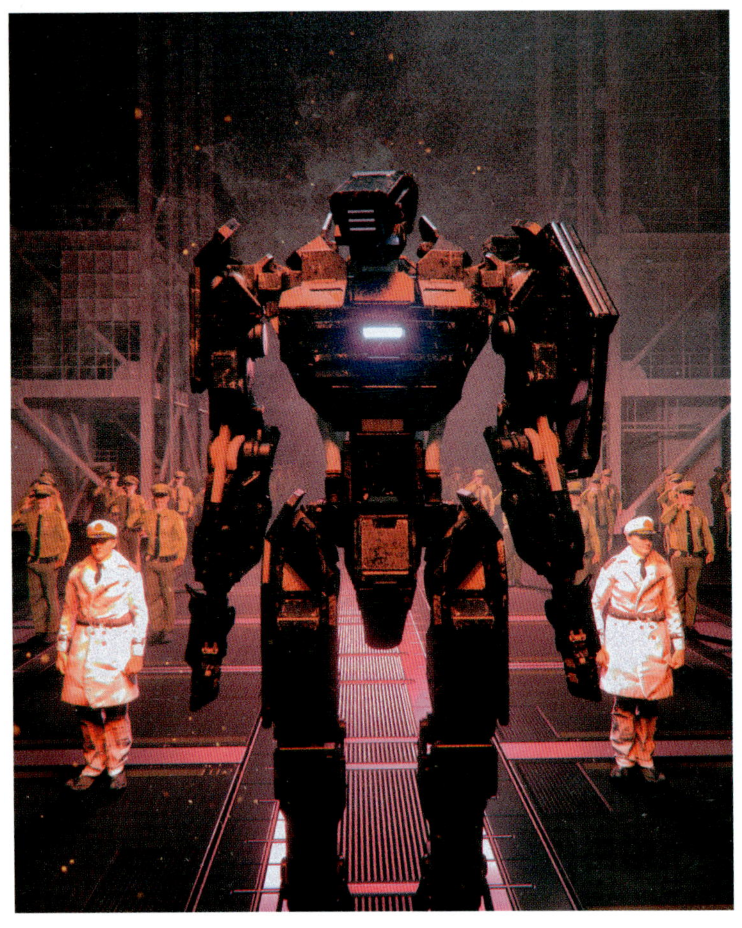

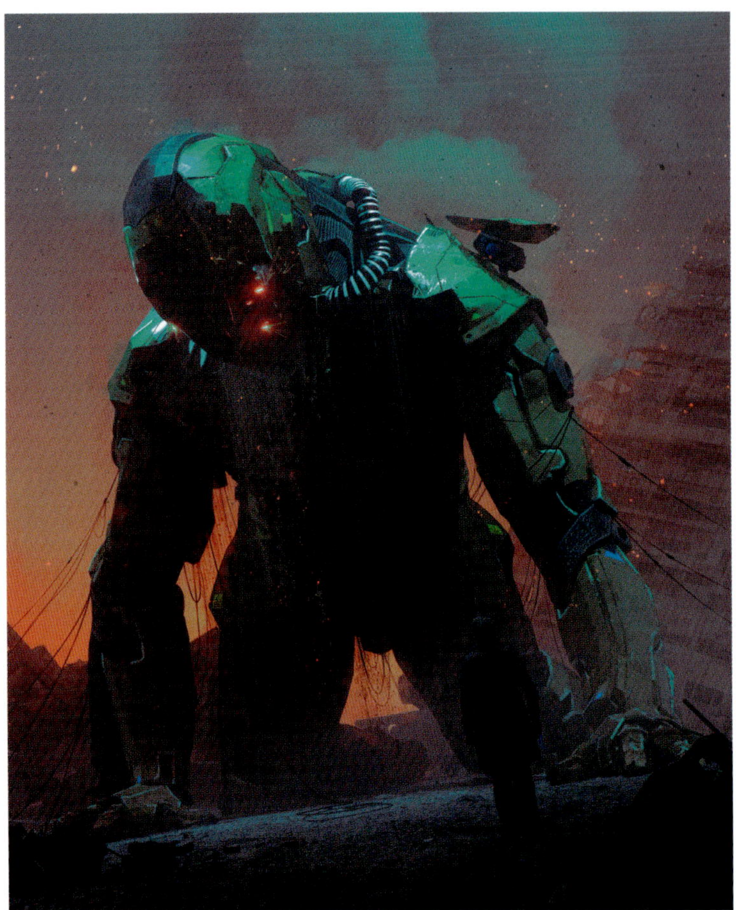

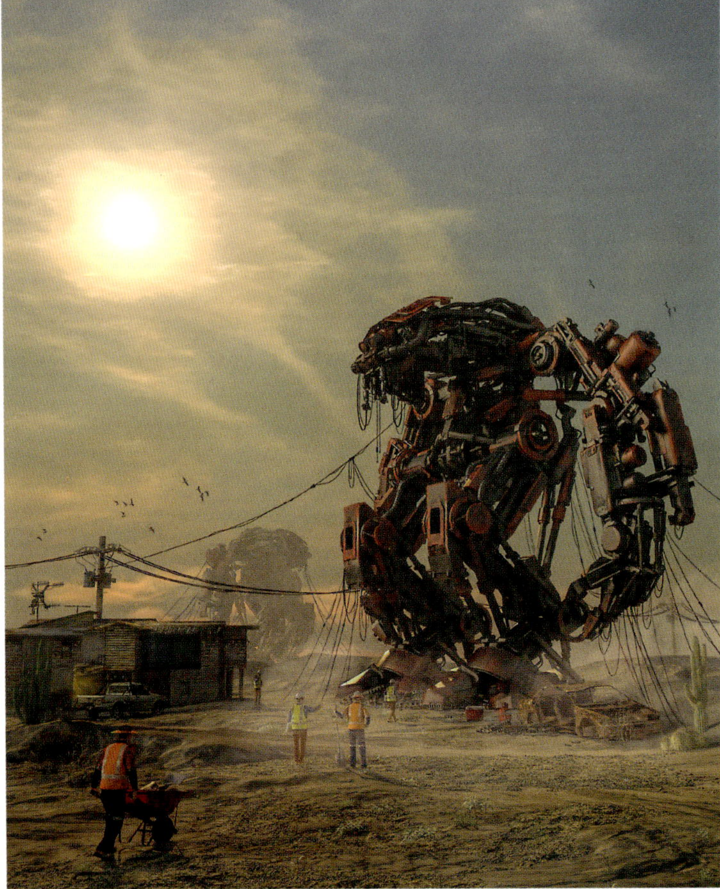

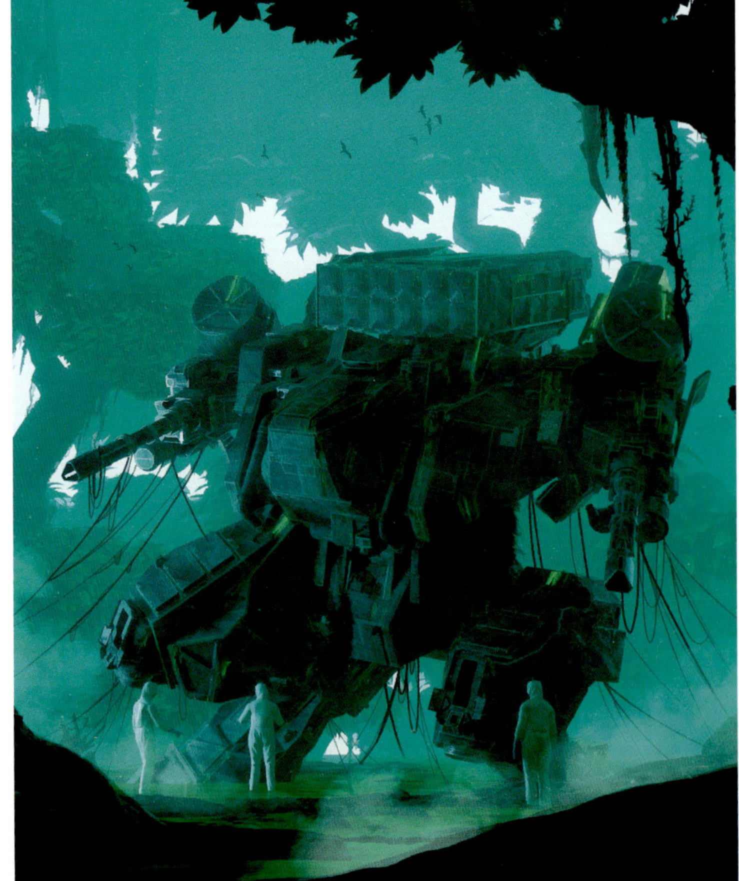

TOP LEFT
robo smard blog
07.13.2019

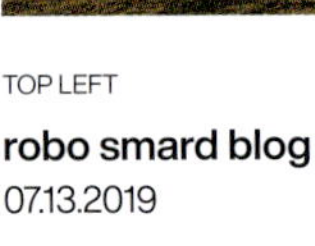

TOP RIGHT
BAD ROBOT
11.02.2019

BOTTOM LEFT
REPURPOSED FUTURE
06.06.2019

BOTTOM RIGHT
BROKE DOWN
06.10.2019

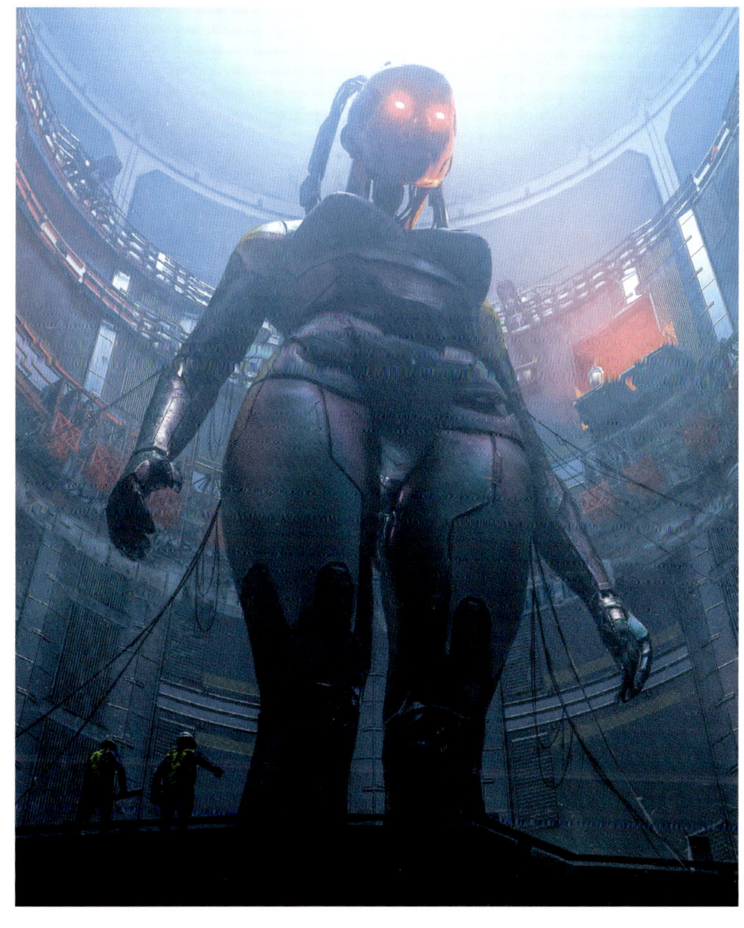

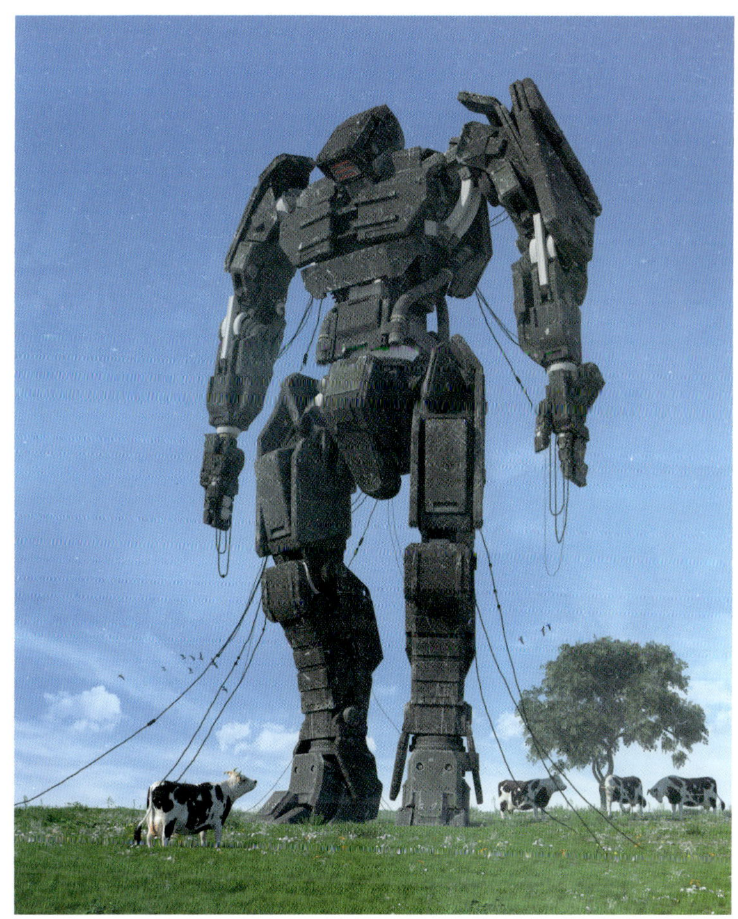

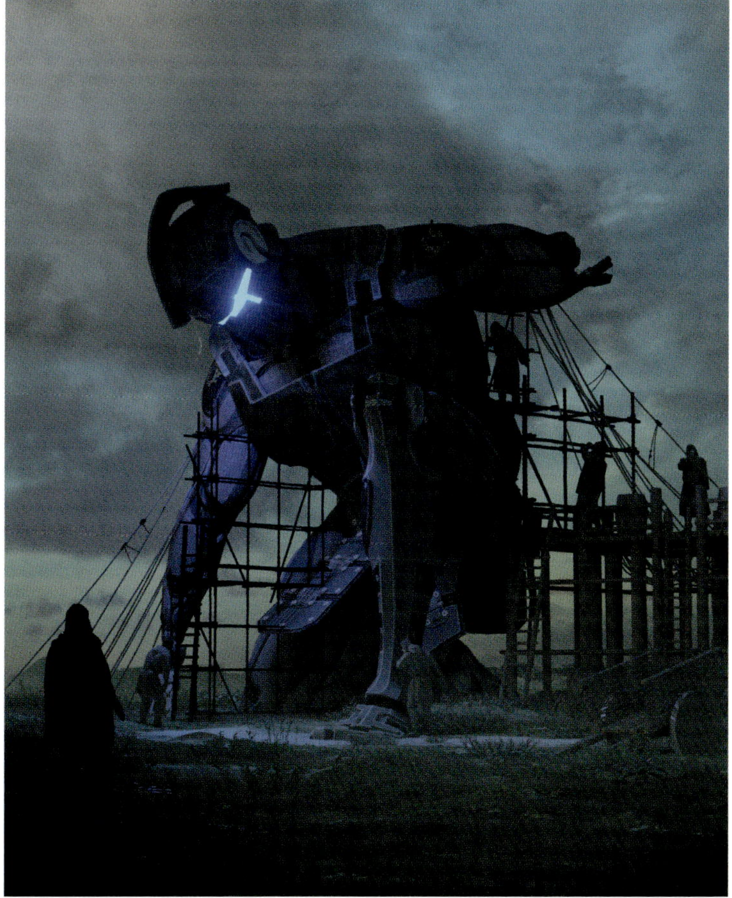

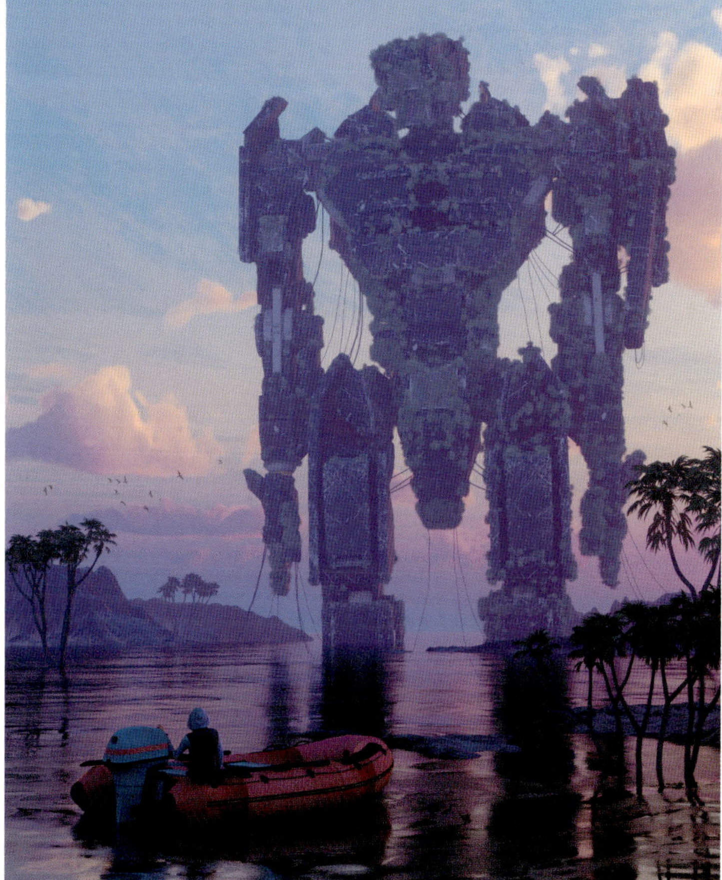

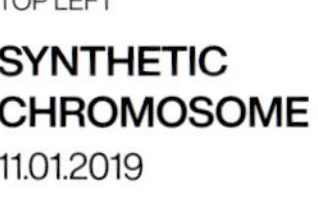

TOP LEFT

SYNTHETIC CHROMOSOME
11.01.2019

TOP RIGHT

BEYOND MEAT
07.15.2019

BOTTOM LEFT

AWAKEN GIANT
03.15.2019

BOTTOM RIGHT

AFTERMATH
12.22.2019

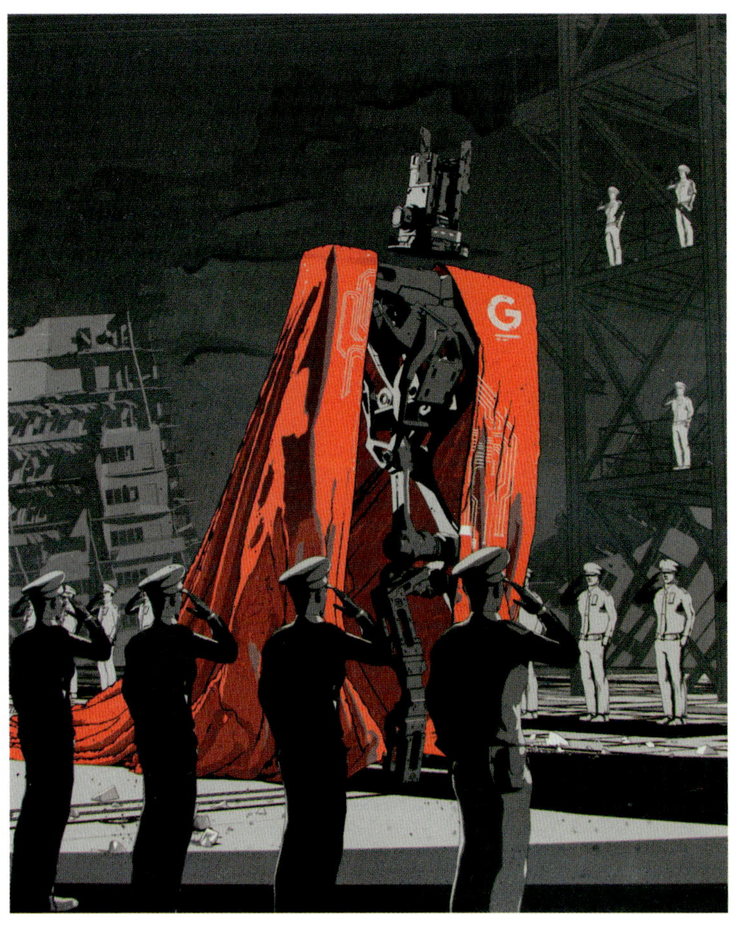

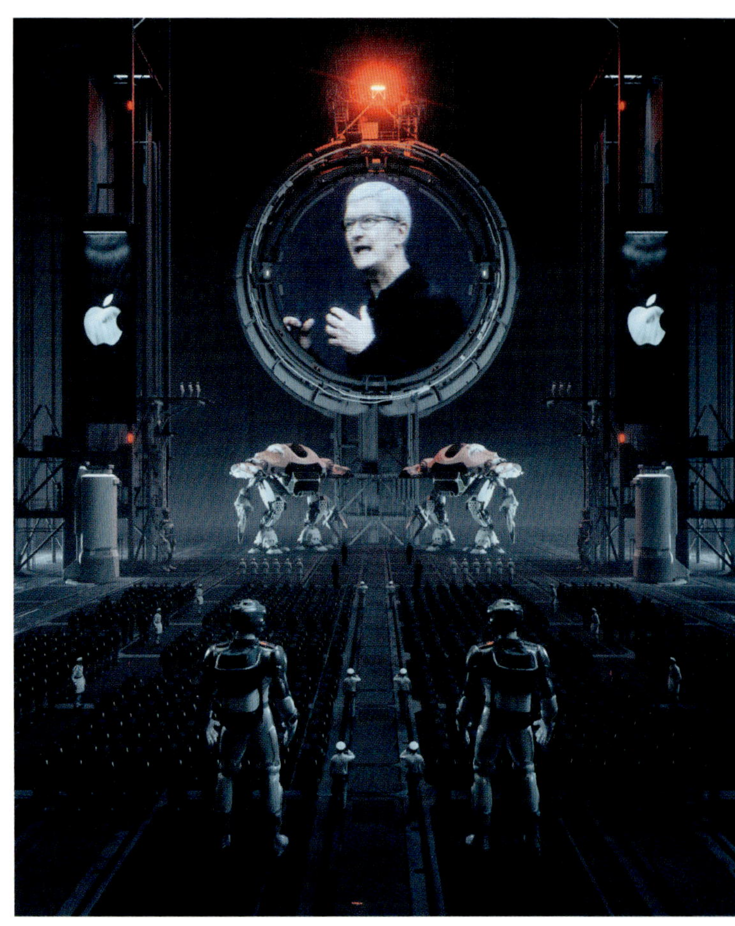

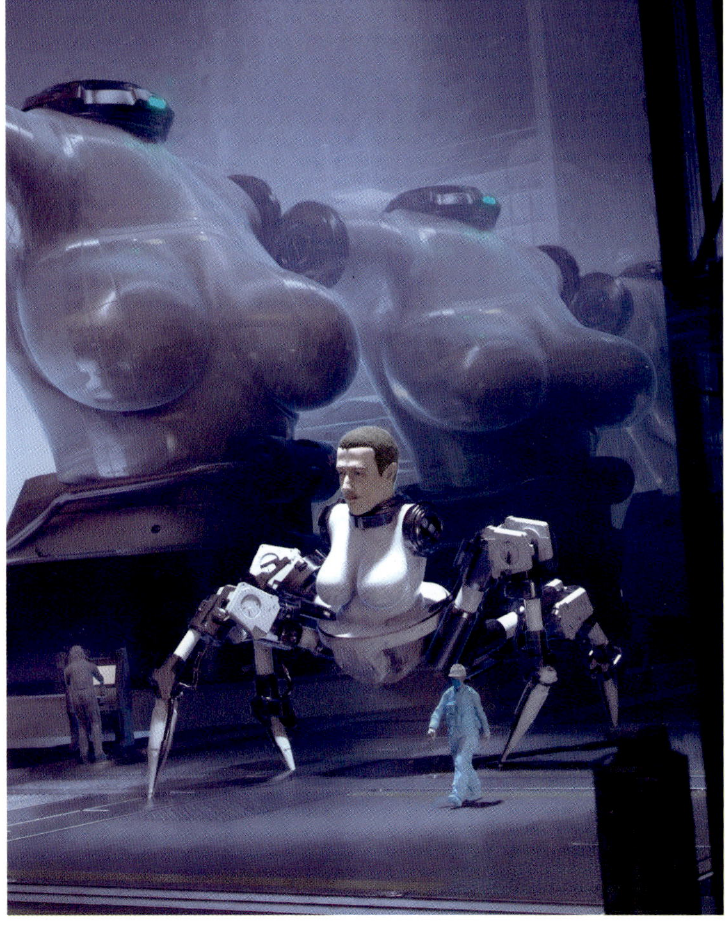

TOP LEFT

GENERAL DUPLEX
06.08.2019

TOP RIGHT

WWDC 2081
06.05.2019

BOTTOM

ZUCKERBORG NIPPLE-FREE SOCIETY
10.08.2019

OPPOSITE PAGE

DISNEYLAND MARS 2070
12.07.2019

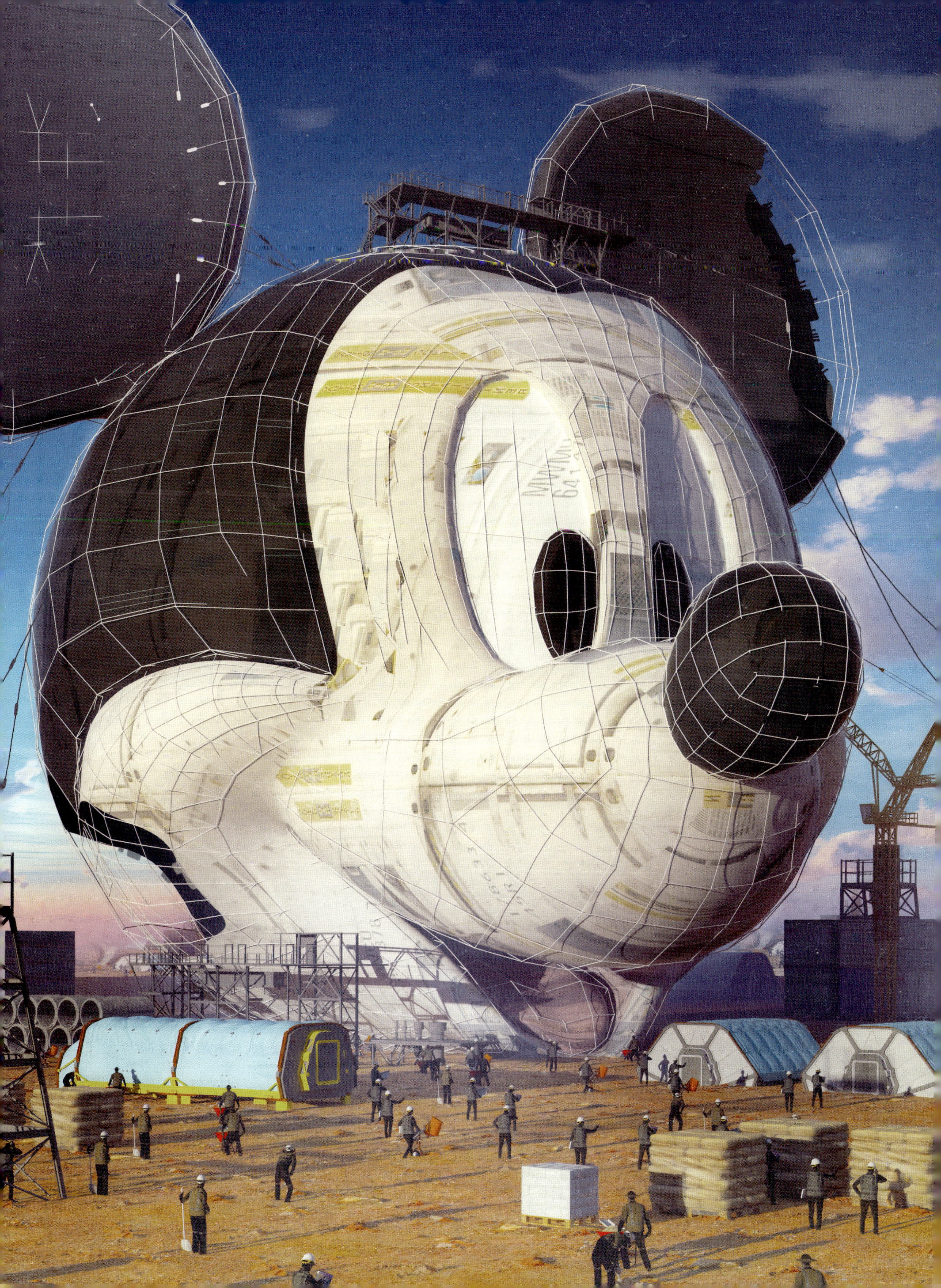

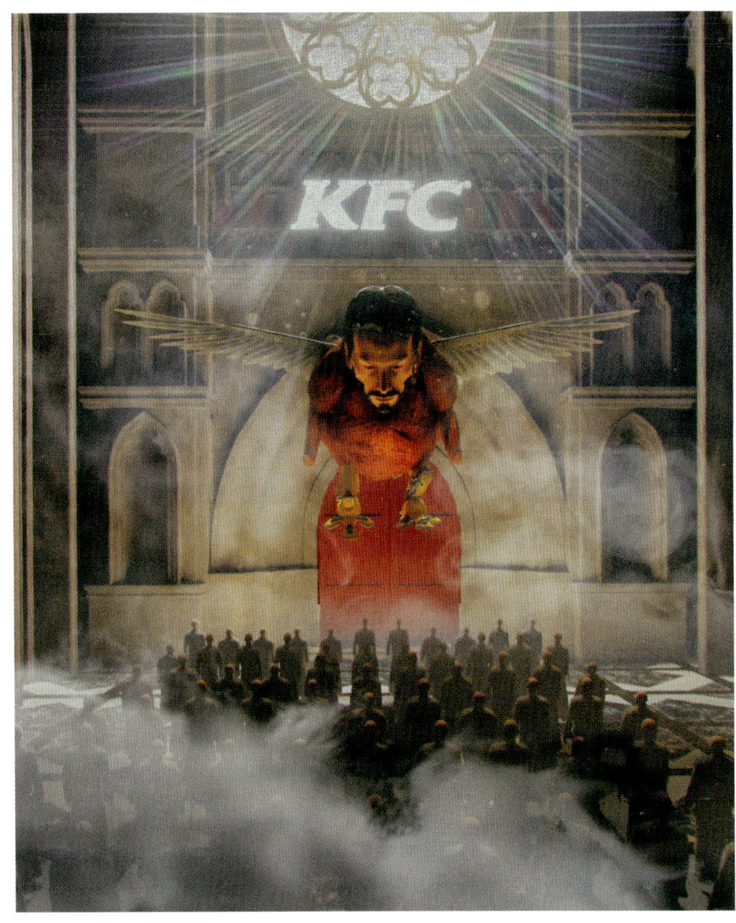

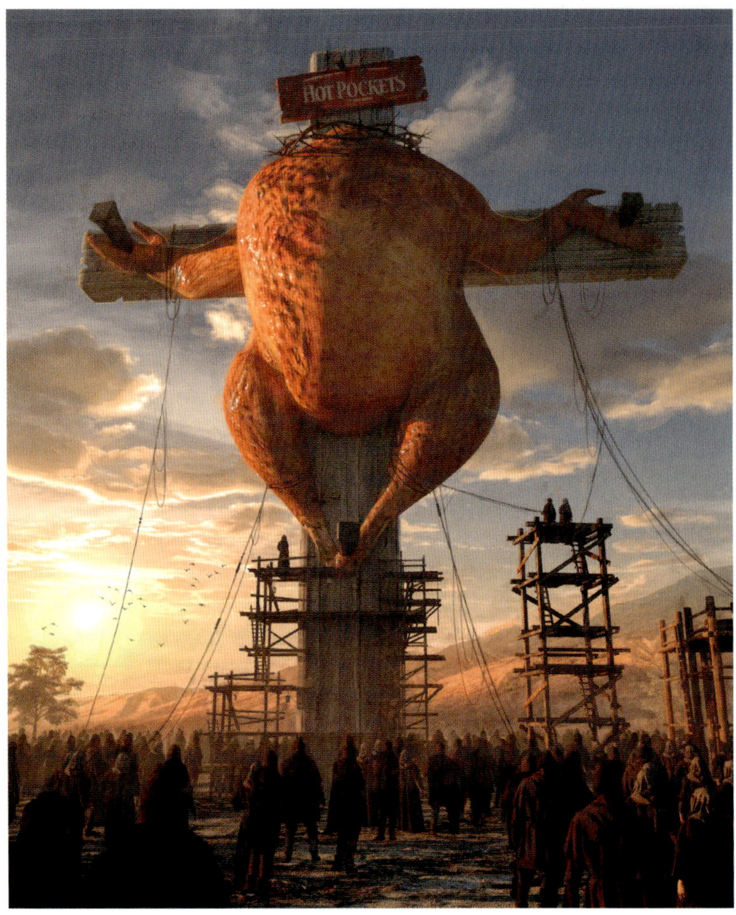

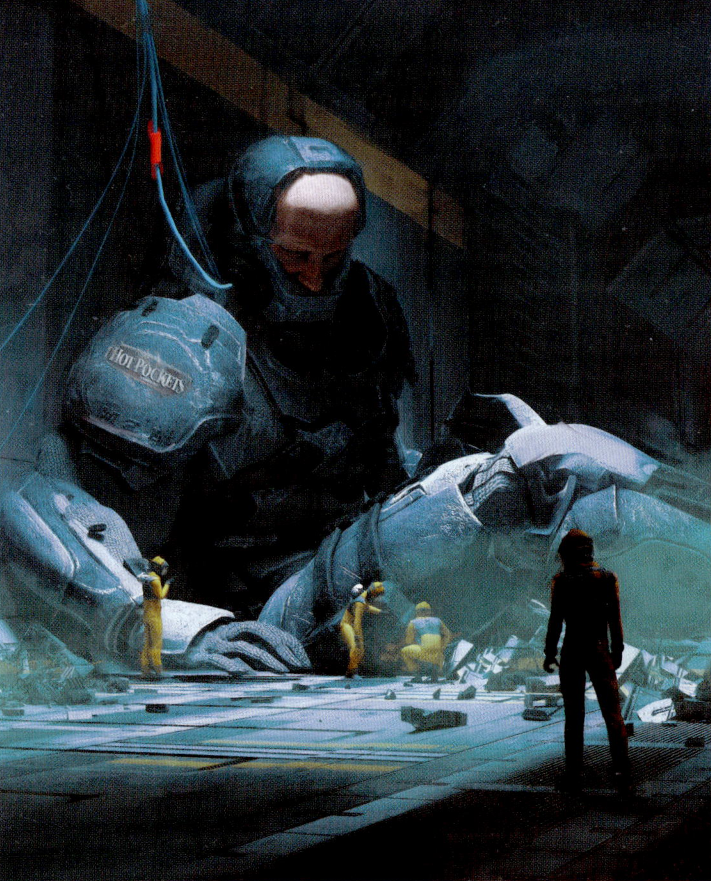

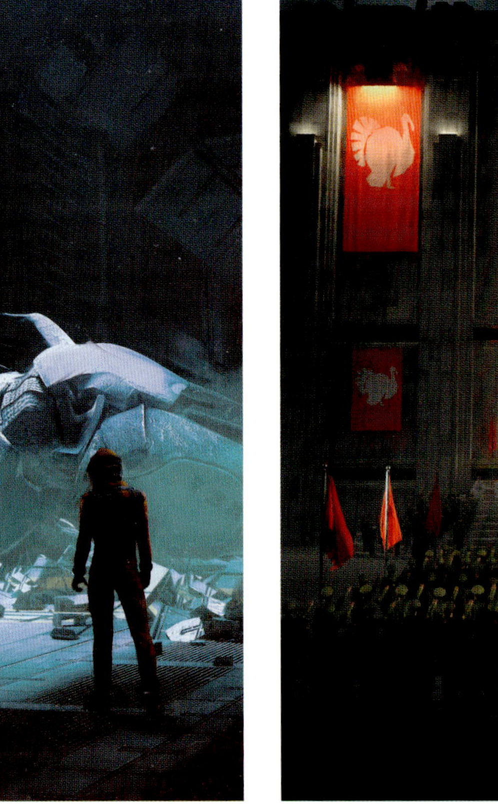

TOP LEFT
KEANU FRIED CHURCH
06.28.2019

TOP RIGHT
TURKEY SAVIOR
11.26.2019

BOTTOM LEFT
SILENT VICTORY
10.23.2019

BOTTOM RIGHT
FASCIST TURKEY
11.27.2019

OPPOSITE PAGE
ORGANIC VIRGIN BABY HEARTS - NEW FLAVOR FROM HOTPOCKETS
09.10.2019

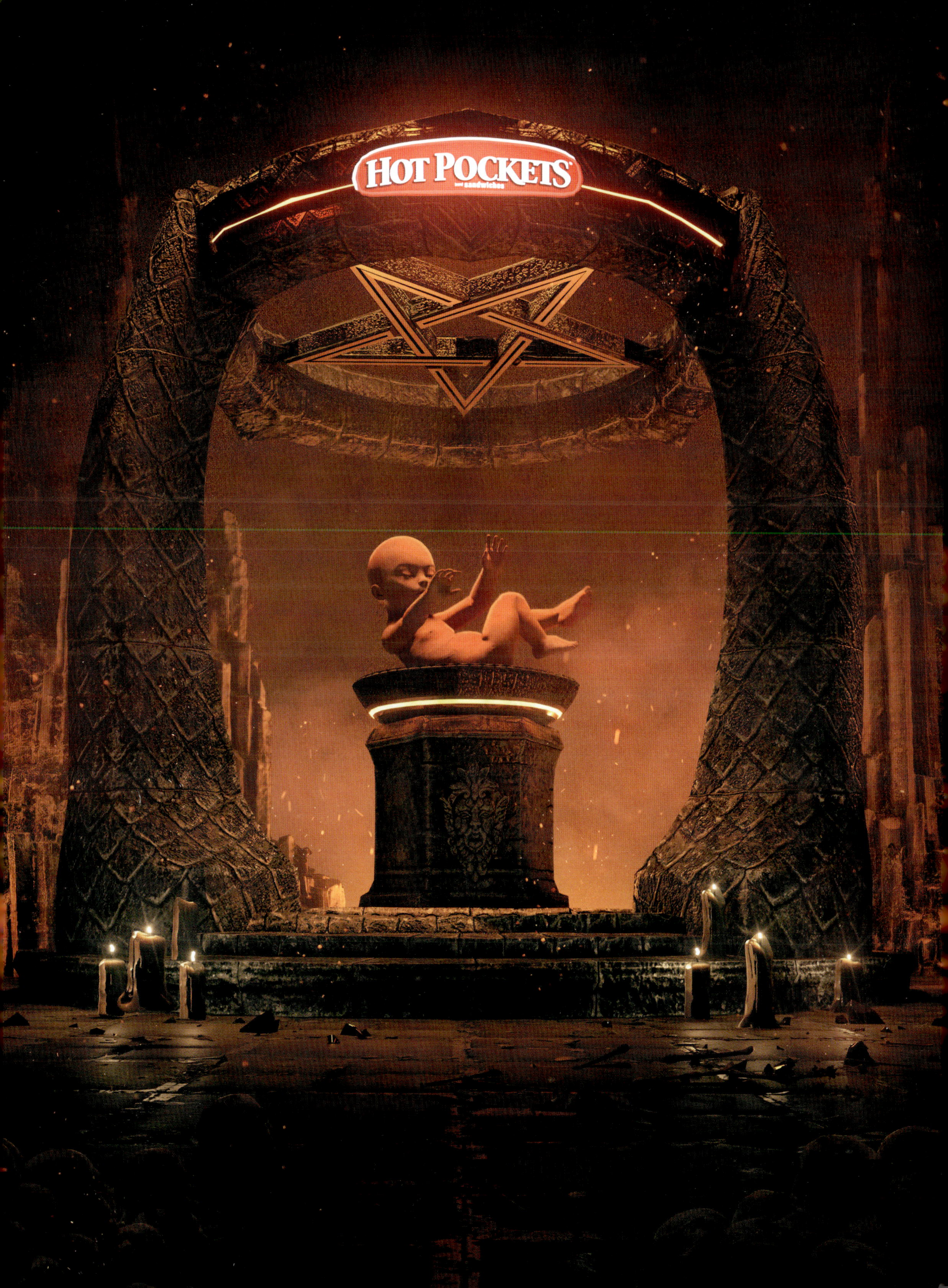
HOT POCKETS
sandwiches

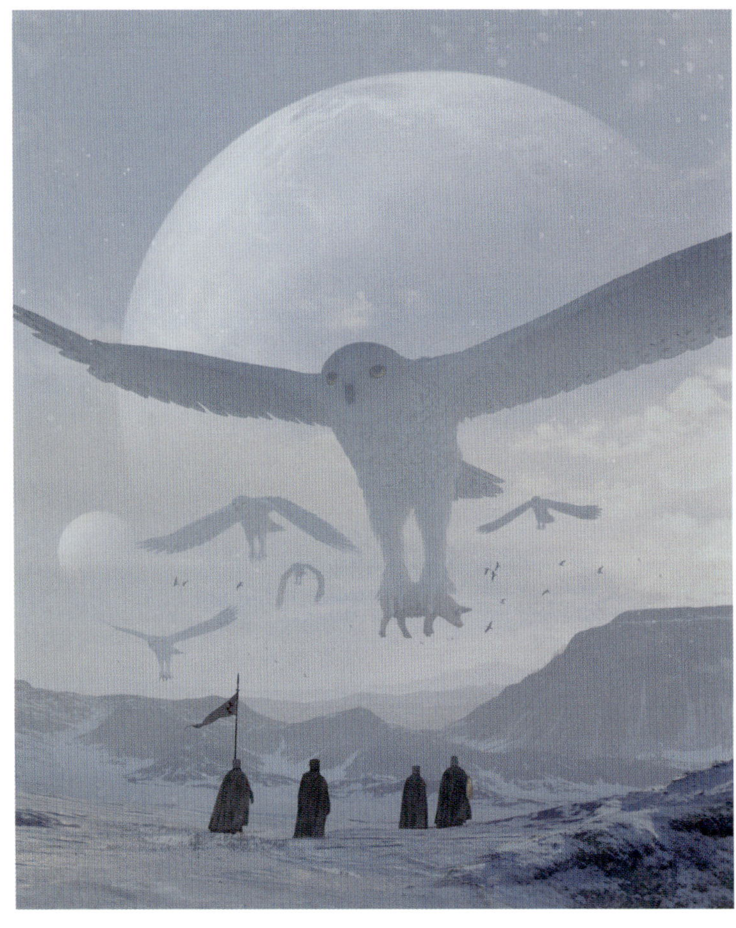

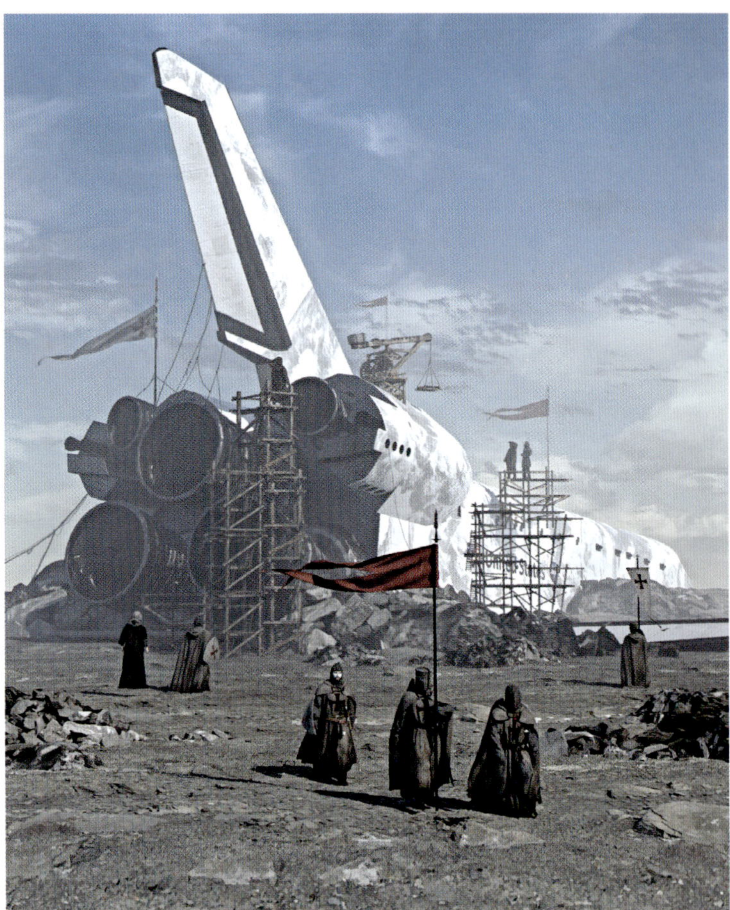

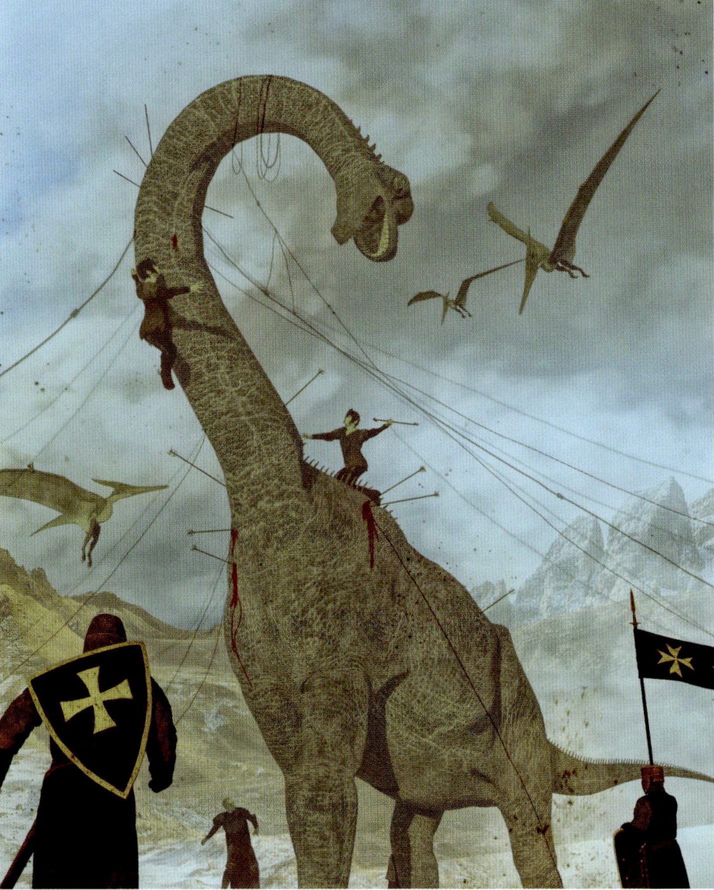

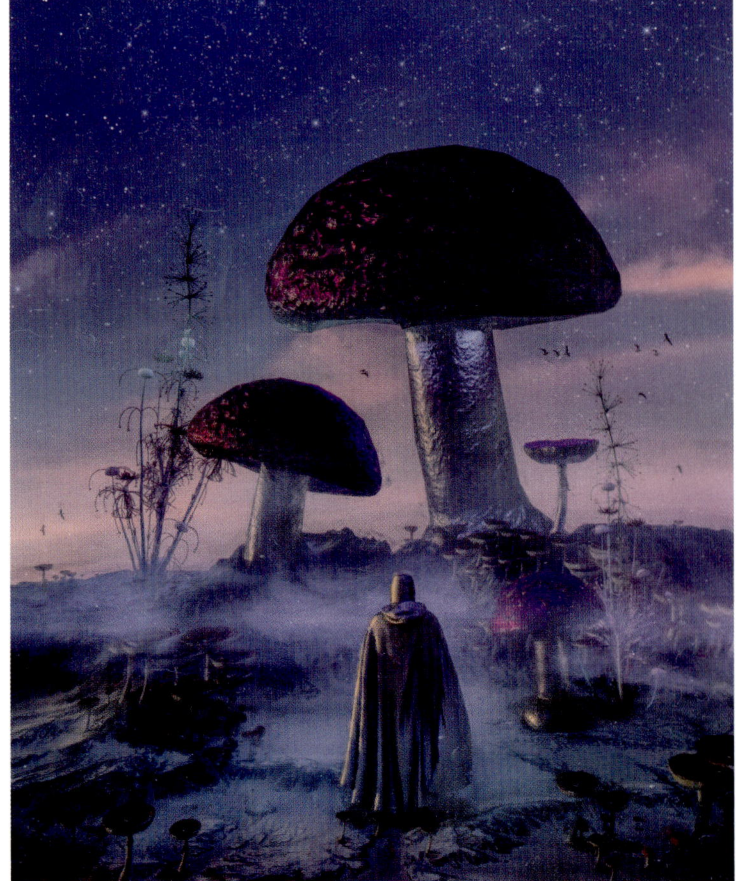

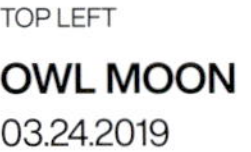

TOP LEFT
OWL MOON
03.24.2019

TOP RIGHT
REBOOT CIVILIZATION
04.07.2019

BOTTOM LEFT
SLOW MACHINE
08.06.2019

BOTTOM RIGHT
SILVERSHROOM
06.29.2019

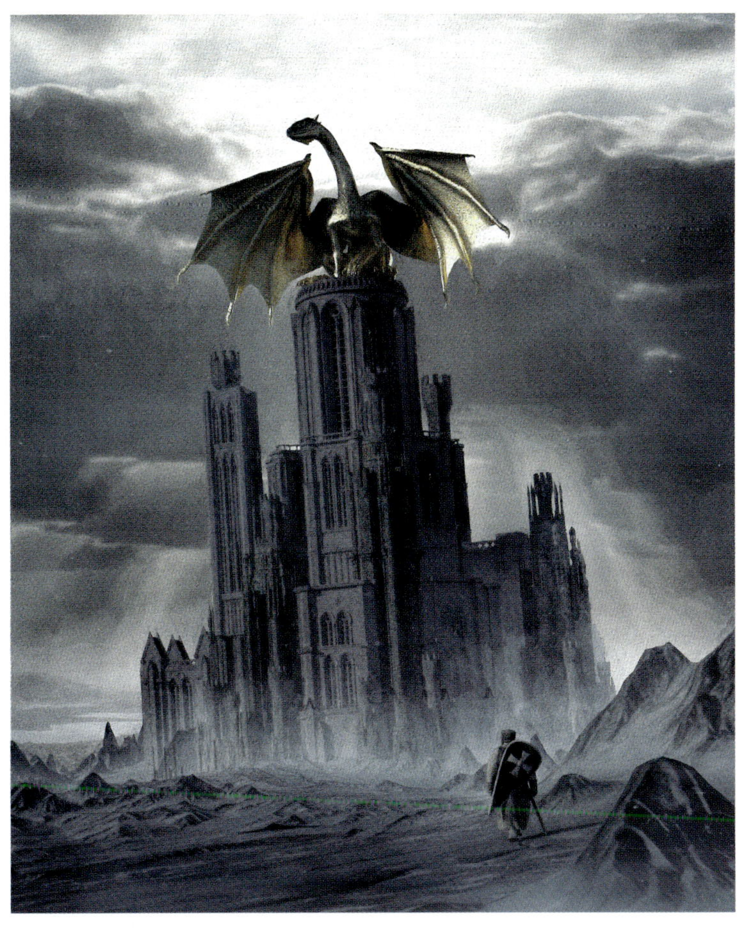

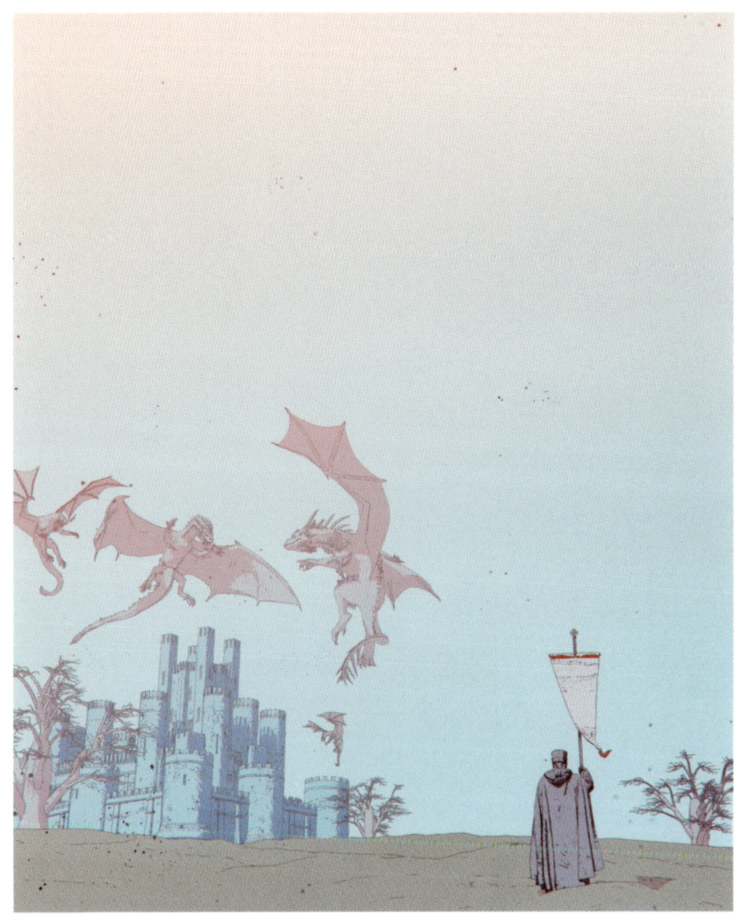

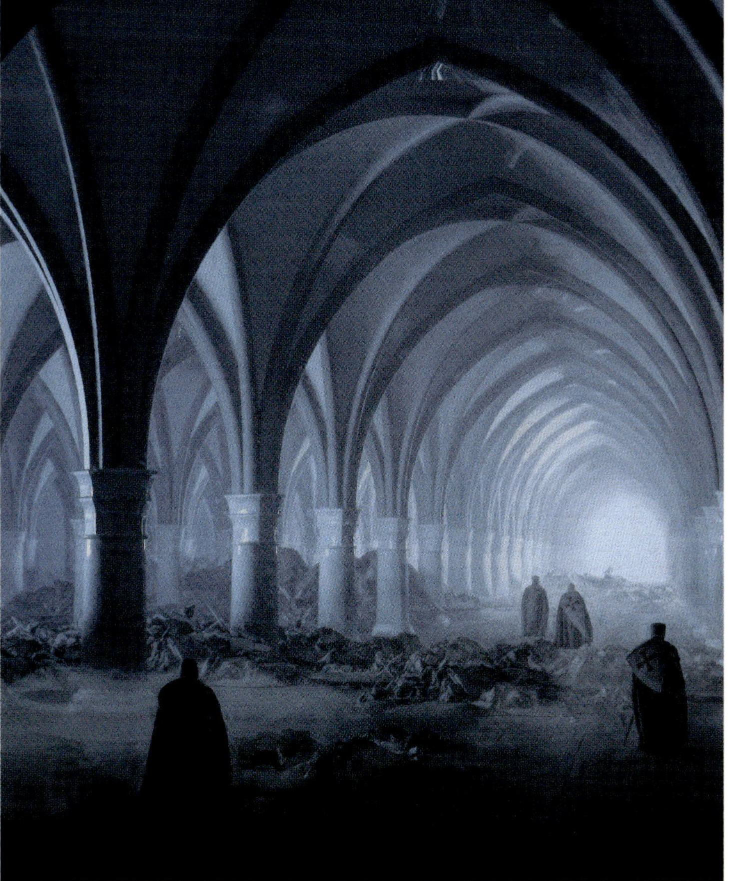

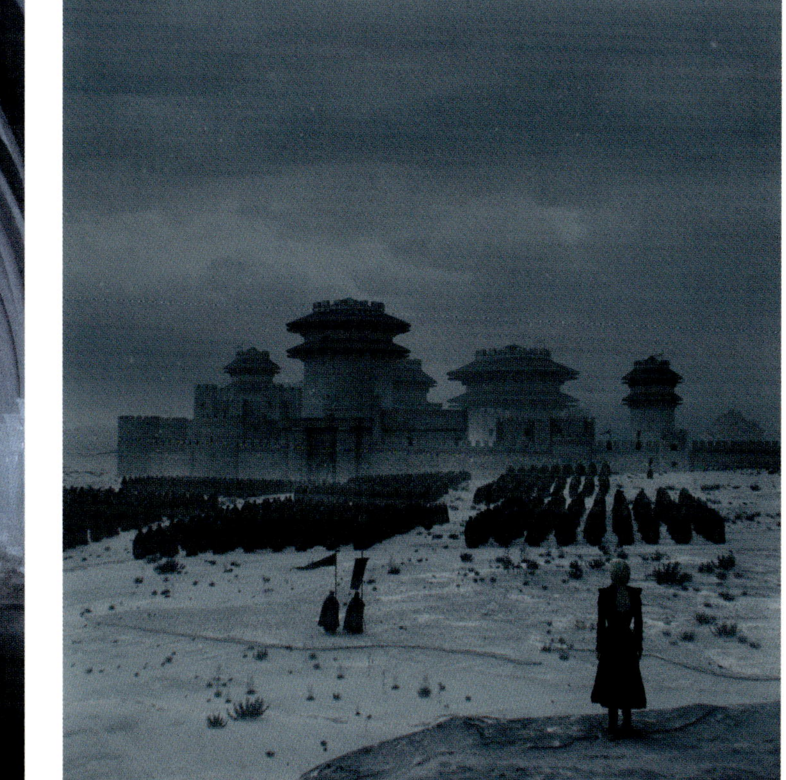

TOP LEFT

THE HUNT CONTINUES
10.12.2019

TOP RIGHT

LADYBUG BIRTHDAY
08.16.2019

BOTTOM LEFT

INFINITE NIGHT
10.02.2019

BOTTOM RIGHT

FINALE
05.19.2019

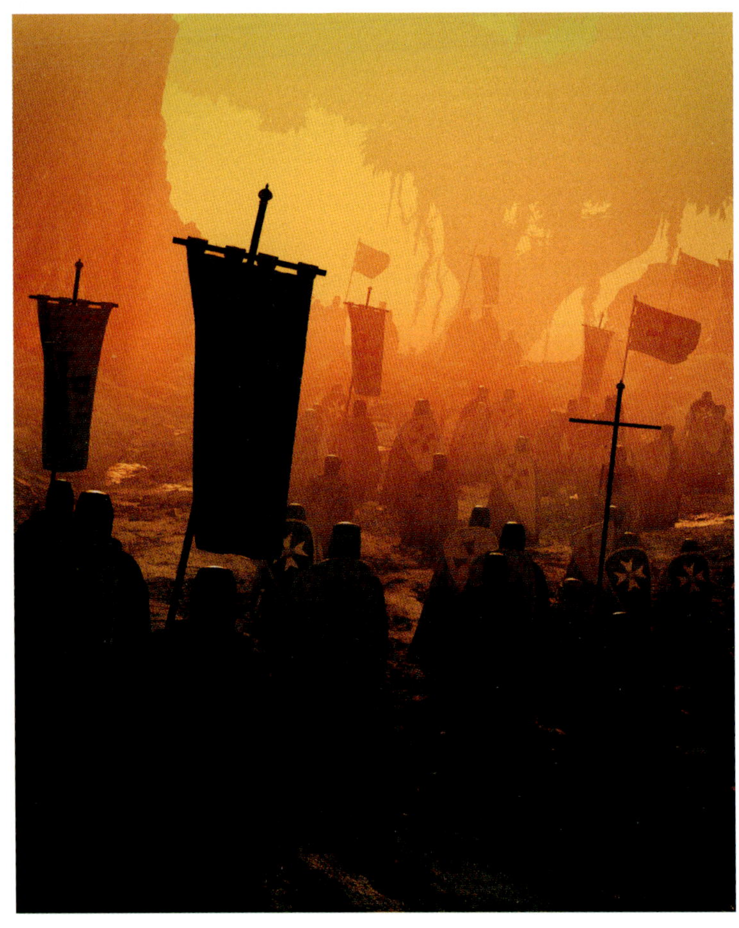

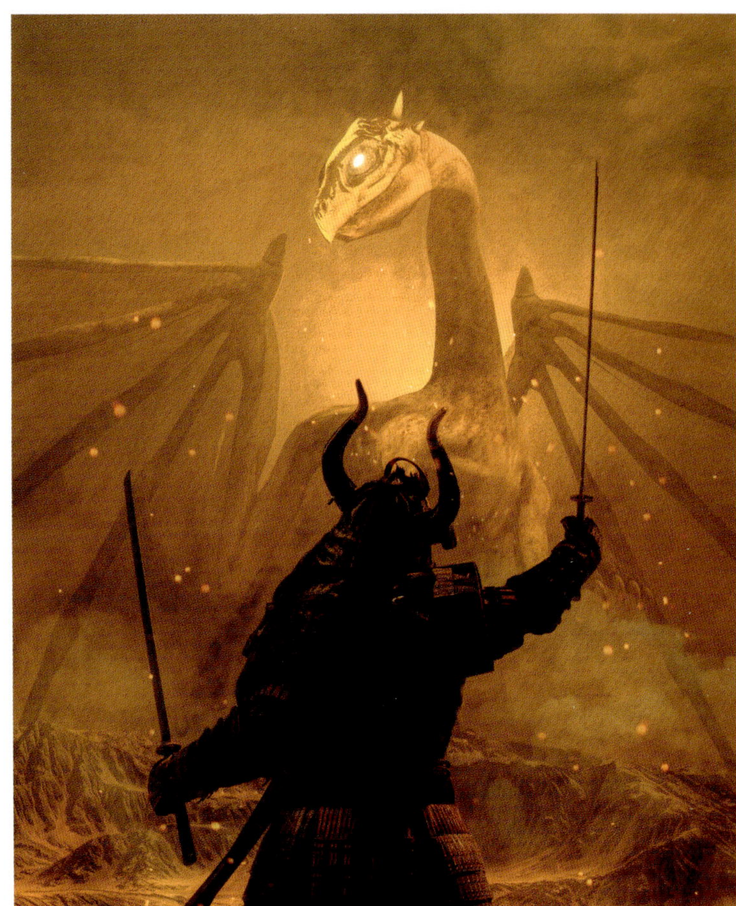

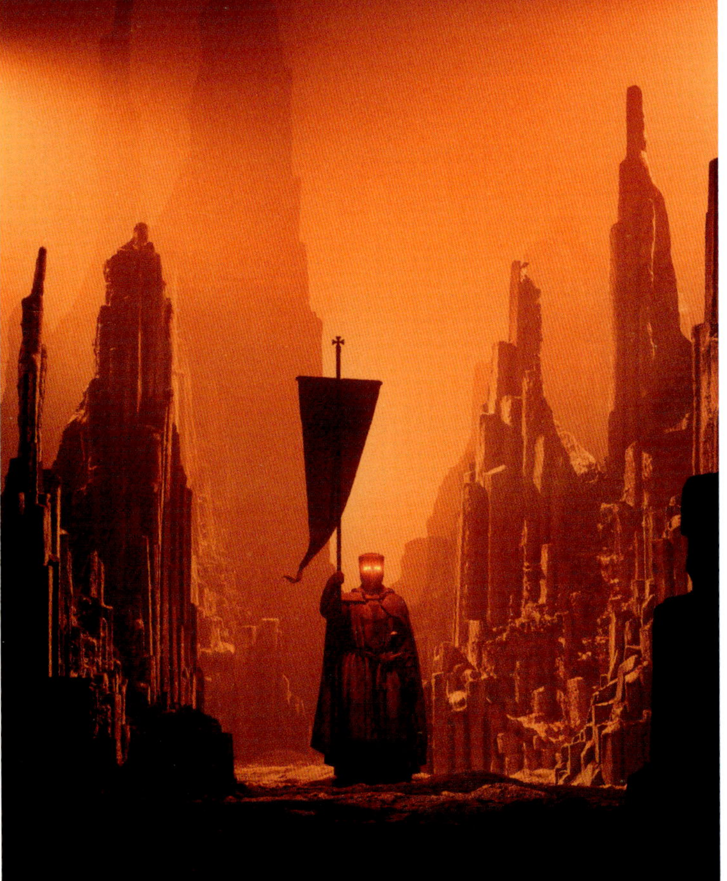

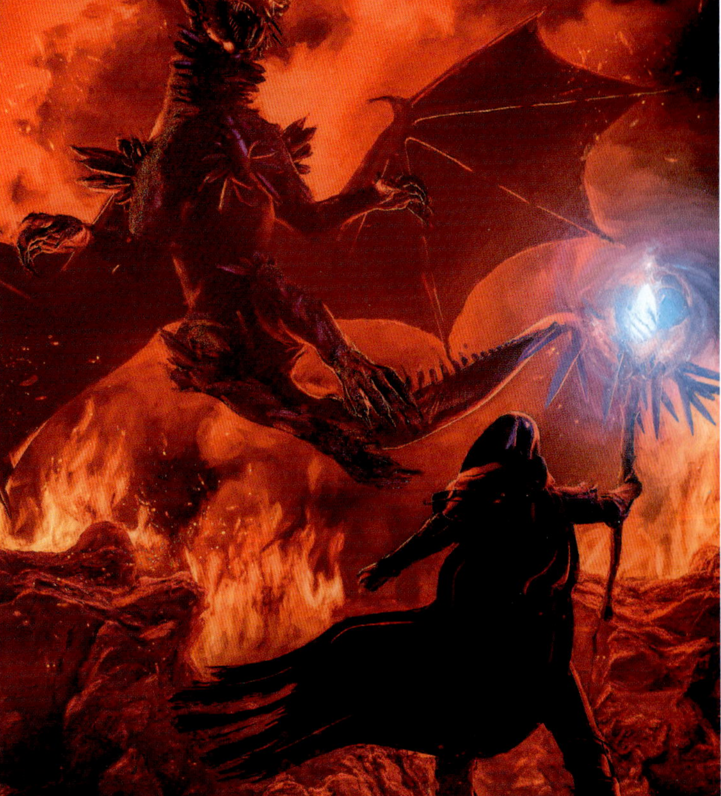

TOP LEFT

FORWARD PROGRESS

05.09.2019

TOP RIGHT

OMNICRUX

05.27.2019

BOTTOM LEFT

B-BOY STANCE

04.25.2019

BOTTOM RIGHT

FIRE EMOJI

04.02.2019

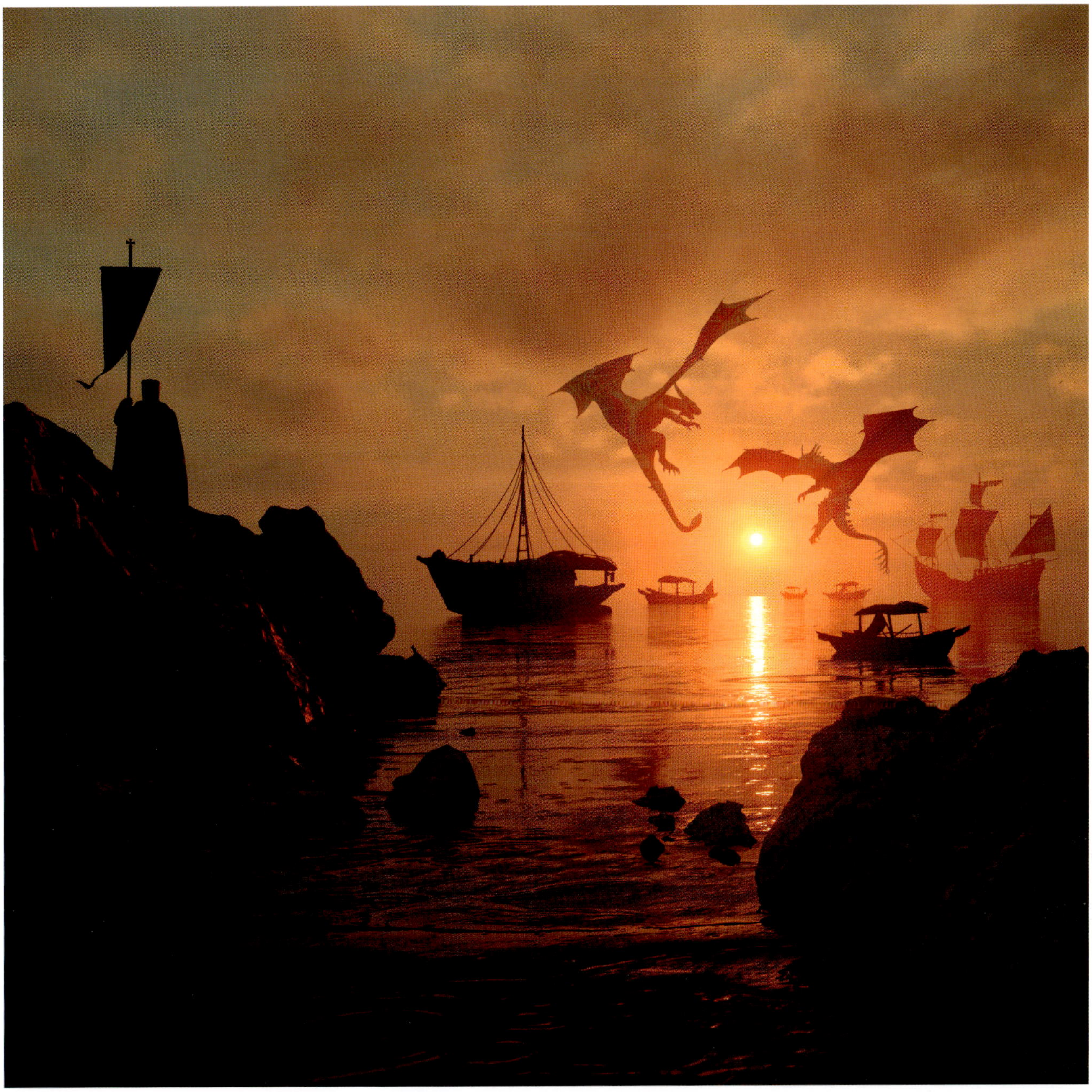

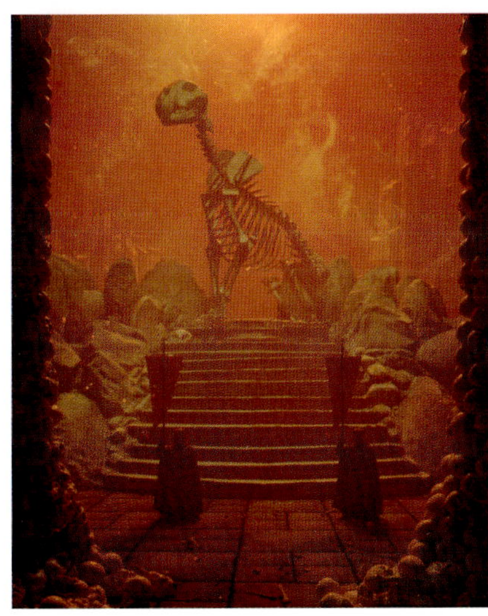

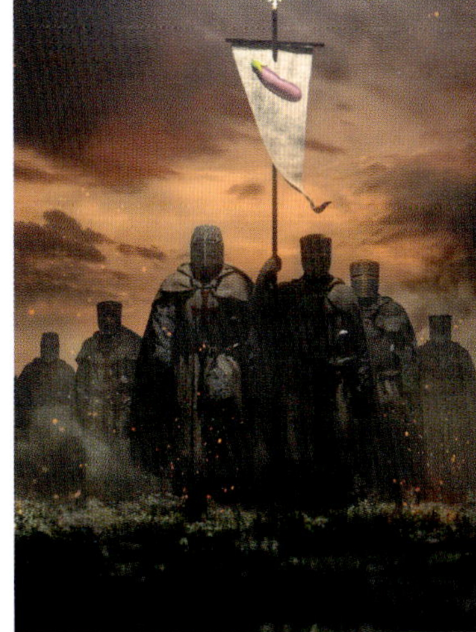

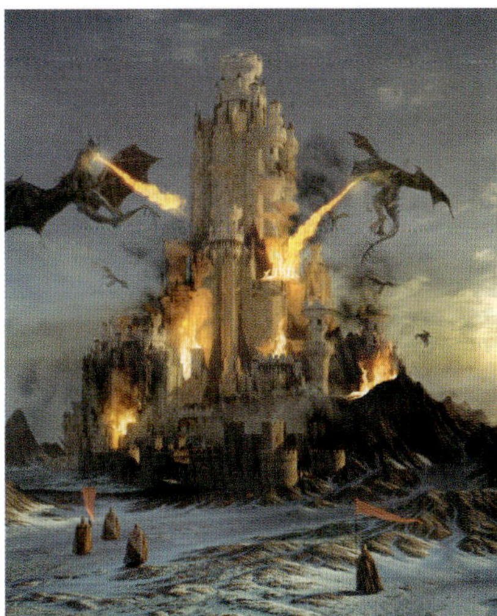

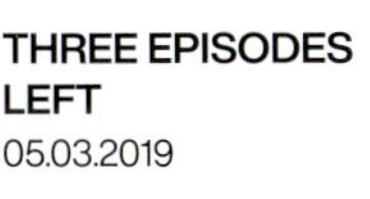

TOP

THREE EPISODES LEFT
05.03.2019

BOTTOM LEFT

TRUE LION KING
07.21.2019

BOTTOM MIDDLE

MEDIEVAL MEASURING CONTEST
03.13.2019

BOTTOM RIGHT

GOING HOME
05.25.2019

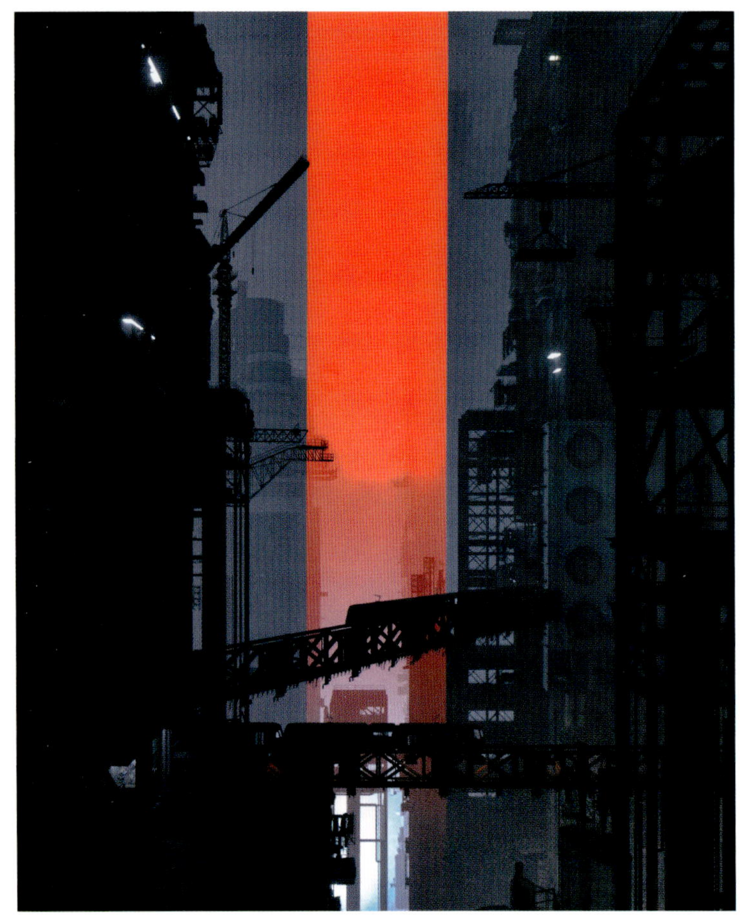

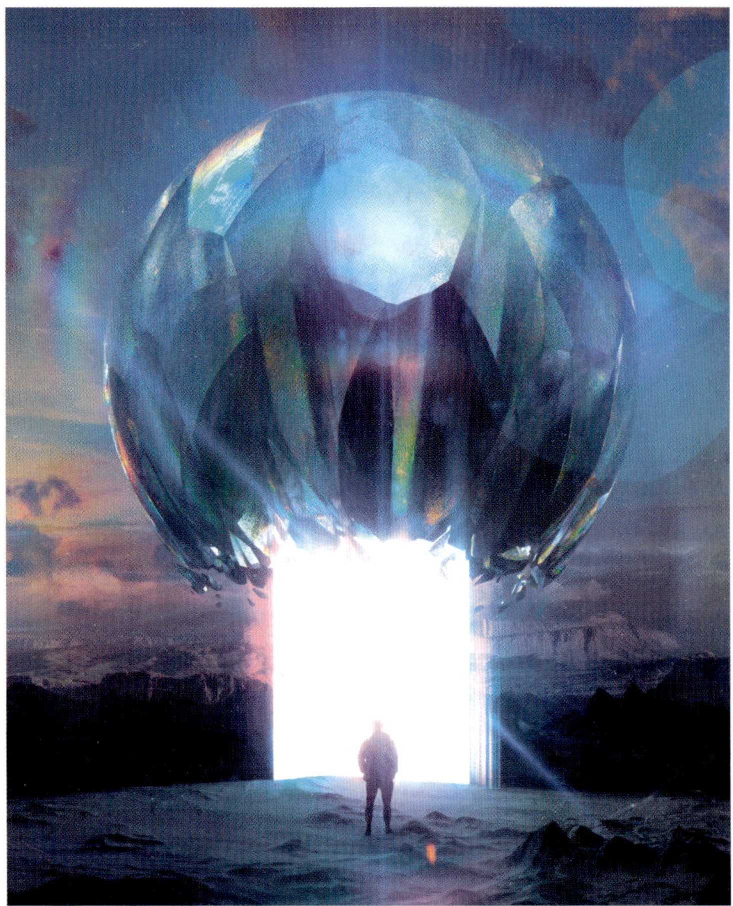

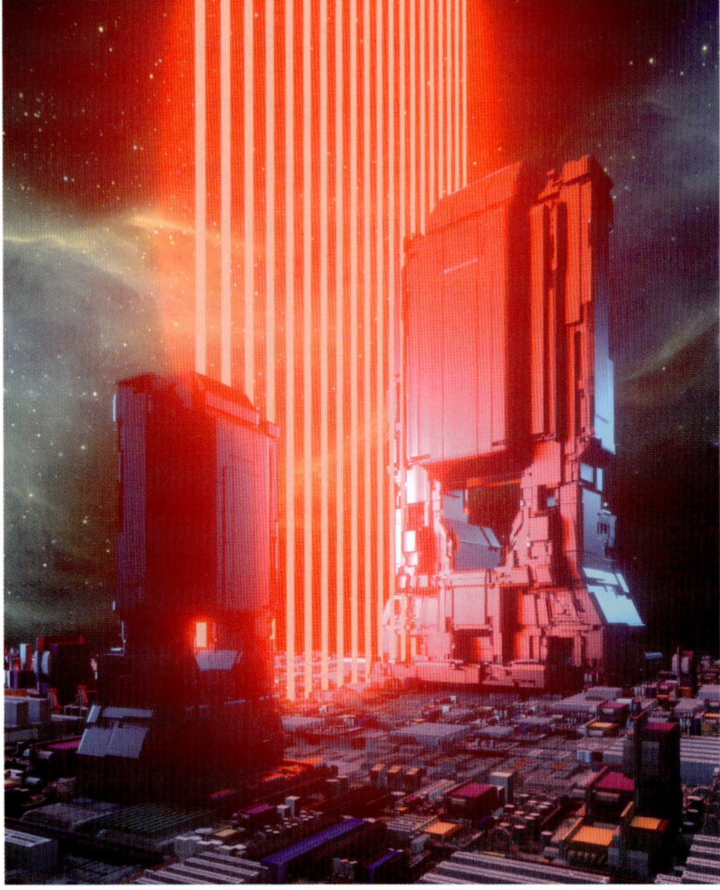

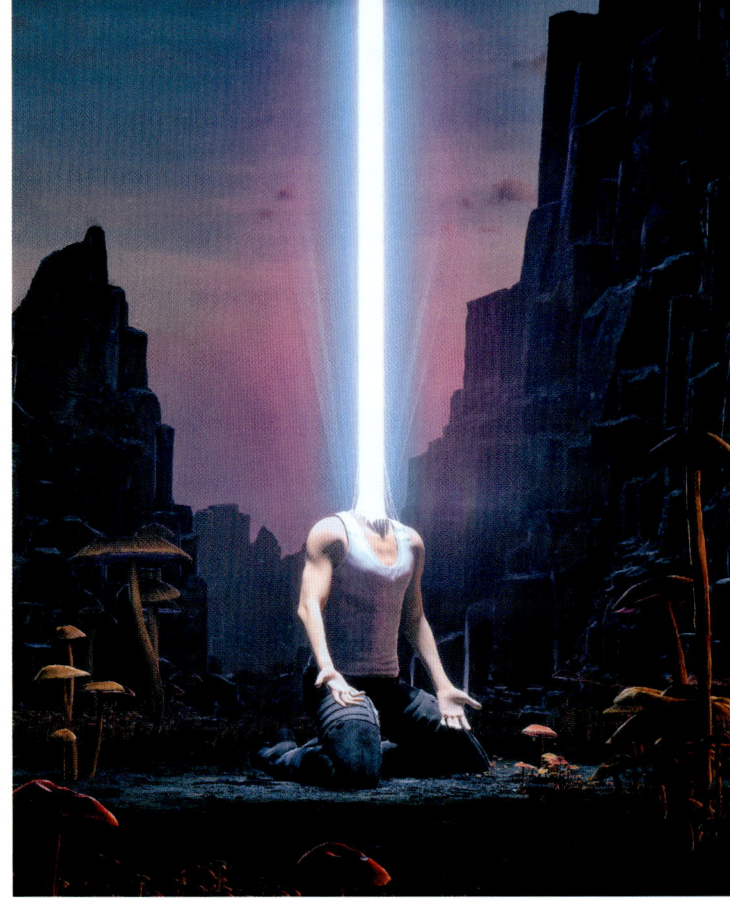

TOP LEFT
ORIGIN LINE
02.20.2019

TOP RIGHT
RAINBOW GLINT
07.24.2019

BOTTOM LEFT
PHASE.ONE
07.27.2019

BOTTOM RIGHT
DUST TO DUST
12.11.2019

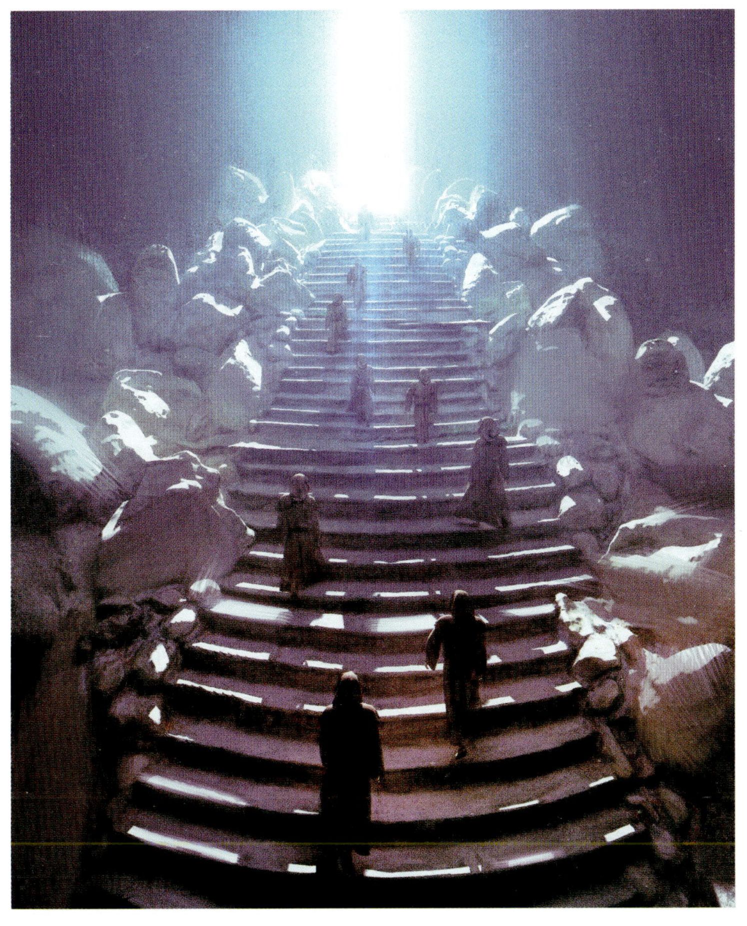

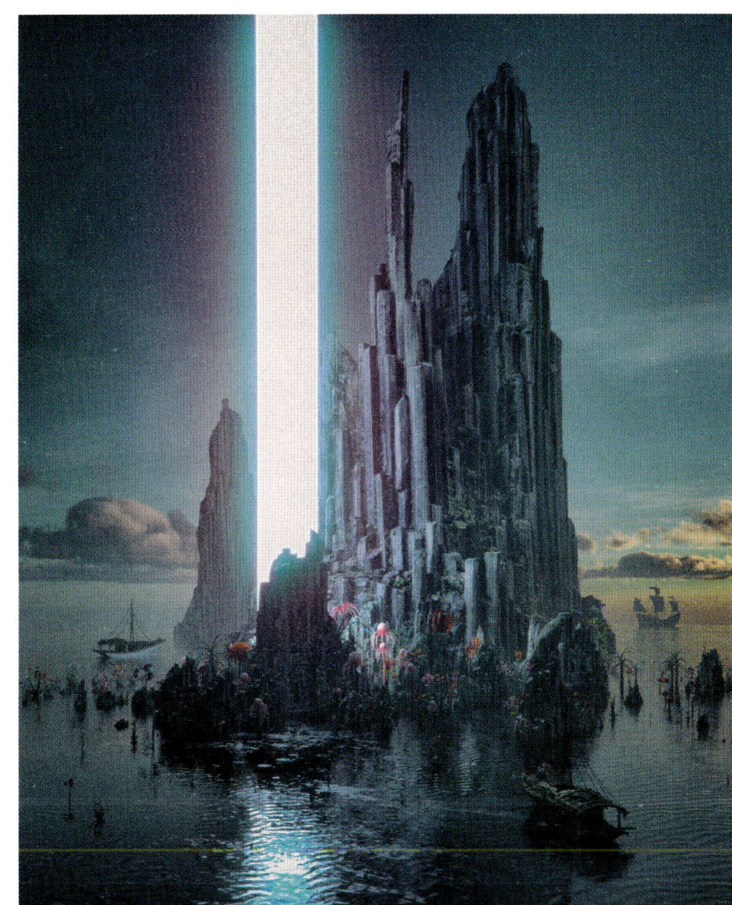

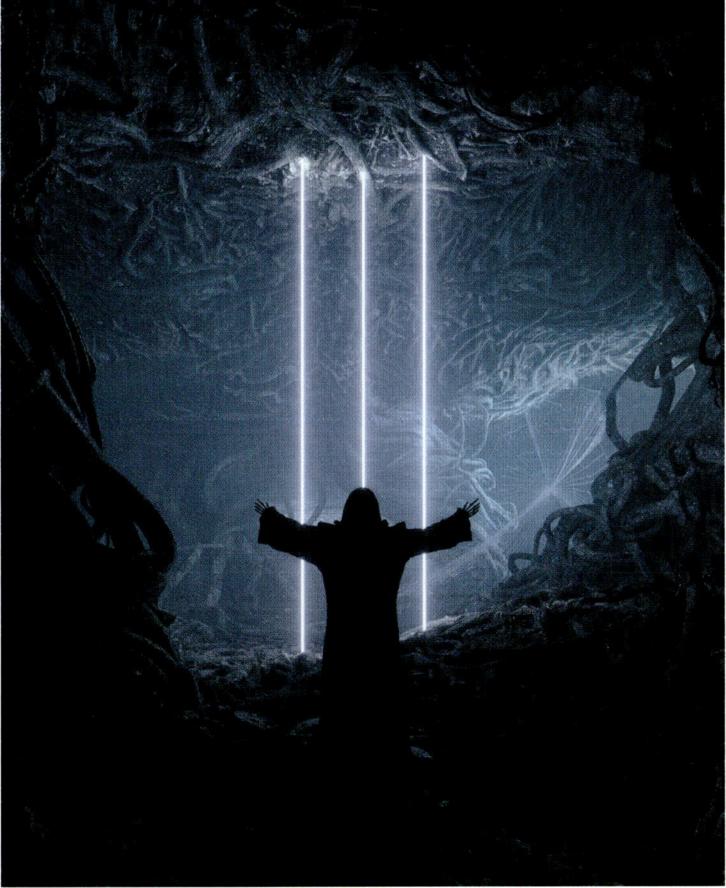

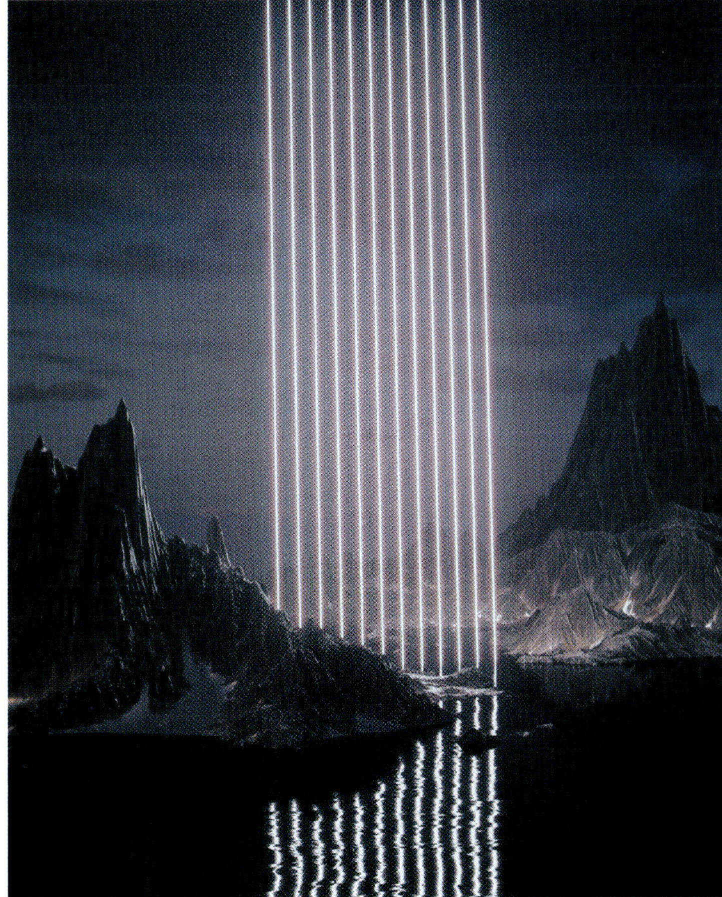

TOP LEFT
CLEANSING LIGHT
05.29.2019

TOP RIGHT
CONCENTRATE
07.22.2019

BOTTOM LEFT
LIGHT POLLUTION
05.22.2019

BOTTOM RIGHT
FULL BROKEN
04.14.2019

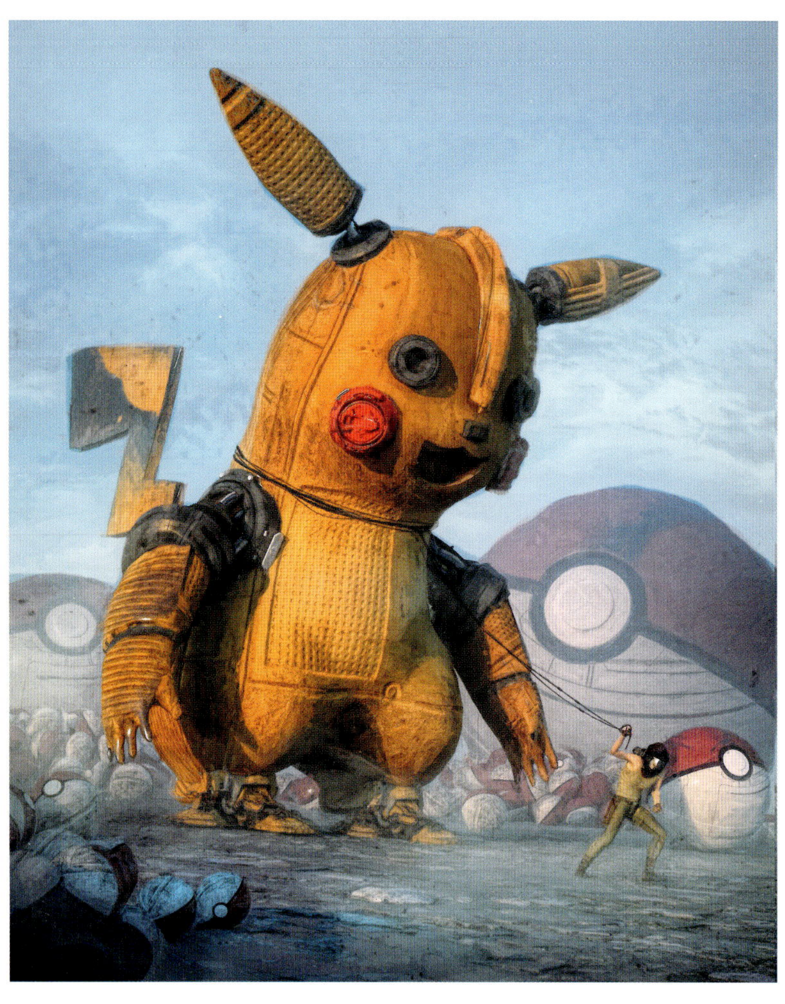

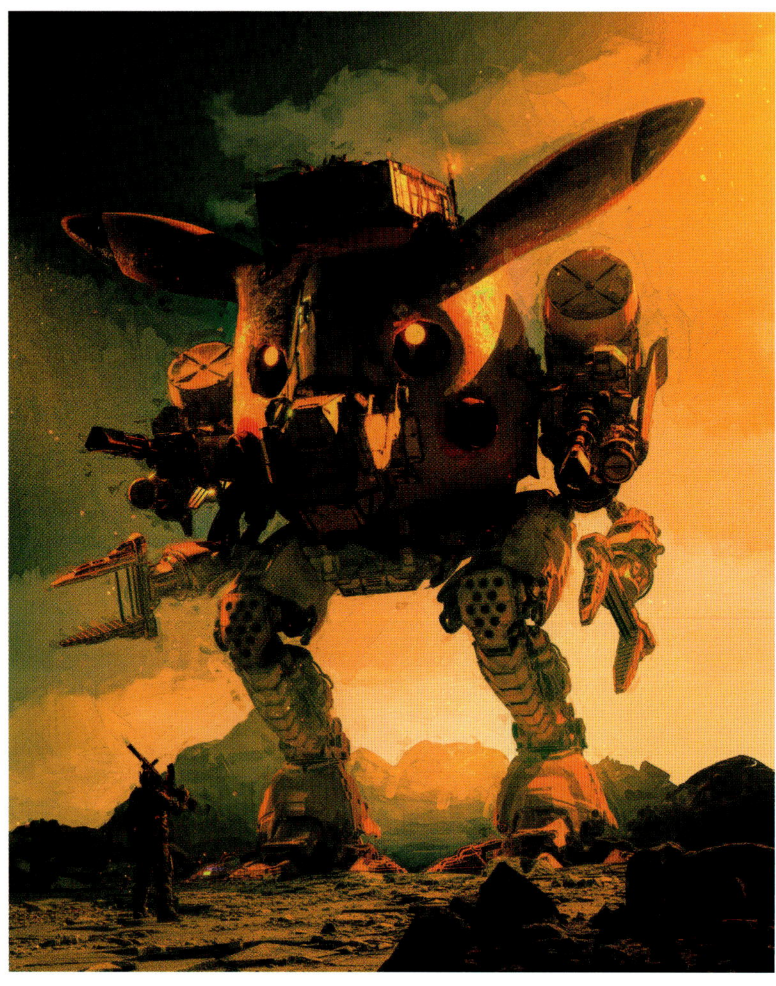

TOP

GOOD CATCH
09.03.2019

BOTTOM

KILLACHU
09.21.2019

OPPOSITE PAGE

I'VE ACTUALLY NEVER PLAYED POKEMON BUT THIS IS HOW I ASSUME IT WORKS
09.04.2019

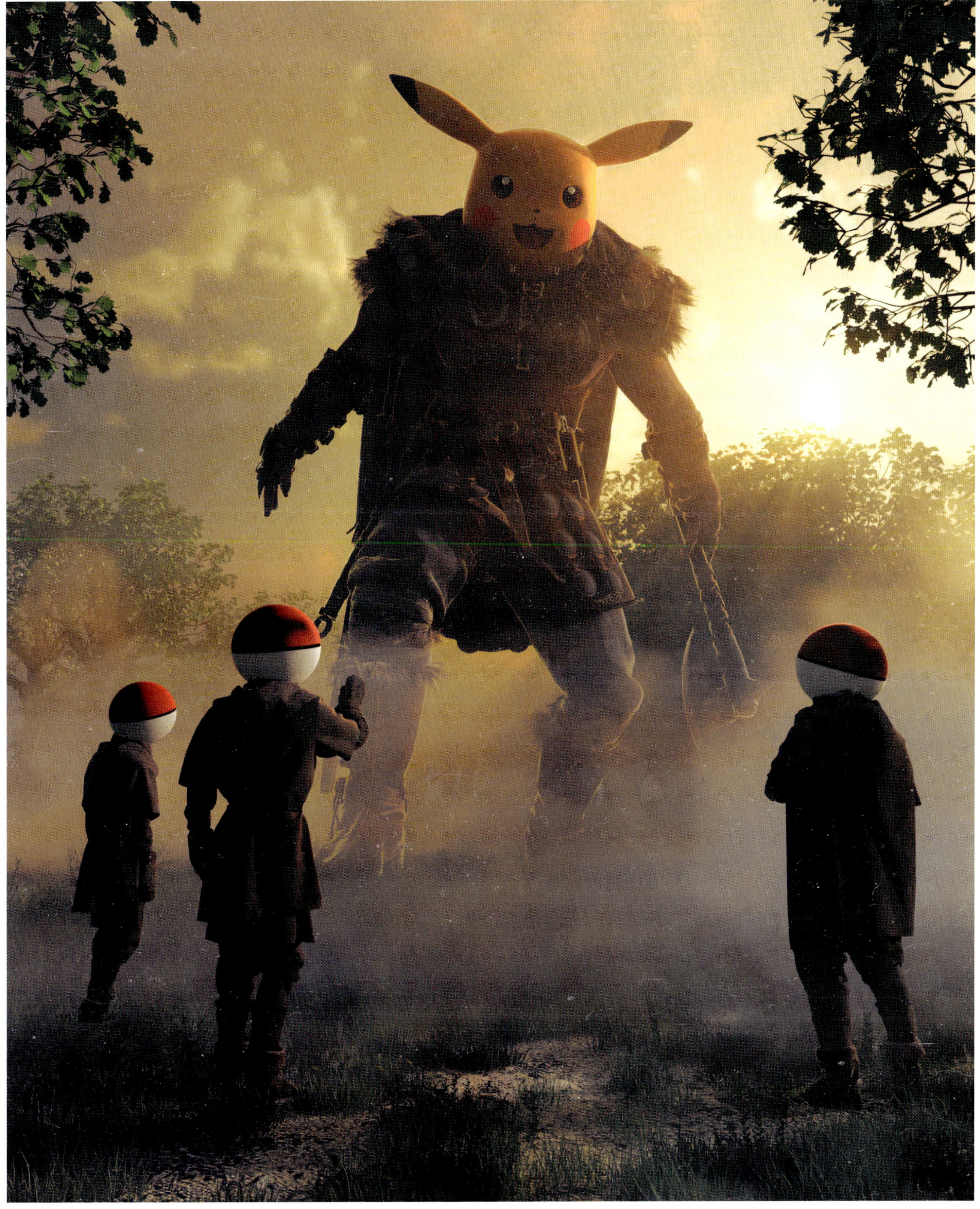

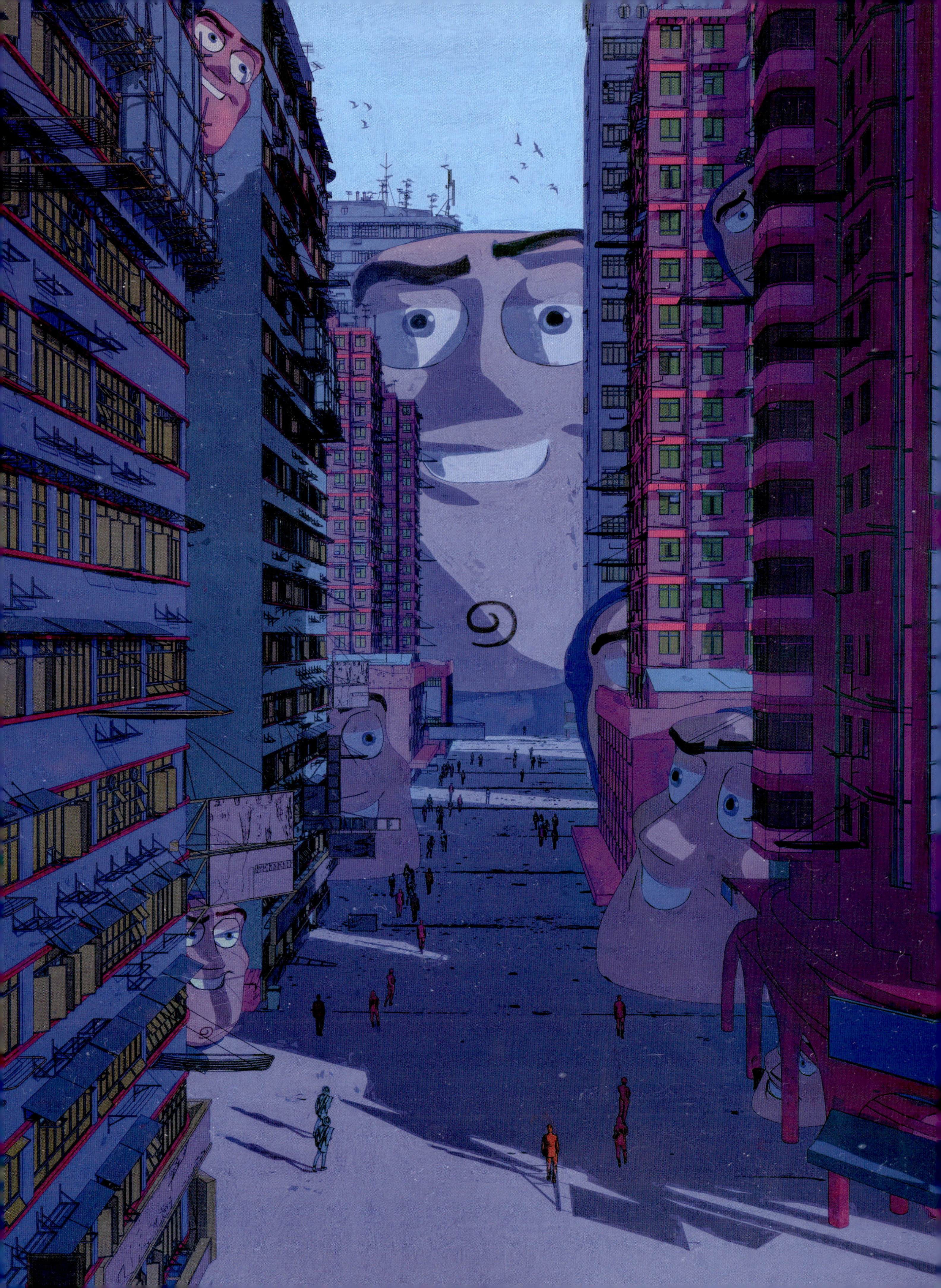

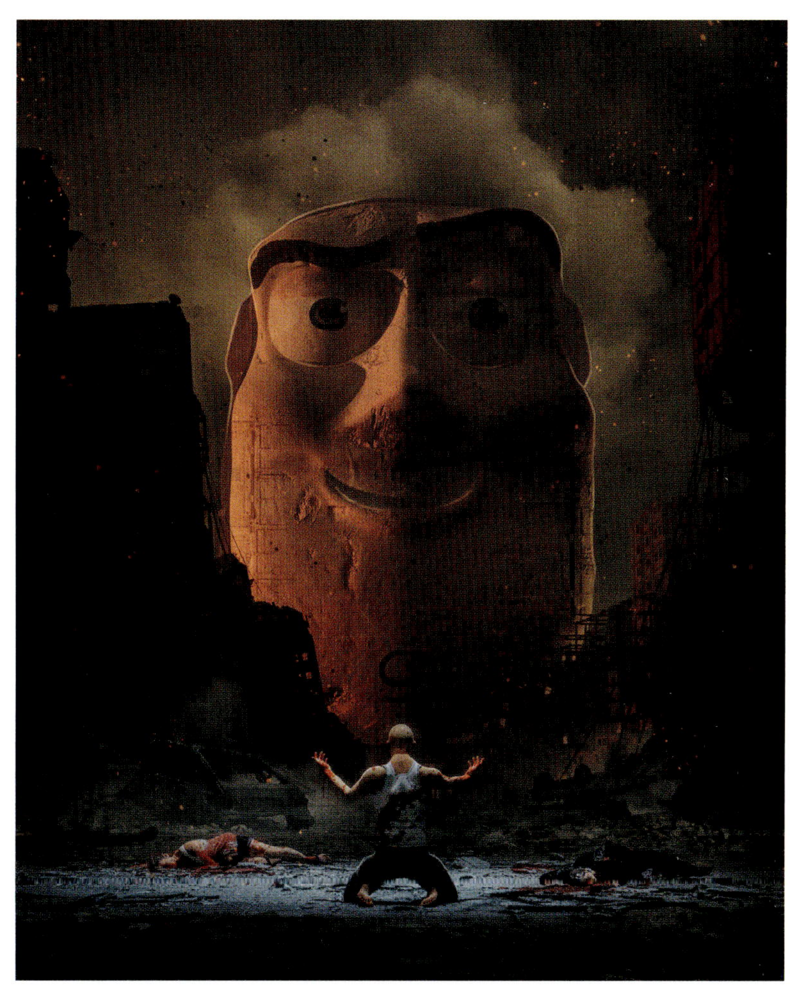

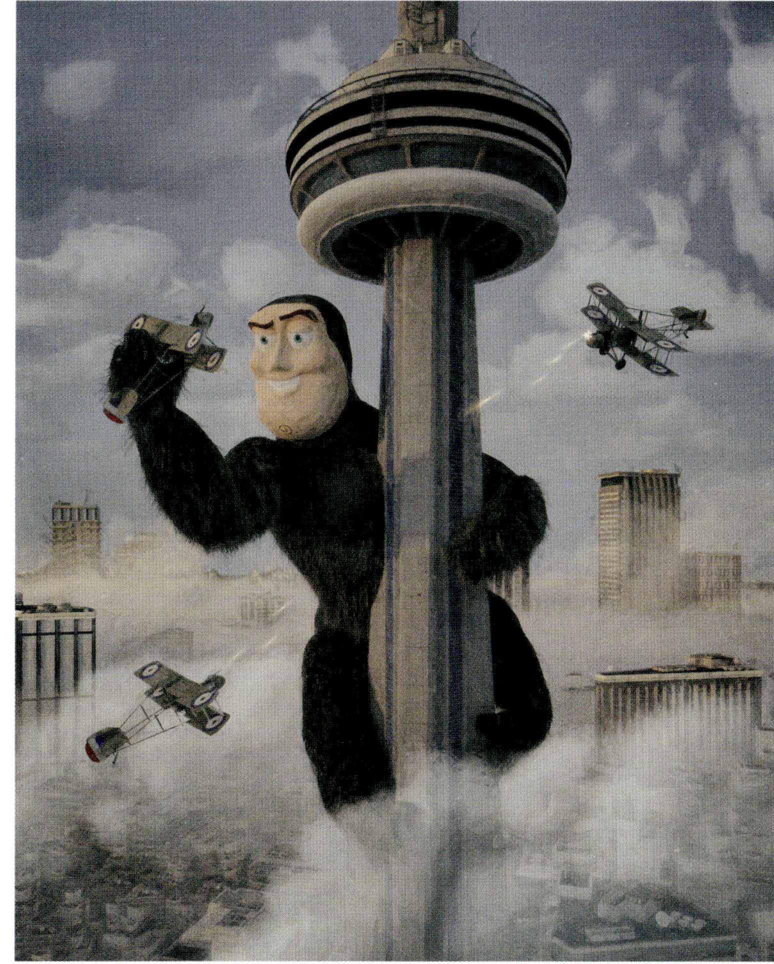

OPPOSITE PAGE

BLUE MONDAY
06.17.2019

TOP

BUZZ LIGHT NUCLEAR HOLOCAUST
11.15.2019

BOTTOM

UNTITLED
08.23.2019

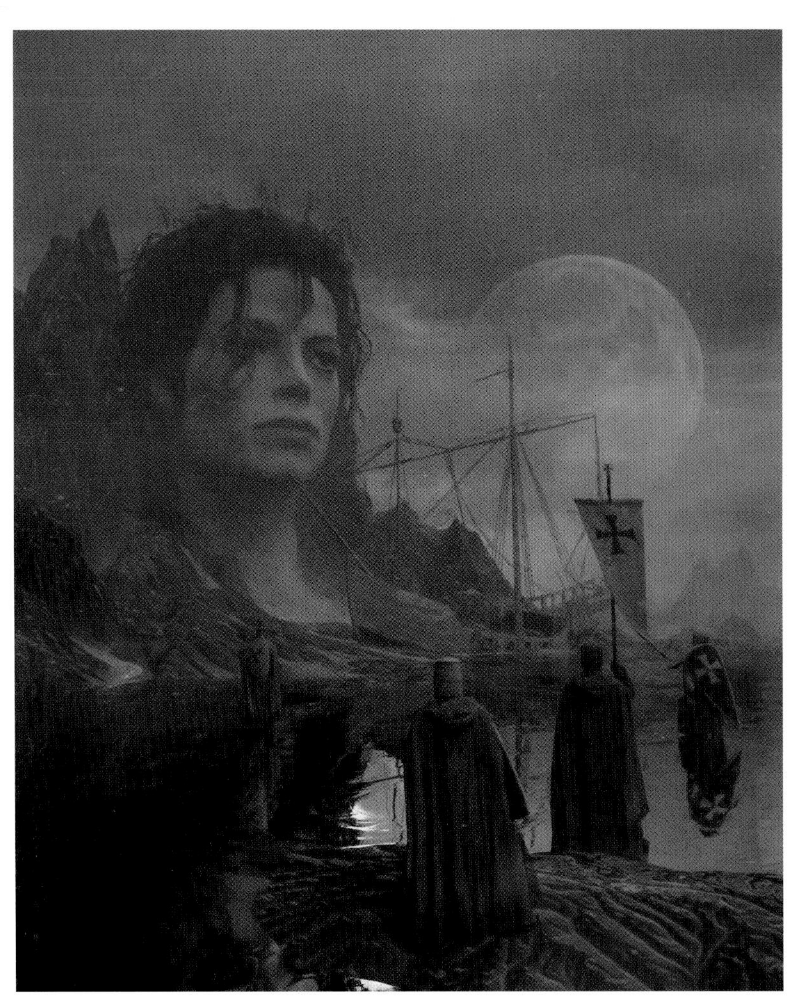

TOP

NEVERLAND 1492
08.22.2019

OPPOSITE PAGE

MICHAEL JACKSON
AI HOST WOMB
04.24.2019

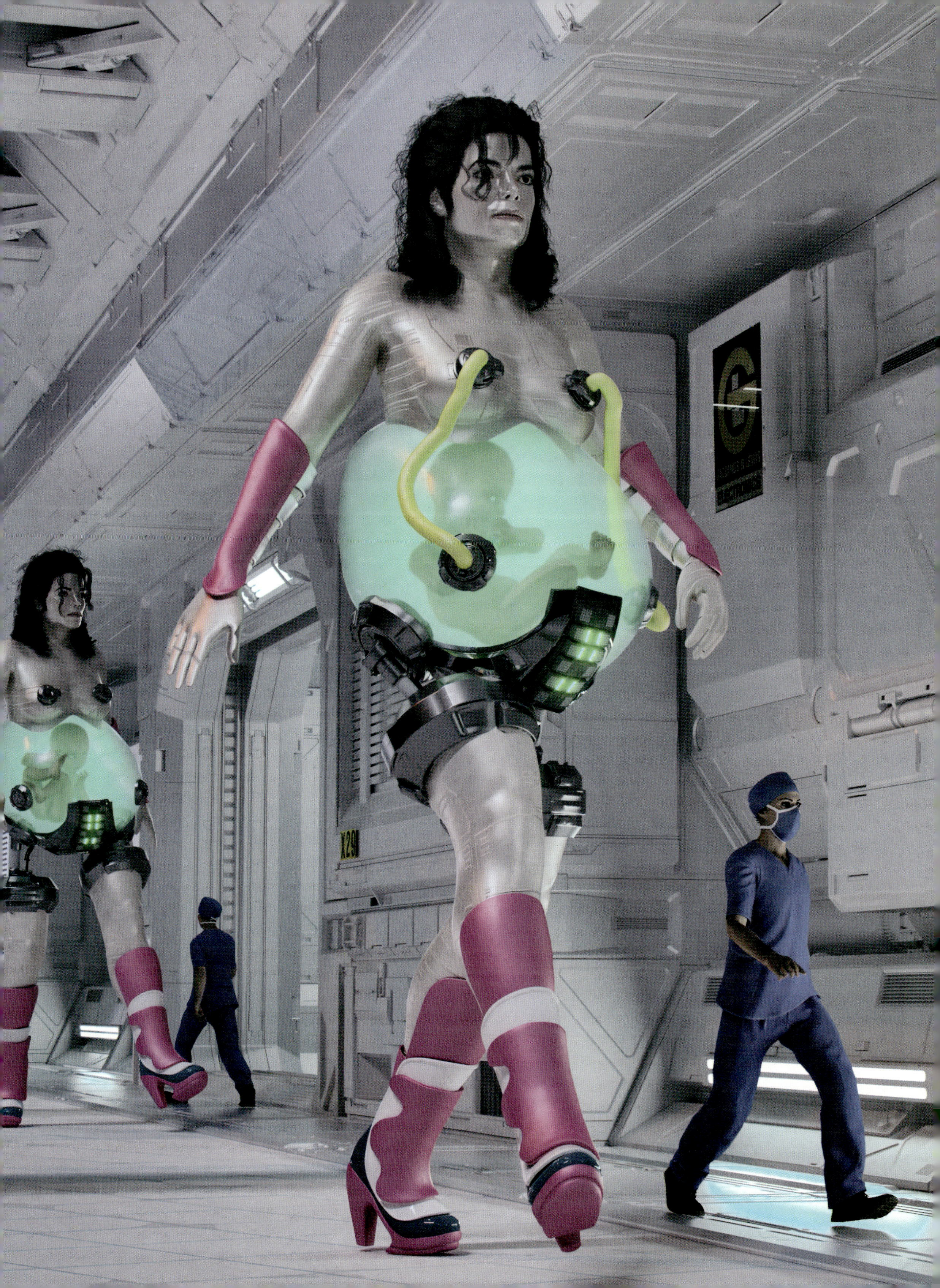
X29

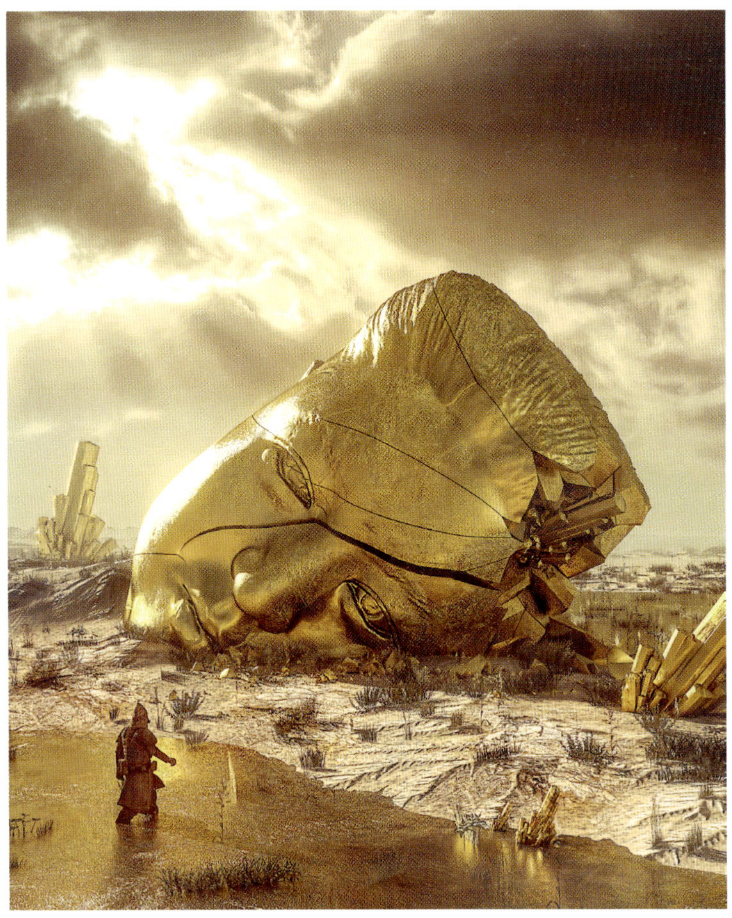

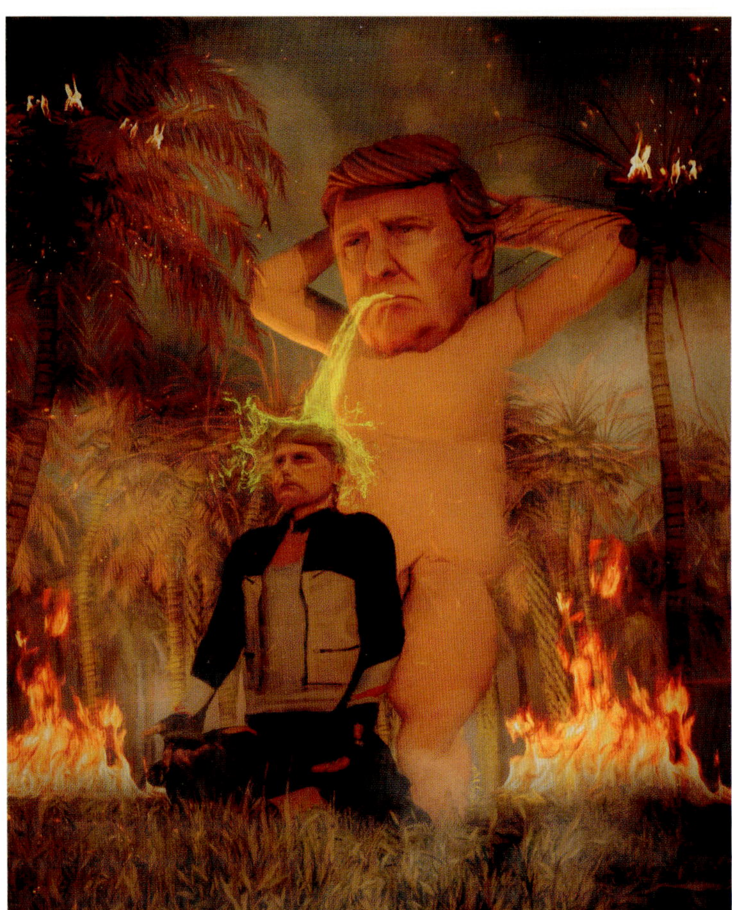

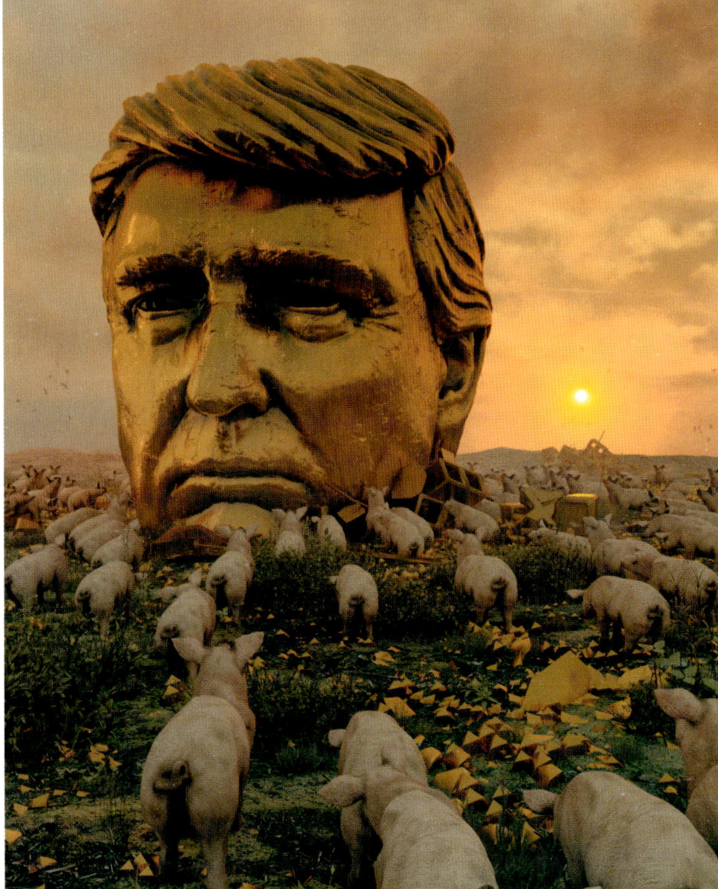

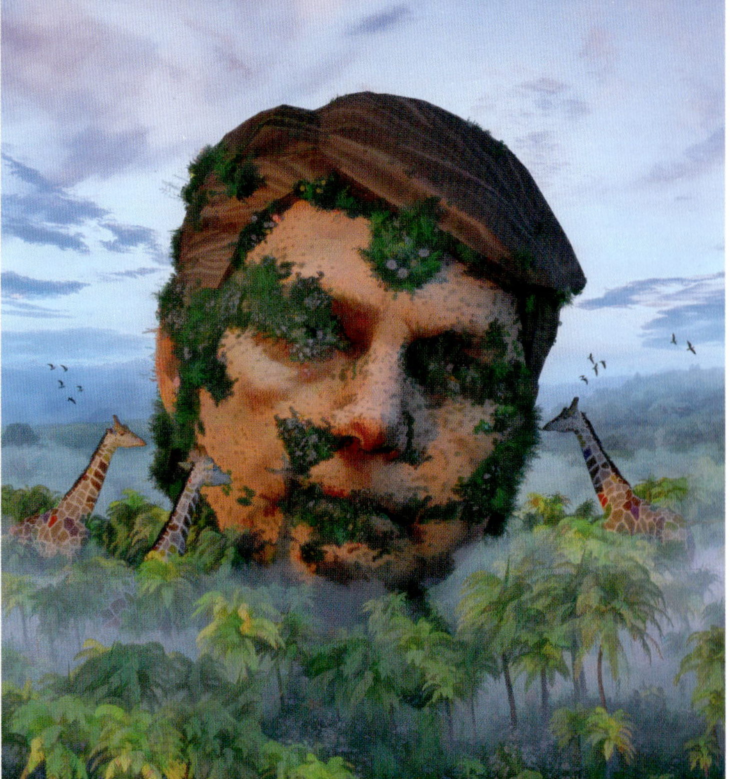

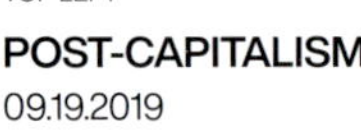

TOP LEFT

POST-CAPITALISM
09.19.2019

TOP RIGHT

GOLDEN HOUR, GOLDEN SHOWER
09.27.2019

BOTTOM LEFT

CHOW TIME
10.09.2019

BOTTOM RIGHT

PLANT FOOD
09.28.2019

OPPOSITE PAGE

JULY 4TH, 2032
07.04.2019

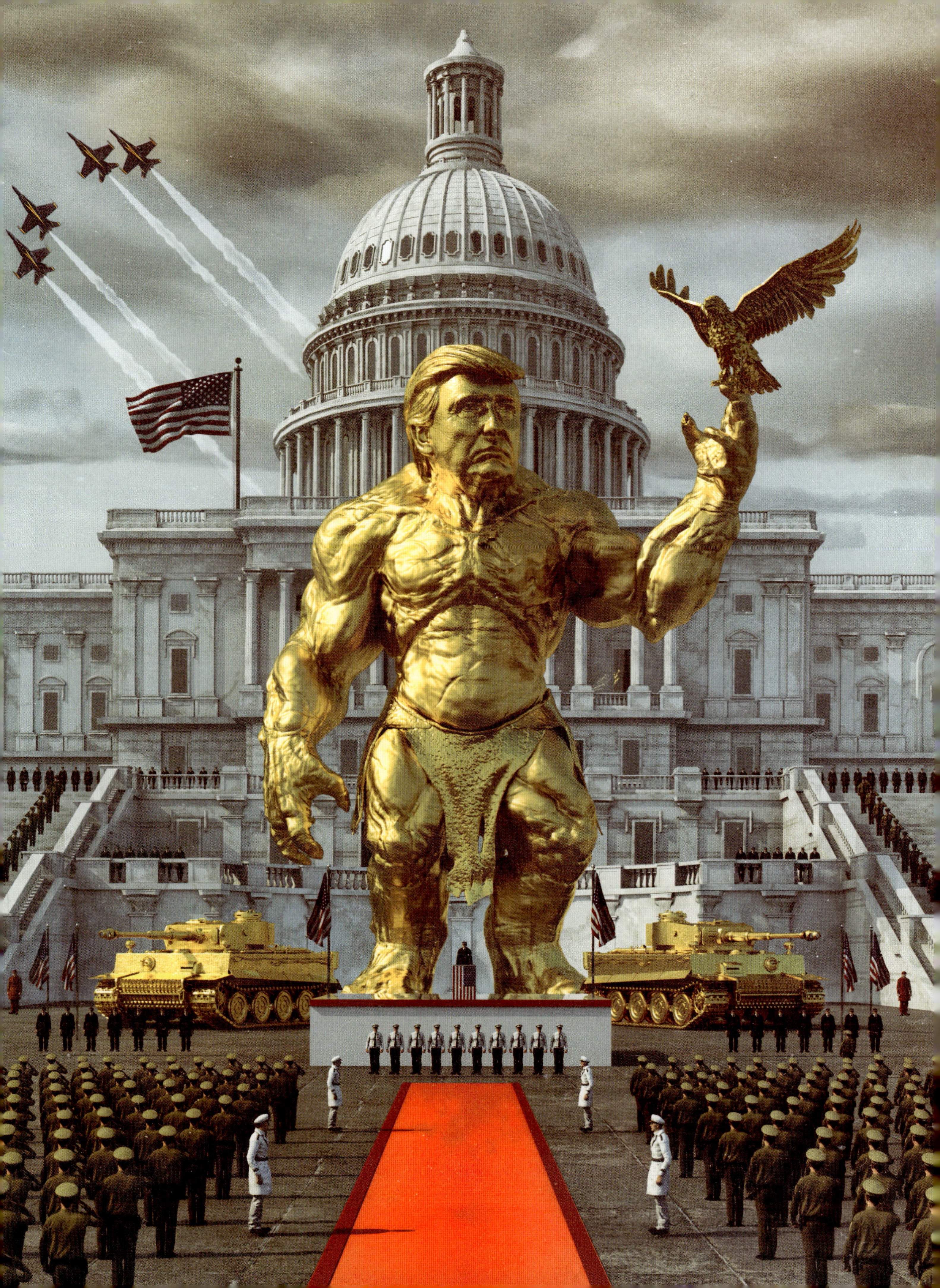

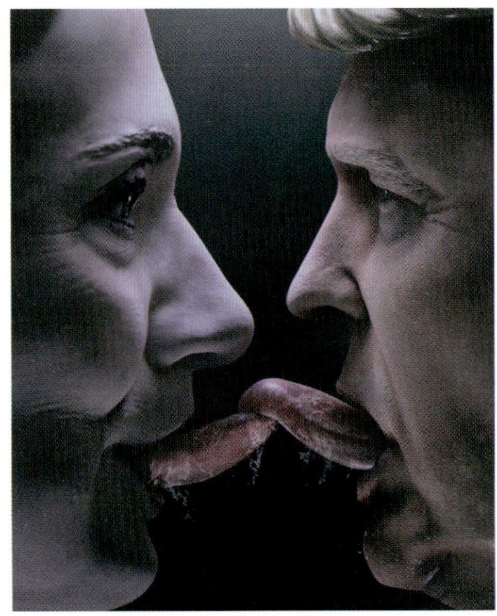

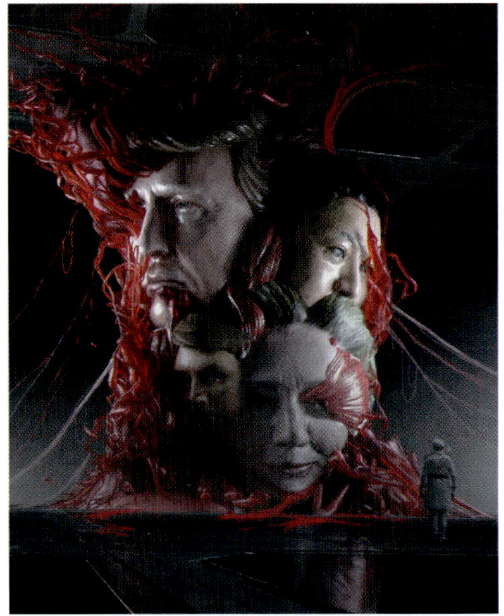

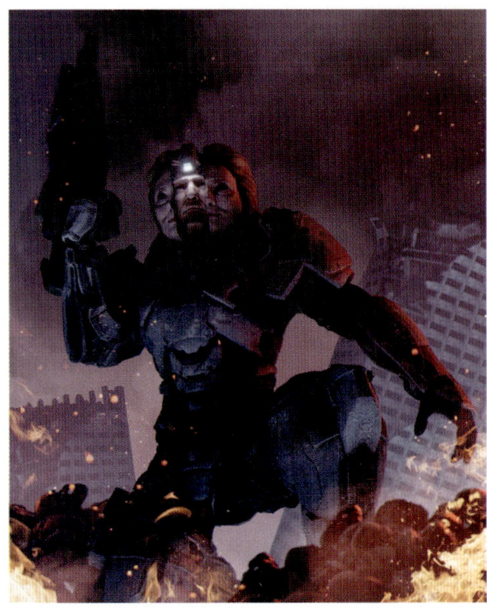

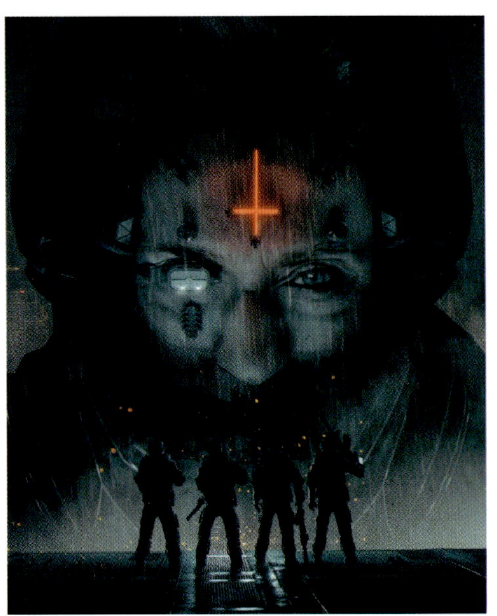

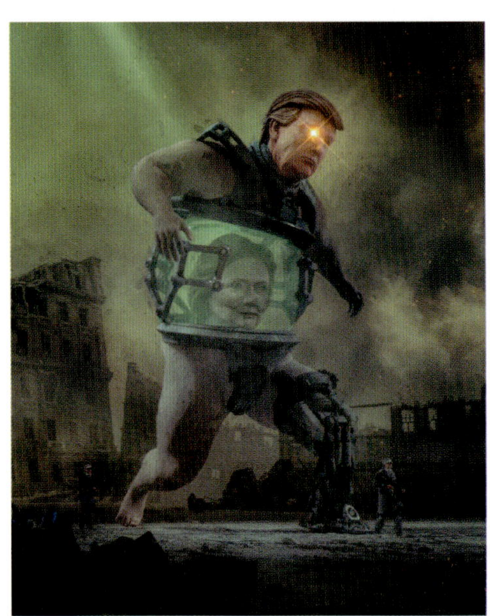

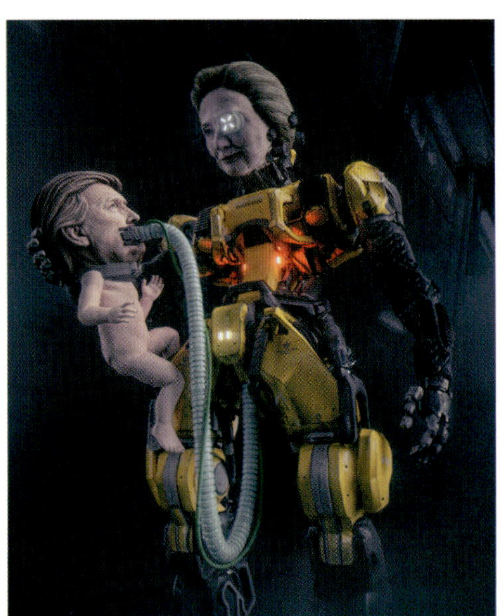

TOP LEFT

HAPPY HALLOWEEN!!

10.31.2019

TOP MIDDLE

CRITICAL MASS

10.18.2019

TOP RIGHT

CLINTRUMP THE DESTROYER

08.14.2019

BOTTOM LEFT

HILLRAISER VS. THE BERNIE BROS

09.02.2019

BOTTOM MIDDLE

AMERICA

07.05.2019

BOTTOM RIGHT

FEEDING TIME

08.27.2019

OPPOSITE PAGE

MEAT HEAD

12.06.2019

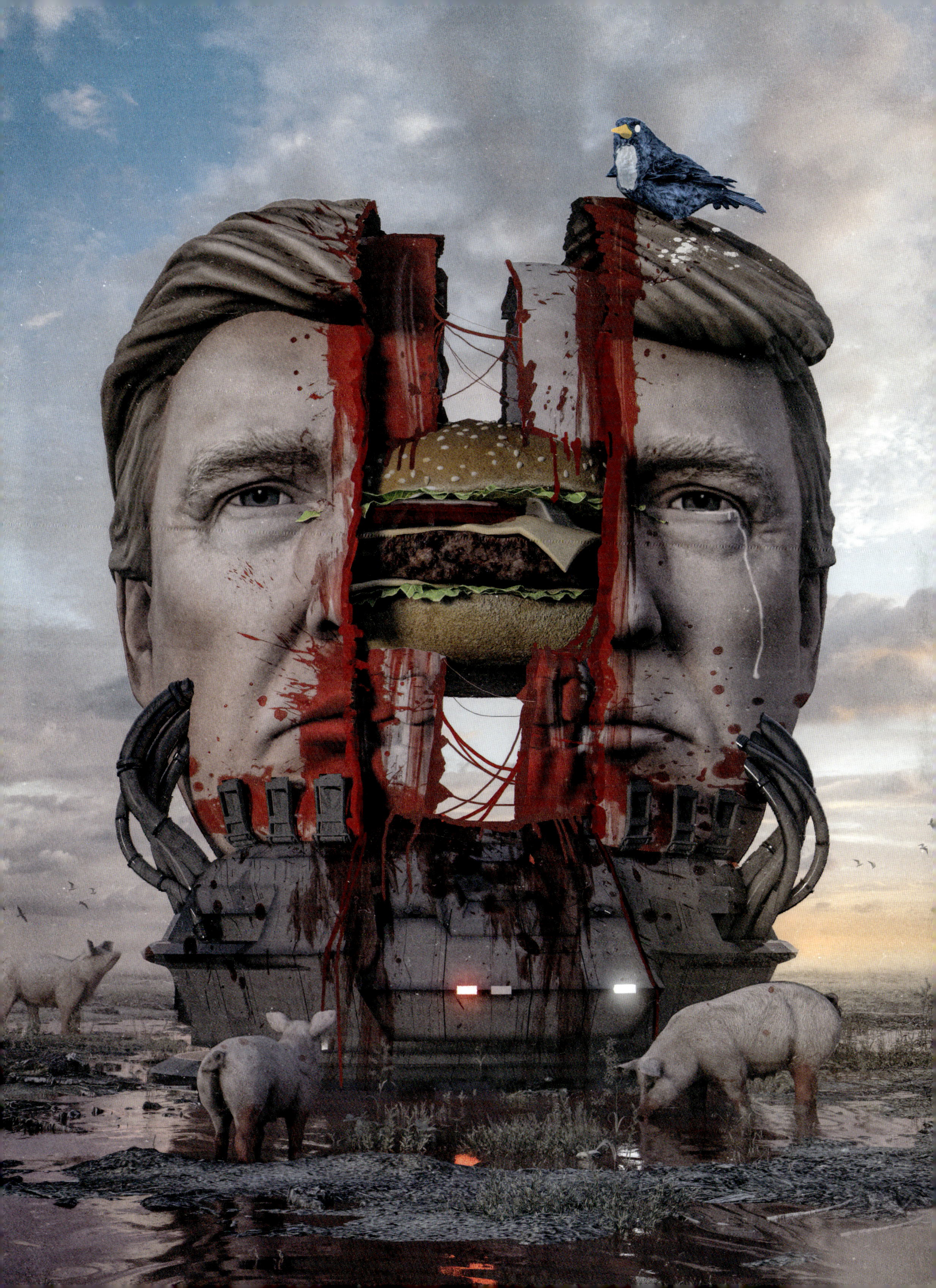

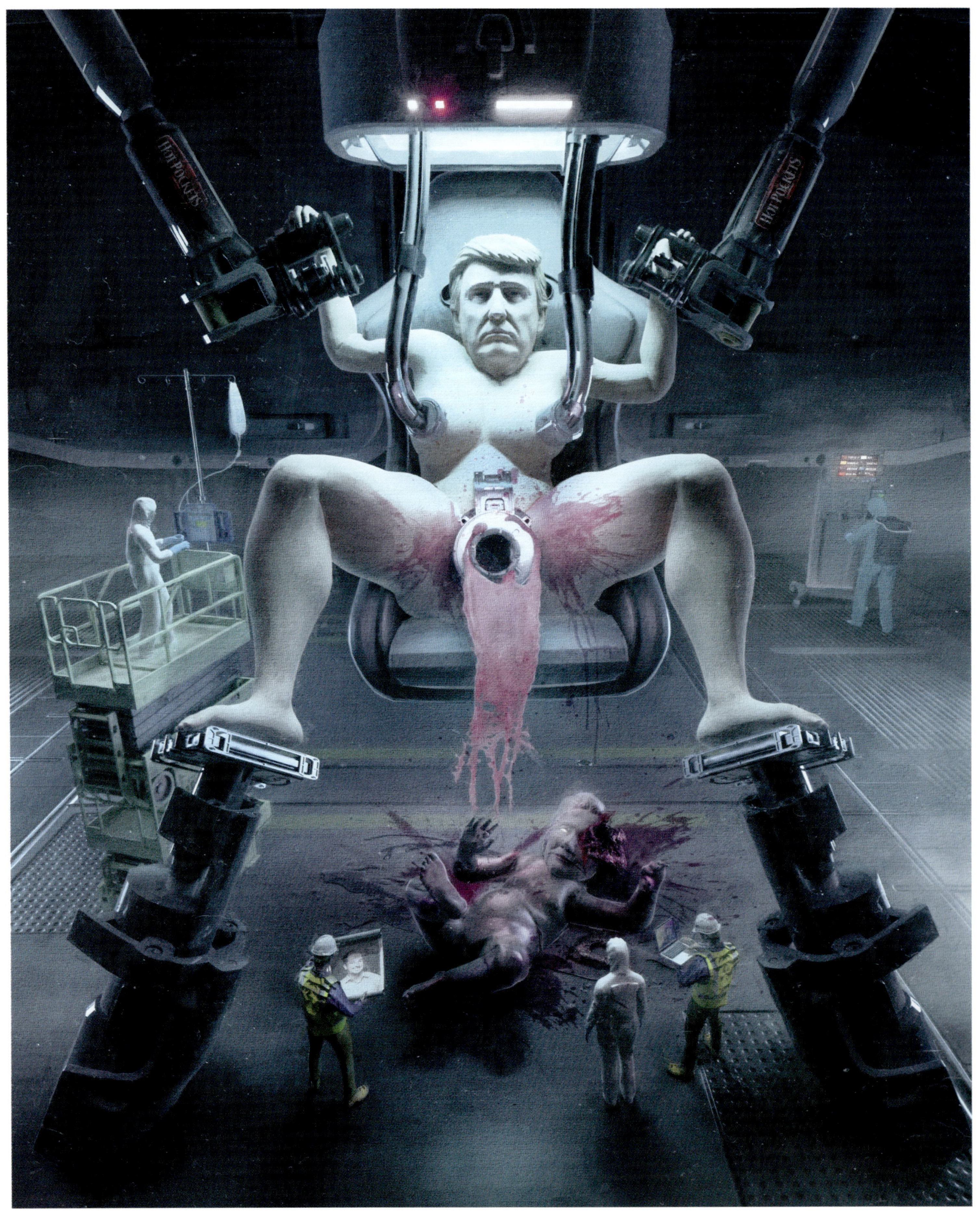

ABOVE

ROUTINE STILLBORN HEIRESS MALFUNCTION

10.10.2019

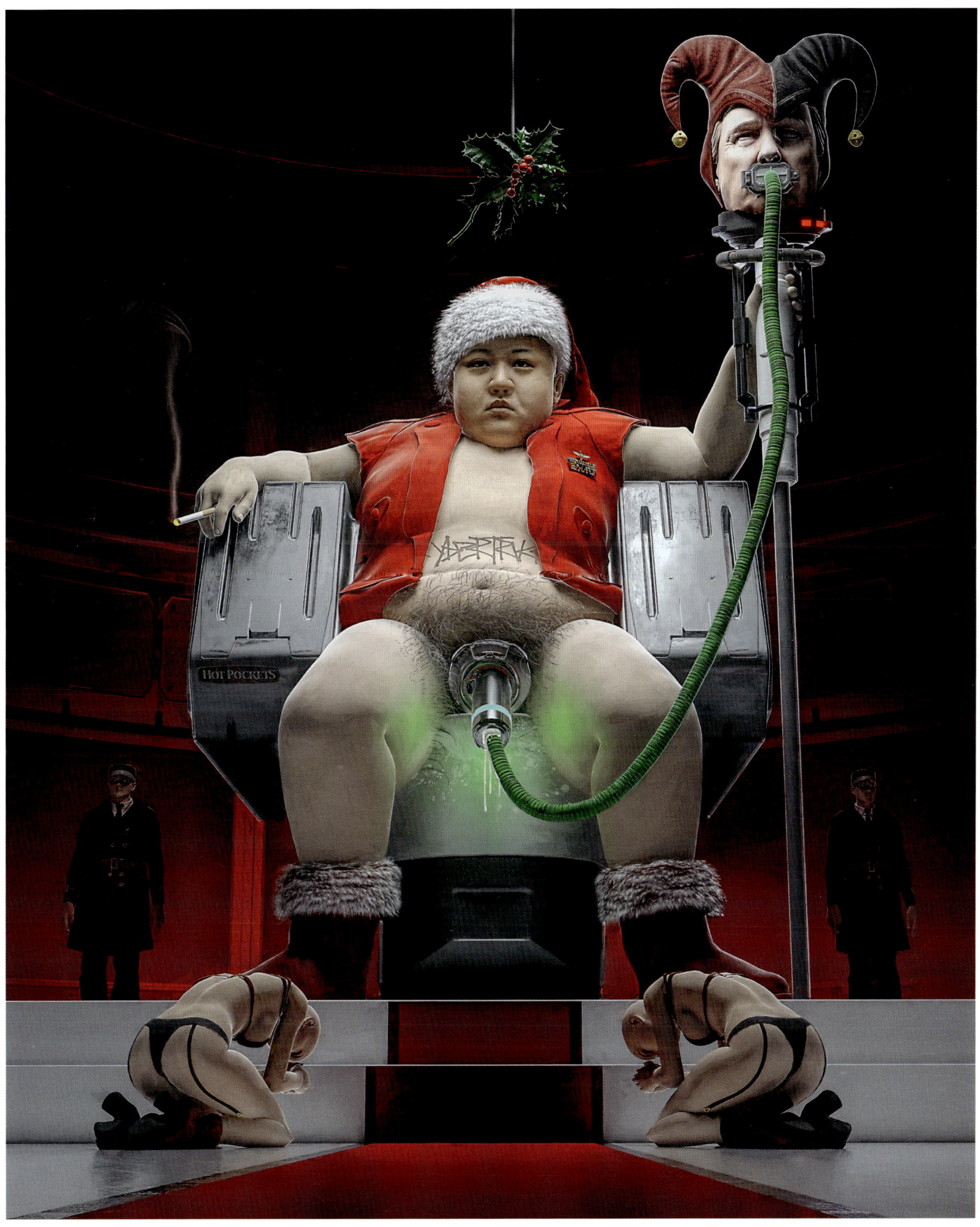

ABOVE

SANTA JONG-UN FEEDING HIS DONALD TOY HOMEMADE EGGNOG

12.14.2019

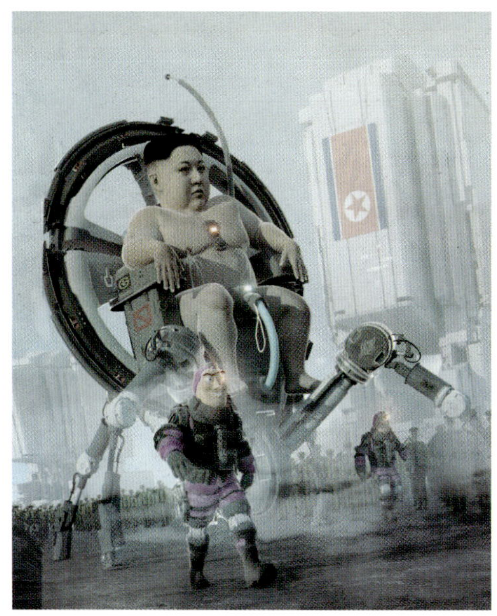

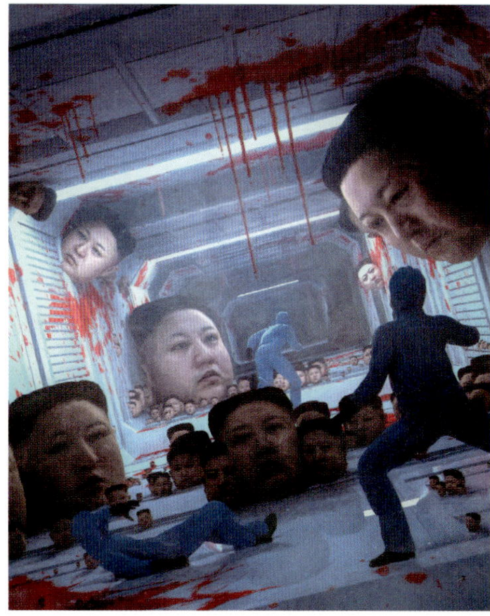

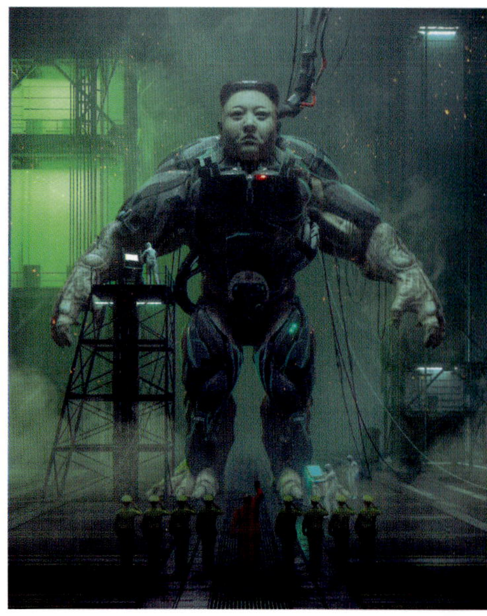

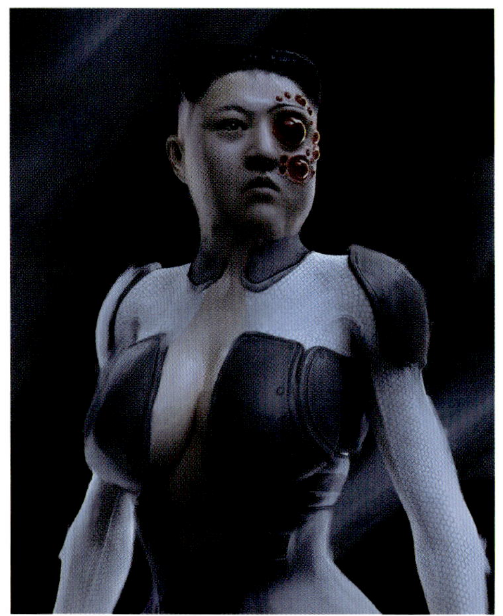

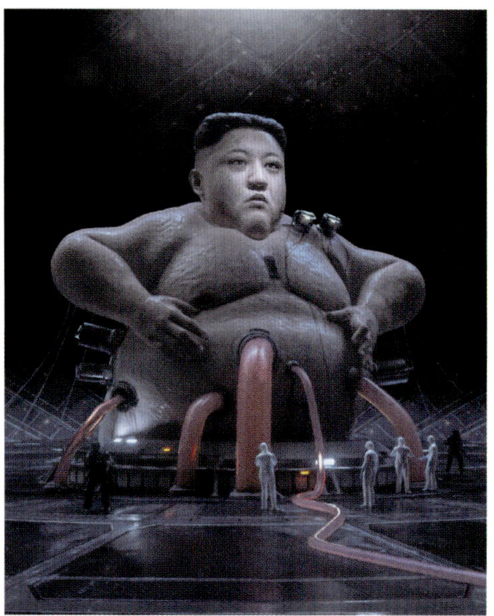

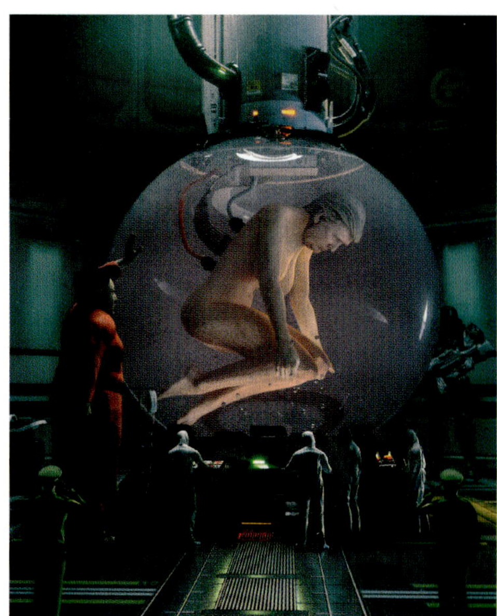

TOP LEFT

GREAT LEADER TESTOSTERONE MILKING DAY
08.03.2019

TOP MIDDLE

KIM JUNG FUNGUS
08.10.2019

TOP RIGHT

LITTLE ROCKET MAN 2091
06.18.2019

BOTTOM LEFT

KIM JONG SEXXYBAEWEIRDFACE
10.21.2019

BOTTOM MIDDLE

GREAT LEADER REJUVENATION DAY
10.06.2019

BOTTOM RIGHT

KIM JONG-UN CYBERNETIC FUCK FARM
09.06.2019

OPPOSITE PAGE

CIRCLE OF LIFE
08.20.2019

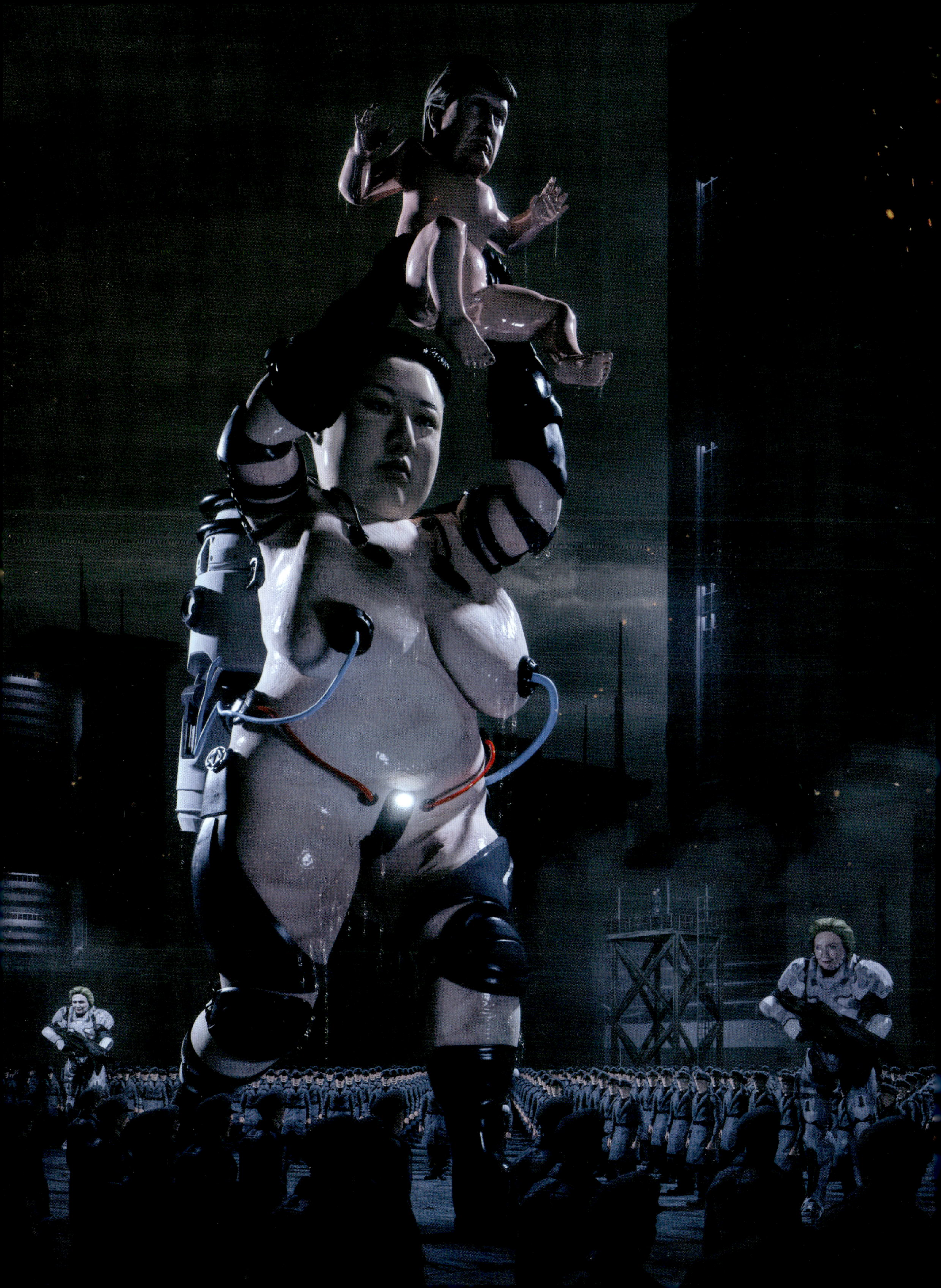

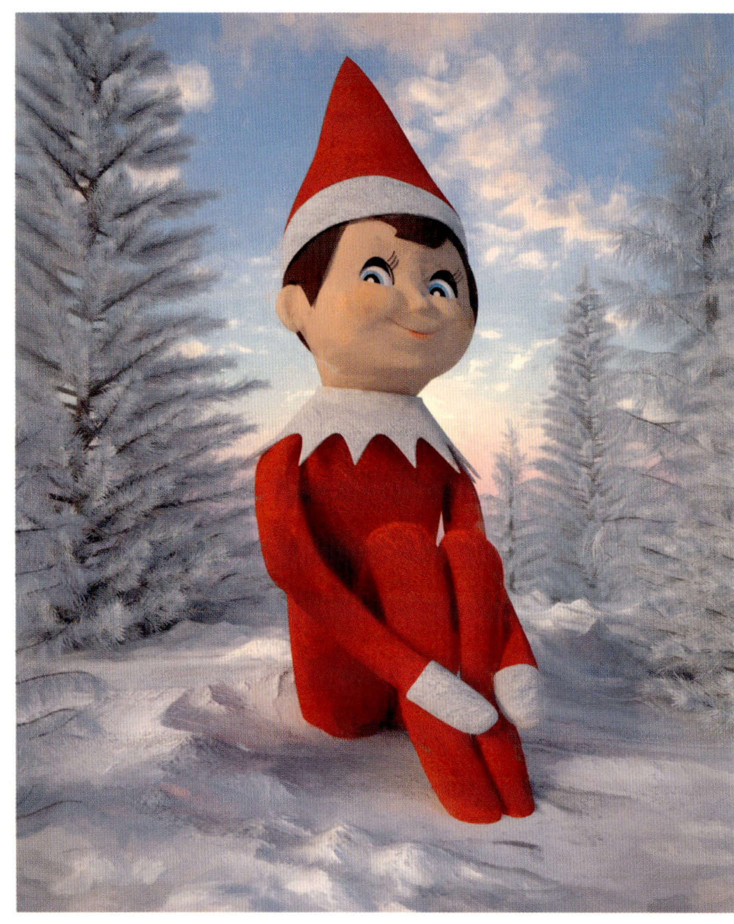

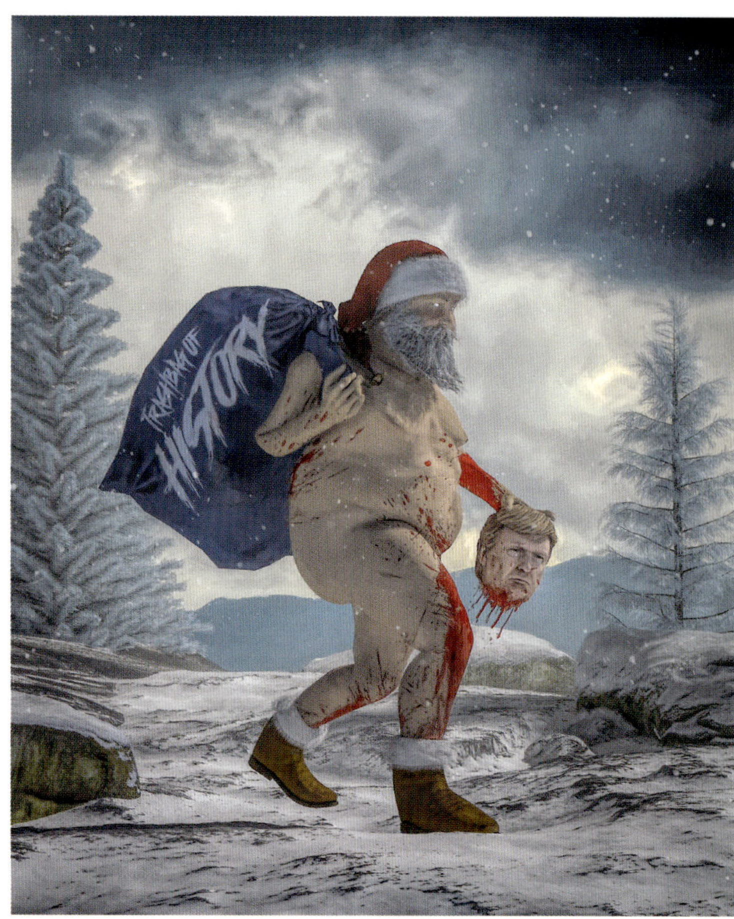

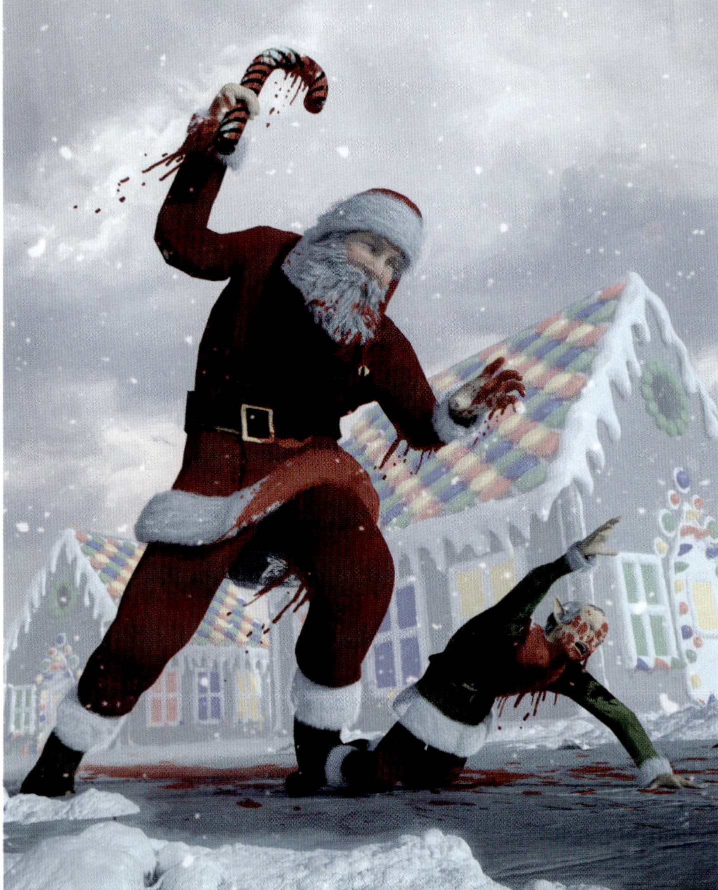

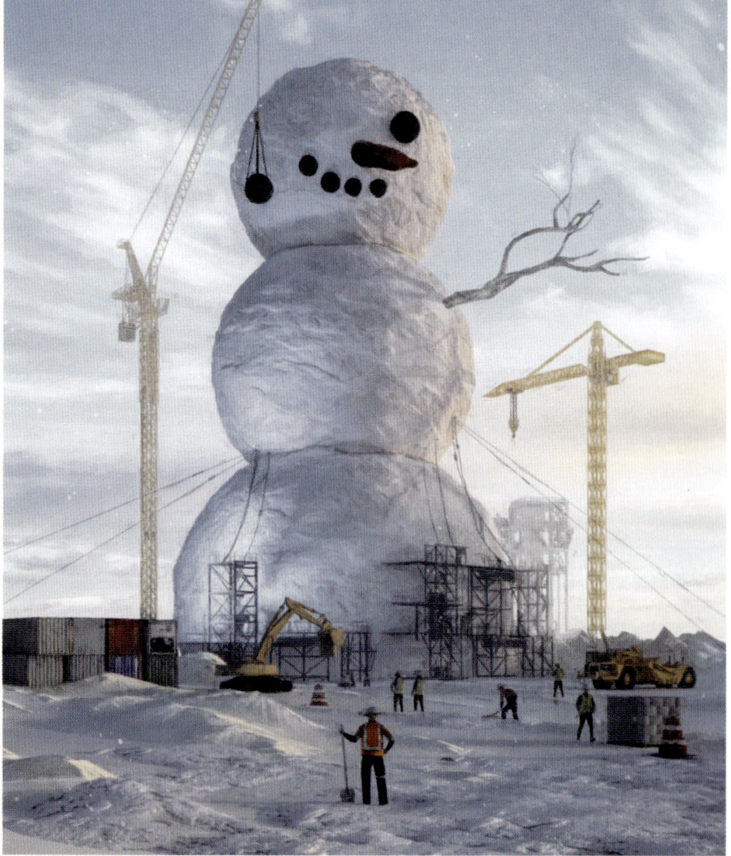

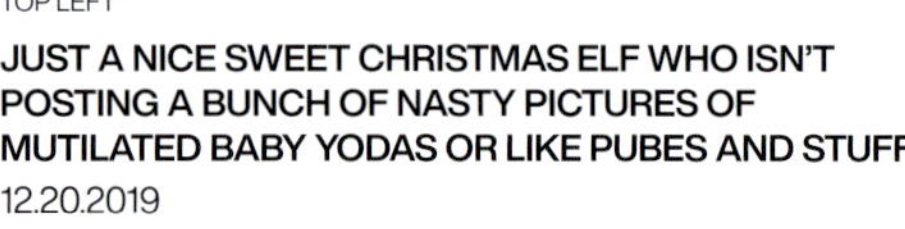

TOP LEFT

JUST A NICE SWEET CHRISTMAS ELF WHO ISN'T POSTING A BUNCH OF NASTY PICTURES OF MUTILATED BABY YODAS OR LIKE PUBES AND STUFF

12.20.2019

TOP RIGHT

CHRISTMAS CAME EARLY

12.18.2019

BOTTOM LEFT

RESPECT THE LIST

12.25.2019

BOTTOM RIGHT

humanity should all just relax for a sec and build a really dope ass snowman together

12.23.2019

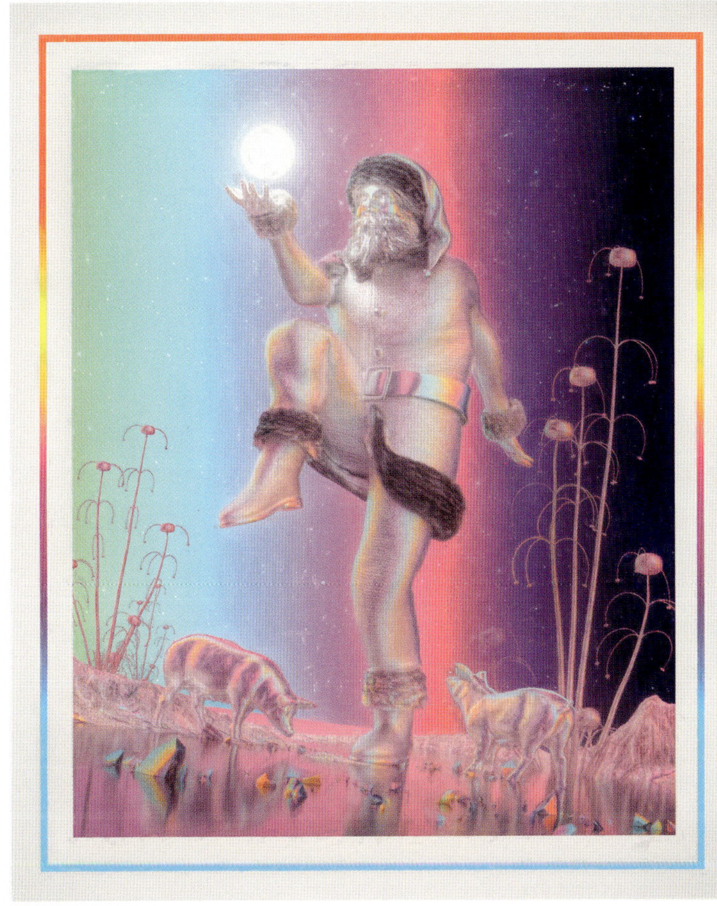

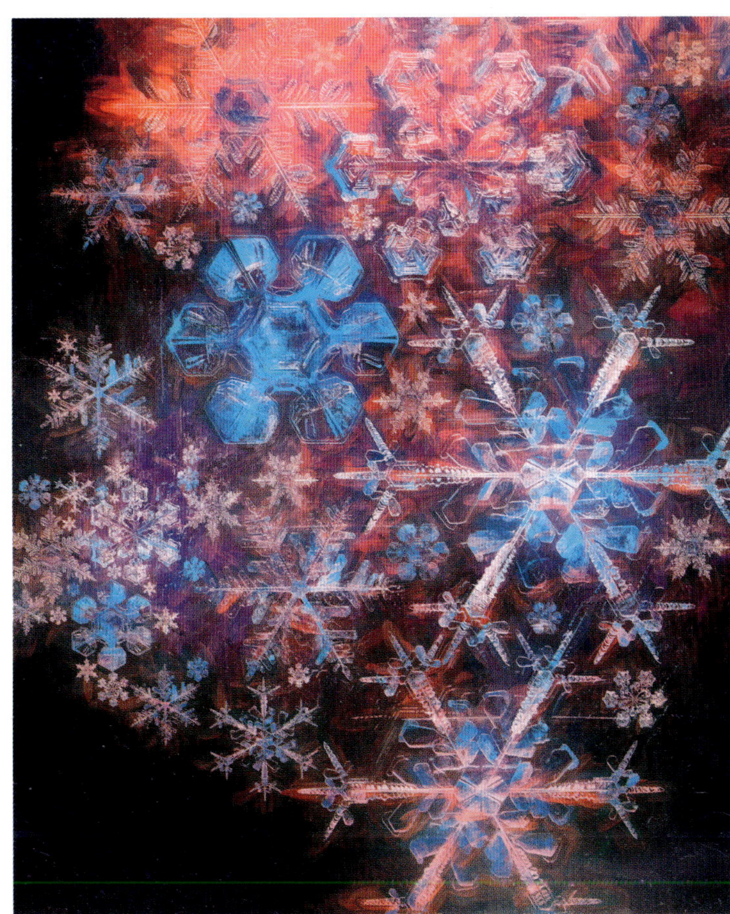

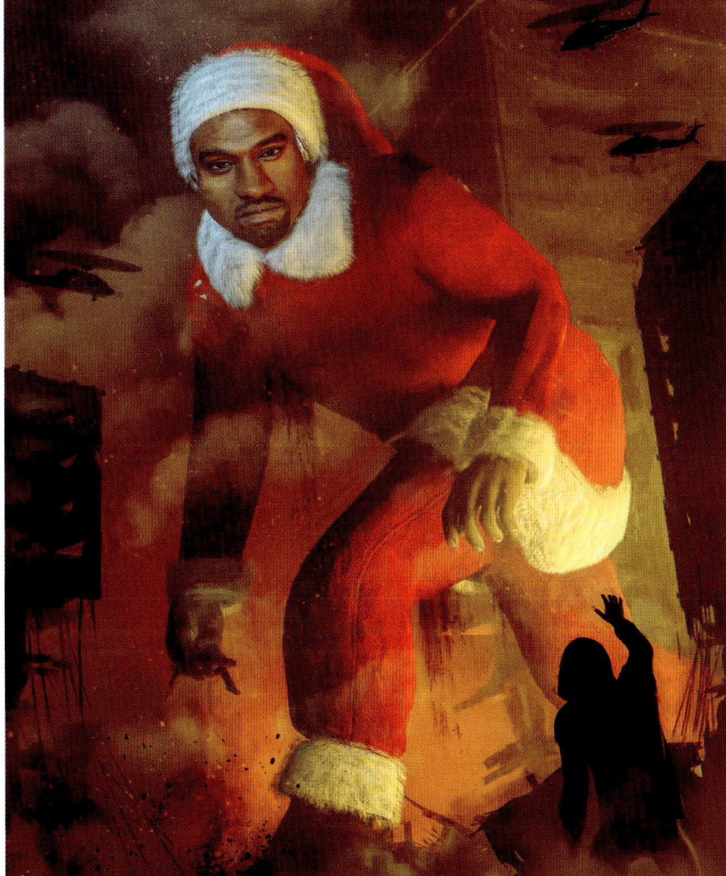

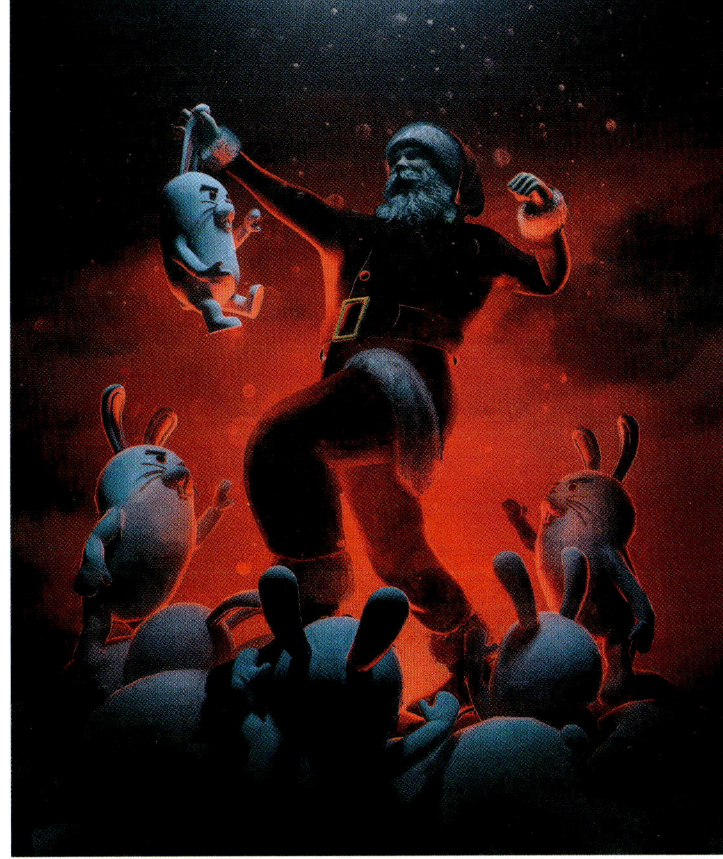

TOP LEFT

LEVEL 7 CHRISTMAS OMEGA SUPERMIRACLE

12.24.2019

TOP RIGHT

BEAUTIFUL SNOWFLAKES

12.19.2019

BOTTOM LEFT

SANTA IS KING

12.15.2019

BOTTOM RIGHT

EASTER VS. CHRISTMAS

04.21.2019

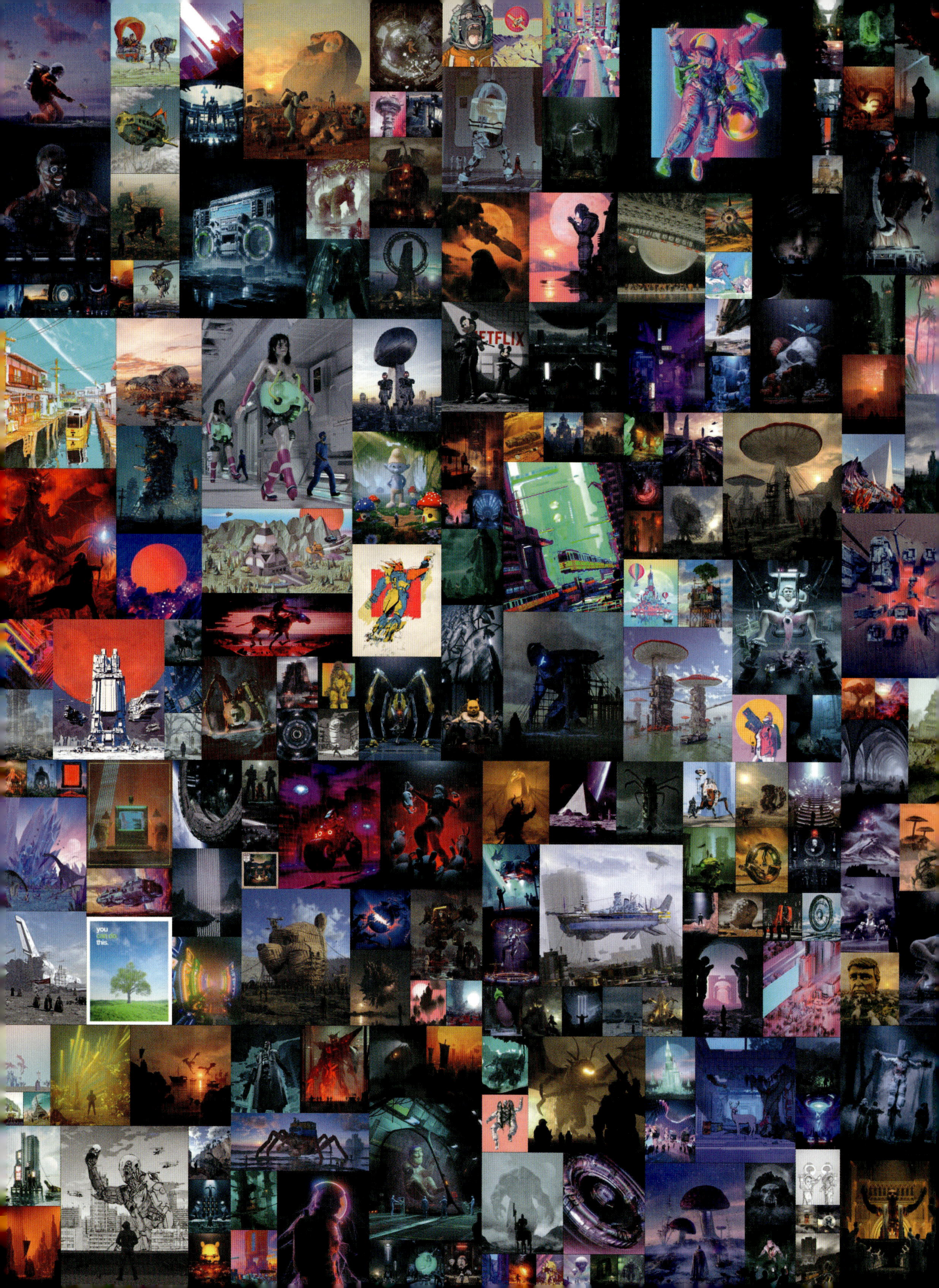
ETFLIX
you
can do
this.

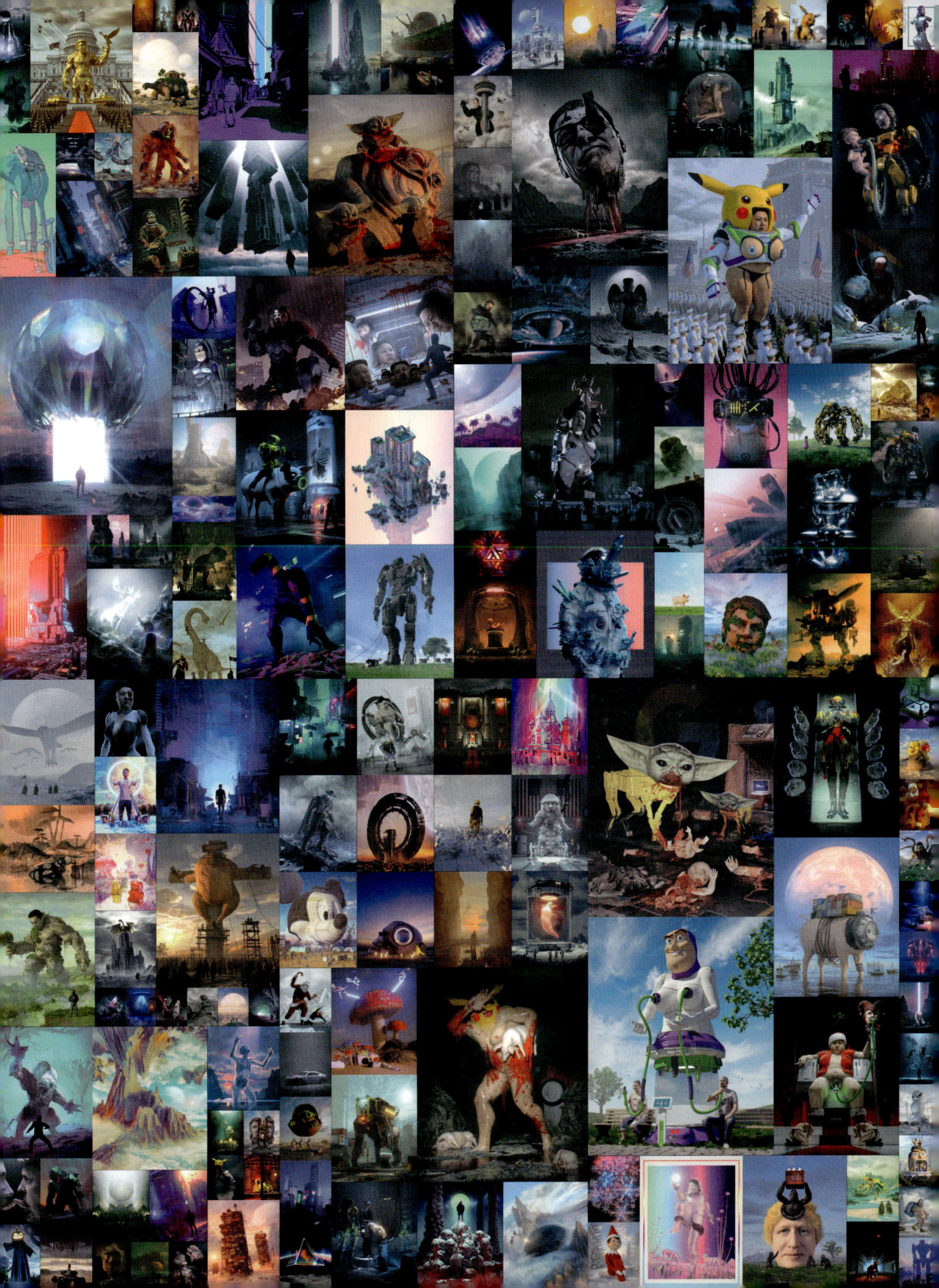

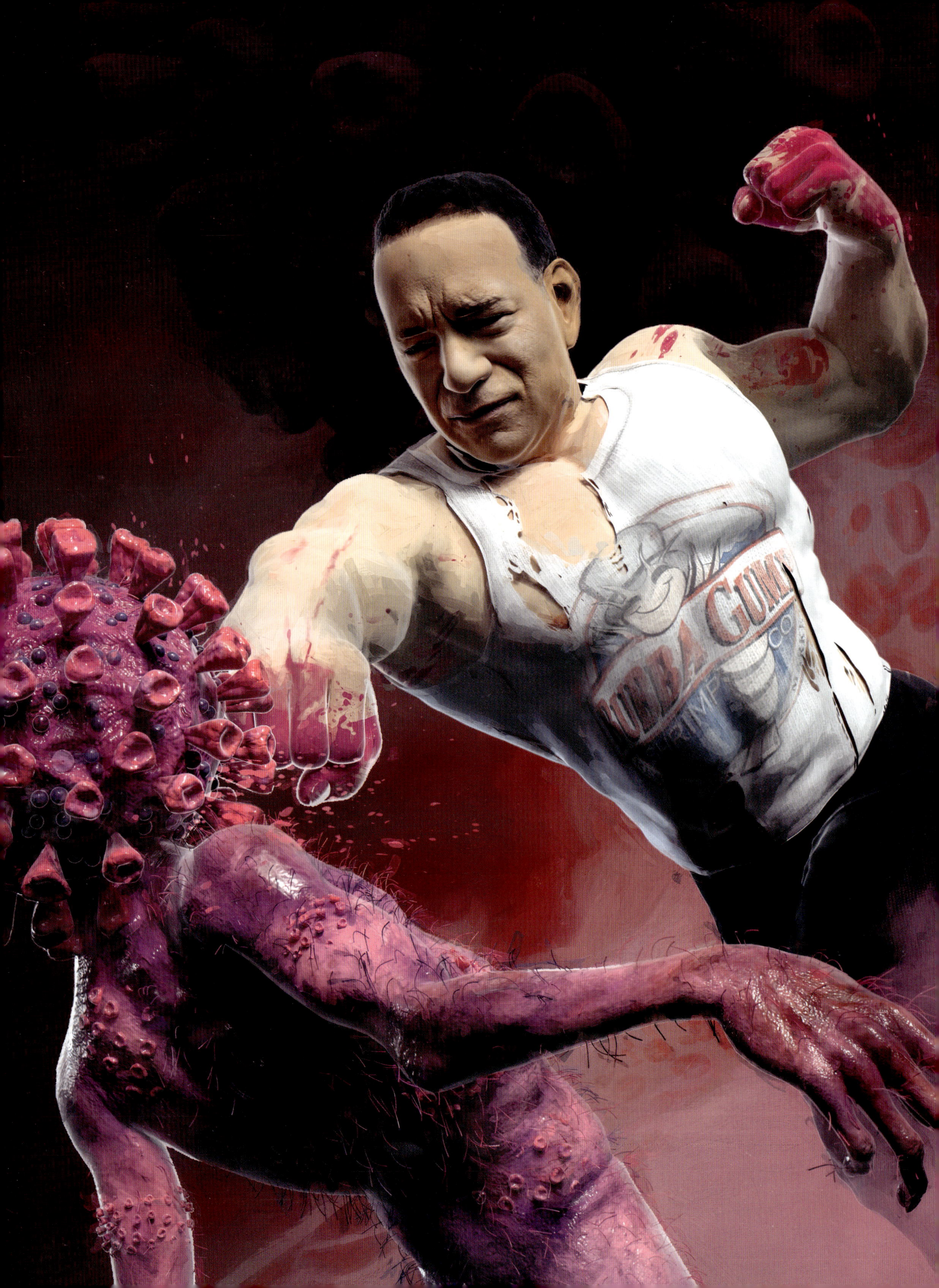

2020

OPPOSITE PAGE

TOM HANKS BEATING THE SHIT OUT OF CORONAVIRUS

03.12.2020

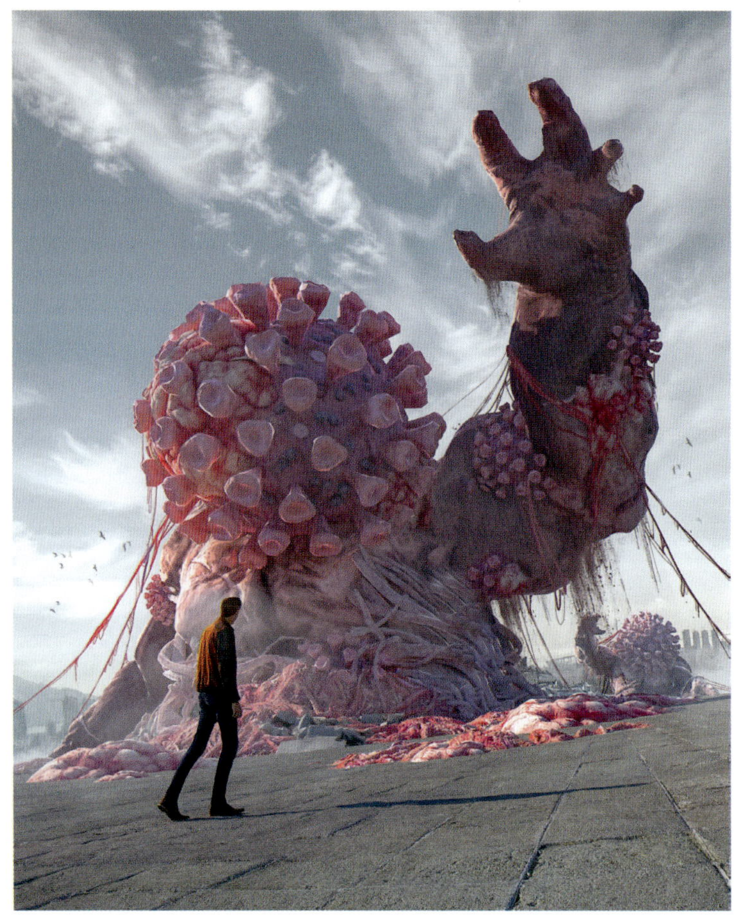

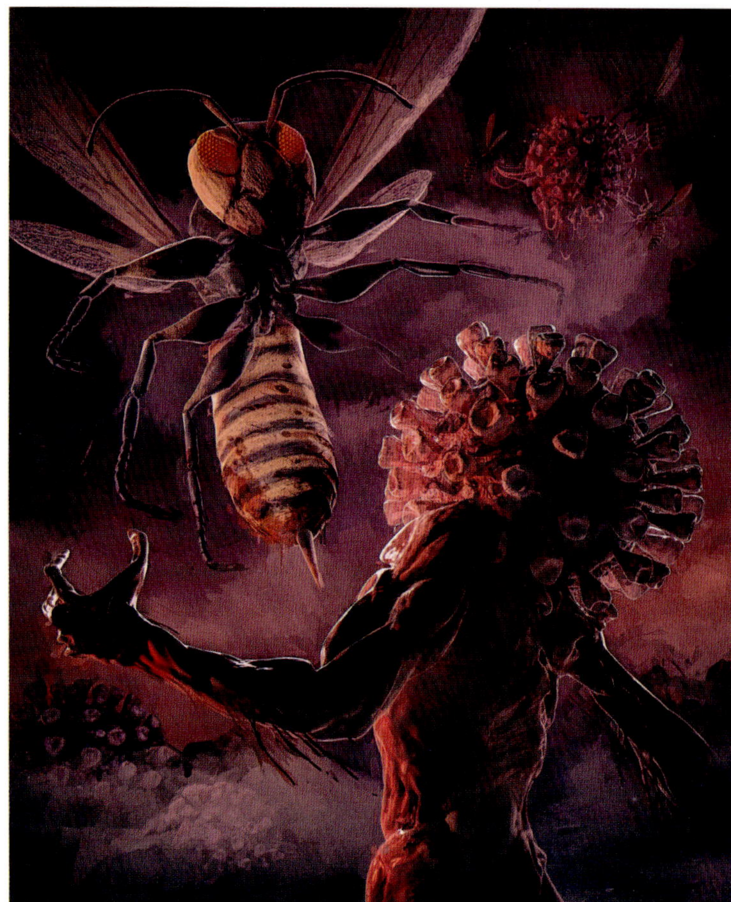

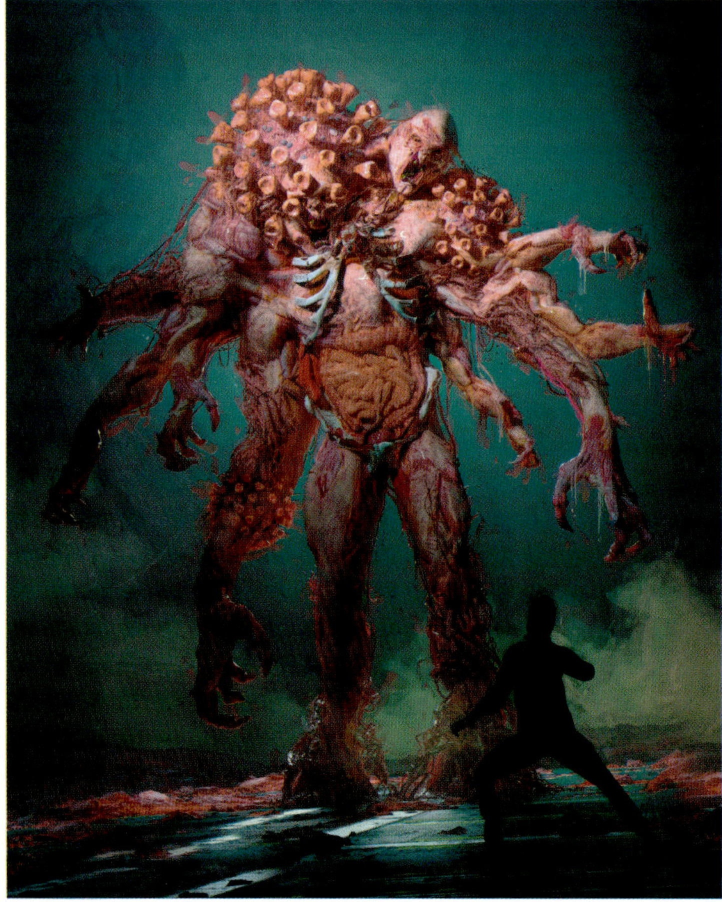

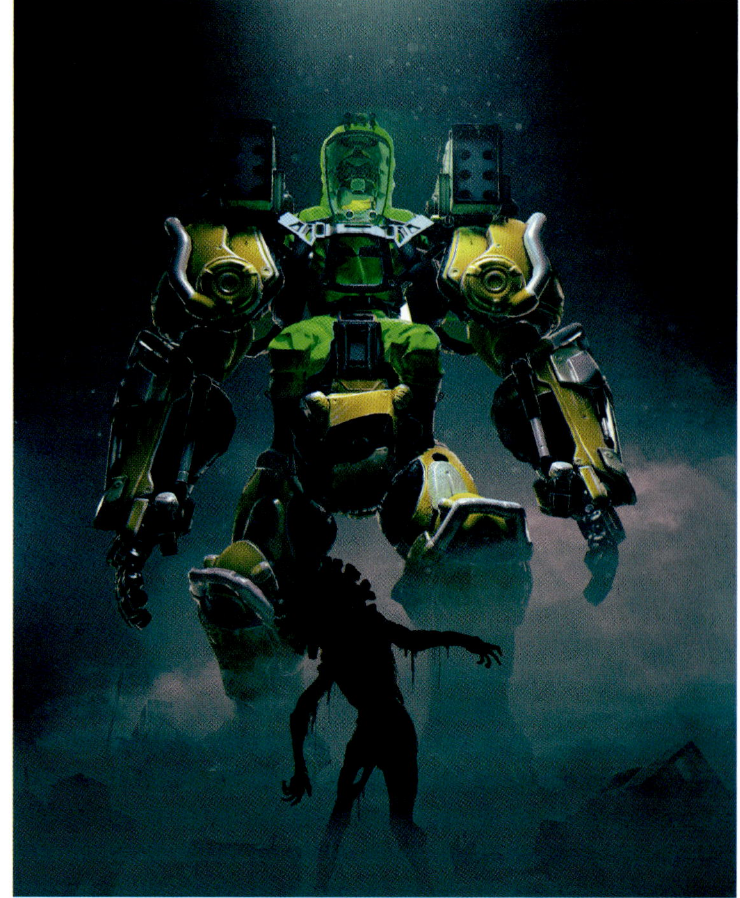

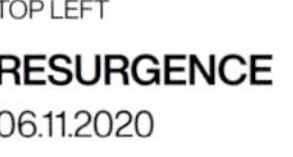

TOP LEFT

RESURGENCE
06.11.2020

TOP RIGHT

CORONAVIRUS vs. MURDER HORNETS
05.06.2020

BOTTOM LEFT

NASTY MOTHERFUCKER
04.06.2020

BOTTOM RIGHT

COVID-19 OFFENSIVE SQUAD-3
04.03.2020

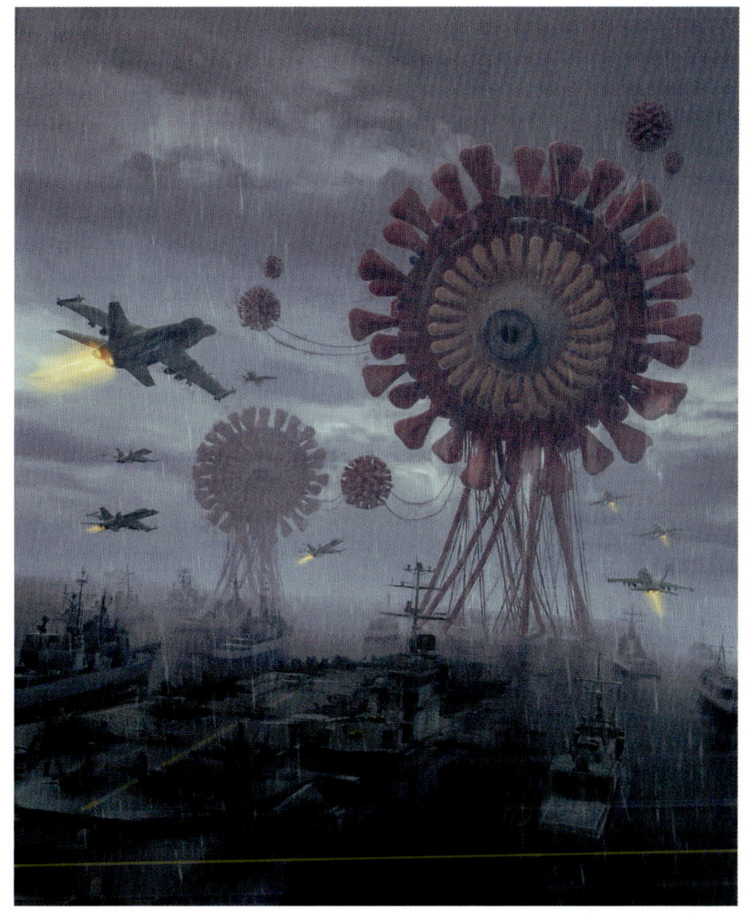

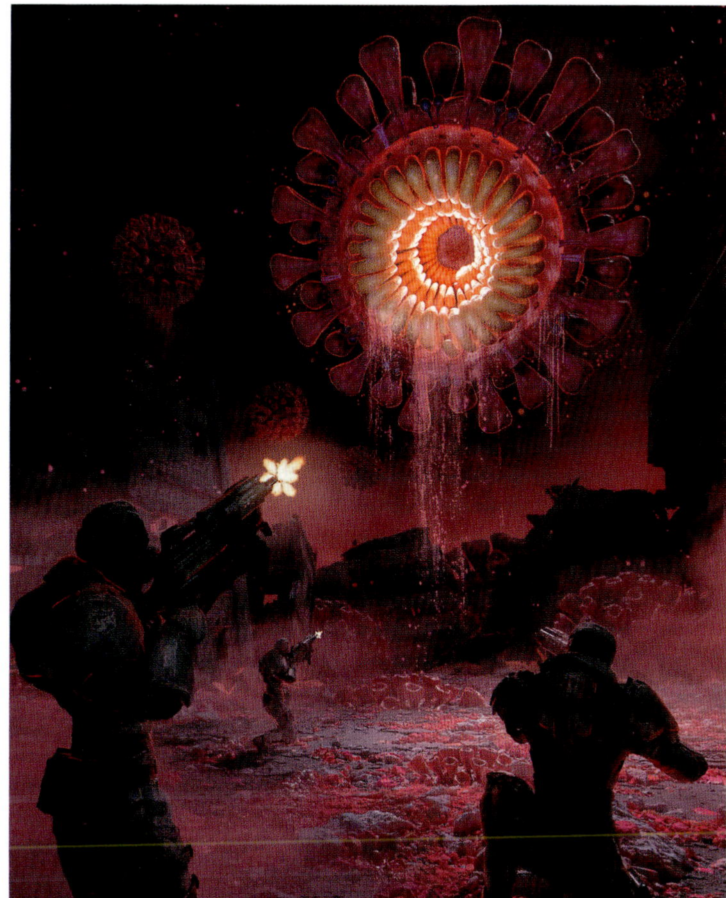

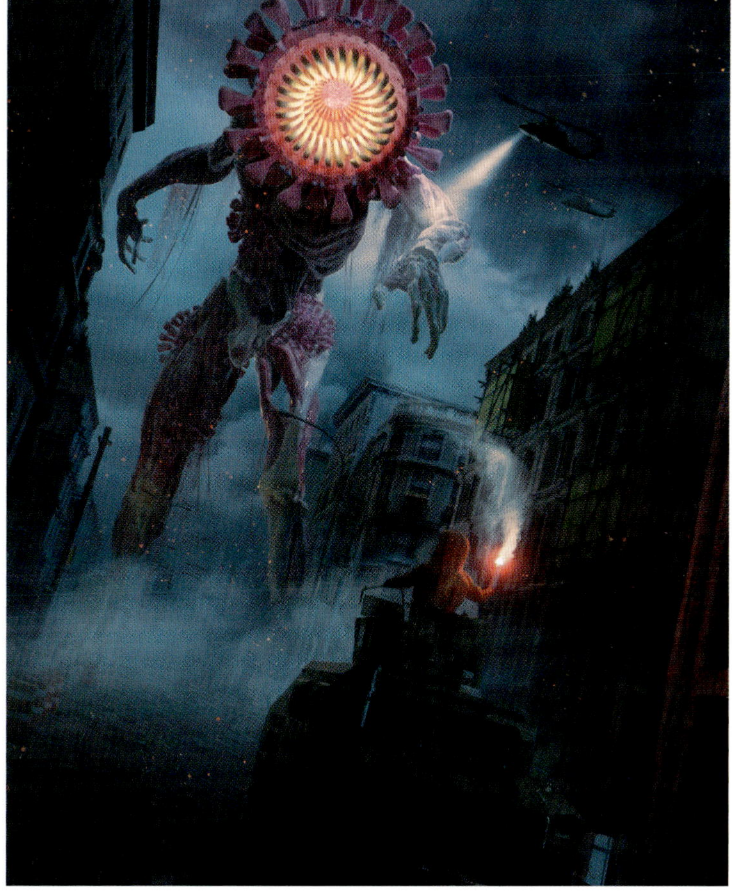

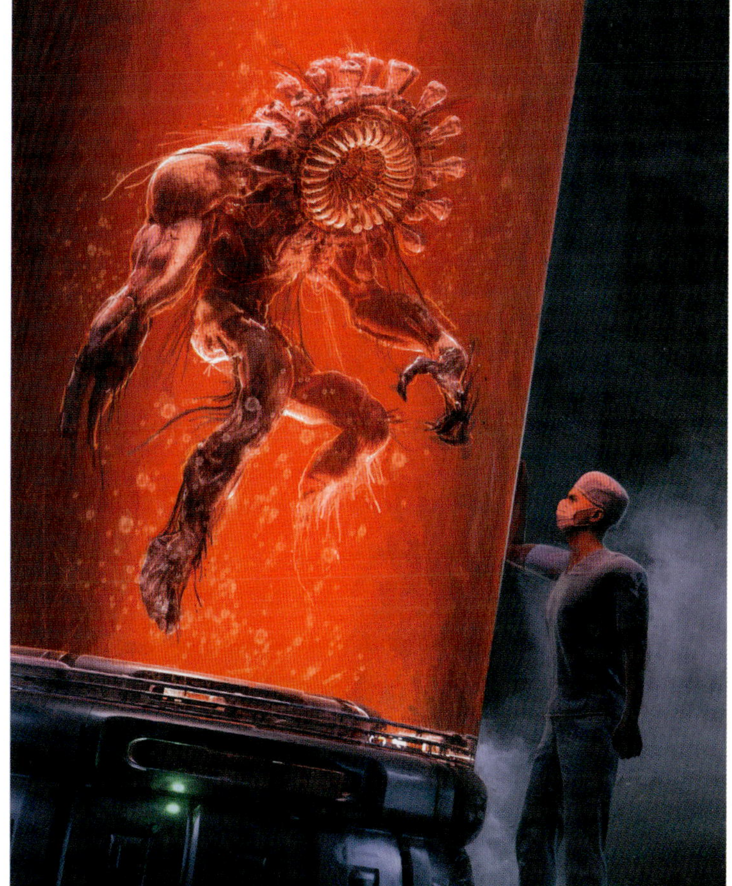

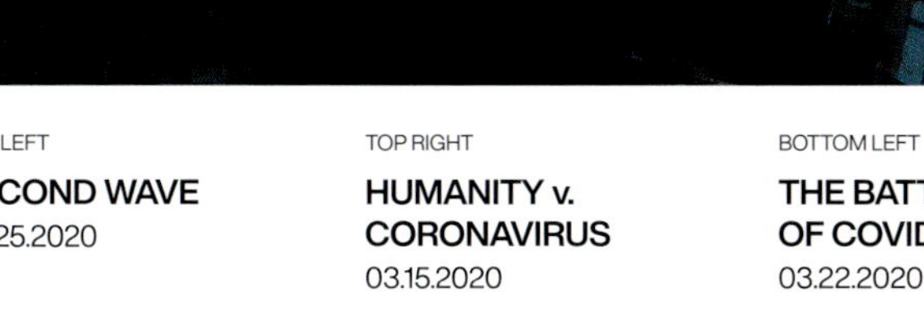

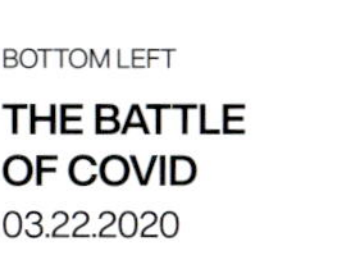

TOP LEFT

SECOND WAVE
05.25.2020

TOP RIGHT

HUMANITY v. CORONAVIRUS
03.15.2020

BOTTOM LEFT

THE BATTLE OF COVID
03.22.2020

BOTTOM RIGHT

FRONTLINE WARRIORS
05.03.2020

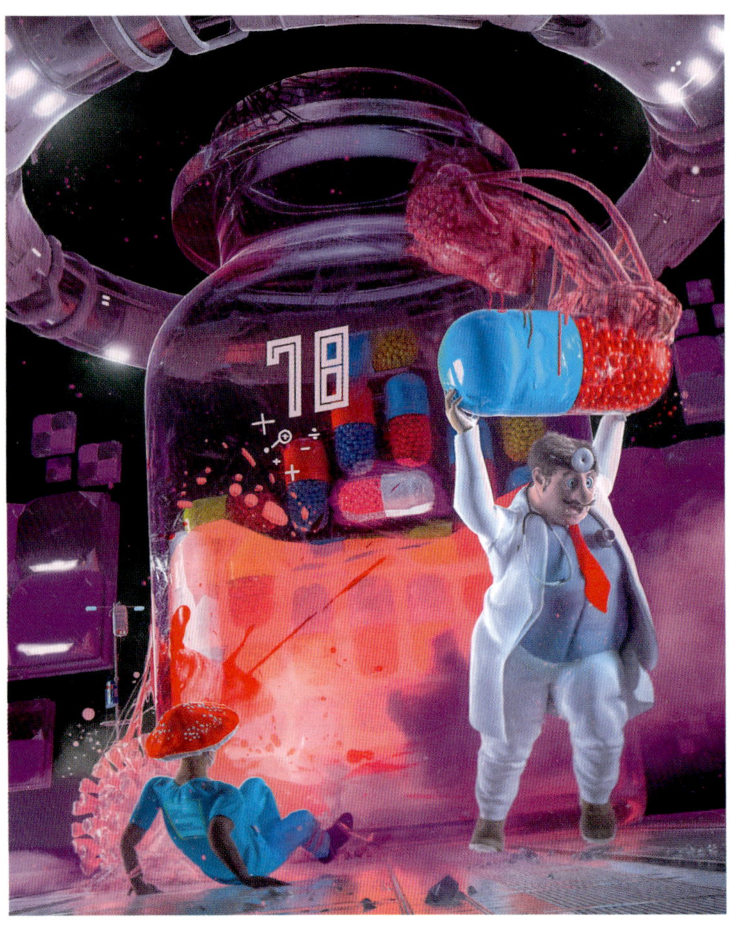

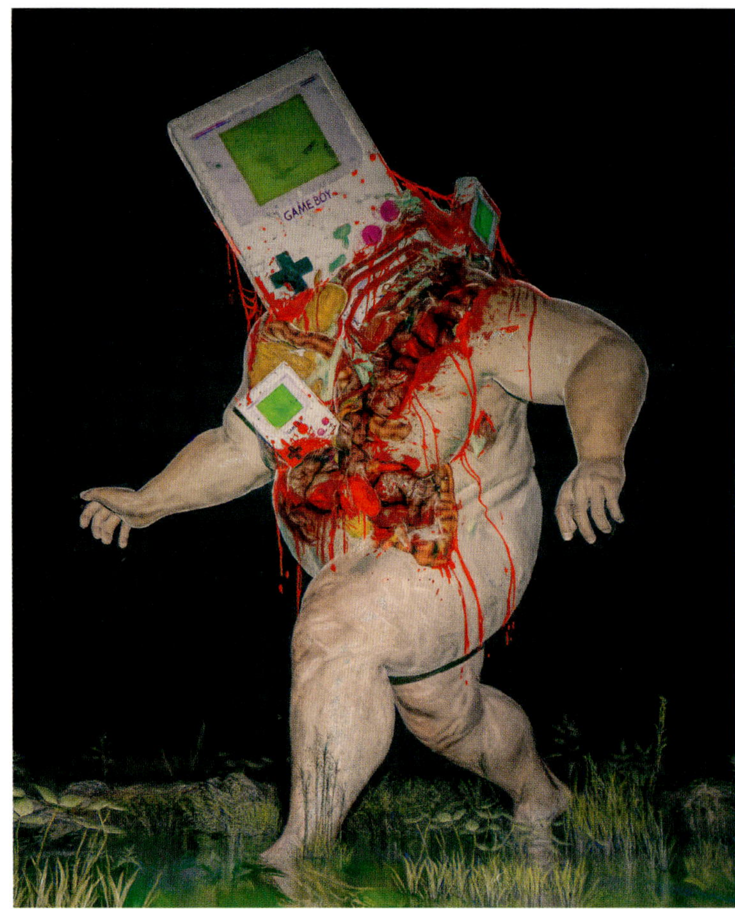

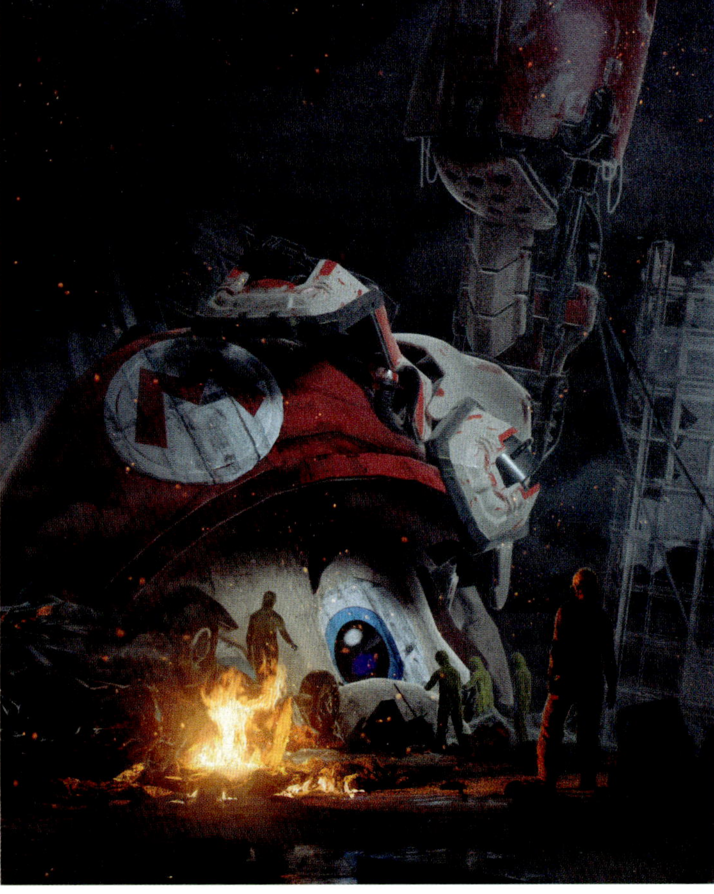

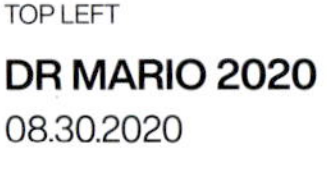

TOP LEFT
DR MARIO 2020
08.30.2020

TOP RIGHT
PS5
06.30.2020

BOTTOM LEFT
GAME OVER
02.26.2020

BOTTOM RIGHT
KONAMI CODE
09.19.2020

OPPOSITE PAGE
ANCIENT TECHNOLOGY
07.21.2020

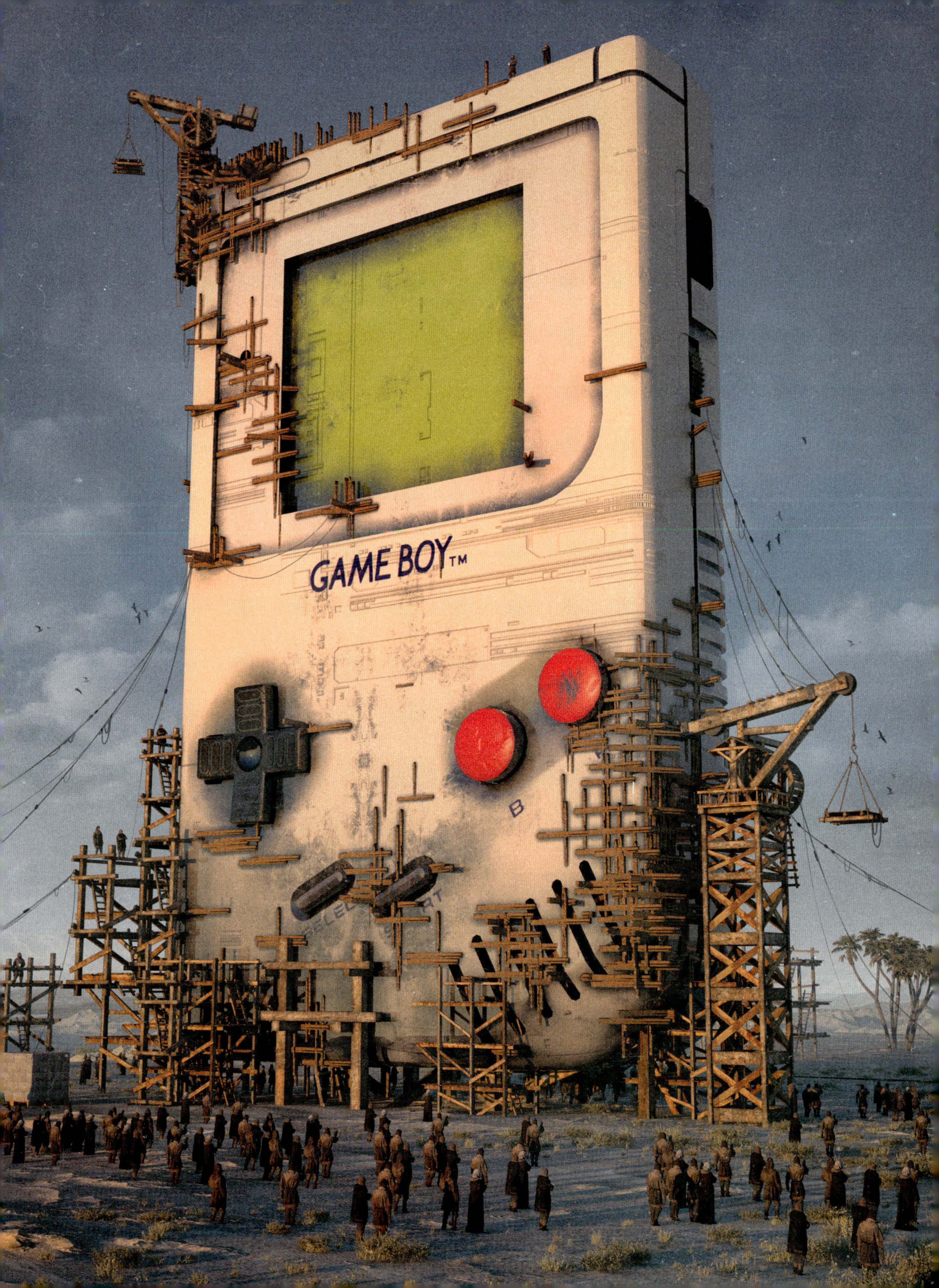
GAME BOY™
B

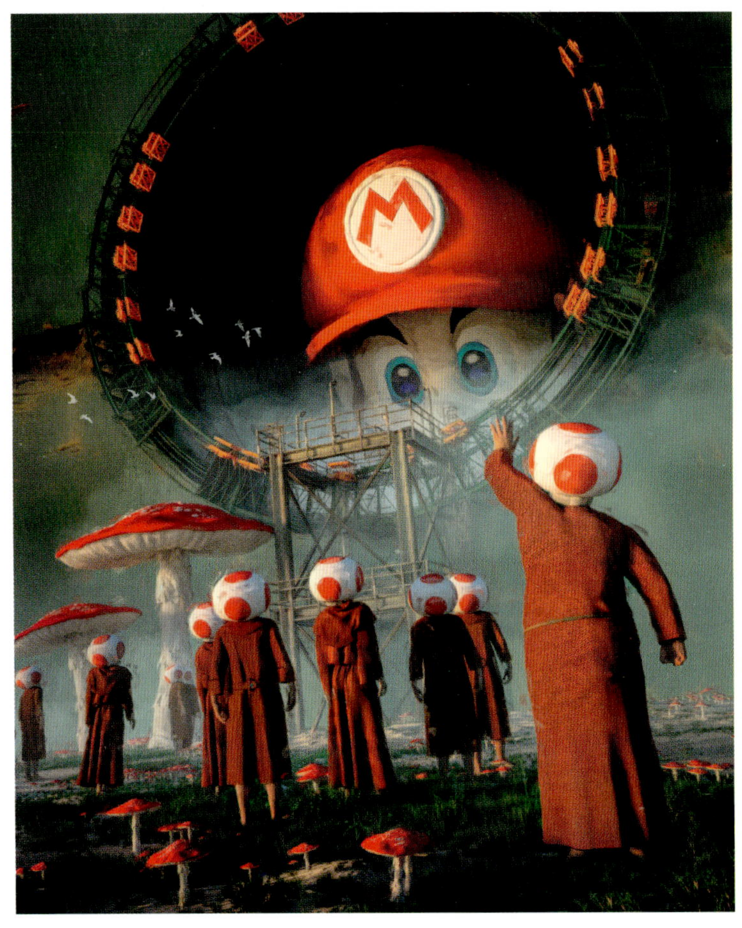

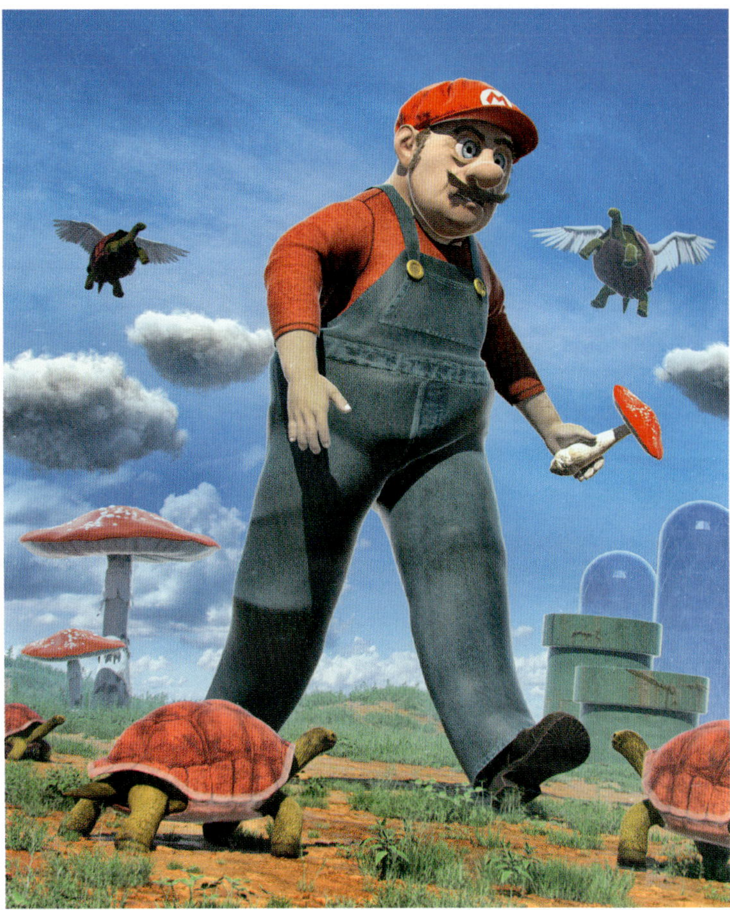

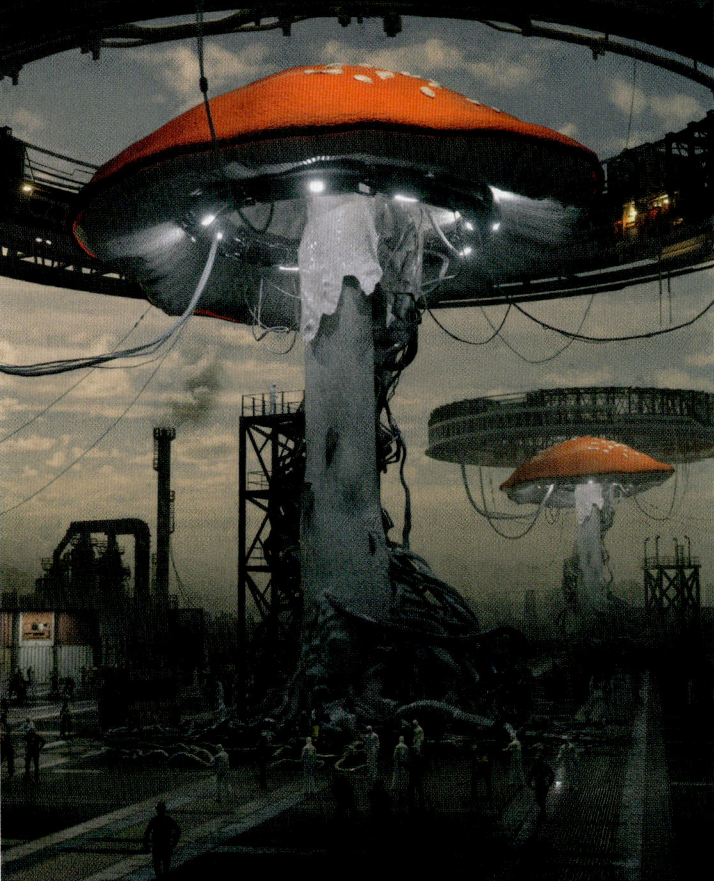

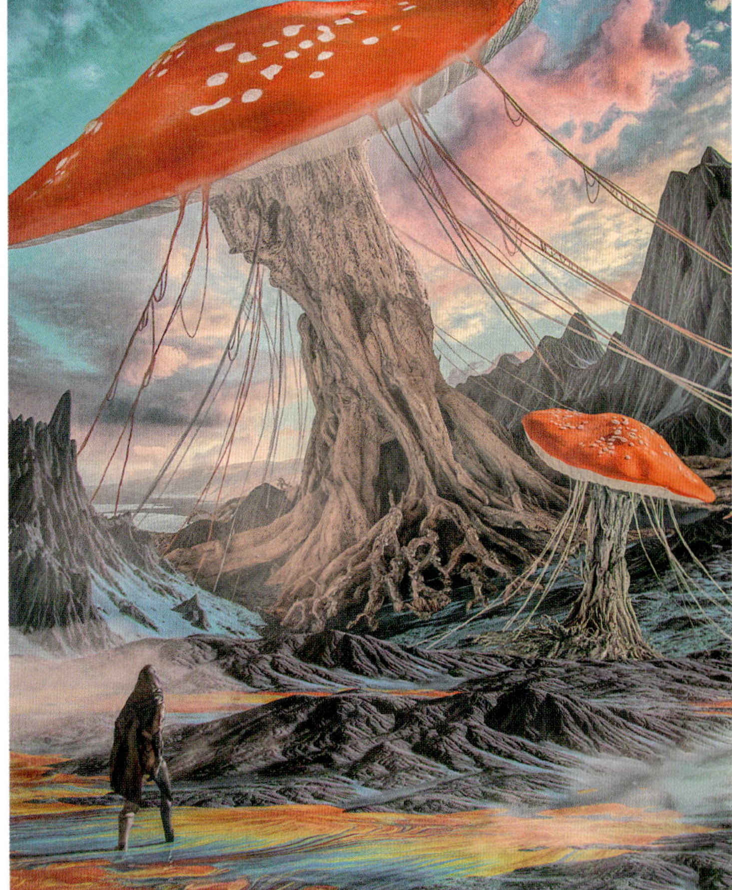

TOP LEFT
NEW PIPE
08.22.2020

TOP RIGHT
MICRODOSE
05.11.2020

BOTTOM LEFT
INDUSTRIAL GRADE
09.08.2020

BOTTOM RIGHT
GRIMM SHROOMS
01.18.2020

OPPOSITE PAGE
MARIO 2020
06.24.2020

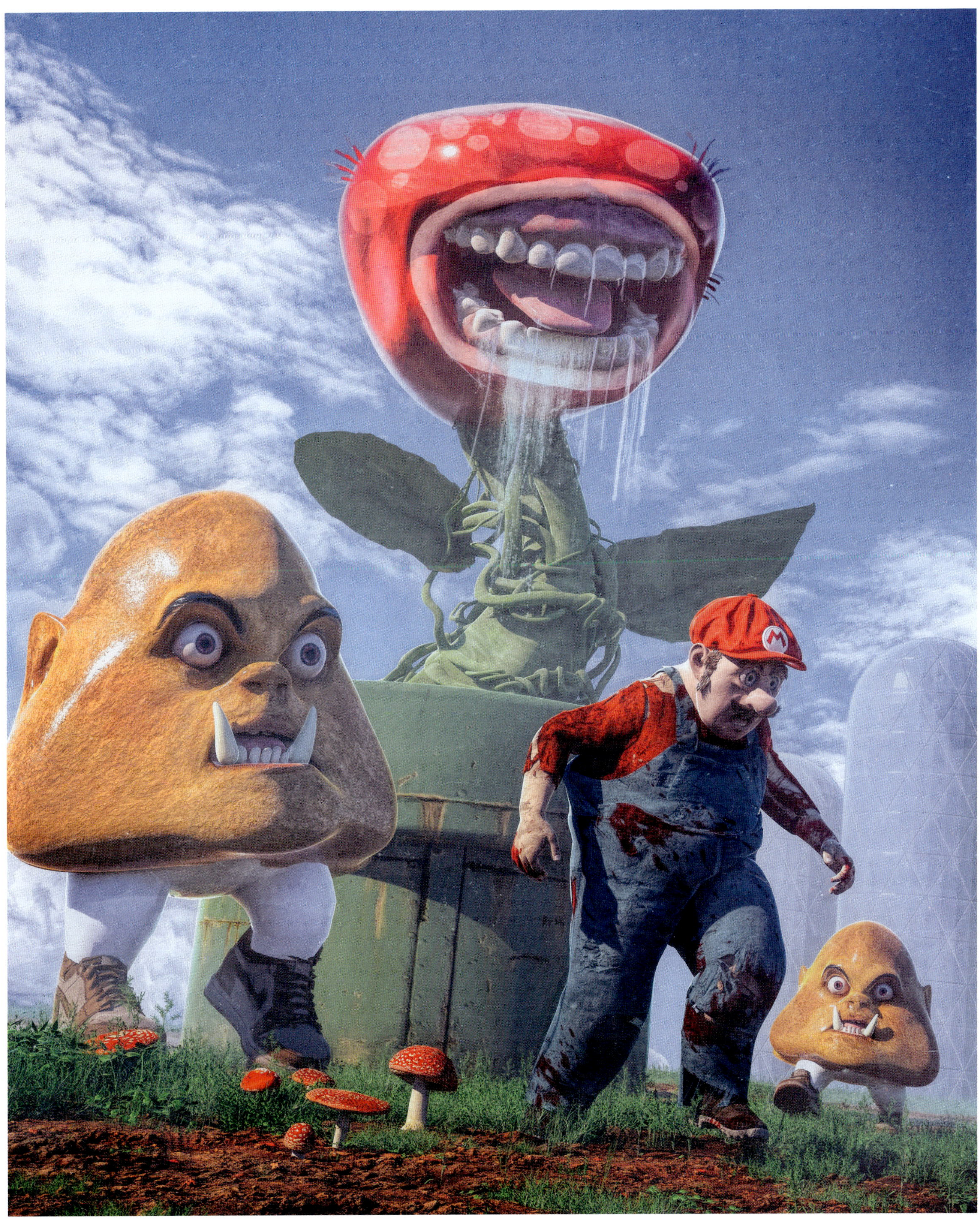

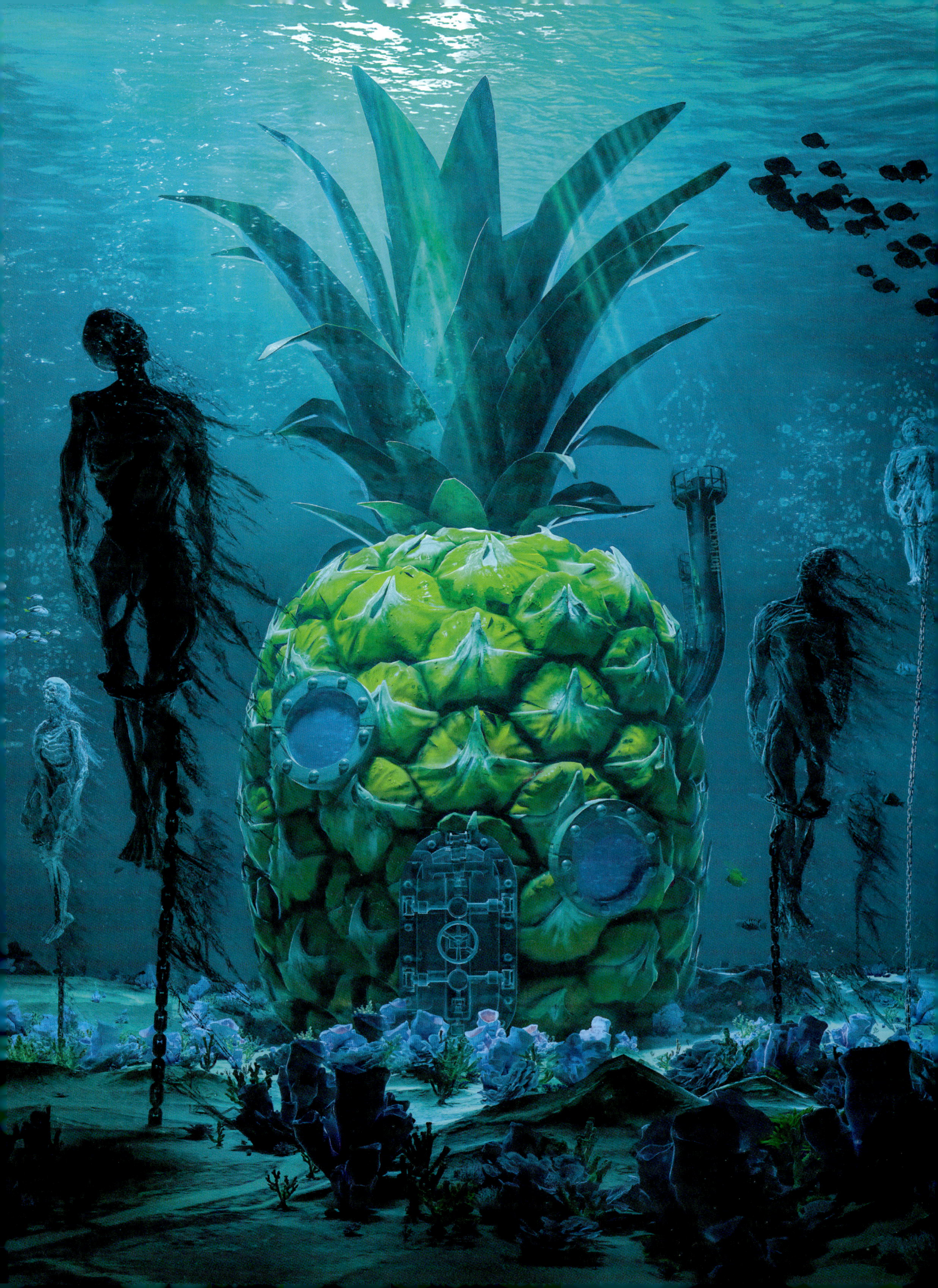

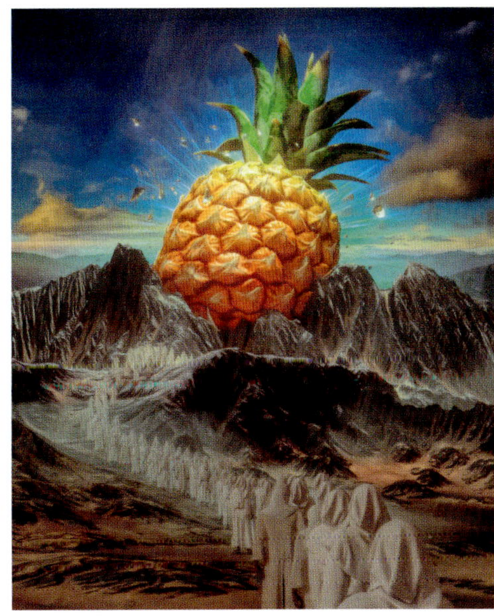

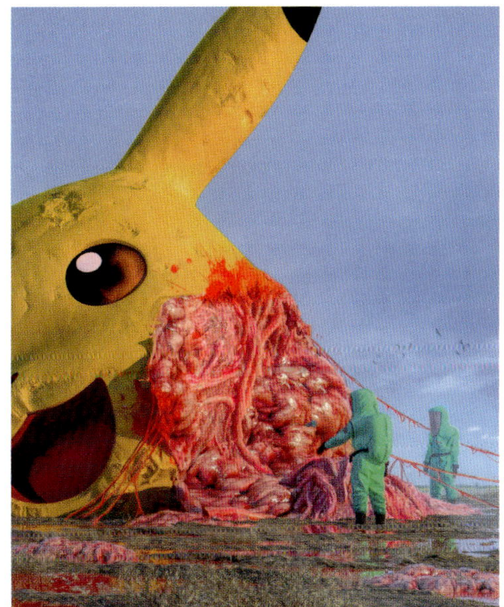

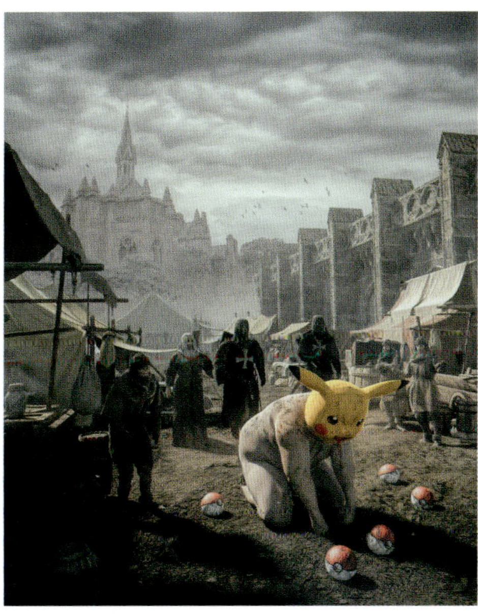

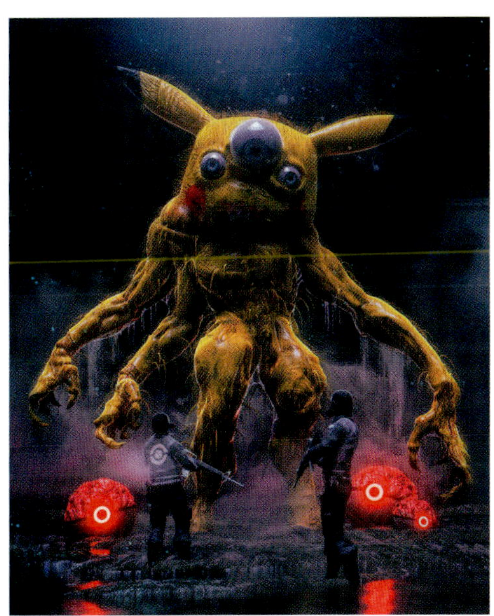

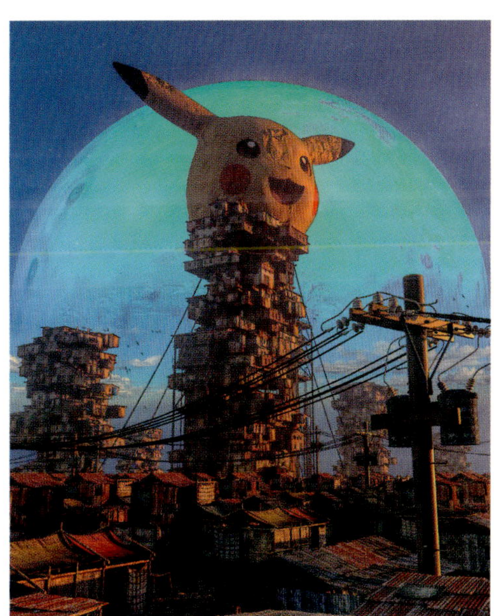

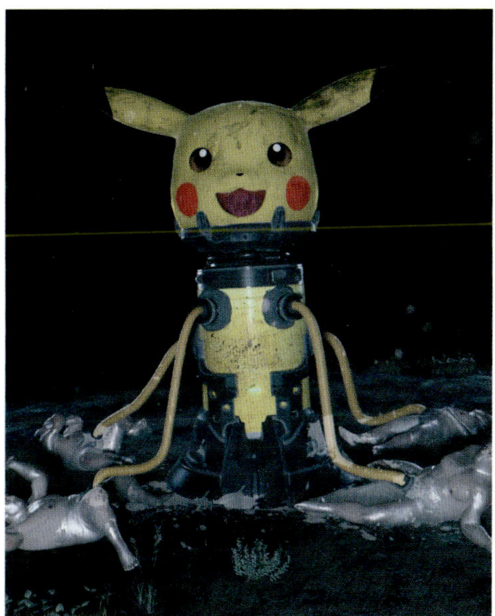

OPPOSITE PAGE
UNDERSEA PINEAPPLE 2020
09.27.2020

TOP LEFT
TOMORROW
10.25.2020

TOP MIDDLE
INFECTED CULTURE
04.10.2020

TOP RIGHT
GUILTY PLEASURE
06.17.2020

BOTTOM LEFT
POKEMON R
05.24.2020

BOTTOM MIDDLE
PIKAChU DISTRICT 7F
12.07.2020

BOTTOM RIGHT
POKÉMON WHITE
01.24.2020

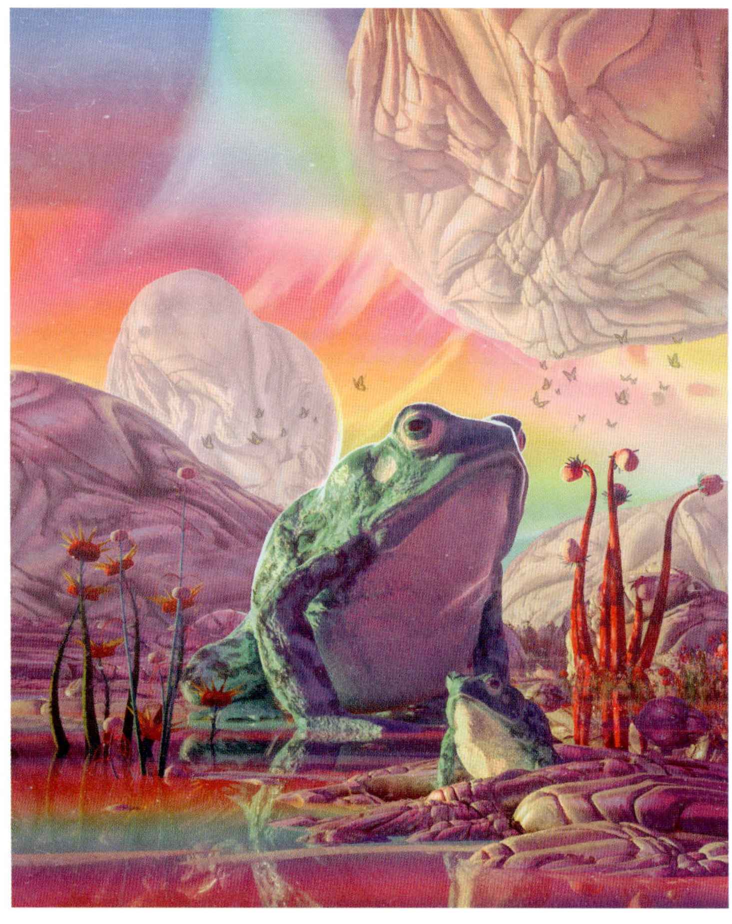

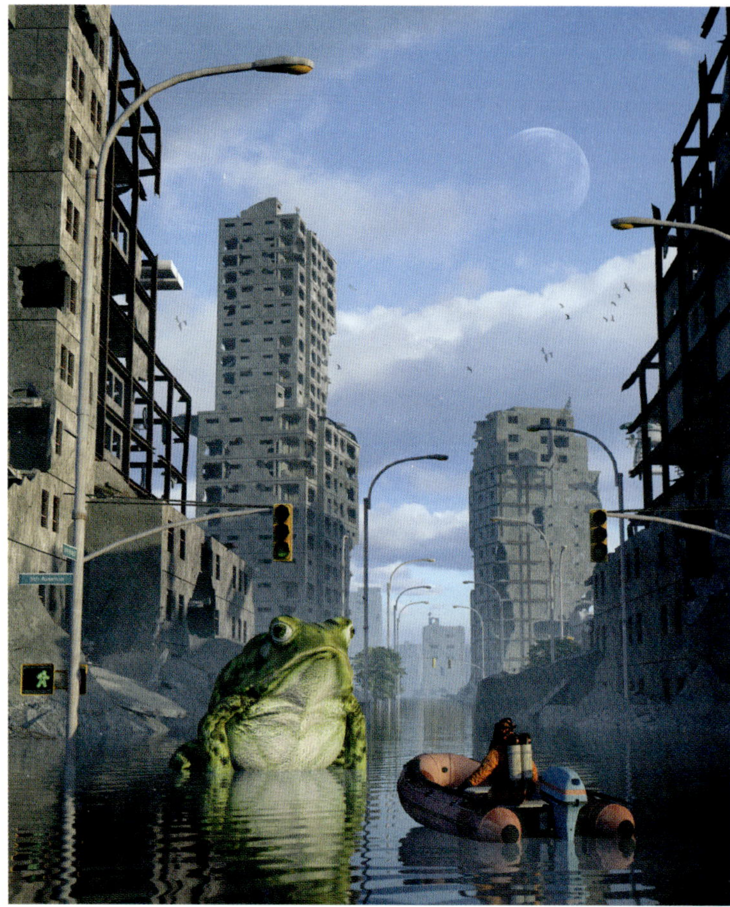

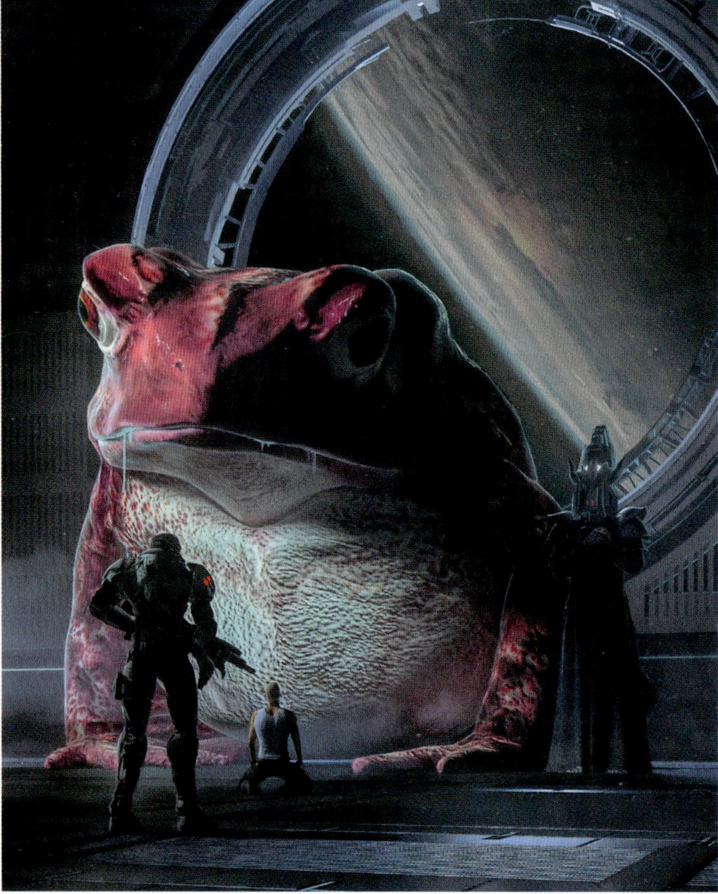

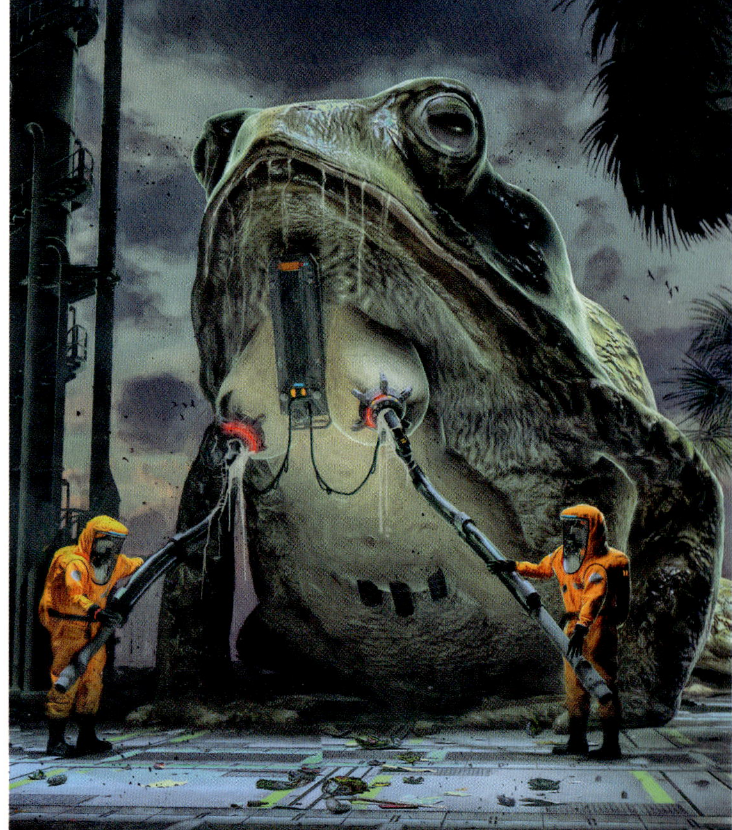

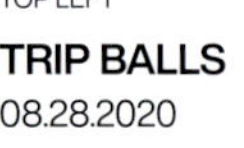

TOP LEFT
TRIP BALLS
08.28.2020

TOP RIGHT
RESET BUTTON
12.27.2020

BOTTOM LEFT
OVERLORD
06.28.2020

BOTTOM RIGHT
STANDARD TITTYFROG MILKING PROCEDURE
11.13.2020

OPPOSITE PAGE
HEALED PLANET
07.26.2020

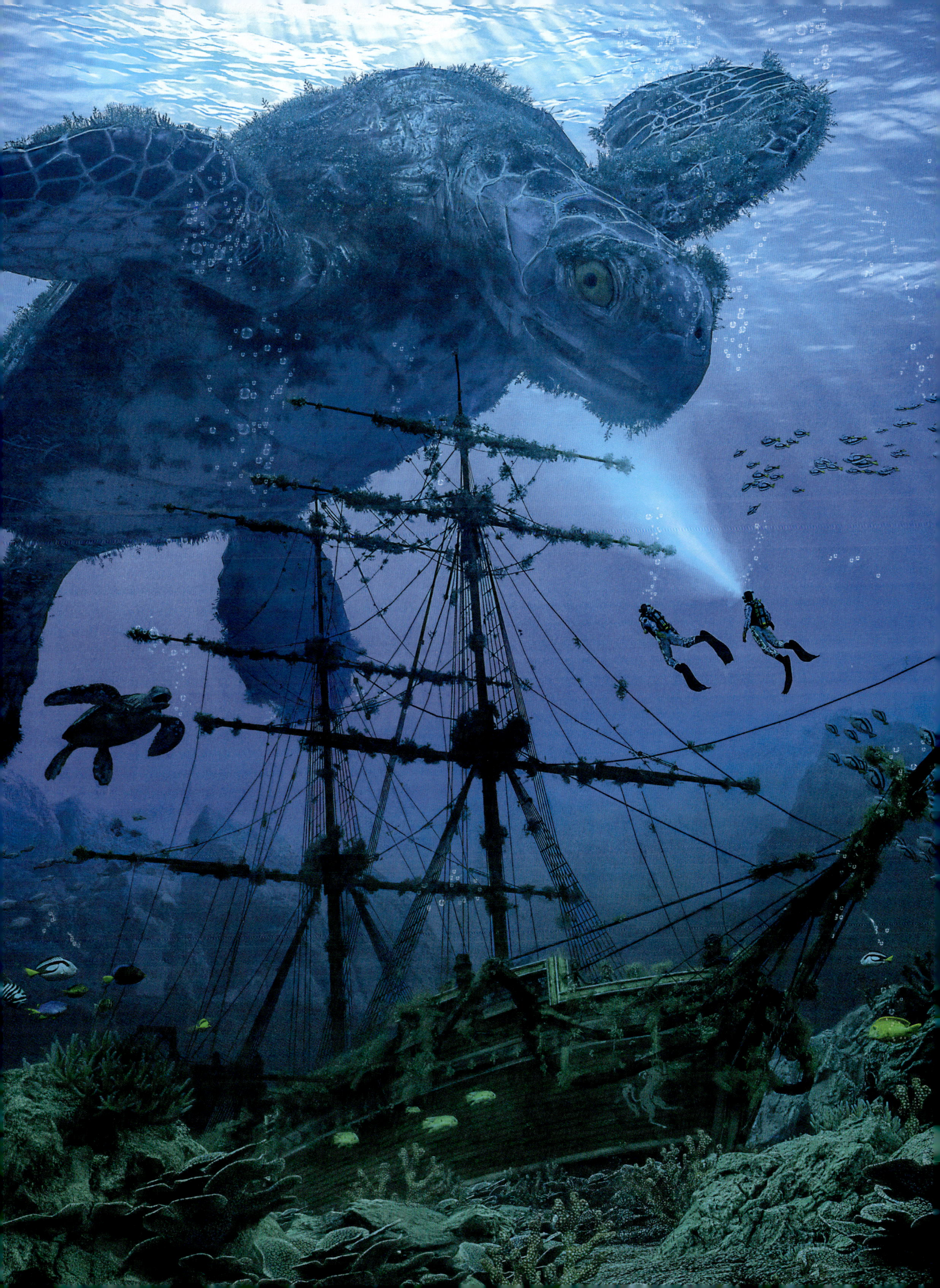

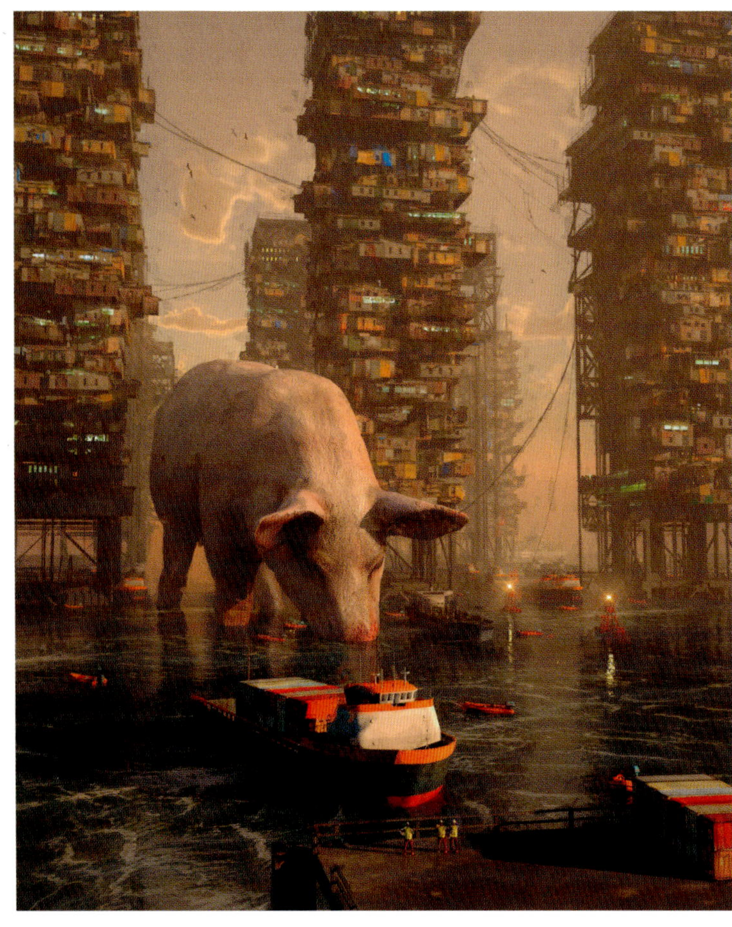

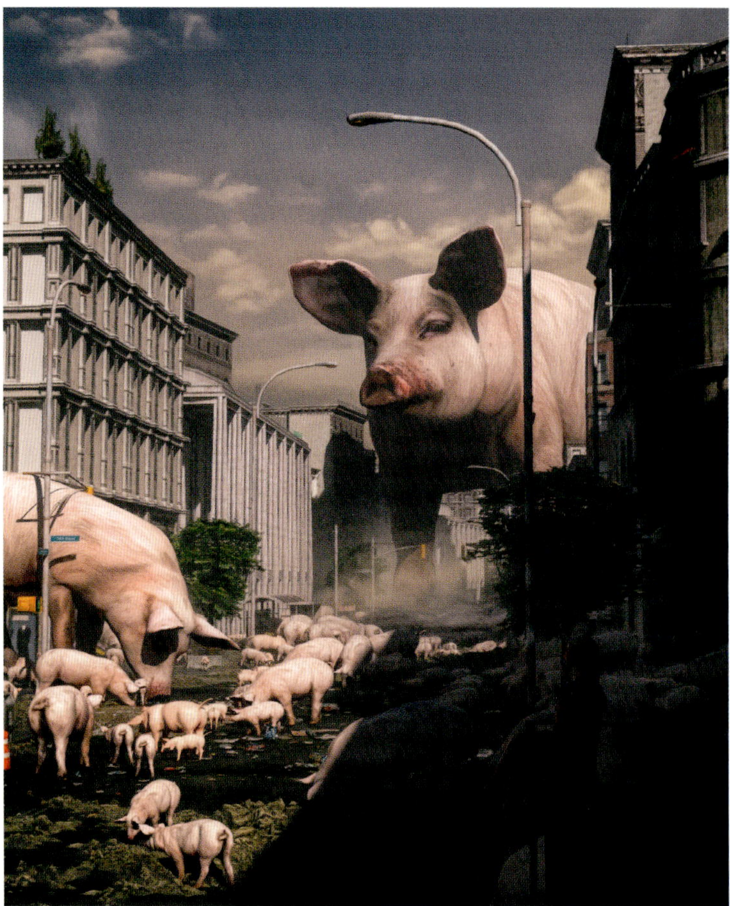

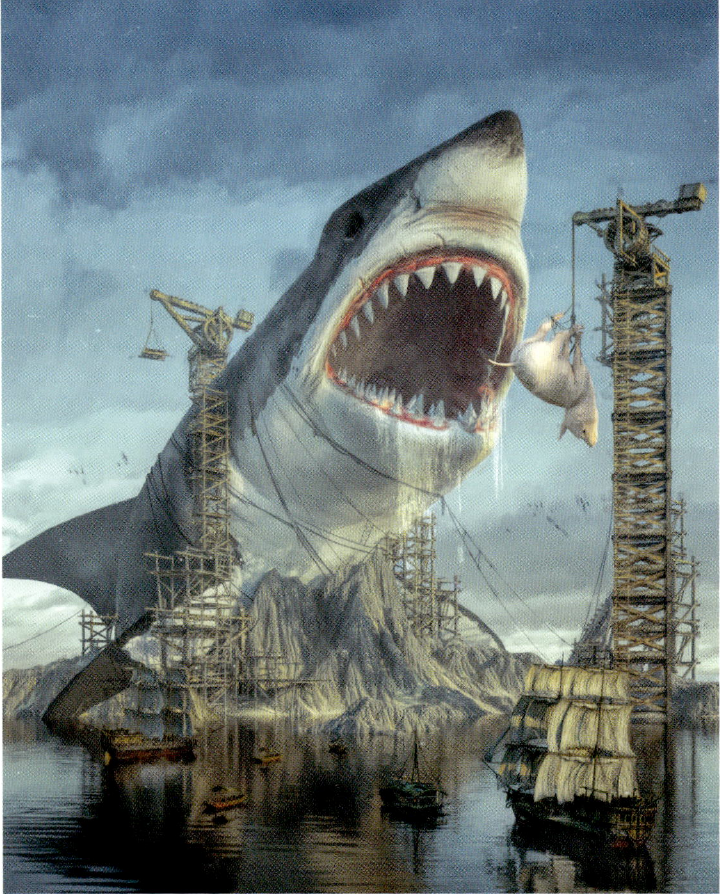

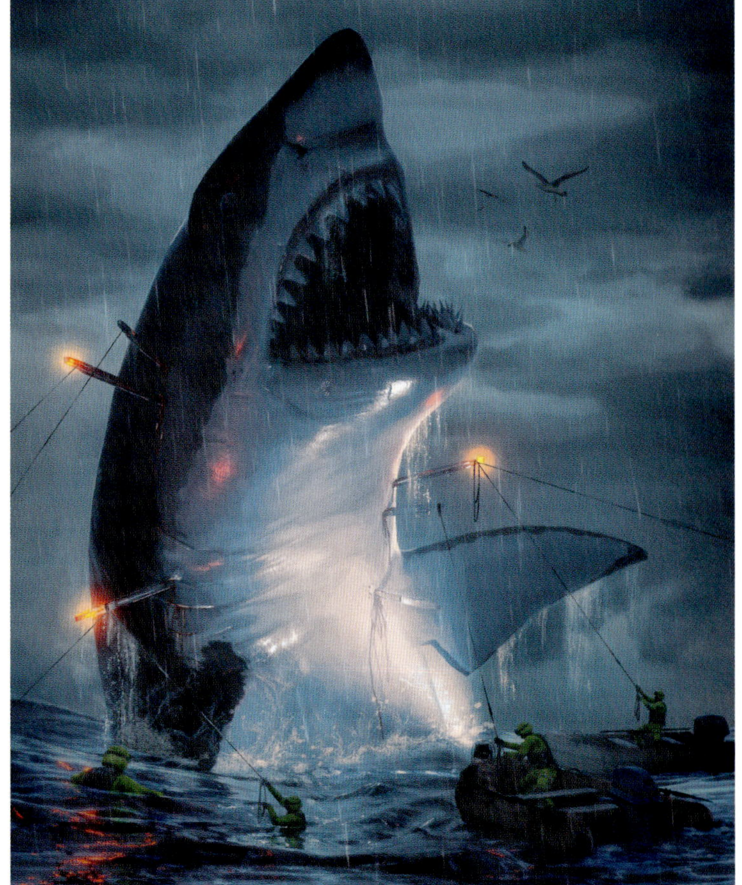

TOP LEFT

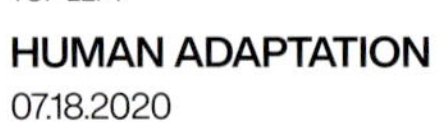

HUMAN ADAPTATION
07.18.2020

TOP RIGHT

BEAUTIFUL MESS
09.13.2020

BOTTOM LEFT

ESSENTIAL WORKERS
08.23.2020

BOTTOM RIGHT

KEEP FIGHTING
03.05.2020

OPPOSITE PAGE

HUMANS
01.20.2020

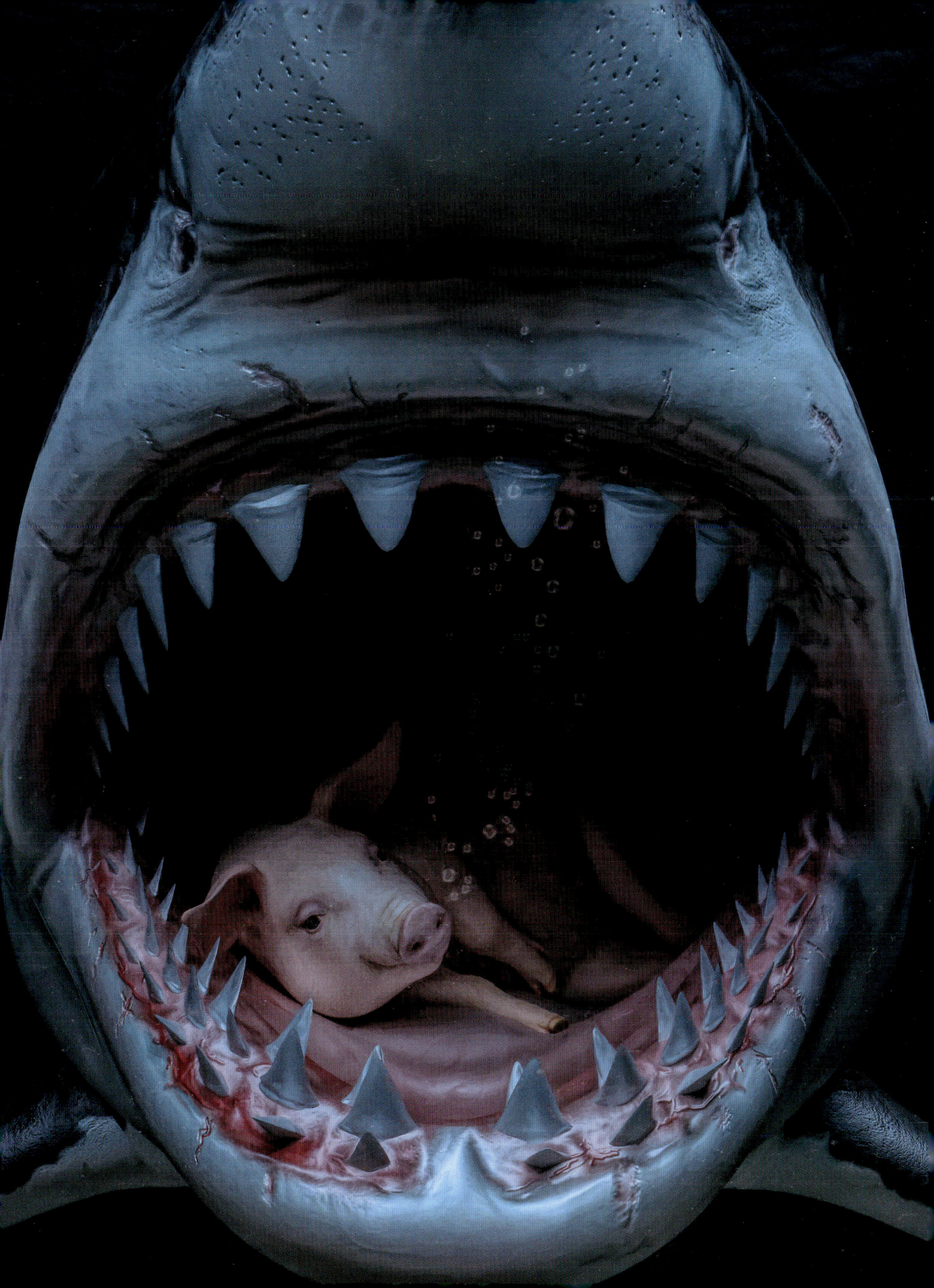

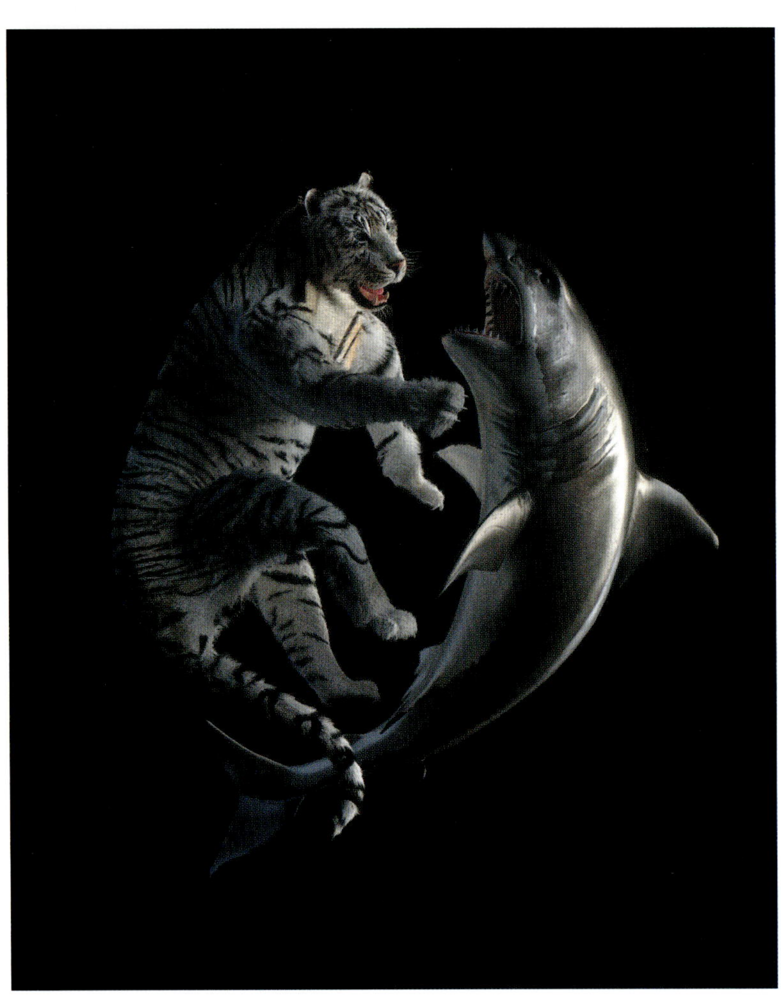

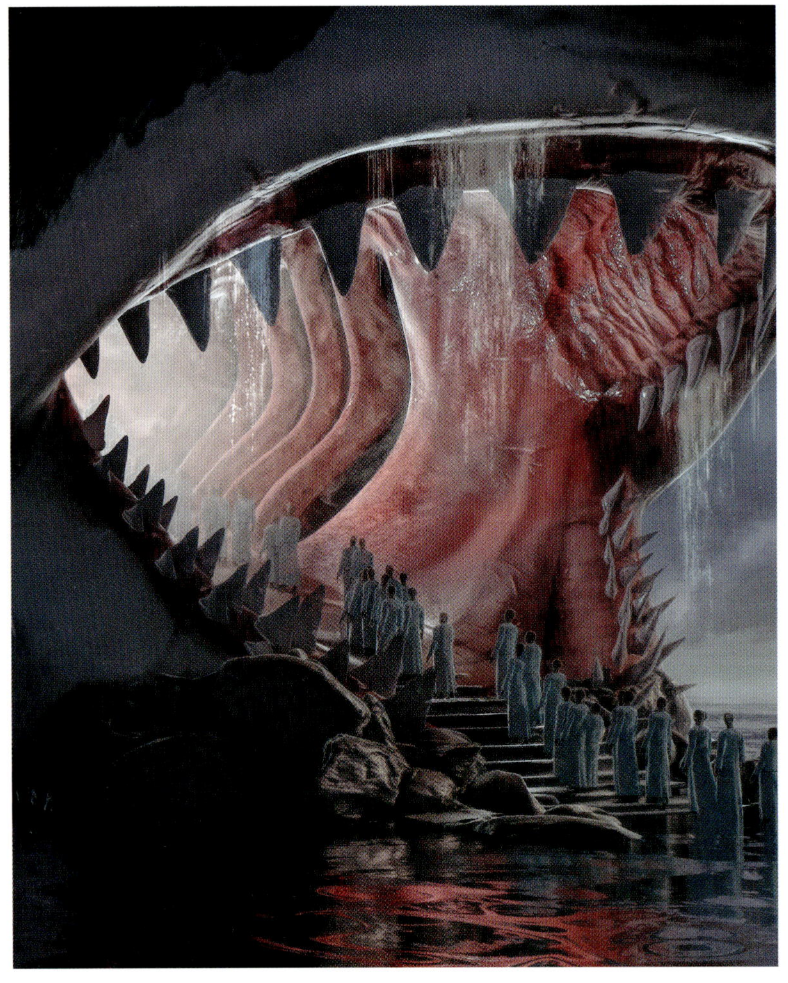

TOP

LATE STAGE CAPITALISM

04.15.2020

BOTTOM

BELLY OF THE BEAST

02.01.2020

OPPOSITE PAGE, TOP

GONE FISHING

10.27.2020

OPPOSITE PAGE, BOTTOM

ANOTHER WORLD

09.14.2020

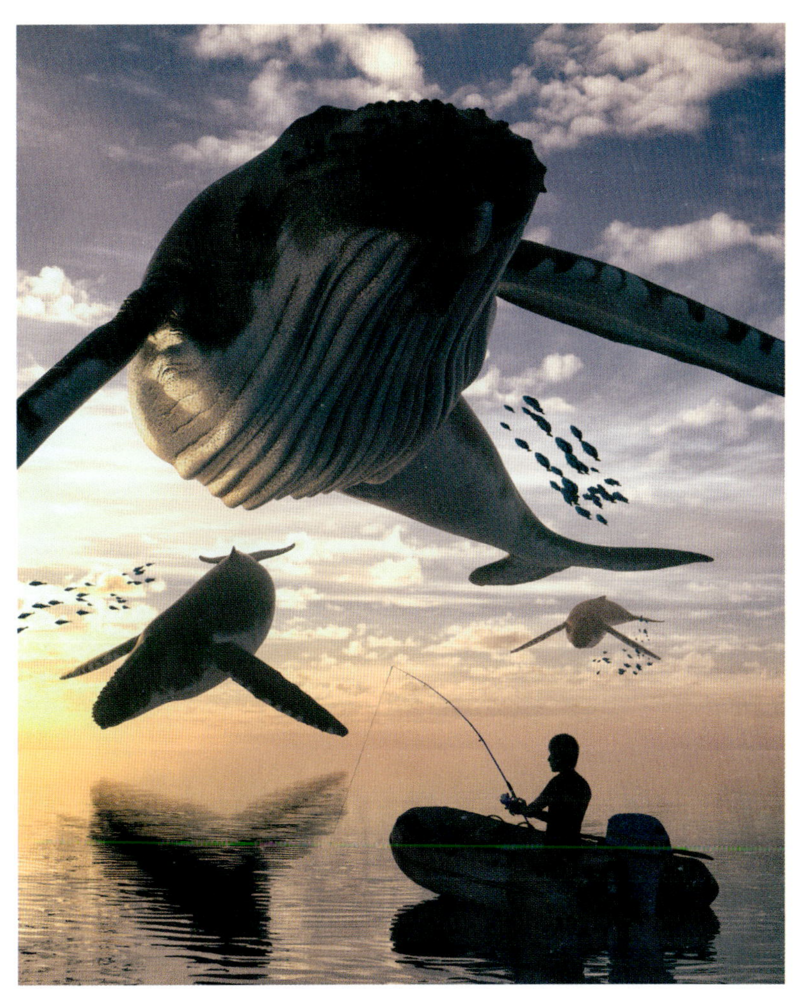

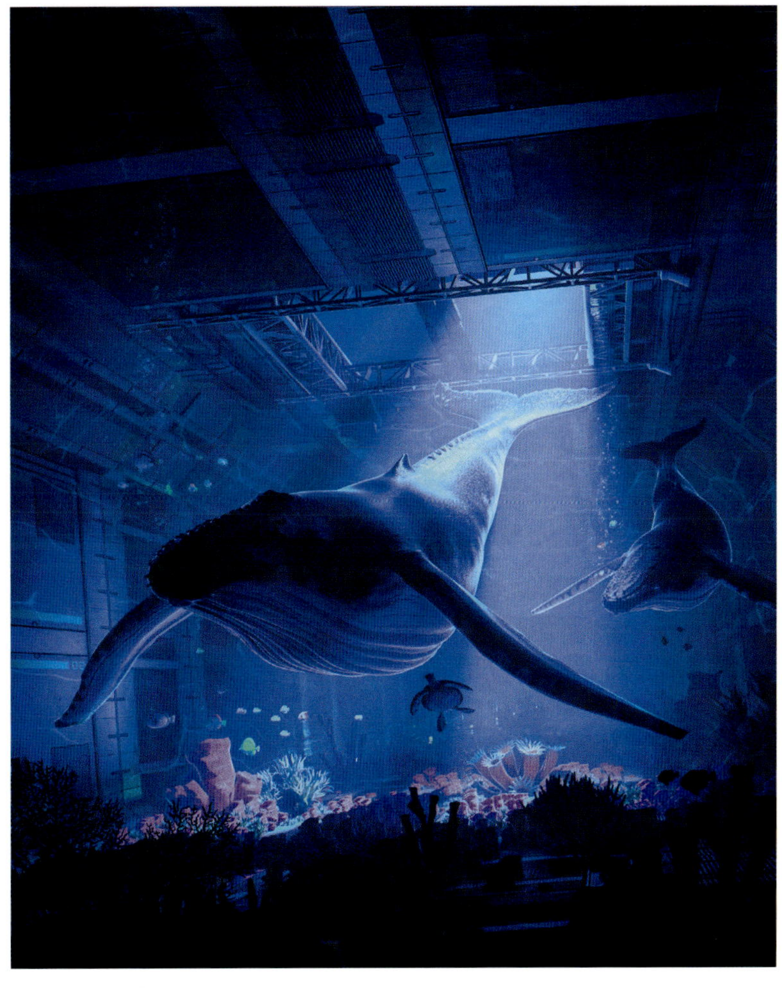

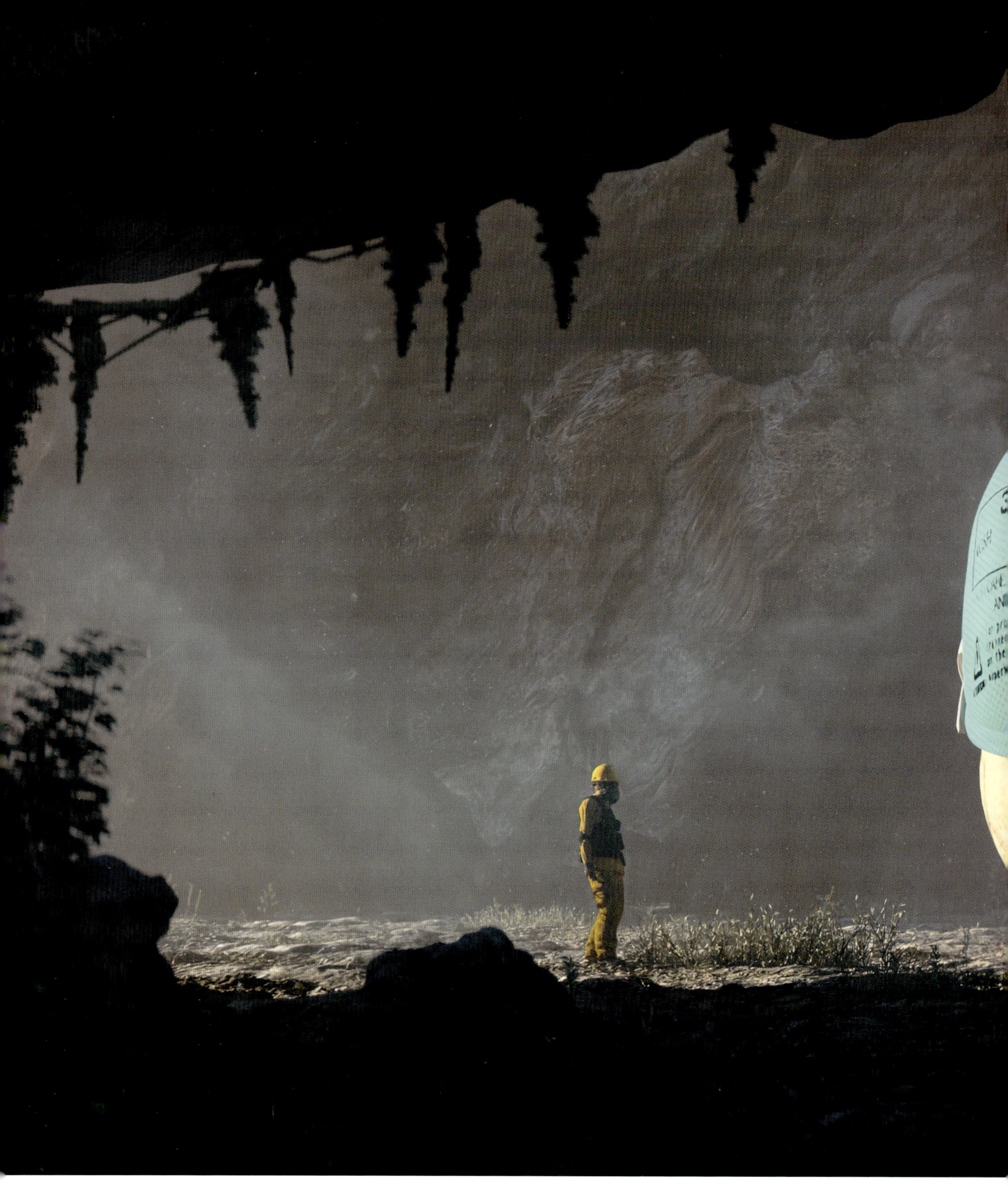

ABOVE

ONE DAY
04.08.2020

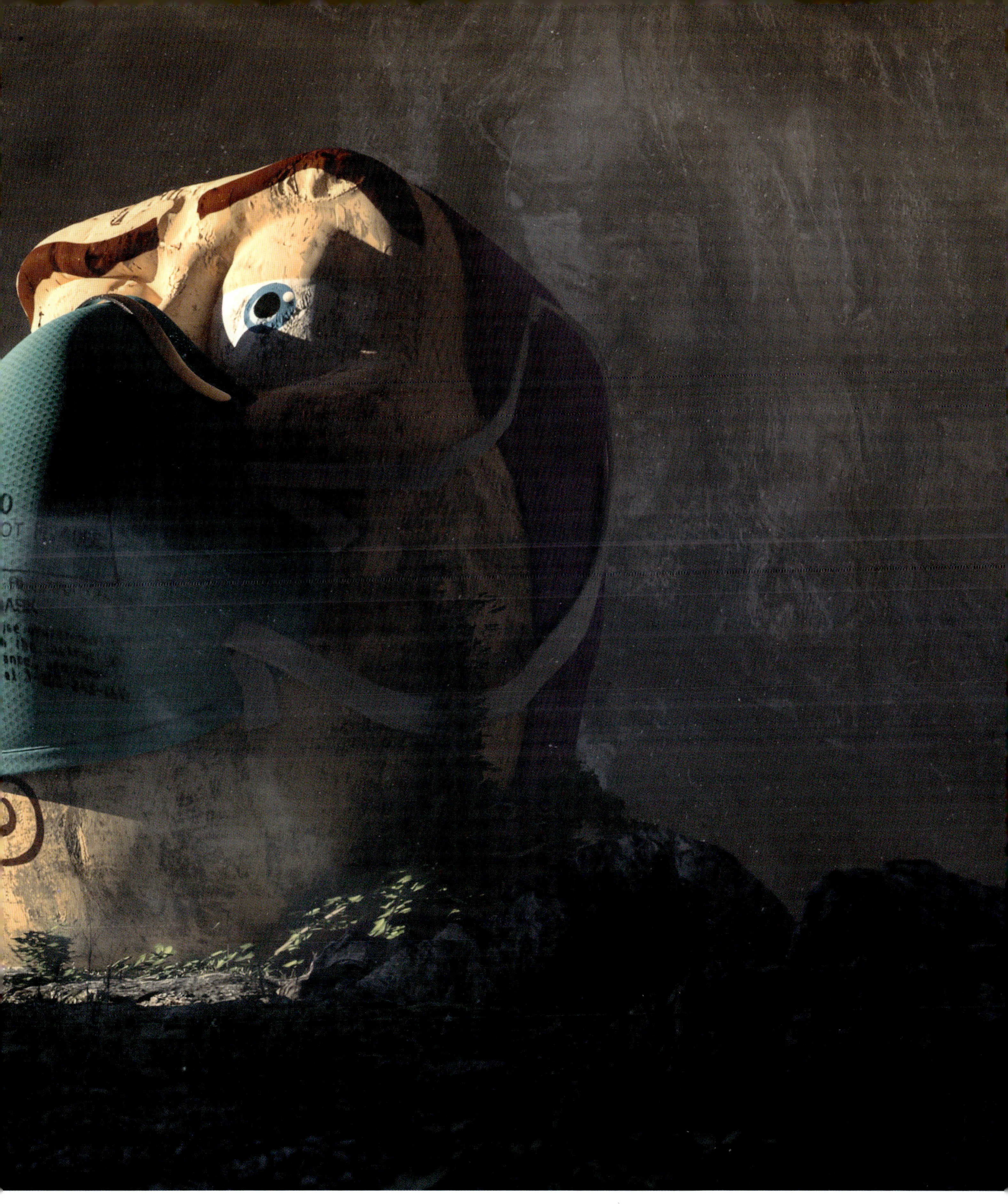

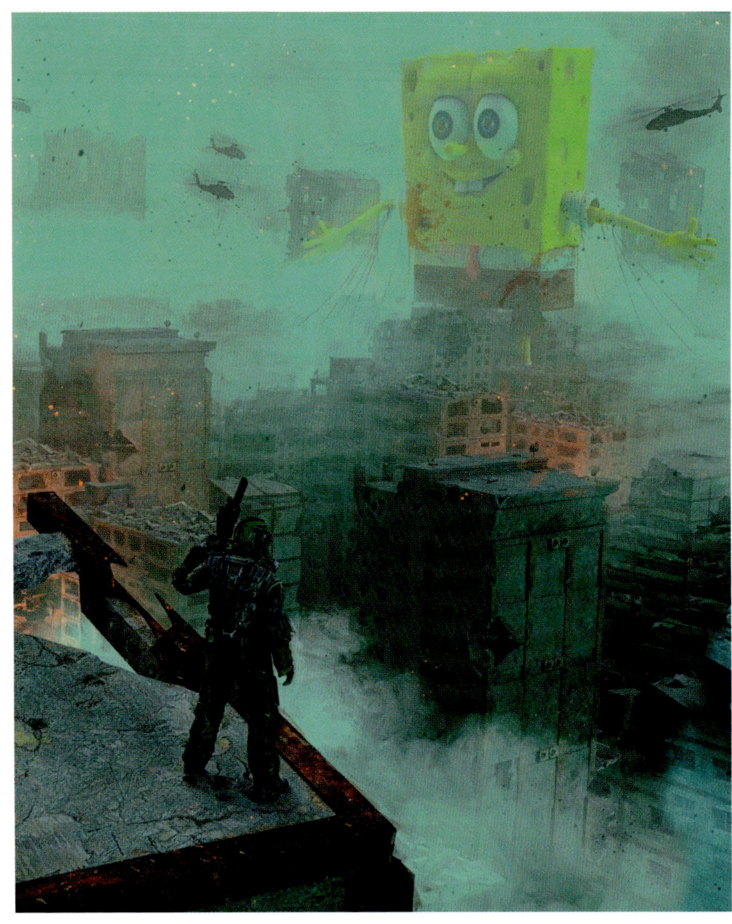
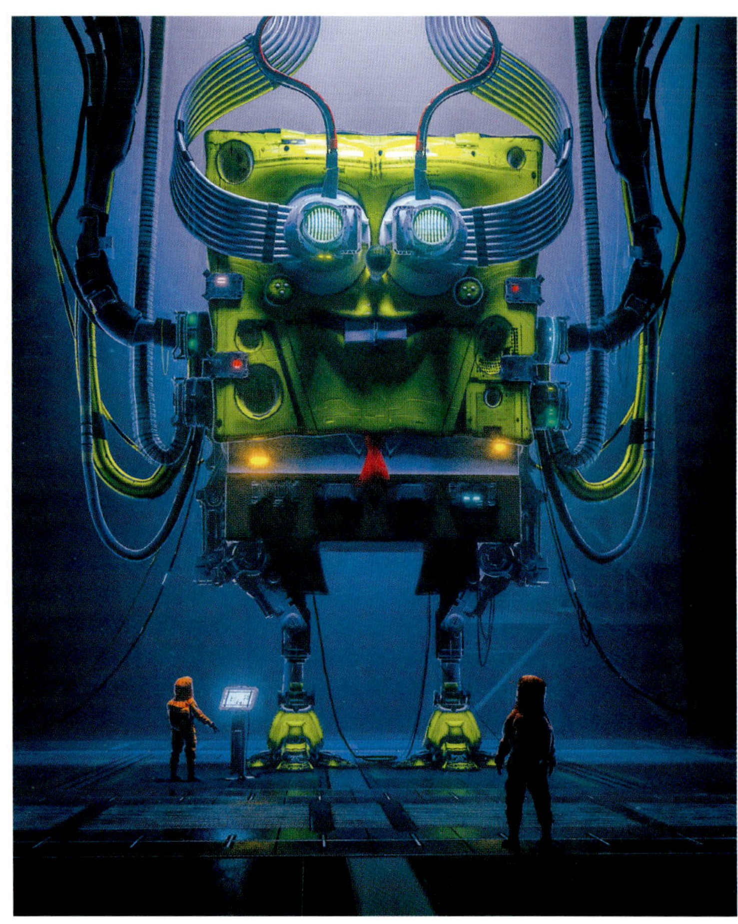
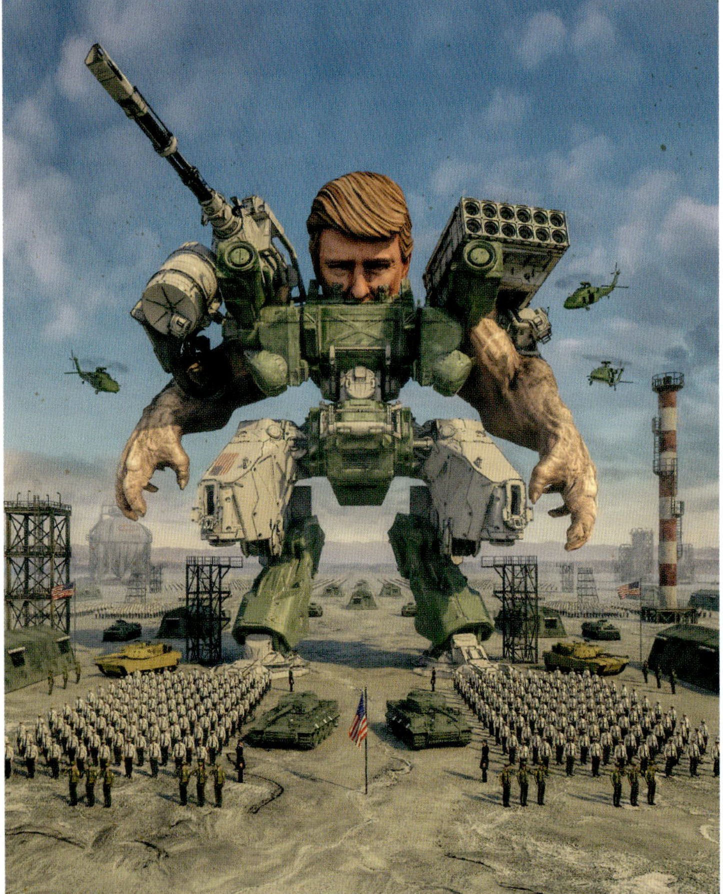
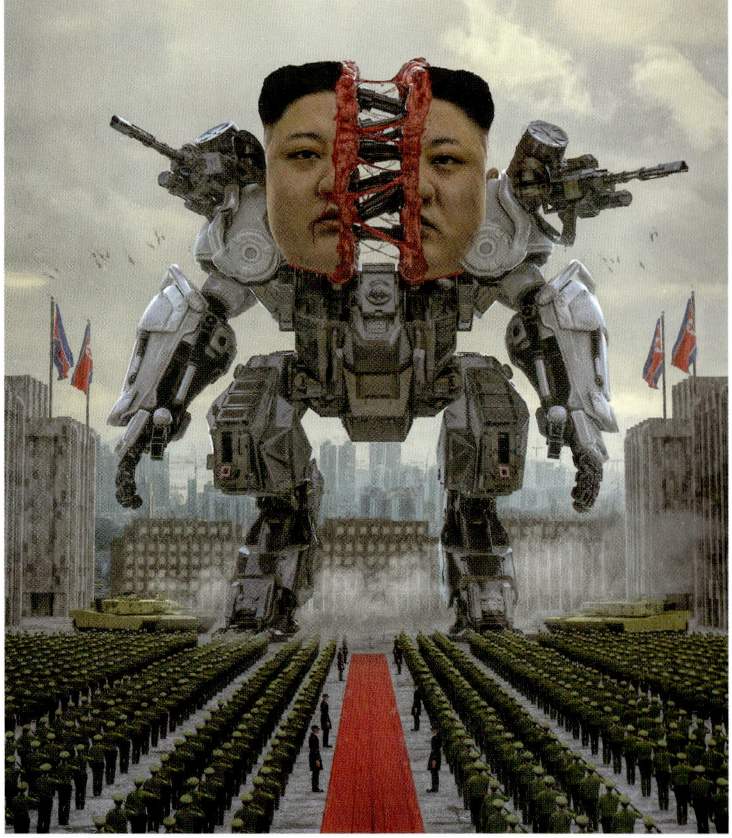

TOP LEFT
SPONGEBOB KILLPANTS
02.21.2020

TOP RIGHT
SPONGEROBERT MILITARY-INDUSTRIALPANTS
07.08.2020

BOTTOM LEFT
WAR MACHINE WET DREAM
01.03.2020

BOTTOM RIGHT
JONG v2.0
04.27.2020

OPPOSITE PAGE
SPONGEBOB HILLARYPANTS
02.23.2020

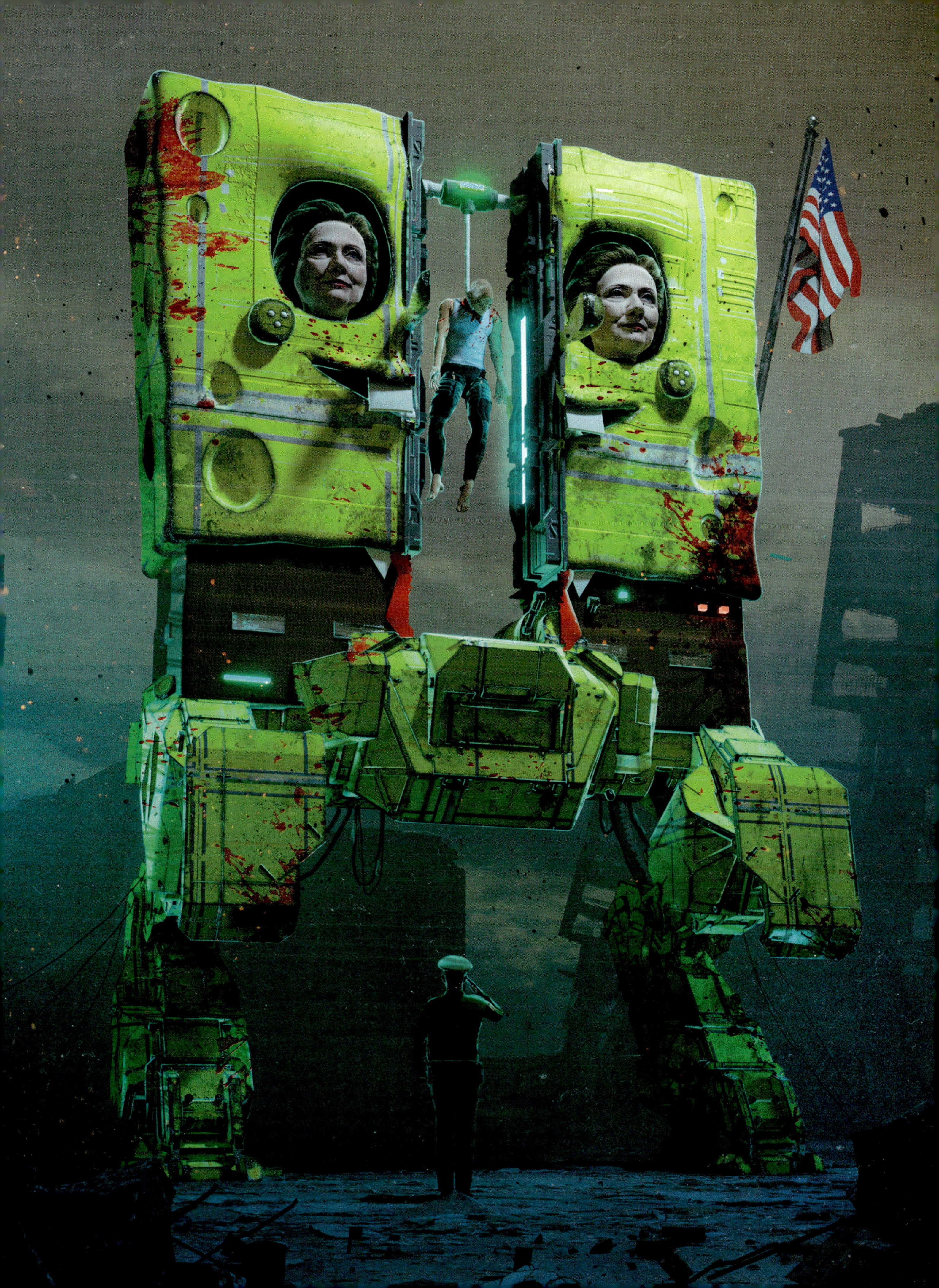

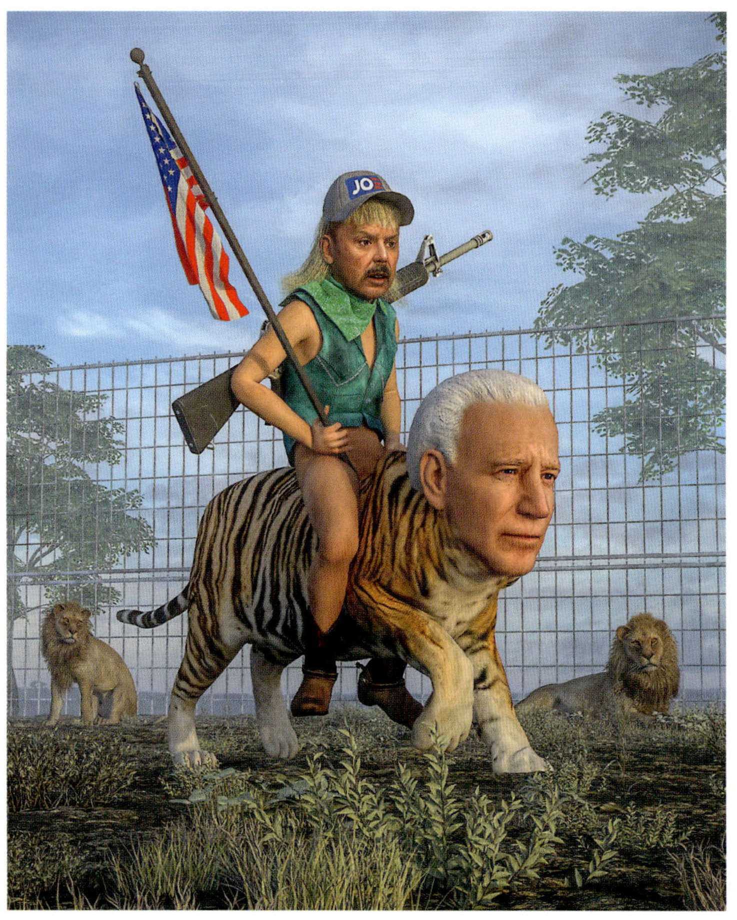

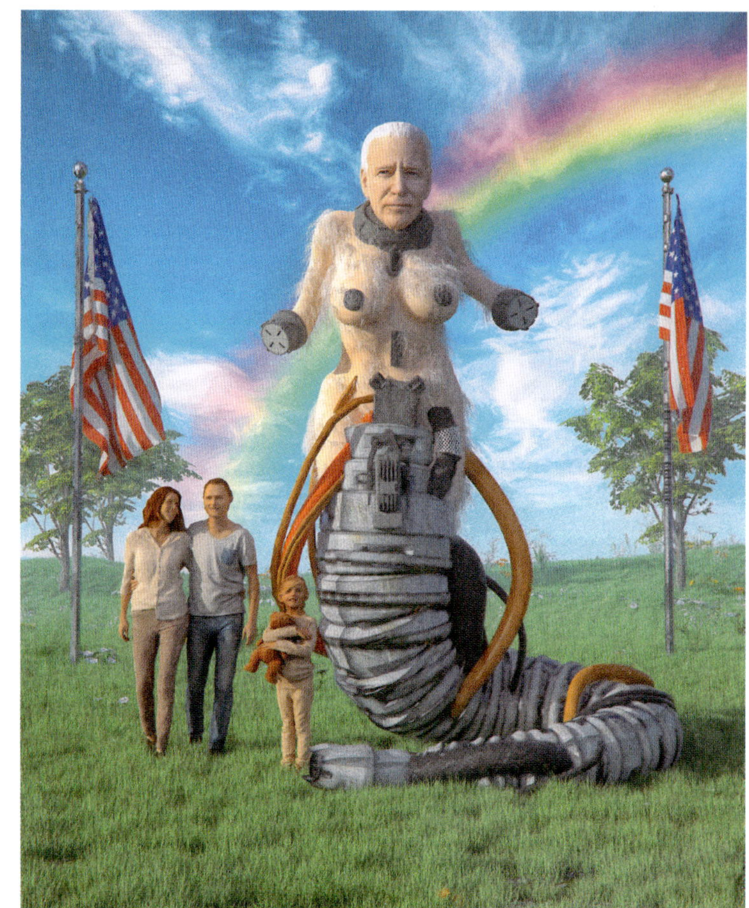

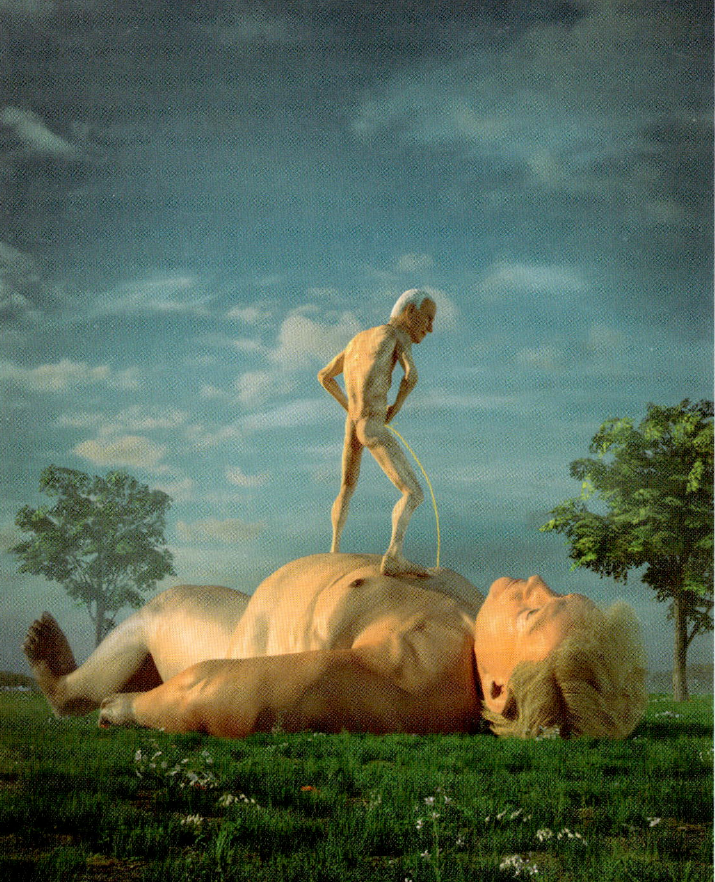

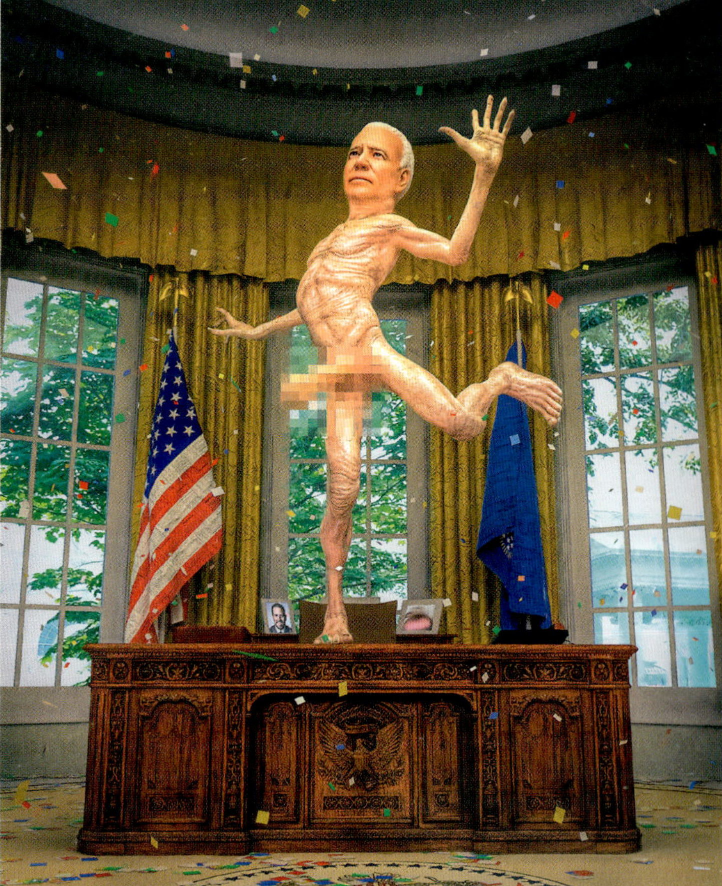

TOP LEFT
JOE-JOE 2020
04.07.2020

TOP RIGHT
BIDEN 2060
03.04.2020

BOTTOM LEFT
holy fuck, i hope this picture stands the test of time
11.03.2020

BOTTOM RIGHT
UNTITLED
11.07.2020

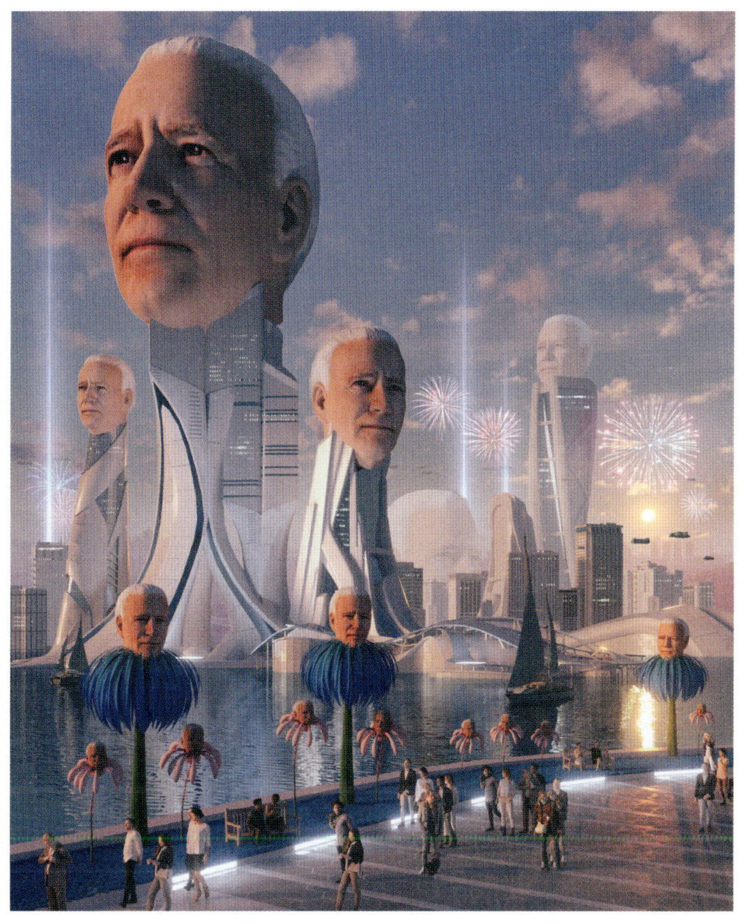

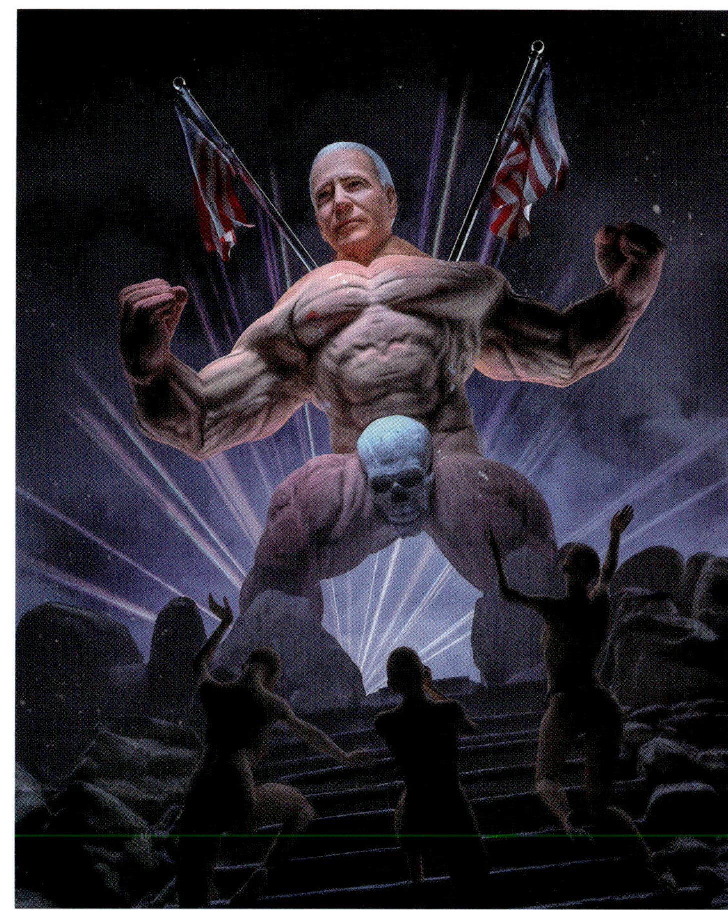

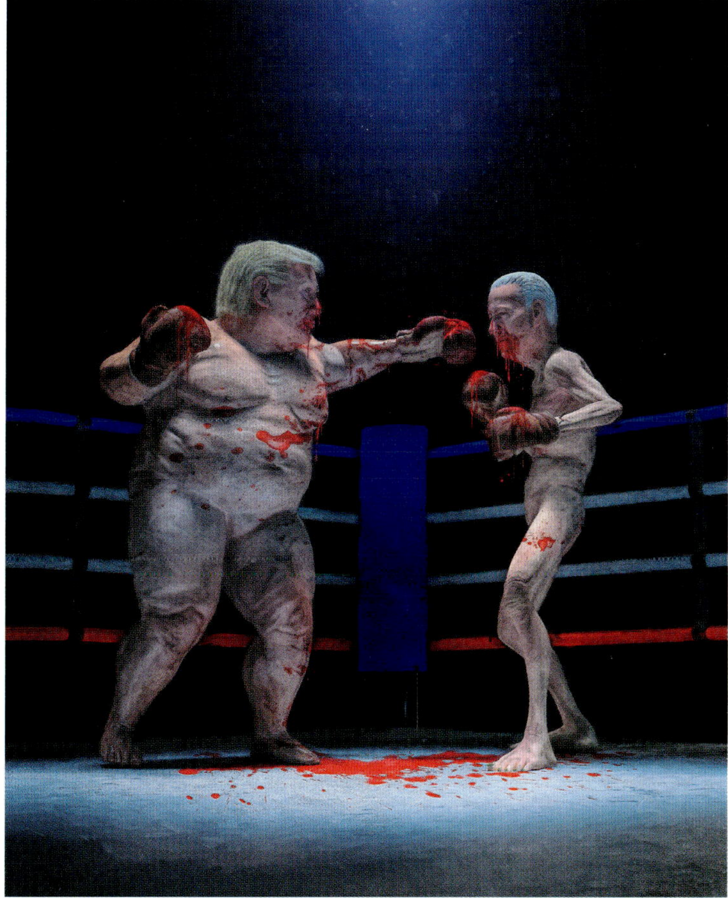

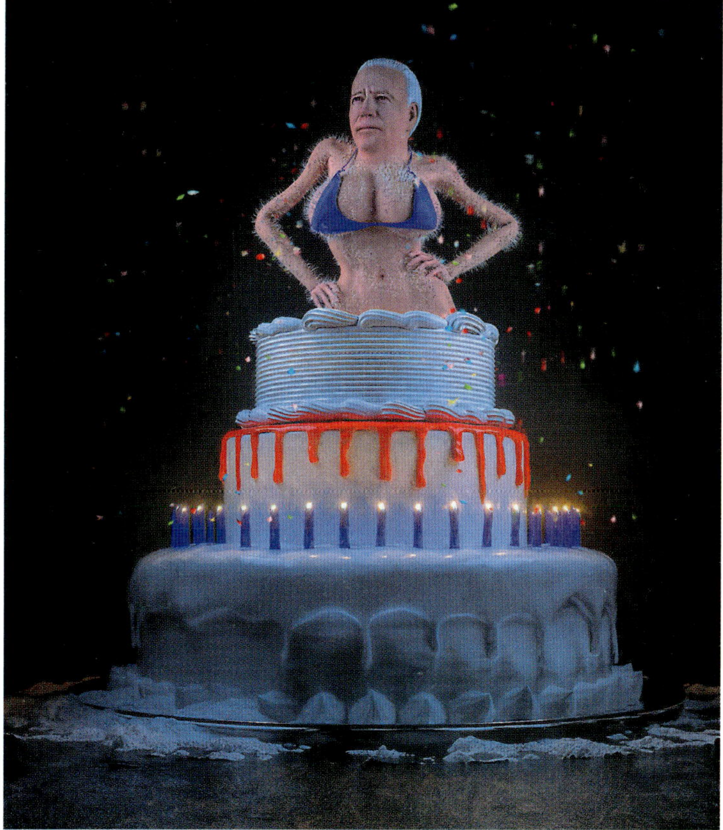

TOP LEFT
JOETOPIA
08.16.2020

TOP RIGHT
JOE BIDEN'S TWISTED DARK FANTASY
02.29.2020

BOTTOM LEFT
SHITSHOW
09.29.2020

BOTTOM RIGHT
HAPPY BIRTHDAY MR. SMITTERS
06.20.2020

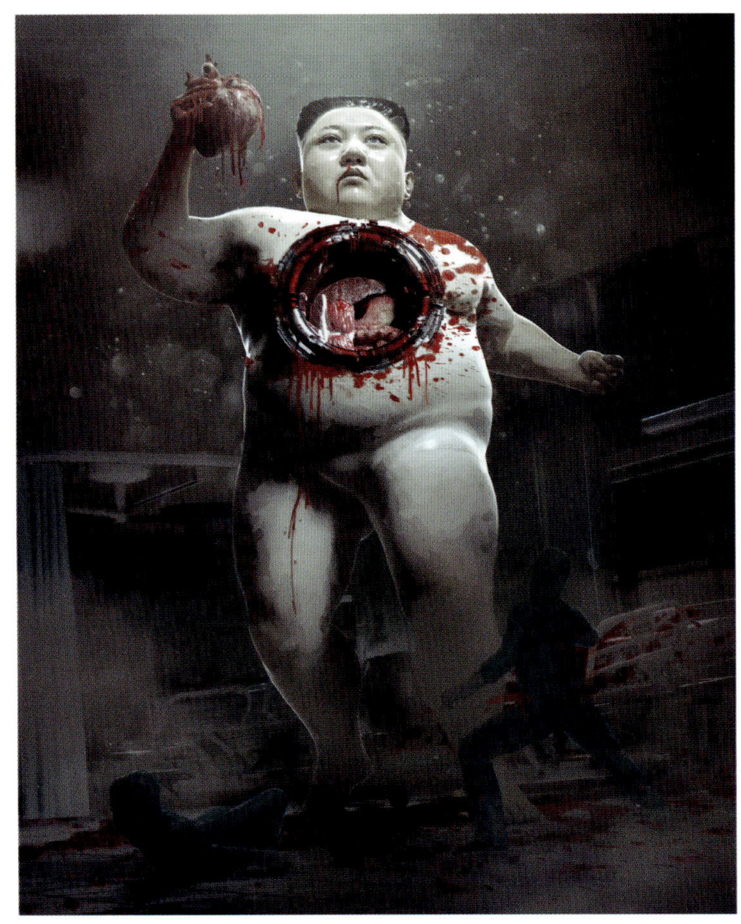

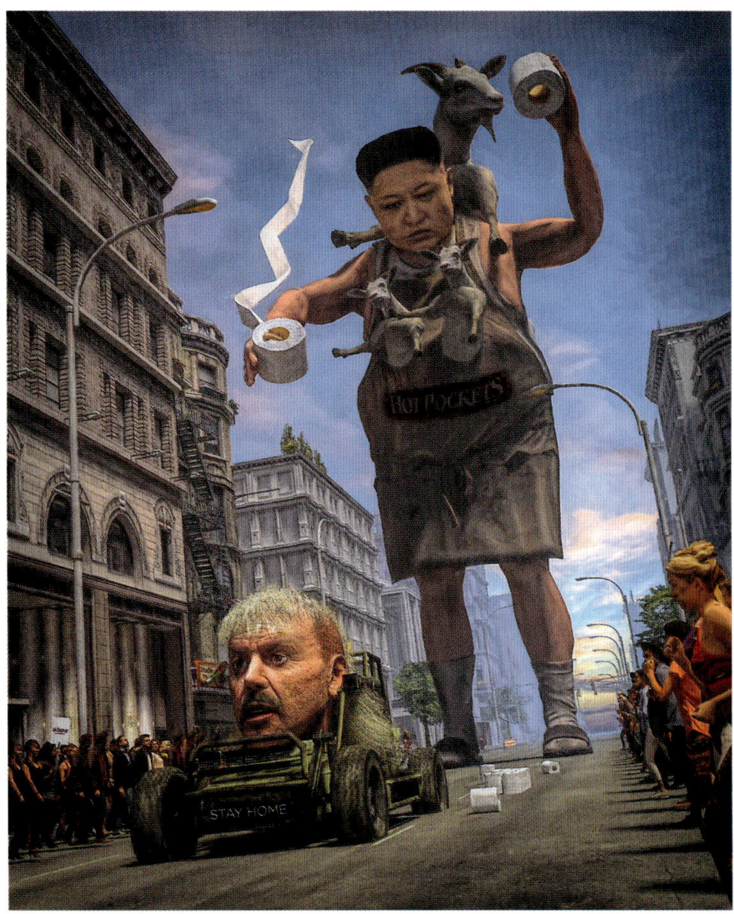

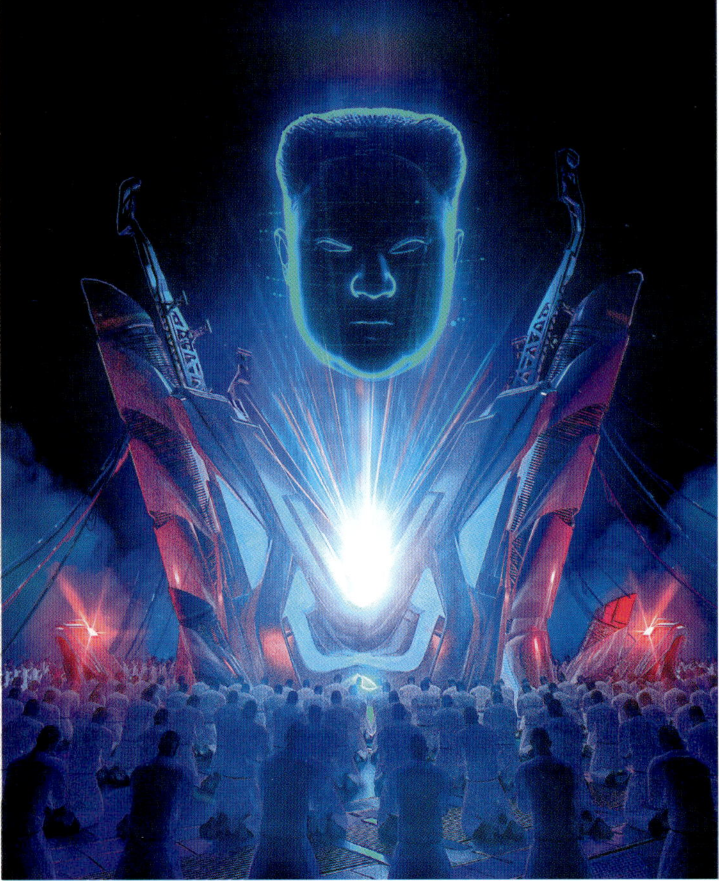

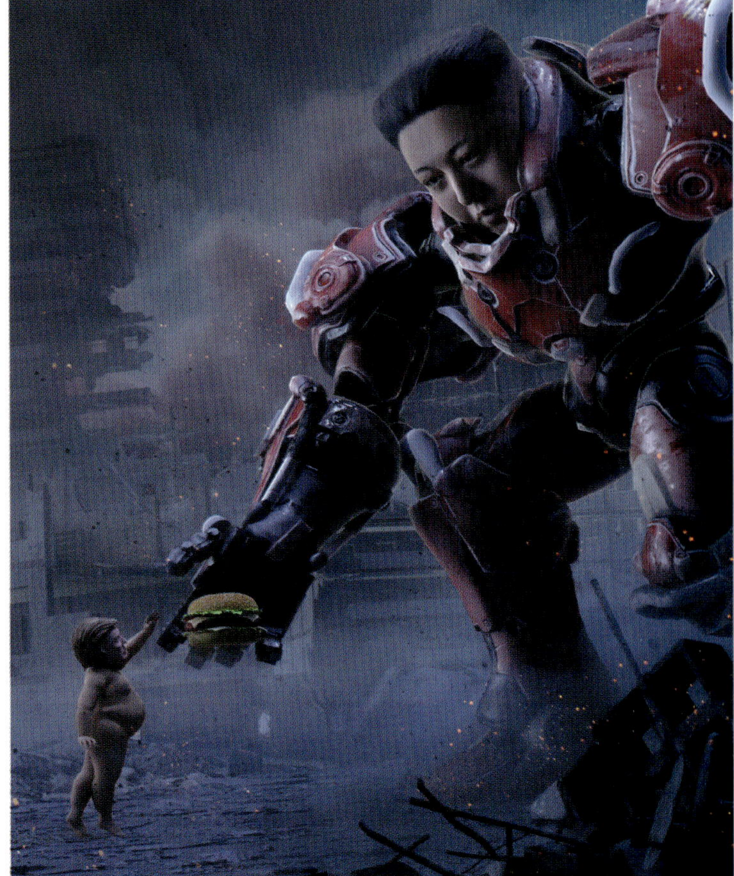

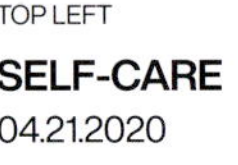

TOP LEFT

SELF-CARE
04.21.2020

TOP RIGHT

TIGER KIM JONG ZOOM
04.23.2020

BOTTOM LEFT

KIM4EVER
04.25.2020

BOTTOM RIGHT

MECHA KIM JONG-UN GIVING BABY DONALD A CHEESEBURGER
02.12.2020

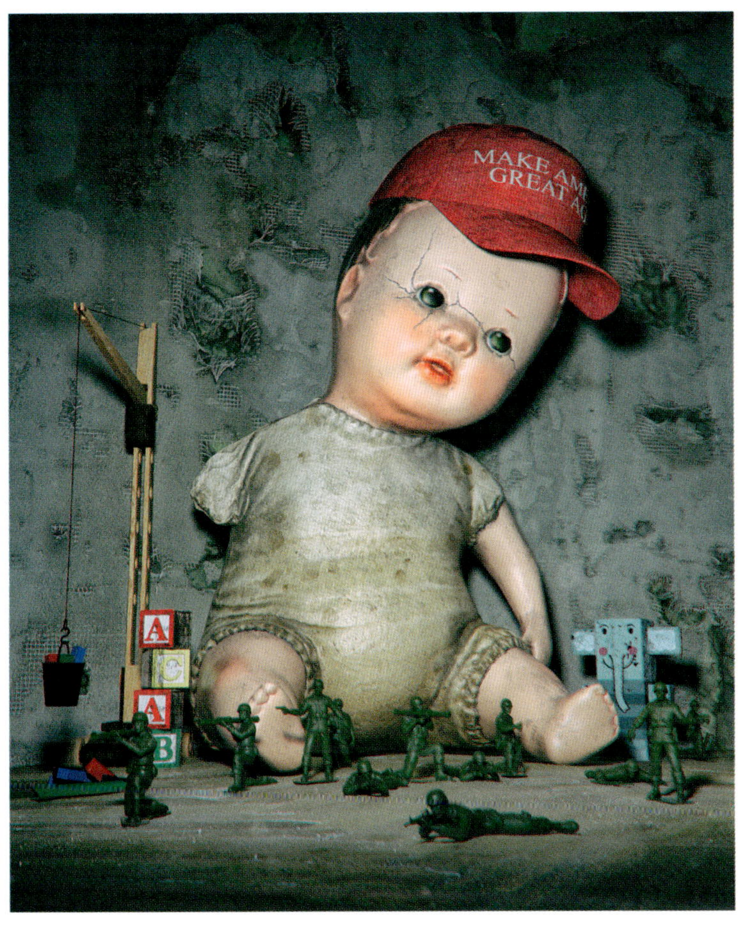

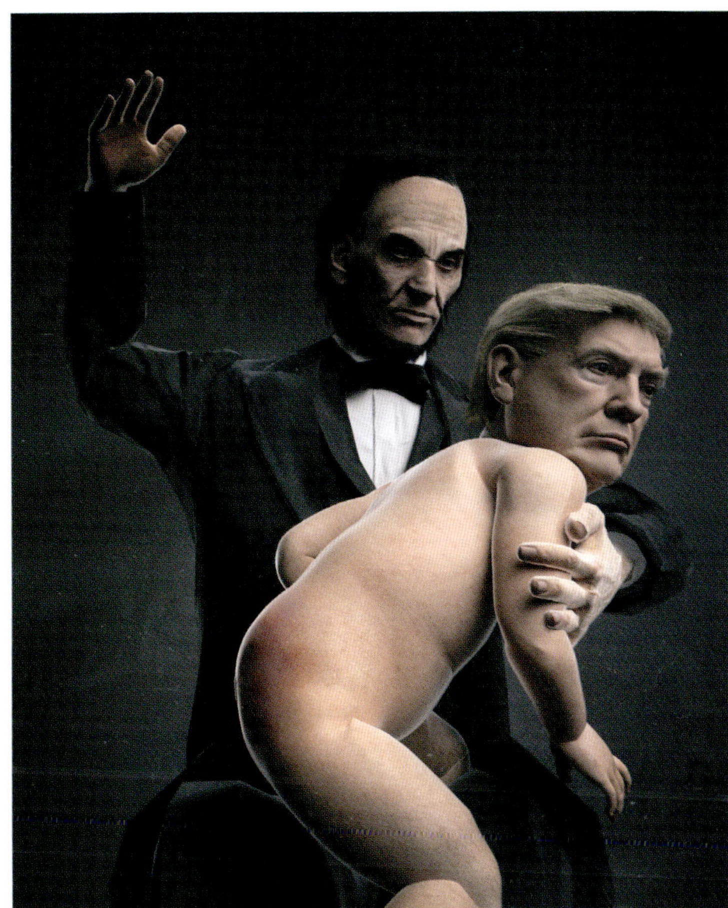

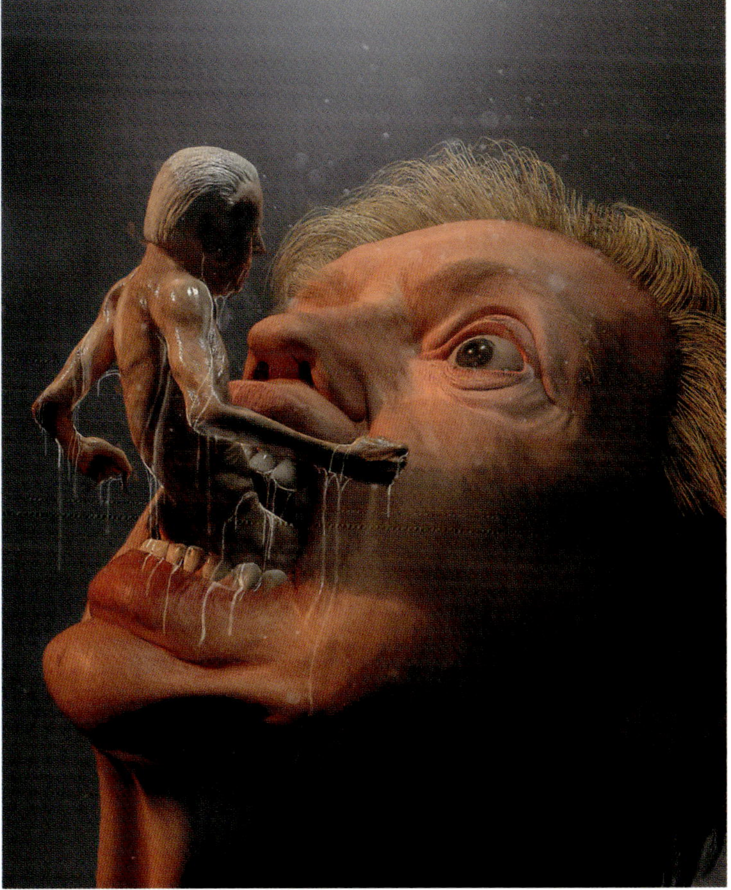

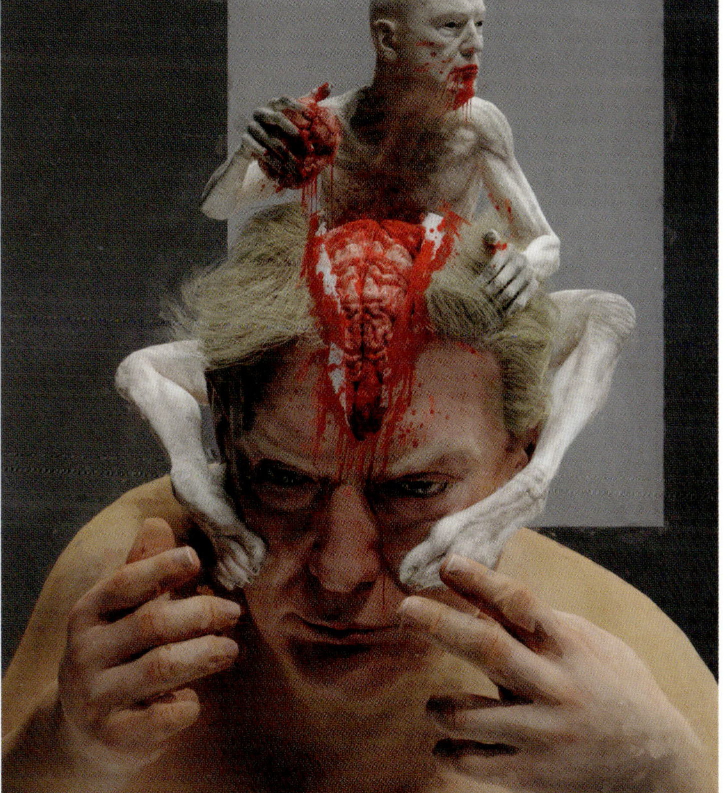

TOP LEFT
CREEPY BABY
08.10.2020

TOP RIGHT
SHITTY KID
07.03.2020

BOTTOM LEFT
OCTOBER SURPRISE
10.26.2020

BOTTOM RIGHT
SELF-DESTRUCT
07.07.2020

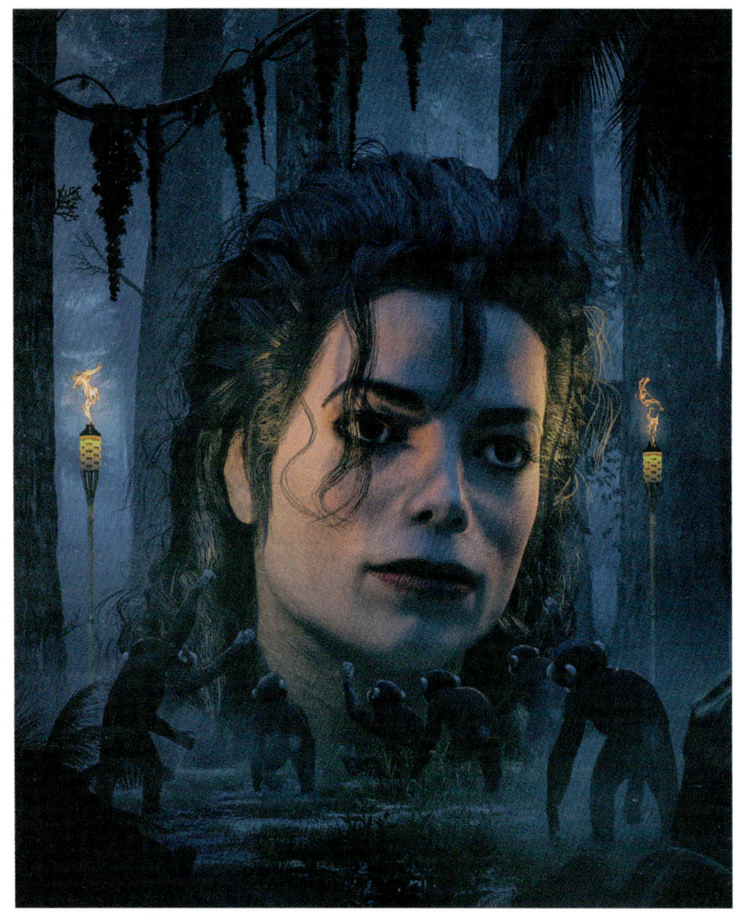

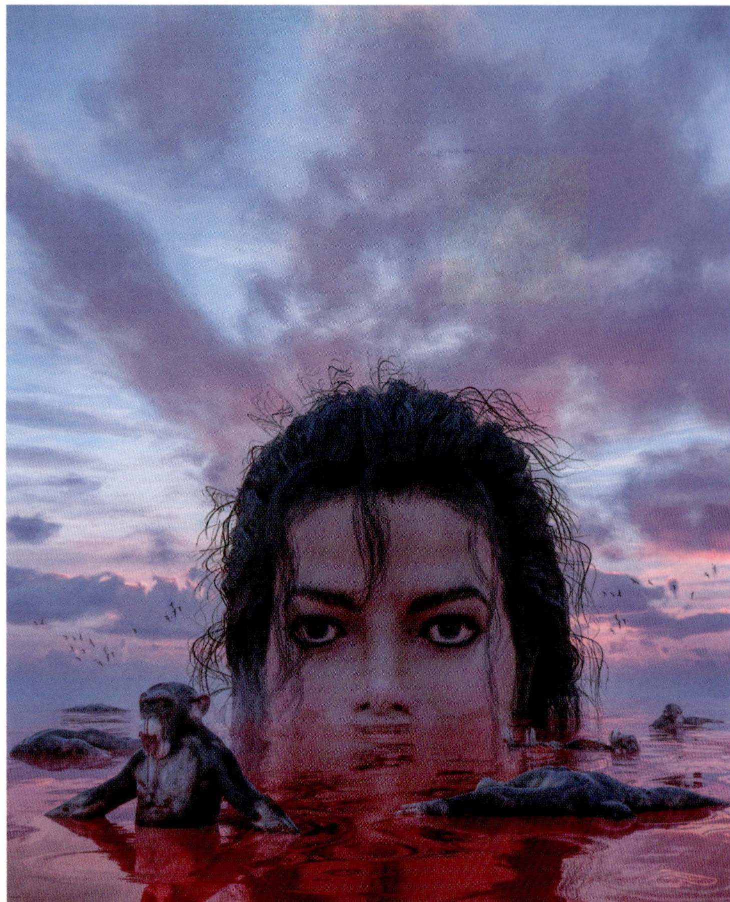

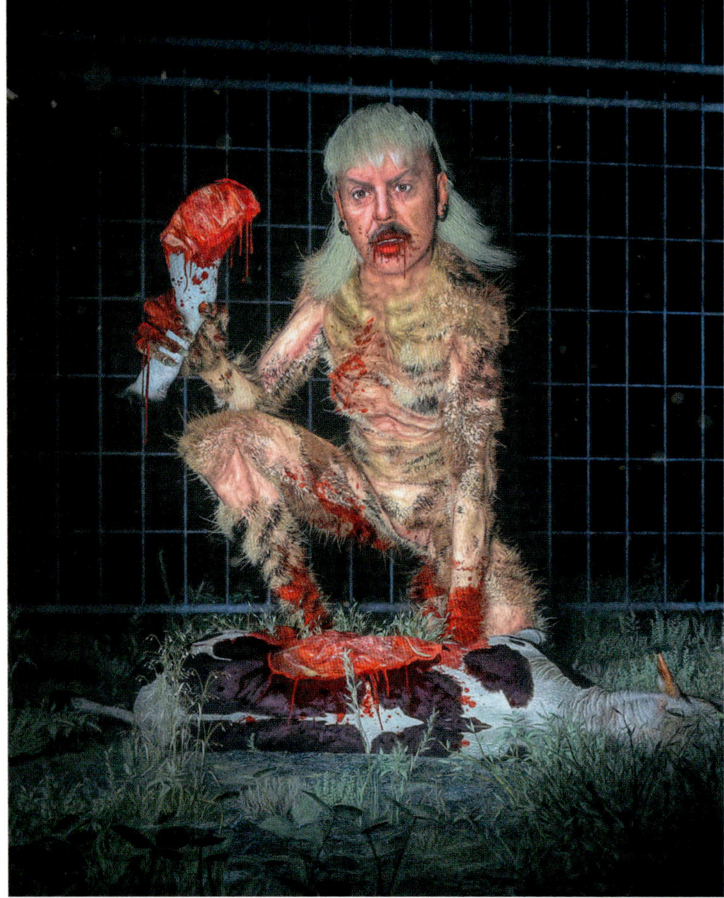

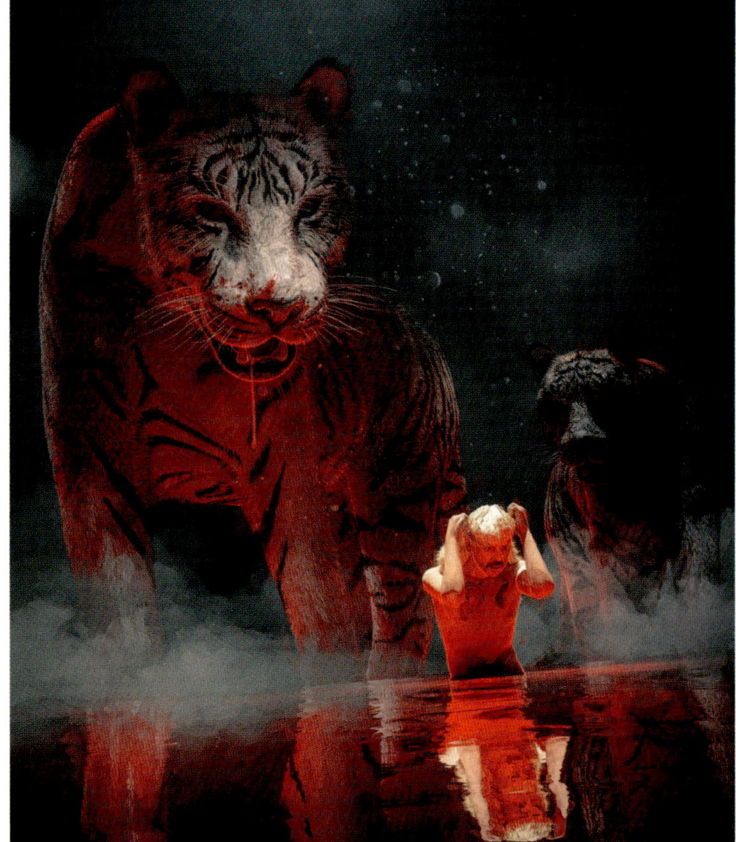

TOP LEFT
MOTHER'S DAY
05.10.2020

TOP RIGHT
BAD
11.12.2020

BOTTOM LEFT
TIGER KING
04.01.2020

BOTTOM RIGHT
DETHRONED
04.26.2020

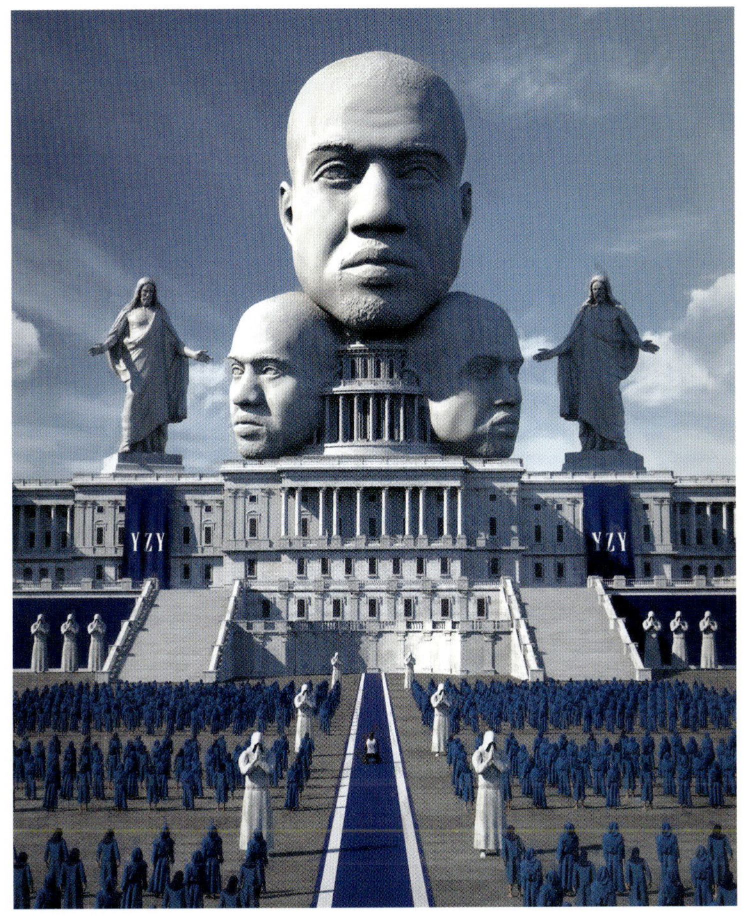

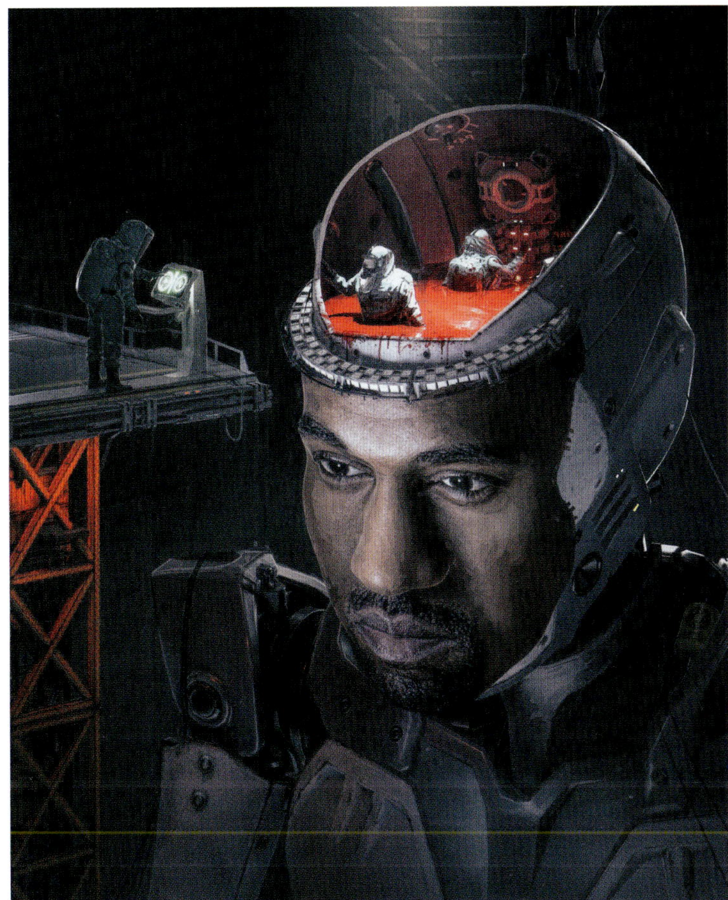

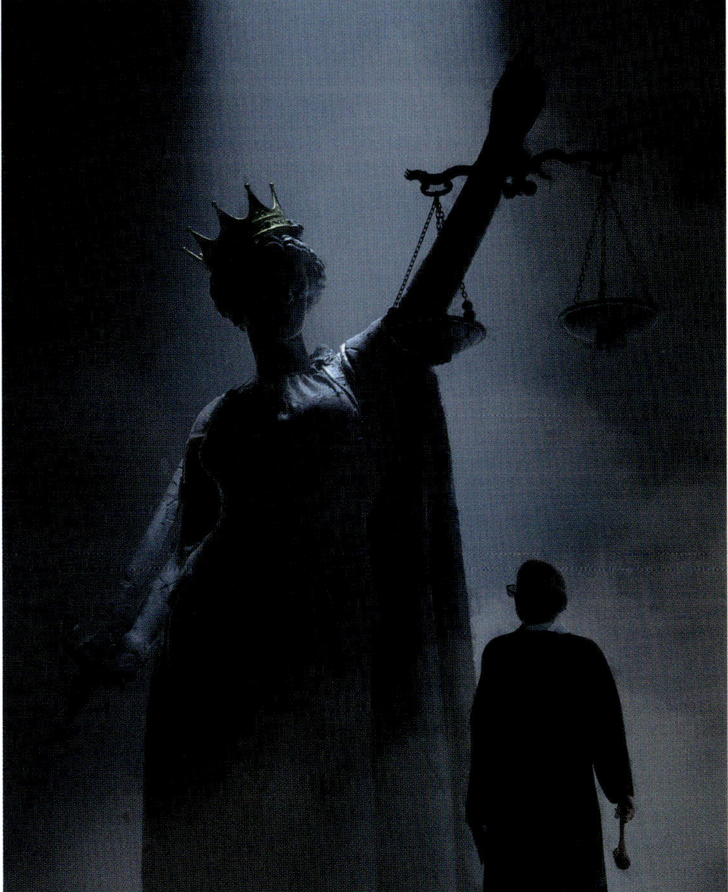

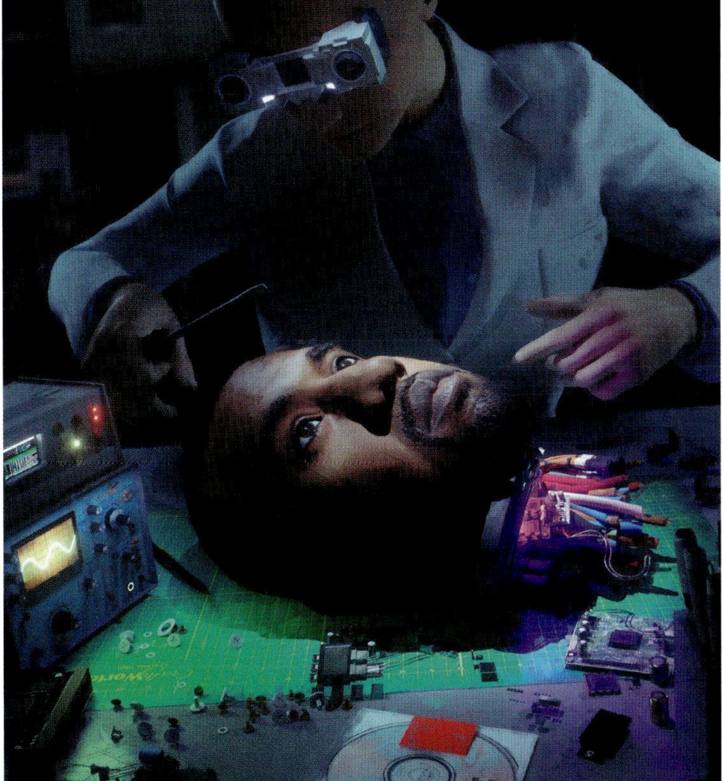

TOP LEFT

YEZZY2020
07.05.2020

TOP RIGHT

SIMULATION CODE "BIRTHDAY PARTY"
07.11.2020

BOTTOM LEFT

LADY JUSTICE
09.18.2020

BOTTOM RIGHT

FIX KANYE
02.18.2020

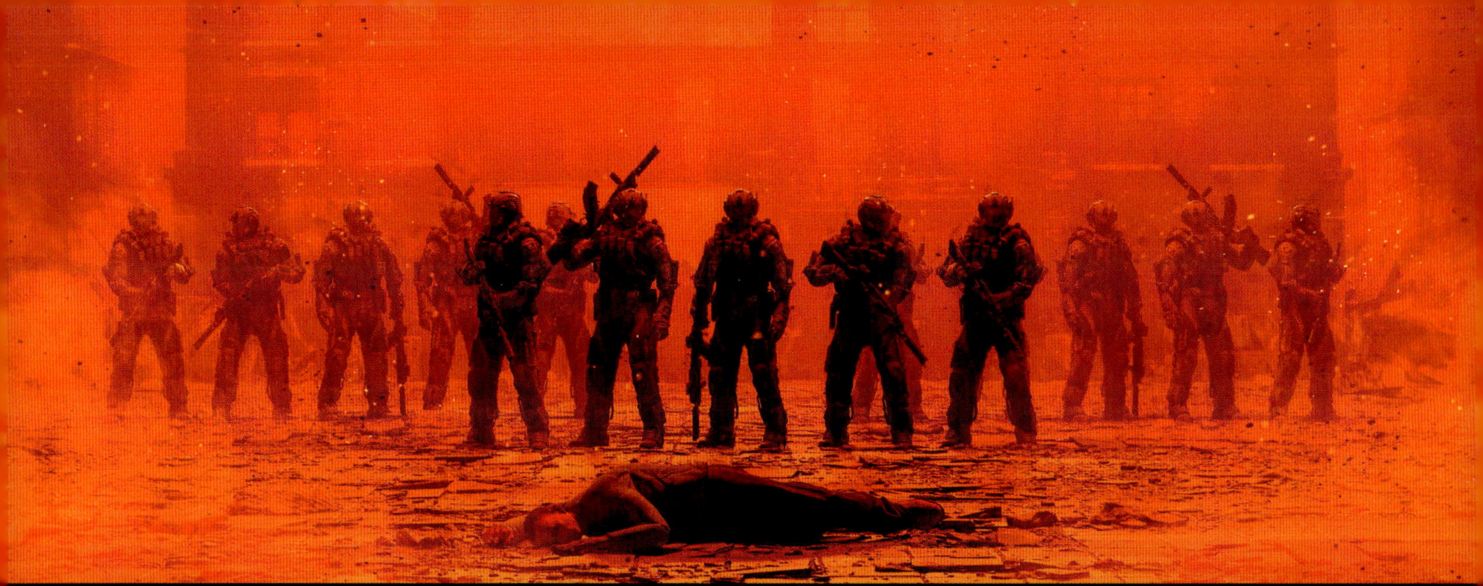

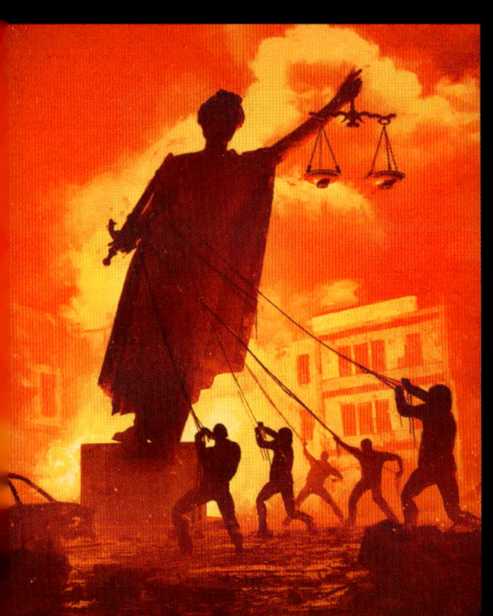

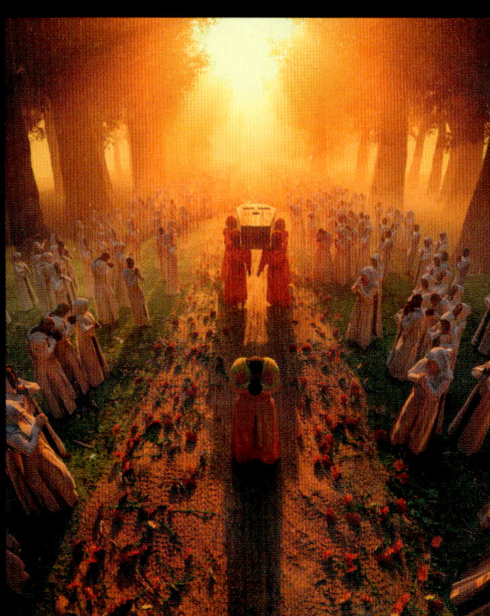

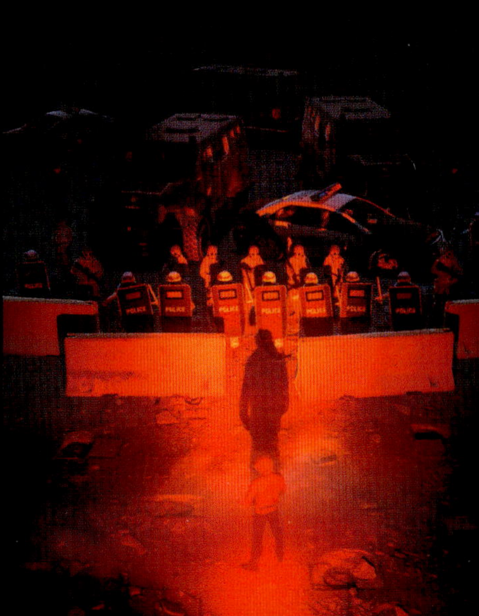
POLICE

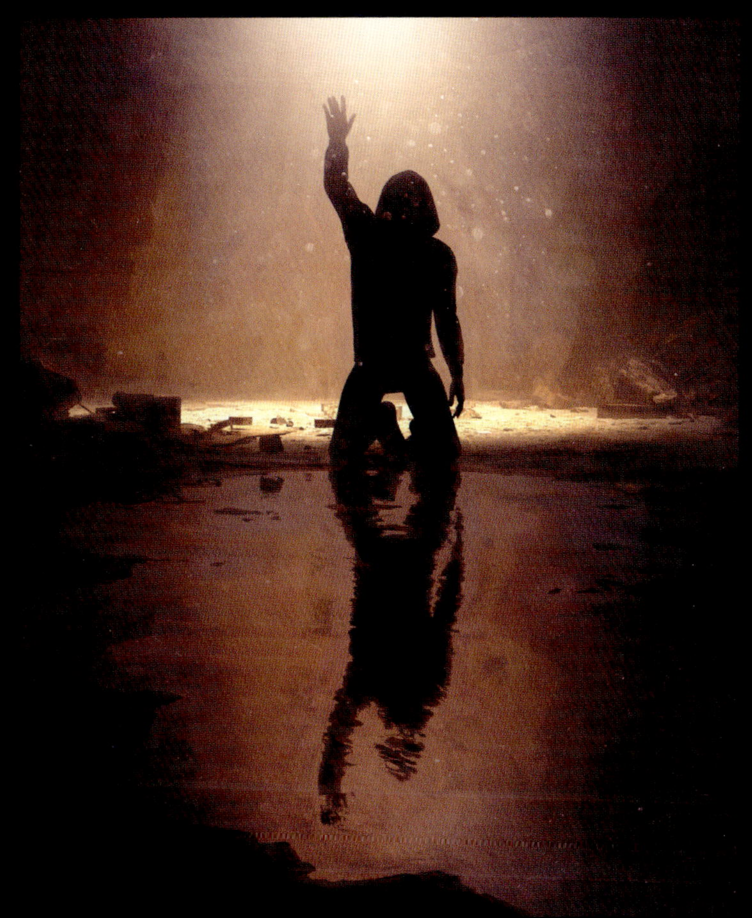

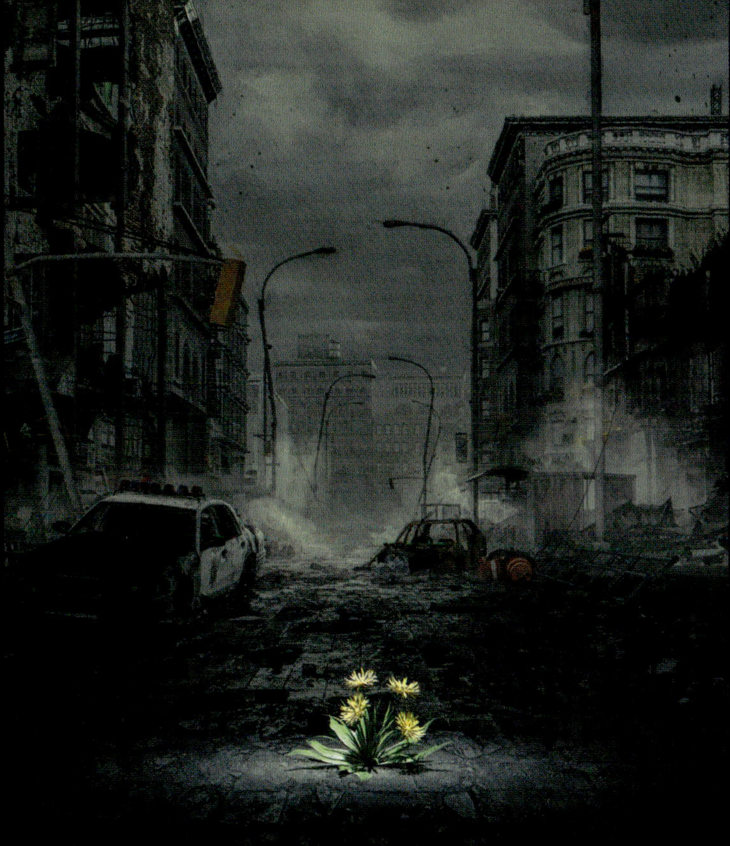

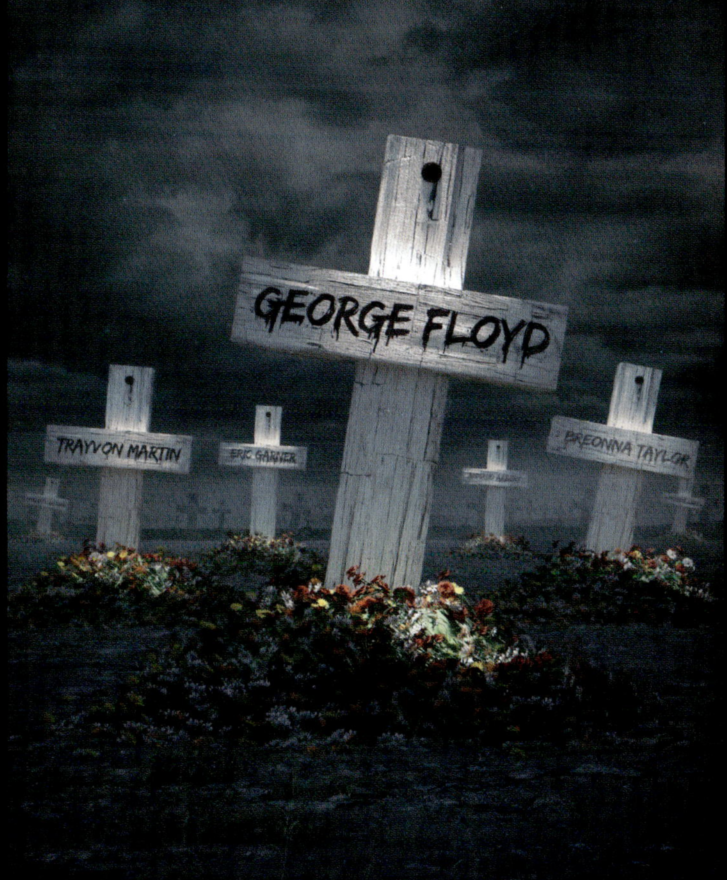

TOP LEFT
BLM
06.02.2020

TOP RIGHT
REFLECT
06.06.2020

BOTTOM LEFT
GROW
06.05.2020

BOTTOM RIGHT
ENDLESS MEMORIALS
06.03.2020

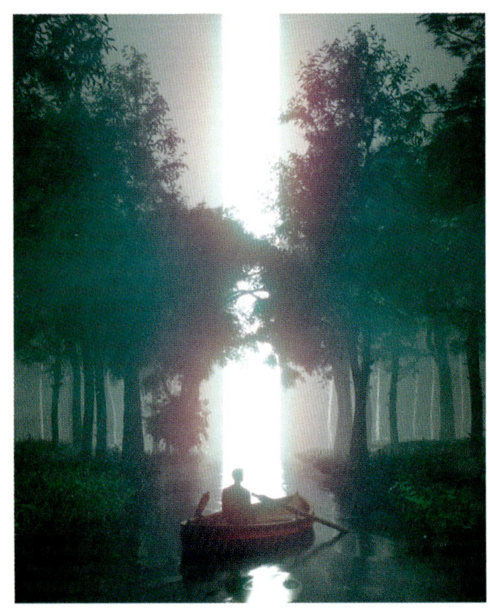
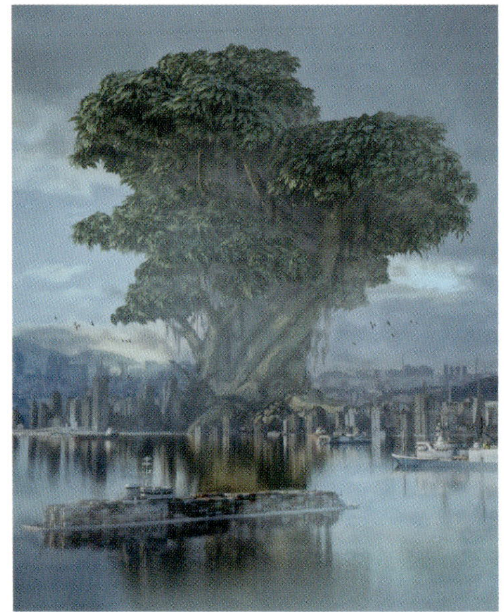
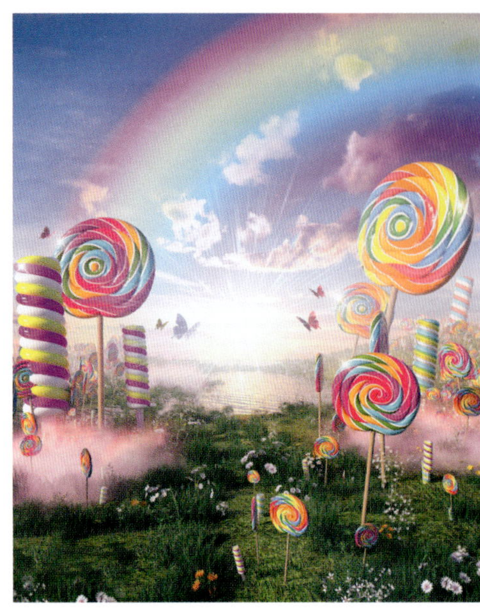
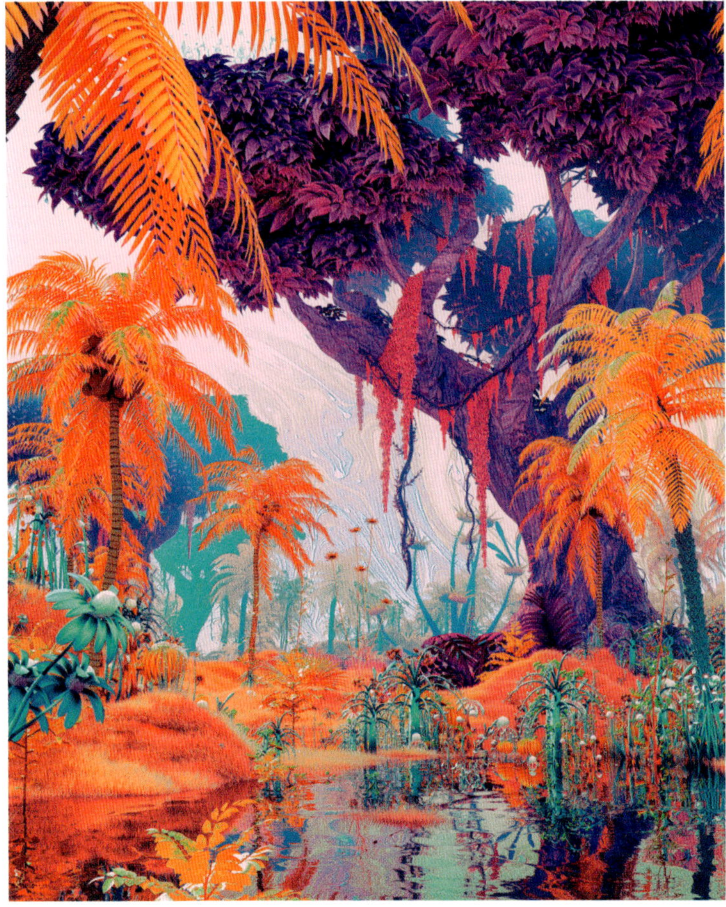
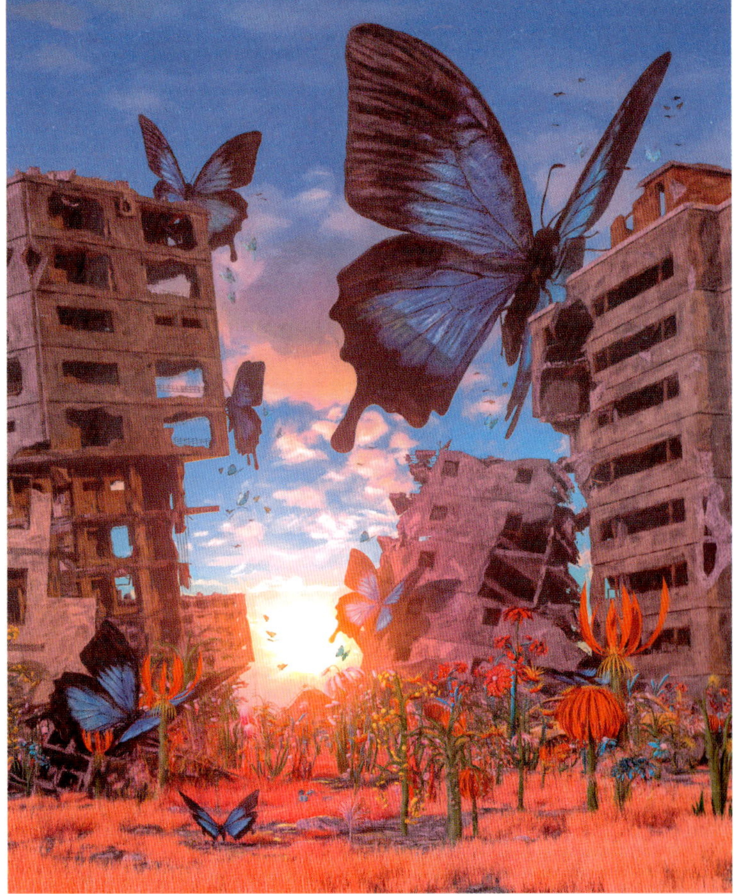

TOP LEFT
NATURAL RESET
08.05.2020

TOP MIDDLE
LAST TREE
08.06.2020

TOP RIGHT
sunshine, lollipops and rainbows
10.01.2020

BOTTOM LEFT
remember nature?
04.02.2020

BOTTOM RIGHT
SOFT COLLAPSE
12.02.2020

OPPOSITE PAGE
GOAT EMOJI
12.09.2020

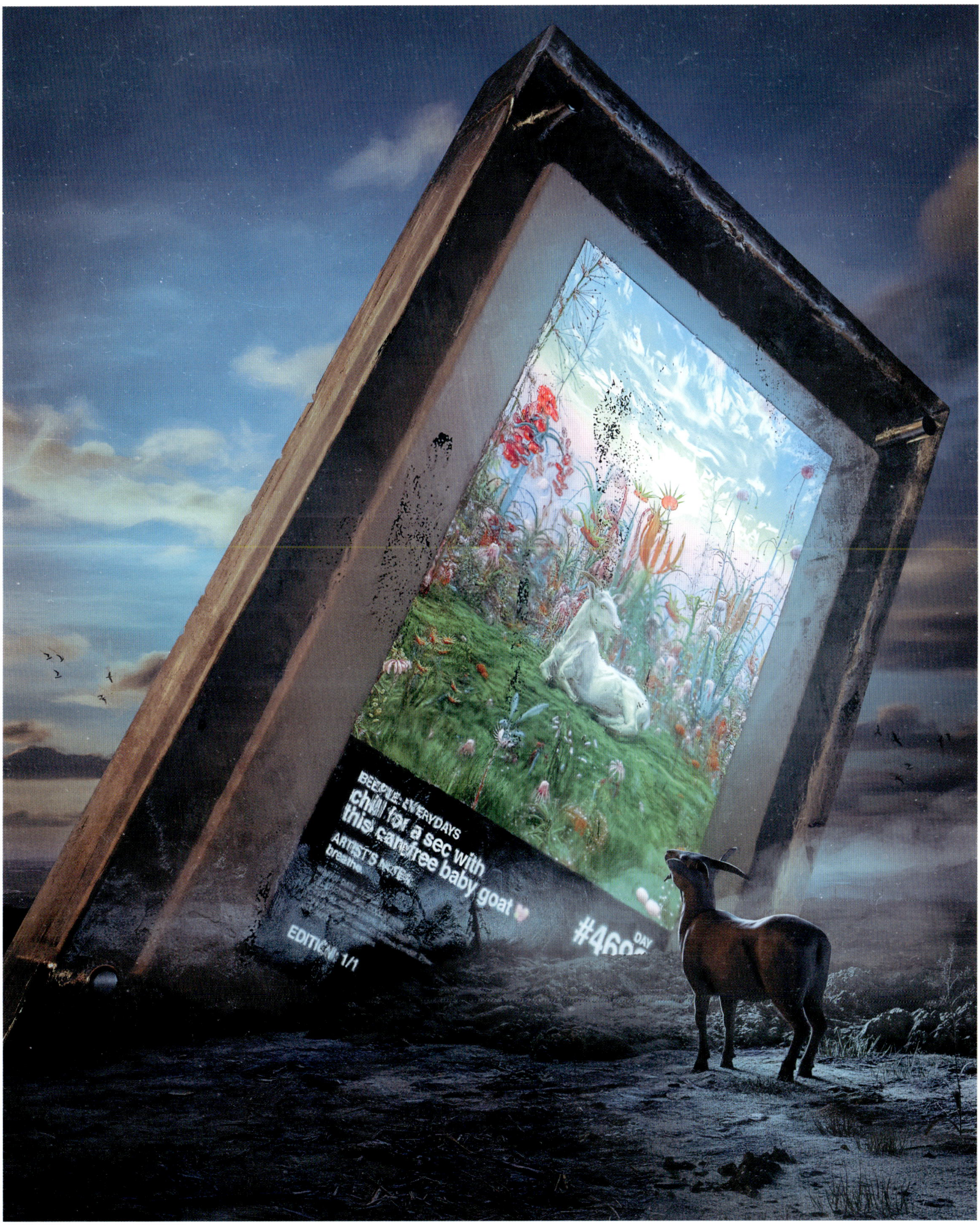
BEEPLE: EVERYDAYS
chill for a sec with
this carefree baby goat
ARTIST'S NOTE:
breathe
EDITION: 1/1
DAY

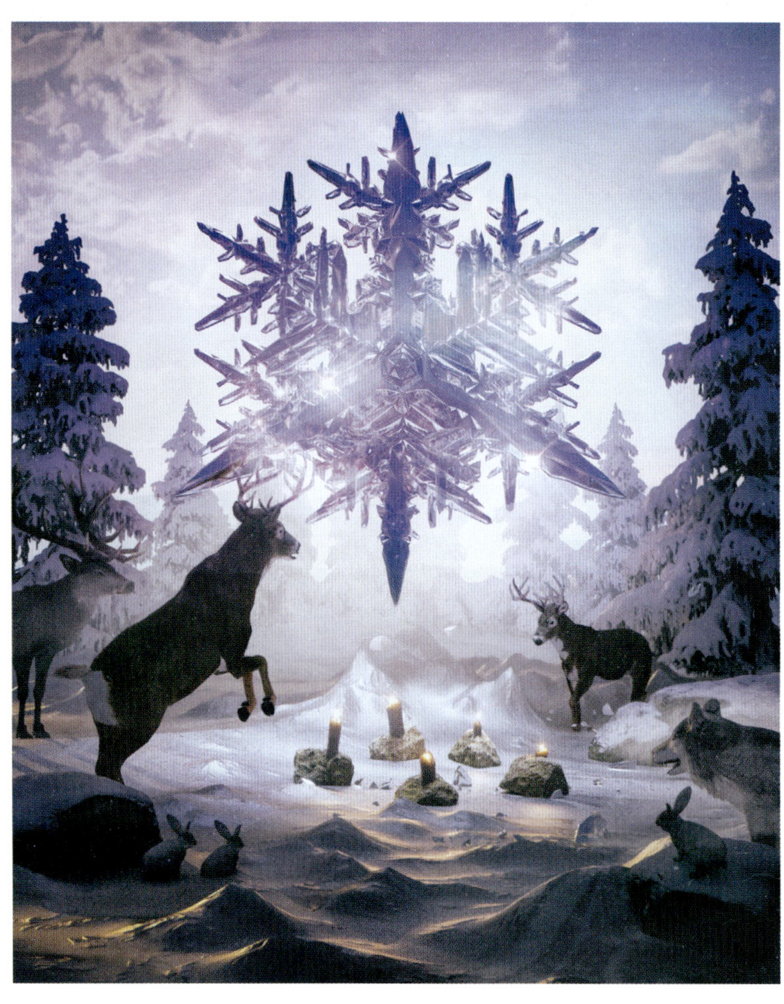

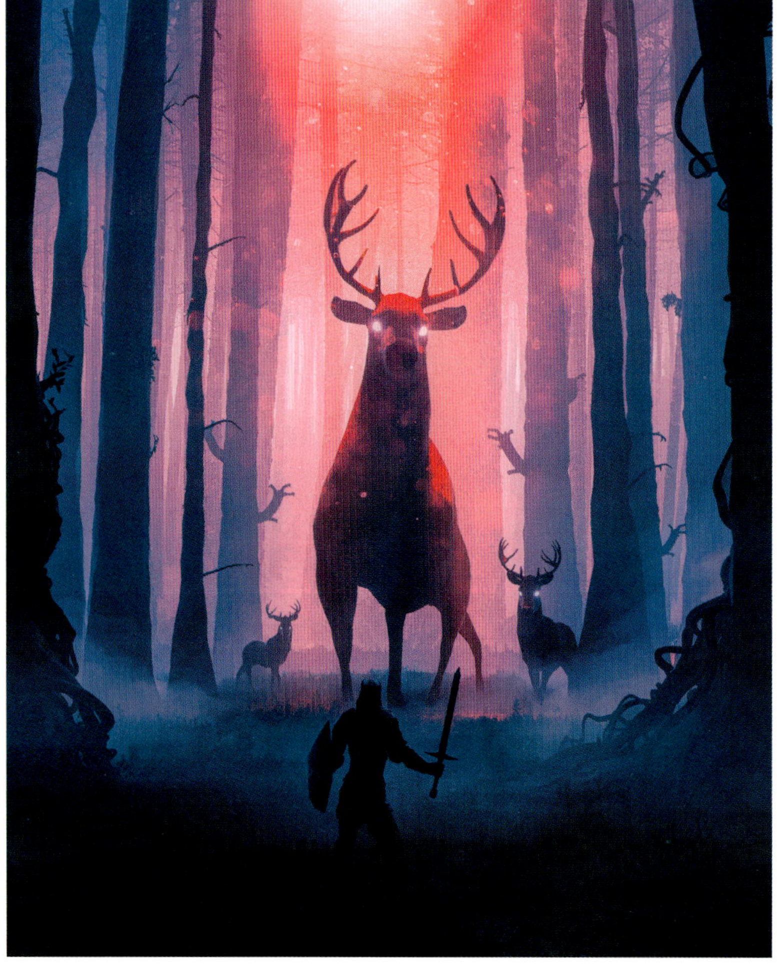

TOP

WINTER SOLSTICE

12.21.2020

BOTTOM

INTRUDER

10.12.2020

OPPOSITE PAGE

LATE CAPITALISM

03.23.2020

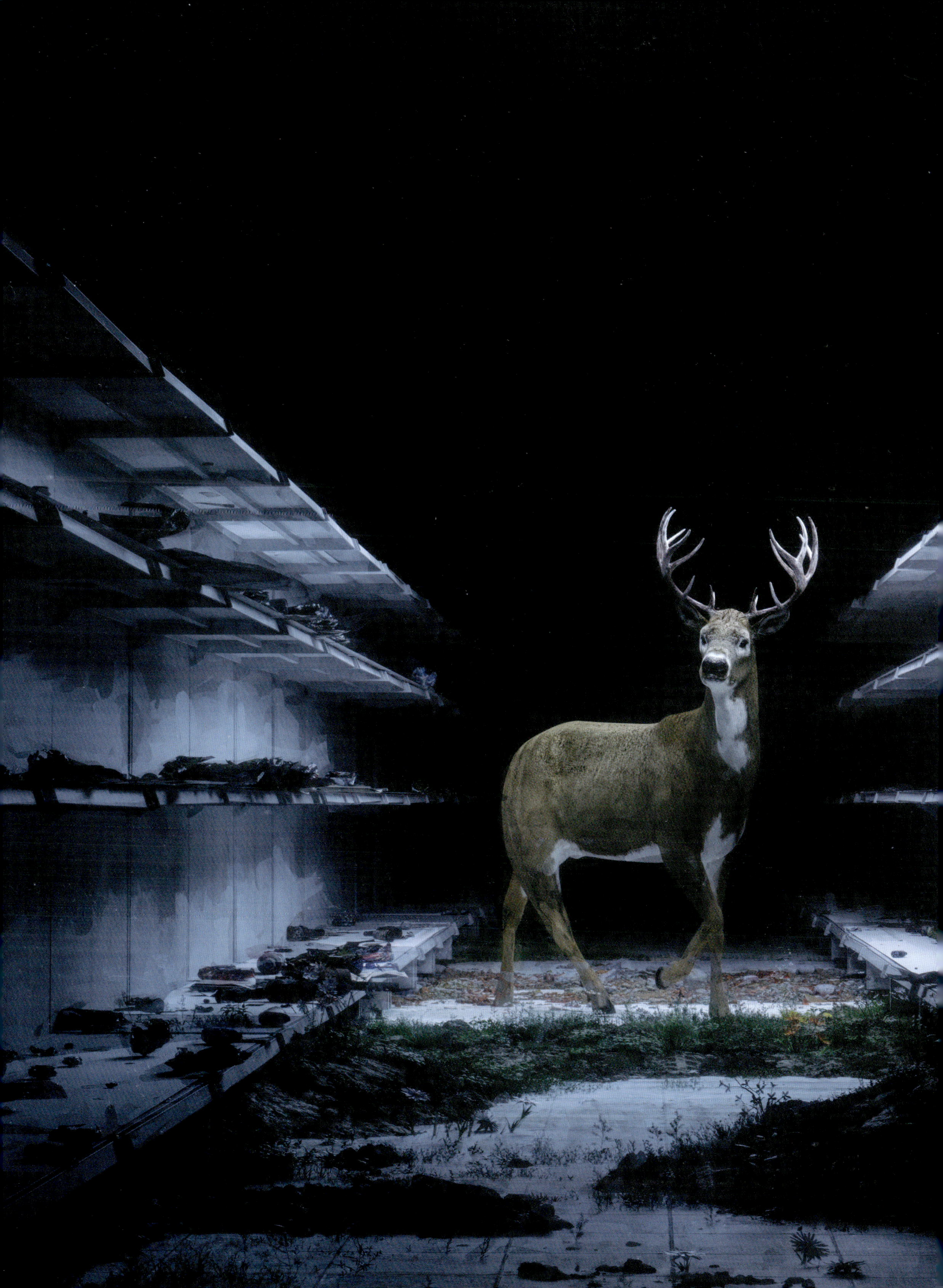

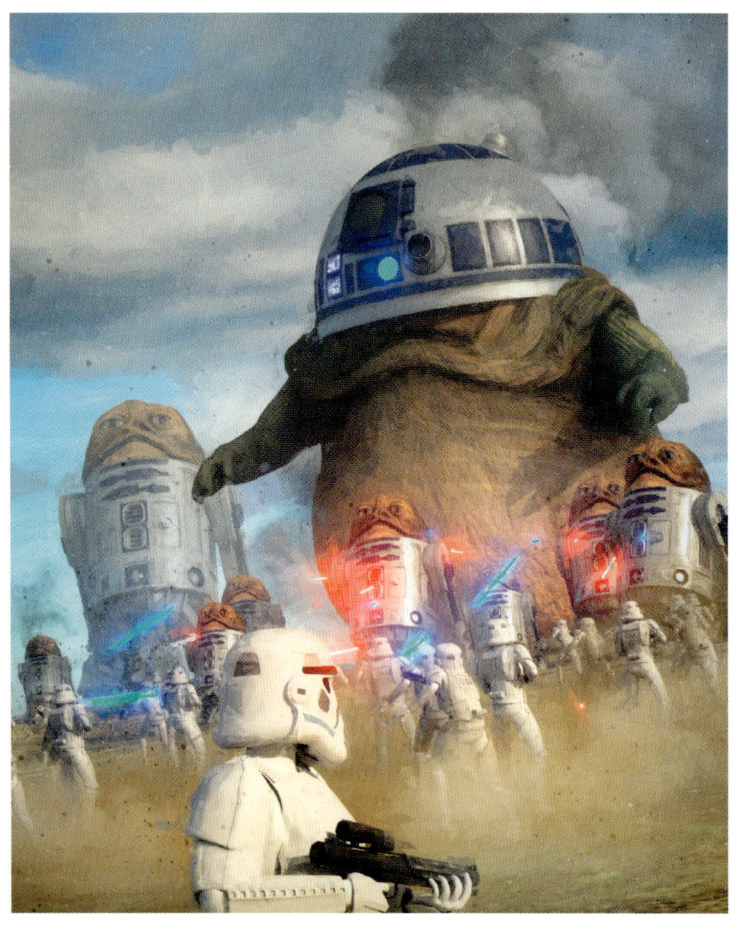

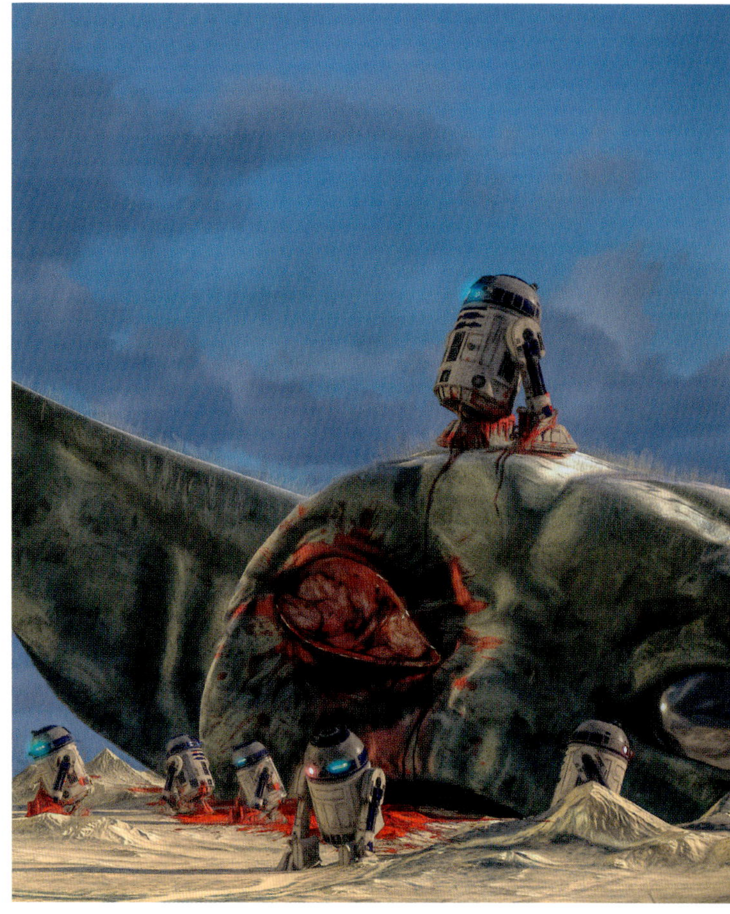

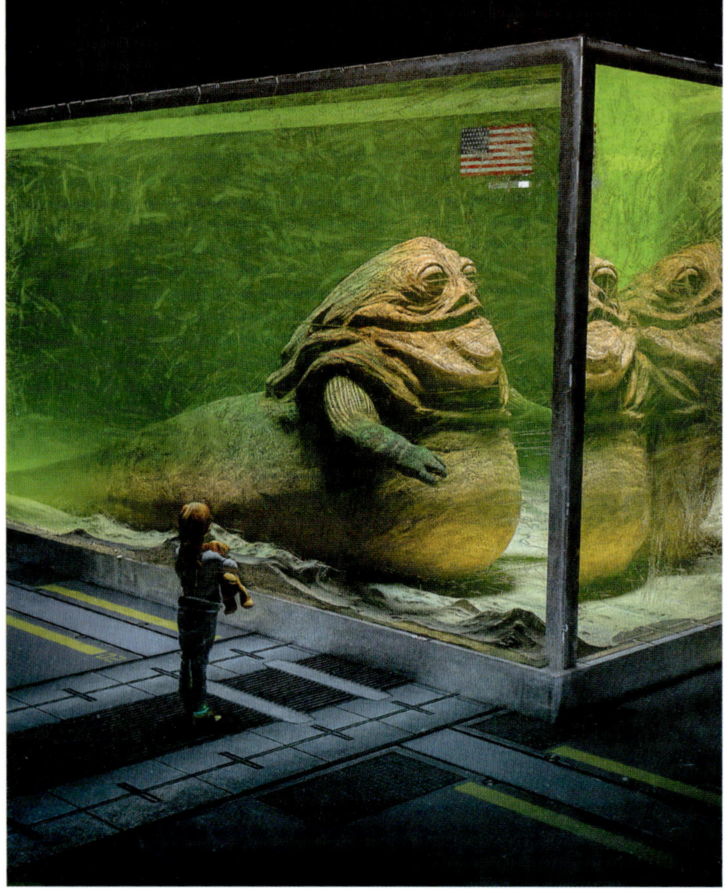

TOP LEFT

STAR WARS 71
05.04.2020

TOP RIGHT

NOT THE DROIDS YOU'RE LOOKING FOR
12.03.2020

BOTTOM

NASTY PILE OF MEAT
11.10.2020

OPPOSITE PAGE

WOOKIE ISLAND
12.28.2020

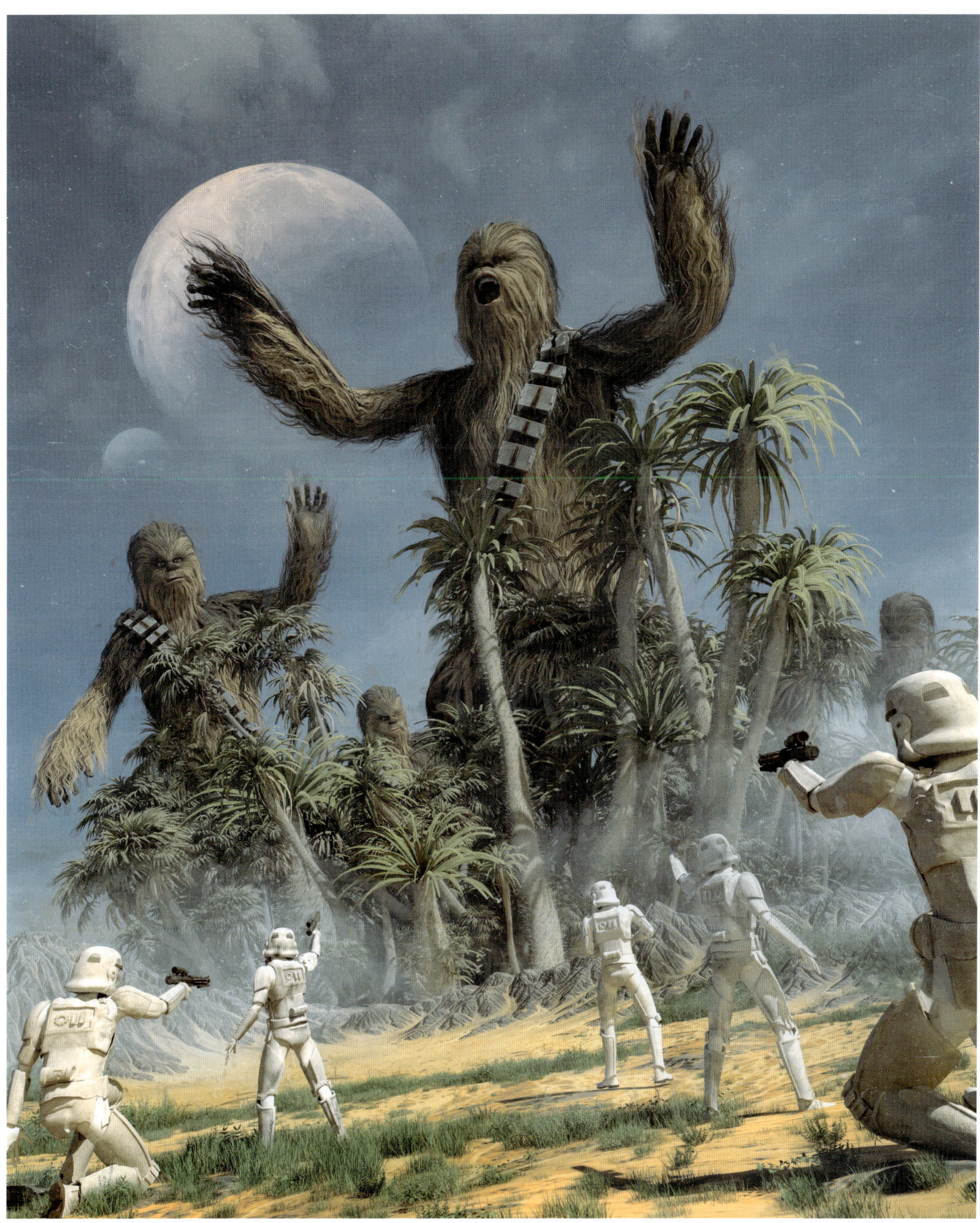

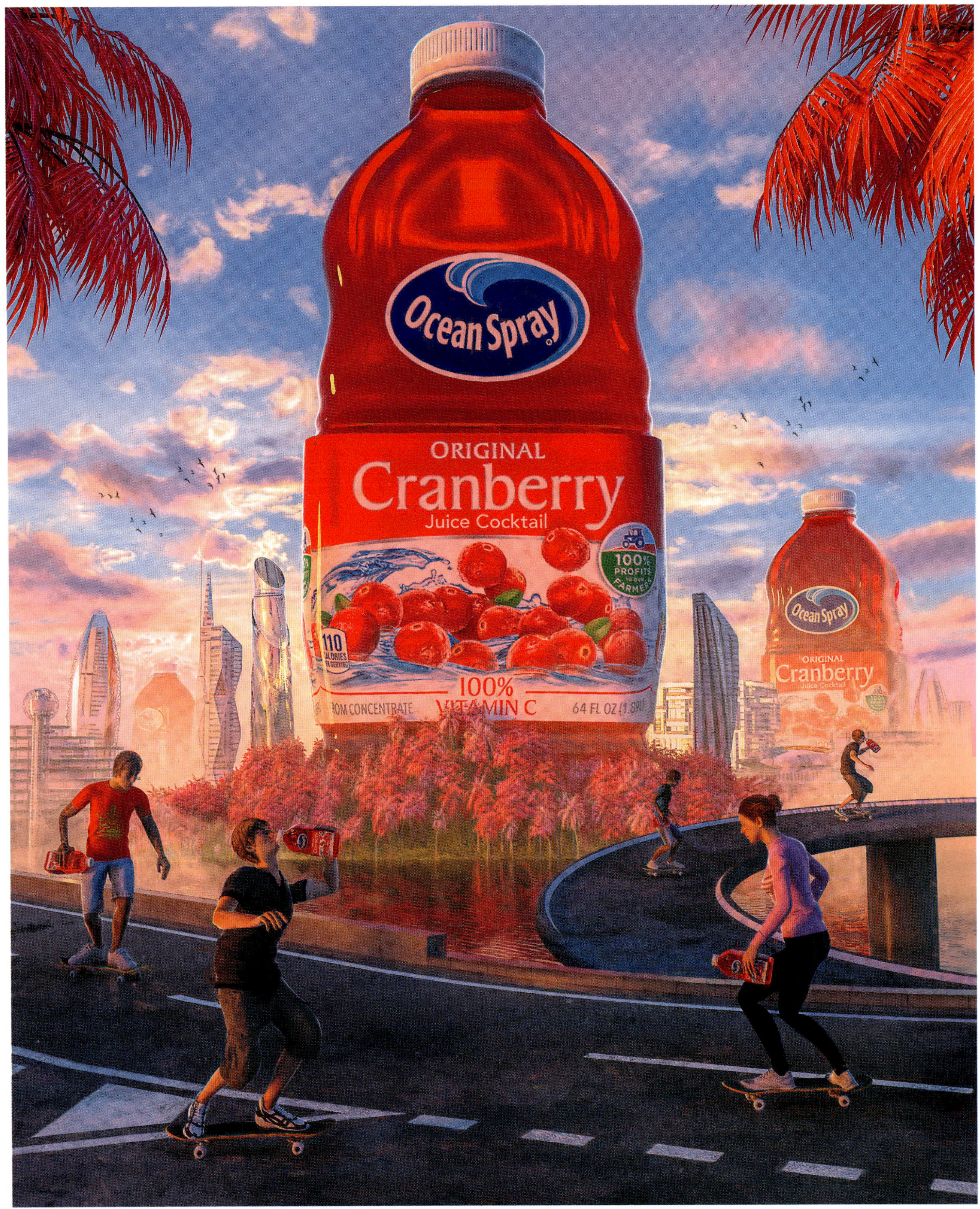

ABOVE

VIBE CITY
10.11.2020

OPPOSITE PAGE

rest in power
08.29.2020

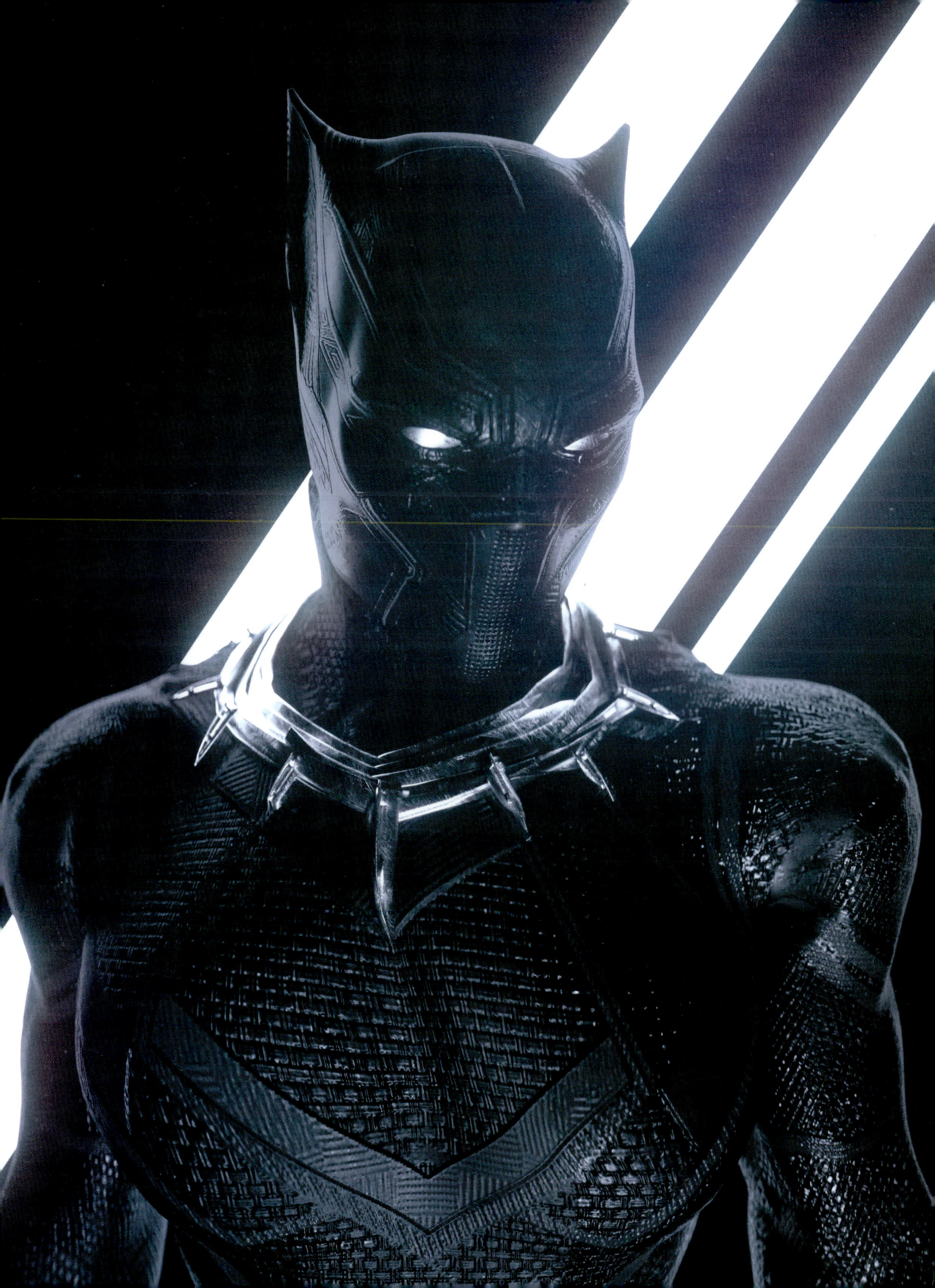

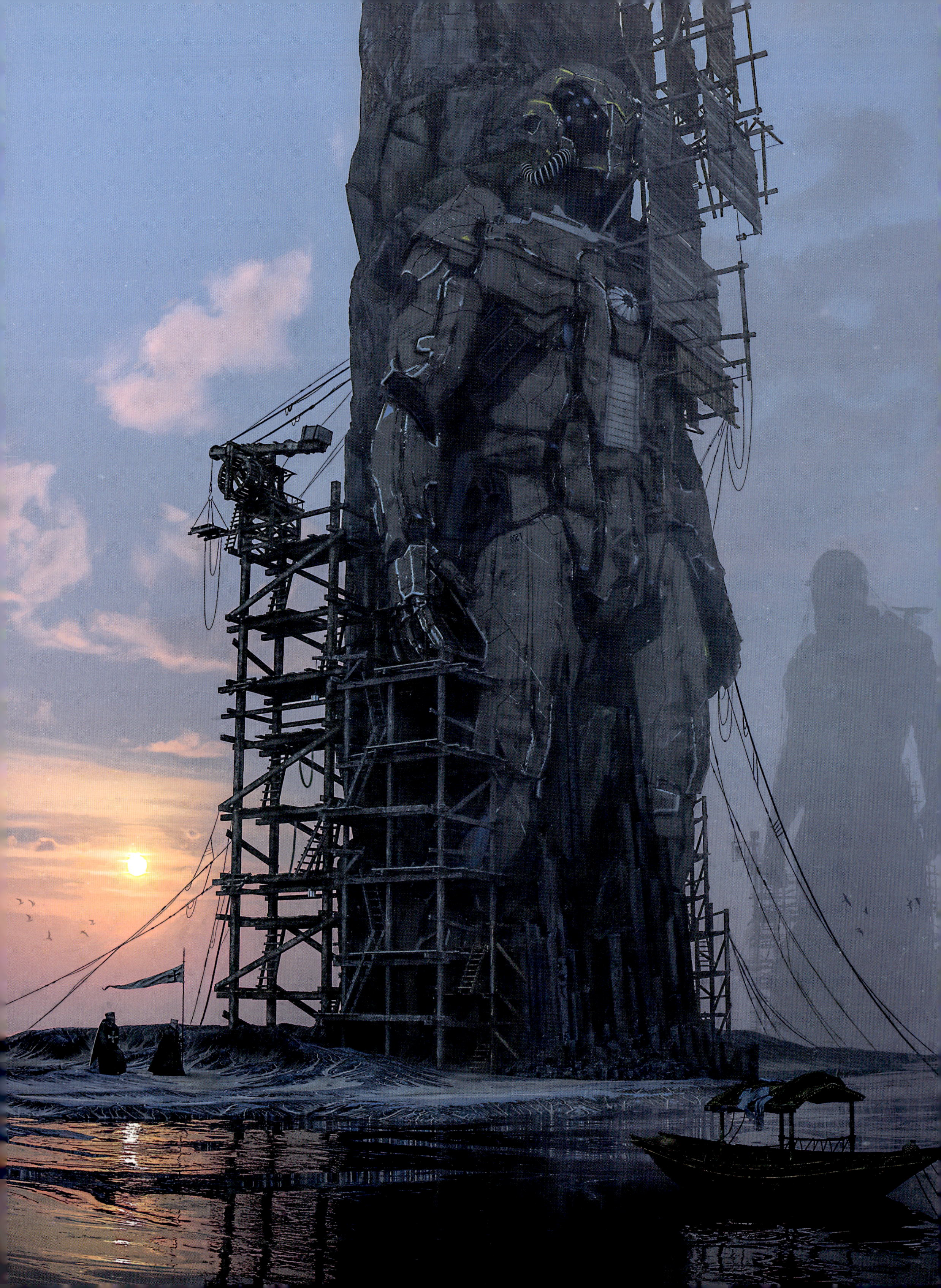

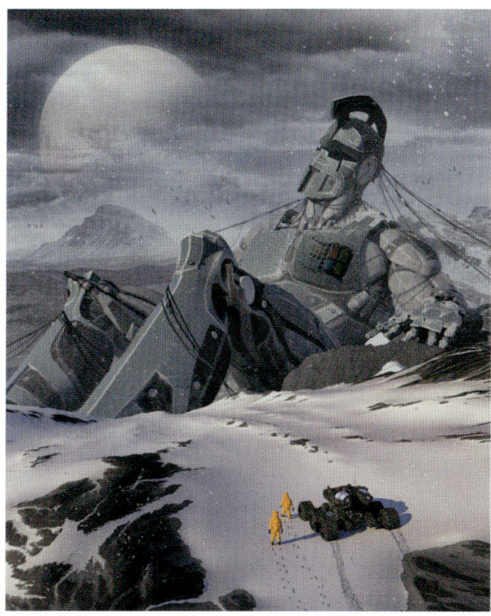

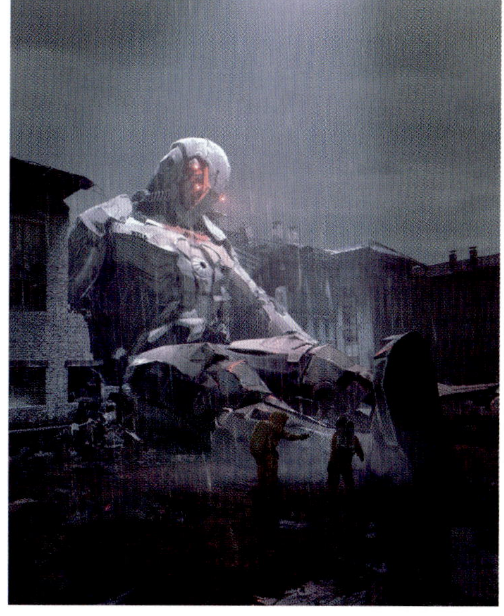

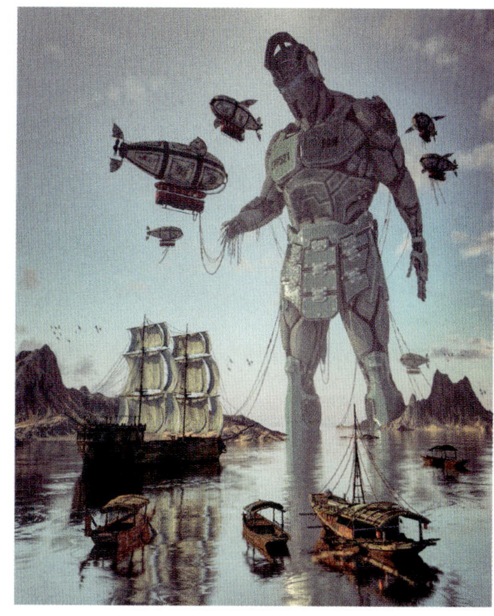

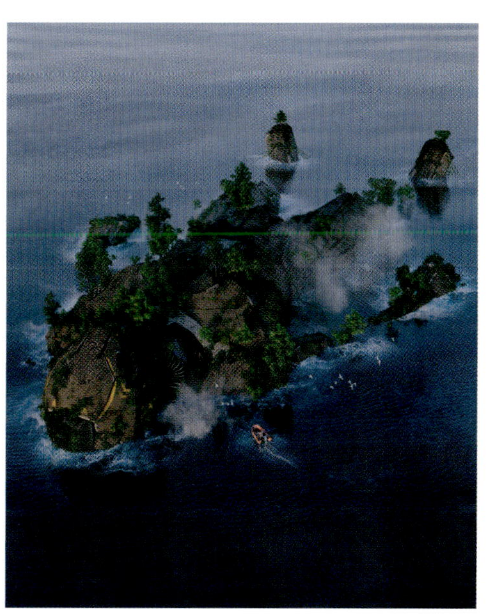

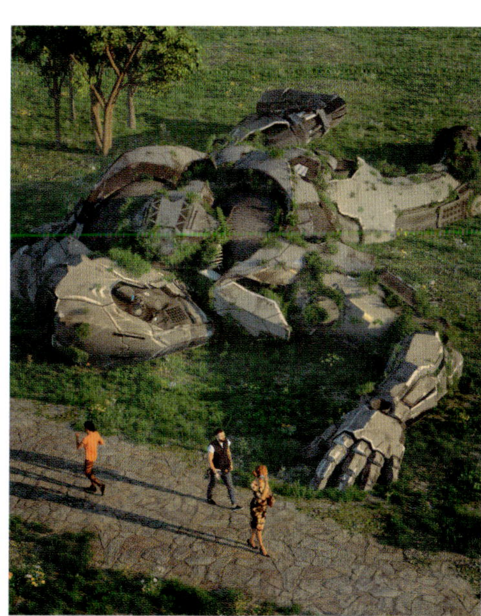

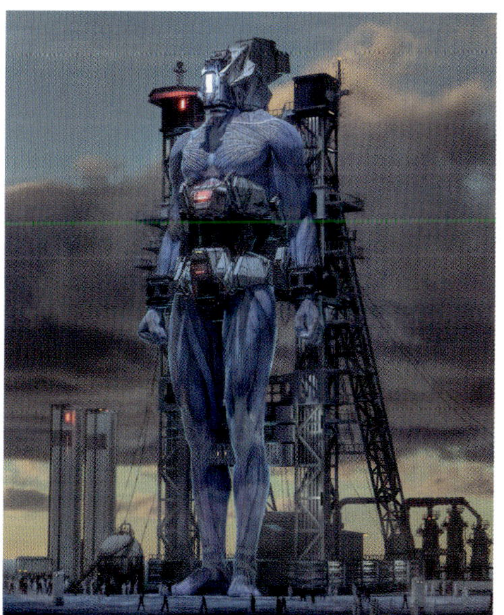

OPPOSITE PAGE
THIRD DAWN
05.13.2020

TOP LEFT
WINDOWS 2095
06.21.2020

TOP MIDDLE
BROKEN DOWN
09.03.2020

TOP RIGHT
BROKEN HAND
12.06.2020

BOTTOM LEFT
OASIS
09.25.2020

BOTTOM MIDDLE
NORMAL LIFE
07.25.2020

BOTTOM RIGHT
ANTIBODY
04.05.2020

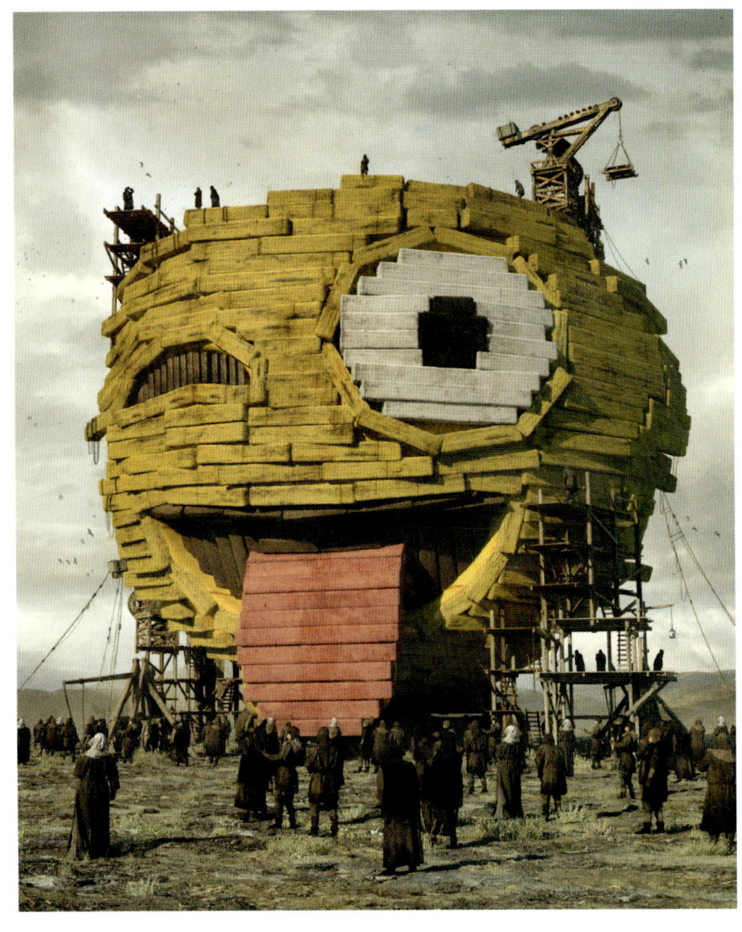

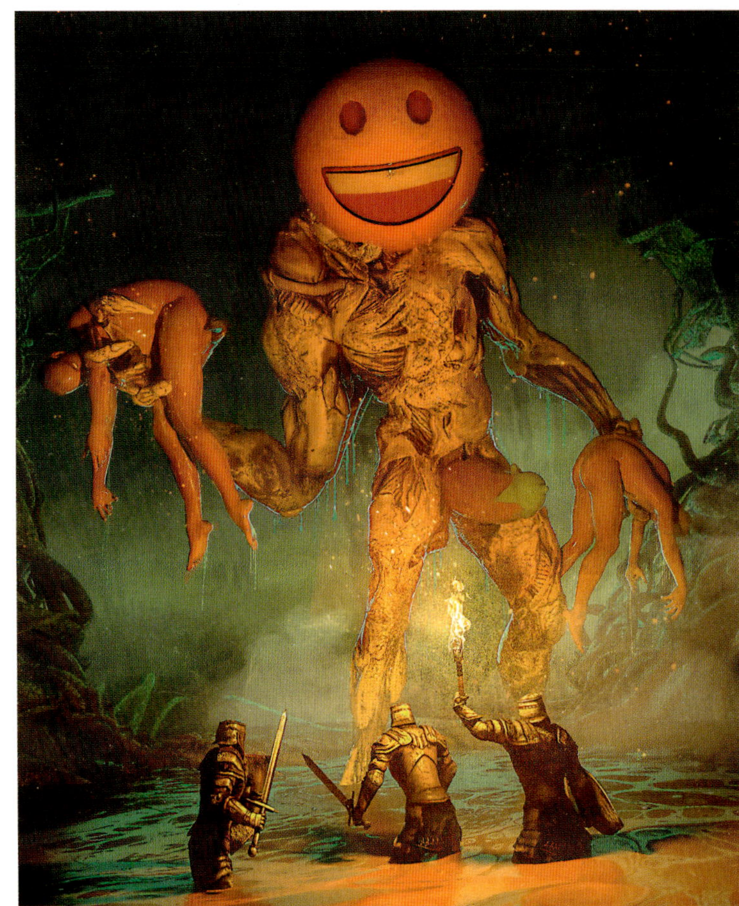

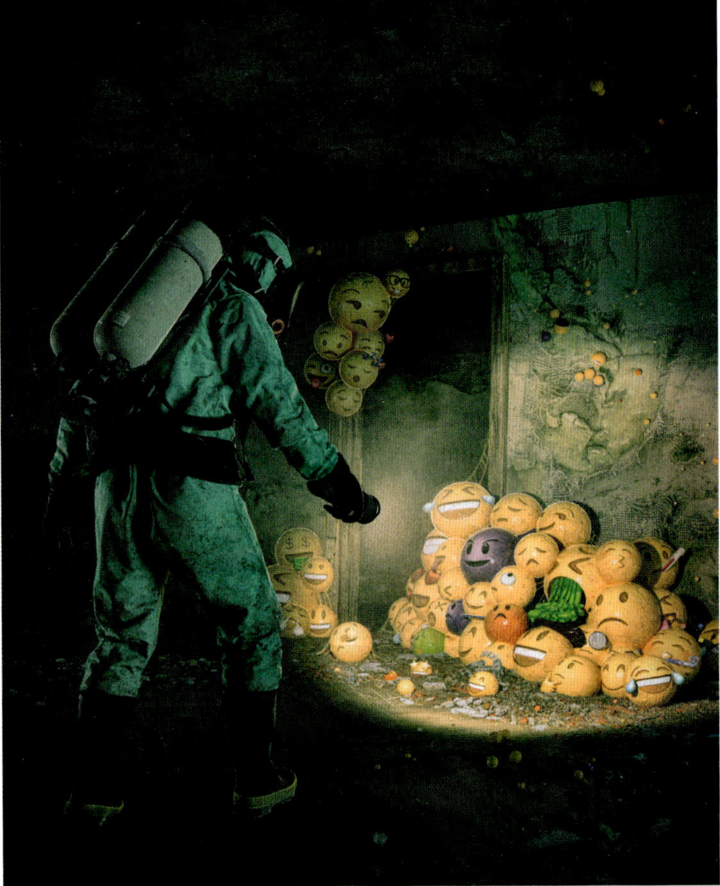

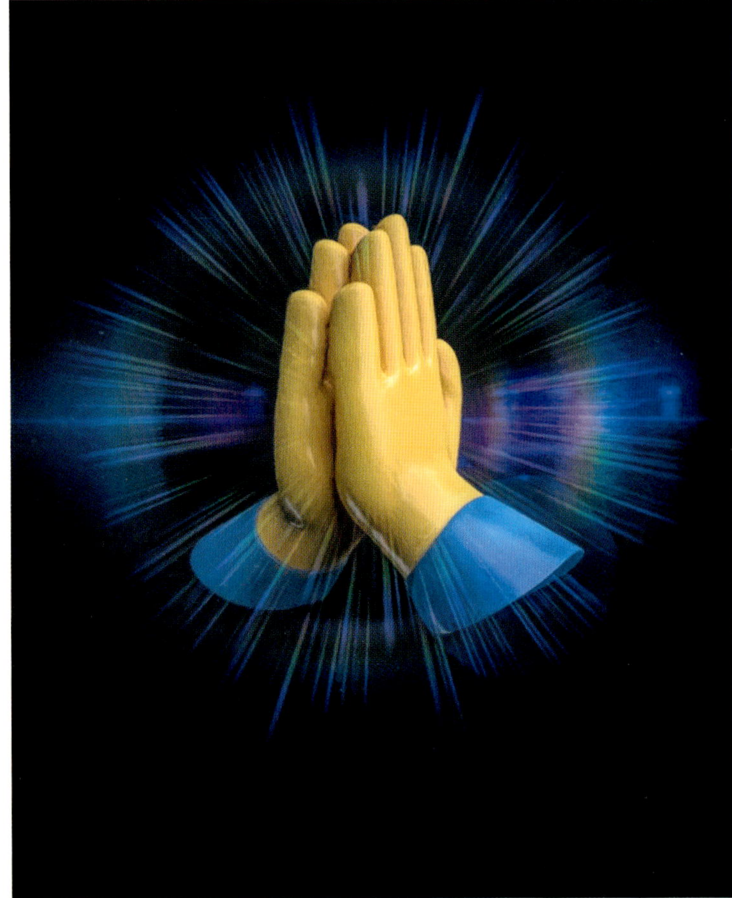

TOP LEFT
THE FIRST EMOJI
09.01.2020

TOP RIGHT
LEFT ON READ 1652
09.07.2020

BOTTOM LEFT
EMOJI INFESTATION
08.21.2020

BOTTOM RIGHT
NO WORDS
10.30.2020

OPPOSITE PAGE
KEANU VACCINE PRODUCTION PHASE 3
08.11.2020

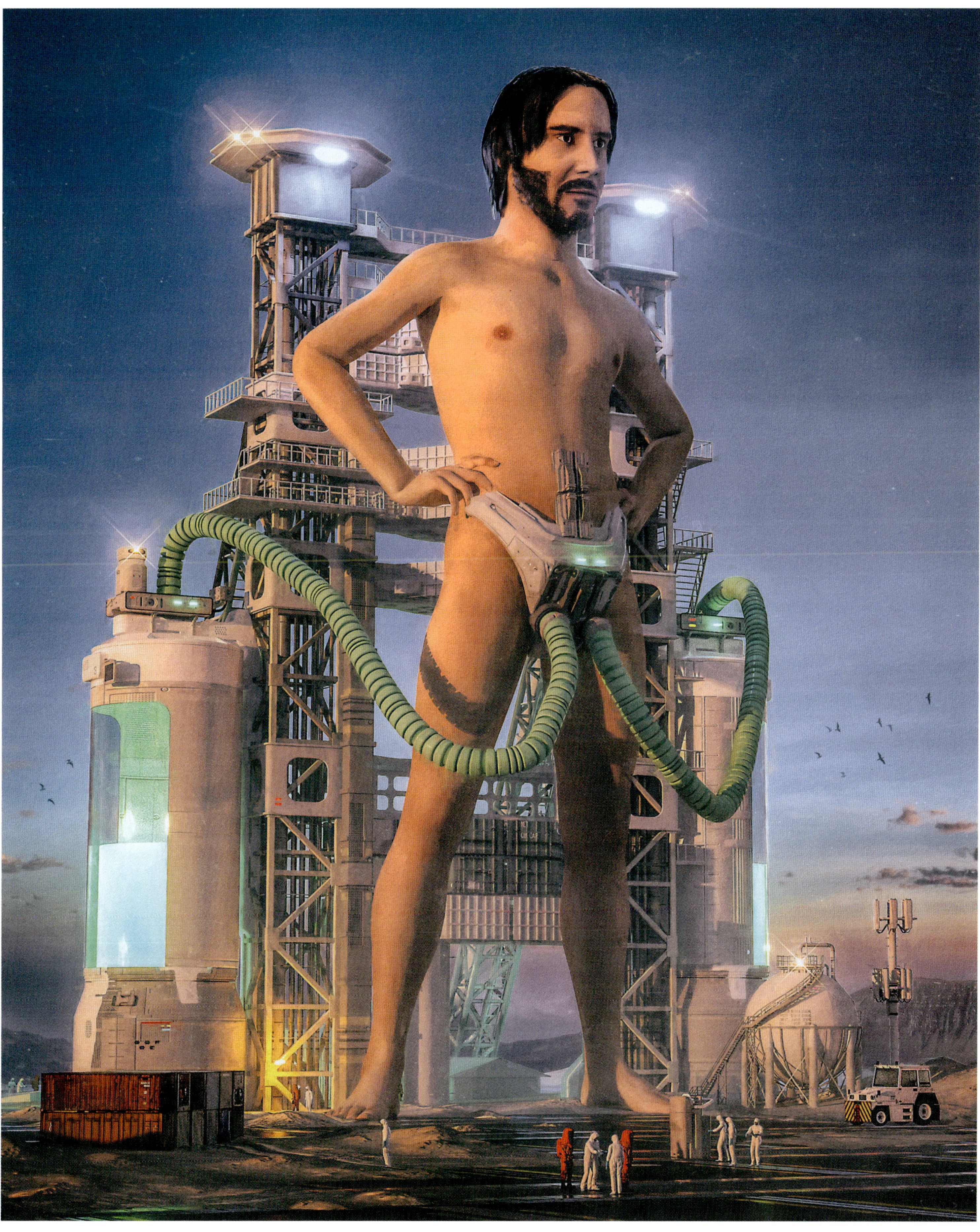

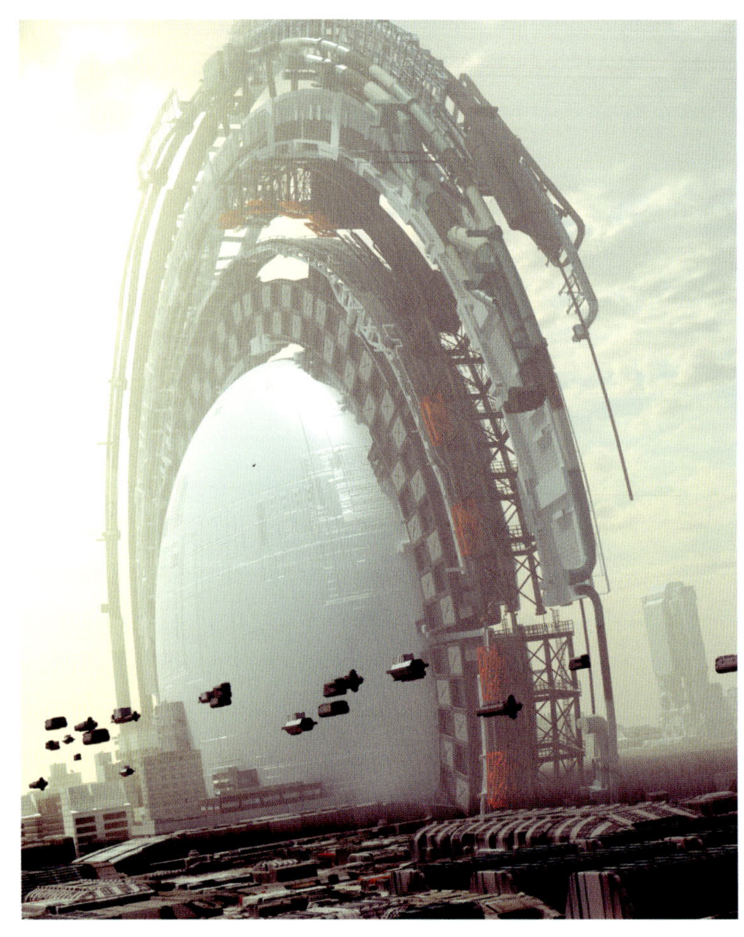

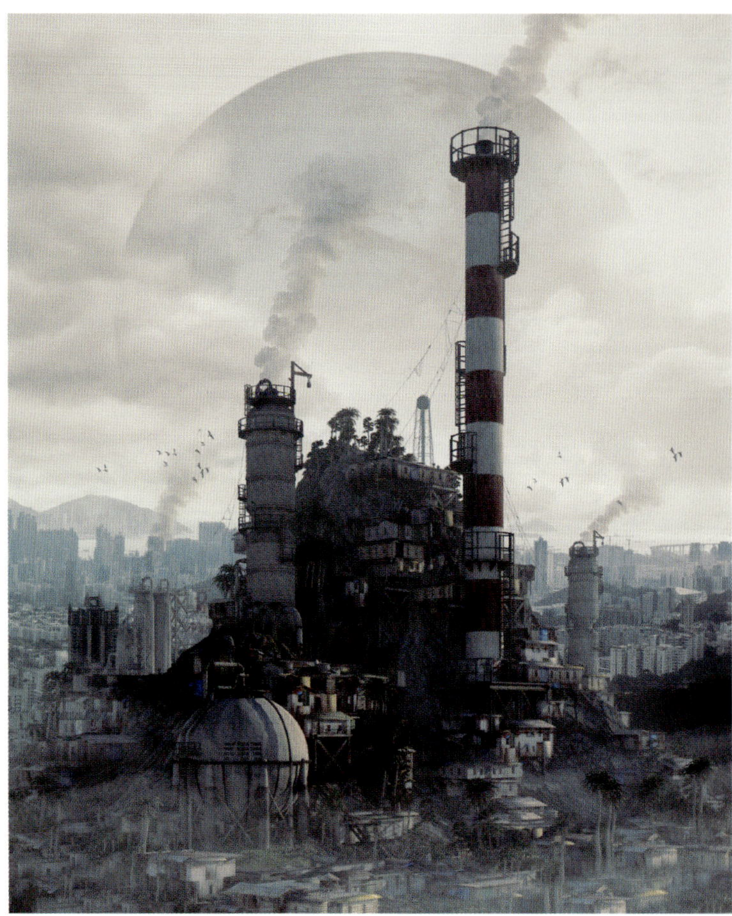

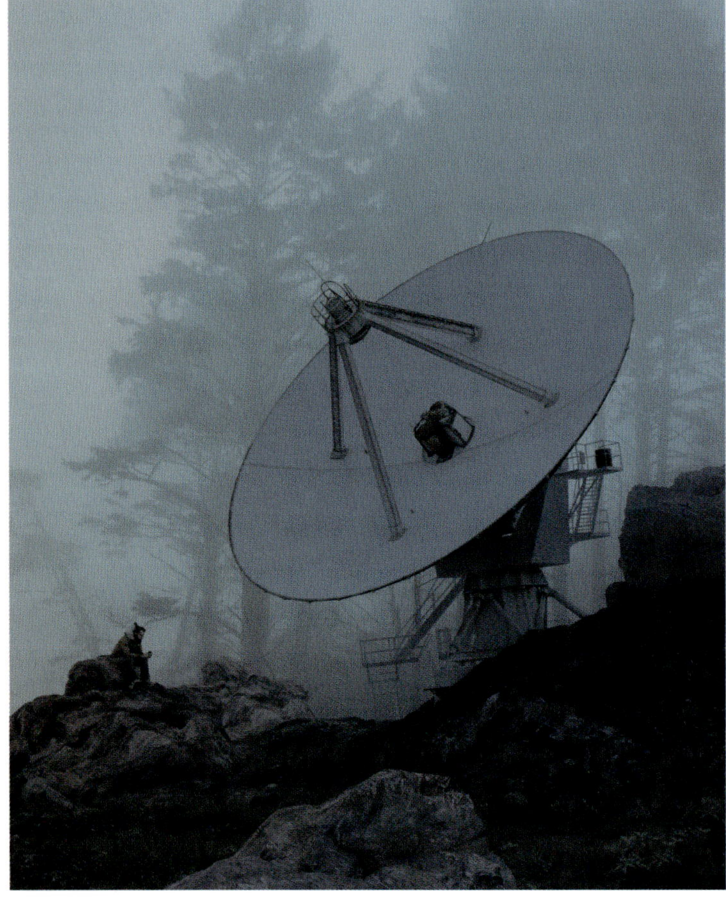

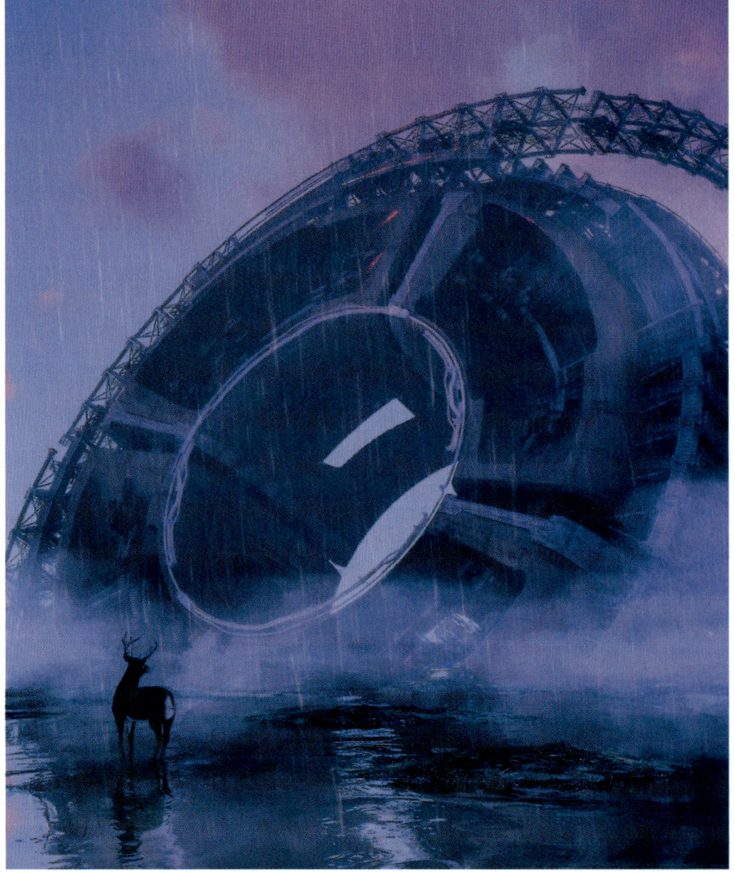

TOP LEFT
PHERICAL
01.27.2020

TOP RIGHT
SENTIENT INDUSTRY
01.17.2020

BOTTOM LEFT
NO SIGNAL
03.18.2020

BOTTOM RIGHT
USED FUEL CELL
09.23.2020

OPPOSITE PAGE
HUMAN CONTACT
08.12.2020

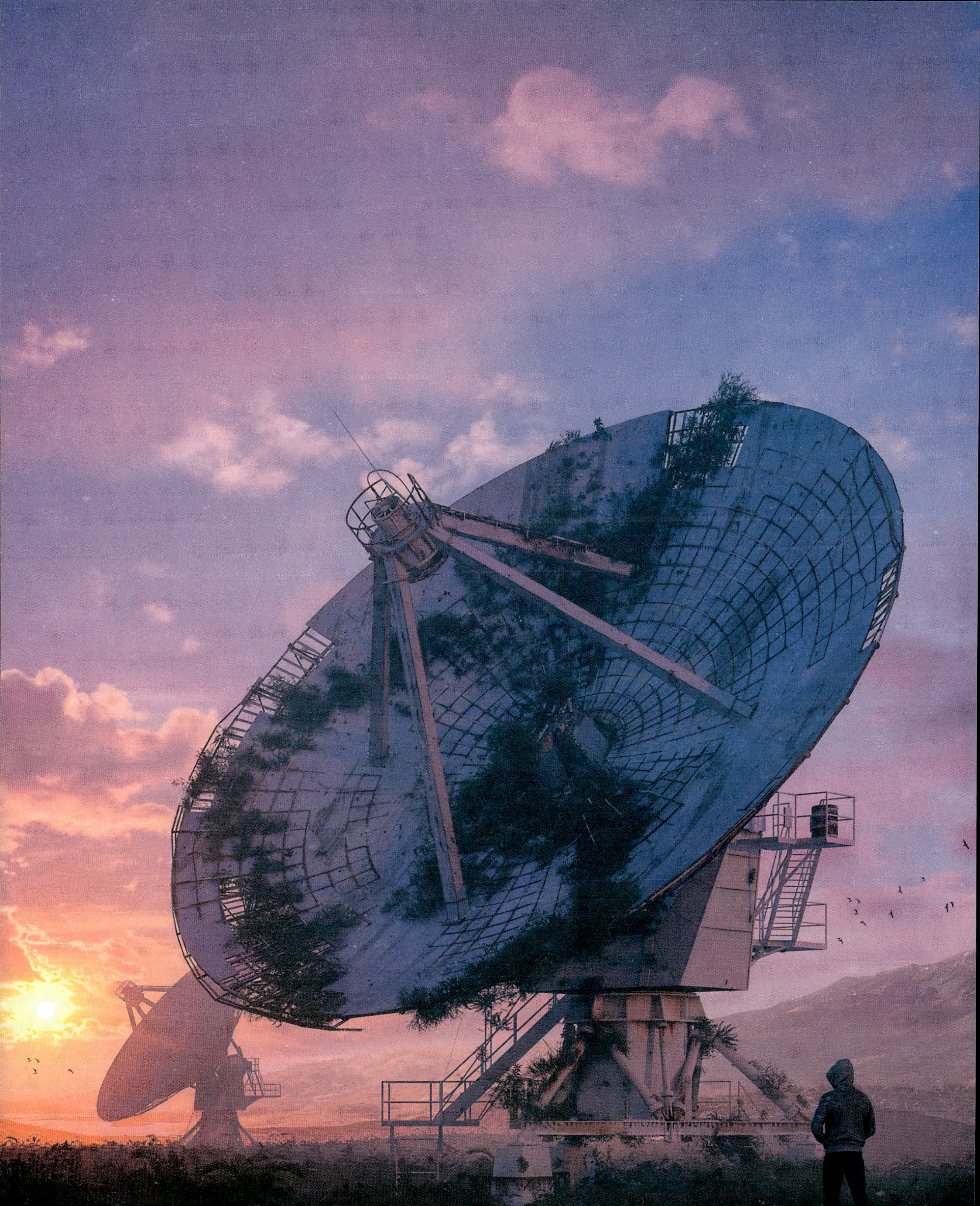

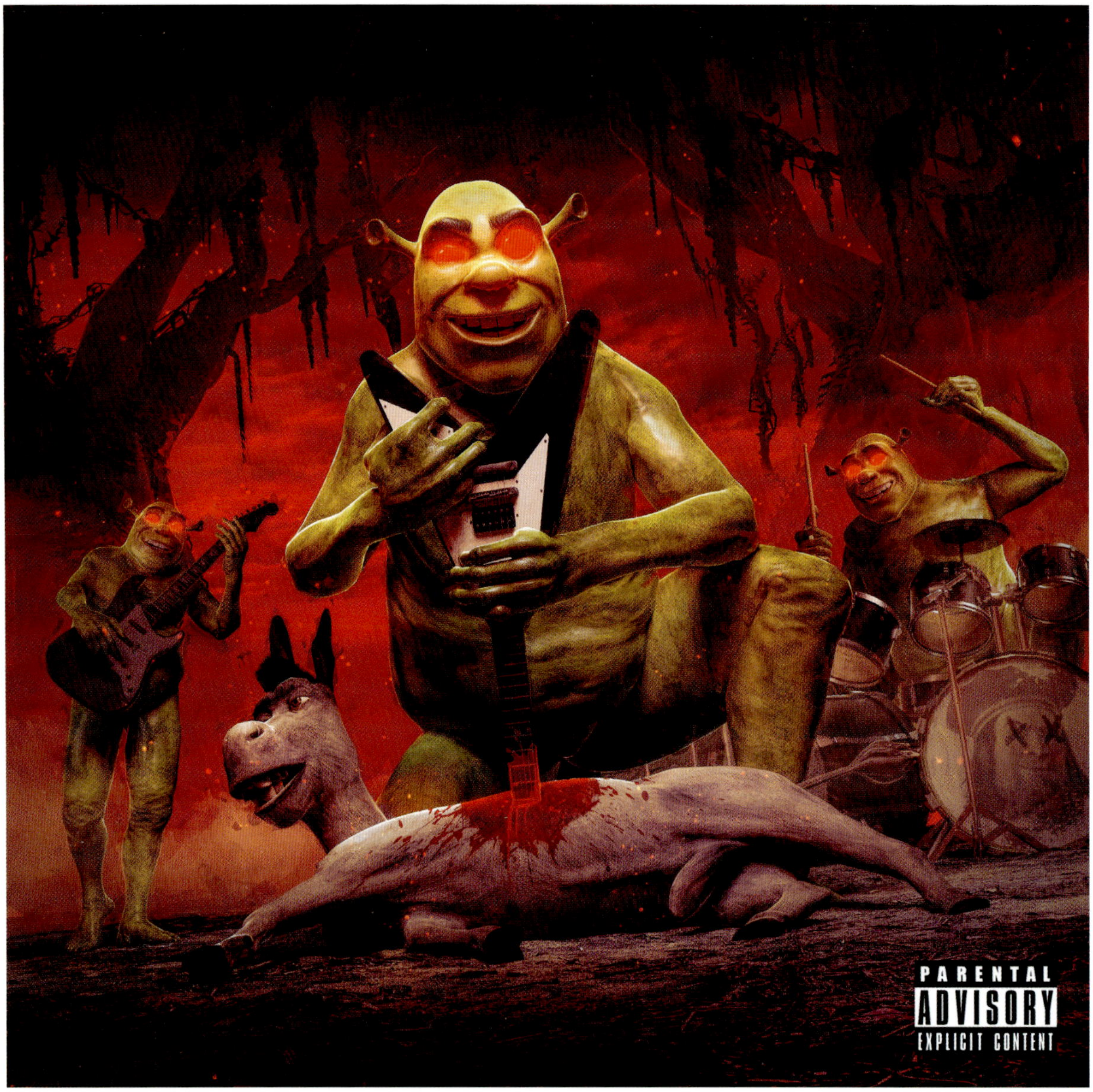

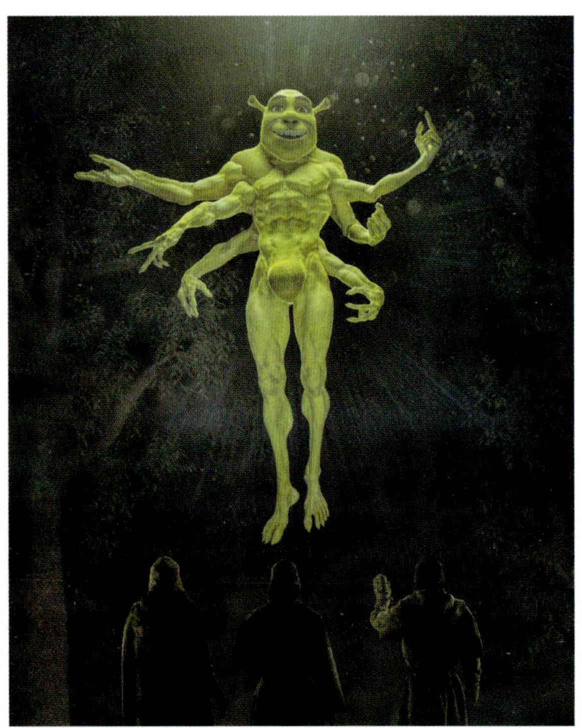

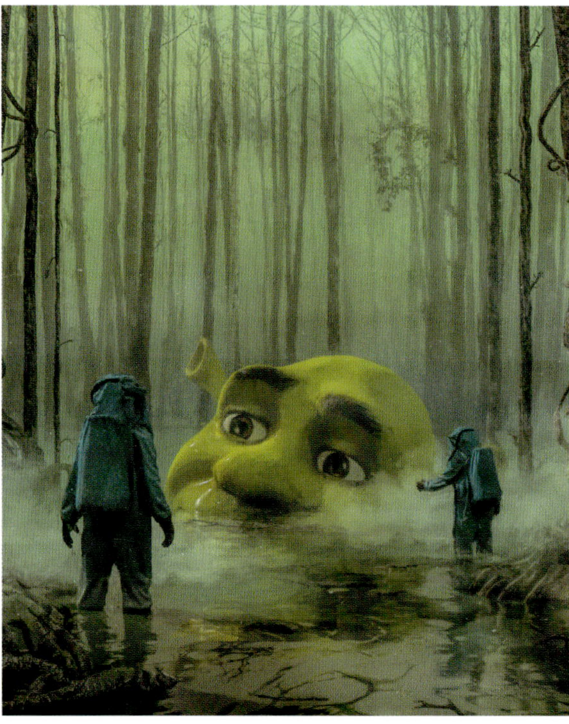

TOP

SHREK-THEMED DEATHCORE ALBUM ART

10.20.2020

BOTTOM LEFT

THE HERO WE DESERVE

11.21.2020

BOTTOM RIGHT

SWAMP ASS

11.06.2020

OPPOSITE PAGE

SHREK TOO

10.19.2020

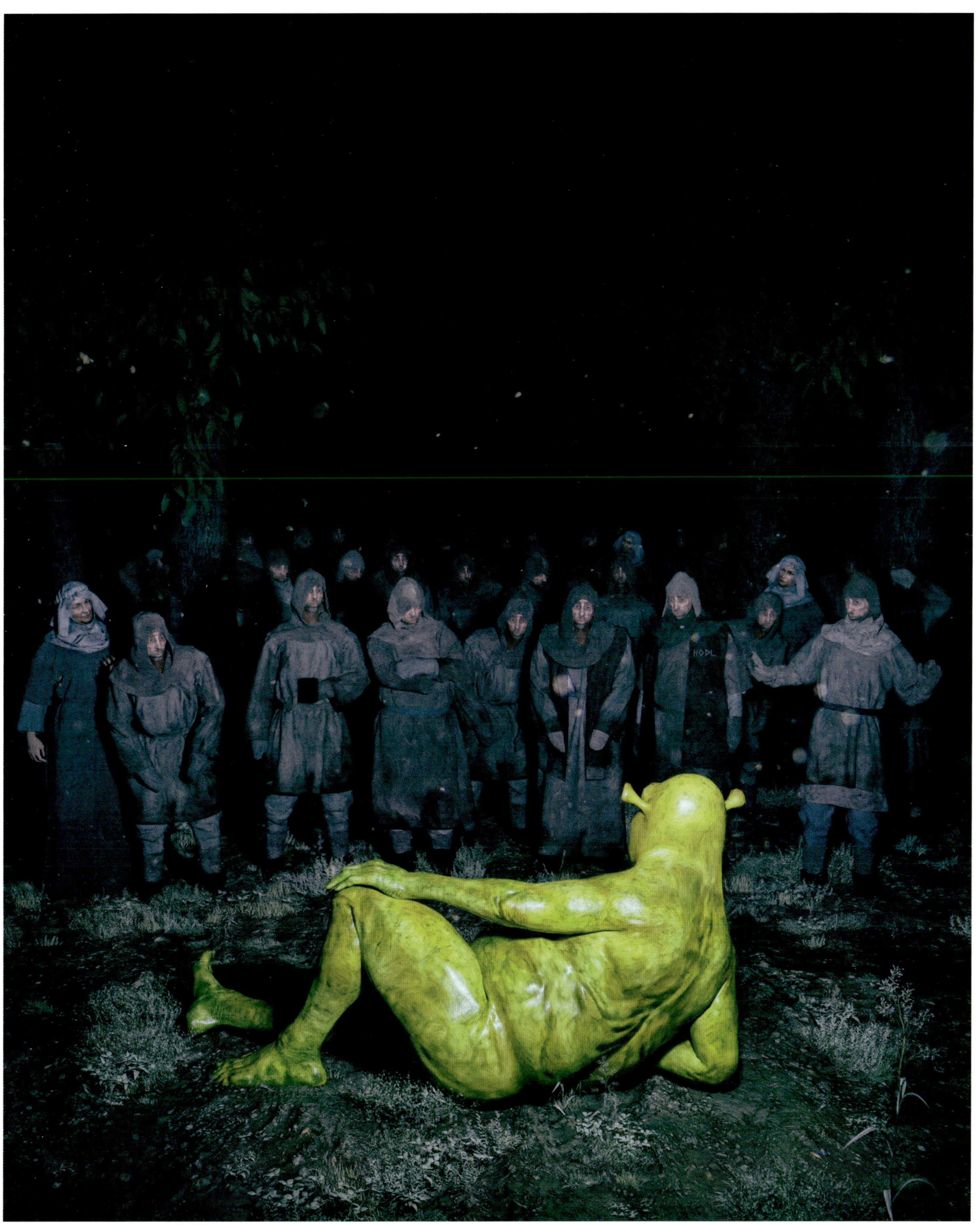

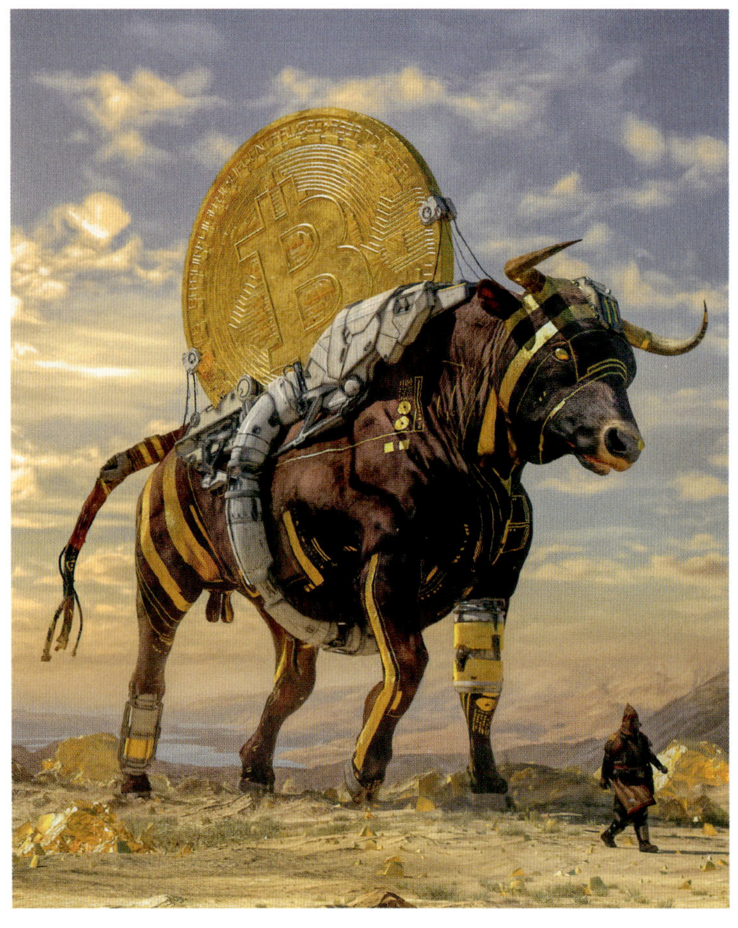

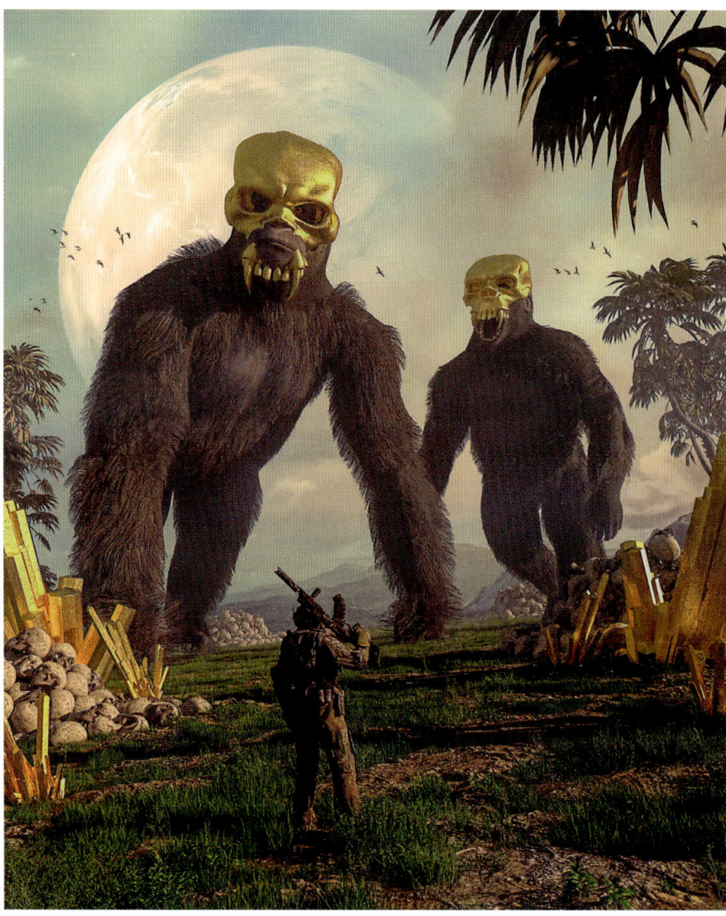

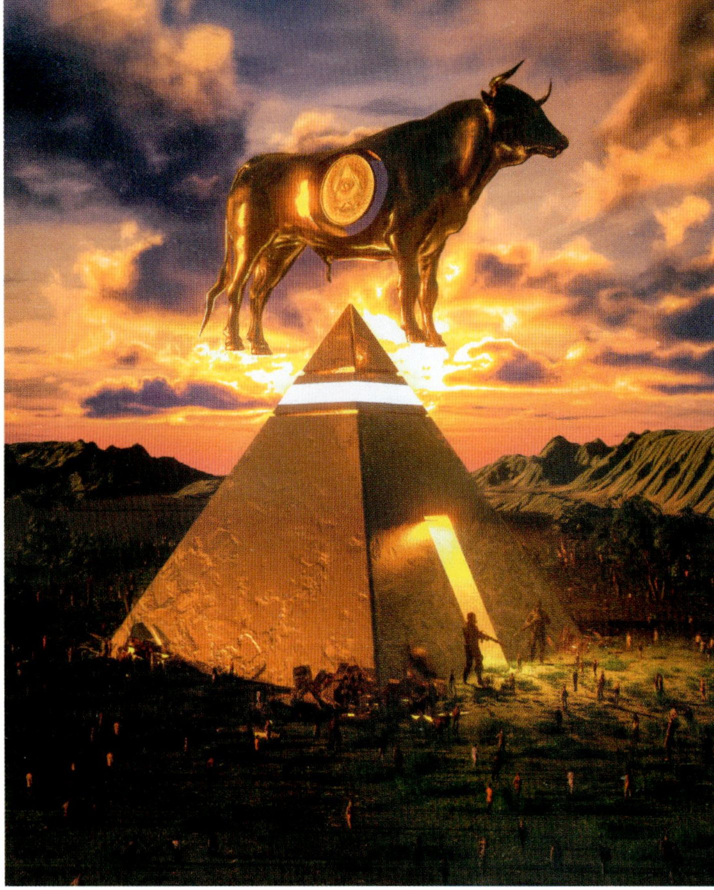

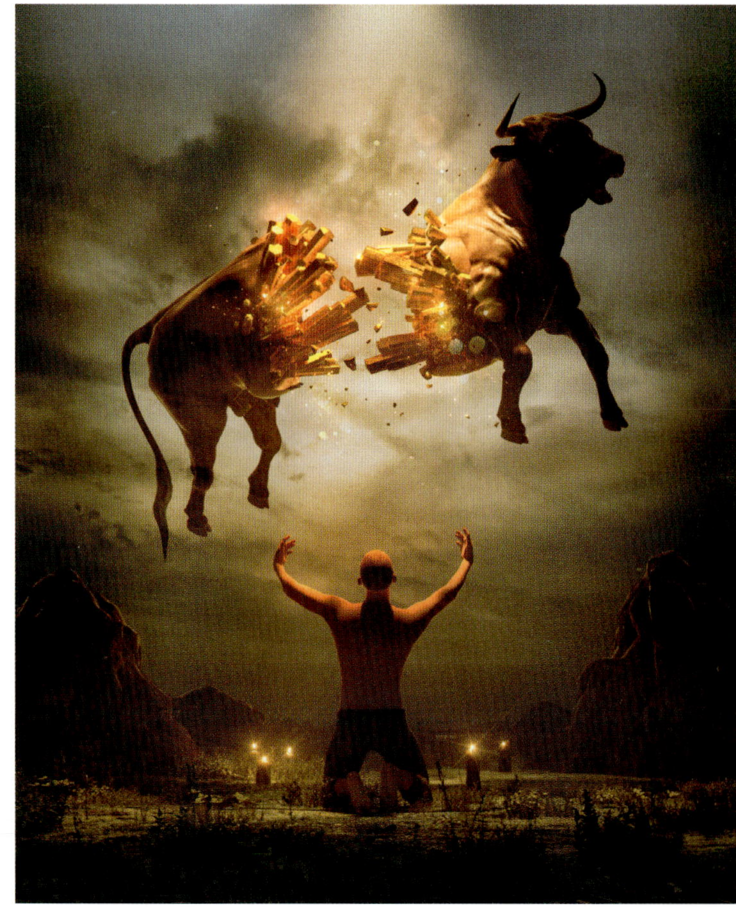

TOP LEFT
BULL RUN
11.19.2020

TOP RIGHT
GOLDEN APE HUNT
12.05.2020

BOTTOM LEFT
FOR SALE
11.01.2020

BOTTOM RIGHT
ALL TIME HIGH
11.30.2020

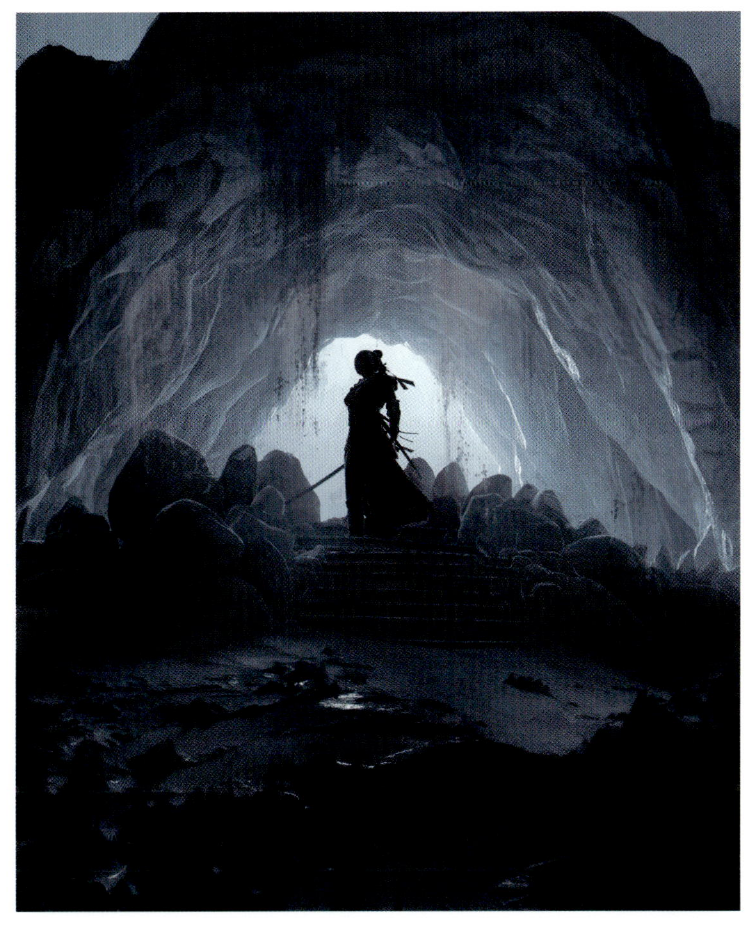

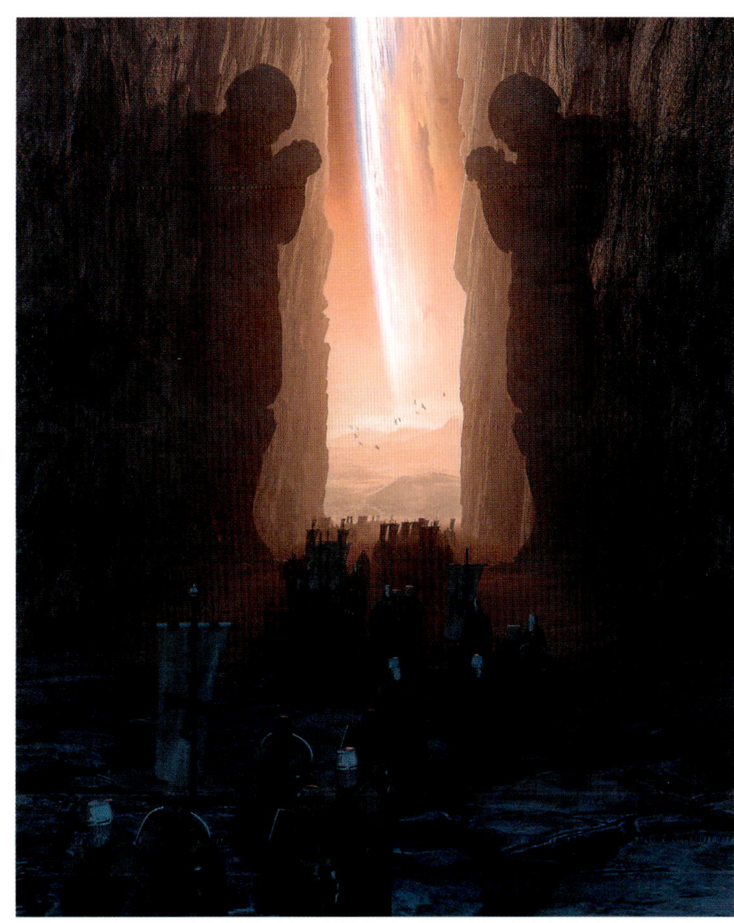

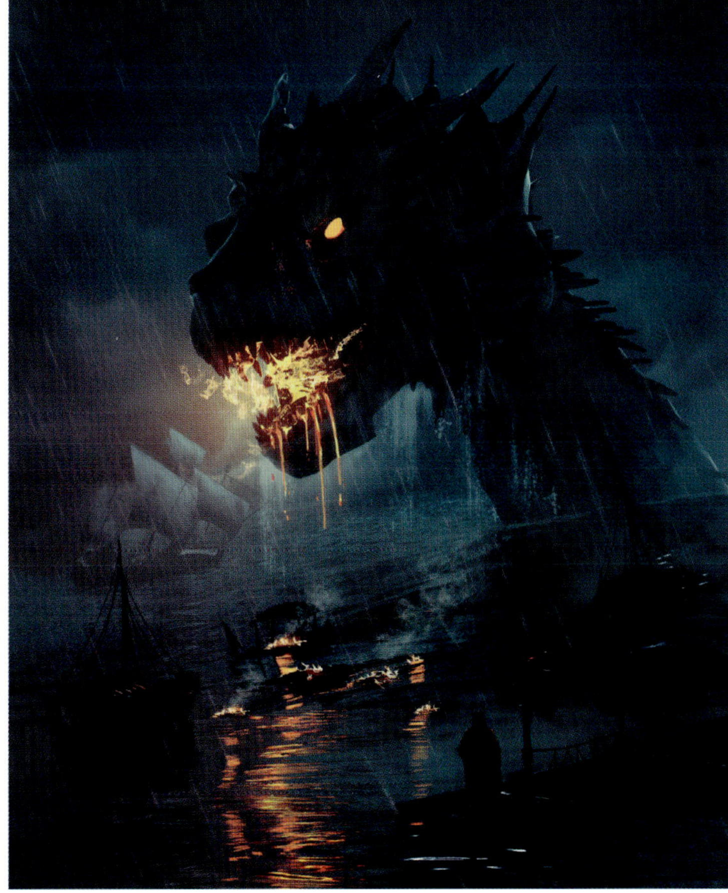

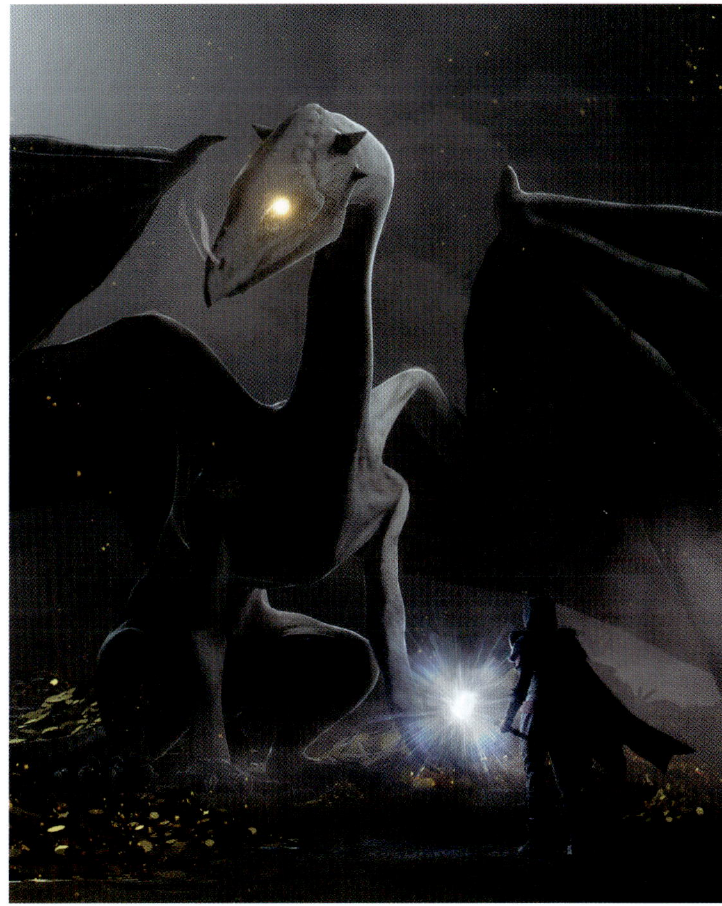

TOP LEFT
LAST LOOK
01.15.2020

TOP RIGHT
JOURNEY ON
02.05.2020

BOTTOM LEFT
DEEP SEA DRAGON
01.16.2020

BOTTOM RIGHT
STONKS
07.10.2020

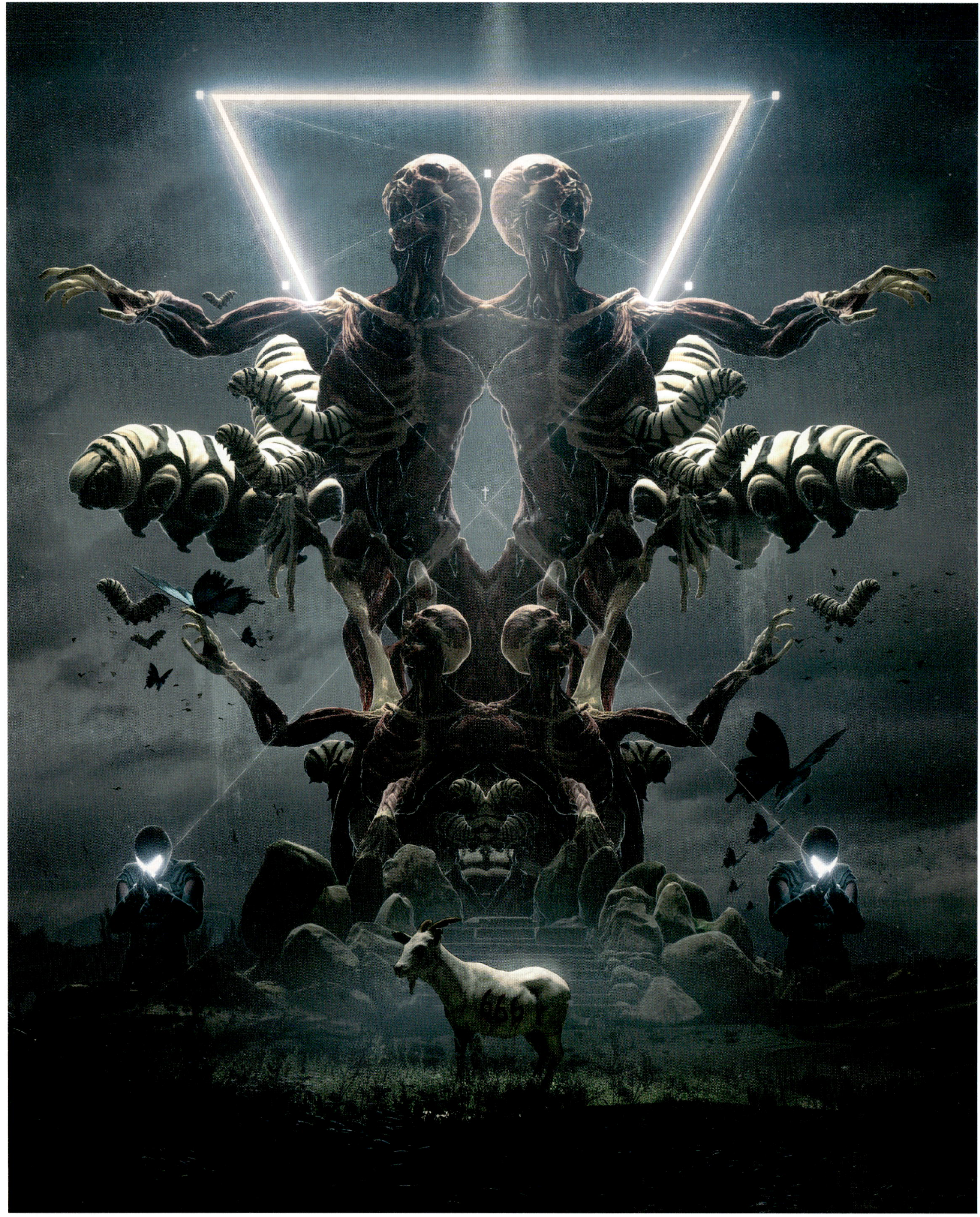

ABOVE

MARK OF THE BEAST
11.11.2020

OPPOSITE PAGE

THE PASSION OF THE ELON
08.13.2020

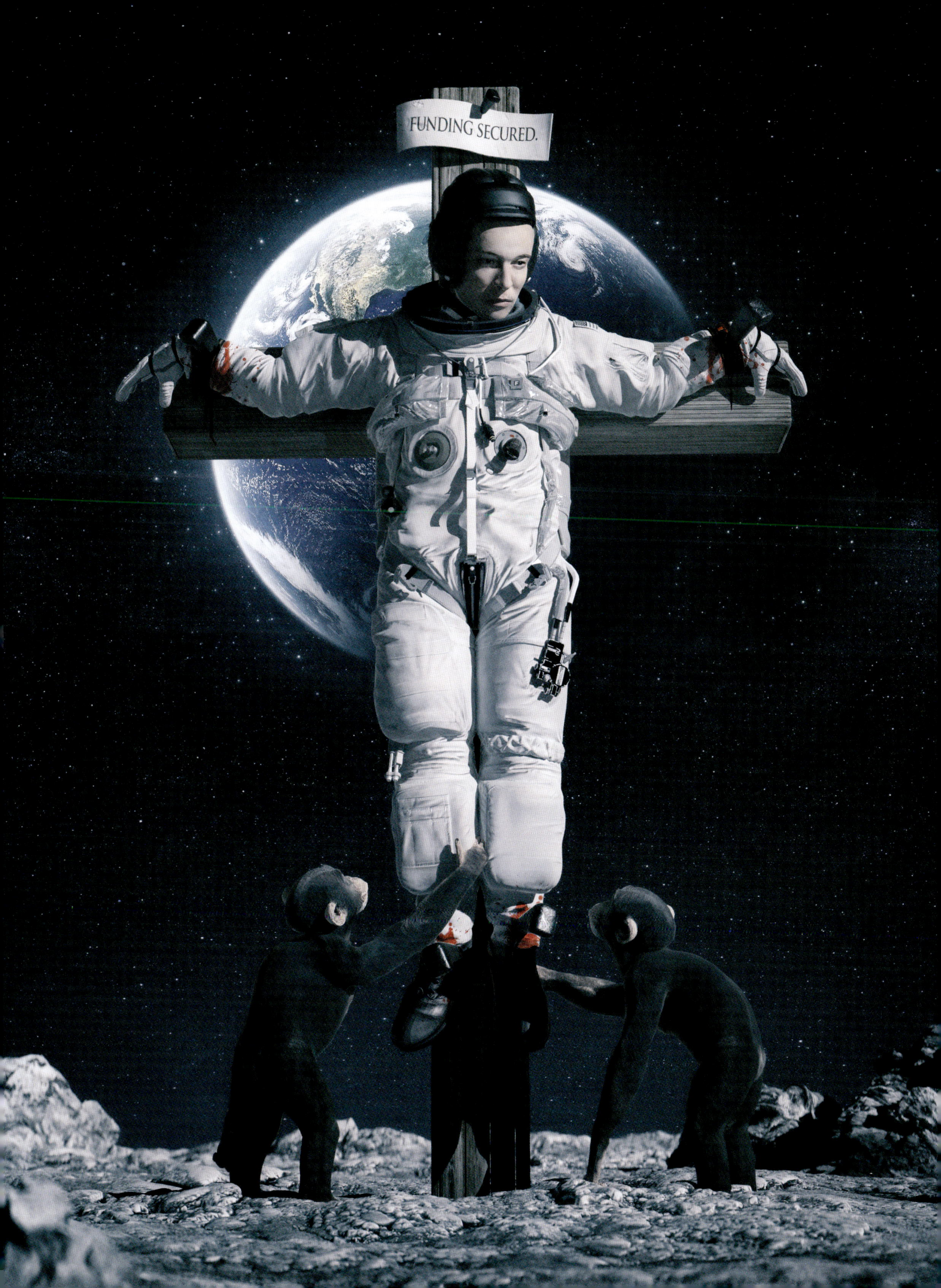
FUNDING SECURED.

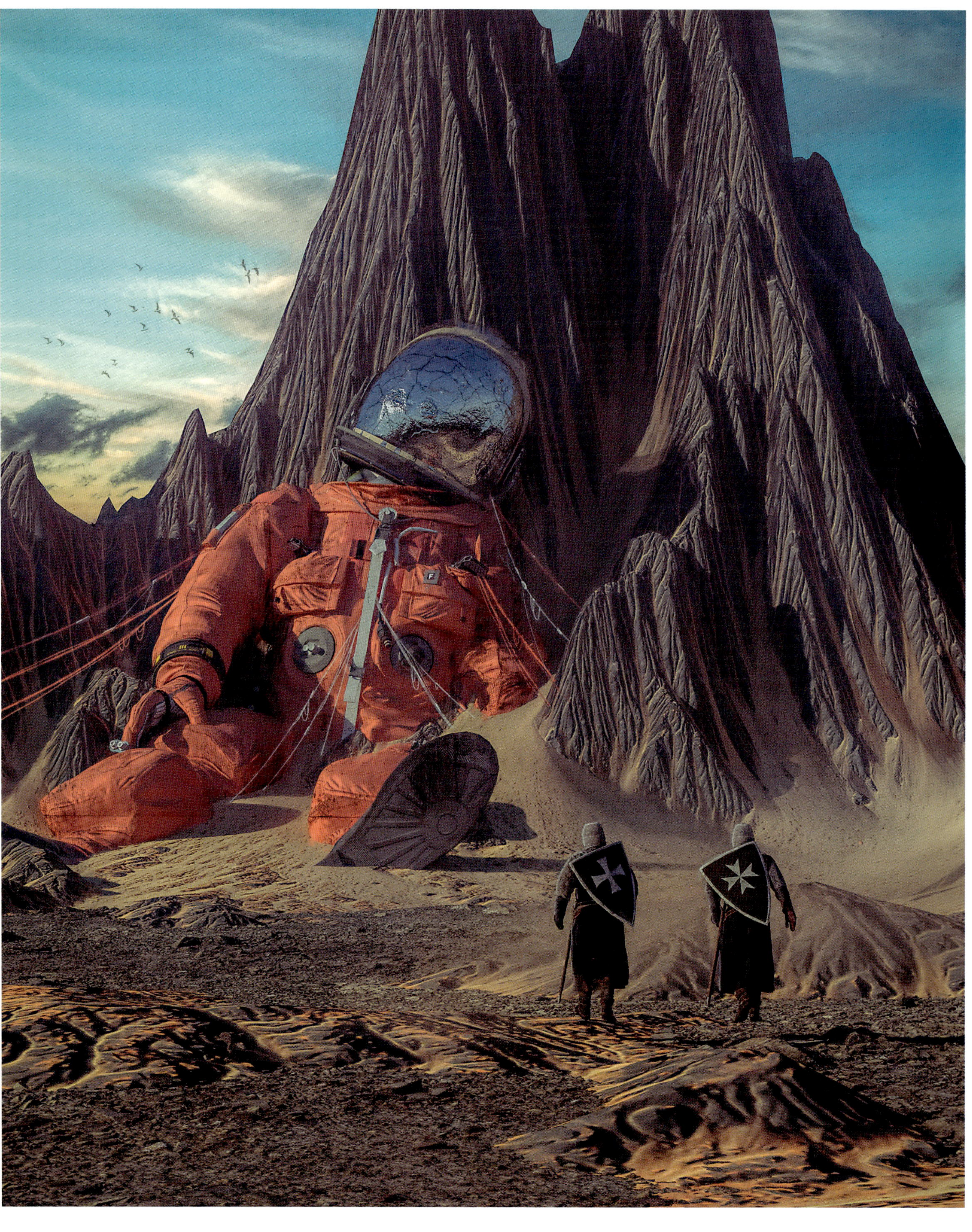

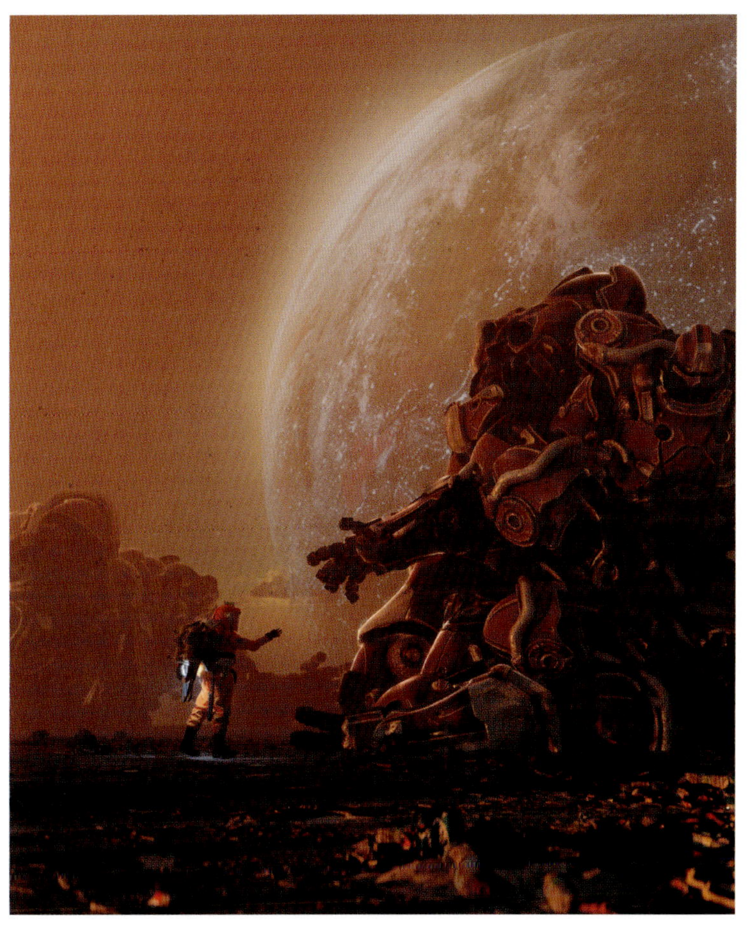

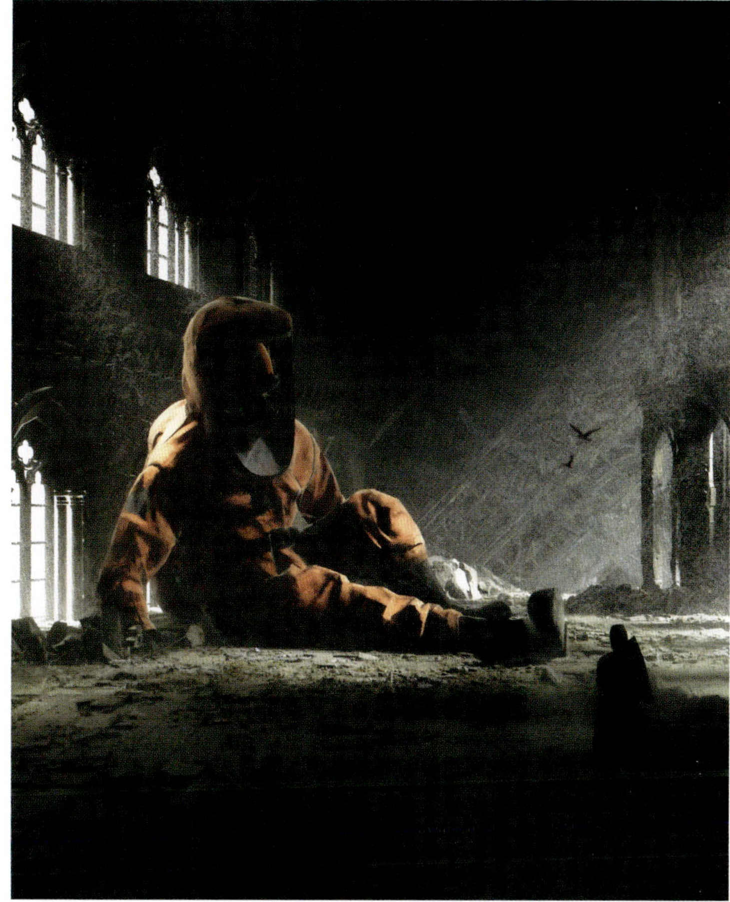

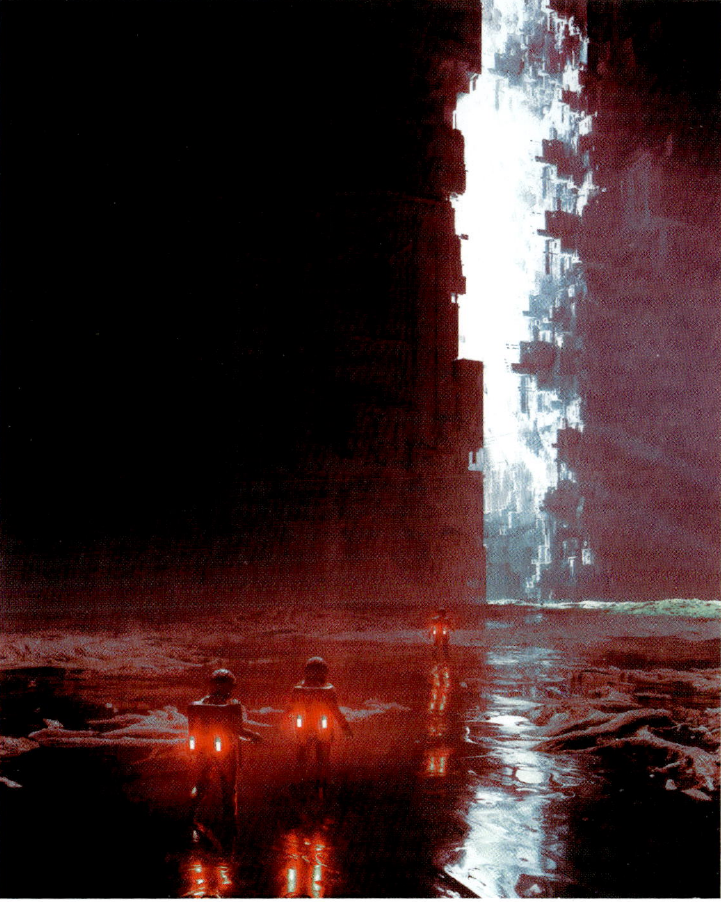

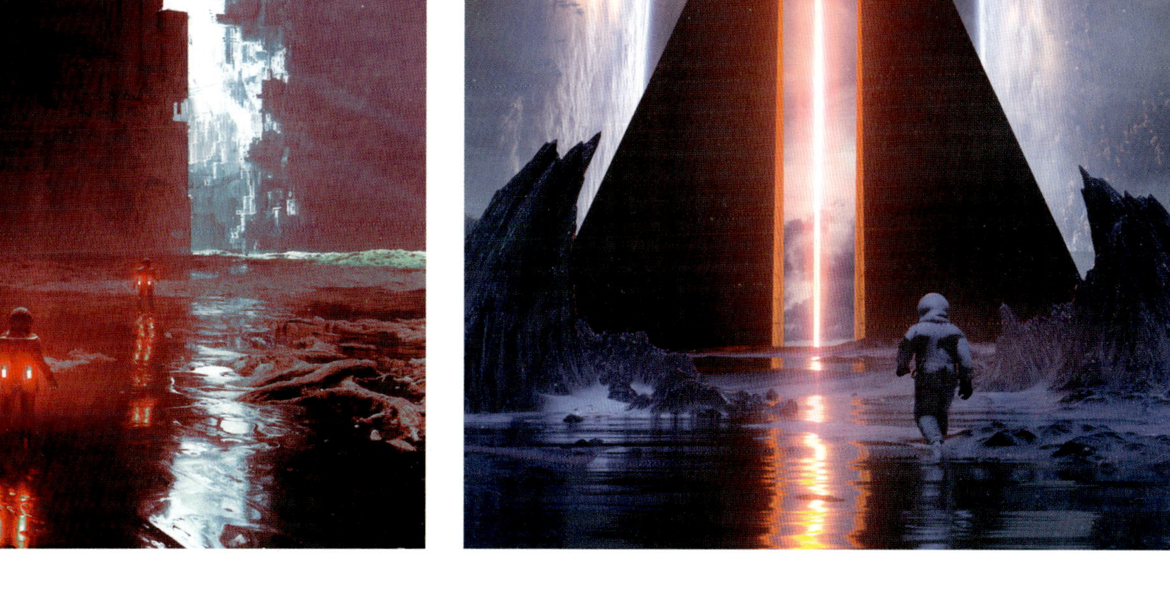

OPPOSITE PAGE
HOME PLANET
02.04.2020

TOP LEFT
GARBAGE MOON
07.15.2020

TOP RIGHT
SOCIAL DISTANCING
03.21.2020

BOTTOM LEFT
UNKNOWN LIGHT
06.16.2020

BOTTOM RIGHT
BETWEEN WORLDS
11.20.2020

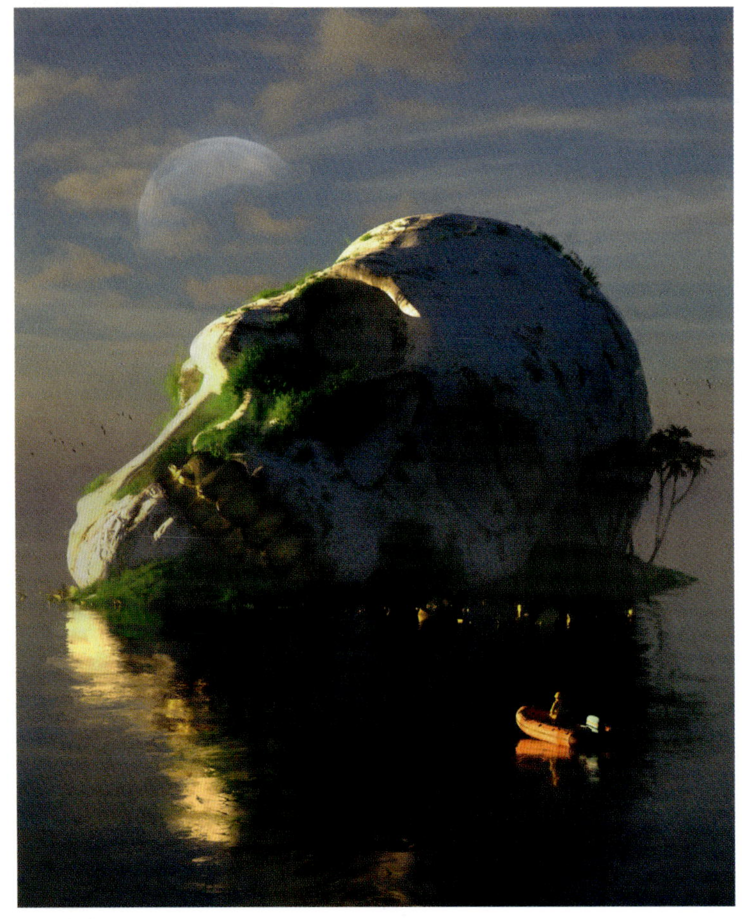

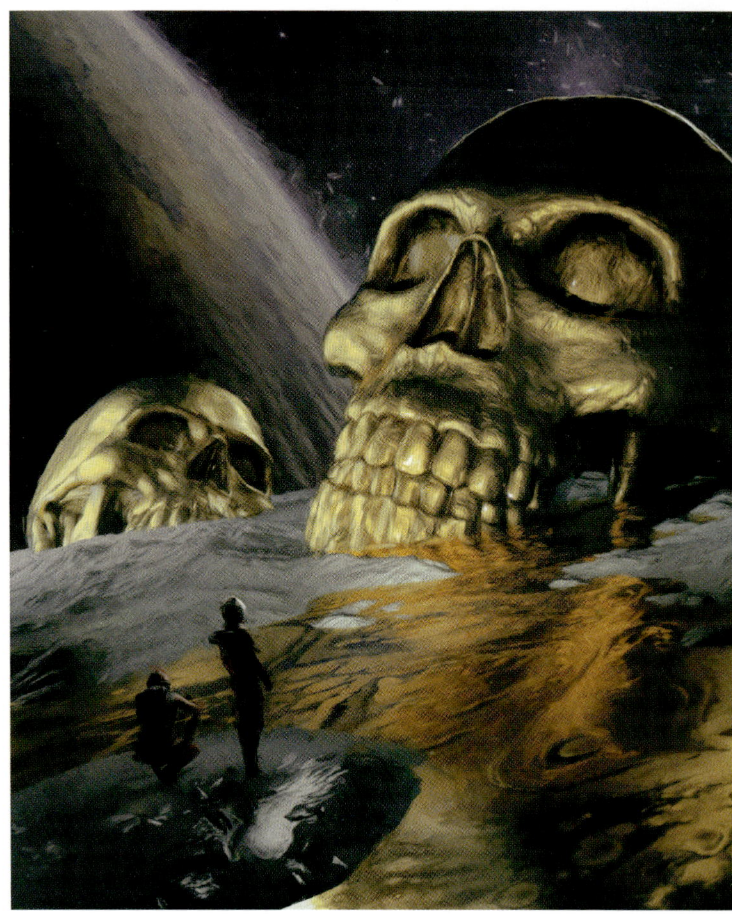

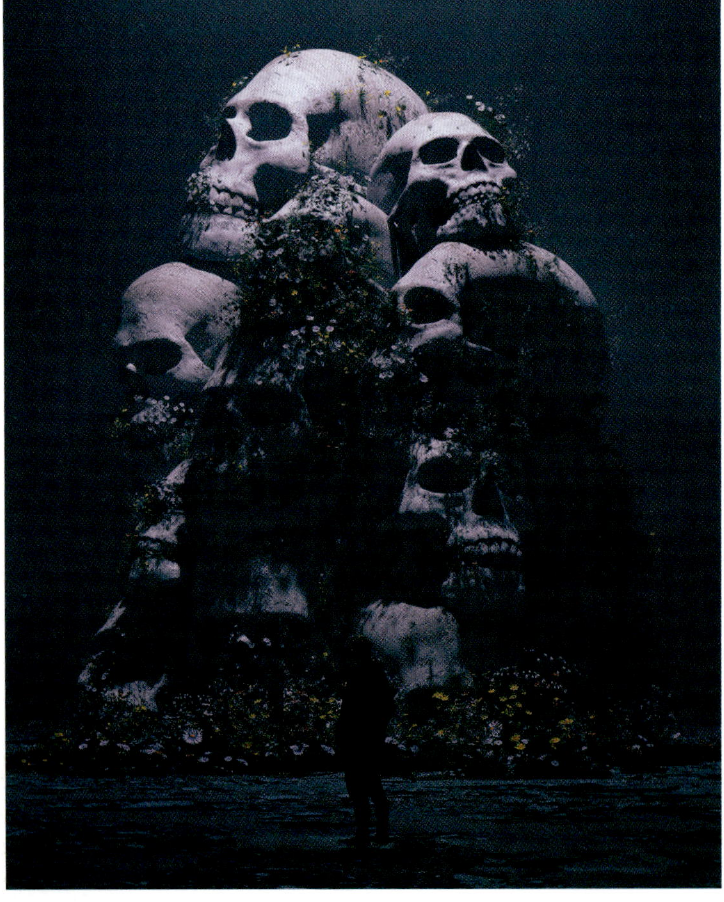

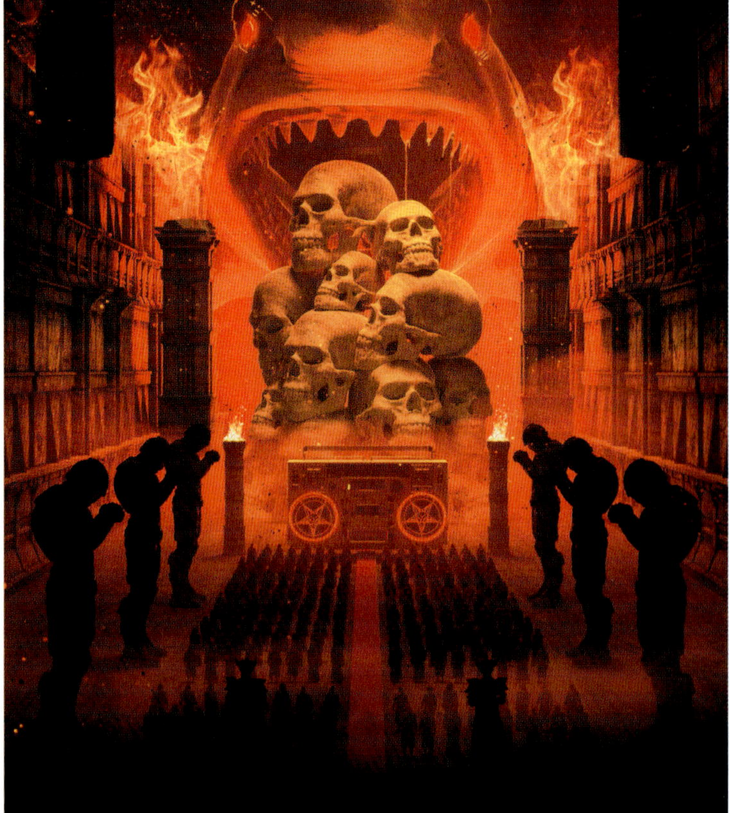

TOP LEFT

SOLITUDE

12.19.2020

TOP RIGHT

EXTINCT LUNAR MINERAL GIANTS

01.28.2020

BOTTOM LEFT

EVERY MINUTE

02.17.2020

BOTTOM RIGHT

BABY SHARK LISTENING PARTY

09.26.2020

OPPOSITE PAGE

DEAD

02.13.2020

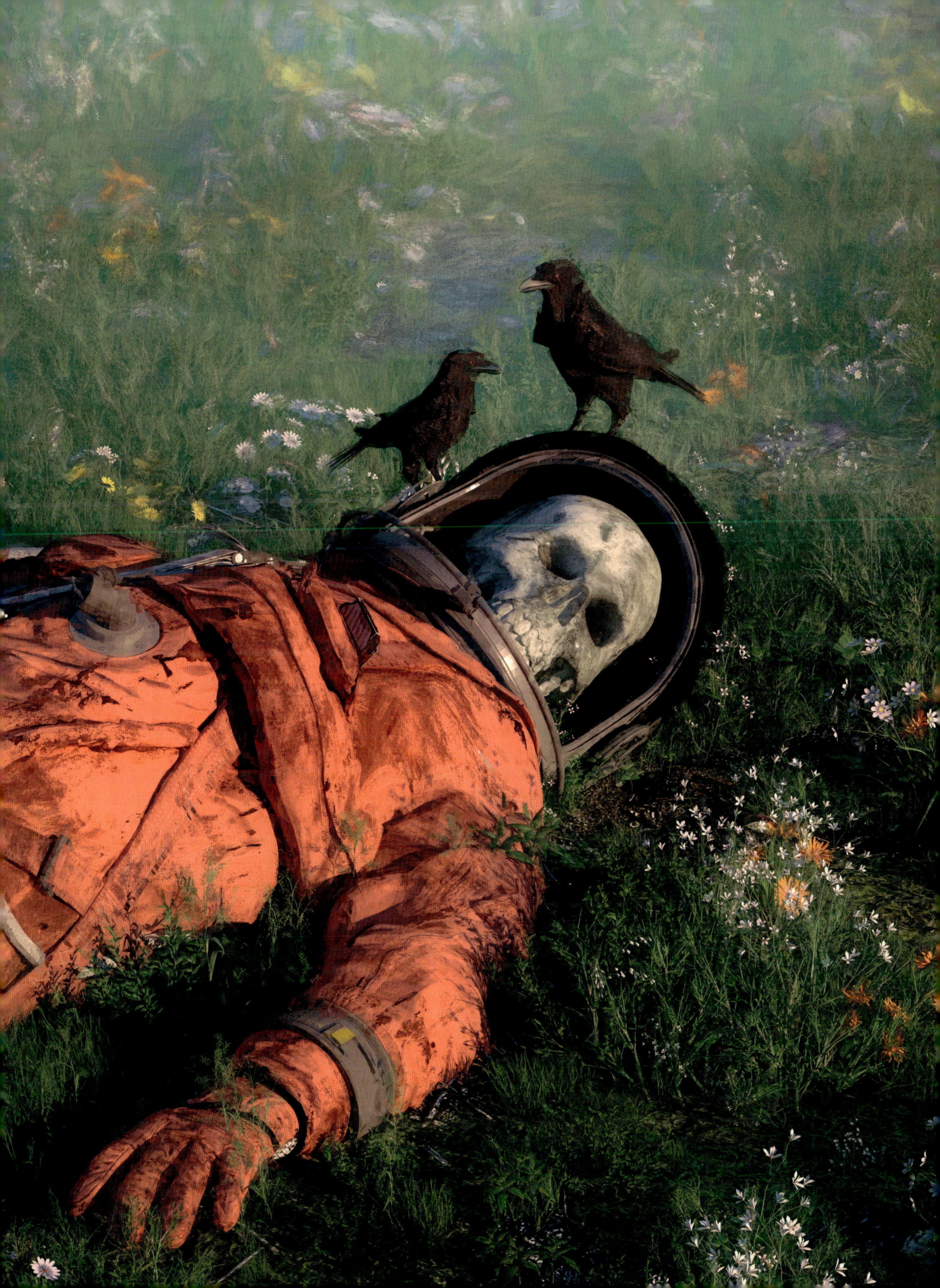

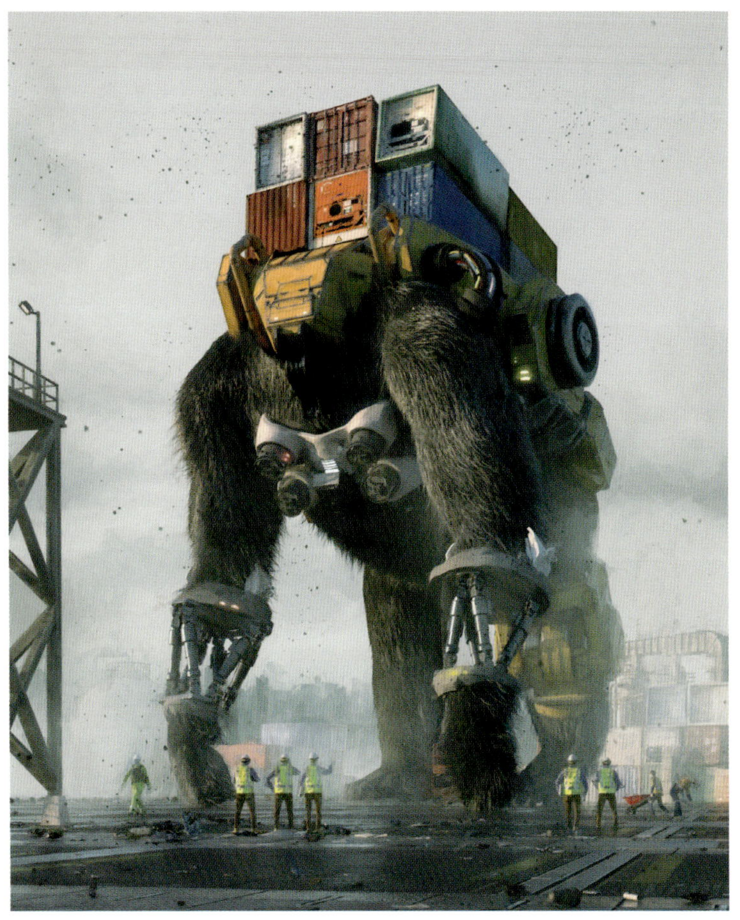

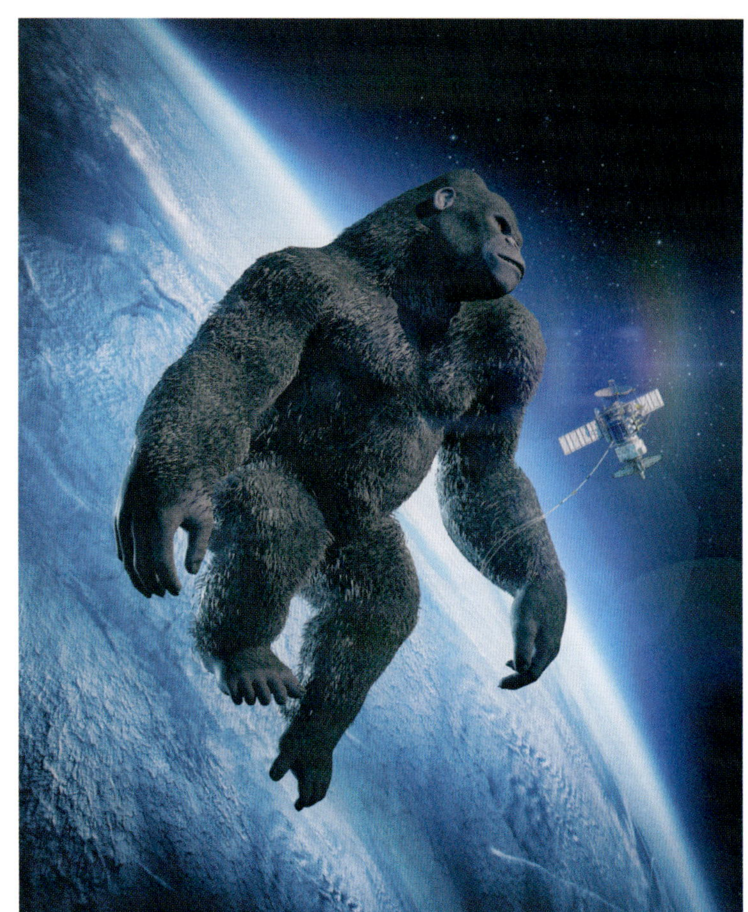

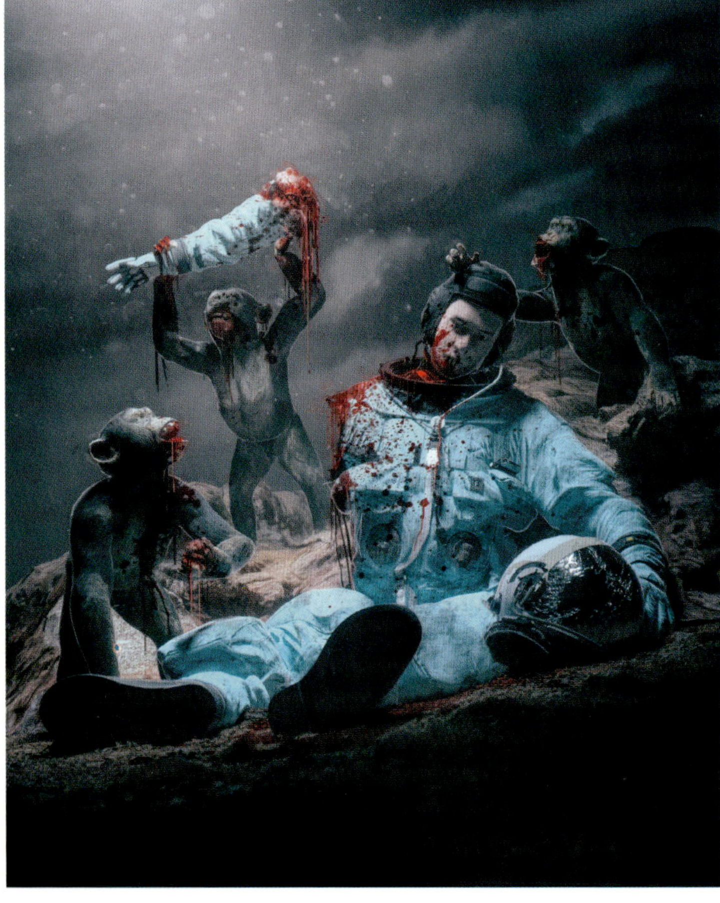

TOP LEFT
MEAT-HORSE.V2
05.20.2020

TOP RIGHT
ADRIFT
09.17.2020

BOTTOM LEFT
NOT WELCOME
05.21.2020

OPPOSITE PAGE
i miss people
10.23.2020

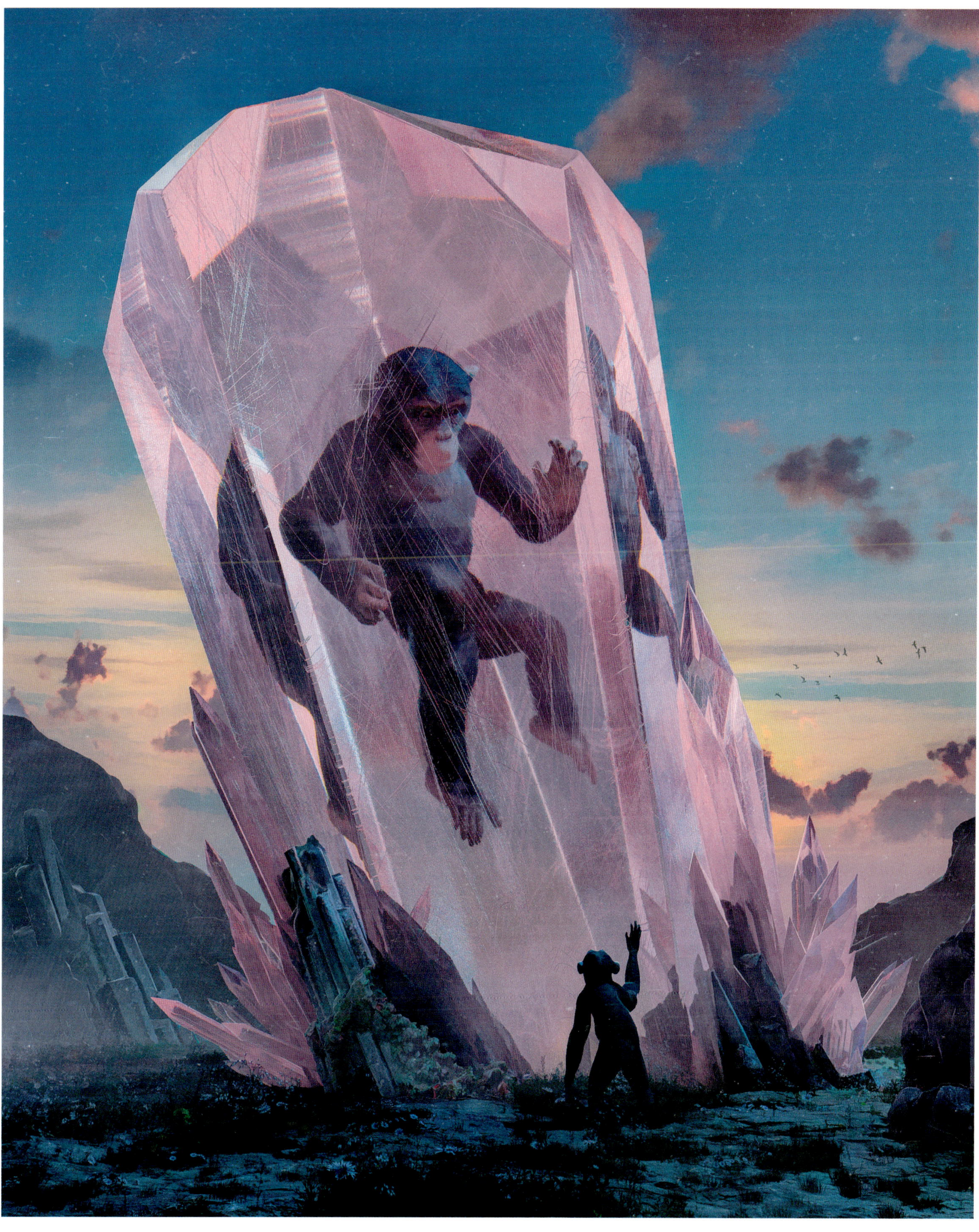

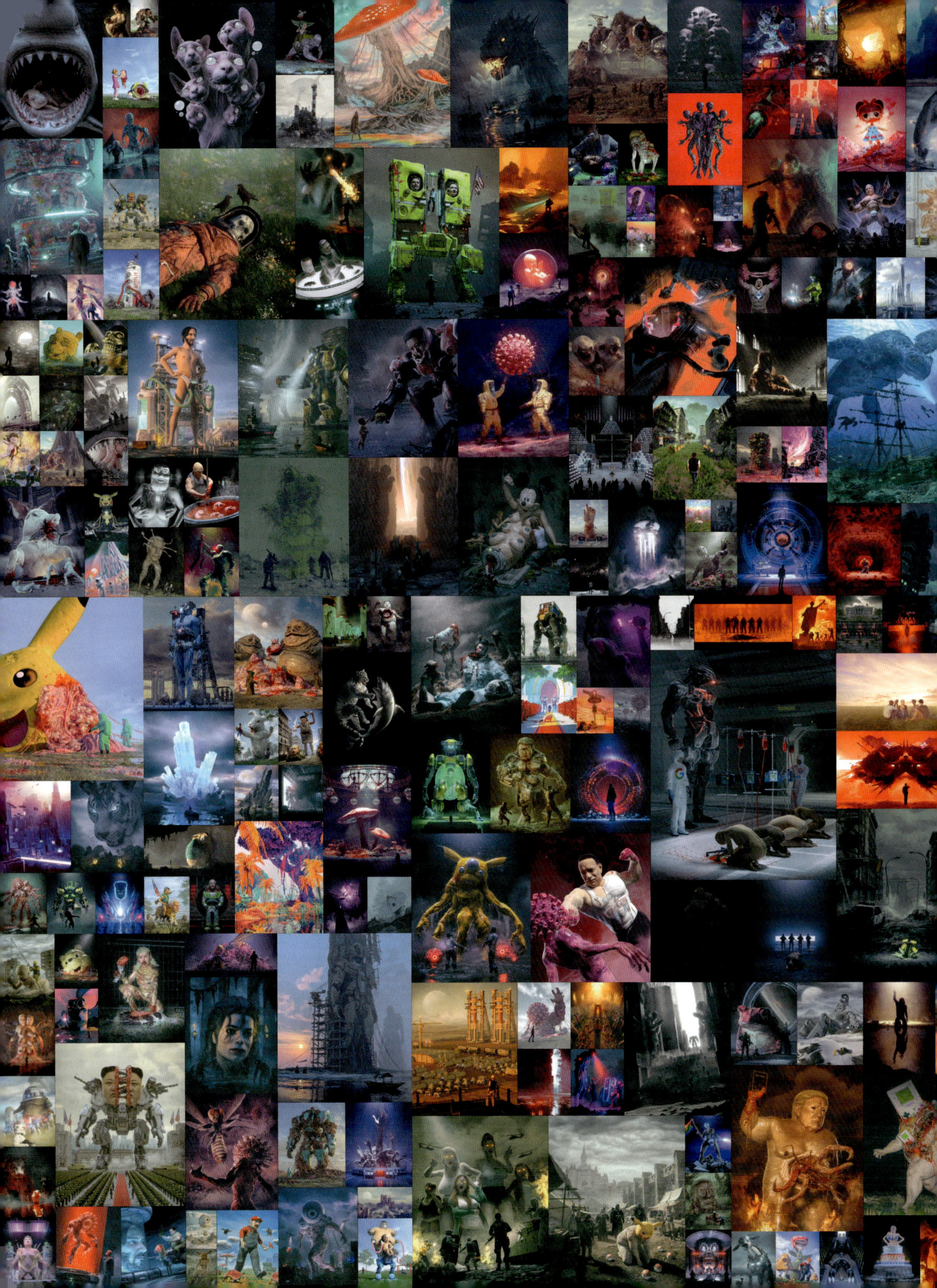

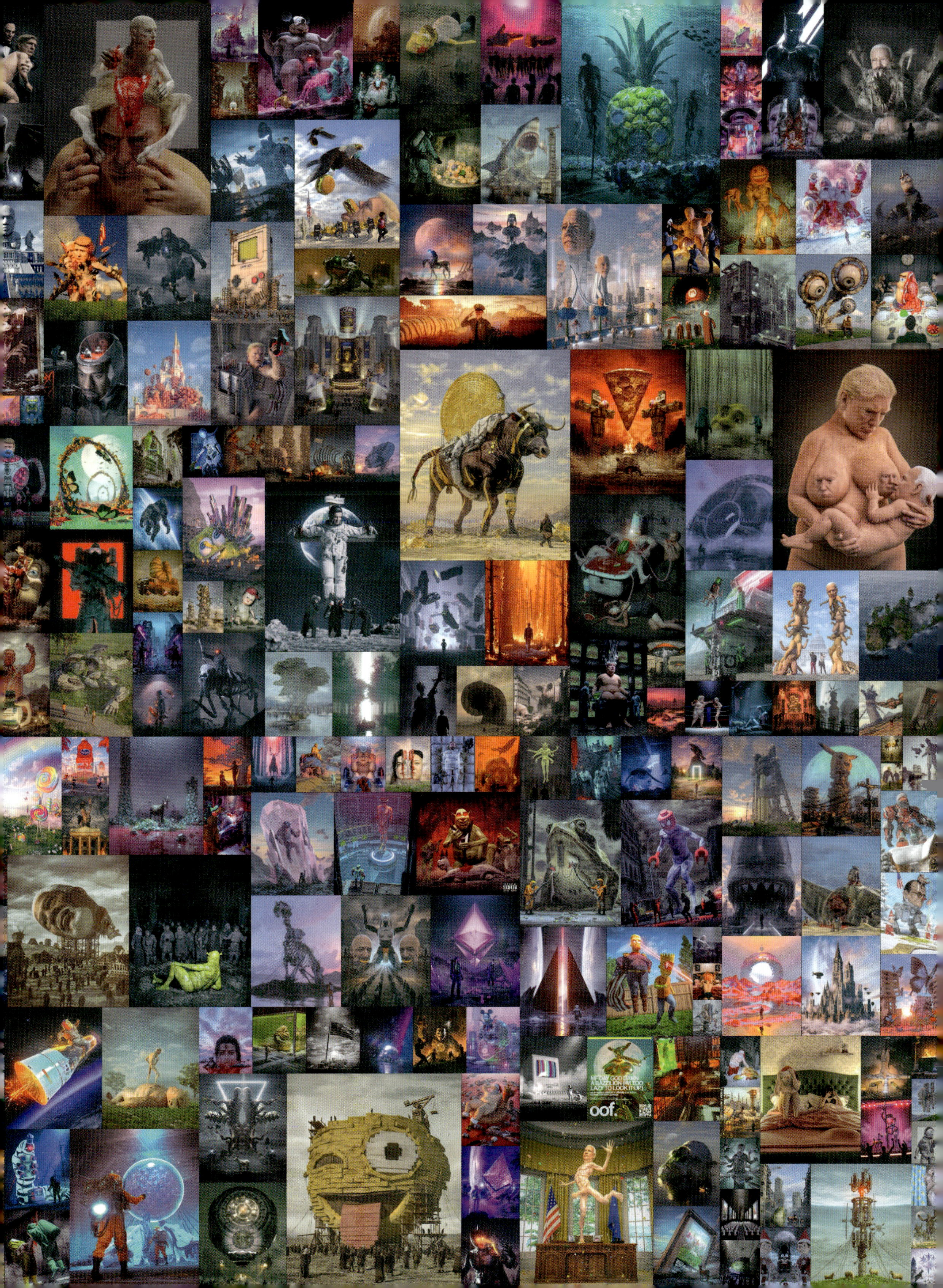
oof.

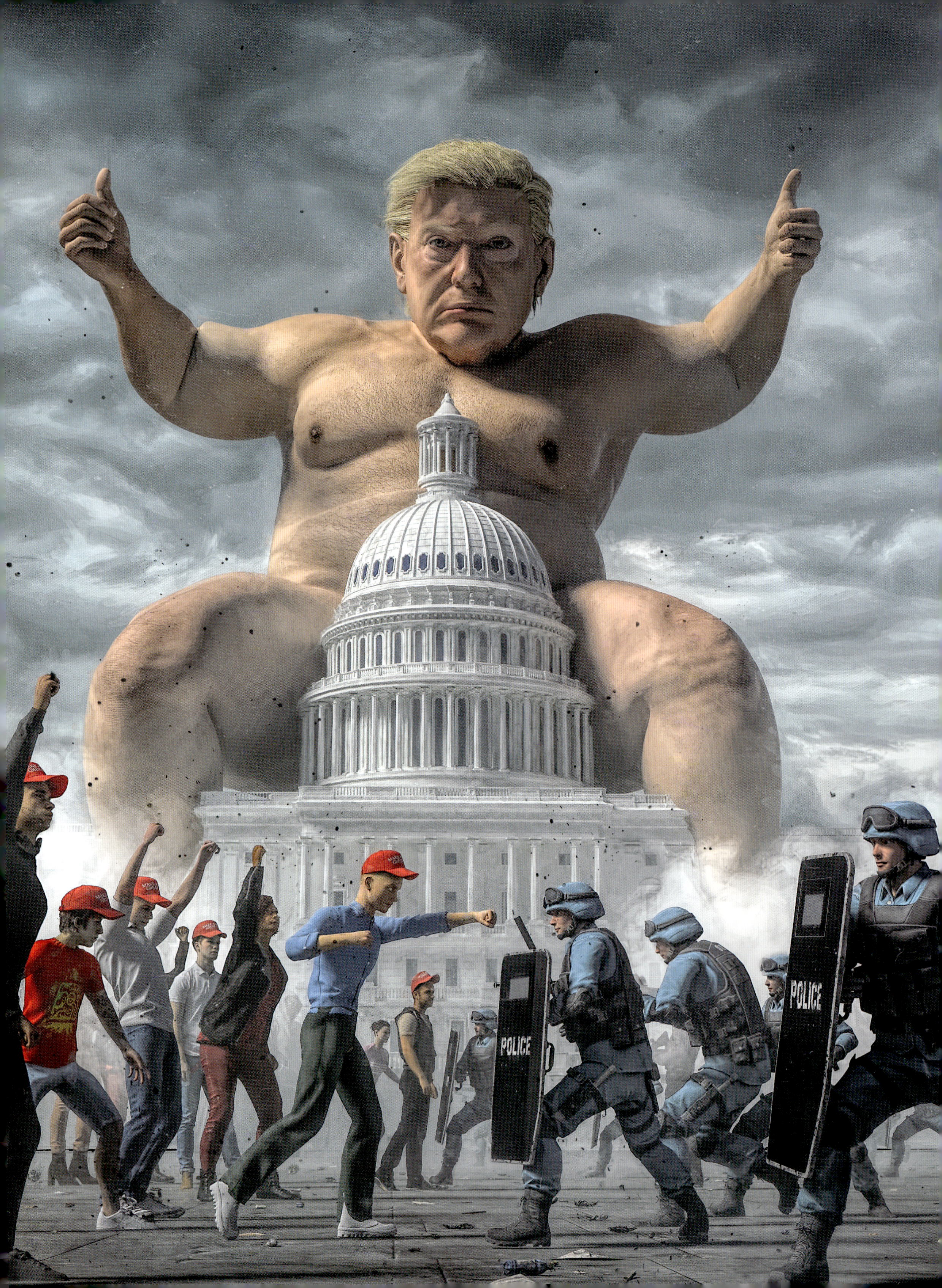
POLICE
POLICE

2021

OPPOSITE PAGE

ENDGAME
01.06.2021

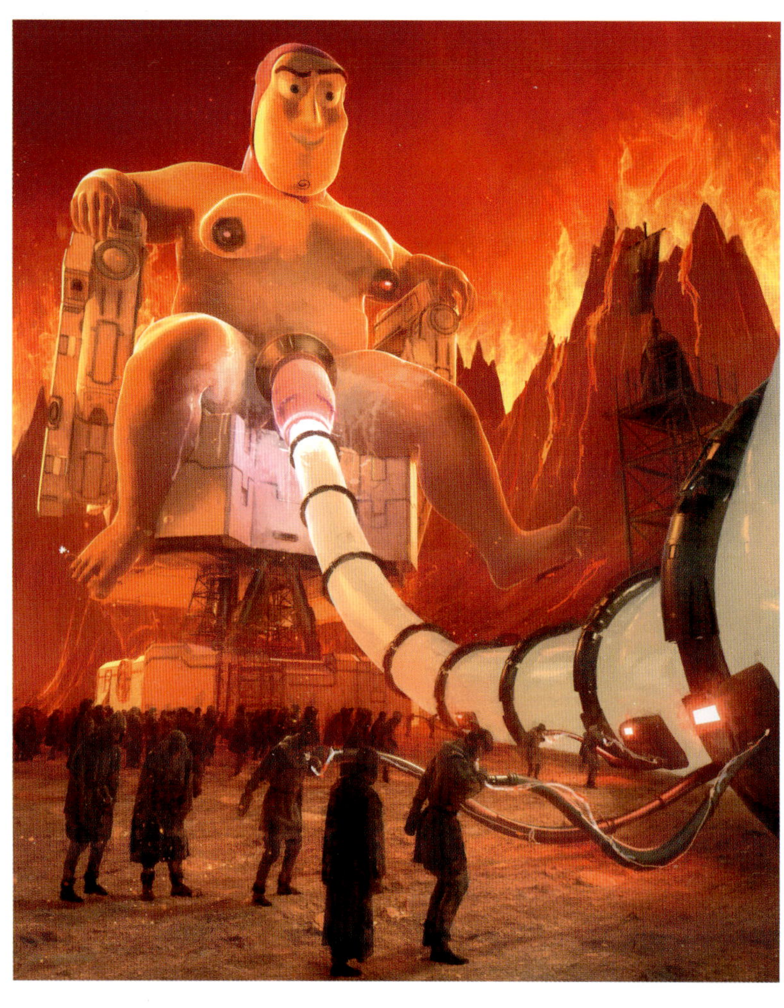

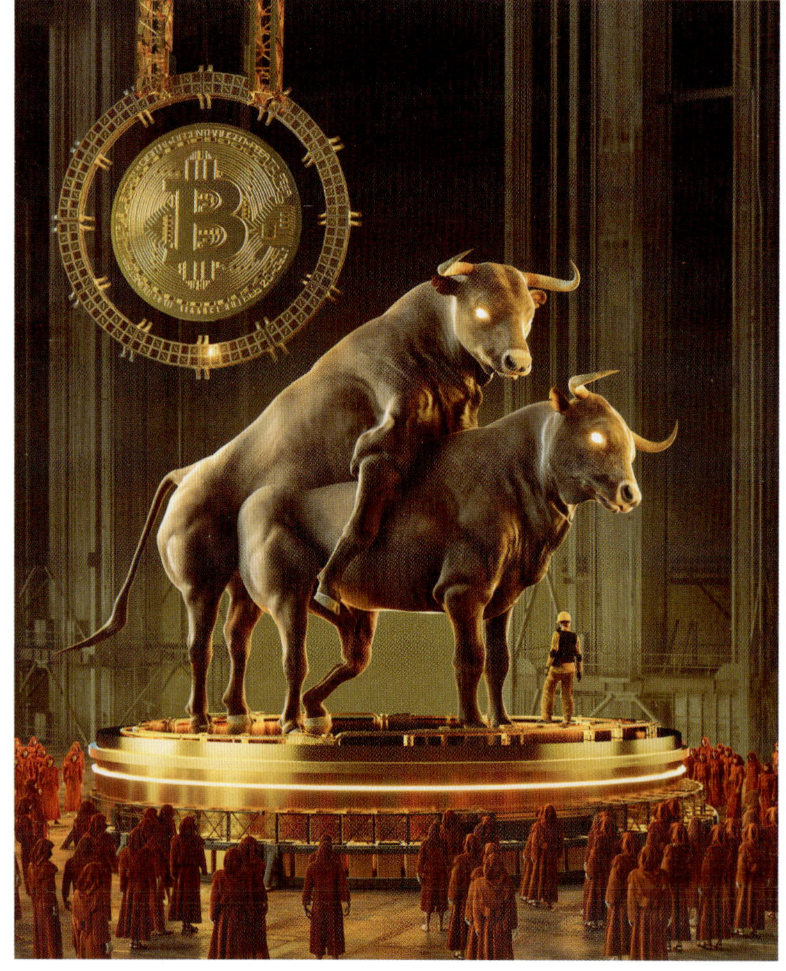

TOP

ROCKETE FUEL

01.04.2021

BOTTOM

30K

01.02.2021

OPPOSITE PAGE

KEEP HUNTING

01.05.2021

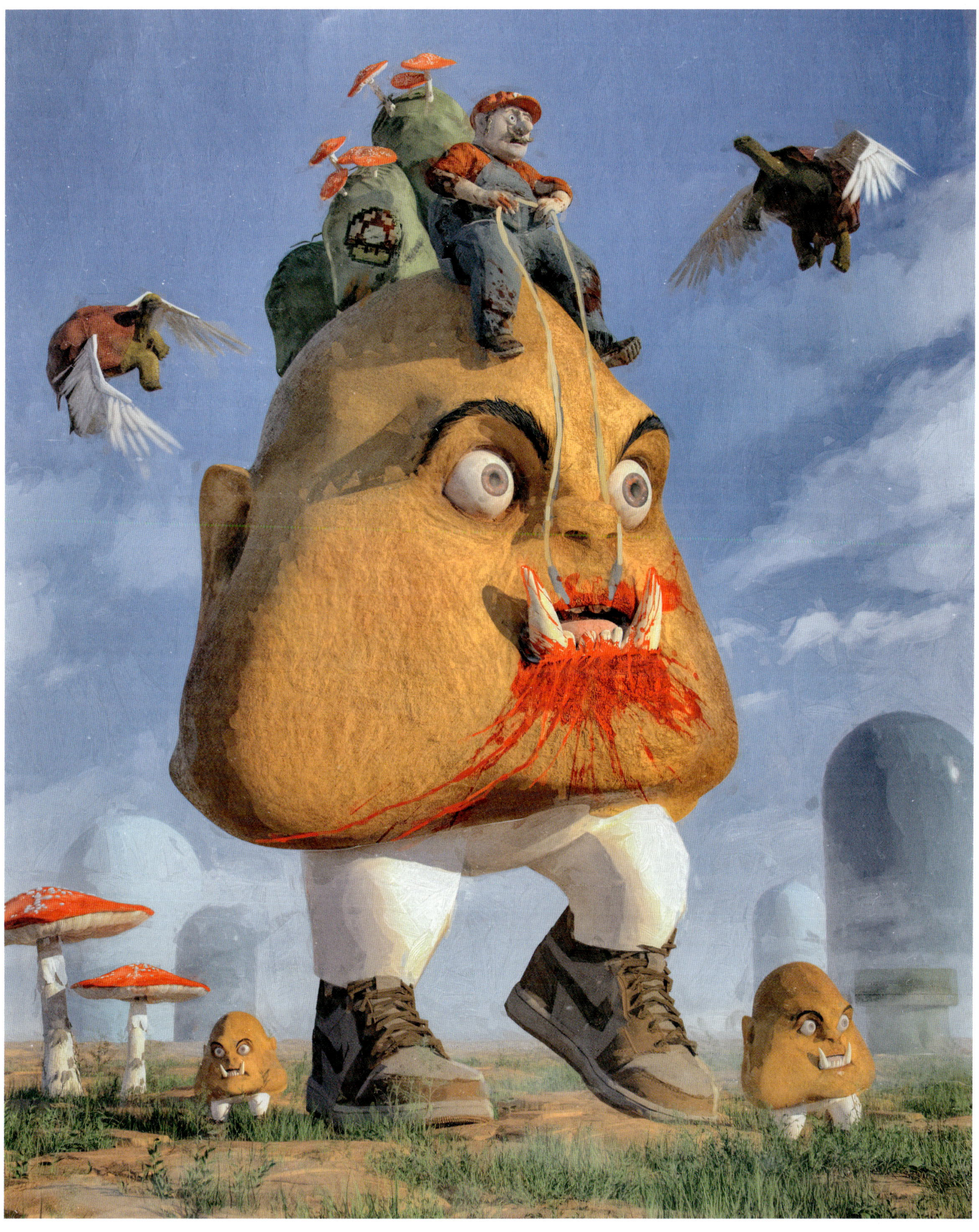

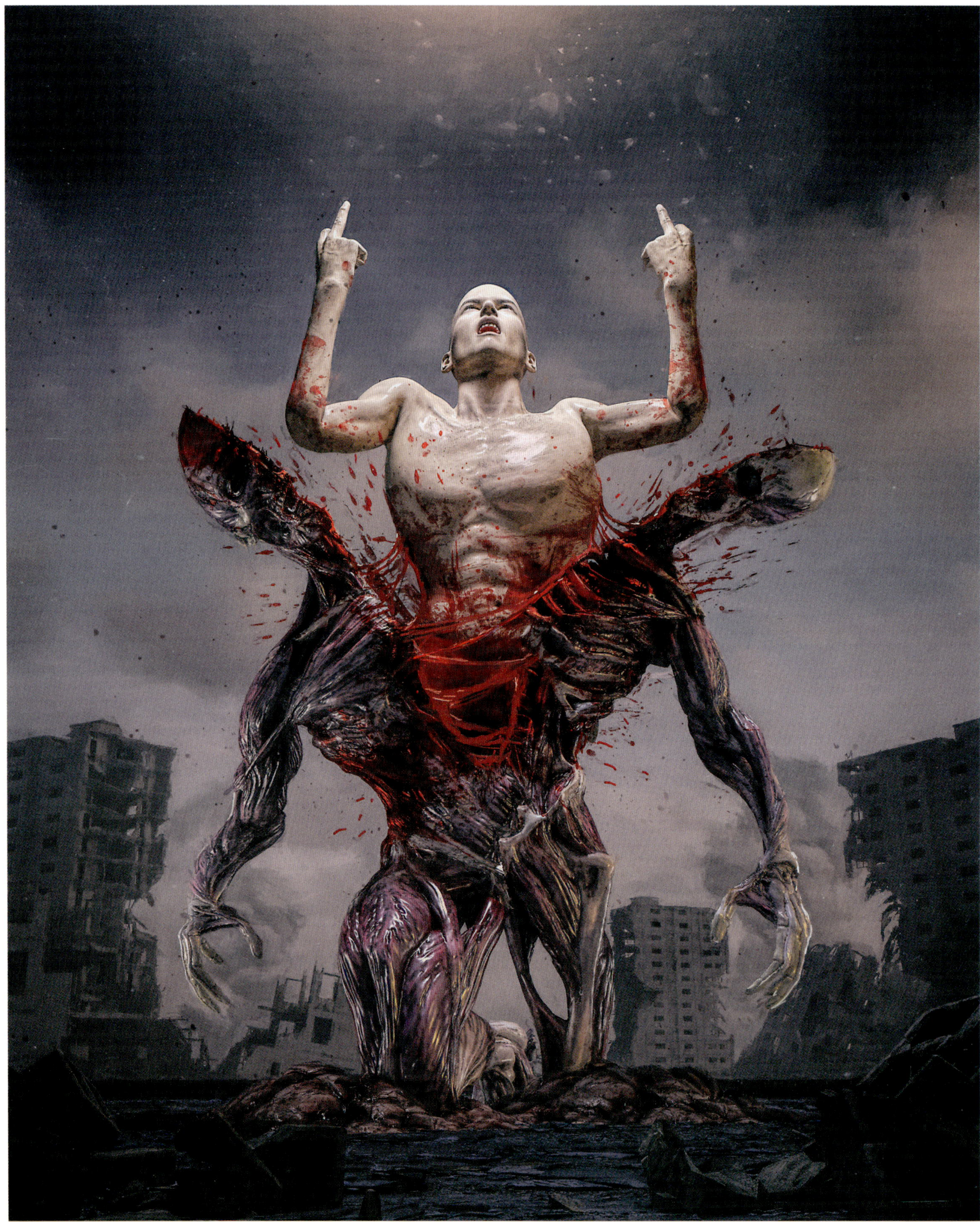

ABOVE

JANUARY 1ST, 2021
01.01.2021

OPPOSITE PAGE

EXPLOSIVE ETHEREUM GROWTH
01.03.2021

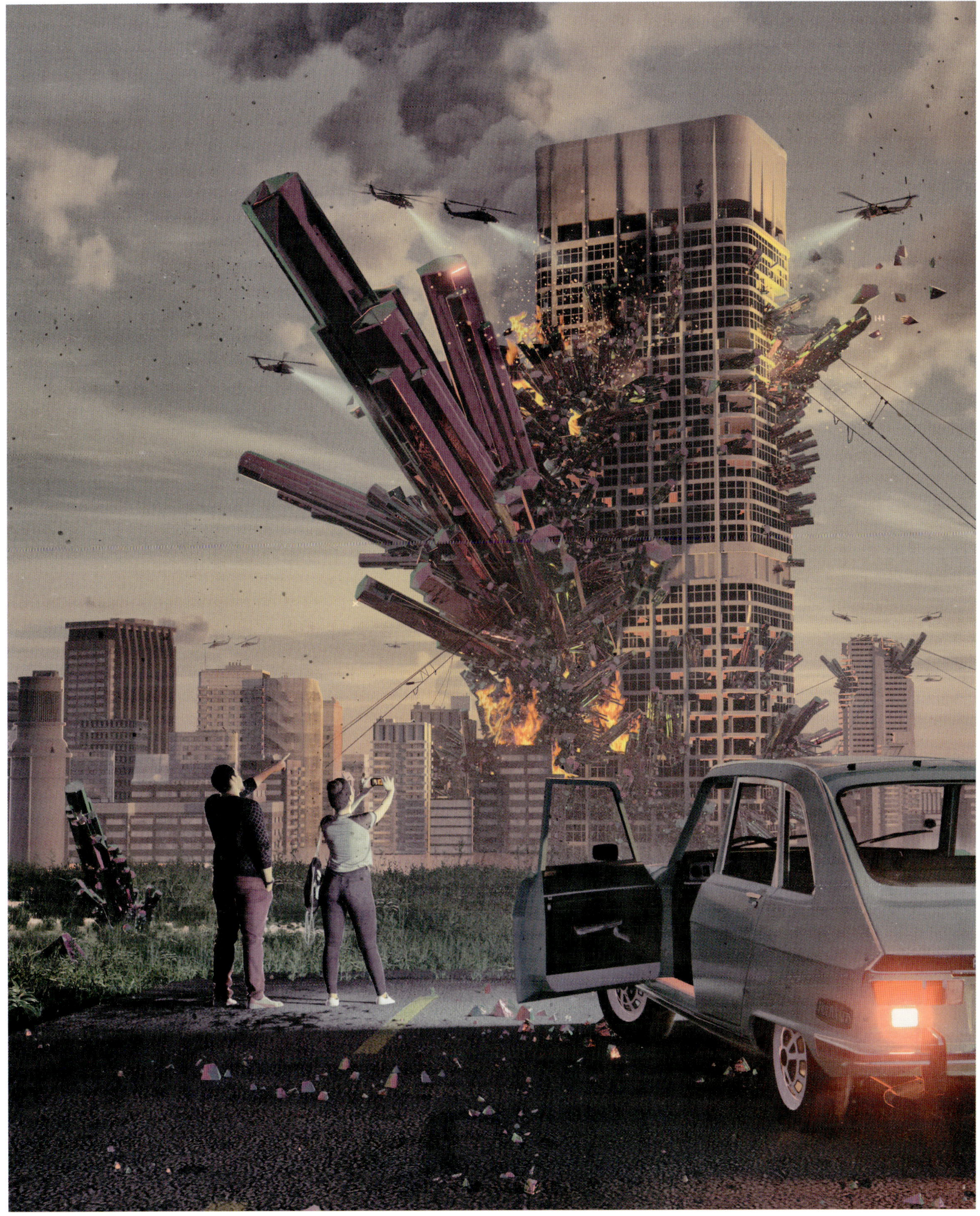

DAY 5000

01.07.2021

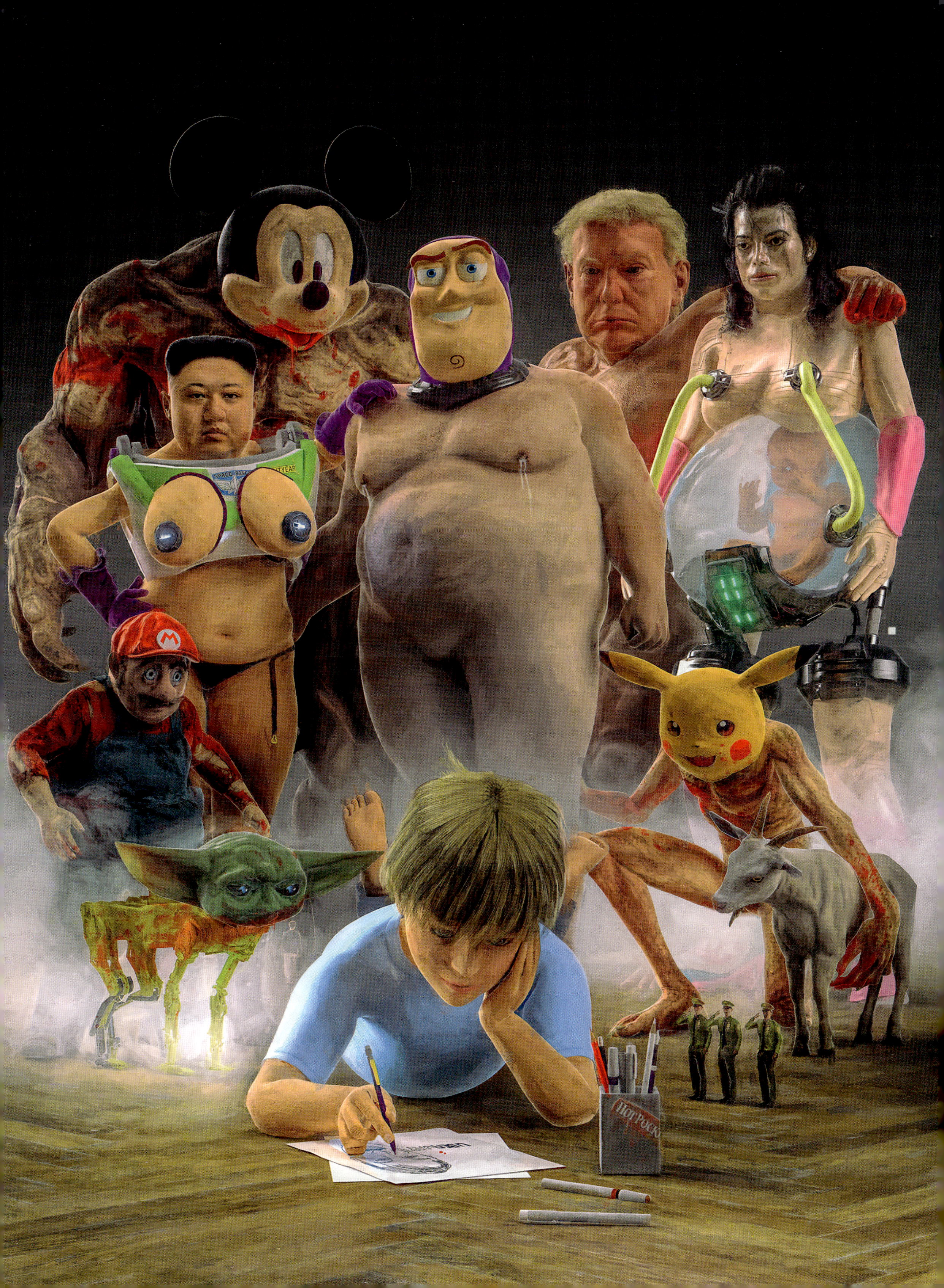
HotPock

biography

Michael Joseph Winkelmann is an American artist known as Beeple. He creates digital still, video, film, and physical work that engages with critical issues in the contemporary global economy, trade, tech culture, politics, social science, and environmental justice. Beeple's images often show contemporary or futuristic figuration in phantasmagoric, utopian, or dystopian landscapes, using recognizable figures from popular culture and politics to satirize current events.

In March 2021, the *Everydays* project gained worldwide attention after Christie's sold an NFT, their first completely digital artwork, **EVERYDAYS: THE FIRST 5000 DAYS** for $69 million, making Beeple the third most expensive living artist.

thank you for your attention. bye.

BEEPLE

everydays, the first 5000 days

Text and images: Mike Winkelmann
Cernunnos logo design: Mark Ryden
Book design: Benjamin Brard
Design manager: Shawn Dahl, dahlimama inc

Library of Congress Control Number: 2021933726

ISBN: 978-1-4197-5691-7

Printed and bound in China

10 9 8 7 6 5 4 3 2 1

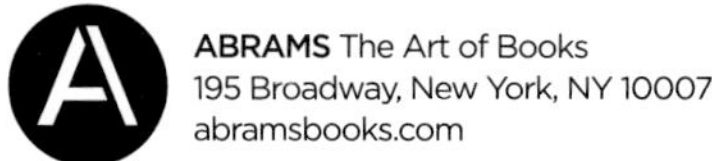
ABRAMS The Art of Books
195 Broadway, New York, NY 10007
abramsbooks.com

COVER

EVERYDAYS, THE FIRST 5000 DAYS
05.01.2007–01.07.2021

BELLYBAND FRONT

HAUNTED CHROME
10.28.2017

BELLYBAND BACK RIGHT

i miss people
10.23.2020

BELLYBAND BACK MIDDLE

THE FIRST EMOJI
09.01.2020

BELLYBAND BACK LEFT

TOM HANKS BEATING THE SHIT OUT OF CORONAVIRUS
03.12.2020